P9-EDQ-506

The Collected Poems of
Robert Penn Warren

Edited by John Burt

With a Foreword by Harold Bloom

Louisiana State University Press
Baton Rouge
1998

Manufactured in the United States of America
First printing
07 06 05 04 03 02 01 00 99 98 5 4 3 2 1

Typeface: Times Roman
Printer and binder: Edwards Brothers, Inc.

Library of Congress Cataloging-in-Publication Data
Warren, Robert Penn, 1905–1989
[Poems]
The collected poems of Robert Penn Warren / edited by John Burt ; with a Foreword by Harold Bloom.
p. cm.
Includes index.
ISBN 0-8071-2333-1 (alk. paper)
I. Burt, John, 1955– . II. Title.
PS3545.A748A17 1998
811'.52—dc21 98-26104
CIP

The Paper in this book meets the guidelines for permanence and durablility of the Committee on Production Guidelines for Book Longevity of the Council on Library Resources. ♾

CONTENTS

Uncollected Poems 1922–1943

Promises

Poems 1954–1956

II.

III.

IV.

V.

VI.

VII.

VIII.

IX.

Uncollected Poems 1943–1989

FOREWORD

Harold Bloom

This extraordinary volume, magnificently edited by John Burt, should establish the permanent place of Robert Penn Warren's poetry in his nation's literary achievement. From 1966 to 1986 Warren wrote much the best poetry composed during those two decades in the United States. During the three years before he died on 15 September 1989, Warren was too ill to continue his high quest for poetic sublimity. Yet between the ages of sixty-one and eighty-one, he had enjoyed a poetic renascence fully comparable to the great final phases of Thomas Hardy, William Butler Yeats, and Wallace Stevens. John Burt's devoted edition gives us the definitive text of all of Warren's poetry, and thus restores an American masterwork, one that will be read, studied, and absorbed, so long as the love for, and understanding of, great poetry survives among us.

The late William K. Wimsatt, formidable scholarly critic and friend of Warren at Yale University, once remarked to me that he found my passion for Warren's later poetry rather surprising, because he thought of Warren as a "dramatic poet" rather than a lyrical one. As my former teacher, Wimsatt frequently had observed that, in his judgment, I tended to undervalue the dramatic elements in modern American poetry. I replied that I recognized in Warren's poetry, from *Incarnations: Poems, 1966–1968* (1968) on, the agonistic spirit that always had marked the sublime ode from Pindar through the Romantics to Yeats. From the start, Warren's characteristic mode had been the dramatic lyric; but after the poet turned sixty he internalized drama, in a great contest with time, with cultural and family history, and above all, with himself. In his long major phase, Warren wrestled with the angel of the poetic sublime and carried away the victory of a new name. "Robert Penn Warren" had meant primarily the novelist of *All the King's Men* (1946) and *World Enough and Time* (1950). Those major fictions endure, but I believe that Warren's name will be more associated with his *Collected Poems,* because scores of them transcend even his finest narratives. This book is Warren's center, and his lasting glory.

Warren had many precursors in American poetry: he paid particular homage to John Greenleaf Whittier and to Herman Melville. Among modern British poets, Hardy meant most to him. But the dominant influence upon Warren's own poetry, from 1922 through 1966, was T. S. Eliot; the spell of *The Waste Land* was not broken before *Incarnations* began to be composed. Until I purchased and read *Incarnations* in 1968, I had thought of Warren's poetry as being admirable but essentially derivative: Eliotic in mode, manner, and argument. Hart Crane, though also strongly affected by Eliot's poetry, fought against it from the start, but Warren needed more than forty years to get beyond Eliot.

Eliot's example both inspired and inhibited Warren. I remember my own surprise when, in January 1973, I received first a postcard and then an exuberant letter from Warren, reacting to a little book I had just published, *The Anxiety of Influence: A Theory of Poetry.* I scarcely had expected Warren to like it, but I was mistaken, and the book, which cost me some old friends, gave me a new one. At our first lunch together, Warren emphasized his uncanny sense of recognizing his own relation to his precursor, Eliot, in my descriptions of the agonistic relationship between strong poets and their inheritors. In the fifteen years that followed, as our friendship developed, we rarely could discuss Eliot—or Ralph Waldo Emerson—without fierce (though amiable) lunchtime disagreements. Eliot and Emerson are profoundly antithetical to one another, and Warren's distaste for Emerson was lifelong and passionate. Strongly *not* a Christian believer, Warren nevertheless had Augustinian convictions as to sin, error, guilt, and history. Himself a man of great humor, ironic tolerance, and considerable wisdom, Warren was probably the most severe secular moralist that I have ever known.

Though he stemmed from Eliot, as poet and as critic, Warren's temperament had little in common with Eliot's. The savage bite of Warren's best novels—*Night Rider* (1939), *At Heaven's Gate* (1943), *All the King's Men,* and *World Enough and Time*—sometimes echoes Eliot's Jacobean diction. Nevertheless, Warren was a great storyteller, whose narrative art had been schooled by Conrad and Faulkner, sensibilities more baroque than Eliotic. The full elaboration of Warren's poetic rhetoric does not enter his poetry until *Incarnations* and the subsequent *Audubon: A Vision* (1969).

While he was teaching his final semester at Yale, Warren was at work upon what became *Or Else: Poem/Poems, 1968–1974,* which still seems to me his finest single volume. A generation younger than the poet, and awed by him (always kind, he nevertheless intimated a force kept in reserve), I listened raptly to his ongoing meditations upon his poetic career. His poetry had ceased in 1943, and was not fully resumed until the late summer of 1954, though the first version of *Brother to Dragons* was published in 1953. Warren remarked that the years from 1943 to 1953 were mostly devoted to the composition of *At Heaven's Gate, All the King's Men,* and *World Enough and Time,* but a kind of undersong intimated personal unhappiness as being an element in his poetic silence. The transitional volumes—*Promises: Poems, 1954–1956* (1957), *You, Emperors, and Others: Poems, 1957–1960* (1960), and the *Selected Poems: New and Old, 1923–1966* (1966)—though admired by many, still seemed much under Eliot's influence. Some of my own gathering thoughts on the nature of poetic influence were greatly stimulated by *Incarnations,* where a new Warren emerged with astonishing intensity.

Warren's new style was hard, riddling, substantive: "My tongue / Was like a dry leaf in my mouth," the poet observes in the particularly good exemplar of this new style, "The Leaf." Blinded in one eye at fifteen, Warren eventually had one glass eye, as well as some perpetual uneasiness should he ever lose the other. I think Warren became aware that this anxiety had some relation to what became his most characteristic metaphor, which is the association of poetic vision with a hawk's sunset flight and with a hawk's own vision. "The Leaf" records a moment of shamanistic identity between the hawk and the reincarnation of the poetic character in Warren: "I saw / The hawk shudder in the high sky." Warren's father had wanted above all to be a poet, but had given up this ambition in order to support his family. Warren's awareness of that renunciation in part explains the piercing outcry: "I, / Of my father, have set the teeth on edge." But this agonistic experience is offset by the blessing that frames the cry:

The world
Is fruitful, and I, too,
In that I am the father
Of my father's father's father. I,
Of my father, have set the teeth on edge.

Warren's father calls to him, and blesses him, "in the moment when the cicada ceases." "Not the cicada," Eliot had written, and, with conscious artistry, Warren achieves his full, post-Eliotic voice, his new style: *teeth set on edge.*

The two great decades of Warren's poetry were very demanding, of the poet and reader alike, and many have not been comfortable with his prophetic style, resonating like a new Isaiah. Yet the power and originality of Warren's finest poems seem to me indisputable. Every lover of Warren's work will have his or her own list of favorites; my ideal anthology of American poetry would begin Warren selections with "The Leaf" and then include, at a minimum: "Birth of Love," "Evening Hawk," "Heart of Autumn," "Red-Tail Hawk and Pyre of Youth," "Myth of Mountain Sunrise," "Mortal Limit," and, of the earlier poems, "Mortmain," "Revelation," and "Bearded Oaks." My choices, though necessarily personal, at least reflect thirty years of rereading and teaching Warren's poetry. Readers new to Warren's work might want to begin with them, though I would invite them also to range freely through this vast and splendid book.

A critic cannot be a prophet, yet my own conception of criticism includes the enterprise of canon making, now a very unpopular labor indeed. Nevertheless, there seems broad agreement these days upon at least some of the modern American poets who will be permanent in our literature: Robert Frost, Wallace Stevens, William Carlos Williams, Marianne Moore, Ezra Pound, T. S. Eliot, Hart Crane, John Crowe Ransom, Theodore Roethke, Elizabeth Bishop, James Merrill, John Ashbery, A. R. Ammons. . . . Robert Penn Warren is clearly of that company. Doubtless there are other extraordinary candidates: I myself would add May Swenson, and the African American poets Jay Wright and Thylias Moss. Such listings can appear idiosyncratic, yet may prove suggestive. The choice of Robert Penn Warren's poetry to help constitute the canon of modern American poetry is, however, neither arbitrary nor idiosyncratic. At their strongest, Warren's poems win their contest with the American Sublime and find a place with Melville's best poems, formidable exiles from our dominant, Emersonian tradition.

Note

The symbol * is used to indicate a space between sections of a poem wherever such spaces are lost in pagination.

Uncollected Poems 1922–1943

Prophecy

You see no beauty in the parched parade,
The quivering, heat-glazed highways mile on mile,
The fields where beauty holds a debt unpaid,
The gray, drab barracks in monotonous, grim file.

You take no joy when dust wraiths dimly curl
Above the winding column crawling on far hills.
You see but short beyond the present whirl
Of circumstance, your little wrongs and petty ills.

But when it all has passed and you have lost
The swinging rhythmic cadence of the marching feet,
Then you will reck as paltry small the cost,
And memory will purge the bitter from the sweet.

Vision

I shall build me a house where the larkspur blooms
    In a narrow glade in an alder wood,
Where the sunset shadows make violet glooms,
    And a whip-poor-will calls in eerie mood.

I shall lie on a bed of river sedge,
    And listen to the glassy dark,
With a guttered light on my window ledge,
    While an owl stares in at me white and stark.

I shall burn my house with the rising dawn,
    And leave but the ashes and smoke behind,
And again give the glade to the owl and the fawn,
    When the grey wood smoke drifts away with the wind.

Crusade

We have not forgot the clanking of grey armors
Along frosty ridges against the moon,
The agony of gasping endless columns,
Skulls glaring white on red deserts at noon;
Nor death in dank marshes by fever,
Flies on bloated bodies rotting by the way,
Naked corpses on the sluggish river,
Sucked from the trampled rushes where they lay.

*

After shouting and trumpets and the crash of splintering lances,
After these and weeping, I can yet remember
How on my castle turret sunset glances,
Touching high windows to a redder amber;
The cenobite's soft hands upon my brow
With cool unpassioned fingers and benediction;
The close hush of the rabble as we made our vow
To win the Tomb of God—that was our mission;
The thronged cathedral where we took our crosses
And prayed away the penance of our sin...

We remember still the sunlight at Marseilles,
The long green wash of breakers swirling in,
Our white ships ready in the open harbor,
The flash of scarlet crosses that we wore
Over glitter and ring of new polished armor...
Shouting shriveling to a whisper from the shore.

Then knightly bodies quiet beneath low stars,
Tattered mail rusting on hot hard sands,
Strange riders startling up the night,
And broken hilts clutched loosely in jewelled hands.

We have now won through these to the Tomb of God;
Here is a hole where once lay sacred bones.
Red crosses have greyed on our hauberks.
Souls may be whiter for gazing on white stones.
Here is the Tomb as when our Lord had risen,
Here is the Tomb, but yonder promised peace.
Can rock and dust presage a fabled heaven?
This low malignant moon gives no surcease
Nor any opiate of forgetfulness
For the sob and choke of remembered sorrow...
We have no solace in this bitter stillness.
We shall be still enough tomorrow.

After Teacups

I was not on the parapets at Cretae
Dreading sails black against the red low moon,
When my ruin overthrew me.
Nor did it claim me with the plunge of Grecian spears
Surging up in dark ships from the sea
That ancient night. There rode no portent of my fears
On the long breeze sweeping in from Cyprus;
Nor later with the rank mists when I fought
Bogged in the marshes, clubbing my arquebus.
I touched on no presentiments
In the whimper of gulls low over our galley

Waiting our bodies, no more than with the Spaniard
Heaving a saber in that fetid valley.
I have not found death snarling in a surge of lances,
In midnight clangor of the mouthing bells,
The legionary shout, the Gothic shields,
The flare and rumble of burning citadels,
Faint moonlight on a taken bastion.
But dissolution clutched me
Descanting in Mme. Atelie's salon
Of balls at Nice and coursing at L'Enprix.
I sipped my tea with marked exactitude,
Refusing claret; speculated on
The bleak breasts of a marble nude,
Noting the while a flutter of trivial hands.
Her eyes were winds down a wintry chasm
Where frozen surf beats rock and frozen sands.
Outside a spring swarmed up the avenues,
Spattering hydrangeas with a gust of bloom.

Midnight

I cannot sleep at night for dread
Of terrible green moons that haunted once
The dark above our marriage bed,
Where night long you lay listening fearfully
To the vulture on the rooftree croaking war;
While on the blackened ceiling you could see
A rocky plain and there your dying lover;
Could see the jackal slinking to the river,
Then red carnival in my victorious tents.
Yet you pretend forgetfulness,
Oblivion to that and like events.
Have you forgot the green Egyptian moon
That leered into the casement where
You sat, wiping bloody fingers through your hair?
Or the lizard on the arras never blinking?
Though your lips now gibber in a prayer
I perceive that you are thinking
Of leprous mists above the muddy Nile
And you, a leper, howling among the tombs;
Of the cold stench of bats in catacombs,
And Tartar gongs or Janizary spears.
Our destiny is goats' blood in a bowl.
Now warlocks and fiends pursue your soul
Down ruined colonnades of years,
While the corpse, here, stares into the grate.
Your gaunt uncomprehending eyes
Clutch at me as I start to rise,

Rattling my newspaper, saying, "It is late."
You draw the pins, release your flood of hair.
Am I doomed to stand thus ever,
Hesitating on the stair?

The Fierce Horsemen

Pitiless, pitiless spoilers,
    Raiding the weeping land,
Wrenching the last frail leaf
    From the dying year's cold hand.

"Why do you ride your wild horses
    Shrieking over our roofs,
Ravage our fair, sweet silence
    With the thunder of their hoofs?"

"Why do we ride down the summer,
    Under hoofs of the wind-hurled rain?
We needs must ride down the summer
    That a spring may come again."

Wild Oats

I am sowing wild oats
    On rocky hills and steep,
And when my harvest whitens
    I shall not be here to reap.

But the four wild winds shall winnow
    And the sun and rain shall reap;
And they shall glut my storehouse,
    But I shall be asleep.

To Certain Old Masters

I have read you and read you, my betters,
    Vivisected every page;
I have diagnosed even the letters,
    Pent each hell in its private cage.

I have hacked you all into pieces
    And stuck you together again,
But my questioning round never ceases;
    No solution at all will you deign.

*

I have seen the man in his volume,
    (I'm as much of a man as you)
But in spite of all my logic,
    One plus one not always makes two.

I have asked you all how it happened.
    I have questioned you one by one,
And each of you pettily jealous,
    Feared to tell how the thing was done.

I have prayed but a crumb of your power,
    But a farthing from you all,
And you gave but a cryptic silence
    From your shelves along the wall.

I might burn you all on my hearthstone
    And watch you flake and glow.
Yes, I will have my vengeance,
    But that were a vengeance low;

For you shall all be forgotten
    On your musty, dust-cloaked shelves,
With your pages flaking and rotten,
    Dead as your masters' dead selves.

For I shall go in the gray of the dawning,
    To the tip of a high, blue hill,
And hear the mist-cowled morning,
    Breathless, awed, and still.

The Golden Hills of Hell

O, fair the Golden Hills of Hell,
    Where lightly rest the purple lilies;
There, as all the saints tell
    Lightly nod the lilies.

Dim beyond the scarlet river,
    Slenderly and slow they nod,
Glimpsed from where the splendors quiver
    On the minarets of God.

False tales the saints tell
    Of the slender lilies;
For I have knelt on the Hills of Hell
    Among the withered lilies.

Three Poems

I. Iron Beach

Beyond this bitter shore there is no going,
This iron beach, this tattered verge of land;
Behind us now the tundra dims with snowing,
In front the seas leap crashing on the strand.
Faintly the sun wheels down its quickened arc
While at our backs with inexorable motion
Earth swings forgotten cities into dark
And night sweeps up across the polar ocean.

This place has its own peace, assuredly.
Here we, once waked by tramcars in the street,
Shall rest in unperturbed austerity,
Hearing the surf interminably beat,
Watching the pole star overhead until
The arctic summer brings the carrion gull.

II. Mrs. Dodd's Daughter

So many are the things that she has learned,
So many, and so bitter was their learning,
That it will take long for this dark she has earned
To quench the smouldering anguish of its earning.

We should perhaps be glad she no more hears,
When faintly the moon streaks in across her bed,
Inconsolable voices of the years
Nocturnally appealing to her dread.

Though now we see her still, as quietly folded
As a white flower in summer after rain,
Yet it will take the roots' long fingers long
To smooth the tortured creases of her brain.

III. Apocalypse

I knew not down what windy nights I fled
Driven by magics of the shuddering moon.
Gigantic and splendid a king slept on his throne;
Before his feet a strangled hound lay dead
Between a board of chess and a broken sheath.
A fire blazed ever without heat or motion;
Heavy bells tolled whose dread reverberation
Hung in the air unheard. I waited death.

*

Hooded, in that tall place a figure came,
Whose voice released the flame and bells; "Thy sword,
O king! Hold now our ancient oath—to game!"
One finger hovered leanly on the board.
I awoke and all that hideous night till dawn
Watched the pale worlds wheel on and faintly on.

Death Mask of a Young Man

I. The Mouse

Down the stair had creaked the doctor's feet
Shuffling. He heard them out thinking it queer
Tomorrow night at nine he would not hear
Feet shuffling out and down into the street
Past the one murky gas jet in the hall,
Past the discarded chair beside his door,
The Steinbach's entrance on the lower floor,
And the cracked patch of plaster on the wall.

Just how that crack came he could never think
To save his life, though he remembered yet
How once a mouse ran in, quick as a wink.
It must have said, "Why here's a hole in the wall!
I'll just whisk in, into the dark, and let
Heavy and terrible feet tramp down the hall."

II. The Moon

Remotely the moon across the window pane,
Was passing, as he had often watched it pass
When nights like this, too tired for sleep, he'd lain
Watching that moon beyond the dirty glass
Slide out of sight as if drawn by a string
Stretched through the stars; then he would count the tread
Of the deliberate clock that soon would bring
The moon past, and a shadow to his bed.

But now forgetful of slow pomp the clock
With slavering fangs and like the haggard dog
Harried the minutes in a desperate flock;
Dully the bell in the cathedral tower,
Mouthing the death of the expiring hour,
Bayed the white moon down to its lair of fog.

Nocturne

Tonight the woods are darkened.
We have forgot our pain,
The pain of hearts that hearkened
To an old abysmal strain,

Creeping up from lost stars
To sear our solitude
And brand these bitter scars
We wear about our wood.

O yes—these paths are haunted,
For we are each a ghost,
A ghost whose wraith is taunted
By memories it lost

And may not find again.
Before lies year on year,
Ruining swales of unreaped grain;
While from those fields we hear

In the wintry cawing raven
Black echoes of our pain.
For the hazel leaf once fallen
Grows never green again.

Adieu Sentimentale

Collect the ashes of this infatuation,
(A metaphor befitting things just past)
And mingle in the urn of recollection
The thought that though not first you may be last;

Perhaps the last, for I, remembering
Nights when your star burned redder than the most,
Shall descant to inexorable spring
Of one somewhat more brutal that we lost.

Since I cannot devise a fit expression
To the requisite gesture of your smile,—my dear,
As epitaph contrive no definition
Of what it is that we are leaving here.

The Romance Macabre

Even tonight, I think, if you would ask,
I could remember what it was you said
When first you pierced beneath my spangled mask
To find the caverned eyes of one long dead.

Even tonight, when once again a spring
Storms gallantly the wintry bastion,
We might rehearse this tale; it will not bring
Tears to the sockets of a skeleton.

Forgive me, Madam, this metaphor macabre,
One scarce incarnate of those glories fled;
For ghost and ghost commune till dawn together,
Haunted by anguish of the lustful dead.

Sonnets of Two Summers

I. Sonnet of a Rainy Summer

It was a rainy summer, you remember;
Rainy, with wind and ruin and swift decay
Of corn grown tall and the wheat unreaped that lay
Between our house and your storm-shattered timber,
Behind whose fractured silhouette the pale
Sun, like a lost desire, falling would break
To terrible dead green along the peak
Of thunder tattered into wind and hail.

Strange now, this rain, not summer's, on the roofs
And windy fingers at the window pane
Stir pitiless remembrance of things I knew—
The scent of wet whitethorn along a lane,
One twisted silver-penny moon, slow hoofs
Plashing the mud as I rode home from you.

II. Sonnet of August Drouth

Eternally our afternoons then stood
On brittle fields, on land seared yellow and dead
Despite the river, that lean like the copperhead
Crawled through dry flats last summer under flood.
Only at night we caught reverberation
Of far and futile thunders on the wind
As echoes of old storm, blowing to mind
Clean rain-washed hills and not this desolation.

*

What winds along what arid lanes will scatter
Seed of that deathy time when nothing grew
But a sultry passion and the feverfew?
Beneath what heavy hills—O tell me now—
Are bound the lightnings that will leap to shatter
This cairn of darkness piled upon my brow!

Praises for Mrs. Dodd

Death squats on the bottom stair
In the drab hall of this drab house,
Smirking at the callers there.

Callers like roaches clutter the hall,
Like roaches in deferential black
For homage to Death who squats by the wall.

At half past nine, like a candle flame,
Neat and obsequious, rubbing his hands;
At half past nine, like a candle flame.

Mother Dodd's soul flickered out at her lips—
A faint blue flicker of choking flame.
Now in and out the daughter slips,

Anxious in flounced and pleated grief
And wondering if her nose is red.
On the door hangs crepe and the garnered sheaf

Symbolic of earthly duties done,
Of broom and rag and mop translated
To the harp and crown Mrs. Dodd has won.

Portraits of Three Ladies

I.

He passed her only once in a crowded street,
A tangent flaring by her petty arc.
She did not hear black spurs clank on his feet
Or under his coat the black emblazoned sark;
For she, of course, knew no mythology
And could not thrill, as others might have done,
To pale and lunar murmurs of the sea
Or gilded savage clarions of the sun.

*

But often that lean smile his lean lips wore
Brutally gashed the drab peace of her mind;
If once at night she stretched upon the floor
Watching the wet moon glisten on the roofs,
It was not to catch on that strange April wind
The scent of damp fern crushed by satyr hoofs.

II.

"Since I can neither move you nor the fate
That parts us here, without recrimination
I beg, my dear, a niche in recollection,
That of your lover unregenerate."
She smiled and left him there to contemplate
His graceful posturings of adoration;
To think; "At least in this one situation
My rhetoric was deft and adequate."

She smiled but found no sudden blade of tears
To cut the strictured cruelty of that smile;
With eyes that were a broken desolation
She faced a shattered night, and all the while
Up to the taciturn and cynic stars
There streamed an immemorial lamentation.

III.

Strangely her heart yet clutched a strange twilight,
One that had lured with dream down a cypressed way
To glens where hairy-haunched and savage lay
The night. Could ever she forget that night
And one black pool, her image in the water,
Or how fat lily stalks were stirred and shifted
By terrible things beneath, and how there drifted
Through slimy trunks and fern a goatish laughter.

Sometimes at dusk before her looking glass
She thought how in that pool her limbs gleamed whitely;
She heard her husband watering the grass
Or his neat voice inquiring,"Supper dear?"
Across the table then she faced him nightly
With harried eyes in which he read no fear.

Autumn Twilight Piece

Now has the brittle incandescent day
Been shattered, spilling from its fractured bowl
The so trite dusk upon a street and soul
That wait their own and evening's decay.
Will not a midnight grant deliverance
Of dusk and all its bitter casuistries;
Nor death, nor dawn whose querulous harmonies
Are torn to day and gorgeous dissonance?

Autumn, we know, is twilight of the year.
This bronze and amber rumor of our death
Stains the far hills and soon to us will bring
The caverned sleep of winter, when beneath
The fennel's frigid roots we shall not hear
Again the bright amphigories of spring.

Admonition to the Dead

Such be the end of all the red and gold;
Such be the end of all the lips and hair......
This thing alone our heritage of old,
Knowledge of this our legacy to despair.
Such be the end.

Convolve in laughter not the lipless bone;
Let us forget your mirth. Such be the end.
Nor weep; but in that land where you are gone
Take rest until all, slow friend by friend,
Come to you there.

Apologia for Grief

Now I remember songs you might have sung,
I can remember words you might have said;
Singing and speech both proper to the young,
For you were young, who now are dead.

Since you are dead with all the other dead,
I am not one to reconsider grief,
To wet with wine my arval bread,
Nor speak too long; I shall be brief.

*

I shall be brief, who have no word
Not fabulous with other tears than mine,
No barbarous tongue you have not heard.
Can I distill the dark in such a sign?

Might I project the image of this hour,
Conceive this symbol fitting to my days,
So few they are,—a ruined and lonely tower
On the wide sand, fired by the sun's last rays?

Alf Burt, Tenant Farmer

Despite that it is summer and the sun
Comes up at four and corn is rank with weed
Old Burt is abed and won't see the plowing done
Nor find a harvest where he laid the seed.

A fatter harvest than he's ever known
He will reap perhaps in field where he is gone—
Harvest of farmlands fairer than our own.
There will the plowshare never bite the stone,

Never will blight fall on the yellow pear,
Nor flood and wind defy the weary hand.
Never will work the plague and weevil there,
Nor yet descend the locust on the land.

Nor pestilence. It is a country where
No frost can come for Old Man Burt to fear.
Perpetual seedtime meets with summer there,
Harvest and spring together in the year.

And if not that at least for him will be
The steadfast earth of a narrow grave and deep
Beneath the fennel and the lean thorntree,
Whose haggard roots will quickly give a sleep.

Heavy as in the midnights of December.
And in that sleep where all things are the same
No dream can fall to stir him to remember
Thistle and drouth and the crops that never came.

Admonition to Those Who Mourn

Now is the hour to rhyme a song for death,
A facile song for him that death has taken;
To formulate what anguish lies beneath
These proper eyes not even death can waken.

From adequate oblivion unto tears
The house is empty now, the portals broken,
The tenant thief has fled; no one there hears
The bells that once so silverly had spoken.

Prepare your faces now and so depart.
The usual feet will bruise the pavement stone;
Let each man fix his hand upon his heart
And measure out the days of flesh and bone,

Until with unequivocal slow tread
He climb alone some hill about twilight—
Then think not long, dear sirs, upon the dead
Lest you, somehow, should envy him the night.

The Mirror

Erect, meticulous within the mirror
My image postured, combing its black hair.
"God," then I thought with sudden terror—
"Tomorrow or next day, some other day,
They'll come and put in a box and carry away
This head with its fine long hair!" O it was droll!
A man regarding with such an anguished stare
His corpse that combed black hair across its skull.

What frigid and especial stars of old
Converged to lead me out into this street,
Leaving my image in the glass, to see
Again and surely in every face I meet
That accurate implacable and cold
Refraction of my own mortality?

Easter Morning: Crosby Junction

The psalms are said and three potted lilies nod
As the preacher's measured plea ascends to God
The Father, to the Son and Holy Ghost.
The words ascend, drift out the windows, are lost

In the April hot sunshine whose intense gold
Has inflamed the maple bud and the sullen cold
Thick crocus whose new fires perfect the spring.
"The Winter today is fled and sweet birds sing

"That to the earth is come the Son of Life,
That Mortality is swallowed up of Life."
(Of a surety after winter there is spring
For joy whereof be it said the sweet birds sing.)

"And so ye all from the body of this death
Shall be sucked up like dew from the earth beneath—"
(The sun sucks up the dew from fields new-plowed)—
"And on such day that which each man hath sowed,

"That shall he reap." (Wherefore let the seed be good
That the yellow corn may fructify when sowed.)
"Rejoice, ye Righteous, Christ from the tomb is come!"
(The crocus, a Christ, breaks its black bulb, the tomb.)

"Now ye that believe on Him are not to die—"
(Through the window the voice importunate and high
Rejects the confutation of the stone
That in the churchyard marks the mortal bone)—

"But inherit life eternal—have ye no fear!"
(Indeed there are no murderers buried here
But godly flesh is rumored to decay,
And if here flourish not the rank green bay

The cedar hath an hungry root and long.
How may we sing who have no golden song,
How may we speak who have no word to say,
Or pray, or pray—who would so gently pray?)

Mr. Dodd's Son

He was born far inland in a little town
That sent no men in ships down to the sea,
And beyond her dusty streets had only known
Green mains of the wheatfield tossing silently.

If in her steeples never there tolled a bell
For lovely keels that left her but to be lost,
At least in chambers of the deep whorled shell
Reverberation lingered like the ghost

Of reminiscent music in a dream.
After the harvest at night in a sultry sleep
He would see his own white body drift and gleam
Down shifting reaches of the grey cold deep.

Before he died unto the sea he came;
He could not speak—as one who suddenly
Hears in the night beyond the coasts of time
Faintly the surges of eternity.

The Wrestling Match

"Here in this corner, ladies and gentlemen,
I now presents 'Mug' Hill, weight two-hundred-ten,
Who will wrestle here tonight the 'Battling Pole,'
Boruff—" who, as insistently the stale

Loud voice behind asserts, is good as hell.
"Is good as hell, I says," and then the bell
Stabs up to life two engines of flesh and bone,
Each like a great and bronze automaton

That by black magic moves stupendously,
Moving with a machine's intensity,
To some obscure and terrible conclusion
Involving us as in an absurd vision

The truculent dull spirit is involved
There to contend above, while is dissolved
In sleep the twisted body on the bed.
The barker said—or was it this he said:

"Ladies and gentlemen, I now present—"
The voice here sank in some obscene intent—
"That which is body so you all may see
The bone and blood and sweat and agony

*

And thews that through the tortured years have striven
To breach the flesh so sure to spill when broken
The only breath, a cry, and the dark blood
That forever we would keep if we but could."

Images on the Tomb

I. Dawn: The Gorgon's Head

Too late returns the measured sun and slow
To mute the night articulate in dream,
For voices like the paling stars did go
Coldly before the dawn whose rigid beam
Now stirs the tangled body to arise.
"Get up, get up. Wash the face, comb the hair,
Put shoes on the feet and take the coat that lies
Crumpled like a brain upon the chair.

"Get up! Go to the mirror on the wall.
See what you are—the eyes and there behind
Grey cells rotting in thought which are the brain.
Blood no more shakes the flesh; in the empty hall
No foot may stir. What if an April wind
Is lost in the smoky avenues again?"

II. Day: Lazarus

Ever in the hot street one walks unseen
Beside you as your heels clack on their way,
Striding beside you, oracular and lean,
Who has not spoken but who will speak some day:
"When the adder coils beneath the shrivelling fern,
And the obscene wheat rots in the bearded head,
Then, in such month alone, I shall return
Bringing remembrance to you from the dead."

And then within the flesh will creep the bone
Mortally cold, while you will wait forever
In a shattered street for the viper, the bearded grain,
Lost in a chasmed land of steel and stone
To wander at noon in a chill daylight and never,
Like Lazarus, be warmed in the sun again.

III. Evening: The Motors

Remorselessly the evening motors pass
Bearing men home down streets where there will be
Doorways and windows where behind the glass
Are lights, and faces that have eyes to see,
Seeing but nothing, ears to hear that hear
Nothing, red lips to cry out that cry not
But speak, speaking quickly, for the fear
Of seeing shadows that they have forgot.

The evening motors pass bearing you home
To words and silence, food, tobacco, sleep—
To sleep, the dark wherein you all are piled,
Poor fragments of the day, until there come
Dreams to release from the troubled heart and deep
The pageantry of thoughts unreconciled.

IV. Night: But a Sultry Wind

If there were storm tonight, if the loud thunder
Contorted the craggy dark, broke terribly
The fabrics of the firmament asunder,
I might rush out, crying,"O come with me!
O come, come out, out in the night again!"
And in the lightning flare would be bodies blown
Naked and white in the windy dark and rain,
The beat of bloody feet on the wet hard stone.

There is no storm tonight, but a sultry wind
Rattles my papers, shifting the slow curtain;
And as I write these lines, in sleep you all
Rise on the arm while in the caverned mind
Remembrance stirs like a weary dream and certain.
But sleep, sleep—white faces turned to the wall.

August Revival: Crosby Junction

Wheat is threshed and cut the heavy clover;
Seedtime with the sinful spring was over.
No more to do and nowhere else to go
They pack the varnished benches, row on row,

Puddling thick air with the yellow palm-leaf fan,
Attentive to history of the Son of Man
Who died for them. On the oaken organ top,
Withered, the red geranium petals drop

*

Slowly, as dropped unto the dust dark blood
Slowly, as drop the words of him who would
The passionate priestly office exercise,
Spreading gaunt arms that he may dramatize

For these, the stiff-necked sinful and Pharisee,
The Cross, the essence of the agony.
So still the bleeding hands extend and still
The Cross subdues the dark Place of the Skull.

Enough—O you behind the pulpit there,
You Peter with bony hands and thinning hair!
Enough, old man! Eat, sleep, for you are old,
And your chronicle too weary to be told.

Wheat is threshed and cut the heavy clover,
But tall the corn stands; harvest is not over.
Let the corn be cut; for bellies there must be bread,
And sleep for men that be not living, not dead.

So wake them not lest they ask too much, too much,
And touch no more the broken feet, nor touch
The piteous brown fingers in the shroud.
Let them so be; and cry no more aloud,

But let the serpent coil in the dry winepress,
The lank hare's foot disturb the withering grass,
Let young foxes be gnawing the hare's worn skull
And the owl hoot from the olive tree on the hill!

Let the city sleep—roofs are white in the moon—
And sleep the young wild head within the stone;
Let the legionary shiver and tramp outside,
Forgetful to-night what manner of man has died!

Pro Sua Vita

Nine months I waited in the dark beneath
Her tired heart for this precious breath,

And month by month since I left her breast
Her breath and blood I have given in waste

Till now at length some peace she has got
That her breath and blood in me have not.

In the strictured nights of glimmering snow
The blood goes quick though the breath is slow,

*

And through the August afternoon
Flees the breath faintly but too soon.

So blood is lost to the brutal gardens
Where the iron petal of dark frost hardens;

And breath, when the storm-black trees bowed under,
Waited the fanged astounding thunder.

Shall I say to my father then
Among the belted best of men:

"Fellow, you tupped her years ago
That tonight my boots might crunch the snow.

"And woman, you show your son to wait
Till the breath and distrait blood abate;

"As my father began the tale of waste
When the sullen head slept on your breast

"So the rigid hills had been forgot
In darkness, if God had wasted not."

The Owl

Here was the sound of water falling only,
Which is not sound but silence musical
Tumbling forever down the gorge's wall.
Like late milkweed that blooms beside the lonely
And sunlit stone, peace bloomed all afternoon.
Where time is not is peace; and here the shadow,
That crept to him across the western meadow
And climbed the hill to mark the dropping sun,
Seemed held a space, washed downward by the water
Whose music flowed against the flow of time.
It could not be. Dark fell along the stream,
And like a child grown suddenly afraid,
With shaking knees, hands bloody on the stone,
Toward the upland gleaming fields he fled.
Light burned against their rim, was quickly gone.

Later he would remember this, and start.
And once or twice again his tough old heart
Knew sickness that the rabbit's heart must know,
When star by star the great wings float,
And down the moonlit track below
Their mortal silken shadow sweeps the snow.
O scaled bent claw, infatuate deep throat!

Tryst on Vinegar Hill

Over Vinegar Hill somehow the sky
Through the long summer seems to lie
More intimately, more blue,
As if from that especial spot it drew
A deep primeval clarity
Up from the heart and desperate sinew
Of niggers who once were buried there.
Their substances may climb the gradual air,
Lifting as moisture calmly after rain,
Up from the burdock leaf and earth-clean bone
In golden atoms to the sun again
—The sun which is their own alone.

Up Vinegar Hill in summertime
A nigger boy and girl will climb
To watch the lazy sun go down,
The supper smoke rise from Squiggtown,
The shadow swell like water over earth
And night hang out a casual first star,
When the heavy crows have beaten north
To roost by the river where the deep woods are.

Niggers are the damnedest breed:
They see such things and do not need
To know they see, or even guess
Within the earth that restlessness
Of thought which arches those obscene
Fat tropic ocean tides, arches the green
Slow channels of the secret leaf; which drops
The nerves' grey filaments to stay the bone,
And whose dishonest artifice unlocks
The oak's tough bole to bud, and subtly props
The crystalline interiors of the stone.
They do not guess that thought which mocks
Itself back to its hungry elements.
They only see, and their ripe innocence
Of laughter from dark lips in twilight now
Spills; no wind, but the low dogwood's intense
White bloom spills on the dew-black bough.

So all night long the girl and boy
Lie side by side on Vinegar Hill
—Yaller gal and big black boy—
And time swings up and westward and away.
Just once they hear the tardy whip-poor-will
To whose uneasy questioning refrain
They have no ready answer but to lay
The lip to lip and heart to heart again.

*

Around them in the summer dark
Timorously huddle then the dead
To humbly watch the lovers and to spread
Their fingers to the little spark
Of warmth the living bodies own.
They know their place—not anxious, not too bold—
Poor ghosts, who once loved laughter and the sun,
And now, when the lazy day is gone,
Still find the ivied earth so cold.

Empire

Phoenician galley and the sweating slave
 over the flat Mediterranean,
 beating by Carthage in the sun.
Pillars of Hercules, gates that gave
 on the deep's grey gardens and the Cornish coast.
Phoenician, Greek, men whom the summer lured
 past Carthage to the waters in the west.
Black galleys beaked to westward like a bird.

Not the beginning, not the end.
They did not know that land and ocean bend
 downward to make the long circuit home.
This much great Cæsar did not know
 when, shield to arm, he leaped the prow
 and over his feet curled the strait's cold foam.
The mad tired eyes, fixed on the wild land
 under his eagles, saw not the long way home,
 the world that closes like a tired closed hand.

Then others came who knew; the man
 from Genoa knew on the high-pooped caraval.
Santa Maria. O white and virginal
 incredible shore where morning breakers ran!
Hendrik Hudson, icicles in his beard,
 northwest by west to the echo of a word.
India. By frozen coasts the bitten spume;
 passage to India, passage home.
Many were hungry, many were cold;
 by rocks, in tall grass, in the deep pinewood,
 by rivers they lay down. Their blood
 toward silence spilled in vagrant westward gold.

You single-hearted and horizon-sick,
 thief from tomorrows, dupe of yesterdays,
 we own no kin with you. Your ways,
 certain, lost, are not our ways; the quick
 lack commerce with the dead whose history
 is commensurate, unnamed.

*

But I would speak
with you, you other. Bastard to memory,
you spawn from no desire... my spotless white
new lamb, got of no sin, born to no wrath,
no home, no repentance.
Always at night
the land-wind lifts. Follow, there is a path
down through the dunes, I recall, which brings
us to the beach. The wind, east, will swerve
only at dawn. Behind us in the duneland
the cicada, cold in the salt grass, sings
no more. I think that we can understand
each other, talking here, while we observe
the foam in calyx on the patient sand.

The Limited

Since there's no help, come, let them kiss and part—
The Pullman step's as good as any place.
It's certain love can scarcely learn the art
To read the mind's construction in the face.
And so he tips the grim white-coated groom,
Consigns her bags to that black hand of doom;
Then slick as death the velvet pistons start,
Like fat blood in a drowning swimmer's heart.

White Proserpine whirled in the cloudy car
While brightness drops from star and star:
Proven—ah, sad sorites of the year—
For him who turns like that mute Orpheus
Again to thrust by all the vulgar dead.
But in his heart the summer's wrath shall roam
With burning eyes, as in the vacant house
The cold and dry-foot cat whose tread
Wheels from last week's newspaper to the broom.

Athenian Death

Born proud and fitful, hot and cold,
Suspicious as a king who sees
In every face unfaith unfold—
Born thus, bred in these qualities,
No wonder, turning, he again
Would turn to seek a steadfast lodgment
For love that was not peace, nor pain,
But a confusion past assuagement.

*

His was the equinoctial heart
Wherein untutored weathers veer
And random violences start:
Blank paroxysms of the year.
Or his the heart that knows no north,
Unpoled, pole-hungering, and spun
In aimless gyre, and little worth
To mark the sure direction.

His eyes pursued the flight of birds
Or read the horizon's hieroglyph;
Grudging as coin, his flattened words
Were paid for innocence, or if,
Unbound as grain, his kindness fell,
The ravening crow, his afterthought,
Revised the yearning furrow well;
And flattery rancor then unwrought.

He is not dead, for dying still,
Each day undoes the death fordone;
Nor living, for his unfed will
Refrains the sustenance of sun.
Young Lucifer! who daily falls
From glimmering pinnacles of light
And daily in the heart's four walls
Erects a hell in heaven's despite.

No traitor he! our brother yet,
So packed of truth and perfidy,
Of rage and charm, that we may get
Thus magnified and perfectly
Our image glassed in grander grace—
Bright parable of paradox.
And thus the passion of his face
Our secret secretly unlocks.

Under the starred and foreign sky,
After the spears made their carouse
And flame played only fitfully,
Timandra crept from out the house
To seek the wild one steel had tamed,
And weeping, held upon her knees
His head, whom men had always named
The *clever Alcibiades.*

Love's Voice

If once we dreamed love had a tongue
Tuned not to flatter but command
Gross ear and grosser thought, and strong
Enough to stay the ravening hand;
Or dreamed that trumpet-lipped loud love
Might shake us where like leaves we hung,
Or throated Joshua-strong might move
The stone—that time, it was not long.

For, no: no breath, no blast, no word
Provoked from sloth or balked from greed
The sty-fat thought, untaught, unstirred,
That slouching but awoke to feed.
For, no: what ear, though keen, had heard
Abroad that breath, that master-sound,
That wristward draws the unhooded bird
Or calls to heel the sullen hound?

Like one alone in a darkened room
Who leans and listens, and translates
What hope has lived despite that gloom
Into a step the ear awaits;
So in the darkness of the breast
The soul then leaned, and hearkened, then
Stretched forth the hands, and took no rest,
And waited, and would lean again,

Would lean like that lucky mariner
Who spied the drifting, berried bough,
Wave-borne yet green (ah! flown was fear
And the heart leaped, for fairer now
Lost leaf than all the groves of Spain),
Or him who hailed the trade-heaved bird,
Bright-winged, coming, going again;
But dreamed that woodland note he heard.

—No answer then: then hope deferred,
Faith fainter, and the absolute
Of joy forgot, reviled, a word
For fools, and nothing but the brute
Disorder for the anarch ear;
And truth stall-trod, and action weaned
Of essence, blind or bloody or
Knee-pawned—But still, sometimes, she leaned,

For faith had guessed all our wild sounds
To purer sense but silence are,
All brutish tumult that confounds
In vanity the unpregnant ear

But quiet to feed a firmer thought
As rank oil feeds the steady flame,
All ignorances violence wrought
But syllables for a clear name;

Or that fair thought antiquity
Bequeathed that sphere replied to sphere
Moving in music's surety,
But music of accord so pure
The cold sense paltered, and the excess
Of joy but spoke to those bright powers
Of mind withdrawn to single bliss:
Could we but dream such fable ours!

Such fable ours! or even snatch
New fable from the scientist's room,
Who marks a world beyond our pitch
Where sounds vibrate, new colors bloom,
Far past the poor ear's, eye's, dull span.
And that had been a happy task
In happier time, for us who scan
The world's blank, eyeless face, and ask,

What evidence in innocence?
What knowledge in the battened lust
Or meat-filled maw or glutted trance?
What glass unwinking gives our trust
Its image back, what echo names
The names we hurl at namelessness?
What thrives but paradox that frames
—And equal, O!—joy or distress?

Such fable ours! However sweet,
That earlier hope had, if fulfilled,
Been but child's pap and toothless meat
—And meaning blunt and deed unwilled,
And we but motes that dance in light
And in such light gleam like the core
Of light, but lightless, are in right
Blind dust that fouls the unswept floor

For, no: not faith by fable lives,
But from the faith the fable springs
—It never is the song that gives
Tongue life, it is the tongue that sings;
And sings the song. Then, let the act
Speak, it is the unbetrayable
Command, if music, let the fact
Make music's motion; us, the fable

*

Then let us turn now—you to me
And I to you—and hand to hand
Clasp, even though our fable be
Of strangers met in a strange land
Who pause, perturbed, then speak and know
That speech, half lost, can yet amaze
Joy at the root; then suddenly grow
Silent, and on each other gaze

Goodbye

That simplest gesture which can touch
Proud face and fair stability
To instability, uncrutch
The crutched-on truth of stone and tree,
Is magic any child may learn,
Or drivelled idiot at play
Who fires the rick and lets it burn
While his coo unseams the season's pay:
It is a magic easy to perform,
And practiced daily on any railroad platform.

Goodbye, and the sad dexterity
Betrays all matter's innocence
From form to mathematic fury,
And on the heart's stroke, disenchants
From smiling substance into shade
The friends you trusted, who have come—
As time, less cleverly, will fade
Those same brave smiles in the old album:
And even the dear landscape dissolves to smoke
Which stings the eyes, and makes the voice choke.

And you have felt the live locks lift
And coil, upon your crimeless head,
And fled your own un-Gorgoning gift,
As some young Gorgon might have fled
Who, kindly yet and new in horror,
By the dawn's first light had leaned to peer
At love, and learned her mortifying power:
In his sculptured eye, the sculptured tear.
You flee, and by your treacherous foot create
Yourself; who fleeing, yet all motion hate.

But are that flight and that fond hate
But your ignorant mathematic's mark,
By which poor chart all lines are straight
And lonely in the mechanic dark;

Which only knows the tangent's curse
Uncurved to hope and never stilled,
And knows no center's hand to nurse
Your course to circuit, thus fulfilled?
Dreaming but home, and not Cathay, you bear
Westward, who would un-Ptolemy despair.

Goodbye, and by that discipline
The heart unstrung and eye unskilled
May learn a surer hope wherein
Those forms whose being love had willed
But self's necessity betrayed
Will rise to pace the unwithering grass,
Unstammering and undismayed,
In their long picnic of blessedness;
Which incorruptible welcome you may find
Familiar, in the sunlit meadows of the mind.

Thirty-Six Poems

The Return: An Elegy

The east wind finds the gap bringing rain:
Rain in the pine wind shaking the stiff pine.
Beneath the wind the hollow gorges whine
The pines decline
Slow film of rain creeps down the loam again
Where the blind and nameless bones recline.

    they are conceded to the earth's absolute chemistry
    they burn like faggots in—of damp and dark—the monstrous bulging
            flame.
    calcium phosphate lust speculation faith treachery
    it walked upright with habitation and a name
        tell me its name

The pines, black, like combers plunge with spray
Lick the wind's unceasing keel
It is not long till day
The boughs like hairy swine in slaughter squeal
And lurch beneath the thunder's livid heel.
The pines, black, snore *what does the wind say?*

        tell me its name

I have a name: I am not blind.
Eyes, not blind, press to the Pullman pane
Survey the driving dark and silver taunt of rain.
What will I find
What will I find beyond the snoring pine?
O eyes locked blind in death's immaculate design
Shall fix their last distrust in mine

    give me the nickels off your eyes
    from your hands the violets
    let me bless your obsequies
    if you possessed conveniently enough three eyes
    then I could buy a pack of cigarettes

In gorges where the dead fox lies the fern
Will rankest loop the battened frond and fall
Above the bare and tushèd jaws that turn
Their insolence unto the gracious catafalque and pall.
It will be the season when milkweed blossoms burn.

    the old bitch is dead
    what have I said!
    I have only said what the wind said
    wind shakes a bell the hollow head

*

By dawn, the wind, the blown rain
Will cease their antique concitation.
It is the hour when old ladies cough and wake,
The chair, the table, take their form again
Earth begins the matinal exhalation

does my mother wake

Pines drip without motion
The hairy boughs no longer shake
Shaggy mist, crookbacked, ascends
Round hairy boughs the mist with shaggy fingers bends.
No wind: no rain:
Why do the steady pines complain?
Complain

the old fox is dead
what have I said

Locked in the roaring cubicle
Over the mountains through darkness hurled
I race the daylight's westward cycle
Across the groaning rooftree of the world.
The mist is furled.

a hundred years they took this road
the lank hunters then men hard-eyed with hope:
ox breath whitened the chill air: the goad
fell: here on the western slope
the hungry people the lost ones took their abode
here they took their stand:
alders bloomed on the road to the new land
here is the house the broken door the shed
the old fox is dead

The wheels hum hum
The wheels: I come I come
Whirl out of space through time O wheels
Pursue down backward time the ghostly parallels
Pursue past culvert cut embankment semaphore
Pursue down gleaming hours that are no more.
The pines, black, snore

turn backward turn backward o time in your flight
and make me a child again just for tonight
good lord he's wet the bed come bring a light

What grief hath the mind distilled?
The heart is unfulfilled
The hoarse pine stilled
I cannot pluck

Out of this land of pine and rock
Of the fallen pine cone
Of red bud their season not yet gone
If I could pluck
(In drouth the lizard will blink on the hot limestone)

  the old fox is dead
  what is said is said
  heaven rest the hoary head
  what have I said!
  . . . I have only said what the wind said
  honor thy father and mother in the days of thy youth
  for time uncoils like the cottonmouth

If I could pluck
Out of the dark that whirled
Over the hoarse pine over the rock
Out of the mist that furled
Could I stretch forth like God the hand and gather
For you my mother
If I could pluck
Against the dry essential of tomorrow
To lay upon the breast that gave me suck
Out of the dark the dark and swollen orchid of this sorrow.

Kentucky Mountain Farm

I. Rebuke of the Rocks

Now on you is the hungry equinox,
O little stubborn people of the hill,
The season of the obscene moon whose pull
Disturbs the sod, the rabbit, the lank fox,
Moving the waters, the boar's dull blood,
And the acrid sap of the ironwood.

But breed no tender thing among the rocks.
Rocks are too old under the mad moon,
Renouncing passion by the strength that locks
The eternal agony of fire in stone.

Then quit yourselves as stone and cease
To break the weary stubble-field for seed;
Let not the naked cattle bear increase,
Let barley wither and the bright milkweed.
Instruct the heart, lean men, of a rocky place
That even the little flesh and fevered bone
May keep the sweet sterility of stone.

II. At the Hour of the Breaking of the Rocks

Beyond the wrack and eucharist of snow
The tortured and reluctant rock again
Receives the sunlight and the tarnished rain.
Such is the hour of sundering we know,
Who on the hills have seen to stand and pass
Stubbornly the taciturn
Lean men that of all things alone
Were, not as water or the febrile grass,
Figured in kinship to the savage stone.

The hills are weary, the lean men have passed;
The rocks are stricken, and the frost has torn
Away their ridgèd fundaments at last,
So that the fractured atoms now are borne
Down shifting waters to the tall, profound
Shadow of the absolute deeps,
Wherein the spirit moves and never sleeps
That held the foot among the rocks, that bound
The tired hand upon the stubborn plow,
Knotted the flesh unto the hungry bone,
The redbud to the charred and broken bough,
And strung the bitter tendons of the stone.

III. History Among the Rocks

There are many ways to die
Here among the rocks in any weather:
Wind, down the eastern gap, will lie
Level along the snow, beating the cedar,
And lull the drowsy head that it blows over
To startle a cold and crystalline dream forever.

The hound's black paw will print the grass in May,
And sycamores rise down a dark ravine,
Where a creek in flood, sucking the rock and clay,
Will tumble the laurel, the sycamore away.
Think how a body, naked and lean
And white as the splintered sycamore, would go
Tumbling and turning, hushed in the end,
With hair afloat in waters that gently bend
To ocean where the blind tides flow.

Under the shadow of ripe wheat,
By flat limestone, will coil the copperhead,
Fanged as the sunlight, hearing the reaper's feet.
But there are other ways, the lean men said:

In these autumn orchards once young men lay dead...
Grey coats, blue coats. Young men on the mountainside
Clambered, fought. Heels muddied the rocky spring.
Their reason is hard to guess, remembering
Blood on their black mustaches in moonlight.
Their reason is hard to guess and a long time past:
The apple falls, falling in the quiet night.

IV. The Cardinal

Cardinal, lover of shade...
Rock and gold is the land in the pulsing noon.
Lover of cedar, lover of shade...
Blue the shadow of cedar on grey limestone,
Where the lizard, devout as an ikon,
Is carved on the stone, throat pulsing on lichen.

At the hour of noon I have seen
The burst of your wings displayed,
Vision of scarlet devised in the slumberous green
...Lover of cedar and shade.

What if the lizard, my cardinal,
Depart like a breath its altar, summer southward fail?
Here is a bough where you can perch, and preen
Your scarlet that from its landscape shall not fade,
Lapped in the cool of the mind's undated shade,
In a whispering tree, like cedar, evergreen.

V. The Jay

Jay, flagrant and military,
Outrageous sergeant in the summer's rout...
Blatant and blue, plunge down the wind and harry
The golden tumble to its last redoubt!
Whip in the traitor leaves that scurry
From those green citadels you kept together,
And call, jay, in the blue weather.

Bright friend of boys and of the truant sun,
It is not long until your call's echo
Stops an old fellow trudging the first snow,
As once the boy who with his dog and gun
Followed the rabbit's track long ago
Stopped, hearing that sudden call, and then
Caught wings that flashed into the red-haw thicket.
Blue cuirassier and summer's lost vidette,
Bright friend of boys, troubler of old men.

VI. Watershed

From this high place all things flow.
Land of divided streams, of water spilled
Eastward, westward, without memento. . .
Land where the morning mist is furled
Like smoke above the ridgepole of the world.

The sunset hawk now rides
The tall light up the climbing deep of air.
Beneath him swings the rooftree that divides
The east and west. His gold eyes scan
The crumpled shade on gorge and crest
And streams that creep and disappear, appear,
Past fingered ridges and their shrivelling span.
Under the broken eaves men take their rest.

Forever, should they stir, their thought would keep
This place. Not love, happiness past, constrains,
But certitude. Enough, and it remains,
Though they who thread the flood and neap
Of earth itself have felt the earth creep;
In pastures hung against the rustling gorge
Have felt the shuddering and sweat of stone,
Knowing thereby no constant moon
Sustains the hill's lost granite surge.

VII. The Return

Burly and clean, with bark in umber scrolled
About the sunlit bole's own living white,
The sycamore stood, drenched in the autumn light.
The same old tree. Again the timeless gold
Broad leaf released the tendoned bough, and slow,
Uncertain as a casual memory,
Wavered aslant the ripe unmoving air.
Up from the whiter bough, the bluer sky,
That glimmered in the water's depth below,
A richer leaf rose to the other there.
They touched; with the gentle clarity of dream,
Bosom to bosom, burned on the quiet stream.

So, backward heart, you have no voice to call
Your image back, the vagrant image again.
The tree, the leaf falling, the stream, and all
Familiar faithless things would yet remain
Voiceless. And he, who had loved as well as most,
Might have foretold it thus, for long he knew

How glimmering a buried world is lost
In the water's riffle, the wind's flaw;
How his own image, perfect and deep
And small within loved eyes, had been forgot,
Her face being turned, or when those eyes were shut
Past light in that fond accident of sleep.

Pondy Woods

The buzzards over Pondy Woods
Achieve the blue tense altitudes,
Black figments that the woods release,
Obscenity in form and grace,
Drifting high through the pure sunshine
Till the sun in gold decline.

Big Jim Todd was a slick black buck
Laying low in the mud and muck
Of Pondy Woods when the sun went down
In gold, and the buzzards tilted down
A windless vortex to the black-gum trees
To sit along the quiet boughs,
Devout and swollen, at their ease.

By the buzzard roost Big Jim Todd
Listened for hoofs on the corduroy road
Or for the foul and sucking sound
A man's foot makes on the marshy ground.
Past midnight, when the moccasin
Slipped from the log and, trailing in
Its obscured waters, broke
The dark algae, one lean bird spoke.

"Nigger, you went this afternoon
For your Saturday spree at the Blue Goose saloon,
So you've got on your Sunday clothes,
On your big splay feet got patent-leather shoes.
But a buzzard can smell the thing you've done;
The posse will get you—run, nigger, run—
There's a fellow behind you with a big shot-gun.
Nigger, nigger, you'll sweat cold sweat
In your patent-leather shoes and Sunday clothes
When down your track the steeljacket goes
Mean and whimpering over the wheat.

"Nigger, your breed ain't metaphysical."
The buzzard coughed. His words fell
In the darkness, mystic and ambrosial.

"But we maintain our ancient rite,
Eat the gods by day and prophesy by night.
We swing against the sky and wait;
You seize the hour, more passionate
Than strong, and strive with time to die—
With Time, the beakèd tribe's astute ally.

"The Jew-boy died. The Syrian vulture swung
Remotely above the cross whereon he hung
From dinner-time to supper-time, and all
The people gathered there watched him until
The lean brown chest no longer stirred,
Then idly watched the slow majestic bird
That in the last sun above the twilit hill
Gleamed for a moment at the height and slid
Down the hot wind and in the darkness hid.
Nigger, regard the circumstance of breath:
Non omnis moriar, the poet saith."

Pedantic, the bird clacked its grey beak,
With a Tennessee accent to the classic phrase;
Jim understood, and was about to speak,
But the buzzard drooped one wing and filmed the eyes.

At dawn unto the Sabbath wheat he came,
That gave to the dew its faithless yellow flame
From kindly loam in recollection of
The fires that in the brutal rock once strove.
To the ripe wheat fields he came at dawn.
Northward the printed smoke stood quiet above
The distant cabins of Squiggtown.
A train's far whistle blew and drifted away
Coldly; lucid and thin the morning lay
Along the farms, and here no sound
Touched the sweet earth miraculously stilled.
Then down the damp and sudden wood there belled
The musical white-throated hound.

In Pondy Woods in the August drouth
Lurk fever and the cottonmouth.
And buzzards over Pondy Woods
Achieve the blue tense altitudes,
Drifting high in the pure sunshine
Till the sun in gold decline;
Then golden and hieratic through
The night their eyes burn two by two.

Eidolon

All night, in May, dogs barked in the hollow woods;
Hoarse, from secret huddles of no light,
By moonlit bole, hoarse, the dogs gave tongue.
In May, by moon, no moon, thus: I remember
Of their far clamor the throaty, infatuate timbre.

The boy, all night, lay in the black room,
Tick-straw, all night, harsh to the bare side.
Staring, he heard; the clotted dark swam slow.
Far off, by wind, no wind, unappeasable riot
Provoked, resurgent, the bosom's nocturnal disquiet.

What hungers kept the house? under the rooftree
The boy; the man, clod-heavy, hard hand uncurled;
The old man, eyes wide, spittle on his beard.
In dark was crushed the may-apple: plunging, the rangers
Of dark remotelier belled their unhouselled angers.

Dogs quartered the black woods: blood black on
May-apple at dawn, old beech-husk. And trails are lost
By rock, in ferns lost, by pools unlit.
I heard the hunt. Who saw, in darkness, how fled
The white eidolon from the fangèd commotion rude?

Letter of a Mother

Under the green lamplight her letter there
Lies among cluttered papers, rusted pens,
Books and handkerchiefs, tobacco tins.
Shuffle of feet ascends the darkened stair.

The son, defined upon the superscription,
Inherits now his cubicled domain,
And reads. Indeed, should he possess again
The loneliness of time's slow mitigation?

Or spell the name, which is himself, and say:
"By now this woman's milk is out of me.
I have a debt of flesh, assuredly,
Which score the mintage of the breath might pay...

"A certain weight of cunning flesh devised
So hunger is bred in the bitter bone
To cleave about this precious skeleton
Held mortmain of her womb and merchandised

*

"Unto the dark: a subtile engine, propped
In the sutured head beneath the coronal seam,
Whose illegal prodigality of dream
In shaking the escheat heart is quick estopped.

"Such is the substance of this legacy:
A fragile vision fed of acrid blood,
Whose sweet process may bloom in gratitude
For the worthier gift of her mortality."

But still the flesh cries out unto the black
Void, across the plains insistently
Where rivers wash their wastage to the sea...
The mother flesh that cannot summon back

The tired child it would again possess
As shall a womb more tender than her own
That builds not tissue or the little bone,
But dissolves them to itself in weariness.

Genealogy

Grandfather Gabriel rode up to town
In black French broadcloth, his hat-brim down,
A gold ring to his finger, hair on his chest,
So he rallied and whored and ginned with the best—
O an elegant son-of-a-bitch, I guess,
Whose boots and bones have fed the elegant grass.

Grandfather Gabriel rode from town
With Grandmother Martha in a white wedding gown.
Wine-Yellow was sunshine then on the corn,
But swollen ran the river, the hills were brown,
And wind in the east, when a son was born.
"A fine little bastard," Gabriel said,
But Martha lay in a strict high bed,
No breath to her body or trouble in her head.

Gabriel, Gabriel, if now together
With Martha you keep any sort of weather
In fragrant hair and dissolute bone adrowse,
Your grandson keeps a broken house.
There's a stitch in his side no plasters heal,
A crack in the firmament, maggots in the meal;
There's a mole in the garden, fennel by the gate,
In the heart a curse of hell-black hate
For that other young guy who croaked too late.

History

Past crag and scarp,
At length way won:
And done
The chert's sharp
Incision:
The track-flint's bite.
Now done, the belly's lack,
Belt tight
—The shrunk sack,
Corn spent, meats foul:
The dry gut-growl.

Now we have known the last,
And can appraise
Pain past.
We came bad ways,
The watercourses
Dry,
No herb for horses.
(We slew them shamefastly,
Dodging their gaze.)
Sleet came some days,
At night no fuel.

And so, thin-wrapt,
We slept:
Forgot the frosty nostril,
Joints rotten and the ulcered knee,
The cold-kibed heel,
The cracked lip.
It was bad country of no tree,
Of abrupt landslip,
The glacier's snore.
Much man can bear.

How blind the passes were!

And now
We see, below,
The delicate landscape unfurled:
A world
Of ripeness blent, and green:
The fruited earth,
Fire on the good hearth,
The fireside scene.
(Those people have no name,
Who shall know dearth
And flame.)

It is a land of corn and kine,
Of milk
And wine,
And beds that are as silk:
The gentle thigh,
The unlit night-lamp nigh.
This much was prophesied:
We shall possess,
And abide
—Nothing less.
We may not be denied.
The inhabitant shall flee as the fox;
His foot shall be among the rocks.

In the new land
Our seed shall prosper, and
In those unsifted times
Our sons shall cultivate
Peculiar crimes,
Having not love, nor hate,
Nor memory.
Though some,
Of all most weary,
Most defective of desire,
Shall grope toward time's cold womb;
In dim pools peer
To see, of some grandsire,
The long and toothèd jawbone greening there.
(O Time, for them the aimless bitch
—Purblind, field-worn,
Slack dugs by the dry thorn torn—
Forever quartering the ground in which
The blank and fanged
Rough certainty lies hid.)

Now at our back
The night wind lifts,
Rain in the wind.
Downward the darkness shifts.
It is the hour for attack.
Wind fondles, far below, the leaves of the land,
Freshening the arbor.
Recall our honor,
And descend.
We seek what end?
The slow dynastic ease,
Travail's cease?
Not pleasure, sure:
Alloy of fact?
The act

Alone is pure.
What appetency knows the flood,
What thirst, the sword?
What name
Sustains the core of flame?
We are
But doom's apparitor.
Time falls, but has no end.
Descend!

The gentle path suggests our feet;
The bride's surrender will be sweet.
We shall essay
The rugged ritual, but not of anger.
Let us go down before
Our thews are latched in the myth's languor,
Our hearts with fable grey.

Resolution

Grape-treader Time,
Bald curator of joys
Burked ere a prime;
Whose guest the weevil is,
Whose will the spider,
Or champing termite, wreaks;
Keen heart-divider
Who deepest vows unspeaks;
The tyrant-friend
Who woe or weal unlocks,
And each will end:
O fangèd paradox!

Your secret pulse
The huddled jockey knows;
Between the bull's
Horns, as the cape flows,
The matador;
The pitcher on his mound,
Sun low, tied score;
The plowman when drouth-bit ground
Deflects the plow;
The cutpurse in the press.
Your pulse, these know;
But all than lovers less.

Than lovers less?
What word had touched the heart

I cannot guess:
It was a place apart,
Of rock and sea,
Salt grass, and the salt wind,
And wind-crooked tree.
Sun gilded sea and land,
The hour past prime.
I spoke of Time. You said:
There is no Time.
Since then some friends are dead;
Hates cold, once hot;
Ambitions thewless grown;
Old slights forgot:
And the weeper is made stone.
We, too, have lain
Apart, with continents
And seas between.
Your words' most brave contents
Came narrowly.
I tried to frame your face
In the mind's eye;
And could, a little space.
Though pondering it,
The chapters glad or sorry,
I can commit
No moral from our story.

Old winnower!
I praise your pacèd power:
Not truth I fear.
How ripe is turned the hour.

Letter from a Coward to a Hero

What did the day bring?
The sharp fragment,
The shard,
The promise half-meant,
The impaired thing,
At dusk the hard word,
Good action by good will marred...
All
In the trampled stall:

I think you deserved better;
Therefore I am writing you this letter.

*

The scenes of childhood were splendid,
And the light that there attended,
But is rescinded:
The cedar,
The lichened rocks,
The thicket where I saw the fox,
And where I swam, the river.
These things are hard
To reconstruct:
The word
Is memory's gelded usufruct.
But piety is simple,
And should be ample.

Though late at night we have talked,
I cannot see what ways your feet in childhood walked.
In what purlieus was courage early caulked?

Guns blaze in autumn and
The quail falls and
Empires collide with a bang
That shakes the pictures where they hang
And democracy shows signs of dry rot
And Dives has and Lazarus not
And the time is out of joint:
But a good pointer holds the point
And is not gun-shy;
But I
Am gun-shy.

Though young, I do not like loud noise:
The sudden backfire,
The catcall of boys,
Drums beating for
The big war,
Or clocks that tick at night, and will not stop.
If you should lose your compass and map
Or a mouse get in the wall,
For sleep try love or veronal,
Though some prefer, I know, philology.
Does the airman scream in the flaming trajectory?

You have been strong in love and hate.
Disaster owns less speed than you have got,
But he will cut across the back lot
To lurk and lie in wait.
Admired of children, gathered for their games,
Disaster, like the dandelion, blooms,
And the delicate film is fanned
To seed the shaven lawn.
Rarely, you've been unmanned;

I have not seen your courage put to pawn.

At the blind hour of unaimed grief,
Of addition and subtraction,
Of compromise,
Of the smoky lecher, the thief,
Of regretted action,
At the hour to close the eyes,
At the hour when lights go out in the houses...
Then wind rouses
The kildees from their sodden ground:
Their commentary is part of the wind's sound.
What is that other sound,
Surf or distant cannonade?
You are what you are without our aid.
No doubt, when corridors are dumb
And the bed is made,
It is your custom to recline,
Clutching between the forefinger and thumb
Honor, for death shy valentine.

Late Subterfuge

The year dulls toward its eaves-dripping end.
We have kept honor yet, or lost a friend;
Observed at length the inherited defect;
Known error's pang—but then, what man is perfect?
The grackles, yellow-beaked, beak-southward, fly
To the ruined ricelands south, leaving empty our sky.

This year was time for decision to be made.
No time to waste, we said, and so we said:
This year is time. Our grief can be endured,
For we, at least, are men, being inured
To wrath, to the act unjust, if need, to blood;
And we have faith from evil bloometh good.

Our feet in the sopping woods will make no sound,
The winter's rot begun, the fox in ground,
The snake cold-coiled, secret in cane the weasel.
In pairs we walk, heads bowed to the long drizzle—
With women some, and take their rain-cold kiss;
We say to ourselves we learn some strength from this.

Ransom

Old houses, and new-fangled violence;
Old bottles but new wine, and newly spilled.
Doom has, we know, no shape but the shape of air.
That much for us the red-armed augurs spelled,
Or flights of fowl lost early in the long air.

The mentioned act: barbarous, bloody, extreme,
And fraught with bane. The actors: nameless and
With faces turned (I cannot make them out).
Christ bled, indeed, but after fasting and
Bad diet of the poor; wherefore thin blood came out.

What wars and lecheries! and the old zeal
Yet unfulfilled, unrarefied, unlaced.
At night the old man coughs: thus history
Strikes sum, ere dawn in rosy buskins laced
Delivers cool with dew the recent news-story.

Defeat is possible, and the stars rise.
Our courage needs, perhaps, new definition.
By night, my love, and noon, infirm of will
And young, we may endeavor definition;
Though frail as the claspèd dream beneath the blanket's wool.

Aged Man Surveys the Past Time

Adept, too late, at art of tears he stands
By gravest orchard in diminished light:
And aged eyes, like twilit rain, their effort
Spill gentlier than herb-issue on a hill.

Grief's smarting condiment may satisfy
His heart to lard the wry and blasphemous theme.
(Once softlier far did Pontius ponder on
His jest before our Lord the steel partook.)

Truth, not truth. The heart, how regular
And sure! How ambidextrous is regret!
Time has no mathematic. Could Orpheus map
The rocky and bituminous descent?

By fruitful grove, unfruited now by winter,
The well-adapted and secular catbird
Whimpers its enmity and invitation.
Light fails beyond the barn and blasted oak.

*

Sweetly trifoliate strumpet spray of green
And crocus-petal, pale, in secret are
April's catalysis: how soon announce
Thy godless summer and the dusty road!

Toward Rationality

Brothers, stones on this moraine of time,
And I, a stone: for you were Xerxes' guests
In littoral picnic by the unfettered brine.
This commentary, perhaps, will discommode.

The cortex-knotty apple draws by blue
Occasion from the lambent air, what?
Perpetual, blithe, armed cap-a-pie, you heard
That modifying sound: ungirt seatone.

Ransack your backward calendar for sages,
Their architectural and russet names,
Or kings who sat with liberal, sunny brow;
Even the postulate zinnia by the path.

Red kine err not, nor under Capricorn
The seaswoop fisher, abler Ptolemy;
The cedar standing close to my house wall
Groans in the long drag of the east wind.

Too happy, happy gentlemen, you freeze
Downward. Shuffle the picturecard mind
And deal: while your kind faces all reflect
The rude Abhorson's spittlebearded grin.

To a Friend Parting

Endure friend-parting yet, old soldier,
Scarred the heart, and wry: the wild plum,
Rock-rent ax-bit, has known with the year bloom,
And tides, the neap and spring, bear faithfully.
Much you have done in honor, though wrathfully.
That, we supposed, was your doom.

O you who by the grove and shore walked
With us, your heart unbraced yet unbetrayed,
Recall: the said, unsaid, though chaff the said
And backward blown. We saw above the lake
Tower the hawk, his wings the light take.
What answer to our dread?

*

Follow the defiles down. Forget not,
When journey-bated the nag, rusty the steel,
The horny clasp of hands your hands now seal;
And prayers of friends, ere this, kept powder dry.
Rough country of no birds, the tracks sly:
Thus faith has lived, we feel.

Letter to a Friend

Our eyes have viewed the burnished vineyards where
No leaf falls, and the grape, unripening, ripes.
It was a dream without fruition as
Without our terror. We have seen it;

And seen the ever-rounding vaulty-structured
Ocean moveless, and the mortised keel
Unmoving o'er the sunlit lichened wave.
That voyage, then each to each we said, had rendered

Courage superfluous, hope a burden.
But living still, we live by them, and only
Thus, or thus, stuttering, eke them out,
Our huddled alms to crammed Necessity.

Fears come, old wranglers out of sleep, and go:
The caterpillar knows its leaf, the mole
Its hummock, who has known his heart, or knows
The trigger of this action, set and sprung?

In this, the time of toads' engendering,
I write to you, to you unfrighted yet
Before the blunt experiment of Time.
Your triumph is not commensurate with stone.

Aubade for Hope

Dawn: and foot on the cold stair treading or
Thump of wood on the unswept hearth-stone is
Comment on the margin of consciousness,
A dirty thumb-smear by the printed page.

Thumb-smear: nay, other, for the blessèd light
Acclaimèd thus, as a ducal progress by
The scared cur, wakes them that wallowed in
The unaimed faceless appetite of dream.

*

All night, the ice sought out the rotten bough:
In sleep they heard. And now they stir, as east
Beyond the formal gleam of landscape sun
Has struck the senatorial hooded hill.

Light; the groaning stair; the match aflame;
The negro woman's hand, horned grey with cold,
That lit the wood; a child's eyes sullen
In the August street—I name some things that shall,

As voices speaking from a farther room,
Muffled, bespeak us yet for time and hope:
For Hope that like a blockhead grandam ever
Above the ash and spittle croaks and leans.

Man Coming of Age

What rime, what tinsel pure and chill,
At dawn defines the new-spied hill?

This brilliance in the night was wrought:
Of dark and cold a dead world caught
Such light that glitters out of thought.

So settles on a dying face,
After the retch and spasm, grace.

(A grace like that did not belong
In the room of no-love, fret, and wrong:
The watchers sat heavy, night was long.)

Now standing on his own doorsill,
He views the woods that crest the hill,

And asks: 'Was it I who roamed to prove
My heart beneath the unwhispering grove
In season greener and of more love?'

And was it he? Now let him stride
With crampèd knee the slant hillside,

Pondering what ways he used to know,
Seeking under the snowy bough
That frail reproachful *alter ego.*

Walker in woods that bear no leaf,
Climber of rocks, assume your grief

And go! lest he, before you tread
That ground once sweetly tenanted,
Like mist, down the glassy gloom be fled.

Croesus in Autumn

If the distrait verdure cleave not to the branch
More powerfully than flesh to the fervent bone,
Should then gruff Croesus on the village bench
Lament the absolute gold of summer gone?

Though this grey guy be no Aurelius
Surveying the ilex and the latin vine,
He might consider a little piteous
The green and fatal tribe's decline;

But in Kentucky against a dwindling sun
The riven red-oak and the thick sweet-gum
Yet hold the northward hills whose final stone
In dark ogive supports the fractured loam.

The seasons down our country have a way
To stir the bald and metaphysic skull,
Fuddling the stout cortex so mortally
That it cries no more, Proud heart, be still, be still.

I bring you but this broken metaphor;
So haul your careful carcass home, old fellow,
More Roman than the doddering emperor
Now green is blown and every gold gone sallow.

So Frost Astounds

I have thought: it will be so
Nothing less

You sat by the window in a dull blue dress;
it was the season when blackbirds go.

Shut to light—too much of light—the classic lids

You were sustained in the green translucence that resides
all afternoon under the maple trees.
I observed your hands which lay, on the lap, supine.

So frost astounds the summer calyxes

And so was locked their frail articulation
by will beneath the pensive skin:
as though composed by the will of an artist on dull blue cloth,
forever beyond the accident of flesh and bone,
or principle of thief and rat and moth,
or beyond the stately perturbation of the mind.

I have thought: this will I find.

The Last Metaphor

The wind had blown the leaves away and left
The lonely hills and on the hills the trees;
One fellow came out with his mortal miseries
And said to himself: "I go where brown leaves drift

"On streams that reflect but cold the evening,
Where trees are bare, the rock is gray and bare,
And scent of the year's declension haunts the air,
Where only the wind and no tardy bird may sing."

He passed by a water, profound and cold,
Whereon remotely gleamed the violent west.
Stark rose a wood about a rocky crest;
Only the wind sang there, as he foretold.

So he took counsel of the heart alone
To be instructed of this desolation,
And when the tongue of the wind had found cessation
After such fashion he lifted up his own.

"The wind has blown the withered leaves away
And left the hills and on the hills the trees.
These thoughts are leaves which are as memories,
Mementoes of the phantom spring's decay

"That bitterly cling if there rise no wind to blow.
I am as the tree and with it have like season."
Again he heard the wind's deep diapason
And spoke again but not in music now.

"Assuredly the planet's tilt will bring
The accurate convulsion of the year—
The budding leaf, the green, and then the sere.
After winter burst the fetid spring,

"After April and the troubled sod
Fell summer on us with its deathy sheaf,
Autumnal ashes then and the brittle leaf
Whereunder fructified the crackling pod.

"Now flat and black the trees stand on the sky
Unreminiscent of the year's frail verdure.
Purged of the green that kept so fatal tenure
They are made strong; no leaf clings mortally."

And hence he made one invocation more,
Hoping for winds beyond some last horizon
To shake the tree and so fulfill its season:
Before he went a final metaphor,

*

Not passionate this, he gave to the chill air,
Thinking that when the leaves no more abide
The stiff trees rear not up in strength and pride
But lift unto the gradual dark in prayer.

Pacific Gazer

Seatide invades
Sandshelf, cove, land verge:
The troublous main unlades
In churn of the muttering gurge.
Day's nimb recedes.

What hope now spent,
On scarp rim that winds gnaw,
A gazer of saddest intent,
Coat bulged in the wind's flaw,
Stares where light went.

Does he seek cease
Of the heart's unprizèd cost?
Can the griding ocean's unease
Or leaning furious blast
Hurt heart appease?

Day's lamp is sped,
As at earth's black misprision,
Yet light, like a steel thread,
Marks taut the cold horizon:
What heart is fed?

Lands of no wrath
Knew, perhaps, his story,
Happier then ere his path
To the billèd promontory
Led, and storm's scath.

Not now again
May heart-friend of days
Gone give handclasp when,
Icy and outbound, his gaze
Bends not to men.

What wrath he owes
Abides in the water's might:
Only the blind blast echoes
His wrath who to black night
Could night oppose.

Calendar

The days draw in:
Southward, the red suns trim
Daily, and dim, and spin
Their bleakening paradigm.
Summer has been.

Now black crows carp
Across the red west home.
Secret, the frost will warp
The oak, and wind thumb
That cold-taut harp.

Do those dead hear
Earth lunge in its dark gyre,
And the grinding orbit veer
Coldward, from the sun's pyre,
More year on year?

Long dead they are:
Do memories they keep
Backpace our calendar
To an age that knew no hap
Of coil, nor jar?

Or is their wrong
Our wrong in the frost's long dark,
And all our young rage strong
Tinct of an elder cark?
The wind takes tongue.

In midnight's poise
Long past our hence-going
Will our hurt in the wind's voice
Speak so to men unknowing
Of our hugged joys

Then overpassed
And frailer than summer's heart
That locked in the burr from frost
With the wanton year may start
And glad time's waste?

Problem of Knowledge

What years, what hours, has spider contemplation spun
Her film to snare the muscled fact?
What hours unbuild the done undone,
Or apprehend the actor in the act?

Loving, with Orphic smile, we yearn
Down the deep backward our feet, we think, have trod:
Or sombrely, under the solstice turn,
We sow where once our mattock cracked the clod.

The rodent tooth has etched the bone,
Beech bole is blackened by the fire:
Was it a sandal smote the troughèd stone?
We rest, lapped in the arrogant chastity of our desire.

Cold Colloquy

She loitered to heed his heart's pouring-out,
Her heart sick within her, she sickening with doubt
That again it might stir, as it once had stirred,
At another's pain snared in gesture or throaty word.
She hearkened, eyeless and sunk like the uncarved stone,
Till the light in his face, an empty candle, was blown:
She hearkened, and all was something once read about,
Or a tale worn glossless in time and bandied about.

She turned, a puzzlement on fair features wrought
That of words so freighted with woe so little she caught.
She turned; with fair face troubled thus would go,
In season of sun when all the green things grow
Or of dry aster and the prattling leaves,
To stand apart, pondering, as one who grieves
Or seeks a thing long lost among the fallen leaves.

For a Self-Possessed Friend

Many of us too often now have granted
Praise for some insolent bright thing;
Our ghosts are simple, we are not haunted
Beyond the moment when those spectres spring
Irresolutely to the mind and fade.
We praise the word, forget the deed;
Praise furred gold leaves in April, not the seed
Tissued of delicate blind agony;

Praise wine, or wit with malice at the heart,
Tolerance in the weak, or innocently
The impeccable unspeaking line of art
In brute stone cut, in paint, in slow bronze cast.
And we who praise so much praise last
The generosity of some calm fool.
But you, my friend... you do not praise at all,
Or praising, stop and seem to cast your eye
Toward some commensurate cold finality
That once you guessed, or dreamed, or read about.
There are some things you do not praise enough;
For instance now, the perilous stuff
Of your own youth. It is not long... beneath
The door, the wind... the candle gone black out.
It is an arrogance to save your breath
Until the time when, self-possessed, you stand
With measured approbation where await,
In darkling kindliness, the bored and bland
Incurious angels of the nether gate.

For a Friend Who Thinks Himself Urbane

I know that you have tried, dear friend,
To make the worse appear the better reason;
But cannot. I know that you have tried to bend
The supple knee, and like the vagrant swallow
To nest in chimneyed hearts of men or follow
The sunshine of consent's good season;
But cannot. Gracious you've tried to cast
The pearl before opinion's tushèd snout;
But cannot. You've tried to greet the last
Bellhop to fortune, the last varnished tout
Of circumstance whose moist palm your palm kissed,
And tried to smile when you suppressed
Some callow gesture of the clumsy heart.
You've tried but cannot, for the better part
Pinches the will, and memories constrain
The ready tongue, bland brow, the careful smile.
You've tried; cannot. But we, among all men,
Share this in secrecy: a little while
And you... O resolute... will try again.

The Garden

On prospect of a fine day in early autumn

How kind, how secret, now the sun
Will bless this garden frost has won,
And touch once more, as once it used,
The furlèd boughs by cold bemused.
Though summered brilliance had but room
In blossom, now the leaves will bloom
Their time, and take from milder sun
An unreviving benison.

No marbles whitely gaze among
These paths where gilt the late pear hung:
But branches interlace to frame
The avenue of stately flame
Where yonder, far more bold and pure
Than marble, gleams the sycamore,
Of argent torse and cunning shaft
Propped nobler than the sculptor's craft.

The hand that crooked upon the spade
Here plucked the peach, and thirst allayed;
Here lovers paused before the kiss,
Instructed of what ripeness is:
Where all who came might stand to try
The grace of this green empery,
Now jay and cardinal debate,
Like twin usurpers, the ruined state.

But he who sought, not love, but peace
In such rank plot could take no ease:
Now poised between the two alarms
Of summer's lusts and winter's harms,
Only for him these precincts wait
In sacrament that can translate
All things that fed luxurious sense
From appetite to innocence.

To One Awake

Shut up the book and get you now to bed.
The cold uncrumpled page will keep
Without your aid
The thought of many a better head
Now drugged and dull in sleep.
Get you to sleep.

*

The sifting darkness like the dust again
Will drift through sockets of the skull, oppress
The throat, the brain;
Bestow as the dim autumnal rain,
Pitiful and passionless,
Its weary kiss.

If in the unclean flesh of sleep are caught
The sightless creatures that uncoil in dream,
Mortal, you ought
Not dread fat larvae of the thought
That in the ogival bone preform
The fabulous worm.

Or say, this hollow hinterland you walk
Is of a swarthy liege your fief,
Whose bitter milk
Is wrung from out a barren stalk,
Whose honey is the sap of grief
And its dark leaf.

Garden Waters

If in his garden all night fell the stream,
Noisy and silver over the moon-dark stone,
It was not so with the voiceless waters of dream,
Monstrously tumbled, falling with no tone.

In this man's garden as in any other
Where decent waters through the night have flowed
Is converse of a musical small clamor,
And men by crags have stopped against the loud

Torn cataract or hollow-bosomed flood
In solace of that full nocturnal tongue
Calling in kinship to the buried blood;
More terrible breaks the torrent with no song.

Though garden waters are not broad or black
Within them still sometimes, I think, is hid
The obscure image of the season's wreck,
The dead leaf and the summer's chrysalid.

To a Face in the Crowd

Brother, my brother, whither do you pass?
Unto what hill at dawn, unto what glen,
Where among the rocks the faint lascivious grass
Fingers in lust the arrogant bones of men?

Beside what bitter waters will you go
Where the lean gulls of your heart along the shore
Rehearse to the cliffs the rhetoric of their woe?
In dream, perhaps, I have seen your face before.

A certain night has borne both you and me;
We are the children of an ancient band
Broken between the mountains and the sea.
A cromlech marks for you the utmost strand

And you must find the dolorous place they stood.
Of old I know that shore, that dim terrain,
And know how black and turbulent the blood
Will beat through iron chambers of the brain

When at your back the taciturn tall stone,
Which is your fathers' monument and mark,
Repeats the waves' implacable monotone,
Ascends the night and propagates the dark.

Men there have lived who wrestled with the ocean;
I was afraid—the polyp was their shroud.
I was afraid. That shore of your decision
Awaits beyond this street where in the crowd

Your face is blown, an apparition, past.
Renounce the night as I, and we must meet
As weary nomads in this desert at last,
Borne in the lost procession of these feet.

Eleven Poems on the Same Theme

To Cleanth Brooks, Jr., and Albert Russel Erskine, Jr.

We stood among the painted trees:
The amber light laved them, and us;
Or light then so untremulous,
So steady, that our substances,
Twin flies, were as in amber tamed
With our perfections stilled and framed
To mock Time's marveling after-spies.

Joy, strongest medium, then buoyed
Us when we moved, as swimmers, who,
Relaxed, resign them to the flow
And pause of their unstainèd flood.
Thus wrapped, sustained, we did not know
How darkness darker staired below;
Or knowing, but half understood.

The bright deception of that day!
When we so readily could gloze
All pages opened to expose
The truth we never would betray;
But darkness on the landscape grew
As in our bosoms darkness, too;
And that was what we took away.

And it abides, and may abide:
Though ebbed from the region happier mapped,
Our hearts, like hollow stones, have trapped
A corner of that brackish tide.
The jaguar breath, the secret wrong,
The curse that curls the sudden tongue,
We know; for fears have fructified.

Or are we dead, that we, unmanned,
Are vacant, and our clearest souls
Are sped where each with each patrols,
In still society, hand in hand,
That scene where we, too, wandered once
Who now inherit new province,
Love's limbo, this lost under-land?

The *then,* the *now*: each cenotaph
Of the other, and contains it, dead.
Or is the soul a hawk that, fled
On glimmering wings past vision's path,
Reflects the last gleam to us here
Though sun is sunk and darkness near
—Uncharted Truth's high heliograph?

Crime

Envy the mad killer who lies in the ditch and grieves,
Hearing the horns on the highway, and the tires scream:
He tries to remember, and tries, but he cannot seem
To remember what it was he buried under the leaves.

By the steamed lagoon, near the carnivorous orchid,
Pirates hide treasure and mark the place with a skull,
Then lose the map, and roar in pubs with a skinful,
In Devon or Barbados; but remember what they hid.

But what was it? But he is too tired to ask it.
An old woman mumbling her gums like incertitude?
The proud stranger who asked the match by the park wood,
Or the child who crossed the park every day with the lunch-basket?

He cannot say, nor formulate the delicious
And smooth convolution of terror, like whipped cream,
Nor the mouth, rounded and white for the lyric scream
Which he never heard, though he still tries, nodding and serious.

His treasure: for years down streets of contempt and trouble,
Hugged under his coat, among sharp elbows and rows
Of eyes hieratic like foetuses in jars;
Or he nursed it unwitting, like a child asleep with a bauble.

Happiness: what the heart wants. That is its fond
Definition, and wants only the peace in God's eye.
Our flame bends in that draft; and that is why
He clutched at the object bright on the bottom of the murky pond.

Peace, all he asked: past despair and past the uncouth
Violation, he snatched at the fleeting hem, though in error;
Nor gestured before the mind's sycophant mirror,
Nor made the refusal and spat from the secret side of his mouth.

Though a tree for you is a tree, and in the long
Dark, no sibilant tumor inside your enormous
Head, though no walls confer in the silent house,
Nor the eyes of pictures protrude, like a snail's, each on its prong,

Yet envy him, for what he buried is buried
By the culvert there, till the boy with the air-gun
In spring, at the violet, comes; nor is ever known
To go on any vacations with him, lend money, break bread.

And envy him, for though the seasons stammer
Past pulse in the yellow throat of the field-lark,
Still memory drips, a pipe in the cellar-dark,
And in its hutch and hole, as when the earth gets warmer,

*

The cold heart heaves like a toad, and lifts its brow
With that bright jewel you have no use for now;
While puzzled yet, despised with the attic junk, the letter
Names over your name, and mourns under the dry rafter.

Original Sin: A Short Story

Nodding, its great head rattling like a gourd,
And locks like seaweed strung on the stinking stone,
The nightmare stumbles past, and you have heard
It fumble your door before it whimpers and is gone:
It acts like the old hound that used to snuffle your door and moan.

You thought you had lost it when you left Omaha,
For it seemed connected then with your grandpa, who
Had a wen on his forehead and sat on the veranda
To finger the precious protuberance, as was his habit to do,
Which glinted in sun like rough garnet or the rich old brain bulging through.

But you met it in Harvard Yard as the historic steeple
Was confirming the midnight with its hideous racket,
And you wondered how it had come, for it stood so imbecile,
With empty hands, humble, and surely nothing in pocket:
Riding the rods, perhaps—or grandpa's will paid the ticket.

You were almost kindly then, in your first homesickness,
As it tortured its stiff face to speak, but scarcely mewed;
Since then you have outlived all your homesickness,
But have met it in many another distempered latitude:
Oh, nothing is lost, ever lost! at last you understood.

But it never came in the quantum glare of sun
To shame you before your friends, and had nothing to do
With your public experience or private reformation:
But it thought no bed too narrow—it stood with lips askew
And shook its great head sadly like the abstract Jew.

Never met you in the lyric arsenical meadows
When children call and your heart goes stone in the bosom;
At the orchard anguish never, nor ovoid horror,
Which is furred like a peach or avid like the delicious plum.
It takes no part in your classic prudence or fondled axiom.

Not there when you exclaimed: "Hope is betrayed by
Disastrous glory of sea-capes, sun-torment of whitecaps
—There must be a new innocence for us to be stayed by."
But there it stood, after all the timetables, all the maps,
In the crepuscular clatter of *always, always,* or *perhaps.*

*

You have moved often and rarely left an address,
And hear of the deaths of friends with a sly pleasure,
A sense of cleansing and hope, which blooms from distress;
But it has not died, it comes, its hand childish, unsure,
Clutching the bribe of chocolate or a toy you used to treasure.

It tries the lock; you hear, but simply drowse:
There is nothing remarkable in that sound at the door.
Later you may hear it wander the dark house
Like a mother who rises at night to seek a childhood picture;
Or it goes to the backyard and stands like an old horse cold in the pasture.

End of Season

Leave now the beach, and even that perfect friendship
—Hair frosting, careful teeth—that came, oh! late,
Late, late, almost too late: that thought like a landslip;
Or only the swimmer's shape for which you would wait,
Bemused and pure among the bright umbrellas, while
Blue mountains breathed and the dark boys cried their bird-throated syllable.

Leave beach, *spiagga, playa, plage,* or *spa,*
Where beginnings are always easy; or leave, even,
The Springs where your grandpa went in Arkansas
To purge the rheumatic guilt of beef and bourbon,
And slept like a child, nor called out with the accustomed nightmare,
But lolled his old hams, stained hands, in that Lethe, as others, others, before.

For waters wash our guilt and dance in the sun:
And the prophet, hairy and grim in the leonine landscape,
Came down to Jordan; toward moon-set de Leon
Woke, while squat, Time clucked like the darkling ape;
And Dante's *duca,* smiling in the blessèd clime,
With rushes, sea-wet, wiped from that sad brow the infernal grime.

You'll come, you'll come! and with the tongue gone wintry
You'll greet in town the essential face, which now wears
The mask of travel, smudge of history;
And wordless, each one clasps, and stammering, stares:
You will have to learn a new language to say what is to say,
But it will never be useful in schoolroom, customs, or café.

For purity was wordless, and perfection
But the bridegroom's sleep or the athlete's marble dream,
And the annual sacrament of sea and sun,
Which browns the face and heals the heart, will seem
Silence, expectant to the answer, which is Time:
For all our conversation is index to our common crime.

*

On the last day swim far out, should the doctor permit
—Crawl, trudgeon, breast—or deep and wide-eyed, dive
Down the glaucous glimmer where no voice can visit;
But the mail lurks in the box at the house where you live:
Summer's wishes, winter's wisdom—you must think
On the true nature of Hope, whose eye is round and does not wink.

Revelation

Because he had spoken harshly to his mother,
The day became astonishingly bright,
The enormity of distance crept to him like a dog now,
And earth's own luminescence seemed to repel the night.

Roof was rent like the loud paper tearing to admit
Sun-sulphurous splendor where had been before
But the submarine glimmer by kindly countenances lit,
As slow, phosphorescent dignities light the ocean floor.

By walls, by walks, chrysanthemum and aster,
All hairy, fat-petalled species, lean, confer,
And his ears, and heart, should burn at that insidious whisper
Which concerns him so, he knows; but he cannot make out the words.

The peacock screamed, and his feathered fury made
Legend shake, all day, while the sky ran pale as milk;
That night, all night, the buck rabbit stamped in the moonlit glade,
And the owl's brain glowed like a coal in the grove's combustible dark.

When Sulla smote and Rome was rent, Augustine
Recalled how Nature, shuddering, tore her gown,
And kind changed kind, and the blunt herbivorous tooth dripped blood;
At Duncan's death, at Dunsinane, chimneys blew down.

But, oh! his mother was kinder than ever Rome,
Dearer than Duncan—no wonder, then, Nature's frame
Thrilled in voluptuous hemispheres far off from his home;
But not in terror: only as the bride, as the bride.

In separateness only does love learn definition,
Though Brahma smiles beneath the dappled shade,
Though tears, that night, wet the pillow where the boy's head was laid
Dreamless of splendid antipodal agitation;

And though across what tide and tooth Time is,
He was to lean back toward that recalcitrant face,
He would think, than Sulla more fortunate, how once he had learned
Something important about love, and about love's grace.

Pursuit

The hunchback on the corner, with gum and shoelaces,
Has his own wisdom and pleasures, and may not be lured
To divulge them to you, for he has merely endured
Your appeal for his sympathy and your kind purchases;
And wears infirmity but as the general who turns
Apart, in his famous old greatcoat there on the hill
At dusk when the rapture and cannonade are still,
To muse withdrawn from the dead, from his gorgeous subalterns;
Or stares from the thicket of his familiar pain, like a fawn
That meets you a moment, wheels, in imperious innocence is gone.

Go to the clinic. Wait in the outer room,
Where like an old possum the snag-nailed hand will hump
On its knee in murderous patience, and the pomp
Of pain swells like the Indies, or a plum.
And there you will stand, as on the Roman hill,
Stunned by each withdrawn gaze and severe shape,
The first barbarian victor stood to gape
At the sacrificial fathers, white-robed, still;
And even the feverish old Jew regards you with authority
Till you feel like one who has come too late, or improperly clothed, to a party.

The doctor will take you now. He is burly and clean;
Listening, like lover or worshiper, bends at your heart;
But cannot make out just what it tries to impart;
So smiles; says you simply need a change of scene.
Of scene, of solace: therefore Florida,
Where Ponce de Leon clanked among the lilies,
Where white sails skit on blue and cavort like fillies,
And the shoulder gleams in the moonlit corridor.
A change of love: if love is a groping Godward, though blind,
No matter what crevice, cranny, chink, bright in dark, the pale tentacle find.

In Florida consider the flamingo,
Its color passion but its neck a question;
Consider even that girl the other guests shun
On beach, at bar, in bed, for she may know
The secret you are seeking, after all;
Or the child you humbly sit by, excited and curly,
That screams on the shore at the sea's sunlit hurlyburly,
Till the mother calls its name, toward nightfall.
Till you sit alone: in the dire meridians, off Ireland, in fury
Of spume-tooth and dawnless sea-heave, salt rimes the lookout's devout eye.

Till you sit alone—which is the beginning of error—
Behind you the music and lights of the great hotel:

Solution, perhaps, is public, despair personal,
But history held to your breath clouds like a mirror.
There are many states, and towns in them, and faces,
But meanwhile, the little old lady in black, by the wall,
Who admires all the dancers, and tells you how just last fall
Her husband died in Ohio, and damp mists her glasses;
She blinks and croaks, like a toad or a Norn, in the horrible light,
And rattles her crutch, which may put forth a small bloom, perhaps white.

Question and Answer

What has availed
Or failed?
The firm decision,
The voices
Lost,
And the choices
Lost,
Elision
Of choice and choice
In the long stammer of chance?
What has availed
Or failed?
Or will avail?
Hawk's poise,
The boxer's stance,
The sail
(O true upon the swollen tack!)
The sprinter's pace,
Moonlit the bomber's bludgeoning grace—
Or looking back,
The stainèd face ?

Pace forth in dawns
Of buds unhinged, and dew;
At dusk pace downs
To view the sea and view,
Immense, the casual land;
For the heart can be held in the hand
And the question held in the hand
And the hour held in the hand:
But never demand
Of the wave-lipped, sea-tongued sand
Answer,
Nor of the gull demand
Answer,
Nor of the noble sky
Where the gull in its integrity

Will move;
Nor answer
Of your true love.

For all—
Each frescoed figure leaning from the world's wall
With tongue too dry and small,
Blunt eye and ignorant hand—
Demand
In truth the true
Answer of you;
And each,
Locked lonely in its valveless speech,
Speaks,
And without resting, seeks
Answer and seeks to speak:
That conversation is not loud.
How painful, intimate, and meek
Before your face are crag and cloud!

For all
Rehearse their own simplicity:
For all—
The wind-heaved gull,
The ocean with its blundering garrulity,
Evening field and morning street—
For all repeat
In mirrored-mirrored-mirror-wise
Unto our eyes
But question, not replies:
All flower from the stalk, and bend,
Like you, with what beseeching hand.

Then let the heart be stone,
And think
On stone,
And think
How once the tribes in dread
From easy-bellied Egypt fled,
And when the conniving sea was past,
Stumbling the waste
Were led,
Not to the desert well
Or green-lipped pool,
Or where moving waters sang
And algae swayed beneath,
But thirsting and accurst—
Tongue black between the teeth
Whence no sweet spittle sprang—
Under the noon's flame
To the rock came:

And think how the Israelite
Struck
And the riven rock
Like a pealing bell rang
And in the general sight
Gave forth to tongue and gut the living stream's delight.

But if not that, then know
At least the heart a bow
Bent,
And the wood's tough nerve unspent,
Cord-kissing notch set now
Upon the cord,
As on the tongue the word
The lover at love has heard:
And once the wide arc is sprung,
Live in the cord's long clang,
Who let the arrow fly
At God's black, orbèd, target eye.

Love's Parable

As kingdoms after civil broil,
Long faction-bit and sore unmanned,
Unlaced, unthewed by lawless toil,
Will welcome to the cheering strand
A prince whose tongue, not understood,
Yet frames a new felicity,
And alien, seals domestic good:
Once, each to each, such aliens, we.

That time, each was the other's sun,
Ecliptic's charter, system's core;
Locked in its span, the wandering one,
Though colder grown, might yet endure
Ages unnumbered, for it fed
Of light and heat flung from the source
Of light that lit dark as it fled:
Wonder of dull astronomers.

No wonder then to us it was!
For miracle was daily food—
That darkness fled through darklessness
And endless light the dark pursued:
No wonder then, for we had found
Love's mystery, then still unspent,
That substance long in grossness bound
Might bud into love's accident.

*

Then miracle was corner-cheap;
And we, like ignorant quarriers,
Ransacked the careless earth to heap
For highways our most precious ores;
Or like the blockhead masons who
Burnt Rome's best grandeur for its lime,
And for their slattern hovels threw
Down monuments of nobler time.

We did not know what worth we owned,
Or know what ambient atmosphere
We breathed, who daily then postponed
A knowledge that, now bought too dear,
Is but ironic residue:
As gouty pang and tarnished vest
Remind the wastrel bankrupt who,
For gut and back, let substance waste.

That all the world proportionate
And joyful seemed, did but consent
That all unto our garden state
Of innocence was innocent;
And all on easy axle roved
That now, ungeared, perturbedly turns,
For joy sought joy then when we loved,
As iron to the magnet yearns.

But we have seen the fungus eyes
Of misery spore in the night,
And marked, of friends, the malices
That stain, like smoke, the day's fond light,
And marked how ripe injustice flows,
How ulcerous, how acid, then
How proud flesh on the sounder grows
Till rot engross the estate of men;

And marked, within, the inward sore
Of self that cankers at the bone,
Contempt of very love we bore
And hatred of the good once known
—So weakness has become our strength,
And strength, confused, can but reject
Its object, so that we at length,
Itching and slumwise, each other infect.

Are we but mirror to the world?
Or does the world our ruin reflect,
Or is our gazing beauty spoiled
But by the glass' flawed defect?
What fault? What cause? What matter for

The hurled leaf where the wind was brewed,
Or matter for the pest-bit whore
What coin her virtue first beshrewed?

O falling-off! O peace composed
Within my kingdom when your reign
Was fulgent-full! and nought opposed
Your power, that slack is, but again
May sway my sullen elements,
And bend ambition to his place.
That hope: for there are testaments
That men, by prayer, have mastered grace.

Terror

"I Volontari Americani Presso Eserciti Stranieri Non Perdono La Cittadinanza."

Il Messaggero, *Roma, Sabato, 27 Gennaio, 1940.*

Not picnics or pageants or the improbable
Powers of air whose tongues exclaim dominion
And gull the great man to follow his terrible
Star, suffice; not the window-box, or the bird on
The ledge, which mean so much to the invalid,
Nor the joy you leaned after, as by the tracks the grass
In the emptiness after the lighted Pullmans fled,
Suffices; nor faces, which, like distraction, pass
Under the street-lamps, teasing to faith or pleasure,
Suffice you, born to no adequate definition of terror.

For yours, like a puppy, is darling and inept,
Though his cold nose brush your hand while you laugh at his clowning;
Or the kitten you sleep with, though once or twice while you slept
It tried to suck your breath, and you dreamed of drowning,
Perjured like Clarence, sluiced from the perilous hatches;
But never of lunar wolf-waste or the arboreal
Malignancy, with the privy breath, which watches
And humps in the dark; but only a dream, after all.
At the worst, you think, with a little twinge of distress,
That contagion may nook in the comforting fur you love to caress.

Though some, unsatisfied and sick, have sought
That immitigable face, whose smile is ice,
And fired their hearts like pitch-pine, for they thought
Better flame than the damp worm-tooth of compromise:
So Harry L. I knew, whose whores and gin
Had dwindled to a slick smile in the drug store
But for the absurd contraption of a plane,

Which flung on air the unformulable endeavor
While heart bled speed to lave the applauded name.
The crash was in an old cornfield; not even flame.

So some, whose passionate emptiness and tidal
Lust swayed toward the debris of Madrid,
And left New York to loll in their fierce idyll
Among the olives, where the snipers hid;
And now the North, to seek that visioned face
And polarize their iron of despair,
Who praise no beauty like the boreal grace
Which greens the dead eye under the rocket's flare.
They fight old friends, for their obsession knows
Only the immaculate itch, not human friends or foes.

They sought a secret which, perhaps, the Moor,
Hieratic, white-robed, pitiless, might teach,
Who duped and dying but for pride, therefore
Hugged truth which cause or conscience scarcely reach.
As Jacob all night with the angelic foe,
They wrestled him who did not speak, but died,
And wrestle now, by frozen fen and floe,
New Courier, in fury sanctified;
And seek that face which, greasy, frost-breathed, in furs,
Bends to the bomb-sight over bitter Helsingfors.

Blood splashed on the terrorless intellect creates
Corrosive fizzle like the spattered lime,
And its enseamed stew but satiates
Itself, in that lewd and faceless pantomime.
You know, by radio, how hotly the world repeats,
When the brute crowd roars or the blunt boot-heels resound
In the Piazza or the Wilhelmplatz,
The crime of Onan, spilled upon the ground;
You know, whose dear hope Alexis Carrel kept
Alive in a test tube, where it monstrously grew, and slept.

But it is dead, and you now, guiltless, sink
To rest in lobbies, or pace gardens where
The slow god crumbles and the fountains prink,
Nor heed the criminal king, who paints the air
With discoursed madness and protruding eye,
Nor give the alarm, nor ask tonight where sleeps
That head which hooped the jewel Fidelity,
But like an old melon now, in the dank ditch, seeps;
But you crack nuts, while the conscience-stricken stare
Kisses the terror; for you see an empty chair.

Selected Poems 1923–1943

To E. C. B. W.

The Ballad of Billie Potts

(When I was a child I heard this story from an old lady who was a relative of mine. The scene, according to her version, was in the section of Western Kentucky known as "Between the Rivers," the region between the Cumberland and the Tennessee. Years later, I came across another version in a book on the history of the outlaws of the Cave Inn Rock, or the Cave-In-Rock. The name of Bardstown in the present account refers to Bardstown, Kentucky, where the first race track west of the mountains was laid out late in the Eighteenth Century.)

Big Billie Potts was big and stout
In the land between the rivers.
His shoulders were wide and his gut stuck out
Like a croker of nubbins and his holler and shout
Made the bob-cat shiver and the black-jack leaves shake
In the section between the rivers.
He would slap you on your back and laugh.

Big Billie had a wife, she was dark and little
In the land between the rivers,
And clever with her wheel and clever with her kettle,
But she never said a word and when she sat
By the fire her eyes worked slow and narrow like a cat
In the land between the rivers.
Nobody knew what was in her head.

They had a big boy with fuzz on his chin
So tall he ducked the door when he came in,
A clabber-headed bastard with snot in his nose
And big red wrists hanging out of his clothes
And a whicker when he laughed where his father had a beller
In the section between the rivers.
They called him Little Billie.
He was their darling.

(It is not hard to see the land, what it was.
Low hills and oak. The fetid bottoms where
The slough uncoiled and in the tangled cane,
Where no sun comes, the muskrat's astute face
Was lifted to the yammering jay; then dropped.
Some cabin where the shag-bark stood and the
Magnificent tulip-tree; both now are gone.
But the land is there, and as you top a rise,
Beyond you all the landscape steams and simmers
—The hills, now gutted, red, cane-brake and black-jack yet.
The oak leaf steams under the powerful sun.
"Mister, is this the right road to Paducah?"
The red face, seamed and gutted like the hill,
Slow under time, and with the innocent savagery
Of Time, the bleared eyes rolling, answers from

Your dream: "They names hit so, but I ain't bin.")

Big Billie was the kind who laughed but could spy
The place for a ferry where folks would come by.
He built an inn and folks bound West
Hitched their horses there to take their rest
And grease the gall and grease the belly
And jaw and spit under the trees
In the section between the rivers.
Big Billie said: "Git down, friend, and take yore ease!"
He would slap you on your back and set you at his table.

(Leaning and slow, you see them move
In massive passion colder than any love:
Their lips move but you do not hear the words
Nor trodden twig nor fluted irony of birds
Nor hear the rustle of the heart
That, heave and settle, gasp and start,
Heaves like a fish in the ribs' dark basket borne
West from the great water's depth whence it was torn.

Their names are like the leaves, but are forgot
—The slush and swill of the world's great pot
That foamed at the range's lip, and spilled
Like quicksilver across green baize, the unfulfilled
Disparate glitter, gleam, wild symptom, seed
Flung in the long wind: silent, proceed
Past meadow, salt-lick, and the lyric swale;
Enter the arbor, shadow of trees, fade, fail.)

Big Billie was sharp at swap and trade
And could smell the nest where the egg was laid,
He could read and cipher and they called him squire
In the land between the rivers.
And he added up his money while he sat by the fire
And sat in the shade while folks sweated and strove,
For he was the one who fatted and throve
In the section between the rivers.
"Thank you kindly, sir," Big Billie would say
When the man in the black coat paid him at streak of day
And swung to the saddle and was ready to go
And rode away and didn't know
That he was already as good as dead,
For at midnight the message had been sent ahead:
"Man in black coat, riding bay mare with star."

(There was a beginning but you cannot see it.
There will be an end but you cannot see it.
They will not turn their faces to you though you call,
Who pace a logic merciless as light,
Whose law is their long shadow on the grass,

Sun at the back; pace, pass,
And passing nod in that glacial delirium
While the tight sky shudders like a drum
And speculation rasps its idiot nails
Across the dry slate where you did the sum.

The answer is in the back of the book but the page is gone.
And grandma told you to tell the truth but she is dead.
And heedless, their hairy faces fixed
Beyond your call or question now, they move
Under the infatuate weight of their wisdom,
Precious but for the preciousness of their burden,
Sainted and sad and sage as the hairy ass, who bear
History like bound faggots, with stiff knees;
And breathe the immaculate climate where
The lucent leaf is lifted, lank beard fingered, by no breeze,
Rapt in the fabulous complacency of fresco, vase, or frieze:

And the testicles of the fathers hang down like old lace.)

Little Billie was full of piss and vinegar
And full of sap as a maple tree
And full of tricks as a lop-eared pup,
So one night when the runner didn't show up,
Big Billie called Little and said, "Saddle up,"
And nodded toward the man was taking his sup
With his belt unlatched and his feet to the fire.
Big Billie said, "Give Amos a try,
Fer this feller takes the South Fork and Amos'll be nigher
Than Baldy or Buster, and Amos is sly
And slick as a varmint, and I don't deny
I lak bizness with Amos fer he's one you kin trust
In the section between the rivers,
And hit looks lak they's mighty few.
Amos will split up fair and square."

Little Billie had something in his clabber-head
In addition to snot, and he reckoned he knew
How to skin a cat or add two and two.
So long before the sky got red
Over the land between the rivers,
He hobbled his horse back in the swamp
And squatted on his hams in the morning dew and damp
And scratched his stomach and grinned to think
How his Pap would be proud and his Mammy glad
To know what a thriving boy they had
In the section between the rivers.
He always was a good boy to his darling Mammy.

(Think of yourself riding away from the dawn,
Think of yourself and the unnamed ones who had gone

Before, riding, who rode away from *goodbye, goodbye,*
And toward *hello,* toward Time's unwinking eye;
And like the cicada had left, at cross-roads or square,
The old shell of self, thin, ghostly, translucent, light as air;
At dawn riding into the curtain of unwhispering green,
Away from the vigils and voices into the green
World, land of the innocent bough, land of the leaf.
Think of your face green in the submarine light of the leaf.

Or think of yourself crouched at the swamp-edge,
Dawn-silence past last owl-hoot and not yet at day-verge
First bird-stir, titmouse or drowsy warbler not yet.
You touch the grass in the dark and your hand is wet.
Then light: and you wait for the stranger's hoofs on the soft trace,
And under the green leaf's translucence the light bathes your face.

Think of yourself at dawn: Which are you? What?)

Little Billie heard hoofs on the soft grass,
But he squatted and let the rider pass,
For he didn't want to waste good lead and powder
Just to make the slough-fish and swamp-buzzards prouder
In the land between the rivers.
But he saw the feller's face and thanked his luck
It was the one Pap said was fit to pluck.
So he got on his horse and cantered up the trace.
Called, "Hi thar!" and the stranger watched him coming,
And sat his mare with a smile on his face,
Just watching Little Billie and smiling and humming
In the section between the rivers.
Little Billie rode up and the stranger said,
"Why, bless my heart, if it ain't Little Billie!"

"Good mornen," said Billie, and said, "My Pap
Found somethen you left and knowed you'd be missen,
And he ain't wanten nuthen not proper his'n."
But the stranger didn't do a thing but smile and listen
Polite as could be to what Billie said.
But he must have had eyes in the side of his head
As they rode along beside the slough
In the land between the rivers,
Or known what Billie was out to do,
For when Billie said, "Mister, I've brung hit to you,"
And reached his hand for it down in his britches,
The stranger just reached his own hand, too.

"Boom!" Billie's gun said, and the derringer, "Bang!"
"Oh, I'm shot!" Billie howled and grabbed his shoulder.
"Not bad," said the stranger, "for you're born to hang,
But I'll save some rope 'fore you're a minute older
If you don't high-tail to your honest Pap

In the section between the rivers."
Oh, Billie didn't tarry and Billie didn't linger,
For Billie didn't trust the stranger's finger
And didn't admire the stranger's face
And didn't like the climate of the place,
So he turned and high-tailed up the trace,
With blood on his shirt and snot in his nose
And pee in his pants for he'd wet his clothes,
And the stranger just sits and admires how he goes,
And says, "Why, that boy would do right well back on the Bardstown track!"

"You fool!" said his Pap, but his Mammy cried
To see the place where the gore-blood dried
Round the little hole in her darling's hide.
She wiped his nose and patted his head,
But Pappy barred the door and Pappy said,
"That bastard has maybe got some friends
In the section between the rivers,
And you can't say how sich bizness ends
And a man ain't sure he kin trust his neighbors,
Fer thar's mortal spite fer him sweats and labors
Even here between the rivers."
He didn't ask Little how he felt,
But said, "Two hundred in gold's in my money belt,
And take the roan and the brand-new saddle
And stop yore blubberen and skeedaddle,
And the next time you try and pull a trick
Fer God's sake don't talk but do hit quick."
So Little Billie took his leave
And left his Mammy there to grieve
And left his Pappy in Old Kaintuck
And headed West to try his luck
And left the land between the rivers,
For it was Roll, Missouri,
It was Roll, roll, Missouri.
And he was gone nigh ten long year
And never sent word to give his Pappy cheer
Nor wet pen in ink for his Mammy dear.
For Little Billie never was much of a hand with a pen-staff.

(There is always another country and always another place.
There is always another name and another face.
And the name and the face are you, and you
The name and the face, and the stream you gaze into
Will show the adoring face, show the lips that lift to you
As you lean with the implacable thirst of self,
As you lean to the image which is yourself,
To set the lip to lip, fix eye on bulging eye,
To drink not of the stream but of your deep identity,
But water is water and it flows,

Under the image on the water the water coils and goes
And its own beginning and its end only the water knows.

There are many countries and the rivers in them
—Cumberland, Tennessee, Ohio, Colorado, Pecos, Little Big Horn,
And Roll, Missouri, roll.
But there is only water in them.

And in the new country and in the new place
The eyes of the new friend will reflect the new face
And his mouth will speak to frame
The syllables of the new name
And the name is you and is the agitation of the air
And is the wind and the wind runs and the wind is everywhere.

The name and the face are you.
The name and the face are always new
And they are you.
Are new.

For they have been dipped in the healing flood.
For they have been dipped in the redeeming blood.
For they have been dipped in Time
And Time is only beginnings
Time is only and always beginnings
And is the redemption of our crime
And is our Saviour's priceless blood.

For Time is always the new place,
And no-place.
For Time is always the new name and the new face,
And no-name and no-face.

For Time is motion
For Time is innocence
For Time is West.)

Oh, who is coming along the trace,
Whistling along in the late sunshine,
With a big black hat above his big red face
And a long black coat that swings so fine?
Oh, who is riding along the trace
Back to the land between the rivers,
With a big black beard growing down to his guts
And silver mountings on his pistol-butts
And a belt as broad as a saddle-girth
And a look in his eyes like he owned the earth?
And meets a man riding up the trace
And looks right sharp and scans his face
And says, "Durn if'n hit ain't Joe Drew!"
"I reckin hit's me," says Joe and gives a spit,

"But whupped if'n I figger how you knows hit,
Fer if'n I'm Joe, then who air you?"
And the man with the black beard says: "Why, I'm Little Billie!"
And Joe Drew says: "Wal, I'll be whupped."

"Be whupped," Joe said, "and whar you goen?"
"Oh, I'm just visiten back whar I done my growen
In the section between the rivers,
Fer I bin out West and taken my share
And I reckin my luck helt out fer fair,
So I done come home," Little Billie said,
"To see my folks if'n they ain't dead."
"Ain't dead," Joe answered, and shook his head,
"But that's the best a man kin say,
Fer hit looked lak when you went away
You taken West yore Pappy's luck
And maybe now you kin bring hit back
To the section between the rivers."
Little Billie laughed and jingled his pockets and said: "Ain't nuthen wrong with my luck."

And said: "Wal, I'll be gitten on home,
But after yore supper why don't you come
And we'll open a jug and you tell me the news
In the section between the rivers.
But not too early fer hit's my aim
To git me some fun 'fore they know my name,
And tease 'em and fun 'em, fer you never guessed
I was Little Billie what went out West."
And Joe Drew said: "Durn if'n you always wuzn't a hand to git yore fun."

(Over the plain, over mountain and river, drawn,
Wanderer with slit-eyes adjusted to distance,
Drawn out of distance, drawn from the great plateau
Where the sky heeled in the unsagging wind and the cheek burned,
Who stood beneath the white peak that glimmered like a dream,
And spat, and it was morning and it was morning.
You lay among the wild plums and the kildees cried.
You lay in the thicket under the new leaves and the kildees cried,
For you all luck, for all the astuteness of your heart,
And would not stop and would not stop
And the clock ticked all night long in the furnished room
And would not stop
And the *El*-train passed on the quarters with a whish like a terrible broom
And would not stop
And there is always the sound of breathing in the next room
And it will not stop
And the waitress says, "Will that be all, sir, will that be all?"
And will not stop
And the valet says, "Will that be all, sir, will that be all?"
And will not stop

For nothing is ever all and nothing is ever all,
For all your experience and your expertness of human vices and of valor
At the hour when the ways are darkened.

Though your luck held and the market was always satisfactory,
Though the letter always came and your lovers were always true,
Though you always received the respect due to your position,
Though your hand never failed of its cunning and your glands always thoroughly knew their business,
Though your conscience was easy and you were assured of your innocence,
You became gradually aware that something was missing from the picture,
And upon closer inspection exclaimed: "Why, I'm not in it at all!"
Which was perfectly true.

Therefore you tried to remember when you had last had whatever it was you had lost,
But it was a long time back.
And you decided to retrace your steps from that point,
But it was a long way back.
It was, nevertheless, absolutely essential to make the effort,
And since you had never been a man to be deterred by difficult circumstances,
You came back.
For there is no place like home.)

He joked them and he teased them and he had his fun
And they never guessed that he was the one
Had been Mammy's darling and Pappy's joy
When he was a great big whickering boy
In the land between the rivers,
And he jingled his pockets and he took his sop
And patted his belly which was full nigh to pop
And wiped the buttermilk out of his beard
And took his belch and up and reared
Back from the table and cocked his chair
And said: "Old man, ain't you got any fresh drinken water, this here ain't fresher'n a hoss puddle?"
And the old woman said: "Pappy, why don't you take the young gentleman down to the spring so he kin git hit good and fresh?"
And the old woman gave the old man a straight look.
She gave him the bucket but it was not empty but it was not water.

Oh, the stars are shining and the meadow is bright
But under the trees is dark and night
In the land between the rivers.
Oh, on the trace the fireflies spark
But under the trees is night and dark,
And way off yonder is the whippoorwill
And the owl off yonder hoots on the hill
But under the trees is dark and still
In the section between the rivers.
And the leaves hang down in the dark of the trees

And there is the spring in the dark of the trees
And there is the spring as black as ink
And one star in it caught through a chink
Of the leaves that hang down in the dark of the trees,
And the star is there but it does not wink.
And Little Billie gets down on his knees
And props his hands in the same old place
To sup the water at his ease;
And the star is gone but there is his face.
"Just help yoreself," Big Billie said;
Then set the hatchet in his head.
They went through his pockets and they buried him in the dark of the trees.
"I figgered he was a ripe 'un," the old man said.
"Yeah, but you wouldn't done nuthen hadn't bin fer me," the old woman said.

(The reflection is shadowy and the form not clear,
For the hour is late, is late, and scarcely a glimmer comes here
Under the leaf, the bough, in its innocence dark;
And under your straining face you can scarcely mark
The darkling gleam of your face little less than the water dark.

But perhaps what you lost was lost in the pool long ago
When childlike you lost it and then in your innocence rose to go
After kneeling, as now, with your thirst beneath the leaves:
And years it lies here and dreams in the depth and grieves,
More faithful than mother or father in the light or dark of the leaves.

But after, after the irrefutable modes and marches,
After waters that never quench the thirst in the throat that parches,
After the sleep that sieves the long day's dubieties
And the cricket's corrosive wisdom under the trees,
After the rumor of wind and the bright anonymities,

You come, weary of greetings and the new friend's smile,
Weary in art of the stranger, worn with your wanderer's wile,
Weary of innocence and the husks of Time,
Prodigal, back to the homeland of no-Time,
To ask forgiveness and the patrimony of your crime;

And kneel in the untutored night as to demand
What gift—oh, father, father—from that dissevering hand?)

"And whar's Little Billie?" Joe Drew said.
"Air you crazy," said Big, "and plum outa yore head,
Fer you knows he went West nigh ten long year?"
"Went West," Joe said, "but I seen him here
In the section between the rivers,
Riden up the trace as big as you please
With a long black coat comen down to his knees
And a big black beard comen down to his guts
And silver mountens on his pistol-butts

And he said out West how he done struck
It rich and wuz bringen you back yore luck."
"I shore-God could use some luck," Big Billie said,
But his woman wet her lips and craned her head
And said: "Come riden with a big black beard, you say?"
And Joe: "Oh, hit wuz Billie as big as day."
And the old man's eyes bugged out of a sudden and he croaked like a sick bull-frog and said: "Come riden with a long black coat?"

Oh, the night is still and the grease-lamp low
And the old man's breath comes wheeze and slow.
Oh, the blue flame sucks on the old rag wick
And the old woman's breath comes sharp and quick,
And there isn't a sound under the roof
But her breath's hiss and his breath's puff,
And there isn't a sound outside the door
As they hearken but cannot hear any more
The creak of the saddle or the plop of the hoof,
For a long time now Joe Drew's been gone
And left them sitting there alone
While the dark outside gets big and still,
For the owl doesn't hoot off there on the hill
Any more and is quiet, and the whippoorwill
Is quiet in the dark of the trees and still
In the land between the rivers.
And so they sit and breathe and wait
And breathe while the night gets big and late,
And neither of them gives move or stir
And she won't look at him and he won't look at her.
He doesn't look at her but he says: "Git me the spade."

She grabbled with her hands and he dug with the spade
Where the leaves let down the dark and shade
In the land between the rivers.
She grabbled like a dog in the hole they made,
But stopped of a sudden and then she said,
"I kin put my hand on his face."
They light up a pine-knot and lean at the place
Where the man in the black coat slumbers and lies
With trash in his beard and dirt on his face;
And the torch-flame shines in his wide-open eyes.
Down the old man leans with the flickering flame
And moves his lips, says: "Tell me his name."
"Ain't Billie, ain't Billie," the old woman cries,
"Oh, hit ain't my Billie, fer he wuz little
And helt to my skirt while I stirred the kittle
And called me Mammy and hugged me tight
And come in the house when hit fell night."
But the old man leans down with the flickering flame
And croaks: "But tell me his name."

"Oh, he ain't got none, fer he just come riden
From some fer place whar he'd bin biden,
And ain't got a name and never had none,
But Billie, my Billie, he had one,
And hit wuz Billie, hit wuz his name."
But the old man croaked: "Tell me his name."
"Oh, he ain't got none and hit's all the same,
But Billie had one, and he wuz little
And offen his chin I would wipe the spittle
And wiped the drool and kissed him thar
And counted his toes and kissed him whar
The little black mark wuz under his tit,
Shaped lak a clover under his left tit,
With a shape fer luck and I'd kiss hit—"
And the old man blinks in the pine-knot flare
And his mouth comes open like a fish for air,
Then he says right low, "I had nigh fergot."
"Oh, I kissed him on his little luck-spot
And I kissed and he'd laff as lak as not—"
The old man said: "Git his shirt open."
The old woman opened the shirt and there was the birthmark under the left tit.
It was shaped for luck.

(The bee knows, and the eel's cold ganglia burn,
And the sad head lifting to the long return,
Through brumal deeps, in the great unsolsticed coil,
Carries its knowledge, navigator without star,
And under the stars, pure in its clamorous toil,
The goose hoots north where the starlit marshes are.
The salmon heaves at the fall, and, wanderer, you
Heave at the great fall of Time, and gorgeous, gleam
In the powerful arc, and anger and outrage like dew,
In your plunge, fling, and plunge to the thunderous stream:
Back to the silence, back to the pool, back
To the high pool, motionless, and the unmurmuring dream.
And you, wanderer, back,
Brother to pinion and the pious fin that cleave
Their innocence of air and the disinfectant flood
And wing and welter and weave
The long compulsion and the circuit hope
Back,
And bear through that limitless and devouring fluidity
The itch and humble promise which is home.
And you, wanderer, back,
For the beginning is death and the end may be life,
For the beginning was definition and the end may be definition,
And our innocence needs, perhaps, new definition,
And the wick needs the flame
But the flame needs the wick.

And the father waits for the son.
The hour is late,
The scene familiar even in shadow,
The transaction brief,
And you, wanderer, back,
After the striving and the wind's word,
To kneel
Here in the evening empty of wind or bird,
To kneel in the sacramental silence of evening
At the feet of the old man
Who is evil and ignorant and old,
To kneel
With the little black mark under your heart,
Which is your name,
Which is shaped for luck,
Which is your luck.)

Variation: Ode to Fear

When the dentist adjusts his drill
And leers at the molar he's going to fill,
Murmuring softly as a mother,
"Just hold tight, it'll soon be over,"
Timor mortis conturbat me.

When the surgeon whets his scalpel
And regards me like an apple,
And the tumor or the wart
Sings, "The best of friends must part,"
Timor mortis conturbat me.

When flushed with morning's genial hope
I slit the crisped envelope
And read the message too oft known,
"Your account $3.00 overdrawn,"
Timor mortis conturbat me.

When I wait on the railway platform
To say goodbye, and the friend's form,
Which was substantial, wavers there
Thinner than smoke upon the air,
Timor mortis conturbat me.

When I think that the national debt
Will blight the children we beget,
And especially blight those of our heirs
Who have the instincts of financiers,
Timor mortis conturbat me.

*

When I read in Charles A. Beard
That the Founding Fathers whom we revered
Were not above a cozy deal
And would skin a pig for the pig's squeal,
Timor mortis conturbat me.

And read that Milton was neurotic
And Saint Joan charmingly psychotic
And Jesus in Gethsemane
Was simply sweating from T.B.,
Timor mortis conturbat me.

When Focke-Wulf mounts, or Zero,
And my knees say I'm no hero
And manly marrow turns to soup
And lunch expertly loops the loop,
Timor mortis conturbat me.

When in the midnight's pause I mark
The breath beside me in the dark,
And know that breath's a clock, and know
That breath's the clock that's never slow,
Timor mortis conturbat me.

O thou, to whom the world unknown
With all its shadowy shapes is shown,
Whose foot makes no sound on the floor,
Who need no latchkey for the door
(Timor mortis conturbat me),

Who gaze from out the chic dummy's gaze,
In the display window, to amaze
The yearning matron by whom you sat
At dinner last night and in her soup spat
(Timor mortis conturbat me),

Who pinch the maiden's tenderest part
But warm no cockles of her heart,
Who snarl the horse's tail, who spill
The bucket fetched by Jack and Jill
(Timor mortis conturbat me),

Whose sleights are slier than Houdini's
And make Puck's pranks look like a ninny's
—Though you were with me *in utero,*
Your own birthday was long ago
(Timor mortis conturbat me),

And though you fawn and follow like Fido,
You'll find other master when I go.
For I'm not the first or last of men

And so I will try to remember when
Timor mortis conturbat me

That various men in various ages
Have dispensed with heroes and with sages,
And managed without our Constitution
Or intercession and absolution
(Timor mortis conturbat me),

And when they walked by grove or shore
Enjoyed the scene, not metaphor,
And when they got it in the gut
Took what comfort they could from a cigarette butt
(Timor mortis conturbat me),

And though they found the going hard
Did without Jesus or the gold standard,
Or lay alone, and reaching over
Could find no hand upon the cover
(Timor mortis conturbat me).

So when I wake I'll pat the head
Of the beast that sleeps beside the bed,
And put on my pants and vest, and go
Down to eat my breakfast, though
Timor mortis conturbet me.

Mexico is a Foreign Country: Five Studies in Naturalism

I. Butterflies Over the Map

Butterflies, over the map of Mexico,
Over jungle and somnolent, sonorous mountains, flitter,
Over the death-gaudy dog whose spangles the sun makes glitter,
And over the red lines which are the highways where you will go.

The highways are scenic, like destiny marked in red,
And the faithful heart inside you purrs like a cat;
While distance drowses and blinks and broods its enormous fiat,
Butterflies dream gyres round the precious flower which is your head.

Their colors are astonishing, and so
Are you, who wrathless, rose, and robed in the pure
Idea, smote, and fled, while benches burned, the clamor:
The black limousine was not detected at Laredo.

*

Tragedy is a dance, as Brutus knew;
But when a little child dies in Jalisco,
They lay the corpse, pink cloth on its face, in the patio,
And bank it with blossoms, yellow, red, and the Virgin's blue.

The pink cloth is useful to foil the flies, which are not few.

II. Siesta Time in Village Plaza by Ruined Bandstand and Banana Tree

If only Ernest now were here
To praise the bull, deride the steer,
And anatomize for chillier chumps
The local beauties' grinds and bumps;

Or if the Baptists would undertake
To dip local sinners in the picturesque lake,
And not too obsessed in spiritual pride,
Bring a nationally advertised insecticide;

Or if Henry Wallace and cortege
Could get this far with friendship's message,
And smile his smile of the bashful Jesus
On these poor Indians and their diseases;

Or even if the Standard Oil
Would come and puncture this parched soil,
And corrupt the pomaded politicos
And load the peons with fresh woes—

But the toothsomer beauties now are sweating
On beds in need of mosquito netting,
While I sweat in the Plaza here
And meditate on my last beer;

And Baptists, Wallace, and Standard Oil
Are too engrossed in their proper toil,
And Ernest twinkles from afar
In his abode where the eternals are;

And all the shutters are down tight,
While my head rocks in the explosive light,
Alone with the bandstand and banana tree
And a poor old dog and the poor dog's flea.

But all at once the peace is shattered,
And all the tranquil hour is tattered:
In a sudden burst of energy
The dog seeks out the banana tree.

*

I watch and applaud the sound idea,
As I meditate on my last beer;
But here even the bladder achieves Nirvana,
And so I sit and think, "mañana."

III. The World Comes Galloping: A True Story

By the ruined arch, where the bougainvillea bled,
And pigeons simmered and shat in the barbaric vine
And made a noise like Plato in the barbaric vine,
He stood: old.
Old, bare feet on stone, and the serape's rose
Unfolded in the garden of his rags;
Old, and all his history hung from his severe face
As from his frame the dignity of rags.

We could not see his history, we saw
Him.
And he saw us, but could not see we stood
Huddled in our history and stuck out hand for alms.

But he could give us nothing, and asked for nothing,
Whose figure, sharp against the blue lake and violet mountains,
Was under the arch, the vine, the violent blue vulgarity of sky.
He ate a peach and wiped the pulp across his gums;
His mouth was no less ruinous than the arch.

Then at the foot of that long street,
Between the pastel stucco and the feathery pepper trees,
Horse and horseman, sudden as light, and loud,
Appeared,
And up the rise, banging the cobbles like castanets,
Lashed in their fury and fever,
Plunged:
Wall-eyed and wheezing, the lurching hammer-head,
The swaying youth, and flapping from bare heels,
The great wheel-spurs of the Conquistador.
Plunged past us, and were gone:
The crow-bait mount, the fly-bit man.

So the old one, dropping his peach-pit, spat;
Regarding the street's astonishing vacancy, said:
"Viene galopando,"—and spat again—"el mundo."

IV. Small Soldiers with Drum in Large Landscape

The little soldiers thread the hills.
Remote, the white Sierra nods
Like somnolent ice cream piled up
To tempt a tourist's taste, or God's.

I saw them in the Plaza when
They huddled there like hens, at dawn,
And forming ranks, took time to gouge
Sleep from their eyes, and spit, and yawn.

Their bearing lacked ferocity.
Their eyes were soft, their feet were splayed,
And dirt, no doubt, behind the ears
Did them no credit on parade.

They did not tell me why they march—
To give some cattle-thief a scare
Or make their captain happy or
Simply take the mountain air.

But now two hours off, they move
Across the scene, and to the eye
Give interest, and focus for
The composition's majesty.

The little drum goes rum-tum-tum,
The little hearts go rat-tat-tat,
And I am I, and they are they,
And *this* is *this,* and *that* is *that,*

And the single pine is black upon
The crag; and the buzzard, absolute
In the sun's great gold eye, hangs;
And leaf is leaf, and root is root;

And the wind has neither home nor hope;
And cause is cause, effect, effect;
And all Nature's jocund atoms bounce
In tune to keep the world intact.

And shrouded in the coats and buttons,
The atoms bounce, and under the sky,
Under the mountain's gaze, maintain
The gallant little formulae

Which sweat and march, and marching, go
On errands which I have not guessed,
Though here I stand and watch them go
From dawn to dark, from East to West,

*

From *what* to *what,* from *if* to *when,*
From ridge to ridge, and cross the wide
Landscape of probability.
They cross the last ridge now, and hide

In valleys where the unprinted dust
Yearns for the foot it does not know;
They march under the same sun,
Appear once more, are gone, but go

Across the high waste of the mind,
Across the distance in the breast,
And climbing hazier heights, proceed
To a bivouac in a farther West.

As I remarked, the little men
Had necks unwashed and manners rude;
They were no cloud of daffodils
As once blest William's solitude.

But when upon my couch I lie
And brood the done, and the undone,
My heart may seize its hint of pleasure
And march beside them in the sun.

V. The Mango on the Mango Tree

The mango on the mango tree—
I look at it, it looks at me,
And thus we share our guilt in decent secrecy

(As once in the crowd I met a face
Whose lineaments were my disgrace
But whose own shame my forehead bore from place to place).

The mango is a great gold eye,
Like God's, set in the leafy sky
To harry heart, block blood, freeze feet, if I would fly.

For God has set it there to spy
And make report, and here am I,
A cosmic Hawkshaw to track down its villainy.

Gumshoe, *agent provocateur,*
Stool, informer, whisperer
—Each pours his tale into the Great Schismatic's ear.

*

For God well works the Roman plan,
Divide and rule, mango and man,
And on hate's axis the great globe grinds in its span.

I do not know the mango's crime
In its far place and different time,
Nor does it know mine committed in a frostier clime;

But what to His were ours, who pay,
Drop by slow drop, day after day,
Until His monstrous, primal guilt be washed away,

Who till that time must thus atone
In pulp and pit, in flesh and bone,
By our vicarious sacrifice fault not our own?

For, ah, I do not know the word
That it could hear, or if I've heard
A breath like *pardon, pardon,* when its stiff lips stirred.

If there were a word that I could give,
Or if I could only say *forgive,*
Then we might lift the Babel curse by which we live,

And I could leap and laugh and sing
And it could leap, and everything
Take hands with us and pace the music in a ring

And sway like the multitudinous wheat
In blessedness so long escheat
—Blest in that blasphemy of love we cannot now repeat.

Promises

Poems 1954–1956

To Rosanna and Gabriel

To a Little Girl, One Year Old, in a Ruined Fortress

To Rosanna

I. Sirocco

To a place of ruined stone we brought you, and sea-reaches.
Rocca: fortress, hawk-heel, lion-paw, clamped on a hill.
A hill, no. Sea cliff, and crag-cocked, the embrasures commanding the beaches,
Range easy, with most fastidious mathematic and skill.

Philipus me fecit: he of Spain, the black-browed, the anguished,
For whom nothing prospered, though he loved God.
His arms, great scutcheon of stone, once at drawbridge, have now languished
Long in the moat, under garbage; at moat-brink, rosemary with blue, thistle with gold bloom, nod.

Sun blaze and cloud tatter, it is the sirocco, the dust swirl is swirled
Over the bay face, mounts air like gold gauze whirled; it traverses the blaze-blue of water.
We have brought you the where geometry of a military rigor survives its own ruined world,
And sun regilds your gilt hair, in the midst of your laughter.

Rosemary, thistle, clutch stone. Far hangs Giannutri in blue air. Far to that blueness the heart aches,
And on the exposed approaches the last gold of gorse bloom, in the sirocco, shakes.

II. Gull's Cry

White goose by palm tree, palm ragged, among stones the white oleander,
And the she-goat, brown, under pink oleander, waits.
I do not think that anything in the world will move, not goat, not gander.
Goat droppings are fresh in the hot dust; not yet the beetle; the sun beats,

And under blue shadow of mountain, over blue-braiding sea-shadow,
The gull hangs white; whiter than white against mountain-mass,
The gull extends motionless on shelf of air, on substance of shadow.
The gull, at an eye-blink, will, into the astonishing statement of sun, pass.

All night, next door, the defective child cried; now squats in the dust where the lizard goes.
The wife of the *gobbo* sits under vine leaves, she suffers, her eyes glare.
The engaged ones sit in the privacy of bemusement, heads bent: the classic pose.
Let the beetle work, the gull comment the irrelevant anguish of air,

*

But at your laughter let the molecular dance of the stone-dark glimmer like joy
in the stone's dream,
And in that moment of possibility, let *gobbo, gobbo's* wife, and us, and all, take
hands and sing: redeem, redeem!

III. The Child Next Door

The child next door is defective because the mother,
Seven brats already in that purlieu of dirt,
Took a pill, or did something to herself she thought would not hurt,
But it did, and no good, for there came this monstrous other.

The sister is twelve. Is beautiful like a saint.
Sits with the monster all day, with pure love, calm eyes.
Has taught it a trick, to make *ciao,* Italian-wise.
It crooks hand in that greeting. She smiles her smile without taint.

I come, and her triptych beauty and joy stir hate
—Is it hate?—in my heart. Fool, doesn't she know that the process
Is not that joyous or simple, to bless, or unbless,
The malfeasance of nature or the filth of fate?

Can it bind or loose, that beauty in that kind,
Beauty of benediction? I trust our hope to prevail
That heart-joy in beauty be wisdom, before beauty fail
And be gathered like air in the ruck of the world's wind!

I think of your goldness, of joy, how empires grind, stars are hurled.
I smile stiff, saying *ciao,* saying *ciao,* and think: this is the world.

IV. The Flower

Above the beach, the vineyard
Terrace breaks to the seaward
Drop, where the cliffs fail
To a clutter of manganese shale.
Some is purple, some powdery-pale.
But the black lava-chunks stand off
The sea's grind, or indolent chuff.
The lava will withstand
The sea's beat, or insinuant hand,
And protect our patch of sand.

*

It is late. The path from the beach
Crawls up. I take you. We reach
The vineyard, and at that path angle
The hedge obtrudes a tangle
Of leaf and green bulge and a wrangle
Bee-drowsy and blowsy with white bloom,
Scarcely giving the passer-by room.
We know that that blossomy mass
Will brush our heads as we pass,
And at knee there's gold gorse and blue clover,
And at ankle, blue *malva* all over
—Plus plants I don't recognize
With my non-botanical eyes.
We approach, but before we get there,
If no breeze stirs that green lair,
The scent and sun-honey of air
Is too sweet comfortably to bear.

I carry you up the hill.
In my arms you are sweet and still.
We approach your special place,
And I am watching your face
To see the sweet puzzlement grow,
And then recognition glow.
Recognition explodes in delight.
You leap like spray, or like light.
Despite my arm's tightness,
You leap in gold-glitter and brightness.
You leap like a fish-flash in bright air,
And reach out. Yes, I'm well aware
That this is the spot, and hour,
For you to demand your flower.

When first we came this way
Up from the beach, that day
That seems now so long ago,
We moved bemused and slow
In the season's pulse and flow.
Bemused with sea, and slow
With June heat and perfume,
We paused here, and plucked you a bloom.
So here you always demand
Your flower to hold in your hand,
And the flower must be white,
For you have your own ways to compel
Observance of this ritual.
You hold it and sing with delight.
And your mother, for our own delight,
Picks one of the blue flowers there,
To put in your yellow hair.

That done, we go on our way
Up the hill, toward the end of the day.

But the season has thinned out.
From the bay edge below, the shout
Of a late bather reaches our ear,
Coming to the vineyard here
By more than distance thinned.
The bay is in shadow, the wind
Nags the shore to white.
The mountain prepares the night.
By the vineyard we have found
No bloom worthily white,
And the few we have found
Not disintegrated to the ground
Are by season and sea-salt browned.
We give the best one to you.
It is ruined, but will have to do.
Somewhat better the blue blossoms fare.
We find one for your hair,
And you sing as though human need
Were not for perfection. We proceed
Past floss-borne or sloughed-off seed,
Past curled leaf and dry pod,
And the blue blossom will nod
With your head's drowsy gold nod.

Let all seasons pace their power,
As this has paced to this hour.
Let season and season devise
Their possibilities.
Let the future reassess
All past joy, and past distress,
Till we know Time's deep intent,
And the last integument
Of the past shall be rent
To show how all things bent
Their energies to that hour
When you first demanded your flower.

And in that image let
Both past and future forget,
In clasped communal ease,
Their brute identities.

The path lifts up ahead
To the *rocca,* supper, bed.
We move in the mountain's shade.
But the mountain is at our back.
Ahead, climbs the coast-cliff track.
The valley between is dim.

Ahead, on the cliff rim,
The *rocca* clasps its height.
It accepts the incipient night.
Just once we look back.
On sunset, a white gull is black.
It hangs over the mountain crest.
It hangs on that saffron west.
It makes its outcry.
It slides down the sky.
East now, it catches the light.
Its black has gone again white,
And over the *rocca's* height
It gleams in the last light.
It has sunk from our sight.
Beyond the cliff is night.

It sank on unruffled wing.
We hear the sea rustling.

It will rustle all night, darling.

V. Colder Fire

It rained toward day. The morning came sad and white
With silver of sea-sadness and defection of season.
Our joys and convictions are sure, but in that wan light
We moved—your mother and I—in muteness of spirit past logical reason.

Now sun, afternoon, and again summer-glitter on sea.
As you to a bright toy, the heart leaps. The heart unlocks
Joy, though we know, shamefaced, the heart's weather should not be
Merely a reflex to solstice, or sport of some aggrieved equinox.

No, the heart should be steadfast: I know that.
And I sit in the late-sunny lee of the watch-house,
At the fortress point, you on my knee now, and the late
White butterflies over gold thistle conduct their ritual carouse.

In whisperless carnival, in vehemence of gossamer,
Pale ghosts of pale passions of air, the white wings weave.
In tingle and tangle of arabesque, they mount light, pair by pair,
As though that tall light were eternal indeed, not merely the summer's
reprieve.

You leap on my knee, you exclaim at the sun-stung gyration.
And the upper air stirs, as though the vast stillness of sky
Had stirred in its sunlit sleep and made a suspiration,
A luxurious languor of breath, as after love, there is a sigh.

*

But enough, for the highest sun-scintillant pair are gone
Seaward, past rampart and cliff borne, over blue sea-gleam.
Close to my chair, to a thistle, a butterfly sinks now, flight done.
By gold bloom of thistle, white wings pulse under the sky's dream.

The sky's dream is enormous, I lift up my eyes.
In sunlight a tatter of mist clings high on the mountain-mass.
The mountain is under the sky, and there the gray scarps rise
Past paths where on their appointed occasions men climb, and pass.

Past grain-patch, last apron of vineyard, last terrace of olive,
Past chestnut, past cork grove, where the last carts can go,
Past camp of the charcoal maker, where coals glow in the black hive,
The scarps, gray, rise up. Above them is that place I know.

The pines are there, they are large, a deep recess,
Shelf above scarp, enclave of rock, a glade
Benched and withdrawn in the mountain-mass, under the peak's duress.
We came there—your mother and I—and rested in that severe shade.

Pine-blackness mist-tangled, the peak black above: the glade gives
On the empty threshold of air, the hawk-hung delight
Of distance unspooled and bright space spilled—ah, the heart thrives!
We stood in that shade and saw sea and land lift in the far light.

Now the butterflies dance, time-tattered and disarrayed.
I watch them. I think how above that far scarp's sunlit wall
Mist threads in silence the darkness of boughs, and in that shade
Condensed moisture gathers at needle-tip. It glitters, will fall.

I cannot interpret for you this collocation
Of memories. You will live your own life, and contrive
The language of your own heart, but let that conversation,
In the last analysis, be always of whatever truth you would live.

For fire flames but in the heart of a colder fire.
All voice is but echo caught from a soundless voice.
Height is not deprivation of valley, nor defect of desire,
But defines, for the fortunate, that joy in which all joys should rejoice.

Promises

To Gabriel

I. What Was the Promise That Smiled from the Maples at Evening?

What was the promise that smiled from the maples at evening?
Smiling dim from the shadow, recessed? What language of leaf-lip?
And the heels of the fathers clicked on the concrete, returning,
Each aware of his own unspecified burden, at sun-dip.
In first darkness hydrangeas float in their spectral precinct.
Beneath pale hydrangeas first firefly utters cold burning.
The sun is well down now, first star has now winked.

What was the promise when bullbats dizzied the sunset?
They skimmer and skitter in gold light at great height.
The guns of big boys on the common go *boom,* past regret.
Boys shout when hit bullbat spins down in that gold light.
"Too little to shoot"—but next year you'll be a big boy.
So shout now and pick up the bird—Why, that's blood, it is wet.
Its eyes are still open, your heart in the throat swells like joy.

What was the promise when, after the last light had died,
Children gravely, down walks, in spring dark, under maples, drew
Trains of shoe boxes, empty, with windows, with candles inside,
Going *chuck-chuck,* and blowing for crossings, lonely, *oo-oo?*
But on impulse you fled, and they called, called across the dark lawn,
Long calling your name, who now lay in the darkness to hide,
While the sad little trains glimmer on under maples, and on.

What was the promise when, after the dying was done,
All the long years before, like burnt paper, flared into black,
And the house shrunk to silence, the odor of flowers near gone?
Recollection of childhood was natural: cold gust at the back.
What door on the dark flings open, then suddenly bangs?
Yes, something was lost in between, but it's long, the way back.
You sleep, but in sleep hear a door that creaks where it hangs.

Long since, in a cold and coagulate evening, I've stood
Where they slept, the long dead, and the farms and far woods fled away,
And a gray light prevailed and both landscape and heart were subdued.
Then sudden, the ground at my feet was like glass, and I say
What I saw, saw deep down, and the fleshly habiliments rent—
But agleam in a phosphorus of glory, bones bathed, there they lay,
Side by side, Ruth and Robert: the illumination then spent.

Earth was earth, and in earth-dark no glow now, therefore I lifted
My gaze to that world which had once been the heart's familiar,
Swell of woods and far field-sweep, in twilight by stream-gleam now wefted,

Railroad yonder and coal chute, town roofs far under the first star.
Then her voice, long forgotten, calm in silence, said: "Child."
Then his, with the calm of a night field, or far star:
"We died only that every promise might be fulfilled."

II. Court-martial

Under the cedar tree,
He would sit, all summer, with me:
An old man and small grandson
Withdrawn from the heat of the sun.

Captain, cavalry, C.S.A.,
An old man, now shrunken, gray,
Pointed beard clipped the classic way,
Tendons long gone crank and wry,
And long shrunken the cavalryman's thigh
Under the pale-washed blue jean.
His pipe smoke lifts, serene
Beneath boughs of the evergreen,
With sunlight dappling between.
I see him now, as once seen.

Light throbs the far hill.
The boughs of the cedar are still.

His years like landscape lie
Spread to the backward eye
In life's long irony.
All the old hoofbeats fade
In the calm of the cedar shade,
Where only the murmur and hum
Of the far farm, and summer, now come.
He can forget all—forget
Even mortgage and lien and debt,
Cutworm and hail and drouth,
Bang's disease, hoof-and-mouth,
Barn sagging and broken house—
For now in the shade, adrowse,
At last he can sit, or rouse
To light pipe, or say to me
Some scrap of old poetry—
Byron or Burns—and idly
The words glimmer and fade
Like sparks in the dark of his head.

*

In the dust by his chair
I undertook to repair
The mistakes of his old war.
Hunched on that toy terrain,
Campaign by campaign,
I sought, somehow, to untie
The knot of History,
For in our shade I knew
That only the Truth is true,
That life is only the act
To transfigure all fact,
And life is only a story
And death is only the glory
Of the telling of the story,
And the *done* and the *to-be-done*
In that timelessness were one,
Beyond the poor *being done.*

The afternoon stood still.
Sun dazzled the far hill.

It was only a chance word
That a chance recollection had stirred.
"Guerrilla—what's that?" I said.
"Bushwhackers, we called 'em," he said.
"Were they on the Yankee side?"
"Son, they didn't have any side.
Just out to plunder and ride
And hell-rake the pore countryside.
Just out for themselves, so, son,
If you happened to run across one,
Or better, laid hand to a passel,
No need to be squeamish, or wrestle
Too long with your conscience. But if—"
He paused, raised his pipe, took a whiff—
"If your stomach or conscience was queasy,
You could make it all regular, easy.

"By the road, find some shade, a nice patch.
Even hackberry does, at a scratch.
Find a spring with some cress fresh beside it,
Growing rank enough to nigh hide it.
Lord, a man can sure thirst when you ride.
Yes, find you a nice spot to bide.
Bide sweet when you can when you ride.
Order halt, let heat-daze subside.
Put your pickets, vedettes out, dismount.
Water horses, grease gall, take count,
And while the men rest and jaw,
You and two lieutenants talk law.
Brevitatem justitia amat.

Time is short—hell, a rope is—that's that."

That was that, and the old eyes were closed.
On a knee one old hand reposed,
Fingers crooked on the cob pipe, where
Last smoke raveled blue up the air.
Every tale has an end, has an end.
But smoke rose, did not waver or bend.
It unspooled, wouldn't stop, wouldn't end.

"By God—" and he jerked up his head.
"By God, they deserved it," he said.
"Don't look at me that way," he said.
"By God—" and the old eyes glared red.
Then shut in the cedar shade.

The head slept in that dusk the boughs made.
The world's silence made me afraid.
Then a July-fly, somewhere,
Like silk ripping, ripped the bright air.
Then stopped. Sweat broke in my hair.

I snatched my gaze away.
I swung to the blazing day.
Ruined lawn, raw house swam in light.
The far woods swam in my sight.
Throbbing, the fields fell away
Under the blaze of day.

Calmly then, out of the sky,
Blotting the sun's blazing eye,
He rode. He was large in the sky.
Behind, shadow massed, slow, and grew
Like cloud on the sky's summer blue.
Out of that shade-mass he drew.
To the great saddle's sway, he swung,
Not old now, not old now, but young,
Great cavalry boots to the thigh,
No speculation in eye.
Then clotting behind him, and dim,
Clot by clot, from the shadow behind him,
They took shape, enormous in air.
Behind him, enormous, they hung there:

Ornaments of the old rope,
Each face outraged, agape,
Not yet believing it true.
Each hairy jaw is askew,
Tongue out, out-staring eye,
And the spittle not yet dry
That was uttered with the last cry.

*

The horseman does not look back.
Blank-eyed, he continues his track,
Riding toward me there,
Through the darkening air.

The world is real. It is there.

III. Gold Glade

Wandering, in autumn, the woods of boyhood,
Where cedar, black, thick, rode the ridge,
Heart aimless as rifle, boy-blankness of mood,
I came where ridge broke, and the great ledge,
Limestone, set the toe high as treetop by dark edge

Of a gorge, and water hid, grudging and grumbling,
And I saw, in mind's eye, foam white on
Wet stone, stone wet-black, white water tumbling,
And so went down, and with some fright on
Slick boulders, crossed over. The gorge-depth drew night on,

But high over high rock and leaf-lacing, sky
Showed yet bright, and declivity wooed
My foot by the quietening stream, and so I
Went on, in quiet, through the beech wood:
There, in gold light, where the glade gave, it stood.

The glade was geometric, circular, gold,
No brush or weed breaking that bright gold of leaf-fall.
In the center it stood, absolute and bold
Beyond any heart-hurt, or eye's grief-fall.
Gold-massy in air, it stood in gold light-fall,

No breathing of air, no leaf now gold-falling,
No tooth-stitch of squirrel, or any far fox bark,
No woodpecker coding, or late jay calling.
Silence: gray-shagged, the great shagbark
Gave forth gold light. There could be no dark.

But of course dark came, and I can't recall
What county it was, for the life of me.
Montgomery, Todd, Christian—I know them all.
Was it even Kentucky or Tennessee?
Perhaps just an image that keeps haunting me.

No, no! in no mansion under earth,
Nor imagination's domain of bright air,
But solid in soil that gave it its birth,
It stands, wherever it is, but somewhere.
I shall set my foot, and go there.

IV. Dark Woods

1. Tonight the Woods Are Darkened

Tonight the woods are darkened.
You have, long back, forgot
What impulse or perturbation
Had made you rise. You went out

Of the house, where faces and light were,
To walk, and the night was black.
The dog whined. He tried to follow.
You picked up some rocks. Rocked him back.

One yelp the brute gave from back there.
Good. So now you were free
To enter the field and dark there
Under your heart's necessity.

Under sparse star-gleam a glimmer
Of pale dust provoked your feet
To pursue the ectoplasmic bisection
Of the dark field-heave, and to meet,

Yonder where woods massed their darkness,
A darkness more absolute.
All right: and in shadow the pale dust,
How soundless, accepted the foot!

Foot trapped in that silken compulsion
Of dust, and dust-softness, and the pale
Path's glimmer in field-darkness,
You moved. Did nerve fail?

Could you stop? No, all's re-enactment.
Trapped in that *déjà-vu,*
Déjà-fait, déjà-fait, you hear whispers,
In the dark, say, "Ah." Say:"You, too?"

Was there a field full of folk there,
Behind you? Threading like mist?
All who, dark-hungry, once had flung forth
From the house, and now persist

In the field-dark to spy on and count you—
They who now rejoice not, nor grieve,
But yet leer in their spooky connivance,
Waiting to pluck sleeve?

You wheel now to face them, but nothing
Is there. Only you. And in starlight,
Beyond the old field and pale cow-track,
The woods wait. They wait. *All right.*

2. The Dogwood

All right: and with that wry acceptance you follow the cow-track.
Yes, it's dark in the woods, as black as a peddler's pocket.
Cobweb tangles, briar snatches. A sensible man would go back.
A bough finds your face, and one eye grieves in the socket.

Midnight compounds with the peeper. Now whippoorwills speak,
Far off. Then silence. What's that? And something blots star—
By your head velvet air-*whoosh,* curdle and shudder of wing-creak.
It is only an owl. You go on. You can guess where you are.

For here is the gum-swamp, the slough where you once trapped the weasel.
Here the dead cow was dumped, and by buzzards duly divested.
All taint of mortality's long since wiped clean as a whistle.
Now love vine threads eyehole, God's peace is by violet attested.

The bones are long lost. In green grass the skull waits, has waited:
A cathedral for ants, and at noon, under white dome, great transept,
They pass in green gloom, under sunlight by leaf mitigated,
For leaf of the love vine shuts eyehole, as though the eye slept.

But now it's not noon, it is night, and ant-dark in that cow skull.
And man-dark in the woods. But go on, that's how men survive.
Went on in the dark, heart tight now as nut in the hull.
Came back in the dark, and home, and throve as men thrive.

But not before you had seen it, sudden at path-turn,
White-floating in darkness, the dogwood, white bloom in dark air.
Like an ice-break, broke joy; then you felt a strange wrath burn
To strike it, and strike, had a stick been handy in the dark there.

But one wasn't handy, so there on the path now, breath scant,
You stood, you stood there, and oh, could the poor heart's absurd
Cry for wisdom, for wisdom, ever be answered? Triumphant,
All night, the tree glimmered in darkness, and uttered no word.

3. The Hazel Leaf

Tonight the woods are darkened.
　　You have forgotten what pain
Had once drawn you forth:
　　To remember it might yet be some pain.
　　But to forget may, too, be pain.

The hazel leaf falls in autumn.
　　It slants athwart the gold air.
Boys come, prompt at nut-fall,
　　To shout and kick up the gold leaves there.
　　Shouts echo in high boughs not yet bare.

*

The hazel leaf falls in autumn.
    Boys go, and no voices intrude
Now at dusk-hour. The foot
    Of only the squirrel stirs leaf of this solitude.
    Otherwise, only shadow may now intrude.

The little green snake by the path-side,
    In May, lifts its jeweled head.
It stares, waves the tongue-wisp.
    What it hears on the path is not now your tread.
    But it still stares with lifted head.

Yes, your tread's now fainter and farther.
    Years muffle a tread, like grass.
Who passed, struck; now goes on.
    The snake waits, head crushed, to be observed by the next to pass.
    He will observe it, and then pass.

Tonight the woods are darkened.
    What other man may go there
Now stares, silent, breath scant,
    Waiting for the white petal to be released in dark air.
    Do not forget you were once there.

V. Country Burying (1919)

A thousand times you've seen that scene:
    Oak grove, bare ground, little white church there,
Bone-white in that light, and through dust-pale green
    Of oak leaf, the steeple pokes up in the bright air.

For it is summer, and once I sat
    At grove-edge beyond the disarray
Of cars in the shade-patch, this way and that.
    They stood patient as mules now in the heat of the day.

Chevrolet, T-Model, a Hudson or two,
    They are waiting like me, and the afternoon glares.
Waiting is all they have come to do.
    What goes on inside is no concern of theirs,

Nor of mine, who have lost a boy's afternoon,
    When summer's so short, oh, so short, just to bring
My mother to bury someone she'd scarce known.
    "I respect her," she'd said, but was that enough of a thing?

Who was she? Who knows? I'd not thought to ask it.
    That kind came to town, in buggy or Ford,
Some butter to swap, clutch of eggs in a basket,
    Gnarled hands in black mittens, old face yellow as a gourd.

*

It's no matter now who lies in the church,
Where heads bend in duty in sparse rows.
Green miles of tobacco, sun-dazzled, stretch
Away. Red clay, the road winds, goes on where it goes.

And we, too, now go, down the road, where it goes,
My mother and I, the hole now filled.
Light levels in fields now, dusk crouches in hedgerows,
As we pass from what is, toward what will be, fulfilled,

And I passed toward voices and the foreign faces,
Knew dawn in strange rooms, and the heart gropes for center,
But should I come back, and come back where that place is,
Oak grove, white church, in day-glare a-daze, I might enter.

For what? But enter, and find what I'd guess:
The odor of varnish, hymnals stacked on a chair,
Light religiously dim by painted paper on window glass,
And the insistent buzz of a fly lost in shadow, somewhere.

Why doesn't that fly stop buzzing—stop buzzing up there!

VI. School Lesson Based on Word of Tragic Death of Entire Gillum Family

They weren't so bright, or clean, or clever,
And their noses were sometimes imperfectly blown,
But they always got to school the weather whatever,
With old lard pail full of fried pie, smoked ham, and corn pone.

It was good six miles to the Gillum place,
Back where the cedar and hoot owl consorted
And the snapping turtle snoozed in his carapace
And the whang-doodle whooped and the dang-whoodle snorted.

Tow hair was thick as a corn-shuck mat.
They had milky blue eyes in matching pairs.
And barefoot or brogan, when they sat,
Their toes were the kind that hook round the legs of chairs.

They had adenoids to make you choke,
And buttermilk breath, and their flannels asteam,
And sat right mannerly while teacher spoke,
But when book-time came their eyes were glazed and adream.

There was Dollie-May, Susie-May, Forrest, Sam, Brother—
Thirteen down to eight the stairsteps ran.
They had popped right natural from their big fat mother,
The clabber kind that can catch just by honing after a man.

*

She must have honed hard, and maybe had to,
For Old Slat Gillum was the kind of a one
Who wasn't designed to cast much shadow
If set a little sideways and not in good strong sun.

But she had her brood, and that was that,
Though you wondered how she had relished her reaming,
For from yellow toenail to old black felt hat,
Gillum was scarcely the type to set a lady dreaming.

In town he'd stop, and say: "Say, mister,
I'll name you what's true fer folks, ever-one.
Human-man ain't much more'n a big blood blister,
All red and proud-swole, but one good squeeze and he's gone.

"Take me, ain't wuth lead and powder to perish,
Just some spindle bone stuck in a pair of pants,
But a man's got his chaps to love and to cherish,
And raise up and larn 'em so they kin git they chance."

So mud to the hub, or dust to the hock,
God his helper, wet or dry,
Old Gillum swore by God and by cock,
He'd git 'em larned before his own time came to die.

That morning blew up cold and wet,
All the red-clay road was curdled as curd,
And no Gillums there for the first time yet.
The morning drones on. Stove spits. Recess. Then the word.

Dollie-May was combing Susie-May's head.
Sam was feeding, Forrest milking, got nigh through.
Little Brother just sat on the edge of his bed.
Somebody must have said: "Pappy, what now you aimin' to do?"

An ice pick is a subtle thing.
The puncture's small, blood only a wisp.
It hurts no more than a bad bee sting.
When the sheriff got there the school-bread was long burned to a crisp.

In the afternoon silence the chalk would scrape.
We sat and watched the windowpanes steam,
Blur the old corn field and accustomed landscape.
Voices came now faint in our intellectual dream.

Which shoe, oh, which, was Brother putting on?
That was something, it seemed, you just had to know.
But nobody knew, all afternoon,
Though we studied and studied, as hard as we could, to know,

*

Studying the arithmetic of losses,
    To be prepared when the next one,
By fire, flood, foe, cancer, thrombosis,
    Or Time's slow malediction, came to be undone.

We studied all afternoon, till getting on to sun.
There was another lesson, but we were too young to take up that one.

VII. Summer Storm (Circa 1916), and God's Grace

Toward sun, the sun flared suddenly red.
    The green of woods was doused to black.
    The cattle bellowed by the haystack.
Redder than ever, red clay was red.
    Up the lane the plowhands came pelting back.

Astride and no saddle, and they didn't care
    If a razor-back mule at a break-tooth trot
    Was not the best comfort a man ever got,
But came huddling on, with jangling gear,
    And the hat that jounced off stayed off, like as not.

In that strange light all distance died.
    You know the world's intensity.
    Field-far, you can read the aphid's eye.
The mole, in his sod, can no more hide,
    And weeps beneath the naked sky.

Past silence, sound insinuates
    Past ear into the inner brain.
    The toad's asthmatic breath is pain,
The cutworm's tooth grinds and grates,
    And the root, in earth, screams, screams again,

But no cloud yet. No wind, though you,
    A half a county off, now spy
    The crow that, laboring zenith-high,
Is suddenly, with wings askew,
    Snatched, and tumbled down the sky.

And so you waited. You couldn't talk.
    The creek-side willows shuddered gray.
    The oak leaf turned the other way,
Gray as fish-belly. Then, with a squawk,
    The henhouse heaved, and flew away,

*

And darkness rode in on the wind.
    The pitchfork lightning tossed the trees,
    And God got down on hands and knees
To peer and cackle and commend
    His own sadistic idiocies.

Next morning you stood where the bridge had washed out.
    A drowned cow bobbled down the creek.
    Raw-eyed, men watched. They did not speak.
Till one shrugged, said he thought he'd make out.
    Then turned, took the woods-path up the creek.

Oh, send them summer, one summer just right,
    With rain well spaced, no wind or hail.
    Let cutworm tooth falter, locust jaw fail,
And if a man wake at roof-roar at night,
    Let that roar be the roar of God's awful Grace, and not of His flail.

VIII. Founding Fathers, Nineteenth-Century Style, Southeast U. S. A.

They were human, they suffered, wore long black coat and gold watch chain.
They stare from daguerreotype with severe reprehension,
Or from genuine oil, and you'd never guess any pain
In those merciless eyes that now remark our own time's sad declension.

Some composed declarations, remembering Jefferson's language.
Knew pose of the patriot, left hand in crook of the spine or
With finger to table, while right invokes the Lord's just rage.
There was always a grandpa, or cousin at least, who had been, of course, a real
        Signer.

Some were given to study, read Greek in the forest, and these
Longed for an epic to do their own deeds right honor:
Were Nestor by pigpen, in some tavern brawl played Achilles.
In the ring of Sam Houston they found, when he died, one word engraved:
        Honor.

Their children were broadcast, like millet seed flung in a wind-flare.
Wives died, were dropped like old shirts in some corner of country.
Said, "Mister," in bed, the child-bride; hadn't known what to find there;
Wept all the next morning for shame; took pleasure in silk; wore the keys to the
        pantry.

"Will die in these ditches if need be," wrote Bowie, at the Alamo.
And did, he whose left foot, soft-catting, came forward, and breath hissed:
Head back, gray eyes narrow, thumb flat along knife-blade, blade low.
"Great gentleman," said Henry Clay, "and a patriot." Portrait by Benjamin
        West.

*

Or take those, the nameless, of whom no portraits remain,
No locket or seal ring, though somewhere, broken and rusted,
In attic or earth, the long Decherd, stock rotten, has lain;
Or the mold-yellow Bible, God's Word, in which, in their strength, they had
also trusted.

Some wrestled the angel, and took a fall by the corncrib.
Fought the brute, stomp-and-gouge, but knew they were doomed in that glory.
All night, in sweat, groaned; fell at last with spit red and a cracked rib.
How sweet were the tears! Thus gentled, they roved the dark land with their old
story.

Some prospered, had black men and lands, and silver on table,
But remembered the owl call, the smell of burnt bear fat on dusk-air.
Loved family and friends, and stood it as long as able,
"But money and women, too much is ruination, am Arkansas-bound." So went
there.

One of mine was a land shark, or so the book with scant praise
Denominates him,"a man large and shapeless,
Like a sack of potatoes set on a saddle," and says,
"Little learning but shrewd, not well trusted." Rides thus out of history, neck fat
and napeless.

One saw Shiloh and such, got cranky, would fiddle all night.
The boys nagged for Texas. "God damn it, there's nothing, God damn it,
In Texas," but took wagons, went, and to prove he was right,
Stayed a year and a day, "hell, nothing in Texas," had proved it, came back to
black vomit,

And died, and they died, and are dead, and now their voices
Come thin, like last cricket in frost-dark, in grass lost,
With nothing to tell us for our complexity of choices,
But beg us only one word to justify their own old life-cost.

So let us bend ear to them in this hour of lateness,
And what they are trying to say, try to understand,
And try to forgive them their defects, even their greatness,
For we are their children in the light of humanness, and under the shadow of
God's closing hand.

IX. Foreign Shore, Old Woman, Slaughter of Octopus

What now do the waves say
    To her, the old woman? She wears peasant black,
Alone on the beach, barefoot, and the day
    Withdraws, and she follows her slow track
Among volcanic black boulders, at sea-edge, and does not look back.
Sea-tongue softly utters among boulders by her track.

Saffron-saddening the mountain, the sun
    Sinks, and from sea, black boulder by boulder,
Night creeps. She stops by the boulders, leans on one,
    And if from black shawl she should unfold her
Old hand to the stone, she would find it yet warm, but it will be colder.
What has soft sea-tongue among black boulders told her?

All day there was picnic and laughter,
    Bright eye and hair tossing, white foam and thigh-flash,
And up from some cold coign and dark lair of water,
    Ectoplasmic, snot-gray, the obscene of the life-wish,
Sad tentacles weaving like prayer, eyes wide to glare-horror of day-wash,
The nightmare was spread out on stone. Boys yelled at the knife flash.

The mountain is black, the sun drops.
    Among the black boulders, slow foam laces white.
Wind stirs, stirs paper of picnic, stops,
    And agleam in imperial ease, at sky-height,
One gull hangs white in contempt of our human heart, and the night.
Pearl-slime of the slaughter, on black stone, glints in last light.

What can the sea tell her,
    That she does not now know, and know how to bear?
She knows, as the sea, that what came will recur,
    And detached in that wisdom, is aware
How grain by slow grain, last sun heat from sand is expended on night air.
Bare flesh of old foot knows that much, as she stands there.

This is not my country, or tongue,
    And my age not the old woman's age, or sea-age.
I shall go on my errand, and that before long,
    And leave much, but not, sea-darkling, her image,
Which in the day traffic, or as I stand in night dark, may assuage
The mind's pain of logic somewhat, or the heart's rage.

X. Dark Night of

Far off, two fields away,
Where dark of the river-woods lay,
I saw him divulged into daylight,
And stand as to look left and right.
You could guess that quick look aside
Like a creature that knows how to hide
And does not debate pride.

Yes, the owner might come riding
With pistol in pocket, or striding
Along with a stout stick in hand,
To say: "Get the hell off my land!"
And the fellow would understand.

The owner would be justified
To clean him out, hoof-and-hide.
He might set your woods on fire,
Or at least mash down barbed wire.
That's all the excuse you require.

I was twelve, and my property sense
Was defective, though much improved since.
The day, anyway, was a scorcher,
So I didn't get up from the porch or
Even whistle the dogs from the shade
To provoke that flap-jawing parade
Of brute holler and whoop through the heat
To set a tooth in tramp-meat.
Didn't lay down my book, or even shout
Back into the house what was out,
How hedge-skulker and creature of night
And son of pellagra and spite
Now stood in our honest daylight.

Now stood, then slowly moved
One step. Stopped to see if he'd proved
That a man could survive half a minute
Outside the woods and not in it.
Looked back once to black safety of shade,
Then was caught in that great suction made
By the world's bright vacancy.
Was drawn by the world's blank eye.
Moved under the light-dizzy sky.

Far off, he is pin-prick size,
A mote dark in your dazzle of eyes.
He moves without truth or dimension
Across that vast space men should shun.
Lost and faceless and far,

Under light's malevolent stare,
In a painful retardation,
He moves toward what destination,
And so passes over
The enormity of clover.
Is now gone. Has passed over.

Now afternoon, strand by gold strand,
Raveled out, and over the land
Light leveled toward time set
For me to get up and forget
Egypt's arrogant dead
Or that Scaevola whom Rome bred.
Yes, time to drop book, and rouse,
And up and leave the house,
And round up the cows.

The cows drift up the lane.
White elder blooms by the lane.
They move in a motion like sleep.
Their jaws make a motion like sleep.
I linger, leaf by leaf.
Dust, pale, powders elder leaf,
And the evening-idle, pale sky
Drains your body light, and dry.
Air moves sweet through pale husk under sky.

But suddenly you are you,
No pale husk the air moves through.
My heart clenched hand-hard as I stood.
The adrenalin tingled my blood.
My lungs made a fish-gasp for air.
Cold prickles ran in my hair.
Beneath elder bloom, the eyes glare.

Couched under elder bloom,
In the honeysuckle he'd made room,
And the white strands regally wreathed
His old head, and the air he breathed
Was heavy with the languishment
Of that too sweet scent.
He was old, rough-grizzled, and spent.

Old and spent, but heaves up his head,
And our eyes thread the single thread
Of the human entrapment, until,
In a voice like a croak from an old well,
He says: "Caint you git on away?"
But I simply can't move away.
He says: "Caint you let a man lay!"

*

I stared down the dank depth and heard
That croak from cold slime. Then he stirred,
Jerked up, stumbled up in his lair,
Like an old mule snagged on barbed wire.
Jerked free, a moment stood there.

A little I stood there alone
To stare down the lane where he'd gone.
Then I turned to follow the cows
Up yonder toward the house,
There to enter and understand
My plate laid by a loving hand,
And to sleep, but not understand
That somewhere on the dark land,
Unable to stop or stand,
On a track no man would have planned,
By age, rage, rejection unmanned,
A bundle of rags in one hand,
Old black felt hat in other hand,
At last he would understand,
And with his old head bare
Move in the dark air.
His head, in the dark air,
Gleams with the absolute and glacial purity of despair.
His head, unbared, moves with the unremitting glory of stars high in the night
heaven there.
He moves in joy past contumely of stars or insolent indifference of the dark air.
May we all at last enter into that awfulness of joy he has found there.

XI. Infant Boy at Midcentury

1. When the Century Dragged

When the century dragged, like a great wheel stuck at dead center;
When the wind that had hurled us our half-century sagged now,
And only velleity of air somewhat snidely nagged now,
With no certain commitment to compass, or quarter: you chose to enter.

You enter an age when the neurotic clock-tick
Of midnight competes with the heart's pulsed assurance of power.
You have entered our world at scarcely its finest hour,
And smile now life's gold Apollonian smile at a sick dialectic.

You enter at the hour when the dog returns to his vomit,
And fear's moonflower spreads, white as girl-thigh, in dusk of compromise;
When posing for pictures, arms linked, the same smile in their eyes,
Good and Evil, to iron out all differences, stage their meeting at summit.

*

You come in the year when promises are broken,
And petal fears the late, as fruit the early frost-fall;
When the young expect little, and the old endure total recall,
But discover no logic to justify what they had taken, or forsaken.

But to take and forsake now you're here, and the heart will compress
Like stone when we see that rosy heel learn,
With its first step, the apocalyptic power to spurn
Us, and our works and days, and onward, prevailing, pass

To pause, in high pride of undisillusioned manhood,
At the gap that gives on the new century, and land,
And with calm heart and level eye command
That dawning perspective and possibility of human good.

2. Modification of Landscape

There will, indeed, be modification of landscape,
And in margin of natural disaster, substantial reduction.
There will be refinement of principle, and purified action,
And expansion, we trust, of the human heart-hope, and hand-scope.

But is it a meanness of spirit and indulgence of spite
To suggest that your fair time, and friends, will mirror our own
Somewhat, and ourselves, for flesh will yet grieve on the bone,
And the heart need compensation for its failure to study delight?

Some will take up religion, some discover the virtue of money.
Some will find liberal causes the mask for psychic disturbance.
Some will expiate ego with excessive kindness to servants,
And some make a cult of honor, having often quite little, if any.

Some, hating all humans, will cultivate love for cats,
And some from self-hate will give children a morbid devotion.
Some will glorify friendship, but watch for the slightest motion
Of eyelid, or lip-twitch, and the longed-for betrayal it indicates.

Success for the great will be heart-bread, and soul's only ease.
For some it will stink, like mackerel shining in moonlight.
At the mere thought of failure some will wet their sheets in the night,
Though some wear it proud as Kiwanis, or manhood's first social disease.

Yes, the new age will need the old lies, as our own once did;
For death is ten thousand nights—sure, it's only the process
Of accommodating flesh to idea, but there's natural distress
In learning to face Truth's glare-glory, from which our eyes are long hid.

3. Brightness of Distance

You will read the official histories—true, no doubt.
Barring total disaster, the record will speak from the shelf.
And if there's disaster, disaster will speak for itself.
So all of our lies will be truth, and the truth vindictively out.

Remember our defects, we give them to you gratis.
But remember that ours is not the worst of times.
We stand convicted of follies rather than crimes—
Yes, we throw out baby with bath, drop the meat in the fire where the fat is.

And in even such stew and stink as Tacitus
Once wrote of, his generals, gourmets, pimps, poltroons,
He found persons of private virtue, the old-fashioned stout ones
Who would bow the head to no blast; and we know that such are yet with us.

He puzzled how virtue finds perch past confusion and wrath;
How even Praetorian brutes, blank of love, as of hate,
Proud in their craftsman's pride only, held a last gate,
And died, and each back unmarred as though at the barracks bath.

And remember that many among us wish you well;
And once, on a strange shore, an old man, toothless and through,
Groped hand from the lattice of personal disaster to touch you.
He sat on the sand for an hour; said *ciao, bello,* as evening fell.

And think, as you move past our age that grudges and grieves,
How eyes, purged of envy, will follow your sunlit chance.
Eyes will brighten to follow your brightness and dwindle of distance.
From privacy of fate, eyes will follow, as though from the shadow of leaves.

XII. Lullaby: Smile in Sleep

Sleep, my son, and smile in sleep.
You will dream the world anew.
Watching you now sleep,
I feel the world's depleted force renew,
Feel the nerve expand and knit,
Feel a rustle in the blood,
Feel wink of warmth and stir of spirit,
As though season woke in the heart's cold underwood.
The vernal work is now begun.
Sleep, my son.
Sleep, son.

*

You will see the nestling fall.
Blood flecks grass of the rabbit form.
You will, of course, see all
The world's brute ox-heel wrong, and shrewd hand-harm.
Throats are soft to invite the blade.
Truth invites the journalist's lie.
Love bestowed mourns trust betrayed,
But the heart most mourns its own infidelity.
The greater, then, your obligation.
Dream perfection.
Dream, son.

When the diver leaves the board
To hang at gleam-height in his sky,
Trajectory is toward
An image hung perfect as light in the mind's wide eye.
So your dream will later serve you.
So now, dreaming, you serve me,
And give our hope new patent to
Enfranchise the human possibility.
Grace undreamed is grace forgone.
Dream grace, son.
Sleep on.

Dream that sleep is a sunlit meadow
Drowsy with a dream of bees
Threading sun, and the shadow
Where you lie lulled by their sunlit industries.
Let the murmurous bees of sleep
Tread down honey in honeycomb.
Heart-deep now, your dream will keep
Sweet in that deep comb for time to come.
Dream the sweetness coming on.
Dream, sweet son.
Sleep on.

What if angry vectors veer
Around your sleeping head, and form?
There's never need to fear
Violence of the poor world's abstract storm.
For you now dream Reality.
Matter groans to touch your hand.
Matter now lifts like the sea
Toward that cold moon that is your dream's command.
Dream the power coming on.
Dream, strong son.
Sleep on.

XIII. Man in Moonlight

1. Moonlight Observed from Ruined Fortress

Great moon, white-westering past our battlement,
Dark sea offers silver scintillance to your sky,
And not less responsive would my human heart be if I
Were duly instructed in what such splendors have meant.

I have thought on the question by other sea, other shore:
When you smoothed the sweet Gulf asleep, like a babe at the breast,
When the moon-lashed old freighter banged stars in Atlantic unrest,
When you spangled spume-tangle on black rock, and seal barked at sea-roar.

Décor must be right, of course, for your massive effect,
But a Tennessee stock-pond is not beneath your contempt,
Though its littoral merely a barnyard with cow-pats unkempt.
No, even a puddle is not too small for respect,

And once on the Cumberland's bluffs I stood at midnight,
With music and laughter behind me, while my eyes
Were trapped in gleam-glory, but the heart's hungry surmise
Faded; so back to the racket and bottle's delight.

Be it sea or a sewer, we know you have never much cared
What sort of excuse, just so you may preen and prink,
With vulgarities to make Belasco blink
And tricks that poor Houdini wouldn't have dared.

So now with that old, anguishing virtuosity
You strike our cliff, and then lean on to Carthage.
We stand on the crumbling stone and ruins of rage,
To watch your Tyrrhenian silver prank the sea.

And thus we enact again the compulsive story,
Knowing the end, the end, and ah, how soon,
But caught in strict protocol of plenilune
And that werewolf thirst to drink the blood of glory.

We stare, we stare, but will not stare for long.
You will not tell us what we need to know.
Our feet soon go the way that they must go,
In diurnal dust and heat, and right and wrong.

2. Walk by Moonlight in Small Town

Through the western window full fell moonlight.
It must have waked me where I lay.
Room objects swam in that spooky day.
I rose, dressed, walked the summer night,
As long years back I had moved in that compulsive light.

Lawns green by day now shimmered like frost.
Shadow, beast-black, in porches lurked.
On house fronts, windowpanes moon-smirked.
Past supper, paper read, lawn hosed,
How white, in the depth of dark rooms now, faces reposed.

Down Main Street, the window dummies blessed,
With lifted hand and empty stare,
The glimmering emptiness of air,
As though lunatically to attest
What hope the daylight heart might reasonably have possessed.

Three boxcars slept, as quiet as cows.
They were so tired, they'd been so far.
SP and *Katy, L & N R R*—
After bumble and bang, and where God knows,
They'd cracked the rust of a weed-rank spur, for this pale repose.

How long ago, at night, up that track,
I had watched the Pullmans flash and fade,
Then heard, in new quiet, the beat my heart made.
But every ticket's round-trip; now back,
I stood and again watched night-distance flee up that empty track.

I crossed the track, walked up the rise.
The school building hulked, ugly as day.
Beyond, the night fields fell away.
Building and grounds had shrunk in size,
And that predictable fact seemed pitiful to my eyes.

And pitiful was the moon-bare ground.
Dead grass, the gravel, earth ruined and raw—
It had not changed. And then I saw
That children were playing, with no sound.
They ceased their play, then quiet as moonlight, drew, slow, around.

Their eyes were fixed on me, and I
Now tried, face by pale face, to find
The names that haunted in my mind.
Each small, upgazing face would lie
Sweet as a puddle, and silver-calm, to the night sky.

*

But something grew in their pale stare:
Not reprobation or surprise,
Nor even forgiveness in their eyes,
But a humble question dawning there,
From face to face, like beseechment dawning on empty air.

Might a man but know his Truth, and might
He live so that life, by moon or sun,
In dusk or dawn, would be all one,
Then never on a summer night
Need he stand and shake in that cold blaze of Platonic light.

3. Lullaby: Moonlight Lingers

Moonlight lingers down the air.
Moonlight marks the window-square
As I stand and watch you sleep.
I hear the rustle where
The sea stirs sweet and sighs in its silvered sleep.
My son, sleep deep.
Sleep deep, son, and dream how moonlight
Unremitting, whitely, whitely, unpetals down the night.
As you sleep, now moonlight
Mollifies the mountain's rigor,
Laves the olive leaf to silver,
And black on moon-pale trunk of the olive
Prints shadow of the olive leaf.
Sleep, let moonlight give
Dark secondary definition to the olive leaf.
Sleep, son, past grief.

I might now close my eyes and see
Moonlight white on a certain tree.
It was a big white oak near a door
Familiar, long back, to me,
But now years unseen, and my foot enters there no more.
My son, sleep deep.
Sleep deep, son, and let me think
How moonlight glimmered down a summer lane to the cedar woods' dark
brink.
Sleep, and let me now think
Of moon-frost white on black bough of cedar,
White moon-rinse on meadow, whiter than clover,
And at moon-dark stone, how water woke
In a wink of glory, slid on to sleep.
Sleep, let this moon provoke
Moonlight more white on that landscape lost in the heart's homely deep.
Son, past grief, sleep.

*

Moonlight falls on sleeping faces.
It fell in far times and other places.
Moonlight falls on your face now,
And now in memory's stasis
I see moonlight mend an old man's Time-crossed brow.
My son, sleep deep,
Though moonlight will not stay.
Moon moves to seek that empty pillow, a hemisphere away.
Here, then, you will wake to the day.
Those who died, died long ago,
Faces you will never know,
Voices you will never hear—
Though your father heard them in the night,
And yet, sometimes, I can hear
That utterance as if tongue-rustle of pale tide in moonlight:
Sleep, son. Good night.

XIV. Mad Young Aristocrat on Beach

He sits in blue trunks on the sand, and children sing.
Their voices are crystal and sad, and tinkle in sunlight.
Their voices are crystal, and the tinkling
Of sadness, like gold ants, crawls on his quivering heart in its midnight.
And the sea won't be still, won't be still,
In that freaking and fracture and dazzle of light.
Yes, somebody ought to take steps and stop it.
It's high time that somebody did, and he thinks that he will.
Why, it's simple, it's simple, just get a big mop and mop it,
Till it's dry as a bone—you sea, you *cretino,* be still!
But he's tired, he is tired, and wants only sleep.
Oh, Lord, let us pray that the children stop singing before he begins to weep.

If he wept, we just couldn't bear it, but look, he is smiling!
He ponders how charming it is to smile, and magnanimous.
And his smile, indeed, is both sweet and beguiling,
And joy floods his heart now like hope, to replace that old dark animus.
So look! at the great concert grand,
He is bowing, and bowing, and smiling now on us,
And smiles at the sea, at the sea's bright applause—
But fame, ah, how sad! Again he sits on the sand,
And thinks how all human rewards are but gauds and gewgaws,
And lets sand, grain by grain, like history slip from his hand.
But his mother once said that his smile was sweet.
Curse the bitch, it is power man wants, and like a black cloud now he mounts to his feet.

He is young and sun-brown and tall and well formed, and he knows it.
He will swim in the sea, the water will break to his will.

Now emerging on shore, he is lethal, he shows it.
Yes, let them beware that brute jaw-jut and eye cold now and still.
Yes, let him beware, beware,
That brother, the elder, who comes to the title.
But a title, *merde!* he will marry a passport,
And dollars, of course—he has blood, though he isn't the heir.
Then sudden as death, a thought stops him chillingly short:
Mais l'Amérique, merde! why it's full of Americans there.
So closes his eyes, longs for home, longs for bed.
Ah, that sweet-haunched new housemaid! But knows he can't get her except in
the dark of his head.

So thinks of a whore he once had: she was dull as a sow,
And not once, never once, showed affection. He thinks he will cry.
Then thinks, with heart sweet, he'll be dead soon now,
And opens his eyes to the blaze and enormousness of the sky.
And we watch him, we watch him, and we
Are lonely, are lonely as death, though we try
To love him, but can't, for we sit on the sand,
Eyes throbbing at merciless brilliance and bicker of sea,
While sand, grain by grain, like our history, slips from his hand.
We should love him, because his flesh suffers for you and for me,
As our own flesh should suffer for him, and for all
Who will never come to the title, and be loved for themselves, at innocent
nightfall.

XV. Dragon Country: To Jacob Boehme

This is the dragon's country, and these his own streams.
The slime on the railroad rails is where he has crossed the track.
On a frosty morning, that field mist is where his great turd steams,
And there are those who have gone forth and not come back.

I was only a boy when Jack Simms reported the first depredation,
What something had done to his hog pen. They called him a God-damn liar.
Then said it must be a bear, after some had viewed the location,
With fence rails, like matchwood, splintered, and earth a bloody mire.

But no bear had been seen in the county in fifty years, they knew.
It was something to say, merely that, for people compelled to explain
What, standing in natural daylight, they agreed couldn't be true;
And saying the words, a man felt, in the chest, a constrictive pain.

At least, some admitted this later, when things had got to the worst,
When, for instance, they found, in the woods, the wagon turned on its side,
Mules torn from trace chains, and you saw how the harness had burst.
Spectators averted the face from the spot where the teamster had died.

*

But that was long back, in my youth, just the first of case after case.
The great hunts fizzled. You followed the track of disrepair,
Ruined fence, blood-smear, brush broken, but came, in the end, to a place
With weed unbent, leaf calm, and nothing, nothing, was there.

So what, in God's name, could men think, when they couldn't bring to bay
That belly-dragging earth-evil, but found that it took to air?
Thirty-thirty or buckshot might fail, but then at least you could say
You had faced it—assuming, of course, that you had survived the affair.

We were promised troops, the Guard, but the Governor's skin got thin
When up in New York the papers called him Saint George of Kentucky.
Yes, even the Louisville reporters who came to Todd County would grin.
Reporters, though rarely, still come. No one talks. They think it unlucky.

Things happen, but they are denied, as when on the road to go out
To the old Pinch'Em Church, a salesman, traveling for Swift, or Armour,
Stepped from his car. The Sheriff said, accident caused by a blowout.
They burned up the car to explain lack of patronage for the embalmer.

If a man disappears—well, the fact is something to hide.
The family says, gone to Akron, or up to Ford, in Detroit.
When we found Jebb Johnson's boot, with the leg, what was left, inside,
His mother said, no, it's not his. So we took it out to destroy it.

Land values are falling, no longer do lovers in moonlight go.
The rabbit, thoughtless of air gun, in the nearest pasture cavorts.
Now certain fields go untended, the local birth rate goes low.
The coon dips his little black paw in the riffle where he nightly resorts.

Yes, other sections have problems somewhat different from ours.
Their crops may fail, bank rates rise, on rumor of war loans be called,
But we feel removed from maneuvers of Russia, or other great powers,
And from much ordinary hope are now disenthralled.

The Catholics have sent in a mission, Baptists report new attendance.
But that's not the point. We are human, and the human heart
Demands language for reality that has no slightest dependence
On desire, or need. Now in church they pray only that evil depart.

But if the Beast were withdrawn now, life might dwindle again
To the ennui, the pleasure, and night sweat, known in the time before
Necessity of truth had trodden the land, and heart, to pain,
And left, in darkness, the fearful glimmer of joy, like a spoor.

XVI. Ballad of a Sweet Dream of Peace

1. And Don't Forget Your Corset Cover, Either

And why, in God's name, is that elegant bureau
Standing out here in the woods and dark?
Because, in God's name, it would create a furor
If such a Victorian piece were left in the middle of Central Park,
To corrupt the morals of young and old
With its marble top and drawer pulls gilt gold
And rosewood elaborately scrolled,
And would you, in truth, want your own young sister to see it in the Park?
But she knows all about it, her mother has told her,
And besides, these days, she is getting much older,
And why, in God's name, is that bureau left in the woods?
All right, I'll tell you why.
It has as much right there as you or I,
For the woods are God's temple, and even a bureau has moods.
But why, in God's name, is that elegant bureau left all alone in the woods?

It is left in the woods for the old lady's sake,
For there's privacy here for a household chore,
And Lord, I can't tell you the time it can take
To apply her own mixture of beeswax and newt-oil to bring out the gloss once more.
For the poor old hands move slower each night,
And can't manage to hold the cloth very tight,
And it's hard without proper light.
But why, in God's name, all this privacy for a simple household chore?
In God's name, sir! would you simply let
Folks see how naked old ladies can get?
Then let the old bitch buy some clothes like other folks do.
She once had some clothes, I am told,
But they're long since ruined by the damp and mold,
And the problem is deeper when bones let the wind blow through.
Besides it's not civil to call her a bitch, and her your own grandma, too.

2. Keepsakes

Oh, what brings her out in the dark and night?
She has mislaid something, just what she can't say,
But something to do with the bureau, all right.
Then why, in God's name, does she polish so much, and not look in a drawer right away?
Every night, in God's name, she does look there,
But finds only a Book of Common Prayer,
A ribbon-tied lock of gold hair,
A bundle of letters, some contraceptives, and an orris-root sachet.
Well, what is the old fool hunting for?

Oh, nothing, oh, nothing that's in the top drawer,
For that's left by late owners who had their own grief to withstand,
And she tries to squinch and frown
As she peers at the Prayer Book upside down,
And the contraceptives are something she can't understand,
And oh, how bitter the tears she sheds, with some stranger's old letters in hand!

You're lying, you're lying, she can't shed a tear!
Not with eyeballs gone, and the tear ducts, too.
You are trapped in a vulgar error, I fear,
For asleep in the bottom drawer is a thing that may prove instructive to you:
Just an old-fashioned doll with a china head,
And a cloth body naked and violated
By a hole through which sawdust once bled,
But drop now by drop, on a summer night, from her heart it is treacle bleeds through.
In God's name, what!—Do I see her eyes move?
Of course, and she whispers,"I died for love,"
And your grandmother whines like a dog in the dark and shade,
For she's hunting somebody to give
Her the life they had promised her she would live,
And I shudder to think what a stink and stir will be made
When some summer night she opens the drawer and finds that poor self she'd mislaid.

3. Go It, Granny—Go It, Hog!

Out there in the dark, what's that horrible chomping?
Oh, nothing, just hogs that forage for mast,
And if you call, "Hoo-pig!" they'll squeal and come romping,
For they'll know from your voice you're the boy who slopped them in dear, dead days long past.
Any hogs that I slopped are long years dead,
And eaten by somebody and evacuated,
So it's simply absurd, what you said.
You fool, poor fool, all Time is a dream, and we're all one Flesh, at last,
And the hogs know that, and that's why they wait,
Though tonight the old thing is a little bit late,
But they're mannered, these hogs, as they wait for her creaky old tread.
Polite, they will sit in a ring,
Till she finishes work, the poor old thing:
Then old bones get knocked down with a clatter to wake up the dead,
And it's simply absurd how loud she can scream with no shred of a tongue in her head.

4. Friends of the Family, or Bowling a Sticky Cricket

Who else, in God's name, comes out in these woods?
Old friends of the family, whom you never saw,
Like yon cranky old coot, who mumbles and broods,
With yachting cap, rusty frock coat, and a placard proclaiming, "I am the Law!"
What makes him go barefoot at night in God's dew?
In God's name, you idiot, so would you
If you'd suffered as he had to
When expelled from his club for the horrible hobby that taught him the nature of law.
They learned that he drowned his crickets in claret.
The club used cologne, and so couldn't bear it.
But they drown them in claret in Buckingham Palace!
Fool, law is inscrutable, so
Barefoot in dusk and dew he must go,
And at last each cries out in a dark stone-glimmering place,
"I have heard the voice in the dark, seeing not who utters. Show me Thy face!"

5. You Never Knew Her Either, Though You Thought You Did, Inside Out

Why now, in God's name, is her robe de nuit
So torn and bedraggled, and what is that stain?
It's only dried blood, in God's name, that you see.
But why does she carry that leaf in her hand? Will you try, in God's name, to explain?
It's a burdock leaf under which she once found
Two toads in coitu on the bare black ground,
So now she is nightly bound
To come forth to the woods to embrace a thorn tree, to try to understand pain,
And then wipes the blood on her silken hair,
And cries aloud, "Oh, we need not despair,
For I bleed, oh, I bleed, and God lives!" And the heart may stir
Like water beneath wind's tread
That wanders whither it is not said.
Oh, I almost forgot—will you please identify her?
She's the afternoon one who to your bed came, lip damp, the breath like myrrh.

6. I Guess You Ought to Know Who You Are

Could that be a babe crawling there in night's black?
Why, of course, in God's name, and birth-blind, but you'll see
How to that dead chestnut he'll crawl a straight track,
Then give the astonishing tongue of a hound with a coon treed up in a tree.
Well, who is the brat, and what's he up to?
He's the earlier one that they thought would be you,
And perhaps, after all, it was true,
For it's hard in these matters to tell sometimes. *But look, in God's name, I am me!*
If you are, there's the letter a hog has in charge,
With a gold coronet and your own name writ large,
And in French, most politely, "Répondez s'il vous plaît."
Now don't be alarmed we are late.
What's time to a hog? We'll just let them wait.
But for when you are ready, our clients usually say
That to shut the eyes tight and get down on the knees is the quickest and easiest way.

7. Rumor Unverified Stop Can You Confirm Stop

Yes, clients report it the tidiest way,
For the first time at least, when all is so strange
And helpers get awkward sometimes with delay.
But later, of course, you can try other methods that fancy suggests you arrange.
There are clients, in fact, who, when ennui gets great,
Will struggle, or ingeniously irritate
The helpers to acts I won't state:
For Reality's all, and to seek it, some welcome, at whatever cost, any change.
But speaking of change, there's a rumor astir
That the woods are sold, and the purchaser
Soon comes, and if credulity's not now abused,
Will, on this property, set
White foot-arch familiar to violet,
And heel that, smiting the stone, is not what is bruised,
And subdues to sweetness the pathside garbage, or thing body had refused.

XVII. Boy's Will, Joyful Labor without Pay, and Harvest Home (1918)

1. Morning

By breakfast time the bustle's on.
In the field the old red thresher clatters.
The old steam tractor shakes and batters.
Sweat pops already in the hot sun.
The dogs are barking, mad as hatters.

*

You bolt your oatmeal, up and go.
The world is panting, the world won't wait.
All energy's unregenerate.
Blood can't abide the status quo.
You run as far as the front gate,

Then stop. For when your hope is displayed
To wait you, you must feast the eye
An instant on possibility,
Before finite constriction is made
To our pathos of rapacity.

2. Work

The hand that aches for the pitchfork heft
Heaves sheaf from the shock's rich disrepair.
The wagoner snags it in mid-air,
Says, "Boy, save yore strength, 'fore you got none left,"
And grins, then wipes the sweat from his hair.

3. The Snake

Daylong, light, gold, leans on the land.
You stoke the tractor. You *gee* and *haw.*
You feed the thresher's gap-toothed maw.
Then on a load-top, high, you stand
And see your shadow, black as law,

Stretch far now on the gold stubble.
By now breath's short. Sweat stings the eyes.
Blue denim is sweat-black at the thighs.
If you make a joke, you waste your trouble.
In that silence the shout rings with surprise.

When you wreck a shock, the spot below
Is damp and green with a vernal gloom.
Field mouse or rabbit flees its doom,
And you scarcely notice how they go.
But a black snake rears big in his ruined room.

Defiant, tall in that blast of day,
Now eye for eye, he swaps his stare.
His outrage glitters on the air.
Men shout, ring around. He can't get away.
Yes, they are men, and a stone is there.

*

Against the wounded evening matched,
Snagged high on a pitchfork tine, he will make
Slow arabesque till the bullbats wake.
An old man, standing stooped, detached,
Spits once, says, "Hell, just another snake."

4. Hands Are Paid

The thresher now has stopped its racket.
It waits there small by the stack it has made.
The work is done, the hands are paid.
The silver dollar's in sweat-cold pocket,
And the shirt sticks cold to the shoulder blade.

Out of the field, the way it had come,
Dragging the thresher's list and bumble,
The tractor now, a-clank, a-shamble,
Grunts down the pike, the long way home.
In dusk, to water now, mules, slow, amble.

The dollar glints on the mantel shelf.
By the coal-oil lamp the man leans his head
Over fried sowbelly and cold corn bread.
He's too sleepy now to wash himself.
Kicks off his brogans. Gets to bed.

The bullbat has come, long back, and gone.
White now, the evening star hangs to preside
Over woods and dark water and far countryside.
The little blood that smeared the stone
Dropped in the stubble, has long since dried.

The springs of the bed creak now, and settle.
The overalls hang on the back of a chair
To stiffen, slow, as the sweat gets drier.
Far, under a cedar, the tractor's metal
Surrenders last heat to the night air.

In the cedar dark a white moth drifts.
The mule's head, at the barn-lot bar,
Droops sad and saurian under night's splendor.
In the star-pale field, the propped pitchfork lifts
Its burden, hung black, to the white star,

And the years go by like a breath, or eye-blink,
And all history lives in the head again,
And I shut my eyes and I see that scene,
And name each item, but cannot think
What, in their urgency, they must mean,

*

But know, even now, on this foreign shore,
In blaze of sun and the sea's stare,
A heart-stab blessed past joy or despair,
As I see, in the mind's dark, once more,
That field, pale, under starlit air.

XVIII. Lullaby: A Motion like Sleep

Under the star and beech-shade braiding,
Past the willow's dim solicitudes,
Past hush of oak-dark and stone's star-glinted upbraiding,
Water moves, in a motion like sleep,
Along the dark edge of the woods.
So, son, now sleep.

Sleep, and feel how now, at woods-edge,
The water, wan, moves under starlight,
Before it finds that dark of its own deepest knowledge,
And will murmur, in motion like sleep,
In that leaf-dark languor of night.
So, son, sleep deep.

Sleep, and dream how deep and dreamless
The covered courses of blood are:
And blood, in a motion like sleep, moves, gleamless,
By alleys darkened deep now
In leafage of no star.
So, son, sleep now.

Sleep, for sleep and stream and blood-course
Are a motion with one name,
And all that flows finds end but in its own source,
And a circuit of motion like sleep,
And will go as once it came.
So, son, now sleep

Till clang of cock-crow, and dawn's rays,
Summon your heart and hand to deploy
Their energies and know, in excitement of day-blaze,
How like a wound, and deep,
Is Time's irremediable joy.
So, son, now sleep.

XIX. The Necessity for Belief

The sun is red, and the sky does not scream.
The sun is red, and the sky does not scream.

There is much that is scarcely to be believed.

The moon is in the sky, and there is no weeping.
The moon is in the sky, and there is no weeping.

Much is told that is scarcely to be believed.

You, Emperors, and Others

Poems 1957–1960

To Max and Carol Shulman

Garland for You

I. Clearly about You

Bene fac, hoc tecum feres.

—On tomb of Roman citizen of no historical importance, under the Empire

Whoever you are, this poem is clearly about you,
For there's nothing else in the world it could be about.
Whatever it says, this poem is clearly true,
For truth is all we are born to, and the truth's out.

You won't look in the mirror? Well—but your face is there
Like a face drowned deep under water, mouth askew,
And tongue in that mouth tastes cold water, not sweet air,
And if it could scream in that medium, the scream would be you.

Your mother preferred the more baroque positions.
Your father's legerdemain marks the vestry accounts.
So you didn't know? Well, it's time you did—though one shuns
To acknowledge the root from which one's own virtue mounts.

In the age of denture and reduced alcoholic intake,
When the crow's dawn-calling stirs memory you'd better eschew,
You will try the cross, or the couch, for balm for the heart's ache—
But that stranger who's staring so strangely, he knows you are you.

Things are getting somewhat out of hand now—light fails on the marshes.
In the back lot the soft-faced delinquents are whistling like snipe.
The apples you stored in the cellar are acerb and harsh as
The heart that on bough of the bosom all night will not ripe.

Burn this poem, though it wring its small hands and cry *alack.*
But no use, for in bed, into your pajama pocket,
It will creep, and sleep as snug as a field mouse in haystack,
And its heart to your heart all night make a feather-soft racket.

II. Lullaby: Exercise in Human Charity and Self-Knowledge

Mr. and Mrs. North and South America, and all the ships at sea, let's go to press.

Greeting of radio broadcast by Walter Winchell

Sleep, my dear, whatever your name is:
Galactic milk spills down light years.
Sleep, my dear, your personal fame is
Sung safely now by all the tunèd spheres,
And your sweet identity
Fills like vapor, pale in moonlight, all the infinite night sky.
You are you, and naught's to fear:
Sleep, my dear.

Sleep, my dear, whatever your face is,
Fair or brown, or young or old.
Sleep, my dear, your airs and graces
Are the inner logic History will unfold,
And what faults you suffer from
Will refract, sand grain in sun-glare, glory of that light to come.
You are you, all will be clear;
So sleep, my dear.

Sleep, my dear, whatever your sex is,
Male or female, bold or shy.
What need now for that sweet nexus
In dark with some strange body you lie by?
What need now to seek that contact
That shows self to itself as merely midnight's dearest artifact?
For you to yourself, at last, appear
Clearly, my dear.

But are you she, pale hair wind-swept,
Whose face night-glistened in sea fog?
Or she, pronouncing joy, who wept
In that desperate noontide by the cranberry bog?
Or only that face in the crowd, caught
And borne like a leaf on the flood away, to which I gave one perturbed
                    thought?
Yes, which are you? Yes, turn your face here
As you sleep, dear.

No, no, dearest, none of these—
For I who bless can bless you only
For the fact our histories
Can have no common bond except the lonely
Fact of humanness we share
As now, in place and fate disparate, we breathe the same dark pulsing air.

Where you lie now, far or near,
Sleep, my dear.

Sleep, my dear, wherever now
Your shadowy head finds place to rest.
Stone or bosom, bed or hedgerow—
All the same, and all the same are blest
If, receiving that good freight,
They sustain it, uncomplaining, till cock-crow makes the dark abate.
Whoever I am, what I now bless
Is your namelessness.

III. Man in the Street

Raise the stone, and there thou shalt find Me,
cleave the wood, there am I.

The Sayings of Jesus

"Why are your eyes as big as saucers—big as saucers?"
I said to the man in the gray flannel suit.
And he said: "I see facts I can't refute—
Winners and losers,
Pickers and choosers,
Takers, refusers,
Users, abusers,
And my poor head, it spins like a top.
It spins and spins, and will not stop."
Thus said the young man I happened to meet,
Wearing his nice new Ivy League flannel suit down the sunlit street.

"What makes you shake like wind in the willows—wind in the willows?"
I said to the man in the black knit tie.
And he said: "I see things before my eye—
Jolly good fellows,
Glad-handers of hellos,
Fat windbags and bellows,
Plumpers of pillows,
And God's sweet air is like dust on my tongue,
And a man can't stand such things very long."
Thus said the young man I happened to meet,
Wearing his gray flannel suit and black knit tie down the sunlit street.

"What makes your face flour-white as a miller's—white as a miller's?"
I said to the man in the Brooks Brothers shirt.
And he said: "I see things that can't help but hurt—
Backers and fillers,
Pickers and stealers,
Healers and killers,

Ticklers and feelers,
And I go to prepare a place for you,
For this location will never do."
Said the nice young man I happened to meet,
Wearing gray flannel suit, knit tie, and Brooks Brothers shirt down the sunlit street.

IV. Switzerland

. . . world-mecca for seekers of pleasure and health. . .

Travel agency brochure

After lunch take the half-destroyed bodies and put them to bed.
For a time a mind's active behind the green gloom of the jalousie,
But soon each retires inside the appropriate head
To fondle, like childhood's stuffed bear, the favorite fallacy.

In their pairings the young, of course, have long since withdrawn,
But they take more time to come to the point of siesta:
There's the beach-fatigue and the first digestion to wait on,
So it's three by the time one's adjusted one's darling, and pressed her.

Here are many old friends you have known from long, long back,
Though of course under different names and with different faces.
Yes, they are the kind of whom you never lose track,
And there's little difference, one finds, between different places.

That's why travel is broadening—you can, for example, expect
The aging alcoholic you once knew in San Diego.
Or the lady theologian who in bed likes best her own intellect:
Lady Hulda House, *Cantab.*— for therapy now trying a dago.

There's the sweet young divorcée whose teacher once said she should write.
There's the athlete who stares at himself in the glass, by the hour.
There's the old man who can't forgive, and wakes in the night:
Forgive—forgive what? To remember is beyond his power.

And the others and all, they all here re-enact
The acts you'd so shrewdly remarked at the very start,
When in other resorts you first met them—many, in fact,
In that high, highly advertised Switzerland of your own heart.

O God of the *steinbock's* great sun-leap—Ice-spike in ice-chasm—
Let down Thy strong hand to all whom their fevers destroy
And past all their pain, need, greed, lip-biting, and spasm,
Deliver them all, young and old, to Thy health, named joy.

V. A Real Question Calling for Solution

There is however one peculiar inconsistency which we may note as marking this and many other psychological theories. They place the soul in the body and attach it to the body without trying in addition to determine the reason why or the condition of the body under which such attachment is produced. This would seem however to be a real question calling for solution.

Aristotle: Psychology *3, 22–23*

Don't bother a bit, you are only a dream you are having,
And if when you wake your symptoms are not relieved,
That is only because you harbor a morbid craving
For belief in the old delusion in which you have always believed.

Yes, there was the year when every morning you ran
A mile before breakfast—yes, and the year you read
Virgil two hours just after lunch and began
Your practice of moral assessment, before the toothbrush and bed.

But love boiled down like porridge in a pot,
And beyond the far snow-fields westward, redder than hate,
The sun burned; and one night much better forgot,
Pity, like sputum, gleamed on the station floor-boards, train late.

When you slept on a board you found your back much better.
When you took the mud baths you found that verse came easy.
When you slept with another woman you found that the letter
You owed your wife was a pleasure to write, gay now and teasy.

There once was a time when you thought you would understand
Many things, many things, including yourself, and learn Greek,
But light changes old landscape, and your own hand
Makes signs unseen in the dark, and lips move but do not speak,

For given that vulture and vector which is the stroke
Of the clock absolute on the bias of midnight, memory
Is nothing, is nothing, not even the memory of smoke
Dispersed on windless ease in the great fuddled head of the sky,

And all recollections are false, and all you suffer
Is only the punishment thought appropriate for guilt
You never had, but wish you had the crime for,
For the bitterest tears are those shed for milk—or blood—not spilt.

There is only one way, then, to make things hang together,
Which is to accept the logic of dream, and avoid
Night air, politics, French sauces, autumn weather,
And the thought that, on your awaking, identity may be destroyed.

VI. The Letter about Money, Love, or Other Comfort, if Any

In the beginning was the Word.

The Gospel according to St. John

Having accepted the trust so many years back,
before seven wars, nine coups d'état, and the deaths of friends and friendships,
before having entered the world of lurkers, shirkers, burkers, tipsters and tips,
or even discovered I had small knack
for honesty, but only a passion, like a disease, for Truth,
having, as I have said, accepted the trust
those long years back in my youth,
it's no wonder that now I admit, as I must,
to no recollection whatever
of wens, moles, scars, or his marks of identification—but do recall my disgust
at odor of garlic and a somewhat perfervid eye-gleam beneath the dark hat of the giver,

Who, as I came up the walk in summer moonlight
and set first foot to the porch step, rose with a cough from beside the hydrangea,
and thrust the thing out at me, as though it were common for any total stranger
to squat by one's door with a letter at night,
at which, in surprise, I had stopped to stare (the address even then but a smudge)
until at the burst of his laugh, like a mirthful catarrh,
I turned, but before I could budge
saw the pattering *V*'s of his shoe tips mar
the moon-snowy dew of the yard,
and be gone—an immigrant type of pointed toe and sleazy insouciance more natural by far
to some Mediterranean alley or merd-spangled *banlieue* than to any boulevard,

Or surely to Dadston, Tenn., and so I was stuck,
for though my first thought was to drop the thing in the mail and forget the affair,
on second glance I saw what at first I had missed, as though the words hadn't been there:
By Hand Only, and I was dumb-cluck
enough to drive over to Nashville next day to find the address, but found
you had blown, the rent in arrears, your bathroom a sty,
and thus the metaphysical runaround
which my life became, and for which I
have mortgaged all, began,

and I have found milk rotting in bottles inside the back door, and
newspapers knee-high
the carrier had left and never got paid for, and once at a question a child up
and ran

Screaming like bloody murder to fall out of breath,
and once in Dubuque you had sold real estate, and left with a church letter,
Episcopal, High, and at the delicious New England farmhouse your
Llewellin setter
was found in the woodshed, starved to death,
and in Via Margutta you made the attempt, but someone smelled gas at the
door
in the nick of time, and you fooled with the female Fulbrights
at the Deux Magots and the Flore,
until the police caught you dead to rights—
oh, it's all so human and sad,
for money and love are terrible things with which to fill all our human
days and nights,
and nobody blames you much, not even I, despite all the trouble I've had,

And still have, on your account, and if it were not
for encroaching age, new illness, and recurring effects of the beating
I took from those hoods in the bar in Frisco for the mere fact of merely
repeating
that financial gossip, and from which I got
this bum gam, my defect in memory, and a slight stutter—
but as I was saying, were it not for my infirm years,
I would try to deliver the letter,
especially since I was moved nigh to tears
myself by the tale you'd been caught
crouched in the dark in the canna bed that pretties the lawn of the
orphanage where it appears
you were raised—yes, crooning among the ruined lilies to a teddy bear,
not what a grown man ought

To be doing past midnight, but be that as it may,
there's little choice for my future course, given present circumstances,
and my conscience is clear, for I assure you I've not made a penny, at least
not expenses,
and so on the basis of peasant hearsay,
at the goatherd's below timber line, I will go up, and beyond the north
face,
find that shelf where a last glacial kettle, beck, or cirque glints
blue steel to sky in that moon-place,
and there, while hands bleed and breath stints,
will, on a flat boulder not
far from the spot where you at night drink, leave the letter, and my
obligation to all intents,
weighted by stones like a cairn, with a red bandanna to catch your eye, but
what

*

Good any word of money or love or more casual
comfort may do now, God only knows, for one who by dog and gun
has been hunted to the upper altitudes, for the time comes when all men will shun
you, and you, like an animal,
will crouch among the black boulders and whine under knife edge of night-blast,
waiting for hunger to drive you down to forage
for bark, berries, mast,
roots, rodents, grubs, and such garbage,
or a sheep like the one you with teeth killed,
for you are said to be capable now of all bestiality, and only your age
makes you less dangerous; so, though I've never seen your face and have fulfilled

The trust, discretion, as well as perhaps a strange shame,
overcomes curiosity, and past that high rubble of the world's wrack,
will send me down through darkness of trees until, having lost all track,
I stand, bewildered, breath-bated and lame,
at the edge of a clearing, to hear, as first birds stir, life lift now night's hasp,
then see, in first dawn's drench and drama, the snow peak go gory,
and the eagle will unlatch crag-clasp,
fall, and at breaking of wing-furl, bark glory,
and by that new light I shall seek
the way, and my peace with God, and if in some taproom travelers pry into this story,
I shall not reduce it to drunken marvel, assuming I know the tongue they speak.

VII. Arrogant Law

This inner life may be compared to the unrolling of a coil...

Henri Bergson: An Introduction to Metaphysics

Have you crouched with rifle, in woods, in autumn,
In earshot of water where at dawn deer come,
Through gold leafage drifting, through dawn-mist like mist,
And the blue steel sweats cold in your fist?
Have you stood on the gunwale and eyed blaze of sky,
Then with blaze blazing black in your inner eye,
Plunged—plunged to break the anchor's deep hold
On rock, where undercurrents thrill cold?
Time unwinds like a falling spool.

Have you lain by your love, at night, by willows,
And heard the stream stumble, moon-drunk, at its shallows,
And heard the cows stir, sigh, and shift space,

Then seen how moonlight lay on the girl's face,
With her eyes hieratically closed, and your heart bulged
With what abrupt Truth to be divulged—
But desolate, desolate, turned from your love,
Knowing you'd never know what she then thought of?
Time unwinds like a falling spool.

Have you stood beside your father's bed
While life retired from the knowledgeable head
To hole in some colding last lurking-place,
And standing there studied that strange face,
Which had endured thunder and even the tears
Of mercy in its human years,
But now, past such accident, seemed to withdraw
Into more arrogant dispensation, and law?
Time unwinds like a falling spool.

VIII. The Self That Stares

John Henry said to the Captain, "A man ain't nothing but a man."

A folk ballad

Have you seen that brute trapped in your eye
When he realizes that he, too, will die?
Stare into the mirror, stare
At his dawning awareness there.
If man, put razor down, and stare.
If woman, stop lipstick in mid-air.
Yes, pity makes that gleam you gaze through—
Or is that brute now pitying you?
Time unwinds like a falling spool.
We have learned little in that school.

No, nothing, nothing, is ever learned
Till school is out and the books are burned,
And then the lesson will be so sweet
All you will long for will be to repeat
All the sad, exciting process
By which ignorance grew less
In all that error and gorgeous pain
That you may not live again.
What is that lesson? To recognize
The human self naked in your own eyes.

Two Pieces after Suetonius

I. Apology for Domitian

He was not bad, as emperors go, not really—
Not like Tiberius cruel, or poor Nero silly.
The trouble was only that omens said he would die,
So what could he, mortal, do? Not worse, however, than you might, or I.

Suppose from long back you had known the very hour—
"Fear the fifth hour"—and yet for all your power
Couldn't strike it out from the day, or the day from the year,
Then wouldn't you have to strike something at least? If you did, would it seem
so queer?

Suppose you were proud of your beauty, but baldness set in?
Suppose your good leg were dwindling to spindly and thin?
Wouldn't you, like Domitian, try the classic bed-stunt
To prove immortality on what was propped to bear the imperial brunt?

Suppose you had dreamed a gold hump sprouted out of your back,
And such prosperous burden oppressed you to breath-lack;
Suppose lightning scorched the sheets in your own bedroom;
And from your own statue storm yanked the name plate and chucked it into a
tomb—

Well, it happened to him. Therefore, there's little surprise
That for hours he'd lock himself up to pull wings from flies.
Fly or man, what odds? He would wander his hall of moonstone,
Mirror-bright so he needn't look over his shoulder to know that he was
alone.

Let's stop horsing around—it's not Domitian, it's you
We mean, and the omens are bad, very bad, and it's true
That virtue comes hard in face of the assigned clock,
And music, at sunset, faint as a dream, is heard from beyond the burdock,

And as for Domitian, the first wound finds the groin,
And he claws like a cat, but the blade continues to go in,
And the body is huddled forth meanly, and what ritual
It gets is at night, and from his old nurse, a woman poor, nonpolitical.

II. Tiberius on Capri

(a)

All is nothing, nothing all:
To tired Tiberius soft sang the sea thus,
Under his cliff-palace wall.
The sea, in soft approach and repulse,
Sings thus, and Tiberius,
Sea-sad, stares past the dusking sea-pulse
Yonder, where come,
One now by one, the lights, far off, of Surrentum.
He stares in the blue dusk-fall,
For all is nothing, nothing all.

Let darkness up from Asia tower.
On that darkening island behind him *spintriae* now stir.
In grot and scented bower,
They titter, yawn, paint lip, grease thigh,
And debate what role each would prefer
When they project for the Emperor's eye
Their expertise
Of his Eastern lusts and complex Egyptian fantasies.
But darkward he stares in that hour,
Blank now in totality of power.

(b)

There once, on that goat island, I,
As dark fell, stood and stared where Europe stank.
Many were soon to die—
From acedia snatched, from depravity, virtue,
Or frolic, not knowing the reason, in rank
On rank hurled, or in bed, or in church, or
Dishing up supper,
Or in a dark doorway, loosening the girl's elastic to tup her,
While high in the night sky,
The murderous tear dropped from God's eye;

And faintly forefeeling, forefearing, all
That to fulfill our time, and heart, would come,
I stood on the crumbling wall
Of that foul place, and my lungs drew in
Scent of dry gorse on the night air of autumn,
And I seized, in dark, a small stone from that ruin,
And I made outcry
At the paradox of powers that would grind us like grain, small and dry.
Dark down, the stone, in its fall,
Found the sea: I could do that much, after all.

Mortmain

I. After Night Flight Son Reaches Bedside of Already Unconscious Father, Whose Right Hand Lifts in a Spasmodic Gesture, as Though Trying to Make Contact: 1955

In Time's concatenation and
Carnal conventicle, I,
Arriving, being flung through dark and
The abstract flight-grid of sky,
Saw rising from the sweated sheet and
Ruck of bedclothes ritualistically
Reordered by the paid hand
Of mercy—saw rising the hand—

Christ, start again! What was it I,
Standing there, travel-shaken, saw
Rising? What could it be that I,
Caught sudden in gut- or conscience-gnaw,
Saw rising out of the past, which I
Saw now as twisted bedclothes? Like law,
The hand rose cold from History
To claw at a star in the black sky,

But could not reach that far—oh, cannot!
And the star horribly burned, burns,
For in darkness the wax-white clutch could not
Reach it, and white hand on wrist-stem turns,
Lifts in last tension of tendon, but cannot
Make contact—*oh, oop-si-daisy,* churns
The sad heart, *oh, atta-boy, daddio's got*
One more shot in the locker, peas-porridge hot—

But no. Like an eyelid the hand sank, strove
Downward, and in that darkening roar,
All things—all joy and the hope that strove,
The failed exam, the admired endeavor,
Prizes and prinkings, and the truth that strove,
And back of the Capitol, boyhood's first whore—
Were snatched from me, and I could not move,
Naked in that black blast of his love.

II. A Dead Language: Circa 1885

Father dead, land lost, stepmother haggard with kids,
Big Brother skedaddling off to Mexico
To make his fortune, gold or cattle or cards,
What could he do but what we see him doing?
Cutting crossties for the first railroad in the region,
Sixteen and strong as a man—was a man, by God!—
And the double-bit bit into red oak, and in that rhythm,
In his head, all day, marched the Greek paradigm:
That was all that was his, and all he could carry all day with him.

Λέγω, λέγεις, λέγει, and the axe swung.
That was that year, and the next year we see him
Revolve in his dream between the piece goods and cheese,
In a crossroads store, between peppermint candy and plow-points,
While the eaves drip, and beyond the black trees of winter
Last light grays out, and in the ruts of the lane
Water gleams, sober as steel. That was that land,
And that was the life, and he reached out and
Took the dime from the gray-scaled palm of the Negro plowhand's hand.

'Εν ἀρχῇ ἦν ὁ λόγος: in the beginning
Was the word, but in the end was
What? At the mirror, lather on chin, with a razor
Big as a corn-knife, or, so to the boy it seemed,
He stood, and said: 'Εν ἀρχῇ ἦν ὁ λόγος.
And laughed. And said: "That's Greek, now you know how it sounds!"
And laughed, and waved the bright blade like a toy.
And laughing from the deep of a dark conquest and joy,
Said: "Greek—but it wasn't for me. Let's get to breakfast, boy."

III. Fox-fire: 1956

Years later, I find the old grammar, yellowed. Night
Is falling. Ash flakes from the log. The log
Glows, winks, wanes. Westward, the sky,
In one small area redeemed from gray, bleeds dully.
Beyond my window, athwart that red west,
The spruce bough, though snow-burdened, looks black,
Not white. The world lives by the trick of the eye, the trick
Of the heart. I hold the book in my hand, but God
—In what mercy, if mercy?—will not let me weep. But I
Do not want to weep. I want to understand.

Oh, let me understand what is that sound,
Like wind, that fills the enormous dark of my head.
Beyond my head there is no wind, the room

Darkening, the world beyond the room darkening,
And no wind beyond to cleave, unclot, the thickening
Darkness. There must be a way to state the problem.
The statement of a problem, no doubt, determines solution.
If once, clear and distinct, I could state it, then God
Could no longer fall back on His old alibi of ignorance.
I hear now my small son laugh from a farther room.

I know he sits there and laughs among his toys,
Teddy bear, letter blocks, yellow dumptruck, derrick, choo-choo—
Bright images, all, of Life's significance.
So I put the book on the shelf, beside my own grammar,
Unopened these thirty years, and leave the dark room,
And know that all night, while the constellations grind,
Beings with folded wings brood above that shelf,
Awe-struck and imbecile, and in the dark,
Amid History's vice and velleity, that poor book burns
Like fox-fire in the black swamp of the world's error.

IV. In the Turpitude of Time: n.d.

In the turpitude of Time,
Hope dances on the razor edge.
I see those ever healing feet
Tread the honed edge above despair.
I see the song-wet lip and tossing hair.

The leaf unfolds the autumn weather.
The heart spills the horizon's light.
In the woods, the hunter, weeping, kneels,
And the dappled fawn weeps in contrition
For its own beauty. I hear the toad's intercession

For us, and all, who do not know
How cause flows backward from effect
To bless the past occasion, and
How Time's tongue lifts only to tell,
Minute by minute, what truth the brave heart will fulfill.

Can we—oh, could we only—believe
What annelid and osprey know,
And the stone, night-long, groans to divulge?
If we could only, then that star
That dawnward slants might sing to our human ear,

And joy, in daylight, run like feet,
And strength, in darkness, wait like hands,
And between the stone and the wind's voice
A silence wait to become our own song:
In the heart's last kingdom only the old are young.

V. A Vision: Circa 1880

Out of the woods where pollen is a powder of gold
Shaken from pistil of oak minutely, and of maple,
And is falling, and the tulip tree lifts, not yet tarnished,
The last calyx, in which chartreuse coolness recessed, dew,
Only this morning, lingered till noon—look,
Out of the woods, barefoot, the boy comes. He stands,
Hieratic, complete, in patched britches and that idleness of boyhood
Which asks nothing and is its own fulfilment:
In his hand a wand of peeled willow, boy-idle and aimless.

Poised between woods and the pasture, sun-green and green shadow,
Hair sweat-dark, brow bearing a smudge of gold pollen, lips
Parted in some near-smile of boyhood bemusement,
Dangling the willow, he stands, and I—I stare
Down the tube and darkening corridor of Time
That breaks, like tears, upon that sunlit space,
And staring, I know who he is, and would cry out.
Out of my knowledge, I would cry out and say:
Listen! Say: *Listen! I know—oh, I know— let me tell you!*

That scene is in Trigg County, and I see it.
Trigg County is in Kentucky, and I have been there,
But never remember the spring there. I remember
A land of cedar-shade, blue, and the purl of limewater,
But the pasture parched, and the voice of the lost joree
Unrelenting as conscience, and sick, and the afternoon throbs,
And the sun's hot eye on the dry leaf shrivels the aphid,
And the sun's heel does violence in the corn-balk.
That is what I remember, and so the scene

I had seen just now in the mind's eye, vernal,
Is altered, and I strive to cry across the dry pasture,
But cannot, nor move, for my feet, like dry corn-roots, cleave
Into the hard earth, and my tongue makes only the dry,
Slight sound of wind on the autumn corn-blade. The boy,
With imperial calm, crosses a space, rejoins
The shadow of woods, but pauses, turns, grins once,
And is gone. And one high oak leaf stirs gray, and the air,
Stirring, freshens to the far favor of rain.

Fatal Interview: Penthesilea and Achilles

Beautiful, bold, shaking the gold glint of sun-foil,
Which light is, scurrying, scouring the plain now, she rides
To distribute man-death, Greek-death—oh, she is the darling
Of war, Troy, and Ares, her black-bristled father, whose toil
Was her dream on the moonlit pillow. She moaned in that dream of
blood-moil.

*

She never remembered her dream at advent of daylight,
But sat with breasts heavy, eyes sad, and the honey tasteless,
And her only pleasure for morning to finger the sword edge
Till from lucky unstitching on thumb-ball one drop blushed to sight;
Then with blood sweet on tongue, she watched bees weave, sun-glinting, and dreamed of night.

Look, look—Greeks flee! For who can withstand Beauty's rage?
Her arrows are spilling afar what will unparch earth now.
Leaping in knee-clip, her courser neighs loud and rolls red eye,
But her heart is yet latched, for only one death can assuage
That heart's deepest need. Yes, let him come forth to her dire tutelage.

From shameful grief, sloth, vanity, and mere pique,
He lifts forth now, spits in his palm for the spear-haft,
Hawks up his phlegm, looms in his darkening selfhood:
Fame-fed, blood-fat as a tick, Ambition's geek.
She leaps from horse, hurls spear; hears laughter, then, from the Greek.

Her mount—how well trained!—waits. She waits, ungirt—
Or at least she has felt so since first the spear flew from handgrip;
And worse, as that Greek grins. He grins. He waits. Will he say:
"Fool girl, get home to your dolls—darn socks, mend a shirt!"
Oh, she couldn't bear that! She'd die, rather. But wonders how much it would hurt.

Where lungs divide to hang belly, the spear-flight first pricks her;
Under breastplate slides weightily in; in blood-darkness shears backbone;
Emerges in sunlight, though briefly; finds the mount waiting, faithful,
And with the same force unallayed it had used to transfix her,
Transfixes the brute, knocks it down; and thus on that pincushion sticks her.

How slow the whole process seemed to the hero who watched it,
Who had dreamed it a thousand times, though without recognition.
How sad all the past years of fame, as he tore off her breastplate
And saw the first globèd sweet handful, then the other that matched it.
His life went like dust on his tongue; he wept, for he knew he had botched it.

"Aie!" he cried out, "I have lolled in a thousand laps,
I have cracked heads by thousands, spilled buckets of blood, like water,
But woe is my soul that it's this sweet blood I spill now,
For this is my True Love—oh, darling, except for mishaps,
You had lain on a bed far softer than this while I mammocked those paps!"

"Aie!" cried Thersites, the foul-mouth, "so it's *aie,* you snot!
What odds, what odds, you splash like a brat in his bathtub.
Oh, you'd kill all the men, debauch all the boys, tup the women,
And if one escapes, you start sniveling—" But further saith not,
For hand of the hero breaks jawbone, and brain-pan is dumped on the spot.

*

Past areas of combat and cultivation, like thunder,
Now History, on the far hill-line, gathers. The hero's great spear-head
Withdraws, and flesh-suction sighs sad, once. The hero waits, rapt,
In blue sun-blaze, on sea-plain. One crow beats up past Scamander,
And will pluck the blue eyes that, puzzled, stare up at blue sky they lie
under.

Some Quiet, Plain Poems

I. Ornithology in a World of Flux

It was only a bird call at evening, unidentified,
As I came from the spring with water, across the rocky back-pasture;
But so still I stood sky above was not stiller than sky in pail-water.

Years pass, all places and faces fade, some people have died,
And I stand in a far land, the evening still, and am at last sure
That I miss more that stillness at bird-call than some things that were to fail
later.

II. Holly and Hickory

Rain, all night, taps the holly.
It ticks like a telegraph on the pane.
If awake in that house, meditating some old folly
Or trying to live an old pleasure again,
I could hear it sluicing the ruts in the lane.

Rain beats down the last leaf of hickory,
But where I lie now rain sounds hint less
At benign sleight of the seasons, or Time's adept trickery,
And with years I feel less joy or distress
To hear water moving in wheel ruts, star-glintless,

And if any car comes now up that lane,
It carries nobody I could know,
And who wakes in that house now to hear the rain
May fall back to sleep—as I, long ago,
Who dreamed dawnward; and would rise to go.

III. The Well House

What happened there, it was not much,
But was enough. If you come back,
Not much may be *too much,* even if you have your old knack
Of stillness, and do not touch
A thing, a broken toy or rusted tool or any such
Object you happen to find
Hidden where, uncontrolled, grass and weeds bend.

The clematis that latches the door
Of the ruinous well house, you might break it.
Though guessing the water foul now, and not thirsting to take it,
With thirst from those years before
You might lean over the coping to stare at the water's dark-glinting floor.
Yes, that might be the event
To change *not much* to *too much,* and more than meant.

Yes, Truth is always in balance, and
Not much can become *too much* so quick.
Suppose you came back and found your heart suddenly sick,
And covered your sight with your hand:
Your tears might mean more than the thing you wept for but did not
understand.
Yes, something might happen there
If you came back—even if you just stood to stare.

IV. In Moonlight, Somewhere, They Are Singing

Under the maples at moonrise—
Moon whitening top leaf of the white oak
That rose from the dark mass of maples and range of eyes—
They were singing together, and I woke

From my sleep to the whiteness of moon-fire,
And deep from their dark maples, I
Could hear the two voices shake silver and free, and aspire
To be lost in moon-vastness of the sky.

My young aunt and her young husband
From their dark maples sang, and though
Too young to know what they meant I was happy and
So slept, for I knew I would come to know.

But what of the old man awake there,
As the voices, like vine, climbed up moonlight?
What thought did he think of past time as they twined bright in moon-air,
And veined, with their silver, the moon-flesh of night?

*

Far off, I recall, in the barn lot,
A mule stamped, once; but the song then
Was over, and for that night, or forever, would not
Resume—but should it again,

Years after, wake me to white moon-fire
On pillow, high oak leaf, and far field,
I should hope to find imaged in what new voices aspire
Some life-faith yet, by my years, unrepealed.

V. In Italian They Call the Bird *Civetta*

The evening drooped toward owl-call,
The small moon slid pale down the sky,
Dark was decisive in cedars,
But dust down the lane dreamed pale,
And my feet stirred that dust there—
Ah, I see that Kentucky scene
Now only behind my shut eyelids,
As in this far land I stand
At the selfsame ambiguous hour
In the heart's ambiguity,
And Time is crumpled like paper
Crushed in my hand, while here
    The thin moon slants pale down the pale sky,
    And the small owl mourns from the moat.

This small owl calls from the moat now.
That other owl answers him
Across all the years and miles that
Are the only Truth I have learned,
And back from the present owl-call
Burns backward the blaze of day,
And the passage of years, like a tire's scream,
Fades now while the reply
Of a dew-damp and downy lost throat spills
To quaver from that home-dark,
And frame between owl-call and owl-call,
Life's bright parenthesis.
    The thin moon slants pale down the pale sky:
    The small owl mourns from the moat.

VI. Debate: Question, Quarry, Dream

Asking what, asking what?—all a boy's afternoon,
Squatting in the canebrake where the muskrat will come.
Muskrat, muskrat, please now, please, come soon.
He comes, stares, goes, lets the question resume.
He has taken whatever answer may be down to his mud-burrow gloom.

Seeking what, seeking what?—foot soft in cedar-shade.
Was that a deer-flag white past windfall and fern?
No, but by bluffside lurk powers and in the fern-glade
Tall presences, standing all night, like white fox-fire burn.
The small fox lays his head in your hand now and weeps that you go, not to return.

Dreaming what, dreaming what?— lying on the hill at twilight,
Still air stirred only by moth wing, and last stain of sun
Fading to moth-sky, blood-red to moth-white and starlight,
And Time leans down to kiss the heart's ambition,
While far away, before moonrise, come the town lights, one by one.

Long since that time I have walked night streets, heel-iron
Clicking the stone, and in dark in windows have stared.
Question, quarry, dream—I have vented my ire on
My own heart that, ignorant and untoward,
Yearns for an absolute that Time would, I thought, have prepared,

But has not yet. Well, let us debate
The issue. But under a tight roof, clutching a toy,
My son now sleeps, and when the hour grows late,
I shall go forth where the cold constellations deploy
And lift up my eyes to consider more strictly the appalling logic of joy.

Ballad: Between the Boxcars (1923)

I. I Can't Even Remember the Name

I can't even remember the name of the one who fell
Flat on his ass, on the cinders, between the boxcars.
I can't even remember whether he got off his yell
Before what happened had happened between the boxcars.

But whether or not he managed to get off his yell,
I remember its shape on his mouth, between the boxcars,
And it was shape that yours would be too if you fell
Flat on your ass, on the cinders, between the boxcars.

*

And one more thing I remember perfectly well,
You go for the grip at the front, not the back, of the boxcars.
Miss the front, you're knocked off—miss the back, you never can tell
But you're flat on your ass, on the cinders, between the boxcars.

He was fifteen and old enough to know perfectly well
You try for the grip at the front, not the back, of the boxcars,
But he was the kind of smart aleck you always can tell
Ends flat on his ass, on the cinders, between the boxcars.

Suppose I remembered his name, then what the hell
Good would it do him now between the boxcars?
But it might mean something to me if I could tell
You the name of the one who fell between the boxcars.

II. He Was Formidable

He was formidable, he was, the little booger,
As he spat in his hands and picked up the Louisville Slugger,
And at that bat-crack
Around those bases he could sure ball the jack,
And if from the outfield the peg had beat him home,
He would slide in slick, like a knife in a nigger.
So we dreamed of an afternoon to come,
In the Series, the ninth-inning hush, in the Yankee Stadium,
Sun low, score tied, bases full, two out, and he'd waltz to the plate with his grin—
But no, oh no, not now, not ever! for in
That umpireless rhubarb and brute-heeled hugger-mugger,
He got spiked sliding home, got spiked between the boxcars.

Oh, his hair was brown-bright as a chestnut, sun-glinting and curly,
And that lip that smiled boy-sweet could go, of a sudden, man-surly,
And the way he was built
Made the girls in his grade in dark stare, and finger the quilt.
Yes, he was the kind you know born to give many delight,
And entering on such life-labor early,
Would have moved, bemused, in that rhythm and rite,
Through blood-throbbing blackness and moon-gleam and pearly thigh-glimmer of night,
To the exquisite glut: *Woman Slays Self for His Love,* as the tabloids would tell—
But no, never now! Like a kid in his first brothel,
In that hot clasp and loveless hurly-burly,
He spilled, as boys may, too soon, between the boxcars.

*

Oh, he might have been boss of the best supermarket in town,
Bright with banners and chrome, where housewives push carts up and down,
And morning and night
Walked the street with his credit *A*-rated and blood pressure right,
His boy a dentist in Nashville, his girl at State Normal;
Or a scientist flushed with *Time*-cover renown
For vaccine, or bomb, or smog removal;
Or a hero with phiz like hewn cedar, though young for the stars of a general,
Descending the steps of his personal plane to view the home-town unveiling.
But no, never now!—battle-cunning, the test tube, retailing,
All, all, in a helter-skeltering mishmash thrown
To that clobber and grind, too soon, between the boxcars.

But what is success, or failure, at the last?
The newspaper whirled down the track when the through freight has passed
Will sink from that gust
To be of such value as it intrinsically must,
And why should we grieve for the name that boy might have made
To be printed on newsprint like that, for that blast
To whirl with the wheels' fanfaronade,
When we cannot even remember his name, nor humbly have prayed
That when that blunt grossness, slam-banging, bang-slamming, blots black the last blue flash of sky,
And our own lips utter the crazed organism's cry,
We may know the poor self not alone, but with all who are cast
To that clobber and slobber and grunt, between the boxcars?

III. He Has Fled

He has fled like electricity down the telegraph wires into
prairies of distance where the single bird
sits small and black against the saffron sky,
and is itself.

He has fled like the glint of glory down the April-wet
rails, toward sunset.

He has fled like the wild goose, north-beaked and star-treading,
with night-hoot too high to be heard by whoever
stands now to brood where the last, lost spur of
the Canadian Pacific ends.

He has retired into the cold chemical combustion where water
at last probes the fibers of the creosote-treated
crosstie.

*

He has retired where the acrid sap of red oak rises under the
iron bark, and he does not now scream at
the saw-bite.

He has retired into the delectable crystallization of sugar
in grape jelly stored twenty years in a cellar,
in a Burgundian drowse.

He has propounded a theorem the refutation of which would devalue
all our anguish.

He has broken past atmospheres, and the lungs breathe rarefaction
of revelation and the head now reels,
like Truth.

He has explored a calculus of your unexpected probabilities,
and what now *is* was never probable,
but only *is,*

For we are in the world and nothing is good enough, which is
to say that the world is here and we are not
good enough,

And we live in the world, and in so far as we live, the world
continues to live in us,

Despite all we can do to reject it utterly, including
this particular recollection, which now I
would eject, reject,
but cannot.

Two Studies in Idealism: Short Survey of American, and Human, History

For Allan Nevins

I. Bear Track Plantation: Shortly after Shiloh

Two things a man's built for, killing and you-know-what.
As for you-know-what, I reckon I taken my share,
Bed-ease or bush-whack, but killing—hell, three's all I got,
And he promised me ten, Jeff Davis, the bastard. 'Taint fair.

*

'Taint fair, a man rides and knows he won't live forever,
And a man needs something to take with him when he dies.
Ain't much worth taking, but what happens under the cover
Or at the steel-point—yeah, that look in their eyes.

That same look, it comes in their eyes when you give 'em the business.
It's something a man can hang on to, come black-frost or sun.
Come hell or high water, it's something to save from the mess,
No matter whatever else you never got done.

For a second it seems like a man can know what he lives for,
When those eyelids go waggle, or maybe the eyes pop wide,
And that look comes there. Yeah, Christ, then you know who you are—
And will maybe remember that much even after you've died.

But now I lie worrying what look my own eyes got
When that Blue-Belly caught me off balance. Did that look mean then
That I'd honed for something not killing or you-know-what?
Hell, no. I'd lie easy if Jeff had just give me that ten.

II. Harvard '61: Battle Fatigue

I didn't mind dying—it wasn't that at all.
It behooves a man to prove manhood by dying for Right.
If you die for Right that fact is your dearest requital,
But you find it disturbing when others die who simply haven't the right.

Why should they die with that obscene insouciance?
They seem to insult the principle of your own death.
Touch pitch, be defiled: it was hard to keep proper distance
From such unprincipled wastrels of blood and profligates of breath.

I tried to slay without rancor, and often succeeded.
I tried to keep the heart pure, though hand took stain.
But they made it so hard for me, the way they proceeded
To parody with their own dying that Death which only Right should sustain.

Time passed. It got worse. It seemed like a plot against me.
I said they had made their own evil bed and lay on it,
But they grinned in the dark—they grinned—and I yet see
That last one. At woods-edge we held, and over the stubble they came with
bayonet.

He uttered his yell, he was there!—teeth yellow, some missing.
Why, he's old as my father, I thought, finger frozen on trigger.
I saw the ambeer on his whiskers, heard the old breath hissing.
The puncture came small on his chest. 'Twas nothing. The stain then got
bigger.

*

And he said: "Why, son, you done done it—I figgered I'd skeered ye."
Said: "Son, you look puke-pale. Buck up! If it hadn't been you,
Some other young squirt would a-done it." I stood, and weirdly
The tumult of battle went soundless, like gesture in dream. And I was dead,
too.

Dead, and had died for the Right, as I had a right to,
And glad to be dead, and hold my residence
Beyond life's awful illogic, and the world's stew,
Where people who haven't the right just die, with ghastly impertinence.

Nocturne: Traveling Salesman in Hotel Bedroom

The toothbrush lies in its case,
Like you in your coffin when
The mourners come to stare
And the bristles grow on your chin.

Oh, the soap lies in the dish,
Dissolving from every pore,
Like your poor heart in the breast
When the clock strikes once, and once more.

The toilet gurgles and whines,
Like History absorbing event,
For process is all, and who cares
What any particular has meant?

Far off, in the predawn drizzle,
A car's tires slosh the street mess,
And you think, in an access of anguish,
It bears someone to happiness,

Or at least to a destination
Where duty is clear, and sleep deep,
And the image of self, in dark standing,
Does not pluck at the hangnail, and weep,

But you're practical, and know
That wherever that place lies
You would find few customers there
For your line of merchandise,

And there's nothing, in fact, really wrong here:
Take a slug of Old Jack neat,
Try a chapter in the Gideon,
Then work on the sales sheet,

*

And vision is possible, and
    Man's meed of glory not
Impossible—oh remember,
    Remember—in life's upshot.

So You Agree with What I Say? Well, What Did I Say?

Albino-pale, half-blind, his orbit revolved
Between his Bible and the cobbler's bench,
With all human complexities resolved
In that Hope past deprivation, or any heart-wrench.

Or so it seemed—and at dusk we'd see him head back
To his place with a can of pork and beans, and some bread,
And once, when he'd lighted his lamp, we spied in the shack
To see him eat beans, then over his book bend his head.

In the summer dusk we would see him heading home,
Past the field where after supper we played baseball
Till the grass got dew-slick and a grounder out of the gloom
Might knock out your teeth, and our mothers began to call.

Past Old Man Duckett out fixing that hinge on his gate,
Past all the Cobb family admiring their new Chevrolet,
Past the moonvines that hid Sue Cramm in the swing with her date,
Whose hand was already up under her dress, halfway—

He would move past us all. And the bat cracked, and the fly
Popped up from our shadow to spin in the high, last light.
Like a little world, the ball hung there spinning, high,
With the side to the setting sun glimmering white.

Mr. Moody is dead long back, and some of the boys
Who played in that ball game dead too, by disease or violence,
But others went on to their proper successes, and joys,
And made contribution to social and scientific improvements,

And with those improvements, I now am ready to say
That if God short-changed Mr. Moody, it's time for Him
To give up this godding business, and make way
For somebody else to try, or an IBM.

Prognosis: A Short Story, the End of Which you Will Know Soon Enough

I. And Oh—

She was into her forties, her daughter slick, sly, and no good;
The son-in-law sweet, booze-bit, much given to talk at twilight,
After tea was removed and drink brought, for he said she alone understood;
And her husband withdrawn in his gloom of success.
Yes, that was her family, she loved them, yes,
But now sat and continued to stare
At the strong hand, white-scrubbed, sprigged with black recalcitrant hair,
And what the voice said she couldn't imagine, or guess,
For the hairs were so black, and a wind to blow
Was gathered below some horizon, and the hairs were so black, and oh,

It was cancer, and oh, felt her face smiling stiff like dried mud,
And went out, felt her thighs as they moved in the street, oh white, and oh,
Moving white in their dark, under silk, under fur, and the multitude
Trod past in their fleshy agitation,
And sun sank, and oh, the flesh clung to bone,
"And, daughter, and oh—" she then tried,
But the daughter said, "Later, I'm doing my hair," and the mother replied,
"So you went to a hotel today with someone,"
And the daughter said sweetly, "But how did you know?"
Said, "Look, how he bruised me—and don't you wish it was you?" And oh,

She wished it, she wished it, and felt her face flaming for shame,
For she knew no word had been uttered, the words only words in her head,
And the daughter's hair, gold, spilled like light, till an anguish without name
Stark shook her. She fled and in twilight found
The son-in-law sitting, first drink not yet downed,
And by fireside said, "Listen—for I—"
But the guests had arrived, they smiled, and the Beast, like a kitten gone shy,
Crept under a chair and from shadow stared forth with no sound,
And the dinner was lovely, they all said so,
And she suddenly saw how all faces were beautiful, hearts pure, and oh,

She loved them, she did, as they glimmered through tears, and wine whirled,
So threw her head back, like a girl laughed for joy, husband watching, and oh,
In dark later his hand was laid on her—in dark, as when, oh, ungirled—
And she shook, she said, "No," but he made headway.
"But the doctor—the doctor—" she tried to say,
Then said it, and oh, she knew she would die,
But he, in that stubborn occupation, made no reply,
For as though provoked at her words, there was sudden essay
Of old force that she long had thought spent, but no,
By blunt bruteness, in love or in hate, she was racked, she was rent, and oh,

*

Time was not Time now—and once as a child she had lain
On the grass, in spring dusk, under maples, to watch the first fireflies,
So prayed now, "God, please—" but *please what* didn't know, so slept, woke again,
And with eyes wide in dark simply stared in the dark there,
One finger yet tangled in his sparse chest-hair,
Which for years, as she knew, had been gray,
And was pitiful of that sad stranger who had come his own difficult way,
And at last, with her anguish exhausted, and past despair,
Dreamed a field of white lilies wind-shimmering, slow,
And wept, wept for joy, beneath the dark glory of the world's name, and oh—

And oh.

II. What the Sand Said

—and God, God, somewhere, *she said,* are lilies, in a field, white,
and let me guess where, where they are, but I don't know, and a slight
wind moves them slow, *and she lay shuddering and white under the dark glory of*
whatever is the world's name, and oh—
what must I dream of, what—*and said,*
If I dream, I shall be real, or really
myself, and oh,
if I am myself, let me lie shuddering and white, please, under the
dark glory of the world's name, and oh—
or at least, not being myself, let whatever
glint in dark my dream is, glimmer like ice,
like steel, like the wickedest
star, please, but let my dream be, being whatever it needs to be in order
to be what it is,
for, dear God, I love
it, and love the world, and I do not grieve to be lost in whatever
awfulness of dark the
world may be, and love is, and oh—
and dawn and dark are the glory we know,
and oh—

I have heard the grain of sand say: I know my joy, I know its name.

III. What the Joree Said, The Joree Being Only a Bird

The joree sang. What does he sing? He says
Joree. But *joree,* what does *joree* mean? It means
Joree, for he sings his sweet sadness of self, and the ways
Of the singing say only himself where the cedar leans
Black on white limestone, oh, listen! Lost in the day-blaze,
Foot set on white stone, stone hot through leather, she came
Down the path, she a girl, and the enormity of sun-blaze consumed her name.

Who was I? Who was I? Oh, tell me my name! But the bird
Only sang, said *joree,* and so she came where the spring
Flowed out from the stone, silver-braiding, brim-swelling, and stirred
The chlorophyll green of pale cress leaf submerged there. So sing,
Say *joree,* for her wrist, lax in water, trailed white, and oh, see,
How sun through closed eyelids is blood and red blood-throb. The bird said
joree,

And in fullness of Time she would say: *All truth comes unwitting,*
For I set heel on worm-head, and relished dawn-stool more than sunrise.
I spat on my shadow in sunlight, and at the sun's setting
Clasped hands on belly. But stared in the dentist's pale eyes
And yearned for the drill-stab, for yes, I loved God, though forgetting
His name. But remembered the joree, so wished she might utter
Herself in that sweet, sad asseverant candor, from black shade, in day-blaze, by
water.

Autumnal Equinox on Mediterranean Beach

Sail-bellyer, exciter of boys, come bang
To smithereens doors, and see if I give a hang,

For I am sick of summer and the insane glitter
Of sea sun-bit, and the wavelets that bicker and titter,

And the fat girls that hang out brown breasts like fruit overripe,
And the thin ones flung pale in rock-shadow, goose-pimpled as tripe,

And the young men who pose on the headlands like ads for Jantzen,
And the old who would do so much better to keep proper pants on,

And all Latin faeces one finds, like jewels, in the sand,
And the gaze of the small, sweet octopus fondling your hand.

Come howl like a prophet the season's righteous anger,
And knock down our idols with crash, bang, or clangor.

*

Blow the cat's fur furry sideways, make dogs bark,
Blow the hen's tail feathers forward past the pink mark,

Snatch the laundry off the line, like youth away,
Blow plastered hair off the bald spot, lift toupee.

Come blow old women's skirts, bring Truth to light,
Though at such age morn's all the same as night.

Come swirl old picnic papers to very sky-height,
And make gulls gabble in fury at such breach of their air-right.

Kick up the bay now, make a mess of it,
Fling spume in our sinful faces, like God's spit,

For now all our pleasures, like peaches, get rotten, not riper,
And summer is over, and time to pay the piper,

And be glad to do it, for man's not made for much pleasure,
Or even for joy, unless cut down to his measure.

Yes, kick the garbage pail, and scatter garbage,
That the cat flee forth with fish-head, the housewife rage,

For pain and pleasure balance in God's year—
Though *whose* is *which* is not your problem here,

And perhaps not even God's. So bang, wind, batter,
While human hearts do the bookkeeping in this matter.

Nursery Rhymes

I. Knockety-Knockety-Knock

Hickory-dickory-dock—
The mouse ran up the clock.
The clock struck one,
And I fell down,
Hickory-dickory-dock.
God let me fall down,
And I tore my nightgown,
And knockety-knockety-knock,
As I lie on the floor,
Someone's at the door—
Hickory-dickory-dock.

*

Hickory-dickory-dock—
The mouse runs up the clock.
My father took me
For a ride on his knee,
Hickory-dickory-dock.
But then things were nice,
With no awful mice,
And no knockety-knockety-knock,
And my head didn't spin
When the strange foot came in—
Hickory-dickory-dock.

Hickory-dickory-dock—
The mouse runs up the clock.
When I'd wake in the night,
Mother held me tight,
Hickory-dickory-dock.
Then dreams were just dreams,
And not, as it now seems,
A knockety-knockety-knock
That walks in at the door
As I lie on the floor—
Hickory-dickory-dock.

Hickory-dickory-dock—
The mouse ran up the clock,
And the clock struck one
And my poor head spun,
Hickory-dickory-dock,
And Ma's deader than mackerel,
And Pa pickled as pickerel,
And oh! knockety-knockety-knock,
God's red eyes glare
From sockets of dark air—
Knockety-knockety-knock.

II. News of Unexpected Demise of Little Boy Blue

Little Boy Blue, come blow your horn,
The sheep's in the meadow, the cow's in the corn.
Little Boy, will you make me stand and call
From first dawn-robin to last dew-fall?
It's no excuse you are young and careless,
With your thing-a-bob little and your little chest hairless,
For people have duties to perform at all ages—
Hurry up, Little Boy, or I'll dock your wages.

*

Come blow your horn, Little Boy Blue,
Or I'll make your bottom the bluest part of you.
Come blow your horn, you Little Gold-bricker,
Or I'll snatch you baldheaded in a wink, or quicker.
Little Boy, you'll get no more ice cream.
Nobody will come when you have a bad dream.
Where is that pretty little horn I gave you?
I simply won't tolerate such behavior.

I should have known you'd be derelict.
From a family like yours what can we expect?
Born of woman, and she grunted like a pig,
Got by man just for the frig,
Dropped in the world like a package of offal,
Demanding love with wail and snuffle,
Lost in the world and the trees were tall—
You Little Wretch, don't you hear me call!

A plague and a pox on such a bad boy.
I know you are hiding just to annoy.
You reflect no credit on the human race.
You stand in need of prayer and grace.
Where's that Little Wretch that tends the sheep?

He's under the haystack, fast asleep.

Well, damn it, go wake him!

No, not I—
I can only walk the green fields, and cry.

III. Mother Makes the Biscuits

Mother makes the biscuits,
Father makes the laws,
Grandma wets the bed sometimes,
Kitty-cats have claws.

Mother sweeps the kitchen,
Father milks the cow,
Grandpa leaves his pants unbuttoned,
Puppy-dogs bark, *bow-wow.*

All do as God intends,
The sun sets in the west,
Father shaves his chin, *scrape-scrape,*
Mother knows best.

*

Clap hands, children,
Clap hands and sing!
Hold hands together, children,
And dance in a ring,

For the green worm sings on the leaf,
The black beetle folds hands to pray,
And the stones in the field wash their faces clean
To meet break of day.

But we may see this only
Because all night we have stared
At the black miles past where stars are
Till the stars disappeared.

IV. The Bramble Bush

There was a man in our town
And he was wondrous wise,
He jumped into a bramble bush
And scratched out both his eyes,

And could not see the pretty sky,
Or how, whenever you throw
A stone into a sparrow-tree,
All wheel like one, and go.

So when he saw he could not see,
And knew the fact was plain,
He jumped back into the bramble bush
And scratched them in again,

And I now saw past the fartherest stars
How darkness blazed like light,
And the sun was a winking spark that rose
Up the chimney of the night,

And like petals from a wind-torn bough
In furious beauty blown,
The stars were gone—and I heard the joy
Of flesh singing on the bone.

Short Thoughts for Long Nights

I. Nightmare of Mouse

It was there, but I said it couldn't be true in daylight.
It was there, but I said it was only a trick of starlight.
It was there, but I said to believe it would take a fool,
And I wasn't, so didn't—till teeth crunched on my skull.

II. Nightmare of Man

I assembled, marshaled, my data, deployed them expertly.
My induction was perfect, as far as induction may be.
But the formula failed in the test tube, despite all my skill,
For I'd thought of the death of my mother, and wept, and weep still.

III. Colloquy With Cockroach

I know I smell. But everyone does, somewhat.
I smell this way only because I crawl down the drain.
I've no slightest idea how you got the smell you've got.
No, I haven't time now—it might take you too long to explain.

IV. Little Boy on Voyage

Little boy, little boy, standing on ship-shudder, wide eyes staring
At unease of ocean, at sunset, and the distance long—
You've stared, little boy, at gray distance past hoping or despairing,
So come in for supper and sleep, now; they, too, will help you grow strong.

V. Obsession

Dawn draws on slow when dawn brings only dawn:
Only slow milk-wash on window, star paling, first bird-stir,
Sweat cold now on pillow, before the alarm's *burr,*
And the old thought for the new day as day draws on.

VI. Joy

If you've never had it, discussion is perfectly fruitless,
And if you have, you can tell nobody about it.
To explain silence, you scarcely try to shout it.
Let the flute and drum be still, the trumpet *toot*less.

VII. Cricket, on Kitchen Floor, Enters History

History, shaped like white hen,
Walked in at kitchen door.
Beak clicked once on stone floor.
Out door walked hen then;
But will, no doubt, come again.

VIII. Little Boy and General Principle

Don't cry, little boy, you see it is only natural
That little red trucks will break, whether plastic or tin,
And some other things, too. It's a general principle
That you'll have to learn soon, so you might, I guess, begin.

IX. Grasshopper Tries to Break Solipsism

Sing *summer, summer,* sing *summer* summerlong—
For God is light, oh I love Him, love is my song.
I sing, for I must, for God, if I didn't, would weep,
And over all things, all night, His despair, like ice, creep.

Tale of Time

Poems 1960–1966

To Eleanor, Rosanna, and Gabriel

Patriotic Tour and Postulate of Joy

Once, once, in Washington,
D.C., in June,
All night—I swear it—a single mockingbird
Sang,
Sang to the Presidential ear,
Wherein it poured
Such criticism and advice as that ear
Had rarely had the privilege to hear.

And sang to every senator
Available,
And some, as sources best informed affirm,
Rose,
Rose with a taste in the throat like bile,
To the bathroom fled
And spat, and faced the mirror there, and while
The bicarb fizzed, stared, feet cold on tile.

And sang to Edgar Hoover, too,
And as it preached
Subversion and all bright disaster, he
Woke;
Woke, then looked at Mom's photo, so heard
No more. But far,
Far off in Arlington, the heroes stirred
And meditated on the message of that bird.

And sang—oh, merciless!—to me,
Who to that place
And to that massive hour had moved, and now
Rose,
Rose naked, and shivered in moonlight, and cried
Out in my need
To know what postulate of joy men have tried
To live by, in sunlight and moonlight, until they died.

Dragon-Tree

The faucet drips all night, the plumber forgot it.
A cat, in coitu, squalls like Hell's honeymoon.
A child is sick. The doctor coughs.
Do you feel, in your heart, that life has turned out as once you expected?

Spring comes early, ice
Groans in the gorge. Water, black, swirls
Into foam like lace white in fury. The gorge boulders boom.
When you hear, in darkness, the gorge boulders boom, does your heart say, "No
comment"?

*

Geese pass in dawn-light, and the news
From Asia is bad, and the Belgians sure mucked up
The Congo. Human flesh is yet eaten there, often uncooked.
Have you sat on a hillside at sunset and eaten the flesh of your own heart?

The world drives at you like a locomotive
In an archaic movie. It whirls off the screen,
It is on you, the iron. You hear, in that silence, your heart.
Have you thought that the headlines are only the image of your own heart?

Some study compassion. Some, confusing
Personal pathology with the logic of history, jump
Out of windows. Some walk with God, some by rivers, at twilight.
Have you tried to just sit with the children and tell a tale ending in laughter?

Oh, tell the tale, and laugh, and let
God laugh—for your heart is the dragon-tree, the root
Feels, in earth-dark, the abrasive scale, the coils
Twitch. But look! the new leaf flaps gilt in the sunlight. Birds sing.

Ways of Day

I have come all this way.
I am sitting in the shade.
Book on knee and mind on nothing,
I now fix my gaze
On my small son playing in the afternoon's blaze.

Convulsive and cantankerous,
Night heaved, and burning, the star
Fell. Oh, what do I remember?
I heard the swamp owl, night-long, call.
The far car's headlight swept the room wall.

I am the dark and tricky one.
I am watching from my shade.
Your tousled hair-tips prickle the sunlight.
I watch you at your sunlit play.
Teach me, my son, the ways of day.

Tale of Time

I. What Happened

It was October. It was the Depression. Money
Was tight. Hoover was not a bad
Man, and my mother
Died, and God
Kept on, and keeps on,
Trying to tie things together, but

It doesn't always work, and we put the body
Into the ground, dark
Fell soon, but not yet, and oh,
Have you seen the last oak leaf of autumn, high,
Not yet fallen, stung
By last sun to a gold
Painful beyond the pain one can ordinarily
Get? What

Was there in the interim
To do, the time being the time
Between the clod's *chunk* and
The full realization, which commonly comes only after
Midnight? That

Is when you will go to the bathroom for a drink of water.
You wash your face in cold water.
You stare at your face in the mirror, wondering
Why now no tears come, for
You had been proud of your tears, and so
You think of copulation, of
Fluid ejected, of
Water deeper than daylight, of
The sun-dappled dark of deep woods and
Blood on green fern frond, of
The shedding of blood, and you will doubt
The significance of your own experience. Oh,
Desolation—oh, if
You were rich!
You try to think of a new position. Is this

Grief? You pray
To God that this be grief, for
You want to grieve.

This, you reflect, is no doubt the typical syndrome.

But all this will come later.
There will also be the dream of the eating of human flesh.

II. The Mad Druggist

I come back to try to remember the faces she saw every day.
She saw them on the street, at school, in the stores, at church.
They are not here now, they have been withdrawn, are put away.
They are all gone now, and have left me in the lurch.

I am in the lurch because they were part of her.
Not clearly remembering them, I have therefore lost that much
Of her, and if I do remember,
I remember the lineaments only beyond the ice-blur and soot-smutch

Of boyhood contempt, for I had not thought they were real.
The real began where the last concrete walk gave out
And the smart-weed crawled in the cracks, where the last privy canted to spill
Over flat in the rank-nourished burdock, and would soon, no doubt,

If nobody came to prop it, which nobody would do.
The real began there: field and woods, stone and stream began
Their utterance, and the fox, in his earth, knew
Joy; and the hawk, like philosophy, hung without motion, high, where the sun-blaze of wind ran.

Now, far from Kentucky, planes pass in the night, I hear them and all, all is real.
Some men are mad, but I know that delusion may be one name for truth.
The faces I cannot remember lean at my bed-foot, and grin fit to kill,
For we now share a knowledge I did not have in my youth.

There's one I remember, the old druggist they carried away.
They put him in Hoptown, where he kept on making his list—
The same list he had on the street when he stopped my mother to say:
"Here they are, Miss Ruth, the folks that wouldn't be missed,

"Or this God-durn town would be lucky to miss,
If when I fixed a prescription I just happened to pour
Something in by way of improvement." Then leaned in that gray way of his:
"But you—you always say something nice when you come in my store."

In Hoptown he worked on his list, which now could have nothing to do
With the schedule of deaths continuing relentlessly,
To include, in the end, my mother, as well as that list-maker who
Had the wit to see that she was too precious to die:

A fact some in the street had not grasped—nor the attending physician, nor God, nor I.

III. Answer Yes or No

Death is only a technical correction of the market.
Death is only the transfer of energy to a new form.
Death is only the fulfillment of a wish.

Whose wish?

IV. The Interim

1.

Between the clod and the midnight
The time was.
There had been the public ritual and there would be
The private realization,
And now the time was, and

In that time the heart cries out for coherence.
Between the beginning and the end, we must learn
The nature of being, in order
In the end to be, so

Our feet, in first dusk, took
Us over the railroad tracks, where
Sole-leather ground drily against cinders, as when
Tears will not come. She

Whom we now sought was old. Was
Sick. Was dying. Was
Black. Was.
Was: and was that enough? Is
Existence the adequate and only target
For the total reverence of the heart?

We would see her who,
Also, had held me in her arms.
She had held me in her arms,
And I had cried out in the wide
Day-blaze of the world. But

Now was a time of endings.

What is love?

2.

Tell me what love is, for
The harvest moon, gold, heaved
Over the far woods which were,
On the black land black, and it swagged over
The hill-line. That light
Lay gold on the roofs of Squigg-town, and the niggers
Were under the roofs, and
The room smelled of urine.
A fire burned on the hearth:
Too hot, and there was no ventilation, and

You have not answered my question.

3.

Propped in a chair, lying down she
Could not have breathed, dying
Erect, breath
Slow from the hole of the mouth, that black
Aperture in the blackness which
Was her face, but
How few of them are really
Black, but she
Is black, and life
Spinning out, spilling out, from
The holes of the eyes: and the eyes are
Burning mud beneath a sky of nothing.
The eyes bubble like hot mud with the expulsion of vision.

I lean, I am the
Nothingness which she
Sees.

Her hand rises in the air.
It rises like revelation.
It moves but has no motion, and
Around it the world flows like a dream of drowning.
The hand touches my cheek.
The voice says: *you.*

I am myself.

The hand has brought me the gift of myself.

4.

I am myself, and
Her face is black like cave-blackness, and over
That blackness now hangs death, gray
Like cobweb over the blackness of a cave, but
That blackness which she is, is
Not deficiency like cave-blackness, but is
Substance.
The cobweb shakes with the motion of her breath.

My hand reaches out to part that grayness of cobweb.

My lips touch the cheek, which is black.
I do not know whether the cheek is cold or hot, but I
Know that
The temperature is shocking.
I press my lips firmly against that death,
I try to pray.

The flesh is dry, and tastes of salt.

My father has laid a twenty-dollar bill on the table.
He, too, will kiss that cheek.

5.

We stand in the street of Squigg-town.
The moon is high now and the tin roofs gleam.
My brother says: *The whole place smelled of urine.*
My father says: *Twenty dollars—oh, God, what*
Is twenty dollars when
The world is the world it is!

The night freight is passing.
The couplings clank in the moonlight, the locomotive
Labors on the grade.
The freight disappears beyond the coal chute westward, and
The red caboose light disappears into the distance of the continent.
It will move all night into distance.

My sister is weeping under the sky.
The sky is enormous in the absoluteness of moonlight.

These are factors to be considered in making any final estimate.

6.

There is only one solution. If
You would know how to live, here
Is the solution, and under
My window, when ice breaks, the boulder
Groans in the gorge, the foam swirls, and in
The intensity of the innermost darkness of steel
The crystal blooms like a star, and at
Dawn I have seen the delicate print of the coon-hand in silt by the riffle.

Hawk-shadow sweetly sweeps the grain.
I would compare it with that fugitive thought which I can find no word for.

7.

Planes pass in the night. I turn
To the right side if the beating
Of my own heart disturbs me.
The sound of water flowing is
An image of Time, and therefore
Truth is all and
Must be respected, and
On the other side of the mirror into which,
At morning, you will stare, History

Gathers, condenses, crouches, breathes, waits. History
Stares forth at you through the eyes which
You think are the reflection of
Your own eyes in the mirror.
Ah, Monsieur du Miroir!

Your whole position must be reconsidered.

8.

But the solution: You
Must eat the dead.
You must eat them completely, bone, blood, flesh, gristle, even
Such hair as can be forced. You
Must undertake this in the dark of the moon, but
At your plenilune of anguish.

Immortality is not impossible,
Even joy.

V. What Were You Thinking, Dear Mother?

What were you thinking, a child, when you lay,
At the whippoorwill hour, lost in the long grass,
As sun, beyond the dark cedars, sank?
You went to the house. The lamps were now lit.

What did you think when the evening dove mourned,
Far off in those sober recesses of cedar?
What relevance did your heart find in that sound?
In lamplight, your father's head bent at his book.

What did you think when the last saffron
Of sunset faded beyond the dark cedars,
And on noble blue now the evening star hung?
You found it necessary to go to the house,

And found it necessary to live on,
In your bravery and in your joyous secret,
Into our present maniacal century,
In which you gave me birth, and in

Which I, in the public and private mania,
Have lived, but remember that once I,
A child, in the grass of that same spot, lay,
And the whippoorwill called, beyond the dark cedars.

VI. Insomnia

1.

If to that place. Place of grass.
If to hour of whippoorwill, I.
If I now, not a child. To.
If now I, not a child, should come to
That place, lie in
That place, in that hour hear
That call, would
I rise,
Go?

Yes, enter the darkness. Of.
Darkness of cedars, thinking
You there, you having entered, sly,
My back being turned, face
Averted, or
Eyes shut, for
A man cannot keep his eyes steadily open
Sixty years.

*

I did not see you when you went away.

Darkness of cedars, yes, entering, but what
Face, what
Bubble on dark stream of Time, white
Glimmer un-mooned? Oh,
What age has the soul, what
Face does it wear, or would
I meet that face that last I saw on the pillow, pale?
I recall each item with remarkable precision.

Would the sweat now be dried on the temples?

2.

What would we talk about? The dead,
Do they know all, or nothing, and
If nothing, does
Curiosity survive the long unravelment? Tell me

What they think about love, for I
Know now at long last that the living remember the dead only
Because we cannot bear the thought that they
Might forget us. Or is
That true? Look, look at these—
But no, no light here penetrates by which
You might see these photographs I keep in my wallet. Anyway,
I shall try to tell you all that has happened to me.

Though how can I tell when I do not even know?

And as for you, and all the interesting things
That must have happened to you and that
I am just dying to hear about—

But would you confide in a balding stranger
The intimate secret of death?

3.

Or does the soul have many faces, and would I,
Pacing the cold hypothesis of Time, enter
Those recesses to see, white,
Whiter than moth-wing, the child's face
Glimmer in cedar gloom, and so
Reach out that I might offer
What protection I could, saying,
"I am older than you will ever be"—for it
Is the child who once
Lay lost in the long grass, sun setting.

*

Reach out, saying: "Your hand—
Give it here, for it's dark and, my dear,
You should never have come in the woods when it's dark,
But I'll take you back home, they're waiting."
And to woods-edge we come, there stand.

I watch you move across the open space.
You move under the paleness of new stars.
You move toward the house, and one instant,

A door opening, I see
Your small form black against the light, and the door
Is closed, and I

Hear night crash down a million stairs.
In the ensuing silence
My breath is difficult.

Heat lightning ranges beyond the horizon.

That, also, is worth mentioning.

4.

Come,
Crack crust, striker
From darkness, and let seize—let what
Hand seize, oh!—my heart, and compress
The heart till, after pain, joy from it
Spurt like a grape, and I will grind
Teeth on flint tongue till
The flint screams. Truth
Is all. But

I must learn to speak it
Slowly, in a whisper.

Truth, in the end, can never be spoken aloud,
For the future is always unpredictable.
But so is the past, therefore

At wood's edge I stand, and,
Over the black horizon, heat lightning
Ripples the black sky. After
The lightning, as the eye
Adjusts to the new dark,
The stars are, again, born.

They are born one by one.

Homage to Emerson, On Night Flight to New York

To Peter and Ebie Blume

I. His Smile

Over Peoria we lost the sun:
The earth, by snow like sputum smeared, slides
Westward. Those fields in the last light gleam. Emerson—

The essays, on my lap, lie. A finger
Of light, in our pressurized gloom, strikes down,
Like God, to poke the page, the page glows. There is
No sin. Not even error. Night,

On the glass at my right shoulder, hisses
Like sand from a sand-blast, but
The hiss is a sound that only a dog's
Ear could catch, or the human heart. My heart

Is as abstract as an empty
Coca-Cola bottle. It whistles with speed.
It whines in that ammoniac blast caused by
The passage of stars, for
At 38,000 feet Emerson

Is dead right. His smile
Was sweet as he walked in the greenwood.
He walked lightly, his toes out, his body
Swaying in the dappled shade, and
His smile never withered a violet. He

Did not even know the violet's name, not having
Been introduced, but he bowed, smiling,
For he had forgiven God everything, even the violet.

When I was a boy I had a wart on the right forefinger.

II. The Wart

At 38,000 feet you had better
Try to remember something specific, if
You yourself want to be something specific, I remember
The wart and the old colored man, he said, *Son*
You quit that jack-off, and that thing go way,
And I said *Quit what,* and he giggled *He-he,* and he
Said, *You is got white skin and hair red as a ter-mater, but*
You is human-kind, but

At 38,000 feet that is hard to remember.

III. The Spider

The spider has more eyes than I have money.
I used to dream that God was a spider, or

Vice versa, but it is easier
To dream of a funnel, and you
The clear liquid being poured down it, forever.

You do not know what is beyond the little end of the funnel.

The liquid glimmers in darkness, you
Are happy, it pours easily, without fume.

All you have to do is not argue.

IV. One Drunk Allegory

Not argue, unless, that is, you are the kind
That needs to remember something specific
In order to be, at 38,000 feet, whatever you are, and once
In New Orleans, in French Town, in
Front of the Old Absinthe House, and it
Was Saturday night, was 2 A.M., a drunk

Crip slipped, and the air was full of flying crutches
Like a Texas tornado exploding with chicken feathers and
Split boards off busted hen-houses, and bingo!—
It was prize money flat on its you-know-what, it
Was like a box of spilled spaghetti, but
I managed to reassemble everything and prop it

Against a lamp post. *Thank you,*
It said in its expensive Harvard-cum-cotton
Voice, then bingo!—
Flat on its you-know-what, on the pavement,
And ditto the crutches. *Prithee,* the voice

Expensively said, *do not trouble yourself*
Further. This is as good a position as any
From which to watch the stars. Then added:
Until, of course, the cops come. I
Had private reasons for not wanting to be
There when the cops came. So wasn't.

Emerson thought that significance shines through everything,

*

And at that moment I was drunk enough to think all this was allegory.
If it was, it was sure-God one drunk allegory, and
Somewhere in the womb-gloom of the DC-8

A baby is crying. The cry seems to have a reality
Independent of the baby. The cry
Is like a small white worm in my brain.

It nibbles with tiny, insistent assiduity. Its teeth
Are almost too soft. Sometimes it merely tickles.

To my right, far over Kentucky, the stars are shining.

V. Multiplication Table

If the Christmas tree at Rockefeller Center were
A billion times bigger, and you laid it
Flat down in the dark, and
With a steam roller waist-high to God and heavy as
The Rocky Mountains, flattened it out thin as paper, but
Never broke a single damned colored light bulb, and they were all
Blazing in the dark, that would be the way it is, but

Beyond the lights it is dark, and one night in winter, I
Stood at the end of a pier at Coney Island, while
The empty darkness howled like a dog, but no wind, and far down
The boardwalk what must have been a cop's flashlight
Jiggled fitfully over what must have been locked store-fronts, then,
Of a sudden, went out. The stars were small and white, and I heard

The sea secretly sucking the piles of the pier with a sound like
An old woman sucking her teeth in the dark before she sleeps.

The nose of the DC-8 dips, and at this point
The man sitting beside me begins, quite audibly, to recite
The multiplication table.

                                        Far below,
Individual lights can be seen throbbing like nerve ends.
I have friends down there, and their lives have strange shapes
Like eggs splattered on the kitchen floor. Their lives shine
Like oil-slicks on dark water. I love them, I think.

In a room, somewhere, a telephone keeps ringing.

VI. Wind

The wind comes off the Sound, smelling
Of ice. It smells
Of fish and burned gasoline. A sheet
Of newspaper drives in the wind across
The great distance of cement that bleeds
Off into blackness beyond the red flares. The air

Shivers, it shakes like Jello with
The roar of jets—oh, why
Is it you think you can hear the infinitesimal scrape
Of that newspaper as it slides over the black cement, forever?

The wind gouges its knuckles into my eye. No wonder there are tears.

VII. Does the Wild Rose?

When you reach home tonight you will see
That the envelope containing the policy
Of your flight insurance is waiting, unopened,
On the table. All had been in order,
In case—but can you tell me,

Does the wild rose know your secret
As the summer silence breathes?

Eastward, the great waters stretch in darkness.
Do you know how gulls sleep when they can't make it home?

Tell me, tell me, does the wild rose— tell me, for

Tonight I shall dream of small white stars
Falling forever in darkness like dandruff, but

Now let us cross that black cement which so resembles the arctic ice of
Our recollections. There is the city, the sky
Glows, glows above it, there must be

A way by which the process of living can become Truth.

Let us move toward the city. Do you think you could tell me
What constitutes the human bond? Do you ever think
Of a face half in shadow, tears—
As it would seem from that muted glitter—in the
Eyes, but

The lips do not tremble.

Is it merely a delusion that they seem about to smile?

Shoes in Rain Jungle

Shoes rot off feet before feet
Rot, and before feet
Stop moving feet
Rot, rot in the
Rain, moving.

Napoleon was wrong, an army
Marches on its feet. If
It has them. If
The feet have shoes.

The Battle of Gettysburg was fought for shoes.
It is hell to die barefoot, unless,
Of course, that is the way you are raised.

They are cheap, but shoes are dear, and

All wars are righteous. Except when
You lose them. This
Is the lesson of history. This—
And shoes. On rotting shoe leather

Men march into history, and when
You get there take a good look around, lost
In the multitudinous gray portieres of beaded
Rain, and say, *"Mot de Cambronne,* this
Is history."

Now you know what it is.

History is what you can't
Resign from, but

There is always refuge in the practice
Of private virtue,
Or at least in heroism, and if

You get stuck with heroism you can, anyway,
When the cameras pop, cover your face,
Like the man who, coming out of the D. A.'s office,
Lifts his hands, handcuffed, to cover his face.

You can do that much.

Melville, ruined, sick, acerb, anent
The Civil War, said: "Nothing
Can lift the heart of man
Like manhood in a fellow-man," and

*

Sociologists should make a study called "Relative
Incidence of Mention of Heroes in News Media
As Index to Gravity of a Situation."

Sociologists can do that much.

And when the rainy season is over
There will be new problems, including
The problem of a new definition of virtue.

Meanwhile talk as little *mot de Cambronne* as
Possible, and remember
There is more than one kind of same.

This last is very important.

Fall Comes in Back-Country Vermont

To William Meredith

(1. One Voter Out of Sixteen)

Deader they die here, or at least
Differently, deeper the hole, and after
The burying, at night, late, you
Are more apt to wonder about the drainage

Of the cemetery, but know that you needn't, for
Here's all hills anyway, or mountain, and the hole
Standard, but if no drainage problem, yet
You may still wake with a kind of psychic

Twitch, as when the nerves in the amputee's
Stump (a saw did it, no doubt) twitch and wonder
How that which has gone off and set up
As a separate self is making out, and whether

It repents of its rashness, and would like
To come back and crawl into bed and be
Forgiven, and even though you, like me,
May forget the name of the dead, in the dark you

Can't help but remember that if there are only
Sixteen voters and one dies, that leaves only
Fifteen, and no doubt you know the story
Of how it began, how he laid his axe down, then

*

Just sat on a log, not saying a word, till
The crew knocked off for the day, and never
Came back (it was cancer), and later you'd see him
Sit on the porch in the sun and throw bread

To the chipmunks, but that was last year, and now
There's the real-estate sign in the yard, and the grass
Not cut, and already one window knocked out,
For the widow's heartbroken and gone, and the bed

Is stripped to the mattress, and the bedpan
Washed with ammonia and put on a high shelf,
And the stuffed lynx he shot now all night glares
At the empty room with a feral vindication,

And does not forgive, and thinks with glee
How cancer is worse than a 30.30, and

(2. The Bear and the Last Person to Remember)

It is well the widow is gone, for here winter's
Not made for a woman lone, lorn, and slow-foot,
And summer already sinks southward, and soon
All over the state the summer people

Will put the lawn mower in the red barn, drain
The plumbing, deny the pain of that heart-pinch
They cannot define, and get out the suitcase
To pack, for last night, in moonlight and high

On the mountain, I heard the first bear-hoot,
As the bear that all day had stripped bushes of the last
Blueberries, felt that hot itch and heaved
Up his black, hairy man-height in moonlight,

Lifted the head and curled back the black lip
To show the white moon-gleam of tusk, and the throat
Pulsed in that call that is like the great owl's,
But more edged with anguish, and then far off,

From a ruined orchard, by the old cellar hole,
In the tang and tawny air-taste of the apple-
Night, the she bear, too, rises,
And the half-crushed apple, forgotten, falls

From the jaw gone slack in that moment before
Her utterance, and soon now, night after night,
On the mountain the moon-air will heave with that hunger,
So that, in that hour, the boys of the village

*

Come out, climb a ridge and reply, and when
Off on the mountain that hoot comes, and nearer,
The girls with them shiver and giggle, not quite
Daring to face that thought that from dark now,

Hot-breathed and hairy, earth-odored and foam-flecked,
Rises, and want to go home, all but one,
Who feels that the night cannot breathe, and who soon,
On the raw mattress, in that house, will cry

Out, but the house is empty, and
Through the window where once the lace curtains hung
And a green shade was but is not,
The moonlight now pours like God, and the sweat

Of her effort goes ice, for she remembers,
So struggles to thrust off that weight that chokes her,
Thrusts herself up on that mattress, and gasping
In that ice and ice-iron of moonlight, with

What breath in that dishevelment
Is possible, says: "But here—it was here—
On this bed that he died, and I'll catch it and die"—
But does not, comes back, comes back until snow flies,

And many years later will be the last person
To remember his name who there on that bed

(3. The Human Fabric)

Had died, but for now let us take some comfort
In the fact that the fifteen surviving voters,
Remembering his name, feel, in the heart,
Diminished, for in this section death

Is a window gone dark and a face not seen
Any more at the P.O., and in the act
Of rending irreparably the human fabric,
Death affirms the fact of that fabric, so what

If at night, in first snow, the hunters pass—
Pale clerks and mechanics from Springfield and Hartford
With red caps and rifles and their pitiful
Blood-lust and histrionic maleness—and passing,

Throw out from the car the empty bourbon
Bottle to lie in the snow by the For-
Sale sign, and snow covers the bottle, will cover
The sign itself, and then the snow plow

*

Will pile up the banks as high as the eaves,
So that skiers who sing past in sports cars at dusk
Cannot see it, nor singing, need yet to know
The truth which at last they will come to need,

That life is of life paradigm, and death
The legend of death, nor need ever to know

(4. Afterwards)

That all night, eaves-high, the snow will press
Its face to the black ice of glass, and by
The white light its own being sheds, stare
Into that trapped cubicle of emptiness which

Is that room, but by that time I
Will not be here, in another place be,
And in my bed, not asleep, will endeavor
To see in my mind the eagle that once,

Above sunset, above the mountain in Stratton,
I saw—on thinnest air, high, saw
Lounging—oh, look!—it turns, and turning,
Shoulders like spray that last light before

The whistling down-plunge to the mountain's shade.
I touch the hand there on the pillow.

The Day Dr. Knox Did It

To William and Rose Styron

I. Place and Time

Heat-blaze, white dazzle: and white is the dust
down the only street of Cerulean Springs,
which is only a piece of country road
mislaid, somehow, among the white houses,

as the houses, too, had got mislaid
among the last big oaks and big tulip trees left
from the old forest-time. But to resume:
heat-dazzle, dust-whiteness—an image in sleep,

*

or in the brain behind the eyeball,
as now, in the light of this other day,
and year, the eyeball, stunned by that inner
blaze, sees nothing, can nothing see

outward whatsoever—only
the white dust of that street, and it
is always August, is 3 P.M.,
the mercury 95, and the leaf

of the oak tree curls at the edge like leather,
and the post master's setter pants in his cave
of cool back under the rotting floor boards
of the P.O.'s high old porch, and every

shade is down in every house,
and the last ash winks in the black kitchen range,
and the iron creaks with contraction in the lonely
new silence of the kitchen. Far off,

when the head of the moccasin parts the green
algae and it slides up out of the slough,
its trail on the stone sizzles dry in a twinkling,
and the lunacy of the cicada knows

now no remission. The sun is white.
It fills the sky with a scream of whiteness,
and my feet move in the white dust.
My feet are bare, I am nine years old,

and my feet in the white dust move, but I move
in a dream that is silver like willow and water
and the glimmer of water on water-dark stone.
I see in my mind that place I will go.

This is the summer of 1914.
I move toward that coolness. Then I hear the sound.

II. The Event

The sound was like one made by a board
dropped from a builder's scaffold to fall
flat and heavy on another
board grounded solid and flat to make

the sound solid. But cottony, too,
as though its own echoes were tangled in it,
in thickness and softness—an effect that was caused,
no doubt, by the fact he had climbed to the barn loft

*

to arrange himself. That summer I'd played
there in that loft, and so knew how
if you lay on your back in the hay, all
you could see was the twilight of spider-web

hung from the rooftree, or maybe one wasp
cruising slow in that gloom with one
sharp glint of light on his hard sheen.
That man—how long had he lain, just looking?

That was the thing that stuck in my head.
I would wonder how long he had lain there, first.

III. A Confederate Veteran Tries to Explain the Event

"But why did he do it, Grandpa?" I said
to the old man sitting under the cedar,
who had come a long way to that place, and that time
when that other man lay down in the hay

to arrange himself. And now the old man
lifted his head to stare at me.
"It's one of those things," he said, and stopped.
"What things?" I said. And he said: "Son—

"son, one of those things you never know."
"But there must be a *why,*" I said. Then he
said: "Folks—yes, folks, they up and die."
"But, Grandpa—" I said. And he: "They die."

Said: "Yes, by God, and I've seen 'em die.
I've seen 'em die and I've seen 'em dead.
I've seen 'em die hot and seen 'em die cold.
Hot lead and cold steel—" The words, they stopped.

The mouth closed up. The eyes looked away.
Beyond the lawn where the fennel throve,
beyond the fence where the whitewash peeled,
beyond the cedars along the lane,

the eyes fixed. The land, in sunlight,
swam, with the meadow the color of rust,
and distance the blue of Time, and nothing—
oh, nothing—would ever happen, and

*

in the silence my breath did not happen. But
the eyes, they happened, they found me, I
stood there and waited. "Dying," he said,
"hell, dying's a thing any fool can do."

"But what made him do it?" I said, again.
Then wished I hadn't, for he stared at me.
He stared at me as though I weren't there,
or as though I were dead, or had never been born,

and I felt like dandelion fuzz blown away,
or a word you'd once heard but never could spell,
or only an empty hole in the air.
From the cedar shade his eyes burned red.

Darker than shade, his mouth opened then.
Spit was pink on his lips, I saw the tongue move
beyond the old teeth, in the dark of his head.
It moved in that dark. Then, "Son—" the tongue said.

"For some folks the world gets too much," it said.
In that dark, the tongue moved. "For some folks," it said.

IV. The Place Where the Boy Pointed

It was ten days after the event
when the son of the man who had lain in the hay
took me back to the loft where we'd once played,
but this time it wasn't to play, though for what

I didn't know, he just said, "Come on,"
and when I came, and there we stood
in the spider-web gloom and wasp-glint light,
he stood, his face white in shadow, and pointed.

I stared at the place, but the hay was clean,
which was strange, for I'd been hearing them tell
how a 12-gauge will make an awful mess
if you put the muzzle in your mouth.

I kept thinking about how the place looked clean.
I kept wondering who had cleaned up the mess.

V. And All That Came Thereafter

But ran from such wondering as I ran
down the street, and the street was dancing a-dazzle,
and the dust rose white in plops round my feet
as they ran toward that stream that was silent and silver

in willow and water, and I would lie
with my eyes shut tight, and let water flow
over me as I lay, and like water, the world
would flow, flow away, on forever. But once

in San Francisco, on Telegraph Hill,
past midnight, alone, and that was
in the time long before that imbecile
tower had there been built, and there I

watched fog swell up from the sea and lean,
and star by star blot the sky out,
and blot the hill, and blot me out
from all relation but to the dry

goat droppings that beneath my feet
pressed the thin soles of my sneakers, as I,
in that swirl of whiteness gone blinder than black,
lifted up my arms, and while distantly

I heard the freighter, savage in fog,
slide past the passage of the Gate,
my own heart, in a rage like joy,
burst. I did not know my name,

nor do I know, even now, the meaning
of another night, by another sea,
when sea-salt on the laurel leaf
in moonlight, like frost, gleamed, and salt

were the tears to my lips on the girl's face, for
she wept, and I did not know why, and thus
entered her body, and in that breathless
instant of poised energy, heard

the sea-sway and the secret grind
of shingle down the glimmering shore.
Later, we lay and heard it. It
from the hollow of earth seemed, but the moon

hung steady as eternity. Now
I sometimes cannot remember her face, nor
the name of the village where we had stayed,
and as for Telegraph Hill, long since

*

gone is the immigrant's goat, and there now
wearers of pin-stripe and of furs by I. Magnin
have swarmed in their hives of glass to admire
from that point of vantage the rising values

of real estate and the beauty of stars,
which yet in fact shine, and if there is fog,
high above the last gray unravelment, shine,
while fog-wrapped, the freighters, and troopships now too,

seaward slide, and hooting, proceed
in darkness, and deeper in darkness blooms
the inward orchid, and agon, blind,
of this, our age, of which I—who

have lied, in velleity loved, in weakness
forgiven, who have stolen small objects, committed
adultery, and for a passing pleasure,
as well as for reasons of sanitation,

inflicted death on flies—am,
like you, the perfect image, and if
once through the blaze of that August I fled,
but toward myself I fled, for there is

no water to wash the world away.
We are the world, and it is too late
to pretend we are children at dusk watching fireflies.
But we must frame more firmly the idea of good.

My small daughter's dog has been killed on the road.
It is night. In the next room she weeps.

Holy Writ

To Vann and Glenn Woodward

I. Elijah on Mount Carmel

(Elijah, after the miraculous fall of fire on his altar, the breaking of the drouth, and the slaughter of the priests of Baal, girds up his loins and runs ahead of the chariot of Ahab to the gates of Jezreel, where Jezebel waits.)

Nothing is re-enacted. Nothing
Is true. Therefore nothing
Must be believed,
But
To have truth

Something must be believed,
And repetition and congruence,
To say the least, are necessary, and
His thorn-scarred heels and toes with filth horn-scaled
Spurned now the flint-edge and with blood spurts flailed
Stone, splashed mud of Jezreel. And he screamed.
He had seen glory more blood-laced than any he had dreamed.

Far, far ahead of the chariot tire,
Which the black mud sucked, he screamed,
Screaming in glory
Like
A bursting blood blister.
Ahead of the mud-faltered fetlock,
He screamed, and of Ahab huddled in
The frail vehicle under the purpling wrack
And spilled gold of storm—poor Ahab, who,
From metaphysical confusion and lightning, had nothing to run to
But the soft Phoenician belly and commercial acuity
Of Jezebel: that darkness wherein History creeps to die.

How could he ever tell her? Get nerve to?
Tell how around her high altar
The prinking and primped
Priests,
Limping, had mewed,
And only the gull-mew was answer,
No fire to heaped meats, only sun-flame,
And the hairy one laughed: "Has your god turned aside to make pee-pee?"
How then on that sea-cliff he prayed, fire fell, sky darkened,
Rain fell, drouth broke now, for God had hearkened,
And priests gave their death-squeal. The king hid his eyes in his coat.
Oh, why to that hairy one should God have hearkened, who smelled like a goat?

Yes, how could he tell her? When he himself
Now scarcely believed it? Soon,
In the scented chamber,
She,
Saying, "Baby, Baby,
Just hush, now hush, it's all right,"
Would lean, reach out, lay a finger
To his lips to allay his infatuate gabble. So,
Eyes shut, breath scant, he heard her breath rip the lamp-flame
To blackness, and by that sweet dog-bait, lay, and it came,
The soft hand-grope he knew he could not, nor wished to, resist
Much longer; so prayed: "Dear God, dear God—oh, please, don't exist!"

II. Saul at Gilboa

Samuel Speaks

1.

From landscape the color of lions.
From land of great stone the color,
At noon-blaze, of the droppings of lions,
But harder than iron and,
By moonlight, bone-white, and the crouched stone seizes,
In its teeth, the night-wind, and the wind
Yelps, the wind
Yowls. From
The district of dry thorn, the ankle
Scarred by thorn. From
The dry watercourses.
Came.

He had been seeking his father's lost asses.

Sought what he found not, but found
Me, for what
We seek we never
Find, find only fate. Which is,
Not the leaf, but the shadow
Of the leaf, turning in air.

Fate is the air we breathe.

He moved toward me, and in that motion
His body clove the bright air.

2.

How beautiful are the young, walking
On the fore-part of the foot, the hair of the head,
Without ointment, glistens, the lower
Lip, though the fat of burnt meat has long since
Been wiped, glistens, and
Eyes with the glister of vision like
The eyes, hunger-whetted, of the eagle
That from the high sky stares.

His hands, by his sides, heavy hang down like hammers.

(Let Amalek shiver in his tent of goat hair.
Let him put belly to belly and no cloth between, not waiting
For the hour when stars, in blackness, are burnished by
The cold wind.)

*

Toward me he walks, I am old.
Dust of desert on him, and thorn-scar, he
Walks, and is the man. He is,
From the shoulder and upward, higher than any among the people.

He comes walking who will make Israel
One among the nations. He walks
In his youth, which is the sweet affront
Of ignorance, toward me, and I
Smile, feeling my face, even in that smile, go stiff as
Fresh goat hide, unflayed, set in sun, goes,
For the people murmur, say
I am old. A king
They would have, and toward me
He walks who will make all things
New. In beauty toward
My knowledge, walks. What
Is in my heart?

I hear my own voice. It says: *My son.*

3.

Before the knowledge in me, he, beautiful, down in the dirt, kneels.
Desert-travel and dry sweat: his odor
Is like old curds and new wine, and it comes to my nostrils.
His head is bowed, and I see the twin plaitings of muscle
At the back of his neck, and how they are grappled,
Olive root in rock, in shoulder-flesh. They grapple
To great bone, new sweat now
Beads in the channel of the back of his neck below
The skull, the skull is a tower of brass
Bent before me. He
Is ignorant, and I pour
Oil on those locks that no new shining need.

The far hills, white light on gypsum, dazzle.
The hills waver like salt dissolving in water. Swim
In the dazzle of my eyes.

4.

I am the past time, am old, but
Am, too, the time to come, for I,
In my knowledge, close my eyes, and am
The membrane between the past and the future, am thin, and
That thinness is the present time, the membrane
Is only my anguish, through which
The past seeps, penetrates, is absorbed into
The future, through which
The future bleeds into, becomes, the past even before
It ceases to be
The future. Am also

The knife edge that divides.

I say to him that the asses of his father that were lost
Are found.

Say to him that at Tabor at
A high place a band of the prophets,
With psaltery and tabret, dancing, will come,
And into him will enter that breath which
Will make him dance.
He will be another man.

Before me, his head is bowed. The oil glistens.

Say he will dance, but I do not say
That that dance is a dance into self-hood—and oh!
Beautiful is ignorance kneeling—and do not
Say how black, when the dance-breath goes out, will be
The blackness, nor say how the young boy
Before him will sit, and strike the harp,
Nor how he at him, because he is young
And the brow smooth, will hurl
The great spear, and the boy will, like smoke, sway,
Slip from his presence, be gone, his foot
Leaving no print among rocks.

He himself will become a friend to darkness, be counseled by wolves.

5.

I do not say that I will anoint against him that boy
Of the smooth brow.

Nor say how, at the hour
When the hosts are gathered, he will,
To Endor, in a mantle not his own,
In dark, come. Enter,
And to the woman of the cave speak, for, in the end,
To know is, always, all. To know
Is, whatever the knowledge, the secret hope within
Hope. So to the cave.

And from death, I,
In shape of shadow, rise,
Stand. He bows down
Before me, and in the fierceness of last joy, I see
That the hair of his bent head is
Now streaked with gray, so say
That the breath of the dance which has passed from him will not
Return. In the dirt,

He falls down.

6.

The woman, who had cried out, "O thou
Art Saul!" and whose life he held in his hand—
She lifts him, gives him to eat.
She feeds him, morsel
By morsel, he like a child.
His jaws move in the labor of grinding by which life is, but
His eyes are in the distance of
Knowledge. He goes

From the cave. But not before
He has cast down the ring, massy of gold, beside her
Who now lies stretched out, eyes closed, face pressed to earth.

She has not stirred. In the silence my voice says:
"Take it, for it
Is of a man who was once a
King." The clink
Of armor, on stone, muted,
From distance and dark outside, comes,
Ceases. "A king," my voice says, "but
Now goes to be

Himself."

7.

I had once poured oil on his head.

It had been in sun-blaze, at
The hour of minimal shadow,
And what shadow fell, fell
Black on stone that swam
White with light.

The cicada was hushed.

He kissed the backs of my hands, rose,
Stood, and was ashamed
Before me, who needs must look upward to his face,
Of his tallness.

The toes of his inordinate sandals
Turned inward somewhat, like
A boy. Of the left foot,
Of the great toe, the nail
Was blackened. Bruised,
In the desert, by stone.

I saw it.

He moved from me in the white light.
The black dwindle in distance which now he
Was, was upheld by
White light as by
A hand. He moved across distance, as across
The broad hand of my knowing.
The palm of my hand was as
Wide as the world and the
Blaze of distance. The fingers
Of my hand itched.

How beautiful are the young, walking!

I closed my eyes. I shuddered in a rage of joy.

8.

The south shoulder of the pass:
And first light, gray, on the right hand,
Came. Not light. Grayness
Not strong enough to cast shadow.

Before redness sudden on east rim, before
The sudden awareness of shadows individual
From eastward, cast by
The random of hunched stones, a stallion,
Far off, neighed, once. I see,
In the shadow of imagination, the beast, dim, large,
Gray as stone. That host
From the shadowy inwardness of which
That brazen *blat* from horn-throat came,
Lower lay, and westwards.

Gilboa is, of that place, the name. There,
With his son whom the sly harpist had loved
With a love surpassing the love of women,
He died. The great torso, a stake
Thrust upward to twist the gut-tangle, towered
Above the wall of Beth-shan, but
With no authority, ha! For the head

Lies at Gilboa. The sky
Is above it, and
The ant has entered
The eye-arch.

9.

The death I have entered is a death
In which I cannot lie down.

I have forgotten, literally, God, and through
The enormous hollow of my head, History
Whistles like a wind.

How beautiful are the young, walking!

If I could weep.

Delight

I. Into Broad Daylight

Out of silence walks delight.
        Delight comes on soundless foot
Into the silence of night,
Or into broad daylight.

Delight comes like surprise.
        Delight will prepare you never.
Delight waits beyond range of your eyes
Till the moment of surprise.

Delight knows its own reason,
        A reason you will never know.
Your will, nor hand, can never seize on
Delight. Delight knows its season.

I have met delight at dawn-crest.
        I have met delight at dove-fall
When sunset reddens the dove's breast.
I may not divulge the rest:

Nor can it be guessed.

II. Love: Two Vignettes

1. Mediterranean Beach, Day after Storm

How instant joy, how clang
And whang the sun, how
Whoop the sea, and oh,
Sun, sing, as whiter than
Rage of snow, let sea the spume
Fling.

Let sea the spume, white, fling,
White on blue wild
With wind, let sun
Sing, while the world
Scuds, clouds boom and belly,
Creak like sails, whiter than,
Brighter than,
Spume in sun-song, oho!
The wind is bright.

*

Wind the heart winds
In constant coil, turning
In the—forever—light.

Give me your hand.

2. Deciduous Spring

Now, now, the world
All gabbles joy like geese, for
An idiot glory the sky
Bangs. Look!
All leaves are new, are
Now, are
Bangles dangling and
Spangling, in sudden air
Wangling, then
Hanging quiet, bright.

The world comes back, and again
Is gabbling, and yes,
Remarkably worse, for
The world is a whirl of
Green mirrors gone wild with
Deceit, and the world
Whirls green on a string, then
The leaves go quiet, wink
From their own shade, secretly.

Keep still, just a moment, leaves.

There is something I am trying to remember.

III. Something is Going to Happen

Something is going to happen, I tell you I know.
This morning, I tell you, I saw ice in the bucket.
Something is going to happen and you can't duck it.
The way the wind blows is the way the dead leaves go.
Something is going to happen, and I'm telling you so.

Something is going to happen, I declare it.
It always happens on days like this, Mother said.
No, I didn't make the world, or make apples red,
But if you're a man you'll buck up and try to bear it.
For this morning the sun rose in the east, I swear it.

*

Something is going to happen, I swear it will.
Men have wept watching water flow,
And feet move fastest down the old track they know.
Look, look!—how light is lying across that hill!
Something may happen today if you don't sit still.

Something is going to happen without a doubt.
If you aren't careful it may happen this very minute.
Have you ever looked in a drawer and found nothing in it?
Have you ever opened your mouth and tried to shout,
But something happened and the shout would not come out?

Something is going to happen whatever you say.
Whether you look out the window or walk in the door
Some things will be less, and other things more.
It's simply no use to turn your head away.
Something is bound to happen on a day like today

To change everything any-which-a-way,
For the sound of your name is only a mouthful of air
And the lost and the found may be found or lost anywhere.
Therefore to prepare you there's one more thing I must say:
Delight may dawn, as the day dawned, calmly, today.

IV. Dream of a Dream the Small Boy Had

All night the small boy kept climbing the tree.
Sleep was the tree. The darkness roared like wind.
Oh, didn't you know that the wind is round, like a ball?
It goes round and round, like going somewhere, but is here.
It goes away and away, but is here, and you hear it.
So I said, *Oh, wind, go away,* and it did, in the dark.

But I didn't know where the wind went, which was bad,
For I was bright-colored like leaves in the blow-away time,
And wind blew me away, I didn't know where, where I was,
And maybe I wasn't, for the colors were gone,
And I dream of the tree in the dark, and no wind,
And the silence swells up to the stars, and the stars
Gasp like fish in a basket, and there is no light, and my bones,
They hang in the tree, shaped like me, and they burn.
Like fireflies or witchwood or foxfire, they shine in the dark,
Or like old kitchen matches gone damp and left in the dark.

Wind has blown me away, all but my bright bones,
Which maybe weren't me to begin with, but only my secret,
And it's awful to have your secret on fire in the dark,
Or maybe there wasn't a secret, just the lie the wind told.
Where I am I don't know now, but hear my own heart

Off somewhere singing. Where? If only I had
My geography book I could do my lesson and find
Where the Andes are and my heart a bird singing.
It must be singing in the high, bright snow, or maybe Asia.

It sings in a foreign language, like pig-latin, or joy.

V. Two Poems About Suddenly and a Rose

1. Dawn

Suddenly. Is. Now not what was *not,*
But what is. From nothing of *not*
Now all of *is.* All is. Is light, and suddenly
Dawn—and the world, in blaze of *is,*
Burns. Is flame, of time and tense
The bold combustion, and
The flame of *is,* in fury
And ungainsayable updraft of that
Black chimney of what is *not,*
Roars. Christmas—

Remember, remember!—and into flame
All those gay wrappings the children fling, then
In hands of *now,* they hold
Presents of *is,* and while
Flame leaps, they, in joy,
Scream. Oh, children,

Now to me sing, I see
Forever on the leaf the light. Snow
On the pine-leaf, against the bright blue
Forever of my mind, like breath,
Balances. Light,

Suddenly, on any morning, is, and somewhere,
In a garden you will never
See, dew, in fracture of light
And lunacy of gleam-glory, glitters on
A petal red as blood, and

The rose dies, laughing.

2. Intuition

Suddenly, suddenly, everything
Happens, it seems. For example, it
Rains—or it does not rain—and suddenly
Life takes on a new dimension, and old pain
Is wisdom—Christ, believe that
And you'll believe anything. But
Everything, some day, is suddenly, and life
Is what you are living, not
What you thought you had lived
All your life, but suddenly
Know you had not—oh, suddenly is what
Mother did not tell, for
How could she when
Suddenly is too sudden to tell, and

The rose dies laughing, suddenly.

VI. Not to Be Trusted

Delight is not to be trusted.
It will betray you.
Delight will undo the work of your hand
In a secret way. You

Cannot trust delight.
As I have told you,
It undoes the ambition of the young and
The wisdom of the old. You

Are not exempt. Though it yet
Has never undone you,
Look! In that bush, with wolf-fang white, delight
Humps now for someone: *You.*

VII. Finisterre

Mist drifts on the bay's face
And the last of day, it would seem, goes under,
But it's hard to tell in this northern place
If this, now, is truly the day's end, or

If, in a new shift of mist,
The light may break through yonder
To stab gold to the gray sea, and twist
Your heart to a last delight—or at least, to wonder.

Incarnations

Poems 1966–1968

To John Palmer

Yet now our flesh is as the flesh of our brethren.
Nehemiah 5:5

John Henry said to the Captain, "A man ain't nuthin but a man."
A Folk Ballad

1. Island of Summer

Island of Summer

I. What Day Is

In Pliny, *Phoenice.* Phoenicians,
Of course. Before that, Celts.
Rome, in the end, as always:
A handful of coins, a late emperor.
Hewn stone, footings for what?
Irrigation, but now not easy
To trace a flume-line.

Later,
Monks, Moors, murderers,
The Mediterranean flotsam, not
Excluding the English, they cut
Down olives, plucked vines up, burnt
The chateau.

All day, cicadas,
At the foot of infinity, like
A tree, saw. The sawdust
Of that incessant effort,
Like filings of brass, sun-brilliant,
Heaps up at the tree-foot. That
Is what day is.

Do not
Look too long at the sea, for
That brightness will rinse out your eyeballs.

They will go gray as dead moons.

II. Where the Slow Fig's Purple Sloth

Where the slow fig's purple sloth
Swells, I sit and meditate the
Nature of the soul, the fig exposes,
To the blaze of afternoon, one haunch
As purple-black as Africa, a single
Leaf the rest screens, but through it, light
Burns, and for the fig's bliss
The sun dies, the sun
Has died forever—far, oh far—
For the fig's bliss, thus.

*

The air
Is motionless, and the fig,
Motionless in that imperial and blunt
Languor of glut, swells, and inward
The fibers relax like a sigh in that
Hot darkness, go soft, the air
Is gold.

When you
Split the fig, you will see
Lifting from the coarse and purple seed, its
Flesh like flame, purer
Than blood.

It fills
The darkening room with light.

III. Natural History

Many have died here, but few
Have names, it is like the world, bodies
Have been eaten by dogs, gulls, rodents, ants,
And fish, and Messire Jean le Maingre,
He struck them, and they fled.

Et les Sarrasins
se retirèrent en une isle qui est devant
le dict chastel—

but little good that, for
The *Maréchal* was hot on them, and

des leurs
y perdirent plus de quatre cent hommes,
que morts, que affolez,

and the root
Of the laurel has profited, the leaf
Of the live-oak achieves a new luster, the mouth
Of the mullet is agape, and my ten-year-old son,
In the island dump, finds a helmet, Nazi—from left
To right, entering at the temple, small and
Perfectly round at the point of entry, neat, but
At egress large, raw, exploding outward, desperate for
Light, air, and openness after
The hot enclosure and intense dark of
That brief transit: this
The track of the missile. Death

Came quick, for history,
Like nature, may have mercy,
Though only by accident. Neither
Has tears.

But at dusk
From the next island, from its pad at
Le centre de recherche d'engins spéciaux, the rocket
Rises, the track of fume now feathers white—spins out, oh whiter—
Rises beyond the earth's shadow, in
Full light aspires. Then,
With no sound, the expected explosion. The glitters
Of flame fall, like shreds of bright foil, ice-bright, from
A Christmas tree, die in earth's shadow, but
The feathers of fume yet hang high, dissolve
White in that last light. The technicians
Now go to dinner.

Beauty
Is the fume-track of necessity. This thought
Is therapeutic.

If, after several
Applications, you do not find
Relief, consult your family physician.

IV. Riddle in the Garden

My mind is intact, but the shapes
of the world change, the peach
has released the bough and at last
makes full confession, its *pudeur*
has departed like peach-fuzz wiped off, and

We now know how the hot sweet-
ness of flesh and the juice-dark hug
the rough peach-pit, we know its most
suicidal yearnings, it wants
to suffer extremely, it

Loves God, and I warn you, do not
touch that plum, it will burn you, a blister
will be on your finger, and you will
put the finger to your lips for relief—oh, do
be careful not to break that soft

*

Gray bulge of fruit-skin of blister, for
exposing that inwardness will
increase your pain, for you
are part of the world. You think
I am speaking in riddles. But I am not, for

The world means only itself.

V. Paul Valéry Stood on the Cliff And Confronted the Furious Energies of Nature

Where dust gritty as
    Hot sand was hurled by
    Sea-wind on the cliff-track
    To burnish the holly-leaf, he

Walked, and white the far sail
    Heeled now to windward, and white
    Cat's-paws up the channel flicked.
    He paused to look, and far down,

Surf, on the Pointe du Cognet,
    Boomed, and clawed white,
    Like vine incessant, up
    That glitter and lattice of air.

Far down, far down, below
    The stone where his foot hung, a gull
    Wheeled white in the flame of
    Air. The white wing scythed

The bright stalks of altitude
    Down, they were cut at the root,
    And the sky keeps falling down,
    Forever it falls down with

A clatter like glass, or delight,
    And his head, like a drum, throbs,
    His eyes, they fly away,
    They scream like gulls, and

Over Africa burn all night,
    But Time is not time, therefore
    His breath stops in his throat
    And he stands on the cliff, his white

*

Panama hat in hand,
For he is Monsieur le Poète,
Paul Valéry is his name,
On a promenade by the sea, so

He sways high against the blue sky,
While in the bright intricacies
Of wind, his mind, like a leaf,
Turns. In the sun, it glitters.

VI. Treasure Hunt

Hunt, hunt again. If you do not find it, you
Will die. But I tell you this much, it
Is not under the stone at the foot
Of the garden, nor by the wall by the fig tree.
I tell you this much to save you trouble, for I
Have looked, I know. But hurry, for

The terror is, all promises are kept.

Even happiness.

VII. Moonrise

The moon, eastward and over
The ridge and rock-blackness, rears.
From the widening throat of the valley,
Light, like a bugle-blast,
Silver, pours at us. We are,
In that silence, stunned.

The faces
Of clients on the café *terrasse*
From shadow lift up. From the shadow
Of sockets, their eyes yearn, and
The faces, in that light, are
Washed white as bone.

Some,
However, have shown more judgment.
They loll in the shadow of laurel.

The air is heavy with blossom.

We wait. We do not even
Know the names of one another.

VIII. Myth on Mediterranean Beach: Aphrodite as Logos

From left to right, she leads the eye
Across the blaze-brightness of sea and sky

That is the background of her transit.

Commanded thus, from left to right,
As by a line of print on that bright

Blankness, the eye will follow, but

There is no line, the eye follows only
That one word moving, it moves in lonely

And absolute arrogance across the blank

Page of the world, the word burns, she is
The word, all faces turn. Look!—this

Is what she is: old hunchback in bikini.

A contraption of angles and bulges, an old
Robot with pince-nez and hair dyed gold,

She heaves along beneath the hump.

The breasts hang down like saddle-bags,
To balance the hump the belly sags,

And under the belly-bulge, the flowers

Of the gee-string garland the private parts.
She grinds along by fits and starts

Beside the margin of the sea,

Past children and sand-castles and
The lovers strewn along the sand.

Her pince-nez glitter like contempt

For all delusion, and the French lad
Who exhibitionistically had

Been fondling the American college girl

Loses his interest. Ignoring him,
The hunchback stares at the horizon rim,

*

Then slowly, as compulsion grows,

She foots the first frail lace of foam
That is the threshold of her lost home,

And moved by memory in the blood,

Enters that vast indifferency
Of perfection that we call the sea.

How long, how long, she lingers there

She may not know, somnambulist
In that realm where no Time may subsist,

But in the end will again feel

The need to rise and re-enact
The miracle of the human fact.

She lifts her head, looks toward the shore.

She moves toward us, abstract and slow,
And watching, we feel the slow knowledge grow—

How from the breasts the sea recedes,

How the great-gashed navel's cup
Pours forth the ichor that had filled it up,

How the wavelets sink to seek, and seek,

Then languishing, sink to lave the knees,
And lower, to kiss the feet, as these

Find the firm ground where they must go.

The last foam crisps about the feet.
She shivers, smiles. She stands complete

In Botticellian parody.

Bearing her luck upon her back,
She turns now to take the lifeward track,

And lover by lover, on she moves

Toward her own truth, and does not stop.
Each foot stumps flat with the big toe up,

But under the heel, the damp-packed sand,

*

With that compression, like glory glows,
And glory attends her as she goes.

In rapture now she heaves along,

The pince-nez glitter at her eyes,
The flowers wreathe her moving thighs,

For she treads the track the blessèd know

To a shore far lonelier than this
Where waits her apotheosis.

She passes the lovers, one by one,

And passing, draws their dreams away,
And leaves them naked to the day.

IX. Mistral at Night

Heat, and cold curdle of wind-thrust, moonlight
To tatters torn, on night-blue the tetter
Of cloud-scud, and in shadow
Of laurel the clash of the dry leaf: and that,
In the moment of long remission when
But a single gust stirs, is
In your sleep, and is as
Unforgettable as what is most deeply
Forgotten—and that, oh,
Will be the last thing remembered, at last, in
That instant before remembering is over. But what
Is it? You must wait

To find out. Hold your breath, count to ten. The world
Is like wind, and the leaves clash. This knowledge
Is the beginning of joy. I

Tell you this as explicitly as I can, for
Some day you may find the information
Of crucial importance.

X. The Ivy

The ivy assaults the wall. The ivy
says: "I will pull you down." Time
is nothing to the ivy. The ivy

Does not sweat at night, for like the sea
it dreams a single dream, it
is its own dream. Therefore,

Peace is the dream's name. The wall
is stone, and all night the stone,
where no stars may come, dreams.

Night comes. You sleep. What is your dream?

XI. Where Purples Now the Fig

Where purples now the fig, flame in
Its inmost flesh, a leaf hangs
Down, and on it, gull-droppings, white
As chalk, show, for the sun has

Burned all white, for the sun, it would
Burn our bones to chalk—yes, keep
Them covered, oh flesh, oh sweet
Integument, oh frail, depart not

And leave me thus exposed, like Truth.

XII. The Red Mullet

The fig flames inward on the bough, and I,
Deep where the great mullet, red, lounges in
Black shadow of the shoal, have come. Where no light may

Come, he the great one, like flame, burns, and I
Have met him, eye to eye, the lower jaw horn,
Outthrust, arched down at the corners, merciless as

Genghis, motionless and mogul, and the eye of
The mullet is round, bulging, ringed like a target
In gold, vision is armor, he sees and does not

Forgive. The mullet has looked me in the eye, and forgiven
Nothing. At night I fear suffocation, is there
Enough air in the world for us all, therefore I

*

Swim much, dive deep to develop my lung-case, I am
Familiar with the agony of will in the deep place. Blood
Thickens as oxygen fails. Oh, mullet, thy flame

Burns in the shadow of the black shoal.

XIII. A Place Where Nothing Is

I have been in a place where
nothing is, it is not
silence, for there are voices, not
emptiness, for there is
a great fullness, it is
populated with nothingness, nothing-
ness presses on the ribs like
elbows angry, and the lump
of nothingness sticks
in the throat like the hard
phlegm, and if, in that dark,
you cough, there is, in that
land of nothingness, no
echo, for the dark has
no walls, or if there is echo,
it is, whatever the original
sound, a laugh. A lamp
by each bed burns, but
gives no light.

Earlier,
I have warned you not to look
too long at the brightness of
the sea, but now—yes—
I retract my words, for
the brightness of that nothing-
ness which is the sea is
not nothingness, but is
like the inestimable sea of

Nothingness Plotinus dreamed.

XIV. Masts at Dawn

Past second cock-crow yacht masts in the harbor go slowly white.

No light in the east yet, but the stars show a certain fatigue.
They withdraw into a new distance, have discovered our unworthiness. It is long since

The owl, in the dark eucalyptus, dire and melodious, last called, and

Long since the moon sank and the English
Finished fornicating in their ketches. In the evening there was a strong swell.

Red died the sun, but at dark wind rose easterly, white sea nagged the black harbor headland.

When there is a strong swell, you may, if you surrender to it, experience
A sense, in the act, of mystic unity with that rhythm. Your peace is the sea's will.

But now no motion, the bay-face is glossy in darkness, like

An old window pane flat on black ground by the wall, near the ash heap. It neither
Receives nor gives light. Now is the hour when the sea

Sinks into meditation. It doubts its own mission. The drowned cat

That on the evening swell had kept nudging the piles of the pier and had seemed
To want to climb out and lick itself dry, now floats free. On that surface a slight convexity only, it is like

An eyelid, in darkness, closed. You must learn to accept the kiss of fate, for

The masts go white slow, as light, like dew, from darkness
Condenses on them, on oiled wood, on metal. Dew whitens in darkness.

I lie in my bed and think how, in darkness, the masts go white.

The sound of the engine of the first fishing dory dies seaward. Soon
In the inland glen wakes the dawn-dove. We must try

To love so well the world that we may believe, in the end, in God.

XV. The Leaf

[A]

Here the fig lets down the leaf, the leaf
Of the fig five fingers has, the fingers
Are broad, spatulate, stupid,
Ill-formed, and innocent—but of a hand, and the hand,

To hide me from the blaze of the wide world, drops,
Shamefast, down. I am
What is to be concealed. I lurk
In the shadow of the fig. Stop.
Go no further. This is the place.

To this spot I bring my grief.
Human grief is the obscenity to be hidden by the leaf.

[B]

We have undergone ourselves, therefore
What more is to be done for Truth's sake? I

Have watched the deployment of ants, I
Have conferred with the flaming mullet in a deep place.

Near the nesting place of the hawk, among
Snag-rock, high on the cliff, I have seen
The clutter of annual bones, of hare, vole, bird, white
As chalk from sun and season, frail
As the dry grass stem. On that

High place of stone I have lain down, the sun
Beat, the small exacerbation
Of dry bones was what my back, shirtless and bare, knew. I saw

The hawk shudder in the high sky, he shudders
To hold position in the blazing wind, in relation to
The firmament, he shudders and the world is a metaphor, his eye
Sees, white, the flicker of hare-scut, the movement of vole.

Distance is nothing, there is no solution, I
Have opened my mouth to the wind of the world like wine, I wanted
To taste what the world is, wind dried up

The live saliva of my tongue, my tongue
Was like a dry leaf in my mouth.

Destiny is what you experience, that
Is its name and definition, and is your name, for

The wide world lets down the hand in shame:
Here is the human shadow, there, of the wide world, the flame.

[C]

The world is fruitful. In this heat
The plum, black yet bough-bound, bursts, and the gold ooze is,
Of bees, joy, the gold ooze has striven
Outward, it wants again to be of
The goldness of air and—oh—innocent. The grape
Weakens at the juncture of the stem. The world

Is fruitful, and I, too,
In that I am the father
Of my father's father's father. I,
Of my father, have set the teeth on edge. But
By what grape? I have cried out in the night.

From a further garden, from the shade of another tree,
My father's voice, in the moment when the cicada ceases, has called to me.

[D]

The voice blesses me for the only
Gift I have given: *teeth set on edge.*

In the momentary silence of the cicada,
I can hear the appalling speed,
In space beyond stars, of
Light. It is

A sound like wind.

2. Internal Injuries

Penological Study: Southern Exposure

To Brainard and Frances Cheney

I. Keep That Morphine Moving, Cap

Oh, in the pen, oh, in the pen,
The cans, they have no doors, therefore
I saw him, head bent in that primordial
Prayer, head grizzled, and the sweat,
To the gray cement, dropped. It dripped,
And each drop glittered as it fell,
For in the pen, oh, in the pen,
The cans, they have no doors.

Each drop upon that gray cement
Exploded like a star, and the Warden,
I heard the Warden saying, "Jake—
You know we're pulling for you, Jake,"
And I saw that face lift and explode
In whiteness like a star, for oh!—
Oh, in the pen, yes, in the pen,
The cans, they have no doors.

A black hole opened in that white
That was the star-exploding face,
And words came out, the words came out,
"Jest keep that morphine moving, Cap,
And me, I'll tough it through,"
Who had toughed it through nigh forty years,
And couldn't now remember why
He had cut her throat that night, and so
Come to the pen, here to the pen,
Where cans, they have no doors,

And where he sits, while deep inside,
Inside his gut, inside his gut,
The pumpkin grows and grows, and only
In such a posture humped, can he
Hold tight his gut, and half believe,
Like you or me, like you or me,
That the truth will not be true.—Oh, Warden,

*

Keep that morphine moving, for
All night beneath that blazing bulb,
Bright drop by drop, from the soaked hair, sweat
Drips, and each drop, on the gray cement,
Explodes like a star. Listen to that
Small sound, and let us, too, keep pulling
For him, like we all ought to, who,
When truth at last is true, must try,
Like him, to tough it through—but oh!—
Not in the pen, not in the pen,
Where cans, they have no doors.

II. Tomorrow Morning

In the morning the rivers will blaze up blue like sulphur.
Even the maps will shrivel black in their own heat,
And metaphors will scream in the shared glory of their referents.
Truth will embrace you with tentacles like an octopus. It
Will suck your blood through a thousand suction-cups, and
The sun utter the intolerable trill of a flame-martyred canary.

Does this suggest the beginning of a new life for us all?

Or is it only, as I have heard an eminent physician remark,
A characteristic phase at the threshold of the final narcosis?

III. Wet Hair: If Now His Mother Should Come

If out of a dire suspicion
She hadn't touched his hair and
Found it yet damp at the roots, she might
Have forgiven the fact he was late,
With supper near over now, and the lamp

On the table already lighted, and shadows
Bigger than people and blacker than niggers swinging
On the board walls of the kitchen, one kid,
The youngest, already asleep,
The head at the edge of
The plate, and tighter than glue
In that hot night, one cheek
To the checked oil-cloth table cover, and grease
Gone gray on the forks—yes, if

*

She hadn't then touched his hair,
She might never have guessed how he'd been in
That durn creek again, and then lied,
And so might never have fetched him that
Awful whack. His face

In the lamplight was white. She

Stood there and heard how,
Maniacal and incessant,
Out in the dark, the
Insects of summer tore
The night to shreds. She
Stood there and tried to think she
Was somebody else. But
Wasn't, so

Put him to bed without supper.

What if tonight when
Again the insects of summer
Are tearing the night to shreds, she
Should come to this room where under the blazing
Bulb, sweat drips, and each drop,
On that gray cement, explodes like
A star? What if she
Should touch his head and now
Find the hair wetter than ever?

I do not think that now she
Would fetch him that awful
Whack—even if

Again he had come late to supper,
Then lied, to boot.

IV. Night: The Motel Down the Road From the Pen

Now in the cheap motel, I lie, and
Belly-up, the dead catfish slides
All night glimmering down the river
That is black and glossy as
Old oil bleeding soundlessly
From the crank-case. Look! the stars

Are there, they shine, and the river
Knows their white names as it flows,
And white in starlight the white belly
Glimmers down the magisterial
Moving night the river is.

*

In this motel, I lie and sweat.
It is summer, it is summer.

The river moves. It does not stop.
It, like night, is going somewhere.

It is going, somewhere.

V. Where They Come to Wait for the Body: A Ghost Story

This is the cheap motel where
They come to wait for the body if they
Are white, and have three dollars to spare,

Which is tough if you had to scrape up to pay
Private for the undertaker because you
Hope he'll make things look better some way,

But won't, for with twenty-three hundred volts gone through,
The customer's not John Barrymore,
And the face he's got will just have to do

Him on out, so load the finished product and go, for
You've long since done with your crying, and now
It's like it all happened long back, or

To somebody else. But referring to Jake, how
Could they schedule delivery, it might be next week,
Or might, if things broke right, be even tomorrow,

But who gives a damn how the cheese, so to speak,
Gets sliced, for nobody's waiting to haul
Jake back to any home cross-roads or creek,

And there's nobody here, nobody at all,
Who knows his name even, but me, and I know
Only the Jake part, but I've got a call

In for five A.M., for I'm due to blow
At half-past, but if he'd be checked out and ready,
If that's not too early for him, he can go

With me, and we roll, and his eyes stare moody
Down a road all different from the last time he passed,
And the new slab whirls at him white now and steady,

*

And what he might recognize snaps by so fast
That hill and stream and field all blur
To a misty glitter, till at last

He shifts on his hams and his stiff hands stir
On his knees, and he says: "That bluff—thar 'tis!
Jest let me off thar, thank you kindly, sir."

And so he drops off at the creek where that bluff is,
And the shadow of woods spills down to the bone-
White slab, and with back to the screech and whizz

Of the traffic, he stands, like he was alone
And noise no different from silence, his face set
Woodsward and hillsward, then sudden, he's gone,

And me, I'm gone too, as I flog the U-Drive-It
Toward Nashville, where faces of friends, some dead, gleam,
And where, when the time comes, you grab the jet.

VI. Night Is Personal

Night is personal. Day is public. Day
Is like a pair of pants you can buy anywhere, and do.

When you are through with day you hang it up like pants on
The back of a chair, and it glows all night in the motel room, but not

Enough to keep you awake. Jake is awake. Oh, Warden,
Keep that morphine moving, for we are all

One flesh, and back in your office, in the dark, the telephone
Is thinking up something to say, it is going to say

It does not love you, for night is each man's legend, and there is no joy
Without some pain. Jake is meditating his joy. He sweats. Oh, Warden,

Keep that morphine moving, for I feel something
Soft as feathers whispering in me, and

Corpuscles grind in your own blood-stream, like gravel
In a freshet, and by this sign know that a congress

Of comets will be convened screaming, they will comb their
Long hair with blue fingers cold as ice, their tears are precious, therefore

My head explodes with flowers like a gangster's funeral, but all this racket won't
Matter, for Jake is awake anyway. Oh, Warden, keep that morphine moving, for

*

When you get home tonight your wife will be weeping. She
Will not know why, for in the multiple eye of the spider, the world bleeds

Many times over, the spider is hairy like a Jewish Jesus, it is soft like a peach
Mercilessly bruised, you have tasted the blood of the spider, and

It smiles, it knows. Jake is awake. Oh, Warden,
Keep that morphine moving, for your father is not really dead, he

Is trying to get out of that box he thinks you put him in, and on the floor by
your bed, in the dark,
Your old dog, like conscience, sighs, the tail feebly thumps, it wants

To be friends again, it will forgive you even if now you
Do take it to the vet, for now is the time, it has suffered enough. Oh, Warden,

Keep that morphine moving, for we've had a frightful summer, sweat
Stings my eyes, salt pills do no good, forest fires rage at night in the mountains.
Warden,

Things have got to change around here. Jake's case is simply
One of many. An investigation is coming, I warn you. And anyway,

Night is personal, night is personal. There are many nights, Warden,
And you have no reason to think that you are above the Law.

VII. Dawn

Owl, owl, stop calling from the swamp, let
Old orange peel and condoms and
That dead catfish, belly white, and
Whitely, whitely, the shed petals
Of catalpa—let all, all,
Slide whitely down the sliding darkness
That the river is, let stars
Dip dawnward down the un-owled air, and sweat
Dry on the sheet.

But
Stars now assume the last brightness, it
Is not yet dawn. Dawn will, it
Is logical to postulate, though not
Certain, come, and the sun then,
Above the horizon, burst
Like a blast of buckshot through
A stained-glass window, for

It is summer, it is summer.

*

Forgive us, this day, our joy.

Far off, a red tractor is crossing the black field.
Iron crushes the last dawn-tangle of ground mist.

Forgive us—oh, give us!—our joy.

Internal Injuries

I. The Event

Nigger: as if it were not
Enough to be old, and a woman, to be
Poor, having a sizeable hole (as
I can plainly see, you being flat on the ground) in
The sole of a shoe (the right one), enough to be

Alone (your daughter off in
Detroit, in three years no letter, your son
Upriver, at least now you know
Where he is, and no friends), enough to be

Fired (as you have just today
Been, and unfair to boot, for
That durn Jew-lady—there wasn't no way
To know it was you that opened that there durn
Purse, just picking on you on account of
Your complexion), enough to be

Yourself (yes, after sixty-eight
Years, just to have to be
What you are, yeah, look
In the mirror, that
Is you, and when did you
Pray last), enough to be,

Merely to be—Jesus,
Wouldn't just *being* be enough without
Having to have the pee (quite
Literally) knocked out of
You by a 1957 yellow Cadillac driven by
A spic, and him
From New Jersey?

Why couldn't it of at least been a white man?

II. The Scream

The scream comes as regular
As a metronome. Twelve beats
For period of scream, twelve
For period of non-scream, there
Must be some sort of clockwork
Inside you to account for such
Perfection, perhaps you have always
And altogether been clockwork, but
Not realizing its perfection, I
Had thought you merely human.

I apologize for the error, but
It was, under the circumstances,
Only natural.

Pneumatic hammers
Are at work somewhere. In the period
Of non-scream, they seem merely a part of the silence.

III. Her Hat

They are tearing down Penn Station,
Through which joy and sorrow passed,

But against the bright blue May-sky,
In the dazzle and sun-blast,

I can see one cornice swimming
High above the hoarding where

Sidewalk superintendents turn now
From their duties and at you stare,

While I, sitting in my taxi,
Watch them watching you, for I,

Ashamed of their insensitiveness,
Am no Peeping Tom with my

Own face pressed directly to the
Window of your pain to peer

Deep in your inward darkness, waiting,
With slack-jawed and spit-wet leer,

For what darkling gleam, and spasm,
Visceral and pure, like love.

*

Look! your hat's right under a truck wheel.
It's lucky traffic can't yet move.

Somewhere—oh, somewhere above the city—a jet is prowling the sky.

IV. The Only Trouble

The only trouble was, you got up
This morning on the wrong side of the bed, and of
Your life. First, you put the wrong shoe on the right
Foot, or vice versa, and next
You quarreled with your husband. No—
You merely remembered a quarrel you had with him before he
Up and died, or did he merely blow, and never
Was rightly your husband, nohow.

                                        Defect of attention
Is defect of character, and now
The scream floats up, and up, like a
Soap bubble, it is enormous, it glitters
Above the city, it is as big as the city,
And on its bottom side all the city is
Accurately reflected, making allowance
For curvature, upside-down, iridescent as
A dream, oh pale!

                              If children were here now,
They would clap their hands for joy.

                                        But,
No matter, for in stunning soundlessness, it
Explodes, and over the city a bright mist
Descends of—microscopically—spit.

V. The Jet Must Be Hunting for Something

One cop holds the spic delicately between thumb and forefinger.
It is as though he did not want to get a white glove dirty.

The jet prowls the sky and Penn Station looks bombed-out.

The spic has blood over one eye. He had tried to run away.
He will not try again, and in that knowledge, his face is as calm as congealing
        bacon grease.

Three construction workers come out from behind the hoarding.

*

The two cops are not even talking to each other, and in spite of
The disturbance you are so metronomically creating, ignore you. They are doing their duty.

The jet prowls. I do not know what it is hunting for.

The three construction workers are looking at you like a technical
Problem. I look at them. One looks at his watch. For everything there is a season.

How long since last I heard birdsong in the flowery hedgerows of France?

Just now, when I looked at you, I had the distinct impression that you were staring me straight in the eye, and
Who wants to be a piece of white paper filed for eternity on the sharp point of a filing spindle?

The orange-colored helmets of the construction workers bloom brilliant as zinnias.

When you were a child in Georgia, a lard-can of zinnias bloomed by the little cabin door.
Your mother had planted them in the lard-can. People call zinnias nigger-flowers.

Nobody wants to be a piece of white paper filed in the dark on the point of a black-enameled spindle forever.

The jet is so far off there is no sound, not even the sizzle it makes as it sears the utmost edges of air.
It prowls the edge of distance like the raw edge of experience. Oh, reality!

I do not know what the jet is hunting for. It must be hunting for something.

VI. Be Something Else

Be something else, be something
That is not what it is, for
Being what it is, it is
Too absolute to be.

If you insist on being
What you are, how can we
Ever love you, we
Cannot love what is—

By which I mean a thing that
Totally is and therefore
Is absolute, for we
Know that the absolute is

*

Delusion, and that Truth lives
    Only in relation—oh!
    We love you, we truly
    Do, and we love the

World, but we know
    We cannot love others unless
    We learn how to love
    Ourselves properly, and we truly

Want to love you, but

For God's sake stop that yelling!

VII. The World Is a Parable

I must hurry, I must go somewhere
Where you are not, where you
Will never be, I
Must go somewhere where
Nothing is real, for only
Nothingness is real and is
A sea of light. The world
Is a parable and we are
The meaning. The traffic
Begins to move, and meaning
In my guts blooms like
A begonia, I dare not
Pronounce its name. —Oh, driver!
For God's sake catch that light, for

There comes a time for us all when we want to begin a new life.

All mythologies recognize that fact.

VIII. Driver, Driver

Driver, driver, hurry now—
Yes, driver, listen now, I
Must change the address, I want to go to

A place where nothing is the same.
My guts are full of chyme and chyle, of Time and bile, my head
Of visions, I do not even know what the pancreas is for, what,

*

Driver, driver, is it for?
Tell me, driver, tell me true, for
The traffic begins to move, and that fool ambulance at last,

Screaming, screaming, now arrives.
Jack-hammers are trying, trying, they
Are trying to tell me something, they speak in code.

Driver, do you know the code?
Tat-tat-tat— my head is full of
The code, like Truth or a migraine, and those men in orange helmets,

They must know it, they must know,
For *tat-tat,* they make the hammers go, and
So must know the message, know the secret names and all the slithery
functions of

All those fat slick slimy things that
Are so like a tub full of those things you
Would find in a vat in the back room of a butcher shop, but wouldn't eat, but

Are not that, for they are you.
Driver, do you truly, truly,
Know what flesh is, and if it is, as some people say, really sacred?

Driver, there's an awful glitter in the air. What is the weather forecast?

3. Enclaves

In the Mountains

To Baudouin and Annie de Moustier

I. Skiers

With the motion of angels, out of
Snow-spume and swirl of gold mist, they
Emerge to the positive sun. At
That great height, small on that whiteness,
With the color of birds or of angels,
They swoop, sway, descend, and descending,
Cry their bright bird-cries, pure
In the sweet desolation of distance.
They slowly enlarge to our eyes. Now

On the flat where the whiteness is
Trodden and mud-streaked, not birds now,
Nor angels even, they stand. They

Are awkward, not yet well adjusted
To this world, new and strange, of Time and
Contingency, who now are only
Human. They smile. The human

Face has its own beauty.

II. Fog

[A]

White, white, luminous but
Blind—fog on the
Mountain, and the mountains

Gone, they are not here,
And the sky gone. My foot
Is set on what I

Do not see. Light rises
From the cold incandescence of snow
Not seen, and the world, in blindness,

Glows. Distance is
Obscenity. All, all
Is here, no other where.

The heart, in this silence, beats.

[B]

Heart—oh, contextless—how
Can you, hung in this
Blank mufflement of white

Brightness, now know
What you are? Fog,
At my knees, coils, my nostrils

Receive the luminous blindness,
And deeper, deeper, it, with the
Cold gleam of fox-fire among

The intricate secrets of
The lungs, enters, an eye
Screams in the belly. The eye

Sees the substance of body dissolving.

[C]

At fog-height, unseen,
A crow calls, the call,
On the hem of silence, is only

A tatter of cold contempt, then
Is gone. Yes, try to remember
An act that once you thought worthy.

The body's brags are put
To sleep—all, all. What
Is the locus of the soul?

What, in such absoluteness,
Can be prayed for? Oh, crow,
Come back, I would hear your voice:

That much, at least, in this whiteness.

Audubon: A Vision

To Allen and Helen Tate

Thou tellest my wanderings: put thou my tears into thy bottle: are they not in thy book?

Psalm 56:8

I caught at his strict shadow and the shadow
released itself with neither haste nor anger. But
he remained silent.

Carlos Drummond de Andrade:
"Travelling in the Family"
Translated by Elizabeth Bishop

Jean Jacques Audubon, whose name was anglicized when, in his youth, he was sent to America, was early instructed in the official version of his identity: that he was the son of the sea captain Jean Audubon and a first wife, who died shortly after his birth in Santo Domingo, and that the woman who brought him up in France was a second wife. Actually, he was the son of Jean Audubon and his mistress during the period when Jean Audubon was a merchant and slave-dealer in Santo Domingo, and the woman who raised him was the wife his father had left behind him in France while he was off making his fortune. By the age of ten Audubon knew the true story, but prompted, it would seem, by a variety of impulses, including some sound practical ones, he encouraged the other version, along with a number of flattering embellishments. He was, indeed, a fantasist of talent, but even without his help legends accreted about him. The most famous one—that he was the lost Dauphin of France, the son of the feckless Louis XVI and Marie Antoinette—did not, in fact, enter the picture until after his death, in 1851.

Audubon: A Vision

I. Was Not the Lost Dauphin

[A]

Was not the lost dauphin, though handsome was only
Base-born and not even able
To make a decent living, was only
Himself, Jean Jacques, and his passion—what
Is man but his passion?

Saw,
Eastward and over the cypress swamp, the dawn,
Redder than meat, break;
And the large bird,
Long neck outthrust, wings crooked to scull air, moved
In a slow calligraphy, crank, flat, and black against
The color of God's blood spilt, as though
Pulled by a string.

Saw
It proceed across the inflamed distance.

Moccasins set in hoar frost, eyes fixed on the bird,
Thought: "On that sky it is black."
Thought: "In my mind it is white."
Thinking: "*Ardea occidentalis,* heron, the great one."

Dawn: his heart shook in the tension of the world.

Dawn: and what is your passion?

[B]

October: and the bear,
Daft in the honey-light, yawns.

The bear's tongue, pink as a baby's, out-crisps to the curled tip,
It bleeds the black blood of the blueberry.

The teeth are more importantly white
Than has ever been imagined.

The bear feels his own fat
Sweeten, like a drowse, deep to the bone.

Bemused, above the fume of ruined blueberries,
The last bee hums.

*

The wings, like mica, glint
In the sunlight.

He leans on his gun. Thinks
How thin is the membrane between himself and the world.

II. The Dream He Never Knew the End Of

[A]

Shank-end of day, spit of snow, the call,
A crow, sweet in distance, then sudden
The clearing: among stumps, ruined cornstalks yet standing, the spot
Like a wound rubbed raw in the vast pelt of the forest. There
Is the cabin, a huddle of logs with no calculation or craft:
The human filth, the human hope.

Smoke,
From the mud-and-stick chimney, in that air, greasily
Brims, cannot lift, bellies the ridgepole, ravels
White, thin, down the shakes, like sputum.

He stands,
Leans on his gun, stares at the smoke, thinks: "Punk-wood."
Thinks: "Dead-fall half-rotten." Too sloven,
That is, to even set axe to clean wood.

His foot,
On the trod mire by the door, crackles
The night-ice already there forming. His hand
Lifts, hangs. In imagination, his nostrils already
Know the stench of that lair beyond
The door-puncheons. The dog
Presses its head against his knee. The hand
Strikes wood. No answer. He halloos. Then the voice.

[B]

What should he recognize? The nameless face
In the dream of some pre-dawn cock-crow—about to say what,
Do what? The dregs
Of all nightmare are the same, and we call it
Life. He knows that much, being a man,
And knows that the dregs of all life are nightmare.

Unless.

Unless what?

[C]

The face, in the air, hangs. Large,
Raw-hewn, strong-beaked, the haired mole
Near the nose, to the left, and the left side by firelight
Glazed red, the right in shadow, and under the tumble and tangle
Of dark hair on that head, and under the coarse eyebrows,
The eyes, dark, glint as from the unspecifiable
Darkness of a cave. It is a woman.

She is tall, taller than he.
Against the gray skirt, her hands hang.

"Ye wants to spend the night? Kin ye pay?
Well, mought as well stay then, done got one a-ready,
And leastwise, ye don't stink like no Injun."

[D]

The Indian,
Hunched by the hearth, lifts his head, looks up, but
From one eye only, the other
An aperture below which blood and mucus hang, thickening slow.

"Yeah, a arrow jounced back off his bowstring.
Durn fool—and him a Injun." She laughs.

The Indian's head sinks.
So he turns, drops his pack in a corner on bearskin, props
The gun there. Comes back to the fire. Takes his watch out.
Draws it bright, on the thong-loop, from under his hunter's-frock.
It is gold, it lives in his hand in the firelight, and the woman's
Hand reaches out. She wants it. She hangs it about her neck.

And near it the great hands hover delicately
As though it might fall, they quiver like moth-wings, her eyes
Are fixed downward, as though in shyness, on that gleam, and her face
Is sweet in an outrage of sweetness, so that
His gut twists cold. He cannot bear what he sees.

Her body sways like a willow in spring wind. Like a girl.

The time comes to take back the watch. He takes it.
And as she, sullen and sunken, fixes the food, he becomes aware
That the live eye of the Indian is secretly on him, and soundlessly
The lips move, and when her back is turned, the Indian
Draws a finger, in delicious retardation, across his own throat.

*

After food, and scraps for his dog, he lies down:
In the corner, on bearskins, which are not well cured,
And stink, the gun by his side, primed and cocked.

Under his hand he feels the breathing of the dog.

The woman hulks by the fire. He hears the jug slosh.

[E]

The sons come in from the night, two, and are
The sons she would have. Through slit lids
He watches. Thinks: "Now."

The sons
Hunker down by the fire, block the firelight, cram food
Into their large mouths, where teeth
Grind in the hot darkness, their breathing
Is heavy like sleep, he wants to sleep, but
The head of the woman leans at them. The heads
Are together in firelight.

He hears the jug slosh.

Then hears,
Like the whisper and *whish* of silk, that other
Sound, like a sound of sleep, but he does not
Know what it is. Then knows, for,
Against firelight, he sees the face of the woman
Lean over, and the lips purse sweet as to bestow a kiss, but
This is not true, and the great glob of spit
Hangs there, glittering, before she lets it fall.

The spit is what softens like silk the passage of steel
On the fine-grained stone. It whispers.

When she rises, she will hold it in her hand.

[F]

With no sound, she rises. She holds it in her hand.
Behind her the sons rise like shadow. The Indian
Snores.

He thinks: "Now."

And knows
He has entered the tale, knows
He has entered the dark hovel
In the forest where trees have eyes, knows it is the tale
They told him when he was a child, knows it
Is the dream he had in childhood but never
Knew the end of, only
The scream.

[G]

But no scream now, and under his hand
The dog lies taut, waiting. And he, too, knows
What he must do, do soon, and therefore
Does not understand why now a lassitude
Sweetens his limbs, or why, even in this moment
Of fear—or is it fear?—the saliva
In his mouth tastes sweet.

"Now, now!" the voice in his head cries out, but
Everything seems far away, and small.

He cannot think what guilt unmans him, or
Why he should find the punishment so precious.

It is too late. Oh, oh, the world!

Tell me the name of the world.

[H]

The door bursts open, and the travelers enter:
Three men, alert, strong, armed. And the Indian
Is on his feet, pointing.

He thinks
That now he will never know the dream's ending.

[I]

Trussed up with thongs, all night they lie on the floor there.
The woman is gagged, for she had reviled them.
All night he hears the woman's difficult breath.

Dawn comes. It is gray. When he eats,
The cold corn pone grinds in his throat, like sand. It sticks there.

Even whiskey fails to remove it. It sticks there.

The leg-thongs are cut off the tied-ones. They are made to stand up.
The woman refuses the whiskey. Says: "What fer?"
The first son drinks. The other
Takes it into his mouth, but it will not go down.

The liquid drains, slow, from the slack side of the mouth.

[J]

They stand there under the long, low bough of the great oak.
Eastward, low over the forest, the sun is nothing
But a circular blur of no irradiation, somewhat paler
Than the general grayness. Their legs
Are again bound with thongs.

They are asked if they want to pray now. But the woman:
"If'n it's God made folks, then who's to pray to?"
And then: "Or fer?" And bursts into laughing.

For a time it seems that she can never stop laughing.

But as for the sons, one prays, or tries to. And one
Merely blubbers. If the woman
Gives either a look, it is not
Pity, nor even contempt, only distance. She waits,

And is what she is,

And in the gray light of morning, he sees her face. Under
The tumbled darkness of hair, the face
Is white. Out of that whiteness
The dark eyes stare at nothing, or at
The nothingness that the gray sky, like Time, is, for
There is no Time, and the face
Is, he suddenly sees, beautiful as stone, and

So becomes aware that he is in the manly state.

[K]

The affair was not tidy: bough low, no drop, with the clients
Simply hung up, feet not much clear of the ground, but not
Quite close enough to permit any dancing.
The affair was not quick: both sons long jerking and farting, but she,
From the first, without motion, frozen
In a rage of will, an ecstasy of iron, as though
This was the dream that, lifelong, she had dreamed toward.

The face,
Eyes a-glare, jaws clenched, now glowing black with congestion
Like a plum, had achieved,
It seemed to him, a new dimension of beauty.

[L]

There are tears in his eyes.
He tries to remember his childhood.
He tries to remember his wife.
He can remember nothing.

His throat is parched. His right hand,
Under the deerskin frock, has been clutching the gold watch.

The magic of that object had been,
In the secret order of the world, denied her who now hangs there.

He thinks: "What has been denied me?"
Thinks: "There is never an answer."

Thinks: "The question is the only answer."

He yearns to be able to frame a definition of joy.

[M]

And so stood alone, for the travelers
Had disappeared into the forest and into
Whatever selves they were, and the Indian,
Now bearing the gift of a gun that had belonged to the hanged-ones,
Was long since gone, like smoke fading into the forest,
And below the blank and unforgiving eye-hole
The blood and mucus had long since dried.

He thought: "I must go."

*

But could not, staring
At the face, and stood for a time even after
The first snowflakes, in idiotic benignity,
Had fallen. Far off, in the forest and falling snow,
A crow was calling.

So stirs, knowing now
He will not be here when snow
Drifts into the open door of the cabin, or,
Descending the chimney, mantles thinly
Dead ashes on the hearth, nor when snow thatches
These heads with white, like wisdom, nor ever will he
Hear the infinitesimal stridor of the frozen rope
As wind shifts its burden, or when

The weight of the crow first comes to rest on a rigid shoulder.

III. We Are Only Ourselves

We never know what we have lost, or what we have found.
We are only ourselves, and that promise.
Continue to walk in the world. Yes, love it!

He continued to walk in the world.

IV. The Sign Whereby He Knew

[A]

His life, at the end, seemed—even the anguish—simple.
Simple, at least, in that it had to be,
Simply, what it was, as he was,
In the end, himself and not what
He had known he ought to be. The blessedness!—

To wake in some dawn and see,
As though down a rifle barrel, lined up
Like sights, the self that was, the self that is, and there,
Far off but in range, completing that alignment, your fate.

Hold your breath, let the trigger-squeeze be slow and steady.

The quarry lifts, in the halo of gold leaves, its noble head.

This is not a dimension of Time.

[B]

In this season the waters shrink.

The spring is circular and surrounded by gold leaves
Which are fallen from the beech tree.

Not even a skitter-bug disturbs the gloss
Of the surface tension. The sky

Is reflected below in absolute clarity.
If you stare into the water you may know

That nothing disturbs the infinite blue of the sky.

[C]

Keep store, dandle babies, and at night nuzzle
The hazelnut-shaped sweet tits of Lucy, and
With the piratical mark-up of the frontier, get rich.

But you did not, being of weak character.

You saw, from the forest pond, already dark, the great trumpeter swan
Rise, in clangor, and fight up the steep air where,
In the height of last light, it glimmered, like white flame.

The definition of love being, as we know, complex,
We may say that he, after all, loved his wife.

The letter, from campfire, keelboat, or slum room in New Orleans,
Always ended, "God bless you, dear Lucy." After sunset,

Alone, he played his flute in the forest.

[D]

Listen! Stand very still and,
Far off, where shadow
Is undappled, you may hear

The tushed boar grumble in his ivy-slick.

Afterward, there is silence until
The jay, sudden as conscience, calls.

The call, in the infinite sunlight, is like
The thrill of the taste of—on the tongue—brass.

[E]

The world declares itself. That voice
Is vaulted in—oh, arch on arch—redundancy of joy, its end
Is its beginning, necessity
Blooms like a rose. Why,

Therefore, is truth the only thing that cannot
Be spoken?

It can only be enacted, and that in dream,
Or in the dream become, as though unconsciously, action, and he stood,

At dusk, in the street of the raw settlement, and saw
The first lamp lit behind a window, and did not know
What he was. Thought: "I do not know my own name."

He walked in the world. He was sometimes seen to stand
In perfect stillness, when no leaf stirred.

Tell us, dear God—tell us the sign
Whereby we may know the time has come.

V. The Sound of That Wind

[A]

He walked in the world. Knew the lust of the eye.

Wrote: "Ever since a Boy I have had an astonishing desire
to see Much of the World and particularly
to acquire a true knowledge of the Birds of North America."

He dreamed of hunting with Boone, from imagination painted his portrait.
He proved that the buzzard does not scent its repast, but sights it.
He looked in the eye of the wounded white-headed eagle.

Wrote: ". . . the Noble Fellow looked at his Ennemies
with a Contemptible Eye."

At dusk he stood on a bluff, and the bellowing of buffalo
Was like distant ocean. He saw
Bones whiten the plain in the hot daylight.

He saw the Indian, and felt the splendor of God.

Wrote: ". . . for there I see the Man Naked from his
hand and yet free from acquired Sorrow."

*

Below the salt, in rich houses, he sat, and knew insult.
In the lobbies and couloirs of greatness he dangled,
And was not unacquainted with contumely.

Wrote: "My Lovely Miss Pirrie of Oackley Passed by Me
this Morning, but did not remember how beautifull
I had rendered her face once by Painting it
at her Request with Pastelles."

Wrote: ". . . but thanks to My humble talents I can run
the gantlet throu this World without her help."

And ran it, and ran undistracted by promise of ease,
Nor even the kind condescension of Daniel Webster.

Wrote: ". . . would give me a fat place was I willing to
have one; but I love indepenn and piece more
than humbug and money."

And proved same, but in the end, entered
On honor. Far, over the ocean, in the silken salons,
With hair worn long like a hunter's, eyes shining,
He whistled the bird-calls of his distant forest.

Wrote: ". . . in my sleep I continually dream of birds."

And in the end, entered into his earned house,
And slept in a bed, and with Lucy.

But the fiddle
Soon lay on the shelf untouched, the mouthpiece
Of the flute was dry, and his brushes.

His mind
Was darkened, and his last joy
Was in the lullaby they sang him, in Spanish, at sunset.

He died, and was mourned, who had loved the world.

Who had written: ". . . a world which though wicked enough
in all conscience is *perhaps* as good
as worlds unknown."

[B]

So died in his bed, and
Night leaned, and now leans,
Off the Atlantic, and is on schedule.
Grass does not bend beneath that enormous weight
That with no sound sweeps westward. In the Mississippi,
On a mud bank, the wreck of a great tree, left
By flood, lies, the root-system and now-stubbed boughs
Lifting in darkness. It
Is white as bone. That whiteness
Is reflected in dark water, and a star
Thereby.

Later,
In the shack of a sheep-herder, high above the Bitterroot,
The light goes out. No other
Light is visible.

The Northwest Orient plane, New York to Seattle, has passed, winking
westward.

[C]

For everything there is a season.

But there is the dream
Of a season past all seasons.

In such a dream the wild-grape cluster,
High-hung, exposed in the gold light,
Unripening, ripens.

Stained, the lip with wetness gleams.

I see your lip, undrying, gleam in the bright wind.

I cannot hear the sound of that wind.

VI. Love and Knowledge

Their footless dance
Is of the beautiful liability of their nature.
Their eyes are round, boldly convex, bright as a jewel,
And merciless. They do not know
Compassion, and if they did,
We should not be worthy of it. They fly
In air that glitters like fluent crystal
And is hard as perfectly transparent iron, they cleave it
With no effort. They cry
In a tongue multitudinous, often like music.

He slew them, at surprising distances, with his gun.
Over a body held in his hand, his head was bowed low,
But not in grief.

He put them where they are, and there we see them:
In our imagination.

What is love?

One name for it is knowledge.

VII. Tell Me a Story

[A]

Long ago, in Kentucky, I, a boy, stood
By a dirt road, in first dark, and heard
The great geese hoot northward.

I could not see them, there being no moon
And the stars sparse. I heard them.

I did not know what was happening in my heart.

It was the season before the elderberry blooms,
Therefore they were going north.

The sound was passing northward.

[B]

Tell me a story.

In this century, and moment, of mania,
Tell me a story.

Make it a story of great distances, and starlight.

The name of the story will be Time,
But you must not pronounce its name.

Tell me a story of deep delight.

Or Else

Poem/Poems 1968–1974

To Cesare and Rysia Lombroso

He clave the rocks in the wilderness, and gave them drink as out of the great depths.
Psalm 78:15

I. The Nature of a Mirror

The sky has murder in the eye, and I
Have murder in the heart, for I
Am only human.
We look at each other, the sky and I.
We understand each other, for

The solstice of summer has sagged, I stand
And wait. Virtue is rewarded, that
Is the nightmare, and I must tell you

That soon now, even before
The change from Daylight Saving Time, the sun,
Beyond the western ridge of black-burnt pine stubs like
A snaggery of rotten shark teeth, sinks
Lower, larger, more blank, and redder than
A mother's rage, as though
F.D.R. had never run for office even, or the first vagina
Had not had the texture of dream. Time

Is the mirror into which you stare.

Interjection #1:
The Need for Re-evaluation

Is this really me? Of course not, for Time
Is only a mirror in the fun-house.

You must re-evaluate the whole question.

II. Natural History

In the rain the naked old father is dancing, he will get wet.
The rain is sparse, but he cannot dodge all the drops.

He is singing a song, but the language is strange to me.

The mother is counting her money like mad, in the sunshine.
Like shuttles her fingers fly, and the sum is clearly astronomical.

Her breath is sweet as bruised violets, and her smile sways like daffodils
reflected in a brook.

The song of the father tells how at last he understands.
That is why the language is strange to me.

*

That is why clocks all over the continent have stopped.

The money the naked old mother counts is her golden memories of love.
That is why I see nothing in her maniacally busy fingers.

That is why all flights have been canceled out of Kennedy.

As much as I hate to, I must summon the police.
For their own good, as well as that of society, they must be put under
surveillance.

They must learn to stay in their graves. That is what graves are for.

III. Time as Hypnosis

For I. A. Richards

White, white in that dawnlight, the world was exploding, white
Light bursting from whiteness. What
Is the name of the world?—for

Whiteness, all night from the black sky unfeathering,
Had changed the world's name, and maybe
My own, or maybe it was all only
A dream I was having, but did not
Know it, or maybe the truth was that I,
Huddling tight in the blankets and darkness and self,
Was nothing, was nothing but what
The snow dreamed all night. Then light:

Two years and no snow in our section, and two years
Is a long time when you are twelve. So,

All day in a landscape that had been
Brown fields and black woods but was now
White emptiness and arches,
I wandered. The white light
Filled all the vertiginous sky, and even
My head until it
Spread bright and wide like another sky under which I
Wandered. I came
To a place where the woods were, stood under
A crazed geometry of boughs black but
Snow-laden and criss-crossed with light, and between
Banks of humped snow and whiteness of ice-fret, saw
Black water slide slow, and glossy as sleep.

*

I stared at the water, and staring, wondered
What the white-bellied minnow, now deep in
Black leaf-muck and mud, thought.
I thought of the muskrat dim in his mud-gloom.

Have you ever seen how delicately
Etched the print of the field mouse's foot in fresh snow is?
I saw the tracks. But suddenly, none. Nothing
But the wing-flurried snow. Then, small as a pin-head, the single
Bright-frozen, red bead of a blood-drop. Have you ever
Stared into the owl's eyes? They blink slow, then burn:
Burn gold in the dark inner core of the snow-shrouded cedar.

There was a great field that tilted
Its whiteness up to the line where the slant, blue knife-edge of sky
Cut it off. I stood
In the middle of that space. I looked back, saw
My own tracks march at me. Mercilessly,
They came at me and did not stop. Ahead,
Was the blankness of white. Up it rose. Then the sky.

Evening came, and I sat by the fire, and the flame danced.

All day, I had wandered in the glittering metaphor
For which I could find no referent.

All night, that night, asleep, I would wander, lost in a dream
That was only what the snow dreamed.

IV. Blow, West Wind

I know, I know—though the evidence
Is lost, and the last who might speak are dead.
Blow, west wind, blow, and the evidence, O,

Is lost, and wind shakes the cedar, and O,
I know how the kestrel hung over Wyoming,
Breast reddened in sunset, and O, the cedar

Shakes, and I know how cold
Was the sweat on my father's mouth, dead.
Blow, west wind, blow, shake the cedar, I know

How once I, a boy, crouching at creekside,
Watched, in the sunlight, a handful of water
Drip, drip, from my hand. The drops—they were bright!

But you believe nothing, with the evidence lost.

Interjection #2: Caveat

For John Crowe Ransom

Necessarily, we must think of the
world as continuous, for if it were
not so I would have told you, for I have
bled for this knowledge, and every man
is a sort of Jesus, but in any
case, if it were not so, you wouldn't know
you are in the world, or even that the
world exists at all—

but only, oh, on-
ly, in discontinuity, do we
know that we exist, or that, in the deep-
est sense, the existence of anything
signifies more than the fact that it is
continuous with the world.

A new high-
way is under construction. Crushed rock has
been spread for miles and rolled down. On Sunday,
when no one is there, go and stand on the
roadbed. It stretches before your eyes in-
to distance. But fix your eyes firmly on
one fragment of crushed rock. Now, it only
glows a little, inconspicuously
one might say. But soon, you will notice a
slight glittering. Then a marked vibration
sets in. You brush your hand across your eyes,
but, suddenly, the earth underfoot is
twitching. Then, remarkably, the bright sun
jerks like a spastic, and all things seem to
be spinning away from the univer-
sal center that the single fragment of
crushed rock has ineluctably become.

At this point, while there is still time and will,
I advise you to detach your gaze from
that fragment of rock. Not all witnesses
of the phenomenon survive unchanged
the moment when, at last, the object screams

in an ecstasy of

being.

V. I Am Dreaming of a White Christmas: The Natural History of a Vision

For Andrew Vincent Corry

[1]

No, not that door—never! But,
Entering, saw. Through
Air brown as an old daguerreotype fading. Through
Air that, though dust to the tongue, yet—
Like the inward, brown-glimmering twilight of water—
Swayed. Through brown air, dust-dry, saw. Saw
It.

The bed.

Where it had
Been. Now was. Of all
Covering stripped, the mattress
Bare but for old newspapers spread.
Curled edges. Yellow. On yellow paper dust,
The dust yellow. No! Do not.

Do not lean to
Look at that date. Do not touch
That silken and yellow perfection of Time that
Dust is, for
There is no Time. I,
Entering, see.

I,
Standing here, breathe the dry air.

[2]

See
Yonder the old Morris chair bought soon
After marriage, for him to rest after work in, the leather,
Once black, now browning, brown at the dry cracks, streaked
With a fungoid green. Approaching,
See.

See it.

The big head. Propped,
Erect on the chair's leather pillow, bald skin
Tight on skull, not white now, brown
Like old leather lacquered, the big nose

Brown-lacquered, bold-jutting yet but with
Nostril-flanges gone tattered in Time. I have not
Yet looked at the eyes. Not
Yet.

The eyes
Are not there. But,
Not there, they stare at what
Is not there.

[3]

Not there, but
In each of the appropriate twin apertures, which are
Deep and dark as a thumb-gouge,
Something that might be taken for
A mulberry, large and black-ripe when, long back, crushed,
But now, with years, dust-dried. The mulberries,
Crushed and desiccated, each out of
Its dark lurking-place, stare out at
Nothing.

His eyes
Had been blue.

[4]

Hers brown. But
Are not now. Now staring,
She sits in the accustomed rocker, but with
No motion. I cannot
Be sure what color the dress once was, but
Am sure that the fabric now falls decisively away
From the Time-sharpened angle of knees. The fabric
Over one knee, the left, has given way. And
I see what protrudes.

See it.

Above,
The dry fabric droops over breastlessness.

Over the shrouded femurs that now are the lap, the hands,
Palm-down, lie. The nail of one forefinger
Is missing.

*

On the ring-finger of the left hand
There are two diamond rings. On that of the right,
One. On Sundays, and some evenings
When she sat with him, the diamonds would be on the fingers.

The rings. They shone.

Shine now.

In the brown air.

On the brown-lacquered face
There are now no
Lips to kiss with.

[5]

The eyes had been brown. But
Now are not where eyes had been. What things
Now are where eyes had been but
Now are not, stare. At the place where now
Is not what once they
Had stared at.

There is no fire on the cold hearth now,
To stare at.

[6]

On
The ashes, gray, a piece of torn orange peel.
Foil wrappings of chocolates, silver and crimson and gold,
Yet gleaming from grayness. Torn Christmas paper,
Stamped green and red, holly and berries, not
Yet entirely consumed, but warped
And black-gnawed at edges. I feel
Nothing. A red
Ribbon, ripped long ago from some package of joy,
Winds over the gray hearth like
A fuse that failed. I feel
Nothing.

Not even
When I see the tree.

*

Why had I not seen the tree before?
Why, on entering, had I not seen it?
It must have been there, and for
A long time, for
The boughs are, of all green, long since denuded.
That much is clear. For the floor
Is there carpeted thick with the brown detritus of cedar.

Christmas trees in our section always were cedar.

[7]

Beneath the un-greened and brown-spiked tree,
On the dead-fall of brown frond-needles, are,
I see, three packages. Identical in size and shape.
In bright Christmas paper. Each with red bow, and under
The ribbon, a sprig of holly.

But look!

The holly
Is, clearly, fresh.

I say to myself:

The holly is fresh.

And
My breath comes short. For I am wondering
Which package is mine.

Oh, which?

I have stepped across the hearth and my hand stretches out.

But the voice:

No presents, son, till the little ones come.

[8]

What shadow of tongue, years back unfleshed, in what
Darkness locked in a rigid jaw, can lift and flex?

The man and the woman sit rigid. What had been
Eyes stare at the cold hearth, but I
Stare at the three chairs. Why—
Tell me why—had I not observed them before? For
They are here.

The little red chair,
For the baby. The next biggest chair
For my little sister, the little red rocker. Then,
The biggest, my own, me the eldest.

The chairs are all empty.

But
I am thinking a thought that is louder than words.
Thinking:

They're empty, they're empty, but me—oh, I'm here!

And that thought is not words, but a roar like wind, or
The roar of the night-freight beating the rails of the trestle,
And you under the trestle, and the roar
Is nothing but darkness alive. Suddenly,
Silence.

And no
Breath comes.

[9]

Where I was,
Am not. Now am
Where the blunt crowd thrusts, nudges, jerks, jostles,
And the eye is inimical. Then,
Of a sudden, know:

Times Square, the season
Late summer and the hour sunset, with fumes
In throat and smog-glitter at sky-height, where
A jet, silver and ectoplasmic, spooks through
The sustaining light, which
Is yellow as acid. Sweat,
Cold in arm-pit, slides down flesh.

*

The flesh is mine.

What year it is, I can't, for the life of me,
Guess, but know that,
Far off, south-eastward, in Bellevue,
In a bare room with windows barred, a woman,
Supine on an iron cot, legs spread, each ankle
Shackled to the cot-frame,
Screams.

She keeps on screaming because it is sunset.

Her hair has been hacked short.

[10]

Clerks now go home, night watchmen wake up, and the heart
Of the taxi-driver, just coming on shift,
Leaps with hope.

All is not in vain.

Old men come out from the hard-core movies.
They wish they had waited till later.

They stand on the pavement and stare up at the sky.
Their drawers are drying stiff at the crotch, and
The sky dies wide. The sky
Is far above the first hysteria of neon.

Soon they will want to go and get something to eat.

Meanwhile, down the big sluice of Broadway,
The steel logs jerk and plunge
Until caught in the rip, snarl, and eddy here before my face.

A mounted policeman sits a bay gelding. The rump
Of the animal gleams expensively. The policeman
Is some sort of dago. His jowls are swart.
His eyes are bright with seeing.

He is as beautiful as a law of chemistry.

[11]

In any case,
I stand here and think of snow falling. But am
Not here. Am
Otherwhere, for already,
This early and summer not over, in West Montana—
Or is it Idaho?—in
The Nez Percé Pass, tonight
It will be snowing.

The Nez Percé is more than 7,000 feet, and I
Have been there. The first flakes,
Large, soft, sparse, come straight down
And with enormous deliberation, white
Out of unbreathing blackness. Snow
Does not yet cling, but the tall stalk of bear-grass
Is pale in darkness. I have seen, long ago,
The paleness of bear-grass in darkness.

But tell me, tell me,
Will I never know
What present there was in that package for me,
Under the Christmas tree?

[12]

All items listed above belong in the world
In which all things are continuous,
And are parts of the original dream which
I am now trying to discover the logic of. This
Is the process whereby pain of the past in its pastness
May be converted into the future tense

Of joy.

Interjection #3: I Know a Place Where All is Real

For Austin Warren

I know a place where all is real. I
have been there, therefore
know. Access is not easy, the way
rough, and visibility extremely poor, especially
among the mountains. Maps
show only the blank space, somewhere
northwest of Mania and beyond Delight,
but if you can manage to elude the natives of
intervening zones, who practice
ghastly rites and have an appetite for human flesh,
you may find a sly track through
narrow and fog-laced passes. Meanwhile
give little credence to tales told
by returning travelers or those
who pretend to be such. But truth,
sometimes, is even more unacceptable
to the casual hearer, and in bars
I have been laughed at for reporting
the simple facts.

In any case,
few travelers do return.
Among those who choose to remain and apply
for naturalization, a certain number
find that they cannot stand the altitude, but these,
upon making their way out, sometimes die of an oppressive
pulmonary complaint as soon as they hit the low country.

VI. Ballad of Mister Dutcher and the Last Lynching in Gupton

He must have been just as old in
days when young as later, his face
as gray and his eyes not gray but
that color there's not even a
name for—all this the same as when,
years later, he'd walk down the street,
and I, a boy, would then see him
in his worn-out gray coat going
twice a day to the depot, where
he'd handle what express came, then
twice a day going back home, the

first time to eat, the last to shut
the door of his small gray house, and
not be seen till tomorrow, and
if ever you said hello, he
might say whatever it was that
you never quite caught, but always
his face had a sort of gray smile
turned more inside than out, as though
there was something he knew but knew
that you'd never know what it was he knew.

He had a small wife whose face was
as gray as the gingham she wore,
or the gray coat that on Sunday
she wore to church, and nobody
could ever imagine what, in
that small gray house, those gray faces
might ever say to each other,
or think, as they lay side by side
while his eyes of that color you
couldn't ever name stared up where
dark hid the ceiling. But we knew
how he'd smile in the dark who knew
that he knew what we'd never know he knew.

But time brings all things to light, so
long after the gray-faced wife was
dead, and the hump of her grave sunk
down to a trench, and the one gray-
faced son dead to boot, having died
one cold winter night in jail, where
the town constable had put him
to sober up—well, long after,
being left all alone with his
knowledge of what we'd never know he knew,

he, in the fullness of time, and
in glory, brought it forth. One hot
afternoon in Hoptown, some fool
nigger, wall-eyed drunk and with a
four-bit hand-gun, tried to stick up
a liquor store, shot the clerk, and,
still broke, grabbed a freight, and was high-
tailing for Gupton, in happy
ignorance that the telephone
had ever been invented. So
when they flagged down the freight, the fool
nigger made one more mistake, up
and drilled one of the posse. That
was that, and in five minutes he
was on his way to the county

seat, the constable driving, but
mighty slow, while back there
in Gupton, in the hardware store,
a business transaction concern-
ing rope was in due process. It
was the small gray-faced man who, to
general astonishment though
in a low, gray voice, said: "Gimme
that rope." Quick as a wink, six turns
around the leader, the end snubbed,
and there was that neat cylinder
of rope the noose line could slide through
easy as a greased piston or
the dose of salts through the widow-
woman, and that was what Mister
Dutcher, all the days, weeks, and years,
had known, and nobody'd known that he knew.

The constable, it sort of seemed,
had car trouble, and there he was
by the road, in the cooling shade
of a big white oak, with his head
stuck under the hood and a wrench
in his hand. They grabbed him before
he even got his head out, which,
you could tell, was not in any
great hurry anyway. Well, what
happened was not Mister Dutcher's
fault, nor the rope's, it was only
that that fool nigger just would not
cooperate, for when the big
bread truck they had him standing on
drew out, he hung on with both feet
as long as possible, then just
keeled over, slow and head-down, in-
to the rope, spilling his yell out
like five gallons of fresh water
in one big, bright, out-busting slosh
in the sunshine, if you, of a
sudden, heave over the crock. So,
that fool nigger managed never
to get a good, clean drop, which was,
you might say, his last mistake. One
man started vomiting, but one
put six .44's in, and that
quieted down the main performer.
Well, that was how we came to know
what Mister Dutcher'd thought we'd never know.

But isn't a man entitled

to something he can call truly
his own—even to his pride in
that one talent kept, against the
advice of Jesus, wrapped in a
napkin, and death to hide? Any-
way, what does it matter now, for
Mister Dutcher is not there to
walk the same old round like a blind
mule hitched to a sorghum mill, is,
in fact, in some nook, niche, crack or
cubby of eternity, stowed
snug as a bug, and safe from all
contumely, wrath, hurt ego, and
biologic despair, with no
drop of his blood to persist in
that howling orthodoxy of
darkness that, like speed-hurled rain on
glass, streams past us, and is Time. At
all events, I'm the one man left
who has any reason at all
to remember his name, and if
truth be told, I haven't got so
damned much, but some time, going back,
I might try to locate the stone
it's on, if grass and ragweed aren't too high.

I might even try to locate
where that black man got buried, though
that would, of course, be somewhat difficult.

VII. Chain Saw at Dawn in Vermont In Time of Drouth

1.

Dawn and, distant, the steel-snarl and lyric
Of the chain saw in deep woods:
I wake. Was it
Trunk-scream, bough-rip and swish, then earth-thud?
No—only the saw's song, the saw
Sings: *now!* Sings:
Now, now, now, in the
Lash and blood-lust of an eternal present, the present
Murders the past, the nerve shrieks, the saw

Sings *now,* and I wake, rising
From that darkness of sleep which
Is the past, and is
The self. It is
Myself, and I know how,

Now far off,
New light gilds the spruce-tops.
The saw, for a moment, ceases, and under
Arm-pits of the blue-shirted sawyer sweat
Beads cold, and
In the obscene silence of the saw's cessation,
A crow, somewhere, calls.

The crow, in distance, calls with the crystalline beauty
Of the outraged heart.

Have I learned how to live?

2.

On the other side of the woods, in the village, a man
Is dying. Wakes
In dawn to the saw's song, thinks
How his wife was a good wife, wonders
Why his boy turned out bad, wonders why
He himself never managed to pay off the mortgage, thinks
Of dawn and the first light spangling the spruces, and how
He leaned on the saw and the saw
Sang. But had not known what
The saw sang. So now thinks:
I have not learned how to die, but

For that thought has no language, has only
The saw's song, in distance: glee of steel and the
Sun-shriek, the scream of castration, the whirl-tooth hysteria
Of *now, now, now!* So
Sweats. What

Can I tell him? I
Cannot tell him how to die because
I have not learned how to live—what man
Has learned how to live?—and I lie

In the dawn, and the thin sheet of summer
Lies on me, and I close my eyes, for
The saw sings, and I know
That soon I must rise and go out in the world where
The heel of the sun's foot smites horridly the hill,
And the stalk of the beech leaf goes limp,
And the bright brook goes gray among boulders,
And the saw sings, for

*

I must endeavor to learn what
I must learn before I must learn
The other thing. If
I learn even a little, I may,
By evening, be able
To tell the man something.

Or he himself may have learned by then.

VIII. Small White House

The sun of July beats down on the small white house.
The pasture is brown-bright as brass, and like brass, sings with heat.
Halt! And I stand here, hills shudder, withdraw into distance,
Leprous with light. And a child's cry comes from the house.

Tell me, oh, where, in what state, did I see the small white house,
Which I see in my mind?—And the wax-wing's beak slices the blue
cedar-berry,
Which is as blue as distance. The river, far off, shrinks
Among the hot boulders, no glister, looks dead as a discarded snake-skin
rubbed off on stone. The house

Swims in that dazzle of no-Time. The child's cry comes from the house.

Interjection #4:

Bad Year, Bad War: A New Year's Card, 1969

*And almost all things are by the law purged
with blood; and without shedding of blood
there is no remission.*

Epistle to the Hebrews, 9:22

That was the year of the bad war. The others—
Wars, that is—had been virtuous. If blood

Was shed, it was, in a way, sacramental, redeeming
Even evil enemies from whose veins it flowed,

Into the benign logic of History; and some,
By common report even the most brutalized, died with a shy

And grateful smile on the face, as though they,
At the last, understood. Our own wounds were, of course, precious.

*

There is always imprecision in human affairs, and war
Is no exception, therefore the innocent—

Though innocence is, it should be remembered, a complex concept—
Must sometimes suffer. There is the blunt

Justice of the falling beam, the paw-flick of
The unselective flame. But happily,

If one's conscience attests to ultimate innocence,
Then the brief suffering of others, whose innocence is only incidental,

Can be regarded, with pity to be sure, as merely
The historical cost of the process by which

The larger innocence fulfills itself in
The realm of contingency. For conscience

Is, of innocence, the final criterion, and the fact that now we
Are troubled, and candidly admit it, simply proves

That in the past we, being then untroubled,
Were innocent. Dear God, we pray

To be restored to that purity of heart
That sanctifies the shedding of blood.

IX. Forever O'Clock

[1]

A clock is getting ready to strike forever o'clock.
I do not know where the clock is, but it is somewhere.

I know it is somewhere, for I can hear it trying to make up its mind to strike.
Somewhere is the place where it is while it is trying to make up its mind.

The sound it makes trying to make up its mind is purely metaphysical.
The sound is one you hear in your bloodstream and not your ear.

You hear it the way a man tied to a post in the yard of the State Penitentiary of Utah
Could hear the mind of the Deputy Warden getting ready to say, "Fire!"

You hear it the way you hear your wife's breathing back in a dark room at home, when
You are away on a trip and wake up in some hotel bedroom and do not know where you are and do not know offhand whose breath you do hear there beside you.

[2]

The clock is taking time to make up its mind and that is why I have time
To think of some things that are not important but simply are.

A little two-year-old Negro girl-baby, with hair tied up in spindly little tits with strings of red rag,
Sits in the red dust. Except for some kind of rag around her middle, she is naked, and black as a ripe plum in the sunshine.

Behind the child is a gray board shack, and from the mud-chimney a twist of blue smoke is motionless against the blue sky.
The fields go on forever, and whatever had been planted there is not there now. The drouth does not see fit to stop even now.

The pin-oak in the yard has been dead for years. The boughs are black stubs against the blue sky.
Nothing alive is here but the child and a dominecker hen, flattened puff-belly down, under the non-shade of the pin-oak.

Inside the gray feathers, the body of the hen pants with the heat.
The yellow beak of the hen is open, and the flattened string-thin tongue looks black and dry and sharp as a pin.

The naked child with plum-black skin is intensely occupied.
From a rusted tin snuff can in the right hand, the child pours red dust over the spread fingers of the left hand held out prone in the bright air.

The child stares at the slow-falling red dust. Some red dust piles precariously up on the back of the little black fingers thrust out. Some does not.
The sun blazes down on the naked child in the mathematical center of the world. The sky glitters like brass.

A beat-up old 1931 Studebaker, of a kind you are too young ever to have seen, has recently passed down the dirt road, and a plume of red dust now trails it toward the horizon.
I watch the car that I know I am the man driving as it recedes into distance and approaches the horizon.

[3]

I have now put on record one thing that is not important but simply is.
I watch the beat-up old green Studebaker moving like a dot into distance trailing its red plume of dust toward the horizon.

I wonder if it will ever get there. The wondering throbs like a bruise inside my head.
Perhaps it throbs because I do not want to know the answer to my wondering.

*

The sun blazes down from the high center of the perfect concavity of sky. The
sky glitters like brass.
A clock somewhere is trying to make up its mind to strike forever o'clock.

X. Rattlesnake Country

For James Dickey

1.

Arid that country and high, anger of sun on the mountains, but
One little patch of cool lawn:

Trucks
Had brought in rich loam. Stonework
Held it in place like a shelf, at one side backed
By the length of the house porch, at one end
By rock-fall. Above that, the mesquite, wolf-waiting. Its turn
Will, again, come.

Meanwhile, wicker chairs, all day,
Follow the shimmering shade of the lone cottonwood, the way that
Time, sadly seeking to know its own nature, follows
The shadow on a sun-dial. All day,
The sprinkler ejects its misty rainbow.

All day,
The sky shivers white with heat, the lake,
For its fifteen miles of distance, stretches
Tight under the white sky. It is stretched
Tight as a mystic drumhead. It glitters like neurosis.
You think it may scream, but nothing
Happens. Except that, bit by bit, the mountains
Get heavier all afternoon.

One day,
When some secret, high drift of air comes eastward over the lake,
Ash, gray, sifts minutely down on
Our lunch-time ice cream. Which is vanilla, and white.

There is a forest fire on Mount Ti-Po-Ki, which
Is at the western end of the lake there.

2.

If, after lunch, at God's hottest hour,
You make love, flesh, in that sweat-drench,
Slides on flesh slicker than grease. To grip
Is difficult.

At drink-time,
The sun, over Ti-Po-Ki, sets
Lopsided, and redder than blood or bruised cinnabar, because of
The smoke there. Later,
If there is no moon, you can see the red eyes of fire
Wink at you from
The black mass that is the mountain.

At night, in the dark room, not able to sleep, you
May think of the red eyes of fire that
Are winking from blackness. You may,
As I once did, rise up and go from the house. But,
When I got out, the moon had emerged from cloud, and I
Entered the lake. Swam miles out,
Toward the moonset. Motionless,
Awash, metaphysically undone in that silvered and
Unbreathing medium, and beyond
Prayer or desire, saw
The moon, slow, swag down, like an old woman's belly.

Going back to the house, I gave the now-dark lawn a wide berth.

At night the rattlers come out from the rock-fall.
They lie on the damp grass for coolness.

3.

I-yee!—

and the wranglers, they cry on the mountain, and waking
At dawn-streak, I hear it.

High on the mountain
I hear it, for snow-water there, snow long gone, yet seeps down
To green the raw edges and enclaves of forest
With a thin pasturage. The wranglers
Are driving our horses down, long before daylight, plunging
Through gloom of the pines, and in their joy
Cry out:

I-yee!

*

We ride this morning, and,
Now fumbling in shadow for *levis,* pulling my boots on, I hear
That thin cry of joy from the mountain, and what I have,
Literally, seen, I now in my mind see, as I
Will, years later, in my mind, see it—the horsemen
Plunge through the pine-gloom, leaping
The deadfall—*I-yee!*—
Leaping the boulder—*I-yee!*— and their faces
Flee flickering white through the shadow—*I-yee!*—
And before them,
Down the trail and in dimness, the riderless horses,
Like quicksilver spilled in dark glimmer and roil, go
Pouring downward.

The wranglers cry out.

And nearer.

But,
Before I go for my quick coffee-scald and to the corral,
I hear, much nearer, not far from my open window, a croupy
Gargle of laughter.

It is Laughing Boy.

4.

Laughing Boy is the name that my host—and friend—gives his yard-hand.
Laughing Boy is Indian, or half, and has a hare-lip.
Sometimes, before words come, he utters a sound like croupy laughter.
When he utters that sound his face twists. Hence the name.

Laughing Boy wakes up at dawn, for somebody
Has to make sure the rattlers are gone before
The nurse brings my host's twin baby daughters out to the lawn. Laughing Boy,
Who does not like rattlers, keeps a tin can
Of gasoline covered with a saucer on an outer ledge of the porch.
Big kitchen matches are in the saucer. This
At the porch-end toward the rock-fall.

The idea is: Sneak soft-foot round the porch-end,
There between rattlers and rock-fall, and as one whips past,
Douse him. This with the left hand, and
At the same instant, with the nail of the right thumb,
Snap a match alight.

The flame,
If timing is good, should, just as he makes his rock-hole,
Hit him.

*

The flame makes a sudden, soft, gaspy sound at
The hole-mouth, then dances there. The flame
Is spectral in sunlight, but flickers blue at its raw edge.

Laughing Boy has beautiful coordination, and sometimes
He gets a rattler. You are sure if
The soft, gasping sound and pale flame come before
The stub-buttoned tail has disappeared.

                                        Whenever
Laughing Boy really gets a rattler, he makes that sound like
Croupy laughter. His face twists.

Once I get one myself. I see, actually, the stub-buttoned tail
Whip through pale flame down into earth-darkness.

"The son-of-a-bitch," I am yelling, "did you see me, I got him!"

I have gotten that stub-tailed son-of-a-bitch.

I look up at the sky. Already, that early, the sky shivers with whiteness.

5.

What was *is* is now *was*. But
Is *was* but a word for wisdom, its price? Some from
That long-lost summer are dead now, two of the girls then young,
Now after their pain and delusions, worthy endeavors and lies, are,
Long since, dead.

                    The third
Committed her first adultery the next year, her first lover
A creature odd for her choosing, he who
Liked poetry and had no ambition, and
She cried out in his arms, a new experience for her. But
There were the twins, and she had, of course,
Grown accustomed to money.

                                Her second,
A man of high social position, who kept a score-card. With her,
Not from passion this time, just snobbery. After that,
From boredom. Forgot, finally,
The whole business, took up horse-breeding, which
Filled her time and even, I heard, made unneeded money, and in
The old news photo I see her putting her mount to the jump.
Her yet beautiful figure is poised forward, bent elbows
Neat to her tight waist, face
Thrust into the cleansing wind of her passage, the face
Yet smooth as a girl's, no doubt from the scalpel
Of the plastic surgeon as well as
From her essential incapacity
For experience.

*

The husband, my friend,
Would, by this time, be totally cynical. The children
Have been a disappointment. He would have heavy jowls.
Perhaps he is, by this time, dead.

As for Laughing Boy, he wound up in the pen. Twenty years.
This for murder. Indians
Just ought to leave whiskey to the white folks.

I can't remember the names of the others who came there,
The casual weekend-ers. But remember

What I remember, but do not
Know what it all means, unless the meaning inheres in
The compulsion to try to convert what now is *was*
Back into what was *is*.

I remember
The need to enter the night-lake and swim out toward
The distant moonset. Remember
The blue-tattered flick of white flame at the rock-hole
In the instant before I lifted up
My eyes to the high sky that shivered in its hot whiteness.

And sometimes—usually at dawn—I remember the cry on the mountain.

All I can do is to offer my testimony.

XI. Homage to Theodore Dreiser

On the Centennial of his Birth

(August 27, 1871)

Oh, the moon shines fair tonight along the Wabash,
From the fields there comes the breath of new mown hay.
Thro' the sycamores the candle lights are gleaming,
On the banks of the Wabash, far away.

The Refrain of "On the Banks of the Wabash, Far Away"
Words by Theodore Dreiser and Paul Dresser
Music by Paul Dresser

1. Psychological Profile

Who is the ugly one slump-slopping down the street?
Who is the chinless wonder with the potato-nose?
Can't you hear the soft *plop* of the pancake-shaped feet?

*

He floats, like Anchises' son, in the cloud of his fine new clothes,
Safe, safe at last, from the street's sneer, toward a queen who will fulfill
The fate devised him by Venus—but where, oh when! That is what he never
knows.

Born with one hand in his pants and one in the till,
He knows that the filth of self, to be loved, must be clad in glory,
So once stole twenty-five dollars to buy a new coat, and that is why still

The left eye keeps squinting backward—yes, history
Is gum-shoeing closer behind, with the constable-hand that clutches.
Watch his mouth, how it moves without sound, he is telling himself his own old
story.

Full of screaming his soul is, and a stench like live flesh that scorches.
It's the screaming, and stench, of a horse-barn aflame,
And the great beasts rear and utter, their manes flare up like torches.

From lies, masturbation, vainglory, and shame,
He moves in his dream of ladies swan-necked, with asses ample and sweet,
But knows that no kiss heals his soul, it is always the same.

The same—but a brass band plays in the distance, and the midnight cricket,
Though thinly, asseverates his name. He seeks amid the day's traffic a sign—
Some horseshoe or hunchback or pin—that now, at last, at the end of this street

He will enter upon his reality: but enters only in-
To your gut, or your head, or your heart, to enhouse there and stay,
And in that hot darkness lie lolling and swell—like a tumor, perhaps benign.

May I present Mr. Dreiser? He will write a great novel, someday.

2. Vital Statistics

[A]

Past Terre Haute, the diesels pound,
Eastward, westward, and under the highway slab the ground,
Like jello, shakes. Deep
In the infatuate and foetal dark, beneath
The unspecifiable weight of the great
Mid-America loam-sheet, the impacted
Particular particles of loam, blind,
Minutely grind.

At that depth and with that weight,
The particles, however minutely, vibrate
At the incessant passage
Of the transcontinental truck freight,
And concerning that emperor whose gut was god, Tacitus

Wrote, "ex urbe atque Italia inritamenta gulae gestabantur. . . ,"
And from both
Adriatic and Tyrrhenian seas, sea-crayfish and bivalve and,
Glare-eyed, the mullet, redder than flame,
Surrendered themselves in delight
To soothe that soft gullet wheredown all honor and empire
Slid slick, and wheels all night
Hummed on the highways to guarantee prompt delivery.

Saliva gathers in the hot darkness of mouth-tissue. The mouth,
Slack, drools at the corners, but ever so little.

All night,
Past Terre Haute, tires, on the concrete, scream, and in that town,
Long before the age of the internal combustion engine, but not
Before that of gewgaw, gilt, and grab, when the war
For freedom had just given place to the war for the dollar,
Theodore Dreiser was born. That was on South Ninth Street, but
The exact address is, of course, lost. He was born
Into the vast anonymity of the poor.

Have you ever
Seen moonlight on the Wabash, far away?

[B]

On the wrong side of the tracks—that was where
He was born, and he never let you forget it, and his sisters
Had hot crotches and round heels.
He knew the gnaw of hunger, and how the first wind of winter feels,
He was born into the age of conspicuous consumption, and knew
How the heart, in longing, numbly congeals.

Nothing could help nothing, not reading Veblen or even Freud, for
The world is a great ass propped high on pillows, the cunt
Winks.

Dreiser,
However, could not feel himself worthy. Not,
At least, of love. His nails,
Most horribly, were bitten. At night,
Sometimes, he wept. The bed springs
Creaked with the shift of his body, which,
In the Age of Faith and of Contempt of the World,
Would have been called a sack
Of stercorry: i. e., that matter the body ejects.

Sometimes he wept for the general human condition,
But he was hell on women.

*

He had never loved any woman, he confessed,
Except his mother, whose broken shoes, he,
In childhood, had once caressed,
In the discovery of pity.

                                        Have you ever
Seen midnight moonlight on the Wabash,
While the diesel rigs boom by?
Have you ever thought how the moonlit continent
Would look from the tearless and unblinking distance of God's wide eye?

3. Moral Assessment

You need call no psychiatrist
To anatomize his pain.
He suffers but the pain all men
Suffer in their human kind.
No—suffers, too,
His nobility of mind.

He denies it, he sneers at it,
In his icy nightmare of
The superlative of self;
Tries to, but cannot theorize past
The knowledge that
Others suffer, too, at last.

He is no philosopher.
His only gift is to enact
All that his deepest self abhors,
And learn, in his self-contemptive distress,
The secret worth
Of all our human worthlessness.

XII. Flaubert In Egypt

For Dorothea Tanning

Winterlong, off La Manche, wind leaning. Gray stones of the gray
      city sluiced by gray rain. And he dreamed

Of desert and distance, sunlight like murder, lust and new colors whose
      names exploded the spectrum like dynamite,
      or cancer. So went there,

*

Who did not know what he was, or could be, though hoping he might
find there his fate. Found
what he found: with head shaven,

One lock at the occiput left, red tarboosh wind-flaunted, rode hard at
the Sphinx, at the "Father of Terrors," which,
in that perspective and distance, lifted slow from
the desert, like a great ship from hull-down.
At its height,
it swung. His cry burst forth.

In the white-washed room, by the light of wicks in three oil-glasses and to
the merciless *screak* of the rebec, with musicians
blind-folded, the dancer, her breasts
cruelly bound to bulge upward and bare, above
pink trousers flesh rippling in bronze, danced
the dance which

He recalls from the oldest Greek vases—the leap on one foot with
the free foot crossed over, the fingers
aquiver, face calm, and
slow centuries sifting like shadow. Light
flickers on whitewash. He finds
the *mons veneris* shaven, arse noble.
That night three *coups,* and once
performs cunnilingus. Fingers clutching her necklace,
he lies. He remembers his boyhood. Her fingers
and naked thighs twitch in sleep.

By day, on the minaret-top, the stork clacked its beak. At the edge of
the carrion-field, the wild dog,
snout blue from old blood,
skulked, and camel bells in the distance.
On the voyage down-Nile, on the slave-boat, old women,
black and slaves too, who had seen all of life, tried
to persuade the young girls, market-bound,
to smile. But once,

On the height of Gebel Abusir, looking down on the Cataract, where
the Nile flung itself to white froth on black granite, he
cried out: "Eureka—the name, it is Emma!"
And added: "Bovary." Pronouncing the *o,*
as recorded by his companion, quite short.

So home, and left Egypt, which was: palms black, sky red, and the river
like molten steel, and the child's hand
plucking his sleeve—*"Baksheesh,*
and I'll get you my mother to fuck"—and the bath-boy

he buggered, this in a clinical spirit and as
a tribute to the host-country. And the chancre, of course,
bright as a jewel on his member, and borne
home like a trophy.

But not to be omitted: on the river at Thebes, having long stared
at the indigo mountains of sunset, he let
eyes fix on the motion of three wave-crests that,
in unison, bowed beneath the wind, and his heart
burst with a solemn thanksgiving to God for
the fact he could perceive the worth of the
world with such joy.

Years later, death near, he remembered the palm fronds—
how black against a bright sky!

Interjection #5: Solipsism and Theology

Wild with ego, wild with world-blame,
He stared at the up-heave and enormity of ocean.
He said: *It does not even know my name.*

Wild with ego, wild with grief,
He stared at the antic small aphid green on the green leaf.
He said: *It has a home, but I—I'm the lost one.*

Wild with ego, wild with despair,
He stared at the icy and paranoid glitter of winter stars.
He said: *They would grind me like grain, small as dust, and not care.*

Wild with ego, wild with weeping,
He stared at the classic shut eyelids of his true love sleeping.
He said: *She sleeps, and the wild boar gashes my groin.*

Wild with ego, wild with wrong,
He stared into the dark pit of self whence all had sprung.
He said: *What is man that I should be mindful of him!*

But was—he was—and even yearned after virtue.

XIII. The True Nature of Time

1. The Faring

Once over water, to you borne brightly,
Wind off the North Sea cold but
Heat-streaked with summer and honed by the dazzle
Of sun, and the Channel boat banging
The chop like a shire-horse on cobbles—thus I,
Riding the spume-flash, by gull cries ringed,
Came.

Came, and the harbor slid smooth like an oil-slick.
It was the gray city, but the gray roof-slates
Sang blue in the sun, and the sea-cliffs,
Eastward, swung in that blue wind. I came thus,
And I, unseen, saw. Saw
You,

And you, at the pier edge, face lifting seaward
And toward that abstract of distance that I
Yet was and felt myself to be, stood. Wind
Tugged your hair. It tangled that brightness. Over
Your breast wind tautened the blue cloth, your skirt
Whipped, your bare legs were brown. Steel
Rang on steel. Shouts
Rose in that language.
Later,

The quiet place. Roses. Yellow. We came there, wind
Down now, sea slopping the rocks, slow, sun low and
Sea graying, but roses were yellow, climbing
The wall, it was stone. The last light
Came gilding a track across the gray water from westward.
It came leveling in to finger the roses. One
Petal, yellow, fell, slow.

At the foot of the gray stone, like light, it lay.
High beyond roses, a gull, in the last light, hung.

The sea kept slopping the rocks, slow.

2. The Enclave

Out of the silence, the saying. Into
The silence, the said. Thus
Silence, in timelessness, gives forth
Time, and receives it again, and I lie

*

In darkness and hear the wind off the sea heave.
Off the sea, it uncoils. Landward, it leans,
And at the first cock-crow, snatches that cry
From the cock's throat, the cry,
In the dark, like gold blood flung, is scattered. How

May I know the true nature of Time, if
Deep now in darkness that glittering enclave
I dream, hangs? It shines. Another
Wind blows there, the sea-cliffs,
Far in that blue wind, swing. Wind

Lifts the brightening of hair.

XIV. Vision Under the October Mountain: A Love Poem

Golding from green, gorgeous the mountain
high hangs in gold air, how
can stone float, it is

the image of authority, of reality—or, is it?—floating
with no weight, and glows, did we
once in the womb dream, dream
a gold mountain in gold
air floating, we in the

pulse and warm slosh of
that unbreathing bouillon, lulled in
the sway of that sweet
syllogism—oh, unambiguous—swung
in the tide of that bliss unbreathed, bathed in
un-self which was self, did we
dream a gold mountain, did
it glow in that faceless unfatuous
dark, did
it glow in gold air in the airless
abstraction of dark, floating high
above our blind eyes with

no lashes yet, unbrined by grief yet, we
seeing nothing, but
what did we dream—a
gold mountain,
floating?

I want to understand the miracle
of your presence here by my side, your
gaze on the mountain. I want

*

to hear the whole story of how
you came here, with
particular emphasis on the development of

the human scheme of values.

XV. Stargazing

The stars are only a backdrop for
The human condition, the stars
Are brilliant above the black spruces,
And fall comes on. Wind

Does not move in the star-stillness, wind
Is afraid of itself, as you have been afraid in
Those moments when destruction and revelation
Have spat at each other like cats, and the mirror
Showed no breath, ha, ha, and the wind,

Far off in arctic starlight, is afraid
To breathe, and waits, huddled in
Sparse blackness of spruces, black glitter in starlight, in
A land, north, where snow already is, and waits:

And the girl is saying, "You do not look
At the stars," for I did not look at
The stars, for I know they are there, know
That if I look at the stars, I

Will have to live over again all I have lived
In the years I looked at stars and
Cried out, "O reality!" The stars
Love me. I love them. I wish they

Loved God, too. I truly wish that.

Interjection #6:
What You Sometimes Feel on Your Face at Night

Out of mist, God's
Blind hand gropes to find
Your face. The fingers
Want to memorize your face. The fingers
Will be wet with the tears of your eyes. God

Wants only to love you, perhaps.

XVI. News Photo

(Of Man Coming Down Steps of Court House after Acquittal on Charge of Having Shot to Death an Episcopal Minister Reported to Be Working Up the Niggers)

[1]

Easy, easy, watch that belly!
Easy—and he lets it down
carefully, not that it is more than
the simple sag of middle age, but

now he knows how precious flesh is,
having with his own hand—finger,
rather—pump gun, finger on trigger of—*wham-mo!*
oh, wham-mo, oh boy—burst
flesh, not his own of course,
open and seen what spills
out, and so now buckles
the belt into flesh, his own, cruelly
in secret expiation perhaps, but also
to hold it preciously together, as you

can plainly see, for he wears no coat, autumn
being warm in Georgia—or is it
Alabama or Mississippi?—and
carries it, the belly, carefully down

the stairs, and descending, lets it
down carefully, step
to step down, like an armful of
crockery, the steps
blind. And his face—

he carries his face down
like, say, a large glass jar full
past brim, by bulge of surface tension, of
a fluid that looks like slightly murky ditch-water, but
can't be that, for obviously it
is too precious to risk spilling
even a single drop of. His
eyes turn inward. He

is innocent, they say
he is innocent, the law
says it too, so why

isn't he happy?

[2]

I wish he were happy, for
so few people manage it, and he
was not working for happiness
for himself, only for

the good of his country, so why
isn't he happy, why
does his tongue taste like an old sock, when
he hasn't had a drink for a week, and

is innocent, for they all say so, for
one bastard had a knife and it was six feet long, and
the other bastard had a French .75
from World War One he stole
off the lawn of the Court House
and was waving it over his head like
a cap pistol, and both

these nigger-loving bastards coming at him, and they
was disguised like preachers but they
was Comminists, and if they was preachers, they
was not Baptists nor even Methodist
preachers, and sure-God not no
Church of Christ preachers, and it was
the Jews and the Romans had Him hung,
them Romans being Roman Catholics, like the song says.

They nailed Him up, the bastards, and He bled for us all.

[3]

I wish he were happy, I
wish everybody were happy, the dead,
they are happy—*wham-mo!* and
you get happy right away—but

coming down the Court House steps, he
is not happy. Nothing
is like he had expected, as now he
moves toward the flash bulbs, his eyes
inward on innocence. But the eyes
of his wife, above him, to the left,
stare out at the flash bulbs in
outrage, for she hates the world. The son,
twelve years old,
is by the father's side.

*

It really is a family picture, even if

from higher up the stairs, friends,
admirers, and well-wishers crane
their heads to horn in
on the act and get in the paper, and
they really deserve to,
even if some are not such close friends, for

they have committed heroism in their hearts.

[4]

This, as he somehow knows, will come later:

Now I tell you, son, I don't care
if niggers in new Buicks gets thicker in Morfee County than
blue-bottle flies round buttermilk, and
if ever nigger south of Mason and Dixon gets bleached till
he's whiter'n a snowfall on the head of a albino old enough
to be drawing Social Security for forty years, and
if ever nigger in this State gets one of them No-Bull
Prizes, which is what they call them Bull-Shit
Prizes, which is what them square-heads in Sweden
gives niggers, but as for me and what I done I know
I done right in my heart and in the eyes of God-a-Mighty,
my only regret being this durn preacher I'm referring to was not
black, even if he wasn't no preacher in the first place,
and now you are nigh grown up and off to
college—now State is a fine place, but I want you to promise me
you won't listen to a single word none of them perfessers
is gonna say against your raising, and not even open
any durn book that says different. You promise?

Yes, sir.

Well, God-damnit, get that look out of
your eyes when you look at me, before I
knock it out!—oh, son, oh, son,
you know I love you, don't you know it, son?

Yes. Yes, sir.

[5]

But now is now, and not later, and nothing
is what he had expected, for where
is the music, where
the flowers, the throwing of blossoms, the
flowing of banners, the black sedan and the gunning
of motorcycles as the State Troopers,
sun on white helmets, wheel
into formation for the escort, and where—yes, where—
is that pure calm of heart he had always longed for?

Yes, where is the kiss of his mother?

And where's the Governor? You'd think
that bastard might show some gratitude after
voting for him and doing all he had done, you'd think
he at least might send the Chief of the Highway Patrol.

But look!—and why should he give a damn now
if some half-ass Governor never comes, for
look!—and it's Robert E. Lee, and—

—yeah, look, and he's wearing
his gray suit and a gray hat to match, and a
sword round his waist, and he's waiting
for me—yeah, for me!—and he's smiling, it must
be a smile, even if I can't see his face good.
Yeah, look! and he's lifting his hand up to take
his hat off—yeah, Jesus!—his hat
off to me—yeah—

—and lifting the hat off, he exposes
the skull to which skin with some hair,
gray, sparsely clings yet, as does
some leathery skin to face-bone, and gray hairs,
sparse too, to chin, and the chin-bone
drops wide open, and the sound
that comes out must be laughter, and Robert

E. Lee is laughing in sunshine, and half
across the state every pine needle
on that side of every pine tree
shrivels up as though hit by a blow torch, and
off in Jackson, Mississippi, or maybe
Montgomery, Alabama, the white paint on
the State House—it pops up and blisters, for Robert

E. Lee, he's laughing, he
shakes all over with laughing, he
rattles like a crap game on a tin roof, he

is laughing fit to kill, or would be
if he weren't dead already. But

there are tears in his eyes, or
at least would be, if
he had any.

Any eyes, I mean.

XVII. Little Boy and Lost Shoe

The little boy lost his shoe in the field.
Home he hobbled, not caring, with a stick whipping goldenrod.
Go find that shoe—I mean it, right now!
And he went, not now singing, and the field was big.

Under the sky he walked and the sky was big.
Sunlight touched the goldenrod, and yellowed his hair,
But the sun was low now, and oh, he should know
He must hurry to find that shoe, or the sun will be down.

Oh, hurry, boy, for the grass will be tall as a tree.
Hurry, for the moon has bled, but not like a heart, in pity.
Hurry, for time is money and the sun is low.
Yes, damn it, hurry, for shoes cost money, you know.

I don't know why you dawdle and do not hurry.
The mountains are leaning their heads together to watch.
How dilatory can a boy be, I ask you?

Off in Wyoming,
The mountains lean. They watch. They know.

XVIII. Composition in Gold and Red-Gold

Between the event and the word, golden
The sunlight falls, between
The brown brook's braiding and the mountain it
Falls, in pitiless plenitude, and every leaf
On the ruined apple tree is gold, and the apples all
Gold, too, especially those

On the ground. The gold of apples
That have fallen flushes to flame, but
Gold is the flame. Gold
Goes red-gold—and the scene:

*

A chipmunk is under the apple tree, sits up
Among gold apples, is
Golden in gold light. The chipmunk
Wriggles its small black nose
In the still center of the world of light.

The hair of the little girl is as brown-gold as
Brook water braiding in sunlight.

The cat, crouching by the gray stone, is gold, too.
The tail of the cat, half-Persian, weaves from side to side,
In infinite luxury, gold plume
Of sea-weed in that tide of light.
That is a motion that puts
The world to sleep.

The eyes of the cat are gold, and

I want to sleep. But
The event: the tiny
Shriek unstitches the afternoon, the girl
Screams, the sky
Tingles crystalline like a struck wine glass, and you
Feel the salt thickening, like grit, in your secret blood. Afterward

There is a difference in the quality of silence.
Every leaf, gold, hangs motionless on the tree, but
There is a difference in the quality of
Motionlessness: unverbed, unverved, they
Hang. On the last day will the sun
Explode? Or simply get too tired?

The chipmunk lies gold among the apples.
It is prone and totally relaxed like ripe
Fruit fallen, and,
Upon closer inspection, you can see
The faint smear of flame-gold at the base
Of the skull. This effect
Completes the composition.

The little girl
Holds the cat in her arms,
Crooning, "Baby, oh, baby." She weeps under
The powerful flood of gold light.

Somewhere, in the shade of alders, a trout
Hangs steady, head against a current like ice.

The eagle I had earlier seen climbing
The light tall above the mountain is

Now beyond sight.

Interjection #7: Remarks of Soul to Body

(On the Occasion of a Birthday Party)

For Sergio and Alberta Perosa

You've toughed it out pretty well, old Body, done
Your duty, and gratified most of my whims, to boot—
Though sometimes, no doubt, against your better judgment,
Or even mine—and are still
Revving over satisfactorily, considering.

Keep doing your duty, yes, and some fine day
You'll get full pension, with your every need
Taken care of, and not a dime out of your own pocket—
Or anybody's pocket, for that matter—for you won't have
Any needs, not with the rent paid up in perpetuity.

But now tonight, to recognize your faithful service,
We've asked a few friends in, with their Bodies, of course—
Many of those Bodies quite charming, in fact—and after
You've drunk and dined, then you and all the other Bodies
Can go for a starlit romp, with the dogs, in the back pasture.

And we, the Owners—of Bodies, not dogs, I mean—
We'll sit by the fire and talk things over, remark
The baroque ironies of Time, exchange
Some childhood anecdotes, then on to the usual topics,
The death of the novel, the plight of democracy, and naturally, Vietnam.

But let us note, too, how glory, like gasoline spilled
On the cement in a garage, may flare, of a sudden, up,

In a blinding blaze, from the filth of the world's floor.

XIX. There's a Grandfather's Clock in the Hall

There's a grandfather's clock in the hall, watch it closely. The minute hand
stands still, then it jumps, and in between jumps there is
no-Time,
And you are a child again watching the reflection of early morning sunlight on
the ceiling above your bed,

Or perhaps you are fifteen feet under water and holding your breath as you
struggle with a rock-snagged anchor, or holding your breath just
long enough for one more long, slow thrust to make the orgasm
really intolerable,
Or you are wondering why you do not really give a damn, as they trundle you
off to the operating room,

*

Or your mother is standing up to get married and is very pretty and excited and is a virgin, and your heart overflows, and you watch her with tears in your eyes, or
She is the one in the hospital room and she is really dying.

They have taken out her false teeth, which are now in a tumbler on the bedside table, and you know that only the undertaker will ever put them back in.
You stand there and wonder if you will ever have to wear false teeth.

She is lying on her back, and God, is she ugly, and
With gum-flabby lips and each word a special problem, she is asking if it is a new suit that you are wearing.

You say yes, and hate her uremic guts, for she has no right to make you hurt the way that question hurts.
You do not know why that question makes your heart hurt like a kick in the scrotum,

For you do not yet know that the question, in its murderous triviality, is the last thing she will ever say to you,
Nor know what baptism is occurring in a sod-roofed hut or hole on the now night-swept steppes of Asia, and a million mouths, like ruined stars in darkness, make a rejoicing that howls like wind, or wolves,

Nor do you know the truth, which is: *Seize the nettle of innocence in both your hands, for this is the only way, and every*
Ulcer in love's lazaret may, like a dawn-stung gem, sing—or even burst into whoops of, perhaps, holiness.

But, in any case, watch the clock closely. Hold your breath and wait.
Nothing happens, nothing happens, then suddenly, quick as a wink, and slick as a mink's prick, Time thrusts through the time of no-Time.

XX. Reading Late at Night, Thermometer Falling

[1]

The radiator's last hiss and steam-clang done, he,
Under the bare hundred-watt bulb that glares
Like truth, blanket
Over knees, woolly gray bathrobe over shoulders, handkerchief
On great bald skull spread, glasses
Low on big nose, sits. The book
Is propped on the blanket.

Thus—
But only in my mind's eye now:

*

                                        and there, in the merciless
Glitter of starlight, the fields, mile
On mile over the county, stretch out and are
Crusted with ice which, whitely,
Answers the glitter of stars.

                                        The mercury
Falls, the night is windless, mindless, and long, and somewhere,
Deep in the blackness of woods, the tendons
Of a massive oak bough snap with the sound of a
Pistol-shot.

                    A beam,
Somewhere in the colding house where he sits,
Groans. But his eyes do not lift. Who,
Long back, had said to me:

"When I was young I felt like I
Had to try to understand how things are, before I died."

[2]

But lived long.

                    Lived
Into that purity of being that may
Be had past all ambition and the frivolous hope, but who now
Lives only in my mind's eye,

                                        though I
Cannot see what book is propped there under that forever
Marching gaze—Hume's *History of England,* Roosevelt's
Winning of the West, a Greek reader,
Now Greek to him and held in his hands like a prayer, or
Some college text book, or Freud on dreams, abandoned
By one of the children. Or, even,
Coke or Blackstone, books forbidding and blackbound, and once I,
Perhaps twelve then, found an old photograph:

                                                    a young man,
In black coat, high collar, and string tie, black, one hand out
To lie with authority on a big book (Coke or Blackstone?), eyes
Lifted into space.

                    And into the future.

                                                Which
Had not been the future. For the future
Was only his voice that, now sudden, said:

*

"Son, give me that!"

He took it from my hand, said:

"Some kinds of foolishness a man is due to forget, son."

Tore it across. Tore
Time, and all that Time had been, across. Threw it
Into the fire. Who,
Years later, would say:

"I reckon I was lucky enough to learn early that a man can be happy in his
obligations."

Later, I found the poems. Not good.

[3]

The date on the photograph: 1890.

He was very young then. And poor.

Man lives by images. They
Lean at us from the world's wall, and Time's.

[4]

Night of the falling mercury, and ice-glitter.
Drouth-night of August and the horned insect booming
At the window-screen.

Ice-field, dusty road: distance flees.

And he sits there, and I think I hear
The faint click and grind of the brain as
It translates the perception of black marks on white paper into
Truth.

Truth is all.

We must love it.

And he loved it, who once said:

"It is terrible for a man to live and not know."

Every day he walked out to the cemetery to honor his dead.
That was truth, too.

[5]

Dear Father—Sir—the "Sir" being
The sometimes disturbed recollection
Of the time when you were big, and not dead, and I
Was little, and all boys, of that time and place, automatically
Said that to their fathers, and to any other grown man,
White of course, or damned well got their blocks
Knocked off.

So, Sir, I,
Who certainly could never have addressed you on a matter
As important as this when you were not dead, now
Address you on it for the last time, even though
Not being, after all my previous and sometimes desperate efforts,
Sure what a son can ever say to a father, even
A dead one.

Indecipherable passion and compulsion—well,
Wouldn't it be sad to see them, of whatever
Dark root, dwindle into mere
Self-indulgence, habit, tic of the mind, or
The picking of a scab. Reality
Is hard enough to come by, but even
In its absence we need not blaspheme
It.

Not that
You ever could, God knows. Though I,
No doubt, have, and even now
Run the risk of doing so when I say
That I live in a profound, though
Painful, gratitude to you for what
You could not help but be: i.e., yourself.

Who, aged eighty, said:

"I've failed in a lot of things, but I don't think anybody can say that I didn't
have guts."

Correct.

And I,
In spite of my own ignorance and failures,
Have forgiven you all your virtues.

Even your valor.

[6]

Who, aged eighty-six, fell to the floor,
Unconscious. Two days later,
Dead. Thus they discovered your precious secret:
A prostate big as a horse-apple. Cancer, of course.

No wonder you, who had not spent a day in bed,
Or uttered a single complaint, in the fifty years of my life,
Cried out at last.

You were entitled to that. It was only normal.

[7]

So disappeared.

Simply not there.

And the seasons,
Nerve-tingling heat or premonitory chill, swung
Through the year, the years swung,

and the past, great
Eater of dreams, secrets, and random data, and
Refrigerator of truth, moved
Down what green valley at a glacier's
Massive pace,

moving
At a pace not to be calculated by the trivial sun, but by
A clock more unforgiving that, at
Its distance of mathematical nightmare,
Glows forever. The ice-mass, scabbed
By earth, boulders, and some strange vegetation, moves
So imperceptibly that it seems
Only more landscape.

Until,
In late-leveling light, some lunkhead clodhopper,
The day's work done, now trudging home,
Stops.

Stares.

And there it is.

It looms.

*

The bulk of the unnamable and de-timed beast is now visible,
Erect, in the thinly glimmering shadow of ice.

The lunkhead
Stares.

The beast,
From his preternatural height, unaware of
The cringe and jaw-dropped awe crouching there below, suddenly,
As if that shimmer of ice-screen had not even been there, lifts,

Into distance,

the magisterial gaze.

[8]

The mercury falls. Tonight snow is predicted. This,
However, is another country.

XXI. Folly on Royal Street before the Raw Face of God

Drunk, drunk, drunk, amid the blaze of noon,
Irrevocably drunk, total eclipse or,
At least, almost, and in New Orleans once,
In French Town, spring,
Off the Gulf, without storm warnings out,
Burst, like a hurricane of
Camellias, sperm, cat-squalls, fish-smells, and the old
Pain of fulfillment-that-is-not-fulfillment, so
Down Royal Street—Sunday and the street
Blank as my bank account
With two checks bounced—we—
C. and M. and I, every
Man-jack skunk-drunk—
Came.

A cat,
Gray from the purple shadow of bougainvillaea,
Fish-head in dainty jaw-clench,
Flowed fluid as thought, secret as sin, across
The street. Was gone. We,
In the shock of that sudden and glittering vacancy, rocked
On our heels.

*

                    A cop,
Of brachycephalic head and garlic breath,
Toothpick from side of mouth and pants ass-bagged and holster low,
From eyes the color of old coffee grounds,
Regarded with imperfect sympathy
La condition humaine—
Which was sure-God what we were.

We rocked on our heels.

                                        At sky-height—
Whiteness ablaze in dazzle and frazzle of light like
A match flame in noon-blaze—a gull
Kept screaming above the doomed city.
It screamed for justice against the face of God.

Raw-ringed with glory like an ulcer, God's
Raw face stared down.

                                        And winked.

                                                            We
Mouthed out our Milton for magnificence.

For what is man without magnificence?

Delusion, delusion!

                                    But let
Bells ring in all the churches.
Let likker, like philosophy, roar
In the skull. Passion
Is all. Even
The sleaziest.

                    War
Came. Among the bed-sheet Arabs, C.
Sported his gold oak leaf. Survived.
Got back. Back to the bank. But
One morning was not there. His books,
However, were in apple-pie order. His suits,
All dark, hung in the dark closet. Drawn up
In military precision, his black shoes,
Though highly polished, gave forth
No gleam in that darkness. In Mexico,
He died.

            For M.,
Twenty years in the Navy. Retired,
He fishes. Long before dawn, the launch slides out.
Land lost, he cuts the engine. The launch

Lifts, falls, in the time of the sea's slow breath.
Eastward, first light is like
A knife-edge honed to steel-brightness
And laid to the horizon. Sometimes,
He comes back in with no line wet.

As for the third, the tale
Is short. But long,
How long the art, and wisdom slow!—for him who
Once rocked on his heels, hearing the gull scream,
And quoted Milton amid the blaze of noon.

Interjection #8:
Or, Sometimes, Night

For Paul Horgan

The unsleeping principle of delight that
Declares the arc of the apple's rondure; of, equally,
A girl's thigh that, as she lies, lifts
And draws full forward in its subtly reversed curve from
Buttock bulge to the now softly closing under-knee nook; and of
The flushed dawn cumulus: the principle
That brackets, too, the breaker's crest in one
Timeless instant, glittering, between
Last upward erg and, suddenly,
Totter and boom; and that,
In a startling burst of steel-brilliant sun, makes
The lone snow-flake dance—
this principle is what,
Intermittently at least and at unlikely moments,
Comes into my mind,
Whether by day or, sometimes, night.

XXII. Sunset Walk in Thaw-Time in Vermont

1.

Rip, whoosh, wing-whistle: and out of
The spruce thicket, beating the snow from
Black spruce boughs, it
Bursts. The great partridge cock, black against flame-red,
Into the red sun of sunset, plunges. Is
Gone.

*

In the ensuing
Silence, abrupt in
Back-flash and shiver of that sharp startlement, I
Stand. Stare. In mud-streaked snow,
My feet are. I,
Eyes fixed past black spruce boughs on the red west, hear,
In my chest, as from a dark cave of
No-Time, the heart
Beat.

Where
Have the years gone?

2.

All day the stream, thaw-flooding, foamed down its gorge.
Now, skyless but for the high-tangled spruce night, it
Moves, and the bulge and slick twining of muscular water, foam-
Slashed and white-tettered, glints now only in
The cold, self-generating light of snow
Strong yet in the darkness of rock-banks.

The boulder
Groans in the stream, the stream heaves
In the deep certainty of its joy, like
Doom, and I,
Eyes fixed yet on the red west, begin to hear—though
Slow and numb as upon waking—
The sound of water that moves in darkness.

I stand, and in my imagination see
The slick heave of water, blacker than basalt, and on it
The stern glint, like steel, of snow-darkness.

3.

On the same spot in summer, at thrush-hour, I,
As the last light fails, have heard that full
Shadow-shimmered and deep-glinting liquidity, and
Again will; but not now.

Now
Here stare westward, and hear only
The movement of darkening water, and from
Whatever depth of being I am, ask
To be made worthy of my human failures and folly, and
Worthy of my human ignorance and anguish, and of
What soul-stillness may be achieved as I
Stand here with the cold exhalation of snow
Coiling high as my knees.

*

Meanwhile,
On the mountain's east hump, darkness coagulates, and
Already, where sun has not touched for hours, the new
Ice-crystal frames its massive geometry.

4.

When my son is an old man, and I have not,
For some fifty years, seen his face, and, if seeing it,
Would not even be able to guess what name it wore, what
Blessing should I ask for him?

That some time, in thaw-season, at dusk, standing
At woodside and staring
Red-westward, with the sound of moving water
In his ears, he
Should thus, in that future moment, bless,
Forward into that future's future,
An old man who, as he is mine, had once
Been his small son.

For what blessing may a man hope for but
An immortality in
The loving vigilance of death?

XXIII. Birth of Love

Season late, day late, sun just down, and the sky
Cold gunmetal but with a wash of live rose, and she,
From water the color of sky except where
Her motion has fractured it to shivering splinters of silver,
Rises. Stands on the raw grass. Against
The new-curdling night of spruces, nakedness
Glimmers and, at bosom and flank, drips
With fluent silver. The man,

Some ten strokes out, but now hanging
Motionless in the gunmetal water, feet
Cold with the coldness of depth, all
History dissolving from him, is
Nothing but an eye. Is an eye only. Sees

The body that is marked by his use, and Time's,
Rise, and in the abrupt and unsustaining element of air,
Sway, lean, grapple the pond-bank. Sees
How, with that posture of female awkwardness that is,

And is the stab of, suddenly perceived grace, breasts bulge down in
The pure curve of their weight and buttocks
Moon up and, in that swelling unity,
Are silver, and glimmer. Then

The body is erect, she is herself, whatever
Self she may be, and with an end of the towel grasped in each hand,
Slowly draws it back and forth across back and buttocks, but
With face lifted toward the high sky, where
The over-wash of rose color now fails. Fails, though no star
Yet throbs there. The towel, forgotten,
Does not move now. The gaze
Remains fixed on the sky. The body,

Profiled against the darkness of spruces, seems
To draw to itself, and condense in its whiteness, what light
In the sky yet lingers or, from
The metallic and abstract severity of water, lifts. The body,
With the towel now trailing loose from one hand, is
A white stalk from which the face flowers gravely toward the high sky.
This moment is non-sequential and absolute, and admits
Of no definition, for it
Subsumes all other, and sequential, moments, by which
Definition might be possible. The woman,

Face yet raised, wraps,
With a motion as though standing in sleep,
The towel about her body, under the breasts, and,
Holding it there, hieratic as lost Egypt and erect,
Moves up the path that, stair-steep, winds
Into the clamber and tangle of growth. Beyond
The lattice of dusk-dripping leaves, whiteness
Dimly glimmers, goes. Glimmers and is gone, and the man,

Suspended in his darkling medium, stares
Upward where, though not visible, he knows
She moves, and in his heart he cries out that, if only
He had such strength, he would put his hand forth
And maintain it over her to guard, in all
Her out-goings and in-comings, from whatever
Inclemency of sky or slur of the world's weather
Might ever be. In his heart
He cries out. Above

Height of the spruce-night and heave of the far mountain, he sees
The first star pulse into being. It gleams there.

I do not know what promise it makes to him.

XXIV. A Problem in Spatial Composition

[1]

Through the high window, upright rectangle of distance:

Over the green interstices and shambling glory, yet bright, of forest,
Distance flees westward, the sun low.

Beyond the distance of forest, hangs that which is blue:
Which is, in knowledge, a tall scarp of stone, gray, but now is,
In the truth of perception, stacked like a mass of blue cumulus.
Blue deepens.

What we know, we know, and
Sun now down, flame, above blue, dies upward forever in
Saffron: pure, pure and forever, the sky
Upward is. The lintel of the high window, by interruption,

Confirms what the heart knows: *beyond* is *forever*—

and nothing moves
Across the glister of saffron, and under the
Window the brook that,
After lalling and lounging daylong by shallow and reach,
Through dapple to glitter, now recessed in
Its premature leaf-night, utters a deeper-toned meditation.

[2]

While out of the green, up-shining ramshackle of leaf, set
In the lower right foreground, the stub
Of a great tree, gaunt-blasted and black, thrusts.

A single
Arm jags upward, higher goes, and in that perspective, higher
Than even the dream-blue of distance that is
The mountain.

Then
Stabs, black, at the infinite saffron of sky.

All is ready.

The hawk,
Entering the composition at the upper left frame
Of the window, glides,
In the pellucid ease of thought and at
His breathless angle,
Down.

*

Breaks speed.

Hangs with a slight lift and hover.

Makes contact.

The hawk perches on the topmost, indicative tip of
The bough's sharp black and skinny jag skyward.

[3]

The hawk, in an eyeblink, is gone.

Can I See Arcturus From Where I Stand?

Poems 1975

To Eleanor, Rosanna, Gabriel

Is was *but a word for wisdom, its price?*
"Rattlesnake Country"

A Way to Love God

Here is the shadow of truth, for only the shadow is true.
And the line where the incoming swell from the sunset Pacific
First leans and staggers to break will tell all you need to know
About submarine geography, and your father's death rattle
Provides all biographical data required for the *Who's Who* of the dead.

I cannot recall what I started to tell you, but at least
I can say how night-long I have lain under stars and
Heard mountains moan in their sleep. By daylight,
They remember nothing, and go about their lawful occasions
Of not going anywhere except in slow disintegration. At night
They remember, however, that there is something they cannot remember,
So moan. Theirs is the perfected pain of conscience, that
Of forgetting the crime, and I hope you have not suffered it. I have.

I do not recall what had burdened my tongue, but urge you
To think on the slug's white belly, how sick-slick and soft,
On the hairiness of stars, silver, silver, while the silence
Blows like wind by, and on the sea's virgin bosom unveiled
To give suck to the wavering serpent of the moon; and,
In the distance, in *plaza, piazza, place, platz,* and square,
Boot heels, like history being born, on cobbles bang.

Everything seems an echo of something else.

And when, by the hair, the headsman held up the head
Of Mary of Scots, the lips kept on moving,
But without sound. The lips,
They were trying to say something very important.

But I had forgotten to mention an upland
Of wind-tortured stone white in darkness, and tall, but when
No wind, mist gathers, and once on the Sarré at midnight,
I watched the sheep huddling. Their eyes
Stared into nothingness. In that mist-diffused light their eyes
Were stupid and round like the eyes of fat fish in muddy water,
Or of a scholar who has lost faith in his calling.

Their jaws did not move. Shreds
Of dry grass, gray in gray mist-light, hung
From the side of a jaw, unmoving.

You would think that nothing would ever again happen.

That is a way to love God.

Evening Hawk

From plane of light to plane, wings dipping through
Geometries and orchids that the sunset builds,
Out of the peak's black angularity of shadow, riding
The last tumultuous avalanche of
Light above pines and the guttural gorge,
The hawk comes.

His wing
Scythes down another day, his motion
Is that of the honed steel-edge, we hear
The crashless fall of stalks of Time.

The head of each stalk is heavy with the gold of our error.

Look! look! he is climbing the last light
Who knows neither Time nor error, and under
Whose eye, unforgiving, the world, unforgiven, swings
Into shadow.

Long now,
The last thrush is still, the last bat
Now cruises in his sharp hieroglyphics. His wisdom
Is ancient, too, and immense. The star
Is steady, like Plato, over the mountain.

If there were no wind we might, we think, hear
The earth grind on its axis, or history
Drip in darkness like a leaking pipe in the cellar.

Loss, of Perhaps Love, in Our World of Contingency

Think! Think hard. Try to remember
When last you had it. There's always

A logic to everything, and you are a part
Of everything, and your heart bleeds far

Beyond the outermost pulsar. Put your mind on
The problem, and under no circumstances look

In the mirror, for you might not
Recognize what you see there, and the night wind

Shuffles a torn newspaper down the street with a sound
Like an old bum's old shoe-soles that he makes

*

Slide on the pavement to keep them from flopping off.
Shut your eyes, think hard, it doesn't really

Matter which end you start from—forward from
The earliest thing you remember, the dapple

Of sunlight on the bathroom floor while your mother
Bathed you, or backward from just now when

You found it gone and cried out, *oh Jesus, no!* Yes,
Forward or backward, it's all the same,

To the time you are sure you last had it. Violets,
Buried now under dead leaves (later snowdrifts), dream

How each, with a new-born, dew-bright eye, will see
You again pass, cleaving the blue air.

Oh, bestiaries!—

Myths, and moraines where the basalt boulders, moonlit, grieve
And the dark little corner under your bed, where God

Huddles tight in the fluff-ball, like a cocoon, that He,
All-knowing, knows the vacuum won't find!

Think hard. Take a deep breath. As the thunder-clap
Dissolves into silence, your nostrils thrill to the

Stunned new electric tang of joy—or pain—like ammonia.

We must learn to live in the world.

Answer to Prayer

A Short Story That Could Be Longer

In that bad year, in a city to have now no name,
In the already-dark of a winter's day, our feet
Unsteady in slip-tilt and crunch of re-freezing snow as if lame,
And two hands ungloved to clasp closer though cold, down a side street

We moved. Ahead, intersecting, stretched the avenue where
Life clanged and flared like a gaudy disaster under
Whatever the high sky wombed in its dark imperative of air,
And where, to meat and drink set, we might soon pretend, or

At least hope, that sincerity could be bought by pain.
But now stopped. She said, "Wait!" And abrupt, was gone
Up the snow-smeared broad stone to dark doors before I could restrain
That sentimental idiocy. Alone,

*

As often before in a night-street, I raised eyes
To pierce what membrane remotely enclosed the great bubble of light that now
The city inflated against the dark hover of infinities,
And saw how a first frail wavering stipple of shadow

Emerged high in that spectral concavity of light, and drew down to be,
In the end, only snow. Then she, again there, to my question, replied
That she had made a prayer. And I: "For what?" And she:
"Nothing much, just for you to be happy." Then cocking her head to one side,

Looked up and grinned at me, an impudent eye-sparkling grin, as though
She had just pulled the trick of the week, and on a cold-flushed
Cheek, at the edge of the grin for an accent, the single snow-
Flake settled, and gaily in insult she stuck her tongue out, and blood rushed

To my heart. So with hands again nakedly clasped, through the soft veil and swish
Of flakes falling, we moved toward the avenue. And later, proceeded,
Beyond swirl and chain-clank of traffic, and a siren's far anguish,
To the unlit room to enact what comfort body and heart needed.

Who does not know the savvy insanity and wit
Of history! and how its most savage peripeteia always
Has the shape of a joke—if you find the heart to laugh at it.
In such a world, then, one must be pretty careful how one prays.

Her prayer, yes, was answered, for in spite of my meager desert,
Of a sudden, life—it was bingo! was bells and all ringing like mad,
Lights flashing, fruit spinning, the machine spurting dollars like dirt—
Nevada dollars, that is—but all just a metaphor for the luck I now had.

But that was long later, and as answer to prayer long out
Of phase. And now thinking of her, I can know neither what, nor where,
She may be, and even in gratitude, I must doubt
That she ever remembers she ever prayed such a prayer.

Or if she remembers, she laughs into the emptiness of air.

Paradox

Running ahead beside the sea,
You turned and flung a smile, like spray.
It glittered like tossed spray in the sunlight.
Yes, well I remember, to this day,
That glittering ambiguity.

*

I saw, when your foot fulfilled its stride,
How the sand, compressed, burst to silver light,
But when I had reached that aureoled spot
There was only another in further flight:
And bright hair, wind-strung, to tease the sun's pride.

Yes, far away and long ago,
In another land, on another shore,
That race you won—even as it was lost,
For if I caught you, one moment more,
You had fled my grasp, up and to go

With glowing pace and the smile that mocks
Pursuit down whatever shore reflects
Our flickering passage through the years,
As we enact our more complex
Version of Zeno's paradox.

Midnight Outcry

Torn from the dream-life, torn from the life-dream,
Beside him in darkness, the cry bursts: *Oh!*
Endearment and protest—they avail
Nothing against whatever is so
Much deeper and darker than anything love may redeem.

He lies in the dark and tries to remember
How godlike to strive in passion and sweat,
But fears to awaken and clasp her, lest
Their whole life be lost, for he cannot forget
That the depths that cry rose from might shrivel a heart, or member.

How bright dawns morning!—how sweetly the face
Inclines over the infant to whom she gives suck.
So his heart leaps in joy, but remembering
That echo of fate beyond faith or luck,
He fixes his studious gaze on the scene to trace

In the least drop spilled between nipple and the ferocious
Little lip-suction, some logic, some white
Spore of the human condition that carries,
In whiteness, the dark need that only at night
Finds voice—but only and always one strange to us.

The day wore on, and he would ponder,
Lifting eyes from his work, thinking, thinking,
Of the terrible distance in love, and the pain,
Smiling back at the sunlit smile, even while shrinking
From recall of the nocturnal timbre, and the dark wonder.

Trying to Tell You Something

To Tinkum Brooks

All things lean at you, and some are
Trying to tell you something, though of some

The heart is too full for speech. On a hill, the oak,
Immense, older than Jamestown or God, splitting

With its own weight at the great inverted
Crotch, air-spread and ice-hung, ringed with iron

Like barrel-hoops, only heavier, massive rods
Running through and bolted, and higher, the cables,

Which in summer are hidden by green leaves—the oak,
It is trying to tell you something. It wants,

In its fullness of years, to describe to you
What happens on a December night when

It stands alone in a world of snowy whiteness. The moon is full.
You can hear the stars crackle in their high brightness.

It is ten below zero, and the iron
Of hoops and reinforcement rods is continuing to contract.

There is the rhythm of a slow throb, like pain. The wind,
Northwest, is steady, and in the wind, the cables,

In a thin-honed and disinfectant purity, like
A dentist's drill, sing. They sing

Of truth, and its beauty. The oak
Wants to declare this to you, so that you

Will not be unprepared when, some December night,
You stand on a hill, in a world of whiteness, and

Stare into the crackling absoluteness of the sky. The oak
Wants to tell you because, at that moment,

In your own head, the cables will sing
With a thin-honed and disinfectant purity,

And no one can predict the consequences.

Brotherhood in Pain

Fix your eyes on any chance object. For instance,
That leaf, prematurely crimson, of the swamp maple

That dawdles down gold air to the velvet-black water
Of the moribund beaver-pond. Or the hunk

Of dead chewing gum in the gutter with the mark of a molar
Yet distinct on it, like the most delicate Hellenistic chisel-work.

Or a black sock you took off last night and by mistake
Left lying, to be found in the morning, on the bathroom tiles.

Or pick up a single stone from the brookside, inspect it
Most carefully, then throw it back in. You will never

See it again. By the next spring flood, it may have been hurled
A mile downstream. Fix your gaze on any of these objects,

Or if you think me disingenuous in my suggestions,
Whirl around three times like a child, or a dervish, with eyes shut,

Then fix on the first thing seen when they open.
In any case, you will suddenly observe an object in the obscene moment of birth.

It does not know its own name. The matrix from which it is torn
Bleeds profusely. It has not yet begun to breathe. Its experience

Is too terrible to recount. Only when it has completely forgotten
Everything, will it smile shyly, and try to love you,

For somehow it knows that you are lonely, too.
It pityingly knows that you are more lonely than it is, for

You exist only in the delirious illusion of language.

Season Opens on Wild Boar in Chianti

To Guerino and Ginevra Roberti

They are hunting the boar in the vineyards.
They halloo and hunt in the pine-glen.
Their voices in distance are music.
Now hounds have the scent, they make music.
The world is all music, we listen:
Men are hunting because they are mere men.

*

Gold light of October falls over
The vineyards and dark bulbs exposed there.
The blood of the great boar has thickened
With grapes, and oak-mast on the ridges.
He is full of years, and now waits where
His tusks gleam white in the dark air.

Since sunrise the halloo and music
Has filled all the vineyards, and wild ground.
Music echoed among the high pine boughs.
It was heard where the oak leaf cast shadow.
Now where rushes are trampled, is no sound.
Dead too, at the tusk-point, the best hound.

In the twilight and silence, now passing
Our door, men pant with the heavi-
ness of their destiny's burden,
Each wondering who will be able
To choose his own ground when the adversary
Encounters him, red eye to red eye.

The boar stood well backed by the river,
His flanks safe in a cavern of rushes.
In front was only the whole world.
But who cares for that, it is simple—
The moiling of dogs and scared dashes,
Men's halloo and stupid fire-flashes?

The delicate, razor-sharp feet, not
Now dancing, now dancing, point starward.
They are lashed to a pole swung from shoulders
So the great head swings weighty and thoughtful
While eyes blank in wisdom stare hard
At the foot-gravel grinding slow forward.

Thus onward they pass in the nightfall,
The great head swinging down, tusks star-gleaming.
The constellations are steady.
The wind sets in from the northeast.
And we bolt up our doors, thus redeeming,
From darkness, our ignorant dreaming.

Old Nigger on One-Mule Cart Encountered Late at Night When Driving Home From Party in the Back Country

Flesh, of a sudden, gone nameless in music, flesh
Of the dancer, under your hand, flowing to music, girl-
Flesh sliding, flesh flowing, sweeter than
Honey, slicker than Essolube, over
The music-swayed, delicate trellis of bone
That is white in secret flesh-darkness. What
The music, it says: *no name, no name!*—only
That movement under your hand, what
It is, and no name, and you shut your eyes, but
The music, it stops. O.K. Silence
Rages, it ranges the world, it will
Devour us, for
That sound I do now hear is not external, is
Simply the crinkle and crepitation,
Like crickets gone nuts, of
Booze in the blood. *Goodnight! Goodnight!*

I can't now even remember the name of the dancer, but

I must try to tell you what, in July, in Louisiana,
Night is. No moon, but stars whitely outrageous in
Blackness of velvet, the long lane ahead
Whiter than snow, wheels soundless in deep dust, dust
Pluming whitely behind, and ahead all
The laneside hedges and weed-growth
Long since powdered whiter than star-dust, or frost, but air
Hot. The night pants hot like a dog, it breathes
Off the blossoming bayou like the expensive whiff
Of floral tributes at a gangster's funeral in N.O.,
It breathes the smell love makes in darkness, and far off,
In the great swamp, an owl cries,
And does not stop. At the sharp right turn,
Hedge-blind, which you take too fast,
There it is: death-trap.

On the fool-nigger, ass-hole wrong side of
The road, naturally: And the mule-head
Thrusts at us, and ablaze in our headlights,
Outstaring from primal bone-blankness and the arrogant
Stupidity of skull snatched there
From darkness and the saurian stew of pre-Time,
For an instant—the eyes. The eyes,
They blaze from the incandescent magma
Of mule-brain. Thus mule-eyes. Then
Man-eyes, not blazing, white-bulging

In black face, in black night, and man-mouth
Wide open, the shape of an *O,* for the scream
That does not come. Even now,
That much in my imagination, I see. But also
The cargo of junk the black face blooms amidst—
Rusted bed-springs on end, auto axle at God-knows-what
Angle up-canted, barbed wire on a fence rail wound,
Lengths of stove pipe beat up. God-yes,
A death-trap. But
I snatch the wheel left in a dust-skid,
Smack into the ditch, but the ditch
Shallow, and so, not missing a beat, I'm out
And go on, and he's left alone on his cart there
Unmoving, and dust of the car's passage settles
White on sweat-sticky skin, black, of the forehead, and on
The already gray head. This,
Of course, under the high stars.

Perhaps he had screamed, after all.

And go on: to the one last drink, sweat-grapple in darkness, then
Sleep. But only until
The hour when small, though disturbing, gastric shifts
Are experienced, the hour when the downy
Throat of the swamp owl vibrates to the last
Predawn cry, the hour
When joy-sweat, or night-sweat, has dried to a microscopic
Crust on the skin, and some
Recollection of childhood brings tears
To dark-wide eyes, and the super-ego
Again throws the switch for the old recorded harangue.
Until waking, that is—and I wake to see
Floating in darkness above the bed the
Black face, eyes white-bulging, mouth shaped like an *O,* and so
Get up, get paper and pencil, and whittle away at
The poem. Give up. Back to bed. And remember
Now only the couplet of what
Had aimed to be—Jesus Christ—a sonnet:
    One of those who gather junk and wire to use
    For purposes that we cannot peruse.

As I said, Jesus Christ. But

Moved on through the years. Am here. Another
Land, another love, and in such latitude, having risen
In darkness, feet bare to cold boards, stare,
Through ice-glitter of glass and air purer
Than absolute zero, into
The white night and star-crackling sky over
The snow-mountain. Have you ever,
At night, stared into the snow-filled forest and felt

The impulse to flee there? Enter there? Be
There and plunge naked
Through snow, through drifts floundering, white
Into whiteness, among
Spectral great beech-boles, birch-whiteness, black jag
Of shadow, black spruce-bulks snow-shouldered, floundering
Upward and toward the glacial assertion that
The mountain is? Have you ever
Had the impulse to stretch forth your hand over
The bulge of forest and seize trees like the hair
Of a head you would master? Well,
We are entitled to our fantasies, for life
Is only the fantasy that has happened to us, and

In God's name. But

In the lyrical logic and nightmare astuteness that
Is God's name, by what magnet, I demand,
Are the iron and out-flung filings of our lives, on
A sheet of paper, blind-blank as Time, snapped
Into a polarized pattern—and I see,
By a bare field that yearns pale in starlight, the askew
Shack. He arrives there. Unhitches the mule.
Stakes it out. Between cart and shack,
Pauses to make water, and while
The soft, plopping sound in deep dust continues, his face
Is lifted into starlight, calm as prayer. He enters
The dark shack, and I see
A match spurt, then burn down, die.

The last glow is reflected on the petal-pink
And dark horn-crust of the thumbnail.

And so I say:
Brother, Rebuker, my Philosopher past all
Casuistry, will you be with me when
I arrive and leave my own cart of junk
Unfended from the storm of starlight and
The howl, like wind, of the world's monstrous blessedness,
To enter, by a bare field, a shack unlit?
Entering into that darkness to fumble
My way to a place to lie down, but holding,
I trust, in my hand, a name—
Like a shell, a dry flower, a worn stone, a toy—merely
A hard-won something that may, while Time
Backward unblooms out of time toward peace, utter
Its small, sober, and inestimable
Glow, trophy of truth.

Can I see Arcturus from where I stand?

Now and Then

Poems 1976–1978

To Andrew Vincent Corry

. . . let the inhabitants of the rock sing . . .
Isaiah 42:11

I. Nostalgic

American Portrait: Old Style

I.

Beyond the last house, where home was,
Past the marsh we found the old skull in, all nameless
And cracked in star-shape from a stone-smack,
Up the hill where the grass was tangled waist-high and wind-tousled,
To the single great oak that, in leaf-season, hung like
A thunderhead black against whatever blue the sky had,

And here, at the widest circumference of shade, when shade was,
Ran the trench, six feet long,
And wide enough for a man to lie down in,
In comfort, if comfort was still any object. No sign there
Of any ruined cabin or well, so Pap must have died of camp fever,
And the others pushed on, God knows where.

II.

The Dark and Bloody Ground, so the teacher romantically said,
But one look out the window, and woods and ruined cornfields we saw:
A careless-flung corner of country, no hope and no history here.
No hope but the Pullman lights that swept
Night-fields—glass-glint from some farmhouse and flicker of ditches—
Or the night freight's moan on the rise where
You might catch a ride on the rods,
Just for hell, or if need had arisen.
No history either—no Harrod or Finley or Boone,
No tale how the Bluebellies broke at the Rebel yell and cold steel.

So we had to invent it all, our Bloody Ground, K and I,
And him the best shot in ten counties and could call any bird-note back,
But school out, not big enough for the ballgame,
And in the full tide of summer, not ready
For the twelve-gauge yet, or even a job, so what
Can you do but pick up your BBs and Benjamin,
Stick corn pone in pocket, and head out
"To Rally in the Cane-Brake and Shoot the Buffalo"—
As my grandfather's cracked old voice would sing it
From days of his own grandfather—and often enough
It was only a Plymouth Rock or maybe a fat Dominecker
That fell to the crack of the unerring Decherd.

*

III.

Yes, imagination is strong. But not strong enough in the face of
The sticky feathers and BBs a mother's hand held out.
But no liberal concern was evinced for a Redskin,
As we trailed and out-tricked the sly Shawnees
In a thicket of ironweed, and I wrestled one naked
And slick with his bear grease, till my hunting knife
Bit home, and the tomahawk
Slipped from his hand. And what mother cared about Bluebellies
Who came charging our trench? But we held
To pour the last volley at face-gape before
The tangle and clangor of bayonet.

Yes, a day is merely forever
In memory's shiningness,
And a year but a gust or a gasp
In the summer's heat of Time, and in that last summer
I was almost ready to learn
What imagination is—it is only
The lie we must learn to live by, if ever
We mean to live at all. Times change.
Things change. And K up and gone, and the summer
Gone, and I longed to know the world's name.

IV.

Well, what I remember most
In a world long Time-pale and powdered
Like a vision still clinging to plaster
Set by Piero della Francesca
Is how K, through lane-dust or meadow,
Seemed never to walk, but float
With a singular joy and silence,
In his cloud of bird dogs, like angels,
With their eyes on his eyes like God,
And the sun on his uncut hair bright
As he passed through the ramshackle town and odd folks there
With pants on and vests and always soft gabble of money—
Polite in his smiling, but never much to say.

V.

To pass through to what? No, not
To some wild white peak dreamed westward,
And each sunrise a promise to keep. No, only
The Big Leagues, not even a bird dog,
And girls that popped gum while they screwed.

Yes, this was his path, and no batter
Could do what booze finally did:
Just blow him off the mound—but anyway,

He had always called it a fool game, just something
For children who hadn't yet dreamed what
A man is, or barked a squirrel, or raised
A single dog from a pup.

VI.

And I, too, went on my way, the winning and losing, or what
Is sometimes of all things the worst, the not knowing
One thing from the other, nor knowing
How the teeth in Time's jaw all snag backward
And whatever enters therein
Has less hope of remission than shark-meat,

And one Sunday afternoon, in the idleness of summer,
I found his farm, and him home there,
With the bird dogs crouched round in the grass
And their eyes on his eyes as he whispered
Whatever to bird dogs it was.
Then yelled: "Well, for Christ's sake—it's you!"

Yes, me, for Christ's sake, and some sixty
Years blown like a hurricane past! But what can you say—
Can you say—when *all-to-be-said* is the *done?*
So our talk ran to buffalo-hunting, and the look on his mother's face,

And the sun sank slow as he stood there,
All Indian-brown from waist up, who never liked tops to his pants,
And standing nigh straight, but the arms and the pitcher's
Great shoulders, they were thinning to old-man thin.
Sun low, all silence, then sudden:
"But, Jesus," he cried, "what makes a man do what he does—
Him living until he dies!"

Sure, all of us live till we die, but bingo!
Like young David at brookside, he swooped down,
Snatched a stone, wound up, and let fly,
And high on a pole over yonder the big brown insulator
Simply exploded. "See—I still got control!" he said.

VII.

Late, late, toward sunset, I wandered
Where old dreams had once been Life's truth, and where
I saw the trench of our valor, now nothing
But a ditch full of late-season weed-growth,
Beyond the rim of shade.

There was nobody there, hence no shame to be saved from, so I
Just lie in the trench on my back and see high,
Beyond the tall ironweed stalks, or oak leaves
If I happen to look that way,

How the late summer's thinned-out sky moves,
Drifting on, drifting on, like forever,
From *where* on to *where,* and I wonder
What it would be like to die,
Like the nameless old skull in the swamp, lost,
And know yourself dead lying under
The infinite motion of sky.

VIII.

But why should I lie here longer?
I am not dead yet, though in years,
And the world's way is yet long to go,
And I love the world even in my anger,
And love is a hard thing to outgrow.

Amazing Grace in the Back Country

In the season of late August star-fall,
When the first crickets crinkled the dark,
There by woods, where oaks of the old forest-time
Yet swaggered and hulked over upstarts, the tent
Had been pitched, no bigger than one of
Some half-bankrupt carnival come
To town with fat lady, human skeleton, geek,
Man-woman and moth-eaten lion, and one
Boa constrictor for two bits seen
Fed a young calf; plus a brace
Of whores to whom menopause now
Was barely a memory, one with gold teeth and one
With game gam, but both
With aperture ready to serve
Any late-lingerers, and leave
A new and guaranteed brand of syphilis handy—yes,

The tent old and yellowed and patched,
Lit inside by three wire-hung gasoline lamps
That outside, through threadbare canvas, were muted to gold.
Here no carnival now—the tabernacle
To the glory of God the Most High, for now corn
Was laid by, business slack, such business as was, and
The late-season pain gnawing deep at the human bone
As the season burned on to its end.

God's Word and His glory—and I, aged twelve,
Sat there while an ex-railroad engineer
Turned revivalist shouted the Threat and the Promise, with sweat
On his brow, and shirt plastered to belly, and
Eyes a-glaze with the mania of joy.

*

And now by my knees crouched some old-fool dame
In worn-out black silk, there crouching with tears
In her eyes as she tugged me to kneel
And save my pore twelve-year-old soul
Before too late. She wept.
She wept and she prayed, and I knew I was damned,
Who was guilty of all short of murder,
At least in my heart and no alibi there, and once
I had walked down a dark street, lights out in houses,
Uttering, "Lust—lust—lust,"
Like an invocation, out loud—and the word
So lovely, fresh-minted.

I saw others fall as though stricken. I heard
The shout of salvation. I stared
In the red-rimmed, wet eyes of the crazy old dame,
Whose name I never remembered, but knew
That she loved me—the Pore Little Lamb—and I thought
How old bones now creaked in God's name.

But the Pore Little Lamb, he hardened his heart,
Like a flint nigger-head rounded slick in a creek-bed
By generations of flood, and suddenly
I found myself standing, then
Ran down an aisle, and outside,
Where cool air and dark filled my lungs, and fifty
Yards off, with my brow pressed hard
On the scaly bark of a hickory tree,
Vomited. Fumbling
In darkness, I found the spring
And washed my mouth. Humped there,

And knowing damnation, I stared
Through interstices of black brush to the muted gold glow
Of God's canvas, till in
The last hymn of triumph rose voices, and hearts
Burst with joy at amazing grace so freely given,
And moving on into darkness,

Voices sang of amazing grace, singing as they
Straggled back to the village, where voice after voice died away,
As singer by singer, in some dark house,
Found bed and lay down,
And tomorrow would rise and do all the old things to do,
Until that morning they would not rise, not ever.

And now, when all voices were stilled and the lamps
Long out in the tent, and stars
Had changed place in the sky, I yet lay
By the spring with one hand in the cold black water
That showed one star in reflection, alone—and lay

Wondering and wondering how many
A morning would I rise up to greet,
And what grace find.

But that was long years ago. I was twelve years old then.

Boy Wandering in Simms' Valley

Through brush and love-vine, well blooded by blackberry thorn
Long dry past prime, under summer's late molten light
And past the last rock-slide at ridge-top and stubborn,
Raw tangle of cedar, I clambered, breath short and spit white

From lung-depth. Then down the lone valley, called Simms' Valley still,
Where Simms, long back, had nursed a sick wife till she died.
Then turned out his spindly stock to forage at will,
And took down his twelve-gauge, and simply lay down by her side.

No kin they had, and nobody came just to jaw.
It was two years before some straggling hunter sat down
On the porch-edge to rest, then started to prowl. He saw
What he saw, saw no reason to linger, so high-tailed to town.

A dirt-farmer needs a good wife to keep a place trim,
So the place must have gone to wrack with his old lady sick.
And when I came there, years later, old furrows were dim,
And dimmer in fields where grew maples and such, a span thick.

So for years the farm had contracted: now barn down, and all
The yard back to wilderness gone, and only
The house to mark human hope, but ready to fall.
No buyer at tax-sale, it waited, forgotten and lonely.

I stood in the bedroom upstairs, in lowering sun,
And saw sheets hang spiderweb-rotten, and blankets a mass
Of what weather and leaves from the broken window had done,
Not to mention the rats. And thought what had there come to pass.

But lower was sinking the sun. I shook myself,
Flung a last glance around, then suddenly
Saw the old enameled bedpan, high on a shelf.
I stood still again, as the last sun fell on me,

And stood wondering what life is, and love, and what they may be.

Old Flame

I never then noticed the rather sausage-like trotters
That toted incomparable glory down the street
Schoolward, for glory's the only thing that matters,
That glory then being twin braids plaited plump and neat,

One over each shoulder with a bewitching twitch
To mark each pace as I followed, drifting, tongue-tied,
Gaze fixed on the sun's stunning paradox which
Gave to blackness a secret flaming that blackness denied.

Tongue-tied—why, yes. And besides, she was somewhat older,
So in nine years no word ever passed, certainly not conversation.
Then I was gone, and as far as I cared, she could moulder,
Braids and all, in the grave, life carved in compressed notation.

A half-century later, stranger on streets back home,
I heard my name, but on turning saw no one I knew.
Then I saw the mouth open and move, of a grisly old dame,
With gingham, false teeth, gray hair, and heard words: "Why, it's you!"

Well, yes, it was me, but who was that pile of age-litter?
"Don't you know me?" it wailed. Then suddenly, by Christ, I did.
So at last conversation—just factual, not joyous or bitter:
Twice widowed, grandmother, but comfortably fixed, she said,

And solstice and solstice will heave on, on its axis earth grind,
And black Cadillacs scarcely hold a funereal pace.
When her name escapes, I can usually call to mind
Sausage-legs, maybe some kind of braids. Never, never, a face.

Evening Hour

There was a graveyard once—or cemetery
It's now more toney to say—just a field without fence
Pretty far from town, on a hill good and gravelly
So rain wouldn't stand to disturb local residents,

Though all were long past the sniffles and rheumatism:
A tract of no real estate value, where flourished not
Even thistle, and the spade at the grievous chasm
Would go *chink* on chipped flint in the dirt, for in times forgot

Here the Indian crouched to perfect his arrowhead.
And there was a boy, long after, who gathered such things
Among shiny new tombstones recording the first-planted dead,
Now and then looking up at a buzzard's high sun-glinting wings,

*

Not thinking of flesh and its nature, but suddenly still
For maybe two minutes; as when, up the rise, a great through-freight
Strove in the panting and clank of man's living will,
Asserting itself in the face of an ignorant date.

Not morbid, nor putting two and two together
To make any mystic, or fumblingly philosophical,
Four, he sometimes kept waiting, if decent the weather,
In a lonely way, arrowheads forgotten, till all

The lights of the town had come on. He did not know
Why the lights, so familiar, now seemed so far away,
And more than once felt the crazy impulse grow
To lay ear to earth for what voices beneath might say.

Orphanage Boy

From the orphanage Al came to
Work on the farm as what you'd call
Hired boy if he got enough to
Call hire. Back at the woodpile chop-
ping stove-lengths, he taught me all the
Dirty words I'd never heard of
Or learned from farm observation,
And generally explained how
Folks went in for fun, adding that
A farm was one hell of a place
For finding fun.

Polite enough,
He'd excuse himself after sup-
per and go sit on the stile with
Bob, the big white farm bulldog, close
At his side, and watch the sun sink
Back of the barn or, maybe in
The opposite direction, the
Moon rise.

It was a copperhead
Bit Bob, and nothing, it looked like,
Would make him better. Just after
Supper one night my uncle stood
On the front porch and handed a
Twelve-gauge to Al, and said, "Be sure
You do it right back of the head."
He never named Bob's name.

*

Al's face
Was white as clabber, but he took
The gun, not saying a word, just
Walking away down the lane to-
ward sunset, Bob too, me follow-
ing. Then, in the woods where it was
Nigh dark, he did it. He gave me
The gun, smoke still in the muzzle,
Said, "Git away, you son-a-bitch,"
And I got away and he lay
On the dead leaves crying even
Before I was gone.

That night he
Never came home and the Sheriff
Never found him.

It was six months
Before I went back in the woods
To the place. There was a real grave
There. There was a wood cross on the
Grave. He must have come back to the
Barn for the shovel and hammer,
And back again to hang them up.

It must have taken nigh moonset.

Red-Tail Hawk and Pyre of Youth

To Harold Bloom

1.

Breath clamber-short, face sun-peeled, stones
Loose like untruth underfoot, I
Had just made the ridge crest, and there,
Opening like joy, the unapprehensible purity
Of afternoon flooded, in silver,
The sky. It was
The hour of stainless silver just before
The gold begins.

Eyes, strangely heavy like lead,
Drew down to the .30-30 hung on my hand
As on a crooked stick, in growing wonder
At what it might really be. It was as though
I did not know its name. Nor mine. Nor yet had known
That all is only
All, and part of all. No wind
Moved the silver light. No movement,

*

Except for the center of
That convex perfection, not yet
A dot even, nameless, no color, merely
A shadowy vortex of silver. Then,
In widening circles—oh, nearer!
And suddenly I knew the name, and saw,
As though seeing, coming toward me,
Unforgiving, the hot blood of the air:
Gold eyes, unforgiving, for they, like God, see all.

2.

There was no decision in the act,
There was no choice in the act—the act impossible but
Possible. I screamed, not knowing
From what emotion, as at that insane range
I pressed the cool, snubbed
Trigger. Saw
The circle
Break.

3.

Heart leaping in joy past definition, in
Eyes tears past definition, by rocky hill and valley
Already dark-devoured, the bloody
Body already to my bare flesh embraced, cuddled
Like babe to heart, and my heart beating like love:
Thus homeward.

But nobody there.

So at last
I dared stare in the face—the lower beak drooping,
As though from thirst, eyes filmed.
Like a secret, I wrapped it in newspaper quickly
And hid it deep
In the ice chest.

Too late to start now.

4.

Up early next morning, with
My father's old razor laid out, the scissors,
Pliers and needles, waxed thread,
The burlap and salt, the arsenic and clay,
Steel rods, thin, and glass eyes
Gleaming yellow. Oh, yes,
I knew my business. And at last a red-tail—

Oh, king of the air!

*

And at that miraculous range.

How my heart sang!

Till all was ready—skull now well scraped
And with arsenic dried, and all flesh joints, and the cape
Like a carapace feathered in bronze, and naturally anchored
At beak and at bone joints, and steel
Driven through to sustain wing and bone
And the clay-burlap body built there within.
It was molded as though for that moment to take to the air—though,
In God's truth, the chunk of poor wingless red meat,
The model from which all was molded, lay now
Forever earthbound, fit only
For dog tooth, not sky.

5.

Year after year, in my room, on the tallest of bookshelves,
It was regal, perched on its bough-crotch to guard
Blake and *Lycidas,* Augustine, Hardy and *Hamlet,*
Baudelaire and Rimbaud, and I knew that the yellow eyes,
Unsleeping, stared as I slept.

Till I slept in that room no more.

6.

Years pass like a dream, are a dream, and time came
When my mother was dead, father bankrupt, and whiskey
Hot in my throat while there for the last

Time I lay, and my heart
Throbbed slow in the
Meaningless motion of life, and with
Eyes closed I knew
That yellow eyes somewhere, unblinking, in vengeance stared.

Or *was* it vengeance? What could I know?

Could Nature forgive, like God?

7.

That night in the lumber room, late,
I found him—the hawk, feathers shabby, one
Wing bandy-banged, one foot gone sadly
Askew, one eye long gone—and I reckoned
I knew how it felt with one gone.

*

And all relevant items I found there: my first book of Milton,
The *Hamlet,* the yellow, leaf-dropping Rimbaud, and a book
Of poems friends and I had printed in college, not to mention
The collection of sexual Japanese prints—strange sex
Of mechanical sexlessness. And so made a pyre for
The hawk that, though gasoline-doused and wing-dragging,
Awaited, with what looked like pride,
The match.

8.

Flame flared. Feathers first, and I flinched, then stood
As the steel wire warped red to defend
The shape designed godly for air. But
It fell with the mass, and I
Did not wait.

What left
To do but walk in the dark, and no stars?

9.

Some dreams come true, some no.
But I've waked in the night to see
High in the late and uncurdled silver of summer
The pale vortex appear once again—and you come
And always the rifle swings up, though with
The weightlessness now of dream,
The old .30-30 that knows
How to bind us in air-blood and earth-blood together
In our commensurate fate,
Whose name is a name beyond joy.

10.

And I pray that in some last dream or delusion,
While hospital wheels creak beneath
And the nurse's soles make their *squeak-squeak* like mice,
I'll again see the first small silvery swirl
Spin outward and downward from sky-height
To bring me the truth in blood-marriage of earth and air—
And all will be as it was
In that paradox of unjoyful joyousness,
Till the dazzling moment when I, a last time, must flinch
From the regally feathered gasoline flare
Of youth's poor, angry, slapdash, and ignorant pyre.

Mountain Plateau

To James Wright

At the center of acres of snow-whiteness
The snag-oak reared, black and old, boughs
Crank. Topmost twigs—pen-strokes, tangle, or stub—fretted
The ice-blue of sky. A crow,
On the highest black, frail, and sky-thrust support,

Uttered

Its cry to the immense distance.

I hear the cry across the immense distance
Of the landscape of my heart.

That landscape now reduplicates, snow-white, the one
In which I once stood. At its center, too, the
Black snag stands.

A crow gleams there up-thrust against the blue sky.

I can make no answer
To the cry from the immense distance,

My eyes fill with tears. I have lived
Long without being able
To make adequate communication.

Star-Fall

In that far land, and time, near the castrated drawbridge where
For four bloody centuries garbage
In the moat's depth had been spilled
To stink, but most at the broiling noontide—
There we, now at midnight, lay.

We lay on the dry grass of August, high
On our cliff, and the odor we caught was of bruised
Rosemary at pathside, not garbage, and sometimes
The salt air of sea, and the only sound to our ears
Was the slap and hiss far below, for the sea has never forgiven
The nature of stone.

We did not lie close, and for hours
The only contact was fingers, and motionless they.
For what communication
Is needed if each alone
Is sunk and absorbed into
The mass and matrix of Being that defines
Identity of all?

*

We lay in the moonless night,
Felt earth beneath us swing,
Watched the falling stars of the season. They fell
Like sparks in a shadowy, huge smithy, with
The clang of the hammer unheard.

Far off in the sea's matching midnight,
The fishing lights marked their unfabled constellations.

We found nothing to say, for what can a voice say when
The world is a voice, no ear needing?

We lay watching the stars as they fell.

Youth Stares at Minoan Sunset

On the lap of the mountain meadow,
At the break of the cliff-quarry where
Venetians had once sawed their stone, soft
Nag of surf far below foot, he
Stares seaward the distance to sunset.

The sky is rose-hearted, immense, undisturbed.
In that light the youth's form is black, without motion,
And birds, gull nor other, have no transaction
In the inflamed emptiness of sky. Mountainward,
No bird cries. We had called once,
But we were too far, too far.

Molten and massy, of its own weight flattened,
The sun accelerates downward, the sea,
From general slate-blue, flaming upward.
Contact is made at the horizon-line.

On that line, one instant, one only,
The great coin, flame-massy and with
The frail human figure thereon minted black,
Balances. Suddenly is gone. A gull
Defiles at last the emptiness of air.

We are closer now. The black
Silhouette, yet small, stares seaward. To our cry
It does not turn. Later,
It will, and turning, see us with a slow
And pitying happiness of recognition born of
A knowledge we do not yet have. Or have forgotten.

He spreads his arms to the sky as though he loves it—and us.

He is so young.

II. Speculative

Dream

Waters, hypnotic, long after moonset, murmur
Under your window, and Time
Is only a shade on the underside of the beech-leaf
Which, upward, reflects a tiny refulgence of stars.

What can you dream to make Time real again?
I have read in a book that dream is the mother of memory,
And if there's no memory where—oh, what—is Time?

So grapple your dream! Like Odysseus the Cunning, who leaped
On the mountainous Ajax, and snug in that lethal embrace, while
Heels slashed at soft knee-backs, rode
Downward the great crash that
Bounced the head of the victim on hard ground, and
Jarred teeth from jawbone, and blood filled
That mouth from its tongue, like a grape-cluster, crushed.

Yes, grapple—or else the Morning Star
Westward will pale, and leave
Your ghost without history even, to wander
A desert trackless in sun-glare.

For the dream is only a self of yourself—and Jacob
Once wrestled, nightlong, his angel and, though
With wrenched thigh, had blackmailed a blessing, by dawn.

Dream of a Dream

Moonlight stumbles with bright heel
In the stream, and the stones sing.
What they sing is nothing, nothing,
But the joy Time plies to feel
In fraternal flux and glimmer
With the stream that does not know
Its destination and knows no
Truth but its own moonlit shimmer.
In my dream Time and water interflow,
And bubbles of consciousness glimmer ghostly as they go.

*

Tell me, tell me, whence came
That stream that sings its un-Timed song.
Tell me, as I lie here nightlong,
And listen and wonder whence my name
Bubbled forth on a moonlit stream
To glitter by the singing stone
A moment before, whirling, it is gone
Into the braiding texture of dream.
In what dark night of history, tell me what moon
Defines the glimmer and froth of self before it is gone.

From what dream to what dream do we
Awake when the first bird stirs to declare
Its glimmering dream of the golden air,
Of green and of dapple?—till finally,
From the twilight spruce thicket, darkening and far,
A thrush, sanctifying the hour, will utter
The glory of diminution. Later,
The owl's icy question shudders the air.
By this time the moonlight's bright heel has splashed the stream;
But this, of course, belongs to the dream of another dream.

First Dawn Light

By lines fainter gray than the faintest geometry
Of chalk, on a wall like a blackboard, day's first light
Defines the window edges. Last dream, last owl-cry
Now past, now is the true emptiness of night,

For not yet first bird-stir, first bird-note, only
Your breath as you wonder what daylight will bring, and you try
To recall what the last dream was, and think how lonely
In sun-blaze you have seen the buzzard hang black in the sky.

For day has its loneliness too, you think even as
First bird-stir does come, first twitter, faithless and fearful
That new night, in the deep leaves, may lurk. So silence has
Returned. Then, sudden, the glory, heart-full and ear-full,

For triggered now is the mysterious mechanism
Of the forest's joy, by temperature or by beam,
And until a sludge-thumb smears the sunset's prism,
You must wait to resume, in night's black hood, the reality of dream.

Ah, Anima!

Watch the great bough lashed by wind and rain. Is it
A metaphor for your soul—or Man's—or even

Mine in the hurricane of Time? Now,
In the gray and splintered light, in the scything

Tail of the hurricane, miles of forest around us
Heave like the sea, and the gray underside of leaf is exposed

Of every tree, non-coniferous. The tall
Pines blackly stagger. Beyond,

The bulk and backdrop of mountain is
Obscured. Can you locate yourself

On the great chart of history?
In the distance a tree crashes.

Empires have fallen, and the stream
Gnashes its teeth with the *klang* of boulders.

Later, sleep. Tomorrow, help
Will come. The Governor promises. Roads will be rebuilt,

And houses. Food distributed. But, meanwhile, sleep
Is a disaster area, too. You have lain down

In the shards of Time and the un-roar of the wind of being,
And when, in the dark, you wake, with only

The *klang* of distant boulders in your ears,
You may wish that you, even in the wrack and pelt of gray light,

Had run forth, screaming as wind snatched your breath away
Until you were nameless—oh, anima!—and only

Your mouth, rounded, is there, the utterance gone. Perhaps
That is the only purity—to leave

The husk behind, and leap
Into the blind and antiseptic anger of air.

Unless

All will be in vain unless—unless what? Unless
You realize that what you think is Truth is only

A husk for something else. Which might,
Shall we say, be called energy, as good a word as any. As when

The rattlesnake, among desert rocks
And Freudian cactus tall in moonlight,

Scrapes off the old integument, and flows away,
Clean and lethal and gleaming like water over moon-bright sand,

Unhusked for its mission. Oh, *neo nato!* fanged, unforgiving,
We worship you. In the morning,

In the ferocity of daylight, the old skin
Will be translucent and abstract, like Truth. The mountains,

In distance, will glitter like diamonds, or salt.
They too will, in that light, seem abstract.

At night I have stood there, and the wide world
Was flat and circular under the storm of the

Geometry of stars. The mountains, in starlight, were black
And black-toothed to define the enormous circle

Of desert of which I was the center. This
Is one way to approach the question.

All is in vain unless you can, motionless, standing there,
Breathe with the rhythm of stars.

You cannot, of course, see your own face, but you know that it,
Lifted, is stripped to white bone by starlight. This is happening.

This is happiness.

Not Quite Like a Top

Did you know that the earth, not like a top on its point,
Spins on an axis that sways, and swings, from its middle?

Well, I didn't know, but do now, and often at night,
After maybe three highballs, I lie in my bed,

In the dark, and try to feel the off-center sensation,
And sometimes if

(In the northern hemisphere, this) my head points north,
I do. Or maybe I do. It is like

So many things they say are true, but you
Can't always be sure you feel them,

Even in dark, in bed, head north.
I have, in shameless dark, sometimes

Wept because
I couldn't be sure something precious was true,

Like they say. Examples could be multiplied. But
Once, in a Pullman berth (upper), I desperately prayed

To God to exist so that I
Might have the exalted horror of denying

Him. But nothing
Came of that project. Nothing. Oh, nothing.

But so young was I then! And maybe the axis of earth
Does not really sway from its center, even if

Ancient Egyptian and modern astronomers say so,
And what good would it do me to have firsthand evidence,

When there's so much that I, lying in darkness, don't know?

Waiting

You will have to wait. Until it. Until
The last owl hoot has quivered to a

Vibrant silence and you realize that there is no breathing
Beside you, and dark curdles toward dawn of no dawn. Until

Drouth breaks, too late to save the corn,
But not too late for flood, and the hobbled cow, stranded

On a sudden islet, gargles in grief in the alder-brake. Until
The doctor enters the waiting room, and

His expression betrays all, and you wish
He'd take his goddam hand off your shoulder. Until

The woman you have lived with all the years
Says, without rancor, that life is the way life is, and she cannot

Remember when last she loved you, and had lived the lie only
For the children's sake. Until you become uncertain of French

Irregular verbs, and by a strange coincidence begin to take Catholic
Instruction from Monsignor O'Malley, who chews a hangnail. Until

You realize, to your surprise, that our Savior died for us all,
And as tears gather in your eyes, you burst out laughing,

For the joke is certainly on Him, considering
What we are. Until

You pick the last alibi off, like a scab, and
Admire the inwardness, as beautiful as inflamed

Flesh, or summer sunrise. Until
You remember that, remarkably, common men have done noble deeds. Until

It grows on you that, at least, God
Has allowed man the grandeur of certain utterances.

True or not. But sometimes true.

The Mission

In the dark kitchen the electric icebox rustles.
It whispers like the interior monologue of guilt and extenuation,
And I wake from a dream of horses. They do not know
I am dreaming of them. By this time they must be long dead.

Behind barbed wire, in fog off the sea, they stand.
Two clumps of horses, uncavorting, like gray stone, stand,
Heavy manes unrustling in the gray sea wind.
The sea is gray. Night falls. Later, the manes will rustle,

But ever so little, in wind lifting off the Bay of Biscay. But no—
They are dead. *La boucherie chevaline,* in the village,
Has a gold horse-head above the door. I wake
From my dream, and know that the shadow

Of the great spruce close by my house must be falling
Black on the white roof of winter. The spruce
Wants to hide the house from the moon, for
The moon's intentions have never been quite clear.

The spruce does not know that a square of moonlight lies cunningly on
The floor by my bed, and I watch it and think how,
On the snow-locked mountain, deep in a fissure
Under the granite ledge, the bear

Huddles inside his fur like an invalid inside
A charity-ward blanket. Fat has thinned on bone, and the fur
Is too big for him now. He stirs in sleep, farts
Gently in the glacial blackness of the cave. The eyes

Do not open. Outside, in moonlight,
The ledges are bearded with ice, and the brook,
Black, crawls under ice. It has a mission, but,
In that blackness, has forgotten what. I, too,

Have forgotten the nature of my own mission. This
May be fortunate, for if I stare at the dark ceiling
And try to remember, I do not have to go back to sleep,
And not sleeping, will not again dream

Of clumps of horses, fog-colored in sea fog, rumps
To the sea wind, standing like stone primitively hewn,
While the fields, gray, stretch beyond them, and distance dies.
Perhaps that lost mission is to try to understand

The possibility of joy in the world's tangled and hieroglyphic beauty.

Code Book Lost

What does the veery say, at dusk in shad-thicket?
There must be some meaning, or why should your heart stop,

As though, in the dark depth of water, Time held its breath,
While the message spins on like a spool of silk thread fallen?

When white breakers lunge at the black basalt cliff, what
Does the heart hear, gale lifting, the last star long gone now,

Or what in the mother's voice calling her boy from the orchard,
In a twilight moth-white with the apple blossom's dispersal?

Yes, what is that undeclared timbre, and why
Do your eyes go moist, and a pain of unworthiness strike?

What does the woman dying, or supine and penetrated, stare at?
Fly on ceiling, or gold mote afloat in a sun-slit of curtains?

Some message comes thus from a world that screams, far off.
Will she understand before what will happen, will happen?

What meaning, when at the unexpected street corner,
You meet some hope long forgotten, and your old heart,

Like neon in shore-fog, or distance, glows dimly again?
Will you waver, or clench stoic teeth and move on?

Have you thought as you walk, late, late, the streets of a town
Of all dreams being dreamed in dark houses? What do they signify?

Yes, message on message, like wind or water, in light or in dark,
The whole world pours at us. But the code book, somehow, is lost.

When the Tooth Cracks—Zing!

When the tooth cracks—zing!—it
Is like falling in love, or like
Remembering your mother's face when she—and you only
A child—smiled, or like
Falling into Truth. This,
Of course, before the pain
Begins. But even
The pain is something—is, you might say,
For lack of a better word,
Reality.

*

Do you
Remember that Jacob Boehme saw
Sunlight flash on a pewter platter on
The table, and his life was totally changed?

Is the name of God nothing more than
The accidental flash on a platter? But what is accident?

I have waked in the dark with the heart-throbbing conviction
Of having just seen some masterly
Shape, but without name. The world
Is suddenly different, then
The pain begins. Sharp as a snapped tooth, it strikes.
And, again, I have waked knowing
That I have only been dreaming,
In classic and timeless precision, of
Winter moonlight flooding a large room where
No spark now winks on the hearth, a broken
Brandy snifter glitters in moonshine by the coffee table, a
Half-burned cigarette butt beside it. And
A woman's slipper lies on its side
On the moon-bleached rug. In moonshine,
Silky as pastel, dust covers all.

It is only a dream, but it must have a name.
Must we totally forget a thing to know it?
Perhaps redemption is nothing more than the way
We learn to live with memories that are no longer remembered.

But it is hard to know the end of a story.

We often pray God to let us have Truth.
It is more important to pray God to help us to live with it.

Especially if your memory is not what it used to be.

Sister Water

. . . and to begin again, the night was dark and dreary, and
The Captain said to his trusty Lieutenant,"Lieutenant,

Tell us a story." And the Lieutenant: "The night was dark and—" And I
Have heard on the creaky stairs at night an old man's

Dragging step approach my door. He pauses for breath, and I
Can hear the chain-rattle of phlegm in the painful intake,

But I never know whose father it is, or son,
Or what mission leads to my locked door. If I

*

Should open it, he might call me by my name. Or yours.
And if he did, then what, what might occur?

And once, not knowing where, in what room, in what city even,
You lay in the dark, and a finger,

Soft as down and with a scent
Unidentifiable but stirring your heart to tears,

Like memory, was laid to your lips. "Now—"
Comes the whisper. But is there a *now* or a *then?*

And you hear in the dark, at street level above
Your basement apartment window, tires hiss on wet asphalt.

You do not know whence they come, nor whither go,
And so lie laughing alone with a sound like a strangled loon-call,

Till, slop-gray, dawn light defines the bars of your window,
And you hear the cough and mastication of

The garbage truck in the next block."God—"
You think, with a stab of joy, "He loves us all. He will not

Let all distinction perish." You cannot pray. But
You can wash your face in cold water.

Memory Forgotten

Forget! Forget it to know it. It sings!
But it is too true to sing its name. Afar,

In a thicket, it sings like
Some unidentified warbler. No, don't move.

If you break a twig, it may stop. But now!—
Oh, light, elate, more liquid than thrush,

It sings. How beautiful it is!—
Now that it is only a memory

Without a name. A shadow of happiness—yes. Did you ever
Wake up at dawn, heart singing, and run out

Barefoot in the dew, and dew blazed like diamonds of light?
Or was it a kiss on the brow, the brush of a feather,

Just as you fell asleep? How long
Has your mother been dead? Or did you, much older,

*

Lie in the tall grass and, motionless, watch
The single white fleck of cloud forever crossing the blue—

As you lay in the summer's gilt aesthetic thralled?
How much do we forget that is ourselves—

Nothing too small to make a difference,
And in the forgetting to make it all more true?

That liquid note from the thicket afar—oh, hear!
What is it you cannot remember that is so true?

Waking to Tap of Hammer

Waking up in my curtain-dark bedroom, I hear,
Cottoned in distance, the tap of a hammer:
Tap-tap. Silence. Then anguish
Of bandsaw on white oak. Yes,
I know what it is. My boy, this early
At his five-tonner at work, the schooner.
I shut eyes and see, rising upright in stocks,
The sanded gray hull. Dew-gleaming,
It swims in the first light. Yearns long Atlanticward.

He lives in a dream of his passion, hands
Never quite still, eyes often fixed on great distance.
You speak, and he seems not to hear. Slowly, then smiles.
He sleeps while the blue prints stare down in the darkness.
Tools gleam when a star spies in..
His head is thrown back in sleep. He dreams
Of sail-crack like a pistol, of spume.
Gulls scream in their hypothetical sky.

Oh, tell me the nature of passion and the fruit thereof!
What would I have otherwise than this truth, even my own dream?
Who have waked in the night from a dream
In which I, like a spirit, hung in the squall-heart—
There saw how, one rag of a spitfire jib forward, the bows
Clambered gray wave-steep, plunged, and emerged,
While through rain-slash and spray-roil,
Behind plexiglass dome, hands on wheel, the face,
Carven, stared forth: gannet-gaze, osprey-eye. Slowly, it smiled.

I dreamed it was smiling at me.

Love Recognized

There are many things in the world and you
Are one of them. Many things keep happening and
You are one of them, and the happening that
Is you keeps falling like snow
On the landscape of not-you, hiding hideousness, until
The streets and the world of wrath are choked with snow.

How many things have become silent? Traffic
Is throttled. The mayor
Has been, clearly, remiss, and the city
Was totally unprepared for such a crisis. Nor
Was I—yes, why should this happen to me?
I have always been a law-abiding citizen.

But you, like snow, like love, keep falling,

And it is not certain that the world will not be
Covered in a glitter of crystalline whiteness.

Silence.

The Smile

Mellow, mellow, at thrush-hour
Swells the note to redeem all—
Sweat and swink and daytime's rancor,
And the thought that all's not worth all.

Blue in distance while the sun dips,
Talus, cliff, and forest melt
Into the promise that soon sleep
Will heal the soul's identity.

If a hand is laid to a hand now,
Hard to soft, or soft to hard,
Can that contact stir the dream,
Long light-lost, of an un-selfed joy?

Yes, perhaps—but remember
Dreams in devious orders thrive.
Nightmare may nook in any bosom,
And saint or mother, in darkness, make outcry.

Nevertheless, our hands have met now
As heels on the darkening gravel grind,
And, star by star, the purpled sky
Defines the season's constellations.

*

What will come will come, and dawn
May breed a dream we may dream real:
Your hand-back, task-tired, pushes up
Damp hair to show the flickering smile.

How to Tell a Love Story

There is a story that I must tell, but
The feeling in my chest is too tight, and innocence
Crawls through the tangles of fear, leaving,
Dry and translucent, only its old skin behind like
A garter snake's annual discard in the ground juniper. If only

I could say just the first word with breath
As sweet as a babe's and with no history—but, Christ,
If there is no history there is no story.
And no Time, no word.
For then there is nothing for a word to be about, a word

Being frozen Time only, and I have dived deep
Where light faded from gold to dark blue, and darker below,
And my chest was filled with a story like innocence,
But I rose, rose up, and plunged into light-blaze brutal as blackness,
And the sky whirled like fireworks. Perhaps I could then have begun it.

If only the first word would come and untwist my tongue!
Then the story might grow like Truth, or a tree, and your face
Would lean at me. If only the story could begin when Time truly began,
White surf and a storm of sunlight, you running ahead and a smile
Back-flung—but then, how go on? For what would it mean?

Perhaps I can't say the first word till I know what it all means.
Perhaps I can't know till finally the doctor comes in and leans.

Little Black Heart of the Telephone

That telephone keeps screaming its little black heart out:
Nobody there? Oh, nobody's there!—and the blank room bleeds
For the poor little black bleeding heart of the telephone.
I, too, have suffered. I know how it feels
When you scream and scream, and nobody's there.
I am feeling that way this goddam minute,
If for no particular reason.

*

Tell the goddam thing to shut up! Only
It's not ringing now at all, but I
Can scrutinize it and tell that it's thinking about
Ringing, and just any minute, I know.
So, you demand, *the room's not empty, you're there?*
Yes, I'm here, but it might start screaming just after
I've gone out the door, in my private silence.

Or if I stayed here I mightn't answer, might pretend
Not to be here at all, or just be part of the blankness
The room is, as the blankness
Bleeds for the little bleeding black heart
Of the telephone. If, in fact, it should scream,
My heart would bleed too, for I know how pain can't find words.
Or sometimes is afraid to find them.

I tell you because I know you will understand.
I know you have screamed: *Nobody there? Oh, nobody's there!*
You've looked up at stars lost in blankness that bleeds
Its metaphysical blood, but not of redemption.
Have you ever stopped by the roadside at night, and couldn't
Remember your name, and breath
Came short? Or at night waked up with a telephone screaming,
And covered your head, afraid to answer?

Anyway, in broad daylight, I'm now in the street,
And no telephone anywhere near, or even
Thinking about me. But tonight, back in bed, I may dream
Of a telephone screaming its little black heart out,
In an empty room, toward sunset,
While a year-old newspaper, yellowing, lies on the floor, and velvety
Dust thick over everything, especially
On the black telephone, on which no thumb-print has,
For a long time now, been visible.

In my dream I wonder why, long since, it's not been disconnected.

Last Laugh

The little Sam Clemens, one night back in Hannibal,
Peeped through the dining-room keyhole, to see, outspread
And naked, the father split open, lights, liver, and all
Spilling out from that sack of mysterious pain, and the head

Sawed through, where his Word, like God's, held its deepest den,
And candlelight glimmered on blood-slick, post-mortem steel,
And the two dead fish-eyes stared steadily ceilingward—well, then,
If you yourself were, say, twelve, just how would you feel?

*

Oh, not that you'd loved him—that ramrod son of Virginia,
Though born for success, failing westward bitterly on.
"Armed truce"—that was all, years later, you could find to say in you.
But still, when a father's dead, an umbrella's gone

From between the son and the direful elements.
No, Sam couldn't turn from the keyhole. It's not every night
You can see God butchered in such learned dismemberments,
And when the chance comes you should make the most of the sight.

Though making the most, Sam couldn't make terms with the fact
Of the strangely prismatic glitter that grew in his eye,
Or climbing the stairs, why his will felt detached from the act,
Or why stripping for bed, he stared so nakedly

At the pore little body and thought of the slick things therein.
Then he wept on the pillow, surprised at what he thought grief,
Then fixed eyes at darkness while, slow, on his face grew a grin,
Till suddenly something inside him burst with relief,

Like a hog-bladder blown up to bust when the hog-killing frost
Makes the brats' holiday. So took then to laughing and could not
Stop, and so laughed himself crying to sleep. At last,
Far off in Nevada, by campfire or sluice or gulch-hut,

Or in roaring S.F., in an acre of mirror and gilt,
Where the boys with the dust bellied-up, he'd find words come,
His own face stiff as a shingle, and him little-built.
Then whammo!—the back-slapping riot. He'd stand, looking dumb.

God was dead, for a fact. He knew, in short, the best joke.
He had learned its thousand forms, and since the dark stair-hall
Had learned what was worth more than bullion or gold-dust-plump poke.
And married rich, too, with an extra spin to the ball;

For Livy loved God, and he'd show her the joke, how they lied.
Quite a tussle it was, but hot deck or cold, he was sly
And won every hand but the last. Then at her bedside
He watched dying eyes stare up at a comfortless sky,

And was left alone with his joke, God dead, till he died.

Heat Lightning

Heat lightning prowls, pranks the mountain horizon like
Memory. I follow the soundless flicker,

As ridge after ridge, as outline of peak after peak,
Is momentarily defined in the

Pale wash, the rose-flush, of distance. Somewhere—
Somewhere far beyond them—that distance. I think

Of the past and how this soundlessness, no thunder,
Is like memory purged of emotion,

Or even of meaning. I watch
The lightning wash pale beyond the night mountains, beyond

Night cumulus, like a stage set. Nothing
Is real, and I think of her, in timelessness: the clutch

In the lightless foyer, the awkward wall-propping, one ear
Cocked for footsteps, all the world

Hates a lover. It seems only a dream, the unsounding
Flicker of memory, even the episode when

Arms, encircling, had clamped arms to sides, the business
Banked on a pillow, head

Back over bed-edge, the small cry of protest—
But meanwhile, paradoxically, heels

Beating buttocks in deeper demand. Then heels stopping
In shudder and sprawl, only whites

Of eyes showing, like death. What all the tension,
The tingle, twist, tangle, the panting and pain,

What all exploitation of orifices and bruised flesh but
The striving for one death in two? I remember—

Oh, look! in that flash, how the peak
Blackens zenithward—as I said, I remember

The glutted, slack look on the face once
And the faintest blood-smear at the mouth's left corner,

And not till next day did I notice the two
Symmetrical half-moons of blue marks tattooed

On my shoulder, not remembering, even then, the sensation
Of the event; and of course, not now, for heat lightning

*

Is thunderless. And thunderless, even,
The newspaper obit, years later, I stumbled on. Yes,

How faint that flash! And I sit in the unmooned
Dark of an August night, waiting to see

The rose-flush beyond the black peaks, and think how far,
Far away, down what deep valley, scree, scar,

The thunder redoubled, redoubling, rolls. Here silence.

Inevitable Frontier

Be careful! Slow and careful, for you now approach
The frontier where the password is difficult to utter—or grasp.

Echo among chert peaks and perilously balanced boulders
Has something to do with it, not to mention your early rearing, with

Its naïve logic. For remember now, this is the frontier
Where words coming out of a mouth are always upside-

Down, and all tongues are sloppily cubical, and shadows of nothing are,
Whatever the hour, always something, and tend to bleed

If stepped on—oh, do keep mindful how
Slick the blood of shadow can be, especially

If the shadow is of nothing. As a corollary,
The shadow of something, yourself for instance,

Provides its own peculiar hazards. You may trip
On it, and start falling upward, screaming,

Screaming for somebody to grab you before you are out
Of reach. Your eyes, too, must be readjusted, for

Here people, owl-like, see only by dark, and grope by day. Here,
People eat in shamefaced privacy, but the great Public Square,

Sparsely planted, is full, in daylight, of gut-wheeze and littered with feces
Till the carts come, and later, *à l'heure sexuelle,* at noon, waiters wheel out

To the café terraces divans of ingeniously provocative designs,
While clients, now clad in filmy robes, emerge from locker-rooms, laughing

Like children at tag. Food is, of course, forbidden, but scented drinks,
And coffee, are served under awnings. Another item:

*

Criminality is rare, but those convicted,
Mystically deprived of the memory of their names, are exiled

To the Isles of the Blest, where they usually end by swallowing their tongues,
This from boredom, for in their language *bliss* and *boredom*

Have the same linguistic root. Yes, many things
Are different here, and to be happy and well-adjusted, you

Must put out of mind much you have been taught. Among others, the names
Of Plato, St. Paul, Spinoza, Pascal and Freud must not be spoken, and when,

Without warning, by day or night, the appalling
White blaze of God's Great Eye sweeps the sky, History

Turns tail and scuttles back to its burrow
Like a groundhog caught in a speeding sportscar's headlight.

Heart of the Backlog

Snug at hearthside, while heart of the backlog
Of oak simmers red in the living pulse of its own
Decay, you sit. You count
Your own heartbeat. How steady, how
Firm! What, ah, is Time! And sometimes

It is hard, after all, to decide
If the ticking you now hear is
A whisk of granules of snow,
Hard and belated on panes, or simply
The old organ, fist-size and resolute,
Now beastlike caught
In your rib-cage, to pace

But go nowhere. It does,
In a ghostly sense, suggest now the sound of
Pacing, as if, in soft litter, curved claws
Were muffled. Or is it
The pace of the muffled old clock in the hall?

You watch the talus-like slide of
Consumed oak from oak yet consuming. Yes, tell me
How many the years that burn there. How delicate, dove-gray
The oak-ash that, tiny and talus-like, slides to unwink
The glowing of oak and the years unconsumed!
What is the color of years your fireplace consumes as you sit there?

*

But think, shut your eyes. Shut your eyes and see only
The wide stretch of world beyond your warm refuge—fields
Windless and white in full moonlight,
Snow past and now steady the stars, and, far off,
The woods-lair of darkness. Listen! is that
The great owl that you, warm at your hearthside, had heard?

How feather-frail, think, is the track of the vole
On new snow! How wide is the world! How fleeting and thin
Its mark of identity, breath
In a minuscule issue of whiteness
In air that is brighter than steel! The vole pauses, one paw
Uplifted in whiteness of moonlight.

There is no indication of what angle, or slant,
The great shadow may silkily accent the beauty of snow,
And the vole, Little One, has neither theology nor
Aesthetic—not even what you may call
Stoicism, as when the diagnostician pauses, and coughs.
Poor thing, he has only himself. And what do you have

When you go to the door, snatch it open, and, cold,
The air strikes like steel down your lungs, and you feel
The Pascalian nausea make dizzy the last stars?
Then shut the door. The backlog burns down. You sit and

Again the owl calls, and with some sadness you wonder
If at last, when the air-scything shadow descends
And needles claw-clamp through gut, heart and brain,
Will ecstasy melting with terror create the last little cry?
Is God's love but the last and most mysterious word for death?

Has the thought ever struck you to rise and go forth—yes, lost
In the whiteness—to never look upward, or back, only on,
And no sound but the snow-crunch, and breath
Gone crisp like the crumpling of paper? Listen!
Could that be the creak of a wing-joint gigantic in distance?

No, no—just a tree, far off, when ice inward bites.
No, no, don't look back—oh, I beg you!

I beg you not to look back, in God's name.

Identity and Argument for Prayer

Having been in this place, I will leave it—
For good and all, I said. In Space: as legs make motion
Like scissors, motors spin, planes
Eat sky with roar gradually diminishing
To silence. In Time:
Like a self-winding watch that
Falls forever in black Spacelessness
Beyond the last stars.
This much I said.
And did. How long ago!

How is it that I am *there* again?
Space and Time our arbitrary illusions: even so,
How odd that my feet fit old foot-tracks, crushing,
Freshly again, the fresh sea-rose, imprinting
The same sea-sand while surf, heaving
At volcanic stone, black, utters
The same old prophecy, which
I knew could never come true. But it did—or did it?
I could never be sure,
But I'm *there,* now again!
Was that what the prophecy said?
Against all sense,
And will?

Thus I stand again making new the old tracks
My tennis shoes made years back, and now,
Astonished, I see that I, this instant, wear old tennis shoes,
And in the same instant become aware of
Old hope, old pain, old evil, old good,
All long forgotten, and
Do not know more than the maple by my window
On which green leaves expand in silence
To unwittingly dream of fall-redness,
As though I had dreamed all the years
This dream of return.
If that is truly what it is.

Yes, I once stood there, and now have
Just dreamed, in painful vividness, of standing
Again *there,* but if
I should, I have it on good authority, that
There is not there any more,
Having dropped through Time into otherness.
But what did happen *there* is—just now
In its new ectoplasmic context—
Happening again, even if
The companion who smiled in that dusk long ago, and

Smiles now again—ah, new innocence,
For now freed from Time—
Is long dead, and I
Am not always readily certain
Of the name now.

For that old *I* is not I any more, though
A ghost somewhat different from that of
The truly perished companion, for the *I* here now
Is not dead, only what
I have now turned into. This
Is the joke you must live with. Have you ever
Seen serpentine Time at the instant it swallowed its tail?

But whatever I am and Truth is, I
Have stood on a high place, yearning
To know what logic of years, and of
Whatever stride, clamber, climb,
Had brought me here to be what I am; downward,
Have seen how wind tossed wildly,
In flicker like gale-spray,
Gray undersides of innumerable leaves
Of the forest below. And whatever
Vision or anguish
Swelled in the heart to be uttered was
By wind crammed in the throat back, and all
I recall is the shadowy thought that
Man's mind, his heart, live only by piecemeal, like mice
On cheese crumbs—the cheese itself, of course,
Being locked in the tin
In God's pantry.

Well, you might, of course, go to bed, and stare
Up at the coagulate darkness and know
How beyond the frail rooftop darkness piles skyward—
Thinking now that at least you are *you,*
Saying *now,* saying *now,* for
Now *now* is all, and you *you.*

At least, for a minute.

This may be taken as an argument for prayer.

Diver

Arrowed, the body flies in light.
The heels flash as water closes.
The board yet quivers where feet struck.

Concentric to the water's wound,
In live geometry the bright-
Born circles widen targetwise
In mathematic accuracy.

Now in the water's inner gleam,
Where no sound comes, and yap and nag
Of the world's old currish annoy is stilled,
The body glides. In timeless peace
The mover that shows no movement moves
Behind the prow of a diver's hands,
And in our watching hearts we know
An unsuspected depth and calm
Of identity we had never dreamed.

But look! The face is up, dark hair
Snaps sidewise to show the boyish grin.
And we smile, too, in welcome back
To all the joy and anguish of
The earth we walk on, lie down in.

Rather Like a Dream

If Wordsworth, a boy, reached out
To touch stone or tree to confirm
His own reality, that wasn't

So crazy. Or even illogical. For
We have all done the same, or at least
Felt the impulse. Right now I feel it, for

I walk in the mountain woods,
Alone, hour sunset, season
When the first maple leaf falls red, the first

Beech leaf gold. Each leaf of each species
Gathers, brooding, beneath it, its film
Of darkness, and waits, and the promise

Of another summer is already a dream. Thus years,
As I stand at this moment, are gathered
In their brooding darkness beneath.

Another summer is now truly a dream
To join those moments, and hours, of joy
That dissolve into glitter, like tears, then gather

*

Each under a brooding leaf, or join
The darkness of conifers, not yet snow-draped.
I stand on stone and am thinking

Of what is no more. Oh, happiness!—often
Unrecognized. But shade hardens, and years
Are darkening under each leaf—old love, old folly,

Old evil and anguish, and the drawstring
Of darkness draws tighter, and the monk-hood
Of darkness grows like a sky over all,

As I stand in the spruce-deep where stars never come.
I stand, hands at sides, and wonder,
Wonder if I should put out a hand to touch

Tree or stone—just to know.

Departure

This is the season when cards are exchanged, or
Addresses scribbled on paper, with ragged edges. Smiles
Are frozen with a mortuary precision to seal friendships. Time is up.

The sun goes earlier low. The last sail, far out,
Looks lonely. And if, toward sunset, at low tide, you walk
Near the shoals, you will find the sea-grass

Combed scrupulously in one direction only
As if some fundamental decision,
Involving us all, had at last been reached, but

Not yet released for announcement. Tomorrow,
We shall sense the direction of history, and now, far away,
In the casino, the first cards are being cut. The dealer

Coughs, the mistral levels in, and you
Again begin to believe what you read in the papers. The market
Wiggles like a cardiogram, or an earthworm on a hot concrete walk, and

In the shadowy corridors luggage, generally expensive, is stacked. Polished
Cowhide glints with a sense of its own destiny, it knows
It is going somewhere soon. That is a truth we must all face.

Heat Wave Breaks

In this motionless sun, no leaf now moves, the stream,
In unwavering reach, mirrors sky's cloudlessness.
On a beech bough, wrapped in the forest's deepest green dream,
The warbler sits ruffled, beak open but music-less.
For some coolness the feathers are ruffled to give air ingress.

In the gasp of silence that follows your new heartbeat
Do you catch the echo of one only just now spent?
Or does Time itself, in that timeless and crystalline heat,
Hang transparent, a concept bleached of all content?
At this moment can you recall what your own life has meant?

Though no leaf moves, and the past dies in the heart,
Though no bird sings, and the sun seems nailed to the sky,
We have hope in the hour when, west, on the cliff's top rampart
The day will redden to flame, like the phoenix, to die,
And darkness come, star by star, to assume the sky.

Will you wake when clouds roll and the roil and lightning make
Again wet leaves twirl on their stems in the green-flaming glare,
And blasphemy of thunder makes the mountain quake?
For what should we pray to our God in the rumble and flare?
That the world stab anew to our hearts in the lightning-stricken air?

Heart of Autumn

Wind finds the northwest gap, fall comes.
Today, under gray cloud-scud and over gray
Wind-flicker of forest, in perfect formation, wild geese
Head for a land of warm water, the *boom,* the lead pellet.

Some crumple in air, fall. Some stagger, recover control,
Then take the last glide for a far glint of water. None
Knows what has happened. Now, today, watching
How tirelessly *V* upon *V* arrows the season's logic,

Do I know my own story? At least, they know
When the hour comes for the great wing-beat. Sky-strider,
Star-strider—they rise, and the imperial utterance,
Which cries out for distance, quivers in the wheeling sky.

That much they know, and in their nature know
The path of pathlessness, with all the joy
Of destiny fulfilling its own name.
I have known time and distance, but not why I am here.

*

Path of logic, path of folly, all
The same—and I stand, my face lifted now skyward,
Hearing the high beat, my arms outstretched in the tingling
Process of transformation, and soon tough legs,

With folded feet, trail in the sounding vacuum of passage,
And my heart is impacted with a fierce impulse
To unwordable utterance—
Toward sunset, at a great height.

Being Here

Poetry 1977–1980

To Gabriel Thomas Penn
(1836–1920)

OLD MAN: You get old and you can't do anybody any good any more.
BOY: You do me some good, Grandpa. You tell me things.

There is in short no absolute time standard.
Van Nostrand's Scientific Encyclopedia,
Fifth Edition, p. 2203

I thirst to know the power and nature of Time. . . .
St. Augustine: Confessions,
Book XI, *Chapter* XXIII
Translated by Albert C. Outler

Time is the dimension in which God strives to define His own Being.

October Picnic Long Ago

"Yassuh, here 'tis," Bumbo said, handing reins to the mister.
Fixed hampers and blankets behind and strapped them tight.
To the surrey helped Mother up, passed the baby to her,
While I, toward seven, kept my sister aright,
And over us all, in a flood, poured the golden October light.

Out of town, clop-clop, *till we found a side-lane that led*
Into woods, where gold leaves flicked a fairy shadow and light
That changed the known shape of a nose or face or head
Till we looked like a passel of circus freaks crammed tight
On four wheels, while the flickering nag was steered by a witch's sleight.

To a stream we came, and well tossed by stones, made crossing.
And there it was—as we might have known Father'd known:
A grass circle, and off to one side, by a boulder, a spring,
All ready for us, and a crude fireplace of stone.
Then quick as a wink, horse unhitched and staked, the big children gone.

All predictable, sure—a Sunday picnic like any
Of that old time when a stable rented an outfit,
That being before the auto had come, or many.
My mother's skirt was blue serge, long and close-fit.
My father's suede shoes were buttoned up high, and a Norfolk jacket.

All predictable—lunch, the baby asleep, children gone
But not far, and Father and Mother gone, hand in hand,
Heads together as though in one long conversation
That even now I can't think has had an end—
But where? Perhaps in some high, cloud-floating, and sunlit land.

But picnics have ends, and just as the sun set,
My mother cried out, "Could a place so beautiful be!"
And my father said, "My ship will come in yet,
And you'll see all the beautiful world there is to see."
"What more would I want," she now cried, "when I love everything I now
see?"

So she swung the baby against the rose-tinted sky,
And a bird-note burst from her throat, and she gaily sang
As we clop-clopped *homeward while the shadows, sly,*
Leashed the Future up, like a hound with a slavering fang.
But sleepy, I didn't know what a Future was, as she sang,

And she sang.

I.

Speleology

At cliff-foot where great ledges thrust, the cave
Debouches, soil level and rank, where the stream,
Ages back, had come boiling forth, and now from alluvial earth
The last of old virgin forest trees rise to cliff-height,
And at noon twilight reigns. No one comes.

I must have been six when I first found the cave-mouth
Under ledges moss-green, and moss-green the inner dark.
Each summer I came, in twilight peered in, crept further,
Till one summer all I could see was a gray
Blotch of light far behind. Ran back. Didn't want to be dead.

By twelve, I was bolder. Besides, now had me a flashlight.
The whole night before couldn't sleep. Daylight. Then breakfast.
The cave wandered on, roof lower and lower except
Where chambers of darkness rose and stalactites down-stabbed
To the heart of my light. Again, lower.

I cut off the light. Knew darkness and depth and no Time.
Felt the cave-cricket crawl up an arm. Switched light on
To see the lone life there, the cave-cricket pale
As a ghost on my brown arm. I thought: *They are blind.*
Crept on. Heard, faintly, below

A silken and whispering rustle. Like what? Like water—so swung
The light to one side. I had crawled out
A ledge under which, far down, far down, the water yet channeled
And sang to itself, and answered my high light with swollen
White bursts of bubble. Light out, unmoving, I lay,

Lulled as by song in a dream, knowing
I dared not move in a darkness so absolute.
I thought: *This is me.* Thought: *Me—who am I?* Felt
Heart beating as though to a pulse of darkness and earth, and thought
How would it be to be here forever, my heart,

In its beat, part of all. Part of all—
But I woke with a scream. The flashlight,
It slipped, but I grabbed it. Had light—
And once more looked down the deep slicing and sluicing
Of limestone where water winked, bubbles like fish-eyes, a song like terror.

Years later, past dreams, I have lain
In darkness and heard the depth of that unending song,
And hand laid to heart, have once again thought: *This is me.*

And thought: *Who am I?* And hand on heart, wondered
What would it be like to be, in the end, part of all.

And in darkness have even asked: *Is this all? What is all?*

When Life Begins

Erect was the old Hellenistic head,
White-thatched in that dark cedar shade,
Curl-tangled the beard like skill-carved stone
With chisel-grooved shadow accenting the white.
The blue gaze fixed on a mythic distance.

That distance, a far hill's horizon, bulged
Past woods into the throbbing blue
Of a summer's afternoon. The silence
There seemed to have substantial life
That was the death of the pulse of Time.

One hand, gnarled, liver-blotched, but sinewed
From wrestling with the sleight of years,
Lay propped on a blue-jeaned knee and wrapped
Around a cob pipe, from which one thread
Of smoke, more blue than distance, rose
To twine into the cedar-dark.

The boy—he felt he wasn't there.
He felt that all reality
Had been cupboarded in that high head,
But now was absorbed into the abstractness
Of that blue gaze, so fixed and far,
Aimed lethally past the horizon's fact.

He thought all things that ever lived
Had gone to live behind that brow,
And in their infinite smallness slept
Until the old voice might wake them again
To strive in the past but passionate

Endeavor—hoofbeat at night, steel-clang,
Boom of the battery to take,
Far smoke seen long before you hear sound,
And before that, too, the gust of grape
Overhead, through oak leaves. Your stallion rears.

Your stallion rears—yes, it is you!

*

With your glasses you spot, from east, from west,
From woods-cover, skirmishers mincing out
On both flanks of that rise. Rifle-fire
Prickles the distance, noiseless, white.
Then a shell bursts over that fanged, far hill,
Single, annunciatory, like
A day-star over new Bethlehem.

In the country-quiet, momentarily
After that event renewed, one lone
Quail calls.

And the old man, once he said
How a young boy, dying, broke into tears.
"Ain't scairt to die"—the boy's words—"it's jist
I ne'er had no chance to know what tail's like."

Hunger and thirst, and the quavering yell
That more than bugle gave guts to a charge,
And once said: "My Mary, her hands were like silk,
But strong—and her mount on his shadow would dance."
Once said: "But things—they can seem like a dream."

Old eyelids shut the horizon out.
The boy sat and wondered when life would begin,
Nor knew that, beyond the horizon's heave,
Time crouched, like a great cat, motionless
But for tail's twitch. Night comes. Eyes glare.

Boyhood in Tobacco Country

All I can dream tonight is an autumn sunset,
Red as a hayrick burning. The groves,
Not yet leafless, are black against red, as though,
Leaf by leaf, they were hammered of bronze blackened
To timelessness. Far off, from the curing barns of tobacco,
Blue smoke, in pale streaking, clings
To the world's dim, undefinable bulge.

Far past slashed stubs, homeward or homeless, a black
Voice, deeper and bluer than sea-heart, sweeter
Than sadness or sorghum, utters the namelessness
Of life to the birth of a first star,
And again, I am walking a dust-silent, dusky lane, and try
To forget my own name and be part of the world.

*

I move in its timelessness. From the deep and premature midnight
Of woodland, I hear the first whip-o-will's
Precious grief, and my young heart,
As darkling I stand, yearns for a grief
To be worthy of that sound. Ah, fool! Meanwhile,
Arrogant, eastward, lifts the slow dawn of the harvest moon.

Enormous, smoky, smoldering, it stirs.
First visibly, then paling in retardation, it begins
The long climb zenithward to preside
There whitely on what the year has wrought.
What have the years wrought? I walk the house.
Oh, grief! Oh, joy! Tonight
The same season's moon holds sky-height.

The dark roof hides the sky.

Filling Night with the Name: Funeral as Local Color

It was all predictable, and just as well.
For old Mrs. Clinch at last lay gut-rigid there
In the coffin, withered cheeks subtly rouged, hair
Frizzled and tinted, with other marks of skill
Of the undertaker to ready his client to meet
Her God and her grave-worm—well, Mrs. Clinch had heard
The same virtues extolled for the likes of her, word for word,
With no word, true or false, that she couldn't exactly repeat.

In piety, a friendly old couple offered
To see Mr. Clinch through the night, cook supper and breakfast.
"When a thing's gonna be," he replied, "git used to it fast."
Thanked them all. Remarked on the grave now flower-coffered.
Shook the preacher's hand. Wiped the tear from a wind-blue eye.
Dropped off at his farm. Not hungry, no supper. Near sundown,
Good clothes still on, went to milk. His forehead pressed down
On the cow's coarse hide. At last, milk rang tinnily.

Milk on ice, he climbed out of Sunday blue serge, and right
Where the box-toed black shoes got set, he hung it above.
Bed pulled back, he stared at the infinite tundra of
Starched sheets by some kindly anonymous hand pulled tight.
He couldn't crawl in. It seemed all was happening still.
So got pen, paper, ink. Sat down to write to his boy,
Far away. But no word would come, and sorrow and joy
All seemed one—just the single, simple word *whip-o-will.*

For the bird was filling the night with the name: *whip-o-will.*

Whip-o-will.

Recollection in Upper Ontario, from Long Before

for Richard Eberhart

Why do I still wake up and not know?—though later
By years, and a thousand miles north, on the Hudson Bay slope,
Lost in forests and lakes, while the embers
In evergreen darkness die, and just
Beyond the black lace of low bough-droop
Sky shows, and stars sown random and rabble and white. The loon
Bursts out laughing again at his worn-out
Joke, and I wonder if it is on me.
That is, if mine could be called one.

Anyway, one kind of a joke is on me, for
There's no locomotive in three hundred miles—and sure,
No express, no old-fashioned, brass-bound eight-wheeler,
To wake up the loon to maniacal stitches.
And if the great owl calls, I know
It can't be because of a locomotive, none near.

When the last ember winks, and the dark,
Crawling near, now means business, and I
Am asleep, then again
The express, now bound hell-for-leather in dream,
The cylinders spewing white steam, comes boiling
Over the hill. Will it come? Really get here, this time?

I don't know for sure. The owl—
He may wake me again
With his same old gargle of question,
The question he ought long back to have answered,
But asks just for fun.
Or to make your conscience ask if it's you who—*who-who*—
Did whatever it was.

But no owl speaks yet, no loon. I sleep on. And again
Old Zack, pore ole white-trash—croker sack dragging—
Is out to scrounge coal off the L & N tracks.
Old Mag at it too, face knobby, eyes bleared,
Mouth dribbling with snuff, skirts swinging
Above the old brogan she's fixed for her clubfoot,
And dragging her own sack for coal.
They don't hear the whistle. Or Zack's
Just stubborn, born democrat, knowing damned well
That the coal, it is his, and by rights.
Then the whistle again, in outrage and anguish.

And now I wake up, or not. If I don't
It blows on like hell, brakes screaming,
And Mag, of a sudden, is down. The brogan she wears

For the clubfoot, it looks like it's caught
In a switch-*V*—the coal chute starts here.
And I stand in a weedy ditch, my butterfly
Net in my hand, my chloroform jar,
Mount box, and canteen strung on me—and Zack,
He keeps pulling. She's up. Zack bends at the brogan.
The whistle goes wild. Brakes scream. I stare.

Zack's up, foot's out! Or is it? A second she's standing,
Then down—now over both rails—
Down for good, and the last
Thing I see is his hands out. To grab her, I reckoned.

Time stops like it's no-Time. Then,
The express, I see it back up. The porters, conductors,
With bed sheets, pile out. I see
The first sheet pass. It sags. It drips. So
Out ditch and over, I'm gone. Look back once
When autos, the sheriff and coroner, come. I look
In my jar: the Gulf State fritillary quiet as a leaf,
Black and gold. Near dark by this time.
I make home, remembering the porter
Who said: "Hell—it's hamburger now!"

I wonder what's coming for supper.

"An accident"—that's what the coroner said, and no tale
For the news-sheet, except a collection
To bury Old Mag. Few came in the rain.
Then on Saturday night, on the street,
It's Zack, now drunk as a coot. He grabs me, he says—
Says: "Yeah, you come spyen on me!
Down thar in the ditch, in them weeds. Well, you're wrong!"

His face, its likker-breath hot on my face—it says:
"I ne'er tetched her! She fell. Nigh got myself kilt
Count of her durn shoe!" Then he,
Old fingers like rusty nails in my biceps: "Stuck up!
You durn little butterfly ketcher—but got enough sense
To haul-ass afore the durn coroner come." So shoved me.

Was gone. And I stood in the crowd of a Saturday night
On a market-town street, years ago,
When farm-folks and tenants, they came in to trade.
I stood there. And something inside me, it grew.

And that night in bed, like a dream but not one, I saw.
Saw inside of Zack's ruin of a shack, and a coal-oil
Lamp flickered, and Zack and his Mag, young now,
Getting ready for bed, them maybe just married.
Saw how she was trying to get off her gear and not show

That foot. Yes, there in my head, I saw it, and saw
How he took it, the foot. Leaned over and kissed it.

And tears gone bright in her eyes.

But all the years later I'd only see
How he'd try not to see it. Then
Blow out the lamp. And if summer,
He'd stare up in darkness. If winter,
And fire on the hearth, lie watching
The shadows dance on the ceiling. And handle himself.
To make himself grab her.

But now, far north, I'm asleep and deep
In the old real dream: the brass-bound express
Comes boiling over the hill, whistle crazy—but that's
Far north, in the woods, and the loon
Begins laughing his crazy fool head off. To wake me.

Stars paled. That was all.

Dawn burst in a riot of glory: chips on the cook-fire,
Smell of bacon, camp struck, canoes waiting easy and yearning.
We glide out, mine first, on the unrippling sheen
Of day's silver and gold, and the paddle dips to a rhythm
That feels like the world's own breath, and behind us
A voice is singing its joy—and is this
The same world I stood in,
In the ditch, years ago,
And saw what I saw?

Or what did I see?

The Moonlight's Dream

Why did I wake that night, all the house at rest?
I could not hear, but knew what each breath meant
In each room. My father's long drag to the depth of his chest.
My mother's like silk or the rustle of lilies that leant
By the garden pool when night breeze was merely a whisper.
But loudest of all, that of my old grandfather,
Who with years now struggled, grumbling, croupy, and slow,
But one night had roused to a blood-yell, dreaming Fort Pillow or Shiloh.

Tonight the house was mouse-still except for some beam
That, whisper or creak, complained of the years it had borne
The weight of reality and the human dream
As the real became more real, and the real more forlorn.
Outside, I wondered why I had come out and where

I would go, and back-looking, now saw the tracks of my bare
Dark footprints set in the moonlit dew like snow,
And thought: *I go where they go, for they must know where we go.*

It was as though they did know the way in a dream
The moonlight was having of all the world that night,
And they followed the path that wandered down to a stream
Where cattle snorted in shadow, their eyes without sight
Staring through the dream that I was, while a whip-o-will
Asserted to moonlight its name, while nameless and still,
I wondered if ever my heart would beat again,
As I wandered the moonlight's dream, past pleasure or past pain.

Across the sweet-clover whiteness, then up the hill
To the darkness that hung from old maples, and lay down to wonder
If I, being part of the moonlight's dream, could be real,
For whatever realness I was, it must lie asleep yonder
In the far, white house that was part of the moonlight's dream, too.
Then blankness. At day-streak, in terror, I woke, ran through
The tangle of clover, corn-balk, the creek, home to bed:
But no breath could I hear, for all seemed still, as still as the dead.

Not dead! Though long years now are, and the creek bulldozed dry,
And their sorrow and joy, their passion and pain and endeavor,
Have with them gone, with whatever reality
They were, or are, by sunlight or moonlight—whatever.
The highway has slicked the spot the white farmhouse once stood.
At sixty per I am whirled past the spot where my blood
Is unwitting of that as of the defunct stream,
Or of the ignorant night I strayed in the moonlight's dream.

The Only Poem

The only poem to write I now have in mind
May not be written because of memory, or eyes.
The scene is too vivid, so tears, not words, I may find.
If perhaps I forget, it might catch me by surprise.

The facts lie long back, and surely are trivial,
Though I've waked in the night, as though at a voice at my ear,
Till a flash of the dying dream comes back, and I haul
Up a sheet-edge to angrily wipe at an angry tear.

My mother was middle-aged, and then retained
Only sweetness of face, not the beauty my father, years later,
Near death, would try to describe, but words blurring, refrained.
But the facts: that day she took me to see the new daughter

*

My friends stashed with Grandma while they went East for careers.
So for friendship I warily handled the sweet-smelling squaw-fruit,
All golden and pink, kissed the fingers, blew in the ears.
Then suddenly was at a loss. So my mother seized it,

And I knew, all at once, that she would have waited all day,
Sitting there on the floor, with her feet drawn up like a girl,
Till half-laughing, half-crying, arms stretched, she could swing up her prey
That shrieked with joy at the giddy swoop and swirl.

Yes, that was all, except for the formal farewell,
And wordless we wandered the snow-dabbled street, and day,
With her hands both clutching my arm till I thought it would swell.
Then home, fumbling key, she said: "Shucks! Time gets away."

We entered. She laid out my supper. My train left at eight
To go back to the world where all is always the same.
Success or failure—what can alleviate
The pang of unworthiness built into Time's own name?

Platonic Drowse

The shaft of paralyzed sunlight.
White cat by the rose bush crouching
Beneath the last blowzy red

Of the season, its eyes, slow
Blinking. Sun-glint gold on
The brown of enameled wasps weaving

Around one gold pear, high-hung.
It is far beyond your reach.
A rooster crows, far, thin.

The sun is nailed to the sky
To bless forever that land
Where only Time dies.

You do not think this is true.
You laugh. Fool, don't you remember?
You lay in the browning, tall

Grass, in unaimed pubescent
Grief, but the grief, it
Shriveled to nothing. Oh, lost!

But your body began to flow
On every side into distance,
Unrippling, silent, silver,

*

Leaving only the steady but pulsing
Germ-flame of your Being, that throbbed
In Platonic joy for the world.

The world, in Platonic drowse, lay.

Grackles, Goodbye

Black of grackles glints purple as, wheeling in sun-glare,
The flock splays away to pepper the blueness of distance.
Soon they are lost in the tracklessness of air.
I watch them go. I stand in my trance.

Another year gone. In trance of realization,
I remember once seeing a first fall leaf, flame-red, release
Bough-grip, and seek, through gold light of the season's sun,
Black gloss of a mountain pool, and there drift in peace.

Another year gone. And once my mother's hand
Held mine while I kicked the piled yellow leaves on the lawn
And laughed, not knowing some yellow-leaf season I'd stand
And see the hole filled. How they spread their obscene fake lawn.

Who needs the undertaker's sick lie
Flung thus in the teeth of Time, and the earth's spin and tilt?
What kind of fool would promote that kind of lie?
Even sunrise and sunset convict the half-wit of guilt.

Grackles, goodbye! The sky will be vacant and lonely
Till again I hear your horde's rusty creak high above,
Confirming the year's turn and the fact that only, only,
In the name of Death do we learn the true name of Love.

II.

Youthful Truth-Seeker, Half-Naked, at Night, Running down Beach South of San Francisco

In dark, climbing up. Then down-riding the sand sluice
Beachward from dune-head. Running, feet bare on
Sand wet-packed and star-stung. Phlegm in lungs loose.
Though now tide turning, spume yet prickling air on

My chest, which naked, splits darkness. On the right hand,
Palisades of white-crashing breakers renew and stretch on
Into unmooned drama and distance.—To understand
Is impossible now. Flight from what? To what? And alone.

Far behind, the glow of the city of men fades slow.
And ahead, white surf and dark dunes in dimness are wed,
While Pacificward, leagues afar, fog threatens to grow,
But on I yet run, face up, stars shining above my wet head

Before they are swaddled in grayness, though grayness, perhaps,
Is what waits—after history, logic, philosophy too,
Even rhythm of lines that bring tears to the heart, and scraps
Of old wisdom that like broken bottles in darkness gleam at you.

What was the world I had lived in? Poetry, orgasm, joke:
And the joke the biggest on me, the laughing despair
Of a truth the heart might speak, but never spoke—
Like the twilit whisper of wings with no shadow on air.

You dream that somewhere, somehow, you may embrace
The world in its fullness and threat, and feel, like Jacob, at last
The merciless grasp of unwordable grace
Which has no truth to tell of future or past—

But only life's instancy, by daylight or night,
While constellations strive, or a warbler whets
His note, or the ice creaks blue in white-night Arctic light,
Or the maniac weeps—over what he always forgets.

So lungs aflame now, sand raw between toes,
And the city grows dim, dimmer still,
And the grind of breath and of sand is all one knows
Of the Truth a man flees to, or from, in his angry need to fulfill

What?—On the beach flat I fall by the foam-frayed sea
That now and then brushes an outflung hand, as though
In tentative comfort, yet knowing itself to be
As ignorant as I, and as feckless also.

*

So I stare at the stars that remain, shut eyes, in dark press an ear
To sand, cold as cement, to apprehend,
Not merely the grinding of shingle and sea-slosh near,
But the groaning miles of depth where light finds its end.

Below all silken soil-slip, all crinkled earth-crust,
Far deeper than ocean, past rock that against rock grieves,
There at the globe's deepest dark and visceral lust,
Can I hear the *groan-swish* of magma that churns and heaves?

No word? No sign? Or is there a time and place—
Ice-peak or heat-simmered distance—where heart, like eye,
May open? But sleep at last—it has sealed up my face,
And last foam, retreating, creeps from my hand. It will dry,

While fog, star by star, imperially claims the night.
How long till dawn flushes dune-tops, or gilds beach-stones?
I stand up. Stand thinking, I'm one poor damn fool, all right.
Then ask, if years later, I'll drive again forth under stars, on tottering bones.

Snowshoeing Back to Camp in Gloaming

Scraggle and brush broken through, snow-shower jarred loose
To drape shoulders, dead boughs, snow-sly and trap-laid,
Snatching thongs of my snowshoes, I
Stopped. At the edge of the high mountain mowing,
I stood. Westward stared
At the half mile of white alabaster unblemished
To the blackness of spruce forest lifting
In a long scree-climb to cliff-thrust,
Where snow, in level striation of ledges, stretched, and the sun,
Unmoving, hung
Clear yet of the peak-snagged horizon—
The sun, by a spectral spectrum belted,
Pale in its ghost-nimb.

The shadow of spruces, magenta,
Bled at me in motionlessness
Across unmarred white of the mowing.

Time died in my heart.

So I stood on that knife-edge frontier
Of Timelessness, knowing that yonder
Ahead was the life I might live
Could I but move
Into the terror of unmarred whiteness under
The be-nimbed and frozen sun.

*

While behind, I knew,
In the garrote of perfect knowledge, that
The past flowed backward: trees bare
As though of all deeds unleafed, and
Dead leaves lost are only
Old words forgotten in snowdrifts.

But the crow in distance called, and I knew
He spoke truth, for

Higher a wash of pale pink suddenly tinted the mowing,
And from spruce-blackness magenta
Leaped closer. But at
That instant, sun-nimb
Made contact with jag-heave of mountain.
Magenta lapped suddenly gray at my feet,
With pink, farther up,
Going gray.

Hillward and sky-thrust, behind me,
Leafless and distanced to eastward, a huge
Beech clung to its last lone twinge
Of pink on the elephant-gray—far under
One star.

Now the track, gone pale in tree-night,
Downward floated before me, to darkness,

So starward I stared
To the unnamed void where Space and God
Flinch to come, and where
Un-Time roars like a wind that only
The dead, unweeping, hear.

Oh, Pascal!
What does a man need to forget?

But moved on, however, remembering
That somewhere—somewhere, it seemed—
Beautiful faces above a hearthstone bent
Their inward to an outward glow.

Remembering, too, that when a door upon dark
Opens, and I, fur-prickled with frost,
Against the dark stand, one gaze
Will lift and smile with sudden sheen
Of a source far other than firelight—or even

Imagined star-glint.

Why Have I Wandered the Asphalt of Midnight?

Why have I wandered the asphalt of midnight and not known why?
Not guilt, or joy, or expectation, or even to know how,
When clouds were tattered, the distance beyond screamed its rage,
Or when fog broke
To clarity—not even to know how the strict
Rearrangement of stars communicated
Their mystic message to
The attent corpuscles hurrying heartward, and from.

Why did I stand with no motion under
The spilt-ink darkness of spruces and try to hear,
In the soundlessness of falling snow,
The heartbeat I know as the only self
I know that I know, while History
Trails its meaning like old cobwebs
Caught in a cellar broom?

Why should I clamber the cliff now gone bone-white in moonlight?
Just to feel blood dry like a crust on hands, or watch
The moon lean westering to the next range,
The next, and beyond,
To wash the whole continent, like spume?
Why should I sit till from the next valley I hear
The great bear's autumnal sex-hoot
Or the glutted owl make utterance?

Why should I wander dark dunes till rollers
Boom in from China, stagger, and break
On the beach in frothed mania, while high to the right
The North Star holds steady enough to be Truth?

Yes, why, all the years, and places, and nights, have I
Wandered and not known the question I carried?
And carry? Yes, sometimes, at dawn,
I have seen the first farmer
Set bright the steel share to the earth, or met,
Snowshoed, the trapper just set on his dawn-rounds,
Or even, long back, on a streetcar
Bound cityward, watched some old workman
Lean over his lunch box, and yawn.

August Moon

Gold like a half-slice of orange
Fished from a stiff Old-Fashioned, the moon
Lolls on the sky that goes deeper blue
By the tick of the watch. Or
Lolls like a real brass button half-buttoned
On the blue flannel sleeve
Of an expensive seagoing blue blazer.

Slowly stars, in a gradual
Eczema of glory, gain definition.

What kind of world is this we walk in?

It makes no sense except
The inner, near-soundless *chug-chug* of the body's old business—
Your father's cancer, or
Mother's stroke, or
The cat's fifth pregnancy.

Anyway, while night
Hardens into its infinite being,
We walk down the woods-lane, dreaming
There's an inward means of
Communication with
That world whose darkling susurration
Might—if only we were lucky—be
Deciphered.

Children do not count years
Except at birthday parties.
We count them unexpectedly,
At random, like
A half-wit pulling both triggers
Of a ten-gauge with no target, then

Wondering what made the noise,
Or what hit the shoulder with the flat
Butt of the axe-head.

But this is off the point, which is
The counting of years, and who
Wants to live anyway
Except to be of use to
Somebody loved?

At least, that's what they say.

Do you hear the great owl in distance?

*

Do you remember a childhood prayer—
A hand on your head?

The moon is lost in tree-darkness.
Stars show now only
In the pale path between treetops.
The track of white gravel leads forward in darkness.

I advise you to hold hands as you walk,
And speak not a word.

Dreaming in Daylight

You clamber up rock, crash thicket, leap
Brook, stop for breath—then standing still, quote

A few lines of verse in the emptiness of silence. Then
Past birches, up bluffside—or near-cliff, it is. Breath

Again short, you crouch, feeling naked to think
That from crevice of stone, from shadow of leaf,

From rotted-out log, from earth-aperture,
Small eyes, or larger, with glitter in darkness, are watching

Your every move. They are like conscience. They are
Like remorse. You don't belong

Here, and that is why, like gastritis
Or migraine, something mysterious

Is going on inside you, but with no name. Do you
Know your own name? Do you feel that

You barely escape the last flicker of foam
Just behind, up the beach of

History—indeed, that you are
The last glint of consciousness before

You are caught by the grind, bulge, and beat of
What has been? Indeed, by

The heaving ocean of pastness? Oh, try
To think of something your life has meant,

While from darkness bright eyes fix now on your strangeness.
They do not know that you are stranger

*

To yourself than to them. Move higher!
For the past creeps behind you, like foam. At last

Rears the stern rock, majestic and snagged, that
The peak is. It thrusts from green growth. Is sky-bare.

You clamber the few mossed shards that frost has ripped off.
Then stop. For no handholds nub the raw pylon. This

Is the end. You think: *I am here.*
You expect to see foam, so white, so silent, snaking

Out from green brush. You wait. You think
That all you can do is to try to remember,

And name by name, aloud, the people you have
Truly loved. And you find that difficult. They are so few.

That night, in your bed, you wake from a dream
Of eyes that from crevice, shade, log, aperture,

Peer. They peer, dark-glistening, like
Conscience. Yes, you are less strange to them

Than to yourself.

Preternaturally Early Snowfall in Mating Season

Three days back, first snow had fallen.
Light, no more than a sprinkling of sugar
Crystalline on brown hickory leaves
And gold-fading beech leaves fallen:
Just like the "breakfast of champions." Upridge,
However, spruces were spangled. The sun,
With remote indifference, heatless,
Fulfilled its shortening arc
From ridge to far ridge in the mountains, grasping
Earth's globe in merciless fingers, the globe
Black-furred. I slept
With foot of sleeping sack near dying coals. Frontiersmen,
I'd read, learned early to beat the chronic curse
Of rheumatism: set wet moccasined feet—which, with wry wit
They said, was just a worse way of going barefoot—
Toward fire to sleep.

Skyward, no stars.

*

Morning, no sun, not even
One leprous wan wen of light; only
Grayness diffused under a dome
Like gray stone crudely set
In gray cement of prehistory,
The dome bulwarked to ride
The horizon's snagged circle. Clouds, like gray stone,
Bellied down: the real thing coming, and soon.

Early, but snowshoes in tote. Pure luck.

On such a day the mind, like sky,
Has no thought; only the sagging promise of itself.
Your mind hangs gray, like the dome of cloud-stone. Hands
Do their tasks, alone, unsupervised:
They are the single point of the world.

This is one name for happiness: the act.

Past midnight, snow on face, I woke.
Re-fed the fire. Crawled back in sack,
Drew tighter the hood, wondered
How is whiteness a darkness, and in that hypnosis,
Slept. Then started up at a blast, wheeze, snort, bleat,
And beat and crash of dead boughs. One moment,
Bewildered. Then knew.

In the world of glitter and dawn-snow whiteness,
My snowshoes at last being dug out, I found the spot.
First, where a doe, by a deadfall, had made her huddle. Then
Where the buck had wrestled and struggled to mount.
There were the poplar boughs, rotten, beat loose by the antlers.
There, scarcely covered by new snow, the marks
Of plunge, stamp, trample, heave, and ecstasy of storm.

It took two days, snowshoeing, to get out,
And rations short the second. My skull
Felt scraped inside as though scrubbed with ammonia,
And I moved through the white world, nothing
Inside the skull but the simple awareness of Being. But
Just once, toward dark, the white world gone gray,
I stopped for breath, and standing, was sure, with leap
Of heart, I was for an instant actually seeing,
Even in that gloom, directly before me, the guessed-at glory.

By that time I must have been pretty beat
From fatigue and hunger. And later
It was hard to get a fire going.

Sila

Sila, for the Eskimo, "is the air, not the sky; movement, not wind; the very breath of life, but not physical life; he is clear-sighted energy, activating intelligence; the powerful fluid circulating 'all around' and also within each individual . . . "

Larousse World Mythology

Upgrade, past snow-tangled bramble, past
Deadfall snow-buried, there—
The ruin of old stonework, where man-heart
Long ago had once lifted
In joy, and back muscles strained. "Stay, Sila!" the boy
Commanded the tawny great husky, broad-chested,
That in harness yet stood, forward-leaning. The boy
Stamped his cross-countries. Stared
At the ruin. Thought:
Two hundred years back—and it might
Have been me.

And wondered what name the man
Might have had. Thought:
Well, summer, I'll come
And hunt for the gravestones. Then thought
How letters that crude must be weathered away—how deeper
A skull must be pulping to earth, and now grinless.
But thought: *At least, I can touch it, whatever*
It is, stone or skull.

Was young, then he thought, *young as me, maybe.*

Then felt muscles tighten and clinch
At a sudden impulse of surprise
To find here the old mark of life that for life
Once had sung, while the axe-edge glittered in sunlight.

Oh, what are the years! his heart cried, and he felt
His own muscles pulsing in joy, just as when
Hands clasp for the lift of the beauty of butt-swell.

Land benched here, great beeches,
Gray, leafless, arising parklike and artful
From snow artificial as Christmas.
"Stay, Sila!" he called, and on level ground now
Slick glided to where the blue gleam of ice-eyes
Looked up in his own, with a knowledge deeper than words.
He snapped harness loose, wrapped cords at his waist, and—
The dog exploded.

*

From behind a beech deadfall, the doe, it had leaped,
Cow-awkward on earth, but magically airy in flight,
And weightless as wind, forelegs airward prowing
To seem as frail as a spider's, but hooves aglitter like glass
To cleave sunlight. Then,
Suddenly knifing the ice-crust as deep
As a trap, while the husky's wide paw-spread
Had opened like snowshoes behind.
Five leaps—and first blood, at a haunch,
Flesh laid back like a hunter's thin knife-slice.

Again, two more leaps, and white slash at belly—
Red line drawn clean on the curve. The boy's order
No use now: "Stay! Damn it, stay!" Until
Hand on harness, at last and too late, for
Red blood dripped now from white fang
To whiteness of snow, and eyes blue as steel drove into
The boy's eyes brain-deep, while, that instant,
All eons of friendship fled.
Then dog-eyes went earthward. The guts
Of the doe slip forth blue on the ice-crust.

The husky, stiff as in bronze cast, waits.

Only one thing to do. Who'd leave the doe there,
Dying slow into sunset, while all the small teeth—
Fox, field mouse, and wildcat—emerge
For their nocturnal feast? So the boy's knees bend,
Break the snow-crust like prayer,
And he cuddles the doe's head, and widening brown eyes
Seem ready, almost, to forgive.

Throat fur is cream color, eyes flecked with gold glintings.
He longs for connection, to give explanation. Sudden,
The head, now helpless, drops back on his shoulder. Twin eyes
Hold his own entrapped in their depth,
But his free hand, as though unaware,
Slides slow back
To grope for the knife-sheath.

The boy could not shut his eyes to the task,
As some fool girl might, but set
Eyes deeper in eyes, as he cradled the head, and gently
Held up the soft chin
To tauten the fullness of throat, and then,
As scrupulous as a well-trained tailor, set
The knife's needle point where acuteness
Would enter without prick of pain, and
Slashed in a single, deep motion.

*

He was sure that the doe
Never twitched.

On snow unconsciously heaped, he let down the head,
Aware even yet of the last embracement of gaze.
He watched, bewitched by the beauty, how blood flowed,
Red petal by petal, a great rose that bloomed where he stood.
How petal on petal, curve swelling past curve,
Gleamed forth at his feet on the snow,
And each petal sparkled with flicker of ice through the crimson,
As rays of last sun found a special glory in smallness.

He lifted his head, knife yet in hand, and westward
Fixed eyes beyond beech-bench to the snow-hatched
Stone thrust of the mountain, above which sky, too,
More majestically bloomed, but petals paler as higher—
The rose of the blood of the day. Still as stone,
So he stood. Then slowly—so slowly—
He raised the blade of the knife he loved honing, and wiped
The sweet warmness and wetness across his own mouth,
And set tongue to the edge of the silk-whetted steel.

He knew he knew something at last
That he'd never before known.
No name for it—no!

He snow-cleaned the knife. Sheathed it. Called: "Come!"
The dog, now docile, obeyed. With bare hands full of snow,
The boy washed him of blood and, comblike,
With fingers ennobled the ruff.

Then suddenly clasping the creature, he,
Over raw fur, past beeches, the mountain's snow-snag,
And the sky's slow paling of petals,
Cried out into vastness
Of silence: "Oh, world!"

He felt like a fool when tears came.

Some sixty years later, propped on death's pillow,
Again will he see that same scene, and try,
Heart straining, to utter that cry?—But
Cannot, breath short.

III.

Empty White Blotch on Map of Universe: A Possible View

The world is that map's white blotch, no charted coast.
The world is a strange shore for shipwreck, the last of choices.
The world is a strange bed to wake in—lost, lost.
The world is an island, strange, full of faceless voices.
What a landfall the world!—on which to be naked cast
By the infinite wind-heave, and wind-shoveled sea, of a father's lust.

Though this island is full of voices, I've never seen
Who sings, or grasped in what language the lyrics are.
I have followed the voices through forests of lethal green,
But the sweeter the note, the note is more far—more far.
Though in dream I see, as I hear that note again,
The wet thigh of a nymph, by a spring, agleam where stars peer in.

In the loneliest places I've wandered. I've clambered, stood
On a ruined cairn raised by lost aboriginals
To honor their dead (but who honored the last?)—and a flood
Of old orations from school I pronounced to the squalls
Of gulls and tern-laughter, as though they understood
My comic charade thus venting youth's view of the noble and good.

And I saw the very delusions before my sight:
Bloody Spartacus or the hair-combing Spartan few,
Or the neat little captain who'd not begun to fight,
Or at Gettysburg, old, angular Abe eschew
The rhetorical ordure which is the patriot's delight.
Oh, yes, I saw them—then all went black, of a sudden, as night.

I have written whole books, with a stone-honed reed on the sand,
Telling truth that should never be told, and what such truths mean.
But who cared? For Truth must accept its reprimand
When the tide comes in like Christ's blood, to wash all clean,
Including the truth that Truth's only a shout, or clapped hand,
At the steel-heeled stomp, steel-throated bark, or a lifted wand.

I have even erected a cross, looped my wrists, hung suspended—
There being no Roman ready with nails for the feet
Or to pierce my side with a spear—as God intended.
As for sponge and vinegar, neither—all incomplete.
But *"lama sabachthani,"* I cried. And attended
The premature dark, the shudder of earth, how all would be ended.

*

But no, no such end. On the blazing tropic sky
The vulture cruised, nor gave me the slightest attention.
At night, wriggling down, I bathed wrists, and crept to lie
In my cave, with no prayer, and no hope of change of condition.
But dreamed, while the surf kept beating its monody,
Of voices beguiling the distance—like pain, their love-stung cry.

Function of Blizzard

God's goose, neck neatly wrung, is being plucked.
And night is blacker for the plethora
Of white feathers except when, in an air-tower beam,
Black feathers turn white as snow. Which is what they are.
And in the blind trajectory travelers scream toward silence.

Black ruins of arson in the Bronx are whitely
Redeemed. Poverty does not necessarily
Mean unhappiness. Can't you hear the creak of bed-slats
Or ghostly echo of childish laughter? Bless
Needle plunging into pinched vein. Bless coverings-over, forgettings.

Bless snow, and chains beating undersides of fenders.
Bless insane sirens of the Fire Department
And Christmas whirl of alarm lights. Bless even
Three infants locked in a tenement in Harlem.
God's bosom is broad. Snow soon will cover the anguished ruin.

Bless snow! Bless God, Who must work under the hand of
Fate, who has no name. God does the best
He can, and sometimes lets snow whiten the world
As a promise—as now of mystic comfort to
The old physicist, a Jew, faith long since dead, who is getting

High-lonesome drunk by the frosted window of
The Oak Room bar in the Plaza. And bless me, even,
With no glass in my hand, and far from New York, as I rise
From bed, feet bare, heart freezing, to stare out at
The whitening fields and forest, and wonder what

Item of the past I'd most like God to let
Snow fall on, keep falling on, and never

Melt, for I, like you, am only a man, after all.

Dream, Dump-heap, and Civilization

Like the stench and smudge of the old dump-heap
Of Norwalk, Connecticut, the residue

Of my dream remains, but I make no
Sense of even the fragments. They are nothing

More significant than busted iceboxes and stinking mattresses
Of Norwalk, and other such human trash from which

Smudge rose by day, or coals winked red by night,
Like a sign to the desert-walkers

Blessed by God's promise. Keep your foot on the gas,
And you'll get to Westport. But

What of my dream—stench, smudge, and fragments?
And behind it all a morning shadow, like guilt, strives.

To say what? How once I had lied to my mother and hid
In a closet and said, in darkness, aloud: "I hate you"?

Or how once, in total fascination, I watched a black boy
Take a corn knife and decapitate six kittens? Did I dream

That again last night? How he said: "Too many, dem"?
Did I dream of six kitten-heads staring all night at me?

All try to say something—still now trying
By daylight? Their blood inexhaustibly drips. Did I wake

With guilt? How rarely is air here pure as in the Montana mountains!
Sometime we must probe more deeply the problem of complicity.

Is civilization possible without it?

Vision

The vision will come—the Truth be revealed—but
Not even its vaguest nature you know—ah, truth

About what? But deep in the sibilant dark
That conviction irregularly

Gleams like fox-fire in sump-woods where,
In distance, lynx-scream or direful owl-stammer

*

Freezes the blood in a metaphysical shudder—which
Might be the first, feather-fine brush of Grace. Such

An event may come with night rain on roof, season changing
And bed too wide; or, say, when the past is de-fogged

And old foot tracks of folly show fleetingly clear before
Rationalization again descends, as from seaward.

Or when the shadow of pastness teasingly
Lifts and you recollect having caught—when, when?—

A glint of the nature of virtue like
The electrically exposed white of a flicker's

Rump feathers at the moment it flashes for the black thicket.
Or when, even, in a section of the city

Where no acquaintance would ever pass,
You watch snowflakes slash automobile lights

As you move toward the first
Illicit meeting, naturally at a crummy

Café. Your pace slows. You see her
Slip from the cab, dash for the door, dark fur coat

Collar up, head down. Inside,
As you order two highballs,

All eyes seem to focus on you. Drinks come, but
There is nothing to say. Hands

Do, damply, clasp—though no bed yet. Each stares
Into the other's eyes, desire like despair, and doom

Grows slow, and fat, and dark, like a burgundy begonia.
Soon you will watch the pale silken flash

Of well-turned ankles beneath dark fur,
As she hurries away on her stolen time, cab-hunting, and the future

Scarcely breathes. Your chest is a great clot. Perhaps then.
Oh, no. It may not happen, in fact, until

A black orderly, white-coated, on rubber soles, enters at 5 A.M.
The hospital room, suds and razor in hand, to shave,

With no word of greeting, the area the surgeon
Will penetrate. The robot departs. No one

*

Comes yet. Do not give up hope.
There is still time. Watch dawn blur the window.

Can it be that the vision has, long back, already come—
And you just didn't recognize it?

Globe of Gneiss

How heavy is it? Fifteen tons? Thirty? More?—
The great globe of gneiss, poised, it would seem, by
A hair's weight, there on the granite ledge. Stop!
Don't go near! Or only on tiptoe. Don't,
For God's sake, be the fool I once was, who
Went up and pushed. Pushed with all strength,
Expecting the great globe to go
Hurtling like God's wrath to crush
Spruces and pines down the cliff, at least
Three hundred yards down to the black lake the last
Glacier to live in Vermont had left to await
Its monstrous plunge.

I pushed. It was like trying
To push a mountain. It
Had lived through so much, the incessant
Shove, like a shoulder, of north wind nightlong,
The ice-pry and lever beneath, the infinitesimal
Decay of ledge-edge. Suddenly,
I leaped back in terror.
Suppose!

So some days I now go again to see
Lichen creep slow up that
Round massiveness. It creeps
Like Time, and I sit and wonder how long
Since that gneiss, deep in earth,
In a mountain's womb, under
Unspeakable pressure, in total
Darkness, in unmeasurable
Heat, had been converted
From simple granite, striped now with something
Like glass, harder
Than steel, and I wonder
How long ago, and how, the glacier had found it.
How long and how it had trundled
The great chunk to globe-shape.

Then poised it on ledge-edge, in balanced perfection.

*

Sun sets. It is a long way
Down, the way darkening. I
Think how long my afternoon
Had seemed. How long
Will the night be?

But how short that time for the great globe
To remember so much!

How much will I remember tonight?

Part of What Might Have Been a Short Story, Almost Forgotten

(octosyllabics)

Fifty-odd years ago if you
Were going to see Shoshone
Falls, the road was not, God knows, slicked
Up for the wheeled hordes of Nature-
Lovers gawking in flowered shirts
From Hawaii, and little bas-
tards strewing candy wrappers as
They come. No—rough roads then, gravel
Sometimes and, too, lonesomeness: no
Pervasive stink of burnt high-test,
Like the midnight memory of
Some act of shame long forgotten
But now back in sickening sweat.

The thunder, in vacant silence,
First grew like a dream of thunder,
Then external palpitation
Of air, not sound. Then, there it is—
The chasmed roar clambers now up
To smite you, as tons of water,
Glinting like steel, if steel could flow,
Plunge over geologic de-
bris to darkening depth where crash-
ing white and foam-stung air prove the
Great natural depth and shadow—
While the red sun of August, mis-
shapen, bloated, sinks to a far
Mountain heave.

The woman went back
To the car. Noise gave her headaches.

*

I watched the chasm darker grow,
And deeper while the white crashing
Momently seemed deeper, deeper,
But paradoxically loud-
er. I found myself drawn to the
Brink, gaze frozen downward. Arms, white,
Wreathed upward, imploring. I tore
My eyes from that compulsion, that
Deepening sound and white fulfill-
ment. I lifted eyes. Stared west. The
Sun, rim down now, flamed to the un-
winged, utmost, blank zenith of sky.
I stared till flame color, blood col-
or, faded to dusking color-
lessness, and the first star, westward
And high, spoke. Then, slowly, night. I
Heard the crash rise merciless, kept
Eyes on that first star. But sudden-
ly, glare of the car's headlights bursts.

Directly on me bursts. Then the
Scream. Then: "Look!" I turned to look and
There it was. On the slant of a
Skyward-broken stratum, among
Sparse scrub, it crouched, the great shoulder
Muscles bunched separate and high,
The noble head outthrust but mas-
sive jaws just clear of earth, upper
Lip drawn slightly back to expose
White glitter of fangs. The eyes, catch-
ing headlight glare, glared at me as
Vented from a skull with blown coals
Packed. The tail, in shadow, slow swung
From side to side. My blood was ice.

But no reason. With insolent,
Contemptuous dignity, its
Curiosity about this
Strange and defenseless beast now at
Last satisfied, it wheeled and took
One leap that, in slow grace, looked more
Like flight into blank darkness past
Lip of the chasm. That was all.

Back in my seat, the brake released,
I let the car coast out on the
Road such as it was. Turned switch. The
Motor snapped to life. My heart was
Slow again. We had seen what we
Had come to see, Nature's beauty,
But not what in the uncoiling

Of Time, Time being what it is,
We would come to see. Now under
White gaze in high darkness of in-
different stars, unknowing, word-
less, we lower swung, lower past
Tormented stone of crags, then in
Black maw of conifer forest:

And there, what beast might, waiting, be.

What beast with fang more white, with claw
More scimitar, with gaze of blaze
More metaphysical, patient
As stone in geological
Darkness, waits, waiting, will wait
Where and how long?—While we,
By other crag, by moonlit field,
By what star-tumbling stream, or through
What soundless snow which wipers groan
To cope with, roads poor-mapped, will move
Toward what foetal, fatal truth
Our hearts had witlessly concealed
In mere charade, hysterical

Or grave, of love.

Cocktail Party

Beyond the haze of alcohol and syntax and
Flung gage of the girl's glance, and personal ambition,
You catch some eye-gleam, sense a faint
Stir, as of a beast in shadow. It may be Truth.

Into what distance all gabble crawls away!
You look, and thirty lips move without sound
As though something had gone wrong with the TV,
And you see, of a sudden, a woman's unheard laugh exposing

Glitter of gold in the mouth's dark ghetto like unspeakable
Obscenity, but not sound. You try
To speak, an urgency like hard phlegm
In your throat, but no sound comes. You quiver, thinking

Of the horror of Truth. It lies in wait—ha, ha!—
A pun—or rises, diaphanous, like
Smoke from the red-stained cigarette butt
Half-crushed in a carved gold ashtray.

*

In wait, it lies. Or like a tumor grows
Somewhere inside your brain. Oh, doctor, please, oh,
Remove it! Expense be damned, I only
See lips moving. I move my lips, but no

Sound comes, not even a lie. Yes, operate, then I
Can hear them—and tell them I love them. At least,
If we are all to be victims of Truth,
Let us be destroyed together in normal communication.

Or maybe I'm only a little drunk. Oh, waiter!

Deep—Deeper Down

By five o'clock—still bright in spring—I'd catch
The first .44 explosion, cottony
In distance, but solid too, as though at the snatch
Of a ripe boll you'd found the hot slug inside, blood-wet. Then lonely

I'd shove back my afternoon chair, get old Lüger, knee-boots,
And the German shepherd and pointer cross-breed that could smell
A cotton-mouth on a bridal wreath as well as on cypress roots,
And head for the bayou, now and then a yell.

For Jim, who'd cursed all day at a desk in town,
Was now free till dark, when his wife drove back.
So we wandered where water was black and slimy, or slickly brown,
And the bough with white blossoms was death—if it reared up its slack.

Two hours, perhaps, is enough to make a man feel
That reality spills into other hours to give
Life fundamental direction, and hand skill
To say, at his whim, *die* or *live.*

Jim and I took turns when a target presented itself.
If the first man missed, the second got two shots for his.
As I took aim I might often feel I was robbing his Self
Of its reason for being. I know what vanity is.

For spring and all summer that was our unspoken duty:
To purge earth of evil, and feel thereby justified.
In our wordless friendship we'd stare at the cleansing beauty
Of the dark arabesque wavering down, belly white as it died.

Long back, that was. Not to come again.
All gone—but dream once showed my own body glimmer down
Past the slick, slimy brush of a form that yet twisted in pain,
Its belly paling in darkness—deep—deeper down.

Sky

Livid to lurid switched the sky.
From west, from sunset, now the great dome
Arched eastward to lip the horizon edge,
There far, blank, pale. The grass, the trees,
Abandoned their kindly green to stretch
Into distance, arsenical now in that
Acid and arsenical light
Streaked yellow like urine.

Farmhouses afar—
They seemed to float, tiny and lost,
Swaying unmoored, forgotten in
That virulence past viridity
That washed, flooded, the world, and seemed
To lift all things, all houses, trees, hills,
From God-ordained foundations.

And
Your head in dizziness swam, while from
Southeast a blackness was towering
Toward you—sow-bellied, brute-nosed, coiling,
Twisting itself in pain, in rage,
And self-rage not yet discharged, and in
Its distant, sweeping downwardness
Uncentered pink flashes flickered pale but
In lethal promise. The sun's red eye
Now from western death glares.

We,
We all, have much endured, buckling
Belts, hearts. Have borne the outrageous
And uncomprehended inclemencies—
Borne even against God's will, or fate's.
Some have survived. We fear, yes. But
What most we fear advances on
Tiptoe, breath aromatic. It smiles.

Its true name is what we never know.

Better Than Counting Sheep

For a night when sleep eludes you, I have,
At last, found the formula. Try to summon

All those ever known who are dead now, and soon
It will seem they are there in your room, not chairs enough

*

For the party, or standing space even, the hall
Chock-full, and faces thrust to the pane to peer.

Then somehow the house, in a wink, isn't there,
But a field full of folk, and some,

Those near, touch your sleeve, so sadly and slow, and all
Want something of you, too timid to ask—and you don't

Know what. Yes, even in distance and dimness, hands
Are out-stretched to glow faintly

Like fox-fire in marshland where deadfall
Rots, though a few trunks unsteadily stand.

Meanwhile, in the grieving susurrus, all wordless,
You sense, at last, what they want. Each,

Male or female, young or age-gnawed, beloved or not—
Each wants to know if you remember a name.

But now you can't answer, not even your mother's name, and your heart
Howls with the loneliness of a wolf in

The depth of a snow-throttled forest when the moon, full,
Spills the spruce-shadows African black. Then you are, suddenly,

Alone. And your own name gone, as you plunge in ink-shadow or snowdrift.
The shadows are dreams—but of what? And the snowdrift, sleep.

The Cross

(A Theological Study)

Once, after storm, I stood at the cliff-head,
And up black basalt the sea's white claws
Still flung their eight fathoms to have my blood.
In the blaze of new sun they leap in cruel whiteness,
Not forgiving me that their screaming lunges
Had nightlong been no more than a dream
In the tangle and warmth and breathless dark
Of love's huddle and sleep, while stars were black
And the tempest swooped down to snatch our tiles.

By three, wind down and sun still high,
I walked the beach of the little cove
Where scavengings of the waves were flung—
Old oranges, cordage, a bottle of beer
With the cap still tight, a baby doll

But the face smashed in, a boom from some mast,
And most desperately hunched by volcanic stone
As though trying to cling in some final hope,
But drowned hours back you could be damned sure,
The monkey, wide-eyed, bewildered yet
By the terrible screechings and jerks and bangs,
And no friend to come and just say *ciao.*

I took him up, looked in his eyes,
As orbed as dark aggies, as bright as tears,
With a glaucous glint in deep sightlessness,
Yet still seeming human with all they had seen—
Like yours or mine, if luck had run out.

So, like a fool, I said *ciao* to him.

Under wet fur I felt how skin slid loose
On the poor little bones, and the delicate
Fingers yet grasped, at God knew what.
So I sat with him there, watching wind abate.
No funnel on the horizon showed.
And of course, no sail. And the cliff's shadow
Had found the cove. Well, time to go.

I took time, yes, to bury him,
In a scraped-out hole, little cairn on top.
And I enough fool to improvise
A cross—

Two sticks tied together to prop in the sand.

But what use that? The sea comes back.

IV.

Truth

Truth is what you cannot tell.
Truth is for the grave.
Truth is only the flowing shadow cast
By the wind-tossed elm
When sun is bright and grass well groomed.

Truth is the downy feather
You blow from your lips to shine in sunlight.

Truth is the trick that History,
Over and over again, plays on us.
Its shape is unclear in shadow or brightness,
And its utterance the whisper we strive to catch
Or the scream of a locomotive desperately
Blowing for the tragic crossing. Truth
Is the curse laid upon us in the Garden.

Truth is the Serpent's joke,

And is the sun-stung dust-devil that swirls
On the lee side of God when He drowses.

Truth is the long soliloquy
Of the dead all their long night.
Truth is what would be told by the dead
If they could hold conversation
With the living and thus fulfill obligation to us.

Their accumulated wisdom must be immense.

On Into the Night

On downward slope gigantic wheels
Of afternoon, how soundless, crunch
Cloud cobbles of bright cumuli
Sparely paving the sky with white dreams of stone.

I lie beside the stream that slides
In the same windless silence beneath
Shadow of birch and beech and alder
Like an image of Time's metaphysic.

*

No insect hums. And taciturn,
The owl's adrowse in the depth of a cedar
To pre-enjoy the midnight's revel.
The thrush-throat only in silence throbs now.

Like film in silence being unspooled
From a defective mechanism,
The film of memory flows with no
Assessment of what it could ever mean.

Shadow and shade of cliff sift down
To darken the dimmest under-leaf,
And in the secret conduits
Of flesh I feel blood darker flow.

Now soon the evening's twitch begins
Beneath the prick of appetite
Or, nameless, of some instinctual tingle.
Bullbat and bat will soon scribble

Their lethal script on a golden sky.
From the apple orchard, a century ruined,
The he-bear will utter his sexual hoot,
Deer will come forth for autumn forage,

On the sleep-dazed partridge the lynx leaps
As the thrush-throat throbs to its last music.
Later, the last of night's voices is heard—
The owl's mystic question that follows his glut.

Then silence again. You sleep. Moonlight
Bathes the world in white silence. No, no!—there's one sound
Defined now by silence. The pump in your breast,
In merciless repetition, declares

Its task in undecipherable metaphor.

No Bird Does Call

Bowl-hollow of woodland, beech-bounded, beech-shrouded,
With roots of great gray boles crook'd airward, then down
To grapple again, like claws, in the breathless perimeter
Of moss, as in cave-shadow darker and deeper than velvet.

And even at noon just a flicker of light,
In summer green glint on darkness of green,
In autumn gold glint on a carpet of gold, for then
The hollow is Danae's lap lavished with gold by the god:

*

But what, through years now, I wake to remember
Is noontide of summer when, from sun-blast and world,
I, in despair, fled deeper and deeper,
To avoid the sight of mankind and the bustle of men,

And first, to that spot, came. No sound,
No movement of leaf, and I lay
In the hollow where moss was a soft depth like shadow.
With closed eyes I fell so slowly—so slow—as though

Into depth that was peace, but not death, and the world far away,
And one noon-ray strayed through labyrinths of leaves,
Revealing to me the redness of blood in eyelids,
And in that stillness my heart beat. The ray

Wandered on. The eyelids were darkened. I slept.
Then late, late, woke. Rose up. Wandered forth.
Came again where men were, and it seemed then that years—
How many?—had passed, and I looked back on life at great distance.

Years now have passed, and a thousand miles lie between,
And long since the time I would go there in every season
To stand in that silence, and hope for no bird, not any, to call.
And now when I wake in the night to remember, no bird ever calls.

Weather Report

In its deep little gorge my brook swells big,
The color of iron rust, and boulders bang—
Ah, where is the sun that yesterday made my heart glad?

Rain taps on the roof of my air-swung workhouse,
On one side in pine-tops above the gorge.
This the code now tapped: *Today is today.*

Where are the warblers that yesterday
Fluttered outside my screen walls, or ignoring
My presence, poured out their ignorant joy to my ignorant heart?

Where are the warblers? Why, yes, there's one,
Rain-colored like gunmetal now, rain-slick like old oil.
It is motionless in the old stoicism of Nature.

Yes, under a useless maple leaf,
The tail with a fringe of drops, like old Tiffany crystal,
And one drop, motionless, hangs at beak-tip.

*

I see that beak, unmoving as death—today
No note of ignorant joy to instruct
My ignorant heart, no promise of joy for tomorrow.

But the code yet taps on my tar-paper roof.
Have I read it aright? *Today is today.*
And earth grinds on, on its axis,

With a creak just this side of silence.
It lurches, perhaps.

Tires on Wet Asphalt at Night

As my head in darkness dents pillow, the last
Automobile, beyond rhododendrons
And evergreen screen, hisses
On rain-wet asphalt. It
Is going somewhere. I cannot
See it, but
It is going somewhere different
From here and now, leaving me
To lie and wonder what is left.

A man and a woman, perhaps they lean
Into cold dimness of gauge-lights, and she
At a flickering gap in my road-cover
Lifts head to catch glimpse of my bedroom windows
That glitter in darkness like
Two dead eyes that nobody has closed.

They do not know that I am here, eyes ceilingward,
Open to darkness. They do not know

That I am thinking of them—
How after the first shake and shudder at sheet-cold, they
Will huddle for warmth in the old
Mechanic hope of finding identity in
The very moment of paradox when
There is always none.

I stare into darkness ceilingward, thinking
How they at last must stare thus. And wonder
Do they, at least, clasp hands.

I think of the hiss of their tires going somewhere—
That sound like the *swish-hiss* of faint but continual
Wavelets far down on the handkerchief beach-patch
In a cove crag-locked and pathless, slotted
Only to seaward and westward, sun low. And I

Felt need to climb down and lie there, that sound
In my ear, and watch the sun sink, in its blaze, below
The blind, perpetual, abstract sea.

What then but climb again up, by stone-jut and scrub-root,
Hearing the loosened talus go tumbling down?
Once up, exhausted, face-down, arms outflung,
I lay clutching old clumps of summer-burned grass.
Was it fear that made me shake then? Or was I
Embracing the world?

It was a long way back home across darkening fields.

That was long ago. Till the hiss of the tires,
Like last wavelets, I had forgotten it.

I wish I could think what makes them come together now.

Timeless, Twinned

Angelic, lonely, autochthonous, one white
Cloud lolls, unmoving, on an azure which
Is called the sky, and in gold drench of light,
No leaf, however gold, may stir, nor a single blade twitch,

Though autumn-honed, of the cattail by the pond. No voice
Speaks, since here no voice knows
The language in which a tongue might now rejoice.
So silence, a transparent flood, thus overflows.

In it, I drown, and from my depth my gaze
Yearns, faithful, toward that cloud's integrity,
As though I've now forgotten all other nights and days,
Anxiety born of the future's snare, or the nag of history.

What if, to my back, thin-shirted, brown grasses yet bring
The heat of summer, or beyond the perimeter northward, wind,
Snow-bellied, lurks? I stare at the cloud, white, motionless. I cling
To our single existence, timeless, twinned.

What is the Voice that Speaks?

What is the voice that speaks? Oh, tongue
Of laurel leaf by my glass door, trying

To tell how long since you lived on a mountain
In Tennessee, free wind inspiring your wisdom?

Or split tongue of *coluber constrictor*—
Black racer to you—who from his hole

In the lawn so valiantly rises to hiss at the cat, aggressive
And spread-clawed? Or the blind man who spat at you

When you put a dime in his cup at Christmas?
(Screw him, a dime is a dime, and suffering no index of virtue.)

Have you heard the great owl in the snow-pine? You know
His question—the one you've never, in anguish, been able to answer.

Yes, think of the wolf-howl, moonlit from mountain. How well
You remember, in warm bed, or season, from darkness that desolate timbre.

What did my mother, ready to die, say? "Son,
I like your new suit." Nor spoke again. Not to me.

And once, long distance, I heard a voice saying:
"I thought that you loved me—" And I:

"I do. But tomorrow's a snowflake in Hell."
And the phone went dead, and I thought of snow falling

All night, in white darkness, across the blindness of Kansas,
And wept, for I thought of a head thrown back, and the moan.

What tongue knows the name of Truth? Or Truth to come?
All we can do is strive to learn the cost of experience.

Language Barrier

Snow-glitter, snow-gleam, all snow-peaks
Scream joy to the sun. Green
Far below lies, shelved where a great *cirque* is blue, bluest
Of waters, face upward to sky-flaming blue. Then
The shelf falters, fails, and downward becomes

*

Torment and tangle of stone, like Hell frozen, where snow
Lingers only in shadow. Alone, alone,
What grandeur here speaks? The world
Is the language we cannot utter.
Is it a language we can even hear?

Years pass, and at night you may dream-wake
To that old altitude, breath thinning again to glory,
While the heart, like a trout,
Leaps. What,
Long ago, did the world try to say?

It is long till dawn.
The stars have changed position, a far train whistles
For crossing. Before the first twitter of birds
You may again drowse. Listen—we hear now
The creatures of gardens and lowlands.

It may be that God loves them, too.

Lesson in History

How little does history manage to tell!
Did the lips of Judas go dry and cold on our Lord's cheek?

Or did tears unwittingly spring to his eyes
As lips found the flesh, torch-lit?

What song, in his screechy voice, and joy, did Boone
At sunset sing, alone in the wild Kentucky Eden?

Who would not envy Cambronne his famous obscenity—
At last, at last, fulfilling identity in pride?

Is it true that your friend was secretly happy when
The diagnostician admitted the growth was, in fact, malignant?

After mad Charlotte Corday had done her work,
Did she dip, trancelike, her hands in the water now staining the tub?

And what did Hendrik Hudson see
That last night, alone, as he stared at the Arctic sky?

Or what, at night, is the strange fulfillment, with anguish entwined,
As you wander the dark house, your wife not long dead?

What thought had Anne Boleyn as the blade, at last, rose?
Did her parts go moist before it fell?

*

And who will ever guess how you, night-waking,
See a corner of moonlit meadow, willows, sheen of the sibilant stream?

And know, or guess, what long ago happened there?
Or know what, in whisper, the water was trying to say?

Prairie Harvest

Look westward over forever miles of wheat stubble.
The roar of the red machines is gone, they are gone.
Their roar has left the heartbeat of silence. The bubble,
Enormous, red, molten, of sun, above the horizon,

Apparently motionless, hangs. Meanwhile, blue mist
For uncountable miles of the shaven earth's rondure arises,
And in last high light the bullbats gyre and twist,
Though in the world's emptiness the sound of their cries is

Nothing. Your heart is the only sound. The sun,
It is gone. Can it be that you, for an instant, forget
And blink your eyes as it goes? Another day done,
And the star the Kiowa once stared at will requite

Man's effort by lust, and lust by the lead-weighted eyes.
So you stand in the infinite circle, star after star,
And standing alone in starlight, can you devise
An adequate definition of self, whatever you are?

V.

Eagle Descending

To a dead friend

Beyond the last flamed escarpment of mountain cloud
The eagle rides air currents, switch and swell,
With spiral upward now, steady as God's will.

Beyond black peak and flaming cloud, he yet
Stares at the sun—invisible to us,
Who downward sink. Beyond new ranges, shark-

Toothed, saw-toothed, he stares at the plains afar
By ghostly shadows eastward combed, and crossed
By a stream, steel-bright, that seems to have lost its way.

No silly pride of Icarus his! All peril past,
He westward gazes, and down, where the sun will brush
The farthermost bulge of earth. How soon? How soon

Will the tangent of his sight now intersect
The latitudinal curvature where the sun
Soon crucial contact makes, to leave him in twilight,

Alone in glory? The twilight fades. One wing
Dips, slow. He leans.—And with that slightest shift,
Spiral on spiral, mile on mile, uncoils

The wind to sing with joy of truth fulfilled.

Ballad of Your Puzzlement

(How not to recognize yourself as what you think you are, when old and reviewing your life before death comes)

Purge soul for the guest awaited.
Let floor be swept, and let
The walls be well garlanded.

Put your lands and recollections
In order, before that hour,
For you, alas, are only

*

Recollections, but recollections
Like a movie film gone silent,
With a hero strange to you

And a plot you can't understand.
His face changes as you look.
He picks the scab of his heart.

He ponders, seems caught in the toils
Of ambiguous regrets,
Like a man with a passion for Truth

Who, clutching his balance-pole,
Looks down the sickening distance
On the crowd-swarm like ants, far below,

And he sways, high on the fated
And human high-wire of lies.
Does he feel the pitiless suction

Their eyes exert on him?
Does he know they wait the orgasmic
Gasp of relief as he falls?

Why doesn't he skyward gaze,
Then plunge—why doesn't he know
The true way to swap lies for Truth?

Then scene flicks to scene without nexus,
And to change the metaphor,
He sometimes seems like a fly

Stuck on the sweet flypaper
To struggle and strain to be free
Even as his senses reel

With the sweetness of deathly entrapment.
This puzzles you, but less than
The scene in the park woods,

Where the blade, flash-bright in darkness,
Slides slick to the woman's heart,
To the very hilt, and her mouth

Makes the shape of an *O* to make
The scream you can never hear.
She falls, and he bursts into tears.

Film blurs, goes black, but then
You see the hero kneeling,
Alone, alone, at prayer.

*

And later, after hiatus,
On a slum street, old now and stooped,
He meets the loathsome beggar

And stares at the sores and filth
With slow-rapt kinship. Draws
Out his last dollar bill, and thrusts

It into the claw-shaped hand—
Reaches out to touch the skin-cancer
That gnaws at a hideous cheek.

Then the flash to a country road
And fields stretching barren to distance.
He stands, gaze upward, then shakes

His fist at the height of sky.
But shrugs, and Chaplinesque,
Trudges on, alone, toward sunset.

Black goes the film, but blackness
Slashed by stab-jabs of white
That remind you of lightning bolts

At night, at a storm in the mountains—
But miniature, and no sound.
There is nothing left but silence

In which you hear your heart beat.
Yes, how many names has Truth?
Yes, how many lives have you lived?

Yes, all, all huddle together
In your Being's squirming nest,
Or perhaps you are only

A wind-dangled mirror's moment
That flickers in light-streaked darkness.
It is hard to choose your dream.

But at last, try to pull yourself
Together. Let floors be swept.
Let walls be well garlanded.

Antinomy: Time and Identity

(1)

Alone, alone, I lie. The canoe
On blackness floats. It must
Be so, for up to a certain point
All comes back clear. I saw,
At dock, the canoe, aluminum, rising ghost-white on blackness.
This much is true. Silent,
As entering air, the paddle, slow, dips. Silent,
I slide forth. Forth on,
Forth into,
What new dimension? Slow
As a dream, no ripple at keel, I move through
The stillness, on blackness, past hope or despair
Not relevant now to illusion I'd once
Thought I lived by. At last,
Shores absorbed in the blackness of forest, I lie down. High,
Stars stare down, and I
See them. I wonder
If they see me. If they do, do they know
What they see?

(2)

Do I hear stars speak in a whisper as gentle as breath
To the few reflections caught pale in the blackness beneath?
How still is the night! It must be their voices.
Then strangely a loon-cry glows ember-red,
And the ember in darkness dims
To a tangle of senses beyond windless fact or logical choices,
While out of Time, Timelessness brims
Like oil on black water, to coil out and spread
On the time that seems past and the time that may come,
And both the same under
The present's darkening dome.

(3)

A dog, in the silence, is barking a county away.
It is long yet till day.

(4)

As consciousness outward seeps, the dark seeps in.
As the self dissolves, realization surrenders its burden
And thus fulfills your fictionality.
Night wind is no more than unrippling drift.
The canoe, light as breath, moves in a dignity
As soundless as a star's mathematical shift

Reflected light-years away
In the lake's black parodic sky.

I wonder if this is I.

(5)

It is not long till day.

(6)

Dawn bursts like the birth pangs of your, and the world's, existence.
The future creeps into the blueness of distance.
Far back, scraps of memory hang, rag-rotten, on a rusting barbed-wire fence.

(7)

One crow, caw lost in the sky-peak's lucent trance,
Will gleam, sun-purpled, in its magnificence.

Trips to California

Two days behind the dust-storm—man's
Fecklessness, God's wrath—and once
Dust on the highway piled so deep
Mules had to drag the car. This

Was Kansas, and in midafternoon
It rained blood for half an hour—
Or what looked red as blood, and what
Bible or folklore would call a rain

Of blood. It never rained any frogs,
Just blood. Then Garden City. What
A hell of a name! Dust heaped aside,
Faces stunned white. Eyes blank like those

Of people picked up in a lifeboat, the only
Survivors. "Whar goen?" This getting gas.
"Californ-ya, hanh? Not me. Out thar
Some day they'll git somethin wuss. I'll jist

Stick whar I knows whut the wust is."
On the road, west, a line of leafless
Black stubs of poplars—this now July—
Against the histrionic sunset.

The last ranch, dust windward to eaves.
Dead mule to lee, bloated like an
Enormous winter squash, green-blue.
This had been buffalo country, herds

*

Stretching for miles, parts of the two
Great herds, the South and the North, the mobile
Commissary for the Indians, but
The hunters took good care of that.

If you got a good "stand," Sharps rifles rang
All day, all night skinners working. Dawn
Then showed the hundred new naked corpses.
Besides, General Sheridan was a realist:

The only good one, he said, is a dead
One—not buffalo, but redskin.
Then plow, stupidity, avarice, did
The rest. But don't worry now. The tame

Continent eastward drops. Inferior
French wine for lunch. California
Waits like the dream it is, and mother
Of dreams. Reality past may be only

A dream, too. But, if so, sometimes
More naked, vivid, commanding than
Even anguish of immediacy,
For that comes piecemeal and guiltless from

Dark humus of history or our
Own fate, which blindly blooms, like a flower.

Auto-da-fé

Beautiful the intricacy of body!
Even when defective. But you have seen
Beauty beyond such watchmaker's craft,
For eyes unshutter in darkness to gleam out
As though to embrace you in holiness.

"...though I give my body to be burned,
And have not..." You know the rest,
And how the "I" is not the "body."
At least, according to St. Paul's text.

Beautiful in whatever sense
The body be, it is but flesh,
And flesh is grass, the season short.
Is a bag of stercory, a bag
Of excrement, the worm's surfeit,
But a bag with movement, lusts, strange
Ecstasies, transports, and strange dreams.
But, oh!—not "I" but "body" screams

When flame licks like a lover. That
Is the pure language of body, purer
Than even the cry, ecstatic, torn out
At the crisis of body's entwinement. That voice
From flame has a glory wilder than joy
To resound forever in heart, mind,
And gut, with thrilled shock and soprano of Truth.

All history resounds with such
Utterance—and stench of meat burned:
Dresden and Tokyo, and screams
In the Wilderness as flame on the wounded
Encroached, and the soft-bellied citizen,
With swollen ego as he tests
The new Cadillac and, half-drunk, piles on-
to the goddam overpass buttress. Then flame.
You can be quite sure he screams. But

Some have not. Witches sometimes,
And saints and martyrs, no doubt in number.
Take Latimer or, evasion all past,
White-bearded Cranmer, who, in slow drizzle,
Outraces the pack, ragtag and bobtail—
Though old, first to the blessèd stake.
Climbs up. Waits. Composed, austere.
Faggots lighted, white beard prickling sudden in
Wisps of brightness, he into fire thrusts
The recreant hand. No, no, not his!—
That traitor in the house.

Or that
Cracked Maid, and her Voices that she, at the last,
Could not betray, though foreknowing the end.
Through dazzle and shimmer of flame-dance, she raptly
Fixed eyes on the tied-stick cross a brutish
Soldier held up. Her cry was a prayer.

Such evidence can scarcely attest
Sure meaning.

But executioners
Might choke flame to smoke to suffocate
Clients quickly. Or sometimes gunpowder in packets,
To belly affixed, made a human grenade
Timed short for the job. This, perhaps,
From some fumbling thought of the holiness or

Beauty of body.

Aspen Leaf in Windless World

Watch how the aspen leaf, pale and windless, waggles,
While one white cloud loiters, motionless, over Wyoming.
And think how delicately the heart may flutter
In the windless joy of unworded revelation.

Look how sea-foam, thin and white, makes its Arabic scrawl
On the unruffled sand of the beach's faint-tilted plane.
Is there a message there for you to decipher?
Or only the joy of its sunlit, intricate rhythm?

Is there a sign Truth gives that we recognize?
Can we fix our eyes on the flight of birds for answer?
Can the bloody-armed augurs declare expediency?
What does dew on stretched wool-fleece, the grass dry, mean?

Have you stood on the night-lawn, oaks black, and heard,
From bough-crotch to bough-crotch, the moon-eyed tree-toad utter,
Again and again, that quavery croak, and asked
If it means there'll be rain? Toward dawn? Or early tomorrow?

We were not by when Aaron laid down his rod
That suddenly twisted, went scaly, and heaved the fanged head,
And when Egypt's high magi probed their own lore for the trick—
Well, the sacred serpent devoured that brood. What, now,

Would you make of that? Yes, we wander our shadowy world
Of miracles, whispers, high jinks, and metaphor.
Yes, why is the wind in the cedar the sub-sob of grief?
And the puppy—why is his tongue on your palm so sweet?

What image—behind blind eyes when the nurse steps back—
Will loom at the end of your own life's long sorites?
Would a sun then rise red on an eastern horizon of waters?
Would you see a face? What face? Would it smile? Can you say?

Or would it be some great, sky-thrusting gray menhir?
Or what, in your long-lost childhood, one morning you saw—
Tinfoil wrappers of chocolate, popcorn, nut shells, and poorly
Cleared up, the last elephant turd on the lot where the circus had been?

Acquaintance with Time in Early Autumn

Never—yes, never—before these months just passed
Had I known the nature of Time, and felt its strong heart,
Stroke by stroke, against my own, like love,
But love without face, or shape, or history—
Pure Being that, by being, our being denies.

Summer fulfills the field, the heart, the womb,
While summerlong, infinitesimally,
Leaf stem, at bough-juncture, dries,
Even as our tireless bodies plunge,
With delicious muscular flexion and heart's hilarity,
White to the black ammoniac purity of
A mountain pool. But black
Is blue as it stares up at summer's depthless azure,
And azure was what we saw beneath
At the timeless instant hanging
At arc-height.

Voices of joy how distant seem!
I float, pubic hair awash, and gaze
At one lone leaf, flame-red—the first—alone
Above summer's bulge of green,
High-hung against the sky.

Yes, sky was blue, but water, I suddenly felt,
Was black, and striped with cold, and one cold claw
Reached ghostly up
To find my flesh, to pierce
The heart, as though
Releasing, in that dark inwardness,
A single drop. Oh, leaf,

Cling on! For I have felt knee creak on stair,
And sometimes, dancing, notice how rarely
A girl's inner thigh will brush my own,
Like a dream. Whose dream?

The sun
Pours down on the leaf its lacquer of Chinese red.

Then, in the lucent emptiness,
While cries of joy of companions fade,
I feel that I see, even in
The golden paradox of air unmoving,
Each tendon of that stem, by its own will,
Release
Its tiny claw-hooks, and trust
A shining destiny. The leaf—it is
Too moorless not to fall. But

Does not. Minutely,
It slides—calm, calm—along the air sidewise,
Sustained by the kiss of under-air.

While ages pass, I watch the red-gold leaf,
Sunlit, descend to water I know is black.
It touches. Breath
Comes back, and I hate God
As much as gravity or the great globe's tilt.

How shall we know the astrolabe of joy?
Shall gratitude run forward as well as back?
Who once would have thought that the heart,
Still ravening on the world's provocation and beauty, might,
After time long lost
In the tangled briars of youth,
Have picked today as payday, the payment

In life's dime-thin, thumb-worn, two-sided, two-faced coin?

Safe in Shade

Eyes, not bleared but blue,
Of the old man, horizonward gazed—
As on horizons and years, long lost, but now
Projected from storage in that capacious skull.

He sat in his big chair propped
Against reddish tatter of
Bole-bark of the great cedar. I,
The boy who on the ground sat, waited.

I waited for him to speak.

I waited for him to come back to me
From the distances he traveled in.
I waited for him to speak. I saw
The cob pipe in the liver-spotted hand
Now propped on a knee, on the washed blue-jeans.
Smoke, frail, slow, blue—as blue
As the jeans but not the eyes—
Rose to thread the cedar-dark.

Around us in our shade and hush
Roared summer's fierce fecundity,
And the sun struck down,
In blare and dazzle, on the myth of the world, but we
Safe in the bourne of distance and shade,
Sat so silent that, from woods coming down

To the whitewashed fence but yards behind me,
I heard the secret murmur and hum
That in earth, on leaf, in air, seethed. Heard
One jay, outraged, scream.
The old blue eyes, they fixed on me.

I waited for him to speak. He spoke.

Into the world hurled,
In later times and other places,
I lived but as man must
In all the garbled world's compulsions,
By fate perforce performed
Acts evil or good, or even
Both in the same gesture, in
That paradox the world exemplifies.

And Time, like wind-tattered smoke,
Blew by for one who, like all men, had flung,
In joy and man's maniacal
Rage, his blood
And the blind, egotistical, self-defining
Sperm into
That all-devouring, funnel-shaped, mad and high-spiraling,
Dark suction that
We have, as the Future, named.

Where is my cedar tree?

Where is the Truth—oh, unambiguous—
Thereof?

Synonyms

(1)

Where eons back, earth slipped and cracked
To leave a great stratum, snag-edged, thrust

As margin to that blind inwardness, water
Now plunges in cosmic racket, sempiternal roar,

White-splintered on masses of stone, deep-domed or spired,
Chaos of white in dark paradox. What is the roar

But a paradox in that
Tumultuous silence—

Which paradox must be a voice of ultimate utterance?

*

(2)

When the last thrush knows the hour past song
Has come, the westward height yet
Stays sallow, and bats scribble
The sky in minuscule murder, which,
From one perspective, is beauty, too.
Time will slip in silence past, like God's breath.

Who will see the first star tonight above the mountain?

(3)

Lean back, one hand on saddle-horn, if you must.
Watch stones and gravel slip and cascade
Down each side of the knife-edge trail.
Just trust your mountain-mount and God,
For there is an end to human judgment.
Unless you stay at home in bed. Look!
Miles west, far down, a river
Crawls, like a blue snake,
Toward Wyoming.

To one side,
On a stunt stub of pine, only one
Raw spray of green visible, a magpie,
Wag-tailed in wind, sits, and with eyes
Like shiny, old-fashioned
Shoe-buttons, observes you.

He has been waiting for something
Funny and disastrous to happen.

(4)

Have you—scarcely more than a boy—been
The last man afield, the old binder
Dragged off, sun low? Have you stood
Among shadowy wheat shocks, the tips
Of stalks showing gold in that last light? Beyond
Shorn earth the sun sags slow red. In distance
One cowbell spills
The empty tinkle of loneliness. A bullfrog,
Brass-bellied, full-throated,
Accents the last silence.

Long later the owl.

Your hands still ache from the pitchfork heft.

Why do you, young, feel tears in your eyes?

*

(5)

Riding in riot and roil of Aegean blue and gold light,
Eastward broad reaching, wind
Northwesterly, force 6, gusting 7, seas smacking
Her quarter, the big yawl, hard-driven,
Thrusts merciless forefoot
Through tasseled silk-swell to swing
Scuppers under, then lifting, wet-waisted, sun-bright. Under
My desperate handgrip the cap-shroud
Strains in joy of its strength and musical hum.

Wind tears at my oilskins, spume
Burns eyeballs, but I can yet see
White flash of glitters blown down the sky
Till one, on a pivot of wing-tip, Nijinski-like, swings
To a motionless, lateral joy, beak north,
While the world, far below, and its tumult fulfill
The mission of mythic and beautiful rage,
In which each of us, a particle, partakes
Of its microscopic part.

Wind down, tonight shall we moor
In a crag-locked bay without
One wavelet to lap the sixty-foot hull,
And wordless, there being no moon, stare up
At the astute complex
Of enormous, white, and foreign stars?

What other eyes have stared there before?

(6)

In the narrow, decrepit old street where day-gleam
Is throttled as tenements shoulder each other for mutual support,
Cab, car, and truck scream
In anguish and anger for space, and fumes burn the eyes,
And swirl, sweat, stink, and foreign tongues abort
Whatever seems human, and nothing human replies.
This, the swelter of summer: at evening on stair,
Street step, cellar step, the old and the sick gasp for air,
And at night, then muggings and rape become sport.

Morning: arrange the principals, for soon—
Action! A middle-aged drunk sits and sways
On curbstone, bottle in hand, tweeds from better days.
Takes a long pull, sags flat, seems fixed till afternoon,
And a grubby old dame, one hand on a cane,
The other, to let down her hulk and sore foot with less pain,
Clutches the iron rail of the old stone
Street-steps. Descends. The great garbage grinder

Screams at its task, but a cab, breaking through,
Flings a kitten aside among filth, where san-men will find her.

But she scrambles out, one leg broken, or two,
To curbside. The boss of the monster, quick as a wink,
Seizes tail, swings her high, choking with laughter to think
How she tries to climb air with mangled, or unmangled, paws.
Still laughing, he holds up the creature so all may look
And relish the joke, but blinded by mirth,
He doesn't see the old dame swing her cane, and the crook
Yanks down his wrist, and despite sore foot, bulk, and girth,
She thrusts the poor prize in the improvised sack of her apron, gives
A long wheeze, and painfully climbs up where she lives.

There's enough laughing now, and the boss flees the public eye.
The drunk staggers up, hiccups, hitches pants,
Takes swig, lifts a half-empty quart to the sky,
And in the rapt voice of a prophet makes utterance:
"Lord God, can't You see the hour to smite!—
Or lost Your nerve, huh? Can't longer tell wrong from right?"

And a little stall-keeper creeps back to his hole in the wall,
Where vegetables, sprinkled, look nigh as fresh as they grow.
Yet one by one, he surveys the condition of all.
Then with edge of his apron, he buffs an apple to glow.

And another. Another. Blind impulse had prompted
The act. —Just what, he could not know.

(7)

There are many things in the world, and I have seen some.
Some things in the world are beautiful, and I
Have seen some. But more things are to come,
And in the world's tangled variety,
It is hard sometimes to remember that beauty is one word for reality.

Swimming in the Pacific

At sunset my foot outreached the mounting Pacific's
Last swirl as tide climbed, and I stood
On the mile-empty beach backed by dune-lands. Turned, saw,
Beyond knotting fog-clots, how Chinaward now
The sun, a dirty pink smudge, grew larger, smokier,
More flattened, then sank.

*

Through sand yet sun-hot, I made to my landmark—
Gray cairn to guard duck pants (not white now), old drawers,
Old sneakers, T-shirt, my wallet (no treasure).
At dune-foot I dressed,
Eyes westward, sea graying, one gull at
Great height, but not white-bright, the last
Smudge of sun being gone.

So I stood, and I thought how my years, a thin trickle
Of sand grains—years I then could
Count on few as fingers and toes—had led me
Again and again to this lonesome spot where
The sea might, in mania, howl, or calm, lure me out
Till the dunes were profiled in a cloud-pale line,
Nothing more,
Though the westering sun lured me on.

But beachward by dusk, drawn back
By the suction of years yet to come—
So dressed now, I wandered the sand, drifting on
Toward lights, now new, of the city afar, and pondered
The vague name of Time,
That trickles like sand through fingers,
And is life.

But suppose, after sorrow and joy, after all
Love and hate, excitement and roaming, failure, success,
And years that had long trickled past
And now could certainly never
Be counted on fingers and toes—suppose
I should rise from the sea as of old
In my twilit nakedness,
Find my cairn, find my clothes, and in gathering fog,
Move toward the lights of the city of men,
What answer, at last,
Could I give my old question? Unless,
When the fog closed in,
I simply lay down, on the sand supine, and up
Into grayness stared and, staring,

Could see your face, slow, take shape.

Like a dream all years had moved to.

Night Walking

Bear, my first thought at waking. I hear
What I think is the first bear this year
Come down off the mountain to rip
Apples from trees near my window—but no,
It's the creak of the door of the shop my son stays in.
Now booted and breeched but bare
From waist, he now stands
Motionless, silent, face up
To the moon, tonight full, now late and zenithward high
Over forests as black as old blood
And the crags bone-white.

My Levis now on, and boots, I wait.
For what? I creep
Behind a parked car and guiltily crouch.

His face, brown but now talc-white in moonlight
Lifts moonward, and I remember how once,
Footloose in Greece, in the mountains, alone, asleep,
He had waked, he said, at a distant dog's howl and
Stood up in a land where all is true.

I crouch as he slowly walks up the track
Where from blackness of spruces great birches
Stand monitory, stand white—
Moving upward, and on, face upward as though
By stars in an old sea he steered.

In silence and shadow and in
The undefinable impulse to steal
What knowledge I, in love, can,
With laggard cunning I trail to the first ridge-crest.
He stops. His gaze
Turns slow, and slower,
From quarter to quarter, over
The light-laved land, over all
Thence visible, river and mowings,
Ruined orchards, ledges and rock-slides,
And the clambering forest that would claim all.

Last, the next range to westward.

High, calm, there the moon rides.
He lifts up his light-bleached arms.
He stands.

Arms down, goes on.

*

I do not guess
How far he will go, but in my
Mixture of shame, guilt, and joy do know
All else is his—and alone.

In shadow, I huddle
Till I can start back to bed and the proper darkness of night.

I start, but alone then in moonlight, I stop
As one paralyzed at a sudden black brink opening up,
For a recollection, as sudden, has come from long back—
Moon-walking on sea-cliffs, once I
Had dreamed to a wisdom I almost could name.
But could not. I waited.
But heard no voice in the heart.
Just the hum of the wires.

But that is my luck. Not yours.

At any rate, you must swear never,
Not even in secret, the utmost, to be ashamed
To have lifted bare arms to that icy
Blaze and redeeming white light of the world.

Passers-By on Snowy Night

Black the coniferous darkness,
White the snow track between,
And the moon, skull-white in its starkness,
Watches upper ledges lean,

And regards with the same distant stare,
And equal indifference,
How your breath goes white in steel air
As you trudge to whither *from* whence.

For from somewhere you rose to go,
Maybe long before daylight withdrew,
With the dream of a windowpane's glow
And a path trodden to invite you.

And, indeed, there may be such place,
Perhaps at next corner or swerve,
Where someone presses a face
To the frost-starred glass, though the curve

Shows yet only mocking moonlight.
But soon, but soon!—Alone,
I wish you well in your night
As I pass you in my own.

*

We each hear the distant friction,
Then crack *of bough burdened with snow,*
And each takes the owl's benediction,
And each goes the way he will go.

Afterthought

The less a poet says about his poems, perhaps the better, but I hazard an afterthought. Upon finishing this book, a reader may feel that a few poems are, in both feeling and style, off the main impulse—accidents, sports, irrelevances; but they are not accidents or sports, and I hope not, in the last analysis, irrelevances.

Rather early, as the book began to take shape in my mind and in some poems, I began to feel that I needed a preliminary poem and another as a sort of coda, both very simple in method and feeling, to serve as a base for the book, or better, as a bracket to enclose the dimly envisaged tangles and complications of the main body. So "October Picnic Long Ago" and "Passers-by on Snowy Night" were composed well before the book had begun to assume anything like its final content and structure.

I may also mention "Empty White Blotch on Map of Universe: a Possible View" and "Ballad of Your Puzzlement," both of which are rather like sore thumbs, at least at first glance. It might be said that both, if taken in isolation, may well be seen not only as peculiar in style, but as having meanings quite contradictory to the tone and intent of the work as a whole. Here, however, it should be remembered that the first, as the title indicates, is only "a Possible View"—a parodic and disintegrating account of the history of man's striving for spiritual values and a sense of community, with only a defeated and pathetic romantic sexual yearning left in the end. This is intended to serve as an introduction to a section chiefly concerned with the issues ironically raised in the poem. It is concerned to serve as a kind of backboard against which the poems of the section are bounced. As for "The Ballad of Your Puzzlement," it has a parenthetic subtitle which is supposed to indicate that this poem, like the other just discussed, may also serve ironically as a backboard for the concluding section. This section is, of course, concerned with the reviewing of life from the standpoint of age. But this is not the place for an attempt at explication. Nor is this the proper author for such explication.

There is one more thing I may mention. The order of the poems is not the order of composition (and certain poems composed during the general period are not included). The order and selection are determined thematically, but with echoes, repetitions, and variations in feeling and tonality. Here, as in life, meaning is, I should say, often more fruitfully found in the question asked than in any answer given. The thematic order—or better, structure—is played against, or with, a shadowy narrative, a shadowy autobiography, if you will. But this is an autobiography which represents a fusion of fiction and fact in varying degrees and perspectives. As with question and answer, fiction may often be more deeply significant than fact. Indeed, it may be said that our lives are our own supreme fiction.

Rumor Verified

Poems 1979–1980

To Peter and Ebie Blume

. . . i' vidi de le cose belle
Che porta il ciel, per un pertugio tondo,
E quindi uscimmo a riveder le stelle.

Dante: Inferno *canto* XXXIV

I. Prologue

Mediterranean Basin

I. Chthonian Revelation: A Myth

Long before sun had toward the mountain dipped,
There downward at crag-fall, bare-footed, bare-hided but for
Beach-decency's minimum, they
Painfully picked past lava, past pumice, past boulders
High-hung and precarious over the sea-edge, awaiting
Last gust or earth-tremor. Below,
Lay the sand-patch, white
As the lace-fringe that, languid and lazy,
Teased from the edge of the sun-singing sea.

Few know what is there:
Sea and sand finger back into cave-shade where
Gothic, great strata,
Once torn in the shudder of earth and earth-agony, had
Down-reached to find footing in depth. Now deep
In arched dusk from the secret strand, the eye
Stares from that mystic and chthonian privacy
To far waters whose tirelessly eye-slashing blue
Commands the wide world beyond that secret purlieu.

After sun, how dark! Or after sun-scimitar, how
Gentle the touch of the shade's hypothetical hand. Farther on,
Farther in!—and on the soft sand he is sure
Of the track. Then looks back
Just once through the dwindling aperture
To the world of light-tangled detail
Where once life was led that now seems illusion of life
And swings in the distance with no more identity than
A dream half-remembered. He turns. His face lifts
To the soaring and scarcely definable nave,
From which darkness downward and endlessly sifts.

Eyes lower: and there,
In that drizzle of earth's inner darkness, she
Stands, face upward, arms up as in prayer or
Communion with whispers that wordlessly breathe—
There in columnar gracility stands, breasts,
In that posture, high. Eyes closed. And in
Such world of shadows, she,
From the light of her own inner being, glows.

*

Slowly, the lifted arms descend, fingers out,
Slightly parted. His eyes find the light of her eyes,
And over immeasurable distance,
Hands out, as though feeling his way in the act,
On the soundless sand he moves in his naked trance.
At last, fingertips make contact.

When in hermetic wisdom they wake, the cave-mouth is dim.
Once out, they find sun sinking under the mountain-rim,
And a last gleam boldly probes
High eastward the lone upper cloud. Scraps of nylon
Slip on like new skin, though cold, and feet
Find the rustle and kitten-tongue kiss of the foam creeping in.

A kilometer toward the headland, then home: they wade out,
And plunge. All wordless, this—
In a world where all words would be
Without meaning, and all they long to hear
Is the gull's high cry
Of mercilessly joyful veracity
To fill the hollow sky.

Side by side, stroke by stroke, in a fading light they move.
The sea pours over each stroke's frail groove.
Blackly, the headland looms. The first star is declared.
It is white above the mountain mass.
Eyes starward fixed, they feel the sea's long swell
And the darkling drag of the nameless depth below.
They turn the headland, with starlight the only light they now know.

At arch-height of every stroke, at each fingertip, hangs
One drop, and the drops—one by one—are
About to fall, each a perfect universe defined
By its single, minuscule, radiant, enshrinèd star.

II. Looking Northward, Aegeanward: Nestlings on Seacliff

Chalky, steel-hard, or glass-slick, the cliff
That you crawl up, inch up, or clamber, till now,
Arms outspread, you cling to rotting scrub roots, and at last
See what you'd risked neck to see, the nub
Of rock-shelf outthrust from the shaded recess where,
From huddle of trash, dried droppings, and eggshell, lifts
The unfeathered pitiless weakness of necks that scarcely uphold
The pink corolla of beak-gape, the blind yearning lifeward.

*

In sun-blast, around and above, weave
The outraged screams that would net your head,
And wings slash the air with gleaming mercilessness,
While for toehold, or handhold, downward you grope,
Or for purchase to pause on and turn to the sun-crinkled sea,
To watch it fade northward into the
Horizon's blue ambiguity. You think
How long ago galleys—slim, black, bronze-flashing—bore
Northward too, and toward that quarter's blue dazzle of distance.
Or of a tale told.

And then think how, lost in the dimness of aeons, sea sloshed
Like suds in a washing machine, land heaved, and sky
At noon darkened, and darkness, not like any metaphor, fell,
And in that black fog gulls screamed as the feathers of gull-wing
From white flash to flame burst. That was the hour
When rooftree or keystone of palaces fell, and
Priest's grip drew backward curls of the king's son until
Throat-softness was tightened, and the last cry
Was lost in the gargle of blood on bronze blade. The king,
In the mantle, had buried his face. But even
That last sacrifice availed naught. Ashes
Would bury all. Cities beneath sea sank.

In some stony, high field, somewhere, eyes,
Unbelieving, opened. They saw, first,
The sky. Stared long. How little
They understood. But, slowly, began,
In new ignorance, the agony of Time.

You think of the necks, unfeathered and feeble, upholding
The pink corolla of beak-gape—that blind yearning lifeward.

II. Paradox of Time

Blessèd Accident

Even if you are relatively young—say,
Nel mezzo del camin—and are not merely as

Blank of curiosity, and soul, as
A computer, you have, in fleeting moments of icy

Detachment, looking backward on
The jigsaw puzzle, wondered how you got where you now are,

And have tried to distinguish between logic
And accident. Are you, after storm, some fragment

Of wreckage stranded on a lost beach, though now perhaps in
The new, benign, but irrelevant, sunlight, in croon and whisper

Too late lulled, as wavelets gently, apologetically,
Approach and retreat on the sand?

Or, pack on back, bare knees scraped and bruised,
One hand somewhat bloody, are you now standing

On the savage crag to survey, at last,
The forest below, where the trail dies, and farther,

Lower, beyond that, the blue and glittering sinuosity
Of the river, where only yesterday you bathed? And beyond,

Fields brown where the plow had been set, houses
Shrinking to pin-point white dots in distance,

The slow bulge of earth purged blue
To join the heavenly blue, no certain

Horizon to be defined? Or what is the
Image that coagulates in your mind

As relevance? But one thing is sure, success,
Particularly of a vulgar order, tends

To breed complacency in the logic of
Your conduct of life. Congratulations! But,

In deepest predawn dark, have you
Grasped out and found the hand, clasped it, and lain

*

Hearing no sound but breath's rhythm near, and,
Gazing toward a ceiling you cannot see but know is there, felt

Slow tears swell, like bursting buds of April, in
Your eyes, your heart, and felt breath stop before

That possibility, doomful, of joy, and the awful illogic of
The tremor, the tremble, of God's palsied hand shaking

The dice-cup? Ah, blessèd accident!

Paradox of Time

I. Gravity of Stone and Ecstasy of Wind

Each day now more precious will dawn,
And loved faces turn dearer still,
And when sunlight is withdrawn,
There, over the mountain's black profile,

The western star reigns
In splendor, benign, arrogant,
And the fact that it disdains
You, and your tenement

Of flesh, should instruct you in
The paradox of Time,
And the doubleness wherein
The fleshly glory may gleam.

Sit on the floor with a child.
Hear laugh that creature so young.
See loom its life-arch, and wild
With rage, speak wild words sprung

From vision, and thus atone
For all folly now left behind.
Learn the gravity of stone.
Learn the ecstasy of wind.

II. Law of Attrition

Learn the law of attrition,
Learn that the mountain's crag-jut,
In that altitude of pride,
Knows the sledge and gnaw of seasons,
Each in its enmity.
Do you know how a particle,
Now rain-washed downward, and down,
Is seized by the stream that boils
And roils in tumultuous white
Of flung spray, down the chasm
To reach falls that, airward, leap,
Then plunge, in incessant thunder,
To the swirl of blind mist below?
Do you know how in the heart
Of the river's majestic, slow
Flow riding, it does not know
Desire or destination?
In the broad estuary
Which, rapt and somnambulistic
Under the glitter of sun,
Moves musing seaward, it
Is borne: to enter unto
The dark inwardness of sea-wisdom
Far from the breakers' roar
And anger hurled against
Whatsoever headland or rock-shore,
And below, below, how far
From the surface agitation
Perceived by sun or star,
It moves in sea-wisdom's will.
Or hangs still, if that is the will.

As aeons pass, in a time
Unpredictable, it may be,
In turn and churn of the globe,
A single, self-possessed grain
Of sand on an unmapped strand,
White but backed by shadow
And depth of rain-jungle, and
The utterance of the victim
When, in nocturnal prowl-time,
It feels the fang at the throat.

Day dawns, and then the sand-grain
Exposes the glaze of a tiny
And time-polished facet that now
Will return from its minimal mirror
The joy of one ray from above,

But no more joy for this than
When tropic constellations,
Wheeling in brilliant darkness,
Strike one ray at that same facet
That, across howling light-years,
Makes what answer it can—
With the same indifferent joy.

For safe, safe in this asylum
Of self that is non-self, it lies
On a beach where no foot may come.

III. One I Knew

At the time of sinew dry
And crank, you may try
To think of a snow-peak glimpsed
Through a sudden aperture
In clouds, and one last sun-shaft
Flung to incarnadine
In glory that far, white
Arrogance before
Clouds close.

Or try,
As you stare at an evening sky,
To put your mind on those
Who once stood
Erect and prophetic in
Age's long irony.
Try to name their names, or try
To think of the nameless ones
You never knew.

I knew
One once, old, old, alone
In his unselfed, iron will,
Who once had said: "To deny
The self is all." So
He sat alone in that spot
Of refuge for life's discards,
His only joy a book or
Thought of the living and dead
He loved. No—one companion
He had, closer than hands,
Or feet: the cancer of which
Only he knew.
It was his precious secret.

*

It was as though he leaned
At a large mysterious bud
To watch, hour by hour,
How at last it would divulge
A beauty so long withheld—
As I once had sat
In a room lighted only by
Two candlesticks, and
Two flames, motionless, rose
In the summer night's breathlessness.
Three friends and I, we sat
With no conversation, watching
The bud of a century plant
That was straining against the weight
Of years, slow, slow, in silence,
To offer its inwardness.
The whiskey burned in our throats.

So the man I knew, in daily
Courtesy, lived until
The day, when, at his desk
In his cramped sitting room, he
Collapsed and, unconscious, slid
To the floor, pen yet in hand.
They revived him only for
The agony of the end.

At last, the injection.

I saw the end. Later,
I found the letter, the first
Paragraph unfinished. I saw
The ink-slash from that point
Where the unconscious hand had dragged
The pen as he fell. I saw
The salutation. It was:
"Dear Son."

The shimmering
White petal—the golden stamen—
Were at last, in triumph,
Divulged. On the dusty carpet.

Small Eternity

The time comes when you count the names—whether
Dim or flaming in the head's dark, or whether
In stone cut, time-crumbling or moss-glutted.
You count the names to reconstruct yourself.

*

But a face remembered may blur, even as you stare
At a headstone. Or sometimes a face, as though from air,
Will stare at you with a boyish smile—which, not
Stone-moored, blows away like dandelion fuzz.

It is very disturbing. It is as though you were
The idiot boy who ventures out on pond-ice
Too thin, and hears here—hears there—the creak
And crackling spread. That is the sound Reality

Makes as it gives beneath your metaphysical
Poundage. Memory dies. Or lies. Time
Is a wind that never shifts airt. Pray only
That, in the midst of selfishness, some

Small act of careless kindness, half-unconscious, some
Unwitting smile or brush of lips, may glow
In some other mind's dark that's lost your name, but stumbles
Upon that momentary Eternity.

Basic Syllogism

Down through the latticework of leaves,
Dark in shade, golden in sunlight,
Through an eyelid half sleeping, the eye receives
News that the afternoon blazes bright.

It blazes in traumatic splendor—
A world ablaze but not consumed,
As though combustion had no end, or
Beginning, and from its ash resumed

The crackling rush of youthful flare.
Far off, a river, serpentine
In flame, threads fields of grass-green glare,
And farther, mountain cliffs incline

To catch the lethal intimation
Of sunset's utterance for climax.
I lie, and think how soon the sun
Its basic syllogism enacts.

I lie, and think how flesh and bone,
And even the soul, in its own turn,
Like faggots bound, on what hearthstone,
In their combustion, flameless, burn.

Sitting on Farm Lawn on Sunday Afternoon

The old, the young—they sit.
And the baby on its blanket

Blows a crystalline
Bubble to float, then burst

Into air's nothingness.
Under the maples they sit,

As the limpid year uncoils
With a motion like motionlessness,

While only a few maple leaves
Are crisping toward yellow

And not too much rust yet
Streaks the far blades of corn.

The big white bulldog dozes
In a patch of private shade.

The afternoon muses onward,
Past work, past week, past season,

Past all the years gone by,
And delicate feminine fingers,

Deft and ivory-white,
And fingers steely, or knobbed

In the gnarl of arthritis, conspire
To untangle the snarl of years

Which are their past, and the past
Of kin who in dark now hide,

Yet sometimes seem to stare forth
With critical, loving gaze,

Or deeper in darkness weep
At wisdom they learned too late.

Is all wisdom learned too late?
The baby lalls to itself,

For it does not yet know all
The tales and contortions of Time.

Nor do I, who sit here alone,
In another place, and hour.

III. Events

Going West

Westward the Great Plains are lifting, as you
Can tell from the slight additional pressure
The accelerator requires. The sun,
Man to man, stares you straight in the eye, and the
Ribbon of road, white, into the sun's eye
Unspools. Wheat stubble behind,
Now nothing but range land. But,
With tire song lulling like love, gaze riding white ribbon, forward
You plunge. Blur of burnt goldness
Past eye-edge on each
Side back-whirling, you arrow
Into the heart of hypnosis.

This is one way to write the history of America.

It was that way that day—oh, long
Ago. I had to slap
The back of my neck to stay awake,
Eyes westward in challenge to sun-gaze, lids
Slitted for sight. The land,
Beyond miles of distance, fled
Backward to whatever had been,
As though Space were Time.

Now do I see the first blue shadow of foothills?
Or is that a cloud line?
When will snow, like a vision, lift?

I do not see, sudden out of
A scrub clump, the wing-burst. See only
The bloody explosion, right in my face,
On the windshield, the sun and
The whole land forward, forever,
All washed in blood, in feathers, in gut-scrawl.

It is, of course, a fool pheasant.

Hands clamping the wheel with a death grip
To hold straight while brakes scream, I,
With no breath, at the blood stare. The ditch
Is shallow enough when the car, in the end, rolls in.

*

Clumps of old grass, old newspaper, dry dirt—
All this got the worst off. Slowly,
Red sunset now reddening to blood streaks,
Westward the car moved on. Blood
Fried on the glass yet stove-hot. For the day—
It had been a scorcher. Later,
Handfuls of dry dirt would scrape off the fried blood.
Eventually, water at a gas station.

Even now, long afterward, the dream.

I have seen blood explode, blotting out sun, blotting
Out land, white ribbon of road, the imagined
Vision of snowcaps.

Nameless Thing

I have no name for the nameless thing
That after midnight walks the house, usually
Soundless, but sometimes a creak on tiptoed stair,
Or sometimes like breath screwed down to a minimum.

But sometimes in silence the effluvium
Of its being is enough, perhaps with a pale,
Not quite sickening sweetness as though left
By funeral flowers, or sometimes like sweat

Under gross armpits. It is the odor of
A real existence lost in the unreality
Of dead objects of day that now painfully try to stir
In darkness. Every stone has its life, we know.

Barefoot, in darkness, I walk the house, a heavy
Poker seized from the hearth. I stand
Just by the door that seems ready to open.
I wait for the first minute motion, first whisper of hinges.

I hold my breath. I am ready. I think of blood.
I fling the door open. Only a square
Of moonlight lies on the floor inside. All is in order.
I go back to bed. I hear the blessèd heart beat there.

But once, on a very dark night, it was almost different.
That night I was certain. Trapped in a bathroom!
I snatched the door open, weapon up, and yes, by God!—
But there I stood staring into a mirror. Recognition

*

Came almost too late. But how could I
Have been expected to recognize what I am?
In any case, that was what happened. I now lie
Rigid abed and hear namelessness stalk the dark house.

I wonder why it cannot rest.

Rumor Verified

Since the rumor has been verified, you can, at least,
Disappear. You will no longer be seen at the Opera,
With your head bowed studiously, to one side a little,
Nor at your unadvertised and very exclusive
Restaurant, discussing wine with the sommelier,
Nor at your club, setting modestly forth your subtle opinion.

Since the rumor has been verified, you can try, as in dream,
To have lived another life—not with the father
Of rigid self-discipline, and x-ray glance,
Not with the mother, overindulgent and pretty,
Who toyed with your golden locks, slipped money on the side,
And waved a witch's wand for success, and a rich marriage.

Since the rumor has been verified, you may secretly sneak
Into El Salvador, or some such anguished spot,
Of which you speak the language, dreaming, trying to believe
That, orphaned, you grew up in poverty and vision, struggling
For learning, for mankind's sake. Here you pray with the sick, kiss lepers.

Since the rumor has been verified, you yearn to hold
A cup of cold water for the dying man to sip.
You yearn to look deep into his eyes and learn wisdom.
Or perhaps you have a practical streak and seek
Strange and derelict friends, and for justification lead
A ragtag squad to ambush the uniformed patrol.

Well, assuming the rumor verified—that may be
The only logical course: at any price,
Even bloodshed, however ruthless, to change any dominant order
And the secret corruption of power that makes us what we seem.
Yes, what is such verification against a strength of will?

But even in face of the rumor, you sometimes shudder,
Seeing men as old as you who survive the terror
Of knowledge. You watch them slyly. What is their trick?
Do they wear a Halloween face? But what can you do?
Perhaps pray to God for strength to face the verification
That you are simply a man, with a man's dead reckoning, nothing more.

Sunset Scrupulously Observed

A flycatcher, small, species not identified, is perched,
Unmoving but for tiny turn and scanning
Twist of head, on the topmost twig, dead,
Of the tall, scant-leafed, and dying poplar. It
Is a black point against the cloud-curdled drama
Of sunset over dark heave
Of the mountain.

The brook, in melodious meditation, unseen,
Moves in its little gorge now brimming
With shadow. The meditation will
Continue nightlong.

The sun itself now gone, rays angle upward
From beyond the mountain. They probe,
Authoritatively, the high clouds.

A jet, military no doubt, appears high, eastward.
It creeps across the sky, ten minutes by my watch,
Uncoiling a white trail, unmoved in unmoving air.
Against paling, skim-milk blue of high sky
That is above cloud-curdle, the jet moves. The trail
Is like a decisive chalk mark that disappears
In penetrating a drift of cloud that is
Heavy, black-bellied, black on edge
Eastward, but westward with
Ragged margin inflamed by the flush of
One high-angled ray. The flush fades slowly
To gold as the jet and white trail emerge
Into that ray, and the previously
Invisible fuselage bursts
On vision, like polished silver. It proceeds
Into the dark cloud now crouching on the horizon, waiting—
Just north of the last struggle of glory.

Nearer, much nearer, five swifts, blunt-bodied like
Five tiny attack planes, zip by in formation,
Wings back-curved and pointed, twitching
In short, neurotic strokes at high speed. Their twitter
Is a needle-sharp, metallic sound.

The first bird, once silhouetted on the dying poplar's top twig,
Is gone. He is gone to fulfill his unseeable and lethal
Obligation, alone.

The evening slowly, soundlessly, closes. Like
An eyelid.

Minneapolis Story

To John Knox Jessup

Whatever pops into your head, and whitely
Breaks surface on the dark stream that is you,

May do to make a poem—for every accident
Yearns to be more than itself, yearns,

In the way you dumbly do, to participate
In the world's blind, groping rage toward meaning, and once,

Long years ago, in Minneapolis,
Dark falling, snow falling to celebrate

The manger-birth of a babe in a snowless latitude,
Church bells vying with whack of snow-chains on

Fenders, there I, down a side street,
Head thrust into snow-swirl, strove toward Hennepin.

There lights and happiness most probably were—
But I was not thinking of happiness, only of

High-quality high-proof and the gabble in which
You try to forget that something inside you dies.

Then—hell!—it's one knee down, half-sprawled, one hand on a hump,
The hump human. Unconscious, but,

With snow scraped off, breath yet, and the putrid stink of
Non-high-quality, and vomit. So run, stumbling,

Toward Hennepin, shouting, "Police!"
"Oh, Christ," the ambulance driver says, "another one!"

"Gonna live?" I ask."Not if he's lucky," the paramedic
Says. Slams door. Tires skid. That's all.

So half a continent, and years, away, and a different
Season too, I sit and watch

The first gold maple leaf descend athwart
My evergreens, and ponder

The mystery of Time and happiness and death.
My friend is just dead. And I wonder why

That old white bubble now arises, bursts
On my dark and secret stream. And why, again waiting alone, I see

*

The nameless, outraged, upturned face, where, blessèd
In shadow, domed architecture of snow, with scrupulous care,

Is minutely erected on each closed eye.
I had wiped them clear, just a moment before.

Mountain Mystery

On the mountain trail, all afternoon,
Gravel, uncertain, grinds under hoof.
On left side, with scrub growth, the cliff hangs.
On right, hypnotic emptiness.

Far down, in distance, a stream uncoils,
Like nothing more than a glittering wire
Tangled in stone-slots, lost on the plain,
In distance dissolved, or down canyon, gone.

You stop. You turn and know what already
You know: snow commanding west ranges, sun
Yet high. Again, eastward turn, and the sun's
Hot hand, fingers spread, is pressed against your shoulders.

Soaring in sunlight, eastward, the eagle
Swings to a height invisible
Except when light catches a bright flash of wing.
You open your lips in infinite thirst for

The altitude's wine. All, all of the past
Is gone. Yet what is the past but delusion?
Or future? In timeless light the world swims.
Alone, alone, you move through the timeless

Light. Toward what? The ranch in the valley,
Some ten miles away—what but delusion?
Alone, but not alone, for if
You lift your eyes, you see, some forty

Feet off, her there—unless, of course,
The track now rounds an abutment, and she
Has ceased to exist, and you are alone
In the world's metaphysical beauty of light.

Only alone do you then think of love.
Eyes shut, you think how, in saddle, that narrow
Waist sways. You think how, when soon the trail straightens,
She will lean back to smile. Her eyes will be bright.

*

You pass the abutment. Beyond, the great mesa
Sinks blue. The world falls away, falls forever.
But she sways in the saddle, turns, smiles, and your heart
Leaps up. Then cries out: *Oh, what is enough?*

That night you will lie in your bed, not alone—
But alone. In dark paradox, you lie
And think of the screaming gleam of the world
In which you have passed alone, lost—

And in dark, lost, lain, hearing frailty of breath beside.

Convergences

By saplings I jerked and swung
Or by vine-twists and rock-snags clung,

Letting myself swing and slide
Down the mountain's near-vertical side

To the *V*-deep gorge below,
Where I caught water's glint and flow,

While last spit on the tongue dried,
And the empty canteen at my side

Clinked dry as Hell at high noon
When rain's not predicted soon,

And the literal sun that hung
At zenith guaranteed the lung

Only air like a blast-furnace blast.
Well, I got down there at last.

Belly-down, I drowned my face
Beneath that clear element's grace

And let arms relax and go
To waver like weeds in the flow,

Till I had to come up for air.
Across the riffle and glint there,

Just as I came to raise
My mouth for sweet breath, that gaze,

Wolfish and slit-eyed, fixed on me.
My blood stiffened up like jelly.

*

There across lips, gray and dry,
A gray tongue-tip warily

Slid back and forth. Slow to heal,
Yellow as piss or orange peel,

From eye-edge to mouth-edge, the slash in
Flesh defined a man born not to win,

But he plunged across the stream—
In that instant less real than a dream

Till he said: "What you got in that sack?"
I'm yet down, he kicked my knapsack.

"Git it off and give it here quick!
You damned little Boy Scout prick—

"Or whatever you are." "But I'm not,"
I yelled, "any durn Boy Scout!"

"Well, prick," he said, and the knife,
At his touch, sprang to sun-flaming life.

My sandwich he ate, but spat
Out the milk. Said: "Christ!" And with that

Had busted my thermos, on stone.
Again spat. Then rose. Was gone.

He splashed back across the stream.
Yes—all had seemed a dream.

I didn't get up, just lay
Staring up at the heart-height of day,

Thinking: "Had me a .38,
And I'd plugged him while he ate."

A buzzard, high, cruised the sky,
I heard a far joree cry.

Then I plunged across as he'd done,
Clambered brush to the ballast-stone

Of the hidden railroad track.
Now I saw him a half-mile back,

A dot in the distance of sun
Where two gleaming rails became one

*

To impale him in the black throat
Of a tunnel that sucked all to naught.

I turned my own way to go
Down a track that I did not yet know

Was the track I was doomed to go
In my biologic flow—

Down the tunnel of year, day, hour,
Where the arch sags lower and lower,

Sometimes darker by day than by night,
Where right may be wrong or wrong right,

Where the wick sparely feeds the flame,
And Hope does not know its own name,

Where sometimes you find that at length
You're betrayed less by weakness than strength,

And though silence, like wax, fills the ear,
Sometimes you think you can hear

The mathematical drip
Of moisture, or shale above slip,

Or rock grind. And your heart gives a cry
For height, for some snow-peak high,

And lighted by one great star.
Then in dark you ask who you are.

You ask that, but yet undefined,
See, in the dark of your mind,

As you once saw, long years back,
The converging gleams of the track

That speared that small dot yonder
So that it was sucked under

The mountain—into that black hollow
Which led where you cannot know.

IV. A Point North

Vermont Thaw

A soft wind southwesterly, something like
The wind in the Far West they call the *chinook,*
About three o'clock, we yet high on the mountain,
Began. Snow softened to burden our snowshoes.

If then you stood perfectly still, so still
You could hear your own heart, each stroke by stroke,
You could hear the forest of spruces—*drip,*
Drip, drip—and you felt that all you had lived was

That sound hung in motionless silence. You held
Your breath to be sure you could hear your own heart
Maintain, with no falter, the rhythm that drops
Now defined. Were you sure you remembered your name?

But there was the *A*-frame, the camp, snow sliding
Down the steep roof-pitch with channels of black
Where all winter your eye had loved whiteness, and now.
Roof-edges dripped in a rhythm that redefined

Life as blankness. In dingy pink pillows of mist,
Sun sank, and you felt it gasping for breath.
You felt it might suffocate, not rise
Again. Inside the *A*-frame you found

Yourself sweating, though only one eye of a coal
Yet winked. You built it up only enough
To cook by, racked up the snowshoes—all this
With no word. What word is to say when the world

Has lost heart, is dripping, is flowing, is counting
Its pulse away? Cooking is but
An irritation. The predinner whiskey
Is tongue-hot but tangless, like rotgut—not what

It is. When you turn on the hi-fi, your friend
Says: "None of that ordure tonight." In silence
You eat—silence except for the eaves-drip.
No need to bank fire on a night like this.

You wake in the dark to the rhythm off eaves.
Can you comfort yourself by thinking of spring?
Of summer's fecundity and body's plunge
Into silvery splash-spray? Of gold and flame

*

In benediction of autumn? Of snow's first
Night-whisper, dawn reddening peak-thrust? No—eaves,
To your heart, say now only one thing. Say: *drip.*
You must try to think of some other answer, by dawn.

Cycle

Perhaps I have had enough of summer's
Swelling complacency, and the endless complex
And self-indulgent daubs and washes of the palette of green.
If only one birch, maple, or high poplar leaf would stir

Even in its sun-glittering green!—but this air
Is paralyzed, and the fat porcupine stops, does not even waddle
Across the lost clearing, where only a chimney now crumbles,
To the log backhouse that by his tooth, long back, is well scored.

He, in characteristic passionlessness, now stands, and
Spine-tips gleam white in sunlight. He waits,
In self-sufficient, armed idleness, memento
Of another age. Birds, in virid heat of shade,

At this hour, motionless, gasp. The beak
Droops open, silent. The sun
Is pasted to the sky, cut crude as a child's collage.
Birds have no instruction in

Cycles of nature, or astronomy. They do not know
That a time for song will, again, come, or time to zigzag
After insects at sunset. They know only the gasping present,
Like an empire unwittingly headed for the dump-heap

Of history. Green hides rock-slide, cliff, ledge. On the mountain,
On one ledge visible, with glasses I see propped, leaning
Back like a fat banker in his club window,
A bear, scratching his belly, in infinite ease, sun or not.

I hear the faint ripple of water
By stones, of which the tops are hot as stove-lids.
I want to lie in water, black, deep, under a bank of shade,
Like a trout. I want to breathe through gills.

But I know that snow, like history, will come. I know that ice-crust
On it will creak and crackle to snowshoes, and that
Breath will be white in air, under sky bluer than
God's Nordic eye. My hearth-wood will be stacked in an admirable row.

In the dark I will wake, on the hearth see last coals glow.

Summer Rain in Mountains

A dark curtain of rain sweeps slowly over the sunlit mountain.
It moves with steady dignity, like the curtain over the
Great window of a stately drawing room, or across a proscenium.

The edge of the drawn curtain of rain is decisive
Like a knife-edge. Soon it will slice the reddening sun across with delicate
Precision. On the yet sunlit half of the mountain miles of massed trees,

Glittering in green as they forever climb toward gray ledges,
Renounce their ambition, they shudder and twist, and
The undersides of leaves are grayly exposed to crave mercy.

The sun disappears. Chairs are withdrawn from the sun-deck.
A whisper is moving through the wide air. The whole event
Is reminding you of something. Your breathing becomes irregular, and

Your pulse flutters. Conversation dies. In silence, you peccantly
Spy on faces that were once familiar. They seem
To huddle together. One has a false face. What,

In God's name, are you trying to remember? Is it
Grief, loss of love long back, loss of confidence in your mission? Or
A guilt you can't face? Or a nameless apprehension

That, doglike, at night, in darkness, may lie at the foot of your bed,
Its tail now and then thumping the floor, with a sound that
Wakes you up? Your palms may then sweat. The wild

Thought seizes you that this may be a code. It may be a secret warning.
A friend is addressing you now. You miss the words. You
Apologize, smile. The rain hammers the roof,

Quite normally. The little group is quite normal too, some
With highballs in hand. One laughs. He is a philosopher.
You know that fact because a philosopher can laugh at

Anything. Suddenly, rain stops. The sun
Emerges like God's calm blessedness that spills
On the refurbished glitter of mountain. Chairs

Are taken again out to the sun-deck.
Conversation becomes unusually animated as all await the glory
Of sunset. You pull yourself together. A drink helps.

After all, it's the sort of thing that may happen to anybody.
And does.

Vermont Ballad: Change of Season

All day the fitful rain
Had wrought new traceries,
New quirks, new love-knots, down the pane.

And what do I see beyond
That fluctuating gray
But a world that seems to be God-abandoned—

Last leaf, rain-soaked, from my high
Birch falling, the spruce wrapped in thought,
And the mountain dissolving rain-gray to gray sky.

In the gorge, like a maniac
In sleep, the stream grinds its teeth,
As I lay a new log at the fireplace back.

It is not that I am cold:
But that I think how the flux,
Three quarters now of a century old,

Has faithfully swollen and ebbed,
In life's brilliantly flashing red
Through all flesh, in vein and artery webbed.

But now it feels viscous and gray
As I watch the gray of the world,
And that thought seems soaked in my brain to stay.

But who is master here?
The turn of the season, or I?
What lies in the turn of the season to fear?

If I set muzzle to forehead
And pull the trigger, I'll see
The world in a last flood of vital red—

Not gray—that cataracts down.
No, I go to the windowpane
That rain's blurring tracery claims as its own,

And stare up the mountain track
Till I see in the rain-dusk, trudging
With stolid stride, his bundle on back,

A man with no name, in the gloom,
On an errand I cannot guess.
No sportsman—no! Just a man in his doom.

In this section such a man is not an uncommon sight.
In rain or snow, you pass, and he says: "Kinda rough tonight."

V. If This Is the Way it Is

Questions You Must Learn to Live Past

Have you ever clung to the cliffside while,
Past star-death at midnight and clouds, the darkness

Curdles and coils, and wind off the sea, caterwauling, swings in
To bulge your shirt belt-free, while claws

Scratch at eyeballs, and snag at loosening stone—
In Hell's own conspiracy with

The five-fathom, lethal, up-lunges of sea-foam fanged white,
That howls in its hunger for blood?

Have you stood by a bed whereon
Your father, unspeakable anguish past, at length

To the syringe succumbs, and your sister's
Nails clench in your biceps? Then, crazed, she cries:

"But it's worse—oh, it's driving pain deeper,
Deeper to hide from praying, or dying, or God—

"Oh, worse!" Or have you remembered the face
Of an old, loved friend, now drowned and glimmering under

Time's windless wash? Then cannot summon the name?
Have you dreamed that you are a child again

And calling in darkness, but nobody comes?
Have you ever seen your own child, that first morning, wait

For the school bus? Have you stood in your garden in autumn,
At some last chore, and in the junipers found

Where a three-foot snake—a big garter, no doubt—
Has combed its old integument off in the convenient prickles?

Would you hold that frayed translucence up,
Beautiful, meaningless, blessed in the mellow light,

And feel your heart stop? And not know why?
Or think that this bright emptiness

Is all your own life may be—or will be—when,
After the fable of summer, a lithe sinuosity

Slips down to curl in some dark, wintry hole, with no dream?

After Restless Night

In darkness we cannot see
How, all night long, slow ages shift and crumble
Into the noble indifference of Eternity,
But all night do see how the dream, anguished or funny, strives
To decode the clutter of our lives.

So, shifting and crumbling too,
We let ourselves flow from ourselves into
The vast programming of the firmament
Or of our secret channeling of blood. But do
We even know the meaning of

A single comet's mathematical prowl?

Nor can we in the silence of night hear
How aeons are de-leafing, year by year,
To build the rotting mulch of History.
So now in the trough of Time, as of earth or water, we
Lie—no wind, no wave,
To stir us in that nocturnal grave,

And consciousness loses faith in itself.

Finally, comes first dawn-streak, sallow
Or slow glow from one small cinder of red
Beyond black trees. If you rise to allow
Nature her due, you may lift a curtain by the bed
To reassure yourself that the world indeed
Exists. Then back to bed,
Where warmth of pillow yet summons your head,
And consciousness for deeper concealment gnaws
Into the fat dark of your skull.
Traffic, far off, begins to whisper, like rumor of Truth.
It is a rumor of which the world is often full.

It is a rumor we might as well take at face value.

You shut your eyes and try
To believe in that possibility.
Meanwhile,
Great plains of grass stretch far
Away, like the pampas in Argentina. In steel-bright air
High snow shines moonlit, and a star
Is blue, not near setting. Somewhere,
Seals bark on a dawn-rock. A foot
Is set soundless to earth in a forest in Asia. Your mother
And father, though in their privileged privacy, turn not
One to the other.

*

They lie sunk in their cogitation.
Perhaps all they have is their future, the past being gone.
I advise no distraction to their frozen agon.
Perhaps each, in prayer for you, is locked alone.

Meanwhile the alarm clock goes off.
It has something to say.
It tells you what you are and what you will be all day.

Meanwhile shut eyes and think of a face you truly love,
Or at least think of something you must do as soon as you can move.

No use falling back. It is now impossible,
No matter how hard you try, to think of truly nothing.

What Was the Thought

The thought creeps along the baseboard of the dark mind.
Through one failed juncture of curtains, the winter moon, full, strikes.
A white line, blade-sharp, streaks the floor,
But sheds no light. You do not see what creeps. What!—
Did it briefly scurry then? Or was that the wind
Momentarily gusting through bare boughs of the season? You think
Of the little heart, more delicate, more
Intricate, than a Swiss watch, beating
Somewhere down in the dark. You cannot, of course,
Hear it. So you listen to your own heart.
It is more gross in the darkness. What
Is it afraid of? It is warm
In its own bed, in its loving flesh. Flesh
Fondles the heart. The heart does not need to creep
Along a baseboard, hungry in the middle
Of the night, in a strange house. You feel
Your heart settle to the old guaranteed rhythm.
You know that constellations also are
Steady about their allotted business. Your children
Are healthy. They do well at school. Your
Wife is faithful. Resolutely,
You try not to wonder
What she thinks about. Suddenly,
You feel like weeping. But
You go to sleep.

Only after first dawn do you wake to the soft bounce
On the bed, and the special throaty mew
Of announcement. Yes, you know
What that means. It is triumph. You
Turn on the light. The pussycat
Crouches at your knees, proud, expecting

Praise. There, blood streaking the counterpane, it lies—
Skull crushed, partly eviscerated.

Dead Horse in Field

In the last, far field, half-buried
In barberry bushes red-fruited, the thoroughbred
Lies dead, left foreleg shattered below knee,
A 30.06 in heart. In distance,
I now see gorged crows rise ragged in wind. The day
After death I had gone for farewell, and the eyes
Were already gone—that
The beneficent work of crows. Eyes gone,
The two-year-old could, of course, more readily see
Down the track of pure and eternal darkness.

A week later I couldn't get close. The sweet stink
Had begun. That damned wagon mudhole
Hidden by leaves as we galloped—I found it.
Spat on it. As a child would. Next day
The buzzards. How beautiful in air!—carving
The slow, concentric, downward pattern of vortex, wing-glint
On wing-glint. From the house,
Now with glasses, I see
The squabble and pushing, the waggle of wattle-red heads.

At evening I watch the buzzards, the crows,
Arise. They swing black in nature's flow and perfection,
High in sad carmine of sunset. Forgiveness
Is not indicated. It is superfluous. They are
What they are.

How long before I go back to see
That intricate piece of
Modern sculpture, white now
By weather and sun, intricate, now
Assuming in stasis
New beauty! Then,
A year later, I'll see
The green twine of vine, each leaf
Heart-shaped, soft as velvet, beginning
Its benediction.

It thinks it is God.

Can you think of some ground on which that may be gainsaid?

Immanence

Stop! Wait! Wherever you are.
Whatever your name. It may well be

At the corner of one of the Fifties and Fifth Avenue,
Where the City of Things gleams brightest, and

Your name does not matter. If you have your credit card.
But sometimes its referent is obscure to you, and then even

The card is no help. Except, of course, for the purchase. Or
The event, in fact, may well be elsewhere, at night,

In bed, and you lost and unsure what
Bed, or breath there beside, and a crusting on

Dong. Like an orchid, now darkness
Swells, benign, benign—or inimical—

In immanence. Yes, something
Plays cat-and-mouse with you, veiled, unrevealed, though you

Sometimes relax, pretend not to notice, thinking
You'll be the cat, and catch

It unawares. Unwary. Trapped
In your stratagem. For if

Its face is seen, name known, it,
Then powerless, like mist, may be shifted by

Whatever slight movement of air, and in anguish
Flee, with a scream of such

Desolation that a heart as horn-scabbed as yours would be stabbed
To pity. But no. You must ponder yet the teasing enigma. But

Suppose you never succeed? Or worse,
The swollen Immanence turns out to be all? Is all? And you,

Yet yearning, torn between fear
And hope, yet ignorant, will, into

The black conduit of Nature's Repackaging System, be sucked.
But that possibility is simply too distressing

To–even–be considered.

The Corner of the Eye

The poem is just beyond the corner of the eye.
You cannot see it—not yet—but sense the faint gleam,

Or stir. It may be like a poor little shivering fieldmouse,
One tiny paw lifted from snow while, far off, the owl

Utters. Or like breakers, far off, almost as soundless as dream.
Or the rhythmic rasp of your father's last breath, harsh

As the grind of a great file the blacksmith sets to hoof.
Or the whispering slither the torn morning newspaper makes,

Blown down an empty slum street in New York, at midnight,
Past dog shit and garbage cans, while the full moon,

Phthisic and wan, above the East River, presides
Over that last fragment of history which is

Our lives. Or the foggy glint of old eyes of
The sleepless patient who no longer wonders

If he will once more see in that window the dun-
Bleached dawn that promises what. Or the street corner

Where always, for years, in passing you felt, unexplained, a pang
Of despair, like nausea, till one night, late, late on that spot

You were struck stock-still, and again felt
How her head had thrust to your shoulder, she clinging, while you,

Mechanically patting the fur coat, heard sobs, and stared up
Where tall buildings, frailer than reed-stalks, reeled among stars.

Yes, something there at eye-edge lurks, hears ball creak in socket,
Knows, before you do, tension of muscle, change

Of blood pressure, heart-heave of sadness, foot's falter, for
It has stalked you all day, or years, breath rarely heard, fangs dripping.

And now, any moment, great hindquarters may hunch, ready—
Or is it merely a poem, after all?

If

If this is the way it is, we must live through it.
Even though the spiked harrow of nightmare until dawn
Rips the humus of experience, and suggests
Your own exit therefrom. Even if you know bliss—
And bliss can seem more absolute than a clock's
Last tick in a dark-shrouded room. Yet

If this is the way it is, let us clamber
Crag-upward from the white-slashed beach and stare
Over the tangled tumult until the soul is absorbed
Into the blue perfection of unnamable distance.
The horizon is our only dream of perfection.

If this is the way it is—and I have stood
Alone, alone, past midnight long, heart empty, in
The dark and unpopulated
Piazza Navona—and I thought: what is the use
Of remembering any dream from childhood? Particularly,
Since any particular moment would be the future all dreams
Had led to. I shut eyes now, but still see
The discarded newspaper, across the Piazza,
In a foreign language, blown
Over stones wise with suffering. The paper
Carries yesterday with it. I hear
It scrape the stones. It carries yesterday
Into tomorrow.

This was only a trivial incident of
My middle years. I do
Not even know why I remember it. But

If this is the way it is, we need, perhaps,
A new concept of salvation, who had long thought
Courage enough to live by. What
Can the sea tell us of a drop we cup in the hand?
What, as the tide slinks away, can a drop,
Caught on the landward side of a pebble,
Tell us of the blind depth of groan out yonder?

VI. But Also

What Voice at Moth-Hour

What voice at moth-hour did I hear calling
As I stood in the orchard while the white
Petals of apple blossoms were falling,
Whiter than moth-wing in that twilight?

What voice did I hear as I stood by the stream,
Bemused in the murmurous wisdom there uttered,
While ripples at stone, in their steely gleam,
Caught last light before it was shuttered?

What voice did I hear as I wandered alone
In a premature night of cedar, beech, oak,
Each foot set soft, then still as stone
Standing to wait while the first owl spoke?

The voice that I heard once at dew-fall, I now
Can hear by a simple trick. If I close
My eyes, in that dusk I again know
The feel of damp grass between bare toes,

Can see the last zigzag, sky-skittering, high,
Of a bullbat, and even hear, far off, from
Swamp-cover, the whip-o-will, and as I
Once heard, hear the voice: *It's late! Come home.*

Another Dimension

Over meadows of Brittany, the lark
Flames sunward, divulging, in tinseled fragments from
That height, song. Song is lost
In the blue depth of sky, but
We know it is there at an altitude where only
God's ear may hear.

Dividing fields, long hedges, in white
Bloom powdered, gently slope to the
Blue of sea that glitters in joy of its being.

Once I lay on the grass and looked upward
To feel myself redeemed into
That world which had no meaning but itself,
As I, lying there, had only the present, no future or past.

*

Yes—who was the man who on the midnight street corner,
Alone, once stood, while sea-fog
Put out last lights, electric or heavenly?
Who knows that history is the other name for death?
Who, from the sweated pillow, wakes to know
How truth can lie? Who knows that jealousy,
Like a chinch-bug under the greenest turf, thrives?
Who learned that kindness can be the last cruelty?

I have shut my eyes and seen the lark flare upward.
All was as real as when my eyes were open.
I have felt earth breathe beneath my shoulder blades.
I have strained to hear, sun-high, that Platonic song.

It may be that some men, dying, have heard it.

Glimpses of Seasons

I. Gasp-Glory of Gold Light

Gasp-glory of gold light of dawn on gold maple—
Now forgotten green bough-loop, fat leaf-droop, and even
The first reddening rondure of August or, slow,
The birth of the grape's yearning bulge, as summer,
Bemused in the dream of the sweetness of swelling,
Forgets to define
The mathematics of Time. But look!
At this moment you stand

On the knife-edge of no-Time.
Or is it not no-Time, but Time fulfilled?

Do not turn your head, the sun no higher will rise.
Do not listen—no heart-beat,
No watch-tick, is here to be heard.
The Self flows away into the unbruised
Guiltlessness of no-Self. Do you imagine you feel

The lips of the world bend to your own?

How long may you stand thus?—though
Such matters of vulgar logic can scarcely apply
To our category of discussion. Dismiss

The topic, and try to think, at the same moment,
Of the living and the dead.

II. Snow Out of Season

Once in October—far too early, far out of phase—dawn
Was nothing but swirl of snow-dimness. How odd
Rose the last, lone bed of zinnias ablaze
Against God, the gray hush, and His willed dissolution!

After white earth and gray sky then came
Nothing you might call a sunset—
Just gray growing grayer to blackness.

More snow that night.

Then dawn: and sun leaped to flame,
Like the biblical strong man to run his race, but I,
Booted, in sheepskin swathed, was more modestly
Out to see the world remade
From this myth of nothingness,
Where now boughs hung heavy, white only, no crimson
Of maple, no willow by destiny yellow. The world,
White in lethalness, gleamed, except
For one thing. You know the berry
Of dogwood? Well,
Sudden on white, as on white velvet deployed,
Uncountable jewels flamed to the sun's flame.

Why should the heart leap? We
Are old enough to know that the world
Is only the world, and the heart
Is like fingers idly outspread while, slowly,
The gray seeds of Time, or gold grain,
Trickle through.

But we often forget.

III. Redwing Blackbirds

How far a-winging to keep this appointment with April!
How much breath left in reserve to fill
The sky of washed azure and whipped-cream cumuli
With their rusty, musical, heart-plumbing cry!

On sedge, winter-bit but erect, on old cattails, they swing.
Throats throb, your field glasses say, as they cling and sing—
If singing is what you call that rusty, gut-grabbing cry
That calls on life to be lived gladly, gladly.

*

They twist, tumble, tangle, they glide and curvet,
And sun stabs the red splash to scarlet on each epaulet,
And the lazy distance of hills seems to take
A glint more green, and dry grass at your feet to wake.

In the vast of night, seasons later, sleet coding on pane,
Fire dead on hearth, hope banked in heart, I again
Awake, not in dream but with eyes shut, believing I hear
That rusty music far off, far off, and catch flash and fleer

Of a scarlet slash accenting the glossy black. Sleet
Continues. The heart continues its steady beat
As I burrow into the tumulus of sleep,
Where all things are buried, though no man for sure knows how deep.

The globe grinds on, proceeds with the business of Aprils and men.
Next year will redwings see me, or I them, again then?
If not, some man else may pause, awaiting that rusty, musical cry,
And catch—how gallant—the flash of epaulets scarlet against blue sky.

IV. Crocus Dawn

Oh, crocus dawn!—premise of promise, what
Will the day bring forth? After all the days

I have waked to in joy or pain, in anxiety or
Expectation, or with the blank check

Of a heart that flutters vacantly in
The incertitude of the future's breath,

Or blast. After the clock that pronounces
The tiny mathematical tick that is your only

Benediction in darkness, what will you wake for? After
Darkness will there come that crocus dawn

With all the shimmer and sheen of the unending promise
We wake to, to live by? Oh, crocus dawn,

May our eyes gleam once more in your light before
We know again what we must wake to be.

English Cocker: Old and Blind

With what painful deliberation he comes down the stair,
At the edge of each step one paw suspended in air,
And distrust. Does he thus stand on a final edge
Of the world? Sometimes he stands thus, and will not budge,

With a choking soft whimper, while monstrous blackness is whirled
Inside his head, and outside too, the world
Whirling in blind vertigo. But if your hand
Merely touches his head, old faith comes flooding back—and

The paw descends. His trust is infinite
In you, who are, in his eternal night,
Only a frail scent subject to the whim
Of wind, or only a hand held close to him

With a dog biscuit, or, in a sudden burst
Of temper, the force that jerks that goddamned, accurst
Little brute off your bed. But remember how you last saw
Him hesitate in his whirling dark, one paw

Suspended above the abyss at the edge of the stair,
And remember that musical whimper, and how, then aware
Of a sudden sweet heart-stab, you knew in him
The kinship of all flesh defined by a halting paradigm.

Dawn

Dawnward, I wake. In darkness, wait.
Wait for first light to seep in as sluggish and gray
As tidewater fingering timbers in a long-abandoned hulk.
In darkness I try to make out accustomed objects.

But cannot. It is as though
Their constituent atoms had gone to sleep and forgotten
Their duty of identity. But at first
Inward leakage of light they will stir

To the mathematical dance of existence. Bookcase,
Chest, chairs—they will dimly loom, yearn
Toward reality. Are you
Real when asleep? Or only when,

Feet walking, lips talking, or
Your member making its penetration, you
Enact, in a well-designed set, that ectoplasmic
Drama of laughter and tears, the climax of which always

*

Strikes with surprise—though the script is tattered and torn?
I think how ground mist is thinning, think
How, distantly eastward, the line of dark woods can now
Be distinguished from sky. Many

Distinctions will grow, and some
Will, the heart knows, be found
Painful. On the far highway,
A diesel grinds, groans on the grade.

Can the driver see color above the far woods yet?
Or will dawn come today only as gray light through
Clouds downward soaking, as from a dirty dishrag?
I think of a single tree in a wide field.

I wonder if, in this grayness, the tree will cast a shadow.
I hold up my hand. I can vaguely see it. The hand.
Far, far, a crow calls. In gray light
I see my hand against the white ceiling. I move

Fingers. I want to be real. Dear God,
To Whom, in my triviality,
I have given only trivial thought,
Will I find it worthwhile to pray that You let

The crow, at least once more, call?

Millpond Lost

Lucent, the millpond mirrors September blue.
Golden, the maples lean, leaf by leaf, to stare down
Through motionless air, where, in water motionless too,
Hangs the mystery of maples, golden but upside-down.

Water brims the old stone of the dam-top
Where the margin is so prettily greened by moss. But the mill,
Now long back, must have rotted away. One by one, old beams may drop,
Though some, mossed and leaning, through vine-ruck, may poke still.

They will drop, one by one, and each individual fact
Will measure out time in a place where Time seems never to die.
But wherever you are, engaged in whatever act,
You cling to the last human dream that a moment can compose infinity.

Try, if you can, to restore the old scene. Can you see
How the great wheel, now gone, would turn, each turn spilling
Sun-flame and silver of water, while, joyfully,
Scrawny flesh of white bodies would plunge to black water, filling

*

The air with maniacal shouts to shake the highest leaf?
As now you stand dreaming, one leaf, slow, releases
Its bough, and golden, luxurious, an image of joy not grief,
Scarcely in motion, descends, till even that motion on water ceases.

Shit! This scene is only imagined. Your whole life
You've not been back, and the boys, they are mostly dead,
Or good as dead, from boredom with job, children, wife,
Or booze, heart failure, cop gunfire or strikebreakers' cracked head.

In darkness, I've tried to imagine the pond after such time-lapse,
Or name the names of the boys who there shouted in joy, once.

Summer Afternoon and Hypnosis

Lulled by stream-murmur and the afternoon's hypnosis
Of summer, guarded by willow shade while the sun
Westward inclines, you lie. The far world's only voice is
The muted music of sheep bells, one by one,

Threading the infinite distance of sunlight and languor.
Yes, lulled thus, your life achieves its honesty,
In which love, hate, lust, courage, cowardice, and anger,
With truth torn at last from lies, emerge from the shadowy

Mist of Time and sequence to seek in Timelessness
Each its lonely and naked reality. And your heart,
Bemused as though in a mirror's icy duress,
Seems to suspend its stroke, and your dry lips part

In a whisper of slow appalment to ask: "Was this
The life that all those years I lived, and did not know?"
Do you really think now the sun's frozen motionless?
Do you really think the stream no longer can flow?

But the heart strikes, and the world resumes its nature,
And Time swirls back like a tide more sousing than Fundy,
And whatever a man has endured he can endure,
And the shadow of that tall pine names night, and by

The moment it touches the mossed stone yonder, you will have roused
Yourself to yourself, and set foot to the mile
That leads to the roof whereunder you find enhoused
The mystery of love's redeeming smile.

VII. Fear and Trembling

If Ever

If ever you come where once it happened,
Pause, even briefly, and try to discover
If the heart now stalls, as once, for a lover,
It did. Or can love at the end, have an end

That is absolute? What if a mysterious
And throttling fist should now squeeze the heart,
And wrench it, and seem to tear it apart
From your bosom—what meaning for you, or for us?

Indeed, what exists in the grab-bag of pastness?
Do all things, in that vatic darkness, wear
Two faces? And frozen in hope—or despair—
Do you guess what may rise from that dark, seething vastness

That was your life? Do contradictory
Voices now at midnight utter
Doom—or promise? Or do voices merely stutter
In pronouncing the future, or history,

So that you, nightlong, in your ignorance, sweat?
What can you do? Listen!—it's true:
Seize the nettle of self, plunge then into
Cold shock of experience, like a mountain lake, and let

Stroke, after stroke, sustain you. And all else forget.

Have You Ever Eaten Stars?

A Note on Mycology

Scene: A glade on a bench of the mountain,
Where beech, birch, and spruce meet
In peace, though in peace not intermingled,
Around the slight hollow, upholstered
In woods-earth damp, and soft, centuries old—
Spruce needle, beech leaf, birch leaf, ground-pine belly-crawling,
And fern frond, and deadfall of birch, grass blade
So biblically frail, and sparse in that precinct where
The sunray makes only its brief
And perfunctory noontide visitation.
All, all in that cycle's beneficence

Of being are slowly absorbed—oh, slowly—into
What once had fed them. And now,
In silence as absolute as death,
Or as vision in breathlessness,
Your foot may come. Or mine,
As when I, sweat-soaked in summer's savagery,
Might here come, and stand
In that damp cool, and peace of process,
And hear, somewhere, a summer-thinned brook descending,
Past stone, and stone, its musical stair.

But late, once in the season's lateness, I,
After drouth had broken, rain come and gone,
And sky been washed to a blue more delicate,
Came. Stood. Stared. For now,
Earth, black as a midnight sky,
Was, like sky-darkness, studded with
Gold stars, as though
In emulation, however brief.
There, by a deer trail, by deer dung nourished,
Burst the gleam, rain-summoned,
Of bright golden chanterelles.
However briefly, however small and restricted, here was
A glade-burst of glory.

Later, I gathered stars into a basket.

Question: What can you do with stars, or glory?
I'll tell you, I'll tell you—thereof
Eat. Swallow. Absorb. Let bone
Be sustained thereof, let gristle
Toughen, flesh be more preciously
Gratified, muscle yearn in
Its strength. Let brain glow
In its own midnight of darkness,
Under its own inverted, bowl-shaped
Sky, skull-sky, let the heart
Rejoice.

What other need now
Is possible to you but that
Of seeing life as glory?

Twice Born

Ah, blaze of vision in the dark hour! Once,
Some fifteen years ago, lightning, the roar
Of summer storm knifing through night forest, ricochet

Of thunder blundering among mountains, and in
Interstices of majestic racket, rain-gust on roof—and I
Was snatched from sleep. I heard
The irredeemable riot, heard
The encirclement of thunder, which, suddenly,
Was sinking to a grumble, far away. So breath
Came back, and the heart resumed normal
Function. But one last and greatest crash, as though
On our roof, as though God
Was not mocked by any easy assumption, the crash
Accompanied by a flash dazzling the dark of the room,
Objects leaping to visibility, plunging at stunned eyes,
Air smelling of electricity. This time, the end, but

Not the end. In silence, light
Was entering the room as though lightning,
Thunderless and constant, prevailed. I
Tore back the curtain, saw. A great dead pine,
Fifty yards off, a torch sky-high now. Nothing
To be done. And no need, only deciduous
Trees near, I found, and rain-drenched, safe enough.

Back from investigation, soaked, and hands
Chilled to the marrow, shoes squishing water, mud
Clear up to blue-jean knees, I tore
Clothes off, toweled blood-heat up, plunged
Into bed. But not to sleep, not even after
The God-ignited torch, dying, left
Only a faint flicker on the walls—and the ceiling
That I stared at with a strange shudder and excitement. But
A calm sweetness was filling the room as darkness grew
And I could not see the ceiling. Then, all
At once, I knew. I knew
The storm, and all therewith, but as
A metaphor.

It was, I knew,
A metaphor for what, long back, I
Had undergone. I saw the fact of that.

In calmness, soon, I slept.

The Sea Hates the Land

Be not deceived by the slow swell and lull of sea lolling
In moonlight off Maine, or by tropical listlessness
Of the Gulf when cesspool slick, or by muted tolling
Of fog-bell when sea scarcely breathes. Deeper process

*

Proceeds, as blood inwardly flows while you sleep. One thing
Remember: the sea hates the land, that arrogant, late
Intruder on solitude's deep coil, no wing
Yet between the unsleeping depth's unabat-

ing fulfillment of self and the undefinable span
Of space forever seeking self's infinite end.
You cannot blame the sea. For you, as a man,
Know that only in loneliness are you defined.

Yes, the cormorant's scream, and even the kiss at midnight,
And the hurly-burly of firmaments and men
Are froth on the surface of deepening need: so by moonlight
Swim seaward, stroke steady, breath deep, remembering when

The self had the joy of selflessness completely
Absorbed in the innocent solipsism of the sea.

Afterward

After the promise has been kept, or
Broken. After the sun

Has touched the peak westward and you suddenly
Realize that Time has cut another notch

In the stick with your name on it, and you wonder
How long before you will feel the need

For prayer. After you have stumbled on the obituary
Of a once-girl, photograph unrecognizable,

Who, at night, used to come to your apartment and do everything but
It. Would fight like a tiger. Then weep.

Never married, but made, as the paper says,
A brilliant career, also prominent in good works. After

You have, in shame, lain awake trying to account for
Certain deeds of vanity, weakness, folly, or

Neurosis, and have shuddered in disbelief. After
You have heard the unhearable lonely wolf-howl of grief

In your heart, and walked a dark house, feet bare. After
You have looked down on the unimaginable expanse of polar

Icecap stretching forever in light of gray-green ambiguousness,
And, lulled by jet-hum, wondered if this

*

Is the only image of eternity. —Ah, menhirs, monoliths, and all
Such frozen thrusts of stone, arms in upward anguish of fantasy, images

By creatures, hairy and humped, on heath, on hill, in holt
Raised! Oh, see

How a nameless skull, by weather uncovered or
The dateless winds,

In the moonlit desert, smiles, having been
So long alone. After all, are you ready

To return the smile? Try. Sit down by a great cactus,
While other cacti, near and as far as distance, lift up

Their arms, thorny and black, in ritual unresting above
Tangles of black shadow on white sand, to that great orb

Of ever out-brimming, unspooling light and glow, queenly for good or evil, in
The forever sky. After you have sat

In company awhile, perhaps trust will grow.
Perhaps you can start a conversation of mutual comfort.

There must be so much to exchange.

VIII. Coda

Fear and Trembling

The sun now angles downward, and southward.
The summer, that is, approaches its final fulfillment.
The forest is silent, no wind-stir, bird-note, or word.
It is time to meditate on what the season has meant.

But what is the meaningful language for such meditation?
What is a word but wind through the tube of the throat?
Who defines the relation between the word *sun* and the sun?
What word has glittered on whitecap? Or lured blossom out?

Walk deeper, foot soundless, into the forest.
Stop, breath bated. Look southward, and up, where high leaves
Against sun, in vernal translucence, yet glow with the freshest
Young tint of the lost spring. Here now nothing grieves.

Can one, in fact, meditate in the heart, rapt and wordless?
Or find his own voice in the towering gust now from northward?
When boughs toss—is it in joy or pain and madness?
The gold leaf—is it whirled in anguish or ecstasy skyward?

Can the heart's meditation wake us from life's long sleep,
And instruct us how foolish and fond was our labor spent—
Us who now know that only at death of ambition does the deep
Energy crack crust, spurt forth, and leap

From grottoes, dark—and from the caverned enchainment?

Chief Joseph of the Nez Perce

Who Called Themselves the Nimipu, "The Real People"

To James Dickey

Made by the same Great Spirit, and living in the same land with our brothers, the red men, we consider ourselves as the same family; we wish to live with them as one people, and to cherish their interests as our own.

Thomas Jefferson: To the Miamis, Powtewataminies, and Weeauki

The more we can kill this year, the less will have to be killed the next war, for the more I see of these Indians, the more convinced I am that they will all have to be killed or be maintained as a species of paupers.

William Tecumseh Sherman

When the last Red Man shall have perished, and the memory of my tribe shall have become a myth among the white men, these shores will swarm with the invisible dead of my tribe, and when your children's children think themselves alone in the field, the store, the shop, upon the highway, or in the silence of the pathless woods, they will not be alone . . . At night when the streets of your cities are silent and you think them deserted, they will throng with the returning hosts that once filled them and still love this beautiful land. The White Man will never be alone.

Chief Sealth of the Duwamish

Note

The Nez Percé (modernly Nez Perce) entered history as the friendly hosts to the explorers Lewis and Clark, and took care of their superfluous possessions when the expedition made the last push to the Pacific. The Nez Perce were a handsome and very vigorous people, but not basically warlike; and in general they refused scalping. They moved about with the offerings of the seasons, digging camas root, taking salmon at the time of their run, and making long hunts, across the Bitterroot Mountains into what is now Montana, for buffalo, which had already disappeared from their land by the time of Lewis and Clark. The Nez Perce, however, were not nomadic in the sense of the Plains Indians and were, for the most part, devoted to their homelands–for old Joseph and his famous son, this being Wallowa, in northeastern Oregon. The lands where the fathers were buried were sacred, and, in their version of immortality, the fathers kept watch on sons to be sure that truth was spoken, and that each showed himself a man.

The first treaty, of 1855, guaranteed the homeland of each band of the Nez Perce (for the Nez Perce were divided into "bands," each with its own organization, and each band being a signatory to the treaty). But after the gold rush of 1860, and the seizure of the guaranteed grants of bands in Idaho, the Federal Government proposed, in 1863, a treaty by which a restricted reservation, centered at Lapwai in Idaho, would include all the Nez Perce. Certain Indians in Idaho, already Christianized to a degree, accepted and signed. But other bands, including that of Joseph, stood on the treaty of 1855 and refused to sign, and remained on their homelands. In 1873, President Grant again guaranteed, in his own hand, Wallowa to Joseph's band, but, under pressure, then turned to the doomed experiment of trying to divide the region between Indians and whites.

In the end, Joseph's band (the young Joseph now being chief) was ordered to the reservation, in the worst season of the year and with little time. They painfully set out to obey overwhelming force, but after an outbreak of violence, in which they had no hand, they were attacked by Federal troops. The troops were routed with heavy loss, but the war had begun with a shot fired on the white flag of the Indians. This occurred on June 17, 1877.

On September 5, 1877, Joseph surrendered to Colonel Miles, in eastern Montana. The terms given by Miles were generous, but these were murderously broken by Sherman, now Commanding General of the U.S. Army. Chief Joseph's life now became a constant struggle for the observation of the terms of Miles, but only after many years and many deaths were his people returned to the high country of the Northwest–though not to Wallowa.

Joseph and 150 Nez Perce were confined on a reservation in northeastern Washington. It seems that Joseph never gave up hope of returning to Wallowa, but in vain. On September 21, 1904, in exile at Colville, Washington, sitting before his fire, he fell dead. The physician of Colville, somewhat unscientifically, filed the report that the chief had died of a broken heart.

Chief Joseph of the Nez Perce

I.

The Land of the Winding Waters, Wallowa,
The Land of the Nimipu,
Land sacred to the band of old Joseph,
Their land, the land in the far ages given
By the Chief-in-the-Sky. Their ponies, crossed
With the strong blood of horses, well-bred, graze
Richly the green blade. Boys, bareback, ride naked,
Leap on, shout "Ai-yah!" Shout "Ai-yee!"–
In unbridled glory. Eagle wing catches sun.
Gleams white. Boys plunge into water, gay as
The otter at gambol, with flat hands slap water
Like beaver tails slapping to warn, then dive,
Beaverlike, to depth, toes leaving the shimmer,
Uncoiling upward, of bubbles. On sandbars
Boys stretch, they yawn, and sun dries the skin
To glints gold, red, bronze. Each year
They go where from seaward salmon, infatuate,
Unfailing at falls-leap, leap great stones. They leap
The foaming rigor of current–seeking, seeking,
In blind compulsion, like fate, the spawn-
Pool that blood remembers. What does our blood,
In arteries deep, heaving with pulse-thrust
In its eternal midnight, remember?
We stir in sleep. We, too, belong
To the world, and it is spread for our eyes.

The salmon leaps, and is the Sky-Chief's blessing.
The Sky-Power thus blessed the Nimipu
And blessed them, too, with
The camas root, good to the tongue, in abundance.

> Their honesty is immaculate and their purity of purpose and their observance of the rules of their religion are most uniform and remarkable. They are certainly more like a nation of saints than a horde of savages.
>
> *Jean Baptiste Le Moyne de Bienville*

It is their land, and the bones of their fathers
Yet love them, and in that darkness, lynxlike,
See how their sons still thrive without fear,
Not lying, not speaking with forkèd tongue.
Men know, in night-darkness, what wisdom thrives with the fathers.

By campfire at night old chiefs tell young boys
How first the"crowned ones," white men with head covered,
Had come, and their great war-chief, with honor,

Clean hands and medals and gifts, had sat
On the blanket with chiefs, and Chief Twisted-Hair
Had drawn on white elk-hide the way west,
Where boomed the Great Water Ill-Tasted–at land's end,
Where storms, winter long, strode those waters, with might.

The white chief went. Returning, said, yes.

> A tremendous wind from the S.W. about 3 Oclock this morning with Lightening and hard claps of Thunder, and hail which continued until 6 Oclock A.M. when it became light for a short time, then the heavens became suddenly darkened by a black cloud.
>
> *The* Journals *of Lewis and Clark*

"I was born at the time of snow. My name—
It was Miats Ta-weet Tu-eka-kas,
The son of my father Tu-eka-kas.
But not my true name. Only after ten snows
Was I, a boy, ready to climb
Alone to the mountain, to lie with no motion
On the stone-bed I made, no food, no water, heart open
To vision. To float as in vision and see
At last, at last, my Guardian Spirit
Come to protect me and give forth my true name.
Three days I lay on the mountain, heart open.
All day stared into bright blue. All night
Into darkening air. Then vision, it came.
But by day, clear. An old man, he stood
And he gave me a name. I learned to say it.

"I went down the mountain. My father I could not
Yet tell. But when the new-named ones, they danced,
Each dancing his new name, I danced. I leaped,
Skyward pointing, exclaiming, *Hin-mah-toó-yah-lat-kekht*—
Thunder-Traveling-to-Loftier-Mountain-Heights. That
Was my name. That made my medicine true.

"My father–Old Joseph, whites called him–had heard
Of the 'New Book of Heaven' the whites had brought
To Lapwai–the Place of the Butterflies–
And how it gave the heart brightness. So went there.
Lapwai was then not named reservation
As later it was for those who sold
Their land to the white man. But no!—
For us never—who sold not the sacred
Bones of our fathers for white-man money,
And food-scraps.

*

"But far in Lapwai, my father
And came there, yet carried the 'New Book of Heaven,'
New in our tongue now. But could he forget
The bones of his fathers, and the Old Wisdom?
Nor eyes of the fathers that watch from darkness?

"So was not at Lapwai, when firewater came. And the killing.

"Again 'crowned heads,' they came, the makers of treaties.
They sought out my father in friendship, with paper and ink."

> For the South Nez Perces; commencing where the southern tributary of the Palouse River flows from spurs of Bitter Root Mountains; thence down said tributary to the mouth of Ti-nat-pan-up Creek, thence southerly to the crossing of the Snake ten miles below the mouth of the Alpowa River; thence to the source of Alpowa River in the Blue Mountains; thence to the crossing of Grande Rond River, midway along the divide between the waters Wol-low-how and Powder Rivers; thence to the crossing of the Snake River fifteen miles below mouth of Powder River; thence Salmon River fifty miles above crossing; then along spurs of Bitter Root Mountains to the place of beginning.
>
> *Nez Perces Cession, 1855*

"I, a boy, stood and watched my father.
His hand reached out. It made the name-mark.
And why not? Not once had we shed white blood
Since the first great war-chief on the blanket had sat
With Twisted-Hair, and had named the land ours.
Now in ink was promised the Winding Waters forever,
Where sacred bones lay, and we knew them sacred.
We were promised also our land fit for snow-time,
For we knew the sacred wheel of the seasons.

"A promise, how pretty!—but our sacred land
They trod. They spat on our earth. It was like
A man's spit on your face. I, then a boy,
I felt the spit on my face. New treaties
They drew up to bind us with thongs. But only
The false Nimipu signed, those who already
Had gone to Lapwai, which was now reservation—
To eat, like a beggar, stale bread of white men.
Yes, they—only they—would sign. No! No!
Not ever my father. Never. Nor I."

> In my opinion the non-treaty Nez Perces cannot in law be regarded as bound by the treaty of 1863 and in so far as attempts to deprive them of a right to occupancy of any land in its provisions are null and void.
>
> *Major H. Clay Wood,*
> *Adjutant to General O. O. Howard*

"How far away, and wavering
Like mist in dawn wind, was the law! You have seen
How mist in creek bottoms to nothing burns
When the sun-blaze strikes. How far away
Sat the Great White Father!
But we heard how in his heart he holds goodness.
His word came to us to give rejoicing."

> Executive Mansion, June 16, 1873
> It is hereby ordered that the tract of country described Nez Perces Cession, 1855 be withheld from entry and settlement as public lands and that the same be set apart as a reservation for the roaming Nez Perces, as recommended by the Secretary of Interior and the Commissioner of Indian Affairs.
>
> *U. S. Grant*

"But it faded like mist in the day's heat."

II.

"But what is a piece of white paper, ink on it?
What if the Father, though great, be fed
On lies only, and seeks not to know what
Truth is, or cannot tell Truth from Lie?
So tears up the paper of Truth, and the liars,
Behind their hands, grin, while he writes a big Lie?

"Yes, what is a piece of white paper with black
Marks? And what is a face, white,
With lips tight shut to hide forkèd tongue?
Too late, too late, we knew what was the white spot
In distance–white cover of cloth, leather-tough,
On wagons that gleamed, like white clouds adrift
Afar, far off, over ridges in sunlight:
But they knew where they went, and we knew.
This knowledge, like lead of a rifle, sagged heavy in flesh—
Healed over, but there. It ached in the night."

> But no recollection of former services could stand before the white man's greed.
>
> *Major J. C. Trimble*

"My father held my hand, and he died.
Dying, said: 'Think always of your country.
Your father has never sold your country.
Has never touched white-man money that they
Should say they have bought the land you now stand on.
You must never sell the bones of your fathers–
For selling that, you sell your Heart-Being.' "

> I think it a great mistake to take from Joseph and his band of Nez Perces Indians that valley [Wallowa].
>
> *General O. O. Howard*

"Into a dark place my father had gone.
You know how the hunter, at dawn, waits,
String notched, where the buck comes to drink. Waits,
While first light brightens highest spruce bough, eyes slitted
Like knife wounds, breath with no motion. My father
Waits thus in his dark place. Waiting, sees all.
Sees the green worm on green leaf stir. Sees
The aspen leaf turn though no wind, sees
The shadow of thought in my heart—the lie
The heel must crush. Before action, sees
The deed of my hand. My hope is his Wisdom.

"Oh, open, Great Spirit, my ears, my heart,
To his sky-cry as though from a snow-peak of distance!"

> It cannot be expected that Indians ... will ... submit without any equivalent to be deprived of their homes and possessions or to be driven off to some other locality where they cannot find their usual means of subsistence. ... It ... is repugnant to the dictates of humanity and the principles of natural justice.
>
> *Oregon Superintendent of Indian Affairs*

"Does a grain of gold, in the dark ground, lie
Like a seed-sprout? What color of bloom
Will it bear? What cunning has it to make
Men rive raw rock where it hides like a murderous secret?
What cunning to lie in innocent brightness
Like wet sand in water? In water, what dives
The deepest—deep, deeper than the lead pellet?

"For all things live, and live in their nature.
But what is the nature of gold?

*

"In the deepest dark what vision may find it?
On its stone-bed of vision what secret name be divulged?
If it could dance in the name-dance, what
Name would gold dance? Would it be–
Death-that-in-darkness-comes-smiling?

"Or is it man's nature this thing not to know?"

> ... to attempt to restrain miners would be like attempting to restrain the whirl wind.
>
> *C. H. Hale, Superintendent of Indian Affairs*
> *for Washington Territory*

"Years fled. But with heart grown small, as from fear,
What man can live forever? True,
We had long back made the promise of peace.
We had sworn no white blood to shed, our tongue was not forkèd.
But now we breathed the stink of the wind of Time,
As when wind comes bad from the death of the promise of peace—
As when on the big plain from upwind taint comes
From the age-dead old buffalo cow that rots in the sun.
You wake at night, not believing the dream's stink.
You try to think: 'I lie here as always,
In my own tepee, at peace with all men.'

"But think of your father's eyes in his darkness.

"The sun rises up. No end to the dream's stink."

> I call him [the Indian] a savage, and I call a savage something wholly desirable to be civilized off the face of the earth.
>
> *Charles Dickens*

"You stand in the sun. You think: 'Am I Joseph?'
You find yourself watching the white man's horse-soldiers,
How they ride two-by-two, four-by-four, how they swing
Into line, charge or stop, dismount.
How the holders of horses fall back, while others
Are forming for skirmish. Or deploying for cover.

"The white horse-soldiers, they mount from the left.
We from right. Can that be a difference?

"Still as a stone, I stand watching, then suddenly know
How the young men watch me. Tears come to my eyes,
For I think how bodies, dead, in moonlight would shine.
I watch how the horse-soldiers wheel into line.
The young men watch me. One finger I touch
To my brow. Trace lines there. Then lay
A hand to my breast. It is hard to stand
And not know what self you have lived with, all years.
Oh, how can such two Truths kiss in your heart?

*

"For now you know what a treaty is–
Black marks on white paper, black smoke in the air.
For the greatest white war-chief—they call him Chief One-Arm–
Chief Howard—now in a loud voice he calls.
At a council of those who would take us away
From our land forever, at last I stood.

"In my weakness, tongue dry to the arch of my mouth,
I stood. My people waited. They waited
For words, for wisdom, to pass my lips—
Lips more dry than dust. Before me, I saw
All the blue coats, the buttons of gold, the black
Coats buttoned up tight
Over bellies that bulged–
White and sweaty, you knew, under that cloth–
And softer than dough. My words
Could not come. I saw
Their lips curl. I saw them,
Behind hands held up, in secret sneer.
'Oh, who will speak!' cried the heart in my bosom.
'Speak for the Nimipu, and speak Truth!'

"But then, my heart, it heard
My father's voice, like a great sky-cry
From snow-peaks in sunlight, and my voice
Was saying the Truth that no
White man can know, how the Great Spirit
Had made the earth but had drawn no lines
Of separation upon it, and all
Must remain as He made, for to each man
Earth is the Mother and Nurse, and to that spot
Where he was nursed, he must,
In love, cling."

> The earth, my mother and nurse, is very sacred to me: too sacred to be valued, or sold for gold or for silver . . . and my bands have suffered wrong rather than done wrong.
>
> *Chief Joseph to the Commissioners of 1876*

"Howard understood not. He showed us the rifle.
The rifle is not what is spoken in peace-talk.
He says we must leave the Winding Waters
Forever, forever—
Or come the horse-soldiers.
We must live afar with a shrunk-little heart,
And dig in the ground like a digger of roots—at Lapwai,
The Place of the Butterflies—how pretty
That name for a reservation to puke on!
Far from the fatherly eyes that stare in darkness.
Far from my father's words—and my promise!

So my chin to my chest dug deep. For I knew
One-Arm's numbers, and all those behind him.
I knew the strange gun that spits bullets like hail.
It sits on its wheels and spits bullets like hail.

"Worse—thirty days only to leave Wallowa,
With horses and herds, our old, young, and sick.
Horses and herds, they swam, though the Snake,
In thaw-flood, snatched off the weak colts, the weak calves,
And whites stole the rest left with poor guard.
But in round boats of buffalo hide, the people
Already were over, four strong horses and riders
To swim with each boat, and push for the shore.

"Even so, our young braves, they swallowed their rage,
Like bile that burns in the belly, and waits.
No, not ours it was who brought the great grief,
But young men of Chief White Bird.
They fled, burned houses, soaked earth with blood."

III.

"But on *our* trail, horse-soldiers in darkness came,
With hope to surprise us. Fools–
With gear jangle and horse fart! Though we needed not that.
At the heart of the night we heard what we heard–
The wailful howl of the sad coyote.
But no coyote! It was our scout.
He lay there in darkness, owl-eyed, deer-eared.
At dawn they came to surprise us.
Surprise!–It was theirs.

"We, who wanted no blood-spill, we sent a white flag.
But we knew not their heart, so young braves
Were stripping for battle. Ponies
Tossed head. Though many braves snored yet. Snored
From firewater the killers had stolen, then sneaked in
For refuge. Like hogs they snored. Vomit flecked lips.

"So what had we? Of braves, had only
Some threescore, and poor-armed, old trade guns
You load at death-lip, old shotguns, or Winchesters
Fewer than ten. Then bows–but bows
With love worked from the horn of wild sheep,
And backed with sheep tendon, and I have seen,
In the thundering chase, a young hunter set
His *flèche* feather-deep to probe the heart
Of the running buffalo bull, and the bull

Stumbles. Our young men, like shadows,
Were gone now, some left, some right, to cover
The draw's depth. To wait peace or war.

"The horse-soldiers stood. The white flag approached,
With the heart's true invitation. But what peace
Can there be when a shot is the only answer?
A man in a white hat, no soldier, fired it.
But how could we know? So soldiers died. From every draw,
Ledge, sage clump, death peered, death came.
Thirsty the sands of the canyon—oh, thirsty!
Death came with the whispering slyness of arrows.
Came with the whistling nag of hot lead.
On a prong-stick you prop your barrel, aim steady.
Not *bang-bang* like soldiers. You husband your powder.

"Then bursts the charge of the braves on their ponies—
The war-whoop, the *whang* of arrows at short-range.
The last of the battle formation is shattered
Like the buffalo herd stampeded at cliff-edge.
The sands redder go. Like old women, some soldiers
Lose mounts. Flee on foot.
In blind corners die.
All flee. Miles we chase them. Coats, weapons, we take.
Scalps never. We touch not the locks of the honored dead.
Now rifles we have, sixty-three by our count.
Now braves hide their bows. Now rifles they have!
And pistols. Ah, the white friend is kind!"

> Before you . . . lies the historic battle ground of the Nez Perce Indian War in which 34 men gave their lives in service for their country.
>
> *Marker on White Bird Battlefield*

"Yes, rifles we had now. But braves so few.
And white men, they swirl down like snowflakes in winter.
Hope we had of the great Looking Glass,
A war-chief with paw of cougar, and cunning
Of fox. We sent word. For he was our blood.
But no, but no, he dreamed he might live
In peace. But soon knew it only
A dream. To his village, horse-soldiers—they came.
They called for surrender. But Looking Glass answered
He was not at war. So a white man fired.
Killed only a baby.

"So Looking Glass, the wise, the brave,
Came to sit in our council of chiefs, the great war-chief!
White fools, they gave him to us, like a present.

*

"Chief Howard, Great One-Arm–his hundreds now come,
With big-bellied belch-gun and those that spit pellets.
Across the Salmon, yet flooding, we teased them, we lured them."

> A safer position was unchoosable, nor one more puzzling and obstructive.
>
> *General O. O. Howard*

"Across the flood-Salmon, like children they came
With all their fool tangle of cables and ferries,
Into our mountains, the trails mud-slick,
Roped pack-mules plunging down cliffside, the forest
In darkness at sun-height. Then we, easy,
Cross over the river. Cross back. On the plain are free
To meet soldiers, scout parties. We meet, and they die.
And in the dark mountains the War-Chief-Who-Prays
Now prayed for supplies. Cut off for three days,
With bellies growling, guts flat, he at last
Made the river with all that aimless tackle and gear.

"At Clearwater, then, we fought them. We held.
For two days we held them, locked in our circle,
While old, young, sick, and women, by travois escaped.
But, oh, not back to the Winding Waters!"

> The Indians fought like devils and were brave as lions.
>
> *Captain Bancroft*
> *(wounded, from hospital at Lapwai)*

"We tried to be brave like men, we tried
To cleanse hearts.
To make acceptable medicine.
But the Great Spirit turned his face away
From the land of the Winding Waters we loved.

"Did he turn his face because of my heart-pride?
Because I was proud to sit in the council
With war-chiefs, the great ones, adept at blood skills?
They knew cunning deceits but never knew soul-fear.
I was proud to sit there, and always my ears
Pricked forward for wisdom, as the wolf pricks ears
At a rustle on soft wind,
For I stored all I heard for the heart's lonely thought,
To be ready, be strong, when the moment came.
Sometimes in battle I took care of those
Too old, too young, or too sick. To give them
Their safety. My Guardian Spirit, it told me.
But I, too, down the length of the death-tube have peered,
Squeezed trigger, seen blood spurt, have rallied
My braves. I knew the joy of the clamor.
I strove to be named by the name of a man.

*

"I have even devised a new death-trap and spoken
In council. And the first chief nodded. Then all."

> The Great Spirit puts it into the heart and head of man to know how to defend himself.
>
> *Chief Joseph*

"But later, ah, later, when men named that war
With my name, my heart in my bosom would tighten.
Would shrink. What praise does man want but his manhood?
We all had manhood, we showed at Clearwater."

> I do not think that I had to exercise more thorough generalship during the Civil War than I did in the march to the battlefield and the ensuing battle with Joseph and his Indians on the banks of the Clearwater.
>
> *General O. O. Howard*

"But what was the good of our sweated blood?–
Howard behind us, the mountain wall eastward.
From Howard no peace terms, and eastward only
Lolo Pass, which crawled up in cloud-heights,
And we knew that Howard would try to cut Lolo.
For me, I would stand, fight, and die, if only
In dream of my sacred land, but the chiefs
In council said *no.* Looking Glass said *no.*
And I heeded their wisdom. What right had I
To die—to leave sick, old, young, women–merely to flatter
My heart's pride? For a true chief no self has. So up,
Up Lolo, track ragged and rocky, crag-dark,
Belabored by deadfall, but with hope
To find at the end of long travail Sitting Bull,
Who now sat safe by the 'skirts of the Old Lady Queen,'
Far northward. He would know us as men.

"Howard, we raced him. Won. But eastward
New soldiers had a fort built to trap us. Now under
White flag we held pow-wow for peace. Meanwhile,
Our scouts smelled a way. Hard and bitter it was.
But the east goes red with dawn—and ho!—
Here only some last coals now dying, all night,
Kept alive for deceit. We had flung out a screen
Of braves behind ledges, rim-rock, tree-growth,
So they dared not leave that fort ill-placed.
Some tried, but not living to hear the gray hornet's song
Before its kiss came.

" 'Fort Fizzle,' they called it. Fort Fizzle it was.
But yet no way to get to the 'Old Lady's Skirts.'

*

"So up Bitterroot, friendly with settlements,
Trading with farmers, for guns, ammunition,
Not killing, laughing together. Then eastward,
Toward grass of the buffalo land, and high sky.
Peace-thinking deceived us. We thought we were free."

IV.

"Near dawn they struck us, new horse-soldiers. Shot
Into tepees. Women, children, old died.
Some mothers might stand in the river's cold coil
And hold up the infant and weep, and cry mercy.
What heart beneath blue coat has fruited in mercy?
When the slug plugged her bosom, unfooting her
To the current's swirl and last darkness, what last
Did she hear? It was laughter.

"And we, we were blind, blind in the bushes,
Rage-blind, hearts burning, hides naked except for
Snatched bandoliers, rifles foolish in hand—but then!
Then the great voice of Looking Glass, White Bird's war-whoop,
Its terrible quaver! We heard, turned,
Saw horse-soldiers laughing, bright milling in firelight.
And, sudden, we knew our darkness a blessing. Few there
Laughed long. Light summoned hot lead from darkness.
Few managed to flee to high cover. Dug holes
In the ground. But our rifles found any that stirred.
And dawn filled the canyon.

"We took their big-bellied gun that belched. We broke it.
New rifles we had, new boots, new coats–
From bodies, white humps gleaming in sunshine,
And now clutching earth as though they had loved her.

"Few laughed as naked they lay there. Our own hearts
Were swollen with rage, but rage like great joy.
And gratefulness. The Chief-in-the-Sky–
He had seen our need. He smiled on us.
He said: 'Know now you are men. Be men!'

"With his help we were men. And scouts out now always."

> I could smell white people, the soldiers, a long way ... My Guardian Spirit instructed that I scout mostly alone. None of the enemies had appeared coming on our last sun's trail ... I watched if antelope acted curious. It might be danger. If prairie birds flew up in distance, it might be buffalo stampeding ... The unexpected shadow against a big rock.
>
> *Yellow Wolf, Scout of the Nez Perce*

"Yes, never again did the sunrise come
Without, at first light, a far shadow on ridge-spine
To wheel, wave blanket, ho! At night had that scout
Snaked nearer and nearer a campfire? The sleeper
Breathed steady. A throat might be slit, and the sleeper
With no breath to moan. For a hand blocked the mouth.
And scouts at distance knew how to direct
The far anger of Enfield, or Spencer, or Sharps.
Men have fallen from saddle before echo came.
Men have fallen face-down in a skillet when cooking.

"All night white men knew eyes to be watching.

"All night scouts wore wolf-skins. In darkness wolves called.

"Past lava, past schist, past desert and sand–
A strange land we wandered to eastern horizons
Where blueness of mountains swam in their blue—
In blue beyond name. The hawk hung high.
Gleamed white. A sign. It gleamed like a word in the sky.
Cleanse hearts and pray. Pray to know what the Sky-Chief
Would now lean to tell. To the pure heart, Truth speaks.

"We dreamed to enter the pass they name Tachee,
The land where Evil Spirits may dwell,
Where water may stink, and a river stink evil,
And the ulcerous earth boils foul.
But we trusted the will of the Sky-Chief to lead us,
To lead us the way of silence and shadow.
We dreamed of the mountain where one drop of dew
At noon yet hangs at the pine-needle tip
And speaks back to no sun. We dreamed.
But no. Not yet.

"To your belly the plant of the camas is kind.
Women gather the root on the camas prairies.
It is a gift from our Great Earth Mother–
But only for us. The white man spits on it,
Blaspheming. And to the white man it gave back,
At last, one word. And Death was the word.
On Camas Meadows we found him. In moon-dark,
In columns of two, as though soldier-saddles we rode.
We sat up as soldiers, as though the friendly
Patrol returning. We knew a patrol out.

"We rode in close. Challenge, at last!
Then war-whoop, the blaze,
Tent canvas tattered by bullets, the death-scream, the mule train
Stampeding after the bell of the lead-mare
Now rung by a brave who had crept in to steal it
And now dashed onward, and on,

Into darkness and distance. Thus
It began. Some ran from their weapons."

> NARRATION: Some were crying. They ran, and one voice called loudly for them to come back to their guns.
> QUERY: Where were the guns of the soldiers who were standing guard?
> NARRATION: The guns were stacked.
> QUERY: You did not really hear the soldiers crying, did you?
> NARRATION: I heard them cry like babies. They were bad scared.
>
> *Interview with Indian Warrior*

"Then Tachee, the door to the friendship of mountains,
And the world of the foot-soundless shadow. Ah, there!–
There the mountains of Yellowstone, silence,
The secret recesses. There the wolf-call
Could be but a wolf in wolf-darkness, calling.
You turn on your side. You sleep. Till dawn.

"What days, what nights, had we come in our harriment?
Long, long the summer, but dawn-ice now blue.
Remember your dead now lonely under
High stars with no name. Snow comes soon. In darkness, awake,
In new mountains, you stare up to see, bright as steel,
Stars wheel in unfamiliar formations. You know not
That sky. Nor that land, nor where foot leads.

"But there was one with us, of white and red blood
Together, but red was his heart, Poker Joe, and he knew
All the sly trails, deceits of the passes. In
That land of mountainous blankness, he scented in darkness,
He tasted the air. We trusted. He knew
The names of the mountains, in darkness
Their whisper he heard.

"And Howard's poor half-wits, with compass and maps,
Had traveled more than their thousand
Miles, steel of horseshoes thin-splitting, boot-leather
No longer saving the callus
From blood-scrape of razor-edge lava, or granite,
Coats threadbare for blasts from northward now fanged, the belly
Already growling in hunger's anxiety."

> As it had been a severer tax upon the energies of officers and men than any period in the late Civil War, surely some method must be found to encourage and properly reward such gallantry and service hardly ever before excelled.
>
> *General O. O. Howard*

"But we, our hearts leaned toward the mountains!
We could never starve in the Sky-Chief's goodness.

"Into that nightmare of chasm and peak,
We plunged. But no nightmare for Joe! How soft
The pine needles, padding the foot arch stone-strained,
Lava-cut! How gentle the silence as when
You wake, and the loving boughs lean! What if
Old One-Arm should come, as sure, in the end?
With new men, new supplies, new spit-guns, new boots?
And we guessed, before word of scouts, that eastward,
Where eye-into-eye mountains see sun come,
Already horse-soldiers were freshly counted
To grind us between a mortar and pestle."

V.

Where east, and north, the mountain wall broke,
Stone fingers, with nails, stretched out at the plain,
And in between fingers were passes that westward
Became a gut-tangle of canyons, ravines, crevasses,
And cliff-sided slits no root could clutch, or bear claw,
And if you looked up, day was only a sky streak.
From high west to high east spine-ridges ran,
Peaks stabbing high beyond blackness
And clamber and shag of conifers. Who,
North or south, could make way that way? Yes,
Poker could, and Joseph, his people.

And Howard,
In blunder and bumble–yes, he was tough.
Would winch wagons—unwheeled front or rear—two hundred
Feet up, or worse. Then down. Then days
Later find he had cut
Across his own trail. Was sometimes, in fact,
As baffled as any idiot kitten that tangles
Itself in a ball of sock-wool, or a trot-line.

The only scouts Howard sent out not later found dead
Were those with news Poker wanted Howard to hear
As he staggered through the insane Absarokas–
That saber-jagged, murderous mania of mountains
And stream-yelping canyons where every
Direction is only a lie—hoping
At last to pin Joseph against Colonel Sturgis,
Who horse-held the plain, waiting, waiting–
For Sturgis, a son dead with Custer, was mad for revenge.

*

Yes, it would be
An operation brilliant in textbooks,
A nutcracker action—depending, of course,
On information and timing. But Howard,
His scouts all found dead or with useless news,
Hung ignorantly north
Near Clark Fork headwaters, waiting to strike.
But Sturgis, in hot haste and heat of revenge, was tricked
South, up the stinking Shoshone, and into the mountains,
Pursuing Joseph and Joe, with trail signs
All subtle but carefully clear,
To find, in the end, a well-trampled spot, a spot
Where ponies outward had circled and circled
To hide all trail thence—or generously give
Too God-damned many. But, ah, plainsward
Sturgis spies dust rise, the bands, of course!
Dust rose, swelling slow in the pale pink of dawn-shine.

So, "Halloo!" shouts Sturgis, hell-bent for the spooks.

For spooks, they were. Dust settles, and nothing
Is there but ripped pine boughs and sage clumps left
By braves now galloping north, and coiling their lariats–
Laughing.

Back now–back at the circle of trampled confusion
Devised by the wicked cunning of Joe or
The instinct of Joseph–or whose?–Sturgis found
The telltale spot where no dew seemed shaken from shyest leaf,
Where pebbles too perfectly showed no streak of mud.
And that, of course, was the route of escape, the magic
Of red men. It gave
On a knife-slice of canyon as dark as a tunnel,
And needle-narrow. It faded back north,
Reversing the track of Sturgis's drive for revenge.

Northward, it led, and Joseph could enter
The mystic path, past Howard, to
Clark's Fork and freedom.

VI.

Now the last dash! The Great Spirit had smiled
On those who knew to endure or die,
And those who knew the joy of expending man's strength
That others might laugh in sunshine, and sing.

*

If you were the eyes of the Eagle of eagles,
And from vast height looked down on the bruised
Thumb-hump of the Little Bear Paw Mountains, then southward,
You'd see a tangle of canyon and coulee
Where water, long back, had sliced at the high plain;
And south then, plains of great grass curried
By wind-comb, or lying gray-green in its slickness
Of windless autumn sunlight, or worn down
By buffalo hoof or tooth-edge to earth's
Inner redness, and dust-devils rising in idle
Swirl, or the white-streaked poison of
Alkali flats, standing stakes of poplars long dead,
And farther, more canyons and coulees black
With shadow as sun saddens westward, and low.
Then, worn down by ages and ice-grind, the Little
Rockies, and, eastward crawling, the glitter
Of rivers, first the Missouri, then
Plains again, lounging and lazy, or plagued by dust-devils.
More mountains, the Moccasins reaching north-south,
The Judiths east-curving, and likewise the Big
Snowy Mountains, and farther some eighty miles,
Another glitter of river, slow, idle, eastward,
The Yellowstone, and from that level,
The bulge, hump, leap of the Great
Granite Peak, from which all earth falls away,
Past glacier, precipice, past rocks ripped
Like wounds from a grizzly's claws.–And there,
Two hundred miles off, slow, slow, in distance,
Almost invisible, even to Your eternal Eye, the advancing
Riffle of dust. They come.

Northward they move.
They move from the Land of the Evil Spirits unharmed.

But dimmer by distance, almost transparent
In late light, unformed as a thumb-smear, blue blur
On the sky's autumnal yellowness: Howard.

Old One-Arm, dogged, devout, knowing
Himself snared in God's cleft stick of justice,
Stirs in the saddle. His heart is military.
Is inflamed with love of glory and
Vanity wounded. He is the butt
Of every newspaper. Like foxfire,
At night in his dream, his quarry flickers, sardonic,
Before him. Does
He hear distant laughter in dream? By God,
Pursue! He will! The old wound
Aches. He thinks of Seven Pines. Well,
Let last leather split, feet bleed, last
Horseshoe be cast. Man

Is born to suffer. He is born to God's will.

But a stern chase, by land or sea,
Is a long chase. He knows that much.
His heart is iron. He has seen much blood. But
Against his will, his ambition, the heart
Melts in his breast. It
Suffers a flame of logic that
Vindictively flares through the straw
Of ambition, and he, in heart-pain, admits
That from Fort Keogh, northeast, Colonel Miles
Might, upward and west, strike a long angle
Of interception.

And receive surrender!

Nausea burns his throat. Acid of bile. What
Then for him, for Howard! For his
Long struggle, unflinching, over a thousand miles,
For anguish, defeats, his dead lying under
Unloving stars? His heart splits in prayer.
He has stood before his regiments on Sunday morning
To pray. Now, in darkness, he prays.

His heart splits,
Like a stone, red-hot, into snow cast.

> If Thou wilt grant my request, do so, I beseech Thee, even at the expense of another's receiving credit of the expedition.
>
> *General O. O. Howard*

He thinks of Miles. He thinks what all men know:
A groveling hem-kisser of the draggled skirts of glory.
He thinks of him. But,
Suddenly, with sad pity.

Orders, identical, go out. One by
Horse, one by boat.—And the heart of Miles at Keogh
Flares like a rocket. A general once—
But only of state militia. Now only
A colonel—regular, but rank reduced. His head goes dizzy
Like a drunkard's whose fingers close on the bottle.
In the infinite black firmament inside
His skull, a star, in explosion, blazes, bursts
In the birth of worlds. He knows now that
God loves him! Bugles blare.
Blare here! Blare there! Distance is nothing.

... something of a glory-chaser, like Custer ...
Major Lewis Merrill

As Joseph drew northward, Howard drew on.
Joseph knew but one word: *north.* And northeast
The Yellowstone flowed, backed westward by yellow-
Gray rim-rock and shortening sunsets. Joseph,
His sick, his old, his young are now driven
Like wraiths in Joseph's iron dream.

Sturgis has his own blood-drenched dream.
His scouts feed his dream.
One more chance! He follows.
Oh, one more chance!

But Joseph drives on. He dreams
Of a break in the western bulwark of rim-rock
That backs the river—dreams
Of an opening, perhaps some creek coming in,
That looks wide and gracious, yet suddenly
Goes narrow, flanked by cliffs and crevasses,
Flange rock and rubble, a place where
One man is twenty—is fifty—if powder holds out. Oh,
For an opening wide, inviting, that,
Suddenly, like a lethal noose,
Tightens. He hacks at his scouts.

There—a gift of the Great Sky-Chief—
It is! And the sick, old, incompetent
Are huddled up-canyon. A few braves
Are set at the opening for bait and delay.

And Sturgis
Gave thanks to God, and struck!

The bait before him fades into the narrowing throttlement.
Poor Sturgis! He never could learn, and now crowded
His horsemen in until, at a burst, from
Flanges, shelves, rim-rocks, ledges, sage clumps,
The unhived lead hums happily honeyward.

Now Joseph long gone up the death-sweet canyon,
Howard arrived to survey the scene.
From saddle, he slowly surveyed it with more than
Professional eye:

> It was the most horrible of places—sage-brush and dirt, and only alkaline water, and very little of that! Dead horses were strewn around, and other relics of the battlefield! A few wounded and dead were there. To all this admixture of disagreeable things was added a cold, raw wind, that, unobstructed, swept over the country. Surely, if anything was needed to make us hate war such after-battle scenes come into play.

Yes, Joseph again gone—and Sturgis
Outfought in spite of men and equipment,
And pursuers unable to breach the inner bulwark of rim-rock!
Now, on the northern horizon, the dust
Of Joseph is lost. Southward, three armies,
In the saw-toothed Absarokas, had, breath-bated, lain
In wait, but Joseph's people, like water,
Like air, like ghosts, had slipped through the clutch of fingers.

But Joseph knew nothing of Miles, and his star.

Miles curses the cavalry, infantry, forward
To follow that flare in his head. In his saddle
Miles reels. The thought—it is ghastly! What if
Howard comes to find him merely holding Joseph at bay?
Then all—all—for naught. For Howard, outranking,
Would receive the surrender. Miles shuts eyes. Sees
In darkness the glare of newspaper headlines,
Far off, in New York. In Washington, too.
Then the merciless masonry of the news story.
Tears come to his eyes. He curses his laggards. And Howard.

On the western shore of the mountains, Joseph
Moves north four days, but slower, slower,
For Howard, in cunning, relaxes his pressure
That Miles, unknown, on the eastern slope
May drive on past, then strike a hook southward.

Joseph, at last, to the Little Bear Paws comes.
He believes himself safe by the "Old Lady's Skirts":

> I sat down in a fat and beautiful country. I had won my freedom and the freedom of my people. There were many empty places in the lodges and the council, but we were in a land where we could not be forced to live in a place we did not want.

Clearly defensible, in the alluvial gulch
Of Snake Creek, beside good water, they
Set themselves down, protected from wind
By bluffs, farther by mountains, tepees now set
In a circle, good hunting handy. Women
Could here dry winter meat, and livestock

Graze widely. But in precaution at each
Tepee a mount was staked. No scouts out, however.
For this was a land of peace. They had peace.

In dawn light this was the pastoral scene Miles saw—
And saw, or thought he saw, how the slope,
Wide, rolling, slightly atilt,
Invited cavalry's thunder. No Howard!
His heart leaped. One charge—and the star!

But Fate, the slut, is flirtatious. What
Miles, in hypnotic passion, did not
See was a network of small, brush-grown coulees,
And a great coulee, moatlike, east and west,
Draining down to the Snake, and top growth
At that distance looked like the leveling plain.
This, Miles could not see, but clear to his sight,
If not to his brain, there was, beyond,
A long ridge, now brown with autumn-bit sage to give
Perfect deception for braves to lie in,
Barrel steady, trigger-finger looped, eye squinting.

How calm the plain looked. In saintly peace
Miles stood in God's love. He knew that God loved him.
For at the debouchment of Bear Paws there was
No perspective to show, in the dip, swell and dip,
That the last east-west cross-ridge, southward,
That looked so easy, lied.
The easiest yet, it looked,
For eastward
It sinks. Ah, how in his dream could he know
That on the far side, on the north,
Before the flat of the village, it dropped sharp
To hoof-trap and haunch-grind that, sudden,
Would crumple the cavalry eastward, and spill it,
Tangled and cramped, directly under
The rifle-pricked ridge beyond,
And the closer spite of the fanged coulee?

That is what the land-lay today indicates.

Miles saw in his head the victory form like a crystal—
With Companies *A, D,* and *K* of Custer's
Old favorite Seventh, with Cheyenne scouts,
Who could not now for scouting be used
For fear of alarm,
As the cutting edge of attack.

His breath comes hard. How slow the bastards find place!
Already the Cheyennes, now slick-skinned and naked
To breech-clout and moccasins, hold back

Pawing mounts, though they pant to ride
For the kill, to make *coup,*
To dab cheek with the blood of a brother.
They yelp in the snow-swirl. Captain Hale jokes:
"My God, have I got to go out and get killed
In such weather?" It was a good joke. But no laughter.

No Howard yet! Miles lifts his arm.
He takes the deep breath. He shouts, "Attack!"

He thought of the half-wits down there, scarce more
Than a hundred. *What were they thinking down there?*

There was only silence down there.

Now is the rhythm of hoof. First, trot:
Down slope, down dip, up ridge-swell,
Then down. Then bursts the hoof-thunder!—
And then the blind surge when the last
Ridge divulges its dire,
Deadly secret, compresses the ranks, swerves horsemen, and spills
The mass to the open before the moat-coulee. Blaze
Now has burst, bursts first
At two hundred, a hundred and fifty, a hundred, then fifty
Long paces, but not long for lead, and the charge,
Like sea-froth at cliff-foot, in blood-spume
Shatters:

Horses rearing in death, the death scream, saddles
Blown empty, lines broken, all officers down, pure panic.
Now Death probes out for the backbone, for shoulders,
At Enfield—at Winchester—at Sharps range,
Snow red, then redder,
And reddening more, as snow falls
From the unperturbed gray purity of sky.

Captain Hale was a prophet: dead in such weather.

> I never went up against anything like the Nez Perces in all my life, and I have been in a lot of scraps.
>
> *James Snell, Scout for Miles*

Miles's infantry made out some better; took losses, of course,
But in dying laid down a ring of investment, which promised a siege.
So the siege settled down,
With slow, systematic shelling of all in the village,
And hunger began its long gut-gnaw.

For Miles, what bastardly luck! A siege—and how long?

*

But luck held for Miles. Under the fire
Of cannon buried howitzerwise, what else
But negotiation? It came—with Miles
Violating a flag of truce to hold Joseph.
But the braves were alert. They, too, grabbed a hostage.
So terms were arranged, Miles's terms mysteriously generous.

Now Howard stands, suddenly, there.

Stood there, commander, enduring the only
Outlet of rage and hatred Miles
Could give vent to: ironical courtesy, cold,
Gray as snot. But Howard,
Whose sweat had soaked sheets in wrestling with God,
Laid his remaining hand on the steel-stiff shoulder
That quivered beneath it. Howard, almost
As soft as a whisper, promises him the surrender.

And hearing his own words, he knew a pure
And never-before-known bliss swell his heart.

Miles laughed with the laughter of friend or brother.
But if Howard smiled, the smile was inward—
A fact unnoticed by Miles, who already
Was deep in his head's dizzy darkness composing
The rhetoric of his official communiqué:

> We have had our usual success. We made a very direct and rapid march across country, and after a severe engagement and being kept under fire for three days, the hostile camp under Chief Joseph surrendered at two o'clock today.

How now would the newspapers blaze! Sherman smile!
And let old Sturgis—a colonel yet—bite his nails.
To hell with his son—all soldiers die.

> I felt the end coming. All for which we had suffered and lost! Thoughts came of Wallowa, where I grew up . . . Then with a rifle I stand forth, saying in my heart, 'Here I will die.'
>
> *Yellow Wolf*

But did not. Lived on. In history.

Five inches of snow now, sky gray, and yonder
One buffalo rug, black on white,
And kept black until Howard, Miles, and the staff
Would arrive when the hour struck.
It would strike.

*

For terms now are firm: rifles stacked
With bandoliers twined. No need now for rifles,
For hunting or honor. They'd go to Keogh
And eat white man's bread, with only the promise
Of Miles that in spring they'd go west to high land
Where mountains are snow-white and the Great Spirit
Spills peace into the heart of man.
Wallowa—no! But another land of pure air,
Blue distance, white peaks, their own lives to live,
And again their own guns, to hunt as man must.
And there they might think of the eyes of the fathers
Yet on them, though across all
The mountains, the distance, the noble disaster.

I believed General Miles or I never would have surrendered.
Chief Joseph

At late afternoon, light failing, Howard
Is called, with his brass, to the buffalo robe that
Lies black against snow. Up from the dry
Brown gravel and water-round stones of the Eagle,
Now going snow-white in dryness, and up
From the shell-churned
Chaos of camp-site, slowly ascends
The procession. Joseph, not straight, sits his mount,
Head forward bowed, scalp lock with otter-skin tied.

Black braids now framed a face past pain.
Hands loose before him, the death-giving rifle
Loose-held across, he comes first.
The bullet scar is on his brow.
Chief Hush-hush-kute, beside him, on foot,
Moves, and that chief speaks, and the head
Of Joseph is bowed, bowed as in courtesy
To words of courage and comfort. But
The head may be bowed to words by others unheard.

Joseph draws in his mount. Then,
As though all years were naught in their count, arrow-straight
He suddenly sits, head now lifted. With perfect ease
To the right he swings a buckskinned leg over. Stands.
His gray shawl exhibits four bullet holes.

Straight standing, he thrusts out his rifle,
Muzzle-grounded, to Howard. It is
The gesture, straight-flung, of one who casts the world away.

Howard smiles as a friend. But
Peremptory or contemptuous,
Indicates Miles. Upon that steel symbol,

The hand of Miles closes. We do not know
What ambiguities throttle his heart.
Miles is sunk in his complex tension of being,
In his moment of triumph and nakedness.

Joseph steps back. His heart gives words.
But the words, translated, are addressed to Howard.

> Tell General Howard I know his heart. What he told me before I have in my heart. I am tired of fighting. Our chiefs are killed. Looking Glass is dead. The old men are killed. It is the young men who say yes or no. He who led the young men is dead. It is cold and we have no blankets. Our little children are freezing to death. I want time to look for my children and see how many of them I may find. Maybe I shall find them among the dead. Hear me, my chiefs, I am tired. Heart is sick and sad. From where the sun now stands, I will fight no more forever.

Then Joseph drew his blanket over his head.

VII.

At Keogh they ate the white man's bread.
The taste was gray to a prisoner's tongue.
Then Bismarck, then Leavenworth, far off in Kansas,
On one side a river. Before ice came, edges
Were streaked, slick, slow. It crawled.
But when sun in its season came back, its wrath
Might suck up green bubbles of slime, to burst.
On the other side a fat lagoon lolled
With dead fish floating, belly-white upward,
And all water foul for cooking or drinking.
As early heat grew, by daylight or night,
Night moonlit or dark, insects unremitting
Were whirring or sizzling like lust in the blood;
Or the sound the lust of murder makes
In the deep of your heart before the stroke.

Ah, when would the terms of the promise be kept!
When would the word of Miles set them
Among promised mountains, far blueness, far whiteness?
How could they know that Miles, whom they trusted,
Was only a brigadier behind whom
Moved forces, faceless, timeless, dim,
And in such dimness, merciless?

> After the arrival of Joseph and his band in Indian Territory, the bad effects of their location at Fort Leavenworth manifested itself in the prostration by sickness at once of two hundred and sixty of the four hundred and ten; and in a few months in the death of more than one quarter of the entire number.
>
> *Report of the Indian Commission of 1878*

Did Joseph now ever think, and with
What twisted irony, of the name—
If he knew it—of that man who
Held life and death in his hands, and who
Had broken the terms of surrender, and sent
Them to Leavenworth to die?
General Sherman, it was, and the name he bore,
That of the greatest Indian chief—
Tecumseh. William Tecumseh Sherman, of course.

> The Great Spirit Chief who rules above seemed to be looking some other way, and did not see what was being done to my people.
>
> *Chief Joseph*

Perhaps Joseph prayed, but could not die.
And living, lived for one thing only—to see
The terms of surrender maintained, and his people
Again in their high land,
Where men love earth and earth loves man,
And men eat food that earth, in love, gives.

With agents, with bosses, Joseph spoke,
With inspectors, with officers, getting no heed.
Only one man, with an uneasy conscience, might
Speak out the truth, and the truth be heard,
And was it integrity, or some
Sad division of self, torn in ambition
And ambition's price, that at last made Miles
The only staunch friend of Joseph for all
The years? In his rising success, did something make Miles
Wonder what was the price of a star?

And was it the friendship of Miles that got Joseph to Hayes
To fill the presidential ear with his old story?
Using Yellow Bull to speak, he spoke
To the Great White Father, but old Hayes
Knew his profession, so Joseph was sent to sit
With busy commissioners to say,
"It makes my heart turn sick when I
Remember all the good, kind words
And broken promises." He told
The bounty white men had sometimes paid

For a red scalp—the going rate,
One hundred dollars per buck, fifty
Per woman, only twenty-five for a child's.

> A party of miners have returned to Owyhee from a raid on Indians with twenty scalps and some plunder. The miners are well.
>
> *The Portland* Oregonian

In the *North American Review,* Joseph's words,
Translated, were published—
The fraud of, the suffering of, his people, the lies,
The thoughts of his heart. Thousands, bored, read.
Some read, remembered. Felt their hearts stir.

VIII.

It took all the years. To the Northwest, but not Wallowa,
At last, honed down by the old torment and Time,
The people came. But on a reservation in Washington,
Joseph sits, can stir thence only by permit.

"They built me a house at Nespelem—
After many had died by the stinking river,
Where death rose on the air of evening
And bellies of dead fish float, bloated white,
In moonlight. In that stinking land we left
Our last dead. Did at last they dream of our mountains?
But mothers remember the names left there,
Still sacred in stink, and children
Remember the names that there sleep. The old
Who there sleep, sleep on the sweetest of pillows—the knowledge
Of what it is to be brave in your time. Their eyes
Fix on us as they lie in their darkness.

"They built me a house—me, a chief,
Who had lifted the death-tube, Winchester or Sharps,
And peered at the blue spot the sight leveled to
In nameless election. I slow squeezed trigger.
The blue spot was still.
For me, a chief—as though I were one
Of the white half-men who scratch in the ground
And at evening slop hogs. For me,
Who had lain on the prairie in starlight
And heard the coyote-wail of the far scout.

*

"No foot of mine ever crossed that doorsill.
I pitched my tepee on earth. I lay there.
At evening I stared at my camp-coals and wondered
If, snared in my error and weakness, I
Had managed at least some pinch of rightness. I prayed
That my father, whose eyes see all, and judge,
Might find some worth in an act of mine,
However slight.

"I sit, coals simmering,
A dying animal humped with no motion under
Darkness of skies that reach out forever
While forever stars spin what patterns
The Great Spirit's heart defines. I—
I only a dot in dimness—think
Of my father and yearn only
That he can think me a man
Worthy the work in dark of his loins.

"But what is a man? An autumn-tossed aspen,
Pony-fart in the wind, the melting of snow-slush?
Yes, that is all. Unless—unless—
We can learn to live the Great Spirit's meaning
As the old and wise grope for it.
And my heart swells when I remember
That day at Snake Creek when Miles surprised us,
And I, herding horses, no gun, ran,
Through bullet-song and scream of the hit ones,
Back to my tepee, but before
I touched, the slot had opened and my own
Wife's hand thrust forth the rifle, and only
One word came: *Fight.* Now all I remember
Is how her eyes gleam in dream-darkness, forever."

At night, coals wink from the heart of years,
But when he rises, the years fall away
Like leaves from a great oak in autumn to show
The indestructible structure.
To a height uncommon to men the head rises
In upward straightness, framed by braids fading,
The face like bronze hardened long back from the mold,
Nose thrusting, the thrust of jawbone, the downward
Decisive will-thrust of lips where they join
On each cheek-side. If you gaze at him,
Eyes you gaze into will seem but to show
The mirror of distance behind you, far,
And the mirror of Time that brings you both here,
And will, in time, part you forever.

Frozen, you stand in that moment of final assessment.

*

He is famous now. Great men have come
To shake his hand in his poverty.
Generals who chased him, ten to one,
With their fancy equipment, Gatling guns,
Artillery. Histories name him a genius.
And even Sherman, who never had fought him
But gave more death than ever his subordinate generals—
Yes, slime-green waters of Leavenworth—wrote:

> The Indians throughout displayed a courage and skill that elicited universal praise; they abstained from scalping; let captive women go free; and did not commit indiscriminate murders of peaceful families ... they fought with almost scientific skill.

Frontiersmen, land-grabbers, gold-panners were dead.
Veterans of the long chase skull-grinned in darkness.
A more soft-handed ilk now swayed the West. They founded
Dynasties, universities, libraries, shuffled
Stocks, and occasionally milked
The Treasury of the United States,
Not to mention each other. They slick-fucked a land.

But as their wealth grew, so Joseph's fame.
As the President's guest, in the White House,
He had shaken Roosevelt's hand. With Miles,
No longer a mere brigadier, he broke
Bread among crystal and silver. Back West
Artists came to commemorate for the future
That noble head. In bronze it was cast:

> In gallery 224 of the American wing of the Metropolitan Museum of Art, accession number 06.313, may be found the bronze portrait of 'Joseph, Chief of the Nez Perce Indians. His Indian name, Hin-mah-toó-yah-lat-kekht, is said to mean Thunder Rolling in the Mountains ... This medallion was taken from life in 1889. Bronze, diameter 17-1/2 in. Signed Olin L. Warner... '
>
> *American Sculpture Catalogue*
> *of the Collection of the Metropolitan*
> *Museum of Art, page 42*

Great honor came, for it came to pass
That to praise the red man was the way
Best adapted to expunge all, all, in the mist
Of bloodless myth. And in the predictably obscene
Procession to dedicate Grant's Tomb, which grandeur
Was now to hold the poor, noble dust of Appomattox,
Joseph, whose people had never taken
A scalp, rode beside Buffalo Bill—
Who had once sent his wife a yet-warm scalp,

He himself had sliced from the pate
Of a red man who'd missed him. Joseph rode
Beside Buffalo Bill, who broke clay pigeons—
One-two-three-four-five—just like that.

Joseph rode by the clown, the magician who could transform
For howling patriots, or royalty,
The blood of history into red ketchup,
A favorite American condiment. By his side
Joseph rode. Did Joseph know
Of the bloody scalp in love's envelope, know
That the dead Grant had once, in the White House,
In his own hand, certified the land
Of the Winding Waters to Joseph's people—
"Forever"—until some western politico, or such,
Jerked him by the nose, like a bull with a brass
Ring there for control?

Not right, not left,
Joseph looked, as hoofs on the cobbles clacked
In the dolor of that procession. He
Was only himself, and the distances
He stared into were only himself.

After all the years back at Nespelem,
In Washington, not the Land of the Winding Waters,
No right to move without written permission,
He wore the poor dress of his people. The great
War-bonnet, whose eagle feathers had gleamed in
Ceremonial grandeur, grander than life,
Lay locked in a box. Only twice
Permission was given him to go to the Winding Waters.

"The grave of my father lay in a land now tilled
By the white man who owned it, but had something human of heart.
No plowshare had wounded the earth where my father slept,
And the mercy of stones was piled to forbid.
I gazed at the stones. My eyes were dim.
I lifted my eyes that they might be washed
In the purity of the distance of mountains.
I thought of the purity of that poor man's heart."

Back at Nespelem, by the campfire,
Did Joseph wonder if the gaze of Old Joseph
Yet fixed on him?

At least, no sacred land had he ever sold.

At last, he said: "I shall see
But one more snow." Face painted, the body,
Adorned for its rank, awaited the shaman

To rise and speak, and lay the tall ghost.
The earthly possessions among friends were scattered.

But this not the end:
Next year at the second death-feast, Yellow Bull,
Now forking the dead hero's war-horse, rehearses
The tale and its greatness. The coffin
Is opened, and that face for the last time seen
By the Real People. But only by them. It is shut,
And thrust beneath the expensive monument
Of white generosity—that seizes all in the end.

More than twenty years passed before the Nimipu
Dug up what was left
Of Old Joseph still in the cornfield, and took it
To a shore of the Winding Waters, and there
Set up, in sight of snowy peaks, their stone. It was theirs.

This was all that remained them,
After Little Bear Paws and Snake Creek's bitter waters.

IX.

To Snake Creek, a century later, I came.

> La Guardia to O'Hare, American Airlines, October 9, 1981, Ticket 704 982 1454 4, Chicago. By Northwest to Great Falls. Met by two friends, Stuart Wright and David Quammen.

Out of Great Falls, north, in the Honda,
Out on the swell of infinite plains,
By wash or coulee here and there slashed,
Vacant of cattle, horse, man, the color
Gray-brown, the season October, not yet
Snowfall. Low ramparts of cloud, dark blue,
Hug the horizon westward like
A mountain range shrunken in distance,
But solid, supporting the arch of the sky.
Correspondingly eastward, the dark blue rampart
Is topped by a lacing of pale, pale gold,
Where sun lies in wait.

Springs forth, and distance
In all directions flees, devouring
The scraggle of villages dropped by history on
Route 87. Far off, a gold clump
Of cottonwood shows ranchstead or waterhole.
Sky shudders from blue to the apex of near-white. Onward,

*

We plunge, northeast, but in our minds see
Only one small black dot,
Which is the Honda creeping slow
Across a large map outspread. Next morning,
At a map-point called Chinook, southward we turn.
Tires now grind gravel. Right, west,
Plains swell to the sweep of arrogant skyline.
Now southwest, the skyline begins to rise, to heave, to crumple,
To darken. There, at last, are
The Little Bear Paw Mountains, lifting
In curves dulled by ages, but some, a few yet,
Snag angrily skyward, snow-smeared. Then eastward
They swing, suck the plain up in blueness. This
Is the hump that had once hidden Miles.

We turn left at the sign. There
Are the modest monuments. First,
A bronze plate, in stone set, and
In relief, a soldier (presumably Miles), and before him
An Indian, tall, half-naked, one arm lifted skyward,
And beneath, the words of Joseph:
"From where the sun now stands, I will fight
No more forever."

There is the map,
Large, enamel on metal, weatherproof:
Analysis of the action. And then,
The large bronze plate on granite propped
By the Republic to honor the name
Of every trooper who, in glory, had died here.

But the troopers who died here, who obediently died
For the ego of Miles, did not rot here. That final
Process was achieved with those who in Custer's
Dream died, when, at the Little Big Horn,
He at last had salted the tail of
That idiot phantasm of immortality.

The map shows here a mass grave
Where, no doubt, red flesh had rotted.
But not all the red flesh, for when the siege-line
Had tightened, and shells began lobbing in,
The Indians tried to dig caves for children,
The women, the old. So shells spared
Later some spade-work for blue-bellies.

You see the heaved earth, now mollified.

Snake Creek loops away, is hidden in thickets
Of last leaves of wild rose, now dusty crimson of leaf,
Branches studded with red hips. You tear through briars

Shoulder-high. Snake Creek is near-dry, only
A string of mossy-green puddles where Joseph,
In the same season,
Had once found water fresh for people and horse herd.

Beyond is the raised alluvial flat
Where tepees stood. There, southward, a steel pipe,
With marker screwed on, defines the spot
Of the tepee of Joseph.

If you climb the slope, say a mile and a half,
Or two, to the point where Miles must first
Have debouched from the Bear Paws, and look north,
You see what he saw—or what erosion has done.
Did he send his Cheyennes
To scout the lay, or did his star dance
In its passionate certainty? No,
Not the Cheyennes—to ruin surprise.
Northward, you see what you guess he saw
In his manic snatch for glory—the village,
The downward plain-sweep, swell and dip, swell and dip,
Cunt-open and panting, inviting the picture-book cavalry stroke.

Now, as you wander brown sage, you find
Steel pipes thrust in where each man died—
If he was white or of consequence.
There are markers screwed on with a name: *Poker Joe,*
Who knew the guile of the Yellowstone,
Ollokot, brother and warrior peerless,
And *Looking Glass,* war-chief, the cunning in council.
And names of the troopers, including the jokester
Captain Hale, who died in such weather.
And you find the spot marked where the buffalo robe
Once lay black on snow, and Howard, with what
Compassion or irony, gestured to Miles.

Alone on that last spot I stood, my friends
Now prowling and far on the high land. No snow
Now on brown grass or red leaf
Or black buffalo robe ceremonially swept
To its blackness. All
Now only a picture there in my head—

And there
He stands, the gray shawl showing
The four bullet holes, and hoofprints seen
In now hypothetical snow,
Marking the way he had come. I,
In fanatic imagination, saw—
No, see—the old weapon

Outthrust, firm in a hand that does not
Tremble. I see lips move, but
No sound hear.

I see him who in how many midnights
Had stood—what seasons?—while the susurrus
Of tribal sleep dies toward what stars,
While he, eyes fixed on what strange stars, knew
That eyes were fixed on him, eyes of
Those fathers that incessantly, with
The accuracy of that old Winchester, rifled
Through all, through darkness, distance, Time,
To know if he had proved a man, and being
A man, would make all those
Who now there slept know
Their own manhood.

He knew—could see afar, beyond all night—
Those ancient eyes, in which love and judgment
Hold equal glitter, and, with no blink,
Strove always toward him. And he—
He strove to think of things outside
Of Time, in some
Great whirling sphere, like truth unnamable. Thus—
Standing there, he might well,
Already in such midnight, have foreknown
The end.

But could not know that, after
The end, his own manhood, burnished
Only in the glow of his endless pity, would shine.

I saw
Vastness of plains lifting in twilight for
Winter's cold kiss, its absoluteness. Thought
Of the squirming myriads far at
My back. Then thought of the mayor
Of Spokane—whoever the hell he may have been.

But suddenly knew that for those sound
Of heart there is no ultimate
Irony. There is only
Process, which is one name for history. Often
Pitiful. But, sometimes, under
The scrutinizing prism of Time,
Triumphant.

I heard shouts of friends, closer.
Now soon they would go back, I too,
Into the squirming throng, faceless to facelessness,
And under a lower sky. But wondered,

Even so, if when the traffic light
Rings green, some stranger may pause and thus miss
His own mob's rush to go where the light
Says go, and pausing, may look,
Not into a deepening shade of canyon,
Nor, head now up, toward ice peak in moonlight white,
But, standing paralyzed in his momentary eternity, into
His own heart look while he asks
From what undefinable distance, years, and direction,
Eyes of fathers are suddenly fixed on him. To know.

I turned to my friend Quammen, the nearer. Called:
"It's getting night, and a hell of a way
To go." We went,
And did not talk much on the way.

Altitudes and Extensions

1980–1984

To our granddaughter, Katherine Penn Scully

Will ye not now after that life is descended down to you, will not you ascend up to it and live?

St. Augustine: Confessions,
Book IV, Chapter XII
Translated by William Watts

I.

Three Darknesses

I.

There is some logic here to trace, and I
Will try hard to find it. But even as I begin, I
Remember one Sunday morning, festal with springtime, in
The zoo of Rome. In a natural, spacious, grassy area,
A bear, big as a grizzly, erect, indestructible,
Unforgiving as God, as rhythmic as
A pile-driver—right-left, right-left—
Slugged at an iron door. The door,
Heavy, bolted, barred, must have been
The entrance to a dark enclosure, a cave,
Natural or artificial. Minute by minute, near, far,
Wheresoever we wandered, all Sunday morning,
With the air full of colored balloons trying to escape
From children, the ineluctable
Rhythm continues. You think of the
Great paws like iron on iron. Can iron bleed?
Since my idiot childhood the world has been
Trying to tell me something. There is something
Hidden in the dark. The bear
Was trying to enter into the darkness of wisdom.

II.

Up Black Snake River, at anchor in
That black tropical water, we see
The cormorant rise—cranky, graceless,
Ungeared, unhinged, one of God's more cynical
Improvisations, black against carmine of sunset. He
Beats seaward. The river gleams blackly west, and thus
The jungle divides on a milk-pale path of sky toward the sea.
Nothing human is visible. Each of us lies looking
Seaward. Ice melts in our glasses. We seem ashamed
Of conversation. Asia is far away. The radio is not on.
The grave of my father is far away. Our host
Rises silently, is gone. Later we see him,
White helmet in netting mystically swathed,
As he paddles a white skiff into the tangled
Darkness of a lagoon. There moss hangs. Later,
Dark now, we see the occasional stab of his powerful

Light back in the darkness of trunks rising
From the side lagoon, the darkness of moss suspended.
We think of the sound a snake makes
As it slides off a bough—the slop, the slight swish,
The blackness of water. You
Wonder what your host thinks about
When he cuts the light and drifts on the lagoon of midnight.
Though it is far from midnight. Upon his return,
He will, you know,
Lie on the deck-teak with no word. Your hostess
Had gone into the cabin. You hear
The pop of a wine cork. She comes back. The wine
Is breathing in darkness.

III.

The nurse is still here. Then
She is not here. You
Are here but are not sure
It is you in the sudden darkness. No matter.
A damned nuisance, but trivial—
The surgeon has just said that. A dress rehearsal,
You tell yourself, for
The real thing. Later. Ten years? Fifteen?
Tomorrow, only a dry run. At
5 A.M. they will come. Your hand reaches out in darkness
To the TV button. It is an old-fashioned western.
Winchester fire flicks white in the dream-night.
It has something to do with vice and virtue, and the vastness
Of moonlit desert. A stallion, white and flashing, slips,
Like spilled quicksilver, across
The vastness of moonlight. Black
Stalks of cacti, like remnants of forgotten nightmares, loom
Near at hand. Action fades into distance, but
You are sure that virtue will triumph. Far beyond
All the world, the mountains lift. The snow peaks
Float into moonlight. They float
In that unnamable altitude of white light. God
Loves the world. For what it is.

Mortal Limit

I saw the hawk ride updraft in the sunset over Wyoming.
It rose from coniferous darkness, past gray jags
Of mercilessness, past whiteness, into the gloaming
Of dream-spectral light above the last purity of snow-snags.

*

There—west—were the Tetons. Snow-peaks would soon be
In dark profile to break constellations. Beyond what height
Hangs now the black speck? Beyond what range will gold eyes see
New ranges rise to mark a last scrawl of light?

Or, having tasted that atmosphere's thinness, does it
Hang motionless in dying vision before
It knows it will accept the mortal limit,
And swing into the great circular downwardness that will restore

The breath of earth? Of rock? Of rot? Of other such
Items, and the darkness of whatever dream we clutch?

Immortality Over the Dakotas

It is not you that moves. It is the dark.
While you loll lax, semisomnolent, inside the great capsule,
Dark hurtles past. Now at the two-inch-thick plane-window glass,
You press your brow, see the furious
Futility of darkness boil past. It can't get in.
It is as though you were at last immortal.

You feel as though you had just had a quick dip
In the Lamb's mystic blood. You laugh into manic darkness.
You laugh at the tiny glow that far, far down
Shines like a glowworm beside an unseeable stone.
It would be a little Dakota town where
Population has not been dipped in the mystic blood.

On a July afternoon you once gassed up
At a town like that: movie, eatery, Baptist church
(Red brick), tourist court, white shotgun bungalows,
Wheat elevator towering over all.
Farms, of course, bleeding out forever.
Most likely the mercury stood at a hundred and one.

Now suddenly through glass, through dark fury, you see
Who must be down there, with collar up on the dirty sheepskin,
Snow on red hunter's cap, earflaps down.
Chores done. But he just can't bring himself to go in.
The doctor's just said he won't last till another winter.

She's sitting inside, white bun of hair neat as ever,
Squinting studiously down through bifocals at what she's knitting.
He knows her fire's getting low, but he can't go in.
He knows that if he did he might let something slip.
He couldn't stand that. So stares at the blackness of sky.
Stares at lights, green and red, that tread the dark of your immortality.

Caribou

Far, far southward, the forest is white, not merely
As snow of no blemish, but whiter than ice yet sharing
The mystic and blue-tinged, tangential moonlight,
Which in unshadowed vastness breathes northward.
Such great space must once
Have been a lake, now, long ages, ice-solid.

Shadows shift from the whiteness of forest, small
As they move on the verge of moon-shaven distance. They grow clear,
As binoculars find the hairline adjustment.
They seem to drift from the purity of forest.
Single, snow-dusted above, each shadow appears, each
Slowly detached from the white anonymity
Of forest, each hulk
Lurching, each lifted leg leaving a blackness as though
Of a broken snowshoe partly withdrawn. We know
That the beast's foot spreads like a snowshoe to support
That weight, that bench-kneed awkwardness.

The heads heave and sway. It must be with spittle
That jaws are ice-bearded. The shoulders
Lumber on forward, as though only the bones could, inwardly,
Guess destination. The antlers,
Blunted and awkward, are carved by some primitive craftsman.

We do not know on what errand they are bent, to
What mission committed. It is a world that
They live in, and it is their life.
They move through the world and breathe destiny.
Their destiny is as bright as crystal, as pure
As a dream of zero. Their destiny
Must resemble happiness even though
They do not know that name.

I lay the binoculars on the lap of the biologist. He
Studies distance. The co-pilot studies a map. He glances at
A compass. At mysterious dials. I drink coffee. Courteously,
The binoculars come back to me.

I have lost the spot. I find only blankness.

But
They must have been going somewhere.

The First Time

Northwest Montana, high country, and downward
The trail, not man-made, too narrow, with boughs
Snatching blue-jean thighs, stubs scraping
At boots. "Hold it!" Old Jack said. Said: "Look!" Backward
Pointed. "Hot elk-turd," he said. "Ain't too many now.
Next cattle come in, then folks, and next
All hellebaloo." Added: "Done come down
For water at sunset. Hold back."

We held.
And soon see upstream the sandbar,
Each elk walking out to its depth, each one
Standing calm in leg riffles, head bowed
Against current, the pale patch of rump
Showing clear in late light, a snort
Now and then, spray bright.

One great bull,
Six cows, one young. "Gal season," Old Jack says,
"Nigh now. Rounden up his take, but now
Just a starter—him the feller he is.
Just look at that rack ride his head in the river.
Now ain't he a pisser!"

The pisser
Heaves up the far bank. Then he, the great one,
Stands back as though to take count. "That rack,"
Jack says, "he'll git it all ready and polished afore
The first fool young he-elk cuts in."

Now,
All up the willows and scrub-brush, but yet
He waits, head erect, profiled
Against snow of a far range, dark bull-cape
Of shoulders now seeming much darker, architecture of antlers,
Above the last line of the far snow, now sharp against sky,
Balanced and noble, with prongs
Thrust into the bronze-red sky as though,
On prong-tangs, to sustain, in that bronze-tinged emptiness, the massive
Sun-ball of flame, now swathed slightly in blue. The sun
Has touched snow before he turns.

That night,
On a broad sand patch at the head of the sandbar, we camped.
I woke in the night, at some distant howl. I saw
Stars immensely reflected in the quiet water. I had never seen
A bull wapiti, wild, before—the
Great head lifted in philosophic

Arrogance against
God's own sky.

Minnesota Recollection

By 3 P.M. the pat of snow-pads had begun
To cling to the windowpane, and in the old kitchen,
Daylight already a dream of dying, the color
Of water sloshed in a used milk can to clean
It. The hired girl
Shook each tin lamp to find it full, or

No. "Not dark as this," Old Grammy, in his musical tangle of
Never-learned English and quite unforgotten Swedish,
Said, "when it took all
We was to haul Old Ma down to the kitchen so
She could die more cheerful, not grave-cold
Between the sheets, and her not yet gone dead."
Who wants to die in a bed already
Colder than frozen ground they'll have to take
Pickaxes to get you into?

Sudden Old Sugfred—Grammy—was gone, or seemed so:
Like sometimes he could be so still, like not there, but
Now two tin lamps were lit, and you could see. He might
Just step outside to the call of nature, and once out,
See snowflakes falling, falling, and ponder on it a half-hour,
Making no move, sunk deep in the world, like a part
Of God's own world, a post, a bare tree, dung heap, or stone.
Gone to the barn, they guessed. *Yes, somebody's got to do it.*
Yeah, cattle's got rights, and if you got cattle,
They's due to be fed and bedded, and the old ax-butt
To bust the ice on the drinking trough.

They piled more wood, heard the clock say what
It would be saying till Earth's last breath: *tick*-and-*tock.*
But what they heard wasn't what they hoped to hear.
Somebody saw the new lantern on its nail.
Done took an old one, Gertie thought. *Or took*
His toy. The big flashlight—they called it that,
He loved it so. Then Gertie gone, soon back,
One hand holding an old lantern, lighted, the other
Old Grammy's toy—but it dead
As a monstrous catfish eye. He'd played
With it too much. No word she said, just screamed.
Her mackinaw just half-jerked on, and screaming, she
Ran out. They did not seem to hear. But felt
It in their throats. The scream
Ran out the open door, darker

Than Death. They lighted lanterns, both lanterns,
Then ran, somebody with the new one. Somebody
Stopped to shut the door. Somebody's
Got to think of that.

In the barn nobody. Ice not cracked. Then outside—
But what are lanterns in a world so wide! Somebody
Fell, and something's broken, one last flare. Worse—
Who could see the window now?
They scattered, trying to see, calling, calling
The name they searched for, or
Simply calling as though the window had a voice to answer.
And suddenly another lantern's gone. It's dry.

If there's one spot, however frail, yet left of hope—
But what can a last lantern do? Oh, the world is wide.
They tried to make a chain of calls, a rope
To hold the human hope together. Oh, why
Is darkness from white snow the darkest thing yet?
Somebody fell in slack blackness. It must
Have felt like a gift. Will tomorrow be
Like today? And was today so goddamned sweet?

Just tell me that.

But suddenly a call again. In last despair?
But then one more. And more, until
The human chain's about to fill the night,
With throats blood-washed and foaming
As the breathed air is knife-edge to suffering past grief.

Then one last call. "The window!"—it said, or seemed to say.
So voices again picked up
The gnarled, untwisting length of rope
Of human hope.

Back at the house one last log faintly glowed.
More wood. Then each sits as before.
Till Gertie screams, tries to run.
They held her down. Then all sit as before.
But one. But he—he fills their heads all night.
He filled the room.

***

By first flame of the prairie dawn they found him.
Snagged on a barbed-wire fence that he'd
Followed the wrong way, hearing no voices, maybe.
At least a mile. His face was calm.
It had, you might say, an innocent expression.

Arizona Midnight

The grief of the coyote seems to make
Stars quiver whiter over the blankness which
Is Arizona at midnight. In sleeping-bag,
Protected by the looped rampart of anti-rattler horsehair rope,
I take a careful twist, grinding sand on sand,
To lie on my back. I stare. Stars quiver, twitch,
In their infinite indigo. I know
Nothing to tell the stars, who go,
Age on age, along tracks they understand, and
The only answer I have for the coyote would be
My own grief, for which I have no
Tongue—indeed, scarcely understand.
Eastward, I see
No indication of dawn, not yet ready for the scream
Of inflamed distance,
Which is the significance of day.
But dimly I do see
Against that darkness, lifting in blunt agony,
The single great cactus. Once more I hear the coyote
Wail. I strain to make out the cactus. It has
Its own necessary beauty.

Far West Once

Aloud, I said, with a slight stir of heart,
"The last time"—and thought, years thence, to a time
When only in memory I might
Repeat this last tramp up the shadowy gorge
In the mountains, cabinward, the fall
Coming on, the aspen leaf gold, sun low
At the western end of the gun-barrel passage
Waiting, waiting the trigger-touch
And the blast of darkness—the target me.

I said, "I'll try to remember as much
As a man caught in Time cannot forget,"
For I carried a headful of summer, and knew
That I'd never again, in the gloaming, walk
Up that trail, now lulled by the stone-song of waters;
Nor again on path pebbles, noon-plain, see
The old rattler's fat belly twist and distend
As it coiled, and the rattles up from dust rise
To vibrate mica-bright, in the sun's beam;
Nor again, from below, on the cliff's over-thrust,
Catch a glimpse of the night-crouching cougar's eyes
That, in my flashlight's strong beam, had burned

Coal-bright as they swung,
Detached, contemptuous, and slow,
Into the pine woods' mounting mass
Of darkness that, eventually,
Ahead, would blot out, star by star,
The slot of the sky-slice that now I
Moved under, and on to dinner and bed.

And to sleep—and even in sleep to feel
The nag and pretensions of day dissolve
And flow away in that musical murmur
Of waters; then to wake in dark with some strange
Heart-hope, undefinable, verging to tears
Of happiness and the soul's calm.

How long ago! But in years since,
On other trails, in the shadow of
What other cliffs, in lands with names
Crank on the tongue, I have felt my boots
Crush gravel, or press the soundlessness
Of detritus of pine or fir, and heard
Movement of water, far, how far—

Or waking under nameless stars,
Have heard such redemptive music, from
Distance to distance threading starlight,
Able yet, as long ago,
Despite scum of wastage and scab of years,
To touch again the heart, as though at a dawn
Of dew-bright Edenic promise, with,
Far off, far off, in verdurous shade, first birdsong.

II.

Rumor at Twilight

Rumor at twilight of whisper, crepuscular
Agitation, from no quarter defined, or something
Like the enemy fleet below the horizon, in
Its radio blackout, unobserved. In a dark cave,
Dark fruit, bats hang. Droppings
Of generations, soft underfoot, would carpet the gravel—
That is, if you came there again. Have you ever felt,
Between thumb and forefinger, texture
Of the bat's wing? Their hour soon comes.

You stand in the dark, under the maples, digesting
Dinner. You have no particular
Financial worries, just nags. Your children
Seem to respect you. Your wife is kind. Fireflies
Punctuate the expensive blackness of shrubbery,
Their prickling glows—here, there—like the phosphorescent
Moments of memory when, in darkness, your head first
Dents the dark pillow, eyes wide, ceilingward.
Can you really reconstruct your mother's smile?

You stand in the dark, heart even now filling, and think of
A boy who, drunk with the perfume of elder blossoms
And the massiveness of moonrise, stood
In a lone lane, and cried out,
In a rage of joy, to seize, and squeeze, significance from,
What life is, whatever it is. Now
High above the maples the moon presides. The first bat
Mathematically zigzags the stars. You fling down
The cigarette butt. Set heel on it. It is time to go in.

Old Dog Dead

1.

Cocker. English. Fifteen years old. Tumor
Of testes. Vet promising nothing. So did it.

Inevitable, but inevitable, too, the
Recollection of the first time, long back,
Seen—puppy-whirl
Of flopping forepaws, flopping ears oversize, stub
Tail awag, eyes bright. And brighter yet,

Dancing in joy-light, the eyes
Of a little girl with her new love. Holding
It up to show. That was what my eyes, open in darkness,
Had now just seen.

And what, no doubt, the eyes now closed beside me
Had, too, been seeing in darkness. With no confirmation needed
To pass between. And now
That breath beside me was at last
Even in sleep. I thought of the possible time
When evenness—in what ears?—
Might be of silence
Only.

Fingering familiar dark, I made
My way out.

2.

Boots on, pullover over
Night shirt, on shoulders camp blanket,
Barberry-ripped—whatever
Came handy in anteroom. Then,
I was standing in starlight, moon
Long since behind the mountain, mountain blackness at my back.
On mossed stone sitting, I, streamward,
Stare, intent
On the stream's now messageless murmur of motion.

The stars are high-hung, clearly
Defined in night's cloudlessness,
But here, below, identity blurred
In the earth-bound waver of water.

Upward again I look. See Jupiter, contemptuous,
Noble, firmly defined,
The month being June, the place Vermont.

3.

I shut eyes and see what
I had not in actuality seen—the
Raw earth, red clay streaked with
Black of humus under
The tall pine, anonymous in
The vet's woodlot.

*

Will I ever go back there? Absurdly,
I think I might go and put, stuck in the clay,
A stone—any stone large enough. No word, just something
To make a change, however minute,
In the structure of the universe.

4.

I think of Pharaoh's
Unblinking gaze across
Sands endless.

If we can think of timelessness, does it exist?

5.

Now Jupiter, southwest, beyond the sagging black spur
Of the mountain, in the implacable
Mathematics of a planet,
Has set. Tell me,
Is there a garden where
The petal, dew-kissed, withereth not?
And where, in darkness, beyond what bramble and flint,
Would iron gate, on iron hinge, move without sound?

Far off, a little girl, little no longer, would,
If yet she knew,
Lie in her bed and weep
For what life is.

6.

Who will be the last to remember tonight?

Perhaps, far off, long later, an old woman,
Who once was the child,
Now alone, waking before dawn to fumble for
Something she painfully knows but cannot lay hand to, in
The unlabeled detritus and trash of Time.

Hope

In the orchidaceous light of evening
Watch how, from the lowest hedge-leaf, creeps,
Grass blade to blade, the purpling shadow. It spreads
Its spectral ash beneath the leveling, last
Gold rays that, westward, have found apertures
From the magnificent disaster of the day.

Against gold light, beneath the maple leaf,
A pale blue gathers, accumulates, sifts
Downward to modulate the flowery softness
Of gold intrusive through the blackening spruce boughs.
Spruces heighten the last glory beyond by their stubbornness.
They seem rigid in blackened bronze.

Wait, wait—as though a finger were placed to lips.
The first star petals timidly in what
Is not yet darkness. That audacity
Will be rewarded soon. In this transitional light,
While cinders in the west die, the world
Has its last blooming. Let your soul

Be still. All day it has curdled in your bosom
Denatured by intrusion of truth or lie, or both.
Lay both aside, nor debate their nature. Soon,
While not even a last bird twitters, the last bat goes.
Even the last motor fades into distance. The promise
Of moonrise will dawn, and slowly, in all fullness, the moon

Will dominate the sky, the world, the heart,
In white forgiveness.

Why You Climbed Up

Where, vomit-yellow, the lichen crawls
Up the boulder, where the rusty needle
Falls from the pine to pad earth's silence
Against what intrusive foot may come, you come—
But come not knowing where or why.
Like substance hangs the silence of
The afternoon. Look—you will see
The tiny glint of the warbler's eye, see
The beak, half-open, in still heat gasp, see
Moss on a cliff, where water oozes.

*

Where or why,
You wonder, wandering, with sweat and pant,
Up the mountain's heave and clamber,
As though to forget and leave
All things, great and small, you call
The past, all things, great and small, you call
The Self, and remember only how once
In the moonlit Pacific you swam west, hypnotized
By stroke on stroke, the rhythm that
Filled all the hollow head and was
The only self you carried with you then.

What brought you back?
You can't remember now,
And do not guess that years from now you may not remember
How once—now—on this high ridge, seeing
The sun blaze down on the next and higher horizon,
You turned, and bumbled for some old logging road
To follow, stumbling, down.

Then all begins again. And you are you.

Literal Dream

(Twenty Years After Reading Tess *and*
Without Ever Having Seen Movie)

You know the scene. You read it in a book.
But did not see what I saw when,
Last night, unseen, I sat, and saw
The bare and tidy room, gone chilly too,
In its English respectability of straitened means.
She rocked in her chair, the old lady,
Bifocals, hair in a bun, neat, gray-streaked, the only
Sound the click of the knitting needles. She
So sat, alone, not seeing me, probably
Just seeing the empty chair I sat in, breath
Soundless. If there was breath. Do we,
Under such circumstances, breathe? When,
Transparent, we sit? She rocked and thought.

Oh, I could read her like the book I'd read!
How handy now came the paying guests
In the room upstairs. A widow
Has to cut her corners when she can.
I knew what she'd picked up. I waited.
Watched. It seemed she'd never look up and see
What I knew she'd see up there. But according to
The law of such circumstances, I
Could not look up until she did. She did.

*

She saw the ceiling spot. Ignored it. Looked
Again. Now bigger, darker, growing, it was
On paint, on whitewash, on paper, whatever
The ceiling was. I can't remember, but
Remember it growing slow, so slow. Her eyes,
They widened in hypnotic slowness.
Her breath, it didn't come until
The stain on her neat ceiling gathered to a
Point.
Which hung forever.
Dropped.

How long would it now take for the tremble
Of finger to sharpen into the instrument
To touch
The spot now on the clean floor? It seemed
Forever. The knitting needles first,
Then the ball of wool, unnoticed, dropped. And then,
The finger, sharpening in massive will,
Suddenly not quivering,
Touched.

It rose.

How slow, how unbelieving, head
Shaking on frail stem of neck, she
Stared.

Her mouth had now made the shape of an *O*.
But no sound came. I stared to see
The shape of sound. It was not there.

I could not make out the color of the stained finger.
But knew. I knew because I'd read the book.
But the blind swirl of eyeless cloud,
Tattered, black-streaked,
In which, that instant, I was up-whirled,
Was in no book, nor ever had been, nor
Such terror.

I woke at the call of nature. It was near day.
Patient I sat, staring through the
Wet pane at sparse drops that struck
The last red dogwood leaves. It was as though
I could hear the plop there. See the leaf quiver.

After the Dinner Party

You two sit at the table late, each, now and then,
Twirling a near-empty wine glass to watch the last red
Liquid climb up the crystalline spin to the last moment when
Centrifugality fails: with nothing now said.

What is left to say when the last logs sag and wink?
The dark outside is streaked with the casual snowflake
Of winter's demise, all guests long gone home, and you think
Of others who never again can come to partake

Of food, wine, laughter, and philosophy—
Though tonight one guest has quoted a killing phrase we owe
To a lost one whose grin, in eternal atrophy,
Now in dark celebrates some last unworded jest none can know.

Now a chair scrapes, sudden, on tiles, and one of you
Moves soundless, as in hypnotic certainty,
The length of table. Stands there a moment or two,
Then sits, reaches out a hand, open and empty.

How long it seems till a hand finds that hand there laid,
While ash, still glowing, crumbles, and silence is such
That the crumbling of ash is audible. Now naught's left unsaid
Of the old heart-concerns, the last, tonight, which

Had been of the absent children, whose bright gaze
Over-arches the future's horizon, in the mist of your prayers.
The last log is black, while ash beneath displays
No last glow. You snuff candles. Soon the old stairs

Will creak with your grave and synchronized tread as each mounts
To a briefness of light, then true weight of darkness, and then
That heart-dimness in which neither joy nor sorrow counts.
Even so, one hand gropes out for another, again.

Doubleness in Time

Doubleness coils in Time like
The bull-snake in fall's yet-leafed growth. *Then*
Uncoils like *Now. Now*
Like *Then.* Oh, it
Was long ago—the years, how many?
Fifty—but now at last it truly
Happens. Only *Now.* Her eyes,

*

From one to another of those who
Stand by, move. You hear,
Almost, the grind in the socket.
The face fixes on each face, and for
Each face constructs
A smile. You hear,
Almost, the grind of the smile
Being manufactured, bit by bit. You hear
The grind of love.

You hear the grind of the smile as you try to smile.

Her eyes, after each effort, fix
On the ceiling of white plaster above them. The pink
Of sunset tints the ceiling. I stare
At the ceiling. It is Infinity.

It roofs all Time.

From his vest pocket the doctor draws
Out the old-fashioned gold-cased watch.
You hear the click as it opens.
Your heart stands still as a stone.
He holds her pulse.

He nods. Slowly. Slowly.

My father, that tall, thin man,
Head sculptured bald and white as marble,
Great Roman nose—he moves first.
He leans above the waiting upturned face.
Lips are laid—you know they are cold—to lips.
Hand touches hand.
I am seeing that *Now.*

By downward age, each child there repeats the act.
The youngest last.

The door opens. Is shut.
The doctor remains within. The nurse
Is no more than an advertising dummy
In a store window.

The little boy in the hall lingers last, is lost.
"Oh, I'm by myself," his voice cries out.

To the waiting room the boy comes.
No word. My father
Sits rigid on a bench. His loneliness
Is what he seems to insist on. As though
He were stone, white stone beneath dark cloth.

It is as though an antique statue,
Exhumed after centuries, were
In modern costume dressed. Why
Didn't I laugh *Then?* I
Feel like laughing *Now.*

His eyes show nothing.
Like stone, too.

The doctor comes in. Nods.

Soundlessly, as though from an ax-butt
Set sudden to temple, the tall man falls
Rigid. Sidewise.

His daughter stoops to hold his rigid hand.

At last, he kisses her hand. Rises:
Face severe, nose out-thrust. Eyes
Glittering, cold.
In dignity shakes hands with the doctor.
Joins him in the hall.

I stand on the gravel of the parking lot, alone.
It is not *Then.*
It is *Now.* For it
Has taken a long time for Truth to become true.

It is autumn, *Now* as *Then,* and the stars
Have begun their wintry tingle.
The moon is full, white, but
Westering above black roofs
Of the little city.
People live there.

I stare at the moon,
And wonder why it has never moved all these years.
I do not know why, nor know
Why my grief has not been understood, nor why
It has not understood its own being.

It takes a long time for it to learn
Its many names: like
Selfishness and *Precious Guilt.*

Snowfall

The whiteness of silence, in silence of squadrons
Of cottony hooves, no creaking of stirrup, no steel-flash—
Over my western hill the white cavalry comes
To blot the last dying crimson that outlines the slope.
Was there a bugle? Or only wind in the spruces?
In the world what music may be that we cannot hear?

Years pass, and always so much to remember, forget: the first
Green to spring in green turf advertising
Earth's old immortality; the first
Whistle of blackbirds, or redwings, arriving,
Numberless, bubbling with music and sperm;
The first time your young face, shame-flushed, looked away
As she leaned hard against the fence-palings between you,
And pressed her new breasts to rise up.

Try hard to remember her name. What was it?
Try hard to remember the eye-gleam, the charming stupidity.

Think how slow was one afternoon's summer swell—
Like swelling of grape, apple, plum—as you lay alone on the hill,
And only the pure opalescence of sky
Filled eye and heart, and all you needed to know
Was the voicelessness you then lay in. But
Afternoons end. But later, remember
The hand you held in late shadow of beeches,
At the hour when no bird-call again comes.

Remember, remember "goodbye" on the station platform—and
Goodbye slips away like a snake in weed-tangle,
For the world is wide and has many phases and faces,
And the end of each summer is autumn's fruit.
What year will you know the fruit that is yourself?

The autumn bough bends with weight glossy and red.
The fat grape bleeds on the tongue, juice and pulp seeking
The throat's dark joy. You will walk again where chestnuts fall,
Dreaming that you, years back, a child, were happy there.

Meanwhile, far north in Vermont
Maples burn in last gold. When leaves fall the gray
Mountain ledges are noble. Deer
Graze where they now can. The bear
Will soon sleep with no dream. The trivial
Snow-swirl now there settles to business, the wind
Rises. Mantled in white,
Southward, two states, it strikes all the miles to the Sound,
Where, as you walk the salt-crusted sand, snowflakes
Die on the bay-swirl of small whitecaps.

*

And salt-crusted sand, under bootsole, creaks.

You do not remember what year was the first,
For many a year has passed. But now, again hillward,
Comes silence of cottony hooves, the wheeling of squadrons,
That tramp out last embers of day, and you

Stand in the darkness of whiteness
Which is the perfection of Being.

III.

New Dawn

To John Hersey and Jacob Lawrence

I. Explosion: Sequence and Simultaneity

Greenwich Time	11:16 P.M.	August 5	1945
New York Time	6:16 P.M.	August 5	1945
Chicago Time	5:16 P.M.	August 5	1945
San Francisco Time	3:16 P.M.	August 5	1945
Pearl Harbor Time	1:16 P.M.	August 5	1945
Tinian Island Time	9:16 A.M.	August 6	1945
Hiroshima Time	8:16 A.M.	August 6	1945

II. Goodbye to Tinian

Now that all the "unauthorized items" are cleared from the bomber, including
The optimistic irrelevance of six packs
Of condoms, and three pairs of
Pink silk panties. Now that
The closed briefing session of midnight
Is over, with no information from Colonel Tibbets, commander, on the
Secret, obsessive question of every crewman—What
Is the cargo? From Tibbets only
That it is "very powerful." Now that
The crew, at the end of the briefing,
Have taken what comfort they can from the prayer
Of their handsome chaplain, a man's man of
Rich baritone—"Almighty Father,
Who wilt hear the prayer of them that love Thee,
We pray Thee to be with those
Who brave the heights
Of Thy heaven..."

And now that around the bomber the klieg lights
Murdering darkness, the flashbulbs, the barking
Of cameramen, the anonymous faces preparing to be famous,
The nag of reporters, the handshakes, the jokes,
The manly embraces,
The scrape of city shoes on asphalt, the tarmac,
The news
From weather scouts out that clouds hovering over
The doomed world will, at dawn,
Probably clear. And,

*

Now down to brass tacks, Lewis,
The flawless co-pilot,
Addresses the crew, "... just don't
Screw it up. Let's do this really great!"

III. Take-off: Tinian Island

Colonel Tibbets, co-pilot beside him,
Lays hand to controls of the plane, which he
Has named for his mother, Enola Gay.

Pocketed secretly in Tibbets' survival vest,
Under the pale green coverall, is the
Metal container of twelve capsules of cyanide,
These for distribution to command if facing capture.

Though a heavy-caliber sidearm would serve.

The tow jeep strains at the leash. Wheels,
Under the weight of 150,000 pounds,
Overweight 15,000, crunch
Off the apron, bound for the runway. Position taken.

"This is Dimples Eighty-two to
North Tinian Tower. Ready for
Takeoff instructions."

So that is her name now. At least in code. Dimples.

"Tower to Dimples Eighty-two. Clear
To taxi. Take off Runway A, for Able."

At 2:45 A.M., August 6, Tinian Time,
Tibbets to Lewis:
"Let's go!"

All throttles full,
She roars down the runway, flicking past
Avenues of fire trucks, ambulances, overload
The last gamble, the runway
Now spilling furiously toward
Black sea-embrace.

Who would not have trusted the glittering record of Tibbets?

*

But even Lewis cries out. Grabs at controls. Tibbets,
Gaze fixed, hears nothing. Time
Seems to die. But
Iron hands, iron nerves, tighten at last, and
The control is drawn authoritatively back. The carriage
Rises to show
The air-slick belly where death sleeps.

This at cliff-verge.

Below, white, skeletal hands of foam
Grope up. Strain up.

Are empty.

IV. Mystic Name

Some 600 miles north-northwest to Iwo Jima, where,
In case of defect developing in the *Enola Gay,*
Tibbets will land, transfer cargo to
The waiting standby plane,
And take over. If not necessary,
No landing, but he will rendezvous
With weather planes and two B-29's
To fly with him as observers.

At 3 A.M., well short of Iwo Jima, code lingo
To Tinian Tower: "Judge going to work"—
To announce innocently the arming
Of the cargo. The cargo,
Inert as a sawed-off tree trunk ten feet long,
Twenty-eight inches in diameter, four and a half tons in weight, lies
In its dark covert.

It is
So quiet, so gentle as it rocks
In its dark cradle, in namelessness. But some
Name it "The Beast," and some,
With what irony, "Little Boy." Meanwhile,
It sleeps, with its secret name
And nature.

Like the dumb length of tree trunk, but literally
A great rifle barrel packed with uranium,
Two sections, forward one large, to rear one small, the two
Divided by a "tamper" of neutron-resistant alloy.
All harmless until, backed by vulgar explosive, the small will
Crash through to

The large mass
To wake it from its timeless drowse. And that
Will be that. Whatever
That may be.

V. When?

When can that be known? Only after
The delicate and scrupulous fingers of "Judge"
Have done their work. After:

1. Plugs, identified by the color green,
   Are installed in waiting sockets
2. Rear plate is removed
3. Armor plate is removed
4. Breech wrench frees breech plug
5. Breech plug is placed on rubber mat
6. Explosive charge is reinserted,
   Four units, red ends to breech
7. Breech plug is reinserted, tightened home
8. Firing line is connected
9. Armor plate is reinstalled
10. Rear plate is reinstalled
11. Tools are removed
12. Catwalk is secured

In that dark cramp of tunnel, the precise
Little flashlight beam
Finicks, fastidious, over all.

Soft feet withdraw.

Later, 6:30 A.M. Japanese Time, last lap to target, green plugs
On the log, with loving care, tenderly, quietly
As a thief, will be replaced by plugs marked
Lethally red.

VI. Iwo Jima

Over Iwo Jima, the moon, now westering, sinks in faint glimmer
Of horizon clouds. Soon
The heartbreaking incandescence of tropic dawn,
In which the *Enola Gay* loiters for contact
With weather scouts and the two B-29's
Which rise to attend her: observers.

Weather reports good from spotters.
Three options: Nagasaki, Kokura, Hiroshima.

But message of one spotter:
"Advise bombing primary"—i.e.,
Hiroshima.

Already preferred by Tibbets.

What added satisfaction it would have been to know that
At 7:31 A.M. Japanese Time, the
All Clear signal sounds over Hiroshima.

VII. Self and Non-Self

Tibbets looks down, sees
The slow, gray coiling of clouds, which are,
Beyond words, the image
Of sleep just as consciousness goes. He looks up, sees
Stars still glaring white down into
All the purity of emptiness. For an instant,
He shuts his eyes.

Shut
Your own eyes, and in timelessness you are
Alone with yourself. You are
Not certain of identity.
Has that non-self lived forever?

Tibbets jerks his eyes open. There
Is the world.

VIII. Dawn

Full dawn comes. Movement begins
In the city below. People
May even copulate. Pray. Eat. The sun
Offers its circular flame, incomparable,
Worship-worthy.

IX. The Approach

Speed 200 miles per hour, altitude
31,060 feet, directly toward the
Target control point of Aioi Bridge. On time. On
Calculation. Polaroid glasses
(Against brilliance of expected explosion)
Ordered on. Color
Of the world changes. It
Changes like a dream.

X. What *That* Is

What clouds remain part now, magically,
And there visible, sprawling supine, unfended, the city.
The city opens itself, opening
As in breathless expectancy.

Crossed hairs of bombsight approach
Aioi Bridge as specified, on time
For the target. Ferebee, bombardier, presses
Forehead devoutly to the cushion of bombsight.
Says,"I've got it."

The bomb is activated:
Self-controlled for the six-mile earthward
Plunge—and at that instant the plane,
Purged of its burden, leaps upward,
As though in joy, and the bomb
Will reach the calculated optimum of distance
Above ground, 1,890
Feet, the altitude determined
By the bomb's own delicate brain.

There,
The apocalyptic blaze of
New dawn

Bursts.

Temperature at heart of fireball:
50,000,000 degrees centigrade.

Hiroshima Time: 8:16 A.M., August 6, 1945.

XI. Like Lead

Of that brilliance beyond brilliance, Tibbets
Was later to report: "A taste like lead."

XII. Manic Atmosphere

Now, after the brilliance,
Suddenly, blindly, the plane
Heaves, is tossed
Like a dry leaf in
The massive and manic convulsion of
Atmosphere, which, compressed, from
Earth, miles down,

Bounces.

The plane recovers.

Again, then, the heave, the tossing.

With recovery.

XIII. Triumphal Beauty

Now, far behind, from the center of
The immense, purple-streaked, dark mushroom that, there, towers
To obscure whatever lies below,
A plume, positive but delicate as a dream,
Of pure whiteness, unmoved by breath of any wind,
Mounts.

Above the dark mushroom,
It grows high—high, higher—
In its own triumphal beauty.

XIV. Home

Later, home. Tinian is man's only home—
The brotherly hug, the bear-embrace, the glory, and
"We made it!"

The music, then solemn
Silence of the pinning of the medal,
The mutual salute. At last,
The gorging of the gorgeous feast
To the point of vomit, the slosh
Of expensive alcohol
In bellies expensively swollen.

XV. Sleep

Some men, no doubt, will, before sleep, consider
One thought: I am alone. But some,
In the mercy of God, or booze, do not

Long stare at the dark ceiling.

IV.

The Distance Between: Picnic of Old Friends

In innocence, and nothing much to remember,
They wandered the green woodland lane,
All others behind them, friends, husband, wife,
And small children who sang
Beside the small tumult of white, singing water,
The picnic now over. They wandered
Deeper and deeper, in purposelessness,
Drifting like breath, more aimless and aimless, old words
Repeating old episodes, old shadows, the drift
Of childhood and years, all the shadowy
Uncoil of Time. All this—

While higher the sky now seemed to withdraw,
And higher rose beeches, then pines.
Till calmly they came
To the glen, where moss-streaked and noble, great cliffs
From ferns rose, and no bird sang. Ten feet
Apart they stopped. Stood. Each fearing
The sudden silence too much to lift eyes.

Of a sudden, she stared. Watched that face, stark and strange, moving,
Through distance, at her.

No resistance: seizure, penetration.

She sat in the rich, sap-bleeding, wild tangle of fern, and wept.
He stood by a beech, some twenty feet off, head down.

After what repair seemed possible, back they wandered,
The path and the world all strange, infinite
The distance between them.

At last, to the others, now starlit, they straggled, straggling
Toward song in the distance.

They tried to sing, too.

True Love

In silence the heart raves. It utters words
Meaningless, that never had
A meaning. I was ten, skinny, red-headed,

Freckled. In a big black Buick,
Driven by a big grown boy, with a necktie, she sat
In front of the drugstore, sipping something

Through a straw. There is nothing like
Beauty. It stops your heart. It
Thickens your blood. It stops your breath. It

Makes you feel dirty. You need a hot bath.
I leaned against a telephone pole, and watched.
I thought I would die if she saw me.

How could I exist in the same world with that brightness?
Two years later she smiled at me. She
Named my name. I thought I would wake up dead.

Her grown brothers walked with the bent-knee
Swagger of horsemen. They were slick-faced.
Told jokes in the barbershop. Did no work.

Their father was what is called a drunkard.
Whatever he was he stayed on the third floor
Of the big white farmhouse under the maples for twenty-five years.

He never came down. They brought everything up to him.
I did not know what a mortgage was.
His wife was a good, Christian woman, and prayed.

When the daughter got married, the old man came down wearing
An old tail coat, the pleated shirt yellowing.
The sons propped him. I saw the wedding. There were

Engraved invitations, it was so fashionable. I thought
I would cry. I lay in bed that night
And wondered if she would cry when something was done to her.

The mortgage was foreclosed. That last word was whispered.
She never came back. The family
Sort of drifted off. Nobody wears shiny boots like that now.

But I know she is beautiful forever, and lives
In a beautiful house, far away.
She called my name once. I didn't even know she knew it.

Last Walk of Season

For the last time, for this or perhaps
Any year to come in unpredictable life, we climb,
In the westward hour, up the mountain trail
To see the last light. Now
No cloud in the washed evening lours,
Though, under drum-tight roof, while each minute's
Mouse-tooth all night gnawed,
The season's first rain had done duty. Dams and traps,
Where the old logging trucks had once made tracks, now gurgle. That
Is the only voice we hear. We do not ask
What burden that music bears.

Our wish is to think of nothing but happiness. Of only
The world's great emptiness. How bright,
Rain-washed, the pebbles shine! A few high leaves
Of birch have golden gone. Ah, the heart leaps
That soon all earth will be of gold:
Gold birch, gold beech, gold maple. That
Is its own delight. Later, nothing visible
Except black conifers will clamber
Up the first white of ridge, then the crag's blank sun-blaze of snow.
Can it be that the world is but the great word
That speaks the meaning of our joy?

We came where we had meant to come. And not
Too late. In the mountain's cup, moraine-dammed, the lake
Lies left by a glacier older than God. Beyond it, the sun,
Ghostly, dips, flame-huddled in mist. We undertake
Not to exist, except as part of that one
Existence. We are thinking of happiness. In such case,
We must not count years. For happiness has no measurable pace.
Scarcely in consciousness, a hand finds, on stone, a hand.

They are in contact. Past lake, over mountain, last light
Probes for contact with the soft-shadowed land.

V.

Old-Time Childhood in Kentucky

When I was a boy I saw the world I was in.
I saw it for what it was. Canebrakes with
Track beaten down by bear paw. Tobacco,
In endless rows, the pink inner flesh of black fingers
Crushing to green juice tobacco worms plucked
From a leaf. The great trout,
Motionless, poised in the shadow of his
Enormous creek-boulder.
But the past and the future broke on me, as I got older.

Strange, into the past I first grew. I handled the old bullet-mold.
I drew out a saber, touched an old bayonet, I dreamed
Of the death-scream. Old spurs I tried on.
The first great General Jackson had ridden just north to our state
To make a duel legal—or avoid the law.
It was all for honor. He said: "I would have killed him
Even with his hot lead in my heart." This for honor. I longed
To understand. I said the magic word.
I longed to say it aloud, to be heard.

I saw the strategy of Bryce's Crossroads, saw
The disposition of troops at Austerlitz, but knew
It was far away, long ago. I saw
The marks of the old man's stick in the dust, heard
The old voice explaining. His eyes weren't too good,
So I read him books he wanted. Read him
Breasted's *History of Egypt.* Saw years uncoil like a snake.
I built a pyramid with great care. There interred
Pharaoh's splendor and might.
Excavation next summer exposed that glory to man's sight.

At a cave mouth my uncle showed me crinoid stems,
And in limestone skeletons of the fishy form of some creature.
"All once under water," he said, "no saying the millions
Of years." He walked off, the old man still with me. "Grandpa,"
I said, "what do you do, things being like this?" "All you can,"
He said, looking off through treetops, skyward. "Love
Your wife, love your get, keep your word, and
If need arises die for what men die for. There aren't
Many choices.
And remember that truth doesn't always live in the number of voices."

*

He hobbled away. The woods seemed darker. I stood
In the encroachment of shadow. I shut
My eyes, head thrown back, eyelids black.
I stretched out the arm on each side, and, waterlike,
Wavered from knees and hips, feet yet firm-fixed, it seemed,
On shells, in mud, in sand, in stone, as though
In eons back I grew there in that submarine
Depth and lightlessness, waiting to discover
What I would be, might be, after ages—how many?—had rolled over.

Covered Bridge

Another land, another age, another self
Before all had happened that has happened since
And is now arranged on the shelf
Of memory in a sequence that I call Myself.

How can you think back and know
Who was the boy, sleepless, who lay
In a moonless night of summer, but with star-glow
Gemming the dewy miles, and acres, you used to go?

You think of starlight on the river, star
By star declaring its motionless, holy self,
Except at the riffle by the sandbar.
You wondered if reflection was seen by the sky's star.

Long, long ago, some miles away,
There was an old covered bridge across that stream,
And if impact of hoof or wheel made the loose boards sway,
That echo wandered the landscape, night or day.

But if by day, the human bumble and grind
Absorbed the sound, or even birdsong
Interfered in its fashion, and only at night might you find
That echo filling the vastness of your mind,

Till you wondered what night, long off, you would set hoof
On those loose boards and then proceed
To trot through the caverning dark beneath that roof.
Going where? Just going. That would be enough.

Then silence would wrap that starlit land,
And you would sleep—who now do not sleep
As you wonder why you cannot understand
What pike, highway, or path has led you from land to land,

From year to year, to lie in what strange room,
Where to prove identity you now lift up
Your own hand—scarcely visible in that gloom.

Re-interment: Recollection of a Grandfather

What a strange feeling all the years to carry
It in your head! Once—say almost
A hundred and sixty-odd years ago, and
Miles away—a young woman carried it
In her belly, and smiled. It was
Not lonely there. It did not see
Her smile, but knew itself part of the world
It lived in. Do you remember a place like that?

How strange now to feel it—that presence, lonely
But not alone, locked in my head.
Are those strange noises
All night in my skull
But fingers fumbling to get out?
He knows few others there or what they talk about.
More lonely than ever he must feel with the new, strange voices.

I hear in dream the insane colloquy and wrangling.
Is that his croak demanding explanation
Of the totally illegal seizure? Then tussle and tangling.
But whence the choked weeping, manic laughter, lips moving in prayer?
It's a mob scene of some sort, and then
Zip and *whish,* like bat wings in dark air,
That sometimes fill the great dome my shoulders bear.
But sometimes silence; and I seem to see
How out of the jail of my head he comes free.
And in twilight,
His lips move without sound, his hands stretch out to me there.
But his face fades from my sight.

Then sometimes I wake, and I know what will wake me.
It's again the fingernails clawing to get out,
To get out and tell me a thousand things to make me
Aware of what life's obligation is. Nails dig at a skull-seam.
They are stronger and sharper each year. Or is that a dream?
Each year more clawlike—as I watch hair go thin and pate gleam.
I strain to hear him speak, but words come too low
From that distance inside my skull,
And there's nothing to do but feel my heart full
Of what was true more than three-score years ago.

Some night, not far off, I'll sleep with no such recollection—
Not even his old-fashioned lingo and at dinner the ritual grace,
Or the scratched-in-dust map of Shiloh, and Bloody Pond,
Or the notion a man's word should equal his bond,
And the use of a word like *honor* as no comic disgrace.
And in our last communal trance, when the past has left no trace,

He'll not feel the world's contempt, or condescending smile,
For there'll be nobody left, in that after-while,
To love him—or recognize his kind. Certainly not his face.

Last Meeting

A Saturday night in August when
Farm folks and tenants and black farmhands
Used to crowd the street of a market town
To do their "traden," and chew the rag,

And to hide the likker from women hung out
Behind the poolroom or barbershop—
If you were white. If black, in an alley.
And the odor of whiskey mixed with the sweat

And cheap perfume, and high heels waggled
On worn bricks, and through the crowd
I saw her come. I see her now
As plain as then—some forty years back.

It's like a flash, and still she comes,
Comes peering at me, not sure yet,
For I'm in my city clothes and hat,
But in the same instant we recognize

Each other. I see the shrunken old woman
With bleary eyes and yellow-gray skin,
And walking now with the help of a stick.
We hug and kiss there in the street.

"Ro-Penn, Ro-Penn, my little tadpole,"
She said, and patted my cheek, and said,
"Git off yore hat so I'll see yore haid."
And I did. She ran her hands through thinning hair.

"Not fahr-red, like it used to be."
And ran her fingers some more. "And thinner,
And sandy color some places too."
Then she rocked her arms like cuddling a child,

And crooned, and said,"Now big and gone
Out in the wide world—but 'member me!"
I tried to say "I couldn't forget,"
But the words wouldn't come, and I felt how frail

Were the vertebrae I clasped. I felt
Tears run down beside her nose,
And a crazy voice, like some half-laugh,
Said, "Chile, yore Ma's dead, yore Pappy ole,

*

"But I'm hangen on fer what I'm wuth."
So we said goodbye, with eyes staring at us
And laughter in some corner, somewhere.
That was the last time we ever met.

All's changed. The faces on the street
Are changed. I'm rarely back. But once
I tried to find her grave, and failed.
Next time I'll promise adequate time.

And find it. I might take store-bought flowers
(Though not a florist in twenty miles),
But a fruit jar full of local zinnias
Might look even better with jimson weed.

It's nigh half a lifetime I haven't managed,
But there must be enough time left for that.

VI.

Muted Music

As sultry as the cruising hum
Of a single fly lost in the barn's huge, black
Interior, on a Sunday afternoon, with all the sky
Ablaze outside—so sultry and humming
Is memory when in barn-shade, eyes shut,
You lie in hay, and wonder if that empty, lonely,
And muted music was all the past was, after all.
Does the past now cruise your empty skull like
That blundering buzz at barn-height—which is dark
Except for the window at one gable, where
Daylight is netted gray with cobwebs, and the web
Dotted and sagged with blunderers that once could cruise and hum?

What do you really know
Of that world of decision and
Action you once strove in? What
Of that world where now
Light roars, while you, here, lulled, lie
In a cunningly wrought and mathematical

Box of shade, and try, of all the past, to remember
Which was *what, what, which.* Perhaps
That sultry hum from the lone bumbler, cruising high
In shadow, is the only sound that truth can make,
And into that muted music you soon sink
To hear at last, at last, what you have strained for
All the long years, and sometimes at dream-verge thought

You heard—the song the moth sings, the babble
Of falling snowflakes (in a language
No school has taught you), the scream
Of the reddening bud of the oak tree

As the bud bursts into the world's brightness.

The Whole Question

You'll have to rethink the whole question. This
Getting born business is not as simple as it seemed,
Or midwife thought, or doctor deemed. It is,
Time shows, more complicated than either—or you—ever dreamed.

If it can be said that you dreamed anything
Before what's called a hand slapped blazing breath
Into you, snatched your dream's lulling nothing-
ness into what Paul called the body of this death.

You had not, for instance, previsioned the terrible thing called love,
Which began with a strange, sweet taste and bulbed softness while
Two orbs of tender light leaned there above.
Sometimes your face got twisted. They called it a smile.

You noticed how faces from outer vastness might twist, too.
But sometimes different twists, with names unknown,
And there were noises with no names you knew,
And times of dark silence when you seemed nothing—or gone.

Years passed, but sometimes seemed nothing except the same.
You knew more words, but they were words only, only—
Metaphysical midges that plunged at the single flame
That centered the infinite dark of your skull; or lonely,

You woke in the dark of real night to hear the breath
That seemed to promise reality in the vacuum
Of the sleepless dream beginning when underneath
The curtain dawn seeps, and on wet asphalt wet tires hum.

Yes, you must try to rethink what is real. Perhaps
It is only a matter of language that traps you. You
May yet find a new one in which experience overlaps
Words. Or find some words that make the Truth come true.

Old Photograph of the Future

That center of attention—an infantile face
That long years ago showed, no doubt, pink and white—
Now faded, and in the photograph only a trace
Of grays, not much expression in sight.

That center of attention, swathed in a sort of white dress,
Is precious to the woman who, pretty and young,
Leans with a look of surprised blessedness
At the mysterious miracle forth-sprung.

*

In the background somewhat, the masculine figure
Looms, face agleam with achievement and pride.
In black coat, derby at breast, he is quick to assure
You the world's in good hands—lay your worries aside.

The picture is badly faded. Why not?
Most things show wear around seventy-five,
And that's the age this picture has got.
The man and woman no longer, of course, live.

They lie side by side in whatever love survives
Under green turf, or snow, and that child, years later, stands there
While old landscapes blur and he in guilt grieves
Over nameless promises unkept, in undefinable despair.

Why Boy Came to Lonely Place

Limestone and cedar. Indigo shadow
On whiteness. The sky is flawlessly blue.
Only the cicada speaks. No bird. I do not know
Why I have these miles come. Here is only *I*. Not *You*.

Did I clamber these miles of distance
Only to quiver now in identity?
You are yourself only by luck, disaster, or chance,
And only alone may believe in your reality.

What drove you forth?—
Age thirteen, ignorant, lost in the world,
Canteen now dry and of what worth
With the cheese sandwich crumbling, and lettuce brown-curled?

Under the ragged shadow of cedar
You count the years you have been in the world,
And wonder what heed or
Care the world would have had of your absence as it whirled

In the iron groove of its circuit of space.
You say the name they gave you. That's all you are.
You move your fingers down your face,
And wonder how many years you'll be what you are.

But what is that? To find out you come to this lonely place.

Platonic Lassitude

Not one leaf stirs, though a high few,
As they hang without motion, shine translucently green
Against the depth of the sky's depthless blue.
The brook is shrunk. It meditates in serene

Silence. You see the warbler's throat palpitate
With heat. That is the only motion you see.
The mountain seems to float, to have no weight.
It may even sway, drift away into infinity,

Like a child's balloon at a circus. No fly, no gnat,
Stirs through the bright unreality of air.
Your lungs seem to have no function, and you have forgot
The substance breathed, and the *near* and the *far* where-

by you locate yourself, and the world
You're in, seem to lose distinction. No utterance
May come again, and the smoke that is curled
From a chimney may never uncurl in greater or lesser distance.

By brookside, by woodsedge, no bird sings or woodpecker taps,
And like the collage of a child to blue paper glued, the sun
Hangs, and you lie in the world's ontological collapse,
And ask if all is accomplished, all now done,

And even the past dissolves like a dream of mist,
Which is a new joy, that unlike the old, cannot end.
So, lulled, you loll in the lap of Time's wave, and the great crest,
With its tattered glory and gleam of foam-fringe, will never descend.

Or will it? To remind you
That nothing defines itself in joy or sorrow,
The crow calls from the black cliff forgotten but beckoning behind you.
Had you forgotten that history is only the fruit of tomorrow?

Seasons

I. Downwardness

Under ledges of snow out-thrust from ledges
Of stone, once ledges of ice, water swells black,
With white whirlpools of sputum at edges.
At the edge of the forest I have seen the year's first bear track.

*

Downstream, a high out-thrust of snow groans, loses structure,
Falls in a smother and splash of white water boiling—
But not from heat. Boulders go grudging and grinding in rupture,
And one, heaved in air, chimes like a bell in that moiling.

After that tumult your ears with silence are tingling.
But, no, not silence. Your ears deceive.
Yes, listen! What seemed such silence is only the singing
Of a thousand driblets and streamlets that receive

Stored snow-waters, ice-waters, earth-waters, freed now in season
On the vast mountain, where they even explore
The most secret channel a root drills in its personal reason.
Here gravity is the only god, and water knows no more

Than the lust for downwardness, and the deepest coil.
But time will change, clouds again draw up buckets, day-
light glitter in the highest leaf like green foil,
And in earth-darkness moisture will climb the lattices of clay.

All night we now hear the desperate downwardness.
All day we have watched the last icicle
Drip, drop by drop, as though from a wound—grow less and less.
Dark comes again. Shut eyes, and think of a sacred cycle.

II. Interlude of Summer

Even in the spruce-dark gorge the last
Fringe of ice is in fatal deliquescence,
And rising waters heave to shoulder a boulder past.
Green will soon creep back in white's absence.

Each day, at mathematically accelerated pace,
The yet unseen sun will flood the eastern notch
With crimson, and you pick up a shoe, and yawn, and face
The morning news-screen of the world's hotchpotch or bloody botch.

Evening by evening, the climactic melodrama of
Day flares from behind the blackening silhouette
Of the mountain for the last and majestic pyre of
What of today you can remember, or forget.

Later and later each day, the eastern notch is now flooded
By dawn, and eyes gaze blankly at the world's disaster
With customary indifference, for you know fate is hooded.
The woodland violet that was your love is replaced by the roadside aster.

*

The faces of the children are now hardening toward definition.
Your own life seems to lose definition, as it did last year.
But garden and grape-arbor have fulfilled your ambition,
And gullet has sucked juice from the golden and tooth-gored pear.

An old friend dies this summer, and now whose carefully
Composed letters will challenge? But your own health is good. Conversation
Turns to New England foliage, which has begun beautifully.
We might come back for a weekend of delightful observation.

After all, aesthetics is a branch of philosophy.

The Place

From shelving cliff-darkness, green arch and nave
Skyward aspire, translucently, to heights
Where tattered gold tags of sunlight twirl, swing,
Or downward sift to the upturned eye. Upward,
The eye probes infinite distance, infinite
Light, while foot, booted, tangled in fern,
Grips stone. Fern
Bleeds on stone.

This
Is the hour of the unbounded loneliness. This
Is the hour of the self's uncertainty
Of self. This is the hour when
Prayer might be a possibility, if
It were. This
Is the hour when what is remembered is
Forgotten. When
What is forgotten is remembered, and
You are not certain which is which.
But tell me:

How had you ever forgotten that spot
Where once wild azalea bloomed? And what there passed? And forgotten
That truth may lurk in irony? How,
Alone in a dark piazza, as the cathedral clock
Announced 3 A.M. to old tiles of the starless city, could you bear
To remember the impossible lie, told long before, elsewhere?
But a lie you had found all too possible.

Self is the cancellation of self, and now is the hour.
Self is the mutilation of official meanings, and this is the place.
You hear water of minor musical utterance
On stone, but from what direction?
You hear, distantly, a bird-call you cannot identify.
Is the shadow of the cliff creeping upon you?
You are afraid to look at your watch.

*

You think of the possibility of lying on stone,
Among fern fronds, and waiting
For the shadow to find you.
The stars would not be astonished
To catch a glimpse of the form through interstices
Of leaves now black as enameled tin. Nothing astounds the stars.
They have long lived. And you are not the first
To come to such a place seeking the most difficult knowledge.

First Moment of Autumn Recognized

Hills haven the last cloud. However white. From brightest blue
Spills glitter of afternoon, more champagne than ever
Summer. Bubble and sparkle burst in
Tang, taste, tangle, tingle, delicious
On tongue of spirit, joyful in eye-beam. We know
This to be no mere moment, however brief,
However blessèd, for
Moment means time, and this is no time,
Only the dream, untimed, between
Season and season. Let the leaf, gold, of birch,
Of beech, forever hang, not vegetable matter mortal, but
In no whatsoever breath of
Air. No—embedded in
Perfection of crystal, purer
Than air. You, embedded too in
Crystal, stand, your being perfected
At last, in the instant itself which is unbreathing.

Can you feel breath brush your damp
Lips? How can you know?

Paradigm of Seasons

Each year is like a snake that swallows its tail.
How long since we have learned, of seasons, the paradigm?
We know how cloud-scut and scud, north-bred, come scouting
The land out for winter, its waiting bulk. Come skirmishing, come scouting.
Then red leaf, gold leaf, then winter's choked road. Spring
Brings hope, even if we have
Ice-dam of river to flood the farmer's cellar. But
We know, too, how the heart, forgetting irony, stares at
The first apple bough to offer blossom,
Parody of snow. We know
The sweetness of the first secret
Tear, not brushed away. Summer

Is manic in strength, or lazy in maple shade and
Dry sweat. Summer dreams of glut. Summer slides
Over night-nakedness like a wave coming in with
The weight of moonlight like ocean beyond. But
On the rattle-trap iron of the slum fire-escape
At night you can see a match flare
To light a marijuana cigarette. And out of boredom
Two fingers penetrate a vagina.

Before long,
Of course, letters addressed to your familiar rural
Tin mailbox cease to arrive there. Now aging widows
In bifocals, with lower jaw slightly quivering, are
Carefully driven north from New York, in
Black sedans, with the price of gasoline no object.
They come to feed the spiritual part upon
The sight of New England foliage in splendor. Some
May even claim descent from Plymouth Rock,
And the saints thereof. Sometimes the chauffeur
Might have an equal claim, but doesn't know it.
But now the ladies are worrying about
Their houses in Florida. Soon,
From the mountains, you can hear the report
Of the authoritative rifle.

Later,
Though you cannot hear it, there will be
The painful bellows of the lungs of an aging man
Who follows, with a burden of supplies on his back,
A snow-choked trail.

If Snakes Were Blue

If snakes were blue, it was the kind of day
That would uncoil in a luxurious ease
As each mica-bright scale exposed a flange of gold,
And slowly, slowly, the golden eyes blinked.

It was the kind of day that takes forever—
As though minutes, minutes, could never be counted—to slide
Among the clouds like pink lily-pads floating
In a crystal liquid pure enough to drink.

And there was no distinction now between
Light and shadow except the mystic and faint
Sense of adaptation of the iris,
As light diminished and the first star shone,

*

And the last veery, hidden in a thicket of alder,
Thought it would break its heart perhaps—or yours.
Let it be yours, then. For such gentle breaking
In that ambiguous moment could not be

Less than a blessing, or the kind of promise
We give ourselves in childhood when first dawn
Makes curtains go gold, and all night's dreams flood back.
They had guaranteed our happiness forever.

And in a way such promises may come true
In spite of all our evil days and ways.
True, few fulfillments—but look! In the distance lift peaks
Of glittering white above the wrath-torn land.

Little Girl Wakes Early

Remember when you were the first one awake, the first
To stir in the dawn-curdled house, with little bare feet
Cold on boards, every door shut and accurst,
And behind shut doors no breath perhaps drew, no heart beat.

You held your breath and thought how all over town
Houses had doors shut, and no whisper of breath sleeping,
And that meant no swinging, nobody to pump up and down,
No hide-and-go-seek, no serious play at housekeeping.

So you ran outdoors, bare feet from the dew wet,
And climbed the fence to the house of your dearest friend,
And opened your lips and twisted your tongue, all set
To call her name—but the sound wouldn't come in the end,

For you thought how awful, if there was no breath there
For answer. Tears start, you run home, where now mother,
Over the stove, is humming some favorite air.
You seize her around the legs, but tears aren't over,

And won't get over, not even when she shakes you—
And shakes you hard—and more when you can't explain.
Your mother's long dead. And you've learned that when loneliness takes you
There's nobody ever to explain to—though you try again and again.

Winter Wheat: Oklahoma

The omelet of sunset vibrates in the great flat pan.
A certain amount of golden grease will spatter.
In distance the tractor is red, but without pride of
The glitter and brightness, with ink scarcely dry on the contract.
But still it makes black earth blacker when it treads with steel heels.

There's a half-mile to tread before it reaches the spot where
The old car waits. The omelet is long done before
The tractor's last blue-gray puff is puffed, and the cranky
Old bones of the driver, in denim swathed, creak down
From the seat of power. Aboard car, he slowly props

Head back, shuts eyes. When they open first stars are out,
Though pale. He hates to go home. It's rough to the lane,
And tough on sciatica. The lane ain't no broadway, nohow.
In the end, there's the tight rectangle of the little lawn-patch, two maples.
He sees the barn, the woodlot, the years. All his,

And his sweat's. The maples are big now. But she's not sitting
To wave when he gets close. Now no smoke in the chimney,
These nights. Well, just grab something, whatever. Then coffee.
A time it was booze. But booze made him wonder
How flesh would peel off cheekbones in earth out yonder, and if

All that gold he'd been so proud to pay good cash for,
For her poor teeth, now gleamed like light in that darkness.
Anyway, a man oughtn't sit and see tears ruin his booze.
He sits alone. Him not one for talking.
His boy writes every Christmas, will sure come next year.

That boy was his boy. Not begrudging sweat. But who
Could be sure about God taking care of His business? Wheat in,
And maybe He'd go skylarkin' off this time,
Like He does sometimes to pleasure Himself,
Whatever He does. And lets

A man's honest sweat just go for nothing.

VII.

Youthful Picnic Long Ago: Sad Ballad on Box

In Tennessee once the campfire glowed
With steady joy in its semi-globe
Defined by the high-arched nave of oaks against
Light-years of stars and the
Last scream space makes beyond space. Faces,

In grave bemusement, leaned, eyes fixed
On the fingers white in their delicate dance
On the strings of the box. And delicate
Was the melancholy that swelled each heart, and timed
The pulse in wrist, and wrist, and wrist—all while
The face leaned over the box
In shadow of hair that in fire-light down-gleamed,
Smoother than varnish, and black. And like
A silver vine that upward to darkness twines,
The voice confirmed the sweet sadness
Young hearts gave us no right to.

No right to, yet. Though some day would,
As Time unveiled,
In its own dancing parody of grace,
The bony essence of each joke on joke.

But even back then perhaps we knew
That the dancing fingers enacted
A truth far past the pain declared
By that voice that somehow made pain sweet.

Would it be better or worse, if now
I could name the names I've lost, and see,
Virile or beautiful, those who, entranced, leaned.
I wish I knew what wisdom they had there learned.

The singer—her name, it flees the fastest!
If only she'd toss back that varnished black screen
Of beautiful hair, and let
Flame reveal the grave cheek-curve, eye-shine,
Then I'd know that much.
If not her name.

Even now.

History During Nocturnal Snowfall

Dark in the cubicle boxed from snow-darkness of night,
Where that soundless paradox summarizes the world,
We lie, each alone, and I reach a finger laid light
To a wrist that does not move, as I think of a body curled—

Is it an inch, or a world, away—a watch-tick
Or a century off? In darkness I compress my eyes
And wonder if I might devise the clever trick
Of making heartbeat with heartbeat synchronize.

Each has come a long way to this wordless and windless burrow,
Each, like a mole, clawing blindly, year after year,
Each clawing and clawing through blindness of joy and sorrow,
And neither knowing how the world outside might appear.

Could one guess the other's buried narrative?
How the other, in weal or woe, might have found
White darkness where, a finger on wrist, one might live
In the synchronized rhythm of heart, and heart, with no sound?

Was it a matter of chance? Or miracle?
Or which is which—for logic laughs at both?
Could it matter less as whiteness and darkness blending fall
And my finger touches a pulse to intuit its truth?

Whistle of the 3 A.M.

At 3 A.M., if the schedule held,
The express blew for the crossing a mile
Out of town, and you woke, and your heart swelled
With the thought that some night in your own dark cubicle,

You would whirl, in sleep or in contempt,
Past some straggle of town with scarcely a streetlight
To show the pale ghost, unloved, unkempt,
Of a place that would shuffle to life with the creak of daylight.

And once at that whistle you from bed crept,
Lifted curtains and wiped the frost from the pane,
And the magisterial headlight swept
Hills snow-white, white woods, white fields, until again

There was nothing but marmoreal moonlight
Defining the structure of night—and your feet
Cold on boards. Did you stare at the sheet's trancelike white-
ness, which held no hint of the world's far fury and heat?

*

Times change, man changes, and thirty-five thousand
Feet down, what whistle wakes any boy
To the world's bliss and rage, and the raging sand
Of the sandblast of History? Am I the boy

Who last remembers the 3 A.M.?
What if some hold real estate nearby,
A good six feet long, but not one of them
Would wake, I guess, to listen, and wonder why

The schedule's gone dead of the 3 A.M..

Last Night Train

In that slick and new-fangled coach we go slam-banging
On rackety ruin of a roadbed, past caterpillar-
Green flash of last light on deserted platforms,
And I watch the other passenger at this
Late hour—a hundred and eighty pounds of
Flesh, black, female, middle-aged,
Unconsciously flung by roadbed jerks to wallow,
Unshaped, unhinged, in
A purple dress. Straps of white sandals
Are loosened to ease the bulge of color-contrasting bare instep.
Knees wide, the feet lie sidewise, sole toward sole. They
Have walked so far. Head back, flesh snores.
I wonder what she has been doing all day in N.Y.

My station at last. I look back once.
Is she missing hers? I hesitate to ask, and the snore
Is suddenly snatched into eternity.

The last red light fades into distance and darkness like
A wandering star. Where that brief roar just now was,
A last cricket is audible. That lost
Sound makes me think, with quickly suppressed
Nostalgia, of
A country lane, late night, late autumn—and there,
Alone, again I stand, part of all.
Alone, I now stand under the green station light,
Part of nothing but years.

I stare skyward at uncountable years beyond
My own little aura of pale-green light—
The complex of stars is steady in its operation.
Smell of salt sedge drifts in from seaward,
And I think of swimming, naked and seaward,
In starlight forever.

*

But I look up the track toward Bridgeport. I feel
Like blessing the unconscious wallow of flesh-heap
And white sandals unstrapped at bulging of instep.

I hear my heels crunch on gravel, making
My way to a parked car.

VIII.

Milton: A Sonnet

No doubt he could remember how in the past
Late carmine had bathed the horizon with its wide kindness.
Not now. In darkness he prayed, and at the last
Moved through the faithful brilliance they called blindness,
Knew burgeoning Space in which old space hummed like a fly,
And Time that devoured itself to defecate
A nobler dimension of that self whereby
The past and future are intrinsicate
To form a present in which the blessèd heart
May leap like a gleaming fish from water into
Sunlight before the joy-flashed curve may dart
Back to the medium of deep wisdom through
A pavane of bubbles like pearls, again to slash
Upward, and upward again, and, in joy, flash.

Whatever You Now Are

In the depth and rustle of midnight, how do you know
What is the dream and who the dreamer? Oh yes,
You fell asleep to the star-bit and murmurous flow
Of the stream beneath your window, but frontierless
Are the stream and the Self conjunct all night long.
How is the difference defined between singer and song?

Is it you that flows from distance, to distance,
With the tune of time and blood intertwined forever?
Or does the dark stream of log-ripple and stone-chance
Define the pattern of your whole life's endeavor?
What elements, shadowy, in that dream interlace
In a region past categories of Time and Space?

Yes, think of the pale transparencies that lave
Stone, riffle, algae, and the moon-bright sandbar,
While music drifts to your shadowy cave
Of consciousness, whoever you now are—
But dawn breaks soon, and that self will have fled away.
Will a more strange one yet inhabit the precinct of day?

Wind and Gibbon

All night, over roof, over forest, you hear
Wind snore, shift, stir, like a dog uncomfortable
In sleep, or dreaming. You think of leg
Twitching. Paw jerking. Claw
Unconsciously scraping the wood floor. You drowse.
Wake. Decide it is only a spruce bough wind-dragging
Across the corner of the house, like a saw. Wind,
Suddenly, stops. Shifts. Again lifts. Has no mind
That could rationally dictate change. Its head
Is like a dried gourd rattling
A few dried seeds within. The wind
Is like a dream of History. Blows where it listeth.

You get up. Wander. Gibbon, you see,
Is on the shelf, volume by volume, solid as masonry. At random,
You seize one. It will be more comforting
Than the morning paper. The paper
Will gabble like paranoia, chitter in a strange tongue like
A capuchin, the organ-grinder's monkey.
You chunk up the fire. You do not hear the wind.

It does not matter where you begin. This is History.
Pick up any volume. Gibbon's hot lava
Seethes over the conical brim of the world whence
Lifts flame-tongue. Glowing,
It flows, like incandescent irony, over
Vineyard, sheepfold (but quickly soothes that
Frizzly tumult), stone hut, villa, the brawny and noble
Cockmaster about to insert the tool of wizardry, that
Moan-maker. It spills
Over empires, imperial palaces, the Crusader
Whose mount is hock-bloody. *In hoc signo.*

History is not truth. Truth is in the telling.

The lava flows on. Before dawn, you sleep. This, in your chair.

Long back the wind has stopped. The world is now white.
You face west. The mountain is white with snow.
From the new sun, back of your house, and thus
Invisible to you, a single
Beam, sky-arrowing, strikes
The mountain to dazzlement.

Delusion? — No!

In atmosphere almost too heavenly
Pure for nourishment of earthbound
Bone, or bone-borne flesh, I stood,
At last past sweat and swink, at crag-edge. Felt
My head swell like the sky that knew
No distance, and knew no sensation but blueness.

In that divine osmosis I stood
And felt each discrete and distinct stroke
Of the heart as it downward fled—
Cliff, cleft, gorge, chasm, and, far off,
Ravine cut in the flattening but still high glitter
Of earth. I saw afar the peek-a-boo of some stream's gleam.

Mind plays strange tricks on us.
One moment I felt the momentous, muscular thrust
Skyward of peak, then the thumb-and-forefinger twist
Of range on range. I entered in.
Was part of all. I knew the
Glorious light of inner darkness burn
Like the fundamental discovery.

Yes, stretch forth your arms like wings, and from your high stance,
Hawk-eyed, ride forth upon the emptiness of air, survey
Each regal contortion
And tortuous imagination of rock, wind, water, and know
Your own the power creating all.

Delusion? — No! For Truth has many moments.

Open your eyes. Who knows? This may be one.

Question at Cliff-Thrust

From the outthrust ledge of sea-cliff you
Survey, downward, the lazy tangle and untangle of
Foam fringe, not on sand, but sucking through
Age-rotten pumice and lava like old fruitcake lost in an angle of
A kitchen closet, the fruit long since nibbled away
By mouse-tooth. This is a day
Of merciless sun, no wind, and
Of distance, slick as oil, sliding infinitely away
To no far smudge of land.
You stare down at your cove beneath.
No blackness of rock shows,
Only the gradual darkening green as depth grows.

In that depth how far would breath
Hold? Down through gull-torn air
You lean forward and stare
At the shelving green of hypnosis.

Who would guess
It would be as easy as this?

A pebble companions your white downward flash.
You do not hear what must be its tiny splash
As, bladelike, your fingertips
Into the green surface slash
And your body, frictionless, slips
Into a green atmosphere,
Where you can hear
Only the nothingness of sound, and see
Only the one great green and unforgiving eye of depth that steadily
Absorbs your being in its intensity.
You take the downward strokes, some two or three.
Suddenly your lungs, aflame, burn.
But there is the beckoning downwardness
That you must fight before you turn, and in the turn
Begin the long climb toward lighter green, and light,
Until you lie in lassitude and strengthlessness
On the green bulge of ocean under the sight
Of one gull that screams from east to west and is

Demanding what?

It Is Not Dead

It is not dead. It is simply weighty with wisdom.
A long way and painful, it has come to become
What it is. In nameless heat under
Nameless pressure, liquefied,
It has tried
To find its true nature, seething in depth and darkness when earth
Was not yet ready to be torn asunder,
But heaved in silence, like throttled thunder.

What eons remained still
To await what cataclysmic birth
That exploded, roared, glowed
To change its liquid mind to hardness like glass, to iron will?
What name had the plowshare that plowed
It wide to the fury of light on a high place?
What determination interminable,
What years, did the crowbar of ice take
To pry from the crag-face

That mass to make
A scythe to reduce some undefined forest to splinters? Then the might
Of the first unmerciful grasp of the glacier, the grind,
The trundling descent in darkness, white
But absolute. What timeless thoughts ground in its downward mind?
Then fingers of water, weak but uncontrollable,
Worked in their tangle of multitudinous will,
Age after age, until
Half in, half out, of my brook it lies,
Honed to perfection, perfect in structure, moss-idle, sunlit.
And, naked, I lie on it,
Brooding on our common destinies.
Against the declaration of sunlight I close my eyes.

All night, it will lie there under the stars,
Attent to the riffle, and I lie, in brotherhood, where I lie,
Hearing the riffle too, though a curtain bars
Me in darkness except in one twisted spot where I spy
A fleeting fracture of the immensity of the night sky.

Sunset

Clouds clamber, turgid, the mountain, peakward
And pine-pierced, toward the
Vulgar and flaming apocalypse of day,
In which our errors are consumed
Like fire in a lint-house—
Not repetitious
But different each day, for day to day nothing
Is identical to eye or soul.
At night, at a late hour, I
Have asked stars the name of my soul.

"Oh, what shall I call my soul in a dire hour?"
But there is no answer from
Heavenly algebra, and you are left with
The implacable gaggles and military squadrons
Of ignorance, which have no
Originality and know
Nothing but repetition, and which
We call constellations.

Who knows his own name at the last?
How shall he speak to a soul that has none?
"Tell me that name," I cried, "that I may speak
In a dire hour." The dire hour
Is the time when you must speak
To your naked self—never
Before seen, nor known.

IX.

Myth of Mountain Sunrise

Prodigious, prodigal, crags steel-ringing
To dream-hoofs nightlong, proverbial
Words stone-incised in language unknowable, but somehow singing
Their wisdom-song against disaster of granite and all
Moonless non-redemption on the left hand of dawn:
The mountain dimly wakes, stretches itself on windlessness. Feels its deep chasm, waking, yawn.

The curdling agony of interred dark strives dayward, in stone strives though
No light here enters, has ever entered but
In ageless age of primal flame. But look! All mountains want slow-
ly to bulge outward extremely. The leaf, whetted on light, will cut
Air like butter. Leaf cries: "I feel my deepest filament in dark rejoice.
I know that the density of basalt has a voice."

How soon will the spiderweb, dew-dappled, gleam
In Pompeian glory! Think of a girl-shape, birch-white sapling, rising now
From ankle-deep brook-stones, head back-flung, eyes closed in first beam,
While hair—long, water-roped, past curve, coign, sway that no geometries know—
Spreads end-thin, to define fruit-swell of haunches, tingle of hand-hold.
The sun blazes over the peak. That will be the old tale told.

Uncollected Poems 1943–1989

Bicentennial

Who is my brother?

1.

Wall Street aflame, strategic police stations
Occupied, the *Times* building a shambles, and
The mayor assassinated—that
Is what you might logically assume, with everything
On four wheels burning rubber over
Every bridge, heading in every
Direction, and every
Public-service thermometer racking up
Ninety-three degrees, and the pollution
Quotient inimitable.—But, no,
Don't worry, it is only
Another Friday afternoon, and July Fourth
Looming up.

It is only an exercise in patriotism.

Everybody is heading for his own version of
Walden Pond, whatever that may be,
And the font of pure American individualism,

And from helicopters, the thruways glitter like striptease sequins
Being ripped off. The death rate,
The car radios report, is unusually low
On the highways today, for a day like today.

2.

On a high slope of the Bitterroot, a shepherd,
Welsh-born, is staring out of his good eye,
As the eagle climbs into the
Invisibility of sky. He shuts his good eye,
And under his feet the

Mountain totters in darkness.

He is trying to recall his childhood.

He tries to remember how his eye got knocked out.

*

3.

Caleb Winthrop, Harvard '53, crew, Porcellian,
Sits in the bar car of the 5:02, Grand Central, and
Shuts his eyes, and
Shudders. He has just downed two highballs,
And he wishes he had not had that martini at lunch.

He will take a cold bath, no matter
What his wife says about getting ready to go out.

Suddenly, he feels very old.

His wife, not yet dressed, thank God, is talking to the new baby-sitter.
His dinner jacket is dutifully laid out, he sees,
As he heads to the bathroom.
He lies in the icy water, shudders, shuts his eyes.

4.

The bateau slides without sound
On the silky water.
The Ojibwa woman's hand reaches out
To pluck the stalk of wild rice.

It will cost you four dollars a pound.

5.

Caleb Winthrop lies in the tub, with closed eyes.
That baby-sitter is very appealing, he thinks.
Spiritual, you might say, with that pale hair hanging glossy
And loose on each side of the long oval face. He hadn't
Noticed her at the time, but now he sees her very clearly.

He opens his eyes, lifts
His head to regard his member floating
Among luxuriant black hairs. A testicle,
Only half visible, is as dark
As a shucked American walnut. The other
Is not visible from his position. The member,
Even in the cold water, is formidable. It comforts him.

"Pore Ole Nig"—that
Was his wife's pet name when she played with it.

She never pronounced the name except in a whisper.
And with no light.

He thinks of the baby-sitter. He bets
"Ole Nig" would be a surprise to her. He thinks how
His wife is getting broad in the bum. "Ole Nig"—
She could still say that, anyway. But last time,
He had, for the first time, been too drunk.

*

He wouldn't drink too much tonight.

But he hoped she would drink enough. Only
In the last years, when she had begun to drink—
To get a kind of impersonal glaze on, but very correct,
Nevertheless—had she begun
To get the way she was now.
Now there wasn't anything she wouldn't do in the dark.
After a party, that was. When they hit the room
She might damned near tear her clothes off.

It was only in this last phase she had
Taken up the pet name.

6.

It was about six when Caleb Winthrop got to Greenwich.
By this time—five by central time—in west Kansas,
The sun wasn't near setting, but
If you look where sunset will be,
You see, far off, a first, faint purple haze begin to rise
From the infinite miles of new wheat stubble.

7.

His name is Murdoch Lancaster, and he was born in Alabama,
Where his father worked in a mill, boiling turpentine,
His father always smelled of turpentine, and his mother
Was distantly related to Nathan Bedford Forrest.
The Forrests were certainly not top drawer.
Except on a battlefield.

He looks from the terrace across the lavish expanse
Of manicured lawn, toward the rose garden.

It is small, but there is no choicer rose garden
In Westchester County. His wife
Is sprinkling some kind of white powder
On the rose plants.

He watches the image of his wife, in filmy
White, with the white powder drifting
Among the roses. She drifts, too,
Among the roses like a ghost.
The sunset is beginning beyond.

She will soon be a ghost, he thinks.

He shuts his eyes and thinks how the image in his head
Will soon be all there is, the only ghost.
That is what he is thinking.

*

He opens his eyes, takes a spaced sip of whiskey, and begins to read.
All he reads now is history. All, except financial reports.
He reads books on American history, sitting in Westchester County
And thinking of Sawynee Crossing, Alabama.

His eyes now rest on a sentence concerning General Forrest:
"During his career, twenty-nine mounts,
Were shot from under him, and he,
With his own hands, killed thirty men,
Perhaps thirty-one."

He wonders if he had ever killed
A man with his own hands. He reckons he must have, but
In a highly impersonal way. He had started
In the killing business as a second lieutenant
And wound up colonel at Bastogne. He had been in the armor.

8.

A woman wearing tight imitation-silk slacks, pink,
And high-heeled black patent-leather pumps, stands
In Yellowstone Park. She is watching a geyser in action.

Her buttocks are as large as full meal sacks.
When she walks, if you are behind her,

They look like two shoats wrasslin' under a rug.

9.

Colonel Lancaster, for that is what he still likes to be called,
Remembers that day after tomorrow
Is the Fourth. He is flying the colors and
It is close to sunset. As he rises,
His glance falls on Randolph, off across the lawn,
In front of the garage, polishing the Rolls.
Old Randolph, he thinks.

He does not think of many people
With innocent trust and affection.
A man who starts out scarcely knowing how to spell
And winds up with his first million at age thirty-five,
Even if his father did smell like turpentine—such a man
Would not be given to easy affection,
Especially since he regarded most men as lazy, trivial, and vain.
But Randolph was "Old Randolph," even if he knew
That most people would call that racist condescension.

"Screw them," he said, out loud.

He likes to talk to Randolph. He likes
To hear Randolph talk.
He had seen Randolph first in France, during the war.

*

Randolph, too, was from south Alabama.

Randolph was very brave. He had seen it.

10.

In the back room of a half-arsoned tenement in the Bronx,
Jesse Kimbrew, black, age eighteen, lies stretched on the floor
With closed eyes. Against the white of his T-shirt,
His muscular arms, with hands folded on the chest,
Look very black.

The syringe lies on the floor.

His mother will try to keep his pork chops warm
A long time. But by midnight,
She gives up.

11.

Murdoch Lancaster goes to lower the flag.
He is as precise as he is hard by nature,
As he had to be to do what he has done in the world.

He folds the flag, a very fine military one, very carefully.

He reckons that Forrest must have shot at this flag.
He reckons that he would have, too, given the circumstances.
A man plays the cards as they fall.

He puts the flag in its chest on the porch.
His wife is still among the roses. More ghostly
Than ever now, she looks. He watches her.
He does not yet know when he will do it.

But he knows he will.

He decides he will do it when she is asleep with the sedative.
Some things had better not be talked about beforehand.
Most things he had done had been done without talking.

She is the only person in the world he had ever really talked to.

But not now.

He walks back to tell Randolph they will not need him until
After the Fourth. He can go
On his vacation tonight, he and his wife.
He can take any car he wants.

After a few paces, he returns to say that the job
On the Rolls looks fine. It sure does.

*

12.

In Lundberg, Minnesota, Spike Oleson comes off
His mother's little front porch and starts
Running down the dusty street,
Toward the sunset, and open country,

He moves in a long, easy stride. He is a miler.
Second in the state high-school meet. He does three miles
Before breakfast, and three miles before supper.
In the summer he works at the A. & P. all day
And studies Latin at night.

He has won a National Merit Scholarship and is going
To Harvard in the fall. His mother is a widow,
But she claims she can scrape through
Until he finishes.

Now, at the end of his stint, in the open country,
He stands, breathing deep and slow, thinking
How he cannot bear to stay in this town.

He cannot bear to look at his mother's hands.

The sight of them ties his guts into a knot.
It is a knot of outrage and guilt.

He does not know why.

13.

From the Nez Percé Pass you can always see snow,
Even on the Fourth of July.

The distant peaks catch the colors of sunset.

14.

By nine-fifteen the baby-sitter has the Winthrop children asleep,
And she has called her new boyfriend. She doesn't know him well yet.

But she knows he is the kind her mother
Would say is too old for her.

After the sound of the motorcycle stops,
He enters from the back of the grounds.
She sees him from the kitchen window and meets him
In the shadow of the garage.
She can hear the telephone from here.

*

15.

In a great cypress swamp in Louisiana, on a tiny islet,
The moss pickers live. Night comes early, for
Here you can rarely see the open sky,
So high the cypresses soar, groining the shadow
Where moss hangs.

Straight up, high before boughs, from a root-footing
Massive in black water, each thrusts. The footing,
Heaving high from black water, looks like
A contorted and internecine death struggle
Of hydras. From a root,
A moccasin drops fatly
Into the black water, and the sound
Is like something overripe. The insects sing all night.

Now, as dark comes on, three moss-pickers huddle
Over a smudge fire, this against insects all night.
They are eating fried fish and corn pone from receptacles
That had once been the tops of lard cans. They have tin cups
Of coffee.

Two men and a woman—their bloodlines a tangle—
Anglo-Saxon, Cajun, *gens de couleur,* Indian (probably Caddo),
Black. Their hands are like crooked and horny claws.
Their eyes are dark and blank in firelight.

Later, the whiskey.

Two, a man and the woman, crawl into
The structure they live in, a dome
Of old beaten tin, waste boards, tar paper, junk.
A slip croker sack, unfolded, hangs
Over the low opening. This against mosquitoes.

The man left alone feeds the smudge fire. He drinks.

There is a fat, plopping sound in the water.
A moccasin has dropped in, somewhere in darkness.

16.

Murdoch Lancaster lies on a cot beside the bed
Where his wife is. He holds her hand
And listens to her breath.
He knows he is right.

She has been tortured long enough, and the doctor,
It is clear, regards this operation as merely ritual
Before the end. The ambulance will come tomorrow.

*

She is all he has got. His son, he is again thinking,
Is a prick. His daughter, he adds, is a cunt.

They are waiting for his money.

Well, he has rewritten his will. It will not please them.
He laughs at his pun.
But it will please the cancer foundation very much.
It will also please Randolph, in scale.

He is now grinning in the dark.

At least, he is very rich.

17.

Moshe Weinstein is so tired he wishes he could close the store now.
However, he knows he can't. He can't ever close decent.
It is the last dime that counts.
He has varicose veins.

He wishes he could get out of this neighborhood.
It is all spades, and they are no good.
But he can get better prices here.

He has been stuck up three times already.
If there is anything he hates, it is spades in Bridgeport, Conn.

You never know to give credit or not.

18.

On the shores of northern Mendocino County,
The body of a dead seal is caught on the rocks.
It is bloated.
It reflects the starlight.

The starlight is a fractured glitter on the long swell
Lifting in from the Pacific.

19.

The panties had been a hassle, but they are in his pocket now.
He had finally got them. He knew his business.
He had worked her into a real condition before he could do it.

He knew when the time had come, and when he
Lifted a foot out, it was like handling a wax dummy.
A wax dummy that could whisper *no, no, no,* but
It was paralyzed, and so
He lifts a foot out like it is an empty shoe.

*

Now the baby-sitter is plastered against the garage wall, in
Shadow. She is good as hung on a meat hook.

Her head is lifted and thrust back against the garage wall.
On each side of the face the pale hair
Hangs down below the shoulders against the wall.
The toes of his old but well-cared-for paratrooper boots
Work rhythmically as they crush the screaming petunias.

The telephone, far off, is ringing.

Well, he'd have one ringing right here, just give him a minute.
It would sure not be ringing long-distance, either.

20.

Releasing the hand of the sleeper, he
Slips off the cot and pads barefoot
Downstairs to his study. His decorations,
Under glass, are hung on the wall. But he
Does not notice them. He
Is feeling for his old service revolver
In the left desk drawer.

The revolver gives almost no glint in the unlighted room.

Its comforting weight seems to fall into his hand
As though it belongs there. He is comforted
In a way not to be named, as when
His command used to stand clean on inspection, or
He patted the setter's head after three quail had hit sage, or
Talked with Randolph, or
In the old days,
Held his wife, wordlessly, on his lap,
Sitting on the terrace at twilight,
With his big hand gently smoothing the smooth hair on her head.

He thinks he may cry.

21.

But he does not. There is a problem.

He sits at the desk, deep in debate.
A shot in the head is positive, but he cannot bear the thought.

He had loved the shape of that small, perfect skull
When he ran his hand over her hair.

The heart will have to do.

*

But he knows this is selfish.
When it comes to himself there will be no debate.

Experimentally, he sets the revolver muzzle between his teeth.
It is like going to the dentist, that hardware in the mouth.

After he takes it out, he laughs.
"Tough tiddy," he says out loud, parodying the old accent of Alabama,
"But you got it to suck."

He sits there a long time, fondling the revolver like a kitten.

He had always like kittens.

22.

Caleb Winthrop has smashed a fender getting into his garage.
Thank God the baby-sitter has her own car.

23.

Moshe Weinstein's store is stuck up tonight just
As he is about to close.

It is the last time it will be stuck up, for
The spade shoots him in the belly.

Moshe Weinstein was a fool to try to save the day's take.

But Moshe Weinstein was a brave man and he did not make the world.

Nor himself.

24.

While is wife is paying off the baby-sitter, Caleb Winthrop
Manages to get upstairs and to bed. His wife is glazed,

He thinks. He keeps his mind firmly fixed on that fact.

He hears her coming up the stairs.

25.

Spike Oleson closes his Horace book.

26.

Murdoch Lancaster is coming up the stairs, barefoot
In his silent and dark house. He knows that nobody
Can hear anything, out here in the country. The staff.
Is all gone.

*

27.

The moss picker who had gone into the dome, now
He comes out alone.
The other man will go in.

The sound of insects is like a raw nerve singing.

28.

The geyser the lady in pink slacks has been staring at
Has not erupted now for a long time. Mud
Lies in concentric circles around the aperture, and
Starlight is reflected therein.

The fat woman, in a motel, is asleep in a pink night garment.
Her mouth is open.

29.

Having done what he has done, Murdoch Lancaster
Kneels at the foot of his bed. " Now I lay me—"
He hears his mind saying, as he set the muzzle
Between his teeth. With the muzzle there,
He laughs at his foolish mind.

The muzzle tastes like smoke.

Otherwise it is like going to the dentist.

But only for an instant.

30.

Mrs. Caleb Winthrop, who is getting broad in the bum,
Is lying on her back, on the bed, not a stitch on.
The bed is tangled and the top sheet kicked off.

Only a little light seeps in, past the curtains,
From the stars light-years away.

She is gazing at the place where the ceiling is,
And panting shallowly in the dark.

It had started out all right, but then,
No matter what she did, the bastard passed out on her.

"Oh, Jesus," she whispers. She does not know what she will do.
No—in a long-range way, she does now know.
She is not so old there won't be something.

She thinks she had better reduce some.

*

"Oh, Jesus," she whispers again, but now she is not thinking
Long range, she is thinking short range:

oh, jesus—oh jesus—oh jesus—oh jesus—
oh jesus—oh—

31.

Somewhere a mother steps soundlessly into a dark room
And leans longer than necessary over
The crib where a baby sleeps.

32.

There are many of us who are awake, and many asleep,

And some of us who are awake now feel
The globe, to which we cling like lichen,
Grind on its axis eastward toward the day,

And the day after that coming day
Will be the anniversary of our freedom.
We have the promise, too,
Of the pursuit of happiness.

33.

It is hard to know what happiness is.
They did not tell us.
That was probably an oversight—and some are happy, and
Many do not think about it.

It all seems a matter of luck.

34.

Even so, we should not forget the virtues of the old ones who,
Backs to a dark continent, stood and set us free from tyranny.

35.

They did not get around to setting us free from ourselves.

A Few Axioms for a Young Man

There are certain profitable things to know, and I
Have been instructed in some. For instance,
In Arizona, where mountains shoot almost vertically
And with complete irrationality up from
The desert floor, lovers, even in moonlight, the most dramatic,
Should never go walking
At night. Rattlers
Are out then, and odds against your welfare
Shift significantly. Changing the level of discourse,
We may say that the moonlit rattler may be taken as symbolic
Of poison lurking in the path of love—
Yes, at its most beautiful. Natives out here
Rarely go out to admire moonlight, and when they do,
Go by automobile.

It is wisdom to stay out of
Sandstone caves. Especially in Kentucky. If,
In a stratified stone, like limestone,
A slip occurs, the slip
Runs with the stratum, which serves as a roof.
But sandstone is plain undependable, even
If Bible Believers maintain that
Floyd Collins (biggest news story ever before Lindbergh!)
Got trapped in his sandcave because he had defied
His ole 'baccy-chawen, hill-billy pappy.
It is best, whatever your theology, to stay out
Of sandcaves even if
You do love yore ole pappy, and he don't chaw.

In hunting bear, never fire when the animal is,
As it were, trapped in a thicket or cedar-tangle with
Only your direction to turn to. A rifle
May jam on the second needed shot and
Your name is mud. In any case,
Always carry a heavy-clobbering side-arm to fall back on.
It is, of course, a good rule, too, never
To go hunting, even for quail,
With a business partner or best friend
Whose wife you have recently laid. She
May have had an attack of conscience.
The more satisfactory the experience for her, the more likely,
In certain sensitive types, the conscience-trouble.

Never propose marriage in magnificent mountain country
(Especially with snow-peaks like a post card), or beside
A thunderous waterfall, in a wooded glen
(Especially when trees are in full autumn color), or when
In truly elegant surroundings (certainly not

If you are not legal owner of same).
It is much safer, from all angles,
To attempt (particularly if you have matrimony
In mind) an ordinary seduction—this
In surroundings deficient in natural beauty or elegance,
And humanly commonplace, or even
Vulgar (like a motel room). You see,
The lady, if in the first type of situation, may confuse
Romantic decor with her own sincerity of heart,
Which would be getting the cart
Before the horse. And this confusion
Is to be encouraged only
In second-rate fiction or the advertising business.

If you are deputy warden (disciplinary officer)
Of a penitentiary, never,
When walking alone in the institution,
Look back. Even for a moment. It might
Give the wrong impression of your character,
And guts. It is best,
Furthermore, to go unarmed as though
You clearly felt no need. Eat,
At least once a week, with
The cons. Gag
At nothing. Show relish. Be friendly, but
Crack few jokes. And, for God's sake, never
Change your mind after any
Declared decision. That is,
Men are like dogs, certainly
In this respect. The marksmanship
Of every towerman should be as perfect as possible.
The rifle, though, should be a last resort, but
In that case, a shot should be to kill.
A mere wound might be taken as incompetence.
Anyway, a lethal hit saves the state money.

A friendly and able warden once told me, after one fag con
Had murdered another at recreation hour, that
He demanded of the towerman nearest
Why he had not fired. The towerman,
Though expert enough, replied that he
Had been afraid of killing an innocent man.
My warden friend stared at him a full minute,
Then exploded: "Jesus Christ!
There ain't no innocent man. Draw yore pay."

When swimming in heavy surf, never
Wait for a breaker to really lean over you.
As it begins to make a marked curve, dive
Into the heart of it, low to undercut it before
It breaks. A strange moment of philosophical quiet is there,

At its heart. This principle
Has more than one application.

When lost in a thick-wooded country always
Work downward as water would. You
Will come out somewhere.

Never expect to be able to will a poem into existence.
It must happen to you because
You are what you are—
With all your defects.

The last item, it should be added,
Is true of death, even of suicide—

And sometimes, love.

Somewhere

Walking down Madison, I suddenly stopped. Stared
Down at the filthy, phthisic, hang-nailed fingers on

My sleeve. Then at the face, looked: dry
And dry-wrinkled cow-patty of age, leached pale, the eyes,

Not yet quite lustreless, set therein. "No, Mister—"
Heaved up from deep and green-dark corridors of phlegm.

"Aint money I'm astin. Ne'er ast no money yit."
So I took my hand out of my pocket. "But you—

What time you got? That's all. Got business
In Stamford. Important, too." And patted

The rag of a coat into parliamentary decorum,
To be worthy of the occasion.

"Eleven," I said, "and Grand Central two blocks down."
"I got a watch," he said, producing same. "It's gold,

Jist it gits cranky," I saw the watch, saw
Him, heard thanks. "My Daddy, he give it me," he said,

"Fer graduation." And was gone. Somewhere.
Somewhere to go. Important. Patted coat. I shut

My eyes. I stood. Got bumped by nameless debris—
Human, no doubt, to stretch a point—seeing

*

Past inner dark, as down a cardboard tube of Time,
The twelve-year-old, far off, the tennis shoes, legs scratched,

Saw dusk of woods, heave of mossed stone, the .22.
In eyes, felt moisture. I blinked, reeled

In the prismatic explosion of soundless light. Thought:
He was going somewhere in joy—that boy.

Who is that boy? I do not know.
I thought, for a moment, I knew, but know only that

Somewhere, far off, is somewhere.

Praise

I want to praise one I love,
Instructress in the heart's glory,
Who whirls through life in a benign fury,
Or walks alone in the high pine grove.

I want to praise one who sheds light
In darkness where the foot can find
No certainty, and the unlit mind
Wavers, and cannot stand upright.

I want to praise one whose angry joy
Is innocence by wisdom hued,
And whose laughter, at its gayest, is brewed
By knowledge the world is only a toy

To all who can summon courage to live
In innocence and pitying rage
At a sickly and self-pitying age
That scorns the true good the world can give.

Aging Man at Noon in Timeless Noon of Summer

Silence—except below leaves gorge-deep
Where my brook makes the muted music of Time:
Not even a petulant bird-call or cheep,
For there's no breath to waste at beak-breathing noontime.

But if music of Time is what the stream
Unfolds in its leafy gorge, the tune,
In its unstructured sweetness seems only a dream
Of Time in timelessness sweetly at last undone.

If upward I look, how translucently
The green sky of leafage lower leans
With a growth of groining intricately
Sustaining a private sphere for our human means,

One in which I feel safe from coil and cark
Of year, or of day, or it even may seem
That the diurnal sequence of light and dark
Is no sequence at all, but dream mirroring heart's dream.

Lord Jesus, I Wonder

Lord Jesus, I wonder if I would recognize you
On the corner of Broadway and Forty-Second—

Just one more glaze-eyed, yammering bum, nobody to listen
But the halt and maimed. My legs are good.

Yet sometimes I've thought of you, sandaled on sand,
Or stub-toed in gravel, dried blood black on a toe-nail,

And you seemed to look beyond traffic, then back with an innocent
Smile, to ask a revealing question

To which I could find no answer. But I suddenly smell
The sweat-putrid mob crowding closer, in pain and emptiness, ready

To believe anything—ignorant bastards. I envy them. Except
Their diseases, of course. For my head roars

With information, true or false, till I feel like weeping
At the garish idiocy of a Sunday School card. At fourteen,

I was arrogantly wrapped up in Darwin, but felt, sometimes,
Despair because I could not love God, nor even know his address.

*

How about this? *God, c/o Heaven—Special Delivery?* Well,
The letter was returned: *Addressee Unknown.* So

I laughed till I vomited. Then laughed again, this time
At the wonder of the world, from dawn to dark, and all

Night long, while stars spoke wisdom in battalions of brilliance.
Sometimes, since then, I have, face up, walked a night road,

Still adolescent enough to seek words for what was in my heart,
Or gut. But words, I at last decided, are their own truth.

There is no use to continue this conversation. We all
Know that. But, for God's sake, look the next blind man you meet

Straight in the eye. Do not flinch at prune-shriveled socket, or
Blurred eyeball. Not that you have

The gift of healing. You will not heal him, but
You may do something to heal something within yourself.

Commuter's Entry in a Connecticut Diary

I finish the *Times.* Shut eyes. My head,
Inside, flickers like TV in a dark hospital room.

This is the world. Or is it? I
Hear the morning curdle of traffic on our pleasant oak-shaded street.

Grab briefcase, kiss wife, discard umbrella,
Hum "Annie Laurie" as I back down the drive in sunshine,

And make ready the plastic smile to greet
The smiles that greet me on the platform of the 8:20.

What is the day but a dream, or the dream but a day?
And what is life but the day and the dream? I sit

In the evening bar car to nurse only one, as I catch
The last gleam on estuary, river, or sail,

And think of a body, white, in the open sea,
With stroke steady sunsetward, and water prismatic in eyes.

Yes, love is reality. Without it what? I clasp
The hand, hear the breath now even and slow, and staring

In darkness, trust I'll not again dream the dream
Of fume and glow, like the city dump, at night

Outside Norwalk, Conn.

You Sort Old Letters

Some are pure business, land deals, receipts, a contract,
Bank statements, dead policies, demand for some payment.
But a beach-party invite!—yes, yes, that tease
Of a hostess and you, withdrawn behind dunes, lay,
With laughter far off, and for contact
Of tongue and teeth, she let you first loosen a breast.
You left town soon after—now wonder what
Might have that day meant.

Suppose you hadn't left town—well, she's dead anyway.
Three divorces, three children, all born for the sludge of the pit.
It was Number One, nice fellow, when she took you to the dunes.
And she gasped, "Bite harder, oh, hard!" And you did,
In the glare of day. When she scrambled up,
She cried: "Oh, you hate me!" And wept,
Like a child. You patted, caressed her.
Cuddled and kissed her. She said: "I'm a shit."

Do you seem to remember that, for a moment, your heart stirred?
You shrug now, remembering how, in the end, she shacked up
With a likker-head plumber, who, now and then,
Would give her a jolt to the jaw, or with heel of a palm
Would flatten lips to the teeth, then slam
Her the works, blood
On her swollen lips—as was common gossip.
You married a little late, and now from this mess
Of old papers words suddenly at you stare:
"You were smart to blow town. Keep your pecker up!"
Signed only: "Yours, maybe." And then:
"P.S. What might have been?"
Of course, she had everything—money, looks,
Wit, breeding, and a charm
Of defenseless appeal—the last what trapped, no doubt,
The three near middle-aged fall-guys, who got only
Horns for their pains. Yes, she threw
All away and, as you've guessed, by struggling
Sank deeper, deeper, into
A slough of self-hate. However, you
Are no psychiatrist, and couldn't say
What or why, as you, far away, lay

By the warm and delicious body you loved
So well, in the dark ashamed of
Recurring speculation, or memory, as though this
Betrayed your love. Years passed. The end, you heard,
Was sleeping pills. You felt some confusion, or guilt,
But how could you be blamed?—Even if
Knees once were grinding sand as sun once smote

Your bare back, or, once in dream, lips,
Bloody, lifted for your kiss.

Aging Painter Sits Where the Great Tower Heaves Down Midnight

I.

Where American magazines
Were sold, we met, she quite clearly
French from toe-tip to the gold hair which,
Even in that shop's windlessness,
Seemed wind-tossed—boy, that's art, I thought—
And eyelids ever so faintly
Shadowed blue, and eyes sea-blue. "Gosh,"
She said, "you're *not* a frog." I blushed
For my accent, then elegantly
Doffed a greasy beret. "No, ma'am—"
And laid the Mississippi on—
"Just hanging round and trying to
Pass till I get the lingo straight."

"We talk it all the time," she said,
"*Maman,* my girl friend, the tutor,
Me. At any important place,
He sure improves your mind. Right now,
It's north to Cluny." And then: "Let's have
A drink outside till *Maman* sends
François. The girls, all they would have
Was Dubonnet. Pernod for me.
My girl, she tasted mine. Verdict:
"*Pas mal.*" The other wried up lips.

Then François came, black leather leg-
gings strapped like World War I. They left
The bill. There went my wine tonight.
Humming off in that black Bentley.

Another day racked up. One more
Poem by Baudelaire to brood on.
To memorize. A snack. A spell
Of grammar. Free! Then heading off
To find *mes vrais mecs,* the bums who
Knew what I'd need for knocking round,
But wouldn't be taught at the Sorbonne,
Come fall, or any studio.
Mes mecs—this time they didn't show.

*

II.

So up the *corniche,* the track back then
Ragged up cliffside to the broad
High plain, where forgotten mountains
Had long been ground down to blunt heaves
Like great molars, white stone deep-streaked
With green and yellow moss as though
They'd never heard of a toothbrush. I
Stood quiet. In nameless distance sheep-
bells tinkled toward sunset and
The slowly deepening wine-glow of
The sea.

Then suddenly I saw
Her stand, one hand laid to a great
And up-thrust stone, motionless. She,
Feeling unseen, stood there in the
Heart's absolute loneness. Sun sea-
ward sank.

How long I stared I do
Not know. Unconsciously, at last,
In criminal, secret silence, I took
One light, earth-kissing step. The sun's
Weight grew. Redder, heavier, it
Sank. She stared as though her sight
Were, in a final hypnosis, fixed.

Was it my will that made her turn?
She looked, but did not move. Only,
Her hand slipped down from the support of
Plinth-thrust. In empty air it hung.
Across the empty air eyes met.
Met without speech. But bodies through tall
And tangled grass, timorous, moved.

Words grew from the emptiness I felt
Myself suddenly to be. They came:
"In God's name how did you get here?"
If words could be less than a mere tinge
Of silence, such were hers: "It's just—
I had to find me some high place
To watch the sun go down into
The sea."

What distance now remained
Between us seemed to be breath-
lessly dying, though each stood stone-still.
"This place, " I said, "is where I come
Whenever I feel like that." So moved,

Took my old place. Sat. Leaned back
On elbows. Watched her face. "But you,"
I stated, "—if you have such a hanker,
Then settle down, I'll lend you a look."

"*Merci*—oh, thanks," she said. Sat down,
Eyes drowning into the limitless
Impersonality of dis-
tance. And now from that limitlessness
Came words: "I'll do my very best
To remember all this exactly. If
I can. You see, we up and leave
Tomorrow."

How long, how long, then the
Two hands, though bodies apart, hung twined—
Hung frail and black against the flat-
tening bulge of flame in which Time dies.

Time died.

When Time came back, at stars
We stared, and knew the truth of sky.

III.

By stars we fumbled down the path.
We passed the shepherd's hovel humped
Like rubble. Through one window saw,
By candlelight on rough boards, the
Red-splotched, maternal hands tilt a
Black pot. Bowl after bowl. Small heads,
Pale-thatched, to gut, or God, were bowed.

We turned away, almost in shame.

She stumbled to a knee. I leaned,
Stretched out my hand, in love, to help.
"Oh, damn!" she said. And I saw her eyes,
Past pain or pity to the highest
Sky lifted. "Oh!" she cried out,
But in no trace of pain. And if tears
Were there, they made even brighter the eye-shine
Lifted in answer to the domed spangle
That wheeled above. In joy, not pain,
She cried: "The world—the world! How can
It be so beautiful?"

*

IV.

We came
To the last mimosa shade before
The *Splendide's* glare. She stopped. Said: "Well,
I hate to lie. But I've just got to say
How I got lost and fell." She giggled.
"That's not a lie—you saw me fall.
But what a whopper for *Maman!*
You ought to hear her, it's a scream
The way she swings those sacred words around—
Lost and *fallen!* And every time
She looks at me like she'd just guessed
The worst." Again, she giggled. "Well,
A half-lie now to make up for all
The truth I've told she took for lies.
Besides, just look—" she showed her knee.
"Just look," she said, "the bruise is real!
Though, shucks—even then—it didn't hurt."

She hid the knee. Laughed once. Was gone
In the darkest shade. I thought for good.
But no—she's here again, offering
The patient whiteness of her face
In shadow. "Kiss me," she said. "But only
Once—but oh, for always!"

V.

That night,
Randomly waking from sleep, I
Suddenly saw—as though in lit-
eral repetition—my handkerchief,
White, maybe not too clean but freshly
Blood-stained, that I, in my star-stung
Delirium, had flung. Had flung
As love's flag to be aimlessly snagged
On a prickly dry thistle to stiffen in that
Ice-white glaze of starlight.

I slept.

VI.

Into Time I slept. Tell me how many
Times in fifty years the sun
Dies! And with its death it drags
Your carcass like a tin can tied
To a dog's tail. Hear the can clink
Hollow and tinny on the stones!

*

Always unique in glory the sun
Dies. Over water best. How many
Times I've dipped my brush, and un-
consciously prayed for the vision that
Makes the true come real, and makes the real
True. We want both things. Yes, once
I dreamed it possible. How long
Ago!

Yet we can try to live
So that the living is a prayer for vision.

VII.

I've no complaints. My daubs, they hang
In the best museums. I sell the damned things.
And now to open the American Wing
Of a gallery great and famous, there is
To be a retrospective hung.

With a young expert I boss the job.
Learned and lively, a gossip, he
Asks did I know—what very few,
Insiders only, he said, knew—
That the will specified me for the first
Exhibit. "Yes, she was cranky—oh, no—
Forgive—I didn't mean that way.
Her taste was famously splendid, far better
Than the deceased Prof's, her husband's. What
I mean by cranky, she named it for him,
And ordered in the will her name,
And any allusion omitted. So
We stand here now in Butterworth Hall.

"Perhaps she was an ironist,
Contemptuous of the fact the Prof's
Learning just made him play everything safe.
So now, for instance, you not being dead
Enough, she gives him a jolt. Ha, ha!
Even if he's dead."

Then, idly, I:
"What was her name?"

And he: "Diana—
Diana Butterworth—oh, no—
Diana Dalton—the Boston fortune."

*

VIII.

The tower from mist thrust up to shed,
Like a last brazen oak leaf down
In darkness, the *bong* that will sum up
What we call life.

Strange, strange, I thought,
How I, for months sometimes, could not
Recall that name. But the face might come,
By day or night, summoned or dreamlike.

At last that great brazen leaf was falling.
I heard the last stroke of the dire
Hour. Thought of images, vision,
Truth. The last note died. Thought
Of all the canvasses my hands,
In hope, in doubt, in desperation,
Had daubed, and wondered what inscru-
table logic destined the fact that those
Daubs now, in those dark rooms, in one
Of those dark hulks of stone, into darkness
Stared.

I felt my femurs stiffen
On cold and damp of stone. I could
Not move. I dreaded dawn's first light.
I did not know what it might say
Of life's long tangle, or, now finally,
Of the lonely world.

Might dawn yet say:
"The world! How can it be so beautiful?"

Was It One of the Long Hunters of Kentucky Who Discovered Boone at Sunset?

The seasons turn like a great wheel
Jogging on whimsies of weather, sometimes
Slipping backward a bit, or even about to heel
Over, paying no attention to chimes

Or clock-tick, seasons themselves being
The great clock to state our fate.
There are many small signs such as seeing
Boot heel-mark in wild mud, or toward the gate

*

And civilization, the grid in snow
Of overshoes, and smoke from the chimney, pale
Against twilight. There will come, you know,
A time for petunias, and loam black under thumbnail.

You feel a mystic reality
In loam's cool touch. But not long later you will lose
Yourself in the glimmering beech wood, high
On the mountain, above you nothing to choose

Between patches of summer sky's heavenly blue
Or green leaf's translucence against blue light,
And later those leaves will hang gold against blue,
And the heart swell to a new delight.

But you might as well remember that deer
In winter have starved before the first bud
Has offered frail sustenance, and the clear-
Eyed lynx forgets not the taste of blood.

Yes, in such ambiguity
The seasons wheel, and our hearts colder
Grow, under every kind of sky,
From early years to years that grow grimly older.

But I think how once in his long, lone wilderness walk
Across Kentucky—alone, sun low, arms crossed to prop his
Face up, they found Boone singing in his tuneless crow-squawk,
In joy just because the world is the way it is.

Goodbye

What lies youth tells itself all from the need
For significant truth to fill the vacuum
Of life's charade, before strangely learning truth,
Or more likely the self-deceiving dramatic trick
Of converting lies to truth by habitude:
And years later tears of salt sincerity
Patter the loam, or undertaker's grass
Of any season. But, of course, sometimes
You may stumble on the real truth and break
Both legs. But that is rare.

It was in the morning
She wanted me to come to say goodbye.
The evening might well seem like something else.
The family was dead against her seeing me,
Not any more: undependable, not a dime,

Given to scribbling, read peculiar subjects,
Wanted to wander universities, and countries,
Here this year, but next year where, and keeping
What company, God knows.

The kiss was formal.
She offered a chair. But slowly retreated thence.
Stood twenty feet away in profile at
The enormous window of her apartment. Yes,
Stood motionless, the profile fine against
The blue mountain. Profile of face, I mean. I felt
A terrible sadness, tears ragged in eyes. Then,
Against the blue mountain, noticed the flatness of breasts,
Not thinking of them as known bare. I noticed,
Also, the previously unnoticed bulge
Of belly, and slight premonitory slump
Of shoulders, and suddenly sadness felt worse—
Like pity, despair, there in the very midst
Of sharp critical vision and prediction.

I did not understand my complex of feeling.
Particularly as she was saying, "Yes,
I'm sorry I ever met you. Ever. If
I hadn't I wouldn't have to go through this
Awfulness, the awfulest part being that
I'll remember you. Always."

She brought me a glass
Of sour mash on ice. She took just coffee.
We talked no more. Though I knew what I should say:
How much all meant. But stared at the whiskey and
Knew that whatever I said would smell like a lie.
Even if it wasn't. And how could I be sure?
But if a lie, why did I feel so awful?

I drank. I stood before her. She lifted her face.
When we kissed, my hand, through summer cloth, felt
That her body was as though bound tight with tape.

Somehow I felt like crying. But not for me.
For the world, perhaps.

When lips had touched, hers
Felt dry and cold and minutely scaly. Felt
Of blood drained dry. I wondered how mine felt.

She shut the door very slowly behind me.
I hoped she might guess how awful I was feeling,
Even though I did not know why I felt awful.
I felt awful all afternoon, but better after
I'd played a game of pick-up basketball
Around 5 P.M.

*

When during the night I woke
I fingered the blind question of really how much
What she had said had meant to her,

Or me?

Remark for Historians

Only Truth is deep as the ocean,
Where green, gold, and blue lights glow,
Dappling total dark where the slimed historian
Makes shine the natural light in his brow.

And still as the ocean depth is Truth
Where horned, slick monsters yet undefined
By science, with suck-plates, arms weaving, and tooth,
Prey on their, or monsters of other, kind.

But do not forget how glitter and glory,
From galley and round-ship to liner and dreadnought,
Have moved on the uncertain surface—and their story
Is often as dim as the depth they, feckless, sought.

Yes, we live for Truth, but what man has been
In its depth and lived to describe that bourn?
And all we know is its sunlit sheen
Or the wind-ripped medium where great waves mourn.

Institute of the Impossible

I often live in the Institute of the Impossible.
My room has what looks like a door
Built into the wall, but is part of the wall.
The neat bathroom has no door at all—
Superfluous, for there one is always alone, twenty-four
Hours a day. Walls and ceilings are glaring white
And giving forth light,
For there is no window,
And the floor
Glitters black like Swedish ice without snow.
It offers no friction. You find it hard not to fall.
So I usually walk on the ceiling or wall,
Like a fly.
Some days I put on best clothes, but there is no place to go.
I scarcely remember what "weather" is, and vaguely know
Of the thing called "sky."

*

Mail comes every day, mysteriously on the bulging pillow
Of the never occupied bed beside one's own—
On which I myself always fear to lie down.
Timorously I always go
For my letter. It has name and address correct, but a blank sheet for the eye.
You ask about food. There's a gorgeous menu
And wine-list affixed to the *soi-disant* door, ready for you
To read. So I nap and dream of wolfing all,
And wake satiated. A telephone, of course, is there,
On an ebony table, low, by an easy chair,
But no directory provided, and even if I call
Some number that surprisingly floats from the deep of my mind,
There's always a voice strange and undefined,
Say, like Grandma on TV saying Mother Goose Rhymes.
Or a professorial tone reading from an unnamed
Novel, and if this is the case,
I find myself—my own name—an actor there, disreputable, base,
And I try to hang up, but sometimes

My hand won't do it, no matter how ashamed
I am till I remember it's fiction—who believes a word?
But sometimes two voices, in near-whisper, are heard—
Male and female, lovers apparently at copulation.
For a hoarse male voice whispers, "The pillow—pull higher." Then no word,
While soft female moans punctuate raw male respiration,
Until she demands, "Further—oh, further!" No sound, no sigh,
Just the tangle of breaths—that is all
Until, sudden, protracted, and small,
Comes the painful, cat-like cry
That drains into silence—but silence like wind on the wires
In an image my heart in its emptiness requires—
Across the continent, dark and vast,
With infinite miles of empty rails, poles leaning beside,
And snow falling slow, not quite enough to hide
The snow-slashed, weak gleam of a town with no name or future or past.

And once, only once, a voice said the Lord's Prayer
In moving reverence—before the air
Was filled with maniacal laughter, then weeping.
And back in the chair I lay, heart torn. But soon sleeping.

For hours I'd sit in the chair, head
In hands, and try to remember—but what?
Until with relief I'd think, "Time for bed."
Though in the clockless and constant light,
Could sleeping ever seem necessary? But I put on pajamas, lie down,
And even in glare, sleep and dream. But no
Dream returns, no matter my struggle, when, awaking,
I rise, look back at the bed, in magic, remade, no wrinkle in sight.
I stretch my body, but find no twinge or aching.
At last I admit I cannot evoke the dream that claimed the night.
*

But perhaps all this is the dream, and elsewhere
I live in the orbit of possibility, where friends
Name my name, and day and dark swap the air,
And seasons change, and I calculate means and ends,
And in a mirror see hair
Going gray, and ponder the problem of Evil and Good, good and bad,
And weakness and strength, and dwell on the golden chances, now missed, I once had.

Winter Dreams

From the edge of the drained beaver swamp,
Where the stumps are pious as monks in their hoods of green moss,
And the lodge a decayed tumble that
For winter was home and food,
And in summer refuge
When the flat tail smote
The pond in alarm—now at the edge,
From a tangle of brush and vine, the she bear
Rises. On hind legs surveys
The gravel road.

Empty.

Beside her, lost in the world,
The cub rises, too.
The world is large and strange.
It is his first summer, and over
The gravel,
Into the forest of spruce,
Mountainward he goes.

Somewhere on that mountain the great father
Of white fangs and short memory wanders. Forages now
For the last fat for winter. But before winter
The sex-hoot will be again heard on the mountain,
Or by the ruined apple trees by a crumbling chimney.
But the she bear will not hear. She has her problem.

That gut-snaring hoot is like the hoot
Of the great owl, and
The season the same.
It can be mistaken for that.
If you are not a bear. The moon is large and white.
The open season comes soon.

Two weeks for bowman and his muscular silence before
Echo of the legal rifle is heard
By the cliffside.
Survivors will sleep in caves, under ledges.

*

The first to reappear in spring
Resemble skeletons waddling in moth-eaten fur coats,
Voracious but not dangerous. But
The bear that has just given birth—
Avoid her.

Once, in spring, I saw a he-bear with the broken shaft
Of the bowman swinging from the
Point of penetration in the left shoulder. What
Was left of the shaft was what the bear's jaws
Had not been able to get at.
The wound was reamed again with every limping lunge forward.

What dreams all winter he may have had?

Breaking the Code

The world around us speaks in code,
Or maybe something like the old Indian sign
Language of the Great Plains—all with a load
Of joy and/or despair. And in all of which you must resign
Yourself to ambiguity, or error. The road
Markers are often missing, or defaced. Is
The message the veery tries at dusk to communicate benign?
Does the first flake of snow from a sky yet blue
Mean *that* or *this?*
Is the owl's old question—*"Who?—who?"*—
Addressed to your conscience, and you?

In dawn light does the scroll-mark of wind-swirl in night snow,
Or later the bleeding icicle tip from the eaves,
Tell you a truth you yearn to know—
Or is it merely an index of the planet's tilt?
And what of the beech's last high leaves
Of hammered gold, or glint of sunlit gilt?

What do the eyes of a mother, dying, say or perceive
As your heart compresses in the torturing twist
Of a fist,
And do you know
Whether you feel a ghastly relief—or grieve—
As with glazed eyes you go
Forth, alone, under winter stars, and try to weep,
And try again, and yet again,
For only undefinable tears will serve such a paradox of pain?
Later, of course, you sleep.
Oh, for the longest sleep!

*

But, no, for later you may see a beloved face
Wreathed in raw rage,
And see a timeless beauty clawed, in a flickering moment, by age.

It is hard to break the code in our little time and space.

Problem of Autobiography
Vague Recollection or Dream?

Was it a long-lost recollection crawling
Out of its fetid darkness, time-smeared,
Worm-smeared, nothing quite clear, all bleared
In ambiguous predawn light, before the calling
Of the first bird announces the idiotic joy of dawn?
You think of footprints on the dewy lawn.

Going away? Not going away?
And you'll never know the face,
For there are no footprints coming in.
Could it be peeled from the mirror in its mirrored place?
A part of you, but a self you never
Knew was you, but from now forever
Will be a part of you, and you go sniffing
Future footprints of identity like a hound, or whiffing
The scent of your dented pillow
To know
What self made it.

Instant on Crowded Street

Knowingly, knowing what secret, but
Unvenomous, even forgiving, the dark glance,
Sideways from dark fur, through
Interstices in the crowd, brushes
Your face, penetrates you, and some
Slow coil twitches in your heart. All seems
To have something to do with memory. With
Perhaps, a lie you once told, and now
Try to forget? A betrayal? Or even worse,
The reproach of a mathematically drafted chart
Of the self you aspired to be, like the scroll
Of a blueprint, scale carefully indicated, flattened
With thumb tacks on the wall of
Your mind?—always there, and you feel
Like weeping in the dark

*

All this, an instant. The glance,
With its forgiving knowledge, suddenly gone. Perhaps,
Never there. The crowd
Closes, and you stand still in the tramp of feet in Time
And think how once you foolishly thought
You knew the most desperate nature of love, how
The heart must welcome suffering, even
Ghastliness, the slimy roots and prickly stalk
That would unfold, in years, white petals with the golden corolla

But you can't stand still, remembering foolish illusion,
With upon you the pressure of the anonymous world.
Particularly since nothing quite seems to explain anything.

You wonder if the wise and forgiving glance ever fixed on your face.

Old Love

I.

At the time when the tulip-tree, even then rare, bloomed
By the edge of the cloistered lane,
They met, and each mildly wondered if ever again
It might be assumed
That such accident would bring them face to face
In another such astutely designed, lovely, and lonely place.
Would they part with a nod of civility—
Or stand with a tentative smile until mutual timidity
Of youth made them pass on? Almost surely not,
For spring sun was reddening westward to gild earth's heave.
But secretly he stubbed the turf with the toe of a boot,
And his tongue went dry, his brain drained. But how could he leave
Without some recognition of her own, and beauty's, worth?
At last in panic, he set heel firmly where boot-toe had scored earth.

He mumbled something. Was gone.
She, too, with no backward look, or word, was gone,
Her gaze idly wandering the gold-flecked hill
As idly as in some store she'd pass someone never known.
But unconsciously now—or half so—she kicked at a stone.

II.

She had married, he later heard. Oh, well, so had he!
And children both. Contentment? Why not?
Yes, a county was like a trap of propinquity,
And memories blur like old mirrors, unsilvering spot by spot.

Twenty-five years later, or so, he said to his bigger son,
"Get out the Ford, I got business over to Tarleton."
They get down the road, gravel then, but in good condition,
Then spotting the county line, the old one's keen eyes
Began to scan road-brush for a gap that might come by surprise.
"Take yore next turn left, up that lane, " he said. "And slow,
For it used to be rough, and a spring's just iron, you know."
"It'd help, " the son said, "if you'd say where you're trying to go."

"Just an old man's craziness, to see if ever yet
Anything's the same," he said. Then: "Hey!—that tulip-tree's gone!"
"Tulip's rare," the son said, "and dollars pay axe-handle sweat."
"Yes, rare," said the old one, slow, "yet it seems they might leave that one."

"What next?" the son asked, but got no reply,
For the hard, blue old eyes were staring at vacancy.
Or was it at something that took the place of the sky?
At last: "On to Tarleton. I used to have friends thereabout,
And might just drop by to see how they're making out.
At Main Street, the light, just turn right and on to the end."
"But that—that's the graveyard!" "Shore is," the old one said,
"And that makes it easy to find a friend,
If it happens at last he's decided he's dead."

Son parked the car and snoozed in the shade,
While his father, weaving from stone to stone, made
His prowling way, just now and then kneeling to peer at
Some name or a date, this or that.
And at last found one where he crouched and lingered.

III.

The waking was wordless, and on the way back
Miles were wordless until they faced sun going low,
And the old man croakingly managed: "I ne'er had no knack
To find words for what was inside, but I want my two boys to know
How I'm grateful to Ma, who give me the get like both you.
Specially since she couldn't make it herself on Number Two."

*

He coughed like something was stuck in his throat.
Tried again. Got it loose. "It's just something I think you ought
To think on, now both's settled down—how a man
Gits so used to his luck he don't give it a thought,
And the years slide on by before he can
Even learn to know
Its name, for he's had to wait
Almost too late
For the knowing to grow."

Upwardness

It is hard to know the logic of mere recollection.
Is Time the nexus? No, for Time does not

Define sequence of recollection, only
Of event, and of event as the death-black humus

In which pale hair-like roots of recollection
Probe in ghostly aim, or aimlessness.

Look! Coming down the street of the little town,
Book-satchel on shoulder, what idle wonderment

In head, the small boy passes homeward, not
Yet knowing where love lived, or what it was.

He gives you a totally blank stare which denies
Your very existence—as you, in the mirror, are often

Inclined to do. There have been mountains. Deserts. Seas.
In moonlit deck-swell there has been head laid to your shoulder,

Hair sweet, name unknown. A lamp has gleamed all night
As print, enchanted, squirmed, live, across the page.

Down Sierra curves, in the old open Buick back,
The standing young man is hurled sidewise, seatward, the gin bottle

Overside. The driver is screaming in ecstasy.
What was happiness? There must have been such a thing.

***

Yes, silently, out of nothing, again it comes true:
Side by side, on night grass lying, one palm to one palm,

And silently, silently, four eyes fixed upward as though
Straining beyond the infinite starwardness.

Uncertain Season in High Country

By the descending mountain track, soundless
At damp impact of foot, a few
Pine-tops tall enough to lift
Into the hover of mist, I came. Horizon,
Encircling the clotted gray dubiety of light we call
The sky, has no definition in curdle
Of cloud and distance. But
You know what is there: bald heavings upward, bold
Peak, bottomless
Ravine. You
Have seen all, the lift
Of monstrous glitterings to
The flame of summer noonlight, depth
At noon dizzy in darkness.
But now, far, far, over what is not
Seen, thunder prowls,
Grumbles. This is the season of
Firmament's, and heart's,
Uncertainty.

Pines thin out, yonder a stump, track widens. Somebody
Must have been at some feeble attempt
At human life. That open area yonder
Must have been a mowing. Dimly,
Like last hope, the track skirts it.
In the middle of the mowing, the cow
Stands. What remains of a cow: udders
Shrunken, backbone sagging, hind quarters
Thin to hide-drape. The beast
Stands under a dying pine.
A tuft of gray grass, unmasticated, hangs from motionless jaw.

South of the beast, the log cabin staggers—
Or seems to stagger. Above mud-plastered rock chimney,
Smoke hovers. It wants to rise. Fails.
I do not stop. I know my fate.

Under a thick clump of larches, I sleep.
At dawn the first few raindrops of
The uncertain season,
Tentative. I manage
A fire. Coffee. A hard day and I'll make it.

Thunder, uncertain,
Rambles the undefinable horizon.

I think of the cow, of the unmasticated snatch of grass.
I speculate on the weather.

The Loose Shutter

All night the loose shutter bangs. This way it won't last
Till morning. Something now bangs in my head. The past
Bangs in my head, hinges rust, hasps rip, all
The slotted crosspieces split. In the morning I'll call

The outfit that used to specialize in such matters
But now always bungles a job, mad as hatters,
For few are expert in repairing old jobs these days,
And the past seems to get out of order a thousand new ways,

And who now plays the decrepit piano downstairs
While the frisky old skeletons scuffle at Musical Chairs,
With old silk and broadcloth in tatters, and sex a debate?
But the party's now over. The last cab horse stamps at the gate.

If that goddam shutter stopped banging, I'd undertake
At least some amateur readjustments, and make
The great banging stop inside my head, and set
Certain matters to rights that now perpetually get

All sequences tangled, wear false faces, deny
All that happened—how at the orgasmic shudder's choked cry
Once ecstasy named the wrong name. The shutter goes *bang*.
What voice? What name? By what thin thread does the past hang?

John's Birches

You stop at the end of the lane, where the birches grow,
And white stems go suddenly black against setting sun,
And from elmsward the last
Dove's grievous utterance spills, fated and slow,
At the death of a day like any other one
To come, or that has already fulfilled itself and passed
Into the timelessness of boyhood. A last
Cowbell trails the herd, the snatch of a gluttonous laggard. Dogs bark.
You watch the sun go down. The birches go white in the dark.

What now might I be expected to remember
That filled my head as I followed the homeward lane?
Was it boyhood fame
Of bat-crack and cheer as the last ember
Of day died? No, only that, star by star, stars asserted their domain
Of infinity, and I strained back my neck to name
The names of a few I then, like a treasure, could name;
And crazily dreamed of a night when I would know all, and, like a star,
My own head, in greeting, would move, nodding near, nodding far.

*

If boyhood is lonely enough, the moss-bearded stone
Communicates wisdom. You are not lonesome at the cool cave-lip,
For back in that dark
The chasmed stream chants, ungleaming, to you alone.
And now you must have known
The joy stars know as, soundless, they slip,
Degree by precise degree, without care or cark,
Each to its place in the great Chart of Being, careless of light or dark.
If you are lonely enough, you will never know lonesomeness,
With day full of leaves that whisper, and night never visionless.

INTRODUCTION TO THE NOTES

A Collected Poems can be one of two things. It can be like an author's autobiography, representing the author's career as it looked from the end of it, with all of the blind alleys and false turns elided (or marked out as necessary lessons and difficult preliminaries). Or it can be like an author's diary, representing the author's intellectual life as it unfolded, with no certainty, but with many provisional intuitions, about how each event will fit into the big picture. A Collected Poems of the first type should include only those poems the poet, at the end of his or her life, felt were worthy to represent that life, and it should represent the texts, in the absence of compelling reasons not to do so, as they stood when the author last gave considered attention to them. A Collected Poems of the second type should include all the poetry the poet published, and it should represent the texts, in the absence of compelling reasons not to do so, as they stood during the period of the poet's career with which they are most strongly associated. In the first case the scholarly editor seeks to establish the author's final intentions for the *oeuvre*, and must make a case either that all of the author's work is of a piece or that the author was able to the end to retain special access to the intentions he or she entertained earlier in life. In the second case the scholarly editor seeks to establish the author's settled intentions at particular periods of his or her career, and must make a persuasive case about what counts as a settled intention of the author and about what counts as a period of the author's career. Warren started, but did not bring to completion, a Collected Poems of the first type, giving to Stuart Wright, who was preparing the edition, a sense of the poems he wished to include and exclude, and interlinearly adding final revisions to many poems. I have consulted the materials from which that edition was to be prepared, and the changes Warren marked have been included in the notes to this edition; but I have chosen, both because I am not certain what shape that volume finally would have taken and because I wish to include all of Warren's published poetry, to compile a Collected Poems of the second type.

My chief reason for choosing the second variety of Collected Poems is my sense of what the first variety would be required to leave out. Warren was known as one of the "Fugitive" poets because of his association with the magazine *The Fugitive,* but only one of the poems from *The Fugitive* ever appeared in his books: "To a Face in a Crowd," which ended the different Selected Poems volumes Warren published in 1943, 1966, 1976, and 1985. In a late poem, "Red-Tail Hawk and Pyre of Youth," Warren describes himself as burning "a book/ Of poems friends and I had printed in college." The book to which he refers is clearly the volume *Driftwood Flames,* but he did not reprint the poems from *Driftwood Flames* in any later volume. While the poems of *Driftwood Flames* are apprentice work, some of the poems from *The Fugitive* retained enough importance in Warren's mind that he included them in *Pondy Woods and Other Poems*, which only the bankruptcy of Payson and Clarke while it was in press prevented from seeing publication, and in several other unpublished collections that Warren pulled together in the 1920's and 1930's, such as *Cold Colloquy,*

Kentucky Mountain Farm and Other Poems and *Problem of Knowledge*. 1931, the year in which "Red-Tail Hawk and Pyre of Youth" is set, seems to have been a poetic turning point for Warren. In the headnote to his unpublished *Problem of Knowledge* (a collection roughly contemporary with *Eleven Poems on the Same Theme*) Warren divides the volume into poems written before and after 1931, noting "a fundamental difference, in both theme and method, between the two groups." If there is a crisis in 1931, there is also a fundamental change in Warren's poetry as well, as he leaves behind the essentially Hardyan ethos of his early poetry for the Marvellian poems of the 1930's.

Whatever the crisis that Warren describes in "Red-Tail Hawk and Pyre of Youth" was—in the poem he alludes to the death of his mother (in 1931, horrifyingly anticipated in "The Return: An Elegy," which Warren was writing at the time of her death) and the bankruptcy of his father—it seems to have turned him ruthlessly against his earlier poetry in ways his more well-known poetic crisis, the ten years of poetic silence in the late 1940's and early 1950's, did not do. A Collected Poems which seeks to follow the poet's final intentions would have to exclude most of this early poetry, some of it of great interest. This volume, by contrast, includes all of the published poems from this early career, as well as the handful of poems Warren later published in magazines or in chapbooks but did not include in books, and the poems that appeared after his last volume. In fact, this volume includes every poem Warren published, including *Audubon* and *Chief Joseph of the Nez Perce* but excluding *Brother to Dragons* and the two brief selections from it that were separately published. (I have in mind ultimately to prepare a parallel text edition of the 1953, 1976, 1979, and 1987 versions of *Brother to Dragons*.) It does not include unpublished poems, although there are many fine unpublished poems among Warren's papers in the Beinecke Library at Yale. (I have made an exception for "Love's Voice," which won the Caroline Sinkler prize from the Poetry Society of South Carolina. Although the poem seems never to have been published, I have treated its winning the Sinkler prize as the moral equivalent of publication, and have followed what seems to be Warren's final version of it, the version he included in the typescript of *Problem of Knowledge*, his unpublished volume of the early 1940's.)

A second reason for choosing to reconstruct Warren's settled intentions at particular periods rather than to reconstruct his final intentions is that the latter project would face tangled questions about how to treat the long, titled sequences of poems (such as "Kentucky Mountain Farm" or "Garland for You") which are such a feature of Warren's work. Because I want to present the sequences as completely as possible, and to preserve the shape Warren gave to his original volumes, the version I am reconstructing is that of the original volumes rather than the later revisions in the 1943, 1966, 1976, or 1985 Selected Poems. I had thought to use the last text of each poem for the copy text, choosing the last revisions to appear in one of the four Selected Poems. But as I began looking at the shape of the original volumes and of the sequences, I realized that I could not use the revised texts in a principled way, for using the revised texts would require me either to break up the sequences or to print versions of the sequences which don't resemble Warren's plans for them at any stage. Indeed, in the final 1985 Selected volume Warren broke up many sequences entirely, or gave the sequence title but included only one poem from it.

Warren's practice in the 1985 volume raises the question of just how much the placing of poems in titled sequences counted in Warren's final intentions for his *oeuvre*. That in 1985 Warren preserved a sequence title even in a case where he only reprinted one section of that sequence suggests that sequences were still part of his vision of his poetry in 1985 and that he broke up the sequences for that volume to save space, not because he had fundamentally changed his mind about them. Even so, the question of which poems were dropped because they no longer had any place in the sequence as Warren thought of it and which were dropped only for reasons of space is an unanswerable one, since choosing to exclude the poem is perforce to concede that it is less central to the intentions of the sequence than are other poems which the poet chose to include. It is unlikely, for instance, that Warren ever would have restored "The Cardinal" to the "Kentucky Mountain Farm" sequence, since he referred disparagingly to that poem in correspondence. But he did restore "Watershed" to that sequence in 1985, after having excluded it for twenty years. It is safest to say that Warren's sense of what the sequences ought to include remained fluid to the end.

If the best evidence of Warren's final intentions about his titled sequences were his practices in the 1985 Selected volume, the question of whether to present the poems in sequences and the question of what to include in them would be a vexed one, and the possibility would arise that the author's settled intentions at particular times of his life and his final intentions for his *oeuvre* would be in stark contradiction to each other. Fortunately, there is other evidence. Although I have not chosen to use the texts which Warren marked up for a Collected Poems as my own copy text, it is clear from those texts, now in the Special Collections of Emory University, that Warren did not reject the idea of printing his poems in the extended sequences in which they had appeared in the earlier volumes. Indeed, in the versions of *Promises* and *Or Else* that he prepared, he planned to include most of the sequences completely and in order, so certainly his intention in shortening the sequences for the Selected Poems volumes was to preserve space, not to effect a wholesale revision of the poems, although in practical terms (since he perforce had to choose some sections of each sequence over others) the selection amounts to a revision anyway. The least I can say is that in restoring the sequences I am not completely ignoring the author's final intentions even though I am attempting to reconstruct his settled intentions at the various earlier stages of his career.

My desire to reconstruct the sequences as they appear in the original volumes also forced me not to use the original publications of the poems in magazines as copy texts. There are several reasons for this. First, sequences were sometimes published piecemeal, often, but not always, with indications that the sections were intended as part of a sequence. "The Owl" was marked as part of "Kentucky Mountain Farm" when it was separately published, but it was never published in any extended version of that sequence. Second, subsets of larger sequences were often published, with the sections in a different order from the one that Warren settled on for the final volume. Third, the extensive revisions of his poetry, which Warren always engaged in between publication in a magazine and the first book publication of every poem, suggest that he thought of the magazine versions as provisional texts, as trial versions. Most of the magazine versions are quite different from the book versions, and in a few cases, such as "The Bramble Bush," Warren seems to have turned the poem in a completely different direction while revising it.

Warren did not simply put together volumes from the poems he had on hand. He paid careful attention to the structure of individual volumes, not only working hard to arrive at a proper arrangement of the poems but also excluding poems that seemed to him to be off the main impulse of the volume, adding poems he had written many years earlier to a volume if they seemed consonant with it, reshaping sequences as his views of them evolved, and even, in the case of "Notes on a Life to be Lived" from *Tale of Time*, breaking up a sequence from one volume entirely and distributing its parts into two later sequences in two later volumes. The discipline and thought Warren put into shaping his volumes is strong evidence that it is the volumes, more than the individual poems, which define the significant stages of his career. Warren's thought about which poems to include, how to group them in sequences, and in what order to present them, gives one insight into which intentions, among the welter of different impulses and intuitions that may have been in play in his poetry at any given time, seemed to the author to be worthy of counting as his settled intentions for that volume.

My choice to use the original volumes as copy texts forced a further decision on me: since Warren continued to revise the poems, sometimes publishing five versions over fifty years, I decided that I had to produce the extensive textual apparatus you see here. Because Warren was a restless reviser at all stages of his career (as a look at the textual apparatus will show you), I have sought to collate all of the published editions of his poems. To save space, wherever I have made an emendation I have provided the collation at that point only in the emendations section, rather than repeating it in the historical collations. In order to save the reader an excessive amount of flipping around in the notes to compare versions, I have simply included my rationale for not emending lines that posed difficulty in the historical collations, rather than segregating disputed readings to a separate section. Because the large majority of Warren's revisions concerned substantives rather than accidentals, I have not diverted substantives and accidentals to separate sections of the notes.

The usual purpose an editor has in compiling a historical collation of a work is to make clear the editor's process of thought in emending the copy text. To some extent that is true of my purpose in this edition as well. But if the Collected Poems is a record of the development of the poet's thought, so, too, is the history of the poet's revisions presented in the notes. Using these notes the reader can reconstruct every version of every poem Warren published.

Reconstructing the published versions of the poems is, however, quite a different thing from representing the poet's local intentions for the work at each stage. A third line of reasoning that induced me to construct Warren's intentions for the individual volumes rather than to construct his final intentions for his *oeuvre* is that for most of his texts the evidence about his settled local intentions is of better quality than the evidence about his final intentions. Warren's several revisions of his work were carried out with varying degrees of care. But the three revisions of his poems (in 1985, 1986, and 1987) that he undertook at the end of his career are so problematic that they cannot be used with confidence.

The thorough going-over Warren gave all of his poems for the 1966 Selected volume seems to have extended to the finest details of punctuation and other matters usually considered "accidentals" rather than "substantives." Furthermore, one can argue that the 1966 revisions are intended not to produce a separate work (as, say, the 1979 *Brother to Dragons* is a separate work from the 1953 *Brother to Dragons*), but to remain as far as possible within the intentions of the earlier versions. (This is how Warren himself described his intentions in the headnote to that volume.) At least it is fair to say that Warren did not attempt to revise the convictions his earlier poems expressed, even when he no longer shared those convictions, and he did not attempt to make poems which had originally appeared in the the twenties and thirties closer in sound to the poetry he was writing in the sixties. But Warren's rethinking of his poems in 1966 is far-reaching enough, and interesting enough, that it is important that the 1966 readings be available in one form or another. Had the 1966 volume been Warren's last, a strong case could have been made for a Collected Poems that follows the author's final intention, and that volume (suitably emended to reflect the flurry of correspondence about typographical errors which followed its publication) would have made a good standard of collation for such a Collected Poems as for both substantives and accidentals. The revisions for the 1976 volume were less thorough, almost always following the 1966 readings for the earlier poetry, and not much changing the later poems. That text, too, might have provided a good basis for a Collected Poems had it been, as it thankfully was not, Warren's last volume.

While the 1966 and 1976 Selected Poems volumes are arguably good representations of the author's intentions regarding substantives and accidentals, the 1985 volume cannot be relied upon for either, since the number of obvious mistakes in that volume argues that the author did not prepare it with the same care he used in preparing the earlier volumes. For instance, Albert Erskine, Warren's editor at Random House, had the setting copy for the earlier sections of the 1985 volume prepared from a cut-up photocopy of the 1976 Selected Poems. Often, in places where the preparer taped in sections unevenly, the typesetter added a stanza break, which Warren did not correct when he examined the galleys for that volume. Even the substantives in the 1985 volume, although they can almost entirely be traced to Warren's own emendations on the galleys, are made carelessly, as if the poet no longer quite understood his earlier poems. His 1985 revision of "The Return" from the sequence "Kentucky Mountain Farm," for instance, seems to forget that the poem is intended to scan, and his most striking revision of "Old Nigger on One-Mule Cart Encountered Late at Night When Driving Home From Party in the Back Country" makes a syntactic mess of the sentence he revises. Thus, while the substantives and accidentals in the 1966 volume represent Warren's view of his poems in 1966, the 1985 volume cannot be assumed to represent either the poet's intentions in 1985 or his final intentions for the poems.

A particularly puzzling set of problems is raised by the 1987 *New and Selected Poems* printed by Eurographica in Helsinki, Finland, in an edition of 350 signed copies edited by Rolando Pieraccini. This was the last volume Warren brought to completion, but, like the 1985 Selected Poems it raises more questions about the author's final intentions than it answers. The volume is very different from other Selected Poems volumes in that the poems are printed in (roughly) chronological order rather than in reverse chronological order (although some poems are out of sequence), and some of the titles are changed. ("Tiberius on Capri," for instance, is changed to "Tiberius on Capri, Autumn 1939," and "Folly on Royal Street Before the Raw Face of God" is changed to "Folly on Royal Street, New Orleans, Before the Raw Face of God.") In addition, many of the poems in the Helsinki volume are substantially revised. Warren did prepare a new typescript for the Helsinki volume (although there is no evidence that he read galley proof for it), so these revisions are undoubtedly Warren's own work. The printing of the Helsinki volume was completed in October, 1986, but when Warren returned to his work to mark up volumes for Stuart Wright's use in preparing a Collected Poems, he seems to have totally forgotten all of the revisions he had prepared less than six months before. I have recorded all of the variants from this volume, but exactly how much authority the Helsinki edition ought to be given is still to my mind an unanswered question. It has weighed with me when there is other evidence tending in the same direction; I have not made emendations on its sole authority.

I have used the alterations (some of them corrections, some of them revisions) that Warren prepared for his unfinished Collected Poems with similar caution, although I have recorded them all in the collations. They too, give only the haziest glimpse into what Warren's final intentions for his poetry would have been. For one thing, all of these alterations date from the late spring of 1987, when Warren's final illness was already far advanced. For another thing, the revisions were clearly not made with the care Warren exercised in 1966. For example, Warren used a copy of the original English edition of *Promises* for the *Promises* section of this project, but he shows no signs of having collated it against his many revisions of the poems from *Promises* in the Selected volumes of 1966, 1976, and 1985. Indeed, many lines that Warren tinkers with are lines he had completely excised from the *Promises* section of all of the later revisions, and many other revisions make no sense against the background of the complicated revision history of those poems. Because it is unclear to me what the final edition would have looked like (since Warren did not bring the project to completion), I have not made emendations on the sole authority of those texts. I have, however, used those emendations to provide supporting evidence for readings for which I have other grounds. Also, since that volume would not have been a Collected Poems in the sense that this one is, in that it would have dropped some poems from some sequences, dropped some other poems entirely, and would not have included the poems Warren published but did not collect, I have treated it merely as a much larger Selected Poems; therefore, my rule about not mixing texts in the sequences from different Selected Poems volumes would apply to this hypothetical text as well. The obvious difficulties presented by the 1985 volume, the Helsinki volume, and the unfinished 1987 Collected Poems project make a third case (in addition to the case about completeness and the case about sequences) for reconstructing Warren's intentions for the individual volumes rather than reconstructing his final intentions for his *oeuvre*.

My collation and proofreading procedures were as follows. I collated the first editions of Warren's poetry collections against the magazine versions of the poems and against the Selected volumes by eye. Then all of the book texts (the poetry collections and the Selected volumes) were scanned into computer files, checked, corrected, and compared by electronic file comparison. Then my team of graduate students again collated the first editions against the magazine versions and against the Selected volumes by eye. Then I collated the pre-publication materials. Due to the heavily worked nature of these materials, this collation sequence was conducted by eye alone. In this stage of collation, the first edition text was used as the standard for collation, and compared against the following layers of revision: the underlayer of the early typescript (preceding magazine publication); the typescript revisions (approximating the magazine publication); the underlayer of the galleys; the galley revisions; the page proofs; the "repros"; and the "blues." As a final check, the magazine versions of the poems were scanned into computer files, checked, corrected, and electronically compared with the first edition texts.

The copy text was transcribed from the archive original, in most cases the first edition galleys, taking advantage of the collational record described above. The transcript was verified word for word against the original, but the points of variation uncovered through collation were also double-checked against the copy text transcription. The remaining post–copy text forms (the Selected volumes, Warren's annotated copies of his collections, and the 1987 Collected Poems materials) were also collated and variations compared to the copy text.

I have not collated the different impressions of the same volume, where they exist, and I have only separately collated the British versions if they were not printed from American plates. I have also not collated separately the special bibliophile editions of Warren's volumes that appeared simultaneously with the trade editions, because they, too, were printed from the same plates, although with additional front and back matter and (in the case of the Franklin Press editions of the the 1976 and 1985 Selected volumes) with reset pages dividing the different sections of the book (telephone conversation with Sam Caggiula at the Franklin Mint, April 26, 1995). I have, however, collated the limited editions which were not simply bibliophile editions of other books, such as the Palaemon Press *Two Poems*, but I have treated emendations based on the texts of limited editions with extreme caution.

I have sometimes relied upon xerox copies of rare printed volumes, but I have returned to the printed texts when I have had questions, and I have marked in the textual notes every occasion where I still find a reading to be troubling. I have not sought to compare all of the appearances of Warren's poems in anthologies. I have not collated the texts in *A Robert Penn Warren Reader,* because Warren did not edit that book, and because the editor followed the texts—in fact, cut-and-pasted the texts (James A. Grimshaw, personal communication, April 11, 1995)—from the 1985 Selected Poems (even including what seem to me to be typographical errors from that volume). I have not collated the beautiful little volume *Six Poems* (Newton, Iowa, 1987), because Warren neither provided a typescript nor read proof for that version. And I have not collated pirated editions, since they have no authority.

I have also examined Warren's copies of his own poetry, both Wright's volumes at Emory University and the volumes at Western Kentucky University (where all of Warren's personal library is preserved). Rosanna Warren made available to me a copy of the 1985 *New and Selected Poems*, found among her mother's papers after her death, which her father had retained for revision. (I have recorded all of those readings, but only adopted them where they seem to be corrections rather than revisions.) In this case, as in the case of other volumes from the personal library, Warren's corrections clarify a number of problematic variants. Warren's marginal corrections in his own copy (now at Western Kentucky University) of the Palaemon Press *Fifteen Poems,* for instance, makes clear that most of what might have been taken for late revisions of Warren's poems are, in fact, typographical errors. I have also read the correspondence with his publishers, which not only includes many corrections and revisions, but provides considerable evidence that Warren sent his poems to Erskine piecemeal and in very early versions.

I have, of course, examined the actual typescripts, not photocopies, of the setting typescripts of the first editions of Warren's volumes of poems. (This turned out to be quite useful: the fact that many but not all of the pages of some typescripts were folded as if for mailing is additional evidence that Warren sent the poems to Albert Erskine at Random House separately, as he composed them, pulling together the volume later.) When I refer to photocopied text in the typescripts, I mean that the setting text was itself a photocopy, not that I have examined a photocopy of it. Warren's habit in the typescripts was to mark whether there was (or was not) a stanza break at the bottom of each page. I have not recorded these marks unless they contradict the volume or bear on an issue about the volume. I have, however, recorded even Warren's trivial typographical errors that Warren corrected where I can imagine they might bear on issues of construing the text. I have recorded all revisions made on the typescripts and on the several sets of galleys, except for printer's errors on the galleys that Warren or his editors caught and corrected. (I make an exception, of course, where the printer's error sheds light on some textual issue, such as in the case of the extra white space before the coda of "Dreaming in Daylight.") I have not corrected consistent misspellings, such as "Sirocco," nor have I regularized the spelling of words Warren spelled several ways (such as "fulfillment"). And I have not generally recorded the designer's notes to the typesetter, except where they shed light on a textual issue.

Because what are marked in the Beinecke Library as the "setting typescripts" in fact reflect very early states of the text—sometimes preceding the magazine versions—and because the poems are heavily revised in Warren's hand on the galleys and page proofs, I have chosen not generally to give the typescript deeper authority than the published text. The typescripts themselves are heavily revised: although these revisions are not always in Warren's hand, they for the most part seem to have been made at his direction, since frequently the changes are accounted for in Warren's correspondence with Random House, and many of these changes simply bring the typescript versions into conformity with the magazine versions. By contrast, most of the revisions that take the poem from the magazine to the book version are made in Warren's hand on the galleys and page proofs.

My copy text, this is to say, is not the "setting typescript" of each volume but the galley proofs as revised and corrected by Warren himself. Any exceptions to this rationale are described in the opening note for the volumes or in the textual notes to the individual poems. There are neither galleys nor typescripts for *Thirty-Six Poems*, for instance, but I did compare the printed text with the typescript drafts of the individual poems, and with the typescripts for the unpublished early volumes *Pondy Woods and Other Poems*, *Cold Colloquy*, *Kentucky Mountain Farm and Other Poems*, and *Problem of Knowledge*. There is a typescript, but no galleys, for *Selected Poems 1923–1943*, but Lambert Davis, Warren's editor at Harcourt Brace, wrote him that he would have the poems set as he received them and would give Warren an opportunity to revise them in proof (Warren had wanted another chance at revising the poems). I have generally followed the first edition rather than the typescript for that volume, on the theory that the differences reflect changes Warren made on the galleys.

I make no case here that published books are generally the product of collaboration between the author and the publisher's editor, since I can well imagine cases in which "collaboration" would not be the proper term to describe this relationship. But Warren's relationship with Albert Erskine, who edited all of the poetry Warren published with Random House (from *Brother to Dragons* and

Promises forward) was very close, and he turned to Erskine for advice about his poems in much the same way that he turned to Allen Tate, Cleanth Brooks, John Palmer, or Harold Bloom, valuing that advice, but not always taking it. It is clear that Erskine gave Warren considerable freedom—allowing him to revise even the titles of his books at very late stages of publication—and that Warren did not have the kind of relationship with Erskine that makes the publisher's editor and the scholarly editor natural enemies. Warren's relationship with other editors—such as with Lambert Davis during the publication of *All the King's Men*—was very different, although even Davis allowed Warren much more freedom about his poetry than about his fiction. On balance, the quality of the relationship between Warren and Erskine suggests that the typescript should not automatically be given deeper authority than the published versions.

I have chosen to treat changes in Warren's use of hyphenated compound words as accidentals, although a high frequency of hyphenated compound words is an idiosyncrasy of Warren's style and the typescripts indicate some pulling and hauling with his editors on the subject. Where the galleys omit a hyphen of this kind that the typescripts include and that the editor has questioned, I have not emended the galley reading unless I had other reasons to do so, although in many cases what seems to have happened is that Warren was persuaded by Erskine's suggestion. Warren had plenty of latitude to reject Erskine's suggestions, and if he took them it is because he thought they were good ones. I have also considered the separation of compound words (such as "wheat field" and "wheatfield") as accidental variants, even though such changes have an effect on the scansion of the lines in which they occur. I have chosen, by contrast, to treat English spellings as substantive variants, since a preference for English spellings is a hallmark of Warren's early style. (I have not regularized those spellings in the text, for the same reason.) Likewise, I have treated Warren's uses of accent marks as substantive variants, since their use is also a hallmark of Warren's early style. Warren's changes to the capitalization of abstract nouns I have also chosen to treat as a substantive variant, since the capitalization often alters the meaning of the word profoundly.

Even some of the accidental variants I have recorded are clearly matters of the house style of the publisher. That all of the poems in *The Fugitive* open with words in all caps, for instance, was a choice of the editor (Warren himself, wearing another hat) rather than of the poet. Some accidentals (the different font for the first letter of every poem in *Encounter,* for instance) I have not recorded, but these are difficult to record accurately in notes and are without doubt not authorial anyway. I have set my horizon of annotation wide enough to include everything that is arguably authorial, as well as some things that are arguably not, but I have not set it so wide as to include everything. Since all of the accidentals are included in the textual collations, the distinction between accidentals and substantives may seem moot, but I do preserve the distinction in the electronic source code of the text.

I have not prepared a separate list of hyphenated words in the text I publish, because I have set the type of this edition in such a way as to ensure that the only hyphens it contains are those that should be preserved in quotation. There is also no need for a list of end-line compounds in the copy texts, for the nature of the verse form, as least as Warren types it, leaves no instances to be resolved.

Some things I have not included may well be second-guessed. For instance, when Warren wrote long lines that ran over the right margin of the printed text, I have not preserved how those lines were broken up. (I will call the point where a long line is broken at the right margin a "line bend.") I have, however, looked at how all of the versions broke up such long lines, in order to make myself sure that the lines really were single long lines rather than, say, a long line followed by an indented shorter one, and I have remarked in the textual notes every case where I felt that this judgment was not a totally obvious one. For example, in the last section of "Ballad: Between the Boxcars," Warren broke up the long lines of the magazine version into separate stanzas in the book version, each of which corresponded to a line in the magazine version. He also transformed the stanzas of the magazine version into several-stanza sections in the book version.

I have not in general recorded how long lines are broken up because Warren worked with a typewriter rather than with a linotype and would not have known how the line would break up in the final typeset version. Of course, where Warren marked line bends in the galley proofs I have made note of it, and in *Incarnations*, where he made how the line bends an issue in the proofs, I have preserved the line bends when the galleys follow the typescript or where Warren corrected the galleys. Even so, there are cases in *Incarnations* where the typesetter did not follow how the typescript broke up long lines and Warren did not correct the line bends on the galleys, so Warren's attention to this detail was intermittent even here. And when the poems from *Incarnations* were reprinted, although the later versions often, even usually, broke up long lines in the same way *Incarnations* did, the practice was not systematically followed. In the cases of other volumes there is still less similarity between how he broke up long lines in the original volume and how he broke them when reprinting the poem in the Selected Poems volumes. I have come to the conclusion that although how long lines were broken up on the page intermittently mattered to Warren, it was even then a feature of book design and not of versification.

Warren's practice was to set the run-over portion of long lines flush with the right margin. (This is not merely a matter of house style, because Warren's typescripts show it as well.) I find that practice ugly and have adopted the more usual practice of indenting the run-over portion of long lines after a line bend. There are those who think that indenting, rather than flushing, the run-over portions of long lines leaves it ambiguous whether the second part is run-over or a new, but indented, line. Context, line numbering, and the deep indentation I have employed suffice to distinguish such cases from cases in which one has two separate lines, with the second one indented. In any event, in the electronic source code of this text, all such cases are individually and unambiguously marked.

I have adopted a similarly relaxed rule with multi-line titles. In most cases, Warren does not seem to have had any particular lineation in mind. The title of the first section of "Mortmain," for instance, was lineated differently in different editions. However, Warren often did mark how such titles were to be broken up, and where he made a point of it I have followed it, except in cases where he forgot that he had made that point when he reprinted the poem. For consistency's sake, I have broken the long titles in the table of contents in the same way they are in the body of the volume, although Warren himself followed no such practice. Where I had evidence that Warren did have a lineation of a title in mind (as for instance in cases where the second line seemed syntactically separate or had the air of a subtitle about it), I have followed that lineation.

I have chosen to set the titles in lower-case type, although most typescripts and many published versions set titles in all caps, and I have adopted a uniform system for setting the titles of sections and subsections of sequences. (Warren did not always do this when he republished his poems, sometimes simply duplicating the style of the earlier volumes.) That said, I have not used the uniform system for "Fall Comes in Back-Country Vermont," because the section breaks in that poem are unusual, sometimes occurring in the middle of lines or sentences, so that the section titles have a *sotto voce* quality. I have also adopted a different rule for subsections of sequences if the subsection has no title other than a number or letter, as in the subsections of "Rattlesnake Country" or "I Am Dreaming of a White Christmas." In these cases, although the magazine versions may have used different systems, the Selected Poems volumes reproduce the different systems adopted for each poem in the first book version. Regularizing these would inevitably involve converting numbered sections to lettered ones (or vice versa), which might make it more difficult for readers to compare the different versions of these texts. Therefore, for these cases I have simply reproduced the system the original book volumes adopted.

I have adopted a few unusual typographical conventions. When I am quoting from the text in the notes, I only include marks of punctuation inside the quotation marks if they exist in the quoted text, which may not be the current custom but at least clearly distinguishes between quoted punctuation marks and those that are grammatical elements of my own text rather than of Warren's.

It is conventional, when one records accidental variants, to use ‸ to represent a place in the variants where a punctuation mark appearing in the lemma is missing from the variants, but not to use it to represent a place in the lemma where a punctuation mark in the variants is missing from the lemma, because it might lead the reader to believe that the glyph ‸ occurs in the copy text. This objection is not a trumping one to me, since in the first place one need only turn to the poem to see whether the glyph appears in it, and Warren never uses that glyph anyway. Therefore, at the price of some redundancy, I have used ‸ on both sides of the square bracket in the notes, partly because the redundancy makes the author's intentions clearer, and partly because the redundancy made it easier for me to find my errors of transcription.

I have also chosen to give a slightly nonstandard look to my emendations. Usually, after the] in an emendation note a siglum indicating the source of the emended reading follows, followed in turn by a semicolon and the copy text reading and any variants discovered in texts between the copy text and the source of the emendation. Because I follow a different copy text for each volume, I have chosen simply to present a historical collation with the copy text reading listed chronologically among the variants, with the argument for my emendation (if necessary) following in parentheses.

I have provided relatively minimal explanatory notes. I have identified persons referred to in the poems only where Warren's biographers have identified them in print or Warren identified them on the typescripts, although in other cases plausible guesses may be made on the basis of Joseph Blotner's magisterial biography. I have noted a few possibly silly things that need no explaining now, but might need explaining later (such as that the phrase "breakfast of champions" is an advertising slogan for a breakfast cereal). And I have identified those of Warren's allusions that I thought might elude my own undergraduate students.

This volume was prepared using the LaTeX typesetting system. The source code for the volume is in ASCII and can be read with any present or future text editor or word processor. The commands I defined for markup of this volume are more or less in plain English and make my local intentions clear in any place where the printed version may be ambiguous. These commands automate many of the features of scholarly editions, such as numbering of lines, sending of line numbers to the textual notes, maintaining the several series of notes that scholarly editions require, and marking cases where stanza breaks might be obscured by page turns. In accordance with the culture of the TeX world, I have gathered these commands into a package and will make them available to anyone who asks for them. Using these commands and the TeX typesetting system, which is available in the public domain for every popular operating system, one can produce scholarly editions of verse texts on a wide variety of platforms from source code that will remain accessible and intelligible when all of the current proprietary word processing programs are a memory. That said, my source code is not precisely an electronic edition, since LaTeX and TeX are typesetting languages, not markup languages like the Standard Generalized Markup Language (SGML). I have designed my LaTeX markup, however, to be easily rewritten in SGML, although I have no plans at the moment to do so.

Acknowledgments

My first acknowledgment is to Mr. Warren himself, without whose help I could not have started this project, and to Eleanor Clark, who kept a keen and helpful eye on this project up to her death. Rosanna and Gabriel Warren have also given constant support to this project. Owen Laster, Mr. Warren's agent, helped this project along in uncountable ways. James A. Grimshaw's bibliography of Warren's works was of inestimable value, since Professor Grimshaw had already tracked down most of the variants. He graciously made available the drafts of his revised bibliography as they developed, keeping me apprised of new versions as they turned up. He also was a generous and thoughtful advisor to this project from the beginning, helping me to think out its many issues. Jon Eller, Susan Staves, Gary Taylor, William Flesch, Anthony Szczesiul, Randolph Runyon, James A. Perkins, Mark Miller, Robert Koppelman, Joseph Blotner, John Lavagnino, and George Franklin helped me think through many textual issues as well. I also owe particular thanks to Joseph Blotner for allowing me to look over his splendid biography of Robert Penn Warren while it was still in draft, and for providing some biographical detail not in his biography. John Lavagnino and Scott Magoon helped me master the LaTeX typesetting system. I also have learned from conversations about Warren with the late Cleanth Brooks and with R.W.B. Lewis, Harold Bloom, and John Hollander. I have had the help of many research assistants at Brandeis University who double-checked many of my collations. These include Stefan Gunther, Gary Roberts, Phil Chassler, Jonathan Kim, Leslee Thorne-Murphy, Michael Schwartz, Lisa Amber Phillips, Sharon Astyk, and Melissa Beauchesne. I have had also the help and support of the staffs of remarkable libraries: Pat Willis and her staff at the Beinecke Rare Book and Manuscript Library at Yale University, Steven Ennis and the Special Collections department at Emory University Library, Riley Handy at the Kentucky Library of Western Kentucky University, Joanne O'Keefe of interlibrary loan at Brandeis, and Kathy Smith at the Jean and Alexander Heard Library at

Vanderbilt University. I also owe thanks to several people I haven't met, who helped me with typesetting issues by answering my questions on the Newsnet news group comp.text.tex. Among these people are David Kastrup, who enabled me to turn all automatic hyphenation off when typesetting verse; Donald Arseneau, whose marn.sty package solved a tricky problem with numbering the lines of verse; and Robin Fairbairns and Frank Mittelbach, who each helped me on a number of technical questions. This work was prepared using shareware software, whose authors provided me considerable assistance. I owe particular thanks to Pete Keleher, whose Alpha text editor I used for collating the different versions of texts as well as for editing the text, and to Tom Kiffe, whose CMacTeX version of the TeX typesetting system I used to set the type. Finally, I had the enthusiastic support of Leslie Phillabaum and John Easterly at Louisiana State University Press, without whose generosity and willingness to take a risk this big book would never have seen print. And I have had excellent editorial and production support from Donna Perreault and Laura Gleason at the Press as well. Whatever mistakes there are in this edition are, of course, my own responsibility.

Research on this project was generously supported by the American Philosophical Society, whose grant enabled me to travel to Emory to examine the materials for Warren's 1987 projected edition of a Collected Poems, and by the Mazer fund of Brandeis University, whose grant enabled me to make countless trips to the Beinecke Library over the summers. A generous grant from the Modern Language Association enabled the Center for Scholarly Editions to inspect this volume, and my inspector, Jonathan Eller, gave me indispensable help and encouragement.

Last of all, but most important, too, I would like to thank Jo Anne Preston, whose encouragement and clear-sightedness and support helped me to bring this project into focus.

ABBREVIATIONS

Abbreviations ending in "TS" are typescripts for the volume in question. Abbreviations ending in "G" are galleys for the volume in question.

- TSP: *Thirty-Six Poems*
- EP: *Eleven Poems on the Same Theme*
- SP43: *Selected Poems 1923–1943*
- P: *Promises*
- YEO: *You, Emperors, and Others*
- SP66: *Selected Poems, New and Old 1923–1966*
- I: *Incarnations*
- A: *Audubon*
- OE: *Or Else*
- SP75: *Selected Poems 1923–1975*
- NT: *Now and Then*
- BH: *Being Here*
- RV: *Rumor Verified*
- CJ: *Chief Joseph of the Nez Perce*
- SP85: *New and Selected Poems 1923–1985*
- *Helsinki*: *New and Selected Poems* (Helsinki, 1985)
- *Emory*: Copies of texts marked up by Warren, now in the library of Emory University.
- *Western Kentucky*: Copies of texts marked up by Warren, now in the library of Western Kentucky University.
- *Clark*: A copy of SP85, found among Eleanor Clark's papers after her death, which was marked up by Warren. The copy is now at Western Kentucky University.

Magazine titles are given in full in the first citation for each poem, but the standard abbreviations for the titles follow in the rest of the notes on each poem.

EMENDATIONS

3 **Prophecy** 10: rhythmic] rythmic *The Mess Kit*, rhythmic *Wright* (revised on proof copy), *Kentucky Poetry Review*

3 **Crusade** 1: We have] WE have *Fugitive*

4 **After Teacups** 1: I was] I WAS *Fugitive*

5 **Midnight** 1: I cannot] I CANNOT *Fugitive*

8 **I. Iron Beach** 1: Beyond] BEYOND *Fugitive*

9 **Death Mask of a Young Man** 1: Down] DOWN *Fugitive*

9 **Death Mask of a Young Man** 1: Remotely] REMOTELY *Fugitive*

10 **Nocturne** 1: Tonight] TONIGHT *Fugitive*

11 **Sonnets of Two Summers** 1: It] IT *Fugitive*

12 **Praises for Mrs. Dodd** 1: Death] DEATH *Fugitive*

14 **Apologia for Grief** 1: Now] NOW *The Measure*

15 **Alf Burt, Tenant Farmer** 1: Despite] DESPITE *Fugitive*

16 **Admonition to Those Who Mourn** 1: Now] NOW *Fugitive*

16 **The Mirror** 1: Erect,] ERECT, *Fugitive*

17 **Easter Morning: Crosby Junction** 1: The] THE *Fugitive*

18 **Mr. Dodd's Son** 1: He] HE *Fugitive*

18 **The Wrestling Match** 1: "Here] ‸HERE *Fugitive* 24: could."] could.‸ *Fugitive*

19 **Images on the Tomb** 1: Too] TOO *Fugitive*

19 **Images on the Tomb** 1: Ever] EVER *Fugitive*

19 **Images on the Tomb** 1: Remorselessly] REMORSELESSLY *Fugitive*

19 **Images on the Tomb** 1: If] IF *Fugitive*, If *Tennesseean*

22 **The Owl** 1: Here] HERE *Poetry*

36 **III. History Among the Rocks** 1: Title] In TSP the title is "History among the Rocks."

49 **Ransom** 12: unrarefied,] unrarified, TSP, unrarefied, SP43, SP66, SP75 14: Strikes] Strokes *SoR,* TSP, SP43TS, Strikes SP43 (and *English*), SP66, SP75 (Despite the authority of SP43TS, "Strokes" does not make sense to me.)

51 **Letter to a Friend** 9: superfluous,] superflous TSP

68 **Crime** 32: like a snail's,] like snail's, SP43, *English* (SP43TS, however, reads "like a snail's"), SP66, SP75 (Here "snails' " might make more sense, since clearly there is more than one picture, but "a snail's" at least has the evidence of SP43TS behind it. Since the eyes of pictures are being compared to the eyes of a snail, not to a whole snail, the SP43 reading must be wrong.)

69 **Original Sin: A Short Story** 5: It acts...moan.] This line is the last line of the first stanza in *KR,* SP43, SP66, SP75, and SP85, but it is the first line of the second stanza in EP, which is clearly just an error. *Anxiety* follows EP. 35: or] *or* EP, *Anxiety*, or *KR,* SP43, SP66, SP75, SP85

77 **Terror** 8: pass] In EP there is a stanza break here, rather than after "definition of terror." The rhyme scheme and the stanzaic structure of the poem argue that EP makes a typographical error here. All the other versions break the stanza after "definition of terror." 35: seek] see EP, seek *Poetry,* SP43, SP66, SP75

81 **The Ballad of Billie Potts** 173: Not] Nor SP43TS, SP43, *English*, Not *PR*, SP66, SP75, SP85 (Despite the witness of SP43TS, "Nor" here makes no sense to me. Perhaps it is a regional idiom unknown to me—as "nor proper" in *PR* for the previous stanza would argue—but if that is so, why did Warren change the reading in SP66 and after?)

109 **I. What Was the Promise That Smiled from the Maples at Evening?** 5: In first darkness hydrangeas float in their spectral precinct.] This line is in fact omitted from P and from PTS, but its appearance in *Encounter,* SP66, and SP75, as well as the fact that its omission mars the stanza structure which the other stanzas show, argues that the omission is an error. An undated letter from Warren to Albert Erskine now in the collection of the Beinecke Library describes the line as having been omitted by accident and asks for it to be restored in future editions.

120 **VIII. Founding Fathers, Nineteenth-Century Style, Southeast U. S. A.** 28: gentled,] $\sim_\wedge$ P, PTS, PG, English, gentled, *Encounter,* SP66, SP75, 15P, SP85. 32: is ruination,] in ruination, P, PTS, PG is ruination *Encounter,* SP66, SP75, 15P, SP85, *Emory*

122 **IX. Foreign Shore, Old Woman, Slaughter of Octopus** 34: much, but not,] much$_\wedge$ but not, P, PTS, PG, English, much, but not, *YR* much—but not, SP66, SP75

125 **1. When the Century Dragged** 15: and the old] and old P, and the old *Encounter,* PTS, SP66, SP75, SP85

127 **XII. Lullaby: Smile in Sleep** 7: of warmth] or warmth P, PTS, PG, English, of warmth *Encounter*, SP66, SP75, SP85, *Emory*

132 **XIV. Mad Young Aristocrat on Beach** 31: *merde!*] *merde*! P, *merde!* SP66, SP75 (Since the exclamation point is italicized in *Mais l'Amérique, merde!* three lines below, it's undoubtedly an error here.)

157 **II. A Dead Language: Circa 1885** 19: 'Εν ἀρχῇ ἦν ὁ λόγος:] 'Εν ἀρχῇ ἦν ὁ λόγος: YEO, SP66, SP75. In all four of these texts the pattern is the same here and in the repetition of the Greek phrase four lines down. Possibly the line is meant to imply that the father's Greek is imperfect. It is more likely, since the breathing marks in the *YR* and *Portrait of a Father* versions are correct, that the error·is the printer's oversight, which Warren did not correct, and therefore I have corrected it. In YEOTS the Greek is penciled in, and the breathing marks are correct. In YEOG the breathing marks are correct, but there are other errors in the Greek, and a marginal query "Greek OK as set?" Warren stapled the magazine pages from *YR* to the second galleys, with instructions to follow that copy.

159 **Fatal Interview: Penthesilea and Achilles** 45: spot.] ~: YEO, ~. *KR*

207 **I. Elijah on Mount Carmel** 9: horn-scaled] horn-sealed SP66, SP66TS, SP66G, horn-scaled *New Leader,* SP75, SP85 (and in the photocopy of SP66 now catalogued as "Draft B" in the Beinecke Library). Warren noticed this error and described it as such in a letter to Albert Erskine of November 11, 1968.

224 **III. Natural History** 6: *une isle*]*un isle* I, *Encounter, une ile* SP75 (I have preserved the archaic spelling of île, although Warren changed it to "ile" on SP75G, but because Warren corrected the article error, I have corrected it here.)

260 **The Dream He Never Knew the End Of [M]** 19: shifts] lifts A, ATS, *Harper's*, shifts SP75, SP85 (Warren described A as a typographical error for "shifts" in a letter to Albert Erskine dated November, 1969. Draft D of *Audubon* indeed does read "shifts." Erskine proposed making a correction in the third printing. SP75G still read "lifts," and Warren corrected it to "shifts" there.)

275 **I Am Dreaming of a White Christmas [1]** 1: door—] door,— OE, door— *Atlantic,* SP75, SP85

287 **Interjection 4: Bad Year, Bad War: A New Year's Card, 1969** 10: no] not OETS, OE, SP75, no *NYRB,* Weber (Despite the fact that OE and SP75 were both printed after the two authorities I cite, the text in OE makes no grammatical sense to me, so I emend.)

297 **XII. Flaubert In Egypt** 48: buggered,] buggared, OE, buggered, *NYRB,* SP75 (revised on SP75G, second set)

309 **XIX. There's a Grandfather's Clock in the Hall** 11: yes,] $\sim_\wedge$ OETS, OE, SP85 (in pencil on SP85TS) ~, *YR*, SP75

326 **Evening Hawk** 16: hieroglyphics] heiroglyphics SP75 (and SP75TS), *Helsinki*, hieroglyphics SP85 (silently corrected by the typesetter)

333 **Old Nigger on One-Mule Cart Encountered Late at Night When Driving Home From Party in the Back Country** 89: night] $\sim_\wedge$ SP75, ~, *NY*, SP85 (revised on SP85G to SP85) (The correction on SP85 back to *NY* argues that SP75, and SP75TS, are wrong.)

385 **Filling Night with the Name: Funeral as Local Color** 16: rang] ran BH, rang *Salmagundi* (For milk to run tinnily is nonsense, but milk can ring tinnily in the pail.)

391 **Grackles, Goodbye** 14: tilt?] tilt. BH, *Salmagundi* tilt? SP85 (in red pen on SP85TS). (The sentence in *Salmagundi* is not grammatically a question, but the sentence in BH and SP85 is.)

395 **Why Have I Wandered the Asphalt of Midnight?** 33: dawn-rounds,] dawn-rounds. BH (and BHTS), dawn-round, *Palaemon*, dawn-rounds, *SoR*, dawn rounds. *Helsinki* (In BH the next few lines form a sentence fragment, but in *SoR* they are grammatically the third element of an ongoing list. Even in BH and *Helsinki* the semantics require the lines to be understood as the third element of a list.)

397 **Dreaming in Daylight** 36: so few.] There are six centered asterisks between this stanza and the next in *Salmagundi.* Five centered asterisks are canceled in BHTS. But there is an annotation requiring a two-line space between this stanza and the next. But when the typewriter did as required, the editor marked it as a printer's error, and Warren wrote "reg. stanza #" in the margin. My sense is that the editor is mistaken, and that Warren forgot his original intention. Since the change arises from a mistake about whether a printer's error has occurred, I have chosen to emend here

398 **Preternaturally Early Snowfall in Mating Season** 5: "breakfast of champions."] breakfast of champions. BH, *NY*, "breakfast of champions." *Emory* (Without the quotation marks it might not be obvious that Warren is quoting an advertising slogan.)

400 **Sila** 60: bend,] ~. BH, ~, SP85 (revised on SP85G to SP85) (The line ends with a comma in *Atlantic*, too, although the word is "broke.")

404 **Function of Blizzard** 22: even,] $\sim_\wedge$ BH, ~, *Antaeus*

411 **Deep—Deeper Down** 5: Lüger] Luger BH, *lüger, SoR*, BHTS (revised to "Lüger" but the typesetter may not have seen the umlaut)

412 **Better Than Counting Sheep** 12: out-stretched] out—stretched, BH out-/stretched *NYRB* (Warren used in BHTS two dashes, usually the sign of an em-dash, and the copy editor and typesetter have understood him so to mean. But the sense requires a hyphen instead, and *NYRB* supports the reading.)

413 **The Cross** 14: baby doll] baby-doll BH, 15P, baby doll *NY*

415 **On Into the Night** 2: how soundless,] soundless, *Salmagundi* how soundless$_\wedge$ BH ("Crunch" is clearly a verb rather than a noun as the punctuation in BH implies, and "soundless" modifies "wheels," not "crunch.")

431 **Acquaintance with Time in Early Autumn** 38: air unmoving,] air unmoving$_\wedge$ BH (and BHTS), motionless air, *NY* (The comma is needed to close the phrase.)

433 **Synonyms** 62: rage,] rage. BH, ~, *Poetry* (Warren does use sentence fragments for emphasis, but not this way. BHTS has "rage.", but it is corrected to "rage," in red pencil in the margin, which, doubtless because of the correction in the next line, the typesetter did not notice.)

439 **Passers-By on Snowy Night** 22: *crack*] crack BH, *crack SoR*, BHTS (Warren did not notice in all this italic type that the galleys lost the emphasis he had placed on "crack" to capture the onomatopoeic quality of the word. Since there's no sign on BHG that he intended to de-emphasize the word, I emend.)

441 **Afterthought** supposed] suppose BH (and BHTS)

450 **II. Law of Attrition** 7: Now rain-washed] Rain-washed *NY*, How rain-washed RV (and RVTS), Now rain-washed *Emory* ("How" makes no sense here.)

451 **III. One I Knew** 9: Clouds close.] In *NY* this line is broken across a stanza break after this text. In RV the line is merely broken across a line break. Because he corrected the same case later in the poem, and because there are only a few such lines broken across stanza breaks in this volume, and because Warren may not have noticed that he missed the first two cases in this poem even as he corrected the third, and because there was

a stanza break in *New Yorker*, RV is probably mistaken in merely having a broken line here rather than one broken across a stanza break. But RVTS merely has a broken line here, too, not a line that straddles a stanza break. RVTS is most likely in error. Drafts D through G (and RVTS) are all photocopies of draft C, which is prepared by the typist who prepared RVTS. Draft B, which is typed on Warren's own machine, breaks the line across the stanza break. In 15P the line is broken across a line break, not across a stanza break. 17: You never knew.] In *NY* this line is broken across a stanza break after this text; RV has only a broken line here. But RVTS breaks the line across a stanza break. Warren did not notice this problem when he was marking up the *Emory* volume, but he did notice the next instance, a few lines down. 15P has only a broken line here. 64: "Dear Son."] In RV this line is broken after this text. In *Emory* he indicates that he wants this line to break across a stanza break. RVTS breaks the line across a stanza break, as does *New Yorker*. In 15P there is only a broken line here.

452 **Small Eternity** 7: which,] but, RV (and RVTS) which, *Emory* ("but" does not make grammatical sense)

459 **Minneapolis Story** 9: a] that RV (and RVTS) a *NYRB*, *Emory* (Minneapolis is clearly not in a snowless latitude. Neither is Bethlehem, but Bethlehem is certainly intended here.)

460 **Mountain Mystery** 30: saddle,] ~∧ RV (and RVTS) ~, *Love*, SP85 (revised on SP85G to SP85)

464 **Vermont Thaw** 33: off] of *APR*, RV (and RVTS) off *Emory* (RV and *APR* must be in error, since eaves don't have rhythm but drops of water off of eaves may.)

473 **The Corner of the Eye** 19: stock-still,] ~∧ RV, RVG ~, RVTS

474 **If** 4: therefrom.] there from. RV (RVTS reads as emended, but is corrected in pencil to RV; however, the RV reading does not make grammatical sense) therefrom. *APR*

482 **Have You Ever Eaten Stars?** 46: Rejoice.] The line straddles the stanza break that follows this text. In RV, and in *NY*, there is merely a broken line here, with the second half set flush to the end of the first half, but a stanza break is clearly indicated on RVTS.

483 **Twice Born** 36: A metaphor.] The line straddles the stanza break that follows this text. In RV there is only a broken line here, with the second half set flush to the end of the first half, but a stanza break is clearly indicated in RVTS.

489 **Chief Joseph of the Nez Perce** subtitle: Nimipu,] *Nimpau— GaR*, *Palaemon*, ~∧ CJ (CJ does not make grammatical sense. The dash in CJ was only removed on the "master pages," in a blue pencil revision, probably by Erskine.) Note: in exile] in the exile CJ 36: subsistence . . .] subsistence . . . CJ, ~. . . . *GaR*, *Palaemon* 36: principles] principals CJ principles *GaR*, *Palaemon*, CJTS

495 **Chief Joseph of the Nez Perce II.** 112: love,] ~∧ CJ ~, *GaR*, CJTS, CJG (The "corrected master pages" read with CJ, although the "master pages" read with CJG. Since the line had to be reset on the master pages to add the close quotation mark, probably the typesetter dropped the comma, and nobody noticed.)

507 **Chief Joseph of the Nez Perce VI.** 268: kept black] kept white *GaR*, *Palaemon*, CJ, CJTS, black *Emory* (hardback) (If the blanket is black, and it is snowing, Joseph would have been keeping the snow off the blanket, keeping it black, rather than piling it on, keeping it white.) 60: have returned] returned CJ have returned *GaR*, *Palaemon*, CJTS (CJG reads as CJ, but no correction accounts for the change.)

518 **Chief Joseph of the Nez Perce VIII.** 127: without written permission,] without permission, CJ, CJG, without written permission *GaR*, *Palaemon*, CJTS (Since there is no indication of a correction on the typescript or on any of the other sets of galleys, CJ is probably an error)

533 **The First Time** 29: far] the far SP85G, far SP85TS, *Clark* (Since there is no correction to account for the change, and since Warren revised the reading in *Clark*, SP85G is probably in error.)

534 **Minnesota Recollection** 16: gone,] ~— SP85 (and SP85TS), ~, *SoR* (The three dashes in SP85 do not make sense.) 33: back,] ~. SP85 (and SP85TS) ~, *SoR* (The next

sentence is a fragment in SP85.)

542 **Literal Dream** 28: hypnotic] hynotic SP85, hypnotic *NY* 41: not] no SP85 (and SP85TS), not *NY* (In the bound "Advance uncorrected proofs" of SP85 Warren marked this line, but it is unclear whether he meant that it should be corrected or that it is correct as it stands.)

544 **Doubleness in Time** 62: nose] nost SP85, nose *NY*, SP85TS, *Clark*

547 **Snowfall** 30: autumn bough bends] autumn bends SP85 (and SP85TS) autumn bough bends *Atlantic*, *Mountain State* (Autumn doesn't itself bend, but boughs may.)

549 **II. Goodbye to Tinian** 27: And,] No stanza break after this text in SP85. Stanza break after this text in *Hiroshima*, *NY*, and SP85TS. (The stanza break is missing from all of the galleys, and since no revision removes it, probably the SP85 reading is an error by the typesetter.)

554 **X. What *That* Is** title] What That Is, SP85, What *That* Is *Hiroshima*, *NY*, SP85TS. (The title alludes back to section IV, where the word is italicized.) Curiously, *NY* underlines rather than italicizes the word.

565 **Muted Music** 12: hum?] ~. SP85 (and SP85TS), *Helsinki*, ~? *GaR83*, *GaR86* (The sentence is grammatically a question.)

576 **History During Nocturnal Snowfall** 20: truth?] ~. SP85 (and SP85TS) ~? *SR* (The sentence is grammatically a question.)

576 **Whistle of the 3 A.M.** 25: A.M..] A.M. *APR*, SP85 (and SP85TS), AM. *London Magazine* (The sense requires a period.)

580 **Wind and Gibbon** 27: wizardry] wizardy SP85, wizardry *SoR*, *Encounter*, SP85TS

587 **Bicentennial** 216: root-footing] root footing *Esquire*, TS, G (added on G) 230: Cajun,] Cajan, *Esquire* Cajun, G, TS (Since the spelling error is not Warren's, I emend it.)

604 **Commuter's Entry in a Connecticut Diary** 15: reality.] ~, *SoR* The capitalization of the next word indicates that a period is intended here.

605 **You Sort Old Letters** 11: It was Number One, nice fellow, when she took you to the dunes.] This line is missing from *Love: Four Versions*, but the next line doesn't make sense without this one.

606 **Aging Painter Sits Where the Great Tower Heaves Down Midnight** 208: light.] ~‸ *GaR* (The sense requires a period here, or perhaps a semicolon.)

616 **Winter Dreams** 25: gut-snaring] gut-snaring TS gut-sharing *SoR* (The TS doesn't have much authority over *SoR* since it isn't a setting copy, but this reading does make much more sense, and all of the several versions read this way.)

619 **Old Love I.** 1: I.] *SR* has sections II and III, but there is no mark for section I.

620 **Old Love II.** 20: thereabout,] There is a stanza break here in *SR*. There are page turns at this point in all of the typescripts in the Beinecke Library, but some of them are marked "No Space." There is no stanza break after this text in *Iowa Review*.

621 **Upwardness** 19: ecstasy.] ecstacy. *PR*

TEXTUAL NOTES

Uncollected Poems 1922–1943

3 **Prophecy** Text: *The Mess Kit (Food for Thought),* ed. Edgar Dow Gilman (Camp Knox, Ky.: Military Training Camps Association [U.S. Army], 1922), p. 41. Variants: Broadside privately printed by Stuart Wright on the occasion of the University of Kentucky's Robert Penn Warren 75th Birthday Symposium, 29–30 October, 1980, *Kentucky Poetry Review*, 16.2–3 (Summer–Fall 1980), p. 5.

3 **Vision** Text: *American Poetry Magazine,* 5 (Dec. 1922), p. 23.

3 **Crusade** Text: *Fugitive,* 2 (June–July 1923), pp. 90–91.

4 **After Teacups** Text: *Fugitive,* 2 (Aug.–Sept. 1923), p. 106.

5 **Midnight** Text: *Fugitive,* 2 (Oct. 1923), p. 142.

6 **The Fierce Horsemen** Text: *Driftwood Flames* (Nashville: The Poetry Guild, 1923), p. 10.

6 **Wild Oats** Text: *Driftwood Flames* p. 17.

6 **To Certain Old Masters** Text: *Driftwood Flames*, pp. 36–37.

7 **The Golden Hills of Hell** Text: *Driftwood Flames*, p. 41. Variant: *The Bookman* (1923), p. 686. (*Bookman* is really an extract from a review of *Driftwood Flames.*)

8 **Three Poems** Text: *Fugitive,* 3 (April 1924), pp. 54–55. Titles are from MS.

8 **I. Iron Beach** Text: *Fugitive,* 3 (April 1924), p. 54 (Fugitive24). Variant: *Driftwood Flames*, p. 30, *Fugitive*, 4 (March 1925), p. 15 (Fugitive25). I have used Fugitive24 rather than Fugitive25 as the proof text because I have decided to retain the sequence "Three Poems." Although "Three Poems" may have been merely a title of convenience on the editor's part (Warren himself was the editor), the poems are not titled in the sequence (the titles are from MS) and all three are sonnets, and linked by theme and mood, so I have chosen not to break the sequence up. The earlier version of I (from *Driftwood Flames*, p. 30) is so different that it is clearer to include it wholesale in the notes than to collate it line for line:

Iron Beach

Beyond this place there is no going.
This iron beach—it is the end of land.
Here I have made my stand;
Behind, the tundra dims with snowing,
Before, the seas leap crashing on the strand.
Assuredly this is an ending.
I shiver in the wind's chill blowing,
And raise a numb and unexpectant hand.
Then looking backward from the sky's last bending,
I see myself yet standing on the sand.

1: bitter] wrathful Fugitive25 1: going,] ~— Fugitive25 2: land;] ~. Fugitive25 4: strand.] sand. Fugitive25 5: arc‸] ~, Fugitive25 9: The sestet of the sonnet in Fugitive25 is so different that it is clearer to quote it wholesale:

Now we have won, dear sirs, to the end of days.
Survey the night and prophesy the rest;
Darkness has hid our track across the snows.
Let no man sink his head upon his breast

But to the north let each a white face raise,
Calling unto whatever gods he knows.

8 **II. Mrs. Dodd's Daughter**

8 **III. Apocalypse**

9 **Death Mask of a Young Man** Text: *Fugitive,* 3 (June 1924), p. 69.

10 **Nocturne** Text: *Fugitive,* 3 (June 1924), p. 70.

10 **Adieu Sentimentale** Text: *Voices: A Journal of Verse,* 3 (July–Aug. 1924), p. 112. Variant: *Voices: A Quarterly of Poetry,* 146 (Sept.–Dec. 1951), p. 10.

11 **The Romance Macabre** Text: *Voices: A Journal of Verse,* 3 (July–Aug. 1924), p. 112.

11 **Sonnets of Two Summers** Text: *Fugitive,* 3 (Aug. 1924), p. 117.

12 **Praises for Mrs. Dodd** Text: *Fugitive,* 3 (Aug. 1924), p. 118. MS. Title: "Praises for Mrs. Dodd Deceased"

12 **Portraits of Three Ladies** Text: *Double Dealer,* 6 (Aug.–Sept. 1924), pp. 191–92.

14 **Autumn Twilight Piece** Text: *Double Dealer,* 7 (Oct. 1924), p. 2.

14 **Admonition to the Dead** Text: *Double Dealer,* 7 (Oct. 1924), p. 2.

14 **Apologia for Grief** Text: *The Measure,* no. 44 (Oct. 1924), p. 12.

15 **Alf Burt, Tenant Farmer** Text: *Fugitive,* 3 (Dec. 1924), p. 154.

16 **Admonition to Those Who Mourn** Text: *Fugitive,* 3 (Dec. 1924), p. 155. The typescript of this poem—not a setting typescript—has the headnote (In Memoriam T.U.S.).

16 **The Mirror** Text: *Fugitive,* 4 (June 1925), p. 16.

17 **Easter Morning: Crosby Junction** Text: *Fugitive,* 4 (June 1925), pp. 33–34.

18 **Mr. Dodd's Son** Text: *Fugitive,* 4 (June 1925), p. 35.

18 **The Wrestling Match** Text: *Fugitive,* 4 (June 1925), p. 37.

19 **Images on the Tomb** Text: *Fugitive,* 4 (Sept. 1925), pp. 89–92. Alternate version of IV: "Firing Line Section." Nashville *Tennesseean,* 27 Sept. 1925, p. 7. In *Tennessean* the odd-numbered lines are indented.

20 **August Revival: Crosby Junction** Text: *Sewanee Review,* 33 (Oct. 1925), p. 439.

21 **Pro Sua Vita** Text: *New Republic,* 11 May 1927, p. 333.

22 **The Owl** Text: *Poetry,* 40 (May 1932), p. 59. This poem was marked in *Poetry* as a section of "Kentucky Mountain Farm" but was never included in any of the book versions of that sequence. Several drafts of this poem in the Beinecke Library are marked as section iv of the sequence, and in the typescript of the unpublished volume *Problem of Knowledge* it also appears as section iv.

23 **Tryst on Vinegar Hill** Text: *This Quarter,* 2 (Jan.–March 1930), pp. 503–4. Variant: *American Caravan IV* Alfred Kreymborg, Louis Mumford, and Paul Rosenfeld, eds. (New York: Macaulay Company, 1931) pp. 392–93. 6: Up from the heart] From the dark heart *American Caravan* 13: summertime] summer time *AmCar* 18: first] white *AmCar* 21: breed:] ~. *AmCar* 27: channels] channel *AmCar* 27: leaf;] ~, *AmCar* 28: bone,] ~; *AmCar* 30: and] or *AmCar* 45: heart again.] No stanza break after this line in *American Caravan.* 47: Timorously‸] Timorous, *AmCar* 51: bold— / Poor] bold / —Poor *AmCar* 52: ghosts,] ~‸ *AmCar* 52: who] that *AmCar* 53: lazy] summer's lazy *AmCar*

24 **Empire** Text: *This Quarter,* 3 (July–Sept. 1930), pp. 168–69. The source text is entirely in italics. In MS this poem is titled "Conquest" 24: bitten] One might think this a printer's error for "bitter," but the MS reads "bitten".

25 **The Limited** Text: *Poetry,* 41 (Jan. 1933), p. 200.

25 **Athenian Death** Text: *Nation,* 31 Oct. 1936, p. 523.

27 **Love's Voice** Text: TS in Beinecke Library (from the unpublished volume *Problem of Knowledge*, which Warren compiled after *Thirty-Six Poems* and before *Eleven Poems on the Same Theme*). On the acknowledgments page of *Problem of Knowledge* Warren describes this poem as among the winners of the Caroline Sinkler Prize from the Poetry Society of South Carolina for 1936, 1937, and 1938. Possibly the Poetry Society

published the poem, but I have not been able to locate a copy. On December 20, 1939, the Poetry Society gave Warren permission to "republish" all three poems (Warren was probably seeking permissions for *Problem of Knowledge*), which implies that they did in fact publish them. And in an invitation the society sent to Warren in 1980 inviting him to their sixtieth anniversary event they also imply that they published the Sinkler Award poems. But the Poetry Society did not publish annuals in those years, and the poems are not reprinted in the Charleston newspapers.

29 **Goodbye** Text: *American Prefaces,* 6 (Winter 1941), pp. 113–14.

Thirty-Six Poems

Thirty-Six Poems (New York: Alcestis Press, 1935) was a limited edition of 165 copies. I have examined a photocopy of number 121, from University Microfilms via the library of the University of Massachusetts at Amherst. The setting typescript is not in the collection at the Beinecke Library, but there are working typescripts of many of the poems there. I have examined the setting typescript for SP43, but will only record its variants where they differ from SP43.

Alcestis Press solicited a volume from Warren on April 27, 1935, noting that they had also published signed limited editions of work by Wallace Stevens, John Peale Bishop, and William Carlos Williams. The work was edited, printed, and shipped by December 3, 1935, and by December 17 Warren was already promising them another manuscript.

33 **The Return: An Elegy** Text: TSP. Variants: *Poetry,* 44 (July 1934), pp. 85–89, SP43, SP66, SP75, SP85. The *Poetry* version shows no indentations. Despite the considerable number of changes in SP85, SP85TS has no revisions from SP75. SP85TS is a photocopy from SP75. There are several drafts of this poem at the Beinecke Library. All are quite different from any of the published versions. One early draft has a second section, after the end of the poem as we now have it, describing the old man, the husband of the speaker's mother, waiting for his son's arrival. 1: rain:] ∼— *Poetry* 2: *Rain in the pine wind shaking the stiff pine*] no italics, *Poetry* 3: whine$_{\wedge}$] ∼, *Poetry* ∼. SP85 (revised on SP85G to SP85) 4: decline$_{\wedge}$] ∼. *Poetry,* SP85 (revised on SP85G to SP85) 5: down the loam] own the loam SP85 (This error appears on SP85G and was not corrected by Warren there.) 7: they are conceded] all are conceded SP85 (revised on SP85G to SP85), line missing in *Poetry.* 8: they burn ... tell me its name] italicized in *Poetry.* 8: —of damp and dark—] ... of damp and dark... *Poetry* 8: flame.] ∼$_{\wedge}$ *Emory* copy of SP85 9: calcium phosphate] calcium-phosphate *Poetry* 9: treachery$_{\wedge}$] ∼: *Poetry* 10: habitation and a name] Stanza break after this line in SP75 (revised on SP75G), SP85. 11: *tell me its name*] This line doubly indented in SP75 (revised on SP75G), SP85 12: spray$_{\wedge}$] ∼, *Poetry* 13: keel$_{\wedge}$] ∼... *Poetry,* ∼. SP85 (revised on SP85G to SP85) 14: *It is not long till day*$_{\wedge}$] It is not long till day, *Poetry* 15: squeal$_{\wedge}$] ∼. SP66, SP75, SP85 15: The boughs ... heel.] Pines lurch beneath the thunder's livid heel;/ The long sough, the rent bough's squeal. *Poetry* 16: And lurch] They lurch SP66, SP75, SP85. 17: *what does the wind say?*] What does the wind say? *Poetry* 19: name:] ∼, *Poetry* 20: Eyes, not blind,] Eyes not blind *Poetry* 22: *What will I find*] What will I find— *Poetry* 24: O eyes] Oh, eyes *Poetry* 25: mine$_{\wedge}$] ∼. *Poetry,* SP85 (revised on SP85G to SP85) 26: give me the nickels...cigarettes] italicized in *Poetry* 28: obsequies$_{\wedge}$] ∼... *Poetry* 31: lies$_{\wedge}$] ∼, *Poetry* 33: and tushèd] and tushed *Poetry,* tushèd SP43TS, tushed SP43, SP66, SP75, SP85 35: will] would *Poetry* 36: the old ... hollow head] italicized in *Poetry* 36: bitch] fox *Poetry* 37: said!] ∼$_{\wedge}$ *Emory* copy of SP85 40: dawn,] ∼$_{\wedge}$ *Poetry* 43: chair,] ∼$_{\wedge}$ *Poetry* 44: Earth] And earth *Poetry,* SP66, SP75, SP85 44: exhalation$_{\wedge}$] ∼. *Poetry,* SP85 (revised on SP85G to SP85) 46: motion$_{\wedge}$] ∼, *Poetry,* ∼. SP85 (revised on SP85G to SP85) 47: shake$_{\wedge}$] ∼. *Poetry,* SP85 (revised on SP85G to SP85) 48: Shaggy mist, crookbacked, ascends] Mist crook-backed and shagged ascends; *Poetry,* Shaggy mist, crookbacked, ascends. SP85 (revised on SP85G to SP85) 50: wind:] ∼$_{\wedge}$ *Poetry* 51: complain?] complain?— *Poetry* 52: Complain$_{\wedge}$] ∼— *Poetry* 54: what have I said] *what have I said! Poetry* 58: rooftree] roof-tree *Poetry* 60: a hundred years ... the old fox is dead]

italicized in *Poetry* 60: they] men *Poetry* 61: hard-eyed] hardeyed *Poetry* 61: hope:] ∼∧ *Emory* copy of SP85 62: ox breath] ox-breath *Poetry* 62: air:] ∼∧ *Poetry* 62: the goad /fell: here] the goad fell: / here *Emory* copy of SP85 65: stand:] ∼∧ *Emory* copy of SP85 66: to the new land/ here is the house] *to the new land // here is the barn Poetry* 69: hum hum] hum— *Poetry* 70: I come I come] I come. *Poetry* I come I come. SP85 (revised on SP85G to SP85) 71: through time O wheels] through time, O wheels! *Poetry* 72: parallels∧] ∼, *Poetry* 73: Pursue past culvert cut embankment semaphore] Pursue past culvert, cut, embankment, semaphore— *Poetry* 73: cut] cut fill SP43TS 74: Pursue down gleaming hours that are no more.] Pursue down time. The pines, black, snore— *Poetry* 76: turn backward . . . light] italicized in *Poetry* 76: o time in your flight] *O time in your flight Poetry,* SP66, SP75, SP85, in your flight SP43 (and SP43TS) 79: hath the mind distilled?] has the mind distilled? SP43 (but SP43TS follows TSP), SP66, SP75, SP85 80: unfulfilled∧] ∼, *Poetry, Emory* copy of SP85 81: stilled∧] ∼. *Poetry,* SP85 (revised on SP85G to SP85) 81: The hoarse pine stilled] An early draft adds in prose here: "the matter is, roughly, this: I have been summoned to the funeral of my mother (a fine woman if I do say it myself) and have departed, dutifully and at considerable expense, the eastern city, where I am engaged in the pursuit of happiness and profit, and now rest, troubled by insomnia, in lower berth, number five" 83: rock∧] ∼, *Poetry* 84: Of the fallen pine cone] line missing SP66, SP75, SP85 84: pine cone∧] pine-cone, *Poetry* 85: Of red bud their season not yet gone] of redbud (its season not yet gone). *Poetry* 87: (In drouth the lizard will blink on the hot limestone)] In drouth the lizard will blink on the hot limestone./ If I could pluck— *Poetry* 88: the old fox is dead . . . days of thy youth] italicized in *Poetry* 90: hoary] *whorey Poetry* 91: said!] ∼∧ *Emory* copy of SP85 92: . . . I have only said] I have only said *Emory* copy of SP85 92: I have only said] *only said Poetry* 94: for time uncoils like the cottonmouth] *look homeward angel let thy heart melt with ruth Poetry* (This version alludes to Milton's "Lycidas.") 96: whirled] whirls *Poetry* 97: pine∧] ∼, *Poetry* 97: rock∧] ∼, *Poetry* 98: furled] furls— *Poetry* 100: mother∧] ∼— *Poetry* 104: Out of the dark . . . sorrow] Out of the dark/ The dark and swollen orchid of this sorrow. *Poetry*

35 **Kentucky Mountain Farm** Text: TSP. Variants: SP43, SP66 (Deletes "The Cardinal," "The Jay," and "Watershed"), SP75 (Same sections as SP66), SP85 (Restores "Watershed"), *Helsinki* (includes only "Rebuke of the Rocks" and "At the Hour of the Breaking of the Rocks"). "The Owl" (above) was marked as a section of "Kentucky Mountain Farm" when it first appeared in *Poetry,* but it was never included in any book version of the entire sequence. The sequence in *Poetry* included, in this order, "The Owl," "The Cardinal," and "Watershed." TSP uses lower case Roman numerals in the section titles. The typescript drafts in the Beinecke Library do not seem to be setting copies.

35 **I. Rebuke of the Rocks** Text: TSP. Variants: *Nation,* 11 Jan. 1928, p. 47, *Literary Digest,* 28 Jan. 1928, p. 32, *Vanderbilt Masquerader,* 10 (Dec. 1933), p. 16, SP43, SP66, SP75, SP85, *Helsinki,* Broadside: The Press at Colorado College, printed on paper handmade by Thomas Leech for the American Poetry Society, April 26, 1985. This poem was not included in SP85 until the second set of galleys, in which a photocopy of the SP75 text is a stapled insert. 2: hill,] ∼— *Nation, Literary Digest* ∼, *Vanderbilt* (I include the reading from *Vanderbilt* even though it is the same as in TSP, because *Vanderbilt* was published after the other magazine versions but before TSP.) 8: old∧] ∼, *Vanderbilt* 11: stone∧] ∼, *Vanderbilt* 14: milkweed.] milk-weed. *Vanderbilt*

36 **II. At the Hour of the Breaking of the Rocks** Text: TSP. Variants: *American Caravan,* ed. Van Wyck Brooks et al. (New York: The Macaulay Company, 1927), p. 803, *Vanderbilt Masquerader,* 10 (Dec. 1933), p. 16, SP43, SP66, SP75, SP85, *Helsinki.* This poem does not appear on SP85G (it is added on the second set), although lines 3–21 are appended to the end of "The Return: An Elegy" by mistake. Warren has a note on SP85G: "The section beginning "Receives the sunlight and the tarnished rain" does *NOT* belong to "The Return: An Elegy"—It belongs to a poem under the general title "Kentucky Mountain Farm" which is being added by Bertha Krantz." 4: sundering∧] ∼, *AmCar, Vanderbilt* 5: seen to stand] seen stand SP66, SP75, SP85, *Helsinki* 11: stricken,] ∼∧

AmCar, Vanderbilt, 12: ridgèd] ridged *AmCar, Vanderbilt,* SP66, SP75, SP85, *Helsinki* 18: tired] weary *AmCar* 20: redbud] red-bud *AmCar, Vanderbilt*

36 **III. History Among the Rocks** Text: TSP. Variants: *New Republic,* 15 Dec. 1928, *Vanderbilt Masquerader,* 10 (Dec. 1933), p. 16, p. 63. SP43, SP66, SP75, SP85. In TSP the title is "History among the Rocks." 6: To startle a cold and crystalline] Startling a crystalline cold *NRep,* To startle a crystalline, cold dream forever. *Vanderbilt* 7: May,] ~∧ *NRep* 9: creek] creed SP43TS 10: the laurel, the sycamore] the sycamore, the laurel *NRep* the sycamore, the laurel, *Vanderbilt* 20: dead. . .] ~— *Vanderbilt,* SP66, SP75, SP85 20: dead. . .] Stanza break after this text in SP43TS 21: Grey] Gray SP66, SP75, SP85 24: mustaches] moustaches *NRep* 24: moonlight.] moonlight,/ Cold musket-barrels glittering with frost. *NRep, Vanderbilt* 25: past:] ~. *NRep* ~; *Vanderbilt*

37 **IV. The Cardinal** Text: TSP. Variants: *Poetry,* 40 (May 1932), p. 60, SP43, Louisville *Courier-Journal,* July 4, 1950, p. 7. 1: shade. . .] ~, *Poetry* 4: Blue] Blue is SP43TS, *Courier-Journal* 4: limestone,] ~∧ *Poetry* 5: ikon,] idon, SP43TS 9: slumberous green. . . / Lover of cedar] slumberous green / . . . Lover of cedar *Poetry* 12: southward fail] westward fall *Poetry* 13: Here] For here *Poetry*

37 **V. The Jay** Text: TSP. Variants: *Saturday Review of Literature,* 11 July 1931, p. 953 (as "Blue Cuirassier"), SP43. 1: Jay,] JAY, *SatR* 2: rout. . .] rout, *SatR* 3: blue,] ~— *SatR* 4: redoubt!] ~, *SatR* 10: Stops an old fellow] Stops some old fellow *Saturday Review* 10: Stops an old fellow . . . dog and gun] These two lines are indented in the English SP43. 11: boy∧] ~, *SatR* 12: ago∧] ~, *SatR* 13: sudden] brilliant *SatR*

38 **VI. Watershed** Text: TSP. Variants: *Poetry,* 40 (May 1932), p. 61, SP43, SP85. This poem was not included in SP85 as late as SP85G, but a photocopy from SP43 is stapled into SP85G second set. 1: flow.] ~: *Poetry* 3: westward,] ~∧ *Poetry* 3: memento. . .] ~; *Poetry* 4: furled] curled *Poetry* 5: above the ridgepole of the world.//] about the ridgepole of the world./ The mist is furled.// *Poetry* 10: crest∧] ~, *Poetry* 16: remains,] ~; *Poetry* 18: creep;] ~, *Poetry* 20: shuddering] shudder *Poetry*

38 **VII. The Return** Text: TSP. Variants: *New Republic,* 15 Jan. 1930, p. 215, SP43, SP66, SP75, SP85 (canceled in SP85TS, but a photocopy from SP75 is added to SP85G second set). 1: Burly] Burley SP43 9: below,] ~∧ *NRep* 12: burned on the quiet stream.] burned, one on, one in, the quiet stream. SP85 (revised on SP85G second set) 13: So,] But, SP66, SP75, SP85 18: for long] for well SP66, SP75, SP85 19: How glimmering] How, glimmering, SP66, SP75, SP85 20: riffle,] riffle or SP66, SP75, SP85

39 **Pondy Woods** Text: TSP. Variants: *Second American Caravan,* ed. Alfred Kreymborg et al. (New York: The Macaulay Company, 1928), pp. 121–22, SP43, SP66, SP75, SP85, *Helsinki.* SP85TS and SP85G did not include this poem. A photocopy from SP75 is added to SP85G second set. 4: grace,] ~∧ *AmCar* 15: road∧] ~, *AmCar* 17: ground.] Stanza break after this line in *AmCar.* 23: saloon,] ~; *AmCar* 26: done;] ~. *AmCar* 28: shot-gun.] shotgun! *AmCar* 33: "Nigger,] ∧~, *AmCar* 34: coughed. His] ~; his *AmCar* 35: darkness,] ~∧ *AmCar* 38: wait;] ~, *AmCar* 40: strong,] ~∧ *AmCar* 41: beakèd] beaked *AmCar,* SP43, SP66, SP75, SP85, *Helsinki* 42: "The] ∧~ *AmCar* 46: lean brown] brown lean *AmCar* 52: *Non omnis moriar,*] 'Non omnis moriar,' *AmCar* 53: grey] gray SP66, SP75, SP85 53: Pedantic,] ~∧ *AmCar* 55: understood,] ~∧ *AmCar* 61: wheat fields] wheatfields *AmCar* 63: Squiggtown.] ~; *AmCar* 65: Coldly; lucid] Coldly. Lucid *AmCar* 70: August] summer's SP75 (revised on SP75G), SP85, *Helsinki.* 71: cottonmouth.] ~, *AmCar* 73: altitudes,] ~∧ *AmCar*

41 **Eidolon** Text: TSP. Variants: *American Review,* 3 (May 1934), pp. 237–38, SP43, SP66, SP75, SP85. In SP85TS this poem follows "Original Sin". 1: woods;] ~. *American Review* 5: clamor] clamour *American Review* 5: throaty,] ~∧ *American Review* 15: unhouselled] unhouseled SP66, SP75, SP85 20: the fangèd] the fanged SP43, SP66, SP75 fangèd SP43TS (Warren added the accent back in pencil on SP85G.)

41 **Letter of a Mother** Text: TSP. Variants: *New Republic,* 11 Jan. 1928, p. 212, *Vanderbilt Masquerader,* 10 (Dec. 1933), pp. 16–17, SP43, SP66. 1: lamplight] lamplight *Vanderbilt* 6: domain,] ~∧ *NRep* 7: possess] regret SP43, SP66 8: of] in SP43,

SP66 12: pay. . .] ∼— SP66 17: dark:] ∼; *NRep* 21: legacy:] ∼, *NRep* 22: blood,] ∼∧ *NRep* 27: sea. . .] ∼, *NRep*, ∼— SP66 28: back∧] ∼. *Vanderbilt* 31: bone,] ∼∧ *NRep*

42 **Genealogy** Text: TSP. Variant: as "Grandfather Gabriel" in *Second American Caravan,* ed. Alfred Kreymborg et al. (New York: The Macaulay Company, 1928), p. 120. The poem is included in SP43TS, but not in SP43. The copy is marked "Gal 24," so the poem was probably removed after the book was set in galleys. The galleys of SP43, however, do not survive. 9: Wine-Yellow] Wine-yellow *Second American Caravan,* SP43TS 9: corn,] ∼; *Second American Caravan* 10: brown,] ∼∧ *Second American Caravan* 11: east,] ∼∧ *Second American Caravan* 22: In the heart] In his heart *Second American Caravan* 22: of hell-black hate] hell-black as hate *Second American Caravan* 23: croaked] died *Second American Caravan*

43 **History** Text: TSP. Variants: *Virginia Quarterly Review,* 2 (July 1935), pp. 353–56, SP43, SP66, SP75. In *VQR* this is section II of "Two Poems on Time." 1: scarp,] ∼∧ *VQR* 2: won:] ∼; *VQR* 5: Incision:] ∼, *VQR* SP66, SP75 8: tight / —The] tight— / The *VQR* 10: foul:] ∼, *VQR,* SP66, SP75 12: Now we] We now *VQR* 14: past.] ∼: *VQR* 22: fuel.] No stanza break after this text in *VQR*. A page turn obscures whether there is stanza break here in TSP. There is a stanza break in SP43TS, and although the readings from SP43 on may derive from a mistake, on balance the odds are that it is *VQR* that is in error. 30: Of] The *VQR* 36: unfurled:] ∼, SP66, SP75 38: green:] ∼; *VQR* ∼, SP66, SP75 51: This much] Thus it *VQR* 53: abide / —Nothing] abide— / Nothing *VQR* 56: fox;] ∼. SP66, SP75 64: Nor] Scarce *VQR* 65: Though] And *VQR* 68: time's] Time's *VQR* 68: time's cold womb;] stanza break after this text, SP43TS 72: bitch/ —Purblind,] bitch—/ Purblind, *VQR* 81: shifts.] sifts. *VQR* 86: descend.] ∼! *VQR* 91: fact?] ∼. *VQR* 94: appetency] appatency SP75G (revised to TSP on SP75G) 99: We are . . . apparitor.] We are the blade, / But not the hand / By which the blade is swayed. SP66, SP75 102: The gentle path . . . be sweet.] These two lines reversed in *VQR* 104: essay] assay *VQR* 105: anger.] ∼: *VQR* 108: grey.] gray. SP66, SP75

45 **Resolution** Text: TSP. Variants: *Virginia Quarterly Review,* 2, (July 1935), pp. 352–53, SP43. As section I of "Two Poems on Time" in *Virginia Quarterly Review*. SP43 deletes the first stanza, but SP43TS retains it. 1: Grape-treader] GRAPE-TREADER *VQR* 3: Burked] Plucked *VQR* 13: Your] Time's SP43 (but SP43TS reads "Your") 22: cutpurse] pickpocket SP43 23: pulse,] ∼∧ *VQR* 27: I] One *VQR* 27: guess:] ∼. *VQR* 28: apart,] ∼: *VQR* 33: The hour past prime.] The hour near prime. *VQR,* Like golden rime. SP43 (but SP43TS follows TSP) 45: narrowly.] hollowly *VQR* 51: I] We *VQR* 52: No moral from our story.] This line is indented in *VQR*.

46 **Letter from a Coward to a Hero** Text: TSP. Variants: *Southern Review,* 1 (July 1935), pp. 92–94, SP43, SP66, SP75. 1: What did] WHAT DID *SoR* 7: marred. . .] ∼— SP66, SP75 10: *I think you deserved better;*] line not italicized in SP66, SP75 23: simple,] ∼∧ *SoR* 31: hang∧] ∼, SP75 (revised on SP75G) 32: democracy] in an early typescript at the Beinecke Library Warren has "the A. F. of L." 34: joint:] ∼, SP66, SP75 36: gun-shy;] ∼. SP66, SP75 44: at night,] all night, SP43 (but SP43TS has "at night,") 48: prefer, I know,] I know, prefer *SoR* 51: speed] strength *SoR* 66: houses. . .] ∼— SP66, SP75 68: ground:] ∼. SP66, SP75 71: cannonade?] Stanza break after this line in SP75 (added on SP75G).

48 **Late Subterfuge** Text: TSP. Variants: SP43, SP66, SP75. 11: act unjust,] unjust act SP66, SP75 12: from evil bloometh] that from evil blooms SP66, from evil may bloom SP75

49 **Ransom** Text: TSP. Variants: *Southern Review,* 1 (July 1935), p. 95, SP43, SP66, SP75. 1: Old houses,] OLD HOUSES, *SoR* 1: violence;] ∼: *SoR* 2: bottles∧] ∼, *SoR*

49 **Aged Man Surveys the Past Time** Text: TSP. Variants: *American Review,* 3 (May 1934), pp. 238–39, SP43. As section I of "Two Poems on Truth" in *American Review*. I have chosen to break up this sequence because Warren did not preserve it in any book version of these poems. It is not linked with "Toward Rationality" in the typescript draft at Beinecke Library. The typescript draft omits the last stanza. 10: sure!] ∼. *American Review* 10: regret!] ∼. *American Review*

50 **Toward Rationality** Text: TSP. Variants: *American Review,* 3 (May 1934), p. 239, SP43. As section II of "Two Poems on Truth" in *American Review.* 7: Perpetual, blithe, armed cap-a-pie,] Perpetual blithe and cap-à-pie, *American Review* 11: liberal,] ~∧ *American Review,* SP43 14: Ptolemy;] ~, *American Review*

50 **To a Friend Parting** Text: TSP. Variants: As "For a Friend Parting" *New Republic,* 26 Dec. 1934, p. 186, SP43, SP66, SP75, as "Old Soldier," read at Allen Tate's 75th birthday celebration, *Vanderbilt Alumnus,* Spring 1975. Warren listed changes in this version in a letter to James A. Grimshaw dated 4 Sept. 1976. 2: Scarred] Though scarred *Vanderbilt* 2: wry:] ~; *NRep* 3: Rock-rent∧] ~, SP43TS 3: ax-bit] axe-bit SP75 5: wrathfully.] ~: *NRep* 7: O you who by the grove and shore walked] Yes you who by grove / and shore have walked *Vanderbilt* 8: your heart] the heart *NRep* 8: unbraced∧] ~, *NRep* 9: the said, unsaid,] the said, the unsaid, SP43, SP66, SP75, *Vanderbilt* 9: though chaff] though like chaff *Vanderbilt* 11: Tower the hawk, his wings the light take.] Tower the hawk, his wings the light take! *NRep* The hawk tower, his wings the light take. SP66, SP75 11: the light] the full light *Vanderbilt* 12: What answer to our dread?] What can be foresaid? SP75 14: rusty] rusted *Poetry* 15: The horny ... now seal;] The horny clasp of hands / that your hands now seal. *Vanderbilt* 16: kept powder dry.] have kept powder dry. *Vanderbilt*

51 **Letter to a Friend** Text: TSP. Variants: *American Review,* 3 (May 1934), p. 236. 4: it;] ~: *American Review* 7: o'er] over SP43 (but SP43TS has "o'er") 16: trigger] carriage *American Review* 17: time of toads' engendering,] season of engendering of toads, *American Review* 19: Time.] time. *American Review* 20: with] to *American Review*

51 **Aubade for Hope** Text: TSP. Variants: *American Review,* 3 (May 1934), pp. 236–37, SP43. 2: is] are *American Review* 5: blessèd] blessed *American Review* 6: Acclaimèd thus,] Thus acclaimed, *American Review* 8: appetite of dream.] horror of their dream. *American Review* 14: negro] Negro SP43 (but SP43TS has "negro") 14: hand,] ~∧ *American Review* 14: grey] gray SP43 (but SP43TS and *English* have "grey") 15: wood; ... that shall,] wood—oh, merciless great eyes / Blank as the sea—I name some things that shall, SP43 19: grandam] grandma SP43 (and *English*) (This is a revision, not a typographical error in SP43—the change is marked in pencil in SP43TS, and the typescript for the unpublished *Problem of Knowledge* reads "grandma.")

52 **Man Coming of Age** Text: TSP. Variants: *Poetry,* 47 (Oct. 1935), pp. 10–11 (grouped with "The Garden" as "October Poems"), SP43, SP66. 2: At dawn defines] By dawn adorns *Poetry* 4: Of dark and cold] From cold and dark *Poetry* 5: out of thought.] past our thought. *Poetry* 13: 'Was it I ...] Quotation is in double quotes in *Poetry,* SP43, *English* (but not SP43TS), and SP66. 15: In season] In a season SP66 17: crampèd] cramped SP66 18: ways] paths *Poetry* 20: reproachful] deceitful *Poetry* 21: Walker] Wanderer *Poetry* 22: grief∧] ~, *Poetry* 25: mist,] ~∧ *Poetry* 25: gloom] glooms *Poetry*

53 **Croesus in Autumn** Text: TSP. Variants: *New Republic,* 2 Nov. 1927, p. 290, *Literary Digest,* 19 Nov. 1927, p. 34, SP43. 2: More] Less *NRep, Literary Digest* 3: Croesus] Crœsus *NRep* 5: grey] gray *NRep, Literary Digest* 5: Aurelius∧] ~, *NRep, Literary Digest* 6: latin] Latin *NRep, Literary Digest* 8: decline;] ~. *NRep, Literary Digest* 10: red-oak] red oak *NRep, Literary Digest* 10: sweet-gum] sweet gum *NRep, Literary Digest* 16: heart,] ~∧ *NRep, Literary Digest* 17: metaphor;] ~, *NRep, Literary Digest*

53 **So Frost Astounds** Text: TSP. Variants: *Poetry,* 44 (July 1934), p. 196, SP43. 1: *it will be so*] *this will be so—Poetry* 2: Nothing] nothing *Poetry* 7: under] beneath *Poetry* 9: *summer*] *garden Poetry* 10: And so ... pensive skin:] They were composed by will which locked the frail / articulation beneath the pensive skin: *Poetry* 12: on dull] on the dull *Poetry* 16: *will I*] *I will Poetry*

54 **The Last Metaphor** Text: TSP. Variants: *New Republic,* 9 Dec. 1931, p. 105, SP43. 4: said to himself:] said: *NRep* 4: I] I'll *NRep* 11: a wood] the wood *NRep* 12: there,] ~∧ *NRep* 13: the] his *NRep* 16: fashion] manner *NRep* 30: Fell summer on us with its deathy sheaf,] Summer fell on us, and the deathy sheaf, *NRep* 37: And hence] Therefore *NRep* 39: season:] ~. *NRep*

55 **Pacific Gazer** Text: TSP. Variants: SP43. 12: unprizèd] unprized SP43 (but SP43TS follows TSP) 24: billèd] billed SP43

56 **Calendar** Text: TSP. Variant: SP43. 3: dim,] Dim, SP43TS 28: in the wind's] in wind's SP43TS

57 **Problem of Knowledge** Text: TSP. Variants: *Southwest Review,* 18 (Summer 1933), p. 417, SP43. 1: What] WHAT *SWR* 4: apprehend] comprehend *SWR* 8: sow] saw *SWR*

57 **Cold Colloquy** Text: TSP. Variant: SP43.

57 **For a Self-Possessed Friend** Text: TSP. Variants: *New Republic*, 27 Nov. 1929, p. 14, SP43, *New English Review Magazine,* NS 2 (Jan. 1949), p. 54. 1: Many] MANY *New English Review* 2: for] to *NRep* 2: thing;] ~. *NRep* 3: simple,] ~— *NRep* 7: leaves] leave *NRep* 13: we who praise so much] we, who praise so much, *NRep* 15: But you, my friend... you do not praise at all,] But there is one who does not praise at all, *NRep* 16: Or^] ~, *New English Review* 16: stop and seem to cast your eye] stops, and seems to turn his eye *New Republic* 18: you] he *NRep* 19: There are some things you do not praise enough;] I think, good friend, you do not praise enough *NRep* 20: For instance] Some things; for instance *NRep* 21: long...] ~— *NRep* 22: wind...] ~— *NRep* 25: await,] ~^ *NRep* 26: kindliness,] ~^ *NRep*

58 **For a Friend Who Thinks Himself Urbane** Text: TSP. Variant: SP43.

59 **The Garden** Text: TSP. Variants: *Poetry,* 47 (Oct. 1935), (grouped with "Man Coming of Age" as "October Poems") pp. 9–10, *Poetry,* 49 (Nov. 1936), pp. 106–7, p. 112, SP43, SP66, SP75, SP85. The *Poetry* versions have no indentations. The *Poetry* versions are identical. Epigraph: *On a fine day in early autumn Poetry* 1: how secret, now the sun] how secretly, the sun *Poetry* 2: Will bless] Has blessed *Poetry* 3: And touch once more,] And touched again, *Poetry* 4: furlèd] furled SP43, SP66,.SP75, SP85 4: cold] frost *Poetry* 6: In blossom,] For blossom, *Poetry* 7: milder sun] a milder sun *Poetry* 8: An] The *Poetry* 9: No marbles ... among] This line not indented in *Poetry*. 9: gaze] gleam *Poetry* 10: hung:] ~; *Poetry* 12: The avenue] An avenue *Poetry* 13: bold] chill *Poetry* 17: The hand ... spade] This line not indented in *Poetry*. 19: before] upon *Poetry* 20: is:] ~. *Poetry* 21: Where all who came ... empery,] Where all who came might stand to prove / The grace of this imperial grove, SP43 (and SP43TS, in a handwritten revision), SP66, SP75, SP85 25: But he ... peace] Line not indented in *Poetry*. 25: But] Then *Poetry* 25: love,] ~^ *Poetry* 29: Only for him] For him alone *Poetry* 30: can] could *Poetry*

59 **To One Awake** Text: TSP. Variants: *Occident* (University of California, Berkeley), 86 (March 1926), p. 13, *New Republic,* 30 May 1928, p. 34. 5: drugged and dull] dull and drugged *Occident* 9: brain; ~, *NRep* 16: larvae] larvæ *NRep* 16: the thought] your thought *Occident* 17: preform] perform *Occident* 19: this hollow] the sable *Occident*

60 **Garden Waters** Text: TSP. Variant: *New Republic,* 7 March 1928, p. 99, SP43. 1: stream,] ~^ *NRep* 9: hollow-bosomed] hollow bosomed *NRep* 16: chrysalid.] *NRep* adds another stanza:

Better for flesh to run out naked and lonely
Where the perfidious surges front the shore;
Those deeps dividing would divulge there only
The comfortless bodies of men who had gone before.

61 **To a Face in the Crowd** Text: TSP. Variants: *Fugitive,* 4 (June 1925), p. 36, SP43, SP66, SP75, SP85. In SP43, SP66, SP75 and SP85 the title is "To a Face in a Crowd."SP85TS and SP85G did not include this poem, but it Warren corrected SP85G to include it. A photocopy of the SP75 text is added to SP85G second set. 1: Brother, my brother,] My brother, brother, *Fugitive* 1: pass?] ~, *Fugitive* 2: glen,] ~^ *Fugitive* 3: among the rocks] among rocks *Fugitive* 8: In dream, perhaps,] In dreams perhaps *Fugitive* 12: the utmost] that ultimate *Fugitive,* that utmost SP43, SP66, SP75, SP85 13: And you must find the dolorous place they stood.] And dolorous you must find the place they stood. *Fugitive* 26: I,] ~^ *Fugitive*

Eleven Poems on the Same Theme

There is no setting typescript at the Beinecke Library, but there are typescript and carbon drafts of many of the poems. I have also examined the typescript of SP43, in which many of these poems appear. I have noted readings from SP43TS only where they differ from SP43.

On the acknowledgments page Warren acknowledges the Poetry Society of South Carolina. On the acknowledgments page of the typescript of *Problem of Knowledge*, an unpublished volume roughly contemporary with EP, Warren acknowledges "the Poetry Society of South Carolina for "Love's Parable," "Question and Answer," and "Love's Voice," which received the Caroline Sinkler Prize in 1936, 1937, and 1938." He does not mention whether they also published the poem.

65 **Monologue at Midnight** Text: EP. Variants: *Virginia Quarterly Review,* 12 (July 1936), p. 395, SP43, SP66, SP75. 1: Among] AMONG *VQR* 10: pleasure;] ~: *VQR* 12: shadows over] shadow o'er *VQR* 12: moved,] ~∧ *VQR* 17: flame] ~, *VQR* 17: gloom] ~, *VQR* 21: The hound, the echo, flame, or shadow . . .] Hound or echo, flame or shadow . . . *VQR* 21: shadow. . .] ~— SP66, SP75 24: stand,] ~∧ *VQR* 28: no dawn.] no-dawn. *VQR*

65 **Bearded Oaks** Text: EP. Variants: *Poetry,* 51 (Oct. 1937), pp. 10–11, SP43, SP66, SP75, SP85, *Helsinki.* In SP85TS the text, which is photocopy from SP75, is moved to after "Revelation". 1: marine,] ~! *Poetry* 6: languorous] langorous *Poetry,* SP43TS 6: light:] ~; *Poetry* 14: hour:] ~; *Poetry* 20: Dark is unrocking,] Unrocked is dark, *Poetry* 22: Descend, minutely whispering down,] Descended, whispered grain by grain, *Poetry* 23: streams,] steams SP66 26: rage, the rage] rage is rage *Poetry* 27: hope is hopeless,] hopeless hope, *Poetry* 27: then fearless] fearless *Poetry* 27: fearless fear,] fearless is fear, *Poetry,* SP66, SP75, SP85, *Helsinki* 29: Our feet. . . fled.] (Our feet. . . fled.) *Poetry* 31: windows,] ~; *Poetry* 34: I do not love you. . . stroke,] That cagèd hearts make iron stroke / I do not love you now the less, *Poetry* 36: revoke.] ~∧ *Poetry* 37: We live in time so little time] So little time we live in Time, *Poetry* 40: eternity.] Eternity *Poetry*

66 **Picnic Remembered** Text: EP. Variants: *Scribner's Magazine,* 99 (March 1936), p. 185, SP43, *New English Review,* 16 (May 1948), pp. 433–34, SP66, SP75, SP85. In SP85TS this poem follows "Bearded Oaks," as in SP75, but both are placed after "Revelation". 1: That] THAT *Scribner's* 1: day,] ~∧ *Scribner's* 3: structures] structure *Scribner's* 5: Seemed quaint disaster] Seemed quaint disasters *Scribner's,* Seemed the quaint disaster SP66, SP75, SP85 7: canceled;] cancelled; *Scribner's,* SP43, *New English Review* 14: marveling] marvelling *Scribner's,* SP43, *New English Review* 16: swimmers,] ~∧ *Scribner's* 18: unstainèd] unstained SP43 (but SP43TS reads "unstainèd"), SP66, SP75, SP85 19: sustained,] maintained, *Scribner's* 21: but half] half but *Scribner's* 21: but half understood.] *Scribner's* adds a stanza after this line:

Our conversation's privilege
Was but to read each other's eyes
For questions and for sure replies:
Leaning, as one who at the verge
Of cliff beneath which sea-birds call
Savors the sweet of space, the fall,
The plunge of sacrificial rage.

25: truth] trust SP85 (revised on SP85G to SP85) 25: betray;] ~: *Scribner's* 41: new province,] a new province, SP66, SP75, a new province: SP85 (revised on SP85G to SP85) 43: The *then,* the *now:*] The then, the now: *Scribner's,* 44: Of the other,] Of other, *Scribner's* 44: contains it, dead.] proclaims it dead. SP66, SP75, SP85

68 **Crime** Text: EP. Variants: *Nation,* 25 May 1940, p. 655, *Living Age,* Jan. 1941, pp. 487–88, SP43, SP66, SP75. 1: killer∧] ~, *Nation* 2: scream:] ~; *Nation* scream. SP66, SP75 6: treasure∧] ~, *Nation* 7: skinful,] skinfull, *Nation* 9: But what was it? But he is too tired to ask it.] And what is hid? But he is too tired to ask it. *Nation,* But what was the treasure he buried? He's too tired to ask it. SP66, SP75 10: woman∧] ~,

Nation 11: wood,] ~? *Nation,* SP66, SP75 19: jars;] ~. *Nation,* SP66, SP75 23: draft;] ~, SP66, SP75 25: Peace, all he asked: past] All he asked was peace. Past SP66, SP75 26: snatched] grasped *Nation* 30: Dark,] ~∧ *Nation, Living Age* 31: silent] still *Nation* 34: with the] with *Nation* 35: at] with *Nation* 37: stammer] stutter *Nation* 39: a pipe] like a pipe *Nation* 40: And in its hutch and hole, as when the earth gets warmer,] And in its hole, as when the earth wakes to the vernal shudder, *Nation,* And in its hole, as when the earth gets warmer, *Living Age* There is no stanza break after this line in *Nation.* 43: puzzled yet,] still confused, *Nation* 44: Names over your name,] Names your name *Nation*

69 **Original Sin: A Short Story** Text: EP. Variants: *Kenyon Review,* 4 (Spring 1942), pp. 179–80, SP43, "Poetry in the Age of Anxiety," (program for Fifth McGregor Room Seminar in Contemporary Prose and Poetry, sponsored by the Schools of English at the University of Virginia, 31 October 1947), SP66, SP75, SP85. In SP85TS this poem follows "The Ballad of Billie Potts". 5: snuffle] sniffle *Anxiety* (revised on Warren's copy to EP) 15: grandpa's] Grandpa's SP66, SP75, SP85 17: mewed;] ~. SP66, SP75, SP75 21: But it] It SP66, SP75, SP85 25: its] it's SP85 (This error appears on SP85G and was not corrected by Warren.) 26: meadows] meadow SP75, SP85 27: bosom;] ~— SP66, SP75, SP85 38: hope,] ~∧ SP66, SP75, SP85 41: lock; you hear] lock. You hear SP66, SP75, SP85

70 **End of Season** Text: EP. Variants: *Nation,* 7 March 1942, p. 286, SP43, *Perspectives USA,* no. 13 (Autumn 1955), pp. 25–26, SP66, SP75. 7: *spiagga,*] *spiaggia*∧*Nation* 13: sun:] ~— SP66, SP75 16: Woke, while squat,] Woke while, squat, SP75 16: squat,] ~∧] *Nation* 18: brow] brown SP43TS 19: *You'll come, you'll come!*] *You'll come, you must! Nation* 21: history;] ~. SP66, SP75 22: And wordless,] Then wordless, SP66, SP75 24: café] cafe *Nation* 33: visit;] ~. SP66, SP75 35: Summer's] The summer's *Nation*

71 **Revelation** Text: EP. Variants: *Poetry,* 59 (Jan. 1942), pp. 202–3, *Angry Penguins*, (Sept. 1943), n.p., SP43, SP66, SP75. 5: Roof was rent like the loud paper tearing to admit] Roof was rent like loud paper tearing to admit SP43 (but SP43TS follows EP), Rent was the roof like loud paper to admit SP66, SP75 7: the submarine glimmer] a submarine glimmer SP66, SP75 10: fat-petalled] fat-petaled *Poetry,* SP66, SP75, ~ *Angry Penguins* (I note this only to note that *Angry Penguins* does not follow *Poetry.*) 17: rent,] racked, SP66, SP75 27: laid∧] laid, SP66, SP75 30: recalcitrant] merciless *Poetry,* recalcitrant *Angry Penguins*, irredeemable SP66, SP75 32: about love,] above love, SP43 (but SP43TS reads "about love,"), SP66, SP75

72 **Pursuit** Text: EP. Variants: *Virginia Quarterly Review,* 18 (Jan. 1942), pp. 57–59, SP43, *Perspectives USA,* no. 13 (Autumn 1955), pp. 23–25, SP66, SP75. 1: The] THE *VQR* 10: innocence is gone.] The typescript worksheets for this poem are not finished, but they show that Warren considered adding another stanza at this point:

Is gone, and where the most prodigal chase
Flags, or your cry, like the lost Babes' lament
Down the autumn aisle when the kindly cut-throat went,
Diminishes. Suppose you know the place:
The street, the house, the attic-hutch, and meet
At that stair-head with your first bridal glance,
Of all his truth, the pious appurtenance
And clutter where such sanctity had seat.
He will not come: and you (lack) (cannot learn) the pure heart to spell
The language of that twisted quilt, the crusted pan on the sill.

11: Wait] Sit *VQR* 11: room,] ~∧ SP43, *Perspectives,* SP66, SP75 16: severe] sever SP43TS 19: regards you] stares stern SP43, *Perspectives,* SP66, SP75 22: heart;] ~. SP66, SP75 23: But] He SP66, SP75 23: impart;] ~, SP66, SP75 28: gleams] gleams white SP66, SP75 31: flamingo,] ~∧ SP43, *Perspectives* 32: question;] ~. SP66, SP75 47: Who admires] Admires SP66, SP75

73 **Question and Answer** Text: EP. Variants: *Poetry,* 57 (Feb. 1941), pp. 288–91, SP43. 6: And the choices / Lost,] lines missing in SP43 25: view] see *Poetry* 28: question] hour *Poetry* 29: hour] question *Poetry* 51: Answer∧] ~, *Poetry* 52: That conversation] Their converse *Poetry* 60: Evening field and morning street—] Stony pasture, starving goat, / Mullein, anemone, / Groaning gallows and the gallows-meat— *Poetry* 67: Then let the heart be stone,] This line starts a new stanza in *Poetry,* and in SP43, but the stanza break is obscured by a page turn in EP. 77: pool,] ~∧ *Poetry* 78: Or where] Where *Poetry* 78: moving waters] the moving water *Poetry* 96: cord,] ~∧ *Poetry*

75 **Love's Parable** Text: EP. Variants: *Kenyon Review,* 2 (Spring 1940), pp. 186–88, SP43, SP66, SP75. 14: Of] On SP43 (but SP43TS reads "Of"), SP66, SP75 18: For miracle] —For miracle *KR* 28: precious] costly *KR* 46: perturbedly] perturbed SP43 (but SP43TS reads "perturbedly"), SP66, SP75 48: yearns.] ~, *KR* 59: very] the very SP66, SP75 61: strength,] ~∧ *KR* 64: each other] each *KR* 67: gazing] grazing *KR* 68: glass'] glass's *KR* 69: What cause? What matter for] What does it matter for *KR*

77 **Terror** Text: EP. Variants: *Poetry,* 57 (Feb. 1941), pp. 285–88, SP43, SP66, SP75. epigraph: 27 Gennaio, 1940.] 27 Gennaio, 1940, XVIII, S. Giovanni Crisostomo *Poetry*. In one of the typescript worksheets in the Beinecke Library, the epigraph continues: "Il Presidente Roosevelt ha dichiarato oggi ai giornalisti, che i cittadini americani, che si arruolino in eserciti stranieri, perderanno la cittadinanza degli Stati Uniti soltanto nel case che pretino un giuramento." 1: Not] NOT *Poetry* 5: mean] means SP66, SP75 8: face,] faces *Poetry* 9: street-lamps,] street-lights, *Poetry* 17: privy breath,] privy-breath, *Poetry* (This is a substantive, not an accidental, because "privy breath" means, "secret breath," whereas "privy-breath" means "breath that smells like a privy." 18: dream,] ~∧ *Poetry* 22: face,] ~∧ SP66, SP75 24: Better] Rather SP43 (though SP43TS reads "Better") 25: Harry L. I knew,] Harry L., my friend, SP66, SP75 26: Had dwindled] Would have dwindled SP66, SP75 27: a plane,] the plane SP66, SP75 30: cornfield;] ~— SP66, SP75 30: flame.] Stanza break after this line in EP obscured by page break. 34: hid;] ~. SP66, SP75 35: North,] ~— SP66, SP75 41: which, perhaps, the Moor,] which fat Franco's Moor, SP43 (but the SP43 TS reads "which, perhaps, the Moor,"), SP66, SP75 48: Courier,] ~∧ *Poetry* 49: in furs,] furred, *Poetry* 60: test tube,] test-tube, *Poetry* 61: But it is dead, . . . an empty chair.] In three of the typescript worksheet versions of this poem in the Beinecke Library this stanza is replaced by the following two stanzas:

But it is dead, that clip of cuddled cell
The fowl gave up to cuddle your content;
And the antiseptic augurs lean to spell
Your fate in other entrails, which are rent
From no brute beast, but man, whose homeless head,
Homesick for terror, bulges, and creates
The diver's nightmare and the weighted tread.
So Civilization, blabbing, emulates
The drivelled Roman in his bloody bath
Who quoted Greek and puddled out his abstract wrath.

Dead, little loss for you who, guiltless, sink
To rest in lobbies, or pace gardens where
The slow god crumbles and the fountains prink,
Nor heed the criminal king, who paints the air
With discoursed madness and protruding eye,
Nor give the alarm, nor ask tonight where sleeps
That head which hooped the jewel Fidelity,
But like an old melon now, in the dank ditch seeps;
But crack nuts, while the conscience-stricken stare
Kisses the terror; for you see an empty chair.

65: eye,] ~— SP66, SP75 70: an empty chair.] In three of the worksheet typescripts the poem continues on for another stanza:

Let lightning groove the granite cheeks which lean
Above your cradle, and the glamor ice
Groan in the months when the lower cirques are green;
Not they, nor wine of altitude, suffice,
While bald allegory, vexed, yelps from the crag;
Nor love of comrades, nor the more prized gewgaw
Of that love's betrayal, which like a china egg
You brood and fluff on in the miteless straw,
Suffices. Huddle apart. Eat what you have
In secret, glut instance and appetite,
Warm gob on the tongue, with saliva sweeter than love;
Clutch the hand which curls, like pathos, in the night;
While the adversary droops, an old horse cold in the pasture,
Or wakes like a mother who tries to remember a childhood picture.

Selected Poems 1923–1943

Although this volume reprints most of the poems from *Thirty-Six Poems* and *Eleven Poems on the Same Theme*, Warren broke up the arrangement of the poems from those volumes, arranging them into two groups. The first, "Late," includes "The Ballad of Billie Potts," "Terror," "Pursuit," "Original Sin: A Short Story," "Crime," "Letter from a Coward to a Hero," "History," "Question and Answer," End of Season," "Ransom," "Aged Man Surveys the Past Time," "Toward Rationality," " To A Friend Parting," "Letter to a Friend," "Aubade for Hope," " Eidolon," "Variation: Ode to Fear," the five sections of "Mexico is a Foreign Country: Five Studies in Naturalism," "Monologue at Midnight," "Bearded Oaks," "Picnic Remembered," "Resolution," "Love's Parable," "Late Subterfuge," "Man Coming of Age," and "The Garden." The second section, "Early," includes "The Return: An Elegy," the seven sections of "Kentucky Mountain Farm," "Pondy Woods," "Letter of a Mother," "Crœsus in Autumn," "So Frost Astounds," "The Last Metaphor," "Pacific Gazer," "Calendar," "Problem of Knowledge," "For a Self-possessed Friend," "For a Friend who Thinks Himself Urbane," "Cold Colloquy," "Garden Waters," and "To a Face in a Crowd." (Notice how even this early in his career Warren adhered to the practice of printing volumes of selected poems roughly in reverse chronological order.) When Warren republished these poems in later Selected Poems volumes, he always treated *Selected Poems 1923–1943* as his first volume of poems, and reprinted the selections (with some deletions) in the order they appear in this volume. When choosing texts from the Selected Poems volumes I have followed Warren's practice of including only those poems which are new with that volume.

I have used the 1944 Harcourt, Brace edition for this volume, but I have also collated the 1954 English edition published by The Fortune Press.

In the published version Warren included the following note to the volume:

> The *Late* poems in this collection have been drawn from among pieces composed during the last eight or nine years. Most of them however, are relatively recent. The *Early* poems belong to the previous decade, some of them going back into student days. R.P.W. *Minneapolis, July 26, 1943.*

In the setting typescript Warren included the following headnote to the volume:

> I feel that I should offer some explanation for the division of material adopted in this book. It is not merely arbitrary—at least, in my own mind—and will not, I trust, appear arbitrary to the reader. The *Late* poems do represent a selection from among pieces composed during relatively recent years, but the date of composition is in itself not the important factor. Rather, the poems in this group were written from an attitude toward poetry—and toward other things—quite different from the attitude behind the *Early* poems. But changes in attitude do not usually come all at once,

> and when the change is going on one may not even be aware of the nature of the process. The awareness comes later. And even when looking back, one can scarcely lay one's finger on the spot on the calendar and say, "That was the time." In fact, three poems in this collection, "Problem of Knowledge," "Calendar," and "Pacific Gazer," though fairly late in date of composition, have been placed in the *Early* group, because in truth they were strays from that period, tardy outcroppings of an old impulse. But the other poems in this group are early, quite literally, one or two of them going back even to undergraduate days.
>
> It is difficult to say on what basis such a selection is made. In one sense, a poem once on paper means—or should mean—nothing to the author. The act of putting it down was an act of disentangling himself from the "meanings" of the material which went into the poem, an act performed in the hope of achieving a new meaning which would be the poem. The author tries to make his selection in terms of the new meaning, but the old meanings live in him so intimately and vindictively that he may the be last man, after all, for the job. It is, however, a job which is always taken out of his hands in the end. R. P. W. *Minneapolis,* July 26, 1943.

The setting typescript differs considerably from the printed text, and although the text is marked up for the typesetter, most of the editorial changes are not marked, which casts some doubt on the superior authority of the typescript over the printed text. The galleys for this volume do not survive. But in a letter of November 2, 1943, Warren's editor at Harcourt Brace, Lambert Davis, suggests that Warren wait until he sees the galleys before making a final decision about what poems to include in the volume, which suggests that Warren made considerable revisions to the volume in proof. The typescript also includes "Genealogy," which SP43 excludes. In most of the cases where SP43 differs from the typescript, the typescript preserves readings from TSP and EP, and in very few cases does Warren in SP66, SP75, or SP85 revise poems from SP43 so as to restore the typescript reading. All of these facts lead me to believe that most if not all of the differences between SP43 and the typescript represent Warren's revisions to the poems. Nothing in the typescript or in the correspondence suggests that any of the revisions are Davis' work; indeed, Davis' correspondence suggests that he was preoccupied at this time with Warren's early drafts of *All the King's Men,* which he revised considerably, and that he gave SP43 less than his full attention. Therefore I have chosen to give SP43 more weight than the typescript where they disagree. I have also collated the unpublished collections, *Kentucky Mountain Farm and Other Poems*, *Pondy Woods and Other Poems*, *Cold Colloquy*, and *Problem of Knowledge*, but because this is a critical rather than a genetic text I have not included those collations here, except when they cast light on an issue in the published volumes.

SP66TS for these poems is photocopy of SP43. SP75TS is photocopy of SP66. SP85TS is cut and taped photocopy of SP75.

81 **The Ballad of Billie Potts** Text: SP43. Variants: *Partisan Review,* 2 (Winter 1944), pp. 56–70, SP66, SP75, SP85. Headnote: SP66, SP75, and SP85 drop the third sentence. Headnote: Rivers,"] Rivers", *English* Headnote: Cave Inn Rock, or the Cave-In-Rock] Cave Inn Rock. *PR* Headnote: where the first] where, it is said, the first SP85 (on SP85G) Headnote: Eighteenth Century.] eighteenth century. *PR*, SP66, SP75, SP85 1: Big] BIG *PR* 2: rivers.] $\sim_\wedge$ SP75, SP85 8: Big] Bib SP85 (This error is on SP85G, but Warren did not notice it.) 12: cat$_\wedge$] $\sim$. SP66, SP75, SP85 13: In the land between the rivers.] SP66, SP75 and SP85 omit this line. 16: when he came in,] SP43TS adds a line after this text: "In the land between the rivers," 19: beller] bellow SP66, SP75, SP85 24: hills$_\wedge$] $\sim$, *PR*, SP43TS 25: uncoiled] uncoils, SP85 (in pencil on SP85TS) 27: Was] Is SP85 (revised on SP85G to SP85) 28: Some] A SP66, SP75, SP85 28: shag-bark] shagbark SP66, SP75, SP85 32: and black-jack yet.] and the black-jack yet. *PR* Stanza break after this line in SP85. Because this is a place where two taped in extracts

from SP75 are joined, probably the stanza break is an error. Warren removed this space in the *Emory* copy of SP85. 33: under the powerful sun.] In the *Emory* copy of SP85, Warren added a stanza break after this line. 35: hill,] hills, *PR* 38: hit] it SP66, SP75 hit SP85 (revised on SP85G to SP85) 40: come by.] come by / In the land between the rivers. *PR*, SP43TS 44: trees^] ~. *PR* 45: In the section between the rivers.] Line omitted from *PR*. 50: words^] ~, SP66, SP75, SP85 51: birds^] ~, SP66, SP75, SP85 55: whence it was torn.] Stanza break after this line in *PR*. A page turn obscures this stanza break in SP43, but it is found in SP43TS, *English*, SP66, SP75, and SP85 58: the range's lip,] the mountain lip, *PR*, the Appalachian lip, SP66, SP75, SP85 61: proceed] they proceed SP66, SP75, SP85 65: laid,] ~. SP66, SP75, SP85 66: squire^] ~, SP66, SP75, SP85 67: In the land between the rivers.] Line omitted from SP66, SP75, and SP85. 68: fire^] ~, SP66, SP75, SP85 74: saddle and was ready to go] saddle, was ready to go, SP66, SP75, SP85 76: dead,] dead / In the section between the rivers. SP43TS 81: call,] ~^ *PR* 84: pace,] who pace, SP66, SP75, SP85 90: grandma] Grandma SP66, SP75, SP85 95: who bear] these who bear SP66, SP75, SP85 99: frieze:] freize: SP43TS 101: piss and vinegar] vinegar SP66, SP75, SP85 103: pup,] pup, / In the land between the rivers. SP43TS 106: the man was] the man who was SP66, SP75, SP85 112: bizness] business SP66, SP75, SP85 113: In the section between the rivers,] Line omitted from *PR*. 114: hit] it SP66, SP75, SP85 117: In addition to snot,] By way of brains, SP66, SP75, SP85 124: his Pap] Pap SP66, SP75, SP85 124: his Mammy] Mammy SP66, SP75, SP85 125: had^] ~. *PR*, SP66, SP75, SP85 126: In the section between the rivers.] Line is omitted from *PR*, SP66, SP75 and SP85. 133: air;] ~: *PR* 137: your face] your own face SP85 (revised on SP85G to SP85) 138: swamp-edge,] ~: SP66, SP75, SP85 144: Which are you?] Which one are you? SP66, SP75, SP85 146: he squatted] squatted SP66, SP75, SP85 147: didn't want] wouldn't SP66, SP75, SP85 151: It was] It's SP85 (revised on SP85G to SP85) 155: humming^] ~. *PR*, SP66, SP75, SP85 156: In the section between the rivers.] Line omitted from *PR*, SP66, SP75, SP85. 158: Why,] ~^ *PR*, SP43TS 160: somethen] somethin *PR*, SP43TS 161: nuthen] nuthin *PR*, SP43TS 161: not proper] nor proper *PR* 161: And he ain't wanten] And Pap don't want SP66, SP75, SP85 162: didn't do a thing] did nothing *PR* 167: known] guessed SP66, SP75, SP85 168: hit] it SP66, SP75, SP85 183: pants^] ~, SP66, SP75, SP85 184: goes,] goes^ / In the section between the rivers, SP43TS 191: "That bastard ... belt,] "Two hundred in gold's in my money belt, SP66, SP75, SP85 195: Fer] For SP43TS 195: labors] labors." *PR*. 196: Even here between the rivers."] Line missing from *PR*. 201: And the next time] And next time SP66, SP75, SP85 202: hit] it SP66, SP75, SP85 202: do hit quick."] Stanza break follows this line in SP66, SP75, SP85. 203: Little] little *PR* 206: luck^] ~, SP66, SP75, SP85 207: And left the land between the rivers,] Line omitted from SP66, SP75, and SP85. 221: the lip to lip,] lip to lip, SP85 (in black pen on SP85TS) 222: identity,] ~. *PR* 226: and the rivers] and rivers *PR* 237: new^] ~, SP85 (in pencil on SP85TS) 238: And they are you.] But they are you, SP85 (Not marked on SP85TS or SP85G. Possibly a typesetter's error on SP85G.) 239: Are new.] And new. SP75, SP85 241: blood.] flood. *PR* 242: Time^] ~. SP66, SP75, SP85 243: Time is only ... priceless blood.] These lines, and the stanza break, are omitted in SP66, SP75, and SP85. 265: looks] squints SP66, SP75, SP85 266: if'n hit] if it SP66, SP75, SP85 267: hit's] it's SP66, SP75, SP85 268: if'n] if SP66, SP75, SP85 268: hit,] it, SP66, SP75, SP85 269: if'n] if SP66, SP75, SP85 270: with the black beard] with black beard *PR* 273: I'm just] just SP66, SP75, SP85 278: if'n] if SP66, SP75, SP85 281: hit] it SP66, SP75, SP85 282: luck] luck." SP66, SP75 283: hit] it *PR* 283: back] back." *PR* 283: And maybe ... rivers."] Lines omitted from SP66, SP75, SP85. 284: To the section between the rivers."] Line omitted from *PR* 285: laughed and jingled] jingled SP66, SP75, SP85 286: home,] ~^ *PR*, SP43TS 290: early^] ~, SP66, SP75, SP85 290: hit's] it's SP66, SP75, SP85 291: git me some fun] git some fun *PR* 294: if'n] if SP66, SP75, SP85 294: wuzn't] wusn't *PR*, wasn't SP66, SP75, SP85 301: and the kildees cried. ... And would not stop and would not stop] In the *Emory* copy of SP85 these lines are changed to: "and the kildees cried, / In spite of all your luck, the kildees were crying. / In spite of all the astuteness of your heart, they cried. / And would not stop and would not stop". 303: For you all luck,] For all your luck, *PR,* SP85 (revised on SP85G to SP85) 304: and would not stop] and would not stop, *PR* 304: And would not stop and would not stop] In the *Emory* copy of SP85, Warren adds a stanza break after this line. 311: all,] ∼‸ SP43TS 314: And the valet . . . stop] Two lines omitted from SP66, SP75, SP85. 323: from the picture,] Stanza break after this line in SP85. Because in SP85TS this is a place where two taped extracts from SP75 are joined, probably the stanza break is an error. In the *Emory* copy of SP85 Warren removed the stanza break. 324: "Why,] ∼‸ *PR* 325: perfectly true.] No stanza break here in SP85, probably again in error since it is not marked in SP85TS or on SP85G. In the *Emory* copy of SP85 Warren added the stanza break back again. 326: had whatever it was] had / Whatever it was SP66, SP75, SP85 327: But it was a long time back.] Line omitted from SP66, SP75. 334: he teased] teased SP66, SP75, SP85 338: rivers,] ∼. SP66, SP75, SP85 339: And he] He SP66, SP75, SP85 345: Pappy, why don't you take] Pappy, take SP66, SP75, SP85 345: it] hit SP66, SP75, SP85 346: And the old woman gave] The old woman gave SP66, SP75, SP85 348: Oh, the stars] The stars SP66, SP75, SP85 351: Oh, on the trace. . . In the section between the rivers.] Six lines omitted from SP66, SP75 and SP85. 352: But under the trees is night and dark,] Line missing in SP43TS. 357: And the leaves hang down in the dark of the trees] The leaves hang down in the dark of the trees, SP66, SP75, SP85 358: trees‸] ∼, SP66, SP75, SP85 359: ink‸] ∼, SP66, SP75, SP85 361: trees,] ∼. SP66, SP75, SP85 362: And the star] The star SP66, SP75, SP85 363: And Little Billie] Little Billie SP66, SP75, SP85 366: gone‸] ∼, *Emory* copy of SP85 366: his face.] Stanza break after this text in SP85 (added on SP85TS) 368: Then set the hatchet in his head.] In the *Emory* copy of SP85 Warren added a stanza break after this text. Warren added the stanza break in pencil in SP85G, but the typesetter did not follow his instructions. 371: bin] been *PR* 373: is late, is late,] is late, SP66, SP75, SP85 374: in its innocence dark;] in innocence dark; SP85 (revised on SP85G to SP85) 379: leaves:] ∼; *PR* 381: mother or father] mother and father *PR* 382: But after. . . anonymities,] Stanza (five lines) omitted in SP66, SP75, SP85. 384: After the sleep] After sleep *PR* 387: You come,] So, SP66, SP75, SP85 388: in art] of art *PR,* SP43TS 388: worn with your] worn in the *PR,* SP43TS 390: Prodigal,] You come, SP66, SP75, SP85 393: oh, father, father] Oh, father, father *PR,* SP43TS 396: year?"] year?‸ *PR* 398: In the section between the rivers,] Line omitted in *PR.* 402: pistol-butts‸] ∼, SP85 (added in pencil on SP85TS) 404: yore] your SP75TS, SP85 404: luck."] luck. *PR,* luck / To the land between the rivers." SP43TS 406: head‸] ∼, SP66, SP75, SP85 408: hit] it SP66, SP75, SP85 410: Oh, the] The SP66, SP75, SP85 418: of the saddle] of saddle SP66, SP75, SP85 418: of the hoof,] of hoof, SP66, SP75, SP85 421: While the dark outside. . . in the dark of the trees and still] These four lines omitted from SP66, SP75, SP85. 425: rivers.] ∼, *PR* 428: stir‸] ∼. SP66, SP75, SP85 429: And she] She SP66, SP75, SP85 432: Where the leaves] Where leaves SP66, SP75, SP85 435: and then she said,] and then said, *PR* 436: "I kin put my hand on his face."] "My hand's on his face." SP66, SP75, SP85 442: says:] ∼; *PR* 442: "Tell me his name."] Stanza break after this line in SP66, SP75, SP85. 444: hit] it SP66, SP75, SP85 447: hit] it SP66, SP75, SP85 449: "But tell me his name."] Stanza break after this line in SP66, SP75, SP85. 450: fer he] he SP66, SP75, SP85 450: just come] jist come SP85 (revised on SP85G to SP85), come *Emory* copy of SP85 451: biden,] ∼. SP66, SP75, SP85 452: And ain't] Ain't SP66, SP75, SP85 452: none,] ∼— SP66, SP75, SP85 454: And hit wuz Billie, hit wuz his name."] And it was Billie, it was his name." SP66, SP75, And hit was Billie, it was his name." SP85 (revised on SP85G to SP85) The *Emory* copy of SP85 adds a stanza break after this text. 455: name.] ∼; SP43TS 456: same,] ∼. *PR* 456: hit's] it's SP66, SP75, SP85 457: wuz] was SP66, SP75, SP85 461: wuz] was SP66, SP75, SP85 462: tit,] ∼‸ *PR* 463: luck‸] ∼, SP85 (added in pencil on SP85TS) 463: hit—] it— SP66, SP75, hit— SP85 (revised on SP85G to SP85) Stanza break after this line in SP66, SP75, SP85. 464: And the] The SP66, SP75, SP85 468: laff] laugh SP66, SP75, SP85 472: burn,] ∼. SP85 (The photocopy which is the basis of SP85TS is unclear here, which is probably the source of the error) 477: marshes] marches SP75G (revised to SP43—a printer's error) 478: and,] ∼‸ *PR,* SP43TS 486: Their innocence of air] The innocence of air SP85 (revised on SP85G to SP85) 489: Back,] Stanza break after this line in SP85. In SP85TS this is a place where two taped extracts from SP75 are joined. But the stanza break is also marked in in pencil. 491: which is home.] Stanza break after this line in SP66, SP75, SP85. 492: And you, wanderer, back,... needs the wick.] These six lines omitted in SP66, SP75, SP85. 498: And the father waits for the son.] Stanza break after this line in SP66, SP75, SP85. 512: for luck,] Stanza break after this line in SP85 (marked in both in pencil and in black pen in SP85TS).

92 **Variation: Ode to Fear** Text: SP43. 36: Focke-Wulf] Fokke-Wulf SP43TS

94 **Mexico is a Foreign Country: Five Studies in Naturalism** Text: SP43. Variants: *Poetry,* 62 (June 1943), pp. 121–22, SP66, SP75. *Poetry,* SP66, and SP75 omit "Siesta Time in Village Plaza by Ruined Bandstand and Banana Tree."

94 **I. Butterflies Over the Map** Text: SP43. Additional variant of this section: *15 Poems*, selected by Rosanna Warren, privately printed for Stuart Wright, 1985. 1: Butterflies,] BUTTERFLIES, *Poetry* 10: Are you, who wrathless, rose, and robed in the pure] Like Brutus, you wrathless rose and, robed in the pure SP66, SP75, 15P. 11: smote,] ~∧ SP75 (revised on SP75G) 16: Virgin's] virgin's SP75

95 **II. Siesta Time in Village Plaza by Ruined Bandstand and Banana Tree** For some reason this section, and this section alone, of this poem, is in a carbon copy in the typescript. It seems to be a late addition to the poem, since unlike all the others the section title is not given in capital letters.

96 **III. The World Comes Galloping: A True Story** 12: out] forth *Poetry*, SP43TS 15: violent] violet SP66 (revised back to SP43 on SP75TS) 17: His mouth] He mouth *English* 32: galopando,] ~∧ SP66, SP75

97 **IV. Small Soldiers with Drum in Large Landscape** 16: take] to take *Poetry* 28: And leaf∧] And leaf, *English* 53: As I remarked ... in the sun] These two stanzas omitted from SP66 and SP75.

98 **V. The Mango on the Mango Tree** Republished separately, *Perspectives USA,* no. 13 (Autumn 1955), pp. 22–23. 6: But] And SP66, SP75 6: place).] place.) *Perspectives USA* 11: I,] ~. *Perspectives USA* 21: clime,] ∧; *Poetry*, *Perspectives USA*, ~. SP66, SP75 22: His] God's SP66, SP75 28: the word] what word SP66, SP75 29: That it could hear,] The mango might hear, SP66, SP75 31: I] it SP66, SP75 36: ring∧] ~, SP66, SP75 38: blessedness] a blessedness SP66, SP75 38: escheat] forfeit— SP66, SP75 39: —Blest] ∧~ SP66, SP75

Promises

Poems 1954–1956

For this volume I have examined the typescript, two sets of galley proofs (they differ slightly), and the plate proofs, all of them in the Beinecke Library, as well as the relevant correspondence with Random House and with Eyre and Spottiswood. The typescript is corrected both in black pencil, in what seems to be Warren's hand, and in red pencil, in what is probably Albert Erskine's. Unless noted otherwise, corrections in the typescript described here are those in black pencil. The typescript seems to have been prepared in one piece on one typewriter, with typed page numbers, although the typescript for the most part follows the magazine versions, with most of the changes being penciled in.

On 23 May 1987, Warren marked up a copy of *Promises* with proposed revisions for Stuart Wright's use. That copy is now at the Special Collections of the Emory University Library. Because Warren clearly did not collate this copy against his later revisions of the poem—indeed, he seems to have forgotten that many of the lines he revised had already been revised in later editions—I have not adopted any emendations on the sole authority of the Emory volume. I cite the emendations from that volume with permission of the Special Collections of the Emory University Library.

Warren prepared the SP66 revisions from a typescript that follows P but the setting copy is a marked up photocopy of P marked up in red pen and green pen. Some revisions were made on the dummy paste-up of SP66. I have not marked in which of these places each SP66 revision was made. The typescript for SP75 is cut and taped text prepared from SP66. The typescript for SP85 is cut and taped text prepared from SP75.

103 **To a Little Girl, One Year Old, in a Ruined Fortress** Text: P. Variants: *Partisan Review,* 23 (Spring 1955), pp. 171–78 (as "To a Little Girl, One Year Old, in Ruined Fortress"), SP66, SP75, SP85. The sequence also appeared in a 1956 private limited edition, *To a Little Girl, One Year Old, In a Ruined Fortress* (here Doggett), which was designed, illustrated, and printed by Jane Doggett in the Department of Graphic Arts, School of Design, Yale University. The sections are untitled in *PR* and in Doggett. Doggett reflects changes made after *PR,* which it cites, but Warren seems to have lost sight of the revisions he made for Doggett when he republished the poem in P. SP85 includes only "Sirocco," and "The Child Next Door."

103 **I. Sirocco** Title] Warren complained in a letter of September 8, 1985, to Stuart Wright that he had misspelled the word for thirty years, and that the correct spelling is "Scirocco." But "Sirocco" is often listed as an alternate spelling, so I have chosen not to emend the title. (The letter to Wright is in the Special Collections of the Vanderbilt University Library.) Warren did not put periods after the Roman numerals in the sequence section titles in Doggett, P, English, SP66, SP75 or SP85. I have done so here in order to treat all sequences in the same way. 2: clamped] set *PR,* Doggett 3: A hill, no. Sea cliff, and crag-cocked, the embrasures] No hill, but a sea-cliff, and crag-cocked embrasures Doggett 3: Sea cliff,] Sea-cliff, *PR,* On a sea cliff, SP66, SP75, SP85. PTS reads "Sea-cliff," but the hyphen is deleted in pencil. There is a red check in the margin of the line that is crossed out in pencil. I read the red check as the editor's query, and the penciled marks as authorial revisions. Therefore I have let the reading from P stand. Where similar cases recur—as they do frequently when Warren employs hyphenated compound words in this volume—I have allowed the reading from P to stand. (Early reviewers of *Promises* complained about Warren's verbal tic of employing hyphenated words. Clearly had he not revised his typescript, he would have given them more to complain about.) 5: anguished,] $\sim_\wedge$ English 7: great scutcheon] a great scutcheon SP66, SP75, SP85 7: at drawbridge,] over the drawbridge, SP66, SP75, SP85 7: have now languished] now have languished PTS (revised to P) have languished SP66, SP75, SP85 8: Long in the moat,] Now long in the moat, SP66, SP75, SP85, Long now in the moat, *Emory* 8: blue,] A red pencil mark in PTS here indicates where to bend the long line at the margin. These marks are for the typesetter to follow in cases where the line cannot be set on one line, but they rarely occur at places where Warren himself bent long lines in the typescript, and they are also not always followed on republication of the poems, so therefore I have treated them as a feature of the design of the book rather than as a feature of the versification of the poem. 9: Sun blaze] Sun-blaze *PR,* Doggett, PTS (revised to P) 9: it is the sirocco,] now the sirocco, SP66, SP75, SP85 10: bay face,] bay-face, *PR,* Doggett, PTS (revised to P) 10: traverses] A red pencil mark in PTS here indicates where to bend the long line at the margin. 11: geometry] the geometry *PR,* Doggett, PTS (revised on PG to P) 11: survives] A red pencil mark in PTS here indicates where to bend the long line at the margin. 11: rigor] rigour English 13: blueness] A red pencil mark in PTS here indicates where to bend the long line at the margin. 14: gorse bloom,] gorse-bloom, *PR,* Doggett, PTS (revised to P)

103 **II. Gull's Cry** 2: oleander,] oleanders, SP66, SP75 4: Goat droppings] Goat-droppings *PR,* Doggett, PTS (revised to P) 5: shadow] shade SP66, SP75 5: of mountain,] of the mountain, SP66, SP75 6: against mountain-mass,] against the mountain-mass, SP66, SP75 7: on shelf] on the shelf *PR,* PTS (revised to P), on a shelf SP66, SP75 7: The gull extends motionless on shelf of air,] The gull, without motion, extends on the shelf of air, Doggett 7: on substance] on the substance SP66, SP75 8: The gull, at an eye-blink] There is a red mark, crossed out in pencil, in the left margin of this line, indicating I think a query about the hyphenation of eye-blink. But nothing is altered in pencil in the line, which leads me to believe that the penciled corrections are Warren's responses to Erskine's queries and are therefore authorial rather than editorial. Such marks are frequent in PTS, and, having noted that Warren often does not take their advice, I won't

record them further. 9: where] A red pencil mark in PTS here indicates where to bend the long line at the margin. There is a note in PTS in red pen, not in Warren's hand, indicating that the run-over parts of long lines should be carried over flush with the right margin. 11: bent:] ~, *PR,* Doggett 12: Let the beetle work,] And the beetle will work, *PR,* Doggett 12: air,] ~. *PR,* Doggett 13: glimmer] A red pencil mark in PTS here indicates where to bend the long line at the margin. 13: at your laughter] in the moment of your laughter *PR,* Doggett, PTS (but PG is revised in pencil to P) 14: moment] instant *PR,* Doggett 14: all,] A red pencil mark in PTS here indicates where to bend the long line at the margin. 14: redeem, redeem!] *redeem, redeem!* SP66, SP75

104 **III. The Child Next Door** 6: day,] ~∧ *PR,* Doggett, PTS (but PG is revised in pencil to P) 7: *ciao,*] *ciaou, PR,* Doggett 8: taint.] PTS has no stanza break after this text, but is corrected in pencil to P, probably in Warren's hand. 14: I trust] We must trust SP66, SP75, SP85 15: wisdom,] truth∧ *PR,* Doggett 16: be] is PTS (penciled revision, but revised back to the P reading in pencil on PG) 17: how] but how SP66, SP75, SP85 18: saying *ciao,* saying *ciao,*] saying *ciaou,* saying *ciaou, PR,* Doggett 18: this is the world.] *This is the world.* SP66, SP75, SP85

104 **IV. The Flower** Variant for this section only: Broadside (Winston-Salem, NC: Palaemon Press, Limited, 1981). 3: fail∧] ~, Doggett 6: lava-chunks] lava chunks *PR,* Doggett. Here Warren added the hyphen in PTS. There is a red check in the margin here, and it is crossed out in pencil. 13: vineyard,] Vineyard, *Palaemon* 13: path angle] path-angle *PR,* Doggett, PTS (revised to P) 17: passer-by] passerby *PR,* Doggett, PTS (revised to P) 18: that blossomy mass] the blossomy mass *PR,* Doggett, SP66, SP75, *Palaemon* 19: pass,] ~. PTS (but revised in pencil on PG to P) 20: And at knee there's gold gorse and blue clover,] And under our feet there's blue clover *PR,* Doggett 20: And at knee there's gold gorse and blue clover,] And knee-high, wild parsley's white lace / Characterizes the place, / And gold thistle, gold gorse, a blue clover PTS (but PG is revised in pencil to P) 21: And at ankle, blue *malva* all over] And the blue stars of *malva* all over. *PR,* Doggett 21: over∧] ~, *Emory* 21: all over / —Plus plants] all over— / Plus plants SP66, SP75, *Palaemon* 22: —Plus] ∧~ *Emory* 22: —Plus ... non-botanical eyes] Lines missing from *PR* and Doggett. 29: sweet and still.] still. SP66, SP75, *Palaemon* 37: gold-glitter] gold glitter PTS (revised to P) 39: And reach out. Yes, I'm well aware] And laugh with joy for the bloom there. *PR,* Doggett (in PTS the line from *PR* appears before rather than in place of the line from P, but it is canceled in pencil in PTS.) 39: Yes,] But∧ PTS (revised to P) 40: That this is the spot,] Yes, this is the spot, *PR,* Doggett 42: first we] we first *PR,* Doggett, PTS (revised on PG to P) 51: Your flower] This flower Doggett 53: compel] compell *PR,* Doggett 55: it∧] ~, *PR,* Doggett 55: delight.] ~, *PR* 61: But the] The Doggett 62: From the] At the *PR,* Doggett 62: bay edge] bay-edge *PR,* Doggett 64: Coming] But it comes *PR,* Doggett, PTS (revised to P) 68: The mountain prepares the night] Stanza break after this line in SP66, SP75 and *Palaemon.* 71: few we have found] few that we have found *PR* 72: disintegrated] distintegrated SP75 77: We find] So we find SP66, SP75, *Palaemon* 84: seasons] season PTS (revised to P) 85: has paced] has *PR,* Doggett 88: reassess] re-assess *PR,* Doggett 90: intent,] ~∧ *PR,* Doggett 96: And in] Yes, in SP66, SP75, *Palaemon* 103: But the mountain] The mountain SP66, SP75, *Palaemon* 103: is at] is now at *Emory* 104: Ahead,] But ahead, SP66, SP75, *Palaemon* 106: cliff rim,] cliff-rim, *PR,* Doggett, PTS (revised to P) 108: It accepts the incipient night.] Stanza break after this line in SP66, SP75, and *Palaemon.* 112: that] the *PR,* Doggett 114: It slides down the sky.] Stanza break after this line in SP66, SP75, and *Palaemon.* 116: white,] ~. *PR,* Doggett, PTS (but PG is revised in pencil to P) 117: And over] Over *PR,* Doggett, PTS (but PG is revised in pencil to P) 118: It gleams in the last light.] Stanza break after this line in SP66, SP75 and *Palaemon.* A page turn obscures whether there is a stanza break in P. (Warren had not yet adopted his convention of marking stanza breaks that are obscured by page turns with an asterisk when P was published.) There is no stanza break in *PR* or Doggett. But there is a stanza break in the English edition. There is no stanza break in PTS, and one is not indicated in PG. The evidence suggests that Warren did not intend a stanza break here in P, and that he

prepared SP66 from the English edition of P. The copy of P at *Emory*, which Warren saved for later revisions, is a copy of the English edition. The galleys of the English edition do not survive, but there is no suggestion in Warren's correspondence with Eyre and Spottiswood that he wished this change. Probably both the SP75 and SP66 readings are in error, and *Palaemon* derives from SP75. 119: It has sunk] Now it sinks SP66, SP75, *Palaemon* 120: Beyond] Below Doggett 123: It will rustle all night, darling.] You will hear it all night, darling. *PR* It will rustle all night, darling. Doggett (Line omitted from SP66, SP75 *Palaemon*)

107 **V. Colder Fire** 6: bright toy,] bauble, *PR* bright thing, Doggett 8: reflex to solstice,] reflex to a solstice, SP66, SP75 8: some aggrieved equinox.] an aggrieved equinox. *PR*, PTS (but PG is revised in pencil to P), aggrieved equinox. Doggett 11: fortress point,] fortress-point, *PR,* Doggett, PTS (revised to P) 11: knee now,] knee, *PR,* Doggett, PTS (revised to P) 16: eternal indeed,] eternal, *PR,* Doggett, PTS (but PG is revised in pencil to P) 19: made a suspiration,] made suspiration, *PR,* Doggett, PTS (revised to P), SP75 23: a butterfly] one butterfly *PR*, Doggett 23: sinks‸] ~, PTS (revised to P) 24: By gold bloom] On gold bloom *PR,* Doggett, By the gold bloom SP66, SP75 27: and there the gray scarps rise] and the gray scarps there rise *PR* and the gray scarps rise Doggett 28: men climb, and pass.] men will pass. *PR*, Doggett, PTS (revised to P) 30: cork grove,] cork-grove, *PR,* Doggett, PTS (revised to P) 31: charcoal maker,] charcoal-maker, *PR,* Doggett, PTS (revised to P) 32: The scarps, gray, rise up.] The gray scarps rise up. *PR*, Doggett, PTS (revised to P) 33: a deep recess,] in a deep recess, Doggett, in a deep recess— SP66, SP75, in a deep recess, *Emory* 34: Shelf above scarp, enclave] On a shelf above scarp, the enclave *Emory* 34: glade] glad PTS (revised to P) 40: in the far light.] in far light. *PR,* Doggett, PTS (revised to P) 41: time-tattered and disarrayed.] time-tattered, disarrayed. Doggett 42: that far scarp's sunlit wall] that scarp's far sunlit wall *PR,* the far scarp's sunlit wall Doggett 44: at needle-tip.] at a needle-tip. *PR,* SP66, SP75, at needle-tip. Doggett In PTS there is a red-pencil check, crossed out in pencil, by every line with a hyphen in it up to this point. But the practice ends with this line. (Clearly the editor had made his point.) 44: It glitters,] Glitters, Doggett 47: conversation,] ~‸ Doggett 48: In the last analysis, be always] Be always at last Doggett 48: truth you would live.] truth you would, at last, live. Doggett 50: caught from] to *PR,* Doggett, PTS (but PG is revised in pencil to P) 52: But defines, for the fortunate, that joy in which all joys should rejoice.] But may define, if you are fortunate, that joy in which all your joys should rejoice. *PR,* Doggett, PTS (revised to P)

109 **Promises** The publication history of this sequence is complex. Two long sequences, each numbered independently, appeared under the name "Promises." The first, which was published in *Yale Review,* 46 (Spring 1957), pp. 321–40, consisted of ten Roman-numeralled sections, including, in order, "Courtmartial," "School Lesson Based on Word of Tragic Death of Entire Gillum Family," "Walk by Moonlight in Small Town," "Moonlight Observed from Ruined Fortress," "Lullaby in Moonlight," "Mad Young Aristocrat on Beach," "Foreign Shore, Old Woman, Slaughter of Octopus," "Dragon Country: To Jacob Boehme," "Lullaby: A Motion Like Sleep," and "Necessity for Belief." The second sequence, also entitled "Promises," appeared in *Encounter*, 8 (May 1957), pp. 3–14, and consisted of thirteen other poems, numbered, like the *YR* sequence, consecutively from 1 (the *Encounter* sequence is numbered with Arabic numerals). The *Encounter* sequence bore the dedication "To Gabriel (born, July 19th 1955)". These poems were, in order, "What Was the Promise That Smiled from the Maples of Evening?" "Gold Glade," "Dark Night Of," "Country Burying: 1919," "Summer Storm (Circa 1916) and God's Grace," the "Dark Woods" subsequence ("Tonight the Woods are Darkened," "The Dogwood," and "The Hazel Leaf"), "Founding Fathers, 19th Century Style, South-East USA," the "Infant Boy at Midcentury" subsequence ("When the Century Dragged," "Modification of Landscape," and "Brightness of Distance") and (as "Lullaby") "Lullaby: Smile in Sleep." The four sections of "Boy's Will, Joyful Labor Without Pay, and Harvest Home (1918)" ("Morning," "Work," "The Snake," and "Hands are Paid") were published in *Botteghe Oscure,* 19 (1957), pp. 203–6, with a note describing the

whole sequence as Number XVIII from a series with the general title *Promises.* The sequence "Ballad of a Sweet Dream of Peace" was published separately, using lower-case letters rather than Roman numerals for the section labels, in *KR,* 19 (Winter 1957), pp. 31–36. In SP66 and SP75 the "Promises" sequence was published with the texts in the same order as in P, except that in both books the final poem, "The Necessity for Belief," was omitted. SP85 did not treat these poems as a sequence, and republished only these texts in this order: from the "Infant Boy at Midcentury" subsequence, "When the Century Dragged," and "Brightness of Distance"; from the "Man in Moonlight" subsequence, only "Moonlight Observed from Ruined Fortress"; then "Dragon Country: To Jacob Boehme," "Lullaby: Smile in Sleep," "Lullaby: A Motion Like Sleep," "School Lesson Based on Word of Tragic Death of Entire Gillum Family," and "Founding Fathers, Early-Nineteenth-Century Style, Southeast U.S.A." For this edition, I am ordering these poems as they appeared in *Promises: Poems 1954–1956.*

109 **I. What Was the Promise That Smiled from the Maples at Evening?** Text: P. Variants: *Encounter,* 8 (May 1957), pp. 3–4, SP66, SP75. The editor suggested on PTS to break the title after "Promise" if it could not fit on one line, but there has been no consistent practice about setting this title. SP66 broke the title after "Maples," and SP75 broke the title after "from." 1: What] WHAT *Encounter* 3: heels] the heels *Encounter* 3: clicked] click SP66, SP75 4: own] old *Encounter* 5: float in their spectral precinct.] float white in their spectral precinct. SP66, SP75 6: hydrangeas] hydrangea *Encounter* 6: first firefly] the first firefly SP66, SP75 7: The sun] Sun PTS (but PG is revised in pencil to P) 7: well down now,] well down, SP66, SP75 7: first star] the first star SP66, SP75, *Emory* 11: when hit bullbat] when the bullbat SP66, SP75 when a bullbat *Emory* 13: Why,] why, *Encounter,* SP66, SP75 17: shoe boxes,] shoe-boxes, *Encounter*, PTS (revised to P) 24: odor] odour *Encounter*, English 31: gray] grey *Encounter,* English 33: deep down, and the fleshly habiliments rent—] deep dow'n—with their fleshly habiliments rent SP66, deep down—with their fleshly habiliments rent, SP75 33: What I saw ... Ruth and Robert:] What I saw, saw deep down—the fleshly habiliments rent, / And bones in a phosphorus of glory were bathed. There they lay, / Side by side, Ruth & Robert *Emory* 34: agleam] a-gleam, *Encounter* 34: But agleam in a phosphorus of glory, bones bathed, there they lay,] But their bones in a phosphorus of glory agleam, there they lay, SP66, SP75 34: phosphorus] phosphorous *Encounter*, English 35: Robert: the illumination then spent.] Robert. But quickly that light was spent. SP66, SP75 36: no glow now,] the glow died, SP66, SP75 38: in twilight by stream-gleam now wefted,] in dusk by stream-gleams now wefted, SP66, SP75 39: coal chute,] coal-chute *Encounter*, PTS (revised to P) 39: far under] under *Encounter* 41: Then his,] And his, SP66, SP75

110 **II. Court-martial** Text: P. Variants: *Yale Review,* 46 (Spring 1957), pp. 321–25 (As "Courtmartial"), SP66 (as "Court-Martial"), SP75 (In PTS the title is "Courtmartial"(but PG is revised in pencil to P) 1: Under] UNDER *YR* 5: C.S.A.] CSA English 6: gray,] grey English 7: Pointed beard clipped the classic way,] Pointed beard clipped the usual way, / Slow-moving, bleared of blue eye, *YR*, Pointed beard clipped the classic way, / Slow-moving, bleared of blue eye, PTS (revised to P) 10: blue jean] blue-jean *YR*, PTS (revised to P) 15: Light throbs ... are still.] These two lines missing from *YR* 20: hoofbeats] hoof-beats *YR* 21: In the calm] In calm *YR* 24: He can forget all—forget] He forgets that, can forget *YR*, But he can forget it—forget PTS (revised to P) 26: Cutworm] Cut-worm *YR* 28: house—] ~, *YR* house. SP66, SP75 29: For now] Now SP66, SP75 31: To light pipe,] To light a pipe, SP66, SP75 33: idly‸] ~, *YR* 42: History,] ~. *YR* 51: were] are *YR* 52: *being done.*] *being-done. YR* 52: *being done.*] The stanza break is obscured by a page turn in P, but there is a stanza break after this line in *YR*, PTS, English, SP66 and SP75. 53: The afternoon stood still.] The afternoon stood still. / The air in the cedar was still. *YR* 55: word‸] ~, *YR* 57: Guerrilla] Guerilla *YR* 58: "Bushwhackers,] "Bushwhackers‸ *YR* 59: "Were they on the Yankee side?"] "Were they on the Yankee side?" / I asked. He spat. Replied: *YR*, PTS (revised to P) 60: "Son, they didn't have any side.] "Son, they didn't have any side. / Didn't care who lived or died. *YR*, PTS (revised to P) 62: pore] poor English 63: themselves, so, son,] themselves. So, son *YR* 65: passel,]

passell, *YR* 66: wrestle] wrassle *YR* 68: He paused, raised his pipe, took a whiff— "If] He paused, raised his pipe, took a whiff. / "If what?" I said then. He said: "If— / But, son, it's a mighty pore *if*— If *YR* 72: Even hackberry does, at a scratch.] There is a stanza break after this text in PG, but it is closed up in a penciled revision. 72: Even hackberry does, at a scratch. Find a spring] Even hackberry does, at a scratch. / But for preference chestnut or white oak, / Or tulip, and if you're in luck, / A spring *YR* 73: it,] $\sim_\wedge$ *YR* 74: Growing rank enough to nigh hide it. / Lord, a man can sure thirst] Growing rank enough to nigh hide it. / Lord, lime-water's sweet when you ride! / A man can sure thurst *YR* 75: can sure thirst] can thirst PTS (revised to P) 77: when you can when you ride.] when you can, when you ride. *YR* 78: heat-daze] the heat-daze SP66, SP75 79: vedettes] videttes *YR*, PTS (revised to P) 84: Time is short—hell, a rope is—that's that."] There is a stanza break here in SP66 and in SP75, and a page turn in both P and *YR*. But there is a stanza break here in PTS and in English. Therefore the stanza break is probably not a mistake. 88: Last smoke] The last smoke SP66, SP75 88: raveled] ravelled *YR*, PTS (revised to P) 89: Every tale has an end, has an end.] Every tale ravels out to an end. SP66, SP75 91: wouldn't stop, wouldn't end.] would not stop, would not end. *YR* 93: they deserved it," he said. / "Don't] they were better off dead. / Don't *YR* 97: The head slept in that dusk the boughs made.] I stared at the old head propped / On the chair-back, where it had dropped. / It slept in that dusk the boughs made. *YR* 102: away.] away / From the dusk where the old head lay. *YR* 104: Ruined lawn, raw house] Raw lawn, ruined house *YR*, PTS (revised to P) 109: Blotting] Out of *YR* 115: Not old now, not old now,] Not old, not old now, *YR* 115: now, but] now—but SP66, SP75 116: cavalry boots] cavalry-boots PTS (revised to P) 124: true.] $\sim$— SP66, SP75 125: Each hairy jaw is askew,] The hairy jaw askew, SP66, SP75

113 **III. Gold Glade** Text: P. Variants: *Encounter,* 8 (May 1957), pp. 5–7, SP66, SP75. In *Emory* the title is III. Gold Glade: The Shagbark. 1: Wandering,] WANDERING, *Encounter* 2: cedar,] cedars, SP66, SP75, *Emory* 3: boy-blankness] in boy-blankness SP66, SP75 4: where ridge broke,] where the ridge broke, SP66, SP75 4: the great ledge,] a great ledge, SP66, SP75 5: set the toe high as treetop by dark edge] set toe high as tree-top by dark edge *Encounter*, PTS (with "my" canceled before "toe," but PG is revised in pencil to P), set my toe high as treetops by the dark edge SP66, SP75, set your toe high as treetop by the dark edge *Emory* (Warren also changed "toe" to "toes" in *Emory*, but erased the change.) 7: in mind's eye,] in my mind's eye, SP66, SP75 10: The gorge-depth] Gorge-depth *Encounter* 11: over] beyond SP66, SP75 11: sky] the sky SP66, SP75, *Emory* 12: yet bright,] bright yet, *Encounter*, PTS (revised to P) 18: center] centre *Encounter,* English 20: Gold-massy] Gold massy PTS (but PG is revised in pencil to P) 20: Gold-massy in air, it stood in gold light-fall,] Gold-massy the beech stood in that gold light-fall. SP66, SP75 21: No breathing of air,] There was no stir of air, SP66, SP75 22: fox bark,] fox-bark, *Encounter*, PTS (revised to P), SP66, SP75 (I usually emend where magazine and selected poems versions agree against the original volume, but the penciled correction in the typescript is explicit.) 24: shagbark] shag-bark *Encounter*, PTS (revised to P) 24: Silence: gray-shagged, the great shagbark] Silence: above and below the gray bole's bark SP75 25: could] could now *Emory* 25: Gave forth gold light.] The air was gold light. SP75 30: Perhaps just an image that keeps haunting me.] Is it merely an image that keeps haunting me? SP66, SP75. The poem ends after this line in SP66 and SP75. 31: in] In *Encounter* 32: Nor] Nor in *Emory*

114 **IV. Dark Woods** In the original publication of this subsequence in *Encounter,* the sections were labeled with small letters in parentheses rather than with small Arabic numerals as in the later publications. *Encounter* also lacks subtitles.

114 **1. Tonight the Woods Are Darkened** Text: P. Variants: *Encounter,* 8 (May 1957), p. 9, SP66, SP75. 1: Tonight] TONIGHT *Encounter* 5: were,] $\sim_\wedge$ *Encounter* 9: One] *One Emory* 13: star-gleam$_\wedge$] $\sim$, *Encounter* 20: foot!] $\sim$. *Encounter* 23: field-darkness,] the field-darkness, SP66, SP75 28: too?] $\sim$! *Encounter* 29: full] dull *Encounter* 31: All who,] All those who, *Encounter*, PTS (but PG is revised in pencil to P) Although PTS follows *Encounter*, Warren's personal copy of *Encounter* is corrected to

P. This provides evidence that PTS consists of a very early version of the poem. 31: once had] had once *Encounter* 33: spy on and count you—] spy on, then greet you— SP66, SP75 34: They] Those *Encounter*, *Emory* 40: *All right.*] All right. *Encounter*

115 **2. The Dogwood** Text: P. Variants: *Encounter,* 8 (May 1957), pp. 9–10, SP66, SP75. 5: whippoorwills] whip-poor-wills PTS (revised to P) 6: star—] ~, *Encounter* 7: curdle] a curdle *Encounter,* SP66, SP75 12: love vine] love-vine *Encounter*, PTS (revised to P) 12: eyehole,] eye-hole, *Encounter*, PTS (revised to P) 14: dome, great transept,] dome and transept SP66, SP75 15: under sunlight] where the sunlight's *Encounter* (Warren restored the *Encounter* reading in pencil in PG, but crossed it out), where sunlight's SP66, SP75 16: love vine] love-vine *Encounter*, PTS (revised to P) 16: eyehole,] eye-hole, *Encounter*, PTS (revised to P) 17: cow skull.] cow-skull. *Encounter*, PTS (revised to P) 19: Went on] You went on SP66, SP75, *Emory* 19: heart tight now as nut] your heart tight as a nut SP66, SP75 21: at path-turn,] at a path-turn SP66, SP75, *Emory* 22: dogwood,] dog-wood PTS (revised to P) 23: Like an ice-break,] Like ice-break, *Encounter*, Like an ice break PTS (the hyphen is canceled in pencil in PTS, but PG is revised in pencil to P) 23: a strange wrath] the strange wrath *Encounter* 25: But one . . . uttered no word.] In *Emory*, Warren has bracketed this stanza and written "Rewrite stanza" in the margin. 25: now,] then, SP66, SP75 26: you stood] and you stood *Encounter*

115 **3. The Hazel Leaf** Text: P. Variants: *Encounter,* 8 (May 1957), pp. 10–11, SP66, SP75. 4: some] somehow *Emory* 10: boughs] hickories SP66, SP75 17: jeweled] jewelled *Encounter,* PTS (revised to P), English 23: passed, struck; now] passes, strikes; and now SP66, SP75 27: may go there] goes there *Encounter*

116 **V. Country Burying (1919)** Text: P. Variants: *Encounter,* 8 (May 1957), pp. 7–8 (as "Country Burying: 1919"), SP66, SP75. 1: A thousand] A THOUSAND *Encounter* 2: little white church] the little white church *Encounter*, PTS (but PG is revised in pencil to P) 4: oak leaf,] oak-leaf, PTS (revised to P) 4: leaf,] leaves, SP75 5: once I] I once *Encounter* 10: are] were PTS (revised to P) 14: oh, so short,] and half gone, SP66, SP75 16: she'd said, but was that enough] she says, but is that enough PTS (but PG is revised in pencil to P) 18: That kind came to town,] They came in to town, *Encounter* (Warren's personal copy of *Encounter*, now in the Beinecke Library, is corrected to P.) 22: rows.] vows. PTS (This is a penciled revision in PTS, so Warren clearly intended it. But he changed it back to "rows." in the galleys.) 24: goes.] ~, SP66, SP75 27: in fields] on fields *Encounter* 27: hedgerows,] hedge-rows, *Encounter* 29: passed toward voices] pass toward the voices PTS (revised to P) 30: center,] centre, *Encounter*, English 31: and come back] come back now SP66, back now, SP75 34: odor] odour *Encounter* English 36: in shadow, somewhere.] There is no stanza break after this text in PG, but it is corrected in pencil to P.

117 **VI. School Lesson Based on Word of Tragic Death of Entire Gillum Family** Text: P. Variants: *Yale Review,* 46 (Spring 1957), pp. 325–28, SP66, SP75, SP85. (In SP85TS this poem appears after "A Motion Like Sleep". SP85TS for this poem is direct photocopy from SP75, not cut and taped photocopy.) 1: They] THEY *YR* 5: It was good six miles . . . dang-whoodle snorted.] This stanza omitted from SP66, SP75, and SP85. 5: It was good six miles] It was a good six mile *YR*, It was a good six miles PTS (revised to P) 6: hoot owl] hoot-owl *YR*, PTS (revised to P) 7: snapping turtle] snapping-turtle *YR* 9: as] s SP85 10: pairs.] ~, *YR,* SP66, SP75, SP85 14: asteam,] a-steam, *YR*, PTS (revised to P) 16: adream] a-dream *YR*, PTS (revised to P) 17: Dollie-May] Dolly-May *YR* 17: Brother—] ~. *YR* 18: Thirteen down to eight] Thirteen to eight *YR*, PTS (but PG is revised in pencil to P) 19: big fat mother,] fat mother. SP66 (a typographical error Warren did not catch, and complains about in a letter to his Random House editor, Albert Erskine, on August 27, 1966, and again on October 24, 1966) big fat mother— SP75, SP85 21: She must have honed . . . a lady dreaming.] These two stanzas omitted in SP66, SP75, and SP85. 26: had relished] got *YR* 27: toenail] toe-nail *YR*, PTS (revised to P) 29: town] ~, *YR* 29: In town he'd stop, and say:] In town, Gillum stopped you, he'd say: SP66, SP75, SP85 30: fer] for *YR* 31: blister,] ~. SP66, SP75, SP85 31: blood blister,]

blood-blister, *YR*, PTS (revised to P) 31: Human-man ain't much more'n a big blood blister,] Human man ain't more'n a big blood-blister, *YR* 34: spindle bone] spindle-bone *YR* 35: cherish,] ~$_\wedge$ *YR* 36: they] their SP66, SP75, they SP85 (revised on SP85G to SP85) 41: wet,] ~. *YR* 45: Dollie-May] Dolly-May *YR* 48: what now] now what SP66, SP75, SP85 48: aimin'] aimin *YR*, PTS (revised to P) 49: ice pick] ice-pick *YR*, PTS (revised to P) 51: bee sting.] bee-sting. *YR*, PTS (revised to P) 52: When] By time *Emory* 52: sheriff] Sheriff *YR* 52: the school-bread] school-bread *YR* 54: windowpanes] window *YR* 55: corn field] corn-field *YR* 56: now faint] faint now *YR*, PTS, PG (but revised in pencil to P in duplicate copy. Warren penciled in the same change in the plate proofs) 57: shoe, oh, which,] shoe—yes, which— SP66, SP75, SP85 60: Though we studied and studied, as hard as we could, to know,] No matter how hard we studied and tried to know, *YR* 61: Studying] And studied *YR* 66: was] would be SP66, SP75, SP85

119 **VII. Summer Storm (Circa 1916), and God's Grace** Text: P. Variants: *Encounter,* 8 (May 1957), p. 8 (as "Summer Storm (Circa 1916) and God's Grace"), SP66, SP75. English uses square brackets rather than parentheses around the date. 1: Toward] TOWARD *Encounter* 3: haystack] hay-stack *Encounter*, PTS (revised to P) 13: you can read] you read *Encounter* 13: eye.] ~, *Encounter* 14: mole, in his sod,] mole in his sod *Encounter* 14: hide,] ~$_\wedge$ *Encounter* 16: silence,] ~$_\wedge$ *Encounter* 17: brain.] ~, *Encounter* 19: cutworm's] cut-worm's *Encounter*, PTS (revised to P) 19: tooth] tooth, it *Emory* 20: And the root,] The root, *Encounter* 23: laboring] labouring *Encounter,* English 24: Is] All *Emory* 25: Snatched,] Is snatched, *Emory* 26: waited.] wait. SP66, SP75 26: couldn't] cannot SP66, SP75 27: shuddered] shudder SP66, SP75 27: gray.] grey. *Encounter,* English 28: oak leaf] oak-leaf PTS (revised to P) 28: leaf turned] leaves turn SP66, SP75 29: Gray] Grey *Encounter,* English 29: Then,] ~$_\wedge$ *Encounter* 30: henhouse] hen-house *Encounter*, PTS (revised to P) 30: heaved, and flew] heaves, and flies SP66, SP75 31: rode] rides SP66, SP75 32: tossed] tosses SP66, SP75 33: got] gets SP66, SP75 36: had washed out.] washed out.*Encounter* 39: thought] guessed SP66, SP75, hoped *Emory* 39: he thought he'd] he might *Encounter*, PTS (revised to P) 41: Oh, send them summer ... of His flail.] This stanza omitted from SP66 and SP75. 43: cutworm] cut-worm *Encounter*, PTS (revised to P) 43: locust jaw] locust-jaw *Encounter*, PTS (revised to P) 45: Grace,] grace, *Encounter* 45: of His flail.] His flail. *Encounter*

120 **VIII. Founding Fathers, Nineteenth-Century Style, Southeast U. S. A.** Text: P. Variants: *Encounter,* 8 (May 1957), pp. 10–11 (as "Founding Fathers, 19th Century Style, South-East U.S.A."), SP66, SP75, *15 Poems*, selected by Rosanna Warren, privately printed for Stuart Wright, 1985, SP85 (as "Founding Fathers, Early-Nineteenth-Century Style, Southeast U.S.A." In SP85TS this poem appears after "School Lesson Based on Word of Tragic Death of Entire Gillum Family".) In PTS the title reads as in *Encounter*, but is corrected to P. 1: They] THEY *Encounter* 1: black coat] black 15P (revised in Western Kentucky copy to P) 2: daguerreotype] dageurrotype *Encounter*, PTS (revised to P) 3: any] and 15P (revised in Western Kentucky copy to P) 4: now remark] remark *Encounter* 6: in crook] in the crook *Encounter*, PTS (revised to P) 7: With finger to table, while right] Finger tip to the table, while the right *Encounter*, PTS (revised to P) 7: right] the right SP66, SP75, 15P right SP85 (revised on SP85G to SP85) 8: or cousin at least,] or cousin, *Encounter* 8: been, of course,] been SP66, SP75, 15P, SP85 8: course,] A red pencil mark in PTS here indicates where to bend the long line at the margin. 10: honor:] honour: *Encounter,* English, honor; SP85 (in pencil on SP85TS) 11: pigpen,] pig-pen, *Encounter*, PTS (revised to P) 12: *Honor.*] *honour. Encounter* 14: were dropped] and were dropped *Encounter*, PTS (revised to P) 15: "Mister,"] "Mister", English 16: Wept all the next morning for shame;] Wept for shame all next morning; *Encounter* Wept all next morning for shame; SP66, SP75, 15P, Wept all the next morning for shame; SP85 (but not corrected to this effect on SP85TS and thus probably a typographical error even though it restores the reading in P) 16: keys] A red pencil mark in PTS here indicates where to bend the long line at the margin. 17: be,"] be", English 17: at the Alamo.] at Alamo. *Encounter* 19: gray] grey *Encounter,* English 19: knife-blade] knife blade *Encounter* 22: seal ring,] seal-ring, *Encounter*, PTS (revised to P) 24: mold-

yellow] mould-yellow *Encounter* 24: God's Word, in which, in their strength, they had also trusted.] God's Word in which they had also trusted. *Encounter*, PTS (revised to P) 24: strength,] A red pencil mark in PTS here indicates where to bend the long line at the margin. 24: had also] also SP66, SP75, 15P SP85 25: corncrib.] corn-crib. *Encounter*, PTS (revised to P) 26: stomp-and-gouge,] Stomp-and-gouge, 15P (revised in Western Kentucky copy to P) 28: were the tears!] then the tears! SP66, SP75, 15P, SP85 28: roved] roved now PTS (revised to P) 28: land] A red pencil mark in PTS here indicates where to bend the long line at the margin. 28: their old story.] their story. *Encounter*, PTS (revised to P), the old story. SP66, SP75, 15P, SP85 29: lands,] acres, SP66, SP75, 15P, SP85 30: owl call,] owl-call, *Encounter*, PTS (revised to P) 30: burnt] brunt 15P (revised in Western Kentucky copy to P) 30: bear fat] bear-fat *Encounter*, PTS (revised to P) 30: dusk-air.] dusk air. *Encounter*, (revised to P) 31: able,] ~— SP66, SP75, 15P, SP85 33: land shark,] land-shark, *Encounter*, PTS (revised to P) 33: book] ~, *Encounter* 33: praise] ~, *Encounter* 34: Denominates] denominates 15P (revised in Western Kentucky copy to P) 34: him,] ~. SP66, SP75, 15P, SP85 34: a man] A man SP66, SP75, 15P, SP85 35: saddle,"] saddle", English 35: and says,] it says, SP66, SP75, 15P, SP85 36: learning] ~, *Encounter* 36: Rides thus] So rides *Encounter*, PTS (but PG is revised in pencil to P) 36: history,] A red pencil mark in PTS here indicates where to bend the long line at the margin. 36: napeless.] shapeless. 15P (revised in Western Kentucky copy to P) 37: saw Shiloh] fought Shiloh SP66, SP75, 15P, SP85 38: nagged] pestered *Encounter*, PTS (revised to P) 39: Texas," but took] Texas" —but took SP66, SP75, 15P, SP85 39: wagons, went,] wagons and went, *Encounter*, PTS (revised to P) 39: right,] ~∧ *Encounter*, PTS (revised to P) 40: day,] ~— SP66, SP75, 15P, SP85 40: Texas,"] Texas", English 40: Texas," had proved it,] Texas," he's proved it, *Encounter*, Texas," he'd proved it, PTS (revised to P), Texas"—had proved it, SP66, SP75, SP85, Texas—had proved it, 15P 40: it,] A red pencil mark in PTS here indicates where to bend the long line at the margin. 41: and now their voices] and their voices *Encounter* 42: last cricket] the last cricket SP66, SP75, 15P, SP85 44: beg us only] beg us for only PTS (revised to P) 44: one] some *Emory* 44: life-cost.] ~, *Encounter* 48: humanness,] ~∧ *Encounter* 48: shadow] A red pencil mark in PTS here indicates where to bend the long line at the margin.

122 **IX. Foreign Shore, Old Woman, Slaughter of Octopus** Text: P. Variants: *Yale Review*, 46 (Spring 1957), pp. 334–336, SP66, SP75. English puts a period after "Octopus." 1: What] WHAT *YR* 3: barefoot,] bare-foot, PTS (revised to P) 6: among] along *YR* 9: one,] ~; SP66, SP75 10: And if from] If from the SP66, SP75 11: stone,] ~∧ *YR*, PTS (but PG is revised in pencil to P) 16: snot-gray,] snot-grey, English 17: glare-horror] the horror *YR* 18: knife flash] knife-flash SP66, SP75 19: the sun drops.] sun drops. *YR* 21: of picnic,] of the picnic, SP66, SP75 22: agleam] a-gleam *YR*, PTS (revised to P) 23: heart,] ~∧ *YR* 24: Pearl-slime] Pearl slime *YR* 25: her,] ~∧ *YR* 28: aware] ~, *YR* 29: last sun heat] the last sun heat SP66, SP75 30: of old foot] of an old foot SP75 (revised on SP75G) 30: that much,] that, *YR* 32: sea-age.] sea's age. SP75 (revised on SP75G)

123 **X. Dark Night of** Text: P. Variants: *Encounter*, 8 (May 1957), pp. 5–7, SP66, SP75. In SP66 and SP75 the title is "Dark Night of the Soul." In PTS the title is "Dark Night Of" but is corrected to P in red ink. 1: Far] FAR *Encounter* 4: as to look] to look SP66, SP75 5: You could guess that] You guessed his *Encounter* 5: aside] ~, *Encounter* 6: hide] ~, *Encounter* 7: does not] doesn't *Encounter* No stanza break after this line in *Encounter*. 17: That's all the excuse you require.] The stanza break after this line is obscured by a page break in P. But there is a stanza break here in PTS. 20: The day, anyway] Anyway, that day *Encounter*, PTS (revised in blue pen, probably by Warren, to P) 23: flap-jawing] flop-jawing *Encounter* 31: Now stood,] There he stood, SP66, SP75 34: Outside the woods] Outside of the woods *Encounter* 50: Is now gone. Has passed over.] Stanza break after this line is obscured by a page break in P. 51: Now afternoon,] Afternoon, now *Encounter*, Afternoon, PTS (revised from "Now afternoon," but PG is revised in pencil to P) 52: Raveled] Ravelled *Encounter*, PTS (revised to P) 53: leveled] levelled *Encounter*, PTS (revised to P) 55: dead] ~, *Encounter* 56: Or that Scaevola

whom Rome bred.] Or what Mucius Scævola did. *Encounter*, Or what Mutius Scaevola did. PTS (revised to P) 57: time to drop book,] I'd drop my book, SP66, SP75 57: rouse,] ~∧ SP75 (The grammar required this change in SP66, too, but Warren missed it and complains about it in a letter to Albert Erskine of October 24, 1966.) 58: And up and leave the house,] Myself and leave the house, SP66, SP75 59: And round up the cows.] To go and round up the cows. SP66, SP75 62: They move in a motion like sleep. / Their jaws make a motion like sleep.] These two lines omitted from SP66 and SP75. 63: Their jaws make a motion like sleep.] *Encounter* adds two lines after this line: They are far ahead up the lane. / My feet dream pale dust up the lane. 65: powders elder leaf,] powders elder leaf. *Encounter* powders the elder leaf, SP66, SP75 66: evening-idle, pale] pale, evening-idle SP66, SP75 67: light,] light-thin, *Encounter* 68: through pale husk] through your husk SP66, SP75 through your pale husk *Emory* 68: under sky.] under the sky. SP66, SP75 69: suddenly] ~, *Encounter* 74: Cold prickles] The cold prickle *Encounter* (*Encounter* also adds a stanza break after this line. PTS adds a stanza break after this line, but penciled revision in PG closes it up.) 75: the eyes glare.] The stanza break after this text existed in PG, but was deleted in the plate proofs. Warren corrected the plate proofs and caught this error. 82: He was old, rough-grizzled, and spent.] Stanza break after this line is obscured by a page break in P. 84: our] my *Emory* 85: the human entrapment,] that human entrapment, *Encounter* 85: until,] ~∧ SP75 (removed on the repros of SP75) 86: In a voice] A voice SP75 86: well,] ~∧ SP75 (removed on the repros of SP75) 87: He says:] Says: SP75 89: He says:] Says: SP75 89: lay!] ~? *Encounter* 90: and heard] where *Encounter* 90: I stared ... he stirred,] The text in PTS (although corrected to P) is substantially different: I stared down the dank depth where / From cold slime the croak rose to air. / I didn't know what I had heard, / Not a human voice. Then he stirred, 91: That croak from cold slime. Then he stirred,] From cold slime the croak rose to air. *Encounter Encounter* also adds two lines after this line: I didn't know what I had heard, / Not a human voice. Then he stirred, 93: on] in *Encounter* 94: Jerked free, a moment stood there.] He jerked free, for a moment stood there. *Encounter*, He jerked free, a moment stood there. PTS (but PG is revised in pencil to P), Jerked free, and a moment stood there. SP66, SP75 95: A little I stood there alone] I stood there a little alone *Encounter*, Then I found myself standing alone PTS (revised in blue pen to "I found myself standing alone" and revised in PG in pencil to P), Then I was left standing alone SP66, SP75 96: To stare] And stared *Encounter* 96: gone.] ~, *Encounter* 97: Then I turned to follow the cows] Then turned to follow the cows *Encounter* He had gone, so I followed the cows SP66, SP75 101: but not understand] but not to understand SP66, SP75 105: age, rage, rejection] age, rage, and rejection SP66, SP75 107: Old black felt hat in other hand] His old black felt hat in the other hand SP66, SP75 108: would] can *Encounter* 108: understand,] ~. SP66, SP75. Stanza break after this line in SP66 and SP75. 109: And with his old head bare] And with his old head bare, *Encounter* Now his old head, bare, SP66, SP75 110: Move] Now moves *Encounter* Moves SP66, SP75 111: His head, in the dark air,] His head moves in the dark air, *Encounter* Line omitted in SP66 and SP75. 112: Gleams] And gleams *Encounter* It gleams SP66, SP75 113: unbared,] bare, *Emory* 113: His head, unbared, moves with] It moves, and is touched by SP66, SP75 113: stars high] A red pencil mark in PTS here indicates where to bend the long line at the margin. 113: heaven] heavens SP66, SP75 114: of the dark air.] of dark air. *Encounter* 114: He moves in joy past contumely of stars or insolent indifference of the dark air.] Stanza break after this line in SP66 and SP75. 115: May we all at last] May we all *Encounter* 115: that awfulness] that last awfulness *Emory*

125 **XI. Infant Boy at Midcentury** In the version published in *Encounter,* the sections of this poem are marked with small letters, rather than with Arabic numerals. There are no subtitles in *Encounter*.

125 **1. When the Century Dragged** Text: P. Variants: *Encounter,* 8 (May 1957), pp. 11–12, SP66, SP75, SP85. 1: When] WHEN *Encounter* 1: stuck] struck *Encounter*, caught PTS (revised to P) 1: center;] centre; *Encounter* 3: velleity] velliety *Encounter*, PTS (revised to P) 4: you chose] then you chose SP66, SP75, SP85, you now chose

Emory 8: And smile] And you smile *Encounter*, PTS (revised to P) 9: at the hour] at hour PTS (revised to P) 10: spread,] blooms, PTS (but PG is revised in pencil to P) 10: in dusk] in our dusk SP66, SP75, SP85 14: fears the late,] fears late, *Encounter*, PTS (revised to P) 14: early∧] ~, *Encounter*, *Emory* 16: had] have *Emory* 17: But to take . . . of human good.] In PTS these two stanzas differ substantially, although they are corrected to P:

But to take and forsake you are here now, and heart will compress
Like stone when we see, with first step, that rosy heel learn
Its awful and apocalyptic power to spurn
Us, and our works and days, and onward, prevailing, pass
To print, in high pride of undisillusioned manhood,
Sand of new century, where you, in your fullness, will stand,
With calm eye and uncurled lip command
That dawning perspective and possibility of human good.

17: now you're] you're now *Encounter* 17: the heart will] heart the will *Encounter* 18: Like stone when we see that rosy heel learn, / With its first step, the apocalyptic power to spurn] Like stone when we see, with first step, that rosy heel learn / Its awful and apocalyptic power to spurn *Encounter* 21: To pause, . . . human good.] In *Encounter* this stanza reads as follows:

To print, in high pride of undisillusioned manhood,
Sand of new century, where you, in your fullness, will stand,
And with calm eye and uncurled lip, command
That dawning perspective and possibility of human good.

21: undisillusioned] unillusioned SP66, SP75, SP85

126 **2. Modification of Landscape** Text: P. Variants: *Encounter,* 8 (May 1957), p. 13, SP66, SP75.The text in PTS is a late revision, since there is a penciled annotation across the top, "New page". 6: mirror our own] mirror own *Encounter* 6: own∧] ~, SP66, SP75 7: Somewhat, and ourselves, for flesh] And ourselves, for the flesh SP66, SP75 8: And the heart need compensation for its failure to study delight?] And the heart grope for justification in the midst of its mortal plight? *Encounter* 12: honor,] honour, *Encounter* 12: having often quite little,] though having quite little, SP66, SP75 13: Some,] ~∧ *Encounter*, PTS (revised to P) 14: And some from self-hate] As some, from self-hate, *Encounter* 16: longed-for] expected *Encounter* 17: and soul's] and the soul's SP66, SP75 19: night,] ~. *Encounter* 20: Though some wear it proud] Some will wear it as proud *Encounter* 20: proud as Kiwanis,] proud as a medal, SP66, SP75 21: Yes, the new age] The new age SP66, SP75 21: as our own once did;] as our own did; *Encounter* as our own more than once did; SP66, SP75 22: nights—sure,] nights,—if *Encounter* 22: sure,] yes, SP66, SP75 23: flesh to idea,] flesh to an idea, *Encounter*, PTS (revised to P) 23: but there's natural distress] there's still natural distress *Encounter*

127 **3. Brightness of Distance** Text: P. Variants: *Encounter,* 8 (May 1957), p. 13, SP66, SP75, SP85. PTS must represent a late revision, since there is a penciled annotation across the top of the page: "new page". 1: true, no doubt.] some true, no doubt. SP85 (revised on SP85G to SP85) 4: lies] lives SP66 (Warren noticed this error, and corrected it in a letter to Albert Erskine of August 30, 1969.) 7: We stand convicted] Our country's convicted SP66, SP75, SP85 7: crimes—] ~, *Encounter* 8: Yes, we throw out baby with bath,] Who throw out baby with bath, *Encounter* We throw out baby with bath, SP66, SP75, SP85 10: Once wrote of,] Wrote of, *Encounter* 11: ones∧] ~, *Emory* 12: such] they *Encounter* 13: puzzled] was puzzled SP75 (revised on SP75G), SP85 13: finds] found SP66, SP75, SP85 14: blank of love, as of hate,] without love or hate, *Encounter*, purged of love or hate, PTS (but PG is revised in pencil to P) 16: and each back] each back SP66, SP75, SP85 17: among us wish] among us now wish *Encounter* 19: Groped hand] Groped a hand SP66, SP75, SP85 19: disaster∧] ~, *Encounter* 22: purged of] past all PTS (but PG is revised in pencil to P) 24: fate,] ~∧ *Encounter*

127 **XII. Lullaby: Smile in Sleep** Text: P. Variants: *Encounter,* 8 (May 1957), pp. 11–12 (as "Lullaby"), SP66, SP75, SP85 (This poem appears in SP85TS after

"Dragon Country: To Jacob Boehme"). 1: Sleep,] SLEEP, *Encounter* 5: nerve expand] nerve and expand *Encounter* 8: season] spring SP66, SP75, SP85 8: heart's cold] winter *Encounter* 9: The vernal work] Your vernal work *Encounter*, PTS (revised to P) 20: then, your] then your, English 22: Dream,] ~∧ English 24: in his sky,] against the sky, SP66, SP75, SP85 26: the mind's wide eye.] his mind's wide eye. SP66, SP75, SP85 29: our hope] the heart *Encounter*, PTS (revised to P) 30: Enfranchise the human] Enfranchise human SP66, SP75, SP85 36: and the shadow] and shadow, *Encounter* and a shadow SP85 (revised on SP85G to SP85) 37: you lie] you may lie SP85 (revised on SP85G to SP85) 39: in honeycomb.] in the honeycomb. *Encounter,* SP66, SP75, SP85, in honeycomb PTS (revised to P) I have not emended here, although both *Encounter* and SP66 add the "the," because Warren often drops articles for poetic purposes, and his doing so here may have been a revision he thought better of rather than an error. 43: Dream, sweet son.] Dream sweet, son. *Encounter*, PTS (but PG is revised in pencil to P) 45: vectors] vestors SP75 46: Around] Round *Encounter* 46: form?] ~. *Encounter* 49: you now] now you SP66, SP75, SP85 51: now lifts] lifts now SP66, SP75, SP85 52: cold moon] strong moon SP85 (revised on SP85G to SP85) 54: Dream, strong son.] Dream strong, son. *Encounter*

129 **XIII. Man in Moonlight** The sections of this poem were not gathered into a subsequence in the *Yale Review* publication, but were separate parts of the "Promises" sequence, with "Walk by Moonlight in Small Town" preceding "Moonlight Observed from Ruined Fortress" and "Lullaby in Moonlight."

129 **1. Moonlight Observed from Ruined Fortress** Text: P. Variants: *Yale Review,* 46 (Spring 1957), pp. 330–31, SP66, SP75, SP85. 1: Great] GREAT *YR* 1: white-westering] white westering *YR* 4: Were duly] Had been duly SP66, SP75, SP85 4: splendors] splendours English 6: breast,] ~. SP85 (not marked in SP85TS or on SP85G; probably a typesetter's error on SP85G) 7: unrest,] ~. SP85 (not marked in SP85TS or on SP85G; probably a typesetter's error on SP85G) 8: seal] seals SP66, SP75, SP85 9: Décor] Decor *YR* 10: stock-pond] stockpond *YR* 11: cow-pats unkempt.] cow-pats, unkempt. SP66, SP75, SP85 12: No, even a puddle is not too small for respect,] Yes, to even a puddle you've been known to pay some respect. SP66, SP75, SP85 14: while my eyes] but my eyes *YR* 15: Were trapped] Trapped *YR* 16: Faded; so back] Faded. So back SP66, SP75, SP85 18: may] might *YR*, PTS (but PG is revised in pencil to P) 20: poor Houdini] even Houdini SP66, SP75, SP85 21: So now] And now *YR,* Now SP66 21: old, anguishing] old anguishing *YR* 21: virtuosity∧] ~, *YR* 24: To watch] And watch *YR* 25: thus] so SP66, SP75, SP85 26: Knowing the end, the end, and ah, how soon,] Knowing of course the end—and ah, how soon— SP66, SP75, SP85 27: in strict protocol] in that protocol SP66, SP75, SP85 28: that werewolf] our werewolf PTS (but PG is revised in pencil to P), SP75 (revised on SP75G), our own werewolf SP85 (revised on SP85G to SP85) 31: soon go] will go *YR*, PTS (revised to P) 32: *YR* adds a stanza here:

The heart is human, splendor can only distress us.
We need to find dialectic paraphrase.
God made all beauty wordless, for His praise.
As we strive to understand, oh, great moon, bless us.

130 **2. Walk by Moonlight in Small Town** Text: P. Variants: *Yale Review,* 46 (Spring 1957), pp. 328–30. SP66, SP75. 1: Through] THROUGH *YR* 6: Lawns green by day] Lawns, green by day, SP75 6: shimmered like frost.] shimmered frost. *YR*, PTS (but revised to "like the frost.", and PG is revised in pencil to P) 8: windowpanes] window panes *YR*, PTS (revised to P) 11: Street, the window dummies] Street window dummies *YR* 13: The glimmering] That glimmering *YR* 14: lunatically] lunaticly PTS (revised to P) 16: boxcars] box cars *YR*, PTS (but PG is revised in pencil to P) 18: *Katy,*] *Kary,* English 19: where God knows,] God knows where, PTS (revised to P) 20: a weed-rank spur,] this weed-rank spur, *YR*, PTS (but PG is revised in pencil to P) 20: this pale repose.] pale repose. *YR* their pale repose. PTS (revised to P) 20: *YR* (and PTS) adds a stanza after this line:

But the main line, double-track, gleamed past.
Those parallels, moon-struck, defied
The laws of space in daytime applied,
And leaving geometry aghast,
Plunged on, past Time, to intersect, in joy, at last.

PTS is corrected in blue pen to P. 21: How long ago,] Yes, long ago, *YR,* But long ago, PTS (but PG is revised in pencil to P), Long, long ago, SP66, SP75 21: up] by *YR* 22: I had] I'd *YR* 22: Pullmans] Pullman SP75 (revised on SP75G—Warren corrected a printer's error, "Pullman's", and the printer misunderstood his correction.) 23: made.] ~, *YR* 24: every ticket's] the ticket is always *YR* 24: back,] ~∧ English 26: track,] tracks, *YR* 28: fell] fled *YR* 30: And that] But that *YR* 35: their play,] that play, *YR* 35: then quiet] and quiet *YR* 39: upgazing] up-gazing *YR* 42: Not] Nor *YR* 43: Nor] Not *YR* 46: a man] man *YR* 47: live so that life,] live so life, *YR* 48: one,] ~— SP66, SP75 50: Need he] Would he *YR*

131 **3. Lullaby: Moonlight Lingers** Text: P. Variants: *Yale Review,* 46 (Spring 1957), pp. 331–32 (as "Lullaby in Moonlight"), SP66, SP75. 1: Moonlight] MOON-LIGHT *YR* 2: window-square] window square *YR* 12: on moon-pale trunk] on the moon-pale trunk SP66, SP75 13: shadow of the olive] the shadow of an olive SP66, SP75 15: Dark secondary] That dark secondary SP66, SP75 17: I might now close my eyes and see] Now I close my eyes and see SP66, SP75 24: down a summer lane] down summer land *YR* 24: How moonlight glimmered down a summer lane to the cedar woods' dark brink.] How a summer lane glimmers in moonlight to the cedar woods' dark brink. SP66, SP75 26: white] bright *YR* 26: on black bough of cedar,] on the black boughs of cedar, SP66, SP75 29: In a wink] In wink *YR,* PTS (revised to P) 29: slid on] then slid on SP66, SP75 36: And now in memory's stasis] And now, in memory's stasis, *YR* 39: Though] For SP66, SP75 40: Moon moves] Now moves SP66, SP75 41: you will wake] you'll be waking SP66, SP75 41: to the day.] to day. *YR* 42: Those] For those *YR,* PTS (but PG is revised in pencil to P) 47: That utterance as if tongue-rustle of pale tide in moonlight:] Their utterance like the rustling tongue of a pale tide in moonlight: SP66, SP75 48: Good night.] Goodnight. *YR,* PTS (revised to P)

132 **XIV. Mad Young Aristocrat on Beach** Text: P. Variants: *Yale Review,* 46 (Spring 1957), pp. 333–34, SP66, SP75. 1: He] HE *YR* 1: sand,] ~∧ English 7: and stop it.] to stop it. *YR* 8: will.] ~∧ English 9: mop it,] mop it *YR* 10: bone—you sea, you *cretino,* be still!] bone, then *cretino,* that sea will be still! *YR,* bone—then you sea, you *cretino,* you'll be still! PTS (revised to P) 15: And his smile,] His smile, *YR* 16: old∧] ~, PTS (revised to P) 17: So look!] And look, *YR,* But look! PTS (revised to P) 19: applause—] ~, *YR* 20: Again] So again *YR,* PTS (revised to P) 22: history∧] ~, *YR* 24: Curse the bitch, it] Curse the bitch! It *YR* 24: and like a black cloud now he mounts] so like a black cloud he mounts *YR* 24: now he mounts] now mounts SP66, SP75 24: now] A red pencil mark in PTS here indicates where to bend the long line at the margin. 28: that brute jaw-jut and eye cold now and still.] at brute jaw-jut and eye cold and still. *YR,* PTS (but PG is revised in pencil to P) 29: Yes, let him beware, beware,] And let him beware, beware— SP66, SP75 30: to] into PTS (revised to P) 31: *merde!*] *c'est merde, YR* 32: blood, though he] blood if he *YR* 33: sudden] chilling *YR,* PTS (revised to P) 33: chillingly] suddenly *YR,* brutally PTS (revised to P) 34: why∧] Why, *YR* 34: there.] ~! *YR* 36: sweet-haunched] sweet-rumped *YR* 36: knows he can't get her] knows she won't have him, *YR,* PTS (revised to P) 36: except] A red pencil mark in PTS here indicates where to bend the long line at the margin. 44: Eyes throbbing at merciless] And eyes throb at the merciless SP66, SP75 48: to] into PTS (revised to P) 48: and be loved] or be loved *YR* 48: themselves,] A red pencil mark in PTS here indicates where to bend the long line at the margin.

133 **XV. Dragon Country: To Jacob Boehme** Text: P. Variants: *Yale Review,* 46 (Spring 1957), pp. 336–38, SP66, SP75, SP85 (SP85TS for this poem is direct photocopy, not cut and taped photocopy, from SP75). 1: This] THIS *YR* 1: and these his own] and

his own *YR*, PTS (but PG is revised in pencil to P) 3: field mist] field-mist *YR* 6: hog pen.] hog-pen. *YR*, PTS (revised to P) 6: God-damn] God-damned *YR*, PTS (revised to P) 9: county] country *YR* 10: merely that,] just that, *YR* 11: they agreed couldn't be true;] they agreed couldn't be true, *YR*, they couldn't believe to be true; SP75 (revised on SP75G), SP85 12: a man] one SP75 (revised on SP75G), SP85 12: a man felt, in the chest, a constrictive pain.] in the chest a man felt a constrictive pain. *YR* 12: felt, in the chest,] felt in the chest SP66, SP75, SP85 13: worst,] ~. *YR* worst— SP66, SP75, SP85 14: found, in the woods,] found in the woods SP66, SP75, SP85 14: wagon turned on] wagon on *YR*, PTS (but PG is revised in pencil to P) 15: trace chains,] trace-chains, *YR* 19: came, in the end,] came in the end SP66, SP75, SP85 20: With weed unbent, leaf calm, and nothing, nothing, was there.] With weed unbent and leaf calm—and nothing, nothing, was there. SP66, SP75, SP85 21: think,] ~∧ SP66, SP75, SP85 22: found that it] found it *YR* 23: buckshot] buck-shot PTS (revised to P) 23: but then at least] but at least *YR* 29: Things happen, ... for the embalmer] This stanza omitted from SP66, SP75 and SP85. 30: Pinch'Em] Pinch 'Em *YR*, English 30: traveling] travelling *YR*, PTS (revised to P), English 30: Swift,] ~∧ PTS (revised to P) 30: Armour,] ~∧ PTS (revised to P) 31: said,] ~∧ *YR* 31: blowout.] blow-out *YR* 35: boot,] shoe, *YR* 35: leg,] foot, *YR* 38: air gun,] air-gun, *YR*, PTS (revised to P) 39: Now certain fields go] Certain fields go now *YR*, Certain fields now go PTS (but PG is revised in pencil to P) 39: birth rate] birth-rate *YR*, PTS (revised to P) 42: on rumor of war loans be called,] loans at rumor of war be called, SP66, SP75, SP85 42: rumor] rumour English 42: called,] ~∧ English 43: maneuvers] manoeuvres English 44: are now] we are now SP66, SP75, SP85 46: But that's not the point.] All that's off the point! SP66, But all that's off the point! SP75 (revised on SP75G), SP85 47: no slightest dependence] not the slightest dependence SP66, SP75, SP85 48: On desire, or need. Now in church they pray only that evil depart.] On desire, or need—and in church fools pray only that the Beast depart. SP66, SP75, SP85 50: and night sweat,] the night sweat *YR*, and night sweat∧ PTS (revised to P), and the night sweat, SP66, SP75, SP85 51: of truth] for truth *YR* 51: and heart,] and our hearts, SP66, SP75, SP85

135 **XVI. Ballad of a Sweet Dream of Peace** Text: P. Variants: *Kenyon Review,* 19 (Winter 1957), pp. 31–36, SP66, SP75. *KR* marks its sections with small letters rather than with numbers, and in SP66 and SP75 the title of section 5 is "You Never Knew Her Either Though You Thought You Did." Warren completely rewrote this poem as a play, but the text is so different from the poem as to constitute a different work. See "Ballad of a Sweet Dream of Peace: A Charade for Easter," with music by Alexei Haieff, *Georgia Review,* 29 (Spring 1975), pp. 5–36. The text in PTS must have been a late addition, since it is marked up "See layout already set" and the paper has been folded and is generally more beatup than the rest of PTS.

135 **1. And Don't Forget Your Corset Cover, Either** Title: Corset Cover,] Corset-Cover, *KR* 6: drawer pulls] drawer-pulls *KR*, PTS (revised to P) 8: Park?] park? *KR* 11: *And why, in God's name,*] *And in God's name, why KR* 19: bring out] A red pencil mark in PTS here indicates where to bend the long line at the margin. 23: *But why, in God's name,*] *But in God's name, why KR* 26: *do.*] ~!*KR* 30: bitch,] ~— SP66, SP75

135 **2. Keepsakes** 3: right.] ~∧ English 4: much,] ~∧ *KR* 4: look] A red pencil mark in PTS here indicates where to bend the long line at the margin. 8: orris-root] corrected in PTS to orris∧ root (but corrected in PG back to P) 10: nothing that's] nothing, that's PTS (revised to P) 13: peers] stares *KR* 13: Prayer Book] prayer book *KR* 17: *tear ducts*] *tear-ducts KR* 19: instructive to you:] Stanza break after this line in SP75. 26: grandmother] grandma *KR* 30: night∧] ~, *KR* 30: the drawer] that drawer *KR* 30: that poor self] the poor self *KR*

136 **3. Go It, Granny—Go It, Hog!** 4: them] A red pencil mark in PTS here indicates where to bend the long line at the margin. 4: dear,] ~∧ *KR* 4: long] now PTS (but PG is revised in pencil to P) 6: *somebody*] ~, *KR* 8: You] Oh *KR* 8: Flesh,] ~∧ *KR* 12: they will sit] they sit *KR*

137 **4. Friends of the Family, or Bowling a Sticky Cricket** subsection title: Friends]

Friend *KR* subsection title: a] A *KR* 4: Law!] ~. *KR* 8: him] A red pencil mark in PTS here indicates where to bend the long line at the margin. But there is a marginal annotation as well: "one line if will go". 11: *in Buckingham Palace!*] *at Buckingham Palace! KR* 14: dark stone-glimmering place,] dark and stone-glimmered place: *KR*, PTS (revised to P)

137 **5. You Never Knew Her Either, Though You Thought You Did, Inside Out** subsection title: Did, Inside Out] Did SP66, SP75 1: *Why now*] *Oh, why, KR* 1: *her*] *the* SP75 1: *robe de nuit*] Warren wrote on SP75G that "this phrase should be in *roman*— since the context is italic." But the correction was not made, and Warren had let it slip both in P and in SP66. 2: *So torn and bedraggled,*] *Of that girl so torn,* SP75 4: try,] A red pencil mark in PTS here indicates where to bend the long line at the margin. But there is a marginal annotation as well: "one line if will go". 7: So now] And so *KR* 8: tree,] ~∧ *KR* 11: oh,] Oh, *KR*

138 **6. I Guess You Ought to Know Who You Are** subsection title: to] To *KR* 2: of course,] or course, *KR* 11: politely,] polite, *KR* 11: Répondez s'il vous] *Respondez vous, s'il vous KR* 11: plaît.] plait. English, *plait. KR* 15: quickest] A red pencil mark in PTS here indicates where to bend the long line at the margin.

138 **7. Rumor Unverified Stop Can You Confirm Stop** subsection title: Rumor] Rumour English 1: clients report it] clients it PTS (revised to P) 2: time∧] ~, *KR* 3: And helpers] And the helpers *KR,* SP66, SP75. A case could be made of an emendation here, since the magazine version and the Selected Poems versions are in agreement against P (and PTS). But Warren does often drop articles for poetic purposes, and on the chance that he revised out the article and changed his mind about it I have chosen not to emend. 3: with delay.] at delay. *KR* 5: who,] ~∧ *KR*, PTS (but PG is revised in pencil to P) 5: great,] ~∧ *KR* 7: state:] ~. *KR* 8: it,] ~∧ *KR*, PTS (but PG is revised in pencil to P) 9: rumor] rumour English 9: astir] a-stir *KR* 10: purchaser] Purchaser SP75 (revised on SP75G) 14: the stone,] stone, SP66, SP75 14: bruised,] ~∧ KR

138 **XVII. Boy's Will, Joyful Labor without Pay, and Harvest Home (1918)** Text: P. Sources: *Botteghe Oscure,* 19 (1957), pp. 203–6, SP66, SP75. The *BotOs* version is set in italic type, and an attached note describes it as Number XVIII from a series with the general title *Promises.* The *BotOs* version also does not title any of the subsections, and marks them only with small letters in parentheses. In SP66 the date in the title is 1919. section title: without] Without SP66

138 **1. Morning** 2: thresher] thrasher PTS (but PG is revised in pencil to P) 5: barking, mad] barking, and mad *BotOs* 11: hope is] hope's *BotOs* 15: pathos of rapacity.] *BotOs* (and PTS) adds two stanzas here (although PTS is corrected to P in blue pen):

Far in that field, how sweet and thin
The life, bright there, fades toward art!
Till on a wagon, high and apart,
A pitchfork gleam—a single tine
That catches sunlight—stabs the heart,

And lets your throat release the shout,
Unlatches foot to leap away,
Gives lung its breath and muscle its play,
And past all scruple flings you out
To join joy's tumult, and the day.

139 **2. Work** The next three subsections represent late revisions in PTS, for there is a penciled annotation, "new page", at the top of the next three pages in PTS. 1: The hand] Your hand *BotOs* 2: Heaves sheaf] Heaves a sheaf SP66, SP75 4: 'fore you got none left,] you won't have none left, *BotOs* 5: grins,] laughs, *BotOs*

139 **3. The Snake** 2: *gee* and *haw.*] gee and haw. *BotOs* 12: with] in *BotOs* 13: doom,] ~∧ *BotOs* 14: scarcely] scarecly *BotOs* 19: around.] round. *BotOs* 23: arabesque] arabesques SP66, SP75 24: stooped, detached,] stooped and detached, *BotOs* 25: says,] says,, English

140 **4. Hands Are Paid** 2: It waits there small] It waits there, small *BotOs* 4: in sweat-cold] in the sweat-cold SP66, SP75 5: shoulder blade.] shoulder-blade. *BotOs*, PTS (revised to P) 11: mantel shelf.] mantel-shelf. *BotOs*, PTS (revised to P) 12: lamp$_{\wedge}$] $\sim$, *BotOs* 13: sowbelly] sow-belly *BotOs*, PTS (revised to P) 17: White now, the evening star hangs] White, hangs the evening star now *BotOs* 18: Over woods] Over the woods English 28: splendor.] splendour. English 30: star,] $\sim$. *BotOs* 36: now,] $\sim_{\wedge}$ *BotOs* 37: In blaze of sun and the sea's stare,] In blaze of sea and the sun's stare, *BotOs*

141 **XVIII. Lullaby: A Motion like Sleep** Text: P. Variants: *Yale Review,* 46 (Spring 1957), p. 339, SP66, SP75, SP85. section title: like] Like SP66, SP75, SP85 1: Under] UNDER *YR* 3: of oak-dark] of the oak-dark *YR*, PTS (revised to P) 3: and stone's] and a stone's SP75, SP85 6: So, son,] So son, *YR*, PTS (revised to P) 7: woods-edge,] woods edge, PTS (The hyphen is canceled in pencil but PG is revised in pencil to P) 12: So, son,] So son, *YR*, PTS (revised to P) 17: In leafage] In the leafage SP75, SP85 18: So, son,] So son, *YR*, PTS (revised to P) 24: So, son,] So son, PTS (revised to P) 25: Till clang] Till the clang SP66, SP75, SP85 25: cock-crow, and dawn's rays,] cock-crow and dawn's rays *YR*, English 27: and know,] and to know, SP66, to know, SP75, SP85 27: in excitement] in the excitement SP66, SP75, SP85 30: So, son,] So son, PTS (revised to P)

142 **XIX. The Necessity for Belief** Text: P. Variants: *Yale Review*, 46 (Spring 1957), p. 340 (as "Necessity for Belief"). In PTS this poem is written as one stanza, but it is corrected in PG. In PTS this poem must be a late addition to the poem, for the title is in all caps (not Warren's practice for this volume, although sometimes his practice elsewhere), the page number is handwritten in pencil, and the sequence section number is added in pencil as well. 1: The] THE *YR*

You, Emperors, and Others

Poems 1957–1960

Typescripts, galleys, and editorial correspondence for this volume are all available in the Beinecke Library. The typed page-headings in YEOTS give an abbreviation of the title of the poem and the page number within the poem. The page numbers within the whole typescript are added in pencil. Because the pages also show different amounts of wear, and some, but not all, are folded in half as if for mailing, and because not all are single-spaced, it seems likely that the poems were typed separately and assembled into a volume later. (Indeed, "Mortmain" appears to have been typed on a different typewriter, or at least with a different ribbon, from the rest.) Every page has a large checkmark, in pencil, written across it, possibly indicating that revisions on that page are finished. The markup for the typesetter is in red pencil, with some in red pen as well. Revisions are in black, red, or blue pencil. (Unless otherwise noted, revisions to YEOTS mentioned in the notes are in black pencil.) I have not recorded obvious typographical errors if Warren corrected them.

Revisions to poems from this volume for SP66 were made in black or red pencil on a typescript that largely followed YEO, but there were later revisions in proof as well. Warren also worked on a cut-up printed text of YEO and solicited advice from Allen Tate and from John Palmer about omitting some poems and resequencing the poems. The setting copy for SP66, however, was a photocopy of YEO, marked up in red and green pen. Some final revisions, including a pasted in stanza in "Clearly About You," occurred on the galleys of SP66.

145 **Garland for You** This sequence was assembled out of poems that had appeared separately in periodicals. In 1959 Warren published in the *Virginia Quarterly Review* a sequence called "Garland for You" which included, in order, "A Real Question Calling for Solution," "Lullabye: Exercise In Human Charity and Self-Knowledge," "The Letter About Money, Love, or Other Comfort, If Any," and "The Self That Stares." In SP66 the sequence from YEO was shortened and rearranged, so that it included, in order, "Clearly About You," "The Letter About Money, Love, or Other Comfort, If Any,"

"Man in the Street," "Switzerland," "A Real Question Calling for Solution," and "Arrogant Law." SP75 follows the ordering of SP66, except that it omits "A Real Question Calling for Solution." SP85 excludes the sequence entirely. In YEO Warren used Arabic numerals in the titles of the sections of sequences. For consistency I have here used Roman numerals, as Warren did in the sequences in his other books and in the sequences from this book when he reprinted them.

145 **I. Clearly about You** Text: YEO. Variants: *Yale Review,* 47 (Summer 1958), pp. 494–95 (as "Garland for You: Poem"), SP66, SP75. *YR* marks this poem as "From *You, Emperors, and Others.*" Epigraph: —On tomb of Roman citizen of no historical importance, under the Empire] —Inscription on the tomb of a Roman citizen of no historical importance, under the Empire. *YR*, Inscription on the tomb of a Roman citizen of no historical importance, under the Empire YEOTS. YEOG corrects the title to the YEO reading in red pen. All of the dashes before the attributions in this poem are added in YEOTS in red pencil. I have removed the dashes throughout the attributions in this sequence to preserve conformity with attributions elsewhere in the volume. 1: Whoever] WHOEVER *YR* 7: And tongue] And the tongue SP66, SP75 7: tastes] crisps *YR*, YEOTS (revised to YEO) 9: mother∧] ~, YEOTS (revised to YEO) 14: memory] memories SP66, SP75 15: You will try the cross, or the couch, for balm for the heart's ache—] You will try the baptismal rebirth as balm for the heart's ache— *YR*, YEOTS (revised to YEO reading in red pen on YEOG) 16: strangely,] queerly, *YR*, YEOTS (revised to YEO reading in red pen on YEOG) 17: marshes.] salt-flat. SP66, SP75 19: The apples you stored in the cellar are acerb and harsh as / The heart that on bough of the bosom all night will not ripe.] *That letter—why doesn't it come!—* You finger your heart that, / At a touch, in the bosom now bleeds, like a plum over-ripe. SP66, *That letter—why doesn't it come!—* you finger your heart that, / At a touch, in the bosom now bleeds, like a plum over-ripe. SP75 20: heart] Heart YEOTS (revised to YEO reading in red pen on YEOG) 21: and cry *alack.*] and try to jerk back. SP66, SP75 23: field mouse] field-mouse *YR*, YEOTS (revised in blue pencil to YEO) 24: make] makes SP66, SP75

146 **II. Lullaby: Exercise in Human Charity and Self-Knowledge** Text: YEO. Variant: *Virginia Quarterly Review,* 35 (Spring 1959), pp. 249–51. epigraph: America,] ~∧ *VQR* attribution: radio broadcast] Radio Broadcast YEOTS (revised to YEO reading in red pen on YEOG) 4: tunèd] tuned YEOTS (revised to YEO) 14: sand grain] sand-grain *VQR*, YEOTS (revised in black pencil to the reading in YEO) 21: seek] know *VQR*, YEOTS (but corrected in red pencil in Warren's handwriting to the reading in YEO. Warren marked up the typescript both in black and in red. The point is that most of the revisions from magazine to YEO readings are made in pencil by Warren on the typescript. Usually the hyphens in compound words from the magazine versions are being deleted. Many of these deletions may be Erskine's doing rather than Warren's, but I have let them stand, since Warren had a relatively free hand in the publication process and could easily have overruled Erskine on these points.) 22: merely] only *VQR*, YEOTS (revised in red pencil to YEO) 23: yourself,] you, *VQR*, YEOTS (but corrected in both red and black pencil to YEO) 28: that] our *VQR* 29: only] merely *VQR*, YEOTS (revised to YEO) 30: gave] A red pencil mark in YEOTS here indicates where to bend the long line at the margin. 38: dark∧] ~, *VQR*, YEOTS (revised in red pencil to YEO) 46: the dark] dark *VQR*

147 **III. Man in the Street** Text: YEO. Variants: *Botteghe Oscure,* 23 (1959), pp. 201–2 (as "Nursery Rhyme: Why are Your Eyes as Big as Saucers?"), SP66, SP75. The *BotOs* version is set entirely in italic type, and lacks the epigraph. In YEOTS this is section IV, and "A Real Question Calling for Solution" is section III. There is a note in YEOG changing the order to the order in YEO. There is no epigraph in YEOTS, but there is a marginal note: "note: epigraph to come." The epigraph is supplied in red pen in YEOG. 3: facts I can't] facts that I can't *BotOs* 8: it spins like a top.] it spins, it spins like a top, *BotOs* 9: spins,] ~∧ YEOTS (revised in red pencil to YEO) 9: and will not] and it will not *BotOs*, YEOTS (but corrected in red pencil to YEO) 10: meet,] ~∧ *BotOs* 11: nice new Ivy league] new gray *BotOs*, new flannel YEOTS (revised to YEO)

12: "What makes you] "Why do you *BotOs* 13: in] with *BotOs* 14: said:] ~; *BotOs* 16: hellos,] helloes, *BotOs*, YEOTS (revised in blue pencil to the reading in YEO. This and other changes in blue pencil seem to be editorial rather than authorial.) 17: windbags] wind-bags *BotOs*, YEOTS (revised in blue pencil to the reading in YEO) 19: is like dust] is dust *BotOs* 20: And] For *BotOs* 21: meet,] ~∧ *BotOs* 22: his gray flannel] gray flannel *BotOs* 23: "What makes your] "Why is your *BotOs* 24: said to the man] said the man *BotOs* 26: Backers and fillers, / Pickers and stealers, / Healers and killers, / Ticklers and feelers,] Snitchers and squealers, / Healers and killers, / Pickers and stealers, / Ticklers and feelers, *BotOs* 32: Said the nice young man] Thus said the young man SP66, SP75 32: meet,] ~∧ *BotOs* 33: down the sunlit street] down the street *BotOs* 33: shirt] A red pencil mark in YEOTS here indicates where to bend the long line at the margin.

148 **IV. Switzerland** Text: YEO. Variants: *Kenyon Review,* 20 (Autumn 1958), pp. 602–3, SP66, SP75. In YEOTS this is section V. The epigraph is in quotation marks in *KR*. epigraph: and] or *KR* attribution: agency brochure] Agency Brochure *KR*, YEOTS (revised to YEO reading in red pen on YEOG) 2: jalousie,] jalousy, *KR* (the spelling is corrected in blue pencil in YEOTS to the reading in YEO) 4: the favorite] some favorite SP66, SP75 6: to come to the point] to reach the point *KR* 6: siesta:] ~. *KR* 9: Here are many old friends you have known from long, long back,] There are many old friends to meet here you've known from long back, *KR,* Here are many old friends to meet you have known from long back, YEOTS (revised to YEO reading in red pen on YEOG), Here's many an old, old friend you have known from long back, SP75 10: Though of course] Though back then *KR* 10: names∧] ~, *KR* 10: faces.] ~, *KR*, YEOTS (revised to YEO reading in red pen on YEOG) 11: Yes, they] But *KR*, YEOTS (revised to YEO reading in red pen on YEOG) 13: That's why] Erskine has written in red pencil beside this stanza "*this is too strained*" 14: once knew] knew once YEOTS (revised in red pencil to YEO) 14: San Diego.] ~, *KR*, YEOTS (revised to YEO reading in red pen on YEOG) 15: Or the lady theologian who in bed likes best her own intellect:] Or the lady theologian, who likes best to bed down with her Intellect: *KR*, YEOTS (revised in red pencil to YEO) 16: *Cantab.*—] Oxon.— *KR* 16: trying] using *KR* 17: divorcée] divorcee YEOTS (revised to YEO) 19: can't] cannot *KR* 20: *Forgive—forgive what?*] Forgive—forgive what? *KR* 20: To remember is] To remember's *KR* 22: you'd] you *KR*, YEOTS (revised to YEO) 24: highly advertised] highly-advertized *KR* 24: of your own heart.] of the heart. *KR*, YEOTS (revised in red pencil to YEO) 25: O God] God YEOTS (revised in red pencil to YEO) 25: sun-leap—Ice-spike in ice-chasm—] sun-leap, ice-cleat in ice-chasm, *KR* sun-leap—Thou spike in ice-chasm— SP66, SP75 26: destroy∧] ~, *KR*, SP75

149 **V. A Real Question Calling for Solution** Text: YEO. Variants: *Virginia Quarterly Review,* 35 (Spring 1959), pp. 249–51, SP66. SP66 deletes the epigraph. In YEOTS this is section III. 1: Don't] DON'T *VQR* 8: toothbrush] tooth brush *VQR*, YEOTS (revised to YEO) 11: much better forgot,] not quickly forgot *VQR*, YEOTS (revised in black pencil to YEO, but the comma was added in red pencil) 12: floor-boards,] floor-tiles, SP66 13: When you slept . . . came easy.] These two lines transposed in *VQR* (and YEOTS (revised to YEO)) 16: teasy.] tease-y. *VQR*, YEOTS (revised to YEO) 22: clock absolute] clock, absolute, SP66 27: wish you had the crime for,] wished you had had the crime for, *VQR*, YEOTS, YEOG (revised to the YEO reading on the author's second copy of the galleys) 27: You never had, but wish you had the crime for,] You cuddle and kiss, and wish you had the crime for, SP66 28: milk—or blood—not spilt.] milk, and blood, not spilt. *VQR* milk, or blood, not spilt. YEOTS (revised to YEO reading in red pen on YEOG) 32: that, on your awaking,] that∧ on your awaking∧ *VQR*, that, on your awaking∧ YEOTS (revised to YEO reading in red pencil on YEOG)

150 **VI. The Letter about Money, Love, or Other Comfort, if Any** Text: YEO. Variants: *Virginia Quarterly Review,* 35 (Spring 1959), pp. 251–55, SP66, SP75. 2: before] Before YEOTS (revised to YEO) 3: tipsters∧] ~, *VQR* 6: having,] ~∧ *VQR* 10: recall] A red pencil mark in YEOTS here indicates where to bend the long line at the margin. 11: at odor] at the odor SP66, SP75 11: hat] A red pencil mark in YEOTS here indicates where to bend the long line at the margin. 13: first foot] foot SP66, SP75 13: porch

step,] porch-step, *VQR*, YEOTS (but corrected in red pencil to YEO) 13: cough] A red pencil mark in YEOTS here indicates where to bend the long line at the margin. 14: common] A red pencil mark in YEOTS here indicates where to bend the long line at the margin. 16: then] A red pencil mark in YEOTS here indicates where to bend the long line at the margin. 16: smudge)∧] smudge), *VQR* 18: budge] ~∧ *VQR* 19: shoe tips] shoetips *VQR*, shoe-tips YEOTS (revised in blue pencil to the reading in YEO) 21: insouciance] A red pencil mark in YEOTS here indicates where to bend the long line at the margin. 22: *banlieue*] A red pencil mark in YEOTS here indicates where to bend the long line at the margin. 22: *banlieue*] banlieu *VQR*, YEOTS (revised to YEO) 23: Dadston,] Dadstown, *VQR*, Gadstown, YEOTS (revised in red pencil to YEO) 24: mail] A red pencil mark in YEOTS here indicates where to bend the long line at the margin. 25: words] A red pencil mark in YEOTS here indicates where to bend the long line at the margin. 27: address,] A red pencil mark in YEOTS here indicates where to bend the long line at the margin. 29: runaround] run-around *VQR*, YEOTS (revised to YEO) 32: door,] A red pencil mark in YEOTS here indicates where to bend the long line at the margin. 33: at a question] at my question SP66, SP75 35: left] A red pencil mark in YEOTS here indicates where to bend the long line at the margin. 36: High,] high, *VQR*, YEOTS (revised to YEO) 36: Llewellin] Llewelyn *VQR*, YEOTS (revised to YEO) 38: Margutta] Marguta *VQR* 43: fill] A red pencil mark in YEOTS here indicates where to bend the long line at the margin. 47: I took] Which I took *VQR*, YEOTS (revised to YEO reading in pencil on YEOG) 47: fact] A red pencil mark in YEOTS here indicates where to bend the long line at the margin. 50: but∧] ~, *VQR* 54: lawn] ~, (revised to YEO) 54: crouched] crouching SP66, SP75 55: teddy bear,] stuffed teddy, *VQR*, YEOTS (revised to YEO) 55: bear,] A red pencil mark in YEOTS here indicates where to bend the long line. 56: midnight,] ~— SP66, SP75 58: penny,] A red pencil mark in YEOTS here indicates where to bend the long line at the margin. 59: so∧] ~, SP66, SP75 59: hearsay,] ~∧ SP66, SP75 60: timber line,] timberline, *VQR*, YEOTS (revised in blue pencil to the reading in YEO) 60: beyond] A red pencil mark in YEOTS here indicates where to bend the long line at the margin. 61: that shelf] the shelf *VQR*, YEOTS (revised to YEO) 61: a last] last *VQR*, YEOTS (revised to YEO in red pen on YEOG) 62: blue steel to sky] blue steel to steel sky SP66, SP75 65: letter,] A red pencil mark in YEOTS here indicates where to bend the long line at the margin. 66: bandanna] bandana *VQR*, YEOTS (but corrected in blue pencil to YEO) 66: eye,] A red pencil mark in YEOTS here indicates where to bend the long line at the margin. 69: comes] A red pencil mark in YEOTS here indicates where to bend the long line at the margin. 71: among the black boulders and whine under] among the black boulders under SP75 (on SP75TS) 71: knife edge] knife-edge *VQR*, YEOTS (revised to YEO), SP66, SP75, the knife-edge SP75 (on SP75TS) 71: night-blast,] the night-blast, SP75TS (revised back to "night-blast," on SP75G) 75: with teeth killed,] with your teeth killed, SP75 76: bestiality,] A red pencil mark in YEOTS here indicates where to bend the long line at the margin. 77: dangerous;] ~, *VQR*, YEOTS (revised to YEO reading in red pen on YEOG) 77: face] A red pencil mark in YEOTS here indicates where to bend the long line at the margin. 79: past] from SP66, SP75 80: through darkness] to the darkness SP66, SP75 80: trees until,] trees, until *VQR*, YEOTS (revised in red pencil to YEO) 81: breath-bated∧] ~, *VQR*, YEOTS (revised in red pencil to YEO) 82: stir,] ~∧ YEOTS (revised to YEO) 82: stir,] A red pencil mark in YEOTS here indicates where to bend the long line at the margin. 83: first dawn's] dawn's first YEOTS (revised to YEO) 83: snow peak] snow-peak *VQR*, YEOTS (revised to YEO) 84: unlatch crag-clasp,] unlatch his crag-clasp, SP75 87: taproom] tap room *VQR*, YEOTS (revised to YEO) 87: travelers] travellers YEOTS (revised in blue pencil to the reading in YEO). 87: pry] A red pencil mark in YEOTS here indicates where to bend the long line at the margin. 88: to drunken] to a drunken SP75 (on SP75TS) 88: know] A red pencil mark in YEOTS here indicates where to bend the long line at the margin.

152 **VII. Arrogant Law** Text: YEO. Variants: *Virginia Quarterly Review*, 35 (Spring 1959), pp. 255–57 (as subsection (a) of "The Self That Stares"), SP66, SP75. The epigraph in *VQR* for the whole "The Self That Stares" subsequence is: *If there are gods,*

you, being righteous,/ Will win reward in heaven; if there are none,/ All our toil is without meaning. The attribution in *VQR* is to "Iphigenia in Aulis, by Euripides." The Euripides quotation (marked "trans. by Charles R. Walker") is the epigraph to "Arrogant Law" in YEOTS, but in YEOG this epigraph is crossed out and the epigraph in YEO is added in red pen. SP66 and SP75 omit the epigraph. 1: with riflė,] with your rifle, SP75 3: dawn-mist] dawn mist *VQR*, YEOTS (revised in red pencil to the reading in YEO (if this is by Erskine—he uses an equal sign—this is one of the rare times he adds rather than deletes a hyphen) 5: and eyed] in the SP75 6: blaze] sun SP75 (revised on SP75G) 8: undercurrents] under-currents *VQR*, YEOTS (revised in blue pencil to the reading in YEO) the undercurrents SP75 9: *Time unwinds like a falling spool.*] In *VQR* all three refrains, indented as in YEO, are set off as if they were separate stanzas from the preceding stanza, and all three refrains read as follows: *Time unwinds like a falling spool:/ All are blockheads in that school.* YEOTS follows *VQR*, except that the refrains are not set off as separate stanzas, and YEOTS is corrected to YEO. 14: hieratically closed,] closed hieratically, *VQR* 22: face,] $\sim_\wedge$ *VQR* 26: more arrogant] a more arrogant SP75

153 **VIII. The Self That Stares** Text: YEO. Variants: *Virginia Quarterly Review,* 35 (Spring 1959), pp. 306–7 (as (b) of "The Self That Stares"). *VQR* here has no epigraph. In *VQR* the whole text is indented, except for the italicized couplets at beginning and end. *VQR* (and YEOTS, although YEOTS is corrected to YEO) opens with these two italicized lines: *Time unwinds like a falling spool:/ All are blockheads in that school. VQR* (together with YEOTS) then add the following stanza (again YEOTS is corrected to YEO):

Have you seen that fool that is your foot
Stray where no angel would follow suit?
Have you seen that knave that is your hand
Slily abrogate your command?
And felt that fatuous dupe, your heart,
Stir, and lift again, and start?
But who are you that you are victim
Of fool's, or knave's, or poor dupe's whim?
You have not learned what experience meant,
Though in that school all is exigent.

That additional stanza, and the two italicized refrains, are crossed out in pencil in YEOTS, so clearly these changes represent very late second thoughts on Warren's part. 3: Stare] Then stare *VQR*, YEOTS (revised to YEO) 9: spool.] $\sim$, *VQR* 10: We have learned little in that school.] And all are dullards in that school, *VQR*, YEOTS (revised to YEO) 11: No, nothing, nothing,] And nothing, nothing$_\wedge$ *VQR*, YEOTS (revised to YEO) 12: and the books] and books *VQR*, YEOTS (revised to YEO) 20: The human self naked in your own eyes.] *VQR* together with YEOTS) adds after this, italicized and placed flush to the left margin, the following two lines: *For Time unwinds like a falling spool: / All, all are blockheads in that school.* YEOTS is corrected to YEO.

154 **Two Pieces after Suetonius**

154 **I. Apology for Domitian** Text: YEO. Variants: *Partisan Review,* 25 (Spring 1958), pp. 223–24, SP66, SP75, *15 Poems*, selected by Rosanna Warren, privately printed for Stuart Wright, 1985. *15 Poems* prints this as a separate poem, not as part of a sequence. 4: might,] There is a marginal suggestion in red pencil in YEOTS to revise this to "might do," but it is crossed out in red pencil. 5: Suppose] Sunppose 15P 5: from long back you had known] you knew from long back *PR* 8: something at least?] something? *PR*, YEOTS (revised to YEO) 8: would it seem] would you think it *PR*, YEOTS (revised to YEO) 9: in?] $\sim$, *PR* 10: thin?] $\sim$, *PR* 11: the classic bed-stunt] his "bed-wrestling" stunt *PR* 14: such prosperous] such a prosperous SP66, SP75, 15P 15: bedroom;] bed room; YEOTS (revised to YEO reading in pencil on YEOG) 16: And from your own statue] Suppose from your statue *PR*, YEOTS (revised in red pencil to YEO) 16: your own statue] your statue YEOTS (revised to YEO reading in pencil on YEOG) 16: storm]

a storm SP66, SP75, 15P 16: name plate] name-plate, *PR*, YEOTS (revised to YEO) 16: chucked] chunked *PR* 17: Therefore,] ~∧ *PR* 20: he needn't] he'd not have to YEOTS (revised to YEO) 20: to know that] to know if *PR* to see if SP66, SP75, 15P 20: know] A red pencil mark after this text in YEOTS indicates where to bend the long line at the margin. 23: in face of] vis-à-vis SP75, 15P 23: assigned] assiduous SP66, SP75, 15P 28: poor,] A red pencil mark after this text in YEOTS indicates where to bend the long line at the margin. 28: nonpolitical.] non-political YEOTS (revised in blue pencil to the reading in YEO)

155 **II. Tiberius on Capri** Text: YEO. Variants: *Partisan Review,* 25 (Spring 1958), pp. 224–25, SP66, SP75, SP85, *Helsinki* (as "Tiberius on Capri, Autumn 1939"). SP85 and *Helsinki* print this as a separate poem, not as part of a sequence. SP66, SP75, SP85, and *Helsinki* mark its sections with Arabic numerals rather than with lowercase letters.

155 **(a)** 1: *All is nothing, nothing all:*] *All is nothing, nothing* all: *Helsinki* 8: the light, far off, of Surrentum.] the lights of far Surrentium. *PR*, YEOTS (In YEOTS there is a penciled query in Erskine's hand: " ptr: please query on galleys. au— The only spelling I can find for this is Surrentum, which breaks the rhythm. Is there a justification of *ium* sp.?" The passage is corrected to the YEO reading in red pen on YEOG) 9: in] at *Helsinki* 12: him∧] ~, *PR* 16: for] beneath *PR* 16: Emperor's] emperor's *PR*, YEOTS (revised to YEO) 18: Eastern] eastern *Helsinki*

155 **(b)** 1: There once,] Long back, *PR*, YEOTS (revised in red pencil to YEO) 1: goat island,] goat-island *PR* 1: I,] ~∧ *PR*, YEOTS (revised to YEO) 2: As dark fell, stood] Once at dark stood *PR* 4: From acedia snatched, from depravity, virtue,] From accidie, frolic, depravity, virtue, *PR*, YEOTS (revised to YEO) 5: Or frolic, not knowing the reason, in rank] Snatched, not knowing the reason, in rank *PR*, YEOTS (revised to YEO) 6: or in bed,] on in bed, *PR* 10: eye;] ~. *Helsinki* 11: forefeeling, forefearing,] fore-feeling, fore-fearing, *PR*, YEOTS (revised to YEO) 17: outcry] out-cry YEOTS (revised in blue pencil to YEO) 18: grain,] ~∧ *Helsinki* 19: stone,] ~∧ *Helsinki* 20: sea:] ~. *Helsinki*

156 **Mortmain** Text: YEO. Variants: *Yale Review,* 49 (Spring 1960), pp. 393–98, SP66, SP75, SP85, *Portrait of a Father,* (Lexington, Kentucky: University Press of Kentucky, 1988) pp. 81–91. The *YR* version does not include the dates in the section titles. The SP85 version includes only the first section, although it keeps the over-title. The *Portrait of a Father* version uses Arabic rather than Roman numerals in the section titles.

156 **I. After Night Flight Son Reaches Bedside of Already Unconscious Father, Whose Right Hand Lifts in a Spasmodic Gesture, as Though Trying to Make Contact: 1955** 1: In] IN *YR* 7: Reordered] Re-ordered *YR*, YEOTS (revised in blue pencil to YEO) 15: History] history *YR* 17: But could not reach that far—oh, cannot!] *YR* places this line at the end of the preceding stanza. Since all of the other versions are in regular stanzas, and since this placement would disorder the rhyme scheme, this must clearly be simply an error in the *YR* version. 24: *One more shot in the locker, peas-porridge hot—*] *YR* omits the stanza break after this line, probably in error. 30: Capitol,] capitol, *Portrait of a Father*

157 **II. A Dead Language: Circa 1885** 1: Father] FATHER *YR,* Mother *Portrait of a Father* Warren learned late in life that his grandfather, W. H. Warren, actually died in 1893, and that the distress of his father's family was caused not by his grandfather's death but by his grandmother's death. Warren provides the details in *Portrait of a Father,* and further details are given in Watkins, *Then and Now.* I have not corrected the text here because I am following the original version printed in YEO. 1: stepmother] step-mother YEOTS (revised in blue pencil to YEO) 2: skedaddling] skeedadling YEOTS (revised to YEO) 5: crossties] cross ties YEOTS (revised in red pencil to YEO) 6: Sixteen∧] ~, *YR* 7: rhythm,] ~∧ *YR* 10: λέγει,] ~: YEOTS (all of the Greek in YEOTS is written in in pencil), YEOG 11: the next year] in the next year *YR* 13: plow-points,] plow points, *YR* 22: corn-knife,] corn knife, *YR* 22: or,] ~∧ *YR*, SP66, SP75 24: sounds!] ~. *YR*

157 **III. Fox-fire: 1956** 1: Years] YEARS *YR* 5: west,] West, YEOTS (revised to YEO reading in red pen on YEOG) 15: wind beyond] wind *YR* 19: His] his YEOTS

(revised to YEO reading in red pen on YEOG) 20: hear now] hear *YR* 21: sits there] sits SP66, SP75 22: dumptruck,] dump-truck, *YR*, YEOTS (revised to YEO), SP66, SP75 23: Bright images, all, of Life's] All the bright images of life's *YR*, All the bright images of Life's YEOTS (revised in red pencil to YEO) 24: book] Greek grammar *Portrait of a Father* 24: own grammar,] own, *Portrait of a Father* 25: Unopened] Unopened now *YR* 29: velleity,] vacuity, SP66, SP75, velleity, *Portrait of a Father*

158 **IV. In the Turpitude of Time: n.d.** 1: In] IN *YR* 3: ever healing] ever-healing *YR*, YEOTS (revised to YEO), SP66, SP75 6: autumn] April *YR* 11: all,] ~^ *YR* 15: what] that *YR*, YEOTS (revised to YEO reading in red pen on YEOG) 15: will fulfill.] would fulfill. SP66, SP75 16: believe] know SP66, SP75, believe *Portrait of a Father* 19: If we could only,] If only we could, SP66, SP75, If we only could, *Portrait of a Father* 19: only,] ~. *YR* 24: become] be *YR* 24: our own song:] our song: SP66, SP75 our own song: *Portrait of a Father*

159 **V. A Vision: Circa 1880** 1: Out] OUT *YR* 3: and the tulip tree lifts, not yet tarnished,] and unshrivelled yet the tulip-tree lifts *YR*, YEOTS (revised first in red pencil to "and the tulip-tree lifts, yet unshriveled," and then in black pencil to YEO) 4: which] whose SP66, SP75, which *Portrait of a Father* 8: fulfilment:] fulfillment: SP75 (on SP75TS) 18: *Listen! I know—oh, I know— let me tell you!*] *Listen! I know, I'll tell you, I'll tell you! YR* 22: limewater,] lime-water, *YR*, YEOTS (revised to YEO) 35: gone. And] gone, and *YR* 36: to] with *YR*

159 **Fatal Interview: Penthesilea and Achilles** Text: YEO. Variant: *Kenyon Review,* 20 (Autumn 1958), pp. 602–3 (as "Penthesilea and Achilles: Fatal Interview"). 2: scurrying, scouring] scurrying and scouring *KR* 5: dream] A red pencil mark after this text in YEOTS indicates where to bend the long line at the margin. 5: Was her dream on the moonlit pillow. She moaned in that dream of blood-moil.] Was her dream on moon-pillow. What forced her moon-moan was such dream of blood-moil. *KR* 8: sword edge] sword-edge *KR*, YEOTS (revised to YEO) 9: sight;] ~. *KR* 10: Then with blood sweet on tongue, she watched bees weave, sun-glinting, and dreamed of night.] Then with blood-taste on tongue, she watched bees weaving sun and dreamed of night. *KR* 10: watched bees] YEOTS reads as YEO, but is corrected in black pencil to "watched bright bees" and then in red pencil back to YEO. In "Mortmain" it appeared as if the red pencil corrections were earlier than the black pencil ones. But it seems as if there were several episodes of correction with red pencil. 10: weave, sun-glinting, and] weaving sun and YEOTS (revised in red pencil to YEO) 11: Look, look—Greeks flee! For who can withstand Beauty's rage?] But now Greeks flee; for few can withstand Beauty's rage. *KR*, YEOTS (revised to "Look now, Greeks flee! For who can withstand Beauty's rage?) 11: Look, look—] Look now, YEOTS (revised to YEO reading in red pen on YEOG) 14: latched, for only] latched–oh, only *KR* 15: That heart's deepest need. Yes,] Her deepest heart-need. So *KR*, Her heart's deepest need. So YEOTS (revised to YEO) 16: shameful] a shameful *KR* 18: selfhood:] self-hood: *KR*, YEOTS (revised in red pencil to YEO) 21: how] yes, how *KR*, YEOTS (revised to YEO) 21: waits.] now waits. *KR*, YEOTS (revised to YEO on YEOG) 21: She waits,] And she waits, *KR* 22: first] once *KR* 22: handgrip;] hand-grip; YEOTS (revised to YEO) 25: wonders] A red pencil mark after this text in YEOTS indicates where to bend the long line at the margin. 27: blood-darkness^] ~, *KR* 30: down;] ~, *KR* 30: pincushion] pin-cushion YEOTS (revised in blue pencil to YEO) 30: pincushion] A red pencil mark after this text in YEOTS indicates where to bend the long line at the margin. 33: her] the *KR* 34: globèd] globed *KR*, YEOTS (revised to YEO) 35: he knew he] A red pencil mark after this text in YEOTS indicates where to bend the long line at the margin. 38: this sweet blood I spill now,] blood and not sperm I spill now, *KR*, YEOTS (revised in red pencil to YEO) 40: mammocked] A red pencil mark after this text in YEOTS indicates where to bend the long line at the margin. 40: paps!] ~. *KR* 42: What odds, what odds,] Blood or sperm, what odds, *KR*, YEOTS (revised in red pencil to YEO) 42: bathtub.] bath-tub. *KR* 44: escapes,] ~^ *KR*, YEOTS (but corrected in blue pencil to YEO) 44: sniveling] snivelling *KR* 44: " But] "But *KR* 45: jawbone,] ~^ *KR* 45: dumped] spilled *KR* 45: dumped] A red pencil mark

after this text in YEOTS indicates where to bend the long line at the margin. 46: combat and cultivation,] combat, or cultivation, *KR* 47: on the far hill-line,] on hill-line, far, *KR*, YEOTS (revised to YEO reading in red pen on YEOG) 50: that, puzzled, stare up at blue sky they lie under.] that in puzzlement start at blue sky they lie under. *KR* 50: sky] A red pencil mark after this text in YEOTS indicates where to bend the long line at the margin.

161 **Some Quiet, Plain Poems** Text: YEO. Variants: *Saturday Review,* 22 Nov. 1958, p. 37, SP66, SP75, SP85. The original publication of this sequence in *SatR* included only the first four sections. The last two sections have separate magazine publications. When Warren republished the sequence in SP75 he dropped "In Italian They Call the Bird *Civetta.*" In SP85 he dropped the whole sequence, publishing "Debate: Question, Quarry, Dream" as a separate poem.

161 **I. Ornithology in a World of Flux** 1: It was] IT WAS *SatR* 1: bird call] bird-call *SatR*, YEOTS (revised to YEO) 2: back-pasture;] back-pasture, *SatR*, YEOTS (but corrected in red pencil to YEO) 3: But so still I stood] But I stopped so still *SatR*, YEOTS (revised to YEO reading in red pen on YEOG), But I stood so still SP75 3: not stiller] YEOTS reads as YEO, but is corrected in red pencil to "not then stiller", and then corrected in black pencil back to YEO. 3: sky] A red pencil mark after this text in YEOTS indicates where to bend the long line at the margin. 4: pass,] go, *SatR*, YEOTS (revised to YEO reading in pencil on YEOG) 6: more that stillness at bird-call] that stillness at bird-call more *SatR*, YEOTS (revised to YEO) 6: things that were to fail later] things to fail later *SatR*, YEOTS (revised in red pencil to YEO)

161 **II. Holly and Hickory** 2: It ticks like a telegraph on the pane.] It makes telegraph-*tac* on the window pane. *SatR*, YEOTS (revised to YEO) 5: I] You *SatR*, YEOTS (revised to YEO) 7: I] you *SatR*, YEOTS (revised to YEO) 7: lie] live YEOTS (revised to YEO) 7: rain sounds hint] rain-sound would hint *SatR,* YEOTS (revised to YEO), rain-sounds hint SP66, SP75 9: And with years I feel less joy or distress] And wherever you are, there's no joy or distress *SatR*, YEOTS (revised to YEO) 10: wheel ruts,] wheel-ruts, *SatR* 11: And if any car] And no car *SatR*, YEOTS (revised to YEO) 12: It carries nobody I could know,] At least with no one whom you could now know, *SatR*, YEOTS (revised to "It bears no one whom I could now know", then corrected in red pencil to YEO) 14: I,] you, *SatR*, YEOTS (revised to YEO)

162 **III. The Well House** Title: The Well-House *SatR* 4: stillness,] single stillness, *SatR* 5: thing,] single thing, *SatR* 5: a broken toy] old toy *SatR* 9: well house,] well-house, *SatR*, YEOTS (revised to YEO) 10: guessing] you guess *SatR* 10: not thirsting] have no thirst *SatR* 11: With thirst] Thirst *SatR*, YEOTS (revised to YEO) 12: You might] Might make you *SatR*, YEOTS (revised to YEO) 12: water's] A red pencil mark after this text in YEOTS indicates where to bend the long line at the margin. 17: suddenly] of a sudden *SatR* 19: wept for] A red pencil mark after this text in YEOTS indicates where to bend the long line at the margin.

162 **IV. In Moonlight, Somewhere, They Are Singing** 1: moonrise] moon-rise YEOTS (revised in blue pencil to YEO) 2: top leaf of the white oak] the top leaf of whiteoak *SatR*, the top leaf of white-oak YEOTS (revised to YEO) 3: from the] past *SatR*, from YEOTS (revised to YEO reading in pencil on YEOG) 5: my sleep] boy-sleep *SatR*, YEOTS (revised to YEO) 5: the whiteness] whiteness *SatR*, YEOTS (revised to YEO) 6: dark maples,] maple-dark, *SatR*, YEOTS (revised to YEO) 8: in] in the *SatR* 10: dark maples] maple-dark *SatR*, YEOTS (revised to YEO) 11: Too young to know] I did not know *SatR*, YEOTS (revised to YEO) 11: what they meant] what it meant SP75 15: bright] A red pencil mark after this text in YEOTS indicates where to bend the long line at the margin. 17: barn lot,] barn-lot, *SatR* 21: Years after,] Now years later, SP66, SP75 22: and] or *SatR* 23: what] whatever *SatR,* SP66, SP75 24: Some life-faith] Some faith in life SP75

163 **V. In Italian They Call the Bird *Civetta*** Text: YEO. Variants: *Prairie Schooner,* 33 (Fall 1959), p. 244, SP66. 1: call,] ~. YEOTS (revised in blue pencil to YEO) 2: sky,] ~. YEOTS (revised in blue pencil to YEO) 3: cedars,] ~∧ *PrS* 4: pale,] ~: *PrS*, YEOTS (revised to YEO) 5: that dust] that pale dust SP66 5: And my feet stirred that dust there—]

My feet had once stirred that dust there, *PrS*, YEOTS (revised to YEO, except the phrase ends with a colon rather than with an em-dash) 5: there—] ~: YEOTS (revised to YEO reading in pencil on YEOG) 6: Ah,] But *PrS*, YEOTS (revised to YEO) 7: eyelids,] ~∧ *PrS* 9: selfsame] self-same YEOTS (revised to YEO) 12: There is a stanza break marking off the refrain both times in *PrS*. 15: now.] ~, SP66 16: That other owl . . . blaze of day,] SP66 extensively rewrites and reorders these lines:

And across all the years and miles that
Are the only Truth I have learned,
That other owl answers him;
So back from the present owl-call
Burns backward the blaze of Time,

22: now] to nothing SP66 23: Of a] From the *PrS*, From that YEOTS (revised to "Of that" on YEOTS, and corrected to YEO reading in red pen on YEOG) 23: spills / To quaver] now / Quavers SP66 24: from] in *PrS*, YEOTS (revised to YEO) 25: And frame] To frame, SP66 25: owl-call,] ~∧ *PrS*

164 **VI. Debate: Question, Quarry, Dream** Text: YEO. Variants: *Yale Review*, 47 (Summer 1958), pp. 498–99, SP66, SP75, SP85. The *YR* version is published with "Garland for You: Poem," the "Three Nursery Rhymes" sequence (including "Knockety-Knockety-Knock," "Little Boy Blue," and "Mother Makes the Biscuits,") as part of a sequence called "from You, Emperors, and Others." 1: Asking] ASKING *YR* 2: canebrake] cane-brake YEOTS (revised in blue pencil to YEO) 6: cedar-shade] cedar shade *YR*, YEOTS (revised to YEO) 7: windfall] dead-fall *YR* (The word is corrected to the YEO reading in YEOTS, but there is a marginal note in pencil in Erskine's hand: "ptr: please Qy on galleys– au– would leaf-fall—a word akin to *Promises* do here, to avoid other connotations of windfall".) 8: powers∧] ~, *YR* 8: in the fern-glade] in fern-glade *YR*, YEOTS (revised to YEO), in the fern glade SP66, SP75, SP85 10: go,] A red pencil mark after this text in YEOTS indicates where to bend the long line at the margin. 12: Still air] Air-stillness *YR*, YEOTS (revised to YEO), The still air SP66, SP75, SP85 12: moth wing,] moth-wing, *YR*, YEOTS (revised to YEO) 12: and last stain] and the last stain SP66, the last stain SP75 (on SP75TS), SP85 20: prepared,] ~. SP85 There is no correction on SP85TS or on any of the galleys, probably this reading is a typographical error on SP85G. 21: debate] then debate *YR* 25: appalling] A red pencil mark after this text in YEOTS indicates where to bend the long line at the margin.

164 **Ballad: Between the Boxcars (1923)** Text: YEO. Variants: *Partisan Review*, 27 (Winter 1960), pp. 70–72, SP66, SP75. *PR* gives the title as "Ballad: Between the Box Cars," and does not give the sections separate titles. In YEOTS the title is "Ballad: Between the Box Cars", but it is corrected to YEO. SP75 drops the date from the title, and drops also the third section of the poem. In YEOTS the date is corrected from 1919 to 1923. In the margin, in red in Erskine's hand is "date of Yankee stadium?" and in pencil "built 1922." If the protagonist had died in 1919, he could not have been imagining himself in Yankee stadium.

164 **I. I Can't Even Remember the Name** 2: boxcars.] box cars. *PR*, YEOTS (revised to YEO) 4: boxcars.] box cars. *PR*, YEOTS (revised to YEO) 6: boxcars,] box cars, *PR*, YEOTS (revised to YEO) 7: shape] the shape *PR* 8: boxcars.] box cars. *PR*, YEOTS (revised to YEO) 9: more] other *PR* 9: And one more thing I remember perfectly well,] And there's one sure thing you had better remember well, SP66, SP75 9: well,] ~— YEOTS (revised to YEO) 10: boxcars.] box cars. *PR*, YEOTS (revised to YEO) 12: boxcars.] box cars. *PR*, YEOTS (revised to YEO) 14: try] go SP66, SP75 14: boxcars,] box cars, *PR*, YEOTS (revised to YEO) 15: smart aleck] smart-aleck *PR*, YEOTS (revised to YEO) 16: Ends] Will end *PR*, SP66, SP75 16: boxcars.] box cars. *PR*, YEOTS (revised to YEO) 18: boxcars?] box cars? *PR*, YEOTS (revised to YEO) 20: boxcars.] box cars. *PR*, YEOTS (revised to YEO)

165 **II. He Was Formidable** 6: like a knife in a nigger.] and mean as a snigger. *PR* 9: Sun low, score tied] Score tied, YEOTS (revised to YEO) 9: plate] A red pencil mark

after this text in YEOTS indicates where to bend the long line at the margin. 11: brute-heeled] steel-heeled SP66, SP75 12: boxcars.] box cars. *PR*, YEOTS (revised to YEO) 16: grade] class *PR*, YEOTS (revised to YEO reading in pencil on YEOG) 16: in dark stare,] in the dark stare, SP66, stare in darkness, SP75 16: stare,] ~∧ YEOTS (revised to YEO) 18: early,] ~∧ *PR*, YEOTS (revised to YEO) 19: bemused,] bemused∧ *PR*, YEOTS (revised to YEO) 20: moon-gleam] moon gleam *PR*, YEOTS (revised in blue pencil to YEO) 20: gleam] A red pencil mark after this text in YEOTS indicates where to bend the long line at the margin. 21: *Woman Slays Self for His Love,* as the tabloid would tell—] *Woman Slays Self For Love,* as the headline would tell *PR*, eyes wet at his contemptuous farewell. YEOTS (revised to *PR*, then to YEO. This provides evidence for a case that the original typescripts that make up YEOTS actually predate the magazine versions.) 21: *for His Love,*] *for Love,* SP66, SP75 21: tabloids would tell—] headline would tell. *PR*, tabloids would tell. YEOTS, YEOG (revised to YEO reading on authors second galleys) 23: hurly-burly,] hurlyburly, *PR*, YEOTS (revised to YEO) 24: boxcars.] box cars. *PR*, YEOTS (revised to YEO) 25: Oh,] Or, SP75 (on SP75TS) 25: supermarket] super-market *PR*, YEOTS (but corrected in blue pencil to YEO) 25: been boss of] managed SP66, SP75 26: carts] A red pencil mark after this text in YEOTS indicates where to bend the long line at the margin. 31: smog removal;] smog-removal; *PR*, YEOTS (revised in blue pencil to YEO) 32: stars] A red pencil mark after this text in YEOTS indicates where to bend the long line at the margin. 33: steps of his] steps to his *PR* 33: personal plane] plane YEOTS (revised to YEO) 35: mishmash] mish-mash *PR*, YEOTS (revised in blue pencil to YEO) 36: boxcars.] box cars. *PR*, YEOTS (revised to YEO) 38: through freight] through-freight *PR*, YEOTS (revised to YEO) 42: newsprint] paper *PR*, YEOTS (revised to YEO) 42: like that,] like that∧ *PR*, YEOTS (revised to YEO) 45: the last blue flash of sky,] the blue sky, YEOTS (revised to YEO) 45: blue flash] blue *PR*, YEOTS (revised to YEO) 47: may] must YEOTS (revised to YEO) 48: clobber and slobber and grunt,] clobber, and clobber, and scream, SP66, clobber, and slobber, and scream, SP75 48: boxcars.] box cars. *PR*, YEOTS (revised to YEO)

166 **III. He Has Fled** *PR* lineates this section very differently from YEO. YEO has four groups of three stanzas each, indenting each of the lines but the first in every stanza. *PR* by contrast treats what YEO treats as stanzas as single long lines, filling the text to the left margin (unlike YEO), and indenting as one does for long lines that run over the physical left margin. It is because YEO and YEOTS break lines in each stanza—always in the same places—in such a way as not to fill the text to the left margin that I believe YEO treats as stanzas what *PR* treats as single lines. The MS and TS drafts of the poem break the lines where YEO does, and do not follow the lineation in *PR*, which argues that Warren always intended the poem to appear as it does in YEO, but that the typesetters at *PR* did not understand his instructions. In YEOTS there is a heavily underlined note to the printer, in red pencil, "this poem to set line for line same indent throughout." YEOTS separated the groups of three stanzas with three centered asterisks, but the asterisks were canceled in pencil, with the annotation "extra # where asterisks have been removed". YEO groups the stanzas into groups of three, separating the groups with extra white space. On YEOG Warren has asked for less white space between the stanzas within groups of three, and for more white space between the groups of three. *PR* groups the long lines into four stanzas of three lines each, except for the fourth, which has four lines, separating the stanzas with centered asterisks. 5: glint] glitter *PR*, YEOTS (revised to YEO) 10: Centered asterisk after this line in *PR* 12: fibers] fibres *PR*, YEOTS (revised to YEO) 13: crosstie.] cross ties. *PR*, YEOTS (revised to YEO) 19: *PR* follows this line with a centered asterisk. A page turn after this line obscures the separation of this group of three stanzas from the next in YEO, but YEOTS confirms the separation. 22: atmospheres, and] atmospheres where *PR* 23: now reels,] reels, *PR*, YEOTS (revised to YEO reading in pencil on YEOG) 25: probabilities,] probability, *PR* 26: *is*] is *PR* 27: *is*,] is, *PR* 28: good enough,] *PR* breaks the line after this phrase. 28: which is / to say] which is to / say YEOTS (revised to YEO) 31: world, and in so far as we live, the world] world and the world *PR* 33: reject] eject *PR*

167 **Two Studies in Idealism: Short Survey of American, and Human, History** Text: YEO. Sources: *Kenyon Review,* 22 (Summer 1960), pp. 337–39, SP66, SP75. YEOTS lacks a running header, and is typed on a different ribbon from the prevailing one in this volume. title: Short] A Short *KR*

167 **I. Bear Track Plantation: Shortly after Shiloh** 4: ten,] ∼∧ YEOTS (revised in red pencil to YEO) 5: 'Taint] It ain't SP66, SP75 9: look,] look— *KR* 13: seems] looks *KR* 15: are—] are! *KR* 18: that look] my look SP66, SP75 20: easy∧] ∼, *KR*

168 **II. Harvard '61: Battle Fatigue** 2: behooves] becomes YEOTS (revised to YEO) 3: Right∧] ∼, *KR* 5: that] such *KR* 9: often] sometimes *KR* 10: hand] my hand SP66, SP75 12: which only] only *KR*, YEOTS (revised to YEO) 16: came] A red pencil mark after this text in YEOTS indicates where to bend the long line at the margin. 17: missing.] ∼, *KR* 20: 'Twas] It was YEOTS (revised to YEO reading in red pen on YEOG) 20: stain] A red pencil mark after this text in YEOTS indicates where to bend the long line at the margin. 21: Why,] ∼∧ *KR* 24: And I] A red pencil mark after this text in YEOTS indicates where to bend the long line at the margin. 25: for the Right,] for Right, YEOTS (revised to YEO reading in pencil on YEOG)

169 **Nocturne: Traveling Salesman in Hotel Bedroom** Text: YEO. Variant: *American Scholar*, 28 (Summer 1959), pp. 306–7.There is a canceled header in YEOTS: "revised". 2: Like you in your coffin when] As you in your coffin will when *American Scholar*, YEOTS (revised to YEO reading in red pen on YEOG) 4: grow] start growing *American Scholar*, YEOTS (revised in red pencil to YEO) 7: Like] As *American Scholar*, YEOTS (revised to YEO reading in red pen on YEOG) 10: Like] As does *American Scholar*, YEOTS (revised to YEO reading in red pen on YEOG) 20: at the] the *American Scholar* 20: weep,] weep; *American Scholar* 24: merchandise,] ∼. *American Scholar*, YEOTS (revised to YEO)

170 **So You Agree with What I Say? Well, What Did I Say?** Text: YEO. Variant: *Delta* (LSU), 14 (1960), p. 1 (as "Do You Agree with What I Say, Well, What Did I Say?") 1: half-blind,] half blind, *Delta*, YEOTS (revised to YEO) 3: all human] all the human YEOTS (revised to YEO) 4: In that Hope past deprivation,] In that Great Hope past pain, *Delta*, YEOTS (revised to YEO) 6: place∧] ∼, *Delta* 13: Old] Ole *Delta* 13: Duckett] Puckett *Delta*, YEOTS (revised to YEO) 15: moonvines] moonvine *Delta* 16: halfway—] half way— *Delta*, YEOTS (revised to YEO) 23: successes,] achievements, YEOTS (revised to YEO) 28: IBM] I.B.M. YEOTS (revised in blue pencil to YEO)

171 **Prognosis: A Short Story, the End of Which you Will Know Soon Enough** Text: YEO. Variant: *Sewanee Review*, 66 (Spring 1958), pp. 252–55 (as "Prognosis").

171 **I. And Oh—** In *SR* this section has an italicized headnote, in parentheses: A Short Story, the End of Which You Will Know Soon Enough. 1: good;] ∼, *SR* 2: sweet, booze-bit,] sweet and booze-bit, *SR* 3: understood;] ∼, *SR* 7: sprigged with] with *SR* 12: street] A red pencil mark after this text in YEOTS indicates where to bend the long line at the margin. 12: oh white,] and oh white, *SR* 14: fleshy] fleshly *SR* 16: And,] ∼∧ *SR* 22: no word] that no word *SR* 23: anguish] A red pencil mark after this text in YEOTS indicates where to bend the long line at the margin. 23: without] that had no *SR* 27: they smiled,] and they smiled, *SR* 27: Beast,] ∼∧ YEOTS (revised to YEO reading in red pen on YEOG) 27: kitten] A red pencil mark after this text in YEOTS indicates where to bend the long line at the margin. 31: tears,] A red pencil mark after this text in YEOTS indicates where to bend the long line at the margin. 32: threw her head back,] threw back her head, *SR* 32: joy,] A red pencil mark after this text in YEOTS indicates where to bend the long line at the margin. 33: on her—in dark, as when, oh, ungirled—] on her, and in dark, as when, oh, ungirled, *SR* 33: when,] A red pencil mark after this text in YEOTS indicates where to bend the long line at the margin. 34: And she shook, she said, "No,"] She shook now, said, "No," *SR* 34: No,] no YEOTS (revised to YEO) 36: Then said] And said *SR* 40: racked,] A red pencil mark after this text in YEOTS indicates where to bend the long line at the margin. 41: not Time now—and once] not now–once *SR* 43: God,] ∼∧ *SR* 43: know,] A red pencil mark after this text in YEOTS indicates where to bend

the long line at the margin. 43: so slept,] so so slept, *SR* 47: who had] who'd *SR* 48: last,] ∼∧ *SR* 49: wind-shimmering, slow,] in slight wind moved slow, *SR*, YEOTS (revised to YEO—"moved" is canceled in black pencil, and the rest of the correction is made in red pencil) 50: glory of] A red pencil mark after this text in YEOTS indicates where to bend the long line at the margin. 50: name,] ∼∧ *SR*

172 **II. What the Sand Said** 1: —and God,] and God, *SR* 1: somewhere, *she said,* are lilies,] somewhere are lilies, *SR* 3: moves] moved YEOTS (revised to YEO reading in red pen on YEOG) 3: *shuddering and white*] *shuddering white SR* 3: *shuddering and white*] A red pencil mark after this text in YEOTS indicates where to bend the long line at the margin. 6: If] if *SR* 13: but let my dream be,] but be, *SR*, YEOTS (revised to YEO) 15: for,] ∼∧ *SR*, YEOTS (revised to YEO) 16: and I do not grieve . . . and dawn and dark] and would be lost in that awfulness of dark which the / world is, and love is, and oh— / and dawn and dark *SR*, and would be lost in whatever awfulness of dark the / world may be, and love is, and oh— YEOTS (revised in a typewritten addition to YEO) 20: and oh—] *SR* omits the stanza break after this line.

173 **III. What the Joree Said, The Joree Being Only a Bird** *SR* gives the title of this section as simply "What the Joree Said." 1: says∧] ∼, *SR*, YEOTS (revised to YEO) 6: stone,] limestone, *SR* 7: consumed] A red pencil mark after this text in YEOTS indicates where to bend the long line at the margin. 8: But the bird∧] The bird, *SR* 9: Only sang, said *joree,* and so she came where the spring] However, sang, said *joree,* And she came where the spring *SR* 10: out from the] from *SR*, from YEOTS (revised to "from the", and finally corrected to YEO reading in red pen on YEOG) 13: The bird] A red pencil mark after this text in YEOTS indicates where to bend the long line at the margin. 13: *joree,*] No stanza break after this text in YEOTS. But since the line runs over the page width it is possible that this is merely a typographical error. Warren did not remark about this on YEOG, where the stanza break appears. And there is a stanza break here in *SR*. 14: fullness] fulness *SR* 20: shade,] A red pencil mark after this text in YEOTS indicates where to bend the long line at the margin.

173 **Autumnal Equinox on Mediterranean Beach** Text: YEO. Variants: *Botteghe Oscure,* 23 (1959), pp. 248–49 (as "Equinox on Mediterranean Beach"), SP66. 3: I am] Changed in blue pencil in YEOTS to "I'm". 4: the wavelets] wavelets *BotOs* 5: that] who *BotOs* 5: overripe,] over-ripe, YEOTS (revised in blue pencil to YEO) 6: flung] drooped *BotOs* 9: Latin] latin *BotOs*, YEOTS (revised to YEO) 10: gaze] stare *BotOs* 13: Blow] Come blow *BotOs* 13: fur furry] fur *BotOs* 13: sideways,] sidewise, *BotOs* 15: youth∧] ∼, *BotOs* 16: off the bald] off bald *BotOs*, YEOTS (revised to YEO reading in red pen on YEOG) 18: such] their *BotOs* 19: Come swirl . . . air-right.] This stanza appears three stanzas down and slightly altered in *BotOs* and YEOTS. The transposition is a correction on YEOTS, although the text of the lines in YEOTS is that in YEO. 22: in] on *BotOs* 23: now all our] now's the time *BotOs* 24: time to] time we must *BotOs* 25: pleasure,] pleasure— SP66 26: Or even for joy, unless cut down to his measure.] Certainly not for joy, unless it's cut down to his measure. SP66 *BotOs* adds a stanza after this line: Come swirl old picnic papers to very sky-height / That the gulls will gabble in fury at breach of their air-right. 27: Yes, kick] Come kick *BotOs*, YEOTS (revised to YEO) 27: garbage,] ∼: YEOTS (revised to YEO) 28: That the cat] Let cat *BotOs*, YEOTS (revised to YEO) 28: with] with a SP66 28: the housewife] housewife *BotOs*, YEOTS (revised to YEO) 30: Though *whose* is *which*] Though whose is which *BotOs* (*BotOs* sets the whole poem in italics.) 31: And] Or *BotOs* 32: bookkeeping] book-keeping *BotOs*, YEOTS (revised to YEO)

174 **Nursery Rhymes** Text: YEO. Variants: *Yale Review*, 47 (Summer 1958), pp. 495–98 (as "Three Nursery Rhymes," including, in order, "Knockety-Knockety-Knock," "Little Boy Blue," and "Mother Makes the Biscuits." "The Bramble Bush" was published separately as "Nursery Rhyme," *Prairie Schooner,* 33 (Fall 1959), p. 244. SP66 reprints only the first three sections, and SP75 and SP85 drop the sequence entirely.

174 **I. Knockety-Knockety-Knock** 1: Hickory] HICKORY *YR* 7: nightgown,] night gown, YEOTS (revised to YEO)

175 **II. News of Unexpected Demise of Little Boy Blue** In *YR* and in YEOTS the title is "Little Boy Blue." The title is corrected to the YEO reading in red pen on YEOG 1: Little] LITTLE *YR* 7: perform] do *YR* 11: Gold-bricker,] Gold-Bricker, *YR*, YEOTS (revised to YEO) 12: baldheaded] bald-headed, *YR*, YEOTS (revised to YEO) 19: Born of woman, . . . for the frig,] These two lines reversed in SP66. 24: Little Wretch,] little wretch, *YR* 25: A plague] In YEOTS there is a stapled-in revision of the text from this point to the end of the poem. The original version in YEOTS reads:

A plague and a pox on such a bad boy.
I know you are hiding just to annoy.
You reflect no credit on the human race.
You stand in need of prayer and grace.
Where's that Little Wretch that tends the sheep?
He's under the haystack, fast asleep.
Well, damn it, go wake him! *No, not I –*
I can only walk the green fields, and cry.

29: Little Wretch] little wretch *YR* 29: tends the sheep?] No stanza break after this line in *YR*. 30: fast asleep.] No stanza break after this line in *YR*. 31: wake him!] No stanza break after this line in *YR*. In other texts the line appears to straddle the stanza break that follows this text. The line that straddles a stanza break is a common feature of Warren's later poetry. Here, in the first instance in the poems, Erskine has marked in the margin of YEOTS: "ptr: # but less than stanza #" and "ptr: indent as indicated."

176 **III. Mother Makes the Biscuits** 1: Mother] MOTHER$_{\wedge}$ *YR* 7: unbuttoned,] $\sim_{\wedge}$ *YR* 8: bark,] $\sim_{\wedge}$ *YR* 11: chin,] $\sim_{\wedge}$ *YR* 13: hand,] $\sim_{\wedge}$ YEOTS (revised to YEO)

177 **IV. The Bramble Bush** In PrS, this poem was entitled "Nursery Rhyme." 11: into] in YEOTS (revised to YEO) 16: of the night, . . . on the bone] PrS and YEOTS replaces the next stanza with the following four stanzas:

And saw a single sparrow fall,
    Then groping down from the sky
God's hand appear, arthritic and old,
    In cranky uncertainty.

I saw the place the sparrow fell,
    Which the poor hand couldn't find,
And as the face leaned closer, I saw
    The reason was it was blind.

So when I think that God has made
    All furious beauty blown
Like petals from a wind-torn bough,
    And our flesh singing on the bone,

But never, never, can see these things,
    I cannot help but begin to
Bewail the fact that God Himself
    Has no bush that He can jump into.

In YEOTS the stanzas from *PrS* are canceled, and the current last stanza is on a stapled attachment. 19: gone—] $\sim$; YEOTS (revised to YEO on YEOG)

178 **Short Thoughts for Long Nights** Text: YEO. Variants: *Botteghe Oscure,* 23 (1959), pp. 199–201, SP66. *BotOs* includes several sections dropped in YEO: "3. Human Nature," "7. A Long Spoon," and "9. Theology." SP66 includes only "Nightmare of Mouse," "Colloquy with Cockroach," "Cricket, on Kitchen Floor, Enters History," and "Grasshopper Tries to Break Solipsism."

178 **I. Nightmare of Mouse**

178 **II. Nightmare of Man** 1: marshaled,] marshalled *BotOs*, YEOTS (revised in blue pencil to YEO) 4: wept,] ~; *BotOs* 4: weep still.] *BotOs* inserts another section after this text:

Human Nature

Even if you scotch it,
You'd still better watch it.

178 **III. Colloquy With Cockroach** The section number in YEOTS is given as 4, but corrected in red pencil to 3.

178 **IV. Little Boy on Voyage** The section number in YEOTS is given as 5, but corrected in red pencil to 4. 2: ocean,] ~∧ *BotOs* 3: despairing,] ~∧ YEOTS (revised to YEO) 4: sleep,] ~∧ *BotOs* 4: grow] A red pencil mark after this text in YEOTS indicates where to bend the long line at the margin.

178 **V. Obsession** The section number in YEOTS is given as 6, but corrected in red pencil to 5. 1: only dawn:] only dawn— *BotOs* 2: bird-stir,] wind-stir, *BotOs* 3: pillow,] ~∧ *BotOs* 4: draws on.] *BotOs* adds another section here:

A Long Spoon

If afraid of water
Don't go to bed with the mermaid's daughter.

179 **VI. Joy** The section number in YEOTS is give as 8, but corrected in red pencil to 6. 4: *toot*less.] toot-less. *BotOs*. *BotOs* adds a section here:

Theology

The old ape is blind—wipe the poor eyes with lace;
The hog is sick—catch his froth in a silver cup;
There is nameless blood on the sidewalk—kiss the place:
For if pain is not pleasing to God, what holds stars up?

179 **VII. Cricket, on Kitchen Floor, Enters History** The section number in YEOTS is given as 10, but corrected in red pencil to 7.

179 **VIII. Little Boy and General Principle** The section number is given as 11 in YEOTS but is corrected in red pencil to 8. 4: begin.] now begin. *BotOs*

179 **IX. Grasshopper Tries to Break Solipsism** The section number is given as 12 in YEOTS but is corrected in red pencil to 9. 2: oh∧] ~, SP66

Tale of Time

Poems 1960–1966

SP66, SP75, and SP85 each opened with a titled section of new poems. In reprinting these sections, I have followed Warren's own habit of referring to them as volumes. In addition to the new poems, SP66 included the following poems and sequences from earlier volumes. From *You, Emperors and Others* SP66 includes "Garland for You" (including "Clearly About You," "The Letter About Money, Love, or Other Comfort, if Any," "Man in the Street," "Switzerland," "A Real Question Calling for Solution," and "Arrogant Law"), "Two Pieces After Suetonius" (including "Apology for Domitian," and "Tiberius on Capri,"), "Mortmain" (including "After Night Flight Son Reaches Bedside of Already Unconscious Father, Whose Right Hand Lifts in a Spasmodic Gesture, as Though Trying to Make Contact: 1955," "A Dead Language: Circa 1885," "Fox Fire: 1956," "In the Turpitude of Time: N.D." and "A Vision: Circa 1880"), "Some Quiet, Plain Poems" (including "Ornithology in a World of Flux," "Holly and Hickory," "The Well House," "In Moonlight, Somewhere, They Are Singing," "In Italian They call the Bird *Civetta*," and "Debate: Question, Quarry, Dream"), "Ballad: Between the Boxcars (1923)" (including "I Can't Even Remember the Name," and "He Was Formidable"), "Two Studies in Idealism: Short Survey of American, and Human, History" (including "Bear Track Plantation: Shortly After Shiloh," and "Harvard '61: Battle Fatigue"), "Autumnal Equinox on Mediterranean Beach," "Nursery Rhymes" (including "Knockety-Knockety-Knock,"

"News of Unexpected Demise of Little Boy Blue," and "Mother Makes the Biscuits"), and "Short Thoughts for Long Nights" (including "Nightmare of Mouse," "Colloquy with Cockroach," "Cricket, on Kitchen Floor, Enters History," and "Grasshopper Tries to Break Solipsism." From *Promises,* SP66 includes "To a Little Girl, One Year Old, in a Ruined Fortress" (including "Sirocco," "Gull's Cry," "The Child Next Door," "The Flower," and "Colder Fire"), and "Promises" (including "What Was the Promise That Smiled from the Maples as Evening?" "Court-Martial," "Gold Glade," "Dark Woods" (including "Tonight the Woods are Darkened," "The Dogwood," and "The Hazel Leaf"), "Country Burying (1919)," "School Lesson Based on Word of Tragic Death of Entire Gillum Family," "Summer Storm (Circa 1916), and God's Grace," "Founding Fathers, Nineteenth-Century Style, Southeast U.S.A.," "Foreign Shore, Old Woman, Slaughter of Octopus," "Dark Night of the Soul," "Infant Boy at Midcentury" (including "When the Century Dragged," "Modification of Landscape," and "Brightness of Distance"), "Lullaby: Smile in Sleep," "Man in Moonlight" (including "Moonlight Observed from Ruined Fortress," "Walk by Moonlight in Small Town," and "Lullabye: Moonlight Lingers"), "Mad Young Aristocrat on Beach," "Dragon Country: To Jacob Boehme," "Ballad of a Sweet Dream of Peace" (including "And Don't Forget Your Corset Cover, Either," "Keepsakes," "Go It, Granny—Go It, Hog!" "Friends of the Family, or Bowling a Sticky Cricket," "You Never Knew Her Either, Though You Thought You Did," "I Guess You Ought to Know Who You Are," and "Rumor Unverified Stop Can You Confirm Stop"), "Boy's Will, Joyful Labor Without Pay, and Harvest Home (1918)" (including "Morning," "Work," "The Snake," and "Hands Are Paid"), and "Lullaby: A Motion Like Sleep". SP66 includes all of SP43 (in the same order as in SP43), excepting "Question and Answer," "Aged Man Surveys the Past Time," "Toward Rationality," "Letter to a Friend," "Aubade for Hope," "Variation: Ode to Fear," "Siesta Time in Village Plaza by Ruined Bandstand and Banana Tree" (from "Mexico is a Foreign Country: Five Studies in Naturalism"), "Resolution," three sections of "Kentucky Mountain Farm" ("The Cardinal," "The Jay," and "Watershed"), "Croesus in Autumn," "So Frost Astounds," "The Last Metaphor," "Pacific Gazer," "Calendar," "Problem of Knowledge," "For a Self-possessed Friend," "For a Friend Who Thinks Himself Urbane," "Cold Colloquy," and "Garden Waters."

The order of poems in the typescript of the first section is slightly different from that in the published volume. After the "Tale of Time" sequence come, in order, "Fall Comes in Back-Country Vermont," "The Day Dr. Knox Did It," "Holy Writ," "Shoes in Rain Jungle," "Homage to Emerson," and "Delight."

Warren appended the following prefatory note, dated at Stratton, Vermont, on March 6, 1966:

> I have published five volumes of poems, not including a long poem presented independently. Here I have gathered, in addition to a considerable number of new pieces, those from the five earlier volumes which seem to lie on the main line of my impulse. Many of the poems in this volume have been revised, some of them drastically. But in revising old poems, I have tried not to tamper with meanings, only to sharpen old meanings–for poems are, in one perspective at least, always a life record, and live their own life by that fact.

(In the Draft A typescript of the prefatory note, "and live their own life by that fact." reads "and to tamper with meanings would be, at the best, to convert a blundering truth into a slick lie.") Warren opened *Tale of Time* with the sequence "Notes on a Life to Be Lived," consisting of, in order, "Stargazing," "Small White House," "Blow, West Wind," "Composition in Gold and Red-Gold," "Little Boy and Lost Shoe," "Patriotic Tour and Postulate of Joy," "Dragon-Tree," "Vision Under the October Mountain: A Love Poem," "Chain Saw at Dawn in Vermont in Time of Drouth," and "Ways of Day." Seven of the ten sections of this sequence he rewrote and inserted at various places (not following the order of "Notes on a Life to Be Lived") in his 1974 book-length sequence

Or Else. I have chosen, as Warren did, to sacrifice "Notes on a Life to Be Lived," to *Or Else.* The sequence "Notes on a Life to Be Lived" as originally published in the *New Yorker* on 12 February, 1966, consisted only of, in order, "Stargazing," "Dragon Tree," and "Composition in Gold and Red-Gold." I have also set the poems from "Notes on a Life to Be Lived," that Warren excluded from *Or Else*— "Dragon-Tree," "Ways of Day," and "Patriotic Tour and Postulate of Joy"— as separate poems, as Warren did when he reprinted the last two poems in SP75. I have put them in the beginning of the volume, as ghosts of "Notes on a Life to Be Lived." In SP75 "Patriotic Tour and Postulate of Joy" and "Ways of Day" appeared after "Shoes in Rain Jungle" and before "Fall Comes in Back-Country Vermont."

In the typescript Erskine points out to the compositor where to bend long lines, but on many occasions Warren changed them on the galleys once he saw how they looked on the page, which argues that the line bends are throughout an element of typographical design rather than an element of the verse. The "setting typescript" is mostly carbon copy (the few actual TS pages are less well typed). They are numbered only within poems. The page numbering is in blue pen in the upper right corner. The typescript is heavily revised in green pen, not in Warren's or Erskine's handwriting. There are also revisions in red pencil, in Erskine's handwriting. Some of these can be accounted for in letters Warren sent to Erskine, and probably they were all done at Warren's direction. Because it was Warren's practice to send poems to Erskine as he completed them, but before he was fully satisfied with them, and because he often wrote to Erskine's secretary with revisions, the markings in green pen were probably made at Warren's direction as well.

In SP66TS all of the titles up to "Fall Comes in Back-Country Vermont" are in all caps and underlined. After that they are in all caps, except for "Elijah on Mount Carmel," which is underlined, "Saul at Gilboa," which is both underlined and in caps, and "Shoes in Rain Jungle," which is in all caps but whose subtitle is both underlined and in caps. There is no clear pattern to how he set the section titles, even within multiple section poems. In "Delight," for instance, up to "Something is Going to Happen" Warren both capitalized and underlined. "Dream of a Dream the Small Boy Had" is capitalized, "The Simplest Greenwood Song" is capitalized and underlined, "Two Poems About Suddenly and a Rose" is capitalized (but its subsections are not), and "Not to Be Trusted" and "Finisterre" are both capitalized and italicized. This is further indication that the typescript was prepared from poems typed at different times. There is a letter in the correspondence with Random House about straightening out the tangle of how to consistently set the titles of sections and subsections. This letter warrants me in simply choosing a consistent pattern for setting titles of sections and subsections, rather than following the different patterns adopted in each book or magazine version.

The setting copy of the sections of SP66 that derive from earlier volumes is marked up photocopies of the earlier volumes, although Warren also worked on typescripts derived from those earlier volumes.

SP66 is the first place where Warren marked cases where the stanza breaks might be obliterated by page turns. He marked them on a dummy paste-up of the volume.

The poems Warren selected for SP85 from this volume appear in SP85 on what seem to be photocopies of originals that were assembled by cutting and taping from photocopies of SP75.

183 **Patriotic Tour and Postulate of Joy** Text: SP66. Variants: *New Yorker,* 22 Jan. 1966, p. 28, SP75. 20: Woke;] ~, *NY* 21: Woke, then looked at] Woke and then kissed *NY*, SP66TS (revised in green pen to SP66)

183 **Dragon-Tree** Text: SP66. Variant: *New Yorker,* 17 Feb. 1966, p. 23 (as "Dragon Tree"). In both publications this poem is a part of the sequence "Notes on a Life to be Lived." 1: the plumber forgot it.] and will not stop. *NY*, SP66TS (revised in green pen to SP66) 2: in coitu,] *in coitu, NY*, SP66TS (but corrected in pen on SP66G to SP66 reading) 5: early,] ~; *NY* 6: gorge. Water,] gorge; water, *NY*, SP66TS (revised in green pen to SP66) 8: heart] The line-bend of the long line is indicated here in red pencil on SP66TS. 9: dawn-light,] dawn light, *NY* 10: mucked up] fucked up SP66TS (but revised

in green pen to SP66 reading) 20: to just sit] just to sit *NY*, SP66TS (revised in red pencil to SP66) 20: tale] The line bend after this word is marked in in red pencil on SP66TS. 22: dragon-tree,] dragon tree, *NY* 24: Twitch. But look! the new leaf flaps gilt in the sunlight.] Stir. But look! The new leaf, in sunlight, flaps gilt. *NY*

184 **Ways of Day** Text: SP66. Variants: *Sewanee Review,* 74 (Summer 1966), p. 592 (as section III of "Three Poems"), SP75. 8: Oh, what] What SP75 (and in the photocopy of SP66 now catalogued as "Draft B" in the Beinecke Library) 9: swamp owl,] swamp-owl, *SR*

185 **Tale of Time** Text: SP66. Variants: *Encounter,* 26 (March 1966), pp. 16–23, SP75, SP85.

185 **I. What Happened** 4: Died,] ~— *Encounter* 9: and oh,] and SP75 (revised on SP75G), SP85 18: realization,] realisation, *Encounter* 25: copulation,] fucking, *Encounter*, SP66TS (revised in green pen to SP66) 28: of deep woods and / Blood on ...] *Encounter* runs these two lines together as one. SP66TS does the same (revised in green pen to SP66). 31: of] of all *Encounter* 32: Desolation—] ~, *Encounter*, SP66TS (revised in pen on SP66G to SP66 reading) 33: rich!] ~. *Encounter* 34: position.] way to fuck. *Encounter*, SP66TS (revised in red pencil to "way to do it.", then in green pen to SP66) 40: eating] aging SP66TS (revised to SP66 in red pen)

186 **II. The Mad Druggist** Text: SP66. Variant: for this section only, *15 Poems*, selected by Rosanna Warren, privately printed for Stuart Wright, 1985. 15P is printed as a separate poem, not as part of a sequence. The poem in 15P is also out of sequence (the poems in 15P are printed in chronological order), following rather than preceding "Composition in Gold and Red-Gold" in 15P. 2: She saw them on the street,] On the street she saw them, *Encounter* 3: away.] ~, SP85 (SP85TS consists of photocopy and cut-and-taped photocopy from SP75. The quality of this page is poor in SP85TS, and Warren had to copy in the punctuation, making an error here, most probably.) 5: in the lurch] left in the lurch *Encounter* 9: Of boyhood contempt,] Of my boyhood contempt, *Encounter* 11: privy] A red pencil mark after this text in SP66TS marks where to bend the long line at the margin. 16: Joy;] ~, *Encounter*, SP66TS (revised in green pen to SP66) 16: high] A red pencil mark after this text in SP66TS marks where to bend the long line at the margin. 17: hear] A red pencil mark after this text in SP66TS marks where to bend the long line at the margin. 17: I hear them and all,] I hear them, and all, *Encounter* 20: we now] they *Encounter*, SP66TS (revised in green pen to SP66) 21: There's] But *Encounter* 23: list] kind SP66TS (revised in red pen to SP66 27: gray] grey *Encounter* 33: physician,] A red pencil mark after this text in SP66TS marks where to bend the long line at the margin.

187 **III. Answer Yes or No** 3: fulfillment] fulfilment *Encounter* , SP66TS (the second "l" is marked in in red pencil and marked out again in green pen), SP66G. 4: *Whose wish?*] Whose wish? SP66TS (revised in green pen to SP66)

187 **IV. The Interim** I have followed Warren's practice of suppressing the subsections of this and the following section of "Tale of Time" in the Table of Contents. In *Encounter* Warren used lower-case italic letters in parentheses, rather than Arabic numerals, to mark the subsections of these poems.

187 **1.** This text in SP66TS is marked "retype to come" in green pen. It is heavily marked up in green pen, red pencil, and blue pencil (the last is the typesetter—marking the division between galleys 7 and 8). In SP66TS Warren used lower case letters for subsection titles. They are changed in green pen on SP66TS to small Arabic numerals. 3: and there would be / The private realization,] *Encounter* (and SP66TS) runs these two lines together as one. SP66TS is corrected in green pen to SP66. 4: realization,] realisation, *Encounter* 6: In that time ... to be, so] *Encounter* (and SP66TS) lineates this stanza this way:

In that time the heart cries out for coherence.
Between the beginning and the end, we must learn the nature of being
In order, in the end, to be, so

SP66TS is corrected in green pen to SP66 9: In the end to be, so] SP85 drops the stanza break after this line. Since there is no correction to this effect on SP85TS or on SP85G, probably this is a typesetter's error on SP85G. 9: be,] *be,* SP85 (revised on SP85G to SP85) 14: now sought] sought now SP66TS (revised in red pencil to SP66) 18: only target / For the total reverence . . .] *Encounter* (and SP66TS) run these two lines together. SP66TS is corrected in green pen to SP66. 19: For the total reverence] For total reverence *Encounter* 23: in the wide / Day-blaze . . .] *Encounter* (and SP66TS) runs these two lines together. SP66TS is revised in green pen to SP66. 26: What is love?] And that was love. SP66TS (revised in red pencil to SP66. An undated letter to Albert Erskine, now in the Beinecke Library, directs this change. Erskine has put a check mark next to Warren's request, in the same red pencil used in the typescript.)

188 **2.** 1: Tell me what love is, for] But tell me SP66TS (revised in red pencil to SP66) 4: On the black land black, and it swagged over] On the black land, black, and swagged over *Encounter*, On the black land, black and over it swagged (revised in red pencil to SP66. Red pencil corrections also propose and reject "heaved" for "it swagged.") 6: Squigg-town,] nigger-town, *Encounter*, SP66TS (revised in pen on SP66G to SP66 reading), Squiggtown, SP75, SP85 9: hearth:] ~; SP85 (again the quality of the photocopy of SP75 used for SP85TS is poor, and Warren has corrected the punctuation mistakenly.) 11: You have not answered my question.] *Encounter* (and SP66TS) eliminates the stanza break before this line, which ends a stanza. A one-line stanza follows, which reads, "I do not want to have to repeat the question." (revised in green pen on SP66TS to SP66)

188 **3.** 2: have breathed,] breathe, *Encounter* 4: that black / Aperture] that / Black aperture *Encounter*, SP66TS (revised in pen on SP66G to SP66 reading) 9: Is black, and life] SP85 adds a stanza break after this line, but in SP85TS this is not a point where the cut and taped extracts from SP75 are joined. This is a page turn in SP85G, and Warren added the mark for a stanza break there, probably in error. 22: *you.*] *You. Encounter*

189 **4.** 3: gray] grey *Encounter* 9: grayness] greyness *Encounter* 14: death,] ~. *Encounter* 17: table. / He,] table. / Secretly. / He, SP85 (added in red pencil on SP85TS)

189 **5.** 1: street of Squigg-town.] street of nigger-town. *Encounter*, SP66TS (but revised to "street." in green pen and corrected in pen on SP66G to SP66 reading), street of Squigg town. SP75 (revised on repros of SP75. Warren also directed that the gap be closed up, but it was not done) street of Squiggtown. SP85 (in pencil on SP85TS) 2: tin roofs] roofs *Encounter*, SP66TS (revised in green pen to SP66) 5: *Is twenty dollars when*] This line is missing from SP66G, but re-entered in red pen. 9: Labors] Labours *Encounter* 11: caboose light] caboose-light *Encounter* 15: to be considered] that must be considered SP66TS (but revised in green pen to SP66)

190 **6.** 4: boulder] boulder now SP85 (revised on SP85G to SP85) 8: coon-hand] A red pencil mark after this text in SP66TS marks where to bend the long line at the margin. 10: I] A red pencil mark after this text in SP66TS marks where to bend the long line at the margin.

190 **7.** 5: Time,] time, SP66TS (revised in green pen to SP66) 8: which,] ~$_\wedge$ *Encounter*

190 **8.**

191 **V. What Were You Thinking, Dear Mother?** section title] What Were You Thinking? SP66TS (revised in green pen to SP66) 2: whippoorwill] whip-poor-will *Encounter*, SP66TS (revised in pen on SP66G to SP66 reading) 3: As] And *Encounter* 5: evening] mourning SP85 (in pencil on SP85TS) 6: of cedar?] of the cedar? SP66TS (revised in pen on SP66G to SP66 reading) 14: in your joyous secret,] your joyous secret, *Encounter*, SP66TS (revised in pen on SP66G to SP66 reading) 20: whippoorwill] whip-poor-will *Encounter*, SP66TS (revised in pen on SP66G to SP66 reading)

191 **VI. Insomnia**

191 **1.** 2: whippoorwill,] whip-poor-will, *Encounter*, SP66TS (revised in pen on SP66G to SP66 reading) 25: I meet that face that last I saw on the pillow, pale?] SP75 and SP85 add a stanza break after this line, setting off the next line as a stanza in its own

right. Warren had this revision in mind as an afterthought, and wrote about it to Albert Erskine, his editor at Random House, on October 24, 1966, but it was too late to include then. He did mark the change in the photocopy of SP66 that is now "Draft B" in the Beinecke Library.

192 **2.** 9: Look, look at these—] But look— *Encounter*, SP66TS (but revised in green pen to "Here, look—", and corrected in pen on SP66G to SP66 reading) 10: no light here penetrates] SP66TS reads as SP66 but is revised in green pen to "no light to us penetrates". SP66G is corrected in pen to SP66 reading. 11: these] the *Encounter*, SP66TS (revised in green pen to SP66) 13: tell] tell you *Encounter*

192 **3.** 4: moth-wing,] moth wing, *Encounter* 5: and so] and so I *Encounter* 6: might] may *Encounter* 7: could,] can, *Encounter* 8: be"—] be," *Encounter* 8: it] you SP75, SP85 (also in the photocopy of SP66 which is labeled "draft B" in the Beinecke Library) 9: Is] Are SP75, SP85 (also in the photocopy of SP66 which is labeled "draft B" in the Beinecke Library) 10: setting.] sinking. *Encounter* 11: "Your hand— / Give it here,] "My hand— / Take my hand, *Encounter* 12: dark and,] dark, and *Encounter*, SP66TS (but revised in green pen to SP66) 13: dark,] ∼∧ SP66TS (revised in pen on SP66G to SP66 reading) 14: home,] home now, *Encounter* 15: And to woods-edge we come,] And we come to wood's edge, *Encounter*, And come to wood's edge, there stand. SP66TS (revised in pen on SP66G to SP66 reading) 15: there stand.] There I stand. SP85 (revised on SP85G to SP85) 24: My breath is difficult.] SP75 omits the stanza break after this line. It is restored in pencil on SP85TS. 25: Heat lightning ranges beyond the horizon.] Heat lighting ranges the far horizon. *Encounter* 25: Heat lightning ranges beyond the horizon.] *Encounter* (and SP66TS) omit the stanza break after this line. (But SP66TS is revised in green pen to SP66.) 26: That, also, is worth mentioning.] That is also worth mentioning. *Encounter*

193 **4.** 5: after pain,] pain past, *Encounter* 6: Spurt] Spurts SP85 (revised on SP85G to SP85) 12: Truth,] Yes, truth *Encounter* 14: But so] So *Encounter* 16: black horizon,] horizon, *Encounter*

194 **Homage to Emerson, On Night Flight to New York** Text: SP66. Variants: *New Yorker,* 16 July 1966, pp. 30–31 (as "Homage to Emerson, on a Night Flight to New York"), SP75. The *NY* version omits "The Wart," and does not give titles to the sections of the sequence. In SP66TS this sequence is moved to near the end of the volume, preceding "Delight." In SP66TS the carbon copy is lighter than those of the rest of SP66TS, and is marked "final version" in red pen. The pages of this sequence in SP66TS are numbered in red ink (the rest are numbered in blue ink). The dedication in SP66TS is "To Peter and Ebe Blume" (but it is corrected in pen on SP66G to the SP66 reading). SP66TS does not title the sections of the sequence, giving them only capital Roman numerals. The sequence is in the SP66TS location in SP66G, but there is a márginal note in Warren's handwriting: "here Emerson and shoes" at the SP66 location. The sequence is moved to its current location and given its section titles (in red pencil) in SP66G and on the dummy paste-up.

194 **I. His Smile** 1: sun:] ∼; *NY* 5: gloom,] ∼∧ SP66TS (revised in pen on SP66G to SP66 reading) 6: page,] ∼; *NY* 13: Coca-Cola] Coca Cola SP66TS (revised in pen on SP66G to SP66 reading) 15: for∧] ∼, *NY* 16: feet∧] ∼, *NY* 19: body] body sweetly *NY*, SP66TS (revised in pen on SP66G to SP66 reading) 25: When I was a boy I had a wart on the right forefinger.] This line absent in *NY.*

194 **II. The Wart** 6: and he / Said,] he / Said, SP66TS (revised on SP66G to reading in SP66),

195 **III. The Spider**

195 **IV. One Drunk Allegory** 3: you are, and] you are—and *NY* 7: crutches∧] ∼, *NY* 9: bingo!—] bingo! *NY* 14: Harvard-cum-cotton] Harvard-*cum*-cotton *NY* 15: bingo!—] bingo! *NY* 20: added:] ∼, *NY* 26: allegory,] ∼— *NY*

196 **V. Multiplication Table** 10: dog,] ∼∧ *NY* 11: boardwalk] board walk SP66TS (revised in pen on SP66G to SP66 reading) 11: flashlight] flash light SP66TS (revised in pen on SP66G to SP66 reading) 18: The multiplication table.] The line appears to

straddle the stanza break that follows this text. That Warren intended this is unmistakable in SP66TS, for he has used the two blank lines he characteristically uses to mark a stanza break, and Erskine has written "indent as typed" in blue pencil. Such lines are a common feature of Warren's later poetry.

197 **VI. Wind** 7: Jello] jello *NY*, SP66TS (revised in pen on SP66G to SP66 reading) 8: jets—oh, why] jets, oh, why *NY*, jets, oh why SP66TS (revised in pen on SP66G to SP66 reading), jets—yes, why SP75

197 **VII. Does the Wild Rose?** 1: tonight$_\wedge$] ~, *NY* 13: so resembles] resembles *NY*, SP66TS (revised in pen on SP66G to SP66 reading) 13: arctic] Arctic *NY*, SP66TS (revised in pen on SP66G to SP66 reading) 15: there must be] and there must be *NY* 18: Do you ever think] How often do you imagine *NY*, How often do you think SP66TS (revised in pen on SP66G to SP66 reading) 19: Of a face] A face *NY* 20: in the / Eyes] brimming in / The eyes, but *NY*, in / The eyes, SP66TS (revised in pen on SP66G to SP66 reading)

198 **Shoes in Rain Jungle** Text: SP66. Variants: *New York Review of Books*, 11 Nov. 1965, p. 10, SP75. The poem is moved to its present location in the dummy paste-up. In SP66TS the title is corrected in green pen from "(Shoes in Rain Jungle, Or:) Some People Can't Tell History From What They Think is Wild Honey". 9: The feet] They *NYRB*, SP66TS (revised in green pen to SP66) 12: are] were *NYRB* 13: They are cheap, but shoes are dear, and] People who are raised barefoot are cheap, / But we who wear shoes are dear, and *NYRB* 16: history.] History. *NYRB*, SP66TS (revised in pen on SP66G to SP66 reading) 18: history,] History, *NYRB* 22: history.] History. *NYRB*, SP66TS (revised in pen on SP66G to SP66 reading) 23: what it is.] what it is: *NYRB*, *New York Review of Books* also omits the stanza break after this line. 28: in] of *NYRB* 37: fellow-man,"] fellow-man" *NYRB* 41: Sociologists can do that much.] *NYRB* omits the stanza break after this line. 45: *mot de Cambronne*] shit *NYRB*, SP66TS (revised in green pen to SP66)

199 **Fall Comes in Back-Country Vermont** In SP66TS there is a note in green ink "not on new page" at every section break. Section breaks are preceded by "2 line #" and followed by "1 line #" also in green ink. Text: SP66. Variants: *New Yorker,* 23 Oct. 1965, pp. 56–57. Because Warren enclosed the section titles in parentheses in all of the published versions of this poem—perhaps because the section breaks sometimes come in the middle the one big sentence in which this poem is mostly written—I have done so here, although I have tried in other sequences to set their section titles in a consistent way. I have also followed Warren's practice of suppressing the section titles for this sequence in the table of contents. The poem bears no dedication in SP66TS, but it is added in red pen in SP66G and in the dummy paste-up.

199 **(1. One Voter Out of Sixteen)** 5: know] you know *NY* 13: rashness,] ~$_\wedge$ *NY* 18: dies,] ~$_\wedge$ *NY*, SP66TS (revised in pen on SP66G to SP66 reading) 23: cancer),] cancer) *NY* 28: heartbroken] heart-broken SP66TS (revised in pen on SP66G to SP66 reading) 29: bedpan] bed-pan SP66TS (revised in pen on SP66G to SP66 reading) 31: now all night glares] glares now all night (revised on SP75G but not adopted in SP75) 34: How cancer is worse] How his cancer was worse SP66TS (but corrected in pen on SP66G to SP66 reading) 34: 30.30] .30-30 *NY*

200 **(2. The Bear and the Last Person to Remember)** 5: lawn mower] lawnmower *NY* 14: tusk,] tush, *NY* 18: tawny] the tawny *NY* 19: she bear,] she-bear, *NY* 30: want] they want *NY* 39: mattress, and] mattress and, *NY* 42: says:] ~, *NY*

201 **(3. The Human Fabric)** 6: Any more] Anymore *NY*, SP66TS (revised in pen on SP66G to SP66 reading) 10: Hartford$_\wedge$] ~, *NY* 12: Blood-lust] Blood lust *NY* 16: snow plow] snowplow *NY*

202 **(4. Afterwards)** 2: glass, and] glass and, *NY* 11: turns, and] turns and, *NY* 12: light] sun-gleam *NY* 14: I touch the hand there on the pillow.] SP75 sets this line off as a separate stanza (and in the photocopy of SP66 now catalogued as "Draft B" in the Beinecke Library Warren indicates the same).

202 **The Day Dr. Knox Did It** Text: SP66. Variants: *Encounter,* 27 (Sept. 1966), pp. 22–24, SP75. The *Encounter* version uses Arabic numerals in the section titles. In SP66TS the dedication is added in red pencil, probably by Erskine, and probably at Warren's direction. Each section title is marked "new page" in green pen.

202 **I. Place and Time** 6: tulip trees] tulip-trees *Encounter*, SP66TS (revised in green pen to SP66) 8: dust-whiteness] dust white *Encounter*, SP66TS (revised in pen on SP66G to SP66 reading) 9: eyeball,] eye-ball, *Encounter*, SP66TS (revised in pen on SP66G to SP66 reading) 11: eyeball,] eye-ball, *Encounter*, SP66TS (revised in pen on SP66G to SP66 reading) 18: post master's] postmaster's *Encounter* 19: floor boards] floorboards *Encounter*

203 **II. The Event** 13: rooftree,] roof-tree, *Encounter*, SP66TS (revised in pen on SP66G to SP66 reading)

204 **III. A Confederate Veteran Tries to Explain the Event** 4: other] younger SP75 (revised on SP75G) 12: But,] ∼‸ *Encounter*, SP66TS (revised in pen on SP66G to SP66 reading) 19: whitewash] white-wash *Encounter*, SP66TS (revised in pen on SP66G to SP66 reading) 22: color] colour *Encounter* 23: nothing—] ∼‸ *Encounter* 25: happen. But] happen, but *Encounter* 38: move‸] SP66TS reads as SP66 but is revised in red ink to ∼, SP66G is revised back to SP66. 39: teeth,] ∼‸ *Encounter*, SP66TS (revised in red pen to SP66) 41: it] the tongue *Encounter* 42: dark,] ∼‸ SP66TS (revised in red pen to SP66)

205 **IV. The Place Where the Boy Pointed** 11: 12-gauge] .12 gauge *Encounter*, SP66TS (revised in pen on SP66G to SP66 reading)

206 **V. And All That Came Thereafter** Section title] And All That Came After SP66TS (the title is changed to its current title in SP66G and on the dummy paste-up, but *Encounter* had the SP66 title to begin with) 10: that was] that SP66TS (revised in pen on SP66G to SP66 reading) 12: there I] I there *Encounter*, SP66TS (revised in pen on SP66G to SP66 reading) 13: watched] saw *Encounter* 46: yet] ye, SP66TS (revised in pen on SP66G to SP66 reading) 47: gray] grey *Encounter* 51: blind, / of this,] of / this, *Encounter*, of / thus, SP66TS (revised in pen on SP66G to SP66 reading) 64: But we must frame more firmly] We must, more firmly, frame *Encounter*, But, more firmly, we must frame the idea of good. SP66TS (revised in green pen from "But we must, more firmly, frame the idea of good.", then given in red pen, then in green pen, "We must frame more firmly the image of good.", and finally corrected in pen on SP66G to SP66 reading), We must frame, then, more firmly SP75 (and in the photocopy of SP66 now catalogued as "Draft B" in the Beinecke Library)

207 **Holy Writ** SP85 drops the sequence title and reprints only "Elijah on Mount Carmel." In SP66TS "and Glenn" is added in red pencil to the dedication.

207 **I. Elijah on Mount Carmel** Text: SP66. Variants: *New Leader,* 26 Sept. 1960, p. 10, SP75, SP85. The epigraph in *New Leader* and SP66TS (revised in green pen to SP66) is "Being a design, in stained glass, for the Cathedral of Saint John the Divine, New York City, showing Elijah, after the miraculous fall of fire on his altar, the breaking of the drouth, and the slaughter of the priests of Baal, as he girds up his loins and runs ahead of the chariot of Ahab to the gates of Jezreel." On SP85G, Warren added the following to the end of the epigraph: "Some commentators interpret the phrase 'turned aside' as rendered here. The body of Jezebel, later, was eaten by dogs." The addition does not appear in SP85, however. 10: blood spurts] blood-spurts *New Leader* 18: fetlock,] ∼‸ *New Leader* 23: soft] white *New Leader* 24: that darkness wherein History creeps to die.] the nether millstone, and upper, of History. *New Leader*, SP66TS (revised in red, and then green, pen to SP66) It is unclear whether there is a stanza break after this line in *New Leader,* because a column break obscures it. A page turn obscures whether there is a stanza break here in SP66TS, but a stanza break is unmistakable in SP66G. 30: And only the gull-mew was answer,] SP85 adds a stanza break after this line, probably in error, since this is a point where two of the cut-and-taped photocopies from SP75 that are used for SP85TS are taped together. 32: turned] stepped *New Leader* 32: pee-pee] peo-pace *New Leader* 34: drouth] the drouth *New Leader* 35: his eyes in] eyes with *New*

Leader, SP66TS (revised in green pen to SP66) 43: lay] and lay *New Leader*, SP66TS (revised in green pen to SP66) 44: his infatuate] the infatuate *New Leader* 48: longer;] ~. SP85 (revised on SP85G to SP85) 48: so prayed:] and prayed: *New Leader* So prayed: SP85 (revised on SP85G to SP85) 48: oh, please] oh please SP66TS (revised to SP66 reading on SP66G 48: Dear God, dear God—oh, please, don't exist!] Dear God, Oh, please—dear God, don't exist! *New Leader*

209 **II. Saul at Gilboa** Text: SP66. Variants: *Yale Review,* 55 (Summer 1966), pp. 481–87 (as "Saul"), SP75. Epigraph] Samuel speaks *YR* The epigraph is in parentheses in SP66 and *YR*.

209 **1.** 1: From] FROM *YR* 19: Of the leaf, turning in air.] *YR* does not have a stanza break after this line. In SP66TS the line, and stanza, were to have continued as follows, but the text is canceled in green pen: "Which is / Not the word spoken, but the silence / Wherein the word ceases, and the silence / Endures like stone."(The stanza break between this text and the next line also was added in green pen.)

209 **2.** The text in SP66TS is heavily marked up in green pen. After the markup, it is essentially the text in SP66. But the original typescript is so different from both *YR* and SP66 (which are closer to each other than either is to the original typescript) that it seems most likely to be a version prior to *YR.* Warren had the habit of sending drafts, sometimes very unfinished drafts, of his poems as he completed them to Albert Erskine at Random House to be held in a file for him, and the two of them seem to have commented upon and revised these drafts extensively. (Warren was also in the habit of sending his poems to John Palmer and to Allen Tate for comment as well, recording their comments on his own drafts. He was particularly interested in their advice about the ordering of poems in extended sequences.) The green pen markup, which is not in Warren's hand, must represent the substance of Warren's conversations with Erskine about the early draft they had in hand. Why they did not work from the more finished version published in *YR* puzzles me. 8: sky stares.] Stanza break added in green pen on SP66TS. 9: hang] hung SP66TS (revised in green pen to SP66) 10: (Let Amalek ... wind.)] Parentheses added in green pen on SP66TS. 14: Toward me he walks, I am old.] Line missing in *YR.* 14: Toward me he walks, ... among the people] This is how SP66TS reads after considerable correction in green pen. The typed lines differ from both SP66 and *YR*:

Toward me he walks, I am old, and my sons,—
Their brains are eaten by vanity as by
Nits, they are nit-headed, and
The muscle of a son's arm that should strike,
Hangs slack as the dugs of an old ewe, and I know
That this who, dust of desert on him
And thorn-scar, walks now, is
The man. As he walks, he is,
From the shoulder and upward, higher than any among the people.

15: him,] ~$_\wedge$ *YR* 15: he / Walks, and is the man. He is,] he is, *YR* 16: He is,] He is$_\wedge$ SP66TS (revised on SP66G to SP66 reading). 17: than any among the people] SP66TS adds, and then cancels in green pen, a stanza after this line: "The Voice is in my ear: *This is the man.*" 20: which is] in SP66TS (revised in green pen to SP66) 23: goes,] ~. *YR* 25: I am old. A king. ... I hear my own voice. It says: "*My son.*"] This is the reading in SP66TS after considerable revision in green pen. The original typescript read:

I am old, a king
They would have, not the Lord and
His Voice. Toward me
He walks who will make all things
New. He walks,
In beauty, toward my knowledge. What
Is in my heart?
I call him my son.

25: old. A king] old, and a king *YR* 29: knowledge,] ∼∧ SP66TS (revised on SP66G to SP66 reading).

210 **3.** 1: he, beautiful, down in the dirt, kneels.] down in the dirt, he, beautiful, kneels. *YR*, down in the dirt, kneels SP66TS (revised to YR in green pen, and corrected in blue pen on SP66G to SP66 reading). 7: sweat now] sweat SP66TS (revised in green pen to SP66) 10: He / Is ignorant, and I pour] This is the reading in SP66TS after correction in green pen. The original typescript read simply "I pour." 13: The far hills,] He is ignorant. The far hills, *YR*, SP66TS (revised in green pen to SP66) 14: Swim] They swim *YR*

211 **4.** 1: I am the past time, ... The membrane between past and future,] This is the reading in SP66TS after considerable revision in green pen. The original typescript read:

I am the past time, I am old, but
Am, too, the time to come, for I close my eyes
And know that time, and am
The membrane between past and future,

1: am old,] I am old, *YR* 4: The membrane] That membrane (revised in green pen to SP66) 15: Tabor∧] ∼, *YR* 15: at Tabor at / A high place] This is the reading in SP66TS after correction in green pen. The original typescript read: "at Tabor a stranger / Will give bread into his hand, and at / A high place" 21: me,] ∼∧ *YR* 21: Before me, his head] This is the reading in SP66TS after correction in green pen. The original typescript read: "His head." 24: Beautiful is] Beautiful, in *YR*, SP66TS (revised in green pen to SP66) 25: will be] is SP66TS (revised in green pen to SP66) 28: Nor how] How SP66TS (revised in green pen to SP66) 29: And the brow] And with brow *YR* 30: sway,] away, (revised in green pen to SP66) 33: He himself will become] Corrected in green pen from "He will be" in SP66TS. 33: counseled] counselled *YR*, SP66TS (revised in pen on SP66G to SP66 reading)

212 **5.** This section division is added in green pen in SP66TS. 7: in the end,] corrected from "now," in green pen in SP66TS. 8: is, always, all.] corrected from "is all" in green pen in SP66TS. 10: So to] corrected from "So now comes to" in green pen in SP66TS. 12: shape] the shape *YR* 12: of shadow, rise,] of shadow, SP66TS (revised in green pen to SP66) 15: is / Now streaked] corrected from "is streaked" in green pen in SP66TS. 16: gray, so say] gray. And so I say *YR* 17: will not / Return] corrected in green pen in SP66TS from "will / Not return." 18: Return. In the dirt,] In *YR* there is no stanza break after this line. The stanza break is added in green pen on SP66TS.

212 **6.** 4: She feeds him, morsel / By morsel, he is like a child.] These two lines missing from *YR*. 14: once a / King] once / A king *YR* 16: muted,] ∼∧ *YR* 17: comes,] ∼. *YR* 19: Now goes to be] corrected in green pen from "Now he goes to be" on SP66TS. 19: Now goes to be] No stanza break after this line in *YR*, SP66TS (revised in pen on SP66G to SP66 reading).

213 **7.** 4: And] But *YR* 8: hands, rose,] hands, *YR* 9: Stood, and was] corrected in green pen in SP66TS from "Stood, was". 17: by stone.] Stanza break after this text is added in green pen in SP66TS. 20: The black dwindle] Corrected in green pen in SP66TS from "Diminishing in distance, moved. The black / Dwindle" 24: knowing.] knowledge. *YR* 24: knowing. / The palm] corrected in green pen in SP66TS from "knowing. / Ignorant, and / The palm". 26: world∧] ∼, *YR* 28: Of my hand itched.] Two lines following this text are deleted in green pen in SP66TS: "Would they close upon the world and crush / The bright distance?" 29: walking!] ∼. *YR* 29: How beautiful are the young, walking!] This stanza added in green pen in SP66TS. 30: I closed my eyes. I shuddered in a rage of joy.] Line missing in *YR*, I closed my eyes and shuddered in a rage of joy. SP66TS (revised in pen on SP66G to SP66 reading) 30: I closed my eyes and shuddered in a rage of joy.] Corrected in green pen in SP66TS from "From heat, in a room of shadow, / I lay. I closed my eyes and shuddered / In a rage of joy."

214 **8.** 1: The south] corrected in green pen in SP66TS from "On the south". 1: pass:] corrected in green pen in SP66TS from "pass," 12: From the ... from horn-throat came,] These two lines added in green pen in SP66TS. 12: which∧] ∼, SP75 13: That] A *YR*

Then, a SP75 (In the photocopy of SP66 now catalogued as "Draft B" in the Beinecke Library the reading is "Then, a".) Warren asked for this revision in a letter to Albert Erskine of November 13, 1966. 13: came,] comes, *YR* 15: Gilboa is, of that place, the name.] Of that place, Gilboa is the name. *YR*

214 **9.**

215 **Delight** "Into Broad Daylight," "It Is Not To Be Trusted," "Something Is Going To Happen," and "Finisterre," appeared together as "Lyrics from "Delight" " in *New York Review of Books,* 1, no. 1, "Special Issue," 1963, p. 18. The poems in *NYRB* appeared entirely in italics. "Dream of a Dream the Small Boy Had," "Love: Two Vignettes" (including "Mediterranean Beach, Day After Storm," and "Deciduous Spring,"), and "Two Poems about Suddenly and a Rose" (including "Dawn," and "Intuition"), appeared together as "Three Poems by Robert Penn Warren," in *Saturday Review,* 13 Aug. 1966, p. 21. They were not marked in *SatR* as being parts of the "Delight" sequence. SP75 drops "Dream of a Dream the Small Boy Had" and "Finisterre." SP85 deletes the sequence, printing "Love: Two Vignettes" (including "Mediterranean Beach, Day After Storm," and "Deciduous Spring"), as a separate poem.In SP66TS this sequence, except for "Finisterre," is folded in half, as for mailing, indicating that it was prepared separately from the rest of the manuscript, and that "Finisterre" was a late addition.

215 **I. Into Broad Daylight** Text: SP66. Variants: *New York Review of Books,* 1, no. 1, "Special Issue," 1963, p. 18, SP75. *NYRB* indents the fourth line of every stanza. 2: on] on a *NYRB* 12: its] its own *NYRB* 16: rest:] ~; *NYRB*, SP66TS (revised in pen on SP66G to SP66 reading) 17: can] may *NYRB NYRB* also sets this last line in roman, to distinguish it from the rest, which is in italic.

215 **II. Love: Two Vignettes** Text: SP66. Variants: *Saturday Review,* 13 Aug. 1966, p. 21, SP75, SP85.

215 **1. Mediterranean Beach, Day after Storm** 1: How] HOW *SatR* 7: sea‸] ~, *SatR*

216 **2. Deciduous Spring** 2: gabbles joy] gabblesjoy *SatR* 6: Now,] *Now,* SP85 (revised on SP85G to SP85) 11: comes back,] comesback, *SatR* 12: gabbling,] gobbling, SP66TS (revised in green pen to SP66) 20: still,] ~‸ *SatR* 20: just a moment, leaves.] Stanza break after this text added in green pen in SP66TS.

216 **III. Something is Going to Happen** Text: SP66. Variants: *New York Review of Books,* 1, no. 1, "Special Issue," 1963, p. 18, SP75. 26: everything‸] ~, *NYRB* 29: Therefore] 'Therefore *NYRB*

217 **IV. Dream of a Dream the Small Boy Had** Text: SP66. Variants: *Saturday Review,* 13 Aug. 1966, p. 21. In SP66TS the section number is added in green pen, so the idea of including this poem in the sequence may have been a late one. The page is also marked "new" in red pen in SP66TS. 1: All] ALL *SatR*

218 **V. Two Poems About Suddenly and a Rose** Text: SP66. Variants: *Saturday Review,* 13 Aug. 1966, p. 21, SP75. In draft A and in SP66TS before this text there is another section inserted, called "The Simplest Greenwood Song":

I lie under the tree.
The leaves are green.
Through the leaves God cannot see.
I am happy under the tree.
I do not want to be seen.

I lie under the tree.
The boughs are bare.
Through the bare boughs God can see.
I am happy under the tree,
Bare bones are a prayer.

The section number (V.) of "The Simplest Greenwood Song" is typed, so it was clearly part of the sequence from an earlier draft. The section number (VI. in SP66TS) of "Two

Poems About Suddenly and a Rose" is added in green pen, so it may be a late addition. Both pages of this section in SP66TS are marked "new" in red pen. "The Simplest Greenwood Song" is crossed out in red pen in SP66G, and removed from the dummy paste-up, but the sequence numbers after it in the dummy paste-up are revised in red pencil to reflect its dropping. It was clearly included in the galley proofs.

218 **1. Dawn** 1: Suddenly.] SUDDENLY. *SatR* 4: Dawn—] ~: *SatR*, SP66TS (revised in green pen to SP66) 9: *not,*] not, *SatR*, SP66TS (revised in green pen to SP66) 13: hands] hand *SatR* 17: Now to me] To me *SatR*, SP66TS (revised in pen on SP66G to SP66 reading) 21: Balances. Light,] No stanza break after this line in *SatR*. 21: Light,] But light, SP75 (and in the photocopy of SP66 now catalogued as "Draft B" in the Beinecke Library) 22: Suddenly, on any morning, is, and somewhere,] Is always light, and suddenly, / On any morning, is, and somewhere, SP75 (and in the photocopy of SP66 now catalogued as "Draft B" in the Beinecke Library)

219 **2. Intuition** In SP66TS this poem is typed on a different typewriter from the rest of the sequence. There is an annotation, "new" in red pen in the upper right corner, and a typed annotation, "Robert Penn Warren" at the bottom of the page. This version is clearly a late addition, although it was added some time before the page numbers were written in in blue pen.

219 **VI. Not to Be Trusted** Text: SP66. Variants: *New York Review of Books,* 1, no. 1, "Special Issue," 1963, p. 18 (as "It Is Not to Be Trusted"), SP75. In SP66TS the section number is corrected in green pen from VI to VII, reflecting the addition of "Two Poems about Suddenly and a Rose" to the sequence. 3: hand] hands *NYRB* 11: Look! In that bush, with wolf-fang white, delight] Look!—in that bush, wolf-fang white, delight *NYRB* 12: someone:] some one: *NYRB*, SP66TS (revised in green pen to SP66) 12: *You.*] *NYRB* sets this in roman, since the body of the poem is in italic.

219 **VII. Finisterre** Text: SP66. Variants: *New York Review of Books,* 1, no. 1, "Special Issue," 1963, p. 18. 1: bay's] boy's SP66TS (revised in red pen to SP66) 2: under,] ~∧ SP66TS (but corrected in pen on SP66G to SP66 reading) 8: at least, to wonder.] at least wonder. *NYRB* 8: to] into SP66TS (revised in red pen in SP66TS)

Incarnations
Poems 1966–1968

The volume *Incarnations* is divided into three volume sections. The first, "I. Island of Summer," consists only of the sequence "Island of Summer." The second, "II. Internal Injuries," consists of the sequence "Penological Study: Southern Exposure," and the sequence "Internal Injuries." The third, "III. Enclaves," consists of the sequence "The True Nature of Time" and the sequence "In the Mountains."

In *Incarnations* the sequence "The True Nature of Time" consisted of "The Faring," and "The Enclave." Warren moved the whole sequence to *Or Else*, where it was section XIII of that book-length sequence. As I did with the "Notes on a Life to be Lived" section of *Tale of Time,* I have sacrificed "Enclaves" to *Or Else* as being the least damaging of the alternatives.

In *Incarnations* itself as well as in the selections republished in SP75, Warren used Arabic numerals in the titles of the sections of the sequences, instead of the capital Roman numerals he used in the titles of sections of sequences in his other volumes, perhaps because he used capital Roman numerals in the titles of the volume sections. Warren did not preserve the volume sections, and broke up all of the sequences as well, in SP85. For consistency with the other volumes, I will be using capital Roman numerals in the titles of sequence sections, as usual, and will use Arabic numerals in the titles of volume sections.

Until a fairly late stage of development—the new title is written in on the setting typescript—this volume was to be called *Internal Injuries, or The True Nature of Joy.* The typescript is a mixture of typescript and photocopy. It is numbered consecutively in typing, and thus is not a collection of drafts sent to Erskine, having been at least consecutively retyped. The corrections on the Author's First Proof are mostly not in Warren's hand, but seem to have been dictated by him, since they reproduce changes in his own hand and typing on the Duplicate Author's Proof.

The issue of where to bend long lines is a vexed one in this volume. The "line bends" are often marked on the typescript, and they are frequently not the places where Warren bent the line when he was typing it. In most of these cases my assumption is that Warren did not think in detail about how to break the line on the printed page until he went over the typescript with Erskine, and therefore I have recorded where a mark directs a line bend rather than where the line bend is typed in in the original where the two differ. When these poems were reset for SP75 and SP85, the typesetters pretty much ignored how the lines were bent in *Incarnations*, and neither Warren nor Erskine seems to have noticed. I have marked enough cases where how the lines are bent differs among the three versions to make the point.

The *Incarnations* section of SP85TS consists of photocopy and cut-and-taped photocopy from SP75.

The American trade (Random House), American limited (Random House), and English (W. H. Allen) editions were set from the same plates. dedication: John Palmer] J. J. E. Palmer ITS (revised on IG to I reading) Both epigraphs are written in pen in ITS and thus were added to the volume late.

1. Island of Summer

223 **Island of Summer** Six of the sections of this sequence appeared as sections of "Ile de Port Cros: What Happened," in *Encounter,* 29 (Oct. 1967), pp. 3–5. The sections were, in this order, "1. What Day Is," "2. Natural History," "3. The Poet Paul Valéry Walked Here And Confronted The Fierce Energies Of The World," "4. Moonrise," "5. A Place Where Nothing Is," and "6. Masts At Dawn." "Ile de Port Cros: What Happened" is dedicated to J. J. E. Palmer. Six more sections of this sequence appeared as sections of "Thoughts in Ruined Garden on Summer Isle," in *Encounter,* 30 (Jan. 1968) pp. 13–15. The sections were, in this order, "1. Riddle in the Garden," "2. Mistral at Night," "3. Where Purples Now The Fig," "4. The Ivy," "5. The Red Mullet," and "6. The Leaf." Until a late stage of the production of the volume the title of the sequence as a whole was "The Summer Island."

223 **I. What Day Is** Text: I. Variants: *Encounter,* 29 (Oct. 1967), p. 3, SP75. I and SP75 are identical. 5: Hewn stone, footings] Hewn stone—footings *Encounter* 6: Irrigation, but] Irrigation—but *Encounter* 7: To trace a flume-line.] The spacing at the beginning of the next line in I, SP75, and *Encounter* is adjusted so as to make this line and the next appear to be one broken line, despite the stanza break that separates them. Warren clearly meant a stanza break to intervene in cases like this, because where a page break would have obliterated the stanza break in cases like this he marked the stanza break with his characteristic centered asterisk, so that it would not be lost. (Also, they are marked as stanza breaks in red pencil on ITS.) Broken lines that straddle stanza breaks are a common feature of this volume and later volumes (there is also an example each in *Tale of Time* and *You, Emperors, and Others*). I have chosen not to increment the line counter for the first fractional line, since Warren's intention is to connect the two fractional lines across the stanza break. Occasionally Warren writes lines that straddle the sectional divisions of poems, and in those cases I have chosen, since I reset the line counter to one for new sections of poems, not to reflect the linkage of the two fractional lines in the line count in such cases. 17: at the] at that *Encounter* 21: gray] grey *Encounter*

223 **II. Where the Slow Fig's Purple Sloth** Text: I. Variants: *New Yorker,* 10 June 1967, p. 145 (as "Where the Slow Fig"), SP75, SP85. 3: soul, the] soul. The *NY* 6: but$_\wedge$] ~, *NY* 9: oh$_\wedge$] ~, *NY* 10: For the fig's bliss, thus.] The line straddles the stanza break following this text. In *NY,* there is no break here, and the stanza break follows "The air" at the end of the line. 11: fig,] ~— *NY* 13: glut,] ~— *NY* 13: inward$_\wedge$] ~, *NY* 14: fibers] fibres *NY*, ITS (revised on IG to I reading) 16: Is gold.] The line straddles the stanza break following this text. In *NY* there is no break here, and the stanza break follows "When you" at the end of the line. 20: Than blood.] The line straddles the stanza break

following this text. In *NY* there is no break here, and the stanza break follows "It fills" at the end of the line.

224 **III. Natural History** Text: I. Variants: *Encounter,* 29 (Oct. 1967) p. 3, SP75 (as "Natural History I" in the text—"Natural History" in the contents—presumably to distinguish it from "Natural History" in *Or Else.* 1: died here,] died, *Encounter* 8: *Maréchal*] *Maréschal Encounter*, Marechal ITS (revised on IG to I reading) 10: *que morts, que affolez,*] The line straddles the stanza break following this text. 12: luster,] lustre, *Encounter*, ITS (revised on IG to I reading) 15: at the temple,] the temple, *Encounter* 25: Has tears.] Here in I and SP75 the line straddles the stanza break following this text. In *Encounter* the line is "Has tears, but" followed by a stanza break (and the rest of the line) but with no straddling of the stanza break by the line. 25: But at dusk / From the next island, from its pad at] At dusk, from the next island, from its pad at *Encounter* 27: *Le centre de recherche d'engins spéciaux,*] *Le Centre de Recherche d'Engins Spéciaux, Encounter* 27: *spéciaux,*] *spécieux,* SP75 (the printer erroneously had "spécious," and Warren corrected it to *spéciaux,* but the printer misread Warren's correction.) 28: fume now feathers] the fume feathers *Encounter*, fume feathers ITS (revised on IG to I reading) 28: white—] There is a line break in *Encounter* after this text, but unlike every other line in the poem the next line does not begin with an initial capital, and thus is probably a run-over from the last line that the compositor has set by mistake as a separate line. 32: bright foil,] foil, *Encounter* 32: ice-bright, from / A Christmas tree, die in earth's shadow, but] ice-bright, / From a Christmas tree falling, they sink / Into earth-shadow, glimmer, then die, but *Encounter.* There is a stanza break after "but" in *Encounter.* 34: yet hang] still shine *Encounter*

225 **IV. Riddle in the Garden** Text: I. Variants: *Encounter,* 30 (Jan. 1968), p. 13, Washington *Post* 6 Dec. 1970, p. C-3, SP75, SP85. The Washington *Post* version is printed in italic type, and uses roman type for emphasis. 4: *pudeur*] pudeur *Encounter*, ITS (revised on IG to I reading) 5: departed$_\wedge$] $\sim$, *Encounter* 16: Gray] Grey *Encounter* 16: fruit-skin of blister,] blister like fruit-skin, SP85 (revised on SP85G to SP85)

226 **V. Paul Valéry Stood on the Cliff And Confronted the Furious Energies of Nature** Text: I. Variants: *Encounter,* 29 (Oct. 1967), p. 4 (as "The Poet Paul Valéry Walked Here And Confronted The Fierce Energies Of The World"), SP75. 3: Sea-wind on the cliff-track] Sea wind on the cliff track *Encounter* 5: and white the far sail / Heeled now to windward,] and to windward afar / The sail heeled white, *Encounter* 6: Heeled now to] Heeled off from SP75 (revised on SP75G) 6: windward,] In a note to Suzanne Baskin at Random House on March 14, 1969, Warren asked that this word be changed to "seaward," but apparently he forgot about this when he actually reprinted the poem. 7: Cat's-paws] Cat's paws SP75 8: to look, and far down,] to look down, and far down *Encounter* 26: But Time is not time,] For Time is not Time, *Encounter* 26: therefore] so *Encounter* 27: throat$_\wedge$] $\sim$, *Encounter* 28: white] panama *Encounter* 29: Panama hat in hand,] Hat white in his hand, *Encounter* 30: Poète,] poète, ITS (revised on IG to I reading) 32: sea, so] sea. Look— *Encounter* 33: He sways high against the blue sky,] Against the blue sky he sways high, *Encounter*

227 **VI. Treasure Hunt** Text: I. Variants: *New Yorker,* 18 March 1967, p. 213 (as "Fairy Story"), SP75. 1: again. If] again, if ITS (revised on IG to I reading) 2: much,] $\sim$: *NY* 4: nor] or *NY* 4: by the fig] at the fig SP75 (revised on SP75G) 6: Have looked, I know. But hurry, for] Have looked. I know. Hurry, for *NY*

227 **VII. Moonrise** Text: I. Variants: *Encounter,* 29 (Oct. 1967), p. 4, Washington *Post,* 6 Dec. 1970, p. C-3. The Washington *Post* version is printed in italic type, and uses roman type for emphasis. 4: bugle-blast,] bugle blast, *Encounter* 7: *terrasse*] terrasse *Encounter* 8: From the shadow] From shadow *Encounter*, ITS (revised on IG to I reading)

228 **VIII. Myth on Mediterranean Beach: Aphrodite as Logos** Text: I. Variants: *Saturday Review,* 25 Feb. 1967, p. 38 (as "Myth on Mediterranean Beach / Venus Anadyomene as Logos"), SP75. In ITS the title is corrected from I to "Myth on Mediterranean Beach: / Aphrodite Anadyomene as Logos (but it is corrected on IG to I reading). 1: From] FROM *SatR* 28: interest.] erection. ITS (revised on IG to I reading) This vari-

ant, and "to seek the crotch" below, lead me to the conclusion that ITS pre-dates *Saturday Review* and follows the draft of works in progress that Warren was in the habit of sending to Albert Erskine at Random House. 29: horizon rim,] horizon-rim, *SatR* 36: How long, how long,] How long, how long *SatR* 43: abstract] bemused *SatR*, ITS (revised in red pencil to I) 44: And watching, we feel the slow knowledge grow—] And as she moves, we watch, we know *SatR*, ITS (revised on IG to I reading) 47: up,] ~. SP75 48: to seek, and seek,] to seek the crotch, ITS (revised on IG to I reading) 49: languishing,] ~‸ *SatR* 49: lave] leave ITS (revised on IG to I reading) 53: She shivers, smiles. She stands complete] She stands forth free. She is complete *SatR*, ITS (revised on IG to I reading) 56: the lifeward] her lifeward *SatR*, ITS (revised on IG to I reading) 64: The pince-nez] And the pince-nez *SatR* 65: The] And *SatR* 65: wreathe] wreath ITS (revised on IG to I reading) 66: blessèd] blessed ITS (revised on IG to I reading) 70: passing,] ~‸ *SatR*, ITS (revised on IG to I reading)

230 **IX. Mistral at Night** Text: I. Variants: *University of Denver Quarterly*, 2 (Spring 1967), p. 32 (as "Mistral at Night on Summer Island: for Alan Swallow"), *Encounter*, 30 (Jan. 1968), p. 13. 1: cold curdle] cold-curdle *Encounter* 4: dry leaf:] In *Encounter* the line straddles a stanza break after this text. 5: when /But a] when but / A *Encounter* 6: gust] leaf *Encounter* 7: sleep,] sleep now, *Encounter* 11: But what / Is it?] But / What is it? *University of Denver Quarterly* In *Encounter* the stanza ends after this text, the "You must wait" in the next line is indented so as to make a line that straddles the stanza break, and there is no stanza break after "You must wait." *University of Denver Quarterly* resembles *Encounter* here, except that there is no stanza break before "You must wait," so that "What is it?" and "You must wait" form a single broken line. ITS is revised in red pencil from the *Encounter* reading to the reading in I.

231 **X. The Ivy** Text: I. Variants: *Encounter*, 30 (Jan. 1968), p. 13, SP75. 2: "I will pull you down."] Single quotes in *Encounter*. 9: stars] star *Encounter*

231 **XI. Where Purples Now the Fig** Text: I. Variants: *Encounter*, 30 (Jan. 1968), p. 13, SP75. In *Encounter* none of the indented lines have initial capitals. 5: all white,] all to white, *Encounter* 9: me] us ITS (revised on IG to I reading)

231 **XII. The Red Mullet** Text: I. Variants: *Encounter*, 30 (Jan. 1968), p. 14, SP75, SP85. 6: Outthrust,] Out-thrust, *Encounter*, ITS (revised on IG to I reading) 9: armor,] armour, *Encounter* 13: lung-case,] ~. *Encounter* 15: Oh, mullet,] Mullet, *Encounter*

232 **XIII. A Place Where Nothing Is** Text: I. Variants: *Encounter*, 29 (Oct. 1967), p. 5, SP75. 6: nothing- / ness presses on the ribs like] loud / it is with nothingness, nothing- / ness presses on the ribs like *Encounter* 8: elbows angry,] elbows, *Encounter* 17: lamp‸] ~, *Encounter* 18: bed‸] ~, *Encounter*, ITS (revised on IG to I reading) 27: the] that *Encounter*

233 **XIV. Masts at Dawn** Text: I. Variants: *Encounter*, 29 (Oct. 1967), p. 5, SP75, SP85. In *Encounter* each stanza is followed by three asterisks set flush with the left margin. The asterisks appear in ITS but are canceled in blue pencil. 1: harbor] harbour *Encounter* 3: a new] new *Encounter* 3: our unworthiness] The magazine versions rarely bend long lines in the same places that the book versions do, and the different book versions of the same poem do not necessarily bend the long lines in the same place either. But at this point in ITS Warren has written "break lines as typed" between these two words. Although I think the line bends are a typographical rather than a poetic device, I have chosen to follow them in this poem, since Warren drew attention to them. In I Warren handled the overrun portions of long, bent lines as he usually did, not by indenting them slightly but by setting them flush to the right margin. (This is also true of the typescript.) This suggests that Warren thought of the bending of long lines as an important part of the design of the volume. 6: evening] Line bend follows this word in ITS. 7: dark‸] ~, *Encounter* 7: white] Line bend follows this word in ITS. SP85, however, bends the line after "nagged the." 7: harbor] harbour *Encounter* 8: you surrender] Warren bent the long line between these two words in ITS, but wrote "run in here," again paying attention to line bends, but treating them as a feature of book design rather than of versification. 9: Your peace] In ITS and IG the long line bends between these words,

but Warren corrected IG to run the text into one line. This suggests that as seriously as he took line bends he still thought of them as an element of the book design and not of the versification. In SP75 the line is bent after "peace." In SP85 the line is bent after "peace is." 11: near] Line bend follows this word in ITS. But in SP85 the line bends after "ash." 12: Receives nor gives] Gives nor receives *Encounter* 14: of] Line bend follows this word in ITS. But in SP85 the line bends after "pier." 15: floats free] The line bend between these words is added in blue pencil in ITS. In the typing, the line bend came after "that". But in IG the line bend comes after "that" too, suggesting that Warren did not always care deeply about where long lines bend. 15: on that surface] on the surface *Encounter* 16: the] Line bend follows this word in ITS. 18: Condenses] Condensed SP85 (revised on SP85G to SP85)

234 **XV. The Leaf** I have followed Warren's practice in the version of this poem in *Incarnations* and in SP75 of using capital letters in brackets in the titles of subsections of "The Leaf." In *Encounter* Warren used small letters in brackets for this, and in SP85 Warren used capital letters not in brackets. None of Warren's volumes show a consistent practice about setting the titles of subsections of sequences when those titles do not appear in the table of contents. Sometimes, as in "Tale of Time," he uses Arabic numerals not in brackets. Sometimes, as in the version of "The Leaf" in SP85, he uses capital letters not in brackets. Sometimes, as in "Audubon," he uses capital letters in brackets. Sometimes, as in "A Problem in Spatial Composition" in *Or Else* and in SP75, he uses Arabic numerals in brackets. Warren's practice is not always consistent within volumes (in *Or Else* Warren uses several different schemes), and it is not always consistent across repetitions of the same poem in different volumes. When confronted with the problem of how to set the titles of sequence sections, I chose to adopt a uniform style, using capital Roman numerals in every title, despite the fact that Warren preserved the Arabic numerals he used for "Island of Summer" when he reprinted the sequence in SP75. But because the titles of subsections like those I am discussing here do not appear in the table of contents (whereas the titles of sections do), and because the letter or number is the only way to refer to them (and the only way they have been referred to in the critical literature), I have adopted the consistently inconsistent policy of simply following the format of the original volume, whatever it is.

234 **[A]** Text: I. Variants: *Encounter,* 30 (Jan. 1968), pp. 14–15, SP75, SP85. The page in ITS is marked "pick up from sample but read," which leads me to suspect that the type was not in fact set from it. 1: the leaf, the leaf] the leaf, that leaf *Encounter* 6: down.] $\sim_\wedge$ ITS (revised on IG to I reading)

234 **[B]** 8: from] by *Encounter* 12: knew.] $\sim$, *Encounter*, $\sim_\wedge$ ITS (revised on IG to I reading) 19: wind] but wind *Encounter* 23: name] only name *Encounter* 23: for] and *Encounter* 25: there, of the wide world,] of the wide world, ITS (revised on IG to I reading)

235 **[C]** 1: fruitful. In] fruiful. In *Encounter* fruitful, In SP75, SP85 (undoubtedly a typographical error in all cases) 2: the gold] that gold *Encounter* 5: oh$_\wedge$] $\sim$, *Encounter*, blessèdly SP75 (revised on SP75G), blessedly SP85 (All of the proofs read with SP85, but no revision in SP85TS accounts for the change, so SP85 is probably in error.) 13: cicada] Line bend follows this word in ITS. There is no line bend in this line in SP85. 13: ceases,] has ceased *Encounter* 13: has called] calls *Encounter*

235 **[D]** 1: The voice blesses me for the only / Gift I have given: *teeth set on edge.*] The voice blesses me for that only gift I have given: *teeth set on edge. Encounter Encounter* also has no stanza break after "on edge." 5: space] spaces *Encounter*

2. Internal Injuries

236 **Penological Study: Southern Exposure** Text: I. Variants: *New York Review of Books,* 12 Sept. 1968, pp. 32–33, SP75. *NYRB* has no dedication, and, like I, uses Arabic numerals in the section titles. *NYRB* Also does not include "Tomorrow Morning," or "Wet Hair: If Now his Mother Should Come." Until a late stage the typescript included a section entitled "We Are Pulling for You, Jake," after "Wet Hair: If Now His Mother Should Come." The section numbers are corrected in pen in ITS to reflect the exclusion of

that section after the typescript was prepared. Until a late stage—it is corrected in pen on ITS—the title was "Penological Study: Southern Style." Since the title in the magazine publication is the same as in I, the typescript may actually be from an earlier version, perhaps from the texts that Warren sent to Albert Erskine as he finished them. ITS has no dedication, but it is added, not in Warren's hand but undoubtedly at his dictation, to IG.

236 **I. Keep That Morphine Moving, Cap** 5: dripped,] ~^ ITS (revised on IG to I reading) 10: and the Warden,] ITS adds a line after this text: "The Warden said, the Warden said," (revised on IG to I reading) 22: forty] thirty *NYRB*, ITS (revised on IG to I reading) 22: years,] ~^ *NYRB*, ITS (revised on IG to I reading) 33: That the truth] The truth ITS (revised on IG to I reading) 33: true.—Oh, Warden,] true. Oh, Warden— *NYRB/*, ITS (revised in red pencil to I) 37: cement,] ~^ SP75 42: oh!] no! SP75

237 **II. Tomorrow Morning** Title] "In the Morning" ITS (revised on IG to I reading)

237 **III. Wet Hair: If Now His Mother Should Come** Title] "Wet Hair" ITS (revised on IG to I reading)

238 **IV. Night: The Motel Down the Road From the Pen** Title] "Night: Waiting in the Cheap Motel" *NYRB*, ITS (revised on IG to I reading) 10: the] that *NYRB* 12: motel,] ~^ *NYRB*

239 **V. Where They Come to Wait for the Body: A Ghost Story** 4: had to] wanted to *NYRB* 7: twenty-three hundred] 100,000 *NYRB*, 90,000 ITS (revised on IG to I reading) 8: John Barrymore,] a John Barrymore, *NYRB*, ITS (revised on IG to I reading) 18: creek,] ~. *NYRB* 22: five A.M.,] 5 A.M., *NYRB* ITS, IG 23: he'd be] he's *NYRB* 24: If that's not too early for him,] And is heading out my road, *New York Review of Books* 31: hams^] ~, *NYRB* 34: is,] ~^ *NYRB* 39: gone,] ~^ ITS (revised on IG to I reading)

240 **VI. Night Is Personal** The stanza divisions in this section in *NYRB* are marked with three asterisks set flush to the left margin. The asterisks are present but crossed out in ITS. 9: and there] In ITS and IG there is a line bend between these words, but it is corrected in pencil to run in on IG. 16: their tears] There is a line bend between these words in ITS and in IG, but on IG it is corrected to run in the line. 17: but] Line bend follows this word in ITS. 18: keep] Line bend follows this word in ITS. 20: the world] there is a line bend between these words in ITS. There is no line bend in IG, and Warren did not have it corrected. 21: it] Line bend follows this word in ITS. 25: and] Line bend follows this word in ITS. 25: you put] you will put *NYRB* 28: now is] nowis *NYRB* 28: suffered] Line bend follows this word in ITS. 30: rage] Line bend follows this word in ITS.

241 **VII. Dawn** 7: let] and *NYRB*, ITS (revised on IG to I reading) 9: But / Stars now assume] Stars / Assume *NYRB*, ITS (revised on IG to I reading) 15: buckshot] buck-shot *NYRB* 16: stained-glass] stained glass ITS (revised on IG to I reading)

242 **Internal Injuries** Text: I. Variants: *Harper's*, (June 1968), pp. 56–58, SP75. *Harper's* gives no titles to the sections of this sequence, marking them only with Arabic numerals follwed by periods. In the table of contents in ITS there is another section, following "The Jet Must Be Hunting for Something," called "Nigger, Nigger, Burning Bright." The section does not appear in ITS.

242 **I. The Event** 3: sizeable] sizable *Harper's* 8: Upriver,] Up-river, *Harper's* Up-river in the pen, SP75 16: sixty-eight] 68 *Harper's*, ITS (corrected in blue pen to I) 27: spic,] spik, *Harper's*, ITS, IG

243 **II. The Scream**

243 **III. Her Hat** 6: hoarding] boarding SP75 (A hoarding is a temporary wooden fence around a building under construction.) 11: insensitiveness,] In ITS this word is corrected in pen from "unsubtlety," which suggests that ITS predates the magazine publication. 17: darkling gleam,] corrected in pen in ITS from "dark gleam there," which suggests that ITS predates the magazine publication.

244 **IV. The Only Trouble** 12: as the city,] as the city^ *Harper's*, ITS (revised on IG to I reading) 16: dream, oh pale!] dream—and as pale! SP75 20: of—microscopically—spit.] of, microscopically, spit. *Harper's*, ITS (revised on IG to I reading)

244 **V. The Jet Must Be Hunting for Something** In *Harper's*, the stanzas in this section are separated by two asterisks set flush with the left margin. 1: spic] spik *Harper's*, ITS (revised on IG to I reading). This suggests that he also intended to correct the spelling in the earlier use of this word, but he didn't do it on IG. 2: a white] his white *Harper's* 4: spic] spik *Harper's*, ITS (revised on IG to I reading) 5: is] Line bend follows this word in ITS. 8: ignore] Line bend follows this word in ITS. 11: For everything] In ITS and IG there was a line bend between these words, but the line is corrected on IG so as to run the line in. 12: flowery hedgerows] In ITS and IG there was a line bend between these words, but the line is corrected on IG so as to run the line in. 13: Just now, when] The last time *Harper's*, ITS (revised on IG to I reading) 13: at you,] at you$_\wedge$ *Harper's*, ITS (revised on IG to I reading) 13: impression] Line bend follows this word in ITS. 14: on] Line bend follows this word in ITS. 15: workers bloom brilliant] There was a line bend in ITS after "bloom" In IG the line bend is after "workers." Warren did not correct the line on IG. This suggests that Warren's attention to line bends was intermittent. I have followed the practice of forcing line bends only where ITS and IG agree. 16: zinnias] Line bend follows this word in ITS. 17: People] Line bend follows this word in ITS. 18: dark] Line bend follows this word in ITS. 19: sizzle] Line bend follows this word in ITS. 20: of experience] There was a line bend between these words in ITS and IG, but IG is corrected so as to run the line in. There is a marginal note: "Make 1 l if possible." 21: It] But it SP75 (revised on SP75G) 21: must] Line bend follows this word in ITS.

245 **VI. Be Something Else** The indented lines in this section do not have initial capitals in *Harper's*. The section numbers of this section and those after it are lowered by one in pen in ITS, indicating that another section has been removed late in the process of publication.

246 **VII. The World Is a Parable**

246 **VIII. Driver, Driver** 2: I] for I *Harper's* 9: last,] last$_\wedge$ ITS (revised on IG to I reading) 11: Jack-hammers] Jackhammers *Harper's* 15: The code,] That code, *Harper's* 15: orange] yellow *Harper's* 18: know the secret names and all] know all SP75 18: slithery] Line bend follows this word in ITS. 20: you / Would find in a vat] you would find / In a vat SP75 21: in a vat in the back room] in the back room *Harper's* 21: but] Line bend follows this word in ITS. 25: What is] In ITS there is a line bend between these words. IG runs the text in, and Warren did not correct it. 25: What] Line bend follows this word in ITS.

3. Enclaves

In SP75 Warren changed the title of this volume section to "In the Mountains," which is perhaps a better title for what is left of this section, with "The True Nature of Time" removed to *Or Else*, than "Enclaves" is. I have kept the title as "Enclaves" only to make it clear that the proof text for this volume is *Incarnations* rather than SP75.

248 **In the Mountains**

248 **I. Skiers** Text: I. Variants: *Northwest Review*, vol. 9, no. 1 (1967), p. 19, Washington *Post*, 6 Dec. 1970, p. C-3, SP75. 5: With the color] With color *Northwest Review*, ITS (revised on IG to I reading) 5: birds$_\wedge$] ~, *Northwest Review* 9: They slowly enlarge to our eyes. Now] SP75 eliminates the stanza break after this line. 10: whiteness] whiteness of snow *Northwest Review*

248 **II. Fog** Text: I. Variants: *Reporter*, 21 Sept. 1967, p. 49 (as "Whiteness of Fog on Wintry Mountains"), SP75. The *Reporter* version is dedicated to Baudouin and Annie de Moustier, and the three subsections are untitled, although the poem is printed in three columns which correspond to the subsections in I and SP75. In SP75, the subsections of this poem are marked with Arabic numerals in brackets rather than with capital letters in brackets.

248 **[A]**

249 **[B]** 1: oh, contextless] contextless SP75

249 **[C]** 5: Yes,] Oh, *Reporter*, ITS (revised on IG to I reading) 6: once you] you once *Reporter*, ITS (revised on IG to I reading) 12: Come back, I would hear your voice:] In *Reporter* there is no stanza break after this line. Since the third section in *Reporter*

breaks the pattern of the other two sections (four tercets followed by a single line) and since the last line in *Reporter* is squeezed at the very bottom of the page, probably there is a compositor's error in *Reporter.*

Audubon: A Vision

Much of this book-length sequence was published in magazines as several separate sequences. All of the subsequence "The Dream He Never Knew the End Of," was published in *Harper's,* Aug. 1969, pp. 73–75 (using Arabic Numerals rather than capital letters for its sections). A sequence entitled "Audubon: A Vision and a Question for You" was published in *New Yorker,* 20 Sept. 1969, pp. 42–43. The *NY* sequence gave section numbers in capital Roman numerals (and small letters in parentheses for its subsections), but no section titles (I will use the first lines as titles, and the titles of the corresponding parts in A where necessary for clarity). It consisted, in order, of "Was not the lost dauphin, though handsome was only" (I [A] in A), "The Sign Whereby He Knew" subsequence (including "His life, at the end, seemed–even the anguish–simple" (IV [A] in A), "Keep store, dandle babies, and at night nuzzle" (IV [C] in A), and "The world declares itself. That voice" (IV [E] in A)), "The Sound of That Wind" subsequence (including "He walked in the world. Knew the lust of the eye"(V [A] in A), and "Night leaned, and now leans" (V [B] in A), "Their Footless Dance" (VI in A), and "Tell me a story" (VII [B] in A). Finally, *Yale Review* published a sequence called "Lyrics from *Audubon: A Vision*" which included "October: and the bear" (I [B] in A) "In this season the waters shrink" (IV [B] in A), " Listen! Stand very still and" (IV [D] in A), and "For everything there is a season" (V [C] in A).

The attributions to the epigraphs are introduced by em-dashes in all of the published editions, but I have not followed that practice here, in order to preserve consistency with epigraphs elsewhere. In A the first attribution is in all caps and the second is in italics; in SP75 both attributions are in all caps. On SP85G Warren instructs the typesetter that the epigraph from de Andrade should be set as verse, with the line endings as they appear here. But the typesetter did not follow Warren's instructions.

The section numbers are Roman numerals without periods in all of the published versions. I have set them differently to preserve consistency with how section numbers are set elsewhere. Introductory Note: without his help] without his help, SP85 (in pencil on SP85TS). The last two sentences in ATS are: "He was, indeed, a fantasist of talent. Legends accreted about him, but the legend that he was the lost Dauphin of France, the son of the feckless Louis XVI and Marie Antoinette—did not, apparently, enter the picture until after his death, in 1851." In earlier versions of the note Warren is less positive that Audubon had nothing to do with the legend about his birth. Warren corrected the note to the A reading on AG.

254 **Audubon: A Vision**

254 **I. Was Not the Lost Dauphin**

254 **[A]** Text: A. Variants: *New Yorker,* 20 Sept. 1969, p. 42, SP75, SP85. In ATS part [A] is a photocopy, titled "Audubon: A Vision and a Question for You", scotch-taped onto the back of a piece of Random House stationery. The section title, "Was Not the Lost Dauphin," is added in blue pen. 2: Base-born] Baseborn *NY* 4: passion—] ~, ATS (but revised on AG to A reading) 7: break;] ~, ATS (but revised on AG to A) 9: outthrust,] out-thrust, ATS (Warren's letter of July 23, 1969 to Erskine notes that he can't settle on a proper treatment of this word—although he deleted the hyphen on AG—and leaves it to Erskine, who deleted the hyphen.) 12: Pulled by a string.] The line straddles the stanza break that follows this text. There is no stanza break, either here or at the end of the line, in *NY*. The stanza break, and line straddle, is marked by cutting of the taped-in text in ATS, and is marked "note #" in blue pencil. 14: hoar frost,] hoarfrost, *NY* 15: Thought:] The quad spaces after "Thought:" and "Thinking" are marked in ATS. There are no such quad spaces in *NY*. 17: Thinking: "*Ardea occidentalis,* heron, the great one."] Thinking: "*Casmerodius albus,* heron, white." *NY*, ATS (but revised on AG to A)

254 **[B]** Text: A. Variants: *Yale Review,* 59 (Autumn 1969), p. 1, SP75, SP85. ATS is typescript for this page. 1: October:] OCTOBER: *YR* 3: tongue, pink as a baby's, out-crisps] tongue, out-crisped ATS (but changed on AG to A). In Warren's letter of July 23, 1969, he leaves it to Erskine's discretion whether to remove or retain the hyphen. Erskine retained it. 3: The bear's tongue ... blueberry.] In a letter received by Albert Erskine on June 20, 1969, Warren proposes that these two lines read "The tongue, pink as a baby's, crisps the extended tip. / It bleeds the black blood of the crushed blue-berry." But further revisions followed on AG. The letter does make it clear, however, that this section was placed here sometime between April 10 (when it was a part of section IV) and June 20. 3: out-crisps] crisps *YR* 4: It bleeds] Bleeds ATS (revised on AG to A) 4: blueberry.] blue berry ATS (revised on AG to A) 9: blueberries,] blue berries, ATS (revised on AG to A) 11: like mica, glint / In the sunlight.] like mica, / Glint in the sunlight. *YR*, glint like mica in the light. ATS (revised on AG to A) 13: Thinks] He thinks ATS (revised on AG to A)

255 **II. The Dream He Never Knew the End Of** Text: A. Variants: *Harper's,* Aug. 1969, pp. 75–77 (as "The Dream He Never Knew the End Of: An Episode from Audubon, 'The Prairie,' ") SP75, SP85. *Harper's* titles the subsections with Arabic numerals rather than capital letters in brackets. ATS is a carbon copy, titled "The Dream He Never Knew the End Of (An Episode from Audubon)" with the section number added in blue pencil.

255 **[A]** 1: the call, / A crow, sweet in distance, then sudden / The clearing:] sudden / The clearing: *Harper's*, ATS (revised in black pencil to the reading in A) 3: cornstalks] corn-stalks *Harper's*, ATS (revised on AG to A) 8: ridgepole,] ridge-pole, ATS (revised on AG to A) 9: stands,] stand, ATS (revised in blue pencil to reading in A) 10: smoke,] ~. ATS (revised in blue pencil to reading in A) 12: axe] axe-edge *Harper's*, ATS (revised on AG to A)

255 **[B]**

256 **[C]** 12: leastwise,] least-wise, *Harper's*, ATS (revised on AG to A)

256 **[D]** 7: bearskin,] bear-skins, *Harper's*, bear-skin, ATS (revised on AG to A) 21: her] his *Harper's*, ATS This change makes a material difference to the poem, since Audubon cannot see the Indian's warning gesture if his back is turned, but the version in *Harper's* is clearly the result of a blunder (see Warren's letter to Howard Moss of August 19, 1969, and his letter to Albert Erskine of the same date). Warren corrected the error in proof. 23: down:] ~. *Harper's*, ATS (revised on AG to A) 24: bearskins,] bear-skins, *Harper's*, ATS (revised on AG to A) 25: stink, the] stink. The *Harper's*, ATS (revised on AG to A) 25: primed and cocked.] *Harper's* and ATS have no stanza break after this line. Warren changed the text on AG to the reading in A.

257 **[E]** 6: the hot] hot SP85 (revised on SP85G to SP85) 11: *whish*] Italics added in blue pen in ATS.

258 **[F]** 2: Behind] And behind *Harper's*, ATS (revised on AG to A) 3: Snores.] The line straddles the stanza break that follows this text. *Harper's* and ATS have no stanza break here, breaking the stanza after "He thinks: ' Now.' " But Warren changed the lineation on AG and called Erskine's attention to it in his letter of July 23, 1969. 3: Snores.] Snores. Or pretends to. SP75, SP85

258 **[G]** 13: Tell] Oh, tell *Harper's*, ATS (revised in blue pencil to reading in A)

258 **[H]** 1: travelers] travellers ATS (Warren's letter of July 23, 1969, left the correct spelling of this word to Erskine)

259 **[I]** 11: slack side] slack SP85 (revised on SP85G to SP85)

259 **[J]** 4: Than] Then SP75 (SP85G reads with SP75 but is corrected to SP85) 22: that he is in the manly state.] of his erection. ATS (but corrected in blue pen, not in Warren's handwriting, to reading in A). The ATS reading is also the reading of the manuscripts. But in an undated letter to Erskine, probably written sometime after April 10 and before April 20, 1969, Warren writes that "Erection is strictly a 20th century semi-polite, semi-technical term," and proposes two alternatives, "So became aware of his pecker at ready" and "So became aware that he was in the manly state." He left the final choice to Erskine. The galleys show the reading in A.

260 **[K]** 7: lifelong,] life-long, *Harper's*, ATS (revised on AG to A) 7: that, lifelong, she had dreamed] that she had, life-long, dreamed ATS (revised on AG to A)

260 **[L]** 6: deerskin] deer-skin *Harper's*, ATS (revised on AG to A)

260 **[M]** 3: Indian,] $\sim_{\wedge}$ *Harper's* 10: snowflakes,] snow flakes, *Harper's*, ATS (revised on AG to A) 17: These] Those *Harper's* 17: he] be ATS 20: shoulder.] In ATS at the bottom of the page at the end of the section is typed "Robert Penn Warren," indicating that the typescript of "The Dream He Never Knew the End Of" was sent to the editor separately.

261 **III. We Are Only Ourselves** Text: A. Variants: SP75, SP85. ATS is a photocopy, with the title added in blue pen. 3: Yes,] Oh, ATS (revised on AG to A)

261 **IV. The Sign Whereby He Knew**

261 **[A]** Text: A. Variants: *New Yorker,* 20 Sept. 1969, p. 42, SP75, SP85. The section title is added in blue pen on ATS. Subsection A is a photocopy of draft D, cut and taped onto the back of a piece of Random House stationery. 2: be,] $\sim_{\wedge}$ SP85 (yet the comma appears in SP85G and is not removed in page proofs. This is a puzzling variant.) 5: blessedness!—] blessedness! *NY* 10: trigger-squeeze] trigger squeeze *NY* (Warren's letter of July 23, 1969, left it to Erskine's choice whether to hyphenate this word.)

262 **[B]** Text: A. Variants: *Yale Review,* 59 (Autumn 1969), p. 1, SP75, SP85. In ATS a typescript of what is now section I:B is taped in here on the back of the same sheet of Random House stationery as section a, as section b (corrected from c) but it is canceled in blue pencil. The current section IV:B follows, on an inserted typed page marked "INSERT as IV-b." Warren's letter of April 10, 1969 to Albert Erskine proposed placing "October: and the bear," "In this season the spring shrinks," and "Listen! Stand very still, and" as sections c, d, and e of IV. But later revisions were to come as well.

262 **[C]** Text: A. Variants: *New Yorker,* 20 Sept. 1969, p. 42, SP75, SP85. In ATS the text is a photocopy from draft D, cut and taped onto the back of a piece of Random House stationery and renumbered (it was subsection b, not c, in draft D). 2: hazelnut-shaped] hazel-nut-shaped *NY*, ATS (revised on AG to A) 3: mark-up] markup *NY* 7: In the height] At the height SP75 (revised on SP75G), SP85 10: campfire,] camp-fire, ATS (revised on AG to A) 11: "God bless you, dear Lucy."] no quotation marks in ATS (revised on AG to A)

262 **[D]** Text: A. Variants: *Yale Review,* 59 (Autumn 1969), p. 2, SP75, SP85. In ATS the text of this subsection is typescript, marked "INSERT as IV–d". A typescript of what is now section IV:B follows, taped onto the same page, but it is canceled. 4: tushed] tusked SP75 (revised on SP75G), SP85 7: The call,] His call, *YR*, That sound, ATS (revised on AG to A)

263 **[E]** Text: A. Variants: *New Yorker,* 20 Sept. 1969, p. 42, SP75, SP85. The text in ATS is a photocopy from draft D, with the section number corrected from c to e. 6: Be spoken?] There is no stanza break after this line in SP85. There is no correction to this effect on SP85TS or SP85G, so it is probably a typesetter's error that Warren did not catch.

263 **V. The Sound of That Wind** Text: A. Variants: *New Yorker,* 20 Sept. 1969, pp. 42–43, SP75, SP85.

263 **[A]** The text of this subsection is a photocopy from draft D. 1: world. Knew] In *NY* there is extra white space after the period, which may serve a poetic purpose. But there is no indication of extra space in ATS here. 2: The quotations are indented so that the lines align with the first letter of the quotation. Because Warren lineated these quotations the same way every time he printed them, I am satisfied that he intended them to be seen not as single very long lines which overflow the right margin, but, despite the lack of initial capitalization, as several indented lines. The typescript is lineated differently from the published version in only one place. But in his letter to Albert Erskine of July 23, 1969, Warren notes that he changed the lineation in this place and expects it to be adhered to. 3: particularly / to acquire a] particularly to acquire / a ATS (revised on AG to A) 5: He dreamed of hunting with Boone, from imagination painted his portrait.] He hunted with Boone, and heard the tale of the old times. ATS (revised in pencil, not in Warren's

handwriting, to the reading in A) 6: proved] knew *NY* ATS (revised to the reading in A in blue pen, not in Warren's handwriting) 7: white-headed] White-headed *NY*, ATS (revised on AG to A) 7: eagle.] Eagle. *NY*, ATS (revised on AG to A) 17: couloirs] *couloirs NY* (Warren's letter of July 23, 1969, left it to Erskine whether to italicize this word.) 26: Nor] Or *NY* 31: honor. Far,] In *NY* there is extra white space after the period. 33: bird-calls] birdcalls *NY* 35: end,] $\sim_{\wedge}$ *NY*, ATS (revised on AG to A) 37: mouthpiece] mouth-piece ATS (revised on AG to A)

265 **[B]** Text: A. Variants: *New Yorker,* 20 Sept. 1969, p. 43, SP75, SP85. 1: So died in his bed, and] Line does not appear in *NY*. The line is added in blue pen, not in Warren's handwriting, in ATS. Warren sent the revision in a letter to Albert Erskine of April 10, 1969. 5: with no sound sweeps] progresses ATS (revised in blue pen, not in Warren's handwriting, to "with no sound swings") In his April 10, 1969, letter to Erskine, he had merely changed the text from "progresses" to "swings". Warren corrected the text to the A reading on AG. 6: mud bank,] mudbank, *NY* 7: root-system] root system *NY* 7: now-stubbed] now stubbed *NY* 12: sheep-herder,] sheepherder, *NY* 12: Bitterroot,] Bitter Roots, ATS (revised in green pencil to "Bitter Root," but in his letter of July 23, 1969, Warren left the correct spelling of this word to Erskine, although on AG he corrected the text to the reading in A) 13: The light goes out.] The candle is blown out. SP85 (revised on SP85G to SP85)

265 **[C]** Text: A. Variants: *Yale Review,* 59 (Autumn 1969), p. 2, SP75, SP85. In ATS, the text is typescript, marked "INSERT as V-e". In Warren's letter of April 10, 1969, Warren had proposed inserting this section as section C of V. 2: the dream] a dream *YR*, ATS (revised on AG to A) 4: such a] that ATS (revised on AG to A) 6: ripens.] ripes. ATS (revised to A on AG)

266 **VI. Love and Knowledge** Text: A. Variants: *New Yorker,* 20 Sept. 1969, p. 43, SP75, SP85. In ATS the text is a photocopy from draft D. The section title is added in blue pen. 7: In air] In an air ATS (revised on AG to A) 8: iron,] $\sim$; *NY* 12: was bowed] bowed ATS (revised on AG to A) 17: One name for it is knowledge.] Its name is knowledge. ATS (revised in pencil in Warren's handwriting to the reading in A)

266 **VII. Tell Me a Story** The text in ATS is a photocopy from draft D, with the section title added in blue pen.

266 **[A]** Text: A. Variants: SP75, SP85, Broadside, Minneapolis: Coffee House Press at Minnesota Center for Book Arts, 1987. 1: a boy,] as a boy, *Coffee House*

267 **[B]** Text: A. Variants: *New Yorker,* 20 Sept. 1969, p. 43, SP75, SP85.

Or Else

Poem/Poems 1968–1974

Warren included the following prefatory note in *Or Else*:

> This book is conceived as a single long poem composed of a number of shorter poems as sections or chapters. It is dated 1968–1974, but a few short pieces come from a period some ten years before, when I was working toward a similar long poem. After a time, however, I was to find that that poem was disintegrating into a miscellany, and so abandoned the project and published the pieces that I wished to preserve under the title "Notes on a Life to Be Lived." More lately, working on this book, I have decided that all except three of those early pieces have a place in the thematic structure of this poem. For the same reason, I have here drawn another poem, "The True Nature of Time," from a more recent volume.

The manuscripts indicate laborious drafting and rethinking of this volume. The working title of the volume was "Essay Toward the Human Understanding." There are two "setting typescripts" in the Beinecke Library, only one of which appears to be much marked up for the typesetter. The dates in the subtitle in the setting typescript are 1968–1973. In the original contents of the typescript "What You Sometimes Feel on Your Face at Night" and "Bad Year, Bad War, a New Year's Card, 1969" are interchanged; "Flaubert in Egypt" is a late, penciled, addition; and "Ways of Day" appears after "Composition in Gold and Red-Gold" but is crossed out. The typescript is for the most part photocopy, and the section numbers are in typing (not merely written in, and not typed later on the photocopy). Warren must have had a fresh typescript made of most of the manuscript at a fairly late stage of the process. Almost none of the markup on the manuscript is clearly in Warren's hand, but the galley corrections are certainly Warren's.

On the galleys of the prefatory note, Warren corrects the closing date of the volume to 1974, and adds the last sentence.

In OE the section numbers do not have periods, although they are followed by a publisher's ornament. In SP75 the section numbers do not have periods. The sections are not numbered in SP85 at all. In OE and SP75 the poem titles are in all caps, and the section titles are in small caps.

Warren prepared the revised copy of this book, which is now in the Special Collections Department of the Woodruff Library at Emory University, on May 23, 1987. I quote from that copy by permission of the Emory University Library.

The section of SP85 from this volume was prepared for the most part from taped-in photocopies from SP75. For some reason I cannot guess, SP85TS begins to use photocopy and taped-in photocopy from OE from part-way through "I Am Dreaming of a White Christmas" to part-way through "Rattlesnake Country," after which it uses SP75 again. Because the revisions for SP85 are often problematic, I have indicated where they were made on SP85TS.

271 **I. The Nature of a Mirror** Text: OE. Variants: *Salmagundi,* (Skidmore College, Saratoga, NY), nos. 22–23 (Spring–Summer 1973), pp. 24–25, SP75, SP85. In OETS there is a canceled sequence title: "Essay on the Human Understanding." 1: eye, and I / Have murder] eye, / And I have murder *Salmagundi*, OETS (revised to OE on OEG) 8: I must tell you] No stanza break after this text in *Salmagundi.*

271 **Interjection #1: The Need for Re-evaluation** Text: OE. Variant: SP75

271 **II. Natural History** Text: OE. Variants: *New Yorker,* 1 April 1972, p. 38, SP75, SP85. 1: rain$_\wedge$] $\sim$, *NY* 5: clearly astronomical.] SP85 omits the stanza break after this line, probably in error, since it breaks the pattern of alternating one and two line stanzas in the rest of the poem. The revision does not appear on SP85TS and is not called for by Warren on any of the galleys. It is probably a typographical error in SP85G. 9: clocks all over the continent have stopped.] the clocks have stopped all over the continent. *NY* 10: old mother] mother *NY* 12: canceled] cancelled *NY*

272 **III. Time as Hypnosis** Text: OE. Variants: *I. A. Richards: Essays in His Honor,* ed. Reuben Brower, Helen Vendler, and John Hollander, (New York: Oxford University Press, 1973), pp. 3–4, SP75. *Richards* includes, in parentheses, the following epigraph: To I. A. Richards, this poem about a country snowfall of far away and long ago, which I hope he will explicate. 6: was all] all was *Richards* 32: field mouse's foot] foot of a field mouse *Emory* 34: the wing-flurried] wing-flurried *Richards*

273 **IV. Blow, West Wind** Text: OE. Variants: *Partisan Review,* 33 (Spring 1966), p. 220, SP66, SP75, SP85. The text of this section in OETS is a corrected photocopied page from SP66. 3: and the evidence,] for the evidence, *PR* 13: with the] the *PR*

274 **Interjection #2: Caveat** Text: OE. Variants: *Sou'wester* (Southern Illinois University), ns 2 (Fall 1973), pp. 62–63, SP75. *Sou'wester* lacks the dedication, but is marked (syllabics). None of the magazine versions of the "interjections" from this volume are labeled as "interjections." The dedication is added in blue pen, not in Warren's hand, on OETS. 6: know] know that OETS (revised to OE on OEG) 7: you are] that you're *Sou'wester* 19: Now, it only / glows a little, inconspicuously] At first, it on- / ly glows a little, not importantly *Sou'wester*, At first, it only / glows a little, inconspicuously OETS (revised to OE on OEG) 21: But soon,] Later, *Sou'wester*, OETS (revised to OE on OEG) 25: twitching. Then,] twitching, then, *Sou'wester*, OETS (revised to OE on OEG) 34: screams] The stanza breaks after this line and the next are added in blue pen in OETS. 35: ecstasy] ecstacy *Sou'wester*

275 **V. I Am Dreaming of a White Christmas: The Natural History of a Vision** Text: OE. Variants: *Atlantic Monthly,* Dec. 1973, pp. 84–90 (as "The Natural History of a Vision"), SP75, SP85. *Atlantic* does not put the section titles in square brackets, and is dedicated "To Andrew V. Corry". OETS is typed with a different typewriter from that used up to here, but the accurate section number is typed, and OETS is a photocopy, as up to here.

275 **[1]** 4: yet—] ~, *Atlantic,* OETS (revised on OETS to OE reading) 5: water—] ~, *Atlantic,* OETS (revised on OETS to OE reading) 17: Entering, see.] The line straddles the stanza break after this text, except in *Atlantic,* where there is neither a line break nor a stanza break at this point. OETS followed *Atlantic* but is corrected in red pencil to the reading in OE. 18: Standing here, breathe the dry air.] The line straddles not only the stanza break but also the section break break after this text. That this is Warren's intention is clearly marked on OETS. Because the line straddles a section break, the straddling will not be reflected in the line count.

275 **[2]** 10: yet] still *Atlantic,* OETS, OEG (revised to OE on second set of galleys) yet, SP85 (revised on SP85G to SP85) 11: tattered in Time.] tattered. SP85 (revised on SP85G to SP85) 16: Is not there.] The line straddles the stanza break and the section break after this text.

276 **[3]** 5: when, long back, crushed,] long back, but SP85 (revised on SP85G to SP85) 6: But now,] Now SP85 (revised on SP85G to SP85) 7: Crushed and desiccated,] Crushed and dessicated, *Atlantic,* OETS (revised to OE on OEG) Desiccated, SP85 (revised on SP85G to SP85) 10: Had been blue.] The line straddles the stanza break and the section break after this text.

276 **[4]**

277 **[5]** 4: where now] where *Atlantic,* OETS (revised to OE on OEG) 5: Is not] Is not now *Atlantic,* OETS (revised to OE on OEG) 7: fire^] ~, SP85 (revised on SP85G to SP85) 8: To stare at.] The line straddles the stanza break and section break after this text. Because the line straddles a section break, the straddle will not be reflected in the line count.

277 **[6]** 6: warped^] ~, *Atlantic,* OETS (revised to OE on OEG) 7: I feel] There is a stanza break after this line in SP85. Because this is a point where two taped-in extracts from SP75 join, probably the stanza break is added in error. 21: always were] were always SP85 (revised on SP85G to SP85)

278 **[7]**

279 **[8]** 19: Breath comes.] The line straddles the stanza break and the section break that follows this text. Because the line straddles a section break, the straddle will not be reflected in the line count.

279 **[9]** 2: Now am] Am *Atlantic* Now am. OETS (Added in blue pen not in Warren's handwriting in OETS, probably misreading Warren's instructions, because he does not imagine himself vanishing and reappearing in the same place, but suddenly finding himself in a different place, Times Square. In OEG Warren deletes the extraneous period.) 5: Of a sudden, know:] The line straddles the stanza break that follows this text. 5: Of a sudden, know:] SP85TS consists of photocopy and taped in photocopy from OE (not from SP75) after this line. 6: Late summer] Summer *Atlantic,* OETS (revised in blue pen not in Warren's handwriting to reading in OE) 11: arm-pit,] armpit, *Atlantic* 12: The flesh is mine.] This stanza omitted in SP85 (revised on SP85G to SP85) 15: south-eastward,] northeastward, *Atlantic,* OETS (revised in orange pencil, not in Warren's hand, to reading in OE) 18: cot-frame,] cot frame, *Atlantic*

280 **[10]** 8: Their drawers are drying stiff at the crotch, and] There is a stanza break in SP85 (but not in SP85TS) after this line. Warren added the stanza break on SP85G, probably mistaking his own intentions. The stanza break does not appear on the page proofs, but Warren has added it in again, marking it as a printer's error.

281 **[11]** 2: But am] Am *Atlantic,* OETS (revised in blue pen to reading in OE) 3: here. Am] here, am *Atlantic,* OETS (revised in blue pen to reading in OE) 5: West] west SP85

(in pencil on SP85TS) 7: Percé] Perce SP85 (in pencil on SP85TS) 9: Percé] Perce SP85 (in pencil on SP85TS) 9: 7,000] 7000 *Atlantic*

281 **[12]** 4: discover the logic of.] make into a poem. OETS (revised in blue pen to reading in OE)

282 **Interjection #3: I Know a Place Where All is Real** Text: OE. Variants: *Teacher & Critic: Essays by and about Austin Warren,* ed. Myron Simon and Harvey Gross, (Los Angeles: Plantin Press, 1976), p. 98 (AW), SP75. OETS is typescript, not photocopy, using the first typewriter. Dedication] (For Austin Warren, who has been there) AW 14: travelers$_\wedge$] ~, AW 16: unacceptable] inacceptable AW, OETS (revised in black pencil in Warren's hand to reading in OE) 24: sometimes] often AW

282 **VI. Ballad of Mister Dutcher and the Last Lynching in Gupton** Text: OE. Variants: *New York Review of Books,* 24 Jan. 1974, p. 35, SP75. *NYRB* has a headnote: (octosyllabics). In OETS the title is corrected to "Mister" from "Mr." in black pencil in Warren's hand. The section number is added in blue ink to OETS. OETS is a photocopy of a typescript typed with the same typewriter first used in OETS. But the typewritten changes are typed with the second typewriter. 4: there's not even a / name for—all this the same as when,] you didn't even / have a name for—the same as when, *NYRB*, you didn't even have / a name for—all the same as when, OETS (revised in typewriting to the reading in OE) 24: on] for *NYRB*, on a OETS (but corrected to OE in red pen) 31: where] where the *NYRB*, OETS (revised in red pen to OE) 49: four-bit] four-hit *NYRB*, OETS (revised in red pen to OE) 61: mighty slow, while back there] mighty damn slow, while back yonder *NYRB* 63: a business transaction concern- / ing rope was in due process. It] a large business transaction con- / cerning rope was in process. It *NYRB*, a business transaction con- / cerning rope was in process. It OETS (revised in typing to OE. The first line in OE is not an octosyllabic line unless you pronounce "business" southern-style, as "bizness.") 71: of rope . . . and years,] which the line could slide through easy / as a greased piston, or the dose / of salts through the widow-woman, / and that was what he, all the years, *NYRB*, OETS (revised in typing to OE) 83: out, which, / you could tell, was not in any / great hurry anyway. Well, what] out. What *NYRB*, OETS (revised to OE on OEG) 106: Mister Dutcher'd thought we'd never know.] we'd all thought we'd never know he knew. SP75 (added in pencil on SP75G) 107: entitled . . . truly] entitled to / something he can call truly OETS (revised in typing to OE) 116: mill,] ~; *Emory* 124: speed-hurled] wind-hurled *NYRB*, OETS (revised in typing to OE) 125: glass,] glass of an airplane window, *Emory* 128: and if . . . aren't too high.]

and I
haven't much, but some time, going
back home, I might take time to prowl
the cemetery to locate
the stone the Dutcher name would be
on, if grass and ragweed aren't too high.
it's on, if grass and ragweed aren't too high.

NYRB The second to last line in *NYRB* is not an octosyllabic, and the last line, apparently a revision printed in *NYRB* by mistake, does not make grammatical sense as it stands. Since the last line of every stanza has ten syllables, the second to last line must be an imperfect version of the last line that found its way into the text, and the last line must be a revision that Warren has imperfectly worked in. 128: and if . . . going back,] and I / haven't much, but some time, going back, OETS (revised in typing to OE)

285 **VII. Chain Saw at Dawn in Vermont In Time of Drouth** Text: OE. Variants: *Sewanee Review,* 74 (Summer 1966), pp. 590–92 (as second part of "Three Poems" sequence, with "Vision Under the October Mountain," and "Ways of Day"), SP66, SP75. The title in *SR* is "Chain Saw in Vermont, In Time of Drouth." The text in OETS is a revised photocopy from SP66.

285 **1.** 2: chain saw] Chain-saw *SR* 4: swish,] -swish, *SR* 5: No—] It is *SR* SP66 (revised in blue ink on OETS) 8: Lash and blood-lust] Blood-lust and lash *SR*, SP66

(revised in red pencil on OETS) 11: that] the *SR* 18: sawyer‸] ~, *SR* 19: Beads] Now beads *SR* 24: Have I learned how to live?] In *SR* this line appears at the beginning of section 2, where it is a separate stanza.

286 **2.** 8: leaned] had leaned *Emory* 24: in] into *Emory*

287 **VIII. Small White House** Text: OE. Variants: SP66, *Saturday Review,* 25 Feb. 1967, p. 38, SP75. In *SatR* the poem is described as extracted from the forthcoming OE, but the text in fact follows the version in SP66. The text in OETS is a revised photocopy from SP66. 2: and‸] ~, *Emory* 4: Leprous with light.] Like paranoia. SP66, *SatR*, OETS (revised to OE on OEG)

287 **Interjection #4: Bad Year, Bad War: A New Year's Card, 1969** Text: OE. Variants: *New York Review of Books,* 13 March 1969, p. 27 (as "Bad Year, Bad War: New Year's Card"), *Sense and Sensibility in Twentieth-Century Writing: A Gathering in Memory of William Van O'Connor,* ed. Brom Weber, (Carbondale: Southern Illinois University Press, 1970), pp. 153–54 (Weber) (as "Bad Year, Bad War: New Year's Card"), SP75. Both *NYRB* and Weber omit the date from the title. In OETS the number in the title is corrected to 4 from 6. OETS is a photocopy of a text prepared on the first typewriter. epigraph] "Without the shedding of blood there is no remission of sins." *NYRB,* Weber, The revised epigraph is pasted onto OETS. The breaks in the lines of the epigraph are indicated on OETS, and since SP75 repeats the same line breaks they are followed here as well. 1: year] end Weber 4: evil enemies] those evil people *NYRB,* Weber, OETS (revised in red pen in Warren's hand to OE) 5: History;] ~, *NYRB,* Weber, OETS (revised to OE on OEG) 6: report‸] ~, *NYRB,* Weber 8: understood.] ~, OETS (revised in red pen to OE) 12: There] there *NYRB* 16: of others, whose innocence is only incidental,] of those incidentally innocent *NYRB,* Weber, OETS (revised in red pen to OE)

288 **IX. Forever O'Clock**

288 **[1]** Text: OE. Variants: *Yale Review,* 63 (Summer 1974), pp. 545–47, SP75. *YR* is the first section of a sequence called "Watch a Clock Closely." ("There's a Grandfather's Clock in the Hall" is the other section.) In OE and *YR* this poem is written in two-line stanzas. In SP75 the stanza breaks are different, although the lineation is the same. (SP75 does not break up the long lines in the same way as OE, however.) On OETS the section number is added in red pencil, which is unusual for OETS, in which most sections were typed with the correct section numbers. OETS is a photocopy of a typescript made on the first typewriter. On OETS is a note to the typesetter, "set line for line and follow ms. for indentation" and "Please indent as typed." Since Warren did not reproduce how he bent the long lines when he republished the poem, and since the line bends do not occur in the same places in the original publication in *YR*, I have chosen to regard the bending of long lines as a feature of the book design rather than of the versification. Warren had this poem retyped for SP75, and in that typescript, as in SP75 itself, the run-over portions of long lines are indented from the left rather than, in Warren's usual practice (and his practice in this poem in its appearances in *YR*, OETS, and OE), flushed to the right. That Warren did not correct the typescript argues that whether the run-over portions of long lines are set flushed to the right or indented from the left was a feature of book design rather than of versification. The consistency with which Warren chooses right justification for run-over portions of lines is thus probably a function of a desire for uniform appearance of the volume, rather than a function of the versification of the poem, else he would have corrected his typist's error here more vigilantly. In *YR* the section numbers are in parentheses without periods, in OE the section numbers are in square brackets without periods, and in SP75 they are not in brackets but have periods. 1: A clock] A CLOCK *YR* 10: bedroom‸] ~, SP75 10: where you are] offhand where you are SP75 10: do not know offhand whose] do not know whose *YR,* SP75 10: there beside you.] there in the dark beside you. *YR* 10: beside you.] The first stanza break in SP75 follows this text.

289 **[2]** 3: two-year-old] two-year old *YR*, OETS, OEG (revised on second set to OE) 3: with hair] with her hair *YR* 3: spindly] splindly OETS (revised to OE on OEG) 4: middle,] ~‸ *YR* 4: red] red-clay SP75 4: in the] in SP75 6: whatever had been] what had been SP75 8: a dominecker] the dominecker *YR* 8: hen, flattened] hen that is flattened

YR 8: down,] $\sim_\wedge$ *YR* 8: of the pin-oak.] The second stanza break in SP75 follows this text. 9: the gray] gray *YR* 9: the heat.] heat. SP75 13: slow-falling] slowly falling *YR* 15: 1931] green 1931 *YR* 15: seen,] $\sim_\wedge$ OETS (revised to OE on OEG) 16: the horizon.] The third stanza break in SP75 follows this text. It is added in pencil on SP75G.

289 **[3]** 5: like brass.] The fourth stanza break in SP75 follows this text. Notice that this stanza break falls in the middle of what in OE is a two-line stanza.

290 **X. Rattlesnake Country** Text: OE. Variants: *Esquire,* Dec. 1973, pp. 206–9, SP75, SP85, *Helsinki.* The section titles in *Esquire* do not have periods. *Esquire* and OETS have no dedication, but *Esquire* has the following epigraph: "It is all a field of vipers, but memory knows the redeeming path". Warren added the dedication on OEG. OETS is a photocopy of a typescript made on the first typewriter, but different darknesses of type show that there was some cutting and pasting on the original.

290 **1.** 1: anger of sun on the mountains,] anger of sun on / The mountains *Helsinki* 2: One little patch of cool lawn:] The line straddles the stanza break that follows this text. In *Helsinki* the line straddles a line break, not a stanza break. 4: Held] Holds *Emory* 5: house porch,] house-porch, *Esquire* 6: wolf-waiting. Its turn / Will, again, come.] wolf-waiting. / Its turn will again come. *Helsinki* 7: Will, again, come.] The line straddles the stanza break that follows this text. In *Helsinki* the line straddles a line break, not a stanza break. 7: Meanwhile, wicker chairs, all day, ... follows] These lines are substantially different in *Helsinki*:

Meanwhile, wicker chairs,
All day, follow the shimmering shade of the lone
Cottonwood, the way that Time,
Sadly seeking to know its own nature, follows

10: sun-dial.] sundial. *Esquire* 11: The sprinkler ejects its misty rainbow.] The line straddles the stanza break that follows this text. In *Helsinki* the line straddles a line break, not a stanza break. 14: under the white] under white *Helsinki* 18: Get heavier all afternoon.] The line straddles the stanza break that follows this text. Because there is a page turn here in *Helsinki*, it is unclear whether there is a stanza break here or not, although the usual practice of *Helsinki* in this poem is to break lines across line breaks where the other versions break them across stanza breaks. 19: When some secret, ... and white.] These lines in *Helsinki* are substantially different:

When some secret high drift of air comes eastward
Over the lake, ash, gray, sifts minutely down on
Our lunch-time ice cream. Which is vanilla. And white.

20: gray,] grey, *Esquire* 21: lunch-time] lunchtime *Esquire* 23: lake there.] lake. SP85 (revised on SP85G to SP85)

291 **2.** 4: Is difficult.] The line straddles the stanza break that follows this text. In *Helsinki* the line straddles a line break, not a stanza break. 6: Lopsided,] $\sim_\wedge$ *Helsinki* 6: blood or bruised cinnabar, because of] blood or bruised / Cinnabar, because of *Helsinki* 7: smoke there] smoke westward there *Helsinki* 8: the red eyes] red eyes *Helsinki* 10: that is] of SP75 that is SP85 of *Helsinki* (It would be a mistake to think of the SP85 as a revision to SP75 that would restore the OE reading, because at this point SP85TS consists of cut-and-taped photocopy from OE. That Warren revised the line in *Helsinki* back to the SP75 reading argues further that the SP85 reading is an error, not a revision. 10: mountain] far mountain *Emory* 12: eyes of fire that / Are] eye of fire that / Is *Emory* 14: But,] $\sim_\wedge$ *Helsinki* 15: When I got out, the moon had emerged from cloud, and I ... Unbreathing medium, and beyond] These lines are substantially different in *Helsinki*:

When I got out, the moon had emerged from cloud,
And I entered the lake. Swam
Miles out. Toward moonset. Motionless,
Awash, metaphysically undone in that silvered
And unbreathing medium, and beyond

17: Toward the moonset.] Toward moonset. SP85 (revised on SP85G to SP85) 21: down,] $\sim_{\wedge}$ *Helsinki* 22: I gave the now-dark lawn a wide berth.] I gave / The now dark lawn a wide berth. *Helsinki*

291 **3.** 1: *I-yee!*—] The line straddles the stanza break that follows this text. There is no stanza break here in SP75, SP85, or *Helsinki*, although there is a broken line, with the next line indented to the line break of this line. OETS is clear that a stanza break is intended here, however. The stanza break appears in SP85TS (since it is photocopied from OE), but it is closed up in pencil on SP85TS, which argues that SP85 is a revision, not at error. 1: and the wranglers... I hear it.] and they cry on the mountain, and waking at dawn-streak, / I hear it. *Esquire*, OETS (but corrected to OE reading, except that the comma after "wranglers" is omitted. The comma is omitted on OEG as well, but is added on the second set of galleys.), and the wranglers, they cry on the mountain, / And waking, at dawn-streak, I hear it. *Helsinki* 2: At dawn-streak, I hear it.] The line straddles the stanza break that follows this text. In *Helsinki* the line straddles a line break, not a stanza break. 2: High on the mountain ... yet seeps down] High / On the mountains, I hear it, for snow-water there, / Snow long-gone, yet seeps down *Helsinki* 3: snow-water there,] there snow-water, *Esquire* 4: raw edges] edges *Esquire* 6: down, long before daylight, plunging] down, long before / Daylight. They plunge *Helsinki* 7: gloom of the pines,] pine-gloom, *Esquire* 8: Cry out:] The line straddles the stanza break that follows this text. In *Helsinki* the line straddles a line break, not a stanza break. 8: *I-yee!*] The line straddles the stanza break that follows this text. In *Helsinki* the line straddles a line break, not a stanza break. 9: *levis,*] Levi's *Esquire* 9: pulling my boots on, I hear] pulling / My boots on, I hear *Helsinki* 10: mountain,] mountains, *Helsinki* 10: what I have,] what once I have, SP85 (revised on SP85G to SP85) 10: what I have, ... it—the horsemen] *Helsinki* is substantially different:

and what
I have, literally, seen now in my mind see, as
Years later I will, in my mind, see it—the horsemen

12: later, in my mind,] later, *Esquire*, OETS (but corrected to OE) 14: deadfall] dead-fall *Esquire* 14: The deadfall ... and their faces] The deadfall—*I-yee!*—and their faces *Helsinki* 16: the shadow] shadow *Helsinki* 16: *I-yee!*—] There is no line break after this text in *Esquire*. 18: the riderless horses, ... glimmer and roil, go] the riderless / Horses, like quicksilver spilled in / Dark glimmer and roil, go *Helsinki* 20: Pouring] Plunging *Helsinki* 20: Pouring downward.] The line straddles the stanza break that follows this text. In SP85 there is no stanza break here, but there is a broken line, with the next line indented to the line break in this line. There is a stanza break in SP85TS (since it is photocopied from OETS), but it is closed up in pencil on SP85TS, which argues that it is a revision, not an error. In *Helsinki* the line also straddles a line break, not a stanza break. 20: The wranglers cry out.] The line straddles the stanza break that follows this text. In *Helsinki* the line straddles a line break, not a stanza break. 20: And nearer.] Nearer *Helsinki*. 20: And nearer.] The line straddles the stanza break that follows this text. In *Helsinki* the line straddles a line break, not a stanza break. 20: But,] $\sim_{\wedge}$ *Helsinki* 21: coffee-scald and to ... croupy] coffee-scald, I hear / Much nearer, not far from my open window, a croupy *Helsinki* 22: my open window,] my window, *Esquire* 23: Gargle of laughter.] The line straddles the stanza break that follows this text. In *Helsinki* the line straddles a line break, not a stanza break. 23: It is Laughing Boy.] In SP85TS the text is again cut-and-pasted photocopy from SP75 (rather than from OETS) after this line.

292 **4.** 1: Laughing Boy is the name that my host—and friend—gives his yard-hand. ... Hence the name.] These lines are substantially different in *Helsinki*:

Laughing Boy is the name that my host—and friend—
Gives his yard-hand. Laughing Boy is Indian—
Or half—and has a hare-lip. Sometimes,
Before words come, he utters a sound like

Croupy laughter. When he utters that sound,
His face twists. Hence the name.

1: yard-hand.] yard hand. *Esquire* 2: has a hare-lip.] has a hare lip. *Esquire* There is a stanza break in SP85 after this text. Because this is a point where two cut-and-taped sections come together, probably the stanza break is introduced by mistake. 4: Hence the name.] There is no stanza break after this text in *Esquire.* 5: wakes] always wakes *Esquire* 7: daughters out to the lawn. Laughing Boy,] daughters / Out to the lawn. Laughing Boy, *Helsinki* 7: lawn. Laughing Boy, / Who] lawn. / Laughing Boy, who SP75, SP85 (There is a mark in OETS before "Laughing" that may indicate a line break, but it looks more to me as if it indicates that there should be a sentence-ending space after the period of the sentence before.) 9: Of gasoline ... rock-fall.] Of gasoline covered with a saucer on an outer ledge / Of the porch. Big kitchen matches by / The saucer. This at the porch end toward the rock-fall. *Helsinki* 13: and as one whips past, / Douse him.] and, / As one whips past, douse him. *Helsinki.* 16: Snap a match alight.] The line straddles the stanza break that follows this text. In *Helsinki* the line straddles a line break, not a stanza break. 17: good,] right, *Helsinki* 17: just as he makes his rock-hole, / Hit him.] just as he makes it / To his rock-hole, / Hit him. *Helsinki* 18: Hit him. ... raw edge.] *Helsinki* is substantially different:

Hit him. The flame
Makes a sudden soft, gaspy sound at
The hole-mouth, then dances there. The flame
Is spectral in sunlight, but flickers blue at its raw edge.

21: its raw edge.] the raw edge of that hole. *Emory* 22: and sometimes / He gets] and / Sometimes gets *Helsinki* 24: soft,] $\sim_\wedge$ *Helsinki* 24: flame come before/ The] flame come / Before the *Helsinki* 25: has disappeared.] disappears. *Helsinki* 25: The stub-buttoned tail has disappeared.] The line straddles the stanza break that follows this text. In *Helsinki* the line straddles a line break, not a stanza break. 25: Whenever] When *Helsinki* 26: really gets] gets *Helsinki* 26: he makes ... earth-darkness.] These lines are substantially different in *Helsinki*:

he makes that sound
Like croupy laughter. His face twists. Once
I got one myself. I see the stub-buttoned tail
Whip through pale flame down into earth-darkness.

29: into] to *Emory* 30: did you see me, I got him!] I got him! *Helsinki* 31: have] had *Helsinki* 31: stub-tailed] stub-buttoned *Helsinki* 32: Already, that early, the sky shivers with whiteness.] Already, that early, / It shivers with whiteness. *Helsinki*

293 **5.** 2: its] it's *Helsinki* 2: Some from ... long since dead.] These lines are substantially different in *Helsinki*:

Some
From that long-lost summer are now dead, two
Of the girls then young, now after their pains and
Delusions, worthy endeavors and lies, are
Long since dead.

5: Long since, dead.] The line straddles the stanza break that follows this text. In *Helsinki* the line straddles a line break, not a stanza break. 6: the next year, her first lover / A creature odd] the next year, / That first lover one odd *Helsinki* 9: a new experience for her. But] a new experience / For her. But *Helsinki* 11: Grown accustomed to money.] The line straddles the stanza break that follows this text. In *Helsinki* the line straddles a line break, not a stanza break. 12: who kept ... just snobbery. After that,] who kept / A score-card. With her, not passion / This time, just snobbery. After that, *Helsinki* 12: score-card.] scorecard. *Esquire* 16: I heard, ... to the jump.] I heard, made / Some unneeded money, and in the old newsphoto / I see her putting her mount to the jump,

Helsinki 17: old news photo I see] yellowed news photo I now see *Esquire* 18: is poised] poised *Helsinki* 24: For experience.] The line straddles the stanza break that follows this text. In *Helsinki*, the section ends here, and section 6 begins with the next line, which is set as a separate line, not as the second half of this one. 24: The husband, my friend,] The husband, *Esquire* 24: my friend,] my old friend, *Helsinki* 24: friend, / Would, by] friend, would / By *Helsinki* 25: time,] $\sim_\wedge$ *Helsinki* 26: Have been ... dead.] Have been a disappointment. Now he / Would have heavy jowls. Perhaps, / He is, by this time, dead. *Helsinki* 28: As for Laughing Boy, he wound up in the pen. Twenty years.] As for Laughing Boy. Twenty years in the pen. *Helsinki* 28: wound up in] went to *Esquire* 30: to] for *Esquire* 31: others who came there, / The casual] others / Who came there, the casual *Helsinki* 32: weekend-ers.] weekenders. *Esquire*, week-enders. *Helsinki* 32: But remember] But *Helsinki* 33: What I remember,] Do remember what I remember, *Helsinki* 34: the meaning inheres in] the meaning / Inheres in *Helsinki* 36: Back into what was *is*.] The line straddles the stanza break that follows this text. In *Helsinki* the line straddles a line break, not a stanza break. 42: usually at dawn] at dawn usually *Esquire*, at dawn *Helsinki* 42: on the] on that *Emory*

294 **XI. Homage to Theodore Dreiser** Text: OE. Variants: *New York Review of Books,* 12 Aug. 1971, p. 24 (as "Homage to Theodore Dreiser on the Centennial of his Birth"), *Homage to Theodore Dreiser*, pp. 3–8 (as "Portrait"), SP75, SP85. *Homage* lacks the epigraph, but prints the words and music to the refrain of "On the Banks of the Wabash, Far Away," with the attribution, on the facing page. *Homage* is also printed in italic type, with roman for emphasis. *Homage* also does not divide "Vital Statistics" into two subsections. OETS is a photocopy of a typescript prepared on the first typewriter. OETS marks where to bend long lines, but the typescript itself does not bend the lines in those places. The division of "Vital Statistics" into two sections is added in red pen on OETS. The section headings have Roman numerals in *NYRB* and *Homage*. The subsections in *NYRB* are lower case letters. The subtitle in *Homage* does not include the date. SP85 includes only section 1, and is entitled "Homage to Theodore Dreiser: Psychological Profile.

294 **1. Psychological Profile** Text: OE. Variant for this section only: *15 Poems*, selected by Rosanna Warren, privately printed for Stuart Wright, 1985 (as "Homage to Theodore Dreiser: Psychological Profile"). 15P is printed out of sequence, after "One I Knew," as the last poem in the volume. 15P includes the epigraph and attribution. 6: knows.] $\sim_\wedge$ SP75 11: gum-shoeing] gumshoeing *Homage* 12: own old story] own story. 15P 13: Full of screaming... always the same.] These two stanzas are interchanged in *Homage*, *NYRB*, and OETS (revised to OE on OEG). These versions are puzzling at this point, since these two stanzas are not in the *terza rima* of the rest of the section. 13: like live flesh] like flesh 15P 14: the screaming,] a screaming, *Homage* 14: of] like *Homage* 14: aflame,] afire, *NYRB*, *Homage*, OETS (revised to OE on OEG) 19: The same—but a brass band plays] But he hears a brass band *NYRB, Homage*, OETS (revised to OE on OEG)

295 **2. Vital Statistics**

295 **[A]** 14: Wrote,] $\sim_\wedge$ *Homage* 16: Tyrrhenian] Tyrrhanean *NYRB* 19: that] the *Homage* 23: All night... town,] Terre Haute lies / On the banks of the Wabash, far away, and tires, / On the concrete, scream. In Terre Haute, *NYRB, Homage* 24: in that town,] there, OETS (revised to OE in red pen) 31: Seen moonlight on the Wabash, far away?] In *Homage* there is no section break following this text, and the line straddles the stanza break that follows this text. OETS originally followed *Homage* here, but was corrected in red pen to the OE reading.

296 **[B]** 1: On the wrong side... his sisters] Dreiser was born on the wrong side of the tracks, and his sisters *NYRB,* He was born / On the wrong side of the tracks, and his sisters *Homage*, OETS (revised in red pen to OE) 4: and how] how *Homage* 4: feels,] $\sim$. SP75 (added on SP75G) 17: stercorry] stercory OETS (revised to OE on OEG)

297 **3. Moral Assessment** 1: You need call no psychiatrist] No psychiatrist need be called *Homage* 3: pain] kind *NYRB, Homage*, OETS (revised in red pencil to OE)

10: Tries to,] And tries, *NYRB, Homage*, OETS (revised to OE on OEG) 16: self-contemptive] self-contempting *NYRB, Homage*

297 **XII. Flaubert In Egypt** Text: OE. Variants: *New York Review of Books,* 8 Aug. 1974, p. 25, SP75. In *NYRB* the poem is broken into sections by lines with centered asterisks. In OE there is extra white space between the stanzas in the same places. In SP75 all of the stanzas are evenly spaced, although it was typeset from a photocopy of OE. OETS is a photocopy of a text prepared on the first typewriter, but the section number is added in blue pen, and the end is marked "Robert Penn Warren," indicating that the text was not prepared with the rest of the volume. The section numbers of all of the poems later in the volume are revised up by one in blue pen, again indicating that the poem was an afterthought. Since the original dates in the subtitle of the volume were 1968–1973, this may be the poem from 1974 that accounts for the change in date. OETS has asterisks marking the sections, but they are crossed out and replaced with marks for two lines of white space. OETS has no dedication, but it is added on OEG. The indented lines are clearly separate lines, rather than the run-over portions of long lines, because Warren indented them all the same distance on his OETS. Normally Warren flushed the run-over portions of long lines to the right margin. 4: names] Names *NYRB* 5: or] of *NYRB* 5: So went there,] There is a centered asterisk after this text in *NYRB.* 14: His cry burst forth.] There is a centered asterisk after this text in *NYRB.* 19: trousers‸] ~, SP75 (revised on SP75G, second set) 26: the] The *NYRB* 30: twitch in sleep.] There is a centered asterisk after this text in *NYRB.* 32: the wild dog,] There is no line break after this text in *NYRB,* or OETS, but it is added in OETS in blue pen. 35: down-Nile,] down the Nile, OETS (revised in blue pen to down Nile, and on OEG to OE) 35: old women,] old-women, *NYRB* 43: quite short.] There is a centered asterisk after this text in *NYRB.* Because this stanza is at the bottom of a page in OE, it is impossible to tell whether there is an extra space between this stanza and the next. I have chosen to add it, to follow the example of other cases. 46: *Baksheesh,*] *Bacsheesh, NYRB* 51: like a trophy.] There is extra white space after this stanza in OE, although there is no centered asterisk in *NYRB.* 58: such joy.] There is a centered asterisk after this text in *NYRB.*

299 **Interjection #5: Solipsism and Theology** Text: OE. Variants: *New Yorker,* 29 Jan. 1972, p. 44, SP75. OETS is a photocopy of a typescript prepared with the first typewriter, but "Interjection #5" is added later, and "XVII" is crossed out at the top, which indicates that this poem until fairly late was a section rather than an interjection. 5: antic‸] ~, *NY* 6: *home, but I—I'm*] *home—but I, I'm NY* 8: winter stars.] stars in winter. *NY* 11: classic‸] ~, *NY* 14: into] at the depth of OETS (revised in red pencil to OE) 16: But was—he was—and even yearned after virtue.] This line does not appear in *NY.* 16: he was] oh, he was OETS (revised in red pencil to OE)

300 **XIII. The True Nature of Time** Text: OE. Variants: *Yale Review,* 58 (Autumn 1968), pp. 74–75, I, SP75. *YR* is titled "A Faring," and the subsections are titled with small letters in parentheses. OETS is a photocopy from I, marked up in red pencil not in Warren's handwriting. I will note the alternations on OETS only where they differ from OE, since in every other case they simply change the reading in I to the reading in OE.

300 **1. The Faring** 1: Once] ONCE *YR* 1: over] over the I 14: lifting] lifted *YR,* I 19: your] the *YR,* I 22: Later,] ~‸ *YR* 26: The last] That last *YR,* I

300 **2. The Enclave** 1: saying. Into] saying, into *YR,* I 2: said. Thus] said, thus *YR,* I 6: sea,] ~‸ *YR* 6: Landward,] ~‸ *YR*

301 **XIV. Vision Under the October Mountain: A Love Poem** Text: OE. Variants: *Sewanee Review,* 74 (Summer 1966), pp. 589–90, SP66, SP75. *SR* is the first part of the "Three Poems," sequence, which includes "Chain Saw in Vermont in Time of Drouth," and "Ways of Day." OETS is a photocopy from SP66, revised in red pen. I record only where it differs from OE. 4: reality—or, is it?] reality, oh—or is it? *SR* 4: or,] oh, SP66 10: lulled in … swung] that lulled / syllogism, swaying / in sweet swill—sweet, unambiguous—swung *SR* 13: the tide of that bliss] that tide of bliss *SR* 22: seeing] saw *SR,* SP66, *Emory* 23: dream—a] dream, a *SR,* SP66, OETS (revised to OE on OEG) 24: mountain,] ~‸ *SR* 27: side, your … you came here, with] side, your gaze / on the

mountain. I want to hear / the whole story of how // you got here, with *SR*

302 **XV. Stargazing** Text: OE. Variants: *New Yorker,* 12 Feb. 1966, p. 30, SP66, SP75, SP85. In *NY* this is the first section of the sequence "Notes on a Life to be Lived," which includes "Dragon Tree," and "Composition in Gold and Red-Gold." OETS is a revised photocopy from SP66. 5: star-stillness,] star stillness, *NY* 12: spruces,] spruce, *NY* 13: waits:] ∼; *NY*

302 **Interjection #6: What You Sometimes Feel on Your Face at Night** Text: OE. Variants: *Yale Literary Magazine,* Nov. 1970, p. [35], SP75. OETS is a photocopy of a typescript prepared on the first typewriter. The interjection number is changed in pencil from 4 to 6.

303 **XVI. News Photo** Text: OE. Variant: *Atlantic Monthly,* June 1974, pp. 72–75. In *Atlantic* all of the words in the epigraph are initially capitalized, and the section numbers are not enclosed in square brackets. OETS is a photocopy of typescript prepared on the first typewriter. The words of the epigraph are all initially capitalized, but those that are not capitalized in OE are revised in red pen to the OE reading. OETS adds parentheses, in red pencil, around the section numbers.

303 **[1]** 3: carefully,] Carefully, *Atlantic*, OETS (revised in red pen to OE) 31: inward. He] There is no stanza break after this text in *Atlantic.* 34: it too, so why] so too, oh, why *Atlantic*, OETS (but revised in red pen to OE)

304 **[2]** 11: French .75 / from World War One he stole] French .75 from / World War I he stole *Atlantic*, French .75 he stole OETS (revised to OE on OEG) 18: Comminists,] Communists, *Atlantic*, OETS (revised in blue pen to OE) 23: them Romans being Roman Catholics, like the song says.] This line added in blue pen in OETS, although it is in *Atlantic*. 23: Catholics,] $\sim_\wedge$ *Atlantic* 24: Him] him *Atlantic*

304 **[3]** 12: The son, ... father's side.] The son, / the little one, twelve years old, is / by the father's side, the big / one above, sullen. (but revised in blue pen to OE) 13: twelve years old, / is by the father's side] fourteen years old, is by / the father's side. *Atlantic*

305 **[4]** 1: This,] Which, OETS (revised in blue pen to OE) 6: *snowfall*] *snow fall* OETS (revised to OE on OEG) 13: *this durn preacher I'm referring to*] *that durn preacher* OETS (revised to OE on OEG) 25: Yes.] ∼, OETS (revised in blue pen to OE)

306 **[5]** 1: now,] $\sim_\wedge$ *Atlantic* 1: now, and not later,] now, OETS (revised to OE on OEG) 8: yes,] oh, OETS (revised in blue pen to OE) 12: that] That OETS (revised to OE on OEG) 13: voting for him and doing all he had done, you'd think] you voting for him and doing all you done. You'd think *Atlantic* 15: he] anybody *Atlantic* 17: look!—] look! *Atlantic* OETS, OEG (revised to OE on second set of galleys) 25: *off to me—yeah—*] The line straddles the stanza break that follows this text. In *Atlantic* the line straddles a line break after this text, not a stanza break. 25: —and lifting] —lifting *Atlantic*, OETS (revised to OE on OEG) 26: with] and *Atlantic*, OETS (revised to OE in blue pen) 27: sparsely clings] clings sparsely *Atlantic* 36: off in Jackson, Mississippi, or maybe / Montgomery, Alabama, the white paint on] off in Jackson, Miss., or maybe Montgomery, Ala., the white paint on *Atlantic*, OETS (revised in red pen to OE)

307 **XVII. Little Boy and Lost Shoe** Text: OE. Variants: *New Yorker,* 12 Feb. 1966, p. 30, SP66, SP75, *15 Poems*, selected by Rosanna Warren, privately printed for Stuart Wright, 1985, SP85. OETS is a revised photocopy from SP66. 15P is out of chronological sequence, following "The Mad Druggist" rather than preceding "Composition in Gold and Red-Gold." 9: Oh,] $\sim_\wedge$ *NY* 15: How dilatory can a boy be, I ask you?] The line straddles the stanza break that follows this text. There is no stanza break or line break here in *NY* or SP66. The stanza break and line break are added in red pen on OETS.

307 **XVIII. Composition in Gold and Red-Gold** Text: OE. Variants: *New Yorker,* 12 Feb. 1966, p. 30, SP66, SP75, *15 Poems*, selected by Rosanna Warren, privately printed for Stuart Wright, 1985. *NY* is the third part of the sequence "Notes on a Life to be Lived," with "Stargazing," and "Dragon Tree." OETS is a revised photocopy from SP66. 10: red-gold—and] red-gold, and *NY* 19: half-Persian,] half Persian, *NY* 21: seaweed] seaweed *NY* 29: wine glass,] wineglass, *NY* 37: among the apples. / It is prone] among / The gold apples. It / Is prone *NY*, SP66 51: tall above] above SP66

309 **Interjection #7: Remarks of Soul to Body** Text: OE. Variants: *New Yorker,* 11 Sept. 1971, p. 46 (as "Address of Soul to Body"), SP75. *NY* has no dedication, but it does have the headnote. OETS is a photocopy of a typescript prepared with the first typewriter. The poem has "Robert Penn Warren" typed at the bottom, indicating that it may have been prepared separately. 16: Owners] owners *NY* 16: Bodies,] ~∧ *NY* 18: Time,] time, *NY* 20: and∧] ~, *NY*

309 **XIX. There's a Grandfather's Clock in the Hall** Text: OE. Variants: *Yale Review,* 63 (Summer 1974), pp. 548–49, SP75, SP85. *YR* is the second part of the sequence "Watch a Clock Closely," the first being "Forever O'Clock." OETS is a photocopy of a typescript prepared with the first typewriter. The section number is added in red pencil. It is the correct section number, so the numbering must have been done after the addition of "Flaubert in Egypt" to the volume. In the typescript it is clear that the poem is written in long lines, not in lines followed by indented groups of lines. OETS is marked "line for line—follow ms for line indentation" not in Warren's handwriting. Warren had the poem retyped for SP75, changing how he bent the long lines, and indenting the over-run portion from the left (as he did with "Forever O'Clock" in SP75) rather than flushing it to the right, which was his usual practice. SP85 also indents the over-run portion of long lines from the left. 1: it jumps,] it jumps *YR* 1: no-Time,] ~. *YR* 3: anchor,] ~∧ *YR* 4: do not really] really do not SP75, SP85 4: damn,] ~∧ *YR* 5: pretty∧] ~, SP75, SP85 10: that you] you *YR* 12: scrotum,] ~. *YR* 14: the now] the SP75, SP85

310 **XX. Reading Late at Night, Thermometer Falling** Text: OE. Variants: *New Yorker,* 11 March 1974, pp. 34–35, SP75, SP85. *NY* marks the subsections with Roman numerals rather than with Arabic numerals in brackets. Subsection 3 does not appear in *NY.* OETS is a photocopy of a typescript prepared with the first typewriter. The section number is correct on OETS. Brackets are added around the section numbers in red pencil on OETS. SP85TS is a cut-and-taped photocopy from SP75 (as is most of the sections of SP85TS for Warren's early poetry), but a typed note ("(To precede, if possible, "Folly on Royal Street in Section from *Or Else*)"), and the lack of the handwritten "Erskine" in the upper left corner argues that the inclusion of this poem in SP85 was a late idea.

310 **[1]** 1: he,] ~— *NY* 2: hundred-watt] 100-watt *NY*, OETS (revised in red pencil on OETS) 3: truth,] revelation, SP85 (revised on SP85G to SP85) 6: nose,] ~— *NY* 7: Thus—] ~, *NY*, OETS (revised to OE in red pen) 8: and there, in] and in *NY*, and there in OETS (This line is typed on a different typewriter in OETS and thus is probably a late revision. It is corrected to OE on OEG.) 9: mile/ On mile over] far / Over OETS (revised to OE in red pen) 16: Pistol-shot.] Pistol shot. *NY*

311 **[2]** In OETS this subsection is a carbon copy, on three-hole paper, not a xerox. 3: frivolous] trivial OETS (revised to OE in blue pen) 4: Lives only in my mind's eye,] In OE the line straddles the stanza break that follows this text. In SP75 and SP85 there is a broken line here, with the second half-line indented to fill out the line, but no stanza break. 4: though I] There is a stanza break in SP75 and SP85 after this text. 5: forever / Marching gaze—Hume's] forever marching gaze— / Hume's *NY*, OETS (revised to OE in red pencil) 6: *England,*]*Great Britain, NY* 6: Roosevelt's] There is a stanza break in SP75 (and SP85TS) after this text. Warren closed up the stanza break on SP85G. 9: text book,] textbook, *NY* 10: Or, even,] Or even *NY* 11: forbidding and blackbound,] forbidding, tattered, and blackbound, *NY*, OETS (revised to OE in red pencil) 19: it] the photograph SP75 (added on SP75G), SP85

312 **[3]** This section is omitted in *NY*. The text in OETS for this section and the next is photocopy. 1: 1890.] 1891 OETS (revised to OE in red pen) 3: They] Some OETS (revised to OE in red pen) 4: Time's] time OETS (revised to OE in red pen)

312 **[4]** 3: window-screen.] window screen. *NY* 4: Ice-field,] Ice field, *NY* 4: road:] ~— *NY* 8: Truth.] ~∧ SP85

313 **[5]** The text in OETS for this section is carbon copy on three hole paper. 1: Sir] sir *NY* (both times) 3: you] your OETS, OEG (revised on second set of galleys) 5: man,] ~∧ *NY* 6: White of course,] (White, of course), *NY* 7: Sir,] sir, *NY* 8: have addressed] address OETS (revised to OE in red pencil) 17: scab.] ~? *NY* 26: i.e.,] i.e. OETS (revised to OE

on OEG) 27: Who,] ∼∧ OETS (revised to OE on OEG) 29: Correct.] The line straddles the stanza break that follows this text. There is neither a line break nor a stanza break here in *NY* or OETS, but OETS is corrected to OE in red pen.

314 **[6]** Photocopy resumes here in OETS. 1: eighty-six,] eighty-five, *NY*, OETS (revised in red pen to OE) 1: to] on OETS (revised in red pen to OE) 4: a horse-apple. Cancer,] an apple, cancer OETS (revised to OE in red pencil) 6: the fifty years of my life,] fifty years, *NY*, forty-five years, OETS (revised to "fifty years," in red pen, finally corrected to OE on OEG)

314 **[7]** 7: pace,] ∼. *NY* 7: Massive pace,] Massive and imperial pace, OETS (but corrected to OE in red pen) 7: moving] It moved *NY* 9: clock more unforgiving] darker clock *NY* 11: ice-mass,] ice mass, *NY* 15: late-leveling] late, levelling *NY* 15: lunkhead] lunk-head OETS (revised in red pencil to OE) 15: clodhopper,] SP85 adds a line after this text: "The clodhopper me," (in typewriting on SP85TS) 17: It looms.] There is no stanza break after this text in *NY.* 19: Erect, in the thinly glimmering shadow of ice.] In OE and SP75 the line straddles the stanza break that follows this text. 19: shadow of ice.] shadow of now sun-thinned ice. SP85 (in pencil in the bound "Advance uncorrected proofs" and again on SP85G) 19: shadow of ice.] SP85 has no stanza break here, but does have a broken line, justifying the next half-line so as to fill out the line. The second half-line actually is adjusted about two characters to the left, so that it in fact does not match the end of the first half-line. The second half-line, added in SP85, is "Somehow yet". SP85 then adds a line that is justified at the left margin. The text of that line is "Alive." A stanza break follows in SP85. The first line of the next stanza, as in OE and SP75, is "The lunkhead", but where in OE and SP75 the text of that line is indented to match the line ending of the last line of the previous stanza, "Erect, in the thinly glimmering shadow of ice." the line in SP85 has a large indentation that doesn't match anything in the text above it. The indentation in SP85 is about the size it would have to be if the half-line were indented to match the line ending of what had been the previous stanza in OE and SP75, however. The typography of SP85 is rather a mess at this point, and it is difficult to figure out exactly what Warren's intentions were, but it looks as if Warren added "Somehow yet / Alive." to the proofs without adjusting the indentation of the next line. I argue that the lines should read this way:

Erect, in the thinly glimmering shadow of now sun-thinned ice.
                                                            Somehow yet
Alive.
      The lunkhead
Stares.

The lines are in fact handwritten in the bound "Advance uncorrected proofs" in a way consistent with my theory, and on SP85G Warren has again inserted the lines and written instructions to set these lines as my theory describes, instructions which the typesetter did not understand. On the SP85 page proofs, the text "Somehow yet alive." appears flush to the left margin, but Warren has corrected it, again in a way consistent with my theory. In the *Emory* copy of SP85 Warren has adjusted the lineation consistently with my theory, and he has changed the line-ending to fall between "Somehow" and "Yet" rather than between "Yet" and "Alive." SP85TS follows SP75. 19: lunkhead] lunk-head OETS (revised in red pencil to OE) 22: The cringe and jaw-dropped awe] The jaw-dropped and cringing amazement OETS (revised in red pen to OE) 23: shimmer of] pellucid OETS (revised in red pen to OE) 23: ice-screen] ice screen *NY* 24: magisterial] noble OETS (revised to OE in red pen)

315 **[8]** In OETS this section is marked "new+ august 9, 1973". 1: snow is predicted. This, / However,] it is snowing. Yes, / This OETS (revised to OE in red pen) 2: another country.] another country. Found in a common atlas. SP85 (revised on SP85G to SP85)

315 **XXI. Folly on Royal Street before the Raw Face of God** Text: OE. Variants: *New York Review of Books,* 7 Jan. 1971, p. 33, SP75, SP85, *Helsinki* (as "Folly on Royal

Street, New Orleans, Before the Raw Face of God"). OETS is a photocopy of a typescript prepared on the first typewriter. The section number XIV, in pen, is crossed out, but the section number added in typewriting is correct. The end is marked "Robert Penn Warren," indicating that this text was prepared separately, with the section number added later. 6: Burst,] ~∧ *Helsinki* 8: fulfillment-that-is-not-fulfillment,] fulfilment-that-is-not-fulfilment, OETS (revised to OE on OEG) 8: so,] There is a stanza break following this text in SP85 and *Helsinki*. Because in SP85TS this is a point where two photocopied extracts from SP75 are taped together, probably the stanza break in SP85 is an error, not a revision, and *Helsinki* follows SP85. 15: bougainvillaea,] bougainvillea, *NYRB*, OETS (revised to OE on OEG) 27: We rocked on our heels.] The line straddles the stanza break that follows this text. In *Helsinki* the line straddles a line break here, but there is no stanza break. 28: ablaze] devoured *NYRB*, OETS (revised in red pen to OE) 29: match flame] match-flame *NYRB* 29: noon-blaze] noon-glare SP75, SP85, *Helsinki* 32: ulcer,] ulcer's, *Helsinki* 33: Raw face stared down.] The line straddles the stanza break that follows this text. In *Helsinki* the line is straddles a line break, but there is no stanza break here. 33: And winked.] The line straddles the stanza break that follows this text. In *Helsinki* the line straddles a line break, but there is no stanza break here. 37: churches] steeples *Helsinki* 40: Even] In *Helsinki* there is no line break after this text. 43: oak leaf.] oakleaf. *NYRB* 53: dawn,] ~∧ *NYRB*, *Helsinki* 56: Eastward,] ~∧ *Helsinki* 58: Sometimes,] ~∧ *Helsinki* 60: As for the third, the tale / Is short.] As for the third, / The tale is short. *NYRB*, OETS, OEG (revised to OE on second copy of galleys)

317 **Interjection #8: Or, Sometimes, Night** Text: OE. Variant: SP75. The text in OETS is typescript, in Warren's own unmistakable typing, on three hole paper. The text is double-spaced, which is unusual for Warren. The dedication is added in red pen. 2: Declares] Prescribes OETS (revised in red pen to "Ordains" then in red pencil to OE)

317 **XXII. Sunset Walk in Thaw-Time in Vermont**

317 **1.** Text: OE. Variants: *Southern Review,* ns 10 (Summer 1974), pp. 590–92, SP75. *Southern Review* marks the subsections with Roman numerals without periods. OETS is a photocopy of a typescript prepared on the first typewriter. The typed section number is correct, but there is a crossed out section number (XVIII) in the upper left corner. OETS marks the subsection numbers with Arabic numerals in parentheses without periods, corrected to Arabic numerals with periods in red pencil. OETS is double-spaced.

318 **2.** 2: high-tangled] high-arching OETS (revised to OE before photocopying) 8: joy, like / Doom,] doom, like Joy, OETS (revised to OE before photocopying)

318 **3.** 5: westward,] ~∧ *SoR* 8: failures] failure *SoR*, OETS (revised in blue pen to OE) 15: massive geometry.] OETS is marked "Robert Penn Warren" after this text, indicating that the last section may perhaps be a late addition.

319 **4.** 12: small son] young son *SoR*, son OETS (revised in blue pen to OE)

319 **XXIII. Birth of Love** Text: OE. Variants: *New Yorker,* 22 July 1974, p. 36 (as "The Birth of Love"), SP75, SP85. OETS is a photocopy of a typescript made on the first typewriter. The section number, which is correct, is typed later. OETS is marked "Robert Penn Warren" at the end, indicating separate preparation. The title on OETS is "The Birth of Love" (but it is corrected to OE in red pen). 9: ten] dozen *NY*, OETS (revised to OE on OEG) 31: whiteness,] ~∧ *NY* 50: that,] ~∧ *NY* 58: into being.] forth. *NY*, OETS (revised to OE in blue ink)

321 **XXIV. A Problem in Spatial Composition** Text: OE. Variants: *Harper's,* April 1975, p. 24, SP75. In *Harpers* the section numbers are without parentheses. OETS is a photocopy of a typescript prepared on the first typewriter. The typed section number is a later addition. OETS is marked "revised: august 9, 1973".

321 **[1]** 11: *beyond* is *forever*—] *beyond is forever*— SP75 11: Confirms what the heart knows: *beyond* is *forever*—] The line straddles the stanza break that follows this text. In *Harper's* the line is broken across a line break here, but there is not stanza break. In fact, the line fragment that follows in *Harper's* may be not a half-line at all, but the

run-over portion of a long line, flushed to the right margin, as is Warren's usual practice with run-over lines.

321 **[2]** 2: right] left OETS (revised to OE in blue pen, and corrected again to OE on OEG) 9: right] left OETS (revised to OE in blue pen, but corrected back to "left" on OEG) 11: at] in *Harper's*, OETS (revised to OE in blue pen) 13: speed.] ~, *Harper's* 13: Hangs with a slight lift and hover.] with slight lift and hover. *Harper's*

322 **[3]**

Can I See Arcturus From Where I Stand?
Poems 1975

Can I See Arcturus From Where I Stand? is the section of new poems that begins *Selected Poems 1923–1975* (SP75). From earlier volumes SP75 includes poems as follows. From *Or Else* SP75 everything but "News Photo." It includes all of *Audubon: A Vision.* From *Incarnations* it includes everything but "Moonrise," "Mistral at Night," and, because it is included in *Or Else,* the sequence "The True Nature of Time" (including "The Faring" and "The Enclave"). From the *Tale of Time* section of SP66 it deletes "Dragon-Tree," "Dream of a Dream the Small Boy Had," and "Finisterre," and, because they have been moved to *Or Else,* seven sections from the "Notes on a Life to Be Lived" sequence ("Stargazing," " Small Red House," " Blow, West Wind," "Composition in Gold and Red-Gold," "Little Boy and Lost Shoe," "Vision Under the October Mountain: A Love Poem," and "Chain Saw at Dawn in Vermont in Time of Drouth"). Of the poems selected from earlier volumes for the rest of *Selected Poems New and Old* (SP66), SP75 includes the following. It includes the entire selection from *You, Emperors, and Others* except for "In Italian They Call the Bird *Civetta,*" "Autumnal Equinox on Mediterranean Beach," the entire sequence "Nursery Rhymes," and the entire sequence "Short Thoughts for Long Nights." It includes all of the selections made for SP66 from *Promises.* It includes all of the selections made for SP66 from *Selected Poems 1923–1943* (SP43), except "Man Coming of Age," and "Letter of a Mother." Random House issued a special limited edition of SP75 as well, but it was printed from the same plates, so I have not collated it separately. A second edition was published in 1977 by the Franklin Library (a division of the Franklin Mint), but the poems were phototypeset from the Random House edition, so I have not collated that edition separately either (telephone conversation with Sam Caggiula of Franklin Mint, April 26, 1995). Worksheets for the "Can I See Arcturus From Where I Stand?" section of SP75 were prepared from photocopies of carbon copies of poems sent individually from Warren to Albert Erskine, some with a note specifying where in the section the poem was to be placed, all of them marked with the poet's typed name. The rest of the volume was prepared from photocopies of earlier volumes, except for a few poems (such as"Forever O'Clock" from *Or Else*) which Warren retyped. The setting copy for the "Can I See Arcturus From Where I Stand?" section is the carbon copy from which the worksheets were made. With a few exceptions the typescripts are all—uncharacteristically for Warren—double-spaced. The corrections on SP75TS are in Warren's hand. Some of the discrepancies between SP75TS and SP75 are carried through right to the galleys, yet the "repros," which Warren touched up, have the SP75 reading, although they are not marked up there. Rather than take these as printer's errors, it seems more likely that there is a further stage of revision here for which I have no record. (Since the page proofs for this volume do not survive, possibly the final changes are there. Warren revised other volumes on the page proofs.) For the rest of SP75 the typescript is photocopied from earlier volumes, back as far as SP66. The corrections on the copy of SP66 follow those on "Draft B" in the Beinecke Library. "Draft B" is a photocopy of SP66 which Warren made soon after the publication of SP66 to make corrections upon. A considerable number of the revisions of older poems for SP75, however, were made on the galleys, as is usual for Warren. I have made notes on the revisions on SP75G (other revisions were either made on Draft B or on the copy of Draft B that served as SP75TS), to demonstrate how late some of the revisions to earlier poems in SP75 took place. The typescript includes an introduction, prepared for the Franklin Library edition:

> This volume is of selected poems arranged in anti-chronological order, covering some fifty years; and therefore a number of poems, published in magazines or volumes, are here omitted. But for each poem finished—including those finished and then rejected and never published in any form—there are the poor limping, malformed creatures, those that never got finished at all, insights that were still-born, emotions that were self-deceptions, lies that you tried to tell yourself, experiments that didn't pan out, mere imitations of fashion.
>
> One of the things I am saying is that to try to write poetry at all, one has to be willing to waste an unpredictable amount of time. How few poems get finished well enough to see print? And for how many may that fact be regretted? If one is more or less seriously concerned to write poetry, the process cannot be like an occasional round of bridge or a Sunday afternoon croquet game. Nor does a poem automatically happen when one sits down at the table and arbitrarily picks up the pencil. The key intuition of a poem may come at any time—walking down the street, lying between sleeping and waking, in the middle of a conversation, standing still in the deep woods. It may start with a commanding or provocative phrase that catches on the mind like a cockleburr, as a mere emotional unease or excitement, or even as an abstract idea. It may start as a scene, before the eyes or recollected. The thing—the important thing—is to be "open" to possibility. In other words, in a very real sense, poetry is a way of living, and not an occupation taken up for mere vanity or idle amusement. It is a process involved in the on-going process of life, but in the on-going process as related to a constant probing and re-evaluation of the past and an inspection of one's ideas and convictions as they have grown out of the past. For we, as human beings, always live, in varying degrees, in three dimensions of Time, the past and future as well as the present; and poetry is one of the complex and fruitful ways in which man can affirm his uniquely human quality for living in more than one dimension. It is an index, and a record, of our capacity for growth in Time. To pursue our notion, the poem is always oriented from our personal past and present toward an unpredictable future—the future of the writer, of the poem, and of the reader. The poem "grows," and in growing it strangely recapitulates our own process of growth. Ultimately, it is an image of that—the process of our personal growth, growth and logical change, for a poem, no more than a life, is haphazard. Unless both happen to be crazy—as can be the case. Or perhaps we should use a more fluid phrase here for "logical change." For instance, "significant association"—just to avoid the mere mechanical implication. Perhaps I am being too abstract here, but if I am, it is because I cannot help having curiosity and over-mastering interest. But how does one's interest become over-mastering? Since I am writing about my poems, I am necessarily writing about myself and the background of an interest. I had a childhood in two rather bookish households, that of my father and that of my maternal grandfather. My father had the habit in our early childhood of reading aloud to the children, frequently poetry—and oh, how I loved "Horatius at the Bridge," by Macaulay. I found that I could even read it myself, for when, at the thousandth time my father flatly refused, I picked up the book and found what the words said. And in the summers, my grandfather sat under a cedar tree [and recited] whatever fragments of poems—or poems—drifted through his head, when he wasn't trying to explain, by a chart drawn in the dust by his stick, some battle of Napoleon

> or of the Civil War, in which he had fought from start to finish. But I felt no need to write poems until I went to college and found myself associated with people, some who had written books of poetry and some of whom had a deep comprehension of it. How much is accident here? It is hard to say. I'll touch on one other fact of boyhood. For the many summers spent on my grandfather's farm, there was almost complete isolation from any child of my age and sex. When there was not my grandfather's conversation or books, there was the woods to wander in, the creatures and the mysterious details of life there, sometimes gone all day with a sandwich in my pocket. It was a world of enforced imagination, the canebreak of the stream and the shadow of woods. Strangely enough, it was not until recent years that a friend, having read this book, remarked to me how much of the imagery was drawn from nature, not the city. I suppose our basic images do come to us early, and who can be other than he is? But as a footnote to that last paragraph, how acutely I remember the *romantic* shock which I encountered, even before I knew the great cities, of the urban poetry of modernity, from Baudelaire to T. S. Eliot. It was, indeed a romantic shock, in its strangeness and newness. And I sometimes feel in my poems a constant interplay and tension between these two kinds of romance.

The epigraph for the volume was added in galleys.

Revisions to these poems for SP85 were made on cut-and-taped passages from SP75. Because the revisions for SP85 are often a vexed question, I have noted the places where they are made on SP85TS.

325 **A Way to Love God** Text: SP75. Variants: *Yale Review,* 65 (Autumn 1975), pp. 71–72, *Times Literary Supplement,* 20 Feb. 1976, p. 199, SP85. The title in both *YR* and *TLS* is "One Way to Love God." SP75TS corrects the title. *TLS* is printed in italic type, with roman for emphasis. SP75TS has a canceled annotation: "REVISED August 12, 1975". 1: Here] HERE *YR* 3: will tell] tells *YR* 8: daylight,] $\sim_\wedge$ *YR* 9: occasions] occassions SP75TS (but revised on SP75G) 11: however,] $\sim_\wedge$ SP75TS, SP75G (but SP75 on repros, and also in an earlier draft included in the editorial material for the volume) 14: my] by *YR* 19: *piazza, place, platz,*] *place, piazza, platz, YR, piazza, platz, TLS* 21: else.] ~, *TLS* 23: Mary of Scots,] Mary Queen of Scots, SP75TS (but revised on SP75G) 37: is] may be SP85 (revised on SP85G to SP85) 37: a] one *YR, TLS*

326 **Evening Hawk** Text: SP75. Variants: *Atlantic Monthly,* Nov. 1975, p. 54 (as the first section of "Two Night Poems"), SP85, *Helsinki.* In *Atlantic Monthly* three indented asterisks separate each stanza. SP75TS has a canceled annotation: "ALBERT: This is to be poem number 4 in NEW POEMS: To follow One Way to Love God". (In both the worksheets and SP75TS, however, it is the second poem. Warren settled on a tentative order for the poems in this section in his letter to Albert Erskine of August 18, 1975.) 5: guttural] gutteral *Helsinki* 11: Look! look!] Look! Look! SP85 (but not on SP85TS or corrected to this reading on any of the galleys; probably a typographical error on the galleys), Look! look!— *Helsinki* 21: in darkness] all night *Atlantic*

326 **Loss, of Perhaps Love, in Our World of Contingency** Text: SP75. Variants: *New Yorker,* 8 Sept. 1975, p. 34. The text in SP75TS is a photocopy of typescript, not of carbon copy. SP75TS is single spaced. 10: shoe-soles] shoe soles *NY* 17: *oh*] *Oh, NY* 21: a new-born,] a newborn, *NY*, new-born, SP75TS (but revised to SP75) 23: where the basalt boulders, moonlit, grieve] where basalt boulders grieve, SP75TS (but revised to SP75) 23: grieve$_\wedge$] ~, *NY* 27: thunder-clap] thunderclap *NY* 28: Dissolves into silence,] Dies away, SP75TS (but revised to SP75) 29: Stunned new] Stunned, new, *NY*

327 **Answer to Prayer** Text: SP75. Variants: *Virginia Quarterly Review,* 51 (Spring 1975), pp. 240–42, *Times Literary Supplement* 28 March 1975, p. 337. *TLS* is printed in italic type. SP75TS is single spaced typescript, on three-hole paper. 3: re-freezing] refreezing *TLS* 8: where, to meat and drink set, we] where we, to meat and drink set, *VQR, TLS,* where, set to meat and drink, we SP75TS (but revised to SP75) 15: the dark hover of

infinities,] dark infinities SP75TS (revised to "dark the hover of infinities," which is nonsense. The typesetter who set SP75G correctly anticipated Warren's intentions to adopt the SP75 reading.) 17: Emerged high] high appeared (but revised to SP75) 26: later,] ~∧ *TLS* 30: peripeteia] peripetia *TLS* 32: one prays.] he prays. *VQR, TLS* 33: meager] meagre *TLS*, lack of SP75TS (but revised to SP75) 37: was] came *TLS* 37: later,] after, *TLS*, back SP75TS (but revised to SP75) 40: ever] once SP75TS (but revised to SP75) 41: Or] And SP75TS (but revised to SP75) 41: if she remembers,] remembering, *VQR, TLS* 41: laughs] may laugh *VQR, Times Literary Supplement*, SP75TS (but revised to SP75)

328 **Paradox** Text: SP75. Variants: *New York Review of Books*, 16 Oct. 1975, p. 35, SP85. In *NYRB* three centered asterisks separate the stanzas.

329 **Midnight Outcry** Text: SP75. Variants: *Atlantic Monthly*, Nov. 1975, p. 55 (as the second section of "Two Night Poems"), SP85, *Helsinki*. *Atlantic* separates each stanza from the next with three indented asterisks. SP75TS has a canceled note: "TO Come in NEW POEMS just after "Paradox"." 7: sweat,] ~. *Helsinki* 16: the ferocious] ferocious *Helsinki* 20: but only and always one strange to us.] one only and always strange to us. SP85 (revised on SP85G to SP85) 21: on,] ~; *Atlantic* 24: even while] though *Atlantic* 24: the sunlit] her sunlit *Helsinki* 25: From] At *Atlantic*

330 **Trying to Tell You Something** Text: SP75. Variants: *New Yorker*, 5 Jan. 1976, p. 26. *NY* omits the dedication.SP75TS corrects the dedication from "To Tinkham Brooks." SP75TS also has a canceled annotation: "ALBERT: Just before "Old Nigger ETC"." (That isn't, however, where the poem was ultimately placed, even in SP75TS.) 7: barrel-hoops,] barrel hoops∧ *NY* 7: only] but *NY* 8: and higher,] and, higher, *NY* 11: fullness] fulness SP75TS, SP75G (correct on repros) 14: high] altitude SP75G (this pencil correction doesn't make grammatical sense, unless Warren intended to replace the whole phrase "high brightness." The change was not adopted on repros.) 18: wind,] ~∧ *NY*

331 **Brotherhood in Pain** Text: SP75. Variants: *American Review*, no. 24 (April 1976), pp. 120–21. 1: Fix your eyes] FIX YOUR EYES *American Review* 2: That] The *American Review*, SP75TS (but revised to SP75) 17: its own name.] What it is. It has no name. *American Review*, SP75TS (but revised on SP75G)

331 **Season Opens on Wild Boar in Chianti** Text: SP75. Variants: *Times Literary Supplement*, 26 Dec. 1975, p. 1530, *Sewanee Review*, 84 (Spring 1976), pp. 300–1. *TLS* and *SR* are titled "Hunting Season Opens on Wild Boar in Chianti." *TLS* is set in italic type. *SR* omits the dedication, which is added in pen in SP75TS. SP75TS has a canceled annotation: "Dear Albert: To go as next to last poem in NEW section. All well. Letter soon. Lo[v]e to all." SP75TS is single spaced. 1: vineyards.] wineyards. SP75TS, SP75G (but revised on second galleys—Erskine asked Warren about this in a letter of October 27, 1975) 2: pine-glen.] pine glen. *TLS*, pine-glens. SP75TS (but revised on SP75G) 3: voices in distance] voices, with distance, *TLS* 4: hounds] the hounds *SR* 5: The world is all music, we listen:] In a world of music we listen. *TLS, SR*, omitted in SP75TS (but revised on SP75G) 6: Men] They *TLS, SR*, SP75TS (but revised on SP75G) 8: The vineyards] Vineyards *TLS, SR*, SP75TS (but revised to SP75) 14: Has] Have *SR* 14: wild ground.] wild-ground. *TLS, SR* 15: pine boughs.] pine grains. *TLS*, pine-boughs. *SR* 17: trampled,] ~∧ *SR* 18: at the tusk-point] at tusk-point *TLS, SR* 18: the best hound.] lies the best hound. *TLS, SR* 29: rushes,] dashes SP75G (but revised on SP75G—a printer's error) 34: thoughtful∧] ~, *TLS, SR* 35: blank in] in blank *TLS, SR*, SP75TS, SP75G (but the repros show SP75) 36: grinding slow] grinding, slow, *TLS, SR* 37: Thus] So *TLS*, SP75TS, SP75G (but the repros have SP75) 37: nightfall,] darkness, SP75TS (but revised on SP75G) 42: darkness,] night∧ SP75TS ~∧ SP75G (but repros follow SP75) 42: ignorant] innocent SP75TS (but revised on SP75G)

333 **Old Nigger on One-Mule Cart Encountered Late at Night When Driving Home From Party in the Back Country** Text: SP75. Variants: *New Yorker*, 8 Dec. 1975, pp. 46–47, SP85. SP75TS is a single-spaced typescript, on three-hole paper. Warren sent a letter to Erskine on June 20, 1975, with several corrections to this poem. These cor-

rections are for the *New Yorker* version. This is more evidence for my claim that Warren sent his typescripts to Erskine at some time before magazine publication. 3: sliding, flesh flowing,] sliding and flowing SP75TS (revised to SP75) 6: white in secret] white and secret in *NY*, SP75TS, SP75G (but repros have SP75) 10: O.K. Silence] *O.K.*—but the silence, *NY* 11: Rages,] It rages, *NY* 13: That sound I do now hear] What sound I now hear *NY* 14: crinkle and crepitation,] crepitation and crinkle, *NY* 16: *Goodnight! Goodnight!*] *Good night! Good night! New Yorker* 17: I can't now even remember] I can't even remember now *NY* 18: in July, in Louisiana,] in Louisiana, in July, *NY* 24: star-dust,] stardust, *NY* 32: There it is: death-trap.] This line is a separate stanza in *NY*. 32: death-trap.] death trap. *NY* 33: On the fool-nigger, ass-hole wrong] On the damn-fool, fool-nigger wrong *NY* Oh the fool-nigger—ass-hole wrong SP85 (This revision, which makes nonsense of the line, is not a typographical error, but a revision made by Warren on SP85G.) 37: skull] that skull *NY*, SP75TS, SP75G (but repros have SP75) 38: pre-Time,] prehistory. SP85 (in black pen on SP85TS) 40: blaze] blaze out *NY*, SP75TS (but revised on SP75G) 44: *O,*] O *NY* 46: But] And *NY* 47: amidst—] ~: *NY* 48: Rusted bed-springs] Rusting bedsprings *NY* 49: wound,] rolled, *NY* 50: stove pipe] stovepipe *NY* 50: beat up.] beat-up. SP85 (revised on SP85G to SP85) 50: God-yes,] There is a stanza break after this text in *NY.* 51: death-trap.] death trap. *NY* 51: But] There is a stanza break after this text in *NY.* 57: sweat-sticky] the sweat-sticky *NY* 60: all.] all, but *NY* 61: And go on ... only until] I have gone on: to the last drink, sweat-grapple in / Darkness, then sleep. That only, however, until *NY* 64: Are experienced, ... or night-sweat,] Are experienced, and the swamp-owl / Utters the last pre-dawn cry, the hour when / Joy-sweat, or night-sweat, SP75TS (revised to SP75) 65: to the last / Predawn cry,] to the last predawn cry, *NY* 70: super-ego] superego *NY* 72: see$_\wedge$] ~, *NY* 73: Floating in darkness above the bed the] In darkness above the bed floating, the *NY* 74: *O,*] O, *NY* 78: a sonnet:] Stanza break after this text in SP75TS (but revised on SP75G). 79: One of those ... peruse.] This couplet is a separate stanza in *NY*. This couplet is not indented in SP85. 81: As I said, Jesus Christ. But] Omitted in *NY*. 82: Moved] But moved *NY* 84: stare,] ~— *NY* 86: zero,] ~— *NY* 95: snow-shouldered,] snow-shrouded, *NY*, SP75TS, SP75G (but repros have SP75) 99: bulge of] swell of *NY*, omitted in SP75TS (but revised to SP75) 99: like the hair] like hair *NY* 101: are entitled] are all entitled *NY*, are are entitled SP75TS (but revised on SP75G) 105: magnet,] mad magnet, SP75TS (but revised to SP75) 106: out-flung] outflung *NY* 108: pattern—] ~?— *NY*, ~, SP75TS, SP75G (but repros have SP75) 116: match] single match *NY* 117: reflected on the petal-pink] reflected, in streaks of petal-pink, *NY* 118: And] On *NY* 120: my Philosopher] Philosopher *NY* 124: blessedness,] blessèdness, *NY* SP75G (correction, but not adopted on repros) 125: To enter, ... to fumble] To enter, by a bare field, / A shack unlit?—entering / Into that darkness to fumble *NY* 128: trust,] thrust, SP75G (but revised on SP75G—a printer's error) 128: name—] ~, *NY*, SP75TS (but revised on SP75G) 129: Like a shell, a dry flower, a worn stone, a toy—merely] A shell, a dry flower, a toy, merely SP75TS (but revised to SP75, except for "toy, merely") 129: Like a shell,] Like shell, *NY* 129: toy—merely] toy, merely *NY* 131: out of] through *NY* 132: small, sober, and] sober, small, *NY* 133: Glow,] ~: *NY*

Now and Then
Poems 1976–1978

Until a late stage of preparation, the typescript included several poems Warren finally chose to omit: "Somewhere," "A Few Axioms for Young Men," "Praise," and the "Bicentennial Ode." NTTS is double-spaced typescript, with some photocopy. There are two sets of corrections on NTTS, one in black pencil (which may be in Warren's hand), one in blue pencil (not in Warren's hand). All corrections which are not marked otherwise are made in black pencil. Since the pages are numbered only within poems (the page numbers for the volume as a whole being added in blue pen later), and since each poem has a canceled annotation at the end listing where it was published (and sometimes adding the author's name), it is reasonable to think of NTTS as typescripts of poems sent to Erskine individually and revised and assembled into a volume later. It may seem tedious to record all of these canceled annotations in the notes, but they prove that even though all of the poems were typed by the same typist, they were typed on separate occasions (since sometimes the typist added the poet's name to the end of the manuscript, and sometimes the typist didn't). Some of the pages are much smudged, and all are folded in the middle, as if for mailing in a 5 x 8 envelope. (The whole typescript could not fit in such an envelope, which again suggests that the typescript was prepared piecemeal.) The typist who prepared these poems—they are all typed on the same machine, and the typing is too good to be Warren's—indented the run-over portion of long lines from the left. (Warren's own usual practice was to flush the run-over portion of long lines to the right.) There are no run-over lines in NT, however, so the question of how they would have been set in type is moot.

Warren prepared the revised copy of *Now and Then* presently in the Special Collections department of the Emory University Library on May 23, 1987. I quote from that volume by permission of the Emory University Library.

The section of poems from this volume in SP85TS consists of photocopied pages from NT. Because the revisions for SP85 are a vexed question, I have indicated the cases where they are made on SP85TS.

I. Nostalgic

339 **American Portrait: Old Style** Text: NT. Variants: *New Yorker,* 23 Aug. 1976, p. 26, *15 Poems*, selected by Rosanna Warren, privately printed for Stuart Wright, 1985, SP85. *NY* and 15P have no periods after the section numbers. 14: window, and woods and ruined cornfields we saw:] window at ruined cornfields and we saw what we saw: *NY*, NTTS (but corrected in blue pencil to NT) 21: Finley] Benton *NY*, NTTS (revised on NTG to NT) 24: bird-note] bird note *NY*, NTTS (revised in blue pencil to NT) 27: twelve-gauge] 12-gauge *NY*, NTTS (revised to NT), twelve-guage 15P 32: often] ofter 15P 53: to live at all.] at all to live. *NY* 57: and powdered] powdered 15P 61: walk,] $\sim_{\wedge}$ *NY*, NTTS (revised in blue pencil to NT) 61: float$_{\wedge}$] to float, *NY*, NTTS (but corrected in blue pencil to NT) 67: pants] coats SP85 (revised on SP85G to SP85) 75: booze] the booze NTTS (revised to NT) 79: or raised / A single dog from a pup.] or even / Raised a single dog from a pup. *NY*, NTTS (revised in blue pencil to NT) 87: one] on SP85 (but not SP85TS and not corrected to this reading on SP85G or the "bound uncorrected proofs" of SP85, and therefore probably a typographical error) 96: on his mother's face,] on his mother's face$_{\wedge}$ *New Yorker*, on his mother's face / When she held the BBs out. SP85 (revised on SP85G to SP85) 100: to] toward *NY*, NTTS (revised on NTG to NT) 102: But,] $\sim_{\wedge}$ *NY*, NTTS (but corrected in blue pencil to NT) 104: bingo!] $\sim$, 15P 110: old dreams] all the old dramas *NY*, old dramas NTTS (revised in blue pencil from "all the old dramas") old dreams NTG 112: a ditch] a stopped-up ditch *NY*, NTTS (revised in blue pencil to NT) 117: happen] happened SP85 (but not on SP85TS and not corrected to this reading on any of the galleys; probably a typographical error) 126: dead yet,] yet dead$_{\wedge}$ *Emory* 129: love is] that's SP85 (revised on SP85G to SP85) 129: outgrow.] NTTS has a canceled annotation: "New Yorker".

342 **Amazing Grace in the Back Country** Text: NT. Variants: *Ohio Review,* 18 (Winter 1977), pp. 32–34, SP85. 8: Man-woman$_{\wedge}$] $\sim$, *Ohio Review*, NTTS (revised to NT) 8: lion,] $\sim_{\wedge}$ *Ohio Review*, NTTS (but corrected in blue pencil to NT) 9: seen] being seen *Ohio Review*, NTTS (revised in blue pencil to NT) 10: calf;] calf or what; SP85 (revised on SP85G to SP85), calf. All this, *Emory* 16: syphilis] syphillis NTTS (revised in red pencil to NT) 17: old] was old *Ohio Review*, NTTS (revised to NT) 19: through] through the *Ohio Review*, NTTS (revised to NT) 25: His glory—] his Glory: *Ohio Review*, NTTS (revised in editorial correspondence), his Glory— NTG (revised to NT on page proofs) 26: engineer$_{\wedge}$] $\sim$, *Ohio Review* 27: revivalist$_{\wedge}$] $\sim$, *Ohio Review* 28: and shirt] shirt SP85 (revised on SP85G to SP85) 30: old-fool] old, fool *Ohio Review*, NTTS (but corrected in blue pencil to NT) 30: dame$_{\wedge}$] $\sim$, *Ohio Review*, NTTS (revised to NT) 34: Before] Before it was *Ohio Review*, NTTS (revised to NT) 41: So] Was so *Ohio*

Review 45: never remembered,] didn't even know, *Ohio Review*, NTTS (revised to NT) 45: knew] I knew *Ohio Review*, NTTS (revised in blue pencil to NT) 47: old] her old *Ohio Review*, NTTS (revised in blue pencil to NT) 65: Voices] The voices *Ohio Review*, NTTS (revised to NT) 67: in some dark house, / Found bed and lay down,] in a dark house, found bed and lay down, *Ohio Review*, NTTS (revised to NT), corrected again to NT on NTG 70: not ever.] ever. NTTS (revised in blue pencil to NT) 72: Long] Were long *Ohio Review*, NTTS (revised to NT) 73: yet] still *Ohio Review*, NTTS (revised in blue pencil to NT) 74: the cold] cold SP85 (revised on SP85G to SP85) 75: alone—] alone,— *Ohio Review*, NTTS (revised to NT) 79: old then.] A canceled annotation follows: "Ohio Review".

344 **Boy Wandering in Simms' Valley** Text: NT. Variants: *Saturday Review,* 29 Oct. 1977, p. 39, SP85. 2: under summer's late molten light / And past] all under the molten light / Of late summer, and past *SatR*, NTTS (revised in blue pencil to NT) 4: Raw tangle of cedar,] Raw cedar, *SatR* 6: long back,] for long years, *SatR*, NTTS (revised to NT) 8: twelve-gauge,] .12 gauge, *SatR*, NTTS (revised to NT) 12: so] but *SatR*, NTTS (revised to NT) 16: a span] two-span *SatR*, NTTS (revised to NT) 18: back to wilderness gone,] gone part of the wilderness, *Saturday Review*, gone back to wilderness, NTTS (revised from "gone back to the wilderness," but corrected on NTG to NT) 19: but] and that *SatR*, NTTS (revised to NT) 20: tax-sale, it] tax-sale. It *SatR* 21: the] the the SP85 24: rats. And] rats, and *SatR*, NTTS (revised to NT) 26: Flung] And flung *SatR*, NTTS (revised to NT) 29: they may be.] Two canceled annotations in NTTS: "Robert Penn Warren" and "Saturday Review".

345 **Old Flame** Text: NT. Variants: Broadside (Winston-Salem, NC: Palaemon Press Limited, 1978). I examined a photocopy of no. 90. 6: drifting, tongue-tied,] drifting and tongue-tied, *Palaemon*, NTTS (revised in blue pencil to NT) 9: besides,] $\sim_\wedge$ *Palaemon*, NTTS (revised to NT) 12: life] her life *Palaemon*, NTTS (revised on NTG to NT) 13: A half-century later,] But in nigh a half-century *Palaemon*, NTTS (revised on NTG to NT) 20: said,] $\sim$. *Palaemon* 22: funereal] funeral *Palaemon* 24: braids. Never, never,] braids. But never, never *Palaemon*, braids, but never, never NTTS (revised in blue pencil to NT) 24: a face.] NTTS has a canceled annotation: "Robert Penn Warren".

345 **Evening Hour** Text: NT. Variant: *Georgia Review,* 32 (Summer 1978), p. 282. 18: fumblingly] blunderingly *GaR*, NTTS (revised on NTG to NT) 18: philosophical,] $\sim_\wedge$ NTTS (revised in blue pencil to NT) 19: kept waiting,] stayed on, *GaR*, NTTS (revised in blue pencil to NT) 24: lay] set *GaR*, NTTS (revised in blue pencil to NT) 24: might say.] Two canceled annotations follow: "Robert Penn Warren" (typed) and "*Georgia Review*" (handwritten, not in Warren's hand).

346 **Orphanage Boy** Text: NT. Variants: *New York Review of Books,* 3 March 1977, p. 12 (as "Orphanage Boy (Octosyllabics)"), *15 Poems*, selected by Rosanna Warren, privately printed for Stuart Wright, 1985. NTTS corrects the title from the magazine to the NT reading. 15P prints this poem out of sequence, since it follows "Heart of Autumn." 3: got enough to / Call hire. Back at the woodpile chop- / ping stove-lengths, he taught me all the] might get enough / To call hire. Back at the wood pile / Chopping stove-lengths, he taught me the *NYRB* 3: woodpile] wood-pile NTTS (revised to NT) 14: bulldog,] bull-dog, NTTS (revised to NT) 21: night$_\wedge$] $\sim$, *NYRB* 28: lane$_\wedge$] $\sim$, *NYRB* 33: Git away, you son-a-bitch] Git on, you son-of-a-bitch *NYRB* 34: away and he lay] on and then he lay *NYRB* 35: crying$_\wedge$] $\sim$, *NYRB* 37: home$_\wedge$] $\sim$, *NYRB* 42: He] Al *NYRB* 44: hang them up.] hang them up. / We'd never known they had been touched. *NYRB* 45: nigh moonset.] A canceled annotation follows in NTTS: "New York Review of Books".

347 **Red-Tail Hawk and Pyre of Youth** Text: NT. Variants: *New Yorker,* 18 July 1977, pp. 32–33, SP85. 9: Eyes, strangely heavy like lead,] This line is indented in *NY.* Possibly Warren intended to have the line straddle the stanza break that precedes it, but all of the indentations in the *NY* version are identical, in that they all follow stanza breaks, but the amount of indentation does not match the length of the preceding lines. Possibly the typesetter did not understand Warren's intentions. The line is not indented in NTTS. 10: .30-30] .30/30 *NY*, .30 30 NTTS (revised to NT) 17: Except for the center of] This line

indented in *NY.* 23: coming] it come SP85 (revised on SP85G to SP85) 36: the bloody] and with the bloody *NY* 39: Thus homeward. // But nobody there. // So at last] Thus homeward. But nobody there. So at last. *NY* 52: Steel rods, ... Oh, yes,] A roll of steel wire, and glass eyes gleaming yellow—oh, yes, *NY* 53: yellow. Oh,] yellow—oh, NTTS (revised in blue pencil to NT) 59: arsenic dried, ... naturally anchored] And with arsenic dried, and all naturally anchored *Emory* 62: bone∧] ~— *Emory* 63: built there] there SP85 (revised on SP85G to SP85) 63: And the clay-burlap body built there within.] Line omitted in *Emory.* 64: It was molded as though for that moment to take to the air—though,] All molded as though for the moment to take to air—though, *Emory* 70: It was regal, perched] Regal, it perched SP85 (revised on SP85G to SP85) 70: its] the *NY*, NTTS (revised on NTG to NT) 71: *Lycidas,*] "Lycidas," *NY*, NTTS (revised in blue pencil to NT) 71: Hardy∧] ~, NTTS (revised to NT) 71: *Hamlet,*] "Hamlet," *NY*, NTTS (revised in blue pencil to NT) 81: Eyes] My eyes *NY*, NTTS (revised to NT) 85: That night in the lumber room,] In the lumber room that night, *New Yorker* 91: *Hamlet,*] "Hamlet," *NY*, NTTS (revised in blue pencil to NT) 103: What left] This line is indented in *NY.* 103: What left] What is left *NY* 108: appear once again—] reappear— *NY* 108: come∧] ~, *NY* 109: rifle swings up, though with / The weightlessness] rifle again swings up, though / With the *NY* 109: though with / The] though / With the NTTS (revised in blue pencil to NT) 111: .30-30] .30/30 *NY*, .30 30 NTTS (revised in blue pencil to NT) 115: that∧] ~, *NY*, NTTS (revised to NT) 118: small∧] ~, *NY*, NTTS (revised to NT) 123: must flinch] flinch *NY* 125: ignorant pyre.] A canceled annotation follows in NTTS: "END".

351 **Mountain Plateau** Text: NT. Variant: *Ironwood 10,* 5, no. 2 (1977), p. 73. The *Ironwood* version has no dedication, but does have the following headnote: (In admiration of James Wright and with the regret that this is not worthy of its mission). NTTS has no dedication, and the dedication is added in pencil on NTG. 2: reared,] rears, *Ironwood* 3: pen-strokes,] pen-stroke, *Ironwood* 3: fretted] fret *Ironwood* 4: The ice-blue of sky. ... to the immense distance.] The ice-blue of sky. The mercury / Is still falling. A crow, / On the highest, black, frail sky-thrust, utters // Its cry to the immense distance. *Ironwood* 5: frail,] ~∧ NTG (revised on NTG to NT) 5: and sky-thrust] sky-thrust NTTS (revised in blue pencil to NT) 10: now reduplicates,] reduplicates, *Ironwood* 13: A crow] But no crow *Ironwood* 13: sky.] ~, *Ironwood* 14: I can make no answer / To the cry from the immense distance,] And there is no answer to the cry I hear from immense distance *Ironwood* 17: Long without being able / To make adequate communication.] Long without being able to make adequate communication. *Ironwood* 18: adequate communication.] Two canceled annotations follow in NTTS: "Robert Penn Warren", and "Ironwood".

351 **Star-Fall** Text: NT. Variants: *Yale Review*, 67 (Spring 1978), p. 419, SP85. 1: In] IN *YR* 1: where∧] ~, *YR*, NTTS (revised to NT) 2: centuries∧] ~, *YR*, NTTS (revised to NT) 2: garbage∧] ~, *YR* 3: depth∧] ~, *YR* 4: at the broiling] at broiling NTTS (revised in blue pencil to NT) 10: hiss∧] ~, *YR*, NTTS (revised to NT) 18: Identity] Nature SP85 (revised on SP85G to SP85) 20: earth] the earth *YR* 20: swing, / Watched the] swing, and watched / The *YR*, NTTS (revised in blue pencil to NT) 21: the season. They fell] the season, that fell *YR*, NTTS (revised in blue pencil to NT) 25: The fishing lights marked] Lights of fishing boats marked SP85 (revised on SP85G to SP85) 28: watching] and watched *YR* 28: the stars] stars SP85 (revised on SP85G to SP85) 28: as they fell.] A canceled annotation follows in NTTS: "Robert Penn Warren".

352 **Youth Stares at Minoan Sunset** Text: NT. Variants: *New York Review of Books,* 30 Sept. 1976, p. 15, SP85. In *Emory*, Warren changes "Minoan" in the title to "Cretan." 1: On the] The *NYRB*, NTTS (revised to NT) 1: meadow,] ~∧ *NYRB*, NTTS (revised to NT) 2: At the break of the cliff-quarry] Breaking at the cliff-quarry *NYRB*, NTTS (revised to NT) 2: cliff-quarry] Cretan cliff-quarry SP85 (in pencil on SP85TS) 13: sea,] ~∧ NTTS (revised to NT) 15: horizon-line.] horizon line. SP85 (in pencil on SP85TS) 18: thereon minted black,] minted black thereon, *NYRB*, NTTS (revised in blue pencil to NT) 20: Defiles] Impairs *NYRB*, NTTS (revised in blue pencil to NT) 22: yet small, stares] small, yet stares *NYRB*, NTTS (revised to NT) 27: it—and us.] us. *NYRB*

II. Speculative

353 **Dream** Text: NT. Variant: *Atlantic Monthly,* Oct. 1977, p. 84 (as the second part of the sequence "Three Poems on Time"). 1: moonset,] moon-set∧ *Atlantic*, NTTS (revised in red pencil to NT) 8: Odysseus∧] ∼, *Atlantic*, NTTS (revised to NT) 17: ghost∧] ∼, *Atlantic* 21: by dawn.] A canceled annotation follows in NTTS: "Atlantic".

353 **Dream of a Dream** Text: NT. Variants: Boston: G. K. Hall, 1976 (a Christmas card), *Southern Review,* ns 13 (Winter 1977), pp. 147–48. 8: but] beyond Hall, *SoR*, NTTS (revised to NT) 8: its own] its Hall, *SoR*, NTTS (revised in blue pencil to NT) 9: interflow,] ∼∧ *SoR* 10: glimmer ghostly] glimmer Hall, *SoR*, NTTS (revised on NTG to NT) 12: un-timed] de-Timed Hall, *SoR*, NTTS (revised in blue pencil to NT) 14: And listen and wonder] Listening, wondering *SoR* 17: whirling, it] it, whirling, Hall, *SoR*, NTTS (revised on NTG to NT) 20: self] Self *SoR* 26: thrush,] thrust, NTTS (revised to NT) 26: hour,] ∼∧ Hall, NTTS (revised to NT) 26: utter] Stanza break after this text in NTG (revised on NTG to NT. The line is at a page-turn in NTTS, and a mark for a stanza break was added there in blue pencil, probably erroneously by Erskine.) 27: diminution.] dimunition, NTTS (revised to NT) 30: another dream.] A canceled annotation follows in NTTS: "Southern Review".

354 **First Dawn Light** Text: NT. Variant: *New Yorker,* 4 April 1977, p. 38. 2: chalk,] ∼∧ *NY* 2: day's first] day's *NY*, first NTTS (revised in blue pencil to NT) 4: night,] ∼. *NY* 6: bring,] ∼— *NY* 9: loneliness∧] ∼, *NY* 9: think∧] ∼, *NY* 14: joy,] joy, and yours, *NY*, NTTS (revised in blue pencil to NT) 14: or by] or *NY*, NTTS (revised in blue pencil to NT) 16: of dream.] A canceled annotation follows in NTTS: "Southern Review".

355 **Ah, Anima!** Text: NT. Variants: *Atlantic Monthly,* Oct. 1977, p. 86 (as the third part of the sequence "Three Poems in Time"), SP85. 8: Pines blackly stagger.] Pine blackly staggers. *Atlantic* 16: Roads will be rebuilt, // And houses. Food distributed] Roads, houses, will be // Rebuilt, food distributed. *Atlantic* 17: And houses. Food] And houses, food NTTS (revised in blue pencil to NT) 17: But,] ∼∧ *Atlantic* 19: In the] On *Atlantic* 19: and the un-roar] and in unroar *Atlantic* 19: being,] Being, *Atlantic* 22: wrack] old wrack *Atlantic* 22: pelt] dark pelt SP85 (revised on SP85G) 22: gray light,] storm, SP85 (revised on SP85G to SP85) 25: mouth, rounded,] round mouth *Atlantic* 25: is there,] is in the night there, SP85 (revised on SP85G to SP85) 25: the utterance] and the utterance NTTS (revised on NTG to NT) 27: and leap / Into the blind] and leap into the / Blind *Atlantic*, and meld / With the blind NTTS (revised to NT) 28: of air.] A canceled annotation follows in NTTS: "Atlantic Monthly".

356 **Unless** Text: NT. Variants: SP85, *Helsinki*. 4: energy, as] energy. As *Helsinki* 6: cactus] cacti *Helsinki* 9: fanged,] Fanged, *Helsinki* 10: worship you.] worship you for what you are. SP85 (in pencil on SP85TS), *Helsinki* 15: At] All *Helsinki* 19: Of desert of which] Of which *Helsinki* 25: is happiness.] A canceled annotation follows in NTTS: "Times Literary Supplement".

357 **Not Quite Like a Top** Text: NT. Variant: *New York Review of Books,* 23 Feb. 1978, p. 34. 2: and swings,] up and down, *NYRB*, NTTS (revised to NT) 5: dark,] ∼∧ *NYRB*, NTTS (revised to NT) 7: northern hemisphere,] Northern Hemisphere, *NYRB* 12: shameless] the shameless *NYRB*, NTTS (revised to NT) 16: (upper),] ∼∧ *NYRB*, NTTS (revised to NT) 24: firsthand] first-hand *NYRB*, NTTS (revised to NT) 25: don't know?] Two canceled annotations follow in NTTS: "Robert Penn Warren", and "New York Review of Books".

358 **Waiting** Text: NT. Variant: *Atlantic Monthly,* Dec. 1976, p. 47. 2: quivered] quavered *Atlantic* 3: that there] there *Atlantic* 4: dawn of no dawn.] dawn. *Atlantic* 6: hobbled cow, stranded // On a sudden islet, gargles in grief in the alder-brake] dog-fox, stranded // On a sudden islet, barks in hysteria in the alder-brake *Atlantic* 10: goddam] God-damned *Atlantic*, NTTS (revised in blue pen—yes, blue pen—to NT) 12: and she cannot ... who chews a hangnail. Until] and she // Had never loved you, had believed the lie only for the sake of the children. Until / You become uncertain of French irregular verbs, // And by a strange coincidence begin to take Catholic instruction from / Monsignor O'Malley, who chews a hangnail. Until *Atlantic* 16: hangnail.] hang-nail. NTTS (revised in black

pencil to NT) 17: to your surprise,] truly, *Atlantic* 22: inflamed // Flesh, or] inflamed flesh // Or *Atlantic* 23: Until / You remember that, remarkably, common men] Until you / Remember, surprisingly, that common men *Atlantic* 24: noble] good *Atlantic* 24: Until // It grows] Until it // Grows *Atlantic* 26: man] us *Atlantic* 27: True or not. But sometimes true.] Line absent in *Atlantic*, True or not. NTTS (revised to NT) 27: sometimes true.] A canceled annotation follows in NTTS: " Atlantic".

359 **The Mission** Text: NT. Variants: *Ohio Review,* 18 (Winter 1977), pp. 30–31, SP85. 1: icebox] ice-box *Ohio Review*, NTTS (revised to NT) 2: monologue] dialogue SP85 (revised on SP85G to SP85) 7: in the] in even the SP85 (revised on SP85G to SP85) 9: wind] new wind SP85 (revised on SP85G to SP85) 9: But‸] ~, *Ohio Review*, NTTS (revised to NT) 17: square] secret square SP85 (revised on SP85G to SP85) 36: lost mission] mission *Ohio Review*, NTTS (revised on NTG to NT) 37: possibility] complexity *Ohio Review*, NTTS (revised to NT) 37: beauty.] A canceled annotation follows in NTTS: "Ohio Review".

360 **Code Book Lost** Text: NT. Variant: *Saturday Review,* 29 Oct. 1977, p. 38. 2: stop,] ~‸ *SatR* 4: fallen?] dropped? *SatR* 8: apple blossom's] apple-blossom's *SatR* 9: that] the *SatR*, NTTS (revised to NT) 10: strike?] start? *SatR* 11: woman dying, or supine and penetrated, stare at?] dying, or screwed, woman stare at? *SatR* 12: curtains?] curtain. *SatR*, NTTS (but corrected on NTG to NT) 13: a world] the world *SatR* 14: understand] get it *SatR*, NTTS (revised on NTG to NT) 15: meaning, when] meaning when, *SatR*, meaning when NTTS (revised in blue pencil to NT) 16: old heart,] heart, *SatR* 18: stoic teeth] teeth *SatR* 20: houses? What do they signify?] houses, and what they imply? *SatR* 22: But the code book, somehow, is lost.] But, somehow, the code book is lost. *SatR* 22: lost.] Two canceled annotations follow in NTTS: "Robert Penn Warren", and "Saturday Review".

360 **When the Tooth Cracks—Zing!** Text: NT. Variant: *Ohio Review,* 18 (Winter 1977), pp. 35–36. 12: pewter] metal *Ohio Review*, NTTS (revised to NT) 16: heart-throbbing] NTTS reads with NT, but is corrected in pencil to "heartthrobbing". There is a question mark in pencil in the margin (presumably Warren is asking Erskine's opinion of the correction), which is crossed out in blue pencil (presumably Erskine is rejecting the correction). NTG reads "heartthrobbing", but there is a query in the margin of NTG about adding back the hyphen, which Warren has OK'd. Warren marked the hyphen in on the page proofs. 26: Brandy snifter] Glass *Ohio Review* 26: in moonshine] in the moonbeam *Ohio Review*, NTTS (revised to NT) 26: coffee table,] coffee-table, *Ohio Review*, NTTS (revised to NT) 27: it. And] it, and *Ohio Review*, NTTS (revised in black pen to NT) 30: Silky as pastel,] Like velvet, *Ohio Review*, Silkily NTTS (but corrected in typing to NT) 30: dust covers all.] There is a stanza inserted after this text in *Ohio Review:* "Oh, tell me the story!" [quotation marks mine] The stanza is canceled in black pen on NTTS. 32: to know it?] There is a stanza break after this text in *Ohio Review. Ohio Review* also includes an additional stanza here: "Memory is like heat-lightning at dusk, no thunder heard." (quotation marks mine)The stanza is canceled—and the stanza breaks before an after it are closed up—in black pen on NTTS. 36: We often] We *Ohio Review*, NTTS (revised in typing to NT) 38: used to be.] NTTS reads with NT. But Warren changed the final period to a comma, and added another line in typing: "And you know Truth is there that you cannot remember." Then both changes were canceled in blue pencil. 38: used to be.] Two identical canceled annotations follow in NTTS: "Ohio Review".

361 **Sister Water** Text: NT. Variant: *New York Review of Books,* 14 Oct. 1976, p. 24. 3: was dark and—] was— *NYRB* 14: Unidentifiable‸] ~, *NYRB* 16: Comes] Came *NYRB* 21: dawn light] dawn-light *NYRB* 26: water.] A canceled annotation follows in NTTS: "New York Review of Books".

362 **Memory Forgotten** Text: NT. 17: thralled?] NTTS is corrected in black pen to "enthralled?" but the NT reading is restored in blue pencil. 22: That liquid note … so true?] NTTS originally ended this way: "Sunlight once flashed on a platter on / A table and all the life of Jacob Boehme changed. Oh, hear // The liquid note from the thicket afar! It is nameless." Warren first crossed out the first sentence in black pen. Then he

crossed out the rest in pencil and typed in the NT reading, forgetting the "it" in the last line. Warren added back the "it" on NTG. 22: so true?] Two canceled annotations follows in NTTS: "END" and "Robert Penn Warren".

363 **Waking to Tap of Hammer** Text: NT. Variant: *Yale Review,* 67 (Spring 1978), p. 418. 1: Waking] WAKING *YR* 1: bedroom,] bed room, NTTS (revised to NT) 4: band-saw] band-saw *YR* 5: early∧] ~, *YR* 6: five-tonner∧] ~, *YR* 9: in the first light.] in first daylight. *YR* 12: and he seems not to hear.] he at first does not hear. *YR* 12: speak,] ~∧ NTTS (revised to NT) 18: fruit] flower *YR*, seed NTTS (revised in blue pencil to NT) 19: this truth,] truth, *YR* 22: spitfire] spit-fire *YR*, NTTS (revised in blue pen to NT) 23: Clambered gray] Climbed the gray *YR* 23: plunged, and emerged,] plunged, emerged, *YR* 26: forth:] forward: *YR* 26: Slowly,] ~∧ *YR* 27: at me.] Two canceled annotations follow: "Robert Penn Warren" and (handwritten) "Yale Review".

364 **Love Recognized** Text: NT. Variant: *Ohio Review,* 18 (Winter 1977), p. 34 (as Love at First Sight). 16: Silence.] A canceled handwritten annotation follows in NTTS "Yale [canceled] Ohio Review used title 'Love at First Sight'."

364 **The Smile** Text: NT. Variant: *Quest/78,* July–Aug. 1978, p. 80. 6: melt] meld *Quest/78*, NTTS (revised to NT) 12: Long] Now long *Quest/78* 12: an un-selfed] a de-selfed *Quest/78*, NTTS (revised in blue pencil to NT, although neglecting to change "a" to "an", and finally corrected to NT on NTG) 19: purpled] purpling *Quest/78* 20: Defines] Accepts *Quest/78* 22: breed a dream] breed a day *Quest/78* 24: smile.] A canceled annotation follows in NTTS: "*Quest* 77".

365 **How to Tell a Love Story** Text: NT. Variants: *Quest/78,* July–Aug. 1978, p. 80 (as "How to Tell a Story"), SP85. NTTS has the title as in *Quest/78*, but corrects to NT. 4: only its] its *Quest/78* 8: story.] ~, *Quest/78*, NTTS (revised in blue pencil to NT) 9: And no Time, no word.] And if there is no Time there is no word, *Quest/78*, NTTS (revised in blue pencil to NT) 15: sky] sea *Quest/78* 15: I could then] then I could *Quest/78*, NTTS (revised in blue pen to NT) 18: Time] all SP85 (revised on SP85G to SP85), *Emory* 18: truly began,] began *Quest/78*, NTTS (revised to NT) 19: ahead and a smile] ahead, a smile *Quest/78* 20: Back-flung] back-flung NTG (revised on NTG to NT) 22: till finally] till SP85 (revised on SP85G to SP85) 22: leans.] Two canceled annotations follow in NTTS: "Robert Penn Warren," and (handwritten) "Quest 77".

365 **Little Black Heart of the Telephone** Text: NT. Variants: *New Yorker,* 23 May 1977, p. 34, SP85, *Helsinki*. 2: *there!*—and] *there!* And *Helsinki* 3: poor∧] ~, *Helsinki* 4: I, too, have] I too have *NY* 6: I am] I'm *Helsinki* 11: any] this *Helsinki* 12: *So,* you demand, *the room's not empty, you're there?*] So, you demand, the room's not empty, you're there? *NY*, NTTS (revised on NTG to NT) 12: *empty, you're*] *empty—you're* *Helsinki* 15: mightn't] might not *Helsinki* 17: blankness] blackness NTTS (revised to NT) 17: blankness / Bleeds for] blankness bleeds / For *Helsinki* 19: scream,] ~∧ *Helsinki* 23: you have] you've *Helsinki* 24: lost in blankness] in blankness *Helsinki* 26: night,] ~∧ *Helsinki* 30: in broad daylight,] now in broad daylight, *NY*, NTTS (but corrected in blue pencil to NT) 30: I'm now] I'm out *NY*, NTTS (revised in blue pencil to NT) 35: floor, and velvety / Dust thick over everything, especially] floor, and / Velvety dust thick / Over everything, especially *Helsinki* 37: black] little black *Helsinki* 37: thumb-print] thumbprint *NY*, *Helsinki* 39: it's] it has *Helsinki* 39: disconnected.] A canceled annotation follows in NTTS: "New Yorker".

366 **Last Laugh** Text: NT. Variant: *New Yorker*, 12 June 1978, p. 80. 6: candlelight] candle light NTTS (revised to NT) 7: fish-eyes] fish eyes *NY* 8: twelve,] eleven, *NY* 11: truce"—that was] truce," was *NY*, NTTS (but corrected in blue pencil to NT) 19: Or∧] ~, *NY* 20: why∧] ~, *NY* 25: hog-bladder] hog bladder *NY* 26: brats'] brat's *NY*, NTTS (revised on NTG to NT) 26: So took then to laughing] Then he just began laughing *NY*, NTTS (revised in blue pencil to NT) 28: campfire] camp fire NTTS (revised to NT) 31: stiff] as stiff *NY* 32: whammo!—] whammo— *NY* 32: back-slapping] backslapping *NY* 32: riot.] ~! *NY* 34: and∧] ~, *NY* 34: stair-hall] stair hall, *NY* 36: ball;] ~, *NY* 38: was, but] was but, *NY* 39: Then∧] ~, *NY* 39: bedside∧] ~, *NY* 40: stare] look *NY* 41: died.] Two canceled annotations follow in NTTS: "Robert Penn Warren", and "New

Yorker".

368 **Heat Lightning** Text: NT. Variants: *Times Literary Supplement,* 5 May 1978, p. 491. There is a canceled annotation at the top of NTTS: "*version number two*". 34: and$_{\wedge}$] ~, *TLS* 36: The newspaper obit, ... Here silence.] The version in *TLS* differs extensively:

That moment when, kneeling, she wept, clutching
His knees till the doctor got in, vindictively,
A good jab of his syringe. How thunderless—
Yes—the newspaper obit years later I stumbled on. How faint
That flash! And I sit in the unmooned
Dark of an August night to see
The flicker and rose-flush beyond
Black peaks, and think how far,
Far away, and down what deep valley and scar
The thunder, redoubled, redoubling, rolls. Here silence.

39: rose-flush] flicker and rose-flush NTTS (revised in blue pencil to NT) 39: peaks, and think how far, / Far] peaks, / And think how far, far NTTS (but corrected in blue pencil to NT) 40: valley, scree,] valley and NTTS (revised on NTG to NT) 40: scar,] ~$_{\wedge}$ NTTS (revised in blue pencil to NT) 41: silence.] A canceled annotation follows in NTTS: "Robert Penn Warren".

369 **Inevitable Frontier** Text: NT. Variant: *New Yorker,* 13 March 1978, p. 36. 3: chert] basalt *NY* 3: boulders] talus *NY*, NTTS (revised to NT) 5: remember$_{\wedge}$] ~, *NY* 6: upside-] ~$_{\wedge}$ *NY* 12: something, yourself for instance,] something—yourself, for instance—*NY* 14: it,] ~$_{\wedge}$ *NY* 17: by dark,] in the dark, *NY* 17: Here,] ~$_{\wedge}$ *NY* 18: in] only in *NY* 18: but] and *NY* 19: full, in daylight, of gut-wheeze and littered with feces] full of gut-wheeze and shamelessly littered with feces *NY* 19: feces] faeces NTTS (revised in blue pencil to NT) 20: come,] ~; *NY* 20: at noon, waiters] waiters *NY* 22: locker-rooms,] locker rooms$_{\wedge}$ *NY*, locker-room, NTTS (revised on NTG to NT) 23: drinks,] ~$_{\wedge}$ *NY* 24: And coffee, are served under awnings. Another item:] And coffee of strange powers served till lights, as though a signal, go the least bit dim. *NY* 24: under awnings] under the dark awnings NTTS (revised to "under dark awnings" on NTTS and to NT on NTG) 25: but] and of peculiar definition, but *NY* 27: tongues,] ~— *NY* 30: well-adjusted,] well adjusted$_{\wedge}$ *NY* 32: Pascal$_{\wedge}$] ~, *NY*, NTTS (revised to NT) 35: burrow$_{\wedge}$] ~, *NY* 36: sportscar's headlight.] sports car's headlights. *NY* 36: headlight.] A canceled annotation follows in NTTS: "New Yorker".

370 **Heart of the Backlog** Text: NT. Variant: *New Yorker,* 30 Jan. 1978, p. 34. In NTTS there is a canceled previous title: "Atheist at Hearthside." 4: heartbeat.] heart-beat. NTTS (revised to NT) 7: now hear] hear now *NY* 12: rib-cage,] rib cage, *NY* 15: litter,] matter, *NY* 18: talus-like] tiny taluslike *NY* 21: talus-like,] taluslike, *NY* 23: fireplace] body *NY* 33: minuscule] miniscule NTTS (revised to NT) 36: what angle, or slant,] any angle by which, or slant, *NY*, NTTS (revised in blue pen to NT) 44: the last stars?] *NY* and NTTS add a line after this text: "But beautiful, too—so beautiful they may bring tears. You shiver,". The line was removed by Warren on NTG. 48: And needles claw-clamp] And claw-clamp goes needling *NY* 48: heart$_{\wedge}$] ~, NTTS (revised to NT) 49: melting] melding *NY*, NTTS (revised in blue pencil to NT) 54: crumpling] tearing *NY*, NTTS (revised to NT) 58: name.] A canceled annotation follows in NTTS: "New Yorker [handwritten:] (different title in mag.)"

372 **Identity and Argument for Prayer** Text: NT. Variant: *Southern Review,* ns 14 (Spring 1978), pp. 306–9 (as "An Argument for Prayer"). 2: In] On NTTS (revised to NT) 12: so,] ~$_{\wedge}$ *SoR*, NTTS (revised to NT) 13: old] the old *SoR* 19: sure,] sure, and perhaps could not understand it. NTTS (revised in blue pencil to NT) 20: *there,*] here, *SoR*, there, NTTS (revised to NT) 23: And] All *SoR* 24: stand$_{\wedge}$] ~, *SoR* 25: years] long *SoR* 25: now,] ~$_{\wedge}$ *SoR* 34: This dream of return.] There is a stanza break in *SoR* after this line. 35: truly

what] what truly *SoR* 35: If that is truly what it is.] A page turn in *SoR* obscures whether there is a stanza break after this line. 36: I once stood there,] I stood there once$_\wedge$ *SoR*, NTTS (revised in blue pencil to NT) 36: now have] have now *SoR*, NTTS (revised in blue pencil to NT) 37: dreamed,] $\sim_\wedge$ *SoR* 50: Of the name now.] Of the name now, / Nor of old emotion. *SoR*, Of the name now, / Nor of my old emotion. (revised to *SoR* on NTTS, and to NT on NTG) 51: any more,] anymore, *SoR*, NTTS (revised to NT) 60: years,] $\sim_\wedge$ *SoR*, NTTS (but revised in blue pencil to NT) 66: whatever / Vision or anguish] whatever anguish NTTS (revised in blue pencil to NT) 71: his heart,] man's heart, *SoR* 73: tin] time NTTS (revised to NT) 75: might,] $\sim_\wedge$ *SoR* 77: rooftop] roof-top *SoR*, NTTS (revised to NT) 78: that$_\wedge$] $\sim$, *SoR*, NTTS (revised to NT) 78: least$_\wedge$] $\sim$, *SoR* 80: Now *now* is all, and you *you.*] Now *now* is all. *SoR*, NTTS (revised to NT) 82: prayer.] A canceled annotation follows in NTTS: "Robert Penn Warren".

373 **Diver** Text: NT. Variant: *Southern Review,* ns 14 (Spring 1978), p. 303. NTTS has a canceled previous title: "Diver and Our Dream of Identity". 2: water] the water *SoR*, NTTS (revised in blue pencil to NT) 9: yap] *yap SoR*, NTTS (revised in blue pencil to NT) 12: shows] show NTTS (revised to NT) 13: a diver's] the diver's *SoR*, diver's NTTS (but corrected in blue pencil to NT) 14: watching] watchful *SoR* 15: unsuspected] undiscovered NTTS (revised in blue pencil to NT) 16: had] have *SoR* 19: in welcome back] to welcome him *SoR*, NTTS (but corrected in blue pencil to NT) 20: To all the joy] Back to the joy *SoR*, NTTS (but corrected in blue pencil to NT) 21: down in.] NTTS adds, then cancels, a further stanza: "Is this the only identity?" 21: down in.] A canceled annotation follows in NTTS: "Robert Penn Warren".

374 **Rather Like a Dream** Text: NT. Variant: *Southern Review,* ns 14 (Spring 1978), pp. 304–5. 19: join$_\wedge$] $\sim$, *SoR* 20: snow-draped.] snow-coped. *SoR*, NTTS (revised to NT) 23: hardens,] coagulates, NTTS (revised in blue pencil to NT) 25: drawstring] draw-string *SoR*, NTTS (revised to NT) 27: grows] closes *SoR* 27: a sky] sky *SoR* 28: spruce-deep] deep NTTS (revised in blue pencil to NT) 29: wonder,] $\sim$— *SoR* 31: just to know.] just to know. / To know what? One's own / Absolute reality? // Perhaps that is what we should all pray for, after all. NTTS (revised to NT) 31: to know.] A canceled annotation follows in NTTS: "Robert Penn Warren".

375 **Departure** Text: NT. Variant: *Ohio Review,* 18 (Winter 1977), p. 34. 11: and now, far away,] but now, *Ohio Review* 16: generally] often *Ohio Review*, NTTS (revised to NT) 18: face.] A canceled annotation follows in NTTS: "Ohio Review".

376 **Heat Wave Breaks** Text: NT. Variant: Broadside (Lexington, Kentucky: King Library Press, Fall 1979). (I examined copy no. 4, of 6, at the Beinecke Library, which follows NT.) 4: music-less.] musicless. NTTS (revised in blue pencil to NT) 5: For some coolness the feathers are ruffled to give air ingress.] For some coolness the feathers are ruffled to give ingress. NTTS (revised in blue pencil from "The feathers are ruffled to give for some coolness ingress." and corrected to NT on NTG) 7: one only just] one just NTTS (revised in blue pencil to NT) 16: Will you . . . lightning-stricken air?] The stanza in NTTS is a late revision, added in typing on a different typewriter. The original stanza in NTTS read:

Will you wake when clouds roll and roil in the lightning-flare?
When blasphemy of thunder makes the mountain quake,
And again wet leaves twirl on their stems in the green-flaming glare?
For what do we pray our God? Is it that He make
All the world stab anew to your heart in the lightning-stricken air?

16: and the roil and lightning make] and roil and the lightning makes NTTS (revised on NTG to NT) 19: should] would NTTS (revised on NTG to NT) 20: air?] A canceled annotation follows in NTTS: "Robert Penn Warren".

376 **Heart of Autumn** Text: NT. Variants: *Atlantic Monthly,* Oct. 1977, p. 84 (as the first part of the sequence "Three Poems in Time"), *15 Poems*, selected by Rosanna Warren, privately printed for Stuart Wright, 1985, SP85, *Helsinki.* 1: gap, fall comes.] gap. Fall comes. *Helsinki* 2: Today,] $\sim_\wedge$ *Helsinki* 3: in perfect formation, wild geese]

wild geese, in perfect formation, *Atlantic* 5: air, fall.] air. *Atlantic* 8: tirelessly] tireless *Helsinki* 8: upon] after *Atlantic* 10: wing-beat.] ∼, *Atlantic* 11: rise,] ∼∧ NTTS (revised to NT) 16: not why I am here.] what more? *Atlantic* 18: same—] ∼?— *Atlantic* 18: and I stand, my face lifted now skyward,] And now I stand, face skyward, *Atlantic* 18: and] And NTTS (revised to NT) 20: tough] feel tough *Atlantic* 23: To unwordable utterance— / Toward sunset, at a great height.] To the unwordable— / Now toward sunset, at a great height. *Atlantic* 24: height.] A canceled annotation follows in NTTS: "Atlantic Monthly".

Being Here

Poetry 1977–1980

The typescript material in the Beinecke Library indicates that this book went through many drafts, and some rethinking about what to include and how to order the poems. Until a late stage of production—very late, since the typescript includes a designed mock-up of the proposed title page—the title of this volume was *Life is a Fable.* Indeed, as late as the time the book was set in galleys it was called *Life is a Fable*, although the title was corrected on the galleys. Like *Now and Then*, the typescript was assembled from photocopies of re-typed copies of poems made after their magazine appearance, with annotations giving the name of the magazine in which they occurred. Unlike *Now and Then*, the typescript seems to have been typed in one piece, and the annotations added for the convenience of the permissions department at Random House. The page numbers have been added—presumably later—in blue pen. The copy is marked up in Warren's hand in black pencil, and in another hand in red pencil. (Unless marked otherwise, all of the mark-up described here is in black pencil.) Like most Warren typescripts BHTS is single-spaced. The dedication to Gabriel Thomas Penn and the dialogue between the old man and the boy appeared on a separate page, and the three epigraphs appeared on another separate page. BHTS gives 1838 as the year of Gabriel Thomas Penn's birth (the error is corrected on the galleys). In the quotation from Augustine, the second word is corrected to "thirst" from "yearn," and the translator's name is added in pencil, not in Warren's handwriting. In one of Warren's own copies at Western Kentucky University, he has corrected the date of Gabriel Thomas Penn's birth to 1837 (copy 310). Some revisions in this book may have come very late indeed. A letter to Erskine of January 28, 1980, refers to changes made in a bound manuscript that Warren kept after returning the copy-edited typescripts. There are revisions not only on the galleys, but also on the page proofs. There are even some corrections on the "blues" for this volume, including some new copy on a card referred to in a note on the cover of the "blues" but now lost. The Secker and Warburg London edition is, except for the title page, printed from the American plates. There is a copy of this book, marked up by Warren with proposed revisions for Stuart Wright's use on May 25, 1987, in the Special Collections Department of the Emory University Library. I quote Warren's notes by permission. Warren has also marked up, slightly, a copy of this book now in the Robert Penn Warren Room of the Library of the Kentucky Museum at Western Kentucky University. I quote that volume too by permission. The setting typescript for the section of SP85 drawn from this volume consisted of taped-in photocopies of passages from BH. Because the revisions for SP85 are sometimes a vexed question, I have indicated where the SP85 revisions are made on SP85TS. Title Page] SP85 omits the dialogue between the old man and the young boy. SP85 capitalizes "time standard" in the quotation from Van Nostrand's Scientific Encyclopedia, and does not capitalize "Time" in the quotation from Augustine.

381 **October Picnic Long Ago** Text: BH. Variants: *Atlantic Monthly,* Oct. 1979, p. 79, *15 Poems*, selected by Rosanna Warren, privately printed for Stuart Wright, 1985. The *Atlantic* version is set in roman type, with italics for emphasis. In the Emory copy Warren has noted that he wished this poem set in roman. Warren did not in the Emory copy change the type of "Passers-by on Snowy Night" to roman, although the two poems in italic type were intended to serve as bookends for the volume. In BHTS the

poem is clearly marked for italic type. In BHG it is set in roman. In 15P the poem is out of published sequence, following "The Cross." 3: To the surrey helped Mother up,] Helped my mother up in the surrey, *Atlantic* 3: her,] ~. *Atlantic* 4: toward seven,] six years old, *Atlantic* 4: my sister] my little sister *Atlantic* 4: aright,] ~. *Atlantic* 5: in] like *Atlantic* 6: side-lane] side lane *Atlantic* 7: flicked a fairy shadow and light] flickered in shadow with light *Atlantic* 10: while] and *Atlantic* 10: was steered] steered *Atlantic* 12: Father'd known:] BHTS mistakenly adds an extra line of vertical space here, but corrects it. 13: off to one side, by a boulder,] off by a boulder, *Atlantic* 14: us,] blankets, *Atlantic* 15: horse unhitched and staked,] the horse unhitched, *Atlantic* 17: a stable] the stable *Atlantic* 19: mother's] Mother's BHTS (revised in red pencil to BH) 20: father's] Father's BHTS (revised in red pencil to BH) 20: father's suede shoes were] father had suede shoes *Atlantic*, BHTS (revised on BHG to BH) 21: gone$_\wedge$] ~, *Atlantic* 22: But not far, and Father and Mother gone,] And Father and Mother had tiptoed away, *Atlantic* 23: long conversation] long close conversation *Atlantic* 25: But where? Perhaps in some high, cloud-floating, and sunlit land.] Underground or perhaps in some floating, high, dreamy, sunlit land. *Atlantic* 27: mother] Mother BHTS (revised in red pencil to BH) 27: out,] ~: *Atlantic* 27: "Could a place so beautiful be!"] "How beautiful can a place be!" *Atlantic* 28: father] Father BHTS (revised in red pencil to BH) 28: said,] ~: *Atlantic* 29: And you'll see all the beautiful world there is to see."] And I'll show you all the world's beautiful things to see." *Atlantic* 30: would] could *Atlantic* 30: she now] she *Atlantic* 30: now see?"] now see?$_\wedge$ BHTS (revised in red pencil to BH) 31: swung the] swung up the *Atlantic* 32: throat, and she gaily sang] throat like a song, and she sang *Atlantic* 32: and she gaily sang] and she sang BHTS (revised on BHG to BH) 33: homeward while the shadows,] along the lane, and the shadows, *Atlantic* 34: Future] future *Atlantic* 34: with a] with *Atlantic* 35: future] Future *Atlantic* 35: sang,] ~. *Atlantic* 36: And she sang.] Line omitted in *Atlantic.* In BHTS there is a canceled annotation, "atlantic." The annotation indicates that BHTS was prepared after the magazine publication. In the almost-final typescript Warren sent to the Beinecke Library on August 27, 1978, the poem ends not with this phrase, but with the following stanza:

Shit—picnics end. And I saw the face on the pillow.
And later, my Father's, like stone, when the pain had passed.
Yes, picnics end, and why should I allow
A fool memory to show me how joy had trespassed
On Truth? Or could it be true that sorrow on joy trespassed?

I.

382 **Speleology** Text: BH. Variant: *New Yorker,* 10 Sept. 1979, p. 47. 1: At cliff-foot where great ledges thrust,] At the foot of the cliff, where the great ledge thrusts, *NY* 2: rank,] ~$_\wedge$ *NY* 2: stream,] stream once *NY* 3: Ages back, had] Had *NY* 3: now$_\wedge$] ~, *NY* 3: earth$_\wedge$] ~, *NY* 4: old] the old *NY* 4: forest trees rise] forest rises *NY* 4: cliff-height,] cliff height. *NY* 5: comes.] comes there. *NY* 6: I first] first I *NY* 6: cave-mouth] cave mouth *NY* 7: the inner dark.] inner darkness. *NY* 8: in] and in *NY* 8: crept further,] further crept, BHTS (revised on BHG to BH) 8: further,] farther, *NY* 9: a gray / Blotch of] the gray blotch / Of *NY* 12: The whole night] And all night *NY*, BHTS (revised on BHG to BH) 12: Daylight.] Then daylight. *NY* 14: down-stabbed] stabbed *NY* 15: my light. Again, lower.] the light I held. Then lower again. *NY* 17: cave-cricket crawl] cave cricket move *NY* 17: light on] the light back on, *NY* 17: light on / To] light / On to BHTS (revised on BHG to BH) 18: To see] And saw *NY* 18: cave-cricket] cave cricket *NY* 19: As a ghost on my brown arm.] On white and velvety stone. *NY* 20: Crept on.] Crept on, light on. *NY* 20: Heard, faintly, below // A silken and] Heard faintly, below, a silken // And *NY* 21: water—so] water. And *NY* 22: to one side.] to one side, and saw. *NY* 22: out / A ledge under] on a ledge / Under *NY* 23: far down, far down,] far down, far below now, *NY* 23: channeled] channelled *NY* 25: unmoving, I lay,] I lay there, unmoving. *NY*, unmoving, I lay there, BHTS (revised on BHG to BH) 26: Lulled as by song in a dream,] Lulled in a sound like song in dream, *NY* 27: a] that *NY* 28: *Me—who am I?* Felt] *Who*

am I? And felt *NY* 29: Heart beating as though to a pulse] My heart beat to the pulse *New Yorker*, Heart beat to a pulse BHTS (revised on BHG to BH) 30: would it] it would *NY*, BHTS (revised on BHG to BH) 31: In its beat, ... a song like terror] This stanza in *NY* is substantially different:

In its beat, part of all. Suppose I stayed there, part of all?
But I woke with a scream. Had I dozed? Scarcely, I managed
To grab the flashlight as it fell. Turned it on, and
Once more looked down the slow slicing of limestone where
Water winked, in bubbles like fish eyes, and song was a terror.

32: The flashlight,] Had I dozed? The flashlight, BHTS (revised to BH) 35: a song] song BHTS (revised on BHG to BH) 36: Years later, ... part of all.] This stanza in *NY* is substantially different:

I never came back. But years later, past dream, have lain
In dark and heard the depth of interminable song,
And laid hand to heart, and once again thought: *This is me.*
And thought: *Who am I?* And with hand on heart have wondered
What it would be like to be, after all, part of all.

36: Years later,] I never went back, but years later, BHTS (revised to BH) 36: I have lain] have lain BHTS (revised to BH) 37: that unending] interminable BHTS (revised on BHG to BH) 40: would it] it would BHTS (revised on BHG to BH) 41: And in darkness have even asked: *Is this all? What is all?*] Line omitted in *NY.* 41: *What is all?*] A canceled annotation follows in BHTS: "new yorker."

383 **When Life Begins** Text: BH. Variants: *Salmagundi,* no. 46 (Fall 1979), pp. 8–9, SP85. 1: the old] the *Salmagundi* 1: head,] ~∧ *Salmagundi* 4: chisel-grooved shadow] chisel-shadow *Salmagundi* 6: That distance, ... The silence] The distance was a far hill's horizon / That bulged, past woods, into the blue / Of a summer's afternoon, and silence *Salmagundi* 7: throbbing] unthrobbing BHTS (revised on BHG to BH) 8: The silence] Our silence SP85 (revised on SP85G to SP85) 9: There seemed] That seemed *Salmagundi* Now seemed SP85 (revised on SP85G to SP85) 10: That] Which *Salmagundi* 11: One hand, gnarled, liver-blotched, but sinewed] One hand, brown liver-blotched and strong *Salmagundi* 14: pipe,] ~∧ *Salmagundi* 19: cupboarded ... into the abstractness] absorbed into the abstractness *Salmagundi* 24: behind] within BHTS (revised on BHG to BH) 26: the old voice] his voice *Salmagundi* 27: past but] old and *Salmagundi* 28: hoofbeat] hoof-beat *Salmagundi*, BHTS (revised to BH) 28: steel-clang,] steel clang, *Salmagundi* 30: Far smoke seen ... How a young boy, dying, broke into tears.] Or how a boy, dying, broke into tears— *Salmagundi* 30: seen long] long seen BHTS (revised to BH) 30: you hear sound,] There is a stanza break after this text in SP85. In SP85TS this is a point where two xeroxed passages from BH are taped together, and it seems likely that the stanza break is merely an error. 33: you!] *you!* SP85 (in pencil on SP85TS), *Emory* 35: woods-cover,] woodscover, BHTS (revised to BH) 42: After that event renewed,] Renewed after that event, BHTS (revised to BH) 43: man, onçe he said] man once said BHTS (revised on BHG to BH). BHG did not, through a printer's error, capture how the line straddled the stanza break, and Warren corrected it. Warren's annotation on the duplicate galleys captures his intentions about lines that straddle stanza breaks: "This is metrically the rest of the line beginning 'Quail calls.' But 'And the old man etc.' is to be moved right, beginning after period following 'calls' and dropped extra space to begin new stanza." 45: "Ain't scairt to die"—the boy's words—"it's jist] "Not afraid to die" — what he said. "It's just *Salmagundi* 46: chance] chanst SP85 (revised on SP85G to SP85) 48: bugle] a bugle *Salmagundi* 48: a charge,] charge. *Salmagundi* 49: silk,] ~— *Salmagundi* 50: strong—] ~, *Salmagundi* 50: dance] prance *Salmagundi* 52: Old eyelids] The blue gaze *Salmagundi* 54: that, beyond the horizon's heave, / Time crouched,] that beyond the horizon crouched / Time, *Salmagundi* 54: heave,] line∧ BHTS (revised to BH) 56: glare.] blaze. *Salmagundi*

384 **Boyhood in Tobacco Country** Text: BH. Variant: *Antaeus,* 30/31 (Summer–Autumn 1978), p. 242 (as "Boyhood in Tobacco Country, at Sunset"). 1: sunset,] ∼∧ *Antaeus* 2: burning.] aflame. *Antaeus* 4: they were hammered of bronze blackened / To timelessness.] hammered in blackened bronze, / into timelessness. *Antaeus* 5: curing barns] curing-barns *Antaeus* 5: tobacco,] ∼∧ *Antaeus* 6: in pale streaking, clings / To the world's dim, undefinable bulge.] in striations, pale, clings to the world's dim rondure. *Antaeus* 8: slashed stubs,] the slashed stubble, *Antaeus* 8: homeward or homeless,] homeless or homeward, *Antaeus* 10: namelessness] nameless *Antaeus* 11: star,] ∼. *Antaeus* 12: And again, I am walking] And I walk down *Antaeus* 13: world. // I move in its timelessness.] twilight that happens, // And will happen. I wait. *Antaeus* 16: Precious] Unassuagable *Antaeus* 17: darkling I] I darkling *Antaeus* 20: smoldering,] and smouldering, *Antaeus,* smouldering, BHTS (revised to BH) 21: paling in retardation, it begins] paling, begins *Antaeus* 21: it begins] begins (revised to BH) (revised on BHG to BH) 22: zenithward∧] ∼, *Antaeus* 25: Tonight / The] Tonight the *Antaeus* 27: the sky.] BHTS has a canceled annotation after this text: "antaeus".

385 **Filling Night with the Name: Funeral as Local Color** Text: BH. Variant: *Salmagundi,* no. 46 (Fall 1979), p. 10 (as "Filling Night With The Name"). The original of which BHTS is a photocopy was typed on a different typewriter from that used in the rest of the volume. 1: predictable,] ∼∧ *Salmagundi,* BHTS (revised to BH) 2: at last lay] lay *Salmagundi* 5: Of] From *Salmagundi* 8: false,] ∼∧ *Salmagundi* 8: couldn't exactly] herself couldn't *Salmagundi* 11: gonna] gotta *Salmagundi,* BHTS (revised to BH) 12: Remarked on] Admired *Salmagundi* 14: farm.] farm gate. *Salmagundi* 14: supper. Near] supper, near *Salmagundi* 15: Good clothes] His good clothes *Salmagundi* 17: Sunday] his Sunday *Salmagundi* 18: Where] Like she'd said, where *Salmagundi* 18: sat,] got set, *Salmagundi* 20: by some kindly anonymous hand] that some kindly, anonymous hand had *Salmagundi* 21: He] But he *Salmagundi* 22: pen, paper, ink. Sat] paper, pen, ink, and sat *Salmagundi,* pen, paper, ink, and sat BHTS (revised to BH) 24: just the single, simple word *whip-o-will.* // For the bird was filling the night with the name: *whip-o-will.* // *Whip-o-will.*] just the name / Of the bird filling night with the name: *whip-o-will.* // *Whip-o-will.* *Salmagundi* 26: *Whip-o-will.*] A canceled annotation follows in BHTS: "salmagundi".

386 **Recollection in Upper Ontario, from Long Before** Text: BH. Variants: Sydney Lea, Jay Parini, and M. Robin Barone, eds., *Richard Eberhart: A Celebration,* (Kenyon Hill Publications, Inc., 1980), n. p., *New England Review,* 2 (Spring 1980), pp. 336–39. 6: random and rabble and white.] random and white. *Eberhart* 6: random∧] ∼, *New England Review* 6: rabble∧] ∼, *New England Review* 12: brass-bound∧] ∼, *Eberhart, New England Review* 13: loon] loons *Eberhart, New England Review* 20: spewing] boiling *New England Review* 22: sure. The owl— / He may wake me again] sure, for I may wake up. / The owl, he may wake me now *Eberhart,* sure. I may wake up. / The owl, he may wake me again *New England Review* 24: question,] ∼— *Eberhart, New England Review* 27: your conscience] conscience *Eberhart* 29: no] nor *Eberhart, New England Review,* BHTS (revised on BHG to BH) 29: on. And] on, and *Eberhart, New England Review* 30: Zack,] Jeff, BHTS (revised to BH) 30: ole] old *Eberhart* 30: white-trash—] ∼, *Eberhart* 30: dragging—] ∼, *Eberhart, New England Review* 33: skirts] and skirt *Eberhart* skirt *New England Review* 34: clubfoot,] club-foot, *Eberhart, New England Review,* BHTS, BHG (but page proofs corrected to BH) 36: Zack's] Jeff's BHTS (revised to BH) 38: That the coal,] That coal, BHTS (revised in red pencil to BH) 40: I wake up, or not.] I may wake up or not. *Eberhart, New England Review,* BHTS (revised to "I wake up or not" and revised again on BHG to BH) 41: It blows on] The whistle keeps blowing *Eberhart,* It keeps blowing *New England Review* 42: And Mag, of a sudden, is down. The brogan she wears] and Old Mag, of a sudden, is down, the brogan she wears *Eberhart* 43: clubfoot,] club-foot, *Eberhart, New England Review,* BHTS, BHG (but page proofs corrected to BH) 44: chute] chute siding *Eberhart* 44: here.] ∼— *Eberhart, New England Review,* BHTS (revised to BH) 46: jar,] ∼. *Eberhart* 47: Mount box,] Mount-box, *Eberhart, New England Review* 47: Zack,] Jeff, BHTS (revised to BH) 48: He keeps

pulling. She's up. Zack bends at the brogan.] He pulls Mag, gets her up, now bends at the brogan. *Eberhart* 48: Zack] Jeff BHTS (revised to BH) 48: pulling. She's] pulling, she's *New England Review* 50: Zack's up ... and the last] But Zack's up, shoe's out. Or is it? But Mag— / Now the strange, it begins. Mag's standing—then down, / Down for good, and over both rails, and the last *Eberhart,* Zack's up, the shoe's out! Or is it? For with Mag— / The strange, it begins. Mag's standing—then down, / Down for good, and over both rails, and the last *New England Review*, Jeff's up, she's out! Or is it? For now, / The strange, it begins. Mag's standing—then down, / Down for good, and over both rails, and the last BHTS (revised to BH) 53: his] Zack's *Eberhart, New England Review*, Jeff's BHTS (revised to BH) 53: reckoned.] reckon. *New England Review*, BHTS (revised to BH) 54: Time stops like it's no-Time. Then,] Time stops a long time. And then *Eberhart,* Time stops like a clock. A long time. Then *New England Review*, BHTS (revised to BH) 57: The first sheet pass. It sags.] Then in the first sheet, the sag. *Eberhart,* The first sheet come. It sags. *New England Review* 60: jar: the] jar, see the *Eberhart,* jar. The *New England Review* 60: fritillary] Fritillary *Eberhart*, BHTS (revised on BHG to BH), Fritillary's *New England Review* 61: Near] It's *New England Review* 61: Near dark by this time.] It's dark by the time *Eberhart* 63: Who said: "Hell—it's hamburger now!"] No stanza break after this line in *Eberhart.* 65: accident"—] accident," *Eberhart* 69: Zack, now drunk] Zack drunk *Eberhart* Zack, drunk *New England Review*, Jeff, drunk (revised to BH) 70: Says:] ~, *Eberhart, New England Review*, BHTS (revised to BH) 73: her!] ~. *Eberhart* 75: rusty nails] nails *Eberhart* 76: butterfly ketcher] butterfly-ketcher *New England Review* 77: haul-ass] haul ass *Eberhart, New England Review*, BHTS (revised to BH) 77: afore] a-fore *New England Review*, BHTS (revised to BH) 77: come.] ~! *Eberhart* 77: So shoved me.] No stanza break after this test in *Eberhart.* 80: farm-folks] farm folks *Eberhart* far-folks BHG (revised on BHG to BH) 81: I stood] Stood *Eberhart, New England Review*, BHTS (revised to BH, first on BHTS, then on BHG) 81: inside me, it grew.] grew in me. / No name for it yet. No face. *Eberhart* 82: And] But *Eberhart* 83: inside of] inside *Eberhart, New England Review*, BHTS (revised on BHG to BH) 83: Zack's] Jeff's BHTS (revised to BH) 83: a coal-oil] coal-oil *Eberhart* 84: Zack] Jeff BHTS (revised to BH) 85: just married.] *Eberhart* has a stanza break after this text. 88: foot. Leaned] foot, leaned *Eberhart* 88: kissed it. // And tears gone bright in her eyes.] kissed it, / And tears gone bright in her eyes. *Eberhart* 90: all the] all *Eberhart, New England Review*, BHTS (revised on BHG to BH) 91: see it.] see. *Eberhart* 92: summer,] $\sim_\wedge$ *Eberhart* 93: darkness. If] darkness, if *Eberhart* 93: winter,] $\sim_\wedge$ *Eberhart* 95: handle] handled *Eberhart* 95: himself.] ~, *Eberhart, New England Review* 96: grab her.] do it. *Eberhart, New England Review* 98: In the old real dream: the brass-bound express] In the real dream: the express *Eberhart* 101: To wake me.] *New England Review* omits the stanza break after this text. 101: To wake me. // Stars] To wake me, / And stars *Eberhart* 104: canoes] the canoes *Eberhart* 106: a rhythm] the rhythm *Eberhart* 109: The same] the same *Eberhart* 112: I see?] A canceled annotation follows in BHTS: "new england review".

388 **The Moonlight's Dream** Text: BH. Variant: *Poetry,* 135 (Nov. 1979), pp. 81–82. The original of which BHTS is a photocopy was typed on the second typewriter. 1: that] at *Poetry* 2: knew$_\wedge$] ~, *Poetry* 3: his chest.] chest. *Poetry* 4: like silk or the rustle] as silky as rustle *Poetry* 5: night breeze] night-breeze *Poetry* 5: was] is *Poetry* 6: all,] $\sim_\wedge$ *Poetry* 7: now struggled,] struggled, *Poetry* 7: slow,] $\sim_\wedge$ *Poetry* 8: But one night had roused to a blood-yell, dreaming Fort Pillow or Shiloh.] But once dreamed forth a yell for blood, at Fort Pillow or Shiloh. *Poetry* 13: out] here *Poetry*, BHTS (revised on BHG to BH) 14: back-looking, now] back-looking now, *Poetry* 16: *I go where they go, for they must know where we go.*] *I must go where they go, for they must know where to go. Poetry* 17: did know the way] knew their way *Poetry* 19: And they followed the path that wandered down to a stream] And I took the path it dreamed, which led to the stream *Poetry*, And I took the path it dreamed that led to a stream BHTS (revised to BH, except that it is "I followed" rather than "they followed", and corrected on BHG to BH) 20: their] and *Poetry*, and their BHTS (revised to BH) 21: Staring] Stared *Poetry*, BHTS (revised to

BH) 24: pain.] ~, *Poetry* 26: and lay] and I lay *Emory* 29: far,] ~∧ *Poetry* 30: woke,] rose, *Poetry*, BHTS (revised on BHG to BH) 31: corn-balk,] the corn balks, *Poetry* 31: creek,] ~— *Poetry* 32: for] and *Poetry* 33: bulldozed] bull-dozed *Poetry*, BHTS (revised to BH) 34: passion and pain and endeavor,] passion, and pain, and endeavor BHTS (revised to BH) 35: gone,] ~∧ *Poetry* 35: with] in *Poetry* 38: spot where my blood / Is unwitting] spot, my blood / Unwitting *Poetry* 40: in] as part of *Poetry* 40: the moonlight's dream.] A canceled annotation follows in BHTS: "poetry".

389 **The Only Poem** Text: BH. Variant: *American Poetry Review,* 8 (July–Aug. 1979), p. 5. In *Emory*, Warren has added a marginal note: "The friends were Allen Tate and Caroline Gordon." 2: May] Will *APR* 2: of memory,] in memory, *APR* 2: eyes.] ~, *APR* 3: I may find.] I find. *APR* 4: If perhaps] If, perhaps, *APR* 4: catch me] catch me then *APR* 5: The facts] But the facts *APR* 5: surely are] are certainly *APR* 8: sheet-edge] sheet *APR* 9: then] only *APR* 10: Only] A *APR* 11: to describe, but words blurring, refrained.] speaking of, could not, then refrained. *APR* 13: My friends stashed] Of my friends left *APR* 13: careers.] ~; *APR* 14: So for friendship] So, for friendship, *APR* 19: Till] So *APR* 19: could swing] swung *APR* 19: prey∧] ~, *APR* 20: That] And the prey *APR* 23: swell.] ~, *APR* 24: away.] ~! *APR* 27: or] nor *APR* 27: what] neither *APR* 28: built into Time's own name?] that is built into Time's name. *APR*, BHTS (revised to BH) 28: own name?] A canceled annotation follows in BHTS: "american poetry review".

390 **Platonic Drowse** Text: BH.

391 **Grackles, Goodbye** Text: BH. Variants: *Salmagundi,* no. 46 (Fall 1979), p. 9 (as "Grackles, Goodbye!"), SP85. Unlike other pages in BHTS, the page for this poem is folded in half, as for mailing. 1: Black] The black *Salmagundi* 1: as,] ~∧ BHTS (revised to BH) 4: stand] stand here *Salmagundi*, stand there BHTS (revised to BH) 5: trance] my trance *Salmagundi*, BHTS (revised to BH) 6: first fall] gum *Salmagundi*, first *Emory* 6: flame-red,] gone flame-red, *Emory* 7: Bough-grip, and seek, through gold light of the season's sun,] High bough-grip and seek, through the windless gold light of fall's sun, *Salmagundi*, High bough-grip and seek, through windless gold light of the season's sun, BHTS (revised to BH) 12: How] Then *Salmagundi* 12: their] the *Salmagundi*, BHTS (revised to BH) 12: obscene fake lawn.] obscene false lawn. *Salmagundi*, BHTS reads as BH, but is corrected to "obscene lawn" (revised on BHG to BH) 13: Who needs] I almost laughed at *Salmagundi*, BHTS (revised to BH) 14: the earth's] earth's *Salmagundi,* SP85 (revised on SP85G to SP85) 15: of fool] of a fool *Salmagundi*, BHTS (revised to BH) 15: of lie?] of a lie? *Salmagundi*, BHTS revised to BH) 16: half-wit] halfwit *Salmagundi*, BHTS (revised to BH) 18: above,] ~∧ *Salmagundi* 19: turn∧] ~, *Salmagundi* 20: Death] death *Salmagundi* 20: the true name] the name *Salmagundi* 20: Love.] love. *Salmagundi*

II.

392 **Youthful Truth-Seeker, Half-Naked, at Night, Running down Beach South of San Francisco** Text: BH. Variants: *Atlantic Monthly,* Dec. 1978, pp. 64–65 (as "Truth-Seeker, Half-Naked, at Night, Running Down Beach South of San Francisco"), *Dialogue,* 12.3 (1979), pp. 54–55, SP85. In *Emory* Warren has written a marginal note: "This poem (illegible) the years 1925 (fall) to spring 1927 when I lived in Berkeley (illegible) and SF and was often at beach (three illegible words) night." 1: Then down-riding] Down-riding *Atlantic* 3: Phlegm] Breath *Atlantic* 4: tide] the tide *Atlantic* 4: air] the air *Atlantic*, BHTS (revised on BHG to BH) 5: which∧] ~, *Atlantic* 5: On] While on *Atlantic* 5: On the right hand,] On right hand BHTS (revised to BH) 7: To] But to *Atlantic* 11: While] And *Atlantic* 11: afar,] far, *Atlantic* 11: fog] the fog now *Atlantic* 11: leagues afar, fog threatens to grow,] fog, leagues afar, now threatens to grow, SP85 (revised on SP85G to SP85) 11: grow,] ~∧ *Atlantic* 12: But on I yet run, face up, stars shining above my wet head] While I run face-up, stars yet shining above my wet head *Atlantic* 14: philosophy∧] ~, *Atlantic* 18: joke∧] ~, *Atlantic* 18: the laughing] a laughing *Atlantic* 22: fullness and threat,] fullness∧ *Atlantic*, fulness and threat, BHTS (revised to BH) 23: unwordable] that unwordable *Atlantic* 24: past—] ~, *Atlantic* 25: by daylight] daylight *Atlantic*, BHTS (revised to BH) 27: ice] the ice *Atlantic* 27: white-night Arctic] the Arctic white-night *Atlantic*, Arctic white-night BHTS (revised to BH) 28: weeps—over] weeps over *Atlantic*,

BHTS (revised to "weeps, over" and corrected on BHG to BH) 29: sand] and sand now *Atlantic* 30: And the city grows dim, dimmer still,] And the city's glow fading dimmer, then dimmer still, *Atlantic* 32: the Truth] the truth *Atlantic,* what SP85 (revised on SP85G to SP85) 32: angry need] need *Atlantic* 33: beach∧] ~, *Atlantic* 33: sea∧] ~, SP85 (revised on SP85G to SP85) 34: That] Which SP85 (revised on SP85G to SP85) 36: and as] as BHTS (revised to BH) 36: as] perhaps as *Atlantic* 36: feckless∧] ~, *Atlantic* 37: So I stare at the stars that remain, shut eyes, in dark press an ear] So I stare at the stars, then shut eyes, and in dark press an ear *Atlantic* 38: sand, cold] sand as cold *Atlantic*, sand cold BHTS (revised to BH) 38: cement,] ~∧ BHTS (revised to BH) 40: depth] earth-depth *Western Kentucky* 40: end.] ~, *Atlantic* 41: Below all silken soil-slip, ... against rock grieves,] And deeper than ocean, or cold-crinkled earth crust, / Past silken soil-slip, past rocks that against rocks grieve, *Atlantic* 41: crinkled] crinkling SP85 (revised on SP85G to SP85) 43: There] Then *Atlantic* 43: dark] darkness *Atlantic* 43: lust,] ~∧ *Atlantic* 44: that churns and heaves?] churn and heave? *Atlantic* 45: Or is] Oh, is *Atlantic* 46: heat-simmered] heat-simmering *Atlantic* 46: heart, like eye,] the heart, like an eye, *Atlantic* 47: sleep at last—it has] sleep, at last it has *Atlantic* 50: dune-tops,] a dune top, *Atlantic*, the dune top, BHTS (revised on BHG to BH) 50: beach-stones?] the beach-stones? *Atlantic* 51: damn] damned *Atlantic* 52: under stars,] under stars, the same old ones, BHTS (revised to BH) 52: tottering] night-tottering *Atlantic* 52: bones.] A canceled annotation follows: "atlantic".

393 **Snowshoeing Back to Camp in Gloaming** Text: BH. Variant: *New England Review,* 1 (Spring 1979), pp. 263–64, *15 Poems*, selected by Rosanna Warren, privately printed for Stuart Wright, 1985. In *Emory* Warren has a marginal note: "Vermont on one of the ski trips." 3: thongs] for thongs *New England Review* 4: mowing, / I stood. Westward] mowing, I / Stood, westward *New England Review* 6: half mile] half-mile *New England Review* 8: to cliff-thrust,] to the cliff-thrust, *New England Review* 9: striation] striations *New England Review* 9: the sun, / Unmoving] the sun, / With spectral spectrum belted, pale in its ghost-nimb, / Unmoving *New England Review* 11: horizon— / The sun, by a spectral spectrum belted, / Pale in its ghost-nimb. // The shadow of spruces,] horizon. / The shadow of spruces, *New England Review* 17: Time died in my heart.] And Time seemed to die in my heart. *New England Review*, BHTS (revised to BH) 19: Timelessness,] timelessness, *New England Review* 20: might] might yet *New England Review* 25: In] With *New England Review* 25: garrote] garrotte *New England Review* 30: crow in distance] crow, in distance, *New England Review* 32: suddenly] had suddenly *New England Review* 33: from] from the *New England Review* 33: spruce-blackness∧] ~, *New England Review* 34: Leaped closer. ... Magenta] Leaped closer, and that instant / The sun-nimb made contact / With jag-heave of mountain, / And magenta *New England Review* 37: suddenly gray] gray *New England Review* 37: feet,] No line break after this text in *New England Review.* 40: sky-thrust, behind me,] sky-thrust, *Emory* 42: Beech] Beech, behind me, *Emory* 42: last lone] last and lone *New England Review* 43: the] bole *New England Review* 45: Now the] The *New England Review* 45: track,] ~∧ BHTS (revised to BH both on BHTS and BHG) 45: gone pale] pale *New England Review* 46: Downward floated] Floated downward *New England Review*, *Emory* 46: darkness,] ~. *New England Review* 47: starward∧] ~, *New England Review* 60: Against the] Against that *New England Review* 63: star-glint.] A canceled annotation follows in BHTS: "new england review".

395 **Why Have I Wandered the Asphalt of Midnight?** Text: BH. Variants: Broadsheet, For Aaron Copland on the occasion of his 78th birthday (Winston-Salem, N.C.: Palaemon Press Limited, 14 Nov. 1978; as "Why?"), *Southern Review,* ns 16 (Spring 1980), pp. 379–80 (as "Why?"), SP85, *Helsinki*. In *Helsinki* the title lacks the question mark. In *Emory*, Warren has written a marginal note: "Summer and early fall in VT." 1: Why have I ... fog broke] These lines are significantly different in *Helsinki*:

Why have I wandered the asphalt of midnight and not
Known why? Not guilt, nor joy, nor expectation,

Nor even to know how, when clouds were tattered,
The night-distance beyond screamed its rage,
Or when completely fog broke

1: not] now BHTS (revised in red pencil to BH) 2: to know how,] how, *Palaemon* 2: Not guilt, or joy, or expectation,] From guilt or joy or expectation, *SoR* 3: tattered, the distance beyond screamed its rage,] tattered and distance screamed its rage, *Palaemon* tattered, and distance screamed its rage, *SoR* 3: were] are SP85 (revised on SP85G to SP85) 3: screamed] screams SP85 (revised on SP85G to SP85) 4: when] even when *SoR* 4: fog broke … heartward, and from.] the fog closed in, the strict / Re-arrangement of stars communicated/ To the attent corpuscles hurrying heartward—and from. *Palaemon* 4: broke] breaks SP85 (revised on SP85G to SP85) 5: To clarity—not even to know how the strict] To clarity, how the strict *SoR* 6: communicated] communicates SP85 (revised on SP85G to SP85), *Helsinki* 8: The attent] Attendant *Helsinki* 8: corpuscles] corpuscles, my own, *Emory* 8: from.] ∼? *SoR* 9: under] beneath *Palaemon, SoR* 10: darkness] blackness *Palaemon* 11: snow,] ∼∧ *Palaemon, SoR*, BHTS (revised to BH) 12: heartbeat] heart beat *Palaemon,* heart-beat *SoR*, BHTS (revised to BH), *Helsinki* 12: self] Self BHTS (revised to BH) 12: only self / I know that I know,] only / Self that I know, *Helsinki* 15: broom?] ∼. *Palaemon* 16: now gone] gone *Palaemon, SoR*, BHTS (revised on BHG to BH) 16: now gone bone-white in moonlight? / Just] now, in moonlight, / Gone bone-white? Just *Helsinki* 17: Just to feel … To wash the whole continent, like spume?] These lines in *Helsinki* are substantially different:

Just to feel
Blood dry like a crust on hands, or
Watch the moon westering to
The next range, the next, and
Beyond,
To wash the whole continent, like spume?

17: a crust] crust *Palaemon, SoR* 17: hands,] my hands, *Palaemon, SoR* 18: lean westering] westering *Palaemon* 19: beyond,] ∼∧ *Palaemon, SoR* 20: whole continent,] continent, *Palaemon* 20: spume?] white spume? *Palaemon* 21: Why should I … sex-hoot] Why should I wait for the bear's sex-hoot from the valley *Palaemon* 21: till] until *Helsinki* 21: from the next valley I hear] I hear from the next valley *SoR*, BHTS (revised on BHG to BH) 22: sex-hoot∧] ∼, *SoR*, ∼? *Helsinki* 24: rollers] In *Emory*, Warren has a marginal note here: "California." 25: China,] Chinaward, *Palaemon, SoR* 25: stagger,] ∼∧ *Palaemon, SoR* 26: frothed mania,] white anger, *Palaemon* 27: Truth?] ∼. *Palaemon* 28: Yes, why, all the years, and places, and nights, have I / Wandered] Yes, why all the years and the places, and nights, have / I wandered *Helsinki* 28: why,] ∼∧ *Palaemon* 28: years,] ∼∧ *Palaemon, SoR* 28: places,] ∼∧ *Palaemon, SoR* 29: not] now *Helsinki* 29: carried?] ∼, *Palaemon* 30: sometimes,] ∼∧ *Helsinki* 30: at] even by *Palaemon, SoR* 31: first farmer] A stanza break follows this text in SP85 and *Helsinki.* Because this is a point in SP85TS where two photcopied extracts are taped together, probably the stanza break was added by mistake. 32: Set bright the steel share to the earth, or met,] Sink steel share in earth, or met, *Palaemon* 32: to the earth,] to earth, *SoR*, to black earth, *Helsinki* 33: Snowshoed,] Snow-shoed, *Palaemon, SoR, Helsinki* 33: just set] set out *Palaemon* 34: streetcar] street car *Palaemon, SoR*, BHTS (revised to BH) 35: cityward,] city-ward, *Palaemon* 35: workman∧] ∼, *Palaemon* 36: lunch box,] lunch-box, *Palaemon* lunchbox∧ *SoR* 36: and yawn.] A canceled annotation follows in BHTS: "in aaron copeland's [sic] birthday collection- copyright returned January 1, 1979".

396 **August Moon** Text: BH. Variant: *New Yorker,* 10 Sept. 1979, p. 47. 1: Gold] Golden *NY*, BHTS (revised on BHG to BH) 1: half-slice] half slice *NY* 2: Old-Fashioned] old-fashioned BHTS (revised on BHG to BH) 5: Lolls like a real] Like a *NY* 5: real brass button half-buttoned] button, real brass, half-buttoned *Emory* 7: Of an expensive seagoing blue blazer.] Of the blue seagoing blazer … *NY*, of a sea-going blue blazer.

BHTS (revised on BHG to BH, but page proofs still have "sea-going" and are corrected to BH) 8: Slowly stars, in a gradual / Eczema of glory, gain definition.] While slowly stars gain definition / In a gradual eczema of glory. *NY* 10: of world] of a world *NY*, BHTS (revised to BH) 10: walk] play *NY*, BHTS (revised to BH) 12: The inner, near-soundless *chug-chug* of the body's old business—] The inner and soundless *chug-chug* of its own old business— *NY* 18: walk] go walking *NY* 18: woods-lane,] woods lane, *NY* 22: only we were] we were only *NY* 28: half-wit] halfwit BHTS (revised to BH) 29: ten-gauge] 10-gauge *NY*, BHTS (revised to BH) 32: the axe-head.] an axe head. *NY* 34: years,] ∼— *NY* 37: Somebody loved? // At least, that's what they say.] Somebody? At least, / That's the way they always say it. *NY* 39: in distance?] in the distance? *NY* 44: pale] sky-pale *NY* 44: treetops.] tree-tops∧ BHTS (revised to BH) 45: white] pale *NY* 45: forward in darkness.] the foot forward / In darkness. *NY* 46: you] you two *Emory* 46: as you] as we *NY* 47: And speak not a word.] And be sure to speak not a word. *NY* 47: a word.] A canceled annotation follows in BHTS: "new yorker".

397 **Dreaming in Daylight** Text: BH. Variant: *Salmagundi*, no. 46 (Fall 1979), pp. 4–5. 2: Brook,] ∼∧ *Salmagundi* 4: Past] Past the *Salmagundi*, BHTS (revised to BH on BHTS and on BHG) 4: near-cliff,] ∼∧ *Salmagundi* 8: with glitter in darkness, are watching] like glittering darkness are watching *Salmagundi* 9: They are like conscience.] Those untamed wild eyes are like conscience. *Emory* 10: don't] do not *Salmagundi* 13: you, but with] you with *Salmagundi* 16: Just behind, . . . on your strangeness.] These lines are substantially different in *Salmagundi:*

Up the beach of History, indeed are
The last glimmer of consciousness before
You sink into the grind, bulge, and beat of what
Has been, into the heaving ocean of pastness?
Try to think of something your life has meant,
As the bright little eyes fix now on your strangeness.

26: you,] ∼∧ *Salmagundi* 27: Rears the stern rock, . . . the raw pylon. This] These lines are substantially different in *Salmagundi:*

The stern rock, majestic and snagged, that the peak is
Thrusts from green growth. Is sky-bare. You manage
The few great mossed shards that frost has ripped off. Then
Stop. For no handholds nub the raw pylon. This

32: snaking] snake *Salmagundi* 33: green brush.] green brush. (two illegible words) tide crawls up. *Emory* 34: remember,] ∼∧ *Salmagundi* 35: you have / Truly loved.] you have truly / Loved. *Salmagundi* 36: that difficult.] this hard. *Salmagundi* 38: log, aperture,] aperture, log, *Salmagundi* 41: to yourself.] A canceled annotation follows in BH: "salmagundi".

398 **Preternaturally Early Snowfall in Mating Season** Text: BH. Variant: *New Yorker,* 10 Sept. 1979, p. 46. 1: fallen. / Light, no more] fallen, light, / Nothing more *NY* 2: sugar∧] ∼, *NY* 4: fallen: / Just like] fallen—all / Like *NY* 6: spruces] the spruces *NY* 9: From ridge to far ridge in the mountains, grasping] From mountain ridge to ridge, grasped *NY* 10: Earth's] The earth's *NY* 12: With foot of sleeping sack near dying coals. Frontiersmen, / I'd read . . . Toward fire to sleep.] These lines are substantially different in *New Yorker:*

With feet of sleeping sack near dying coals.
Frontiersmen, I knew, had early learned
To delay the chronic curse of rheumatism:
Set wet moccasins toward fire to sleep.

14: wet] your wet BHTS (revised on BHG to BH) 14: moccasined] mocassined BHTS (revised in red pencil to BH) 17: Skyward, no stars.] I stared upward. There were no stars. *NY* 18: not even / One leprous] not even one / Leprous *NY* 19: light;] ∼, *NY* 20: a dome

/ Like] a / Dome, like *NY* 24: horizon's snagged circle.] mountain rims. *NY* 24: like] wordless as *NY* 25: down:] ~— *NY* 25: and soon.] In *NY* there is no stanza break after this text. 26: Pure luck.] Pure luck, or accident. *NY* 27: day the mind, like sky,] day, mind, like the sky, *NY* 28: thought;] ~: *NY* 29: hangs gray, like the dome of cloud-stone.] hangs like the dome of stone. *NY* 30: unsupervised:] ~; *NY* 32: act.] deed. *NY* 33: snow on face, I woke. / Re-fed the fire. Crawled back in sack,] with snow on face / I woke. Refed fire, crawled back in sack, *NY* 36: and∧] ~, *NY* 37: Slept.] At last slept. *NY* 37: a blast, wheeze,] blasting wheeze, *NY*, a blasting, wheeze, BHTS (revised on BHG to BH) 39: Bewildered. Then knew.] Wondered. Then, in the silence, knew. *NY* 40: In the world of glitter and] Later, in the glittering world of *NY* 41: My snowshoes at last being dug out,] Snowshoes at last dug out, *NY*, My snowshoes at last dug out, BHTS (revised on BHG to BH) 42: a doe,] the doe, *NY* 44: poplar] polar *NY* 44: the antlers.] antlers. *NY* 45: new] fresh *NY* 46: trample, heave,] heave, trample, *NY* 49: scraped] scraped and clean *NY* 51: Being.] being. *NY* 51: But∧] ~, *NY* 52: gone] going *NY* 53: and∧] ~, *NY* 53: was sure,] thought, *NY* 56: By] But by *NY* 56: I must have been pretty beat] I was pretty well beat *NY* 57: From fatigue and hunger.] In *NY* the poem ends with this text. 58: to get] getting BHTS (revised to BH) 58: a fire going.] A canceled annotation follows in BHTS: "new yorker".

400 **Sila** Text: BH. Variants: *Atlantic Monthly,* March 1980, pp. 70–71, SP85. In BHTS the text of the first two pages (up to "To tauten the fullness of throat, and then,") is typescript, not photocopy. Epigraph: Sila, for the Eskimo, "is] "He is *Atlantic*, "Sila, for the Eskimo, is BHTS (revised on BHG to BH) Epigraph] In *Atlantic* the final ellipses are preceded by a period. 1: snow-tangled] snow-tangle of *Atlantic* 2: Deadfall ... muscles strained.] Ruin of old stonework, where man-heart had once lifted / In joy, and back strained. *Atlantic* 4: Long ago] Long back BHTS (revised to BH) 5: strained.] straining. *Emory* 6: Commanded] Now commands *Western Kentucky* 6: tawny∧] ~, *Atlantic* 7: yet stood, forward-leaning.] stood yet leaning forward. *Atlantic* 9: Thought:] *Atlantic* deletes the line break after this text. 9: Thought:] His thought: *Western Kentucky* 12: what name the man / Might have had.] what name / The man's name might have been. *Atlantic*, what name the man's name / Might have been. BHTS (revised to BH.) 14: *summer,*] ~∧ *Atlantic* 16: how∧] ~, *Atlantic* 16: deeper∧] ~, *Atlantic* 19: *is,*] ~— *Atlantic* 20: then he] he then *Atlantic* 20: thought, *young*] thought. *Young Atlantic* 20: *Was young,* then he thought, *young as me,*] *Was young,* then he thought. *Young as me,* BH (revised to "*Was young.* Then he thought, *Young as me,* and finally corrected on BHG to BH) 21: clinch] clinch, coil *Atlantic* 24: the] an *Atlantic* 24: in sunlight.] In *Atlantic* there is no stanza break after this text. 25: *years!*] ~? *Atlantic* 25: his heart cried, and he felt] he demanded, and felt *Atlantic* 28: Land] He lifted his gaze. Land *Atlantic*, BHTS (revised to BH) 28: benched] is benched SP85 (revised on SP85G to SP85) 29: arising parklike] parklike arising, *Atlantic* 29: artful] ~, *Atlantic* 31: Sila!] ~, *Atlantic* 32: Slick glided] Slick-glided SP85 (revised on SP85G to SP85) 33: in] to *Atlantic* 34: wrapped cords at his waist, and— / The dog exploded.] slipped out of cross-countries, / Wrapped cords at his waist, and— / The dog exploded. SP85 (revised on SP85G to SP85) 34: at his] at *Atlantic* 36: behind] under *Western Kentucky* 38: airward prowing] prowing airward *Atlantic* 39: To seem as] As *Atlantic* 39: but] and *Atlantic* 39: aglitter] in glitter *Atlantic* 41: ice-crust] ice crust BHTS (revised on BHG to BH) 43: snowshoes behind.] snowshoes in long leaps behind. *Atlantic* 44: Five leaps—and first blood,] Four leaps and first blood *Atlantic* 45: like] as though in SP85 (revised on SP85G to SP85) 46: Again, two more leaps,] Two leaps again *Atlantic* 46: belly] white belly *Atlantic* 47: drawn] coming *Atlantic* 47: The boy's] No *Atlantic* 48: No] Of *Atlantic* 48: Stay! Damn] Stay, damn *Atlantic* 51: and eyes] and now eyes *Atlantic* 51: drove into / The] drove / Into the *Atlantic* 52: that] for an *Atlantic* 54: went] go SP85 (revised on SP85G to SP85) 55: ice-crust.] In *Atlantic* there is no stanza break after this text. 57: Who'd] Who could *Atlantic* 59: wildcat] wild cat BHTS (revised to BH) 60: bend,] broke, *Atlantic* 61: Break] Broke *Atlantic* 63: ready, almost, to forgive.] almost about to forgive. *Atlantic*, BHTS (revised to "almost to forgive.", corrected finally on BHG to BH) 63: to

forgive.] In *Atlantic* there is no stanza break after this text. 64: Throat fur is cream color, eyes flecked with gold glintings.] Line omitted in SP85 (in pencil on SP85TS). 64: is] was *Atlantic* 65: longs] longed *Atlantic* 66: drops] dropped *Atlantic* 66: on] to *Atlantic* 66: Twin] The twin *Atlantic* 67: Hold his own entrapped] Entrapped his own *Atlantic* 69: Slides] Slid *Atlantic* 70: knife-sheath.] knife sheath. *Atlantic* 71: task,] fact, *Atlantic* 72: As some fool girl might,] Knowing some fool girl would do that, *Atlantic* 74: Held] Gently held *Western Kentucky* 74: soft] sweet *Atlantic*, BHTS (revised to BH) 75: fullness] fulness BHTS (revised to BH) 75: then,] ∼. BHTS (revised to BH) 76: well-trained tailor,] tailor well trained, *Atlantic*, well trained tailor, BHTS (revised in red pencil to BH) 77: needle point] needle-point *Atlantic* 78: enter without ... motion.] almost without prick of pain, then slashed / In a single deep motion. *Atlantic* 80: sure that the doe / Never twitched.] sure / That the doe never stirred. *Atlantic* 82: On snow unconsciously heaped, he let down the head,] He laid down the head on snow unconsciously heaped like a pillow, *Atlantic* 83: embracement] entrapment *Atlantic* 84: He watched, bewitched by the beauty, how blood flowed,] Then watched, bewildered by beauty of blood flowing, *Atlantic* 85: bloomed] grew *Atlantic* 85: stood.] ∼, *Atlantic* 87: feet on the snow,] feet, *Atlantic* 88: flicker of] flickering *Atlantic* 88: crimson,] ∼∧ *Atlantic* 89: a special] special *Atlantic* 90: He] Then *Atlantic* 90: knife yet] knife *Western Kentucky* 90: knife yet in hand,] in hand knife yet, BHTS (revised to BH) SP85G reads with BH but is corrected to "knife in hand yet,". The correction was not made on the second set of galleys, and it appears neither on the page proofs nor in SP85. 90: hand,] hand hung, *Atlantic* 91: Fixed eyes beyond beech-bench to the snow-hatched] Stood staring beyond the beech bench to the high snow-hatched *Atlantic* 91: snow-hatched] high snow-hatched BHTS (revised to BH) snow-thatched *Emory*. (Had *Atlantic* and BHTS also not read "snow-hatched" I might have emended this reading, since "snow-thatched" —covered with a thatched roof of snow—seems to make more sense than "snow-hatched"—covered with hatchmarks made of snow.) 92: the mountain,] mountain, *Atlantic* 92: above which sky, too,] there where the sky *Atlantic* 92: sky, too,] sky too BHTS (revised to BH) 93: More majestically bloomed, but petals paler as higher—] Majestically petaled, but paler as higher *Atlantic* 93: but petals paler] but shows petals paler *Western Kentucky* 93: paler] gone paler *Emory* 94: The rose] Made the rose *Atlantic* 95: so slowly—] slowly— *Atlantic* 96: He] Had *Atlantic* 96: blade of the knife] blade *Atlantic* 96: honing,] ∼∧ *Atlantic* 99: at last / That he'd never before known. / No name for it—no!] at last that he'd never yet known. / But no name for it—no! *Atlantic* 100: before known.] known before. BHTS (revised on BHG to BH) 102: Sheathed] He sheathed *Atlantic* 103: now docile,] quiet and docile, *Atlantic* 103: With bare hands full of snow, / The boy] And with bare hands, / With snow, the boy *Atlantic*, Bare hands full of snow, / The boy *Emory* 104: washed him of blood] of blood washed him BHTS (revised to BH) 105: the ruff.] the ruff. / The dog licked his hands. *Atlantic* 106: Then suddenly clasping the creature, he, / Over raw fur, past beeches,] On impulse he clasped the dog close to his breast, / And over the raw fur, the beeches, *Atlantic* 106: creature, he,] creature close to his heart, BHTS (revised to "creature," and finally corrected on BHG to BH) 109: Cried out into vastness / Of silence: "Oh, world!"] Into the vastness of silence, / Cried out: "Oh, world!"*Atlantic* 109: Cried out into vastness] He cried out into the vastness BHTS (revised to "He cried out into vastness" on BHTS and to BH on BHG) 109: Cried] Cries SP85 (revised on SP85G to SP85) 113: Again will see ... breath short.] He saw the same scene. Would have called / The same words. If he could— / But breath was so short. *Atlantic* 115: breath short.] A canceled annotation follows in BHTS: "atlantic".

III.

403 **Empty White Blotch on Map of Universe: A Possible View** Text: BH. Variant: *Atlantic Monthly,* June 1980, p. 58. In *Emory* the whole poem is crossed out in pencil, with "*BAD* omit this poem" written across the top. But on the facing page it says in pencil, "But in light of "Afterthought" this must be *kept.*" And the "*BAD* omit this poem" is itself crossed out. At the top of the page and at the bottom is written "KEEP." 3: lost,] lost, oh, *Atlantic* 4: island,] ∼∧ *Atlantic* 5: world!—] world∧— BHTS (revised

on BHG to BH) 10: the note is more far—more far.] the more far—oh, more far! *Atlantic* 12: The wet thigh of a nymph, by a spring, agleam where stars peer in.] A spring, a nymph crouching, a glimmer of thigh in starlit wet sheen. *Atlantic* 13: stood] and stood *Atlantic* 14: lost aboriginals] the aboriginal *Atlantic* 16: squalls] squall *Atlantic, Emory* 18: thus venting] as I vented *Atlantic* 19: And I saw the very delusions before my sight:] And delusions sprang even before my actual sight, *Atlantic* 20: hair-combing] hair-combed *Atlantic* 22: old,] ~$_\wedge$ *Atlantic* 25: I have] I've *Atlantic* 25: reed$_\wedge$] ~, *Atlantic* 27: Truth] truth *Atlantic*, BHTS (revised to BH) 28: in$_\wedge$] ~, *Atlantic* 28: clean,] ~— *Atlantic* 29: only] but *Atlantic* 29: shout,] ~$_\wedge$ *Atlantic* 29: hand,] ~$_\wedge$ *Atlantic* 30: steel-throated] the steel-throated *Atlantic* 35: I cried.] cried I. *Atlantic* 37: no,] ~— *Atlantic* 37: the] a *Atlantic* 41: the surf] surf *Atlantic* 42: love-stung cry.] A canceled annotation follows in BHTS: 'atlantic'. Also, in pencil, in Warren's hand, " PRETERNaturally Early Snowfall in / Mating Season / SILA".

404 **Function of Blizzard** Text: BH. Variant: *Antaeus,* 30/31 (Summer–Autumn 1978), p. 242. 3: an air-tower] a tower *Antaeus* 4: are.] ~, *Antaeus* 10: in] into *Antaeus* 10: coverings-over, forgettings.] all covering-over, all forgetting. *Antaeus*, all coverings-over, forgettings. BHTS (revised to BH) 11: snow,] ~. *Antaeus* 13: alarm lights.] alarm-lights. *Antaeus* 15: soon will] will soon BHTS (revised on BHG to BH) 15: ruin.] ashes. *Emory* 16: Who] who *Antaeus* 16: hand of / Fate,] hand / Of Fate, *Antaeus* 25: forest,] ~$_\wedge$ *Antaeus* 25: wonder] wonder painfully *Antaeus* 26: Item] Items *Antaeus* 26: the] my *Antaeus* 27: falling on,] falling on, and on, *Antaeus* 28: after all.] A canceled annotation follows in BHTS: "antaneus".

405 **Dream, Dump-heap, and Civilization** Text: BH. Variants: *Southern Review,* ns 16 (Spring 1980), pp. 382–83 (as one of "Two Poems about Old Norwalk Dump"), *Life,* April 1981, p. 102. Both of the poems (the other is "Entry in a Connecticut Commuter's Diary") are in the table of contents to BHTS, but "Entry in a Connecticut Commuter's Diary" is crossed out. In BHTS, the title begins with "2.", but the section number is crossed out. The running header at the top of the page is "2. Two dreams, his and mine", possibly at one time the title of the sequence. 2: Connecticut,] Conn., *SoR*, BHTS (revised to BH) 5: iceboxes] ice-boxes *SoR*, BHTS (revised to BH) 7: night, / Like] night, sometimes. / It was like *SoR* 11: my] my own *SoR* 12: it] them *SoR* 12: guilt,] ~$_\wedge$ BHTS (revised to BH) 14: you"?] you." *SoR* 15: Or how] Or *SoR* 16: corn knife] corn-knife *SoR* 16: Did I dream // That again last night?] Did I // Dream that dream again, last night? *SoR* 17: dem"?] dem." *SoR* 18: of] of the *SoR* 19: try] trying *SoR* 19: still] and still *SoR* 20: inexhaustibly drips.] yet dripping? *SoR*, inexhaustably drips. BHTS (revised to BH) 20: Did I wake // With guilt? How] Did I wake with guilt? // How *SoR* 21: Montana mountains!] The editor has marked "Do not justify line" at the end of this line in BHTS, to prevent the typesetter from bending the long line. 22: Sometime] Some time BHTS (revised to BH) 23: without it?] A canceled annotation follows in BHTS: "southern review".

405 **Vision** Text: BH. Variants: Washington *Post Book World,* 12 Aug. 1979, p. 1, SP85, *Helsinki.* 2: its] in its *Post Book World* 2: you] do you now *Post Book World*, you now BHTS (revised to BH) 2: know] guess *Helsinki* 2: ah,] ~! *Post Book World* 4: That] Of your mind, that *Post Book World*, BHTS (revised to BH), A *Helsinki* 5: fox-fire] foxfire *Post Book World* 6: lynx-scream or direful owl-stammer] lynx scream or owl stammer *Post Book World* 7: shudder—which / Might] shudder— / Which might *Post Book World*, BHTS (revised on BHG to BH) 9: An event ... descends, as from seaward.] *Post Book World* is substantially different:

An event may well come in your deepest
Moment of loneliness, with rain on the roof,

As the season changes, and bed too wide. Or even
At moments of irrational depression. But

May come at any time, when, for instance,
The past is de-fogged and foot tracks

Of old folly show fleetingly clear, before rationalization
Again descends as from seaward.

BHTS is also substantially different:

An event may well come in your deepest
Moment of loneliness, rain on the roof

With the season's change, and bed too wide; or even
At moments of irrational depression. But

May come at any time, when, say,
The past is de-fogged and foot tracks

Of old folly show fleetingly clear, before rationalization
Again descends, as from seaward.

(but BHTS is corrected to BH) 10: wide; or,] wide. Or, *Helsinki* 11: foot tracks] foot-tracks *Helsinki* 13: Or when the shadow of pastness] Or even, when again the shadow of the past *Post Book World*, Or even, again when the shadow of pastness BHTS (revised to BH) 14: Lifts and you recollect having caught—when, when?—] Lifts, and you remember having caught *Post Book World* 16: electrically] eletrically *Helsinki* 18: Or when, even,] Or even *Post Book World* 19: pass,] come, *Post Book World* 20: slash] slash at *Post Book World* 20: lights] headlights *Post Book World* 21: first / Illicit meeting,] first illicit / Meeting, *Helsinki* 25: up,] $\sim$. (revised in red pencil to BH) 29: clasp—] clutch, *Post Book World*, clasp. Ungloved, *Helsinki* 30: desire like] like *Post Book World* 32: Soon$_{\wedge}$] $\sim$, *Post Book World* 33: well-turned] the well turned *Post Book World*, well turned BHTS (revised in red pencil to BH) 34: and the future // Scarcely breathes.] and // The future scarcely breathes. *Helsinki* 35: Your chest is a great clot. Perhaps then. / Oh, no. It may not happen, in fact, until] Your chest is a clot. Perhaps / Soon. No, it may not happen, in fact, until *Helsinki* 35: then.] now. *Post Book World* 37: enters at] at *Post Book World* 37: at 5 A.M. / The hospital room,] at / 5 A.M., the hospital room, *Helsinki* 38: The hospital] Enters the hospital *Post Book World* 38: shave,] $\sim_{\wedge}$ BHTS (revised to BH) 39: word of greeting,] greeting, *Post Book World* 40: The robot departs.] He goes away. *Post Book World* 41: hope. / There is] hope. There / Is *Helsinki* 42: window.] windows. *Post Book World* 43: that the] that *Post Book World* 43: come—] already come— *Post Book World*, BHTS (revised to BH) 43: already come— / And you] already / Come—and you *Helsinki* 44: didn't] did not *Helsinki* 44: recognize it?] A canceled annotation follows in BHTS: "Book week, of washington post, august 12, 1979".

407 **Globe of Gneiss** Text: BH. Variant: *Salmagundi,* no. 46 (Fall 1979), pp. 6–7. 1: Fifteen tons? Thirty? More?—] Ten tons? Twenty? Or more?— *Salmagundi* 2: gneiss,] $\sim_{\wedge}$ *Salmagundi* 3: hair's weight,] hair-weight, *Salmagundi* 3: ledge.] ledge-edge. *Salmagundi*, BHTS (revised to BH) 4: near!] $\sim$. *Salmagundi* 4: Don't,] $\sim_{\wedge}$ *Salmagundi* 5: For God's sake, be] Be *Salmagundi* 8: to crush / Spruces and pines] through spruces / And pines *Salmagundi* 10: yards down] yards *Salmagundi* 11: await] wait *Salmagundi*, BHTS (revised to BH) 12: Its] The *Salmagundi* 12: monstrous plunge.] Two lines follow in *Salmagundi,* but a page turn there obscures whether they are preceded by a stanza break or not: Suppose it had gone when I pushed / And the ledge-edge with it—and me. 16: Shove,] $\sim_{\wedge}$ *Salmagundi* 16: shoulder,] $\sim_{\wedge}$ *Salmagundi* 16: wind$_{\wedge}$] $\sim$, *Salmagundi* 17: infinitesimal / Decay of] infinitesimal decay / Of *Salmagundi* 18: ledge-edge.] BHTS reads as BH, but is corrected to "ledge". It is corrected back to BH on BHG 18: Suddenly,] And suddenly, *Salmagundi* 19: terror. / Suppose!] terror. Suppose! *Salmagundi* 21: go] come *Salmagundi* 22: Lichen ... I sit] Moss creeping slow up that rondure, like Time, / And I sit *Salmagundi* 25: that] the *Salmagundi* 27: in total / Darkness ... granite,] in total darkness, / In unmeasurable heat, had been converted / From granite, *Salmagundi* 32: I wonder] wonder *Salmagundi* 33: How long ago, and how,] When and how *Salmagundi* 33: it.] $\sim$, *Salmagundi* 34: How long and how] How long, and how, *Salmagundi* 34: it had trundled / The great chunk to globe-shape.] had it trundled globe into globe. / Or had water done that? And how? *Salmagundi* 36: Then

poised it on ledge-edge, in balanced perfection] This one-line stanza is deleted in *Salmagundi.* 42: that time for the great globe] the hours will the great globe have *Salmagundi* 43: much!] ~? *Salmagundi* 44: tonight?] A canceled annotation follows in BHTS: "salmagundi".

408 **Part of What Might Have Been a Short Story, Almost Forgotten** Text: BH. Variant: *Georgia Review,* 33 (Spring 1979), pp. 86–88 (as "Part of a Short Story"). *GaR* has no headnote. In BHTS there is a note to the typesetter in purple pencil: "pick up from sample pg. 82 (Don't pick up last line)". 1: ago∧] ~, *GaR* 5: Lovers gawking] loving gawkers *GaR* 5: in flowered] flowered BHTS (revised to BH) 8: roads] back *GaR* 18: clambers now] clambering *GaR* 23: prove] proved *GaR* 26: bloated,] boated, BHTS (revised on BHG to BH) 26: sinks] sank *GaR* 27: Mountain heave.] The line straddles the stanza break that follows this text. Warren noted that there should be a stanza break's space on BHG. 27: heave.] rim. *GaR* There is no stanza break after this text in *GaR.* 28: headaches.] A page turn obscures whether there is a stanza break here in *GaR.* 34: downward. Arms, white,] down. White, white arms *GaR*, down. Arms, white, white, BHTS (revised on BHG to BH) 35: Wreathed upward, imploring.] Wreathing upward, implored. *GaR* 37: fulfill-] fulfil- BHTS (revised to BH) 39: flamed] flames BHTS (revised to BH) 39: flamed to the un- / winged, utmost, blank zenith of sky.] inflames, to the / Unwinged zenith's blankness, the sky. *GaR* 41: I stared till] Stared until *GaR* 45: kept] There is a stanza break after this text in *GaR.* 46: But sudden- / ly,] Suddenly, / The *GaR* 47: bursts.] burst. *GaR*, BHTS (revised to BH) 48: bursts.] burst. *GaR*, BHTS (revised to BH) 52: great] greater *GaR* 54: outthrust] out-thrust *GaR*, BHTS (revised to BH) 56: drawn slightly] slightly drawn *GaR* 60: slow swung] swung slow *GaR* 63: its] A page turn here in *GaR* obscures whether there is a stanza break after this text or not. There is no stanza break here in BH. 68: flight∧] ~, *GaR* 68: blank darkness past / Lip of the chasm.] the blank darkness / Of the chasm's lip. *GaR* 72: Road∧] ~, *GaR* 73: snapped] puffed *GaR* 81: lower past] lower, past *GaR* 82: crags,] ~; *GaR* 83: forest:] ~. *GaR* There is no stanza break after this text in *GaR.* 84: And there, what beast might, waiting, be.] And what beast might there wait. *GaR*, And what beast might there, waiting, be. BHTS (revised to BH) 88: stone∧] ~, BHTS (revised on BHG to BH) 88: in geological / Darkness, waits,] in a roar that seems like / Silence, waiting *GaR* 89: Darkness, waits, waiting, will wait] The line in BH is not octosyllabic. 90: Where and how long?—While we,] Where and however long?—While we, *GaR.* The line in BH is not octosyllabic. 91: crag,] crags, *GaR* 93: which] the *GaR* 94: roads poor-mapped, will move] on roads poor-mapped, move *GaR* 96: had witlessly concealed] unguiltily conceal *GaR* 97: In mere charade, hysterical // Or grave, of love.] Beneath the pretense of life's jollity. *GaR* 98: of love.] A canceled annotation follows in BHTS: "GaR".

410 **Cocktail Party** Text: BH. Variants: *Southern Review*, ns 16 (Spring 1980), p. 381, SP85. 3: some] some some BHTS (revised to BH) 3: eye-gleam,] glimpse, or *SoR* 5: away!] ~? *SoR* 7: with the] with *SoR*, BHTS (revised on BHG to BH) 8: you see, of a sudden,] you, sudden, see *SoR* 8: laugh∧] ~, *SoR* 10: not] not a *SoR* 12: throat,] throats, *SoR* 12: comes. You] comes, you *SoR* 13: ha!—] ~!∧ *SoR* 14: A pun—or rises,] BHTS reads as BH, but is corrected to "Or rises,". BHG is corrected to BH. 16: Half-crushed] Half crushed *SoR* 16: ashtray.] ash tray. *SoR*, BHTS (revised to BH) 17: lies. Or] lies—or *SoR* 17: grows] grown *SoR* 18: doctor,] Doctor, *SoR* 19: Expense] Expense and pain *SoR* 20: lips moving.] moving lips. *SoR* 22: and tell] tell *SoR* 25: waiter!] A canceled annotation follows in BHTS: "southern review".

411 **Deep—Deeper Down** Text: BH. Variant: *Southern Review,* ns 16 (Spring 1980), pp. 377–78. (as "Deeper"). 2: The first .44 explosion, cottony] Echo of the first .44 fired, cottony *Emory* 4: boll] cotton boll *SoR* 4: the hot slug inside,] a hot slug, *SoR* 4: lonely∧] ~, *SoR* 7: cotton-mouth on a] cottonmouth in *SoR* 8: now] with now *SoR* 9: town,] ~∧ BHTS (revised to BH) 9: cursed] been slaving *SoR* 10: now free] free now BHTS (revised on BHG to BH) 10: dark,] ~∧ *SoR* 10: wife drove back.] wife, from her job, drove back. *SoR* 11: slickly brown,] brown, *SoR* 12: death—] ~, *SoR* 12: up its slack.] There is a marginal note in red pencil here on BHG: "Do not justify line". 13: Two] But two *SoR*

15: hand] his hand *SoR* 16: To say, at his whim,] That few command, and that says, at his will, *SoR* 18: If the first man missed,] But if the first missed, *SoR* 18: his.] this. *SoR* 19: As I took aim] Taking aim, *SoR* 20: being. I] being, for I *SoR* 21: spring and all summer] a spring and a summer, *SoR* 21: unspoken] basic *SoR*, BHTS (revised on BHG to BH) 21: duty:] pact: BHTS (revised on BHG to BH) 22: evil,] ~∧ *SoR* 23: friendship∧] ~, *SoR* 23: beauty] reward of our act, BHTS (revised on BHG to BH) 24: Of the dark] As the dark BHTS (revised on BHG to BH) 24: wavering] wavered BHTS (revised on BHG to BH) 24: white∧] ~, *SoR* 25: Long back, that was.] But that was long back. *SoR* 26: glimmer] glimmering *SoR* 26: down∧] ~, *SoR* 27: Past the slick, slimy brush of a form that yet twisted in pain,] Brushed lightly once by a slick, slimy form yet twisting in pain, *SoR* 28: Its] And its *SoR* 28: down.] A canceled annotation follows in BHTS: "southern review".

412 **Sky** Text: BH. Variant: *New Yorker,* 7 April 1980, p. 38. 3: lip the horizon edge,] find the horizon as base *NY* 4: There∧] ~, *NY* 14: From God-ordained foundations.] In BH the line straddles the stanza break that follows this text. There is no stanza break here in *NY*. 14: And] Stanza break after this line in *NY*. 19: discharged,] ~— *NY* 23: from] from its *NY* 23: Now from western death glares.] In BH the line straddles the stanza break that follows this text. There is no stanza break here in *NY*. 23: We,] Stanza break after this line in *NY*. 28: fear,] ~— *NY*. 29: advances on] Stanza break after this line in *NY*. 30: It smiles.] No stanza break after this line in *NY*. 31: know.] There are two canceled annotations in BHTS: "not out yet - spt. 10" and (in pencil) "New Yorker".

412 **Better Than Counting Sheep** Text: BH. Variant: *New York Review of Books*, 9 Nov. 1978, p. 27. 1: For] On *NYRB*, BHTS (revised on BHG to BH) 3: dead now,] dead, *NYRB* 5: For the party,] To go around, *NYRB* 6: Chock-full,] Chock full, *NYRB* 6: faces] some faces *NYRB* 6: pane] panes *NYRB* 6: peer.] peer in. *Emory* 7: in] like *NYRB* 9: sleeve,] ~∧ *NYRB* 10: Want something of you, ... to glow faintly] Want something of you, though you don't know what—for even // In distance and dimness the hands are out- / Stretched to glow faintly *NYRB* 11: hands∧] ~, BHTS (revised to BH) 12: Are] They are BHTS (revised to BH) 14: Rots,] Sump-rots, *NYRB* 14: trunks] tree trunks *Emory* 14: unsteadily] uneasily *NYRB* 15: grieving susurrus, all wordless,] grieving, though wordless, susurrus, BHTS (revised to "grieving susurrus, though wordless," and finally corrected to BH on BHG) 15: all wordless,] though wordless∧ *NYRB* 16: You sense,] Indeed, you know, *NYRB* 18: if] do *NYRB* 19: mother's name,] mother's, BHTS (revised on BHG to BH) 19: But now you can't answer, not even your mother's name, and your heart] And you can't now—not even your mother's—and your heart *NYRB* 21: moon, full,] full moon∧ *NYRB* 22: Spills the spruce-shadows African black.] Makes coniferous shadows like ink. *NYRB* 22: African black.] like ink. BHTS (revised on BHG to BH) 22: Then you are, ... plunge] Then you are alone, // And your name strangely gone as you plunge *NYRB* 24: The] And the *NYRB* 24: sleep.] A canceled annotation follows in BHTS: "new york review of books."

413 **The Cross** Text: BH. Variants: *New Yorker*, 2 Oct. 1978, p. 36, *15 Poems*, selected by Rosanna Warren, privately printed for Stuart Wright, 1985, SP85. The *NY* and SP85 versions have no subtitle. The subtitle is deleted in *Emory*. 1: cliff-head,] cliff head, *NY* 3: eight fathoms] fathoms 15P 3: fathoms] fathoms up SP85 (revised on SP85G to SP85) 4: leap] leaped *NY* 5: Not forgiving ... breathless dark] Unforgiving that nightlong their screaming lunge / Had been only a dream in the tangled warmth *NY* 9: snatch] snatch at *NY* 10: By three, wind down] Wind, by three, down, *NY* 12: flung—] ~: *NY* 14: cap] top *NY* 16: And∧] ~, *NY* 16: hunched] huddled *NY*, BHTS (revised on BHG to BH) 17: hope,] ~— *NY* 18: back∧] ~, *NY* 18: sure,] ~— *NY* 19: wide-eyed,] wide-eyed and *NY* 20: screechings∧] ~, *NY* 20: jerks∧] ~, *NY* 22: up,] up and *NY*, BHTS (revised to BH) 22: eyes,] ~∧ *NY* 26: had run out.] In *NY* there is no stanza break after this line. 28: Under wet fur I felt] I felt, under wet fur, *NY* 29: the delicate] delicate *NY* 30: grasped, at] grasping at *NY* 31: wind abate.] Stanza break after this text in SP85. This is probably an error, since there is a page turn at this point in SP85TS. 32: showed.] ~∧ *NY* 33: And∧] ~, *NY* 36: top.] ~, *NY* 37: I enough fool] such a fool as *NY* 39: prop]

stick *NY* 40: But what use that?] For what was the use? *NY*, But what was the use? BHTS (revised to "But what the use?" on BHTS and finally to BH on BHG) 40: back.] A canceled annotation follows in BHTS: "new yorker".

IV.

415 **Truth** Text: BH. Variant: *Yale Review*, 68 (Summer 1979), pp. 541–42. 1: Truth] TRUTH *YR* 4: By the wind-tossed elm] This line indented one character, apparently mistakenly, in BHTS. Corrected in red pencil. 5: grass well groomed.] the grass well mowed. *YR*, grass well mowed. BHTS (revised on BHG to BH) 8: History,] ∼∧ *YR* 9: over again,] over∧ *YR* 9: plays on us. . . . the tragic crossing. Truth] *YR* is substantially different:

Its shape
Of shadow or sunlight, and its utterance
The whisper we strive forever to catch,
Or the blasting scream of a locomotive
Desperately blowing for a crossing. Truth

14: upon] on *YR* 17: He] he *YR* 19: dead∧] ∼, *YR* 22: fulfill] fulfill their *YR* 23: immense.] A canceled annotation follows in BHTS: "YR".

415 **On Into the Night** Text: BH. Variant: *Salmagundi*, no. 46 (Fall 1979), pp. 11–12. 1: On] on BHTS (revised in red pencil to BH) 1: slope∧] ∼, *Salmagundi* 2: Of] Of the *Salmagundi* 4: Sparely paving] That pave *Salmagundi*, BHTS (revised to BH) 4: dreams] dream *Salmagundi*, BHTS (revised to BH) 10: cedar] spruce *Salmagundi* 12: only in silence throbs now.] throbs in silence yet. *Salmagundi*, throbs only in silence yet. BHTS (revised on BHG to BH) 13: Like] Like in *Salmagundi* 14: mechanism,] ∼∧ *Salmagundi* 16: mean.] have meant. *Salmagundi* 17: of cliff] of the cliff *Salmagundi* 21: Now] But *Salmagundi* 23: of some] some *Salmagundi* 30: to its last music.] to music, at last. *Salmagundi*, BHTS (revised on BHG to BH) 32: that follows] to follow *Salmagundi* 34: no!—] ∼∧— *Salmagundi* 37: metaphor.] A canceled annotation follows in BHTS: "salmagundi"

416 **No Bird Does Call** Text: BH. Variant: *American Poetry Review*, 8 (Jan.–Feb. 1979), p. 3. 1: Bowl-hollow of woodland,] The woodland bowl-hollow, *APR* 1: beech-shrouded,] beech shrouded, BHTS (revised in red pencil to BH) 2: With roots] Roots *APR* 2: crook'd] humped *APR* 2: then down] and down then *APR* 4: darker and deeper] darkness, deeper *APR* 5: noon∧] ∼, *APR* 5: light,] light down, *APR* 6: summer] summer a *APR* 6: green,] moss, *APR* 7: for then] for *APR* 8: The hollow is] Now the hollow was *APR* 8: with] in *APR*, BHTS (revised on BHG to BH) 9: what,] ∼∧ BHTS (revised to BH) 10: Is] Is a *APR* 10: when,] ∼∧ *APR*, when I, BHTS (revised on BHG to BH) 10: from sun-blast and world,] from the world and the sun-blast, I 11: I, in despair,] Bearing despair, *APR*, In despair, BHT (revised on BHG to BH) 11: deeper,] deeper, directionless, *APR*, BHTS (revised on BHG to BH) 12: men,] ∼. *APR* men, and my own, *Emory* 13: And first, to that spot, came.] And came the first time to that spot. *APR* 15: shadow.] ∼, *APR* 16: With] And *APR* 16: I] and *APR* 16: fell so] fell *APR* 16: so slow] oh, slowly *APR* 18: labyrinths . . . my heart beat.] the labyrinth of upper / Green to make me see redness of blood in shut eyelids, / And I heard my heart beat in that stillness. *APR* 18: labyrinths of leaves,] the labyrinth of leaves, BHTS (revised on BHG to BH) 21: on. The eyelids] on, and the eyelids *APR* 22: woke.] awoke. *APR* 23: Came again] Came *APR* 23: seemed then that . . . had passed,] seemed / That years had passed, *APR* 25: between,] ∼. *APR* 26: long] years *APR* 27: hope] pray *APR* 27: not any,] even, *APR* 28: now∧] ∼, *APR* 28: night to remember,] night, *APR* 28: calls.] A canceled annotation follows in BHTS: "american poetry review".

417 **Weather Report** Text: BH. Variant: *New England Review*, 1 (Spring 1979), p. 262. In the table of contents in BHTS, this title is added in black pen. 1: gorge] chasm *New England Review* 5: pine-tops] pine tops *New England Review* 5: gorge.] chasm. *New England Review* 6: This is the code now tapped:] The only code being tapped is this: *New England Review*, The code now tapped is this: BHTS (revised on BHG to BH) 9: presence,] ∼∧ *New England Review* 10: yes,] ∼— *New England Review* 11: like

gunmetal now,] now like gunmetal, *New England Review* 13: useless] single, useless *New England Review* 15: hangs at] hung at the *New England Review*, hung at BHTS (revised on BHG to BH) 18: joy for] joy *New England Review* 19: the code yet] yet the code *New England Review*, BHTS (revised on BHG to BH), the code of last raindrops yet *Emory* 19: my] the *New England Review* 21: And] Yes, *New England Review* 21: grinds on, on its axis,] grinds on its axis, *New England Review* 22: of silence.] In *Emory*, Warren adds a stanza break after this line. 23: perhaps.] A canceled annotation follows in BHTS: "new england review".

418 **Tires on Wet Asphalt at Night** Text: BH. Variant: *American Poetry Review*, 8 (Jan.–Feb. 1979), p. 4. In *Emory* Warren has crossed out the poem in pencil. At the end he has written "arbitrary end of original stimulus to poem—not relevant to this poem. Bad poem." But there are revisions too. It is not clear whether Warren revised the poem and then junked it, or junked it and thought better. 1: head] ~, *APR* 1: dents] dents the *APR* 2: Automobile,] ~∧ BHTS (revised on BHG to BH) 2: rhododendrons] rhododendron *APR* 3: screen,] ~∧ BHTS (revised on BHG to BH) 5: Is going somewhere. ... what is left.] It is going somewhere. I cannot see it, but / It is going somewhere different from here and now. / Leaving me to lie and wonder what is *me.* 9: To lie and wonder what is left.] To lie and wonder. *Emory* 10: perhaps they lean] they are perhaps leaning forward *APR*, they lean perhaps forward BHTS (revised to BH) 11: Into cold dimness of gauge-lights, and she] Into the cold dimness of gauge-lights, and she BHTS (revised to BH) 11: Into] In the *APR* 11: she∧] one, *APR* 12: road-cover∧] ~, *APR* 13: catch glimpse of] glimpse *APR* 14: That glitter ... has closed.] Glitter in darkness like two dead eyes that do not close. *APR* 15: nobody has closed.] do not close. BHTS (revised on BHG to BH) 16: here, eyes ceilingward,] here with ceilingward *APR* 17: Open to darkness. They do not know] Eyes open to darkness. *APR* 18: That] They do not know that *APR* 19: How∧] ~, *APR* 19: after the] after *APR* 19: at] of *APR* 21: of finding] to find *APR*, BHTS (revised on BHG to BH) 22: when] There is no line break after this word in *APR*. 24: I stare ... hands.] I stare ceilingward in darkness and think of them staring. / Do they, at least, clasp hands? *APR* 24: darkness ceilingward, thinking] ceilingward darkness and think BHTS (but corrected to BH) 25: must] may *Emory* 25: stare thus.] stare. BHTS (revised on BHG to BH) 27: somewhere—] ~. *Emory* In *Emory* there is a line drawn between this line and the next, indicating perhaps that he intends to end the poem with this line. 28: faint] tired *APR* 29: handkerchief] handkerchief-size *APR* 30: slotted / Only to] slotted only / To *APR* 32: Felt need ... abstract sea.] Climbed down and lay there, that sound in my ear, and watched / Sun sink, in its blaze, below the horizon line. *APR* 33: the sun] sun BHTS (revised on BHG to BH) 35: then] to do *APR* 35: climb again] again climb *APR* 36: loosened] sparse, loosened *APR* 37: face-down, ... summer-burned grass.] face-down I lay, arms outflung, / Hands clutching the clumps of summer-burned grass. *APR* 39: shake then?] shake? *APR* 41: across] across the *APR* 42: That] It BHTS (revised on BHG to BH) 42: That was long ago. ... together now.] It was long ago. Till the hiss / Of tires I had forgotten it. *APR* 44: now.] A canceled annotation follows in BHTS: "american poetry review".

419 **Timeless, Twinned** Text: BH. Variant: *New England Review*, 1 (Spring 1979), p. 265. 1: lonely,] ~∧ *New England Review* 2: unmoving,] ~∧ *New England Review* 2: on an] on *New England Review* 3: light,] ~∧ *New England Review* 4: may] will *New England Review* 4: nor a single blade twitch, // Though autumn-honed, of the cattail] nor twitch // A single blade, now autumn-honed, of cat-tail *New England Review* 5: cattail] cat-tail BHTS (revised to BH) 5: pond.] ~, *New England Review* 6: since here] since *New England Review* 7: now] here *New England Review* 8: a·transparent] like a transparent *New England Review* 8: flood,] ~∧ BHTS (revised on BHG to BH) 9: it,] ~∧ *New England Review* 11: forgotten] forgot *New England Review* 12: Anxiety born of] Anxiety of *New England Review*, BHTS (revised to BH) 12: the nag] nag *New England Review* 13: thin-shirted,] ~∧ BHTS (revised to BH) 14: perimeter northward,] northern rim, *New England Review* 15: lurks?] ~. *New England Review* 15: white, motionless. I cling] white and motionless∧ I cling *New England Review* 16: single] one *New*

England Review 16: twinned.] A canceled annotation follows in BHTS: "new england review".

420 **What is the Voice that Speaks?** Text: BH. Variant: *Yale Review,* 68 (Summer 1979), pp. 542–43. 1: What] WHAT *YR* 7: so valiantly rises] rises valiantly up *YR* 9: put a dime] put but a dime *YR* 9: at] for *YR* 11: snow-pine?] snow pine? *YR* 11: You know . . . been able to answer.] It asks you a question— / But one that you've never, in anguish so long, been able to answer. *YR* 12: in anguish,] in anguish so long, BHTS (revised to BH) 13: from mountain.] from the mountain *YR* 14: from] in *YR* 14: that desolate timbre.] the desolate timbre! *YR* 19: do. But] do, but *YR* 19: tomorrow's a] tomorrow's not worth a *YR* 23: Truth? Or Truth] truth? or truth *YR* 24: experience.] A canceled annotation follows in BHTS: "YR".

420 **Language Barrier** Text: BH. Variant: *Southern Review,* ns 15 (Autumn 1979), p. 997 (as "Language Problem"). 1: snow-peaks] snow peaks *SoR* 2: Far below lies, shelved] Lies below, far shelved *SoR* 4: waters,] water, *SoR* 5: fails, and downward becomes] falls, and becomes *SoR* 7: Alone, alone,] Then down. Though alone. *Emory* 12: that] the *SoR* 12: breath thinning again] again breath thinning BHTS (revised on BHG to BH) 12: again to] with *SoR* 12: glory,] $\sim_\wedge$ *SoR* 13: While the heart, . . . try to say?] And heart palpitating for Truth. / What, long ago, did the world try to say? *SoR* 14: Leaps.] Leaps for Truth. BHTS (revised on BHG to BH) 17: position,] positions, *SoR* 17: train whistles . . . gardens and lowlands] train whistles for crossing. / You may again drowse before the first twitter of birds. / Listen—we hear now the creatures of gardens and lowlands. *SoR* 18: Before the first twitter . . . again drowse.] You may again drowse before the first / Twitter of birds. BHTS (revised on BHG to BH) 20: and lowlands.] No stanza break after this text in *SoR*. 21: too.] A canceled annotation follows in BHTS: "southern review".

421 **Lesson in History** Text: BH. Variant: *American Poetry Review,* 8 (July–Aug. 1979), p. 5 (as "Lessons In History"). In BHTS the title is "Lessons of History" but the title is corrected to BH. 1: tell!] ~? *APR* 2: Did the] Did *APR* 3: Or did, . . . torchlit?] Or did tears spring, unwitting, to / His eyes as lips found torch-lit flesh? *APR* 5: Boone$_\wedge$] ~, *APR* 6: sunset$_\wedge$] ~, *APR* 6: the wild Kentucky Eden?] Kaintuck's Eden wilderness? *APR* 7: Cambronne] Cambron *APR*, BHTS (revised to BH) 7: his famous obscenity—] as he uttered his famous word. *APR* 8: At last, at last,] At last—at last— *APR* 8: fulfilling identity in pride?] fulfilled in identity of pride? *APR* 9: happy . . . malignant?] happy when the / Diagnostician admitted, in fact, the growth was malignant? *APR* 11: mad] the mad *APR* 11: work,] $\sim_\wedge$ *APR* 12: dip, trancelike, her hands] dip her hands *APR* 15: fulfillment,] fulfilment BHTS (revised to BH) 15: fulfillment, with anguish entwined,] joy with your pain intertwined, *APR* 17: Anne] Ann *APR* 17: as the blade, at last, rose?] as, at last, the axe rose? *APR* 17: blade] axe BHTS (revised on BHG to BH) 18: before] just before *APR* 19: guess] know *APR* 19: night-waking,] at night waking, *APR* 20: sibilant] whispering *APR* 21: And know, or guess, what long ago happened there?] And who know, or guess, what, long ago, happened there? *APR* 21: And know, or guess, what long ago happened there?] In *APR* and in *Emory* this line is deleted. 22: say/] A canceled annotation follows in BHTS: "APR".

422 **Prairie Harvest** Text: BH. Variant: *Salmagundi,* no. 46 (Fall 1979), pp. 4–5. 3: heartbeat] heart beat *Salmagundi*, heart-beat BHTS (revised to BH) 6: For] From *Salmagundi* 7: in last] in the last *Salmagundi* 9: Nothing. Your heart is the only sound.] Nothing, and the only sound is your heart. *Salmagundi* 10: Can it be that you, for an instant,] Did you, for an instant, *Salmagundi* 10: forget] forgot BHTS (revised to BH) 11: And blink your eyes as it goes? Another day done,] And shut your eyes? And another day is thus done *Salmagundi*, And blinked your eyes as it went. Another day done, BHTS (revised to BH) 12: the Kiowa] that the Kiowa *Salmagundi* 12: the Kiowa once] once the Kiowa BHTS (revised to BH) 12: requite] acquit *Salmagundi*, BHTS (revised to BH) 13: by lust,] to lust, *Salmagundi*, BHTS (revised to BH) 13: lust by] lust to *Salmagundi*, BHTS (revised to BH) 16: whatever] what *Salmagundi* 16: are?] A canceled annotation follows in BHTS: "salmagundi".

V.

423 **Eagle Descending** Text: BH. Variant: *Vanderbilt Poetry Review,* 4, nos. 1–2 (1979), p. 29. In *Emory* the whole poem is crossed out in pencil, with "Cut" in the margin and "not good" across the bottom. *Vanderbilt Poetry Review* lacks the dedication. 2: switch and swell,] their switch and swell$_\wedge$ *Vanderbilt Poetry Review*, their switch and swell, BHTS (revised on BHG to BH) 3: With spiral upward now,] Turned into spiral$_\wedge$ *Vanderbilt Poetry Review* 4: cloud,] $\sim_\wedge$ BHTS (revised on BHG to BH) 5: invisible to us,] to us invisible$_\wedge$ *Vanderbilt Poetry Review* 7: at the plains] at plains *Vanderbilt Poetry Review* 10: No silly pride of Icarus his!] No fool, no Icarus he! *Vanderbilt Poetry Review* 11: gazes,] stares, *Vanderbilt Poetry Review* 12: of earth] of the earth *Vanderbilt Poetry Review* 15: Soon crucial contact makes,] makes crucial contact$_\wedge$ *Vanderbilt Poetry Review* 17: He leans.—And] He leans. And *Vanderbilt Poetry Review* 19: fulfilled.] A canceled annotation follows in BHTS: "vanderbilt poetry review".

423 **Ballad of Your Puzzlement** Text: BH. Variant: *Georgia Review,* 34 (Spring 1980), pp. 11–13. Headnote: when old and reviewing your life before death comes] when old and reviewing your past life, while waiting for death. *GaR* In BHTS the headnote was originally set as a subtitle, appearing with the title in the table contents. There are four annotations in purple pencil on BHTS. Next to the title is "pick up from sample pg. 79". Next to the headnote is "set–Don't pick up". Next to the first nine stanzas of the poem is "pick up from sample pg. 79". Next to the tenth stanza is "pref start". These are notes to the typesetter, which I do not normally record, except that here they have bearing on whether the headnote is really a subtitle or not. The first page of BHTS (up to "Even as his senses reel"), although a photocopy related to those from the rest of the volume, is folded in half, as if for mailing, and may be a late replacement of an earlier draft. The second and third pages in BHTS are typescript, not photocopy, and have typed headers: "ballad of your puzzlement—Second version." 8: Like a movie$_\wedge$film gone silent,] Like an old silent movie film BHTS (revised to BH) 18: crowd-swarm$_\wedge$] $\sim$, *GaR* 19: sways,] $\sim_\wedge$ *GaR* 28: flicks] skips *GaR*, jumps BHTS (revised on BHG to BH) 29: And to change the metaphor,] And—to change the metaphor— *GaR* 31: flypaper] fly-paper BHTS (revised to BH) 40: an] a BHTS (revised to BH) 42: he bursts into tears.] tears fill his eyes. *GaR* 47: old now] now old *GaR*, BHTS (revised on BHG to BH) 48: loathsome] loathesome BHTS (revised to BH) 51: bill, and thrusts] bill. Thrusts *GaR* 52: hand—] $\sim$. *GaR*, BHTS (revised on BHG to BH) 65: and] with *GaR* 70: all huddle] all, huddled *GaR* 72: or perhaps you are only] And Reality is only *GaR*, BHTS (revised on BHG to BH) 76: But$_\wedge$] $\sim$, *GaR*

426 **Antinomy: Time and Identity** Text: BH. Variants: *Yale Review,* 68 (Summer 1979), pp. 540–41, SP85 (as "Antinomy: Time and What Happened"), *Helsinki* (As "Antimony: Time and Identity"). Warren changed the title of the poem in SP85 on SP85G. SP85 removes the parentheses around the section numbers. In *Emory* there is a marginal note: "One Poem." There is a note in purple pencil to the typesetter on BHTS: "pick up all from sample pp. 80+81". 1: Alone ... What they see?] These lines are substantially different in *YR*:

ALONE, alone, I lie. The canoe floats on blackness.
It must be so, for up to a certain point
I remember all clearly. Then perhaps things go out of joint.
Or even of jointure. I saw the canoe
At the dock, aluminum riding ghost-white on blackness.
This much is true. Silent, as entering air,
The paddle slow dips. Silent, I slide forth. Forth on,
Forth into, what dimension?
Slow as a dream, no ripple at keel, I move through
The stillness, on blackness, past hope or despair
Not relevant now to illusions I once thought I lived by. At last,
All shores lost in blackness of forest, I lie down. High,

Stars stare down, and I
See them. I wonder if they see me.
If they do, do they know what they see?

4: All comes back clear. I saw,] All comes back clear. Then things may go out of joint. / Or even of jointure. I saw, BHTS (revised to BH) 5: aluminum,] ~∧ BHTS (revised on BHG to BH) 5: rising ghost-white on blackness. / This] rising ghost-white / On blackness. This *Helsinki* 15: in the] in BHTS (revised on BHG to BH) 15: down. High,] down. / High. *Helsinki* 21: caught pale] caught, pale, *Helsinki* 22: must] *must* *YR* 23: loon-cry] loon cry *YR* 25: windless fact or logical choices, / While out of Time, Timelessness brims] windless fact, / Or logical choices, while out of Time, / Timelessness brims *Helsinki* 26: Time,] ~∧ *YR* 27: coil out] coil *YR* 27: to coil out and spread / On the time that seems past and the time that may come,] to coil out and / Spread on the time that seems past and / The time that may come, *Helsinki* 29: And both the same under / The present's darkening dome.] And both / The same under the present's darkening dome. BHTS (revised on BHG to BH) 29: both] all *YR* 29: under / The present's] under the present's *YR* 31: silence,] ~∧ *Helsinki* 32: till] before *Helsinki* 33: As consciousness ... your fictionality.] These lines are substantially different in *Helsinki*:

As consciousness outward seeps, the dark seeps
In. As the self dissolves, realization surrenders
Its burden, and thus fulfills
Your own fictionality.

36: unrippling] uprippling BHG (revised on BHG to BH) 37: light as breath, moves in a dignity] like breath, moves with the soundless dignity *YR* 38: As soundless as a star's mathematical shift] Of a star's ineluctable shift *YR* 40: parodic sky.] under-sky *YR* 41: I wonder if this is I.] This stanza is omitted in *YR*. 42: It is not long till day.] This entire section omitted in *YR*. 43: Dawn bursts like the birth pangs of your, and the world's, existence.] Dawn bursts like the birth pangs of / Your and the world's existence. *Helsinki* 43: bursts] will burst *YR*, BHTS (revised to BH) 43: like] with *YR* 43: your,] yours, *YR* 43: your, and the world's,] yours and the world's BHTS (revised on BHG to BH) 44: creeps] will creep *YR*, BHTS (revised to BH) 45: Far back, scraps of memory hang, rag-rotten, on a rusting barbed-wire fence.] Far back, scraps of memory hang, / Rag-rotten, on a rusting barbed-wire fence. *Helsinki* 45: hang,] will hang, BHTS (revised to BH) 45: hang, rag-rotten,] will hang like rags rotten *YR* 46: One crow, ... in its magnificence.] A crow, alone and icy at zenith, will gleam sun-purpled in its magnificence. *YR* 47: magnificence.] A canceled annotation follows in BHTS: "YR".

427 **Trips to California** Text: BH. Variant: *New York Review of Books*, 19 July 1979, p. 24. 1: dust-storm] dust storm *NYRB* 3: piled so deep] so deep piled *NYRB* 7: blood,] ~∧ *NYRB* 14: goen] going *NYRB* 15: Not me.] Well, I ain't. *NYRB* 16: jist] jest *NYRB* 17: Stick] "Stick *NYRB* 17: knows whut] know what *NYRB* 19: now July] July *NYRB* 20: histrionic sunset.] molten red of sunset. *NYRB* 21: to eaves.] to the eaves. *NYRB* 22: to lee,] to the lee, *NYRB* 24: had been] had once been *NYRB* 24: This had been buffalo country, herds] Once buffao country this, herds BHTS (revised to BH) 29: you] they *NYRB* 29: "stand,"] stand, *NYRB* 30: working. Dawn] working, and dawn *NYRB* 31: showed] showing *NYRB* 32: Besides,] ~∧ BHTS (revised to BH) 34: One—not] One, meaning not *NYRB* 34: not buffalo, but redskin.] not buffalo by redskin. BHTS (revised to BH) 35: avarice,] ~∧ *NYRB* 37: eastward drops.] drops eastward *NYRB* 40: Reality past may be only ... like a flower.] Reality past is only a dream too. *NYRB* The poem ends after this line in *NYRB*. 43: immediacy,] reality, BHTS (revised on BHG to BH) 46: flower.] A canceled annotation follows in BHTS: "new york review of books".

428 **Auto-da-fé** Text: BH. Variant: *New Yorker*, 31 December 1979, p. 28. In the table of contents to BHTS, "Aging Man In Woodland in Timeless Noon of Summer" follows this poem, but it is crossed out in pencil. 9: St.] Saint BHTS (revised on BHG to BH) 17: But, oh!] Oh, no! *NY* 31: half-drunk] half drunk *NY* 32: to] To *NY* 34: Witches∧] ~, *NY* 38: bobtail—] ~, *NY*, BHTS (revised on BHG to BH) 39: blessèd] blessed *NY*

41: beard prickling] beard then prickling *NY*, BHTS (revised to BH) 41: sudden in / Wisps] sudden / In wisps *NY*, BHTS (revised on BHG to BH) 43: recreant] offensive *NY*, BHTS (revised on BHG to BH) 47: flame-dance,] ~∧ *NY* 51: Sure meaning.] The line straddles the stanza break that follows this text. Warren reminds the typesetter to put a stanza break here in BHG. 57: body.] Two canceled annotations follow in BHTS: "not out" and (in pencil) "New Yorker".

430 **Aspen Leaf in Windless World** Text: BH. Variant: *Poetry*, 135 (Nov. 1979), pp. 83–84. 2: loiters, motionless,] loiters motionless *Poetry* 2: Wyoming.] ~, *Poetry* 5: how sea-foam, thin and white,] how the sea-foam, white, *Poetry* 8: sunlit, intricate rhythm?] sunlit intricacy? *Poetry* 12: wool-fleece] woolfleece *Poetry*, BHTS (revised on BHG to BH) 13: oaks black,] in blackness of oaks, *Poetry* 13: heard,] ~∧ *Poetry*, BHTS (revised to BH) 14: tree-toad] tree toad *Poetry* 18: scaly,] scaley, *Poetry*, BHTS (revised to BH) 19: trick—] ~. *Poetry* 20: now,] then, *Poetry*, BHTS (revised to BH) 21: you make] you've made *Poetry*, BHTS (revised to BH) 21: our shadowy world] our world *Poetry*, BHTS (revised to BH) 22: high jinks] high-jinks *Poetry* 27: sun then rise] sun rise *Poetry* 29: menhir?] ~∧ *Poetry* 29: gray menhir?] In *Poetry* a stanza break follows this text, doubtless in error. 31: popcorn] tramped popcorn *Poetry* 32: been?] A canceled annotation follows in BHTS: "poetry".

431 **Acquaintance with Time in Early Autumn** Text: BH. Variant: *New Yorker*, 10 Sept. 1979, pp. 46–47 (as "Acquaintance with Time in Autumn"). 1: passed] past *NY* 2: Time,] ~∧ *NY* 2: heart,] ~∧ *NY* 3: Stroke by stroke,] Pulse, stroke by stroke, *NY* 4: face, or shape, or history—] face or shape or history: *New Yorker* 5: our being] Being *NY* 8: bough-juncture] bough juncture *NY* 10: flexion] flection *NY* 11: black ammoniac] black and ammoniac *NY* 14: beneath∧] ~, *NY* 15: At] For *NY* 15: instant] instant of *Emory* 15: hanging] we hung *NY* 17: how distant seem!] now distant seem∧ *NY* 18: I float] As I float *NY* 18: gaze] stare *NY* 19: flame-red—the first—alone] flame red, alone *NY* 20: Above] Above the *NY* 24: Reached ghostly . . . Oh, leaf,] These lines are substantially different in *NY*:

Of nameless depth reached ghostly up
To find my flesh and pierce the heart, as though releasing,
In that dark inwardness, a single drop. Oh, leaf,

30: notice] now notice *NY* 33: The sun] The leaf hangs motionless. The sun *NY* 35: Then, in the lucent emptiness,] Then by its own will, on the lucent emptiness, *NY* 36: fade,] seem to fade, *NY* 39: stem, by its own will, / Release / Its tiny claw-hooks, and trust] stem release / Its tiny claw-hook, and trust *NY* 42: The leaf] But the leaf *NY*, BHTS (revised on BHG to BH) 42: is] seems *NY* 43: not to fall. But / Does not. Minutely, / It] not to fall. And does / Not. Instead, / It *NY* 45: calm, calm] oh, calm *NY* 47: the red-gold leaf,] the red-gold, *NY*, red-gold, BHTS (revised on BHG to BH) 49: It touches. Breath / Comes back, and I hate God] It touches, and breath comes back, and I hate God *NY* 50: Comes] Come BHTS (revised to BH) 51: great globe's] world's *NY* 55: Still ravening] Ravening *NY* 55: might,] ~∧ BHTS (revised on BHG to BH) 58: the payment] and payment *NY* 59: dime-thin, thumb-worn, two-sided,] dime-thin, two-sided, *New Yorker* 59: coin?] a canceled annotation follows in BHTS: "new yroker".

432 **Safe in Shade** Text: BH. Variants: *Georgia Review*, (Summer 1980), pp. 313–14, SP85. 2: man,] ~∧ *GaR* 2: gazed] fixed BHTS (revised to BH) 3: lost,] ~∧ *GaR* 6: reddish] reddish, scrofulous BHTS (revised to BH) 6: tatter] tetter BHTS (revised to BH) In *Emory*, Warren changed this to "tetter," then changed it back to "tatter." Since the two words don't have similar meanings, Warren's hesitations indicate that he was attracted as much to the sound as to the sense. But since in BHTS the cedar bark was "scrofulous" as well, "tetter" made sense there. 8: who on the ground sat, waited.] on the ground, sat. Waited. *GaR* 14: on the] on *GaR* 17: Rose to thread the cedar-dark.] SP85 omits the stanza break after this line. Since there is no correction on SP85TS and all of the galleys read with SP85, the SP85 reading is probably a typesetter's error. 21: we∧] ~, *GaR* 23: Sat so silent] So silent sat BHTS (revised to BH) 24: whitewashed] white-washed

GaR 29: He spoke.] In *Emory* Warren adds a line after this text: "And now I speak." 30: Into] Now into SP85 (in blue pen on SP85TS) 36: gesture,] act, SP85 (revised on SP85G to SP85) 39: flung,] ~∧ *GaR*, BHTS (revised on BHG to BH) 44: high-spiraling,] ~∧ *GaR* 45: that / We have,] that we / Have BHTS (revised to BH)

433 **Synonyms** Text: BH. Variant: *Poetry*, 135 (Nov. 1979), pp. 76–80. In *Poetry* there is a dedication: "To A. T. for whom beauty and reality were synonymous." A. T. is probably Allen Tate. *Poetry* does not enclose the section numbers in parentheses. 1: back,] ~∧ *Poetry* 3: blind] dark *Poetry* 5: White-splintered] White splintered *Poetry* 5: masses of stone,] stone masses, *Poetry* 6: What is the roar] And deafness *Poetry* 7: But a] A *Poetry* 8: silence—] ~, *Poetry* 9: Which paradox] Which *Poetry* 9: utterance?] ~. *Poetry* 9: ultimate utterance?] *Poetry* adds another line after this text: "It must be speaking Truth." In BHTS the line is "This must be the speaking of Truth." BHG corrects to BH. 10: When the] After the *Poetry*, After BHTS (revised to BH) 13: which,] ~∧ *Poetry* 14: From one perspective, is beauty,] Is another word for beauty, *Poetry* 17: saddle-horn,] ~∧ *Poetry* 17: must.] ~, *Poetry*, BHTS (revised on BHG to BH) 18: Watch] And watch *Poetry*, BHTS (revised on BHG to BH) 21: judgment.] ~∧ *Poetry* 22: at home in bed.] at home. *Poetry* 28: spray] splay *Poetry* 28: visible,] showing, *Poetry* 29: sits,] ~∧ *Poetry* 30: old-fashioned] black old-fashioned *Poetry* 31: Shoe-buttons,] Shoebuttons∧ *Poetry* 32: for something] In *Poetry* there is no line break after this text. 35: afield,] a-field, *Poetry* 38: stalks] stalk *Poetry* cut stalks *Emory* 38: in that last] in last *Poetry* 39: In distance∧ / One cowbell spills] In / Distance, one cow-bell spills *Poetry* 40: cowbell] cow-bell BHTS (revised to BH) 41: bullfrog,] bull-frog, *Poetry*, BHTS (revised to BH) 41: empty tinkle] tinkle *Emory* 44: later∧] ~, *Poetry* 45: pitchfork heft.] pitch-fork shaft. *Poetry* 46: young,] so young, *Poetry*, BHTS (revised to BH) 52: tasseled silk-swell] tasselled silk swell *Poetry* 52: silk-swell] silk swell BHTS (revised on BHG to BH) 55: strength] strength-proud *Poetry*, strength-pride BHTS (revised to BH) 56: oilskins,] oil-skins, *Poetry* 57: Burns eyeballs,] Burns the eyeballs, *Poetry* 58: White] The white *Poetry* 59: Nijinski-like,] Nijinski like, *Poetry* 60: motionless,] ~∧ *Poetry* 61: tumult∧] ~, BHTS (revised to BH) 64: its] a *Emory* 72: In the narrow, ... he could not know] This whole section is crossed out in *Emory*, and the rest of the sections are renumbered accordingly. 78: the swelter of summer: at] summer swelter: and at *Poetry*, summer swelter: at BHTS (revised on BHG to BH) 79: the old and the sick] old and sick *Poetry* 79: air,] ~. *Poetry* 80: And at night, then muggings] Night then: and mugging *Poetry* 81: soon—] ~, *Poetry* 82: Action!] ~. *Poetry* 84: afternoon,] mid-afternoon. *Poetry* 87: Clutches] Clutching *Poetry* 88: Street-steps. Descends.] Street-steps, descends. *Poetry* 89: cab,] cad, BHTS (revised to BH) 93: choking] almost choking *Poetry* 94: paws.] paws, / Not knowing what waits in the teeth of the laughing steel jaws. *Poetry* 95: he holds,] holds *Poetry* 97: see the old dame swing] see how the old dame swings *Poetry*, BHTS (revised to BH) 98: bulk,] hulk, *Poetry* 99: She thrusts the poor prize] Has the prize *Poetry* 100: climbs] clambers *Poetry* 101: eye.] ~, *Poetry* 101: The drunk] And the drunk *Poetry* 103: Takes swig,] Takes a swig, *Poetry* 103: lifts a] lifts up his *Poetry* 105: You] you *Poetry*, BHTS (revised to BH) 105: smite!— / Or] smite! / —Or *Poetry* 106: Or lost Your nerve, huh? Can't longer tell wrong from right?"] —Or lost your nerve? Or can't longer tell wrong from right?" *Poetry* 110: apron, he buffs an apple] apron polishes apples *Poetry* 111: And another. ... he could not know.] These two lines omitted in *Poetry*. 113: world,] ~∧ *Poetry* 116: tangled variety,] tangle and variety, *Poetry* 117: hard sometimes] hard *Poetry* 117: reality.] A canceled annotation follows in BHTS: "poetry".

436 **Swimming in the Pacific** Text: BH. Variant: *American Poetry Review*, 8 (Jan.–Feb. 1979), p. 5. 3: backed by] and the *APR* 3: Turned, saw,] Turned then, and saw, *APR* 5: grew] grow *APR* 5: smokier,] ~∧ BHTS (revised to BH) 6: More flattened, then sank.] Flatter. Then sank. *APR*, Flatter, then sank. BHTS (revised on BHG to BH) 6: flattened, then] flattened. Then *Emory* 7: to] for *Emory* 8: Gray] A Gray *APR* 9: my wallet (no treasure).] and my wallet, no treasure. *APR* 10: dune-foot∧] ~, *APR* 14: stood,] ~∧ *APR* 15: sand grains] sand-grains *APR* 15: then could] could then *APR* 16: few as] fewer than *APR* 16: toes—] toes, plus a couple— *Emory* 17: where / The sea might,] where

the sea / Might, *APR* 18: might,] night, BHTS (revised in red pencil to BH) 18: mania,] ∼∧ *APR* 19: cloud-pale line,] No line break after this text in *APR* 21: on.] on. And on. *Emory* 22: dusk,] sunset, *APR* 25: now new, of the city afar,] lights of the city in distance, *APR* 25: new,] newly bright, *Emory* 26: of Time,] No line break after this text in *APR*. 27: That trickles ... is life.] that trickled like sand, and was life. *APR*, that trickles like sand, / And is life. BHTS (revised on BHG to BH) 29: after sorrow] after all the sorrow *APR* 31: years] grains *APR*, BHT (revised on BHG to BH) 32: now could certainly never] now certainly could not *APR*, certainly now could never BHTS (revised on BHG to BH) 33: counted] readily counted *APR* 34: as of old / In my twilit nakedness,] as of old in my nakedness, *APR* 35: nakedness,] ∼∧ BHTS (revised to BH) 37: Move] Wander *APR* 37: city of men, / What answer, at last,] city of men, what answer at last∧ *APR* 39: question?] questions? *APR* 40: in,] ∼∧ *APR* 42: stared and,] stared, and *APR* 43: Could see] Saw *APR* 44: dream all] dream that all *APR* 44: moved to.] A canceled annotation follows in BHTS: "american poetry review".

438 **Night Walking** Text: BH. Variant: *American Poetry Review*, 8 (July–Aug. 1979), p. 48. 1: *Bear,* my first thought at waking.] *Bear*∧ my first thought, as waking, *APR*, BHTS (revised on BHG to BH, except for a comma after "thought", and corrected on page proofs to BH) 2: What I think ... but no,] First bear off the mountain ripping apples / From trees near my window—but no, *APR*, What I think is first bear off the mountain rip apples / From trees near my window—but no, BHTS (revised on BHG to BH) 5: in.] ∼, *APR* 6: Now] Who *APR* 7: he now] now *APR* 9: late and zenithward] late zenithward *APR* 10: Over forests ... white.] Over forests as black as old blood and the crags bone-white. *APR* 11: bone-white.] There is no stanza break after this text in *APR*. 12: Levis] *levis APR*, BHTS (revised to BH), *Levis* BHG (revised on BHG to BH) 13: For what? ... crouch.] For what? As I creep behind a parked car and guiltily crouch. *APR* 15: His face, brown] Face brown, *APR*, BHTS (revised to "Face, brown—") There is a canceled marginal query here in red pencil: "See other TS / Syntax?" The line is corrected to BH on BHG. 15: moonlight∧] ∼, *APR* 16: Lifts moonward,] Moonward he lifts, BHTS (revised to BH) 16: remember] think *APR* 18: He had waked, he said, at a distant dog's howl and] At a distant howl he had waked and *APR* 19: is] was *APR* 22: Stand monitory, stand white—] Stand white and monitory— *APR* 23: upward, and on,] on upward, *APR* 25: In silence ... can,] In silence and shadow, in my / Undefinable impulse to steal what knowledge I, in love, may, *APR* 25: and in / The undefinable] and my / Undefinable BHTS (revised on BHG to BH) 27: can,] may, BHTS (revised to BH) can steal, *Emory* 28: With laggard cunning I trail to] Now I with laggard cunning trail him to *Emory* 35: And the] The *APR* 35: all.] ∼: *APR* 35: all.] No stanza break after this text in *APR* 37: High, calm, there the moon rides.] High there the moon rides calm. *APR*, BHTS (revised on BHG to BH) 38: He] The boy *Emory* 40: Arms down, goes on.] He goes on. *APR*, Goes on. BHTS (revised on BHG to BH) 43: joy∧] ∼, *APR* 44: All else ... I stop] All else is his, and alone. In shadow / I huddle till, in solitude, I / Can start back to bed and the proper darkness of night. // But alone now in moonlight, I stop *APR* 48: opening] opened *APR* 49: as sudden,] sudden, *APR* 49: as sudden, has come from long back—] as sudden as any black brink opens up— *Emory* 50: once I] I *APR*, BHTS (revised on BHG to BH) 51: Had dreamed] Had once dreamed *APR*, Once had xreamed BHTS (revised on BHTS in red pencil to "Once had dreamed" and on BHG to BH) 51: almost could] could not *APR* 52: But could not ... hum of the wires.] I heard no voice in the heart, just the hum of the wires. *APR* 54: Just the hum of the wires.] Not even echo of moon-bemused surf far below. *Emory* 58: bare arms] arms up *APR* 59: redeeming white] transforming *APR* 59: world.] A canceled annotation follows in BHTS: "american poetry review".

439 **Passers-By on Snowy Night** Text: BH. Variant: *Southern Review*, ns 16 (Spring 1980), pp. 378–79 (as "Passersby on Snowy Night"). Because Warren intended this poem and "October Picnic Long Ago," to serve as bookends to *Being Here*, I have preserved the italic type in both cases, although the magazine versions were in roman type. The title in BHTS is "Passersby on Snowy Night" but it is corrected to BH. A penciled annotation on the top of the page, in Warren's hand, reads "*right-hand page*". 2: snow track] snow-track

SoR 3: moon,] ~∧ *SoR* 3: starkness,] ~∧ *SoR* 5: regards∧] ~, *SoR* 11: windowpane's] window pane's BHTS (revised to BH) 14: Perhaps] And perhaps *SoR* 17: mocking] the mocking BHTS (revised on BHG to BH) 20: you] on *SoR* 23: benediction,] ~∧ *SoR* 24: And] As *SoR* 24: go.] A canceled annotation follows in BHTS: "southern review".

441 **Afterthought** The Afterthought is numbered two pages out of sequence with BHTS (although it is corrected in pencil to the proper numbers), and probably comes from an earlier version in which there were two more pages. impulse] impulse found here BHTS (revised to BH) irrelevances; but they] irrelevances. A few poems may indeed, seem off the main impulse, but they BHTS (revised to BH) another∧] ~, BHTS (revised on BHG to BH) Passers-by] Passersby BHTS (revised to BH) seen∧] ~, BHTS (revised to BH) intent] thrust BHTS (revised to BH) "The Ballad of Your Puzzlement"] The actual title of the poem is "Ballad of Your Puzzlement". supposed] suppose BH (and BHTS) of course, concerned with the reviewing] of course, concerned with the reviewing of section is obviously, concerned with the reviewing BHTS (but corrected to BH. This takes place at a page turn. The second page of the Afterward clearly comes from a different draft from the first page.) The order of the poems is] The order of the poems here is BHTS (revised to BH) general period] period here specified (revised to "period specified" on BHTS and to BH on BHG) are not included] are not included, and some not even finished. BHTS (but corrected to BH) selection] selection here BHTS (revised to BH) thematically,] thematically, not in a rigorously logical sequence BHTS (revised to BH)

Rumor Verified

Poems 1979–1980

Until a late stage of development—including RVTS, and even up to the first set of "repros," in fact—this book was to be called *Have You Ever Eaten Stars?* RVTS even includes a mock-up of the title page with that title. The volume underwent at least eight stages (up to Draft G) of revision prior to RVTS, and even RVTS shows considerable evidence of having been assembled piecemeal. All of RVTS is on three-hole paper. Most of it is a photocopy of Draft C, which was typed with a carbon ribbon on round-cornered typing paper. Some is typed with a cloth ribbon on corrasable bond. (Unless noted otherwise, all of the poems originate from Draft C.) All are typed single-spaced, as is Warren's usual practice. All of the page numbers in RVTS are added in pencil in the upper right corner, and the pages, after the first, of poems with more than one page, have the title typed in the upper left corner, with the page number within the poem, indicating that even the poems from draft C may have been typed separately. Most of the pages have been folded in half for mailing, again indicating that the typescript was assembled from poems typed separately. (The few pages that were not folded in half are indicated below.) Corrections on RVTS are sometimes in black pen (in what seems to be Warren's hand), and in pencil (in what seems to be Albert Erskine's).

The poems Warren extracted from this volume for SP85 appear as marked-up photocopy from RV in SP85TS. In RV the run-over portions of long lines are, unusually for Warren, set indented from the left. On SP85TS Warren had those run-over portions set flush with the right margin, as he usually did. Because the revisions Warren did for SP85 are often problematic, I have recorded whether they appear as revisions on SP85TS, in order to distinguish between readings which originate as revisions and readings which originate as errors.

Warren's markup of the Emory copy of this book is not dated, but since it is marked "Stuart's copy" inside the front cover, it presumably was marked up in May, 1987, with the other books. dedication] Ebie SP85 (and SP85TS), *Emory*, Ebe RV, RVTS epigraph: i'] io RV, i' SP85 (revised on SP85TS) epigraph: de le] delle RV de le SP85 (revised on SP85TS) epigraph: stelle.] ~, RV, ~. SP85 (and SP85TS) (Because these are Dante's words, not Warren's, and because Warren discovered and corrected his misquotation, I have followed SP85 here rather than RV.)

I. Prologue

445 **Mediterranean Basin** Although both "Chthonian Revelation: A Myth" and "Looking Northward, Aegeanward: Nestlings on Seacliff" appear in SP85, they are not part of a sequence there, and "Looking Northward, Aegeanward: Nestlings on Sea-cliff" appears separately in *Helsinki*.

445 **I. Chthonian Revelation: A Myth** Text: RV. Variants: *Yale Review,* 70 (Autumn 1980), pp. 95–96, SP85. The section is typed on corrasable bond in RVTS, and there is a canceled annotation in pencil on the top right corner: "revised Feb. 1981". The pages have been folded in thirds, as if for mailing in a business envelope. The first page has a typed annotation, circled in pencil, on the last line: "Yale Review". 1: sun] the sun *YR* 3: minimum,] minimal, *YR* 3: they] we *YR* 4: past lava, past pumice,] past pumice, past lava, *YR*, RVTS (revised in pencil to RV) 4: boulders,] ~‸ *YR* 8: lace-fringe] lace fringe *YR* 10: Few] We *YR* 11: cave-shade] a cave-shade RVTS (revised in pencil on RVG to RV) 13: earth-agony,] earth's agony, *YR* 14: Down-reached] Reached down *Emory* 15: from] of *YR* 15: the eye / Stares from that] you stare out / From the *YR* 17: tirelessly] pitilessly RVTS (revised in pencil to RV) 18: Commands the wide world beyond that secret purlieu.] Is the only promise the light of the sun now makes you. *YR* 18: the wide world] so far off wide worlds *Emory* 19: sun,] sun-blaze, *YR* 21: he is] you are *YR* 22: looks] look *YR* 25: life was led] you led life *YR* 27: He turns. His face] You turn. Your face *YR* 30: there,] ~‸ *YR* 33: Communion] In communion RVTS (revised in red pen to RV) 34: There in columnar gracility stands,] Stands in columnar gracility, *YR* 36: shadows, she,] shadows, *YR* 37: From the light] In the light *YR* 39: parted. His eyes] parted, and your eyes *YR* 41: out,] ~‸ *YR* 41: his way in the act,] the way in your act, *YR* 42: he moves in his] you move in your *YR* 43: fingertips] finger-tips *YR* 44: they] you *YR* 44: cave-mouth] cave mouth *YR* 45: they] you *YR* 45: mountain-rim,] mountain's rim, *YR* 46: a] the *YR* 46: gleam boldly] beam goldly *YR* 48: and feet] and your feet *YR* 49: creeping] coming *YR* 49: in.] on. RVTS (revised in pencil to RV) There is no stanza break after this text in RVG, but the galleys are corrected to RV. 50: they] you *YR* 52: world] word RVG (revised in pencil on RVG to RV) 53: they] you *YR* 55: Of] In RVTS (revised in pencil on RVG to RV) 55: mercilessly joyful] merciless *YR* 56: To fill] That fills *YR*, RVTS (revised in pencil on RVG to RV) 56: the hollow sky.] In RVTS the stanza break that follows is marked with four asterisks, but they are canceled in pencil, with the penciled annotation "reg. verse #". 57: they] we *YR*, RVTS (revised in pencil to RV) 61: they] we *YR*, RVTS (revised in pencil to RV) 62: the nameless] nameless SP85 (revised on SP85G to SP85) 63: They] We *YR*, RVTS (revised in pencil to RV) 63: they now] we *YR*, we now RVTS (revised in pencil to RV) 64: fingertip,] finger-tip, *YR* 67: enshrinèd] enshrined *YR*, RVTS (revised in pencil on RVG to RV)

446 **II. Looking Northward, Aegeanward: Nestlings on Seacliff** Text: RV. Variants: *New Yorker*, 3 Nov. 1980, p. 50, SP85. In *NY* the title is "Looking Northward, Aegeanward: Nestlings on Sea Cliff."On the contents page of RVTS, the title is "Northward, Ageanward: Nestlings on Seacliff" (but it is corrected to RV in black pen). The same title appears on the poem in RVTS, but is corrected to RV in red pencil. RVTS is typed with a carbon ribbon, and there is a typed annotation, canceled in pencil, in the upper right corner: "version June 10, 1980". That the poem is part of a sequence is not clear on RVTS, because the "2." is added in pencil. In *Helsinki* the title is "Looking Northward, Aegeanward: Nestlings on Sea-Cliff." 1: the cliff / That you] the cliff is / What you *NY* 5: rock-shelf] rock shelf *NY* 5: outthrust] out-thrust RVTS (revised in pencil to RV) 6: droppings,] dropplings, RVG (revised in pencil on RVG to RV) 6: eggshell, lifts] egg-shell, lift RVTS (revised in pencil to RV) 7: unfeathered‸] ~, *NY*, *Helsinki* 7: uphold] upheld *Helsinki* 8: The pink] That pink *Helsinki* 8: gape,] ~— *NY* 12: toehold,] ~‸ *NY*, toe-hold, RVTS (revised in pencil to RV), *Helsinki* 12: handhold,] ~‸ *NY*, hand-hold, RVTS (revised in pencil to RV), *Helsinki* 12: grope,] ~. *NY* 13: Or for purchase to pause on and turn to the sun-crinkled sea,] Breathless, at last you find a place to breathe . . . / Or even to pause on, and turn to the sun-crinkled sea. *NY* 13: Or for purchase . . . of a tale told.] These lines are typed with cloth ribbon and taped into RVTS. 13: purchase]

surface RVTS (revised in pencil to RV) 14: into the / Horizon's] into / The horizon's *NY* 16: How long ago galleys] How, long back, the galleys *NY* 17: Northward$_\wedge$] ∼, *NY* 17: toward] toward RVG (revised to "into" in pencil on RVG, then corrected back to "toward") 17: that quarter's] the quarter's RVTS (revised in pencil on RVG to RV) 17: that quarter's blue dazzle of distance.] the blue daze of distance. *NY* 19: And then think how, lost in the dimness of aeons, sea sloshed] And you think, in dimness of aeons, how once the sea sloshed *NY* 19: aeons,] eons, RVTS (revised in pencil to RV) 19: sea sloshed] seas sloshed *Helsinki*, sea had sloshed *Emory* 20: washing machine,] dishpan, *NY*, washing-machine, *Helsinki* 20: sky] the sky *NY* 22: gulls screamed . . . When rooftree] gulls screamed / As the feathers of gull wing from white flash / To flame burst. Yes, that was the hour/ The rooftree *NY* 22: screamed$_\wedge$] ∼, *Helsinki* 24: fell,] ∼$_\wedge$ *NY* 24: fell, and] In *Helsinki* there is a stanza break after this text. 25: Priest's] A priest's *NY*, The priest's RVTS (revised in black pen to RV) 25: curls] the curls SP85 (revised on SP85G to SP85) 25: king's] King's *NY*, RVTS (revised in black pen to RV) 25: until] till RVTS (revised in black pen to RV 26: Throat-softness] The soft throat RVTS (revised in black pen to RV) 27: king,] King, RVTS (revised in black pen to RV) 27: king, / In the mantle, had buried his face.] The King's / Mantle buries his face. *NY* 28: In the mantle,] In his mantle, SP85 (revised on SP85G to SP85) 28: buried] hidden RVTS (revised in black pen to RV) 28: But even / That last sacrifice] But even that last / Sacrifice RVTS (revised in black pen to RV) 29: availed naught.] meant nothing. *NY* 30: Cities beneath sea sank.] Cities / Beneath sea sank. *NY* 31: stony, high field] stony field *NY* 32: saw,] ∼$_\wedge$ SP85 (Because there is no correction on SP85TS and all of the galleys read with SP85, SP85 is probably a typesetter's error.) 32: They saw, first, / The sky.] They saw, / First, the sky. *NY* 34: understood.] ∼! *Helsinki* 34: But, slowly,] But$_\wedge$ slowly$_\wedge$ *NY* 35: agony] nature SP85 (revised on SP85G to SP85) 36: of the necks,] of necks, SP85 (revised on SP85G to SP85) 36: unfeathered and feeble,] unfeathered, feeble, *NY* 37: beak-gape—] ∼, RVTS (revised in black pen to RV) 37: lifeward.] A typed annotation, circled in pencil, follows in RVTS: "New Yorker".

II. Paradox of Time

The divider page for this volume section in RVTS lists the poems it includes.

448 **Blessèd Accident** Text: RV. Variant: *Yale Review*, 70 (Summer 1981), p. 554. The accent mark was added to the title on RVG. 1: say,] ∼$_\wedge$ *YR* 6: jigsaw] jig-saw *YR*, RVTS (revised in pencil to RV) 18: bathed?] ∼. *YR*, RVTS (revised in pencil to RV) 19: where the plow] where plow *YR* 29: predawn] pre-dawn *YR*, RVTS (revised in pencil to RV) 35: That] The *YR* 37: dice-cup?] ∼. *YR*, RVTS (revised in pencil to RV) 37: accident!] ∼. *YR*

449 **Paradox of Time** Text: RV. Variant: *New Yorker*, 11 May 1981, p. 36. RVTS has a typed annotation, circled in pencil, on the bottom of the first page: "New Yorker - all sections".

449 **I. Gravity of Stone and Ecstasy of Wind** 14: Hear laugh that creature] Hear laughter of that thing *NY*, Hear laugh that thing RVTS (revised in pencil on RVG to RV), Hear the laugh of that creature *Emory* 15: loom its life-arch,] its life-arch loom, *Western Kentucky* 15: loom] how looms *Emory* 15: life-arch, and$_\wedge$] life-arch$_\wedge$ and, *NY*

450 **II. Law of Attrition** 2: Learn] Know *NY*, RVTS (revised in black pen to RV) 3: that] its *NY*, what RVTS (revised in black pen to RV) 4: Knows the] Must know *Emory* 11: airward, leap,] airward, will leap, *NY*, RVTS (revised in pencil on RVG to RV) 14: how$_\wedge$] ∼, *NY* 18: In the broad . . . somnambulistic] Then think how in the broad / Estuary, somnambulistic *NY* 18: In] To RVTS (revised in pencil to RV), Now in *Emory* 19: Which, rapt] Rapt *Emory* 21: Moves musing seaward, it] Musing, musing seaward, it *NY* 21: Moves musing seaward, it / Is borne: to enter unto] It moves musing seaward. / It is borne to enter unto *Emory* (In RV the estuary moves seaward and the fragment is borne in it, in *Emory* both verbs apply to the fragment, and in *NY* "borne" applies clearly to the fragment but "musing seaward" could apply to either.) 23: The dark] dark *Emory* 26: rock-shore,] ∼. *Emory* 27: And] Now *Emory* 29: Perceived] Unperceived *Emory* (In RV and *NY* sun or star perceives the surface agitation; in *Emory* sun or star does not

perceive the particle.) 30: will.] ~, *NY* 36: strand,] ~— *Emory* 37: White] A strand white *Emory* 38: and] where *Emory* 42: dawns,] ~^ *NY* 42: sand-grain] sand grain *NY* 46: above,] ~. *Emory* 47: But no more joy] But there's no more joy *Emory* 47: for] from *NY* 47: this] that RVTS (revised in black pen to RV) 50: that same] that *NY* 51: That,] And the facet, *NY* 54: this] the *NY*, that RVTS (revised in black pen to RV), such *Emory*

451 **III. One I Knew** Text: RV. Additional variant for this section only: *15 Poems*, selected by Rosanna Warren, privately printed for Stuart Wright, 1985. 15P is presented as a separate poem, not as part of a sequence. 15P is out of sequence, following "What Voice at Moth-Hour." 3: snow-peak] snow peak *NY* 5: clouds,] ~^ *NY* 5: sun-shaft] sun shaft *NY* 29: Only he knew.] *Western Kentucky* adds a line after this text: He, alone, in the world knew. 35: A beauty so long withheld—] There is a stanza break after this text in *NY*. 36: once had] had once *NY*, RVTS (revised in pencil on RVG to RV) 38: and / Two flames,] two / Flames, *Emory* 40: summer night's] night's summer *Emory* 48: knew,] ~^ *NY* 49: Courtesy, lived^] Courtesy^ lived, *New Yorker* 50: day,] ~^ *NY* 51: his cramped sitting room] his sitting room *Emory* 55: end.] ~^ RVTS (revised in pencil on RVG to RV) 55: The agony of the end.] There is no stanza break after this text in *NY* or RVTS. But RVG is corrected in pencil to RV. 63: was:] ~^ *NY* 65: petal—the golden stamen—] petal, the golden stamen^ *NY*, petal, and golden stamen, RVTS (revised in pencil to RV) 67: carpet.] In the MS that Warren sent to the *NY* the poem ends as follows:

Divulged. On the dusty carpet.
What more is there to say?

Especially if it
Is assimilated to
The tearless pity for,
And sad admiration of,
The blind struggles of man, who, blindly
Is caught in the complex toils
Of his own blind humanity

452 **Small Eternity** Text: RV. On the contents page of RVTS the title is "Eternity" (but it is corrected in pencil to RV). In RVTS the title is also "Eternity" (but is corrected in pencil to RV). 15: airt.] In RVTS Warren has written "(airt)" in the margin after this line, perhaps to indicate to the typesetter that he really does mean to use the word.

453 **Basic Syllogism** Text: RV. Variant: *Atlantic Monthly*, June 1981, p. 71. 1: lattice-work] lattice-work RVTS (revised in black pen to RV) 2: shade,] shadow, *Atlantic* 3: half sleeping,] half-sleeping, *Atlantic* 4: afternoon blazes bright.] afternoon's blaze is bright. RVTS (revised in black pen to RV. The "is" is not crossed out in pen, but is circled in red pen, then canceled in pencil. There is a question mark in red pencil in the margin next to this line.) 8: ash] own ash *Atlantic* 9: flare.] glare. RVTS (revised in black pen to RV) 11: glare,] flare, RVTS (revised in black pen to RV) 11: glare,] ~. *Emory* 12: mountain cliffs] mountain-cliffs *Atlantic* 19: bound,] ~^ RVG (revised in pencil on RVG to RV) 19: hearthstone,] hearth-stone, RVTS (revised in pencil to RV)

454 **Sitting on Farm Lawn on Sunday Afternoon** Text: RV. Variant: *Washington Post Magazine*, 3 Aug. 1980, p. 8. RVTS has a typewritten annotation, crossed out in pencil, in the upper right corner: "final version May 20, 1980". There is another typewritten annotation, circled in pencil, at the bottom of the first page: "Washington Post (magazine)". 13: bulldog] bull-dog RVTS (revised in pencil to RV) 24: in dark now] now in dark *Emory*

III. Events

The divider page in RVTS again lists all the poems in the section, but it includes "You Sort Old Letters," calls "Convergences" "Tramp and Boy Meet in Woodland", and includes (added in black pen) "Aging Painter." All are corrected in pencil to reflect the contents of RV.

455 **Going West** Text: RV. Variants: *New Yorker*, 19 Jan. 1981, p. 40, SP85. In the contents page of RVTS "Going West" is added in in black pen, and "You Sort Old Let-

ters" is crossed out in pencil. RVTS is a carbon copy, typed on the typewriter used for "Chthonian Revelation." There is a typed annotation, canceled in pencil, across the top of the page: "GOING WEST IS TO BE PLACED AS THE FIRST POEM IN SECTION III (EVENTS) TO TAKE THE PLACE OF "YOU SORT OLD LETTERS, NOW DISCARDED". The pages are numbered 17a and 17b, so this poem was obviously added to the volume after the page numbers were added to RVTS (since "You Sort Old Letters" can be typed on one page). 6: behind,] long behind, SP85 (in pencil on SP85TS) 10: eye-edge] eye edge *NY*, RVTS (revised in pencil to RV) 21: As though Space were Time.] No stanza break after this text in SP85. On SP85TS, Warren indicates that he wishes to close up the stanza break after this text. In the "Setting typescript, revised, incomplete" (folder 3025 in the Beinecke Library's Warren collection) this poem is represented by a xerox of a typescript, and in that copy there is no stanza break after this line. I have decided not to emend here, since evidence that Warren went back and forth about this line, and decided the question the other way in SP85, doesn't conclusively establish that the received reading is incorrect. 24: lift?] lift there? SP85 (revised on SP85G to SP85) 37: Slowly,] $\sim_{\wedge}$ SP85TS (revised on SP85G to SP85) 40: day—] $\sim$, SP85 (in pencil on SP85TS) 41: had been] had sure been SP85 (in pencil on SP85TS) 42: blood.] $\sim_{\wedge}$ RVTS (revised in pencil on RVG to RV) 44: afterward,] afterwards, SP85 (in pencil on SP85TS) 45: blotting out] blotting *NY* 47: Vision of snowcaps.] Vision of snowcaps, white in their purity. SP85 (in typewriting on SP85TS)

456 **Nameless Thing** Text: RV. Variant: *American Poetry Review*, (March–April 1981), p. 4. 2: walks] walls *APR* 3: on] on a *APR* 4: sometimes] something *APR* 4: screwed down to a minimum.] to a minimum shuttered. *APR*, RVTS (revised in pencil on RVTS to "to a minimum screwed down." and on RVG to RV.) 6: with] in *APR* 7: as though] seemingly *APR*, RVTS (revised in pencil on RVG to RV) 8: or sometimes] sometimes *APR* 11: now] how RVTS (revised in pencil on RVG to RV) 15: the] a *APR* 20: blessèd heart beat] blessed breath *APR*. The accent is marked on RVTS but added again in pencil on RVG. 28: abed$_{\wedge}$] $\sim$, *APR* 29: rest.] A typewritten annotation, circled in pencil, follows in RVTS: "American Poetry Review".

457 **Rumor Verified** Text: RV. Variant: *Antaeus*, (Winter–Spring 1981), pp. 401–2 (as "The Rumor"), SP85. 4: Nor at ... sommelier,] Nor at the Four Seasons, discussing wine with the *sommelier, Antaeus* 9: x-ray] X-ray *Antaeus*, RVTS (revised in pencil to RV) 10: overindulgent] over-indulgent *Antaeus*, RVTS (revised in pencil to RV) 14: El Salvador,] Guatemala, *Antaeus*, RVTS (revised to "San Salvadór," in black pencil, then to RV in pencil) 15: trying to believe] believing, *Antaeus*, RVTS (revised in pencil to RV) 19: A] The *Antaeus* 22: friends,] companions, *Antaeus* 22: for justification] in the end *Antaeus* 23: ragtag] rag-tag *Antaeus*, RVTS (revised in pencil to RV) 24: assuming the rumor verified] assume the rumor has been verified *Antaeus* 25: course:] $\sim$, *Antaeus* 26: bloodshed, however ruthless,] ruthless bloodshed, *Antaeus* 28: verification] an order *Emory* 29: in face of the rumor,] in the face of rumor, *Antaeus*, in the face of the rumor, SP85 (in pencil on SP85TS) 31: slyly.] slily. RVTS (revised in red pencil to RV) 31: Of knowledge.] Of their knowledge. *Antaeus* 33: pray to God for strength] may pray God for courage *Antaeus* 34: simply] only *Antaeus* 34: dead reckoning, nothing more.] blind guesses, after all. *Antaeus* 34: nothing more.] A typewritten annotation, circled in pencil, follows in RVTS: "Antaeus".

458 **Sunset Scrupulously Observed** Text: RV. Variant: *New Yorker*, 27 July 1981, p. 36. 3: Twist] Shift *NY*, Turn RVTS (revised in pencil on RVG to RV) 3: topmost] topmast RVTS (revised in red pencil to RV) 5: Is a black point] Is tiny and black *NY*, RVTS (revised in pencil to "Is a point of black" on RVTS and to RV on RVG) 6: over dark] over the dark *NY* 11: nightlong.] night-long. RVTS (revised in pencil to RV) 17: trail,] train, RVTS (revised in pencil to RV) 17: unmoved] seemingly motionless *NY* 18: high] highest *NY* 20: mark that] mark, which *NY* 26: as the jet] as jet *NY* 30: Into the] Into a *NY* 32: swifts,] sweeps, *NY*, flycatchers, RVTS (revised in pencil to RV) 35: at high speed. ... metallic sound.] at high speed, uttering / A twitter of needle-sharp, metallic sound. *NY*, RVTS (revised in pencil on RVG to RV) 37: first bird,] flycatcher, *NY*, bird,

RVTS (revised in pencil on RVG to RV) 37: top] topmost *NY* 38: to fulfill his] on his *NY*, RVTS (revised in pencil on RVG to RV) 40: soundlessly,] $\sim_\wedge$ *NY*

459 **Minneapolis Story** Text: RV. Variant: *New York Review of Books*, 16 July 1981, p. 40. The dedication is added in pencil on RVG. There is an annotation, handwritten in black pen, circled in pencil, at the bottom of the first page in RVTS: "NEW YORK REVIEW OF BOOKS". 6: blind,] $\sim_\wedge$ *NYRB* 6: meaning,] Truth, *NYRB* 9: babe] Babe *NYRB* 10: vying] vied *NYRB* 11: there I, down a side street,] and down a side street, I, *NYRB* 12: Hennepin.] Hennepin Avenue. *Emory* 13: There] Where *NYRB* 13: most probably] undoubtedly *NYRB* 14: But I was not thinking of happiness,] I not thinking of happiness however, *NYRB* 18: but,] $\sim_\wedge$ *NYRB* 20: stumbling,] $\sim_\wedge$ *NYRB* 22: "Oh, Christ," the ambulance driver says, "another one!"] Ambulance finally. Driver: "Oh, Christ, another one!" *New York Review of Books*, RVTS (revised in pencil to RV) 27: leaf] leaves *NYRB* 31: bubble now arises, bursts] bubble, this instant, bursts *NYRB* 31: bubble] bubble, a memory, *Emory* 31: now] how RVTS (revised in pencil to RV) 31: bursts / On my dark and secret] bursts on my dark / And secret RVTS (revised in black pen to RV) 32: stream. And why, again waiting alone, I see] stream, and waiting, alone, I see *NYRB* 33: where,] $\sim_\wedge$ *NYRB* 34: domed] a domed *Emory* (*Emory* makes better grammatical sense than RV or *NYRB*, but dropping articles is often a characteristic of Warren's style, and on the chance that *Emory* is a revision rather than a correction I have chosen not to emend.) 36: I had wiped] I had just wiped *Emory*

460 **Mountain Mystery** Text: RV. Variants: *Love: Four Versions* (Winston-Salem, NC: Palaemon Press, 1981), Broadside (Winston-Salem, NC: Palaemon Press, 1981), SP85. 3: On left side, with] On the left side, past *Emory* 3: scrub growth,] scrub-growth, *Love*, *Palaemon* 4: On right,] On the right, *Emory* 8: canyon,] $\sim_\wedge$ *Palaemon* 9: You stop. You turn and know what already] You rein in. Turn. And know what already *Palaemon* 12: is pressed against] presses against *Love*, is laid to RVTS (revised in pencil on RVG to RV), *Palaemon* 15: catches] snatches *Love* 17: all$_\wedge$] $\sim$, *Love*, *Palaemon* 20: the timeless // Light.] timelessness // Of light. *Palaemon* 22: away] off *Love* 22: delusion?] delusion, too? *Love* 25: off,] ahead, *Love* 29: alone$_\wedge$] $\sim$, *Love* 37: alone—] $\sim$. *Palaemon* 38: paradox,] $\sim_\wedge$ *Love* 41: in dark, lost, lain,] And now in dark, lost, you lie, *Emory* 41: beside.] there beside. *Palaemon*

461 **Convergences** Text: RV. Variant: *Sewanee Review*, 89 (Summer 1981), pp. 311–14. In the contents of RVTS, the title of this poem is "Tramp and Boy Meet in Woodland" (but it is corrected in pencil to RV). "Aging Painter Where the Great Tower Heaves Past Midnight" [sic] is added in black pen to the contents after this poem in the contents to RVTS, but it is crossed out in pencil. RVTS is also titled "Tramp and Boy Meet in Woodland," but the title is corrected to RV in pencil. There is a typed annotation, canceled in pencil, in the upper right corner: "new version May 28, 1980". 2: clung,] $\sim$. RVTS (revised in pencil on RVG to RV) 3: Letting] To let *Emory* 4: near-vertical] near vertical *SR* 5: *V*-deep] V-deep *SR* 6: flow,] $\sim_\wedge$ *SR* 7: last spit] the last spit *SR* 7: on the tongue] on my tongue *Emory* 9: high] nigh *SR* 12: guaranteed the] guaranteed to the *Emory* 14: last.] least. RVTS (revised to RV in black pen) 15: Belly-down,] $\sim_\wedge$ RVTS (revised in pencil to RV) 16: grace$_\wedge$] $\sim$, *Emory* 19: Till I had to come up for air. … Where the arch sags lower and lower] In *Emory* Warren replaces these lines with the following text, on a typed insert with many corrections:

Till I had to come up for air.
Then, just over the riffle and glint there,
Just as I came to raise
My head for breath, that gaze–
That gaze wolfish and slit-eyed fixed on me.
My blood stiffened up like jelly,
Even if, across lips gray and dry,
A gray tongue-tip warily
Now slid back and forth. Slow to heal,

And yellow as piss or orange peel,

From ear-edge to mouth-edge, a long slashing
Marked a man not born for winning.

But, sudden, he plunged through the stream
To hang over me like a bad dream,

Till he said: "What you got in that sack?"
I'm still down, so he kicked my knapsack.

"Git it off and give it here, quick!
You damned little Boy Scout prick." [*sic*]

Or whatever you are" "But I'm not [*sic*]
I yelled, "any durn Boy Scout!"

"Well, prick," he said then, and a clasp-knife,
At some touch, like a blaze, jumped to life.

He ate my sandwich, but spat
Out the milk. Said, "Christ!" And with that,

He busted my thermos on stone.
Spat again. Got up. Was gone.

I just lay there. I just seemed to lie
And stare up, far up, at the sky.

I thought: "Had me a .38
I'd plugged him while he ate."

A buzzard hung high in the air.
A joree calle [sic] somewhere.

Then I plunged across as he'd done.
Clambered up to the ballast stone

Of the hidden railroad track.
Now I saw him a half-mile back,

A dot in the dazzle of sun
Where the two gleaming rails became one.

And there, the tunnel's black throat
Would suck in that last gleam, that dot.

I turned my own way to go
Down a track that I could not yet know

Was the track I was bound to go
I [sic] my biologic flow—

Down that tunnel of year, day, hour,
Where the arch sags lower and lower,

22: that gaze,] and gaze, RVTS (revised in pencil to RV) 25: lips,] ~$_\wedge$ *SR*, RVTS (revised in pencil on RVG to RV) 26: tongue-tip] tongue tip RVTS (revised in pencil to RV) 28: Yellow] Bright *SR*, RVTS (revised in pencil on RVG to RV) 28: peel,] ~$_\wedge$ *SR* 30: win,] ~$_\wedge$ *SR* 32: dream$_\wedge$] ~, *SR* 35: quick!] ~, *SR* 36: damned] durn *SR* 42: "Christ!"] "Christ"! RVTS (revised in pencil to RV) 49: Thinking:] ~, *SR* 51: sky,] ~. *SR* 59: in] at *SR*, RVTS (revised in pencil on RVG to RV) 62: a track that] the track *SR*, the track that RVTS (revised in pencil on RVG to RV) 70: Hope] your hope *Emory* 73: though] when *SR*, RVTS (revised in pencil to RV) 76: shale above slip,] hear shale slip, *Emory*, shale slip$_\wedge$ RVTS (revised in black pen to RV) 77: And] So *Emory* 78: high,] ~$_\wedge$ *SR* 80: are.] ~, RVG (revised in pencil on RVG to RV) 81: but yet] but *SR* 82: See,] ~$_\wedge$ *SR*, You see, *Emory* 82: of] on *SR* 85: speared that small dot] spread the small dot *SR* 85: that] the RVTS (revised in pencil on RVG to RV) 88: know.] A penciled, circled annotation follows in RVTS: "Sewanee Review".

IV. A Point North

The divider page in RVTS lists the poems in the sequence.

464 **Vermont Thaw** Text: RV. Variant: *American Poetry Review*, (March–April 1981), p. 3. On the bottom of the first page in RVTS there is a typewritten annotation, circled in pencil: "American Poetry Review". 3: About ... to burden our snowshoes.] Began about three o'clock, we yet high on the mountain, / Snow soon softened to burden our snowshoes. *Emory* 5: If then] And if *APR* 6: each stroke] stroke *APR* 8: all you had lived was // That sound hung in motionless silence. You held] all Time, and your life, // Was like that in motionless silence, and held you *APR* 11: the rhythm] that rhythm *APR*, RVTS (revised in pencil on RVG to RV) 11: rhythm that drops] rhythm by drops *Emory* 12: your name?] your own name? *Emory* 13: the camp, snow sliding] the snow now sliding *Emory* 16: Roof-edges] Roof-edge *APR* 16: a rhythm] the rhythm *APR* 17: Life as blankness. In dingy pink pillows of mist, / Sun sank,] Life. And the sun, in pink pillows of mist, / Sank, *APR* 19: not rise] never to rise *Emory* 20: you found] you now found *Emory* 22: it up] up *APR* 24: world // Has lost heart,] World has // Lost heart, *Emory* 26: Its pulse] Itself *APR*, Its own pulse *Emory* 27: predinner] pre-dinner *APR*, RVTS (revised in pencil to RV) 28: rotgut] rot-gut *APR*, RVTS (revised in pencil to RV) 32: No need to bank fire] No banking the fire *APR* 34: Can you comfort yourself by thinking of spring?] Try to comfort yourself by thinking of spring. *APR* 35: and body's] and the *APR* 36: splash-spray?]~. *APR* 37: autumn?] ~. *APR* 37: Of snow's] of the snow's *Emory* 38: Night-whisper, dawn reddening peak-thrust? No—eaves,] Night-whisper and dawn light on peak-top. But eaves, *APR* 38: eaves,] ~$_\wedge$ RVTS (revised in pencil on RVG to RV) 39: now only one thing. Say: *drip.*] say one thing. Say: *drip.* Say: *drip. APR* 40: some other answer,] some answer, *APR*

465 **Cycle** Text: RV. Variant: Broadside in conjunction with the Robert Penn Warren 75th Birthday Symposium, University of Kentucky, 29–30 Oct. 1980 (Lexington, KY: King Library Press, Oct. 1980). The King Library version indents the second and fourth lines of every stanza. 4: one birch,] one leaf, birch *Emory* 8: backhouse that by his tooth, long back, is] backhouse which his tooth, long back has *Emory* 8: backhouse] back-house King Library, RVTS (revised in pencil to RV) 9: He, in] He, only in King Library, RVTS (revised in pencil on RVG to RV) 21: ledge. On the mountain,] ledge on the mountain. King Library, ledge, on the mountain RVTS (revised in pencil on RVG to RV) 22: On one ledge visible, with glasses I see propped, leaning] On one ledge, by glasses visible, I see him propped, leaning *Emory* 22: On one ledge] Only on one ledge King Library, RVTS (revised in pencil on RVG to RV) 23: window,] ~— *Emory* 24: A bear,] One bear, King Library, RVTS (revised in pencil on RVG to RV) 24: A bear, scratching his belly, in infinite ease, sun or not.] The bear, scratching his belly, in infinite ease. *Emory* 26: By stones,] On stones, *Emory* 26: stones,] ~$_\wedge$ King Library 32: hearth-wood] firewood King Library 33: I will wake, on the hearth see last coals glow.] I will wake to see on the hearth, last coals glow. *Emory* 33: glow.] A typewritten annotation, circled in pencil, follows in RVTS: "University of Kentucky Libraries".

466 **Summer Rain in Mountains** Text: RV. Variant: *Antaeus*, 40/41 (Winter/Spring 1981), pp. 403–4. 4: is decisive / Like] is as decisive / As *Antaeus*, is decisive / As RVTS (revised in pencil on RVG to RV) 6: mountain$_\wedge$] ~, *Antaeus* 8: ambition, they] ambition, and *Antaeus*, ambition. They *Emory* 10: sun-deck.] sun deck. *Antaeus* 21: up?] ~. *Antaeus* 22: be a code.] be code. *Emory* 24: The rain] Rain *Emory* 24: roof,] ~$_\wedge$ *Antaeus* 26: highballs] highball *Antaeus* 29: God's calm blessedness] God's blessedness *Emory* 30: the refurbished glitter] the icy glitter *Emory* 31: sun-deck.] sun deck. *Antaeus* 32: await] wait *Antaeus*, RVTS (revised in pencil on RVG to RV) 35: And does.] A typewritten annotation, circled in pencil, follows in RVTS: "Antaeus".

467 **Vermont Ballad: Change of Season** Text: RV. Variants: *Salmagundi*, nos. 50–51 (Fall 1980–Winter 1981), pp. 13–14 (as "Vermont Ballad: Season Change"), SP85. At the bottom of the first page is a typewritten annotation, circled in pencil, "Salmagundi". 2: wrought] sought *Salmagundi*, RVTS (revised in pencil on RVG to RV) 4: see$_\wedge$] ~, *Emory* 5: gray$_\wedge$] ~, *Emory* 12: fireplace back.] fire-place back. *Salmagundi*, fireplace-

back. SP85 (revised on SP85G to SP85) 13: cold:] ~, *Salmagundi* 16: swollen^] ~, *Salmagundi* 21: soaked] webbed RVTS (revised in black pen to RV) 22: master] the master *Salmagundi* 23: season,] ~^ *Salmagundi* 29: No, I] No, no, I'll *Salmagundi* 29: windowpane] pane *Salmagundi*, window pane RVTS (revised in black pen to RV) 32: rain-dusk,] ~^ RVTS (revised in black pen to RV) 34: name,] ~^ *Salmagundi* 36: sportsman—] ~, *Salmagundi* 38: Kinda] kinda *Salmagundi*

V. If This Is the Way it Is

The divider page in RVTS lists the poems in the section.

468 **Questions You Must Learn to Live Past** Text: RV. Variant: *Salmagundi*, nos. 50–51 (Fall 1980–Winter 1981), pp. 11–12 (as "Question You Must Learn To Live Past"). 1: cliffside] cliff-side *Salmagundi* 3: Curdles] Thickens RVTS (revised in black pencil to RV) 4: claws] its claws *Salmagundi* 5: snag at loosening stone—] at fingers clutching the stone— *Salmagundi*, at fingers clutching at stone— RVTS (revised in black pen to RV) 7: lethal,] ~^ *Salmagundi* 7: sea-foam^] sea-may, *Salmagundi* 9: whereon^] ~, *Salmagundi* 10: Your father, unspeakable anguish past, at length] Unspeakable anguish past, your father at length *Salmagundi* 12: biceps? Then,] biceps, then *Salmagundi* 12: she cries:] cries: *Salmagundi* 13: deeper,] ~^ *Salmagundi* 14: Deeper to hide from praying, or dying, or God—] Inside to hide from praying or God or dying— *Salmagundi*, Inside to hide deeper from praying, or dying, or God— RVTS (revised in black pen to RV) 15: "Oh] ^Oh *Salmagundi* 15: Or have you remembered the face / Of an old,] Have you remembered / The face of an old, *Salmagundi* 19: calling] you call *Emory* 20: own child,] child, *Salmagundi* 23: three-foot snake—a big garter, no doubt—] long three-foot—or longer—a big garter, no doubt— *Salmagundi* 24: Has] Had *Salmagundi* 29: will be—when, / After the fable] will be / When after the fable *Salmagundi* 30: summer, a lithe] summer the lithe *Salmagundi* 31: dark,] ~^ *Salmagundi* 31: no dream?] A typewritten annotation, circled in pencil, follows in RVTS: "Salmagundi".

469 **After Restless Night** Text: RV. Variants: *Salmagundi*, nos. 50–51 (Fall 1980–Winter 1981), pp. 15–16. At the bottom of the first page in RVTS there is a typewritten annotation, circled in pencil: "Salmagundi". 4: do see] see *Salmagundi* 4: funny,] gay, *Salmagundi*, RVTS (revised in black pen to RV) 6: So,] ~^ *Salmagundi*, RVTS (revised in pencil to RV) 9: channeling] seepage *Salmagundi* 9: But do / We] But we do / Not *Salmagundi* 11: prowl?] ~. *Salmagundi* 12: Nor] Now RVTS (revised in black pen to RV) 13: aeons] eons *Salmagundi*, RVTS (revised in pencil to RV) 18: And consciousness loses] Whenever consciousness loses *Emory* 22: you may lift a curtain ... back to bed,] you may lift a curtain and peer / To reassure yourself the world exists. Then back to bed *Salmagundi* 22: by the bed] and peer RVTS (revised in black pen to RV) 26: And consciousness ... skull.] And consciousness deeper shrivels in the hollow dark of skull, *Salmagundi*, And consciousness deeper gnaws into the fat dark of your skull, RVTS (revised in black pen to RV) 28: Traffic,] Though traffic, *Salmagundi* 28: like rumor] like a rumor *Emory* 42: cogitation.] meditation. *Salmagundi* 44: agon.] agon of love. *Emory*

470 **What Was the Thought** Text: RV. Variant: *Salmagundi*, nos. 50–51 (Fall 1980–Winter 1981), pp. 12–13. In RVTS the title is "What Was the Thought?" There is a typed annotation in the upper left corner in RVTS: "last version May 28, 1980". 4: creeps. What!—] may be creeping. What— *Emory* 4: What!—] ~^— RVTS (revised in pencil to RV) 7: heart, ... to your own heart,] heart, more delicate than a Swiss watch, / Beating somewhere down in the dark. You cannot, of course, / Hear it. So you listen to your own heart. *Salmagundi* 8: Intricate,] ~^ RVTS (revised in pencil to RV) 13: loving flesh. ... to creep] loving flesh. It does not creep *Salmagundi* 16: night, in a strange house.] night. *Emory* 17: guaranteed] mechanistic *Salmagundi* 18: constellations also are] the constellations are *Salmagundi* 19: allotted] assigned *Salmagundi* official *Emory* 30: pussycat] cat *Salmagundi* 33: eviscerated.] A typed annotation, circled in pencil, follows in RVTS: "Salmagundi".

471 **Dead Horse in Field** Text: RV. Variants: *American Poetry Review*, March–April 1981, p. 5, SP85. 1: In the last ...] *APR* is substantially different from RV and SP85:

In the last, far field, half-buried in barberry bushes, red-fruited,
The thoroughbred lies dead, left foreleg shattered below knee,
A 30.06 in heart. In distance,
I see the gorged crows rise ragged in wind. The day after death
I went for farewell, and the eyes were already gone—
That the work of beneficent crows. Eyes gone,
The two-year-old could, of course, more readily see
Down the track of pure and eternal darkness.

A week later I didn't get close. The sweet stink
Had begun. That damned wagon-mudhole, hidden
By leaves as we galloped—I found it.
Spat on it. Just as a child would.
Next day the buzzards. How beautiful in air,
Carving the slow and concentric downward pattern of vortex, glint
On wings. From the house, now with glasses, I see
The squabbles and pushing. The waggle of wattle-red heads.

At evening I watch the buzzards, the crows,
Arise. They swing black in Nature's flow and perfection
Against the sad carmine of sunset.
Forgiveness is not indicated. They are
What they are.

How long before I go back to find
An intricate piece of fake modern sculpture,
White now by weather and sun, assuming in stasis
New beauty. Then,
Say two years after that, the green twine of vine,
Each leaf heart-shaped, soft as velvet,
Or a baby's kiss, beginning
Its benediction.

It thinks it is God.

4: 30.06] .30-30 SP85 (revised on SP85G to SP85) 6: had gone] went RVTS (revised in pencil on RVG to RV) 8: beneficent] beneficient RVG (revised in pencil on RVG to RV) 27: now$_\wedge$] ~, SP85 (revised on SP85G to SP85) 28: By weather and sun, intricate, now] line omitted in SP85. Clearly a mistake, since the line is present in SP85TS, is not canceled there, and does not appear in any of the proofs. 36: gainsaid?] A typed annotation, circled in pencil, follows in RVTS: "APR".

472 **Immanence** Text: RV. Variant: *Georgia Review*, 34 (Winter 1980), pp. 732–33. RVTS is a photocopy of an original typed on a different typewriter from the prevailing one, in Warren's inimitable typing. There is a canceled annotation in red pencil in the upper left corner: "retypedck". 4: Where the City] In RVTS there is a red pencil arrow in the left margin by this line. 5: matter. . . . and then even] matter, for you are you. Even if / The name's referent is sometimes obscure, and then even *GaR* 7: card] credit card *GaR* 7: no help.] Corrected in pencil on RVG to "no fundamental help." The RV reading is restored on the Master Page Proofs. 7: Except, of course,] Except *GaR* 7: Or / The event,] Corrected in pencil on RVG to "The / Event,". 10: and a crusting on // Dong.] and sperm crusting // On dong. *GaR* 12: inimical] is it inimical? *GaR* 13: immanence.] Immanence. *GaR*, RVTS (revised in red pencil to RV, with an annotation, "lc" in the left margin) 17: unawares.] unaware RVG (revised in pencil on RVG to RV) 18: stratagem] strategem *GaR* 20: Then] Now *GaR* 21: slight movement of air,] movement of air exists, *GaR* 23: a heart] even a heart *GaR* 23: stabbed / To pity. But no.] stabbed to pity. / But no *GaR*, RVTS (revised in pencil on RVG to RV) 24: You must ponder yet the teasing enigma. But] Not yet. You must ponder the teasing enigma. But *GaR*, Not yet. You must ponder yet the teasing enigma. But RVTS (revised in pencil on RVG to RV) 26: you,] ~$_\wedge$ RVTS (revised in pencil to RV) 27: torn] yet torn *GaR* 29: System,] Plant, *GaR* 31: To–even–be

considered.] To, even, be contemplated. *GaR*, To, even, be considered. RVTS (revised in pencil on RVG to RV)

473 **The Corner of the Eye** Text: RV. Variants: *Atlantic Monthly*, April 1981, p. 97 (as "At the Corner of the Eye"), SP85 2: gleam,] quiver, *Atlantic* 3: stir.] glint. *Atlantic* 3: fieldmouse,] ∼‸ RVG (revised in pencil on RVG to RV) 4: snow‸ while,] snow, while‸ RVTS (revised in pencil to RV) 8: makes,] ∼‸ *Atlantic* 18: despair,] desire, RVG (revised in pencil on RVG to RV) 18: nausea, till one night, late,] nausea. Until one night late, *Emory* 18: late, late‸] late, late, *Atlantic* 19: and again felt] and again remembered—felt SP85 (in pencil on SP85TS) 20: How her head had thrust] Her head thrusting SP85TS (revised on SP85G to SP85) Her head thrust SP85 20: you,] ∼‸ RVTS (revised in pencil to RV), SP85 (SP85TS reads with RV but on SP85 page proofs the reading is corrected to SP85, doubtless to preserve grammatical consistency with the changes in the next line in SP85.) 21: Mechanically patting] Were mechanically patting RVTS (revised in pencil to RV) 21: Mechanically patting the fur coat, heard sobs, and stared up] Mechanically pat the fur coat, hear sobs, and stare up SP85 (in pencil on SP85TS) 22: Where tall buildings, frailer than reed-stalks, reeled among stars. // Yes, something there] Where tall buildings reeled, frail as reeds, among stars. Yes, something // There *Atlantic*, RVTS (revised in pencil on RVG to RV) 22: reeled] reel SP85 (in pencil on SP85TS) 23: Yes, something there at eye-edge lurks,] At eye-edge there lurks, *Atlantic* 27: great hindquarters may hunch,] may hunch the great hind-quarters, RVTS (revised in pencil to RV)

474 **If** Text: RV. Variant: *American Poetry Review*, March–April 1981, p. 5. RVTS is a photocopy of an original typed on a different typewriter from the prevailing one, in Warren's own typing. There is a canceled annotation in red pencil in the upper right margin: "retyped ck". 4: if you know bliss— / And bliss can seem] through bliss, / Which can seem *APR* 6: Yet] But *APR* 9: Over the tangled] Over tangled *APR* 10: Into] In *APR* 11: perfection.] Truth. *APR* 13: past midnight long,] long past midnight, *Emory* 13: empty, in / The dark and unpopulated] empty, / In the middle of the dark and unpopulated *APR* 15: Navona] Navonna RVTS (revised in pencil to RV) 15: and I thought: what is the use] what is the use *APR* 16: any dream] a dream *APR* 17: Since any particular moment would be the future all dreams / Had led to. I shut eyes now, but still see] Since that was the future all dreams had led to. / I shut eyes now, but still see *APR* 17: would be] was RVTS (revised in pencil on RVG to RV) 19: newspaper, across the Piazza, / In a foreign language, blown] The discarded newspaper blown *APR* 24: To] Into *APR* 25: This was only ... But] This stanza missing in *APR*. 29: concept of salvation,] definition of Self, *APR* 29: had] have *APR* 32: as the tide] as tide *APR* 34: groan] groan, or fulfilmet, [sic] *Emory* 34: yonder?] ∼. RVTS (revised in pencil on RVG to RV) 34: yonder?] A penciled annotation, circled in pencil, follows in RVTS: "American Poetry Review".

VI. But Also

The divider page for this section in RVTS lists the poems it includes. "Crocus Dawn" is listed as a separate poem, immediately preceding the "Glimpses of Seasons" sequence, but is moved in pencil to its present position as the fourth section of that sequence.

475 **What Voice at Moth-Hour** Text: RV. Variants: *New Yorker*, 19 Jan. 1981, p. 34, *15 Poems*, selected by Rosanna Warren, privately printed for Stuart Wright, 1985, SP85. There is a typed, canceled annotation in the upper right corner of RVTS: "March 4–6, 1980". 4: moth-wing] moth wing *NY* 7: steely] steady *NY* 10: a] the *NY* 11: stone‸] ∼, *NY* 12: while] till *NY* 13: dew-fall,] dewfall‸ *NY* 13: I now / Can hear] now / I can hear *NY* 15: again know] again can know *NY* 18: bullbat,] bull-bat, RVTS (revised in pencil to RV) 18: off,] ∼‸ *NY* 19: and‸] ∼, *NY* 20: *It's late! Come home.*] A typewritten annotation follows, circled in pencil, "New Yorker".

475 **Another Dimension** Text: RV. Variants: *American Poetry Review*, March–April 1981, p. 4 (as "Death Of Time"), SP85, *Helsinki*. There is a typed, canceled annotation in the upper left corner of RVTS: "last version May 6, 1980". 2: divulging,] ∼‸ *Helsinki* 2: tinseled] tinselled *APR*, RVTS (revised in pencil to RV) 7: long hedges,] the hedges, *APR* 8: to the] to *APR* 10: Once I lay ... no future of past.] This entire stanza missing in *APR*. 13: no future or past.] no future, no past. *Helsinki* 14: street corner,] street-corner,

APR 15: sea-fog] sea fog *APR* 19: that] the *APR* 20: chinch-bug] ~, *APR*, chich-bug RVTS (revised in pencil to RV) 22: flare] flame *APR*, RVTS (revised in pencil on RVG to RV) 26: heard it.] A typed annotation, circled in pencil, follows in RVTS: "American Poetry Review (under old title)".

476 **Glimpses of Seasons** Text: RV. Variant: *Southern Review*, ns 17 (Summer 1981), pp. 551–54.

476 **I. Gasp-Glory of Gold Light** 7: mathematics] mathematic *SoR*, RVTS (revised in pencil on RVG to RV) 7: Time.] ~; *SoR* 10: not no-Time,] no-Time, RVTS (revised in pencil on RVG to RV) 16: bend] slow bend *SoR* 21: dead.] A typed, canceled annotation follows in RVTS: "(see 2.)"

477 **II. Snow Out of Season** 5: then came] came RVTS (revised in black pen to RV) 10: biblical] Biblical *SoR* 11: sheepskin] sheep-skin *SoR*, RVTS (revised in pencil to RV) 12: remade] re-made RVTS (revised in pencil to RV) 14: boughs] bough *SoR* 16: White] ~, *SoR*, RVTS (revised in pencil on RVG to RV) 17: know] know how *SoR* 18: dogwood?] dogwood flames? *SoR* 19: white velvet] white of velvet *SoR*, RVTS (revised in pencil on RVG to RV) 21: leap? We / Are] leap? / We are RVTS (revised in pencil on RVG to RV) 25: seeds] seed RVTS (revised in pencil to RV) 27: forget.] A typed, canceled annotation follows in RVTS: "(see 3.)".

477 **III. Redwing Blackbirds** 1: a-winging] awinging *SoR*, a -winging RVTS (revised in pencil to RV) 4: their] your RVTS (revised in pencil to RV) 4: cry!] ~? *SoR* 5: on old] and RVTS (revised to "and old" in black pen on RVTS and to RV on RVG) 5: cattails] cat-tails *SoR*, RVTS (revised in pencil to RV) 10: stabs] fans *SoR*, RVTS (revised in pencil on RVG to RV) 13: seasons later,] seasons RVG (revised in pencil on RVG to RV) 14: I again / Awake, not in dream] I wake, and again, / Not in dream *SoR*, RVTS (revised in pencil on RVG to RV) 15: believing] believe *SoR*, RVTS (revised in pencil on RVG to RV) 17: the] that *SoR* 20: knows how deep.] knows / how deep. *SoR* 21: Aprils] April *SoR* 22: or I them,] or I, them RVTS (revised in pencil on RVG to RV)

478 **IV. Crocus Dawn** In the contents of RVTS this poem is listed as a separate poem, preceding the sequence "Glimpses of Seasons" (but it is changed to the fourth part of that sequence in pencil). In RVTS the section number in the title is added in pencil, with instructions to set the title as a section of a sequence, and the paper, unlike the paper of the rest of the sequence, is not folded in half. 12: to live by?] live by? RVTS (revised in pencil to RV) 13: gleam once more] once more gleam *SoR*

479 **English Cocker: Old and Blind** Text: RV. Variants: *Kentucky Poetry Review*, 16.2–3 (Summer–Fall 1980), p. 4, SP85. There is a canceled annotation on the upper right corner of RVTS: "final version September 22, 1980". 3: edge] abyss-edge *Kentucky Poetry Review*, RVTS (revised in pencil on RVG to RV) 15: remember] you remember *Kentucky Poetry Review* 19: sweet] sad, sweet *Kentucky Poetry Review*, RVTS (revised in pencil to RV) 20: a halting] that halting *Kentucky Poetry Review* 20: paradigm.] A typewritten annotation, circled in pencil, follows in RVTS: "Kentucky Poetry Review".

479 **Dawn** Text: RV. Variant: *American Poetry Review*, March–April 1981, p. 5. In RVTS there is a canceled annotation in the upper right corner: "final December 4–5, 1979". The page in RVTS is not folded in half. 1: Dawnward,] ~$_\wedge$ *APR* 1: darkness,] ~$_\wedge$ *APR* 2: as sluggish] a sluggish RVG (revised in pencil on RVG to RV) 3: tidewater] tide-water *APR*, RVTS (revised in pencil to RV) 3: long-abandoned] long abandoned RVTS (revised in pencil to RV) 6: gone to sleep] gone sleep *APR* 10: chairs—] ~, *APR*, RVTS (revised in pencil on RVG to RV) 10: they will] will RVTS (revised in pencil on RVG to RV) 15: well-designed] well designed (revised in pencil to RV) 18: how ground] how the ground *APR* 25: driver] driver, I wonder, *APR* 27: dishrag?] dish-rag? *APR* 36: You] you *APR* 37: call?] A typewritten annotation, circled in pencil, follows in RVTS: "American Poetry Review".

480 **Millpond Lost** Text: RV. In the contents of RVTS, and in RVTS, the title of this poem is "Mill Pond Lost" (but it is corrected in black pen to RV). 1: millpond] mill pond RVTS (revised in pencil to RV) 4: maples,] ~$_\wedge$ RVTS (revised in pencil on RVG to RV) 6: is so prettily greened by moss.] by moss is so prettily greened. RVTS (revised in pencil

to RV) 7: may drop,] drop RVTS (revised in pencil on RVG to RV) 11: act,] ~∧ RVTS (revised in pencil to RV) 15: while,] ~∧ RVTS (revised in pencil to RV) 15: joyfully,] ~∧ RVTS (revised in pencil to RV) 17: leaf?] ~. RVTS (revised in pencil to RV) 24: booze,] from booze, RVTS (revised in pencil on RVG to RV) 24: strikebreakers'] strike-breakers RVTS (revised in pencil to RV) 25: such time-lapse,] such a time-lapse, *Emory*

481 **Summer Afternoon and Hypnosis** Text: RV. Variant: *New Yorker*, 18 Aug. 1980, p. 34 (as "Summer Afternoons and Hypnosis"). RVTS has a typed, canceled annotation in the upper right corner: "March 5, 1980". 8: torn at last from lies,] at last from lies torn, *NY*, RVTS (revised in pencil on RVG to RV) 10: reality. And] reality, and *NY*, RVTS (revised in pencil on RVG to RV) 13: appalment] appallment *NY* 13: ask:] ~, *NY* 15: sun's] sun *NY*, RVTS (revised in pencil on RVG to RV) 17: heart] heart again *NY* (there is a canceled query in red pencil in the right margin here: "again/? cf N. Yr". 18: like a tide] in a tide *NY* 19: whatever a man] what man *NY*, whatever man RVTS (revised in black pen to RV) 21: the] that *NY* 24: smile.] A typed annotation, circled in pencil, follows in RVTS: "New Yorker".

VII. Fear and Trembling

The divider page in RVTS includes the titles of all the poems in the section.

482 **If Ever** Text: RV. Variant: Bradford Morrow, ed., *Conjunctions: I* (A Festschrift in Honor of James Laughlin, Publisher of New Directions), n.v. (Winter 1981–1982), p. 98. 4: love∧] ~, *Conjunctions: I* 9: the] that *Conjunctions: I*, RVTS (revised in pencil on RVG to RV) 11: or despair] of despair *Conjunctions: I* 13: Do contradictory . . . or promise?] Do voices now, slily, / Contradictory at midnight, doom utter— / Or promise? *Conjunctions: I*, Do voices now, / Contradictory, at midnight doom utter— RVTS (revised to "Do contradictory, / Voices now, at midnight doom utter—" on RVTS and to RV on RVG. 15: Or do voices merely] Or do voices merely RVG (revised in pencil to "Or merely" on RVG. But Warren also wrote in the line on the bottom of the page to make his intentions clear, and there he wrote in the RV reading. The "master galleys" have the RV reading written in. 15: Doom–or promise?] Or promise? *Conjunctions: I*, RVTS (revised in pencil on RVG to RV) 17: So] so *Conjunctions: I* 17: in your ignorance,] Corrected in pencil on RVG to "in ignorance,".

482 **Have You Ever Eaten Stars?** Text: RV. Variants: *New Yorker*, 6 July 1981, p. 38 (as "Stars"), SP85. *NY* has no "stage directions" and is set without indentations. In RVTS, the subtitle is in parentheses. RVTS is not folded. 1: Scene: A] A *NY*, Spot: A RVTS (revised in pencil to RV) 2: a bench] the bench *NY* 3: peace] amity RVTS (revised in pencil to RV) 4: hollow,] ~∧ *NY* 5: In woods-earth damp, and soft, centuries old—] In woods-earth, damp and soft-centuries old, *NY* 5: soft,] what RVTS (revised in pencil to RV) 6: Spruce needle, beech leaf, birch leaf, ground-pine belly-crawling,] Spruce needle, beech-, birch-leaf, ground pine belly-crawling,. *NY*, RVTS (revised in pencil to RV) 7: fern frond,] fern-frond, RVTS (revised in pencil to RV) 7: deadfall] dead fall RVTS (revised in pencil to RV) 8: biblically] Biblical *NY* 9: sunray] sun ray *NY*, sun-ray RVTS (revised in pencil to RV) 10: visitation.] ~— *NY*, ~, RVTS (revised in pencil on RVG to RV) 11: all in] all, in RVTS (revised in pencil to RV) 12: Of being are slowly absorbed] Of being slowly absorbed *NY*, Of being absorbed slowly RVTS (revised in pencil on RVTS to "Of being slowly absorbed" and finally corrected in pencil on RVG to RV) 12: absorbed—oh, slowly,—into] absorbed, oh, slowly, into *NY* 18: here come] come here *NY* 19: cool,] coolth, *NY*, RVTS (revised in pencil on RVG to RV) 20: somewhere,] ~∧ RVTS (revised in pencil to RV) 21: stair.] ~. . . . *NY* 23: drouth] drought *NY* 24: been] thus RVTS (revised in pencil to RV) 30: There,] ~∧ *NY* 31: gleam,] glow, RVTS (revised in pencil to RV) 31: rain-summoned,] rain summoned, RVTS (revised in pencil to RV) 35: stars] them *NY* 35: Later, I gathered stars into a basket.] In *NY* the poem ends after this text. 47: to you but that / Of seeing life as glory?] to you? RVTS (revised in pencil on RVG to RV)

483 **Twice Born** Text: RV. Variant: *Sewanee Review*, 89 (Winter 1981), pp. 22–23. 4: and∧] ~, *SR* 5: rain-gust] rain gust *SR*, RVTS (revised in pencil to RV) 27: toweled] towelled *SR*, RVTS (revised in pencil to RV) 30: Only a faint] Only faint *SR* 31: That I

stared at] I stared at *SR* 31: with a strange] with strange *SR* 33: Then,] ~∧ *SR*, RVTS (revised in pencil to RV) 34: once,] ~∧ RVTS (revised in black pen to RV) 36: A metaphor.] In RV the line is broken here into half-lines. In *SR* the line straddles a stanza break after this text. 38: that.] ~∧ RVTS (revised in pencil on RVG to RV) 39: slept.] A typewritten annotation, circled in pencil, follows in RVTS: "Sewanee Review".

484 **The Sea Hates the Land** Text: RV. Variant: *Vanderbilt Poetry Review*, 5 (1980), p. 40. 3: Of the Gulf when cesspool slick, or by muted tolling] Of the Gulf's cess-pool slick, or by night-muted tolling *Vanderbilt* 3: cesspool] cess-pool RVTS (revised in pencil to RV) 4: Deeper process] The deeper process *Vanderbilt*, RVTS (revised in pencil on RVG to RV) 9: undefinable] infinite *Vanderbilt* 12: Know that only in loneliness are you defined.] Know that loneness is the lonely man's only friend, *Vanderbilt* 12: are you] can you be RVTS (revised in pencil on RVG to RV) 13: Yes, the cormorant's] And the cormorant's *Vanderbilt* 13: and even] or even *Vanderbilt* 14: And] Or *Vanderbilt* 14: hurly-burly] hurlyburly *Vanderbilt*, RVTS (revised in pencil to RV) 14: men∧] ~, *Vanderbilt* 15: need: so by moonlight] need; by moonlight *Vanderbilt* 16: stroke steady, breath deep,] stroke by stroke steady, *Vanderbilt* 18: of the sea.] of sea. *Vanderbilt* 18: sea.] A typewritten annotation, circled in pencil, follows in RVTS: "Vanderbilt Poetry Journal".

485 **Afterward** Text: RV. Variants: *American Poetry Review*, March–April 1981, p. 4, SP85. In RVTS the bottom of the first page has a typewritten annotation, circled in pencil: "American Poetry Review". 3: peak westward] western peak *APR* 7: stumbled on the obituary/ Of] stumbled on / The obituary of *APR* 8: photograph unrecognizable,] photograph now unrecognizable, *APR*, SP85 (in pencil on SP85TS) 9: Who, at night, used to come] Who used to come at night *APR* 11: but made, as the paper says, / A brilliant career,] but, as the paper says, / Made a brilliant career SP85 (in pencil on SP85TS) 16: unhearable] unbearable, SP85 (in pencil on SP85TS) 19: Icecap] Ice-cap *APR*, RVTS (revised in pencil to RV) 19: stretching forever] stretching SP85 (in pencil on SP85TS) 20: And,] ~∧ *APR* 21: Ah,] Oh, *APR* 21: monoliths,] ~! *APR*, RVTS (revised in pencil on RVG to RV) 22: Such frozen thrusts] Such thrusts *APR* 22: in upward anguish of fantasy,] in anguished fantasy towering, *APR* 23: creatures,] ~∧ SP85 (in pencil on SP85TS) 24: Raised!] ~. *APR*, RVTS (revised in pencil on RVG to RV) 27: desert,] ~∧ *APR* 31: ritual unresting] unresting ritual *APR* 33: Of ever out-brimming, unspooling light and glow,] Of glowing light, *APR* 33: out-brimming,] unreeving, RVTS (revised in pencil on RVG to RV) 34: The forever sky.] The absolute sky. *APR*, RVTS (revised in pencil on RVG to RV) 35: awhile,] a while, *APR*, RVTS (revised in pencil to RV)

VIII. Coda

The divider page in RVTS lists the poem in this section.

487 **Fear and Trembling** Text: RV. Variants: *Georgia Review*, 35 (Spring 1981), p. 13, SP85, *Helsinki*. 2: summer] autumn *GaR*, season RVTS (revised in pencil to RV) 2: its] a RVTS (revised in black pen to RV) 2: fulfillment.] fulfilment. *GaR*, RVTS (revised in pencil to RV), ~, *Helsinki* 3: bird-note] bird note *GaR*, RVTS (revised in pencil to RV) 8: whitecap?] white-cap? *GaR*, RVTS (revised in pencil to RV) 8: Or] or RVTS (revised in black pen to RV) 11: glow with] translate *GaR*, RVTS (revised in pencil on RVG to RV) 12: of the lost] of lost *GaR*, *Helsinki* 12: Here now nothing grieves.] Nothing here now, at the last moment, grieves. *Helsinki* 14: Or find his own voice in the towering gust now from northward?] Or must find his voice only in towering gusts now from northward? *Helsinki* 15: is it in joy or pain and madness? / The gold leaf] is it in pain and madness, / Or joy? The gold leaf *GaR*, RVTS (revised in pencil on RVG to RV) 15: or pain] or in pain *Emory* 18: our labor] all labor *GaR*, RVTS (revised in pencil on RVG to RV) 18: spent—] ~?— *GaR*, AVTS (revised in pencil on RVG to RV) 19: Us who now know that only] Who know now that, only RVTS (revised in pencil to RV) 19: ambition∧] ~, RVTS (revised in pencil to RV) 20: and leap] leap *GaR*, RVTS (revised in pencil on RVG to RV) 21: grottoes,] grottos, *GaR*, RVTS, ~∧ *Helsinki* 21: dark—] ~, RVTS (revised in pencil to RV) 21: enchainment?] ~! *GaR*, RVTS (revised in pencil on RVG to RV)

Chief Joseph of the Nez Perce

Text: CJ. Variants: *Georgia Review*, 36 (Summer 1982), pp. 269–313, Privately Printed edition (probably by Palaemon Press), 1982. The drafts in the Beinecke Library indicate laborious revision. There are at least eleven drafts (marked A–I) prior to the setting typescript. The penciled revisions on CJG are clearly in Warren's hand.

Warren marked up two copies of this poem for Stuart Wright's use, one hardback and one softcover. Both are now at the Special Collections Department of Emory University, and I quote them with permission. The two marked copies are quite different from each other, but they have enough in common that it is not safe to conclude that one is a kind of supplement to the other. There is no clear evidence of which copy is the earlier, or whether one was understood as replacing the other. In the paperback copy there is a typewritten note referring to it as the revised text, but it is unclear whether that means revised relative to CJ or revised relative to the hardback copy. It seems most likely that Warren simply did not remember that he had already marked up one copy for Wright, and marked up each completely independently of the other, not keeping a systematic record of what he had changed.

The privately printed edition of CJ, copyright 1982, was apparently printed by Palaemon Press. Five lettered copies were produced. I have collated copy C, which was signed by Warren and is now in the Special Collections Department of the Heard Library at Vanderbilt University. I quote that edition by permission. title: Perce$_\wedge$] ~, *GaR* subtitle: Nimipu,] *Nimpau— GaR*, *Palaemon*, ~$_\wedge$ CJ (CJ does not make grammatical sense.) The name of the tribe is "Nimpau" as late as the mockup of the title page included in CJTS, and the correction to "Nimipu" is made on CJTS. epigraphs] *GaR* lacks the epigraphs on the title page, but the quotation from Jefferson appears between the title and the beginning of section I. *Palaemon* follows *GaR* in this. In *GaR* and *Palaemon* the attribution of the Jefferson quotation bears, in parentheses, the date: (January 7, 1802). This epigraph is in roman type in *GaR* and *Palaemon*, but all of the quotations in the text in both editions are in italics. In CJ all of the epigraphs and all of the epigraphs, the explanatory note, and all of the inset quotations are in italics. I have ignored how attributions are formatted in CJ, CJTS, *Palaemon*, and *GaR*, in the interest of presenting them in a manner consistent with attributions in other volumes. Note] In *GaR* and *Palaemon* the introductory note is substantially different:

> The Nez Percé (more modernly Nez Perce) first entered history with the visit of Lewis and Clark and their great expedition to the Pacific. The explorers were received in great friendship, and the Indians even took care of supplies and gear when Lewis and Clark made the last dash to the ocean. They swore never to harm a white man, and, until forced, never did. The Nez Perce were larger than usual among Indians, strong and active but not warlike, great breeders of horses. Unlike the Plains Indians, they were not nomadic, but they did follow a certain cycle according to seasons: buffalo hunting, digging camas roots, taking salmon in season. Their religion, which was regarded very seriously and was highly ethical made their land sacred, for there, from their graves, the fathers (they believed in a version of immortality) constantly watched their sons to be sure that they were men. To lie was a disgrace. The war of 1877 was provoked when two Federal treaties (1855 and 1873), which guaranteed to the Nez Perce in perpetuity their sacred homeland, were broken by the whites. In 1904, after the disaster, now back in the Northwest (but not in his own land, a prisoner on a reservation in the state of Washington), Chief Joseph died sitting at his campfire. The reservation physician reported the death as caused by a broken heart.

In CJTS the note and the epigraphs are typed on a different typewriter from that used in the body of the text. Presumably the current form of these texts is a late addition. Note: Percé] Perce CJG (revised in pencil to CJ) Note: scalping] to take scalps CJTS (revised in pencil on CJG to CJ) Note: for the most part] in general (revised in pencil in Warren's handwriting to CJ) Note: But after the gold rush] But the gold rush CJTS (revised in pencil in Warren's hand to CJ) Note: grants of bands] lands of bands CJTS, CJG (but "master pages" set of galleys is corrected in pencil to CJ) Note: other bands] certain bands CJTS (revised in pencil in Warren's hand to CJ) Note: 1855$_{\wedge}$] $\sim$, CJTS (revised in pencil in Warren's hand to CJ) Note: 1873,] $\sim_{\wedge}$ CJTS (revised in pencil in Warren's hand to CJ) Note: This occurred on] Thus the war began on CJTS (revised in pencil on CJG to CJ) Note: deaths$_{\wedge}$] $\sim$, CJTS (revised in pencil in Warren's hand to CJ) Note: in exile] in the exile CJTS, CJ

492 **Chief Joseph of the Nez Perce** title] On the first page of the poem proper (as opposed to the title page), *GaR*, *Palaemon*, and CJTS give the title as "Chief Joseph."

492 **I.** Section titles in *GaR* and *Palaemon* are Roman numerals followed by periods. In CJ they lack the periods, although they have periods (deleted by the designer) in CJTS. I have added periods to preserve consistency with numbered section titles in other volumes. CJTS is double-spaced, which is not Warren's usual practice. 2: Nimipu,] *In-an-toin-mi*, *GaR*, *Palaemon*, CJTS (revised in pencil on CJTS to "*Nimipu*," and to the unitalicized reading in CJ in pencil on the "master pages") 3: Land sacred to the band of old Joseph,] Line omitted in *GaR*, *Palaemon*, and CJTS (revised in pencil to CJ). 4: the far ages] the ages *GaR*, *Palaemon* 4: given$_{\wedge}$] $\sim$, *GaR*, *Palaemon* 7: bareback,] bare-back, *GaR*, *Palaemon* 8: shout$_{\wedge}$] $\sim$, *GaR*, *Palaemon* 8: Shout$_{\wedge}$] $\sim$, *GaR*, *Palaemon* 9: Eagle wing] Eaglewing *GaR*, *Palaemon* 12: beaver tails] beaver-tails *GaR*, *Palaemon* 12: slapping to warn,] slapped in warning, *GaR*, *Palaemon* 15: Boys stretch, ... To glints gold,] Boys lie, and sun dries the skin. / It glints golden, *GaR*, *Palaemon* 17: seaward salmon,] seaward surge salmon, *GaR*, *Palaemon* 18: leap great stones. They leap / The foaming rigor of current—] leap stones, leap the foaming / rigor of current— *GaR*, *Palaemon* 18: leap great] leaping great CJTS (revised in pencil on CJG to CJ) 21: What does our blood, ... for our eyes.] These lines missing from *GaR* and *Palaemon*. 27: thus blessed] blessed *GaR*, *Palaemon* 27: Nimipu] Nimpau *GaR*, *Palaemon*, CJTS (revised in pencil to CJ) 29: camas root,] camas-root, *GaR*, *Palaemon* 29: Jean Baptiste Le Moyne de Bienville] In *GaR* and *Palaemon* all of the attributions are preceded by an em-dash, but are not in small caps. In CJ all of the attributions are in small caps but are not preceded by an em-dash. I have changed them from small caps to preserve consistency with attributions in other volumes. In CJTS the quotations are underlined, to indicate italic type. The decision to set the attributions in small caps was made by the designer, on CJTS. The designer also makes it clear that the quotations are to be set as prose. 31: lynxlike,] lynx-like, *GaR*, *Palaemon* 33: forkèd] the forkèd *Palaemon*, forked CJG (CJG lacks the accent, but it is added in pencil) 34: thrives with the fathers.] is theirs. *GaR*, *Palaemon* 35: young boys] boys *GaR*, *Palaemon* 40: west,] $\sim_{\wedge}$ *GaR*, *Palaemon*, CJTS (revised in pencil on CJG to CJ) 41: Ill-Tasted—] $\sim$, *GaR*, *Palaemon*, CJTS (revised in pencil to CJ) 42: Where] How *GaR*, *Palaemon*, CJTS (revised in pencil to CJ) 42: winter long,] winter-long, *GaR*, *Palaemon* 43: A.M.] a.m. *Palaemon* 44: "I was born] CJG consistently omits the quotation marks at the beginning of stanzas in speeches by Joseph. Warren has written in the margin in pencil at this point, "Bert: Speeches of Joseph should be in quotes. Note that each verse paragraph (stanza) begins with quotation marks but has none at end *unless* Joseph no longer speaks." On CJTS, Erskine had noted for the typesetter that the quotation marks should hang in the left margin so that the first letters of all of the lines should be aligned. The typesetter seems to have erroneously omitted all of the quotation marks. Since the error is consistent, and does not follow CJTS, I will not note it further, although it occurs wherever Joseph speaks. The quotation marks are restored on the "repros." The quotation marks do appear in *Palaemon*, but they are not hung in the left margin. 50: On] Upon *GaR*, *Palaemon* 50: stone-bed I made,] stone-bed, *GaR*, *Palaemon* 57: But] Came *GaR*, *Palaemon* 58: I learned to say it.] Omitted in *GaR* and *Palaemon* 58: to say it.] it to say. CJTS (revised in pencil to CJ) 63: Thunder-Traveling-to-Loftier-Mountain-Heights. That] The-Thunder-that-strikes-up-from-Water. That *GaR*, *Palaemon*, CJTS (revised in pencil to CJ) 66: 'New Book of Heaven'] New Book of Heaven *GaR*, *Palaemon* 69: Lap-

wai ... money,] Then Lapwai was reservation for many— / But not for us who sold not the sacred / Bones of their fathers for white-man money, *GaR*, *Palaemon* 69: Lapwai ... New Book of Heaven,] These lines are a taped-in addition, typed on a different typewriter, in CJTS. 74: And food-scraps.] And food-scraps. Then firewater came there. The killing. *GaR*, *Palaemon* 75: "But far ... 'New Book of Heaven,'] "So back to the Winding Waters, my father, / He fled. Yet carried the New Book of Heaven, *GaR*, *Palaemon*, But longed for the Winding Waters, my father, // And came there, yet carried the 'New Book of Heaven, CJTS (revised in pencil on CJG to CJ) 77: now.] writ. CJTS (revised in pencil to CJ) 77: now. But could he forget?] writ, but forgot not *GaR*, *Palaemon* 78: Wisdom?] ~. *GaR*, *Palaemon* 79: darkness?] ~. *GaR*, *Palaemon* 80: "So was not at Lapwai, when firewater came. And the killing.] Omitted in *GaR*, *Palaemon*, and CJTS (revised in pencil to CJ). 81: Again] New *GaR*, *Palaemon* 82: sought out my father in friendship,] came with their hats on, *GaR*, *Palaemon* 82: paper‸] ~, *GaR*, *Palaemon* 82: Blue Mountains;] Blue Mountains, *GaR* 86: first great] great *GaR*, *Palaemon* 87: had named the land ours.] called the land ours always. *GaR*, *Palaemon* 90: We were promised ... of the seasons.] Omitted in *GaR* and *Palaemon*. 92: A promise, how pretty!] *Promises, promises* *GaR*, *Palaemon*, CJTS (revised in pencil to CJ) 93: earth. It was like ... face.] earth, as though / They spat on our faces. *GaR*, *Palaemon*, as though // A man spits on your face. CJTS (revised in pencil to CJ) 96: drew] draw *GaR*, *Palaemon* 97: Nimipu] Nimpau *GaR*, *Palaemon*, CJTS (revised in pencil to CJ) 98: which was now] and *GaR*, *Palaemon*, CJTS (revised in pencil to CJ) 98: reservation—] reservation— / Lapwai, the Place of the Butterfly— *GaR*, *Palaemon* 101: In my opinion ... null and void.] The extract as it reads makes no grammatical sense, but I can't think of a simple, plausible emendation which would remedy it. 104: creek bottoms] creek-bottoms *GaR*, *Palaemon* 106: Father!] Father! He burns like the sun, *GaR*, *Palaemon* 107: But] And CJTS (revised in pencil to CJ) 107: But we heard ... to give rejoicing."] And we heard how goodness in his heart holds. / But only that word, like mist came to us, not fact." *GaR*, *Palaemon* 108: rejoicing."] Quotation marks added in pencil in CJTS. 109: "But it faded like mist in the day's heat."] Omitted in *GaR* and *Palaemon*. The quotation marks are added in pencil in CJTS.

495 **II.** 2: great, be] Great, is *GaR*, *Palaemon*, CJTS (revised in pencil to "great, is" but corrected in pencil on CJG to CJ) 9: forkèd] the forkèd *GaR*, *Palaemon*, CJTS (revised in pencil to CJ) 11: leather-tough,] hide-tough, *GaR*, *Palaemon* 14: But they knew where they went, and we knew.] Line missing in *GaR* and *Palaemon* 15: lead of a rifle,] lead, *GaR*, *Palaemon*, CJTS (revised in pencil to CJ) 15: flesh—] ~, *GaR*, *Palaemon*, CJTS (revised in pencil to CJ) 20: white-man] white man's *GaR*, *Palaemon*, CJTS (revised in pencil to CJ) 22: fathers— ... Heart-Being.' "] fathers.' " *GaR*, *Palaemon* 23: that,] ~‸ CJTS (revised in pencil to CJ) 27: brightens] gilds *GaR*, *Palaemon*, CJTS (revised in pencil to CJ) 31: The aspen leaf turn though no wind, sees] Omitted in *GaR* and *Palaemon*. 35: open,] ~‸ *GaR*, *Palaemon* 42: water,] ~‸ *GaR*, *Palaemon* 45: of gold?] of gold? We know not. *GaR*, *Palaemon*, CJTS (revised in pencil to CJ) 48: name-dance,] ~‸ *GaR*, *Palaemon* 49: gold dance?] be danced? *GaR*, *Palaemon* 49: Would it be— ... *smiling?*] Would it be / *Keyox-hipaca -? iske -? ilaka -? win*— / Which means, 'Death that in darkness comes smiling'? *GaR*, *Palaemon*, Would it be— / 'Death-that-in-darkness-comes-smiling'— / *Keyox-hipaca -? iske -? ilaka -? win'?* CJTS (revised in pencil to CJ, except that the English phrase is not italicized in CJTS, and corrected in pencil on CJG to CJ) 51: whirl wind.] whirlwind. *GaR*, *Palaemon* 51: C. H.] S. H. *GaR*, *Palaemon*, CJTS (revised in pencil to CJ) 53: can live forever?] forever can live? *GaR*, *Palaemon* 57: death of the promise of peace—] death of peace— *GaR*, *Palaemon* 58: from upwind] downwind *GaR*, *Palaemon* 69: while others / Are forming] with others / Forming *GaR*, *Palaemon* 72: difference?] No stanza break after this text in *GaR* or *Palaemon*. On CJG Warren has written in "(stanza space)" at this point, to make his intentions clear. 73: "Still] ‸~ *GaR* 75: in moonlight would shine.] shine in moonlight. *GaR*, *Palaemon*, CJTS (revised in pencil to CJ) 81: such two] two *GaR*, *Palaemon*, two such CJTS (revised in pencil on CJG to CJ) 89: My] And my *GaR*, *Palaemon*, CJTS (revised in pencil to CJ) 91: more dry] drier *GaR*, *Palaemon* 92: the black] and black *Emory*

(paperback) 93: tight] No line break after this text in *GaR* and *Palaemon*. 94: bulged—] ∼, *GaR*, *Palaemon* 95: sweaty,] ∼∧ *GaR*, *Palaemon* 95: under that] under black *Emory* (paperback) 95: cloth—] ∼, *GaR*, *Palaemon* 96: My words . . . I saw them,] My words could not come, / I saw their lips curl. I saw them, *GaR*, *Palaemon* 99: in secret sneer.] in the secret sneer. *Emory* (paperback) 100: the heart] my heart *GaR*, *Palaemon*, CJTS (revised in pencil to CJ) 101: 'Speak for the Nimipu, and speak Truth!'] 'For the Nimpau, will speak and speak Truth!' *GaR*, *Palaemon* 101: Nimipu,] Nimpau, CJTS (revised in pencil to CJ) 106: how the] how once the *GaR*, *Palaemon*, CJTS (revised in pencil to CJ) 107: Had made the earth but had drawn] That made the earth had drawn *GaR*, *Palaemon* 107: had drawn] drawn CJTS (revised in pencil to CJ) 111: he must,] No line break after this text in *GaR* or *Palaemon*. 112: cling."] cling.∧ CJTS, CJG (revised on "master pages" to CJ) 112: of 1876] of the Treaty of 1876 *GaR*, *Palaemon*, CJTS (revised in pencil to CJ) 113: Howard understood not.] Could Howard understand? *GaR*, *Palaemon* 116: forever—] No line break after this text in *GaR* or *Palaemon*. 119: like a digger of roots] like a squaw *GaR*, *Palaemon*, CJTS (revised in pencil to CJ) 126: hail.] vomit. *GaR*, *Palaemon* 127: spits] spit CJTS (revised in pencil to CJ) 127: hail.] vomit. *GaR*, *Palaemon* 128: Wallowa,] Winding Waters, *GaR*, *Palaemon*, CJTS (revised in pencil to CJ) 130: Snake,] ∼∧ *GaR*, *Palaemon*, CJTS (revised in pencil on CJG to CJ) 131: In] Was in *GaR*, *Palaemon*, CJTS (revised in pencil on CJG to CJ) 131: thaw-flood, snatched off the weak colts, the weak calves,] thaw-flood and snatched off the weak colts and calves, *GaR*, CJTS (revised in pencil on CJG to CJ) thaw-flood and snatched off weak colts and calves, *Palaemon* 132: left] that we left *GaR*, *Palaemon*, CJTS (revised in pencil to CJ) 133: But in] In our *GaR*, *Palaemon*, CJTS (revised in pencil on CJG to CJ) 138: was∧] ∼, *GaR*, *Palaemon* 138: the great grief.] the grief. *GaR*, *Palaemon*, CJTS (revised in pencil to CJ) 139: young] the young *GaR*, *Palaemon* 139: White Bird.] Kicking Bird. *GaR*, *Palaemon*, CJTS (revised in pencil to CJ)

499 **III.** 1: trail, horse-soldiers in darkness came,] trail the horse-soldiers came, and in darkness *GaR*, *Palaemon*, trail the horse-soldiers came, in darkness CJTS (revised in pencil on CJG "trail, horse-soldiers, in darkness, came∧", and corrected on the "master pages" to CJ) 2: And] With *GaR*, *Palaemon*, CJTS (revised in pencil on CJG to CJ) 3: gear jangle] gear-jangle *GaR*, *Palaemon* 3: horse fart!] horse-fart! *GaR*, *Palaemon* 4: heard—] ∼, *GaR*, *Palaemon*, CJTS (revised in pencil on CJG to CJ) 8: At dawn they came to surprise us.] In *GaR* and *Palaemon* this line and the next are a single line, broken across the line-break. 9: It was theirs.] No stanza break after this text in *GaR* or *Palaemon*. 10: "We,] ∧We, *GaR*, *Palaemon* 11: young braves] our young men *GaR*, *Palaemon* 16: Of braves, had only] Had only *GaR*, *Palaemon*, CJTS (revised in pencil to CJ) 17: Some threescore,] Some braves, threescore∧ CJTS (revised in pencil to CJ) 17: threescore,] three score, *GaR*, *Palaemon* 18: shotguns,] shot guns, *GaR*, *Palaemon* 19: Then] The rest held *GaR*, *Palaemon*, CJTS (revised in pencil to CJ) 23: *flèche*] flèche *GaR*, *Palaemon*, CJTS, CJG (revised in pencil on "master pages" to CJ) 25: Stumbles.] Stumble. *GaR*, *Palaemon* 25: shadows,] ∼∧ *GaR*, *Palaemon*, CJTS (revised in pencil to CJ) 30: Can there be] Can be *GaR*, *Palaemon* 32: So soldiers died.] Soldiers died. *GaR*, *Palaemon* 32: draw,] crevasse, *GaR*, *Palaemon*, CJTS (revised in pencil to CJ) 33: sage clump,] sage-clump, *GaR*, *Palaemon* 34: Thirsty the sands] Thirsty are sands *GaR*, *Palaemon*, CJTS (revised in pencil to CJ) 38: You husband] You must husband *GaR*, *Palaemon* 42: the buffalo herd] fool buffalo *GaR*, *Palaemon* 44: Flee on foot.] Line break after this text omitted in *GaR* and *Palaemon*. 47: honored] brave *GaR*, *Palaemon*, CJTS, CJG (revised in pencil on "master pages" to CJ) 49: hide] break *GaR*, *Palaemon*, CJTS (revised in pencil to CJ) 49: rifles they have!] CJTS reads as CJ but is corrected in pencil to: "they have rifles!" CJG is corrected in pencil to CJ. 50: Before you . . . lies] Before you to the westward lies *GaR*, *Palaemon*, CJTS (revised in pencil to CJ) 51: braves] men *GaR*, *Palaemon* 53: Hope we had of] Hope had we of *GaR*, *Palaemon* 54: cougar,] grizzly, *GaR*, *Palaemon*, puma, CJTS (revised in pencil to CJ) 55: was our blood.] of our blood was. *GaR*, *Palaemon* 58: To his] For to his *GaR*, *Palaemon*, CJTS (revised in pencil on CJG to CJ) 58: horse-soldiers—they] horse-soldiers, they *GaR*,

Palaemon 61: Killed only a baby.] In *GaR*, *Palaemon*, and CJTS there is no stanza break here, rather this line and the next are two half-lines, broken over a line break, with the second half-line set flush to the end of the first. CJTS is corrected in pencil to CJ. 64: like a present] a present, *Emory* (hardback) 66: belch-gun] belch gun *GaR*, *Palaemon*, CJTS (revised in pencil to CJ) 67: the Salmon, yet flooding,] the flood-Salmon *GaR*, *Palaemon*, the Salmon, now flooding, CJTS (revised in pencil on CJG to CJ) 68: like children they] thoughtless, they *GaR*, *Palaemon*, they CJTS (revised in pencil to CJ) 73: are] were *GaR*, *Palaemon* 74: We meet, and they die.] We met, and they died. *GaR*, *Palaemon*, We met, and they die. CJTS (revised in pencil to CJ) 78: Made the river] Crossed over the river *Emory* (paperback) 78: that aimless tackle] their fool tackle *GaR*, *Palaemon*, that fool tackle CJTS (revised in pencil to CJ) 78: and gear.] No stanza break after this text in *GaR*, *Palaemon*, or CJTS, but CJTS is corrected in pencil to CJ. 80: two] three *GaR*, *Palaemon*, CJTS (revised in pencil to CJ) 80: our circle] their circle *GaR*, *Palaemon*, CJTS (revised in pencil to CJ) 81: sick, and women,] women, and sick, *GaR*, *Palaemon*, CJTS (revised in pencil to CJ) 84: To cleanse hearts.] The line break after this text is omitted in *GaR* and *Palaemon*. 102: knew] know *Palaemon* 103: named by the name] named the name *GaR*, *Palaemon*, CJTS (revised in pencil to CJ) 104: devised a new death-trap] dreamed of a new death-trap *GaR*, *Palaemon* 105: the first chief] first one *GaR*, *Palaemon*, first chief CJTS (revised in pencil to CJ) 111: mountain wall] mountain-wall *GaR*, *Palaemon*, CJTS (revised in pencil to CJ) 113: Lolo Pass,] Pass Lolo, *GaR*, *Palaemon*, CJTS (revised in pencil to CJ) 119: women] squaws *GaR*, *Palaemon*, CJTS (revised in pencil to CJ) 119: merely to flatter] to flatter *GaR*, *Palaemon*, CJTS (revised in pencil to CJ) 123: of long travail] of the long travail *GaR*, *Palaemon* 125: He would] For he would *GaR*, *Palaemon*, CJTS (revised in pencil to CJ) 127: had a fort built] had forts *GaR*, *Palaemon*, CJTS (revised in pencil to CJ) 130: goes] turns *GaR*, *Palaemon*, CJTS (revised in pencil on CJG to CJ) 131: Here only ... for deceit.] Here only coals dying and pony turds dew-damp / Until the sun hits them. *GaR*, *Palaemon*, Here only some last coals dying, kept in deceit, / And pony turds dew-damp / Until the sun hits them. CJTS (these lines on a taped-in insert in CJTS) CJG is corrected in pencil to CJ. 134: that fort ill-placed.] that fool fort they had built. *GaR*, *Palaemon*, CJTS (revised in pencil to "that fort they had ill-placed." CJG is corrected in pencil to CJ.) 135: song / Before its kiss came.] song. *GaR*, *Palaemon* 135: song / Before its kiss came.] No stanza break after this text in *GaR* and *Palaemon*. 137: " 'Fort Fizzle,'] Fort Fizzle, *GaR*, *Palaemon*, "Fort Fizzle, CJTS (revised in pencil on CJG to CJ) 138: yet no way] no way *GaR*, *Palaemon*, CJTS (revised in pencil to CJ) 138: to get to] to *Emory* (paperback) 139: Bitterroot,] Butternut, *GaR*, *Palaemon*, CJTS (revised in pencil to CJ) 141: eastward,] southward, *GaR*, *Palaemon*, CJTS (revised in pencil to CJ) 143: deceived] fooled *GaR*, *Palaemon*

503 **IV.** 1: Near dawn] At dawn *GaR*, *Palaemon*, CJTS (revised in pencil on CJG to CJ) 1: horse-soldiers. Shot / Into teepees.] horse-soldiers. / Shot into teepees. *GaR* 2: Women,] Squaws, *GaR*, *Palaemon*, CJTS (revised in pencil to CJ) 8: It was laughter.] It was, of course, laughter. *GaR*, *Palaemon*, CJTS (revised in pencil to CJ) 14: bright milling] milling *GaR*, *Palaemon*, milling bright CJTS (revised in pencil on CJG to CJ) 15: Few there ... And dawn filled the canyon.] *GaR* and *Palaemon* are substantially different:

Few
Laughed longer. Few from the light escaped. Those few to high cover.
Dug holes in the ground. But our rifles
Found any that stirred. And light filled the canyon.

CJTS is substantially different:

Few
Laughed long. Few from the light lived to flee.
Those few to high cover.
Dug holes in the ground. But our rifles
Found any that stirred. And light filled the canyon.

CJTS is corrected in pencil to:

Few there
Laughed long. Light summoned hot lead from darkness.
Few managed to flee to high cover.
Dug holes in the ground. But our rifles
Found any that stirred. And dawn filled the canyon.

CJG is corrected in pencil to CJ. 22: bodies, white humps] bodies then white humps *GaR*, *Palaemon*, bodies now white humps CJTS (revised in pencil to CJ) 22: humps] humps left *Emory* (hardback) 23: And now clutching] Clutching *GaR*, *Palaemon*, And clutching CJTS (revised in pencil to CJ) 24: as naked they] as they *GaR*, *Palaemon* 25: but rage] with rage *GaR*, *Palaemon*, CJTS (revised in pencil to CJ) 29: And scouts out now always.] And our scouts always out. *GaR*, CJTS (revised in pencil to: "And scouts now always out.") CJG is corrected in pencil to CJ. 29: a long way∧ …] a long way. … *GaR*, *Palaemon* 29: trail∧ …] ~. … *GaR*, *Palaemon* 29: The unexpected] the unexpected *GaR*, *Palaemon* 29: Perce] Perces *GaR*, *Palaemon*, CJTS (revised in pencil to CJ) 35: blocked the] lay on *GaR*, *Palaemon* 40: eyes to be] that eyes would be *GaR*, *Palaemon* 59: "To your belly the plant of the camas is kind.] Line omitted in *GaR* and *Palaemon* 60: Women] "Squaws *GaR*, *Palaemon*, Squaws CJTS (revised in pencil on CJG to CJ) 68: a patrol out.] No stanza break after this text in *GaR*, *Palaemon*, or CJTS (CJTS corrected in pencil to CJ). 69: at last!] No line break after this text in *GaR* or *Palaemon* 70: blaze,] ~∧ CJTS (revised in pencil to CJ) 71: Tent canvas tattered] Tents tettered *GaR*, *Palaemon*, Tents in tetter CJTS (revised in pencil to: "Tent canvas in tetter") CJG is corrected in black pen in Warren's hand to CJ. 78: there!—] ~∧— *GaR*, *Palaemon* 79: silence,] and the silence, *GaR*, *Palaemon* 80: wolf-call] wolf call *GaR*, *Palaemon* 82: Till dawn.] Sleep till dawn. *GaR*, *Palaemon*, CJTS (revised in pencil to CJ) 86: High stars] Stars *GaR*, *Palaemon*, CJTS (revised in pencil on CJG to CJ) 86: In darkness, awake,] Awake. *GaR*, *Palaemon*, CJTS (revised in pencil to CJ) 87: mountains,] ~∧ *GaR*, *Palaemon*, CJTS (revised in pencil to CJ) 93: blankness,] nightmare, *GaR*, *Palaemon* 99: boot-leather / No longer] leather / Of boots no longer *GaR*, *Palaemon* 99: callus] callous *GaR*, *Palaemon* 101: razor-edge] razor-edged *Emory* (hardback) 102: from northward] northward *GaR*, *Palaemon* 102: fanged,] nourished, *GaR*, *Palaemon* 103: General O. O. Howard] General O. O. Howard, Report *GaR*, *Palaemon*, CJTS (revised in pencil to CJ) 106: nightmare] mare's nest *GaR*, *Palaemon*, CJTS (revised in pencil to CJ) 106: chasm and peak,] chasms and peaks, *GaR*, *Palaemon* 107: nightmare] mare's nest *GaR*, *Palaemon*, CJTS (revised in pencil to CJ) 108: The pine needles] Is the pine-needle *GaR*, *Palaemon* 108: the foot arch] to foot-arch *GaR*, *Palaemon* 116: a mortar] mortar *GaR*, *Palaemon*, CJTS (revised in pencil to CJ)

506 **V.** 1: mountain wall] mountain-wall CJTS (revised in pencil to CJ) 5: root] roots *GaR*, *Palaemon*, CJTS (revised in pencil to CJ) 7: spine-ridges ran] ran spine-ridges with *GaR*, *Palaemon* 8: blackness] the darkness *GaR*, *Palaemon* 11: Poker could, and Joseph, his people.] Poker, yes, Joseph, his people, they could. *GaR*, *Palaemon*. In *GaR*, *Palaemon*, and CJTS, the line straddles the stanza break that follows this text, but CJTS is corrected in pencil to CJ. 18: any] an *Emory* (hardback) 18: idiot] young *GaR*, *Palaemon*, fool *Emory* (paperback) 19: Itself] Himself *GaR*, *Palaemon* 20: sent out] had out *GaR*, *Palaemon* 23: mania] nightmare *GaR*, *Palaemon*, CJTS (revised in pencil to CJ) 24: stream-yelping] stream-yelling *GaR*, *Palaemon* 25: is only] is *GaR*, *Palaemon* 26: At last to pin Joseph] To pin Joseph at last *GaR*, *Palaemon* 27: waiting—] ~. *GaR*, *Palaemon*, CJTS (revised in pencil to CJ) 28: a son] his son *Emory* (hardback) 28: mad] made CJG (revised in pencil on CJG to CJ) (This is a printer's error, corrected on the "master pages," but since it makes grammatical sense I note it here.) 29: it would] that it would CJTS (revised in pencil to CJ) 29: be∧] ~, CJTS (revised in pencil to CJ) 31: nutcracker] nut-cracker *GaR*, *Palaemon* 33: useless] worse than useless *Emory* (hardback) 33: His scouts … ignorantly north] His scouts all found dead, hung ignorantly north, *GaR*, *Palaemon*, CJTS (revised in pencil to CJ) 36: But Sturgis,] While Sturgis, *GaR*, *Palaemon*

38: with trail signs . . . a well-trampled] signs carefully clear, / To a well-trampled *GaR*, *Palaemon* 38: signs∧] ~, CJTS (revised in pencil to CJ) 39: clear,] ~∧ CJTS (revised in pencil to CJ) 40: find, in the end,] find in the end CJTS (revised in pencil to CJ) 41: ponies outward had circled] ponies had circled *Emory* (paperback) 42: thence—] ~, *GaR*, *Palaemon*, CJTS (revised in pencil to CJ) 43: many. But] many—but *GaR*, *Palaemon*, CJTS (revised in pencil to CJ) 44: spies] spied *GaR*, *Palaemon* 44: rise, the] rise—the *GaR*, *Palaemon* 44: bands,] ~∧ CJTS (revised in black pen on CJG to CJ) 46: So,] ~∧ *GaR*, *Palaemon*, CJTS (revised in pencil to CJ) 46: spooks.] ~, *GaR*, *Palaemon* 47: For] And *GaR*, *Palaemon*, CJTS (revised in pencil to CJ) 47: spooks,] ~∧ *GaR*, *Palaemon*, CJTS (revised in black pen on CJG to CJ) 48: sage clumps] sage-clumps *GaR*, *Palaemon*, CJTS (revised in pencil to CJ) 49: lariats—] ~. *GaR*, *Palaemon* 50: Laughing.] But taking time for their laughter. *GaR*, *Palaemon* 55: pebbles] a pebble *GaR*, *Palaemon*, no pebble CJTS (revised in pencil to CJ) 58: tunnel,] ~∧ *Emory* (hardback) 59: And needle-narrow. It] Needle-narrow, it *Emory* (hardback) 59: And needle-narrow . . . revenge.] And needle-narrow, and fading back north. / It faded north, reversing the track of Sturgis' revenge. *GaR*, *Palaemon* 60: Sturgis'] Sturgis and his *Emory* (hardback) 60: revenge.] No stanza break after this text in *GaR* and *Palaemon*. 61: it led, and Joseph could enter] it led Joseph to enter *GaR*, *Palaemon*, CJTS (revised in pencil to CJ) 63: Fork] Ford *GaR*, *Palaemon*, CJTS (revised in pencil to CJ)

507 **VI.** 9: plain;] ~, *GaR*, *Palaemon*, CJTS (revised in pencil on CJG to CJ) 10: south then,] south, then *GaR*, *Palaemon*,CJTS (revised in pencil to CJ) south there were, *Emory* (hardback) (The comma does not make grammatical sense but it is clearly marked.) 16: flats, standing] flats, with standing *Emory* (hardback) 17: And farther, more canyons and coulees black] Line omitted in *GaR* and *Palaemon* 20: and,] ~∧ *GaR*, *Palaemon*, CJTS (revised in pencil to CJ) 20: crawling,] ~∧ *GaR*, *Palaemon*, CJTS (revised in pencil to CJ) 28: bulge, hump, leap] bulge, the hump, the leap *GaR Palaemon* 29: falls away,] away falls, *GaR* away falls ∧ *Palaemon* 33: Your eternal] the Eternal *Emory* (hardback) 34: Riffle of dust. They come.] In *GaR*, *Palaemon*, and CJTS, this line and the first line of the next stanza are a single line, broken into two half-lines after "come." CJTS is corrected in pencil to CJ. 39: Howard.] Howard comes. *Emory* (hardback) 41: cleft stick] ambiguity *GaR*, *Palaemon* 42: Stirs] He stirs *GaR*, *Palaemon*, CJTS (revised in pencil to CJ) 42: military.] ~, *Emory* (hardback) 46: sardonic,] ~∧ *GaR*, *Palaemon* 51: Let] Let the *GaR*, *Palaemon* 51: split,] split on shoes, *Emory* (paperback) 51: feet] let feet *GaR*, *Palaemon*, CJTS (revised in pencil to CJ) 51: last] the last *GaR*, *Palaemon* 52: Horseshoe] Horse-shoe *GaR*, *Palaemon* 58: Melts in his breast. It] Line omitted in *Emory* (paperback) 62: Keogh,] McKoegh *GaR*, *Palaemon*, CJTS (revised in pencil to CJ) 72: Now,] ~∧ *GaR*, *Palaemon* 73: His heart . . . cast.] This stanza missing in *GaR* and *Palaemon*. 80: Keogh] McKoegh *GaR*, *Palaemon*, CJTS (revised in pencil to CJ) 83: regular,] ~∧ CJTS (revised in pencil to CJ) 83: regular, but rank reduced.] reduced. *GaR*, *Palaemon* 91: but] only *GaR*, *Palaemon*, CJTS (revised in pencil to CJ) 91: *north.*] north. *GaR*, *Palaemon* 91: northeast] northward *GaR*, *Palaemon*, CJTS (revised in pencil to CJ) 94: driven] driven onward *GaR*, *Palaemon*, CJTS (revised in pencil to CJ) 98: One more . . . hacks at his scouts.] The lines are substantially different in *GaR* and *Palaemon*:

Only once, westward, the bulwark of rim-rock
Breaks where a creek flows in, and in
That narrowness, flanked by crevasses,
Flange rock, and rubble, one man is twenty—
Is fifty—if powder holds out. So Joseph
Drives on. Oh, for that opening wide
That suddenly, like a lethal noose,
Tightens! he hacks at his scouts.

In CJTS these lines are a taped-in insert. 98: One more chance! He follows. / Oh, one more chance!] One more chance! CJTS (revised in pencil on CJG to CJ) 101: in] on CJTS (revised in pencil to CJ) 105: Goes narrow,] Narrows, CJTS (revised in pencil on CJG to

CJ) 108: that,] but *Emory* (paperback) 110: Tightens.] Would tighten. *Emory* (hardback) Drawn tight. *Emory* (paperback) 111: There . . . up-canyon] There it is, and the incompetent / Are huddled up-canyon. *GaR*, *Palaemon* 111: a gift] as a gift CJTS (revised in pencil to CJ) 112: It is! And] It is, and CJTS (revised in pencil to CJ) 114: bait and delay . . . throttlement.] bait—and Sturgis, / Gave thanks to God, and struck! The bait / Faded before him into the narrowing throttlement. *GaR*, *Palaemon*, bait—and Sturgis / Gave thanks to God, and struck! // The bait before him fades into the narrowing throttlement. (In CJTS "bait—and Sturgis," is corrected in pencil to "bait and delay—and Sturgis,". CJG is revised in pencil to CJ.) 119: until, at a burst, from] until suddenly from *GaR*, *Palaemon*, until, suddenly, from CJTS (revised in pencil to CJ) 120: Flanges, shelves] Flanges, *GaR*, *Palaemon* 120: sage clumps,] sage-clumps, *GaR*, *Palaemon*, CJTS (revised in pencil to CJ) 121: hums happily honeyward.] hummed honeyward. *GaR*, *Palaemon* 122: Now] With *GaR*, *Palaemon*, CJTS (revised in pencil to CJ) 126: gone—and Sturgis] gone, Sturgis *GaR*, *Palaemon*, gone, and Sturgis CJTS (revised in pencil to CJ) 128: the inner bulwark] the bulwark *GaR*, *Palaemon*, CJTS (revised in pencil on CJG to CJ) 128: rim-rock!] ~. *GaR*, *Palaemon* 129: Now,] ~‸ *GaR*, *Palaemon*, CJTS (revised in pencil to CJ) 130: is] was *GaR*, *Palaemon* 130: Southward,] ~‸ *GaR*, *Palaemon*, CJTS (revised in pencil to CJ) 131: saw-toothed] rugged *GaR*, *Palaemon*, CJTS (revised in pencil to CJ) 131: Absarokas,] Ansarokas‸ *GaR*, *Palaemon*, Absarokas‸ CJTS (revised in pencil to CJ) 133: the clutch] that clutch *Emory* (hardback) 134: nothing] not *GaR*, *Palaemon*, CJTS (revised in pencil to CJ) 135: the cavalry,] cavalry, *Emory* (hardback) 136: that flare] the flare *GaR*, *Palaemon* 136: flare in his head.] flare of that star. *GaR*, *Palaemon*, flare. CJTS (revised in pencil to CJ) 137: is] was *GaR*, *Palaemon*, CJTS (revised in pencil on CJG to CJ) 138: him] Miles *GaR*, *Palaemon* 140: Would receive] Receives *GaR*, *Palaemon* 140: shuts eyes.] shuts his eyes. *GaR*, *Palaemon* 143: merciless masonry] masonry *GaR*, *Palaemon* 148: Miles, unknown, on] Miles, on *Emory* (paperback) 148: slope‸] ~, *Emory* (paperback) 151: "Old Lady's Skirts":] Old Lady's skirts. *GaR*, *Palaemon*, Old Lady's skirts: CJTS (revised in pencil to CJ) 156: Women] Squaws *GaR*, *Palaemon*, Here squaws CJTS (revised in pencil to CJ) 157: Could here dry] Could dry CJTS (revised in pencil to CJ) 167: in hypnotic] in his hypnotic *GaR*, *Palaemon* 169: moatlike,] moat-like, *GaR*, *Palaemon* 170: and top growth] the growth *GaR*, *Palaemon*, CJTS (revised in pencil to CJ) 171: At that distance looked like the leveling plain.] At its top with the look of the levelling plain. *GaR*, *Palaemon*, At its top with the look of the leveling plain. CJTS (revised in pencil to CJ) 172: This,] ~‸ *GaR*, *Palaemon*, CJTS (revised in pencil to CJ) 173: there was, . . . to give] there was / A long ridge overlooking the village, behind it, / Now brown with autumn-bit sage that gave *GaR*, *Palaemon*, CJTS (revised in pencil to CJ) 176: trigger-finger] finger *GaR*, *Palaemon*, CJTS (revised in pencil on CJG to CJ) 176: squinting.] No stanza break after this text in *GaR* or *Palaemon*. *GaR* and *Palaemon* also add four lines here:

What made Miles here blind? But did see the horse herd,
And brilliantly thought how he would,
With second-rate cavalry, strike a stampede there
While wings of infantry closed on the flanks of the village.

180: the dip,] that dip, *GaR*, *Palaemon*, CJTS (revised in pencil to CJ) 181: That the last east-west cross-ridge, southward,] The last ridge southward (revised in pencil to: "That last cross-ridge southward") CJG is corrected in pencil to CJ. 181: That the last . . . that, sudden,] These lines are substantially different in *GaR* and *Palaemon*:

The last ridge, which on his, the south, side, looked easy—
The easiest yet, eastward sinking.
Ah, how in his dream could he know
That on the far side it dropped sharp
To hoof-trap and haunch-grind, and sudden

186: That on the far side, . . . dropped sharp] That on the far side it dropped sharp CJTS (revised in pencil to CJ) 191: ridge beyond,] ridge *GaR Palaemon*, CJTS (revised in pencil to CJ) 192: coulee?] ~. *GaR*, *Palaemon* 193: That is what the land-lay today indicates.] This stanza omitted in *GaR* and *Palaemon*. 197: Who could not now ... attack.] As the cutting edge of attack. *GaR*, *Palaemon*, CJTS (revised in pencil on CJG to CJ) 198: alarm, / As the cutting edge of attack.] alarm. *Emory* (paperback) 202: hold back / Pawing mounts, though they pant to ride] paw, panting to ride *GaR*, *Palaemon*, CJTS (revised in pencil to CJ) 208: But no laughter.] Laughter. *GaR*, *Palaemon*, CJTS (revised in pencil to CJ) 210: shouts,] ~: *GaR*, *Palaemon*, CJTS (revised in pencil to CJ) 210: "Attack!"] No stanza break after this text in *GaR*, *Palaemon*, or CJTS. A stanza break is added in pencil at this point in CJG. 211: half-wits] fools *GaR*, *Palaemon* 213: only silence] silence only *GaR*, *Palaemon* 216: hoof-thunder!—] real thunder!— *GaR*, *Palaemon*, hoof's thunder!— CJTS (revised in pencil to CJ) 217: the last / Ridge divulges] the last ridge / Divulges CJTS (revised in pencil to CJ) 217: the last ... compresses the ranks,] the ridge's dire secret / Compresses the ranks, *GaR*, *Palaemon* 218: Ridge divulges ... and reddening more, as snow falls] In *Emory* (hardback) Warren has marked both sides in pencil. This seems to be a passage he intended to rewrite thoroughly but did not. 218: dire,] ~$_\wedge$ CJTS (revised in pencil on CJG to CJ) 219: Deadly secret,] Secret, CJTS (revised in pencil on CJG to CJ) 220: to] in *GaR*, *Palaemon*, CJTS (revised in pencil on CJG to CJ) 220: Blaze ... then fifty] Then / The blaze bursts, bursts first / At a hundred and fifty, a hundred, then fifty *GaR*, *Palaemon* 225: Shatters:] No stanza break after this text in *Emory* (hardback). There is a page turn after this text in *GaR*, and in *Palaemon*, but the line in both cases straddles the stanza break after this text, so Warren is clearly revising the poem here rather than correcting an error carried over from *GaR*. In CJTS there is no stanza break here, but the line is broken into two half-lines at this point. On CJTS corrections in pencil add the stanza break and make the second half-line into a separate line. 226: the death scream,] man's death scream, *Emory* (hardback) 229: Enfield—at Winchester—] Enfield,—at Winchester,— *GaR* Enfield—, at Winchester—, *Palaemon*, Enfield, at Winchester, CJTS (revised in pencil to CJ) 229: range,] ~. *GaR*, *Palaemon* 230: Snow red, ... of sky.] These lines missing in *GaR* and *Palaemon*. 232: unperturbed gray purity of sky.] sky's unperturbed gray purity. CJTS (revised in pencil to CJ) 233: I never ... Scout for Miles] This quotation missing in *GaR* and *Palaemon*. It is stapled in at this point in CJTS. 234: made out some better;] fare some better. *GaR*, *Palaemon* 234: took losses, of course,] Some died, *GaR*, *Palaemon* 235: But in dying ... settled down,] But in dying had ringed the camp with a ring / Of investment, which promised a siege, and revenge / For the grisly first charge. So the siege settles down, *GaR*, *Palaemon* 237: village,] CJTS reads with CJ, but is corrected in pencil to: "village$_\wedge$ / By the newly arrived artillery of Miles," CJG is corrected in pencil to CJ. 238: began] begins *GaR*, *Palaemon* 239: Miles,] ~$_\wedge$ *GaR*, *Palaemon*, CJTS (revised in pencil to CJ) 239: bastardly] lousy *GaR*, *Palaemon* 242: But] Except *GaR*, *Palaemon* 244: They, too, grabbed a hostage.] They grabbed hostage, too. *GaR*, *Palaemon* 245: mysteriously] strangely *GaR*, *Palaemon* 245: generous.] No stanza break after this text in *GaR* or *Palaemon*. 246: Now Howard stands, suddenly, there.] Suddenly, Howard stands there. *GaR*, *Palaemon*, For Howard stands, suddenly, there. *Emory* (hardback), But Howard stands, suddenly, there. *Emory* (paperback) 251: soaked] wet *GaR*, *Palaemon* 253: That quivered beneath it.] In *Emory* (hardback) Warren adds a stanza break after this text. 254: As soft as a whisper, promises him the surrender.] As soft as a whisper, speaks. / Howard promises him the surrender. *Emory* (hardback) 254: surrender.] No stanza break after this text in *GaR*, *Palaemon*, or CJTS. A stanza break is added in pencil at this point in CJG. 255: And hearing his own words, he knew] Howard, hearing his own words, knew *Emory* (hardback) 256: swell] swell in *GaR*, *Palaemon*, CJTS (revised in pencil to CJ) 257: Miles laughed] After that, affability ruled the roost. / Miles laughed *GaR*, *Palaemon* 261: communiqué:] communique: *GaR*, *Palaemon* 264: To hell with] Fuck *GaR*, *Palaemon*, CJTS (revised in pencil to CJ) 264: up$_\wedge$ ...] up. ... *GaR*, *Palaemon* 264: 'Here I will die.'] "Here I will die." *GaR*, *Palaemon* 265: But did not. Lived on. In history.] Stanza missing in *GaR*, *Palaemon*, and CJTS (revised in pencil to CJ). 269: struck.] No line break after this text in *GaR* and *Palaemon*. 270: strike.] No stanza break after this text in *GaR* or *Palaemon*. 273: They'd go] Those who had borne them would go *Emory* (hardback) 273: Keogh] McKoegh *GaR*, *Palaemon*, CJTS (revised in pencil to CJ) 274: And eat] To eat *Emory* (hardback) 275: high land] the land *Emory* (hardback) 277: heart of man.] heart of a man. *Emory* (hardback) 278: another] some *GaR*, *Palaemon*, CJTS (revised in pencil to CJ) 283: distance,] miles, *GaR*, *Palaemon*, CJTS (revised in pencil to CJ) CJG reads as CJTS but is corrected again in black pen to CJ. 283: the noble disaster.] and the noble disaster. *GaR*, *Palaemon*, CJTS (revised in pencil to CJ) CJG reads as CJTS but is corrected again in black pen to CJ. 284: failing, Howard] failing according / To season and latitude, Howard *GaR*, *Palaemon* 285: that] that yet *Emory* (hardback) 286: black] brushed black *GaR*, *Palaemon*, CJTS (revised in pencil to CJ) 290: Chaos ... otter-skin tied.] Chaos of camp-site, the procession / Slowly ascends. Joseph / Not straight, sits his mount, / Head bowed, scalp lock with otter-skin tied. *Emory* (hardback) 292: with otter-skin tied.] tied with otter skin. *GaR*, *Palaemon*, CJTS (revised in pencil to CJ, but CJG reads as CJTS and is corrected again in pencil to CJ) No stanza break after this text in *GaR*, *Palaemon*, or CJTS (revised in blue pen to CJ). 293: now] here *GaR*, *Palaemon*, CJTS (revised in pencil to CJ) 293: a face] that face *Emory* (hardback) 296: The bullet scar is on his brow.] Line missing in *GaR*, *Palaemon*, and CJTS, but the following is added in pencil in CJTS: "A bullet scar is across his brow.". CJG is corrected in black pen in Warren's hand to CJG. 302: Then,] Then, suddenly, *GaR*, *Palaemon*, CJTS (revised in pencil to CJ) 304: suddenly sits,] sits, *GaR*, *Palaemon*, CJTS (revised in pencil to CJ) 305: a buckskinned] his buck-skinned *GaR*, *Palaemon*, a buck-skinned CJTS (revised in pencil on CJG to CJ) 307: thrusts] thrust *GaR*, *Palaemon*, CJTS (revised in pencil to CJ) 307: rifle,] ~. *GaR*, *Palaemon*, CJTS (revised in pencil to CJ) 308: is] was *GaR*, *Palaemon*, CJTS (revised in pencil to CJ) 310: Howard ... Indicates Miles.] Peremptory or contemptuous, Howard / Indicates Miles. *GaR*, *Palaemon*, CJTS (revised in pencil to CJ) 313: We do not know / What ambiguities throttle his heart.] Omitted in *Emory* (hardback) 314: throttle his heart.] Stanza break after this text in CJTS. CJG is corrected in pencil to CJ. 316: nakedness.] No stanza break after this text in *GaR*, *Palaemon*, or CJTS. CJG is corrected in pencil to CJ. 318: words, translated, are addressed] words are addressed *GaR*, *Palaemon* 319: Then Joseph drew his blanket over his head.] Line missing in *GaR*, *Palaemon*, and CJTS (revised in pencil to CJ).

516 **VII.** 1: Keogh] McKoegh *GaR*, *Palaemon*, CJTS (revised in pencil to CJ) 2: The taste was gray] Found the taste gray *GaR*, *Palaemon* 4: Before ice came, edges / Were streaked,] Before ice came, / It was streaked, *Emory* (hardback) 6: in its season came back, its wrath] in season came back, that heat *Emory* (hardback) 8: side$_\wedge$] ~, *Emory* (paperback) 10: drinking.] drink. *GaR*, *Palaemon*, CJTS (revised in pencil on CJG to CJ) 12: insects unremitting] unremitting, the insects *GaR*, *Palaemon*, CJTS (revised in pencil on CJG to CJ) 13: blood;] ~, *GaR*, *Palaemon* 14: Or the sound ... before the stroke.] Omitted in *Emory* (hardback). 17: word] promise *Emory* (hardback) 18: Among promised mountains] Among mountains *Emory* (hardback) 19: How could] Could *GaR*, *Palaemon*, CJTS (revised in pencil on CJG to CJ) 19: whom they] whom now they *GaR*, *Palaemon*, CJTS (revised in pencil on CJG to CJ) 21: dim,] ~? *Emory* (hardback) 22: merciless?] ~. *Emory* (hardback) 23: Did Joseph ... of course.] Stanza missing in *GaR* and *Palaemon*. 23: now ever] ever now *Emory* (hardback) 24: irony,] ~$_\wedge$ CJTS (revised in pencil to CJ) 28: die?] ~. CJTS (revised in pencil to CJ) 31: Tecumseh. William Tecumseh Sherman, of course.] Tecumseh, of course. CJTS (revised in pencil on CJG to CJ) 31: The Great Spirit Chief ... to my people.] Quotation missing in *GaR* and *Palaemon*. 33: And living,] But *GaR*, *Palaemon* 35: Again] Living again *GaR*, *Palaemon*, CJTS (revised in pencil to CJ) 37: gives.] No stanza break after this text in *GaR*, *Palaemon*, or CJTS, but there is a mark in blue pencil in CJTS which may be a correction. 38: spoke,] would speak, *Emory* (hardback) 40: with an uneasy conscience] out of what conscience *Emory* (hardback) 41: speak out] speak *Emory* (hardback) 45: The only staunch friend] The only friend *Emory* (hardback) 47: price of a star?] price of stars on his shoulder? *Emory* (hardback) 48: Joseph] him *GaR* 49: To fill the presidential ear with his old story?] To tell the presidential ear his old, old story? *GaR* 52: his profession,] all the tricks, *GaR*

57: white men had sometimes paid] white men, long back, had paid *Emory* (hardback) 60: woman,] squaw, *GaR*, *Palaemon*, CJTS (revised in pencil on CJG to CJ) 60: child's.] child. *GaR*, *Palaemon*, CJTS (revised in pencil to CJ) 61: In the ... were published—] In the words of old war-comrade Yellow Bull, / In a great magazine his words were published. *GaR*, *Palaemon*, Translated by old war-comrade Yellow Bull, / Joseph's words were in a magazine—his story, CJTS (revised in pencil to CJ) 63: suffering of,] suffering of‸ *Emory* (hardback) 65: Some] But some *Emory* (hardback)

518 **VIII.** 1: To the Northwest, but not Wallowa,] But to the Northwest, not Wallowa, *GaR*, *Palaemon*, To the Northwest, not Wallowa, CJTS (revised in pencil on CJG to CJ) 2: torment] torments *GaR*, *Palaemon* 3: But on a reservation in Washington,] On a reservation, *GaR*, *Palaemon* 8: white,] ~‸ *GaR*, *Palaemon*, CJTS (revised in pencil to CJ) 11: names left] names of some left *GaR*, *Palaemon*, CJTS (revised in pencil on CJG to CJ) 17: me,] for me, *GaR*, *Palaemon* 18: Sharps,] Spencer, *GaR*, *Palaemon* 19: leveled to] levelled with *GaR*, *Palaemon* 20: election. I] election, as I *GaR*, *Palaemon*, CJTS (revised in pencil on CJG to CJ) 20: squeezed trigger.] squeezed the trigger. *GaR*, *Palaemon* 23: Of the white half-men] Of those white men, those half-men *Emory* (hardback) 23: ground‸] ~, *GaR*, *Palaemon* 25: in] at *GaR*, *Palaemon*, CJTS (revised in pencil to CJ) 26: the far scout] our far scout. *Emory* (hardback) my far scout *Emory* (paperback) 29: wondered‸] ~, *GaR*, *Palaemon* 33: Might find ... of his loins.] *GaR* and *Palaemon* are substantially different:

Might give approval to some act of mine,
However slight. I sit, but all
I yearn for is that he thinks me a man
Worthy the work in dark of his loins.

33: Might find some worth in an act of mine,] Might find worth in some act of mine CJTS (revised in pencil on CJG to CJ) 34: However slight.] No stanza break or line break after this text in CJTS (revised in pencil to CJ) 48: and wise] and the wise *GaR*, *Palaemon* 51: ran,] ~‸ *GaR*, *Palaemon*, CJTS (revised in pencil to CJ) 58: night,] ~‸ *GaR*, *Palaemon*, CJTS (revised in pencil to CJ) 61: structure,] structure, the height. *GaR*, *Palaemon*, CJTS (revised in black pen on CJG to CJ) 63: by braids fading,] by his black braids now fading, *Emory* (hardback) 65: the thrust] the long thrust *GaR*, *Palaemon*, CJTS (revised in black pen on CJG to CJ) 70: mirror of Time] mirror Time *GaR*, *Palaemon* 77: name] named *GaR*, *Palaemon* 79: ever his subordinate] ever his *GaR*, *Palaemon*, ever subordinate *Emory* (hardback) 80: slime-green] the slime-green *GaR*, *Palaemon*, CJTS (revised in pencil on CJG to CJ) 82: skull-grinned] now skull-grinned *Emory* (hardback) 83: soft-handed] soft-palmed *GaR*, *Palaemon* 85: occasionally] to the last drop *GaR*, *Palaemon* 93: commemorate for the future] commemorate *Emory* (hardback) 94: wing] Wing *GaR*, *Palaemon* 94: 'Joseph, ... Olin L. Warner... '] This passage is doubly indented in *GaR* and *Palaemon*. 94: 'Joseph,] "Joseph, *GaR*, *Palaemon* 94: Perce] Percé *GaR*, *Palaemon* 94: mountains ...] mountains. ... *GaR*, *Palaemon* 94: 17-1/2] $17\frac{1}{2}$ *GaR*, *Palaemon* 94: Signed‸] ~: *GaR*, *Palaemon* 94: Warner‸ ... '] Warner. ... " *GaR*, *Palaemon* 94: American Sculpture Catalogue] American Sculpture: A Catalogue *GaR* 94: Art, page 42‸] Art (p. 42). *GaR*, *Palaemon*, CJTS Art, P. 42 CJG (but "master pages" are marked for revision, and "corrected master pages" read as CJ) 96: red man] redman *GaR*, *Palaemon* 103: yet-warm scalp,] yet-bloody scalp‸ *GaR*, *Palaemon*, scalp, yet bloody and warm, CJTS (revised in pencil to CJ) 105: red man] redman *GaR*, *Palaemon* 113: the bloody scalp] that bloody scalp *Emory* (hardback) 114: the dead] dead *GaR*, *Palaemon* 114: had once, in the White House,] once in the White House had, *GaR*, *Palaemon* 117: western politico, or such,] patriot shit *GaR*, *Palaemon*, patriot CJTS (revised in pencil to CJ) 119: control?] No stanza break or line break after this text in *GaR* or *Palaemon*. In CJTS there is a stanza break here, but the line straddles the stanza break. CJTS is corrected in pencil to CJ. 121: looked,] ~‸ *GaR*, *Palaemon* 121: as hoofs] as the hoofs *GaR*, *Palaemon*, CJTS (revised in pencil on CJG to CJ) 125: years‸] ~, *GaR*, *Palaemon* 126: In Washington, not the Land of the Winding Waters,] Line missing in *GaR* and *Palaemon.* 129: had gleamed] had once gleamed *GaR*, *Palaemon*, CJTS (revised in pencil on CJG to CJ) 131: twice] once *GaR*, *Palaemon*, CJTS (revised in pencil to CJ) 132: go to the Winding Waters.] go and look at the Winding Waters. *Emory* (hardback) 133: lay] now lay *GaR*, *Palaemon* 141: campfire, / Did Joseph] campfire did / Joseph *GaR*, *Palaemon* 148: lay the tall ghost.] Stanza break after this text in *Emory* (hardback) 152: hero's] warrior's *GaR*, *Palaemon* 154: Is] Was *GaR*, *Palaemon* 155: is] was *GaR*, *Palaemon* 158: Nimipu / Dug] people / Of In-an-toin-mu dug *GaR*, *Palaemon*, CJTS (revised in pencil to: "people/ Of Nimipu dug") CJG is corrected in pencil to CJ. 163: This] This much *GaR*, *Palaemon*

522 **IX.** 1: Airlines,] Air Lines, *GaR*, *Palaemon* 3: plains,] ~∧ *GaR*, *Palaemon* 4: wash or coulee] washes or coulees *GaR*, *Palaemon* 5: man,] or man, *GaR*, *Palaemon* 10: But solid,] Solid, *GaR*, *Palaemon* 12: a lacing] an edging *GaR*, *Palaemon* 13: lies] lay *GaR*, *Palaemon* 13: wait.] No line break or stanza break after this text in *GaR* or *Palaemon.* 14: Springs] Sprang *GaR*, *Palaemon* 15: flees] fled *GaR*, *Palaemon* 19: Onward,] We plunge on. *GaR*, *Palaemon* 20: We plunge,] Plunge on, *GaR*, *Palaemon* 21: one] our *GaR*, *Palaemon* 21: dot, ... outspread.] dot creeping slow / Across a large map outspread. *GaR*, *Palaemon* 23: outspread.] Stanza break after this text in *Emory* (hardback) 27: to rise, to heave, to crumple,] to heave, *GaR*, *Palaemon* 27: to heave,] heave, CJTS (revised in pencil to CJ) 29: lifting] mostly *GaR*, *Palaemon* 33: hump] ridge *GaR*, *Palaemon* 33: had once] once had *GaR*, *Palaemon*, CJTS (revised in pencil on CJG to CJ) 38: half-naked,] naked, *GaR*, *Palaemon*, CJTS (revised in pencil to CJ) 40: stands,] ~∧ *GaR*, *Palaemon*, CJTS (revised in pencil to CJ) 40: I will fight] I fight *GaR*, *Palaemon* 41: forever."] In *GaR*, *Palaemon*, and CJTS, the line straddles the stanza break that follows this text. CJTS is corrected in pencil to CJ. 48: who obediently died] and died *GaR*, *Palaemon*, obediently died CJTS (revised in pencil to CJ) 49: That final / Process] Their rotting— / That process *GaR*, *Palaemon* 51: at] by *GaR*, *Palaemon*, CJTS (revised in pencil to CJ) 52: at last had] at last *GaR*, *Palaemon* 53: That idiot phantasm] His idiot phantasm *Emory* (hardback) 54: shows here] shows, too, *GaR*, *Palaemon* 56: all the red] all red *GaR*, *Palaemon* 57: Had] Was *GaR*, *Palaemon* 59: So shells ... blue-bellies.] And shells spared the later / Spade-work from blue-bellies. *GaR*, *Palaemon* 60: Later some spade-work for blue-bellies.] Spade-work for blue-bellies later. CJTS (revised in pencil to: "Later spade-work for blue-bellies." CJG is corrected in pencil to CJ.) Later some spade-work. *Emory* (hardback) 63: rose,] roses, *GaR*, *Palaemon* 63: leaf,] ~. *Emory* (hardback) 64: Branches studded] Branches are studded *Emory* (hardback) 65: near-dry,] near dry, *GaR*, *Palaemon* 66: Joseph, / In the same season,] Joseph *GaR*, *Palaemon* 68: horse herd.] horse-herd. *GaR*, *Palaemon* (CJTS reads with CJ, but is corrected in pencil to: "horse flesh." CJG is corrected in black pen to CJ.) 71: spot] location *GaR*, *Palaemon*, CJTS (revised in pencil to CJ) 73: say] say south *GaR*, *Palaemon* 76: or what erosion has done.] or what years have left. *GaR*, *Palaemon* 79: In its passionate certainty?] In passionate certainty? *Emory* (hardback) 79: No, ... you see] Northward, / You see *GaR*, *Palaemon*, CJTS (revised in pencil to CJ) 80: Not the Cheyennes—to ruin surprise.] This line in pencil in CJTS. 80: Cheyennes] Cheyenne scouts CJTS (revised in pencil on CJG to CJ) 80: to ruin surprise.] to ruin his surprise. *Emory* (hardback) 80: surprise. / Northward, you] surprise. Northward, / You CJTS (revised in pencil on CJG to CJ) 82: his manic snatch] his snatch *Emory* (hardback) 83: plain-sweep,] plainsweep, *GaR*, *Palaemon* 85: Now, as you wander brown sage, you find] Now if you wander old sage you will find *GaR*, *Palaemon* 85: you find] you will find CJTS (revised in pencil on CJG to CJ) 87: of consequence.] of any consequence. *GaR*, *Palaemon* 89: guile] tricks *GaR*, *Palaemon* 91: war-chief, the cunning] war-chief and cunning *GaR*, *Palaemon*, war-chief, fox-cunning CJTS (revised in pencil to CJ) 93: in such weather.] "in such weather." *Emory* (hardback) 95: on snow,] on the snow, *GaR*, *Palaemon*, CJTS (revised in pencil to CJ) 97: friends∧] ~, CJTS (revised in pencil on CJG to CJ) 98: far∧] ~, *GaR*, *Palaemon* 101: To its blackness.] To keep blackness. *Emory* (hardback) 102: a picture there] a picture *GaR*, *Palaemon*, CJTS (revised in pencil on CJG to CJ) 102: in my head—] The line straddles the stanza break that follows this text in *GaR*, *Palaemon* and CJTS. CJTS

is corrected in pencil to CJ. 103: And] and *GaR*, *Palaemon* 106: In now hypothetical snow, / Marking the] Backward in that hypothetical / Snow marking the *GaR*, *Palaemon*, Approaching in that hypothetical / Snow, marking the CJTS (revised in pencil to: "In that hypothetical snow, / Marking the") CJG is corrected in pencil to CJ. It is possible, but not certain, that Warren intended to erase his cancellation of "that". 110: Outthrust,] Out-thrust, *GaR*, *Palaemon* 111: but / No sound hear.] but I / Hear no sound. *Emory* (hardback) 112: sound hear.] The line straddles the stanza break that follows this text in *GaR* and *Palaemon*. 113: I see] See *GaR Palaemon* 113: how many] what *GaR*, *Palaemon*, CJTS (revised in pencil on CJG to CJ) 114: seasons?—] ~∧— *GaR*, *Palaemon*, CJTS (revised in pencil on CJG to CJ) 119: that old] his old *Emory* (hardback) 124: Their own manhood. ... The end.] In *GaR* and *Palaemon* the text is substantially different:

Their own manhood. This, even though
He, standing there, might well, in midnight, have foreknown
The end.

125: He knew ... of things outside] CJTS is substantially different:

He knew, could see, beyond all,
Old eyes in which love and justice, in equal glitter,
And with no blink, strove toward him.
And he—he strove to think of things outside

CJTS is corrected in pencil to:

He knew, could see, afar, beyond all,
Those eyes in which love and justice, in equal glitter,
And with no blink, strove always toward him.
And he—he strove to think of things outside

CJG is corrected to CJ with a typewritten insert. 131: truth unnamable.] nameless Truth. CJTS (revised in pencil to: "truth CJTS." The "master pages" are corrected in pencil to CJ.) 132: Standing there, he might well,] Even though he standing there, might well, CJTS (CJG is corrected in a typewritten insert to CJ.) 133: such] this CJTS (revised in pencil on CJG to CJ) 134: The end.] No stanza break or line break after this text in *GaR* or *Palaemon*. 136: manhood,] manhood might, *GaR*, *Palaemon*, CJTS (revised in pencil on CJG to CJ) 137: in the glow] in glow *GaR*, *Palaemon* 137: would shine.] shine. *GaR*, *Palaemon*, CJTS (revised in pencil on CJG to CJ) 137: shine.] The line straddles the stanza break that follows this text in *GaR* and *Palaemon*. 142: Then thought] I thought *GaR*, *Palaemon* 142: the mayor] some mayor *Emory* (hardback) 142: mayor / Of Spokane—whoever] mayor of / Spokane—whoever *GaR*, *Palaemon*, mayor of Spokane— / Whoever CJTS (revised in pencil to CJ) 149: prism] glass *GaR Palaemon* 150: Triumphant.] The line straddles the stanza break that follows this text in *GaR*, *Palaemon*, and CJTS (revised in pencil to CJ). 159: canyon,] canyon now, *GaR*, *Palaemon*, CJTS (revised in pencil on CJG to CJ) 160: head now up,] head up, *GaR*, *Palaemon*, even head up, CJTS (revised in pencil on CJG to CJ) 161: his] this *GaR*, *Palaemon* 162: His own heart] His heart *GaR*, *Palaemon* 162: look∧] ~, *GaR*, *Palaemon* 164: of fathers] of the fathers *GaR*, *Palaemon* 165: I turned ... on the way.] Stanza missing in *GaR* and *Palaemon*.

Altitudes and Extensions
1980–1984

Altitudes and Extensions is the new portion of Warren's last volume of selected poems, *New and Selected Poems 1923–1985* (which will be referred to here as SP85). In addition to the poems of *Altitudes and Extensions* SP85 included the following selections. From *Rumor Verified* it included "Chthonian Revelation: A Myth," "Looking Northward,

Aegeanward: Nestlings on Seacliff," "Going West," "Rumor Verified," "Mountain Mystery," "Vermont Ballad: Change of Season," "Dead Horse in Field," "The Corner of the Eye," "What Voice at Moth-Hour," "Another Dimension," "English Cocker: Old and Blind," "Have You Ever Eaten Stars?" "Afterward," and "Fear and Trembling." From *Being Here* it included "When Life Begins," "Grackles, Goodbye," "Youthful Truth-Seeker, Half-Naked, at Night, Running Down Beach South of San Francisco," "Why Have I Wandered the Asphalt of Midnight?" "Sila," "Vision," "Cocktail Party," "The Cross," "Antinomy: Time and What Happened," and "Safe in Shade." From *Now and Then* it included "American Portrait: Old Style," "Amazing Grace in the Back Country," "Boy Wandering in Simms' Valley," "Red-Tail Hawk and Pyre of Youth," "Star-Fall," "Youth Stares at Minoan Sunset," "Ah, Anima!" "Unless," "The Mission," "How to Tell a Love Story," "Little Black Heart of the Telephone," and "Heart of Autumn." From *Can I See Arcturus From Where I Stand?* it included "A Way to Love God," "Evening Hawk," "Paradox," "Midnight Outcry," and "Old Nigger on One-Mule Cart Encountered Late at Night When Driving Home from Party in the Back Country." Since SP85 deletes so many of the poems Warren included in SP75, it is easier to work back volume by volume listing what Warren included than it is to list what he excluded from SP75. From *Or Else* SP85 included "The Nature of a Mirror," "Natural History," "Blow, West Wind," "I Am Dreaming of a White Christmas: The Natural History of a Vision," "Rattlesnake Country," "Homage to Theodore Dreiser: Psychological Profile," "Stargazing," "Little Boy and Lost Shoe," "There's a Grandfather's Clock in the Hall," "Reading Late at Night, Thermometer Falling," "Folly on Royal Street Before the Raw Face of God," and "Birth of Love." (Notice that SP85, unlike SP75, makes no attempt to treat *Or Else* as a sequence, and even breaks up the sub-sequence "Homage to Theodore Dreiser.") SP85 includes all of *Audubon: A Vision.* From *Incarnations* SP85 preserves in no case the sense that any of the poems are in a sequence, and includes only "Where the Slow Fig's Purple Sloth," "Riddle in the Garden," "The Red Mullet," "Masts at Dawn," and "The Leaf." From *Tale of Time* SP85 includes the "Tale of Time" sequence (including "I. What Happened," "II. The Mad Druggist," "III. Answer Yes or No," "IV. The Interim," "V. What Were You Thinking, Dear Mother," and "VI. Insomnia"), "Elijah on Mount Carmel," and "Love: Two Vignettes" (including "1. Mediterranean Beach, Day After Storm," and "2. Deciduous Spring."—Notice that SP85 does not follow a consistent policy about whether to use Roman or Arabic numerals in the titles of poems in sequences or sub-sequences). From *You, Emperors, and Others* SP85 includes only "Tiberius on Capri," "Mortmain," (of which it includes only "After Night Flight Son Reaches Bedside of Already Unconscious Father, Whose Right Hand Lifts in a Spasmodic Gesture, as Though Trying To Make Contact: 1955"), and "Debate: Question, Quarry, Dream." From *Promises* SP85 includes the "To a Little Girl, One Year Old, in a Ruined Fortress" sequence (but includes only "I. Sirocco" and "II. The Child Next Door"), the "Infant Boy at Midcentury" sequence (including "1. When the Century Dragged" and "2. Brightness of Distance"), "Man in Moonlight," "Dragon Country: To Jacob Boehme," "Lullaby: Smile in Sleep," "Lullaby: A Motion Like Sleep," "School Lesson Based on Word of Tragic Death of Entire Gillum Family," and "Founding Fathers, Early-Nineteenth-Century Style, Southeast U.S.A." (Notice that this is not the order in which these poems appear in *Promises.*) From SP43, SP85 includes "The Ballad of Billie Potts," "Original Sin: A Short Story," "Eidolon," "Revelation," "Bearded Oaks," "Picnic Remembered," "The Garden," "The Return: An Elegy," the "Kentucky Mountain Farm" sequence (including "I. Rebuke of the Rocks," "II. At the Hour of the Breaking of the Rocks," "III. History Among the Rocks," "IV. Watershed," and "V. The Return"—and "Watershed" for the first time since SP43), "Pondy Woods," and "To a Face in a Crowd."

MSS drafts for SP85, in which the tentative title of the section of new poems is "Directions and Altitudes," indicate that Warren intended SP85 to be even more selective than it turned out to be. It would have included no poem written earlier than "The Ballad of Billie Potts" (of 1943), for instance. As late as the galleys it did not include "Pondy Woods," "To a Face in a Crowd," or any of "Kentucky Mountain Farm" other than "History Among the Rocks." The earliest draft of the table of contents describes a volume that would have been quite different from SP85, including several unfamiliar poems entitled "Boot Tracks," "Back-Country Vermont," "Who?," "Magic," "Whip-poor-will," and "With or Without Compass?" It would also have included the uncollected "Problem of Autobiography: Vague Recollection or Dream," "Winter Dreams," "Was It One of the 'Long Hunters' Who Discovered Boone at Sunset?," "Instant on Crowded Street," "Institute of the Impossible" (which was a part of the volume as late as the bound "Advance uncorrected proofs," and appeared after "Sunset" there—Warren finally deleted it on SP85G), "Old Love" (under the title "The Tulip Tree is Rare Now"), "You Sort Old Letters," and "Aging Painter Sits Where Great Tower Heaves Down Midnight." Some poems appear under unfamiliar titles. "Muted Music," for instance, is "The Sound Truth Makes" (and also "Sunday Afternoon in Summer in Old Barn"), "Whatever You Now Are," is "Self," "Small Eternity," is "Fragments to Make Eternity," and "Mortal Limit" is "Was it a 'Rough-Leg'?". Warren did considerable rearranging of the draft contents before he settled upon an arrangement that pleased him, and as late as the advance uncorrected proofs the volume included "With or Without Compass?" immediately before "Last Night Train." (Warren deleted it on SP85G.)

The setting typescript of the *Altitudes and Extensions* section of SP85 is a single-spaced typescript. The pages are folded across the middle, as for mailing, and are numbered in pencil, as would accord with Warren's usual practice of assembling volumes from poems separately typed. In addition at the upper left corner of each poem appears an annotation in the following form: "A-5 – 2 pages." This indicates that the poem in question (in the example, "The First Time") is the fifth poem in the first section of the book. Often the typed annotation is revised in pencil. ("The First Time," for instance, started out as b-2.) Other than noting here that this demonstrates that the arrangement of poems in *Altitudes and Extensions* was not set until a very late stage of the manuscript, I will not further note these annotations.

The setting typescript of the rest of SP85 consists of photocopy from earlier volumes, except that all of the poems from volumes before SP75 are taken from SP75. "Watershed" in "Kentucky Mountain Farm" was not taken from SP75, of course, and the typescript breaks off at the end of "History Among the Rocks" (with "The Return" from "Kentucky Mountain Farm" canceled at the bottom of the page). Because the revisions for SP85 are vexed, I have noted the cases where the revisions were made on SP85TS. Since most of the revisions for SP85 were not made on SP85TS, and since each page of SP85TS except for the *Altitudes and Extensions* section has "Erskine" written in black ink at the top of the page, the cutting and pasting may have been done at Random House, with Warren doing the bulk of the revising on galleys. I have examined both slightly-differing sets of galley proofs, page proofs, revised page proofs, repros, blues, and the author's bound advance uncorrected proofs.

Warren's marked-up copy, now in the Special Collections Department of the Emory University Library, is marked "Corrected Copy" but is not dated. I quote Warren's annotations from that volume by permission of the Emory University Library. This copy is referred to in the notes as *Emory*, when annotations to *Altitudes and Extensions* are in question, and as *Emory copy of SP85* when annotations to other parts of SP85 are in question.

Rosanna Warren discovered among her mother's papers after her death another copy of SP85 that had been marked up by her father. I have transcribed the annotations Warren made to that copy and forwarded it to the Robert Penn Warren collection at Western Kentucky University. Because there are other copies of SP85 that belonged to Warren in that collection, I will refer to that copy here as *Clark* (for Eleanor Clark). Warren listed the pages he corrected on the half-title page of *Clark*, with a note: "N.B. These pages in need of correction are *only* for *Altitudes and Extensions*." I take this to mean that Warren was well aware of the errors in other parts of the book (as for instance the errors in "The Ballad of Billie Potts" and "Old Nigger on One-Mule Car Encountered Late at Night When Driving Home from Party in the Back Country") but did not choose to correct them in *Clark.* For the most part the annotations in *Clark* seem to be revisions rather than corrections (for instance, in one place he proposed and then erased an alteration), so I have not adopted them except where they are backed up by evidence from the typescripts and drafts. The revisions in *Clark* do not correspond to those in *Emory* or to those in *Helsinki.* Even in the one place in *Clark* where Warren clearly was correcting an error ("nost" for "nose" in "Doubleness in Time"), he did not correct that error in *Emory.*

SP85 must be distinguished from the Eurographica *New and Selected Poems* (Helsinki: Eurographica, 1985), referred to hereafter as *Helsinki.* Although *Helsinki* bears the copyright date of 1985, it did not in fact appear until 1987. There are no new poems in *Helsinki,* but Warren did prepare a fresh typescript for it, and most of its poems are extensively revised. Indeed, he typed new versions of all of the poems for this volume himself, then sent the typescript to Louise Webb, his typist, to prepare a cleaner copy for Eurographica's use (I have examined both typescripts). Unlike most of Warren's Selected volumes, the poems in *Helsinki* appear in more or less chronological order, with a few significant variations. *Helsinki* includes the following poems, in this order: the "Kentucky Mountain Farm" sequence (including "Rebuke of the Rocks" and "At the Hour of the Breaking of the Rocks"), "Pondy Woods," "Bearded Oaks," "Tiberius on Capri, Autumn 1939," "Folly on Royal Street, New Orleans, Before the Raw Face of God," "Rattlesnake Country," "Midnight Outcry," "Evening Hawk," "Heart of Autumn," "The Little Black Heart of the Telephone," "Unless," "Why Have I Wandered the Asphalt of Midnight?" "Fear and Trembling," "Vision," "Looking Northward, Aegeanward: Nestlings on Sea-Cliff," "Antimony: [sic] Time and Identity," "Another Dimension," "Sunset," "Hope," "Youthful Picnic Long Ago: Sad Ballad on Guitar," "Delusion?—No!" "The Place," "Rumor at Twilight," "It is Not Dead: The Great Smooth Boulder," "Mortal Limit," "Question at Cliff-thrust," "Picnic of Old Friends," "Muted Music," "Far West Once," "Why You Climbed Up," "Immortality Over the Western Dakotas," "Caribou as Viewed from Air," and "Three Darknesses."

The two typescripts of *Helsinki* in the Beinecke Library—Warren's typing and Mrs. Webb's typing—have the poems in a different order, but there is no particular pattern in either case, and they seem, as in Warren's usual practice, to be sheafs of independent poems which he intends to put in order at a later time. epigraph: Will ye not now after that life is descended down to you, will not you ascend up to it and live?] Will ye not after that life is descended down to you, will you not ascend up to it and live. SP85TS (revised on SP85G to SP85)

I.

529 **Three Darknesses** Text: SP85. Variants: *New Yorker*, 7 Feb. 1983, pp. 40–41, *Helsinki.* In *Helsinki* the section numbers are Arabic numerals in parentheses.

529 **I.** 1: here to trace,] here, *NY* 2: begin,] $\sim_\wedge$ *NY* 6: as rhythmic as / A pile-driver] rhythmic / As a pile-driver *Helsinki* 7: pile-driver] pile driver *NY* 7: right-left, right-left] right, left, right, left *NY* 8: Slugged] Slugs *Helsinki* 9: Heavy, bolted, barred, must have been] Heavy, battered, bolted, must be *Helsinki* 11: near, far,] far, *Helsinki* 12: wandered,] $\sim_\wedge$ *NY*, wander, *Helsinki* 13: the air] air *Helsinki* 14: children,] little children, *Helsinki* 15: continues.] continued. *NY* 15: You think of the / Great paws like iron on iron.] You think of the great paws / Like iron on iron. *Helsinki* 19: bear$_\wedge$] $\sim$— *Helsinki* 19: The bear / Was trying to enter into the darkness of wisdom.] Omitted in *NY*. 20: Was trying to enter into the darkness of wisdom.] Is he trying to enter into the darkness of wisdom? *Helsinki*

529 **II.** 1: Up Black Snake ... we see] Up Black Moccasin River, at anchor in black tropical water, we see *NY* 2: That black tropical water,] That tropical blackness of water, *Helsinki* 3: cranky,] crazy, *Helsinki* 4: God's more cynical ... carmine of sunset. He] God's more / Cynical improvisations, black / Against carmine of sunset. He *Helsinki* 4: cynical / Improvisations, black] cynical improvisations— / Black *NY* 6: and thus / The jungle] and / Thus the jungle *Helsinki* 7: on a milk-pale ... lies looking] on a milk-pale / Path of sky toward the sea. Nothing / Human is visible. On deck each of us lies looking *Helsinki* 7: milk-pale path of sky ... white helmet mystically swathed,] *NY* is

substantially different:

milk-pale path of sky
Toward the sea. Nothing human is visible.
Each of us lies looking seaward. Ice
Melts in our glasses. We are ashamed of conversation.
Asia is far away. The grave of my father is far away.
The radio is not on. The host rises silently, is gone.
Later we see him, white helmet in netting mystically swathed,

9: Seaward. Ice melts in our glasses. We seem ashamed] Seaward. The river gleams blackly west. / Ice melts in our glasses. We seem ashamed *Helsinki* 10: The radio ... Our host] The radio is / Silent. The grave of my father is far away. Our host *Helsinki* 12: Rises silently, is gone. Later we see him,] Rises silently. Is gone. Later, we see him, *Helsinki* 15: There moss hangs.] Moss hangs there. *NY* 18: side lagoon,] side-logoon, *Helsinki* 18: darkness of moss] dark moss *NY* 19: a snake makes ... water. You] a snake makes as it slides off a bough— / The slop, the slight swish, the blackness of water. You *NY* 20: slop,] plop, *Helsinki* 21: The blackness of water. You / Wonder what your host thinks about] Curled blackness of water. You wonder what / Your host, in his blackness, is thinking about *Helsinki* 22: host thinks] host now thinks *NY* 23: drifts on the lagoon of midnight. / Though it is far from midnight.] drifts on the / Lagoon of his midnight. *Helsinki* 23: of midnight.] like midnight. *NY* 24: Though it is far ... you know,] Upon his return, he will, you know, *NY* 26: deck-teak] deck teak *NY* 27: Had] Has *NY*, Has now *Helsinki*

530 **III.** 1: nurse] hospital nurse *Helsinki* 1: still here.] here. *NY* 3: here∧] ∼, *Helsinki* 4: darkness.] darkness of switch-click. *NY* 4: No matter. / A] No / Matter. A *NY* 5: nuisance,] ∼∧ *NY*, nuisance, sure— *Helsinki* 6: said that.] said. *NY* 6: A dress rehearsal, ... a dry run.] *Helsinki* is substantially different:

A dress rehearsal
For the real show? You ask yourself that. Later.
Ten years? Fifteen years? Tomorrow
Only a dry run.

7: yourself,] ∼∧ SP85TS, SP85G (added in pencil on second set) 8: thing. Later.] thing, some morning. *NY* 10: A.M.] A.M. *Helsinki* 11: To] For *Helsinki* 11: western.] Western. *NY*, *Helsinki* 13: virtue,] ∼∧ *NY*, *Helsinki* 14: Of moonlit] Of the moonlit *NY*, SP85TS (revised in black pen to SP85) 14: desert. ... Black] Of moonlit desert. Black *Helsinki* 17: remnants of forgotten] remnants of / Forgotten *Helsinki* 17: nightmares,] nightmare, *Helsinki* 19: triumph. ... They float] triumph. Far / Beyond all the world, the mountains lift. Snow / Peaks float into moonlight. They float *Helsinki* 19: sure that virtue] sure virtue *NY* 22: unnamable] unnameable *NY* 23: Loves] Must love *NY* 23: Loves the world. For what it is.] Loves the world for what it is. *Helsinki*

530 **Mortal Limit** Text: SP85. Variants: *Sewanee Review*, 91 (Fall 1983) p. 566, *Helsinki*. 5: were the Tetons. Snow-peaks] tower the Tetons. Those peaks *Helsinki* 5: Snow-peaks] Those snow-peaks *SR*, SP85TS (revised on SP85G to SP85) 6: dark] stark *Helsinki* 7: see∧] ∼? *SR*, SP85TS (revised in pencil to SP85), *Helsinki* 8: New ranges] Will new ranges *Helsinki* 8: mark] mask *Helsinki* 9: having tasted ... vision before] having tasted atmosphere's thinness at the mortal height, / Will that speck hang motionless in dying vision before *Helsinki* 11: limit,] ∼∧ *Helsinki* 12: that will restore] to restore *Helsinki* 14: Items,] ∼∧ *SR* 14: dream] dreams *Helsinki*

531 **Immortality Over the Dakotas** Text: SP85. Variants: *Grand Street*, 2 (Summer 1983), p. 74, *Helsinki* (as "Immortality Over the Western Dakotas"). 2: loll∧] ∼, *Grand Street* 3: two-inch-thick] two-inch thick SP85TS (revised in pencil to SP85), *Helsinki* 5: darkness] dark *Helsinki* 8: into] down into *Helsinki* 9: far, far down] far, far, down *Grand Street*, SP85TS (revised in pencil to SP85), *Helsinki* 10: glowworm] glow-worm *Grand Street*, SP85TS (revised in pencil to SP85), *Helsinki* 12: not been]

not yet been *Grand Street* 15: shotgun] shot-gun *Grand Street*, SP85TS (revised in pencil to SP85), *Helsinki* 16: elevator] elevators *Grand Street*, *Helsinki* 18: Most likely the mercury stood at a hundred and one.] The mercury, most likely, at a hundred and one. *Helsinki* 19: through glass,] through-glass, SP85TS (revised in pencil to SP85) 20: the dirty] a dirty *Grand Street* 21: earflaps] ear-flaps *Grand Street*, SP85TS (revised in pencil to SP85), *Helsinki* 22: just can't] can't *Helsinki* 25: at what she's knitting.] at her knitting. *Helsinki* 28: So stares] So he stares *Grand Street*

532 **Caribou** Text: SP85. Variants: *New Yorker*, 30 Nov. 1981, p. 46 (as "Caribou Near Arctic"), *We Alaskans* (Anchorage *Daily News* magazine), Feb. 20 1982, pp. H8–9, *Helsinki* (as "Caribou As Viewed From Air"). 1: Far, far southward,] Now southward, behind us, *NY*, *We Alaskans* 1: southward,] $\sim_\wedge$ *Helsinki* 2: As snow of no blemish, but whiter than ice yet sharing] As snow with no blemish but sharing *NY*, *We Alaskans* 2: yet] but *NY*, *Helsinki*, *We Alaskans* 3: blue-tinged, tangential] blue tangential *NY*, *We Alaskans* 3: moonlight,] $\sim_\wedge$ *NY*, *We Alaskans* 4: unshadowed] shadowless *NY*, *We Alaskans* 4: vastness$_\wedge$] $\sim$, SP85TS (revised in pencil to SP85) 4: northward.] ever northward. *Helsinki* 5: Such] That *NY*, What *We Alaskans* 5: once / Have been a lake, now,] once have been a lake. / Now, *NY*, *We Alaskans* 7: shift] now drift *NY*, *We Alaskans* 8: distance. They grow clear, / As binoculars find] distance; grow / Clear as binoculars find *Helsinki* 8: As they move on the verge] On the verge *NY*, *We Alaskans* 8: of moon-shaven] of the moon-shaven *NY*, *We Alaskans* 8: grow clear,] grow$_\wedge$ *NY*, *We Alaskans* 8: clear,] $\sim_\wedge$ SP85TS (revised on SP85G to SP85) 9: hairline] hair-line SP85TS (revised in pencil to SP85), *Helsinki* 10: the purity] the white purity *NY*, *We Alaskans* 11: each / Slowly detached] each slowly / Detached *NY*, *We Alaskans* 12: anonymity / Of forest, each hulk] anonymity of forest, each hulk *NY*, *We Alaskans* 20: could, inwardly,] inwardly, could$_\wedge$ *NY*, *We Alaskans* 21: antlers,] $\sim_\wedge$ SP85TS (revised in pencil to SP85) 22: Blunted and awkward,] Spoon-awkward, *NY*, *We Alaskans* 23: to / What mission] to what/ Mission *NY*, *We Alaskans* 25: it] this *NY*, *We Alaskans* 27: as pure / As a] as pure as / A *NY*, *We Alaskans* 28: Their destiny / Must resemble] What they know must / Resemble *NY*, *We Alaskans* 29: happiness$_\wedge$] $\sim$, *NY* 30: that] its *NY*, *We Alaskans* 32: He glances ... back to me.] *NY* and *We Alaskans* are considerably different:

He
Glances at mysterious dials. I
Drink coffee. The binoculars
Courteously come back to me.

35: I have lost the spot. I find only blankness.] The line straddles the stanza break that follows this text. 35: only blankness.] There is neither a line nor a stanza break after this text in *NY* or *We Alaskans*. 35: But] There is a stanza break after this text in *Helsinki*.

533 **The First Time** Text: SP85. 5: Pointed.] He pointed *Clark* 17: now.] here. SP85TS (revised on SP85G to SP85) 24: fool young he-elk] fool SP85TS (revised on SP85G to SP85) 32: sustain,] $\sim_\wedge$ SP85TS (revised on SP85G to SP85) 32: emptiness,] $\sim_\wedge$ SP85TS (revised on SP85G to SP85)

534 **Minnesota Recollection** Text: SP85. Variant: *Southern Review*, ns 19 (Spring 1983), pp. 345–47. 2: windowpane,] window pane, SP85TS (revised in pencil to SP85) 2: and in the old kitchen, ... a dream of dying,] daylight already / A dream dying in the old kitchen, *SoR* 7: in his musical ... took all] in his / Never unlearned Swedish, said, "When it took all *SoR* 10: Old] Ole *SoR* 12: her] you *SoR*, SP85TS (revised on SP85G to SP85) 12: dead."] In SP85TS the quotation continues, ending after the next sentence. SP85G is revised to SP85. 15: Pickaxes] Pick-axes *SoR*, SP85TS (revised in pencil to SP85), 16: Old] Ole *SoR* 16: so:] $\sim$, *SoR* 18: lit,] $\sim_\wedge$ *SoR* 19: Just step] Have just stepped *SoR* 20: See] Sees *SoR* 20: ponder] pondered *SoR* 20: half-hour,] half hour, *SoR* 25: *ax-butt*] *axe-butt SoR* 26: *trough.*] *tank. SoR* 27: wood,] wood on, *SoR* 28: *tick*-and-*tock.*] *tick-tock. SoR* 29: And] But *SoR* 30: lantern on] lantern hanging on *SoR* 31: *an old*] *the ole SoR* 31: Gertie thought.] thought. *SoR*, SP85TS (revised on

SP85G to SP85) 33: Then Gertie gone, soon back,] Gert disappeared. Came back, *SoR* 34: an] the *SoR* 34: lantern, lighted] lantern *SoR* 35: but it dead] dead *SoR*, but dead SP85TS (revised on SP85G to SP85) 37: word∧] ~, SP85TS (revised in pencil to SP85) 38: just] was *SoR* 39: But felt / It in] They felt it / In *SoR* 40: The] Their *SoR*, SP85TS (revised on SP85G to SP85) 41: Ran] Was *SoR* 42: both lanterns,] both, *SoR*, both of them SP85TS (revised on SP85G to SP85) SP85G has a penciled annotation: "otherwise not clear". 43: ran, somebody with the new one.] ran. *SoR* 47: are lanterns in a world so wide!] is a pair of lanterns in the world so dark? *SoR* 48: something's] something *SoR* 49: window now?] window? *SoR* 51: or / Simply calling as] or simply calling / As *SoR* 53: And suddenly another lantern's gone. It's dry.] Line omitted in *SoR*. A page turn obscures whether there is a stanza break or not at this point in *SoR*. 55: the world is wide.] *SoR* adds a line after this text: They're scattered so, a call was almost lost. *SoR* 57: To hold ... so goddamned sweet?] These lines are substantially different in *SoR*:

To hold the human hope together, though some
Fell in slick blackness. It felt like a gift. Will a dream
Wake them to their despair? What if you wake?
Tomorrow's like today. And was
Today so Goddam sweet?

61: goddamned] god-damned SP85TS (revised in pencil to SP85) 65: chain's about to] chain to *SoR* 68: Then] But *SoR* 68: "The window!" ... picked up.] It said—or seemed to say— / "The window!" So voices again picked up *SoR* 68: said,] ~∧ SP85TS (revised in pencil to SP85) 70: length] piece *SoR* 71: hope.] hope, a link of chain. *SoR*, ~, SP85TS hope, SP85G (revised on SP85G second set to SP85) 72: house∧] ~, *SoR* 74: Till Gertie screams, ... as before.] These two lines omitted in *SoR*. 74: screams, tries] screamed and tried SP85TS (revised on SP85G to SP85) 75: all sit] each sits SP85TS (revised on SP85G to SP85) 76: But he—he] He *SoR* 77: ***] ***** *SoR* 78: prairie dawn ... voices, maybe.] prairie dawn, blizzard now past, / They found him. Snagged on a barbed wire fence / That he'd followed the wrong way. *SoR*

536 **Arizona Midnight** Text: SP85. Variant: *New England Review and Bread Loaf Quarterly*, (Spring 1984), p. 417. 2: blankness] blackness *New England Quarterly* 4: Protected by the looped rampart of anti-rattler horsehair rope,] Line omitted in *New England Quarterly*. 4: horsehair] horse-hair SP85TS (revised in pencil to SP85) 14: indication of dawn, not yet ready for the scream] indication yet of dawn that will utter its scream *New England Quarterly*

536 **Far West Once** Text: SP85. Variants: *New Yorker*, 9 April 1984, p. 44, *Helsinki*. 2: time] moment *NY* 3: When only in memory] In memory when only *NY* 7: passage∧] ~, *NY* 8: Waiting, waiting the trigger-touch] As though waiting, waiting, the trigger-flick *NY* 9: darkness—] ~, *NY*, SP85TS (revised on SP85G to SP85), *Helsinki* 14: trail,] ~∧ *NY* 15: again∧] ~, *Helsinki* 16: rattler's fat belly] rattler's belly *NY* 18: vibrate∧] ~, *Helsinki* 18: To vibrate mica-bright, in the sun's beam;] To vibrate loose dust in the bright sun; *NY* 19: over-thrust,] overthrust, *NY*, over-trust, *Helsinki* 20: glimpse] blaze *Helsinki* 21: in] at *Helsinki* 21: burned] shone *NY* 22: Coal-bright∧] ~, *Helsinki* 22: Coal-bright as they swung,] Their coal-bright glitter as they turned, *NY* 23: Detached, contemptuous,] Contemptuous, detached, *NY* 24: pine woods'] pinewoods' *NY* 28: under,] ~— *NY*, *Helsinki* 32: waters; then] waters. Then *NY* 35: years since,] after years, *NY* 40: fir,] spruce, *NY* 41: far, how far—] far off, how far? *NY* 42: or waking] And I have waked *NY* 42: stars,] ~∧ *NY* 43: Have heard ... threading starlight,] To such redemptive music threading / Starlight, distance to distance, *NY* 45: Able yet,] And able yet, *NY*, And found myself able yet, *Helsinki* 46: years, / To touch again the heart,] years, to touch, / Again, the heart, *NY* 47: To touch again the heart,] To feel my heart touched again, *Helsinki* 47: at a dawn] at the dawn *NY* 48: Of dew-bright Edenic promise, with,] Of dew-bright Eden's promise—with, *NY* 49: birdsong.] bird-song. *Helsinki*

II.

538 **Rumor at Twilight** Text: SP85. Variants: *New Yorker,* 19 July 1982, p. 32, *Helsinki*. 3: horizon,] ~∧ *NY* 4: blackout,] black-out, SP85TS (revised in pencil to SP85), *Helsinki* 4: cave,] ~∧ *NY* 5: Dark fruit,] Back on your land, like dark fruit, *NY* 7: there again.] there. As you never do. *NY* 7: ever felt, / Between] ever / Felt, between *NY* 8: texture] the texture *NY* 10: under the maples,] under maples, *NY* 15: Their prickling glows] That prickling glow *NY* 16: head first] head *NY* 18: smile?] The stanza break after this text is missing in SP85G, but is restored on SP85G second set. 20: elder] hedge *NY* 21: the massiveness of moonrise] massive moonrise *NY* 22: lone] long *NY* 22: lane,] ~∧ *NY* 23: and squeeze, significance from, / What life is, whatever it is. Now] and squeeze significance / From whatever life is—whatever. *NY* 23: squeeze,] ~∧ SP85TS (revised on SP85G to SP85), *Helsinki* 25: High above the maples the moon presides.] High over your maples, the moon now presides. *NY* 27: It is time] Time *Helsinki*

538 **Old Dog Dead** Text: SP85. Variant: *Nation*, 3 Dec. 1983, pp. 572–73 (as "Old Dog"). SP85TS is a taped-in photocopy of *Nation*.

538 **1.** 15: at last / Even in] even / In *Clark*

539 **2.** 1: pullover] pull-over *Nation*, SP85TS (revised in pencil to SP85) 2: camp] a camp *Clark* (but erased). (I include this to make it clear that some of the annotations in *Clark* are probably revisions, not corrections, despite how Warren described them on the half-title page. This looks to me like a revision that Warren thought better of.) 4: anteroom.] ante-room. *Nation*, SP85TS (revised in pencil to SP85)

539 **3.** 4: Black] Blackness *Nation*, SP85TS (revised on SP85G to SP85)

540 **4.** 2: across / Sands endless.] across the / Endless sand. *Nation*, SP85TS (revised in black pen to SP85)

540 **5.**

540 **6.** 2: off, long later,] off, *Nation*, SP85TS (revised in black pen to SP85) 3: the] a *Nation*, SP85TS (revised in black pen to SP85)

541 **Hope** Text: SP85. Variants: *Yale Review*, 73 (Spring 1984), p. 430, *Helsinki*. In the manuscript tentative table of contents for SP85 in the Beinecke Library, Warren lists this poem as appearing in the December 6 [1983?] *Atlanta Journal*, but I have been unable to find it there. There is no credit to the *Atlanta Journal* on the acknowledgements page of SP85. 1: In the orchidaceous light of evening] In the tangled bloom of light at evening *Helsinki* 1: evening∧] ~, *YR* 2: Watch how, from the lowest hedge-leaf, creeps,] Watch from the lowest hedge-leaf creep, SP85TS (revised on SP85G to SP85), Watch from the lowest hedge-leaf how creeps, *Helsinki* SP85TS has a penciled annotation here: " 'purpling shadow' is the subject of verb 'creeps' " 2: how,] ~∧ *YR* 2: hedge-leaf,] hedgeleaf∧ *YR* 2: creeps,] creep, *YR* 3: Grass blade] From grass blade *Helsinki* 3: to blade,] to grass blade, *YR*, *Helsinki* 3: shadow.] shadows. *YR* 3: It spreads] They spread *YR* 4: Its] In *YR* 5: that, westward,] that westward *Helsinki* 6: disaster of the day.] disaster of day. *YR* 8: sifts∧] ~, *YR* 10: Of] Old SP85G (This is clearly a printer's error. Warren re-inserted "of" at the end of the previous line, not noticing the error in "Old" in this line. On SP85G second set he revised the reading to SP85.) 10: gold intrusive through the blackening] gold, intrusive but sparse, through blackening *YR* 11: heighten the last glory beyond by] heighten last glory by *YR* 13: placed] pressed *YR* 15: That] Such *YR*, The SP85TS (revised on SP85G to SP85), This *Helsinki* 17: While cinders in the west die,] While, westward, cinders fade, *YR* 19: bosom∧] ~, *YR* 20: intrusion] intrusions *YR* 20: or lie, or both.] or lie. *YR*, SP85TS (revised on SP85G to SP85), *Helsinki* 22: not even a last bird twitters,] even a last thrush note dies, *YR* 24: in all fullness,] in fulness, *YR*, in all fulness SP85TS (revised in pencil to SP85) 25: the world, the heart,] the world, the roofs, the heart, *YR*

541 **Why You Climbed Up** Text: SP85. Variants: *Georgia Review*, 37 (Fall 1983), p. 565, *Sewanee Review*, 91 (Fall 1983), pp. 567–68, *Helsinki*. Warren's copy of *GaR* in the Beinecke Library shows several revisions, but they are not adopted in SP85. 1: the lichen] lichen Warren's copy of *GaR* 2: where] and *SR* 2: the rusty] rusty Warren's copy of *GaR* 2: needle] needles *GaR*, *SR* 3: Falls] Fall *GaR*, *SR* 4: Against] For *SR* 5: But

come not] But not *SR* 9: half-open,] half open, *GaR* 9: The beak, half-open, in still heat gasp, see] Line omitted in *SR*. 11: Where or why, ... sweat and pant,] Where or why, you wonder—/ Wandering in sweat and pant *SR* 15: things,] ∼∧ *SR* 15: you call] which you call *SR*, Warren's copy of *GaR* 16: The past, all things, great and small, you call] Line omitted in *Helsinki*. 16: all] and all *SR* 16: things,] ∼∧ *SR* 16: you call] which you call *SR*, Warren's copy of *GaR* 17: Self,] ∼∧ *GaR* (revised to SP85 on Warren's copy of *GaR*), self, *SR* 17: remember] remembering *GaR*, and remembering Warren's copy of *GaR* 18: Pacific] ocean *GaR*, *SR*, *Helsinki* 18: swam west,] westward swam, *GaR* 20: head∧] ∼, *SR* 21: then.] there. *SR* 23: You can't remember now, ... To follow, stumbling, down.] *SR* is substantially different:

You can't remember now,
As in the future you may not remember
How on this high ridge,
Seeing the sun blaze toward the higher horizon westward,
You turned and, bumbling, hunted
For some old logging road, or such,
To follow, stumbling, down.

23: now,] ∼— *Helsinki* 24: do not guess ... blaze down] do not know how later, on a high ridge, / Seeing sun blaze down *GaR* (Warren's copy of *GaR* corrects "how later," to "how,—now later,"), Any more than years from now / You might imagine how / Long back, on this high ridge, / Seeing the sun blaze down *Helsinki* 25: once—now—on] once, SP85TS (revised on SP85G to SP85) 27: You turned,] You'll turn, *GaR* 27: turned,] ∼∧ *Helsinki* 27: bumbled] bumble *GaR* 29: Then all begins again. And you are you.] Then all will begin again. And you be you. *Helsinki* 29: begins] began *SR*

542 **Literal Dream** Text: SP85. Variant: *New Yorker*, 2 Jan. 1984 (as "Literal Dream (Twenty Years After Reading 'Tess ...' and Without Ever Having Seen the Movie)"). 3: saw∧] ∼, *NY* 4: room,] ∼∧ *NY* 4: chilly∧] ∼, *NY* 8: needles. She / So sat,] needles. Or / Did I hear that noise? Anyway, she / So sat, *NY* 13: rocked∧] ∼, *NY* 14: the book] the old book *NY* 17: when] where *NY* 20: But∧] ∼, *NY* 23: ceiling spot.] spot on the ceiling. *NY* 25: whitewash,] white-wash, SP85TS (revised in pencil to SP85) 34: now take] take now *NY* 36: To touch] To touch with? To touch *NY* 39: then,] ∼∧ *NY* 41: Suddenly∧] ∼, *NY* 47: *O*.] O. *NY* 49: not there.] No stanza break after this text in *NY*. 50: of] on *NY* 54: up-whirled,] upwhirled, *NY* 57: I woke at the call of nature.] I woke. *NY* 61: plop there.] plop out there. *NY*

544 **After the Dinner Party** Text: SP85. 10: has quoted] quotes SP85TS (revised on SP85G to SP85) 11: one∧] ∼, SP85TS (revised on SP85G to SP85) 11: grin,] ∼∧ SP85TS (revised on SP85G to SP85) 12: unworded] wordless SP85TS (revised on SP85G second set to SP85) 19: crumbling of ash] ash crumbling SP85TS (revised on SP85G to SP85)

544 **Doubleness in Time** Text: SP85. Variant: *New Yorker*, 24 Oct. 1983, p. 46 (as "Marble"). 1: Doubleness] Paradox *NY* 1: Time] *time NY* 2: bull-snake] bull snake *NY* 3: like *Now*.] like *now*. *NY* 4: *Then*.] *then*. *NY* 7: *Now*.] *now*. *NY* 11: The face] Face *NY* 16: love.] *love*. *NY* 21: Infinity.] *infinity*. *NY* 22: Time.] *time*. *NY* 24: Out the] The *NY* 26: Your heart.] Heart. *NY* 28: He nods. Slowly. Slowly.] *NY* adds a line after this line: He stares into my father's eyes. 32: waiting∧] ∼, *NY* 32: upturned] up-turned SP85TS (revised in pencil to SP85) 32: face.] ∼, *NY* 33: Lips are laid] Lips laid *NY* 35: *Now*.] *now*. *NY* 37: youngest last.] youngest, of course, last. *NY* 42: is lost.] lost. *NY* 43: "Oh, I'm by myself," his voice cries out.] "Oh, I'm all alone," his voice calls. / "I'm by myself." / I heard him *NY* 52: *Then?*] *then? NY* 53: *Now*.] *now*, / The picture is so funny. *NY* 56: Nods.] Slowly nods. *NY* 57: Soundlessly,] Soundless, *NY* 57: ax-butt] axe-butt *NY*, SP85TS (revised in pencil to SP85) 58: sudden] suddenly *NY*, SP85TS (revised on SP85G to SP85) 59: Rigid. Sidewise.] Sidewise. Rigid. *NY* 61: last,] ∼∧ *NY* 62: out-thrust. Eyes] outthrust, eyes *NY* 67: It is not *Then*.] It was, but is not *then*. *NY* 68: *Now*.] *now*. *NY* 69: Truth] truth *NY*

69: true.] *true. NY* 70: It is autumn, ... People live there.] *NY* is substantially different:

It is autumn *now* as *then,* gravel underfoot,
And the stars have begun
Their wintry tingle.
The moon is full and white but westering
Near black roofs
Of the little city. People live here.

76: moon.] moon. *Now. NY* 77: And wonder] I wonder *NY* 78: nor] or *NY* 79: nor] or *NY* 83: *Precious Guilt.*] *precious guilt. NY*

547 **Snowfall** Text: SP85. Variants: *Atlantic Monthly*, March 1983, pp. 86–87, Broadside (Charlestown, WV: Mountain State Press, 1984). (I have examined a photocopy of no. 36, which has some handwritten corrections, apparently in Warren's hand.) 3: my] the *Atlantic* 6: In the world what music may be that we cannot hear?] What music exists in the world that we cannot hear? *Atlantic, Mountain State* 8: to spring] new sprig *Atlantic, Mountain State* 9: immortality;] imbecility; *Mountain State* 10: redwings,] red-wings SP85TS (revised in pencil to SP85), *Mountain State* 12: away$_\wedge$] ~, *Atlantic* 13: you,] ~$_\wedge$ *Atlantic, Mountain State* 17: slow was one afternoon's summer] long was one afternoon's slow summer *Atlantic* 21: voicelessness] voiceless emptiness *Atlantic* 21: then] now *Atlantic* 22: But later, remember / The hand you held in late shadow of beeches,] Remember the hand / You later held in the shadow of beeches *Atlantic*, Remember the hand / You later held in the shadow of beeches, *Mountain State* 24: bird-call] bird call SP85TS (revised in pencil to SP85) 25: goodbye] good-bye *Atlantic* 25: station] railroad *Atlantic, Mountain State* 26: *Goodbye*] *Good-bye Atlantic* 26: slips] slid *Atlantic, Mountain State* 26: weed-tangle,] wee-tangle, *Mountain State* (revised to SP85) 29: that] which *Mountain State* 31: pulp seeking / The throat's] pulp / Seek your throat's *Atlantic* 32: will walk] walk *Atlantic, Mountain State* 33: Dreaming that you, years back,] And dream that years back you, *Atlantic, Mountain State* 34: Meanwhile, far] Far *Atlantic, Mountain State* 34: north$_\wedge$] ~, *Atlantic* 34: Vermont$_\wedge$] ~, *Atlantic, Mountain State* 35: When] And when *Atlantic, Mountain State* 37: now can.] can now. *Atlantic*, SP85TS (revised on SP85G to SP85), *Mountain State* 39: now there settles] settles *Atlantic* there settles *Mountain State* 39: the wind] and wind *Atlantic, Mountain State*, wind *Clark* 42: sand, snowflakes / Die on the bay-swirl of small whitecaps.] sand, / Snowflakes hiss on the tangle of whitecaps. *Atlantic* sand, / Snowflakes die on the bay-swirl of whitecaps. *Mountain State* 43: small whitecaps.] whitecaps. SP85TS (revised on SP85G to SP85) 44: And salt-crusted sand, under bootsole, creaks.] This stanza omitted in *Atlantic*, SP85TS, and *Mountain State*, but it is written in, in pencil, in the bound "Advance uncorrected proofs". It is missing, however, as late as the page proofs, where it is typed in. 46: But now, again hillward, / Comes silence] But / Again the silence *Atlantic* 46: But now, again] But, now again *Mountain State* 47: wheeling of squadrons,] wheeling squadrons, *Atlantic, Mountain State* (but *Mountain State* is revised to: wheeling squadrons$_\wedge$) 48: That tramp] Tramp *Atlantic, Mountain State* 48: out last] out the last *Atlantic, Mountain State* 49: in the darkness] in darkness *Atlantic* 50: is] seems *Atlantic*

III.

549 **New Dawn** Text: SP85. Variants: In *Hiroshima* (New York: Limited Editions Club, 1983) (as "New Dawn: Hiroshima"), *New Yorker*, 14 Nov. 1983, pp. 46–48. In *Hiroshima, NY*, and SP85 the section titles are in Arabic numerals, but I have changed them to Roman numerals for the sake of consistency with other sequences. *Hiroshima* also lacks the dedication. SP85TS is a photocopy of *Hiroshima* with the title and dedication typed in.

549 **I. Explosion: Sequence and Simultaneity** In *NY* all of the "Augusts" except the first, are replaced by ditto marks, the day of the month is not repeated except where it changes, and all the years, except the first, are replaced by ditto marks.

549 **II. Goodbye to Tinian** 2: six packs] six-packs *NY* 3: condoms,] ~$_\wedge$ *NY* 23: asphalt, the tarmac,] the tarmac, *Hiroshima*, *NY*, SP85TS (revised in typing to "the asphalt, the tarmac," then revised on SP85G to SP85)

550 **III. Take-off: Tinian Island** 5: pale green] pale-green *NY* 6: cyanide,] ~. *NY* 8: heavy-caliber] heavy-calibre *Hiroshima*, *NY*, SP85TS (revised in pencil to SP85) 18: off] off on *NY* 22: All throttles] Throttle *Emory* 22: full,] full forward, *NY* 25: the runway] and runway *Hiroshima*, *NY*, SP85TS (revised on SP85G to SP85) 27: Black] The black *Hiroshima*, *NY*, SP85TS (revised on SP85G to SP85) 32: nerves,] ~$_\wedge$ *NY* 37: white,] ~$_\wedge$ *NY*

551 **IV. Mystic Name** 2: *Enola Gay,*] "Enola Gay," *NY* 7: two] the two *NY* 7: B-29's] B-29s *NY* 8: fly with him as] fly as *Clark* 11: To announce innocently] Innocently to announce *Hiroshima*, *NY*, SPS85TS (revised on SP85G to SP85) 14: Twenty-eight inches] Over two feet *NY* 14: four and a half] five *NY* two and a half *Hiroshima*, SP85TS (revised in typing to SP85) 25: sections,] ~— *NY*

552 **V. When?** 3: After:] ~$_\wedge$ *NY* 8: frees] frees from SP85TS (revised in pencil to SP85) 11: reinserted,] inserted, *NY*, re-inserted, SP85TS (revised in pencil to SP85) 12: reinserted,] re-inserted *Hiroshima*, SP85TS (revised in pencil to SP85) 14: reinstalled] re-installed *Hiroshima*, SP85TS (revised in pencil to SP85) 15: reinstalled] re-installed *Hiroshima*, SP85TS (revised in pencil to SP85) 22: A.M.] ~, *NY*

553 **VI. Iwo Jima** 4: *Enola Gay*] "Enola Gay" *NY* 5: the two B-29's$_\wedge$] two B-29s, *NY* 14: a.m.] a.m., *NY* 14: Time, the / All Clear signal] Time, the all-clear / Signal *NY*, Time, / All Clear *Hiroshima*

553 **VII. Self and Non-Self** 8: Shut / Your own eyes,] Shut your own / Eyes, *NY*

553 **VIII. Dawn**

554 **IX. The Approach**

554 **X. What *That* Is** title: What *That* Is] What That is, SP85, What *That* Is *Hiroshima*, *NY* (*NY* underlines "that" rather than italicizing it.) 1: part now,] now part, *Clark* 3: opening] offers itself, *NY* 6: Bridge$_\wedge$] ~, *NY* 6: time$_\wedge$] ~, *NY* 10: activated:] ~, *NY* 12: Plunge—] ~, *NY* 16: Above ground,] Aboveground, *NY*

555 **XI. Like Lead** 2: report: "A taste like lead."] report a taste "like lead." *NY*

555 **XII. Manic Atmosphere**

555 **XIII. Triumphal Beauty**

556 **XIV. Home** 4: The music,] Then music, *NY*

556 **XV. Sleep** 3: do not] No stanza break after this text in *Hiroshima*, *NY*, or SP85TS. SP85G is revised to SP85.

IV.

557 **The Distance Between: Picnic of Old Friends** Text: SP85. Variants: *Sewanee Review*, 90 (Fall 1982), pp. 497–98 (as "The Distance Between"), *Helsinki* (as "Picnic of Old Friends"). The title in SP85TS is "Picnic of Old Friends" and is not revised until the page proofs. 1: and nothing much] with innocent nothings *SR* 6: over.] eaten. *SR* 8: more aimless] aimless *SR* 9: episodes,] memories, *SR* 10: all the] and the *SR* 13: beeches, then pines.] beeches and pines. *SR*, SP85TS, SP85G (revised to SP85 on page proofs) 15: where$_\wedge$] ~, *SR*, *Helsinki* 15: noble, great cliffs ... Ten feet] noble, / Great cliffs from ferns rose, and no / Bird sang. Ten feet *Helsinki* 19: Of a sudden, ... at her.] This stanza omitted in *SR*, SP85TS, SP85G and *Helsinki*. It was typed in on the page proofs on Warren's typewriter. 21: No resistance:] No protest, no resistance: *SR*, No protest, resistance none: SP85TS, SP85G (revised to SP85 on page proofs), *Helsinki* 21: penetration.] No stanza break after this text in *SR*. *SR* adds four lines after this text, but a page turn obscures whether they end with a stanza break:

At division, no moan, no gasp at heave: nor at breast
Torn bare. Only when, hair seized, the white throat
Was drawn back for
A last swollen thrust. Then stillness like death.

In SP85TS there are three lines added here, which end with a stanza break:

At division no moan, no gasp at heave: nor at breast torn bare.
Only when, hair seized, the white throat was drawn back for
A last swollen thrust. Then stillness of death.

These lines are canceled in pencil in SP85TS. 22: fern, and wept. / He stood by a beech,] fern / And wept. He / Stood by a beech, *SR*, fern, / And wept. He, by a last beech, *Helsinki* 23: beech, some] beech, / Some *Helsinki* 23: head down.] stood, head down. *Helsinki* 24: wandered,] ~. *SR* 25: all strange, infinite] all seemed strange. And strange *SR* 26: between them.] between them. No word to say. *SR* 27: last,] ~∧ *SR*, *Helsinki* 27: straggled, straggling] straggled. *SR* 28: Toward song in the distance.] They moved toward song in the distance. *SR* 29: They tried to sing, too.] This text omitted in *SR*.

558 **True Love** Text: SP85. Variants: *Love: Four Versions* (Winston-Salem, NC: Palaemon Press, 1981), *Southern Review*, ns 19 (Spring 1983), pp. 343–45, *New Statesman,* 26 Oct. 1984, p. 32. 1: In silence the heart raves. It utters words] Let the heart rave. In silence. With words *SoR*, Let the heart rave. But in silence. It utters words *Love: Four Versions* 2: that] which *Love: Four Versions* 3: red-headed,] ~∧ SP85TS (revised in pencil to SP85) 4: Freckled.] Well freckled. *Love: Four Versions* 5: boy,] ~∧ *SoR*, *Love: Four Versions* 7: nothing like / Beauty. It] nothing / Like beauty. It *Love: Four Versions* 8: heart.] blood. *Love: Four Versions* 9: Thickens] Purifies *SoR*, *Love: Four Versions* 9: your blood.] the heart. *Love: Four Versions* 9: It] But it *SoR*, *Love: Four Versions* 11: pole,] ~∧ *SoR*, *Love: Four Versions* 12: saw] even looked at *Love: Four Versions* 12: me.] ~, *SoR*, *Love: Four Versions* 13: How] For how *SoR*, *Love: Four Versions* 13: world with that brightness?] world? *SoR*, *Love: Four Versions* 14: She] She even *Love: Four Versions* 15: thought] though *Love: Four Versions* 17: slick-faced.] ~, *SoR*, *Love: Four Versions* 18: barbershop.] barber shop. *SoR*, *Love: Four Versions* 19: is] was *Love: Four Versions* 20: Whatever he was he] Whatever that was, he *SoR*, *Love: Four Versions* 21: big white farmhouse] big house *SoR*, great brick farmhouse *Love: Four Versions* 21: maples] oaks *Love: Four Versions* 21: twenty-five] twenty *Love: Four Versions* 21: years.] ~∧ *SoR* 24: good,] ~∧ *Love: Four Versions* 25: married,] ~∧ *SoR* 26: tail coat,] tail-coat, *Love: Four Versions* 27: There were // Engraved] There // Were engraved *Love: Four Versions* 30: would cry] cried *SoR*, *Love: Four Versions* 31: That last word] The word *SoR*, *Love: Four Versions*, That word *New Statesman*, SP85TS (revised on SP85G to SP85) 33: drifted off.] disappeared. *SoR*, *Love: Four Versions* 33: shiny boots] shiny riding boots *Love: Four Versions* 36: called] named *Love: Four Versions* 36: didn't even know she] didn't know that she *SoR*, didn't know she even *Love: Four Versions*

559 **Last Walk of Season** Text: SP85. Variant: *Love: Four Versions* (Winston-Salem, NC: Palaemon Press, 1981). 1: time,] ~∧ *Love: Four Versions*, SP85TS (revised in pencil to SP85) 1: this∧] ~, *Love: Four Versions*, SP85TS (revised in pencil to SP85) 2: Any year to come . . . Dams and traps,] *Love: Four Versions* is substantially different:

Any other year, we climb, in the westward hour,
The mountain trail to see last light.
Now no clouds in the washed evening lour,
Though under drum-tight roof, while mouse-tooth of Time all night
Gnawed, we heard the season's first rain doing duty. Dams and traps,

9: the old logging] logging *Love: Four Versions* 10: do not ask] No line break after this text in *Love: Four Versions*. 11: that music bears.] bears that music. *Love: Four Versions* 15: Ah, the heart leaps] Yes, who grieves *Love: Four Versions* 16: That soon . . . of our joy?] The rest of the stanza is substantially different in *Love: Four Versions*:

That soon all earth is gold, gold birch, gold beech! Ah, what delight!
Later, nothing but black conifers clamber
White snow-blaze of snow up ridge to crag.
Can it be that the world's empty being is but the word
That speaks the mysterious meaning that is our joy?

24: moraine-dammed,] moraine-damned, *Love: Four Versions* 26: Ghostly,] Spectrally, *Love: Four Versions* 27: exist,] $\sim_\wedge$ *Love: Four Versions* 28: We are thinking of happiness.] Are we thinking of happiness? *Love: Four Versions*

V.

560 **Old-Time Childhood in Kentucky** Text: SP85. 27: Pharaoh's] Pharoah's SP85TS (revised in pencil to SP85) 33: what] What SP85TS (revised in pencil to SP85) 43: seemed,] $\sim_\wedge$ SP85TS (revised in red pencil to SP85)

561 **Covered Bridge** Text: SP85. Variant: *Southern Review*, ns 19 (Spring 1983), pp. 29–31 (as "Old Covered Bridge"). SP85TS is also entitled "Old Covered Bridge" but is revised in pencil to SP85. 21: you would] might you *SoR* 22: boards$_\wedge$] $\sim$, *SoR* 26: And you would sleep—who now do not sleep] And you, a boy, would sleep. Who now, no boy, do not sleep *SoR* 30: now lift up] lift up now *SoR* 31: hand—scarcely] hand, scarcely *SoR*, hand scarcely SP85TS (revised on SP85G to SP85) 31: gloom.] *SoR* adds a line after this text: It hangs there motionless in what benediction, or doom.

562 **Re-interment: Recollection of a Grandfather** Text: SP85. Variant: *Atlantic Monthly*, Feb. 1985, p. 48. 1: all the] all through the *Atlantic* 3: and / Miles away] and miles / Away *Atlantic* 4: carried it / In] carried / It in *Atlantic* 5: and smiled. It was] in secret caressed it, / And smiled. It was *Atlantic* 7: itself part] itself a part *Atlantic* 8: remember a place] remember / A place *Atlantic* 9: presence,] being, *Atlantic* 10: But not alone, ... to get out?] These lines are substantially different in *Atlantic*:

But not alone, snow locked from the world in my head
As I lie stiff in my sleepless bed!
Is one of the strange noises
Trapped in my skull only
The lonesome fingers scrabbling to get out?

14: He knows] For he knows *Atlantic* 15: More lonely than ever he must feel with the new, strange voices.] How lonely each night he must feel with newer, stranger voices. *Atlantic* 16: I hear in dream ... from my sight.] This stanza is substantially different in *Atlantic*:

In dream I try to identify his tone
Caught in the insane colloquy and wrangling
About what was true or not true, done or not done,
But I can't place his voice in the tussling and tangling,
And certainly not when the weeping starts, mad laughter,
Or the *zip* and *whish* which like bat wings in dark air—
All locked in the something dome my shoulders bear.
But sometimes just silence comes, and a dreamy twilight.
I see his lips, soundless, move, old hands stretched to me there.
Then his face fades from my sight.

28: Then] Yes, *Atlantic* 30: To get out] Get out *Atlantic* 31: Aware of ... three-score years ago.] These lines are substantially different in *Atlantic*:

Aware of what life's obligation is, or what life's all about.
I feel edges sharper each year dig at my skull.
Or is it only a dream? Then in daylight too comes dream
As I stand at the mirror and watch hair grow thin and pate gleam,
I stand there and strain to hear words, but the voice is too low,
And there's nothing to do but feel my heart full
Of recollection of more than seventy years ago.

37: three-score] three score SP85TS (revised in pencil to SP85) 38: no such] no *Atlantic* 39: lingo and at dinner] lingo, or at dinner *Atlantic* 40: and Bloody] and the Bloody *Atlantic* 41: Or the notion ... disgrace.] And the use of a word like *honor* as no comic disgrace, / Or the notion a man's word should equal his bond. SP85TS (revised on SP85G to SP85) 41: Or the notion a man's word should equal his bond,] Line omitted in *Atlantic*. 42: And the use of a word like *honor* as no comic disgrace.] Or the use of words like *honor* without shame. *Atlantic* 43: our last] that last *Atlantic* 44: not feel] not again feel *Atlantic* 44: contempt,] ~∧ *Atlantic* 45: left,] ~∧ *Atlantic* 45: after-while,] endless after-while∧ *Atlantic* 46: or recognize his kind. Certainly not his face.] or know the lineaments of his face. *Atlantic*

563 **Last Meeting** Text: SP85. Variant: *American Poetry Review*, 13 (July–Aug. 1984), p. 22. 2: folks] folk *APR* 3: market town] market-town *APR* 4: traden,] graden∧ *APR* 5: hung out] they hung out *Clark* 6: poolroom] pool room *APR*, SP85TS (revised in pencil to SP85) 6: barbershop] barber shop *APR*, SP85TS (revised in pencil to SP85) 8: with the sweat] with sweat *APR* 10: bricks,] brick, *APR* 13: flash,] ~— *APR* 13: and] but *APR* 20: kiss∧] ~, *APR* 23: I'll] I *APR* 24: did. She ran her hands through thinning] did, and hands ran through the thinning *APR* 25: fahr-red,] ~∧ *APR* 26: And ran her fingers some more.] She said, and ran her fingers. *APR* 27: sandy color] gone sandy-color *APR* 28: arms∧] ~, *APR* 29: crooned,] ~∧ *APR* 29: said,] ~: *APR*, SP85TS (revised in pencil to SP85) 30: 'member me] 'membersme *APR* 30: in the wide world] wide in the world *APR* 31: say∧] ~: *APR* ~, SP85TS (revised in pencil to SP85) 34: Tears] The tear *APR*, The tears SP85TS (revised on SP85G to SP85) 36: Said,] ~: *APR*, SP85TS (revised in pencil to SP85) 36: Chile, yore Ma's] Yore Ma *APR* 37: fer] for *APR* 38: us∧] ~, *APR* 40: That] And that *APR* 40: last time] last *APR* 44: Next time I'll promise adequate time.] Next time, by God, I'll take adequate time. *APR* 46: miles),] ~)∧ SP85TS (revised on SP85G to SP85) 47: fruit jar] fruit-jar *APR* 49: It's nigh] Now *APR*

VI.

565 **Muted Music** Text: SP85. Variants: *Georgia Review*, 37 (Summer 1983), p. 247, *Georgia Review*, 40 (Fall 1986), p. 818, *Helsinki*. 5: barn-shâde,] barn-depth, *GaR83*, *GaR86* 7: And muted] Muted *GaR83*, *GaR86* 7: was all] is all *GaR83*, *GaR86* 9: barn-height—which is dark] barn-height, a region dim *GaR83*, *GaR86* 20: *what, which.*] *what∧ which. GaR83*, *GaR86* 21: bumbler,] ~∧ *GaR83*, *GaR86* 21: high∧] ~, *GaR83*, *GaR86* 22: that truth can make,] truth makes, *GaR83*, *GaR86* 25: long years,] years, *GaR83*, *GaR86* 28: has taught] could teach *GaR83*, *GaR86*

566 **The Whole Question** Text: SP85. Variant: *American Poetry Review*, 11 (Nov.–Dec. 1982), p. 47. 1: rethink] re-think SP85TS (revised in pencil to SP85) 3: midwife] the midwife *APR* 8: Paul] —was it Calvin?— *APR* 16: And] Or *APR* 20: infinite] inward *APR* 20: skull; or lonely,] skull, or lonely, lonely *APR* 24: wet] first *APR* 27: yet find] find *APR*, SP85TS (revised on SP85G to SP85) 27: one] way *APR*

566 **Old Photograph of the Future** Text: SP85. Variant: *Encounter*, 64 (Feb. 1985), p. 23. 1: center] centre *Encounter* 2: doubt,] ~∧ SP85TS (revised on SP85G to SP85) 5: center] centre *Encounter* 6: the woman] a woman *Encounter*, a woman, SP85TS (revised in pencil to SP85) 6: who,] ~∧ SP85TS (revised in pencil to SP85)

567 **Why Boy Came to Lonely Place** Text: SP85. Variant: *New England Review and Bread Loaf Quarterly*, 5:1–2 (Autumn/Winter 1982) p. 163. 4: Not] No *New England Review* 8: believe in] know *New England Review* 10: Age thirteen,] Thirteen, *New England Review* 12: crumbling,] ~∧ *New England Review* 15: heed] need *New England Review* 21: you come] you now come *Clark*

568 **Platonic Lassitude** Text: SP85. 18: collage of a child] collage by a child *Clark*

568 **Seasons** Text: SP85. Variants: *Georgia Review*, 37 (Summer 1983), pp. 750–51, *Georgia Review*, 40 (Fall 1986), pp. 816–17.

568 **I. Downwardness** 1: out-thrust] outthrust *GaR83*, *GaR86* 2: black,] ~∧ *GaR83*, *GaR86*, SP85TS (revised in pencil to SP85) 5: out-thrust] outthrust *GaR83*, *GaR86* 10: But,] ~∧ *GaR83*, *GaR86* 15: personal] deep personal *GaR83*, *GaR86*

569 **II. Interlude of Summer** 3: heave] rise *GaR83*, *GaR86* 6: yet unseen] yet-unseen *GaR86* 8: hotchpotch] hotch-potch *GaR83*, *GaR86*, SP85TS (revised in pencil to SP85) 10: from behind] up from beyond *GaR83*, *GaR86* 11: last and majestic] majestic *GaR83*, *GaR86* 12: today] the day *GaR83*, *GaR86* 13: later and later∧] later and later, *GaR83*, *GaR86* 14: blankly] vacantly *GaR83 GaR86* 19: grape-arbor] grape arbor

GaR83, *GaR86* 22: challenge? But your own health] challenge you? Your health *GaR83*, *GaR86* 22: good.] In SP85 one might think that the line is broken into two half-lines after this word, but closer inspection reveals that there is merely a line bend after this word. 24: weekend] week-end SP85TS (revised in pencil to SP85)

570 **The Place** Text: SP85. Variants: *New Yorker*, 25 July 1983, p. 26, *Helsinki*. 1: green] the green *Helsinki* 4: upturned] uplifted *Helsinki* 8: Bleeds on stone.] The line straddles the stanza break that follows this text. In *Helsinki* there is no line straddle here, although there is a stanza break; what is the second half-line in the other versions is set as a separate line. 8: This ... of self.] This is the hour of the self's uncertainty / Of self. *Helsinki* 18: But tell me:] The line straddles the stanza break that follows this text. In *Helsinki* there is no line straddle here, and this line is the first line of the following stanza, not the last line of this one. In *Helsinki* what is the second half-line in other versions is set as a separate line. 18: had you ever forgotten] did you ever forget *Helsinki* 19: And what there passed? And forgotten] And therefore forgot *Helsinki* 20: may lurk in irony? ... all too possible.] *Helsinki* is substantially different:

            may first lurk in irony? Or have you forgotten
How you, once alone at 3 A.M. in a dark piazza, as the
Cathedral clock announced the fact to the tiles of the
Old city, remembered the
Impossible lie, told long before, elsewhere?
But a lie, you now realized, that had proved all too possible.

21: piazza,] *piazza, Clark* (There is a marginal note here in *Clark*: "*underscore word–* Italian.) 21: piazza, ... to old tiles] piazza, at 3 A.M., as the cathedral clock / Announced to old tiles *NY* 26: this is] this *Helsinki* 27: minor] a minor *Helsinki* 29: distantly,] distinctly, *Helsinki* 29: bird-call] birdcall *NY* 32: stone,] $\sim_\wedge$ *NY* 33: fern fronds,] ferns *Helsinki* 33: fronds,] $\sim_\wedge$ *NY*, SP85TS (revised in pencil to SP85) 34: to find you.] to find you. Then stars. *Helsinki* 36: interstices] the interstices *Helsinki* 37: enameled tin. ... difficult knowledge.] *Helsinki* is substantially different:

                    enameled tin. Nothing
Astounds the stars. They have long lived.
And you are not the first to come
To such a place, seeking the most difficult knowledge.

37: enameled] enamelled *NY* 37: astounds] can astound *NY*

571 **First Moment of Autumn Recognized** Text: SP85. Variant: *Yale Review*, 73 (Spring 1984), p. 429. 7: blessèd,] $\sim_\wedge$ SP85TS (revised in pencil to SP85) 8: means time,] means Time, *YR* 9: Only the dream, untimed, between] Or part thereof, only / The dream, untimed, between *YR* 14: purer / Than air.] purer than air. *YR* 16: your] you *YR*

571 **Paradigm of Seasons** Text: SP85. Variants: *Ploughshares*, 9:2–3 (1983) pp. 11–12, *London Magazine*, vol. 24, no. 7 (Oct. 1984), pp. 39–40 (as "Paradigm of Seasons in Vermont"). 3: cloud-scut and scud,] cloud- scud and scut, *Ploughshares* (The space after "cloud-" in *Ploughshares* is meant to indicate that the prefix "cloud" applies to both "scud" and "scut.") 4: winter, its waiting bulk.] winter's waiting bulk. *London Magazine* 4: come scouting.] flanking. *Ploughshares* 5: then winter's] the winter's *Ploughshares* 5: road.] red. *London Magazine* 6: have] have an *Clark* 9: apple bough] apple-bough *Ploughshares* 9: to offer blossom,] to offer *Ploughshares*, *London Magazine*, SP85TS (revised on SP85G to SP85) 16: of moonlight] of the moonlight *Ploughshares*, *London Magazine*, SP85TS (revised on SP85G to SP85) 18: can] could *London Magazine* 19: marijuana] marajuna *London Magazine*, SP85TS (revised in pencil to SP85) 20: Two fingers penetrate a vagina.] The line straddles the stanza break that follows this text. In *Ploughshares* the second half-line is indented, but not enough to be flush with the end of the first half-line. In *London Magazine* the line is indented, but too much to be flush with the end of the first half-line. 22: mailbox] mail box *Ploughshares*, *London Magazine*, SP85TS (revised in pencil to SP85) 22: aging] ageing *London Magazine* 27: splendor]

splendour *London Magazine* 29: saints] peasantry *Ploughshares* 32: Their houses] The house *Ploughshares, London Magazine,* SP85TS (revised on SP85G to SP85) 33: mountains,] mountain$_{\wedge}$ *Ploughshares* 34: Of the authoritative rifle.] The line straddles the stanza break that follows this text. In *Ploughshares* there is neither a line break nor a stanza break after this text. In *London Magazine* the line straddles the stanza break, but the second part is indented too far to be flush with the end of the first half-line.

572 **If Snakes Were Blue** Text: SP85. Variants: *Atlantic Monthly,* Oct. 1982, p. 46, *London Magazine,* vol. 24, no. 7 (Oct. 1984), pp. 41-42. 1: blue,] $\sim_{\wedge}$ *Atlantic, London Magazine,* SP85TS (revised in pencil to SP85) 6: minutes, minutes, could never] minutes could never, never, *Atlantic* 13: a thicket] thickets *Atlantic* 16: ambiguous moment] ambiguousness *Atlantic* 18: give] make *Atlantic* 19: back.] $\sim_{\wedge}$ *Atlantic, London Magazine,* SP85TS (revised on SP85G to SP85) 20: They had] That *London Magazine, Atlantic,* SP85TS (revised on SP85G to SP85) 20: forever.] $\sim$: *Atlantic* 21: promises] promise *Atlantic* 23: fulfillments] fulfilments *London Magazine,* SP85TS (revised in pencil to SP85) 23: In the distance] In distance *Atlantic*

573 **Little Girl Wakes Early** Text: SP85. Variant: In *Fifty Years of American Poetry: A Tribute to Marie Bullock* (Winston-Salem, NC: Palaemon Press, 1984). 4: no] or *Palaemon* 5: breath$_{\wedge}$] $\sim$, *Palaemon* 6: and no] no *Palaemon* 8: housekeeping.] housekeeping. *Palaemon,* SP85TS (revised in pencil to SP85) 9: the dew] dew *Palaemon* 10: And climbed] Climbed *Palaemon* 13: awful,] $\sim_{\wedge}$ *Palaemon,* SP85TS 14: where now] where *Palaemon* 15: Over the stove,] Now at the stove, *Palaemon* 17: you—] $\sim$, *Palaemon,* SP85TS (revised on SP85G to SP85) 18: hard—] $\sim$, *Palaemon,* SP85TS (revised on SP85G to SP85) 20: ever to explain to] to find to explain *Palaemon* 20: try$_{\wedge}$] $\sim$, *Palaemon*

574 **Winter Wheat: Oklahoma** Text: SP85. Variants: *New England Review and Bread Loaf Quarterly,* 6 (Spring 1984), p. 416, *London Magazine,* vol. 24, no. 7, pp. 40–41. 3: red,] $\sim_{\wedge}$ *New England Review* 4: brightness, with ink scarcely dry] brightness when ink was scarce dry *New England Review, London Magazine,* SP85TS (revised on SP85G to SP85) 5: still it makes black earth blacker when] still makes blacker black earth where *New England Review* 11: open$_{\wedge}$] $\sim$, *New England Review* 14: In the end, there's the tight rectangle of the little lawn-patch, two maples.] There's the tight little white rectangle on lawn patch, two maples. *New England Review,* In the end, there's the tight little rectangle of lawn-patch, two maples. *London Magazine,* SP85TS (revised on SP85G to SP85) 15: woodlot] wood lot *New England Review* 15: All his,] All is his, *New England Review* 16: sweat's.] sweat. *New England Review* 18: just] he'll just *New England Review* 19: A time] For a time *New England Review* 20: cheekbones in earth out yonder,] cheek-bones out yonder, *New England Review* 21: pay good] pay in good *New England Review* 24: He sits alone.] He's alone *New England Review* 24: Him] Nobody comes by, him *New England Review* 26: That boy ... just go for nothing.] These lines are substantially different in *New England Review*:

That boy was sure Pa's boy. Stuck to his sweat. But you couldn't
Be so sure about God. Get the winter wheat in, and maybe
He'd up and take a notion to pleasure Himself,
Whatever that was, and like sometimes just go
Skylarkin' off. And to hell with a man's sweat.

VII.

575 **Youthful Picnic Long Ago: Sad Ballad on Box** Text: SP85. Variant: *Helsinki* (as "Youthful Picnic Long Ago: Sad Ballad on Guitar"). 1: once] once, at night, *Helsinki* 5: Last scream space makes beyond space.] Last soundless scream space makes beyond space. SP85TS (revised on SP85G to SP85), Last soundless scream Space makes beyond space. *Helsinki* 7: On the fingers] On fingers *Helsinki* 15: The voice] That voice *Helsinki* 19: parody] parady *Helsinki* 24: that voice] words of that voice *Helsinki* 30: varnished] gleaming *Helsinki* 32: eye-shine,] $\sim$. *Helsinki* 33: Then I'd know that much / If not her

name. // Even now.] If not her name. // Then I'd know, at least, that much // Even now. *Helsinki*

576 **History During Nocturnal Snowfall** Text: SP85. Variant: *Sewanee Review*, 91 (Fall 1983), p. 565 (as "Personal History"). 1: boxed] curtained *SR* 1: from snow-darkness of night,] from the snow-dark night, *SR* 2: Where that] Whose *SR*, Where the SP85TS (revised on SP85G to SP85) 3: We lie, each alone,] We lie wrapped in white, *SR* 5: inch,] ~‸ *SR* 5: world,] ~‸ *SR* 8: heartbeat with heartbeat] heart-beat with heart-beat SP85TS (revised in pencil to SP85) 10: clawing] clawingly, *SR* 12: knowing] knows *SR* 13: one] either *SR*, SP85TS (revised on SP85G to SP85) 13: the other's] other's *SR*, SP85TS (revised on SP85G to SP85) 15: White darkness] This white darkness *SR* 15: one] they *SR* 16: and heart,] or lungs, *SR* 19: darkness blending] darkness *SR* 19: darkness‸] ~, *Clark* 19: blending‸] ~, *Clark* 19: fall‸] ~, *SR* 20: a pulse] the pulse *SR*, SP85TS (revised on SP85G to SP85)

576 **Whistle of the 3 A.M.** Text: SP85. Variants: *American Poetry Review*, 13 (July–Aug. 1984), p. 22 (as "Whistle of the Three A.M. Express"), *London Magazine* vol. 24, no. 7 (Oct. 1984), p. 37. 1: A.M.,] am, *London Magazine* 4: night‸] ~, *APR* 9: once at that whistle you from bed] once, at that whistle, you, from bed, *APR* 12: Hills snow-white,] Snow-white hills, *APR* 17: change, man] change. Man *APR* 18: down, what whistle wakes any boy] down would the jet's flight wake any boy *APR* 21: A.M.?] am? *London Magazine* 22: What if some hold real estate nearby, / A good six feet long,] Indeed—some hold real estate nearby, / In plots of six feet, *APR* 24: wake, I guess, to listen, and] wake to listen and *APR* 25: schedule's gone] schedule is *APR* 25: a.m..] In SP85TS (and all the way up to the bound "Advance uncorrected proofs") this poem follows:

With or Without Compass?

Just before night-fold of eyelids have you ever imagined
That the day just dead shows footprints that lead
To you now, this moment in which Time itself hangs darkly agleam
Like some last raindrop at twig-tip in unstirring air
Of the belly-drag night pelt of undecipherable cloud?

What tracks have led to this moment whence no track
Henceforward may ever again be made? Looking back, could you count
Footprints, one by one, here made? Could you say how love
Might lead to hate? Hate to love? Hope to despair?
And apathy to the clang of decision like

Red iron caught in the slam-bang of hammer and anvil?
But what of footprints of years long before, invisible now,
That had wandered on thistle, strayed among stones? Had felt
The fondling of grasses dew-wet, or gold-starred? Or known
The silence of century-packed pine needles in twilight at noontide?

Over what terrain, or through what texture of sorrow or joy, had
A compass hand-held in knowledge, or heart-held in none,
Dictated the track you followed to this place and hour
As you lie beneath the ineluctable weight
Of darkness, and ponder what might be the nature of dawn?

If dawn.

The poem was revised extensively on SP85G, and then canceled.

577 **Last Night Train** Text: SP85. Variant: *New Yorker*, 7 April 1980, pp. 38–39. 1: new-fangled] newfangled *NY* 10: color-contrasting] contrasting *NY*, SP85TS (revised on SP85G to SP85) 11: They / Have walked so far.] They have walked / So far. *NY* 17: into] in *NY* 18: that brief] the brief *NY* 19: cricket] cricket only *NY* 22: there,] ~‸ *NY* 23: Alone, again I stand,] Alone I stood, *NY* 23: stand,] stood, SP85TS (revised on SP85G to SP85) 30: of swimming,] of the joy of swimming, *NY* 31: In starlight forever.] *NY* and SP85TS add a stanza here:

By habit, I put hand in pocket, find keys there.
Bemused, I stare at them, and gradually
Grow aware of their preciousness. I discover
The blessedness of the world. Ah, Time! Why so short?

In SP85TS the last exclamation point is replaced by an em-dash. The stanza is canceled on SP85G. 32: But I] I *NY*, SP85TS (revised on SP85G to SP85) 35: on gravel,] on the gravel, *NY* 36: a parked car.] the parked car. *NY*

VIII.

579 **Milton: A Sonnet** Text: SP85. Variant: *Forum: A Journal of the Humanities and Fine Arts*, 17.3–18.1 (Summer/ Fall 1979), p. 6 (as "Milton"). *Forum* concludes with the following annotation: "March 27–29, 1982" (which makes no sense to me). The same date appears on the typescript in the Beinecke Library. Possibly the issue of *Forum* did not appear until that much later date. In SP85TS the title is "Milton" (revised on SP85G to SP85). 2: had bathed] bathed *Forum* 3: at the last] at last *Forum* 4: Moved] He moved *Forum* 5: burgeoning] bourgeoning SP85TS (revised in pencil to SP85) 9: present] Present *Forum* 9: blessèd] blessed *Forum* 14: and upward again, and, in joy, flash.] and upward again in joy flash. *Forum*

579 **Whatever You Now Are** Text: SP85. Variant: *Nation*, 7 May 1983, p. 583 (as "Self"). In SP85TS the title of this poem is "Self" (revised on SP85G to SP85). 1: midnight,] ~∧ *Nation*, SP85TS (revised in pencil to SP85) 2: Oh∧] ~, *Nation*, SP85TS (revised in pencil to SP85) 2: yes,] ~∧ SP85TS (revised in pencil to SP85) 5: the Self] Self *Nation* 6: defined] divided *Nation* 7: Is it] Can it be *Nation* 7: to distance,] to distance∧ *Nation* 9: stone-chance?] stond-chance? *Nation* 15: music drifts to your] music seems to drift from a *Nation* 16: consciousness,] consciousness you inhabit, *Nation*

580 **Wind and Gibbon** Text: SP85. Variants: *Southern Review*, ns 19 (Spring 1983), pp. 349–51, *Encounter*, 64 (Feb. 1985), p. 22. 1: night,] ~∧ *SoR* 2: Wind∧] ~, SP85TS (revised on SP85G to SP85) 2: stir,] ~∧ *SoR* 3: leg] the leg *SoR* 3: leg / Twitching. Paw] leg twitching. / Paw *SoR* 4: jerking.] ~, *SoR* 11: dried] dry *SoR* 14: solid] There is a line break in *SoR* after this text. 17: paranoia] a paranoiac *SoR* 28: Moan-maker.] Merciless moan-maker. *SoR*, *Encounter*, SP85TS (revised in pencil to SP85) 30: *signo.*] *signum.* *SoR*, *Encounter* (but Warren's copy of *Encounter* in the Beinecke Library is revised to SP85), SP85TS (revised in pencil in the bound "Advance uncorrected proofs". 32: dawn,] Line break after this text in *SoR*. 32: This,] ~∧ *SoR* 35: back of your house, and thus / Invisible to you,] invisible to you, *SoR*, *Encounter*, SP85TS (revised on SP85G to SP85)

581 **Delusion? — No!** Text: SP85. Variants: *Sewanee Review*, 91 (Fall 1983), pp. 566–67, *Helsinki*. 2: Pure for] For *Helsinki* 3: bone-borne flesh,] flesh bone-borne, *SR*, bone-bound flesh, *Helsinki* 10: Cliff,] Past cliff, *SR* 14: momentous,] ~∧ *Helsinki* 15: then the] then *SR*, SP85TS (revised on SP85G to SP85) 19: the fundamental discovery.] the discovery of selfhood. *SR*, SP85TS a discovery of selfhood. (revised on SP85G to SP85), *Helsinki* 20: Yes, . . . has many moments.] *SR* is substantially different:

Or stretched forth arms like wings, and from the highest stance,
Hawk-eyed, rode forth upon the emptiness of air, surveyed
Each regal contortion
And torturous imagination of rock, wind, and water, and knew
My own the power that was creating all.
Delusion?—No! For Truth has many moments.

SP85TS follows *SR*, except that it corrects "torturous" to "tortuous" and adds a stanza break after "that was creating all." The text is revised on SP85G to SP85, except that again Warren has "torturous" rather than "tortuous". On SP85G second set the word is "tortuous". 20: Yes, . . . Each regal contortion] *Helsinki* is substantially different:

Or stretched forth arms like wings,
And from that highest stance, hawk-eyed,
Rode forth upon the emptiness of air, surveyed
Each regal contortion

23: tortuous] torturous *Helsinki* 23: know] knew *Helsinki* 24: Your own the power creating all.] My own the power that was creating all. *Helsinki* 25: Truth] truth *Helsinki*

581 **Question at Cliff-Thrust** Text: SP85. Variants: *Southern Review*, ns 19 (Spring 1983), pp. 351–52, *London Magazine* vol. 24 no. 7 (Oct. 1984), pp. 38–39, *Helsinki*. 1: outthrust] out-thrust *SoR*, *London Magazine*, SP85TS, SP85G (revised to SP85 on page proofs), *Helsinki* 2: Survey, downward, the] Survey the *SoR*, *London Magazine*, SP85TS (revised on SP85G to SP85), *Helsinki* 3: Foam fringe,] Foam-fringe, *Helsinki* 3: sand,] ~∧ *SoR* 4: pumice and lava] pumice *Helsinki* 4: lava∧] ~, *SoR* 4: fruitcake] fruit-cake *Helsinki* 4: an angle] angle *SoR* 5: nibbled] all nibbled *SoR* 7: and / Of distance,] and of / Distance, *Helsinki*, *London Magazine* (revised to SP85 on Warren's copy of *London Magazine* in the Beinecke Library) 8: Of distance,] Distance, *SoR*, SP85TS (revised in pencil in the bound "Advance uncorrected proofs") The correction is repeated on the page proofs. 16: hypnosis.] No stanza break after this line in *SoR*. 17: would] could *SoR*, *London Magazine* 18: It] That it *SoR* 27: green and unforgiving eye of depth] green eye of depth *Helsinki* 27: eye of depth] eye *SoR* 32: you turn, and in the turn] you turn, / And in the turn *Helsinki* 33: climb] journey *Helsinki* 36: and is] No stanza break after this line in *SoR*. 37: what?] ~. *SoR* 37: what?] *SoR* adds a second half-line, broken across a stanza break, after this text: Demanding what?

582 **It Is Not Dead** Text: SP85. Variants: *New Yorker*, 7 Feb. 1983, p. 40, *Helsinki* (as "It Is Not Dead: The Great Smooth Boulder"). 2: painful,] ~∧ *NY*, *Helsinki* 4: liquefied,] liquified, SP85TS (revised in pencil to SP85) liquidified, *Helsinki* 6: depth ... asunder,] depth and / Darkness when earth was not / Yet ready to be torn asunder, *Helsinki* 7: asunder,] ~∧ *NY* 8: silence,] ~∧ *NY* 9: eons] aeons *Helsinki* 9: remained still] still *NY* 10: await what] wait the *NY* 10: birth∧] ~— *NY* 12: its liquid mind] its mind *NY* 12: to hardness like glass, to iron] to hardness, to iron *Helsinki* 12: to iron will?] an iron will? *NY* 13: had] has *NY* 15: What determination interminable,] Line omitted in *NY*. 16: years,] ~∧ *NY* 16: crowbar] crow-bar, crow-bar, SP85TS, SP85G (revised to SP85 on SP85G second set), *Helsinki* 16: ice take / To pry] ice / Take to pry *NY* 17: from] loose from *NY* 17: crag-face] crag face *NY* 18: That mass ... first unmerciful] An edged mass to scythe an undefined / Forest to splinters? Then in what night, / And with what might, / Came the first unmerciful *NY* 19: some] an SP85TS (revised on SP85G to SP85), *Helsinki* 19: Then the might / Of] Then / What might of *Helsinki* 20: the first unmerciful] the unmerciful *Helsinki* 20: the grind, / The trundling descent] the grind / And trundling descent *Helsinki* 21: white / But absolute.] how white / In its absolute night? *Helsinki* 22: absolute.] ~? *NY* 22: in its] its *NY* 22: ground in its downward mind? / Then fingers of water,] in its downward mind / Ground before fingers of water, *Helsinki* 23: uncontrollable,] uncountable, *NY* 24: will,] ~∧ *NY* 25: age,] ~∧ *Helsinki* 26: Half in,] Half-in, *NY* 26: half out,] half-out∧ *NY* 27: sunlit.] ~, *NY* 28: And,] ~∧ *Helsinki* 31: night,] ~∧ *NY*, *Helsinki* 32: and I lie, in brotherhood, where I lie,] and I, in brotherhood, lie abed where I lie, *NY*, and I lie, / In brotherhood, where I lie, *Helsinki* 33: riffle∧] ~, *NY* 35: the night] night *NY* 35: immensity of the night sky.] immensity / Of night sky. *Helsinki*

583 **Sunset** Text: SP85. Variants: *Ploughshares*, 9:2–3 (1983), p. 13, *Helsinki*. 1: Clouds clamber, turgid, the mountain,] Clouds, turgid, clamber the mountain, *Helsinki* 2: pine-pierced,] pine-speared, *Helsinki* 5: Like fire] As by fire *Helsinki* 5: lint-house—] No line break after this text in *Ploughshares*, SP85TS (revised on SP85G to SP85), and *Helsinki*. 9: at a late hour,] at the last hour, *Helsinki* 11: "Oh, what shall I call my soul in a dire hour?"] *Oh, what shall I call my soul in a dire hour?* *Helsinki* 20: that] who *Helsinki* 21: "Tell me that name," I cried, "that I may speak / In a dire hour."] *Tell me that name!* I cried, *that I may speak / In a dire hour.* *Helsinki* 22: In] in *Ploughshares* 23: the time when] whatever time *Ploughshares* 24: self—never / Before seen, nor known.] self—never before / Seen, and yet unknown. *Ploughshares* 25: seen, nor] seen. Nor *Helsinki* 25: nor known.] In SP85TS "Institute of the Impossible" appears as the next poem, but it is canceled in SP85G.

IX.

584 **Myth of Mountain Sunrise** Text: SP85. Variant: *New England Review and*

Bread Loaf Quarterly, 6 (Spring 1984), p. 417. 2: nightlong,] night-long, *New England Review* 3: unknowable, but] mysterious but *New England Review* 7: dayward,] toward day, *New England Review* 8: entered∧] ~, *Clark* 11: in dark] in the dark SP85TS (revised in pencil to SP85) 12: I know that] I know *New England Review*, SP85TS (revised on SP85G to SP85) 13: spiderweb,] spider-web, *New England Review*, SP85TS (revised in pencil to SP85) 14: glory!] ~? *New England Review* 14: sapling,] sapling stem, *New England Review*, SP85TS (revised on SP85G to SP85) The correction is repeated on the page proofs. 16: sway that no geometries] and the sway no geometries *New England Review* 16: sway that] sway SP85TS (revised on SP85G to SP85) 17: end-thin,] ends thin∧ *New England Review* 17: fruit-swell] the fruit-swell *New England Review* 18: The sun] But sun *New England Review* 18: blazes] glazes SP85G (revised on SP85G to SP85) I normally do not note printer's errors that Warren corrected on galleys, but since this one could conceivably have made sense in context, and since Warren originally did not spot the error (correcting it to "gazes"), the error may cast light on a textual issue. 18: That will be the old tale told.] Thus will the old tale be told. *New England Review*

Uncollected Poems 1943–1989

Typescripts for these poems are in the collection of the Beinecke Library, but it is unclear in most cases whether they are setting typescripts or drafts. I have collated them only where it is clear that they are setting typescripts, or where I needed some evidence about a disputed reading, such as whether there is a stanza break at a point where a page break in the magazine version would have obscured it.

587 **Bicentennial** Text: *Esquire,* Dec. 1976, pp. 132–35, 200–1. There are several typescripts of this poem, as well as galley proofs (cited here as G) of the *Esquire* version, in the collection of the Beinecke Library. G differs from *Esquire* in several places, but G may be the "author's set," and in other cases where Warren had both a master set and an author's set of galleys he marked them up slightly differently, which means that G does not automatically have authority over *Esquire.* The Beinecke collection includes a typescript which was probably the poem as it was originally going to appear in a later book version. Since that typescript is marked "III. Prayerful", it was probably going to open a third section of *Now and Then.* (Indeed, the manila folder in which that section appears, upon which Warren has written "Bicentennial Ode in *Esquire* but not in book", lists a number of other titles of poems from *Now and Then.*) It is marked "Out A E" in black marker, probably by Albert Erskine. That version would have been dedicated to James Dickey, and would have had the following additional epigraph, from Blake's "Visions of the Daughters of Albion":

For the soft soul of America, Oothoon, wander'd in woe,
Along the vales of Leutha seeking flowers to comfort her . . .

Because this typescript was prepared not for *Esquire* but for *Now and Then*, I have chosen to cite not this but the earlier typescript in folder 3952 in the Beinecke Library collection as "TS". 37: very old.] There is a column break in the *Esquire* text at this point which obscures whether there is a stanza break or not, but there is a stanza break in G. 46: four] two G 77: phase she had] A column break obscures whether there is a stanza break or not after this text in *Esquire*, but there is no break in G. 109: Sawynee Crossing, Alabama.] There is a page turn in G after this text, but there is a stanza break here in the typescripts as well. 149: on the floor] There is a column break here in the *Esquire* text, but there is no stanza break in G. 184: three miles.] There is a page turn in the *Esquire* text after this test, but there is no stanza break in G. 184: three miles] a mile G (revised on G to *Esquire*) 185: three miles] a mile G (revised on G to *Esquire*) 192: stint,] mile, G (revised to *Esquire*) 208: window∧] ~, G (but not TS or *Esquire*) 215: Where moss hangs.] There is a page turn after this text in G, but there is a stanza break in the typescripts after this test as well. 222: and the sound] There is a column break in *Esquire* after this text, but there is no stanza break in G or the typescripts. 224: moss-pickers] moss pickers G, moss-pickers

TS 229: bloodlines] blood lines G, TS 237: sack, unfolded, hangs] is unfolded to hang G (revised to *Esquire*) 248: tomorrow.] There is no stanza break after this text in G, but there is in TS and in *Esquire*. 256: dark.] No stanza break after this text in G, but it is added on G, and appears on TS as well. 286: against the wall.] There is a column break after this text in *Esquire*, but there is no stanza break in G. 287: well-cared-for] well cared for TS, G 315: over her hair.] There is no stanza break after this text in G, but there is one after the equivalent of this text (TS slightly differs) in TS. 319: Experimentally, he] He G (revised to "He experimentally") 324: like a kitten.] There is a page break after this text in *Esquire* and, as it happens, on G, but the stanza break is penciled in on G. (There is no stanza break, however, on TS.) 329: close.] The stanza break after this text is added on G. 333: the world.] The stanza break after this text is added on G. 351: therein.] No stanza break after this text in G. 358: mind.] The stanza break after this text is added on G. 359: like smoke.] There is a column break here in *Esquire,* but there is a stanza break here in G. 360: dentist.] The stanza break after this text is added on G. 392: and] though G (revised to *Esquire* on G) 397: from ourselves.] G continues on for two more sections, although they are canceled:

35.

No, they didn't—but that is no reason for forgetting
That the dream they dreamed was not merely a system for
The distribution of goods and the maintenance of order

36.

Who is my brother?

599 **A Few Axioms for a Young Man** Text: *Two Poems* (Winston-Salem, NC: Palaemon Press Limited, 1979). Variant: *Georgia Review,* 31 (Winter 1977), pp. 785–87. 1: profitable things to know,] things one should know, *GaR* 2: some.] some of them. *GaR* 3: mountains] the mountains *GaR* 5: lovers, even in moonlight ... At night. Rattlers] lovers, even in / The most dramatic moonlight, even hand in hand, / Should not go walking at night. Rattlers *GaR* 8: Are] Come *GaR* 8: odds] the odds *GaR* 9: the level] our level *GaR* 10: taken as] called *GaR* 11: love—] ∼, *GaR* 12: Yes, at its] When things are *GaR* 13: moonlight,] the moonlight *GaR* 15: It is wisdom ... as a roof.] It is wisdom to stay out of sandstone caves, / Especially in Kentucky. If a slip occurs / In stratified stone, like limestone, the slip / Runs with the stratum, which serves as a roof. *GaR* 20: plain] just plain *GaR* 20: even / If Bible Believers maintain that] even though / True Believers maintain that *GaR* 25: It is best, ... even if] It is best to stay out of sandcaves even if *GaR* 27: pappy,] Pappy, *GaR* 29: cedar-tangle] cedar tangle *GaR* 29: with / Only your direction to turn to. A rifle] and can only / Turn in your direction. A rifle *GaR* 31: on the second needed shot] for the second shot *GaR* 35: To go hunting, ... attack of conscience.] To go out with a business partner or / A best friend whose wife you have recently laid. / She may have had an attack of conscience. *GaR* 39: the experience for her,] for her the recent experience, *GaR* 40: certain] some *GaR* 41: in] in a *GaR* 41: country / (Especially with snow-peaks like a post card), or beside] country, / Especially with snow peaks like a post card, beside *GaR* 43: glen$_\wedge$] ∼, *GaR* 44: (Especially ... of same).] Especially when the trees are in full autumnal color, or when in / Elegant and expensive surroundings, certainly not / If you are not the actual owner of same. *GaR* 47: from all angles,] in regard to all consequences, *GaR* 48: matrimony / in mind) an ordinary seduction—this] matrimony in mind) / An ordinary seduction, this *GaR* 50: beauty or elegance,] beauty *GaR* 52: like a motel room] like a room in a motel *GaR* 53: if in] in *GaR* 54: heart,] heart and appetite, *GaR* 55: the cart ... advertising business.] the cart before the horse. / This is advisable only in fiction or advertising. *GaR* 59: deputy warden] deputy-warden *GaR* 62: back. Even] back, even *GaR* 63: character, ... The marksmanship] character. / It is best to go unarmed, as though you clearly felt no need. / Eat with the cons at least once

a week. / Try not to gag at anything. Show relish. Moreover, / Never change your mind about any declared decision. / That is, remember that men are like dogs, certainly / In some respects. The marksmanship *GaR* 75: towerman] tower-man *GaR* 75: possible.] humanly possible. *GaR* 76: The rifle, ... to kill.] Shooting should be a last resort, but / In that resort, a shot should never be fired except to kill. *GaR* 78: A mere wound ... money.] These two lines (and the stanza break) are missing in *GaR*. 80: one fag con] one con *GaR* 82: He demanded ... innocent man.] He asked a tower-man why he had not fired. / The tower-man, a real expert, replied that he / Was afraid of killing an innocent man. *GaR* 86: My warden friend] My friend *GaR* 88: Draw yore pay.] You're fired! *GaR* 89: When swimming] Swimming *GaR* 90: really lean] lean high *GaR* 91: As it begins ... one application.] Dive into its heart, low, to undercut it before it breaks. / There is a strange moment of quiet there. / This principle has more than one application. I / Advise you to think it over. *GaR* 96: thick-wooded] wooded *GaR* 100: happen] merely happen *GaR* 103: The last item, ... love.] The last item is, it should be added, / True of death—and sometimes love. *GaR*

601 **Somewhere** Text: *Southern Review*, ns 14 (Spring 1978), pp. 305–6. Variant: *Times Literary Supplement*, 20 Jan. 1978, p. 64. The *Times Literary Supplement* text is in italic type, with roman for emphasis. 3: Then$_\wedge$] ~, *TLS* 3: looked: dry / And dry-wrinkled] looked: / Dry and dry-wrinkled, *TLS* 4: age, leached pale,] age, *TLS* 5: yet quite] quite *TLS* 5: "No, Mister—"] "Aint money"—the words *TLS* 6: phlegm$_\wedge$] ~, *TLS* 7: "Aint money I'm astin.] "Not money, I'm astin. *TLS* 8: "But you—] "Jist one thing— *TLS* 10: Important, too.] Important. *TLS* 13: "Eleven,"] "Eleven", *TLS* 14: watch,"] watch", *TLS* 15: Jist it gits cranky,"] Jist gits cranky." *TLS* 16: thanks.] him. *TLS* 16: "My Daddy, he give it me,"] "My Daddy give it me" *TLS* 17: "Fer graduation." And was gone.] "Fer graduation long back." Was gone. *TLS* 19: I stood.] Stood. *TLS*

602 **Praise** Text: *Atlantic Monthly,* June 1978, p. 45. Variant: *New England Review*, 2.2 (Winter 1979), p. 232.

603 **Aging Man at Noon in Timeless Noon of Summer** Text: *Southern Review*, ns 15 (Autumn 1979), p. 996.

603 **Lord Jesus, I Wonder** Text: *Two Poems* (Winston-Salem, NC: Palaemon Press, 1979).

604 **Commuter's Entry in a Connecticut Diary** Text: *Southern Review,* ns 16 (Spring 1980), pp. 383–84.

605 **You Sort Old Letters** Text: *Love: Four Versions* (Winston-Salem, NC: Palaemon Press, 1981). Variant: *American Poetry Review*, 11 (Nov.–Dec. 1982), p. 47. 4: behind] beyond *APR* 5: With] The *APR* 7: now] and now *APR* 8: have that day meant] that day have meant *APR* 12: And she gasped, "Bite harder, oh, hard!"] And gasped: "Harder, bite harder!" *APR* 14: "Oh, you hate me!"] "Oh, don't you hate me!" *APR* 14: wept,] ~$_\wedge$ *APR* 17: Do you seem ... she shacked up] Do you seem to remember that, for a moment, / Your heart stirred? But you shrug now, remembering / How, in the end, she shacked up *APR* 23: as was common gossip.] There is a stanza break after this text in *APR*. 24: late, and now from this mess] late—and now in this mess *APR* 25: words suddenly at you stare:] words at your stare: *APR* 27: "Yours, maybe." And then: / "P.S. What might have been?"] "Yours, maybe." *APR* 27: "Yours, maybe."] Stanza break after this text in *APR*. 30: and a charm] a charm *APR* 32: fall-guys,] fall guys, *APR* 33: she threw ... Sank deeper, deeper, into] she threw all away. / And as you've guessed, by struggling / Sank deeper and deeper into *APR* 36: However, you] Stanza break after this text in *APR*. 41: speculation, or memory,] speculations, *APR* 43: guilt,] ~— *APR* 46: in dream,] in a dream, *APR*

606 **Aging Painter Sits Where the Great Tower Heaves Down Midnight** Text: *Georgia Review*, 35 (Winter 1981), pp. 768–74. Section numbers in *GaR* are in Arabic numerals, but I have used Roman numerals to preserve consistency with other sequences. There are ten distinct versions of this poem in the Beinecke Library, including a setting typescript for the *GaR* version. Strangely, although the envelope included with the typescript describes it as the typescript for the *GaR* version, it has been marked up by Albert

Erskine. It has also been folded several times, as if for distinct mailings in ordinary business envelopes, but the envelope with the typescript is a 9 x 11 envelope. Because this is marked as a setting typescript, I have collated it, but because there is clearly a missing set of galleys and several clear cases where the typescript is in error, I have not given it trumping authority over *GaR*. 8: *not*] not TS (but the word is italicized in other typescripts, so presumably TS is in error) 27: Bentley.] A page turn in *GaR* obscures whether there is a stanza break here. But there is a stanza break in the setting typescript. 63: eyes met.] A page turn in *GaR* obscures whether there is a stanza break following this text, but there is no stanza break in the setting typescript. 82: oh, thanks,] oh, I mean thanks TS 111: wheeled] swing TS 113: so beautiful?"] The line straddles not only the stanza break, but also the section break, that follows this text. 116: *Splendide's*] *Splendid's* TS (but other typescripts have *Splendide's*) 127: I've told] I'd tell TS 130: didn't hurt."] A page turn in *GaR* obscures whether there is a stanza break after this text but there is one in TS. 136: for always!"] The line straddles not only the stanza break but also the section break that follows this text. In the TS there is a further section here (although the line again straddles the stanza and section break, and does so at the end of the section as well) canceled in red pencil by Albert Erskine:

That
Was that. Now gone for good. I watched
Her run. Traverse the *Splendide's* glare.

She limped somewhat

137: That night,] Later that night, TS 151: the can clink] how the can clinks TS 192: thought,] A page turn in *GaR* obscures whether there is a stanza break following this text, but there is not one in TS.

611 **Was It One of the Long Hunters of Kentucky Who Discovered Boone at Sunset?** Text: *Sewanee Review*, 90 (Fall 1982), pp. 498–99. One of the typescripts of this poem in the Beinecke Library seems to be a version later than *SR*, since it is marked "rejected for *New and Selected Poems 1975–1984*".

612 **Goodbye** Text: *Atlanta Magazine* [GA], Nov. 1982, p. 78

614 **Remark for Historians** Text: Frances C. Blessington and Guy Rotella, eds., *The Motive for Metaphor: Essays on Modern Poetry* (Boston: Northeastern University Press, 1983), p. xi.

614 **Institute of the Impossible** Text: *Grand Street*, 2 (Spring 1983), pp. 29–31. 61: awaking,] A page turn in *Grand Street* obscures whether there is a stanza break after this text or not. But there is no stanza break in TS.

616 **Winter Dreams** Text: *Southern Review*, ns 19 (Spring 1983), pp. 348–49. 28: for that.] A page turn in *SoR* obscures whether or not there is a stanza break after this line. But there is no stanza break in the typescript.

617 **Breaking the Code** Text: *Southern Review*, ns 19 (Spring 1983), pp. 352–53. Variant: *The Nation*, 7 May 1983, p. 583. 5: ambiguity, or error.] error or ambiguity. *Nation* 8: Does the first flake . . . and you?]

Is the owl's old question—"Who-who"—
Addressed to your conscience, and you?
Does the first flake of snow from a sky yet blue
Mean *that* or *this?*

11: Addressed to your conscience, and you?] A page turn in *SoR* obscures whether there is a stanza break after this line, but there is a stanza break in *Nation*. 26: undefinable] the undefined *Nation* 26: such a paradox] such paradox *Nation* 26: pain?] ~. *Nation* 31: a timeless] timeless *Nation*

618 **Problem of Autobiography Vague Recollection or Dream?** Text: *Sewanee Review*, 91 (Fall 1983), p. 568.

618 **Instant on Crowded Street** Text: *New England Review and Bread Loaf Quarterly*, 6 (Spring 1984), p. 415.

619 **Old Love** Text: *Sewanee Review*, 92 (Summer 1984), pp. 348–50. *SR* has sections II and III, but there is no mark for section I. Variant: *Iowa Review*, vol. 15, no. 1 (Winter 1985), pp. 20–21 (as "Tulip-Tree in Bloom"). *Iowa Review* is not divided into sections.

619 **I.** 10: heave.] heaven. *Iowa Review* (The fact that Warren did not correct this in *Iowa Review* when he did correct something else argues for the *Iowa Review* reading. But the TS of both "Old Love" and "Tulip-Tree in Bloom" in the Beinecke Library reads "heave," and the rhyme requires it anyway.) 13: worth?] ~. *Iowa Review* (revised in Warren's copy in the Beinecke Library to ~?)

620 **II.** 7: good condition,] A page turn in *SR* obscures whether there is a stanza break here or not, but there is no stanza break here in the typescript in the Beinecke Library or in *Iowa Review*. 7: condition,] ~; *Iowa Review* 9: surprise.] There is a page turn after this text in *Iowa Review* but no stanza break is indicated in the typescripts or in *SR*. 12: It'd] I'd *Iowa Review* (revised in Warren's copy of *Iowa Review* in the Beinecke Library to "It'd") 19: took] had taken *Iowa Review* 19: of the sky?] There is a stanza break after this text both in *Iowa Review* and in the TS of "Tulip-Tree in Bloom," although there is no stanza break in either "Old Love" or the TS of "Old Love." 30: lingered.] lingered. Then woke his son. *Iowa Review*. *Iowa Review* ends at this point (but the typescript goes on to the conclusion in *SR*). There is an annotation in Warren's hand in his copy of *Iowa Review* in the Beinecke Library: "This poem never republished".

620 **III.** 3: no knack] A page turn in *SR* obscures whether there is a stanza break after this text. But there is no stanza break here in TS.

621 **Upwardness** Text: *Partisan Review*, 51:4–52:1 (1984–1985), p. 611.

622 **Uncertain Season in High Country** Text: *Southern Review*, ns 21 (Spring 1985), pp. 428–29.

623 **The Loose Shutter** Text: *New Yorker*, 18 March 1985, p. 42.

623 **John's Birches** Text: *New Yorker*, 12 Aug. 1985, p. 26. Warren's copy of the *NY* in the Beinecke Library has the jocular annotation "Not by the John Birch Society!!" In MS this poem is titled "Recollection."

EXPLANATORY NOTES

14 **Apologia for Grief** 7: arval] from the fields.

23 **Tryst on Vinegar Hill** 1: Vinegar Hill is the site of an African-American cemetery in Warren's home town of Guthrie, Kentucky (Personal Communication, Ms. Melba Smith, Guthrie, Kentucky).

25 **The Limited** 1: Since there's no help, come, let them kiss and part—] The line alludes to Drayton's sonnet "Since there's no help, come let us kiss and part."

25 **Athenian Death** 32: Erects a hell in heaven's despite.] The line alludes to Blake's "The Clod and the Pebble." But the sense—not only of this line but also of the poem's treatment of Alcibiades more generally—alludes to the lines to which Blake's own poem alludes, Milton's Satan's claim in Book I of *Paradise Lost* that the mind is its own place, and in itself can make a heaven of hell, a hell of heaven. 44: Timandra] According to Plutarch, Alcibiades' mistress in exile, who took care of his body after his assassination.

33 **The Return: An Elegy** 76: turn backward . . . just for tonight] These lines are from "Rock Me to Sleep," by Elizabeth Akers Allen (1832–1911). The Allen poem actually reads "Backward, turn backward, O Time, in your flight, / Make me a child again just for to-night!"

39 **Pondy Woods** 1: Pondy Woods is a large, swampy, wooded area near Guthrie, Kentucky. The lynching in prospect in this poem, and the lynching in Warren's much later poem "Ballad of Mister Dutcher and the Last Lynching in Gupton," are both loosely based on the actual lynching, in Guthrie, of Primus Kirby in June, 1926 (Letter from Melba Smith of Guthrie Kentucky, May 3, 1995). Details may be found in the *Clarksville Leaf-Chronicle,* 15 June 1926, p. 1. Some of the details of the Kirby case are very different from the case here. Kirby, an ex-convict, was sought for murdering his wife, and injuring his aunt, with an axe. He had just been released from prison after serving a one-year sentence for a previous assault upon his wife. He also shot a deputy named Ed Bringhurst in resisting capture. He was lynched in broad daylight on College Hill (not in Pondy Woods) by a mob that seized him from the sheriff and the constable as they were bringing him to Elkton after his arrest. As in "The Ballad of Mister Dutcher," the hanging was bungled, and Kirby was actually killed by numerous bullets fired at his hanging body. See also the account of the Kirby case in Watkins, *Then and Now* (University Press of Kentucky, 1982), pp. 64ff. 23: Blue Goose saloon] There really was a Blue Goose Saloon in Squiggtown. See Watkins, *Then and Now*, p. 73. 52: *Non omnis moriar,*] I shall not die totally. The phrase is from Horace *Odes* III.30.6. 63: Squiggtown, also called "Squigg," was the predominantly African-American neighborhood in Warren's home town of Guthrie, Kentucky.

41 **Letter of a Mother** 16: Mortmain] legally, a gift in perpetuity or an inalienable possession; figuratively the control of the present by the past. 18: Coronal seam] the joint along the top of the skull. 20: Escheat] a property that has reverted to the state upon the failure of its owner. 20: Estopped] legally, a bar to alleging or denying a fact because of one's own previous actions or words to the contrary; stopped up (archaic).

42 **Genealogy** 1: Grandfather Gabriel] Not, apparently, Warren's real grandfather, Gabriel Penn. But why then the obviously inflammatory name? 8: Grandmother Martha] Warren's real grandmother, the wife of Gabriel Thomas Penn, was born Mary Elia Mitchell, according to Mary Mexico Penn (Personal Communication, Joseph Blotner).

49 **Ransom** 6: The mentioned act] lust in action, according to Shakespeare.

50 **Toward Rationality** 20: Abhorson] an executioner in Shakespeare's *Measure for Measure.*

53 **Croesus in Autumn** 15: stout cortex] Warren may be punning on "Stout Cortez" from Keats's sonnet on Chapman's Homer.

55 **Pacific Gazer** 4: gurge] whirlpool 13: griding] scraping

70 **End of Season** 14: the prophet] John the Baptist 15: de Leon] Ponce de Leon 18: the infernal grime.] Virgil wipes Dante's face with rushes in the opening canto of the *Purgatorio.*

77 **Terror** 1: "I Volontari Americani Presso Eserciti Stranieri Non Perdono La Cittadinanza."] The American volunteers serving in foreign armies do not lose their citizenship. 25: Harry L.] Harry Lyle, a classmate of Warren's at Clarksville High School (see Watkins, *Then and Now* [University Press of Kentucky, 1982], p. 66). 32: Madrid] Warren has in mind the Spanish Civil War. 41: the Moor,] Franco's campaign started in Morocco. There may be a more specific reference, but possibly the point is that those who fought against the Russians in Finland and who had earlier fought alongside the Russians in Spain have as little concrete stake in the struggle as Moorish soldiers do in fighting for Franco. 50: Helsingfors] Helsinki. Warren has in mind the Russo-Finnish Winter War of 1939–1940. 57: Piazza, Wilhelmplatz] That is to say, in Italy, or Germany. 58: Onan] who, in Genesis, spilled his seed upon the ground. 59: Alexis Carrel] 1873–1944, the inventor of a perfusion pump which enabled a human heart to remain alive outside of the body. 64: criminal king,] Macbeth

81 **The Ballad of Billie Potts** 2: an old lady who was a relative of mine] Mrs. Anna Barker, Warren's great-aunt, according to Warren's note on a letter (filed with the poem in the Beinecke Library) from Ronald L. Nelson of May 13, 1985. Many writers—but not Warren himself, who thought the story was European—treat the Billie Potts story as historical. Two books, *Outlaws of Cave-in-Rock* and *Satan's Ferryman*, retell the story. There is a treatment of the story in Ronald L. Nelson, "In Search of Billy Potts," *The Springhouse*, May–June 1985, pp. 12–20. There was a "Potts Inn" near the Cave-in-Rock, but the evidence linking that Squire Potts to the one of the common folktale is uncertain. The Cave-in-Rock and the Potts Inn are not located in the Land Between the Rivers, but across the Ohio River in what is now Hardin Country, Illinois. 38: "They names hit so, but I ain't bin."] The point is that Paducah is only a few miles away. 185: Bardstown] site of a famous racing track.

92 **Variation: Ode to Fear** 36: When Focke-Wulf mounts, or Zero,] German and Japanese fighter planes of World War II.

95 **II. Siesta Time in Village Plaza by Ruined Bandstand and Banana Tree** 1: Ernest] Hemingway 9: Henry Wallace] Then vice-president of the United States.

96 **III. The World Comes Galloping: A True Story** 32: Viene galopando el mundo.] Everybody comes galloping. (The poet translates this more literally: It comes galloping, the world.)

97 **IV. Small Soldiers with Drum in Large Landscape** 56: William] Wordsworth, in "I Wandered Lonely as a Cloud."

98 **V. The Mango on the Mango Tree** 12: Hawkshaw] I have been unable to trace this allusion, although presumably Hawkshaw is a detective or spy. 38: escheat] having reverted to the state by forfeit.

103 **I. Sirocco** 2: Rocca: La Rocca, an abandoned fortress near Porto Ercole in Italy. Warren lived there with Eleanor Clark and their new daughter Rosanna in 1954.

103 **II. Gull's Cry** 10: *gobbo*] hunchback

110 **II. Court-martial** 5: Captain, cavalry, C.S.A.,] Gabriel Penn, although opposed both to slavery and to secession, was captain of Company H of the 15th Tennessee Cavalry, and in that capacity court-martialed and hanged "bushwhackers" in Tennessee. Legal proceedings by the families of the bushwhackers after the war caused Penn to move to Kentucky (see Watkins, *Then and Now* [University Press of Kentucky, 1982], p. 28). 83: *Brevitatem justitia amat.*] Justice loves brevity.

117 **VI. School Lesson Based on Word of Tragic Death of Entire Gillum Family** 5: Gillum place,] Apparently this poem depends upon an actual event, hazy memories of which Watkins uncovered in Guthrie while he was writing *Then and Now*, although the

family name was Millen or Millum and the victims were the murderer's brother, sister-in-law, mother, and father, not his children; however, as Warren told R. W. B. Lewis, if he had had children, one of them would certainly have been named Dollie-May.

120 **VIII. Founding Fathers, Nineteenth-Century Style, Southeast U. S. A.** 23: Decherd] A rifle.

123 **X. Dark Night of** 56: Scaevola] Mucius Scaevola, a legendary Roman, said to have held his hand in flame to demonstrate his indifference to pain.

126 **2. Modification of Landscape** 18: like mackerel shining in moonlight.] The nineteenth century Virginia politician John Randolph said of Edward Livingston that "he is a man of splendid abilities but utterly corrupt. He shines and stinks like a rotten mackerel by moonlight." Some historians mistakenly believe that Randolph's gibe was directed at Henry Clay.

130 **2. Walk by Moonlight in Small Town** 18: *SP* and *Katy, L & N R R*—] The Southern Pacific; Missouri, Kansas, and Texas; and Louisville and Nashville railroads.

132 **XIV. Mad Young Aristocrat on Beach** 10: *cretino*] cretin 34: *Mais l'Amérique, merde!*] But America, shit!

133 **XV. Dragon Country: To Jacob Boehme** 1: Title: Jacob Boehme] German mystic, 1575–1624. 27: Todd County] Guthrie, Warren's birthplace, is in Todd County, Kentucky.

155 **Tiberius on Capri (a)** 1: Capri] The Roman Emperor Tiberius, 42 B.C.– 37 A.D., a noted libertine, spent the last years of his reign on the island of Capri. 12: spintriae] male prostitutes

155 **Tiberius on Capri (b)** 2: where Europe stank.] At the outbreak of World War II.

156 **I. After Night Flight Son Reaches Bedside of Already Unconscious Father, Whose Right Hand Lifts in a Spasmodic Gesture, as Though Trying to Make Contact: 1955** 1: For "mortmain," see explanatory note to "Letter of a Mother."

157 **II. A Dead Language: Circa 1885** 10: Λέγω, λέγεις, λέγει,] "I read, you read, he reads." R. F. Warren is memorizing the conjugation of the verb. 19: 'Eν ἀρχῇ ἦν ὁ λόγος:] "In the beginning was the Word," the opening words of the Gospel of John.

159 **V. A Vision: Circa 1880** 19: Trigg County,] Robert Franklin Warren moved to Guthrie, in Todd County, from Cerulean Springs, in Trigg County. Warren spent summers as a child at Cerulean Springs. Gabriel Penn, Warren's maternal grandfather, also settled in Trigg County in 1881 (see Watkins, *Then and Now* [University Press of Kentucky, 1982], p. 22).

164 **I. I Can't Even Remember the Name** 1: I can't even remember the name] Kent Greenfield could, though, and told Watkins that the protagonist of this poem was named Larry Grizzard (see Watkins, *Then and Now* [University Press of Kentucky, 1982], p. 100).

169 **Nocturne: Traveling Salesman in Hotel Bedroom** 26: Old Jack] Jack Daniel's whiskey 27: Gideon] The Gideons are an organization that places bibles in hotel bedrooms for travelers to use.

170 **So You Agree with What I Say? Well, What Did I Say?** 21: Mr. Moody] A real person, says Watkins, *Then and Now* (p. 91).

173 **Autumnal Equinox on Mediterranean Beach** 7: Jantzen] a swimwear manufacturer

186 **II. The Mad Druggist** 21: the old druggist] A real person, according to Watkins (*Then and Now* [University Press of Kentucky, 1982], p. 94). 22: Hoptown] Hopkinsville, where there is a state mental asylum.

187 **Interim 1.** 14: Whom we now sought] Ms. Cecilia (Seeley) Bradshaw, according to Watkins (*Then and Now* [University Press of Kentucky, 1982] p. 54).

198 **Shoes in Rain Jungle** 21: *Mot de Cambronne*] Word of Cambronne, which is to say, shit. When at Waterloo the British demanded of Pierre-Jacques Cambronne, the commander of the Imperial Guard, that he surrender, Cambronne replied "Merde."

202 **I. Place and Time** 2: Cerulean Springs] Watkins argues that Dr. Knox is Dr. Sterling Price Quinsenberry, a dentist of Cerulean Springs, who killed himself on 16 June 1916 (*Then and Now* [University Press of Kentucky, 1982], p. 107).

206 **V. And All That Came Thereafter** 12: that imbecile / tower] Coit tower 26: another sea,] the Mediterranean 42: I. Magnin] an elegant retailer

224 **III. Natural History** 7: *Et les Sarrasins se retirèrent en une isle qui est devant le dict chastel—*] And the Saracens retreated to an island which is under the said castle. The quotation, according to Warren's notes, is from the *Livre des faits du bon Messire Jean le Mangre, du Boucicault.* 8: The *Maréchal*] the Maréchal du Boucicault. 10: *des leurs y perdirent plus de quatre cent hommes, que morts, que affolez,*] four hundred men of them were lost, who died or were washed away.

235 **The Leaf [C]** 11: By what grape?] "In those days they shall no longer say: 'The fathers have eaten sour grapes, and the children's teeth are set on edge.' But every one shall die for his own sin; each man who eats sour grapes, his teeth shall be set on edge." Jeremiah 31:29–30.

271 **I. The Nature of a Mirror** 6: I stand / And wait.] Possibly an allusion to Milton's sonnet "When I consider how my life is spent."

282 **VI. Ballad of Mister Dutcher and the Last Lynching in Gupton** 1: In the early manuscript the title is "Ballad of Mister Crutcher and the Last Lynching in Guthrie." Like "Pondy Woods" this poem follows some of the details of the Primus Kirby lynching of June 1926. On a note at the bottom of an early typescript of "Caveat," Warren writes "Ray Crutcher's father tied noose (only skill) for lynching in Guthrie (last one)—no danger of intrusion on privacy and legal action by any Crut[c]her. all dead. Ray, etc." 7: I, a boy] Warren had already finished college when the Kirby lynching took place. 47: Hoptown] Hopkinsville. But the story here does not at all follow the Kirby case. 112: death to hide?] Warren refers to the New Testament Parable of the Talents, but his language is that of Milton's Sonnet on his blindness.

291 **Rattlesnake Country 3.** 9: *levi's*] Slang term for blue jeans, from Levi Strauss and Company.

295 **Vital Statistics [A]** 14: "ex urbe atque Italia inritamenta gulae gestabantur. . . ,"] "Gullet-teasers are brought from the city and from Italy. . . ,"

300 **1. The Faring** 1: Once over water] Joseph Blotner quotes Eleanor Clark's account of her joyous impatience on this occasion early in their courtship in *Robert Penn Warren* (New York, 1997).

311 **Reading Late at Night, Thermometer Falling [2]** 26: Later, I found the poems. Not good.] Two of Robert Franklin Warren's poems were published in *Local and National Poets of America,* ed. Thomas W. Herringshaw (n.p.: 1890). Watkins, in *Then and Now* [University Press of Kentucky, 1982], suggests that this may have been a subscription publication, and he also reprints both poems.

315 **XXI. Folly on Royal Street before the Raw Face of God** 1: Drunk, drunk, drunk, amid the blaze of noon,] A parody of Samson's first line in Milton's *Samson Agonistes*: Dark, dark, dark, amid the blaze of noon. 12: C. and M.] In the MS draft of this poem, which is called "Spring Off the Gulf," Warren uses "Cannon and Manson" here, rather than "C. and M.'.

326 **Loss, of Perhaps Love, in Our World of Contingency** 15: while your mother/ Bathed you,] In fact an early memory of Warren's own. See Joseph Blotner, *Robert Penn Warren* (New York: 1997).

327 **Answer to Prayer** 1: city to have now no name] Minneapolis, probably. 36: Nevada dollars] From slot machines, of course, but Warren has in mind Nevada as a center for divorce as well as for gambling.

329 **Midnight Outcry** 12: Inclines over the infant] If this poem is rooted in autobiography, it revisits some of the scenes of "To a Little Girl, One Year Old, in a Ruined Fortress."

330 **Trying to Tell You Something** 21: truth, and its beauty] a dark parody of Keats' "Ode on a Grecian Urn."

333 **Old Nigger on One-Mule Cart Encountered Late at Night When Driving Home From Party in the Back Country** 4: Essolube] A brand of motor oil. 27: N.O.] New Orleans 79: The sonnet Warren is quoting has been preserved in the Beinecke Library (folder 3357):

In late afternoon, he stops in the road's red dust,
Or the red mud, stalled there, cart's tongue, wheel's rim,
(Iron or wood ruined by the rot or rust)
Broken at last; then passing, we see him
Bend, and the mule droop, and over his head
The bright leaves, if autumn, fly, or summer, the sun
Beats, winter, the rain; he stands in the red
Dust, red mud, his motion the same, the one
Motion always, which we know but cannot name
—Sudden like the flung headlight glare in dark
That seasonless gesture to mind comes, the same
Motion that stuns the eternal, empty air:
    One of the poor with a cart of junk to use
    For purposes which we cannot peruse.

(I have deleted an alternative draft of the first two lines of the sestet: We always recall but cannot name / —Sudden to mind like the flung headlight glare.)

339 **American Portrait: Old Style** 21: Harrod or Finley or Boone,] James Harrod (1742–1793), a Kentucky pioneer, founder of Harrodsburg, the first white settlement in Kentucky. James Bradley Finley (1781–1856), Methodist evangelist in Kentucky and Ohio. 23: K] Warren's childhood friend Kent Greenfield. 33: Plymouth Rock, Dominecker] Kinds of chicken. 34: Decherd] An imaginary Decherd: Decherds were rifles, not BB guns. 59: Piero della Francesca] Italian painter, 1420?–1492 105: David at brookside] during the fight with Goliath

342 **Amazing Grace in the Back Country** 7: geek] A carnival side-show attraction; someone who bites the heads off chickens.

345 **Evening Hour** 1: a graveyard once—or cemetery] There is a difference. A graveyard is small, densely populated, and attached to a church or synagogue. Cemeteries are larger, landscaped, and freestanding. There have been graveyards since there have been people. Cemeteries are an invention of the early nineteeth century. What Warren describes here is clearly a cemetery.

347 **Red-Tail Hawk and Pyre of Youth** 89: I knew how it felt with one gone.] Warren lost one eye in an accident in his youth. 92: a book / of poems friends and I had printed in college] Probably *Driftwood Flames*.

351 **Star-Fall** 1: drawbridge] The landscape seems to be that of "To a Little Girl, One Year Old, in a Ruined Fortress."

368 **Heat Lightning** 12: of her,] Joseph Blotner calls this poem, which is tied to Warren's learning of the death of his first wife, "a Cinina-flashback."

372 **Identity and Argument for Prayer** 6: self-winding watch] Self-winding watches were wound when a weighted crank inside was turned by the arm's natural motions. It's hard to see how a self-winding watch falling in black Spacelessness would continue to self-wind.

381 **October Picnic Long Ago** 20: Norfolk jacket.] A loose-fitting, single-breasted jacket, box-plaited in front and back, and belted.

383 **When Life Begins** 1: Hellenistic head] This is the poet's grandfather, Gabriel Thomas Penn.

386 **Recollection in Upper Ontario, from Long Before** 30: Zack,] Throughout the setting typescript Warren has corrected the name from "Jeff." This raises the tantalizing possibility that the derelict here is the same person Warren describes in *Jefferson Davis Get his Citizenship Back.* But BHTS is a later text than either of the magazine versions, in which the derelict is named Zack. 31: L & N] Louisville and Nashville Railroad

396 **August Moon** 13: Your father's cancer, or / Mother's stroke] Warren's actual parents died in those ways.

398 **Preternaturally Early Snowfall in Mating Season** 5: breakfast of champions] Wheaties, the breakfast cereal, advertised itself as "The Breakfast of Champions."

403 **Empty White Blotch on Map of Universe: A Possible View** 7: this island is full of voices] Like the island of *The Tempest,* although in most ways this island resembles that of *Robinson Crusoe.* 20: Spartan few] At the battle of Thermopylae. 21: neat little captain] John Paul Jones.

405 **Vision (Being Here)** 18: the city] The context suggests Minneapolis in the dark days toward the end of Warren's first marriage.

411 **Deep—Deeper Down** 5: Lüger] A German military pistol.

412 **Sky** 15: Your head in dizziness swam] The language suggest's Milton's description of the birth of Sin from the head of Satan in *Paradise Lost.*

412 **Better Than Counting Sheep** 8: field full of folk,] Possibly echoes the opening of *Piers Plowman.*

413 **The Cross** 23: aggies] a kind of marble, from the children's game of marbles.

421 **Lesson in History** 7: Cambronne] Upon being ordered to surrender at Waterloo, Cambronne replied "*Merde.*" 11: Charlotte Corday] The assassin of Marat. 13: Hendrik Hudson] Henry Hudson, his son, and seven others were set adrift in a small boat in Hudson's Bay by mutineers on 22 June 1611. They were never seen again. 17: Anne Boleyn] Second wife of Henry VIII; beheaded 1536.

427 **Trips to California** 1: dust-storm] Warren has in mind the catastrophic dust-storms, caused by bad agricultural practices, of the Depression era "Dust Bowl." 32: General Sheridan] Philip Henry Sheridan (1831–1888), an aggressive cavalry commander during the Civil War, succeeded W. T. Sherman as commmander in chief of the army in 1884.

428 **Auto-da-fé** 27: Dresden and Tokyo] Both cities were fire-bombed during the Second World War. 28: Wilderness] During the battle of the Wilderness, 4–5 May 1864, a forest fire broke out, incinerating the wounded. Warren describes this scene both in *Brother to Dragons* and in his novel *Wilderness.* 36: Latimer] Hugh Latimer (1485–1555), reformer, Bishop, political and religious figure during the reigns of Henry VIII and Edward VI, was burned at the stake by Mary Tudor. 37: Cranmer] Thomas Cranmer (1489–1556), reformer, theologian, archbishop of Canterbury, ally of Henry VIII, was burned at the stake by Mary Tudor. 45: Cracked Maid] Possibly the "Maid of Kent," hung, not burned, by Henry VIII, but more likely Joan of Arc.

433 **Synonyms** 59: Nijinski] Vaslav Nijinski (1890–1950), the great ballet dancer.

Rumor Verified epigraph]

I saw, through a round opening,
the beautiful things that heaven bears,
and came forth to see again the stars

448 **Blessed Accident** 2: Nel mezzo del camin—] "In the middle of the way" The phrase opens Dante's *Divine Comedy.*

451 **III. One I Knew** 18: One once] The poet's father, Robert Franklin Warren.

495 **Chief Joseph of the Nez Perce II.** 85: Howard] Oliver Otis Howard (1830–1909), who commanded the Union XI Corps during the Civil War, and headed the Freedmen's Bureau during Reconstruction (for which Howard University was named after him), also made a famous treaty with the Apache chief Cochise and befriended his son Geronimo.

499 **Chief Joseph of the Nez Perce III.** 124: 'skirts of the Old Lady Queen,'] in Canada. The 'Old Lady Queen' is Victoria.

503 **Chief Joseph of the Nez Perce IV.** 37: Enfield, or Spencer, or Sharps.] Varieties of rifle.

503 **Chief Joseph of the Nez Perce IV.** 88: Stars wheel in unfamiliar formations.] Joseph has traveled east, but he has not traveled far north or south. The formations in which the stars wheel would still be familiar.

507 **Chief Joseph of the Nez Perce VI.** 9: Where water, long back, had sliced at the high plain] Warren has in mind how the landforms were shaped by catastrophic floods at the end of the Ice Ages, when Lake Missoula, a lake of glacial origin in the valley of the Clark Fork, broke through the ice-dam that created it. 50: Seven Pines] Howard lost an arm at the battle of Seven Pines, May 31, 1862. 62: Miles] Nelson A. Miles (1839–1925), later general-in-chief of the Army. Warren's portrayal of him here accords with his portrayal of Miles in *Jefferson Davis Gets His Citizenship Back.* During the Civil War, Miles fought in every major battle of the Army of the Potomac and was four times wounded, winning the Congressional Medal of Honor. Warren, like many Southerners, is critical of Miles' conduct as custodian of the imprisoned Jefferson Davis after the Civil War, but the *Dictionary of American Biography* argues that Miles was ultimately "vindicated when the true facts became known and the bitterness engendered by the war had passed." During the Indian Wars, Miles defeated both Sitting Bull and Geronimo, and was in command of the U.S. forces at the Wounded Knee massacre of 1891. Miles also commanded the troops which put down the Pullman strike of 1894. But it was also Miles who investigated and reported abuses of Filipino insurgents by American soldiers during the insurrection in 1902. The point is that while Miles is not a sympathetic figure, he is by no means the clown that Warren portrays him as both here and in *Jefferson Davis Gets His Citizenship Back.*

507 **Chief Joseph of the Nez Perce VI.** 241: cannon buried howitzerwise,] So as to elevate the muzzle, allowing the cannon to fire with a high arc, like a howitzer. 318: He] Ollokot, brother of Joseph [Warren's note]

516 **Chief Joseph of the Nez Perce VII.** 20: brigadier] But Warren has earlier said that Miles was only a colonel. But he may have been promoted very soon after the victory over Joseph. Warren refers to that victory as "the price of a star," referring to the brigadier general's star.

516 **Chief Joseph of the Nez Perce VII.** 47: price of a star?] a brigadier's star 48: Hayes] Rutherford Hayes, President of the United States from 1877 to 1881. 52: Knew his profession,] A sly reference to the so-called Compromise of 1877, by which Hayes fraudulently obtained the Presidency.

518 **Chief Joseph of the Nez Perce VIII.** 103: a yet-warm scalp,] William Frederick Cody (1846–1917), known as "Buffalo Bill" for killing 4,280 head of Buffalo to feed construction crews of the Kansas Pacific Railroad during 1867–1868, scalped the Cheyenne warrior Yellow Hair in Sioux County, Nebraska, on 17 July 1876. After his years as a hunter, and as a scout for the Fifth Cavalry, Cody staged a famous Wild West show, with a troupe that included Annie Oakley and Chief Sitting Bull.

542 **Literal Dream** 1: You know the scene.] The scene in *Tess of the D'Urbervilles* in which Tess's murder of Alec is discovered. The movie referred to in the epigraph is the Roman Polanski version.

560 **Old-Time Childhood in Kentucky** 13: the first great General Jackson] Andrew Jackson, this is to say, not Stonewall. 19: Bryce's Crossroads] Brice's Crossroads, 10 July 1864, a cavalry battle in which Nathan Bedford Forrest's cavalry drove off superior forces under Samuel D. Sturgis. Warren's grandfather Gabriel Thomas Penn was probably there. This is the same Sturgis whom Chief Joseph tricks in *Chief Joseph of the Nez Perce.* 20: Austerlitz] Napoleon's decisive 1 December 1805 victory over larger Austrian and Russian forces commanded by Kutuzov, who was later his opponent at Borodino. 28: Excavation next summer] of the tomb of Tutankhamen by Howard Carter in 1922.

562 **Re-interment: Recollection of a Grandfather** 40: Bloody Pond] Scene of heavy fighting on the first day of the battle of Shiloh, April 6 1862.

563 **Last Meeting** 11: I see her now] The TS of the poem in the Beinecke Library is dedicated to Geraldine Carr, who is probably the person the speaker encounters here.

570 **The Place** 18: How had you ever forgotten that spot / Where once wild azalea bloomed? And what there passed?] This is clearly an autobiographical memory, but Warren does not elaborate it enough to identify it. 21: Alone in a dark piazza,] Another unidentifiable but clearly autobiographical allusion.

571 **Paradigm of Seasons** 2: learned, of seasons, the paradigm?] Warren has in mind learning grammatical paradigms, such as the Greek verbs his father recited in "Mortmain." 25: price of gasoline no object.] The early 1980's were a period of acute gasoline shortages.

579 **Whatever You Now Are** 6: How is the difference defined between singer and song?] Possibly an allusion to Yeats's poem "Among School Children,"

580 **Wind and Gibbon** 30: *In hoc signo.*] According to Eusebius, the Emperor Constantine was moved to convert to Christianity by a vision of a cross, with the motto "In hoc signo vinces" (In this symbol, conquer), at the battle of Milvian Bridge in 312, in which he defeated his brother-in-law Maxentius and conquered Rome.

587 **Bicentennial** 22: a shepherd,] One-eyed, watching a distant eagle, trying to remember his childhood, living in the Bitterroots (always a talismanic location for Warren), who could this shepherd be, despite his Welsh birth, but Warren himself? On the other hand, in an unpublished poem of 1981 called "Mythology" Warren describes meeting a Welsh-born shepherd in Montana, although that shepherd is not missing one eye. 30: Porcellian,] An elite "finals club" at Harvard. 119: Bastogne] Site of the heroic stand by General McAuliffe and his men during the Battle of the Bulge in December 1944. 230: Cajun,] a descendent of French-speaking people deported from Acadia (now Nova Scotia) by the British in 1755. 230: *gens de couleur,*] racially mixed French-speaking people from New Orleans and environs.

599 **A Few Axioms for a Young Man** 22: Floyd Collins] The media hoopla surrounding Floyd Collins' entrapment in a cave near Nashville in 1925 is the basis of Warren's 1959 novel *The Cave.*

606 **Aging Painter Sits Where the Great Tower Heaves Down Midnight** 27: Bentley] An elegant motorcar.

INDEX OF TITLES AND FIRST LINES